Active Learning Exercise 10b: Does Output Per Person Depend on Hu
Augmented Solow Model of Growth)

Active Learning Exercise 10c: Is Trade Good or Bad for the Envi

Active Learning Exercise 11a: Central Limit Theorem Convergence for β ...
Regression Model

Active Learning Exercise 11b: Bootstrap Analysis of the Convergence of the Asymptotic Sampling Distributions for Multiple Regression Model Parameter Estimators

Active Learning Exercise 12a: The Role of Institutions ("Rule of Law") in Economic Growth

Active Learning Exercise 12b: Is Trade Good or Bad for the Environment? (Completion)

Active Learning Exercise 12c: The Impact of Military Service on the Smoking Behavior of Veterans

Active Learning Exercise 12d: The Effect of Measurement-Error Contamination on OLS Regression Estimates and the Durbin/Bartlett IV Estimator

Active Learning Exercise 14a: Analyzing the Food Price Sub-Index of the Monthly U.S. Consumer Price Index

Active Learning Exercise 14b: Estimating Taylor Rules for How the U.S. Fed Sets Interest Rates

Active Learning Exercise 16a: Assessing the Impact of 4-H Participation on the Standardized Test Scores of Florida Schoolchildren

Active Learning Exercise 16b: Using Panel Data Methods to Reanalyze Data from a Public Goods Experiment

Active Learning Exercise 17a: Conditional Forecasting Using a Large-Scale Macroeconometric Model

Active Learning Exercise 17b: Modeling U.S. GNP

Active Learning Exercise 18a: Modeling the South Korean Won–U.S. Dollar Exchange Rate

Active Learning Exercise 18b: Modeling the Daily Returns to Ford Motor Company Stock

Active Learning Exercise 19a: Probit Modeling of the Determinants of Labor Force Participation

FUNDAMENTALS OF APPLIED ECONOMETRICS

by

RICHARD A. ASHLEY
Economics Department
Virginia Tech

John Wiley and Sons, Inc.

Vice President & Executive Publisher	George Hoffman
Project Editor	Jennifer Manias
Assistant Editor	Emily McGee
Editorial Assistant	Erica Horowitz
Associate Director of Marketing	Amy Scholz
Marketing Manager	Jesse Cruz
Marketing Assistant	Courtney Luzzi
Executive Media Editor	Allison Morris
Media Editor	Greg Chaput
Senior Production Manager	Janis Soo
Associate Production Manager	Joyce Poh
Assistant Production Editor	Yee Lyn Song
Cover Designer	Jerel Seah
Cover Photo Credit	©AveryPhotography/iStockphoto

This book was set in 10/12 Times Roman by Thomson Digital and printed and bound by RR Donnelley. The cover was printed by RR Donnelly.

This book is printed on acid-free paper. ∞

Founded in 1807, John Wiley & Sons, Inc. has been a valued source of knowledge and understanding for more than 200 years, helping people around the world meet their needs and fulfill their aspirations. Our company is built on a foundation of principles that include responsibility to the communities we serve and where we live and work. In 2008, we launched a Corporate Citizenship Initiative, a global effort to address the environmental, social, economic, and ethical challenges we face in our business. Among the issues we are addressing are carbon impact, paper specifications and procurement, ethical conduct within our business and among our vendors, and community and charitable support. For more information, please visit our Web site: www.wiley.com/go/citizenship.

Library of Congress Cataloging-in-Publication Data

Ashley, Richard A. (Richard Arthur), 1950-
Fundamentals of applied econometrics / by Richard Ashley. – 1st ed.
p. cm.
Includes index.
ISBN 978-0-470-59182-6 (hardback)
1. Econometrics. 2. Econometrics–Statistical methods. 3. Econometrics–Data processing. I. Title.
HB139.A84 2012
330.01'5195–dc23 2011041421

Printed in the United States of America

10 9 8 7 6 5 4 3 2 1

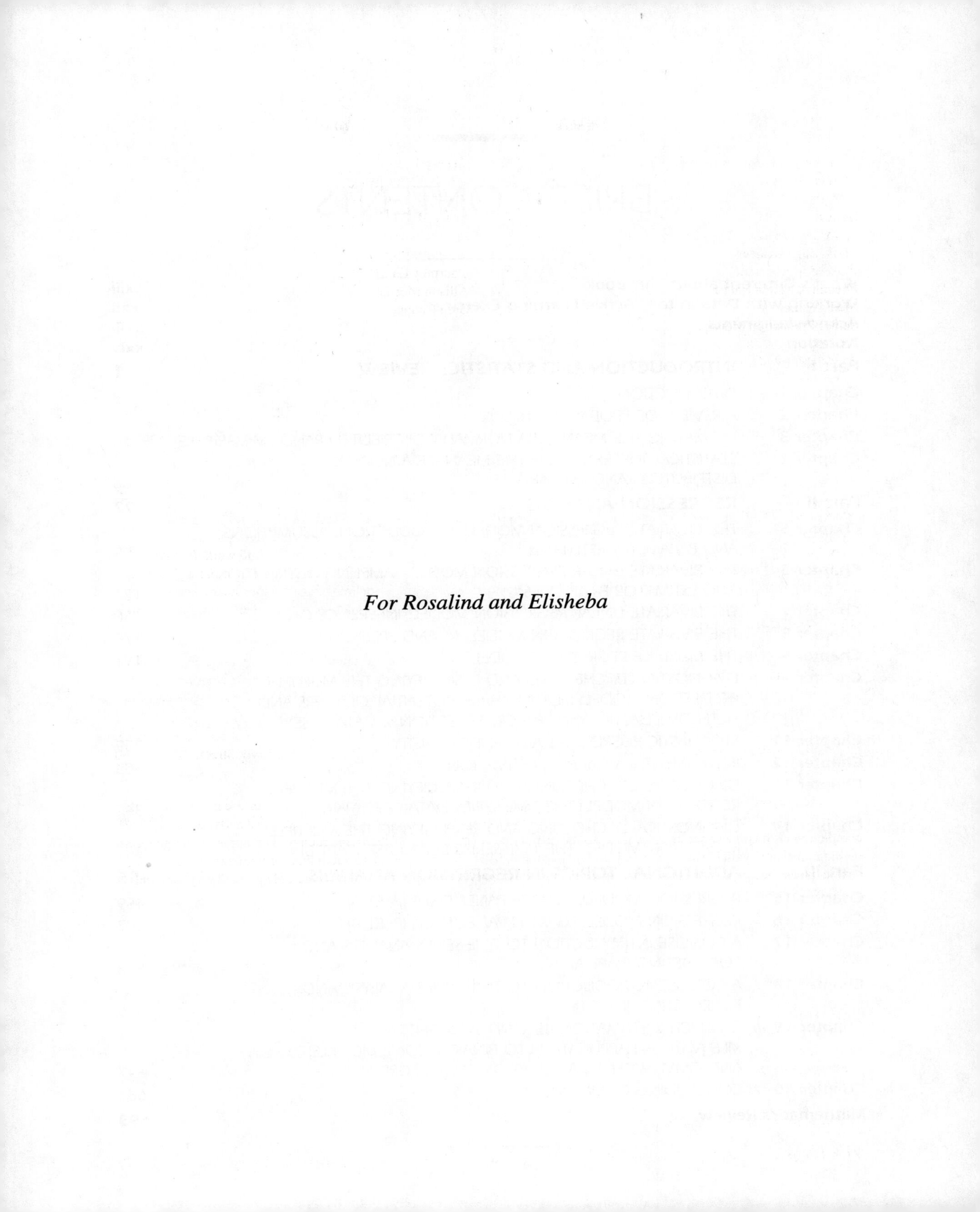

For Rosalind and Elisheba

BRIEF CONTENTS

TABLE OF CONTENTS

[1] Uses data from Dollar, D., and A. Kraay (2002), "Growth Is Good for the Poor," *Journal of Economic Growth 7*, 195–225.

[2] Uses data from Mankiw, G. N., D. Romer, and D. N. Weil (1992), "A Contribution to the Empirics of Economic Growth," *The Quarterly Journal of Economics 107(2)*, 407–37. Mankiw et al. estimate and test a Solow growth model, augmenting it with a measure of human capital, quantified by the percentage of the population in secondary school.

[3] Uses data from Frankel, J. A., and A. K. Rose (2005), "Is Trade Good or Bad for the Environment? Sorting Out the Causality," *The Review of Economics and Statistics 87(1)*, 85–91. Frankel and Rose quantify and test the effect of trade openness $\{(X+M)/Y\}$ on three measures of environmental damage (SO_2, NO_2, and total suspended particulates). Since trade openness may well be endogenous, Frankel and Rose also obtain 2SLS estimates; these are examined in Active Learning Exercise 12b.

[4] Uses data from Acemoglu, D., S. Johnson, and J. A. Robinson (2001), "The Colonial Origins of Comparative Development," *The American Economic Review 91(5)*, 1369–1401. These authors argue that the European mortality rate in colonial times is a valid instrument for current institutional quality because Europeans settled (and imported their cultural institutions) only in colonies with climates they found healthy.

[5] See footnote for Active Learning Exercise 10c.

[6] Uses data from Bedard, K., and O. Deschênes (2006), "The Long-Term Impact of Military Service on Health: Evidence from World War II and Korean War Veterans." *The American Economic Review 96(1)*, 176–194. These authors quantify the impact of the provision of free and/or low-cost tobacco products to servicemen on smoking and (later) on mortality rates, using instrumental variable methods to control for the nonrandom selection into military service.

WHAT'S DIFFERENT ABOUT THIS BOOK

THE PURPOSE OF THE KIND OF ECONOMETRICS COURSE EMBODIED IN THIS BOOK

Econometrics is all about quantifying and testing economic relationships, using sample data which is most commonly not experimentally derived. Our most fundamental tool in this enterprise is simple multiple regression analysis, although we often need to transcend it, in the end, so as to deal with such real-world complications as endogeneity in the explanatory variables, binary-choice models, and the like.

Therefore, the econometrics course envisioned in the construction of this book focuses on helping a student to develop as clear and complete an understanding of the multiple regression model as is possible, given the structural constraints – discussed below – which most instructors face. The goals of this course are to teach the student how to

- Analyze actual economic data so as to produce a statistically adequate model
- Check the validity of the statistical assumptions underlying the model, using the sample data itself and revising the model specification as needed
- Use the model to obtain reasonably valid statistical tests of economic theory – i.e., of our understanding of the economic reality generating the sample data
- Use the model to obtain reasonably valid confidence intervals for the key coefficients, so that the estimates can be sensibly used for policy analysis
- Identify, estimate, and diagnostically check practical time-series forecasting models

The emphasis throughout this book is on empowering the student to thoroughly understand the most fundamental econometric ideas and tools, rather than simply accepting a collection of assumptions, results, and formulas on faith and then using computer software to estimate a lot of regression models. The intent of the book is to well serve both the student whose interest is in understanding how one can use sample data to illuminate/suggest/test economic theory *and* the student who wants and needs a solid intellectual foundation on which to build practical experiential expertise in econometric modeling and time-series forecasting.

REAL-WORLD CONSTRAINTS ON SUCH A COURSE

The goals described above are a very tall order in the actual academic settings of most basic econometrics courses. In addition to the limited time allotted to a typical such course – often just a single term – the reality is that the students enter our courses with highly heterogeneous (and often quite spotty) statistics backgrounds. A one-term introductory statistics course is almost always a course prerequisite, but the quality and focus of this statistics course is usually outside our control. This statistics course is also often just a distant memory by the time our students reach us. Moreover, even when the statistics prerequisite course is both recent and appropriately focused for the needs of our course, many students need a deeper understanding of basic statistical concepts than they were able to attain on their first exposure to these ideas.

In addition, of course, most undergraduate (and many graduate-level) econometrics courses must do without matrix algebra, since few students in their first econometrics course are sufficiently comfortable with this tool that its use clarifies matters rather than erecting an additional conceptual barrier. Even where students are entirely comfortable with linear algebra – as might well be the case in the first term of a high-quality Ph.D.-level econometrics sequence – a treatment which eschews the use of linear algebra can be extremely useful as complement to the kind of textbook typically assigned in such a course.

Therefore the design constraints on this book are threefold:

1. The probability and statistics concepts needed are all developed within the text itself: in Chapters 2 through 4 for the most fundamental part of the book (where the regression explanatory variables are fixed in repeated samples) and in Chapter 11 for the remainder of the book.
2. Linear algebra is not used at all – nary a matrix appears (outside of a very occasional footnote) until Appendix 19.1 at the very close of the book.[1]
3. Nevertheless, the focus is on teaching an understanding of the theory underlying modern econometric techniques – not just the mechanics of invoking them – so that the student can apply these techniques with both competence and confidence.

FINESSING THE CONSTRAINTS

This book deals with the linear algebra constraint by focusing primarily on a very thorough treatment of the bivariate regression model. This provides a strong foundation, from which multiple regression analysis can be introduced – without matrix algebra – in a less detailed way. Moreover, it turns out that the essential features of many advanced topics – e.g., instrumental variables estimation – can be brought out quite clearly in a bivariate formulation.[2]

The problem with the students' preparation in terms of basic probability theory and statistics is finessed in two ways. First, Chapter 2 provides a concise review of all the probability theory needed for analyzing regression models with fixed regressors, starting at the very beginning: with the definition of a random variable, its expectation, and its variance. The seamless integration of this material into the body of the text admits of a sufficiently complete presentation as to allow students with weak (or largely forgotten) preparation to catch up. It also provides textbook "backup" for an instructor, who can then pick and choose which topics to cover in class.

[1] The necessary elements of scalar algebra – i.e., the mechanics of dealing with summation notation – are summarized in a "Mathematics Review" section at the end of the book.

[2] This strategy does not eliminate the need for linear algebra in deriving the distribution of S^2, the usual estimator of the variance of the model error term. That problem is dealt with in Chapter 4 using a large-sample argument. Occasional references to particular matrices (e.g., the usual X matrix in the multiple regression model) or linear algebraic concepts (e.g., the rank of a matrix) necessarily occur, but are relegated to footnotes.

Second, the treatment here frames the linear regression model as an explicit parameterization of the conditional mean of the dependent variable – plus, of course, a model error term. From this point of view it is natural to initially focus (in Chapters 3 and 4) on what one might call the "univariate regression model":

$$Y_i = \alpha + U_i \quad U_i \sim \text{NIID}(0, \sigma^2)$$

The estimation of the parameters α and σ^2 in this model is essentially identical to the typical introductory-statistics-course topic of estimating the mean and variance of a normally distributed random variable. Consequently, using this "univariate regression model" to begin the coverage of the essential topics in regression analysis – the least squares estimator, its sampling distribution, its desirable properties, and the inference machinery based on it – provides a thorough and integrated review of the key topics which the students need to have understood (and retained) from their introductory statistics class. It also provides an extension, in the simplest possible setting, to key concepts – e.g., estimator properties – which are usually not covered in an introductory statistics course.

Bivariate and multiple regression analysis are then introduced in the middle part of the book (Chapters 5 through 10) as a relatively straightforward extension to this framework – directly exploiting the vocabulary, concepts, and techniques just covered in this initial analysis. The always-necessary statistics "review" is in this way gracefully integrated with the orderly development of the book's central topic.

The treatment of stochastic regressors requires the deeper understanding of asymptotic theory provided in Chapter 11; this material provides a springboard for the more advanced material which makes up the rest of the book. This portion of the book is ideal for the second term of an undergraduate econometrics sequence, a Master's degree level course, or as a companion (auxiliary) text in a first-term Ph.D. level course.[3]

A CHAPTER-BY-CHAPTER ROADMAP

After an introductory chapter, the concepts of basic probability theory needed for Chapters 3 through 10 are briefly reviewed in Chapter 2. As noted above, classroom coverage of much of this material can be skipped for relatively well prepared groups; it is essential, however, for students with weak (or half-forgotten) statistics backgrounds. The most fundamentally necessary tools are a clear understanding of what is meant by the probability distribution, expected value, and variance of a random variable. These concepts are developed in a highly accessible fashion in Chapter 2 by initially focusing on a discretely distributed random variable.

As noted above, Chapter 3 introduces the notion of a parameter estimator and its sampling distribution in the simple setting of the estimation of the mean of a normally distributed variate using a random sample. Both least squares estimation and estimator properties are introduced in this chapter. Chapter 4 then explains how one can obtain interval estimates and hypothesis tests regarding the population mean, again in this fundamental context.

Chapters 3 and 4 are the first point at which it becomes crucial to distinguish between an estimator as a random variable (characterized by its sampling distribution) and its sample realization – an ordinary number. One of the features of this book is that this distinction is explicitly incorporated in the notation used. This distinction is consistently maintained throughout – not just for estimators, but for all of the various kinds of random variables that come up in the development: dependent

[3] Thus, in using this book as the text for a one-term undergraduate course, an instructor might want to order copies of the book containing only Chapter 1 through 12 and Chapter 20. This can be easily done using the Wiley "Custom Select" facility at the customselect.wiley.com Web site.

variables, model error terms, and even model fitting errors. A summary of the notational conventions used for these various kinds of random variables (and their sample realizations) is given in the "Notation" section, immediately prior to Part I of the book. In helping beginners to keep track of which variables are random and which are not, this consistent notation is well worth the additional effort involved.

While Chapters 3 and 4 can be viewed as a carefully integrated "statistics review," most of the crucial concepts and techniques underlying the regression analysis covered in the subsequent chapters are first thoroughly developed here:

- What constitutes a "good" parameter estimator?
- How do the properties (unbiasedness, BLUness, etc.) embodying this "goodness" rest on the assumptions made?
- How can we obtain confidence intervals and hypothesis tests for the underlying parameters?
- How does the validity of this inference machinery rest on the assumptions made?

After this preparation, Part II of the book covers the basics of regression analysis. The analysis in Chapter 5 coherently segues – using an explicit empirical example – from the estimation of the mean of a random variable into the particular set of assumptions which is here called "The Bivariate Regression Model," where the (conditional) mean of a random variable is parameterized as a linear function of observed realizations of an explanatory variable. In particular, what starts out as a model for the mean of per capita real GDP (from the Penn World Table) becomes a regression model relating a country's output to its aggregate stock of capital. A microeconometric bivariate regression application later in Chapter 5 relates household weekly earnings (from the Census Bureau's Current Population Survey) to a college-graduation dummy variable. This early introduction to dummy variable regressors is useful on several grounds: it both echoes the close relationship between regression analysis and the estimation of the mean (in this case, the estimation of two means) and it also introduces the student early on to an exceedingly useful empirical tool.[4]

The detailed coverage of the Bivariate Regression Model then continues with the exposition (in Chapter 6) of how the model assumptions lead to least-squares parameter estimators with desirable properties and (in Chapter 7) to a careful derivation of how these assumptions yield confidence intervals and hypothesis tests. These results are all fairly straightforward extensions of the material just covered in Chapters 3 and 4. Indeed, that is the raison d'être for the coverage of this material in Chapters 3 and 4: it makes these two chapters on bivariate regression the *second* pass at this material. Topics related to goodness of fit (R^2) and simple prediction are covered in Chapter 8.

Chapter 9 develops these same results for what is here called "The Multiple Regression Model," as an extension of the analogous results obtained in detail for the Bivariate Regression Model. While the mathematical analysis of the Multiple Regression Model is necessarily limited here by the restriction to scalar algebra, the strategy is to leverage the thorough understanding of the Bivariate Regression Model gained in the previous chapters as much as is possible toward understanding the corresponding aspects of the Multiple Regression Model. A careful – albeit necessarily, at times, intuitive – discussion of several topics which could not be addressed in the exposition of the Bivariate Regression Model completes the exposition in Chapter 9. These topics include the issues arising from over-elaborate model specifications, underelaborate model specifications, and multicollinearity. This chapter closes with several worked applications and several directed applications ("Active Learning Exercises," discussed below) for the reader to pursue.

[4] Chapter 5 also makes the link – both numerically (in Active Learning Exercise 5d) and analytically (in Appendix 5.1) – between the estimated coefficient on a dummy variable regressor and sample mean estimates. This linkage is useful later on (in Chapter 15) when the fixed-effects model for panel data is discussed.

By this point in the book it is abundantly clear how the quality of the model parameter estimates and the validity of the statistical inference machinery both hinge on the model assumptions. Chapter 10 (and, later, Chapters 13 through 15) provide a coherent summary of how one can, with a reasonably large data set, in practice use the sample data to check these assumptions. Many of the usual methods aimed at testing and/or correcting for failures in these assumptions are in essence described in these chapters, but the emphasis is not on an encyclopedia-like coverage of all the specific tests and procedures in the literature. Rather, these chapters focus on a set of graphical methods (histograms and plots) and on a set of simple auxiliary regressions which together suggest revisions to the model specification that are likely to lead to a model which at least approximately satisfies the regression model assumptions.

In particular, Chapter 10 deals with the issues – gaussianity, homoscedasticity, and parameter stability – necessary in order to diagnostically check (and perhaps respecify) a regression model based on cross-sectional data. Robust (White) standard error estimates are obtained in a particularly transparent way, but the emphasis is on taking observed heteroscedasticity as a signal that the form of the dependent variable needs respecification, rather than on FGLS corrections or on simply replacing the usual standard error estimates by robust estimates. The material in this chapter suffices to allow the student to get started on a range of practical applications.[5]

The remaining portion of Part II – comprising Chapters 11 through 14 – abandons the rather artificial assumption that the explanatory variables are fixed in repeated samples. Stochastic regressors are, of course, necessary in order to deal with the essential real-world complications of endogeneity and dynamics, but the analysis of models with stochastic regressors requires a primer on asymptotic theory. Chapter 11 provides this primer and focuses on endogeneity; Chapter 12 focuses on instrumental variables estimation; and Chapters 13 and 14 focus on diagnostically checking the nonautocorrelation assumption and on modeling dynamics.

Each of these chapters is described in more detail below, but they all share a common approach in terms of the technical level of the exposition: The (scalar) algebra of probability limits is laid out – without proof – in Appendix 11.1; these results are then used in each of the chapters to rather easily examine the consistency (or otherwise) of the OLS slope estimator in the relevant bivariate regression models. Technical details are carefully considered, but relegated to footnotes. And the asymptotic sampling distributions of these slope estimators are fairly carefully derived, but these derivations are provided in chapter appendices. This approach facilitates the coverage of the basic econometric issues regarding endogeneity and dynamics in a straightforward way, while also allowing an instructor to easily fold in a more rigorous treatment, where the time available (and the students' preparation level) allows.

Chapter 11 examines how each of the three major sources of endogeneity – omitted variables, measurement error, and joint determination – induces a correlation between an explanatory variable and the model error. In particular, simultaneous equations are introduced at this point using the simplest possible economic example: a just-identified pair of supply and demand equations.[6] The chapter ends with a brief introduction to simulation methods (with special attention to the bootstrap and its implementation in Stata), in the context of answering the perennial question about asymptotic methods, "How large a sample is really necessary?"

Chapter 12 continues the discussion of endogeneity initiated in Chapter 11 – with particular emphasis on the "reverse causality" source of endogeneity and on the non-equivalence of

[5] In particular, see Active Learning Exercises 10b and 10c in the Table of Contents. Also, even though their primary focus is on 2SLS, students can begin working on the OLS-related portions of Active Learning Exercises 12a, 12b, and 12c at this point.

[6] Subsequently – in Chapter 12, where instrumental variables estimation is covered – 2SLS is heuristically derived and applied to either a just-identified or an over-identified equation from a system of simultaneous equations. The development here does not dwell on the order and rank conditions for model identification, however.

correlation and causality. Instrumental variables estimation is then developed as the solution to the problem of using a single (valid) instrument to obtain a consistent estimator of the slope coefficient in the Bivariate Regression Model with an endogenous regressor. The approach of restricting attention to this simple model minimizes the algebra needed and leverages the work done in Chapter 11. A derivation of the asymptotic distribution of the instrumental variables estimator is provided in Appendix 12.1, giving the instructor a graceful option to either cover this material or not. The two-stage least squares estimator is then heuristically introduced and applied to the classic Angrist-Krueger (1991) study of the impact of education on log-wages. Several other economic applications, whose sample sizes are more feasible for student-version software, are given as Active Learning Exercises at the end of the chapter.

Attention then shifts, in a pair of chapters – Chapters 13 and 14 – to time-series issues. Because Chapters 17 and 18 cover forecasting in some detail, Chapters 13 and 14 concentrate on the estimation and inference issues raised by time-series data.[7] The focus in Chapter 13 is on how to check the non-autocorrelation assumption on the regression model errors and deal with any violations. The emphasis here is not on named tests (in this case, for serially correlated errors) or on assorted versions of FGLS, but rather on how to sensibly respecify a model's dynamics so as to reduce or eliminate observed autocorrelation in the errors. Chapter 14 then deals with the implementation issues posed by integrated (and cointegrated) time-series, including the practical decision as to whether it is preferable to model the data in levels versus in differences. The "levels" versus "changes" issue is first addressed at this point, in part using insights gained from simulation work reported in Ashley and Verbrugge (2009). These results indicate that it is usually best to model in levels, but to generate inferential conclusions using a straightforward variation on the Lag-Augmented VAR approach of Toda and Yamamoto (1995).[8] On the other hand, the differenced data is easier to work with (because it is far less serially dependent) and it provides the opportunity (via the error-correction formulation) to dis-entangle the long-run and short-run dynamics. Thus, in the end, it is probably best to model the data both ways.[9] This synthesis of the material is carefully developed in the context of a detailed analysis of an illustrative empirical application: modeling monthly U.S. consumption expenditures data. This example also provides a capstone illustration of the diagnostic checking techniques described here.

The last portion of the book (Part III) consists of five chapters on advanced topics and a concluding chapter. These five "topics" chapters will be particularly useful for instructors who are able to move through Chapters 2 through 4 quickly because their students are well prepared; the "Concluding Comments" chapter – Chapter 20 – will be useful to all. Chapters 15 and 16 together provide a brief introduction to the analysis of panel data, and Chapters 17 and 18 together provide a concise introduction to the broad field of time-series analysis and forecasting. Chapter 19 introduces the two main alternatives to OLS for estimating parametric regression models: maximum likelihood estimation (MLE) and the generalized method of moments (GMM). Each of these chapters is described in a bit more detail below.

A great deal of micro-econometric analysis is nowadays based on panel data sets. Chapters 15 and 16 provide a straightforward, but comprehensive, treatment of panel data methods. The issues, and requisite panel-specific methods, for the basic situation – with strictly exogenous explanatory variables – are first carefully explained in Chapter 15, all in the context of an empirical example. This material

[7] Most of the usual (and most crucial) issues in using regression models for prediction are, in any case, covered much earlier – in Section 8.3.

[8] See Ashley, R., and R. Verbrugge (2009), "To Difference or Not to Difference: A Monte Carlo Investigation of Inference in Vector Autoregression Models." *International Journal of Data Analysis Techniques and Strategies1(3)*: 242–274 (ashley-mac.econ.vt.edu/working_papers/varsim.pdf) and Toda, H. Y., and T. Yamamoto (1995), "Statistical Inference in Vector Autoregressions with Possibly Integrated Processes," *J. Econometrics 66*, 225–250.

[9] The "difference" versus "detrend" issue comes up again in Section 18.1, where it is approached (and resolved) a bit differently, from a "time-series analysis" rather than a "time-series econometrics" perspective.

concentrates on the Fixed Effects and then on the Random Effects estimators. Then dynamics, in the form of lagged dependent variables, are added to the model in Chapter 16. (Many readers will be a bit surprised to find that the Random Effects estimator is still consistent in this context, so long as the model errors are homoscedastic and any failures in the strict exogeneity assumption are not empirically consequential.) Finally, the First-Differences model is introduced for dealing with endogeneity (as well as dynamics) via instrumental variables estimation. This IV treatment leads to an unsatisfactory 2SLS estimator, which motivates a detailed description of how to apply the Arellano-Bond estimator in working with such models. The description of the Arellano-Bond estimator does not go as deep (because GMM estimation is not covered until Chapter 19), but sufficient material is provided that the student can immediately begin working productively with panel data.

The primary focus of much applied economic work is on inferential issues – i.e., on the statistical significance of the estimated parameter on a particular explanatory variable whose inclusion in the model is prescribed by theory, or on a 95% confidence interval for a parameter whose value is policy-relevant. In other applied settings, however, forecasting is paramount. Chapters 17 and 18, which provide an introduction to the broad field of time-series analysis and forecasting, are particularly useful in the latter context. Chapter 17 begins with a careful treatment of forecasting theory, dealing with the fundamental issue of when (and to what extent) it is desirable to forecast with the conditional mean. The chapter then develops the basic tools – an understanding of the sample correlogram and the ability to invert a lag structure – needed in order to use Box-Jenkins (ARMA) methods to identify, estimate, and diagnostically check a univariate linear model for a time-series and to then obtain useful short-term conditional mean forecasts from it. These ideas and techniques are then extended – in Chapter 18 – to a variety of extensions of this framework into multivariate and nonlinear time-series modeling.

Up to this point in the book, regression analysis is basically framed in terms of least-squares estimation of parameterized models for the conditional mean of the variable whose sample fluctuations are to be "explained." As explicitly drawn out for the Bivariate Regression Model in Chapter 5, this is equivalent to fitting a straight line to a scatter diagram of the sample data.[10] Chapter 19 succinctly introduces the two most important parametric alternatives to this "curve-fitting" approach: maximum likelihood estimation and the generalized method of moments.

In the first part of Chapter 19 the maximum likelihood estimation framework is initially explained – as was least squares estimation in Part I of the book – in terms of the simple problem of estimating the mean and variance of a normally distributed variable. The primary advantage of the MLE approach is its ability to handle latent variable models, so a second application is then given to a very simple binary-choice regression model. In this way, the first sections of Chapter 19 provide a practical introduction to the entire field of "limited dependent variables" modeling.

The remainder of Chapter 19 provides an introduction to the Generalized Method of Moments (GMM) modeling framework. In the GMM approach, parameter identification and estimation are achieved through matching posited population moment conditions to analogous sample moments, where these sample moments depend on the coefficient estimates. The GMM framework thus directly involves neither least-squares curve-fitting nor estimation of the conditional mean. GMM is really the only graceful approach for estimating a rational expectations model via its implied Euler equation. Of more frequent relevance, it is currently the state-of-the-art approach for estimating IV regression models, especially where heteroscedastic model errors are an issue. Chapter 19 introduces GMM via a detailed description of the simplest non-trivial application to such an IV regression model: the one-parameter, two-instrument case. The practical application of GMM estimation is then illustrated using a

[10] The analogous point, using a horizontal straight line "fit" to a plot of the sample data versus observation number, is made in Chapter 3. And the (necessarily more abstract) extension to the fitting of a hyperplane to the sample data is described in Chapter 9. The corresponding relationship between the estimation of a parameterization of the conditional median of the dependent variable and estimation via least absolute deviations fitting is briefly explained in each of these cases also.

familiar full-scale empirical model, the well-known Angrist-Krueger (1991) model already introduced in Chapter 12: in this model there are 11 parameters to be estimated, using 40 moment conditions.

Even the simple one-parameter GMM estimation example, however, requires a linear-algebraic formulation of the estimator. This linear algebra (its only appearance in the book) is relegated to Appendix 19.1, where it is unpacked for this example. But this exigency marks a natural stopping-point for the exposition given here. Chapter 20 concludes the book with some sage – if, perhaps, opinionated – advice.

A great deal of important and useful econometrics was necessarily left out of the present treatment. Additional topics (such as nonparametric regression, quantile regression, Bayesian methods, and additional limited dependent variables models) could perhaps be covered in a subsequent edition.

WITH REGARD TO COMPUTER SOFTWARE

While sample computer commands and examples of the resulting output – mostly using Stata, and very occasionally using Eviews – are explicitly integrated into the text, this book is not designed to be a primer on any particular econometrics software package. There are too many different programs in widespread use for that to be useful. In any case, most students are rather good at learning the mechanics of software packages on their own. Instead, this book is more fundamentally designed, to help students develop a confident understanding of the part they often have great difficulty learning on their own: the underlying theory and practice of econometrics.

In fact, generally speaking, learning how to instruct the software to apply various econometric techniques to the data is not the tough part of this topic. Rather, the challenge is in in learning how to decide which techniques to apply and how to interpret the results. Consequently, the most important object here is to teach students how to become savvy, effective users of whatever software package comes their way. Via an appropriate amount of econometric theory (which is especially modest up through Chapter 10), a sequence of detailed examples, and exercises using actual economic data, this book can help an instructor equip students to tackle real-world econometric modeling using any software package.

In particular – while no knowledgeable person would choose Excel as an econometrics package – it is even possible to teach a good introductory econometrics course using Parts I and II of this book in conjunction with Excel. The main limitation in that case, actually, is that students would not themselves be able to compute the White-Eicker robust standard error estimates discussed in Chapter 10.[11]

An instructor using Stata, however, will find this book particularly easy to use, in that the appropriate implementing Stata commands are all noted, albeit sometimes (in Part I) using footnotes. It should not be at all difficult, however, to convert these into analogous commands for other packages, as the essential content here lies in explaining what one is asking the software to do – and why. Also, all data sets are supplied as comma-delimited (*.csv) files – as well as in Stata's proprietary format – so that any econometric software program can easily read them.

WITH REGARD TO STATISTICAL TABLES

Where a very brief table containing a few critical points is needed in order to illustrate a particular point, such a table is integrated right into the text. In Table 4-1 of Chapter 4, for example, a tabulation of a handful of critical points for the Student's t distribution exhibits the impact on the length of an estimated 95% confidence interval (for the mean of a normally distributed variate) of having to estimate its variance using a limited sample of data.

[11] And, of course, it is well known that Excel's implementation of multiple regression is not numerically well-behaved.

In general, however, tables of tail areas and critical points for the normal, χ^2, Student's t, and F distribution are functionally obsolete – as is the skill of reading values off of them. Ninety-nine times out of a hundred, the econometric software in use computes the necessary p-values for us: the valuable skill is in understanding the assumptions underlying their calculation and how to diagnostically check these assumptions. And, in the one-hundredth case, it is a matter of moments to load up a spreadsheet – e.g., Excel – and calculate the relevant tail area or critical point using a worksheet function.[12]

Consequently, this book does not included printed statistical tables.

SUPPLEMENTARY MATERIALS

A number of supplementary materials are posted on the companion Web site for this book, www.wiley.com/college/ashley. These include:

- Active Learning Exercises listed in the Table of Contents, including their accompanying data sets and any computer programs needed. Answer keys for these Exercises are posted also.
- Answer keys for all of the end-of-chapter exercises.
- Windows programs which compute tail areas for the normal, χ^2, t, and F distributions.
- PowerPoint slides for each chapter.
- Image Gallery – equations, tables, and figures – in JPEG format for each chapter. Sample presentation files based on these, in Adobe Acrobat PDF format, are also provided for each chapter.

HETEROGENEITY IN LEARNING STYLES

Some students learn best by reading a coherent description of the ideas, techniques, and applications in a textbook. Other students learn best by listening to an instructor work through a tough section and asking questions. Still other students learn best by working homework exercises, on their own or in groups, which deepen their understanding of the material. Most likely, every student needs all of these course components, in individually specific proportions.

In recognition of the fact that many students need to "do something" in order to really engage with the material, the text is peppered with what are here called "Active Learning Exercises." These are so important that the next section is devoted to describing them.

[12] The syntax for the relevant Excel spreadsheet function syntax is quoted in the text where these arise, as is a citation to a standard work quoting the computing approximations used in these worksheet functions. Stand-alone Windows programs implementing these approximations are posted at Web site www.wiley.com/college/ashley.

WORKING WITH DATA IN THE "ACTIVE LEARNING EXERCISES"

Most chapters of this textbook contain at least one "Active Learning Exercise" or "ALE." The titles of these Active Learning Exercises are given in the Table of Contents and listed on the inside covers of the book. Whereas the purpose of the end-of-chapter exercises is to help the student go deeper into the chapter material – and worked examples using economic data are integrated into the text – these Active Learning Exercises are designed to engage the student in structured, active exercises.

A typical Active Learning Exercise involves specific activities in which the student is either directed to download actual economic data from an academic/government Web site or is provided with data (real or simulated) from the companion Web site for this book, www.wiley.com/college/ashley. (This Web site will also provide access to the latest version of each Active Learning Exercise, as some of these exercises will need to be revised occasionally as Web addresses and content change.) These exercises will in some cases reproduce and/or expand on empirical results used as examples in the text; in other cases, the Active Learning Exercise will set the student working on new data. A number of the Active Learning Exercises involve replication of a portion of the empirical results of published articles from the economics literature.

The Active Learning Exercises are a more relaxed environment than the text itself, in that one of these exercises might, for example, involve a student in "doing" multiple regression in an informal way long before this topic is reached in the course of the careful development provided in the text. One could think of these exercises as highly structured "mini-projects." In this context, the Active Learning Exercises are also a great way to help students initiate their own term projects.

ACKNOWLEDGMENTS

My thanks to all of my students for their comments on various versions of the manuscript for this book; in particular, I would like to particularly express my appreciation to Bradley Shapiro and to James Boohaker for their invaluable help with the end-of-chapter exercises. Thanks are also due to Alfonso Flores-Lagunes, Chris Parmeter, Aris Spanos, and Byron Tsang for helpful discussions and/ or access to data sets. Andrew Rose was particularly forthcoming in helping me to replicate his very interesting 2005 paper with Frankel in *The Review of Economics and Statistics* quantifying the impact of international trade on environmental air quality variables; this help was crucial to the construction of Active Learning Exercises 10c and 12b. I have benefited from the comments and suggestions from the following reviewers: Alfonso Flores-Lagunes, University of Florida, Gainesville; Scott Gilbert, Southern Illinois University, Carbondale; Denise Hare, Reed College; Alfred A. Haug, University of Otago, New Zealand; Paul A. Jargowsky, Rutgers-Camden; David Kimball, University of Missouri, St. Louis; Heather Tierney, College of Charleston; Margie Tieslau, University of North Texas; and several others who wish to remain anonymous. Thanks are also due to Lacey Vitteta, Jennifer Manias, Emily McGee, and Yee Lyn Song at Wiley for their editorial assistance. Finally, I would also like to thank Rosalind Ashley, Elizabeth Paule, Bill Beville, and George Lobell for their encouragement with regard to this project.

NOTATION

Logical and consistent notation is extremely helpful in keeping track of econometric concepts, particularly the distinction between random variables and realizations of random variables. This section summarizes the principles underlying the notation used below. This material can be skimmed on your first pass: this notational material is included here primarily for reference later on, after the relevant concepts to which the notational conventions apply are explained in the chapters to come.

Uppercase letters from the usual Latin-based alphabet – *X*, *Y*, *Z*, etc. – are used below to denote observable data. These will generally be treated as random variables, which will be discussed in Chapter 2. What is most important here is to note that an uppercase letter will be used to denote such a random variable; the corresponding lowercase letter will be used to denote a particular (fixed) realization of it – i.e., the numeric value actually observed. Thus, "*X*" is a random variable, whereas "*x*" is a realization of this random variable. Lowercase letters will *not* be used below to denote the deviation of a variable from its sample mean.

The fixed (but unknown) parameters in the econometric models considered below will usually be denoted by lowercase Greek letters – α, β, γ, δ, and so forth. As we shall see below, these parameters will be estimated using functions of the observable data – "estimators" – which are random variables. Because uppercase Greek letters are easily confused with letters from the Latin-based alphabet, however, such an estimator of a parameter – a random variable because it depends on the observable data, which are random variables – will typically be denoted by placing a hat ("^") over the corresponding lowercase Greek letter. Sample realizations of these parameter estimators will then be denoted by appending an asterisk. Thus, $\hat{\alpha}$ will typically be used to denote an estimator of the fixed parameter α and $\hat{\alpha}^*$ will be used to denote the (fixed) realization of this random variable, based on the particular values of the observable data which were actually observed. Where a second estimator of α needs to be considered, it will be denoted by $\tilde{\alpha}$ or the like. The only exceptions to these notational conventions which you will encounter later are that – so as to be consistent with the standard nomenclature – the usual convention of using $\bar{Y}$ and S^2 to denote the sample mean and variance will be used; sample realizations of these estimators will be denoted $\bar{y}$ and s^2, respectively.

The random error terms in the econometric models developed below will be denoted by uppercase letters from the Latin-based alphabet (typically, *U*, *V*, *N*, etc.) and fixed realizations of these error terms (which will come up very infrequently because model error terms are not, in practice, observable) will be denoted by the corresponding lowercase letter, just as with observable data.

When an econometric model is fit to sample data, however, one obtains observable "fitting errors." These can be usefully thought of as estimators of the model errors. These estimators – which will be random variables because they depend on the observable (random) observations – will be distinguished from the model errors themselves via a superscript "fit" on the corresponding letter for the model error. As with the model errors, the sample realizations of these fitting errors, based on particular realizations of the observable data, will be denoted by the corresponding lowercase letter.

The following table summarizes these notational rules and gives some examples:

	Random Variable	Realization
observable data (*i*th observation)	X_i, Y_i, Z_i	x_i, y_i, z_i
parameter estimator	$\hat{\alpha}$, $\hat{\beta}$, $\hat{\mu}$, $\bar{Y}$, S^2	$\hat{\alpha}^*$, $\hat{\beta}^*$, $\hat{\mu}^*$, $\bar{y}$, s^2
model error (*i*th observation)	U_i, V_i	u_i, v_i
model fitting error (*i*th observation)	U_i^{fit}, V_i^{fit}	u_i^{fit}, v_i^{fit}

Part 1

INTRODUCTION AND STATISTICS REVIEW

This section of the book serves two functions. First – in Chapter 1 – it provides a brief introduction, intended to frame the topic of econometrics and to convey a sense of how this book is organized and what it intends to accomplish. Second, Chapters 2 through 4 provide a concise review of the main statistical foundations necessary for understanding multiple regression analysis at the level presented here. These chapters are intended to be sufficiently detailed as to provide a self-contained refresher on all of the statistical concepts and techniques used up through the treatment, in Chapter 10, of diagnostically checking a multiple regression model with fixed regressors. Additional statistical material – necessary for understanding regression models in which the explanatory variables (regressors) cannot be treated as fixed – is developed in Chapter 11.

On the other hand, the material in Chapters 2 through 4 is not intended to substitute for an introductory statistics course: presuming that you have taken an appropriate prerequisite course, much of the material in these chapters should be review. Consequently, you should expect your instructor to assign a good deal of this material as outside reading, covering in class only those topics – perhaps including the distribution of a weighted sum of random variables or the optimality properties of estimators – which are often not emphasized in an introductory statistics course. In any case, you are strongly encouraged to read these chapters carefully: virtually all of the terms, ideas, and techniques reviewed in these chapters are used later in the book.

1

Introduction

1.1 PRELIMINARIES

Most of the big questions in economics are, in the end, empirical questions. Microeconomic theory predicts that an increase in the minimum wage will cause unemployment to increase. Does it? Trade theory predicts that an expansion of international trade at least potentially makes everyone better off. Does it? Macroeconomic theory predicts that an increase in government spending on goods and services will cause output to increase – or not, depending on the theory. Does it? And so forth.

People can (and do) argue vociferously about these and similar issues based on theoretical aesthetics or on political/philosophical prejudices, but what matters in the end is how well these predictions measure up when confronted with relevant data. This book provides an introduction to the econometric tools which are necessary for making that confrontation valid and productive.

These same econometric tools are also crucially useful to policymakers who need quantitative estimates of model parameters so that they can predict the impact of proposed policy changes, and to forecasters who want to predict future values of economic time-series. In both of these cases, the estimates and predictions are themselves almost useless without explicit estimates of their imprecision, but, again, this book provides an introduction to the tools used to provide those estimates.

Modern econometrics software packages – such as Stata and EViews – make the required data manipulations very easy once you "know the ropes" for a given program. Indeed, no one really needs to work through a textbook in order to use such software to apply various econometric methods. The problem is that econometric techniques are sharp-edged tools: very powerful, and therefore dangerous when used indiscriminately. It is almost trivially easy to use the software to obtain econometric results. But all that the software really does is mindlessly evaluate formulas and print out the results in nicely formatted columns. Ensuring that the sample data is consistent with the statistical assumptions underlying these formulas, and meaningfully interpreting the numerical output, is a different story: the computing equipment and software is pretty clueless in this arena. Thus, the mechanical aspect of obtaining econometric results is fairly straightforward – the problematic part is learning how to obtain results which are as high in quality as possible (given the raw materials available) and how to gauge just how useful the results are – or are not. *That* requires skills born of understanding how these tools work. And that is what this book is intended to help you begin developing.

1.2 EXAMPLE: IS GROWTH GOOD FOR THE POOR?

A decade ago a World Trade Organization conference was considered newsworthy only by the likes of the *The Wall Street Journal* and *The Economist*. Nowadays, the host city prepares for large-scale demonstrations and occasional rioting. Various groups are bitterly divided as to whether the net impact of the expansion of world trade in the 1990s was a good thing for the majority of the world's population, even though economic theory is fairly unequivocal in predicting that globalization leads to an expansion in world economic output.

Obviously, there is a lot more involved in human well-being than per capita real output, but surely this is a constructive place to start. In a 2002 journal article, Dollar and Kraay at the World Bank[1] addressed the issue of whether or not the real growth induced by globalization in the 1980s and 1990s was good for the world's poor. They used data on each of 92 countries to model the relationship between its per capita real GDP growth rate – "$meangrow_1$" ... "$meangrow_{92}$" – during this period and the corresponding growth rate in per capita real GDP received by the poorest 20% of its population, "$poorgrow_1$" ... "$poorgrow_{92}$".[2]

They began by examining a scatterplot or of the data. This corresponds to graphing each observation on "*poorgrow*" against the corresponding observation on "*meangrow*" for each of the 92 countries. Once the data is entered into a computer program, this is very easy. For example, using Stata, the command "scatter *poorgrow meangrow*" produces the scatterplot in Figure 1-1.

Alternatively, using EViews, one can create an essentially identical scatterplot by creating a group containing the data on *poorgrow* and *meangrow* and selecting the view/graph/scatter/simple_scatter menu option (Figure 1-2).

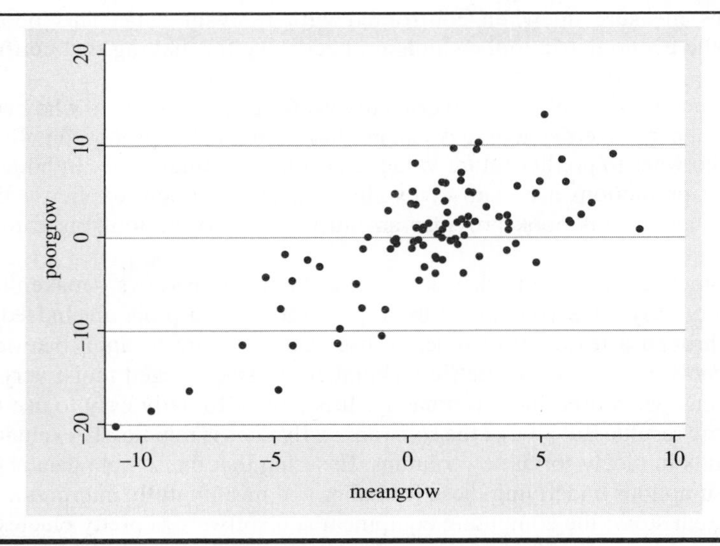

Figure 1-1 Stata Scatterplot of $poorgrow_i$ versus $meangrow_i$ Data.

[1] Dollar, David and Aart Kraay (2002), "Growth Is Good for the Poor," *Journal of Economic Growth 7,* pp. 195–225; a working paper version and their data can be found at www.worldbank.org/research/growth.

[2] Dollar and Kraay also modeled the level of per capita real GDP for the poor in each country, but here only the data on growth rates are used; a detailed discussion of this issue is given in Ashley (2008), "Growth May Be Good for the Poor, But Decline Is Disastrous: On the Non-Robustness of the Dollar-Kraay Result," *International Review of Economics and Finance 17,* 333–338.

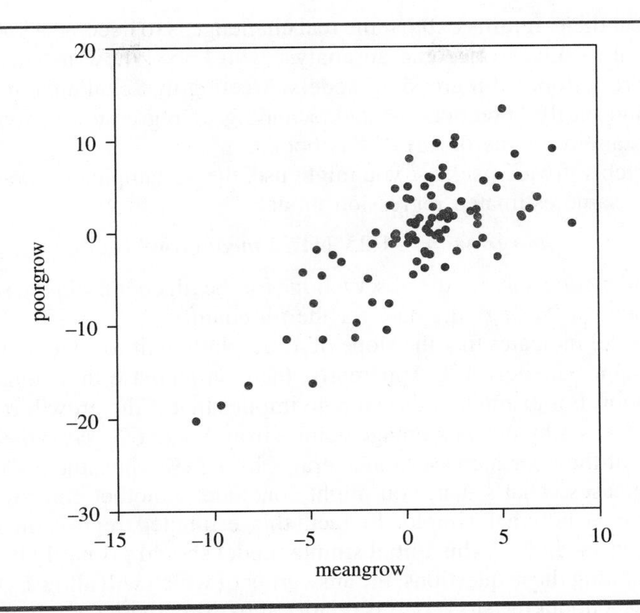

Figure 1-2 EViews Scatterplot of $poorgrow_i$ versus $meangrow_i$ Data

Other econometrics software packages (SAS, MINITAB, etc.) all provide similar functionality and produce similar output; only the form of the necessary commands will differ from one computer program to another. In the chapters to come, Stata output or EViews output will occasionally be quoted so that you can get used to both the differences and the similarities; most typically, it will be Stata commands which are quoted, however, because this is usually clearer than trying to describe EViews menu options.

Evidently, there is a direct relationship between *poorgrow* and *meangrow*: the countries with higher values of *meangrow* clearly tend to have higher values of *poorgrow*. Thus, these scatterplots make it obvious that the poor in these countries do benefit from real growth in the sense that per capita real GDP for the poorest 20% of each country clearly grows faster in countries whose average per capita real GDP growth rate is higher. But do the poor share proportionately in this growth, or does the growth mainly improve real per capita incomes for the middle and upper classes? If the slope of a straight line representing this relationship is one, then the poor do share proportionately when a country's growth rate increases, and such an increase has no average impact on the distribution of income across individuals in a country. In contrast, if the slope of the line corresponding to this relationship is less than one, then an increase in the growth rate makes the poor better off in absolute terms but makes them worse off in terms of their relative share of national output.

A scatterplot is clearly effective in uncovering and displaying the direct relationship between *poorgrow* and *meangrow*, but – as you will find out for yourself in working Active Learning Exercise 1b (available at www.wiley.com/college/ashley) – it is not so effective in addressing this question about the slope of the relationship: a quantitative model for *poorgrow* is necessary in order to say anything credibly useful about the slope of this relationship.

That is where the regression modeling techniques covered in this book shine. The issue is *not* how to estimate a regression model. Indeed, once the data are entered into an appropriate computer program, obtaining an estimated regression model is so easy that one hardly need take an econometrics course to figure it out. Using EViews, for example, a handful of mouse clicks does the job; using Stata, one need only enter "regress *poorgrow meangrow*" on the command line; the task is similarly almost trivial using SAS, MINITAB, or other commercially available software packages.

What's the big deal then? It turns out that the real challenge is to become a knowledgeable user of econometrics software – i.e., to become an analyst who knows how to adequately specify and meaningfully interpret estimated regression models. Meeting that challenge requires a thorough – partly theoretical and partly "practical" – understanding of regression analysis. Helping you to develop that understanding is the object of this book.

Regardless of which software package you might use, the 92 sample observations in this data set yield essentially the same estimated regression model:

$$poorgrow_i = -1.25 + 1.31\, meangrow_i + u_i^{\text{fit}} \tag{1-1}$$

where $poorgrow_i$ and $meangrow_i$ are the observations for the ith country in the sample and u_i^{fit} is the error the model makes in "fitting" the data for the ith country.

This estimated model indicates that the slope of a straight line fit to the data in the scatterplot for this relationship is approximately 1.3. Apparently, then, an increase in a country's growth rate is quite good for the poor. For example, this estimate implies that if the growth rate in per capita real GDP in a country increases by one percentage point – from 5% to 6%, say – then the growth rate of per capita real GDP of the poor increases, on average, by 1.31%; thus, the poor's share of national income actually increases. That's that, you might conclude – another controversy settled.

Unfortunately, life is not that simple. In fact, this estimated regression model raises more questions than it answers! Indeed, this initial simple model should primarily be viewed as a useful framework for stimulating those questions, the answering of which will allow us to credibly quantify what can in fact be said about the slope of this relationship using these data. In particular, this initial estimated model raises the following questions:

- Because $meangrow_i$ enters the estimated model with a positive coefficient, it would appear that there is indeed a direct relationship between the growth rate of per capita real GDP in a country and the growth rate of per capita real GDP that goes to the poor in that country. Does the model based on this relationship do a reasonably good job of explaining the variation in $poorgrow_i$ across the 92 countries? How could we know?
- Given that there are only 92 observations, is this estimate of the slope coefficient a high-quality estimate – i.e., one that does a good job of using this limited amount of data? How can we conceptualize this concept of estimator "goodness" in such a way that we might be able to convince ourselves that this is, in fact, a good estimate? What things would we need to investigate, check, and maybe correct in our model as part of a process which will provide us with a reasonable level of assurance that this estimate of the slope coefficient is as accurate as it can be?
- And how accurate **is** this slope coefficient estimate, anyway? In particular, is it sufficiently precise that we have obtained credible evidence that the "actual" slope of this relationship differs from one? Is it sufficiently precise that we have obtained credible evidence that the actual slope even differs from zero? What things would we need to assume about the data in order to quantify the strength of this evidence? How can we use the sample data to check whether or not these assumptions are sufficiently reasonable approximations in this instance that our results with regard to these two propositions about the slope are credible?

By the end of Chapter 10 you will have learned how to answer all these questions. Indeed, we will revisit this example in Section 10.8 and apply the new tools developed at that point to ferret out what this data set actually does have to say about whether or not growth is good for the poor. In fact, the results obtained at that point will shed a disturbing new light on Dollar and Kraay's upbeat conclusion that the poor share equiproportionately in recent macroeconomic growth.[3]

[3] Your results in Active Learning Exercise 1c (available at www.wiley.com/college/ashley) will foreshadow these Chapter 10 results.

1.3 WHAT'S TO COME

Chapter 2 provides a concise summary of the probability concepts needed in order to understand regression modeling. In Chapter 3 these concepts are used to tackle the quintessential basic statistics problem: the estimation of the mean and variance of a normally distributed random variable. In Chapter 4 these results are used to develop the relevant statistical inference machinery for testing hypotheses and for obtaining confidence intervals in that context. Estimating the mean of a normally distributed random variable turns out to be equivalent to estimating the intercept in a very simple regression model with no explanatory variables. Chapters 5 through 8 extend the estimation and inference results of Chapters 3 and 4 to a more interesting (and much more useful) regression model in which the sample variation in the dependent variable is modeled as being due to sample variation in a single explanatory variable. In Chapter 9 these results are extended – somewhat informally, because matrix algebra is not used in this book – to the full multiple regression model, in which the dependent variable's sample variation is taken to be due to sample fluctuations in a number of explanatory variables. An ongoing theme of Chapters 3 through 9 is that the properties of the parameter estimators and the validity of the statistical inference machinery hinge on the satisfaction of a set of assumptions which underlie the statistical framework being used. The spirit of the enterprise, however, is that we do not make these assumptions blindly – rather, we use the sample data itself to examine the validity of these assumptions for the case at hand. Chapters 10 and 13 describe simple, practical methods for operationalizing this examination, for models involving cross-sectional and time-series data, respectively.[4]

The scope of this book is limited almost entirely to single-equation modeling. In some economic modeling contexts, however, this limitation is quite restrictive. One salient example is when one models equilibrium price and quantity in a market. In this situation the sample behavior of these two variables is jointly determined by a pair of simultaneous equations, one for demand and one for supply. Even where our interest centers firmly on just one equation – e.g., for the observed price – in such a setting it must be recognized that the observed quantity sold is actually jointly determined with the price: this simultaneous determination of the two variables notably affects our ability to estimate the model parameters.

Such simultaneity is an example of the "endogenous regressors" problem examined in Chapter 11, but it is by no means the only example: problems with regressor endogeneity can arise whenever explanatory variables are corrupted by substantial amounts of measurement error, or when important explanatory variables have been inadvertently omitted from the model, or when the fluctuations in the regressor are partly driven by the fluctuations in the dependent variable rather than solely vice-versa. In fact, it is fair to say that many of the toughest challenges in applied economics stem from endogeneity issues such as these. The material in Chapter 11 enables the reader to understand the nature of the parameter estimation problems that arise with endogenous regressors; Chapter 12 introduces the most common econometric procedure – instrumental variables estimation – used to deal with these problems.

The quantity of data available for applied economic analysis has expanded dramatically in the past couple of decades, primarily due to the creation of large "panel data" sets. A cross-section of 92 countries provides the analyst with just 92 observations for estimating model parameters. But if one has a panel of five years of annual data on each country, suddenly the estimation sample increases to 460 observations! Similarly, a modern household-survey data set might contain observations on each household for only a few years, but have survey data on thousands of households. These data bonanzas become a mixed blessing, however, once one recognizes that the 92 countries (and the

[4] Checking the assumptions needed for dealing with time-series data requires the additional probability theory material covered in Chapter 11, so it is delayed a bit.

thousands of household respondents) are actually all different. Chapters 15 and 16 cover the methods which have been developed for confronting this heterogeneity in panel data sets.

Chapter 17 starts out by examining the theoretical issue "What constitutes a good forecast?" and goes on to provide a concise introduction to what is called "time-series analysis." This is a substantial area which is actually distinct from the "time-series econometrics" covered in Chapters 13 and 14 . In both frameworks, a time-series is a sequence of observations ordered in time, such as quarterly GDP observations for a particular country. In "time-series econometrics" the focus is on estimating the parameters in a relationship – the form of which is usually suggested by economic theory – in which a substantial number of regressors are typically posited to explain the sample variation in the dependent variable. By way of contrast, in "time-series analysis" the focus is on using the data itself to specify the form of the model, but the dependent variable is typically modeled as depending only on its own recent past, and perhaps the recent past of a couple of other variables. This latter approach is not always as useful for testing the predictions of economic theory, but it turns out to be surprisingly effective at producing short-term forecasting models. Chapters 17 and 18 survey this very practical field.

Up through Chapter 18 the emphasis here is on least-squares estimation of the parameters in regression models; Chapter 19 widens this purview to include two very important alternatives to least-squares estimation: the maximum likelihood and the generalized method of moments approaches. These approaches make it possible to analyze regression models in contexts which would otherwise be infeasible. For example, suppose that the object is not to explain or forecast the numerical value of an economic variable, but rather to model the determinants of a binary choice: e.g., a household might decide to enter the labor force and look for a job – or not. This binary decision is not itself a number, yet it can be extremely useful to quantitatively model the degree to which observable numerical economic variables (such as educational attainments, the level of the minimum wage, etc.) impact this decision. Surprisingly, this can be done – by applying the maximum likelihood estimation framework to an extension of the regression modeling framework developed in Chapters 5 through 18.

Chapter 20 ends the book with some general advice; you might find this chapter worthy of a first look early on. Also, you might at this point want to look at Active Learning Exercise 1b (available at www.wiley.com/college/ashley), which illustrates how even so seemingly straightforward a tool as a scatterplot can yield surprisingly deceptive conclusions.

Active Learning Exercise 1a: An Econometrics "Time Capsule"

Instructions:

1. Read the fictional account (appended) of what you might hope will be a quite atypical day in your first applied economics job. This day calls for econometric expertise and skills of the kind you will be developing through your work with this book, expertise and skills which you probably do not have at this time.
2. Fill out the simple survey form at the end of this fictional account, indicating to what degree you feel capable at the present time of dealing with the indicated challenge. Be forthright in your answer: no one but you will ever read it.
3. Put your completed form aside in a safe place or – if your instructor has so indicated – bring it to class. In the latter case, your instructor will supply an envelope in which you can seal your form, indicating only your name on the outside of the envelope. Your instructor will collect, store, and (on the last day of class) return your envelope.

4. You can view this exercise as a message from yourself now to yourself at the end of the term. I hope that after you work with this exercise, you will see a substantial opportunity to use your encounter with the material presented in this book in such a way as to increase your power to act in the world. And, when you open this "time capsule" several months from now, I hope that you will discover that your power to use sample data to meaningfully quantify economic relationships has indeed substantially increased.

Time: 5:30 p.m.
Date: January 16, 2009
Location: A cramped, but not windowless, cubicle somewhere in the World Bank building in Washington, D.C.

Scenario:
Three months into your first real job – as a junior analyst at the World Bank – you are (you think) reaching the end of a long day. You look up as your boss drifts distractedly into your cubicle and stares absently out the window at the not-very-distant burning buildings lighting up the darkening cityscape. She begins to speak,

"Well, the good news is that the bulk of the rioting is moving off to the north now and they're pretty sure they can douse those fires before they reach here."

After working for this woman for three months, you are ready with the right response:

"And the bad news?"

"The bad news is that the three of us are stuck here until they can free up another helicopter to lift us over to Arlington."

"The three of us?"

"Yeah. You, me, and the Director. It seems that you were too wrapped up in your project to pay any attention to the evacuation alarms. And I was stuck listening to the Director whine on and on about her obsession with how all this conflict and rioting is actually fueled by a resolvable misunderstanding about the facts of economic reality rather than by any essential difference in values between us and the folks out there kicking up the fuss."

"Resolvable misunderstanding? Are you nuts? Those 'folks' you're talking about are literally wreaking havoc all over the city!"

"Yeah, well, the whole dispute hinges on a belief by the rioters that the globalization and economic growth that we've been so busy promoting has actually made poor people poorer and increased income inequality all over the world – especially where it's been most successful. But our Director is certain that this belief is factually incorrect. Her theory is that if we could puncture the belief system by *showing* that the reality is just the opposite, then the rioting would collapse."

At this point you see a glint starting up in your boss's eye and you know you're in for trouble. Obviously, it was no accident that she has turned up here in your cubicle ... She goes on,

"In fact, the Director just gave me this url for a Web site with just the data needed to make her point – figures on average per capita income and per capita income for the poorest 20% of the population in a bunch of countries. Why don't you go look at it? Maybe you can use it to show that per capita income for the poorest people in each country goes up right in pace with average per capita income!"

Suddenly, even a helicopter ride over a burning city is starting to sound attractive. But before you can interrupt, she continues excitedly,

"You'll need to retrieve the data. That won't be so hard. But it won't be in the right format to get into Stata; you'll have to import it into Excel first. Then you can make a scatterplot to look for a relationship, but that won't let you test the hypothesis that the coefficient in the relationship is really one. Hmmm, and if you run a regression so you can estimate the coefficient and actually test whether it is really one, no one will believe you unless you've diagnostically checked your model. We'd better get this right the first time: if it turns out that your results are an artifact of an invalid statistical test, we'll be worse off than before... "

At this point you break in, "But what if the relationship is different for Third World countries than for developed ones or for countries that trade a lot versus countries that don't – won't that mess it all up?"

This stops her in her tracks for a minute, but she is not to be dissuaded: "Oh, that's okay. You can control for the development issue with a dummy variable for whether the observation refers to a Third World country. And that Web site has each country's total exports and imports in it – you can use the ratio of the sum of those to GDP as a measure of how much the country trades. That means you'll have to rely on multiple regression, though – simple scatterplot won't allow you to control for those things. You couldn't get real inferences out of a scatterplot anyway. Better still make them, though – they really help communicate what the relationships look like in a simple way."

"Wait a minute," you respond, " you mean I'm supposed to start on this *now*?"

"Right. *Now.* I need this analysis by 9:00. The Director is so sure that this will work out that she has scheduled an emergency meeting with the President for 9:30. We've got to be out of here by then anyway, or else we're toast along with the building."

"I thought you said they thought they could control the fires before they reached here!"

"Well, I exaggerated that a bit; I thought it might distract you from listening to me... "

Okay, so maybe your real life won't be quite that dramatic five years from now. And the President (much less the rioters) might not be all that willing to even look at your results. Nevertheless, circle your response to the following statement (using the 1 to 10 scale given) and then take a few minutes to write a brief paragraph on the following sheet describing your reaction to this assignment by your new boss.

Given what I know now (and plenty of time) I could do a reasonable job of handling this assignment as my boss has described it.

1. You're kidding. I have no idea how to do what she is suggesting. And what is this business about "dummy variables" and "diagnostically checking" a regression model to make sure my results are not an "artifact of an invalid statistical test"?
2.
3.
4.
5.
6.
7.
8.
9.
10. All right – given what I now know, I basically see how to do this at the level she has set up the problem, but I will want a substantial salary raise afterward, especially if this saves the city.

2

A Review of Probability Theory

2.1 INTRODUCTION

This chapter provides a brief review of the probability concepts needed in order to understand econometric modeling at the level presented in this book.[1] The word "review" used here is intended to convey the impression that a typical reader will have been exposed to much of this material before. That's good! "Exposed" is not the same thing as "mastered," however, and mastery is by no means assumed here or in the chapters to follow. You should be neither surprised nor dismayed to find that some of the material in this chapter is either new or treated in greater depth than in your previous encounters with it.

This material in this chapter is of two sorts: vocabulary and techniques.

Under the "vocabulary" heading, the goal in this chapter is to help make sure that you have a firm grasp of the meaning attached to such terms and concepts as

- The expected value of a random variable
- The population variance of a random variable
- The covariance of a pair of random variables
- Statistical independence
- The normal distribution
- The Central Limit Theorem

An understanding of these concepts is essential to all of the work below on parameter estimation and statistical inference. Indeed, a treatment of econometrics not founded on an understanding of these terms would be the equivalent of a course on writing and analyzing poetry without any concepts of rhyme or meter.

Under the "technique" heading, the goal here is to review the basics on how to calculate expectations in general and population variances in particular. The chapter culminates with the derivation of the distribution of a weighted sum of normally distributed random variables. This result is essential preparation for obtaining the sampling distributions of regression model parameter estimators later on. In fact, it is more than preparation: most of the essential derivations in the remainder of the book are really just variations on this one.

[1] Basic mathematical concepts (summation notation and a bit of material on taking partial derivatives) are briefly reviewed in the Mathematics Review section at the end of the book. A review of integral calculus is not included because – despite the presence of a few integrals below in the discussion of continuous random variables – integration itself plays only a very minor role here.

The fact of the matter is that this chapter is not as fun or interesting as Chapter 1. In fact, it is not as engaging as the chapters to follow, either. It is actually one of the most important chapters in the book, however, because this is where we get together on what the words and concepts mean, and this is where the basic techniques underlying the analysis to follow are developed.

2.2 RANDOM VARIABLES

Randomness represents our ignorance. Each time we observe ("pick" or "draw") a random variable – for example, by flipping a coin or by surveying households – the value we observe (its "realization") is typically different. But that's not what makes it random. Fundamentally, what makes a variable random is that we do not know what the value of the realization will be until we make the observation. Generally this is because there is some aspect of the mechanism generating this value which we do not (perhaps cannot) explicitly quantify.

Suppose, for example, that we survey 20 people as to their weekly wage income. These 20 people might all have identical incomes, yet it is quite likely that the 20 reported wage incomes will vary noticeably. This kind of random variation is sensibly called "measurement error." A few of the people will honestly misremember their income: one person because she might be suffering from a cold that day, another because he just came from an argument with his employer. And a number of the rest will more or less knowingly inflate their reported income, to varying degrees, based on their feelings about themselves, the interviewer, or some other aspect of the situation. If we observe a large number of such people – all with identical actual incomes – we might be able to say quite a bit about this measurement error. Still, we simply cannot know ahead of time exactly what income the next person will report. It is therefore random.

Alternatively, we might abstract from measurement error – by requiring each respondent to bring a pay stub along to the interview, for example – and still observe noticeable variation in the reported weekly wage income values, in this case because actual incomes differ across the individuals. What will the income value be for a 21st respondent? We cannot know until he enters the interview room and hands over his pay stub. Again, if we observe a large number of people, we can say quite a bit about the likely variation in weekly wage income; still, we can't know ahead of time exactly what income the next person will report – it is therefore random.

Note that we might observe or measure other aspects of each respondent – age, weight, gender, education level, etc. – and these data might allow us to use the techniques described in this book to do a pretty good job of modeling how weekly wage income depends on these observable variables. If we have an opportunity to first observe or measure these other attributes of the next respondent, then our model might allow us to predict this next respondent's income with some degree of accuracy. In that case, the weekly wage income of the next respondent would be less random – in a sense to be conceptualized later in this chapter – than if either the model or the observed attributes were unavailable. Indeed, in many cases the point of econometric modeling is to reduce the randomness of economic variables (conditional on observed explanatory variable data) in precisely this way.[2]

There are two kinds of random variables: discrete and continuous. We begin with a consideration of discrete random variables because they are mathematically simpler: almost everyone finds summation easier to understand than integration, and double sums vastly more comprehensible than double integrals. Yet virtually all of the key concepts – expectations, the population mean and variance of a single random variable, the population covariance of a pair of random variables, etc. – can be amply described using discrete variables. Indeed, the main reason continuous random

[2] But not always. For example, one's objective might be to test a theoretical hypothesis that one or another of these observed aspects is (or is not) a significant determinant of weekly wage income, in which case the randomness reduction, while potentially important, is not the central point of the modeling effort.

variables are also treated in this chapter is that we need to understand gaussian random variables, which are continuous.[3]

2.3 DISCRETE RANDOM VARIABLES

A discrete random variable can take on any one of a given, usually finite, set of values. In this instance it is convenient to think of the world taking on m possible states, in each of which the random variable takes on some specified value:

Discretely distributed random variable:

$$\begin{aligned} Y &= c_1 \text{ with probability } p_1 \\ &= c_2 \text{ with probability } p_2 \\ &\quad \text{(etc.)} \\ &= c_m \text{ with probability } p_m \end{aligned} \tag{2-1}$$

Here, for example, the random variable Y takes on value c_1 in state 1, value c_2 in state 2, and so forth. The m possible states can be numbered as we wish; it is convenient to number them in such a way that $c_1 \leq c_2 \leq \dots \leq c_m$. The value of Y is no longer random once it is observed; below, the value of such a "realization" of Y is distinguished from Y itself by using the lower-case letter, y.[4]

The number p_j is called "the probability of state j" and the set of numbers $\{p_1 \cdots p_m\}$ is called "the probability distribution of Y." Here we will use the "frequentist" interpretation of probability[5] and define p_j to be the fraction of the realizations of Y which would be observed in state j over an arbitrarily large collection of realizations. Clearly, that interpretation implies that $0 \leq p_j \leq 1$ for all j.

Evidently, then (for $m \geq 6$) the probability of observing realizations of Y in the closed interval $[c_3, c_6]$, say, is just $p_3 + p_4 + p_6$. Because the probability of observing Y *somewhere* in its allowed interval must equal one, the sum of the probabilities must be one – i.e., $\sum_{j=1}^{m} p_j = 1$.[6] The standard terminology for this is that the probability distribution is normalized to one.

The classic example of a discrete random variable is the number of dots showing on a six-sided die. Clearly, $m = 6$ in this case and, if the die is "fair," one would expect the p_i to be essentially equal to 1/6. But many – indeed, almost all – measured economic variables are in fact discretely distributed. For example, aggregate employment is tabulated in thousands, and most national income accounting data is only calculated to the nearest million dollars. Indeed, in view of the fact that currency for paying out a quantity less than \$0.01 does not even exist, all dollar-denominated economic variables are inherently discretely distributed.

The probability distribution contains all that can be known about the random variable Y prior to observing it, but we are often not interested in all that can be known: in many instances all that we want or need to know about a random variable is how large it is and how random it is. These two

[3] Summation notation – including all that you need to know about double sums – is covered in the Mathematics Review section at the end of the book.

[4] This notational convention is fairly standard in the literature and will be used consistently throughout this book; see the "Notation" section, immediately after the preface, for a complete description.

[5] E.g., see John Freund (1971), *Mathematical Statistics* Prentice-Hall, Englewood Cliffs, p. 36.

[6] Summation notation will be used quite extensively in this book. The reader is urged to consult the Mathematics Review section at the end of the book for a summary of the necessary background in both single and double summation notation. Note that a good way to tackle any expression involving summation notation is to write it out explicitly with the upper limit set to 2 or 3. For example, with $m = 2$ this expression reduces to $p_1 + p_2 = 1$.

aspects of a random variable are conceptualized by its expected value and its variance, each of which is defined and discussed below. **The importance of these two concepts cannot be overstated: almost everything we will do from here on involves your ability to understand and manipulate these two quantities.**

For a discrete random variable, the expected value or expectation is very simple: it is just the value that the random variable takes on in each state of the world, weighted by the probability with which that state occurs:

$$\text{Expected value of } Y \equiv E[Y] \equiv \mu_Y \equiv \sum_{j=1}^{m} c_j\, p_j = c_1\, p_1 + c_2 p_2 + \ldots + c_m p_m \tag{2-2}$$

By custom, the Greek letter μ is used to denote $E[Y]$, with an appropriate subscript appended where one wants or needs to emphasize which random variable is at issue.

Note that the expected value of Y is an inherently *fixed* number which can be calculated directly from the probability distribution of Y and the set of values $(c_1 \ldots c_m)$ that Y takes on in the m states: no observations on Y (i.e., sample data) are needed! For example, if Y is the number of dots showing on a six-sided (crooked) die with $p_1 = 3/6, p_2 = 1/6, p_3 = 2/6$, and $p_4 = p_5 = p_6 = 0$, then $c_1 = 1,\ c_2 = 2,\ \ldots\ c_6 = 6$, and $E[Y]$ is just $1(3/6) + 2(1/6) + 3(2/6)$, or $\frac{11}{6}$.

The expected value of Y is also called the "population mean of Y," which is often abbreviated to just "the mean of Y." Particularly in view of this common abbreviation for $E[Y]$, it is essential to carefully distinguish $E[Y]$ from $\bar{y}$, the "sample mean of Y":

$$\text{Sample Mean of } Y \equiv \overline{Y} \equiv \frac{1}{N}\sum_{i=1}^{N} Y_i \tag{2-3}$$

The expected value of Y, as we have seen, is a fixed, non-random quantity – it is just a weighted sum of the m possible values the random variable Y can take on. In contrast, $\overline{Y}$ is itself a random variable, equal to $\frac{1}{N}$ times the sum of N (random) drawings from the probability distribution of Y.

A thorough analysis of the probability distribution of $\overline{Y}$ (its "sampling distribution") is the principal focus of Chapter 3. For now, note that once each of these N drawings from the probability distribution of Y is actually observed, it is a specific fixed number: $c_1,\ c_2,\ c_3,\ \ldots$ or c_m. These N fixed (non-random) realizations of Y – here denoted $y_1 \ldots y_N$ – yield the fixed (non-random) value

$$\bar{y} = \frac{1}{N}\sum_{i=1}^{N} y_i \tag{2-4}$$

which is one realization of the random variable $\overline{Y}$. Thus, the observed value $\bar{y}$ is one drawing of the random variable $\overline{Y}$ from its sampling distribution.

It is useful to think of the expected value of Y as part of a fixed, objective reality: "truth," as it were. We ordinarily do not know the value of $E[Y]$, because in practice the probability distribution of Y is usually unknown. The single available realization of the random variable $\overline{Y}$, then, is our imperfect attempt to know this "truth" using N sample observations on Y. In Chapters 3 and 4, the properties of $\overline{Y}$ as an estimator of $E[Y]$ and the specific sense in which a sample realization of it allows us to "know" $E[Y]$ are described in detail.

Because the random variable Y takes on m possible values, the question "how large is Y?" is a non-trivial one. In general it is reasonable to use the population mean of Y, $E[Y]$ to quantify the size of Y, even though (for a discretely distributed random variable) it will generally not be equal to the value of any possible realization of Y. One way to motivate this interpretation is to observe that if c_i is the amount person A wins from person B in a game of chance when state i occurs, then $E[Y]$ is both the maximum entrance fee for the game which person A should be willing to pay and the minimum entrance fee which person B should require in order for both players to perceive the game as "fair."

The other major question one usually needs to ask about a random variable is "how random is it?" As noted above, the answer to this question is typically formulated in terms of the variance of the random variable. To deal with this, we need to consider the expected value of a function of a random variable.

Suppose that $\varphi(Y)$ is some given function of the random variable y. $\varphi(Y)$ might be the cube of Y or its square root, to give two specific examples. Because Y is a random variable, its value is unknown until it is realized. Consequently, as the value of $\varphi(Y)$ obviously depends on the value of Y, its value is in general random also. Thus, the sensible measure of the size of $\varphi(Y)$ is its expectation, $E[\varphi(Y)]$. Calculating the expectation of the random variable $\varphi(Y)$ is essentially the same as calculating the expected value of any other random variable: it is the sum of all the possible values the random variable can take on, weighted by how probable each value is. More precisely, $E[\varphi(Y)]$ is the weighted sum of the value $\varphi(Y)$ takes on in each possible state, weighted by the probability of that state's occurring:

$$E[\varphi(Y)] \equiv \sum_{j=1}^{m} \varphi(c_j)p_j = \varphi(c_1)p_1 + \varphi(c_2)p_2 + \ldots + \varphi(c_m)p_m \tag{2-5}$$

For example, if Y is again the number of dots showing on a six-sided die with $p_1 = 3/6$, $p_2 = 1/6$, $p_3 = 2/6$, and $p_4 = p_5 = p_6 = 0$, then $c_1 = 1$, $c_2 = 2$, ... , $c_6 = 6$, and $E\left[\sqrt{Y}\right]$ is just $\sqrt{1}(3/6) + \sqrt{2}(1/6) + \sqrt{3}(2/6)$, or 1.313 in this case.

Where the function $\varphi(Y)$ is Y raised to the integer power k, $E[\varphi(Y)] = E[Y^k]$ is called "the kth moment of Y around 0." Thus, $\mu_Y = E[\varphi(Y)]$ is also the first moment of Y around 0. Higher-order moments around zero are seldom used, however, because it is typically more convenient to instead consider what are called "central moments." The kth central moment of Y is defined as

$$E\left[(Y - \mu_Y)^k\right] = \sum_{j=1}^{m} \left(c_j - \mu_Y\right)^k p_j \tag{2-6}$$

Observe that as in any expectation, the expected value of $(Y - \mu_Y)^k$ is just the value that this random variable takes on in the jth state – i.e., $(c_j - \mu_Y)^k$ – weighted by the probability that state j occurs, and added up over all the possible states that can occur.

It is instructive to observe that the first central moment is always zero:

$$\begin{aligned} E[(Y - \mu_Y)] &= \sum_{j=1}^{m} (c_j - \mu_Y)p_j = \sum_{j=1}^{m} (c_j p_j - \mu_Y p_j) \\ &= \sum_{j=1}^{m} c_j p_j - \sum_{j=1}^{m} \mu_Y p_j \\ &= \sum_{j=1}^{m} c_j p_j - \mu_Y \sum_{j=1}^{m} p_j \\ &= \mu_Y - \mu_Y = 0 \end{aligned} \tag{2-7}$$

Thus, the expected value of the deviation of any random variable from its own expectation is zero. This is actually a handy result, which will be useful on a number of occasions in the chapters to come.

More important, however, notice the logical structure of this derivation: it is very typical. We start by applying the definition of the quantity to be evaluated – the expectation of a particular function of a discrete random variable, in this case – and then use the available properties (the rules for manipulating sums, in this case) to rewrite the resulting expression in terms of known quantities: the expressions defining μ_Y and the normalization condition on the probability distribution in this case.

Because it is always 0, the first central moment is of little intrinsic interest. The second central moment, in contrast, is overwhelmingly important, because it quantifies the randomness in Y:

$$\begin{aligned}\text{Variance of } Y &\equiv \text{var}[Y] \equiv \sigma_Y^2 \equiv E\left[(Y-\mu_Y)^2\right] \\ &= \sum_{j=1}^{m}(c_j-\mu_Y)^2 p_j = (c_1-\mu_Y)^2 p_1 + (c_2-\mu_Y)^2 p_2 + \cdots + (c_m-\mu_Y)^2 p_m\end{aligned} \tag{2-8}$$

One can interpret the variance of Y as a measure of the dispersion of Y around its mean value due to the differing values Y takes on in the various states. Put another way, the variance of Y is quantifying the size of the average squared discrepancy between Y and its population mean, μ_Y. Clearly, if Y is not very random, then its value is pretty much the same regardless of which state occurs. Thus, its average squared deviation from μ_Y will be small: i.e., its variance is small. In contrast, if Y is very random, then its value varies quite a bit, depending on which state is realized. Consequently, its expected squared deviation from μ_Y is large: i.e., its variance is large.

$E[(Y-\mu_Y)^2]$ is more precisely called the *population* variance of Y. As with the discussion of the population mean versus the sample mean given above, it is important to clearly distinguish the population variance of $Y\left(\sigma_Y^2\right)$ from its sample variance $\left(S_Y^2\right)$, an estimator of σ_Y^2 based on a sample of N drawings from the distribution of Y. In particular, note that σ_Y^2 is a fixed quantity determined by the probability distribution of Y. For example, if Y is once again the number of dots showing on a six-sided die with $p_1 = 3/6, p_2 = 1/6, p_3 = 2/6$, and $p_4 = p_5 = p_6 = 0$, then the population variance of Y is just

$$\sigma_Y^2 = \left(1-\frac{11}{6}\right)^2\left(\frac{3}{6}\right) + \left(2-\frac{11}{6}\right)^2\left(\frac{1}{6}\right) + \left(3-\frac{11}{6}\right)^2\left(\frac{2}{6}\right) = \frac{174}{216} = .806$$

In contrast, the sample variance of Y is

$$S_Y^2 = \frac{1}{N-1}\sum_{i=1}^{N}\left(Y_i-\overline{Y}\right)^2 \tag{2-9}$$

a random variable whose distribution will be discussed in Chapter 4; substituting N observed realizations of Y and the corresponding realization of $\overline{Y}$ – i.e., $y_1 \ldots y_N$ and $\overline{y}$ – into this expression yields a single drawing from this distribution, the fixed number s_Y^2, which is a realization of the random variable S_Y^2.

The population "standard deviation" of a random variable is just the square root of its population variance:

$$\text{Standard Deviation of } Y \equiv \sqrt{\text{var}(Y)} \equiv \sigma_Y \equiv \sqrt{E\left[\left(Y-\mu_{Y_y}\right)^2\right]} = \sqrt{\sum_{j=1}^{m}\left(c_j-\mu_y\right)^2 p_j} \tag{2-10}$$

and similarly for the analogous sample quantity. Because the standard deviation is monotonically related to the variance, both of these can be viewed as a measures of randomness. In some circumstances – such as in stating a confidence interval, as defined and analyzed in Chapter 4 – it is more convenient to use standard deviations and avoid the notation for the square root.

2.4 CONTINUOUS RANDOM VARIABLES

Where Y can take on any value in a subset of the real line, it is said to be continuously distributed on this interval. In this case probabilities, expectations, and the population mean and variance of a random variable are all defined in much the same way as for a discrete random variable. The only difference is that the mathematics involved is more sophisticated, fundamentally because the points on a subset of the real line are so closely packed that the limiting concept of integration must be used rather than simply summing over m discrete states.

As noted in the previous section, virtually all economic data are actually discretely distributed, although continuous random variables often provide an excellent approximation. Moreover, much of our subsequent work will actually only involve expectations of random variables, irrespective of whether those expectations are taken over discrete or continuous random variables. Consequently, one might be tempted – for simplicity's sake – to frame everything in terms of discrete random variables. This is not possible, however. Continuous random variables must be described here to some extent because the statistical inference machinery we will use to test hypotheses about the coefficients in our models is framed in terms of normally distributed random variables, which are continuously distributed over the real line.

For clarity's sake, however, the key propositions developed later in this chapter will be proven only for discrete random variables. And the expression given below for the expectation of a function of a continuous random variable (leading to expressions for the population mean and variance) is motivated informally by analogy with the corresponding result for a discrete random variable, rather than being rigorously derived.

Thus, even a brief summary of integral calculus is not necessary here, except to note that the integral of a positive function

$$\int_a^b f(Y)dY = \text{area beneath } f(Y) \text{ from } Y = a \text{ to } Y = b \tag{2-11}$$

corresponds to the area underneath a graph of the function:[7]

Supposing, then, that Y is a random variable which is continuously distributed over the entire real line, it follows that a particular realization of Y can take on any value in the interval $[-\infty, \infty]$. Just as the probability distribution summarizes all that we can know about the value of a discrete random variable before it is observed, what we can know about a random variable Y which is continuously distributed is summarized in its probability density function. This density function – denoted $f(Y)$ here – quantifies how relatively likely various values of Y are. If $f(Y)$ looks like Figure 2-1, for example, then one is likely to observe realizations of Y around -2 and around 3, but realizations of Y exceeding five should be fairly rare.

The probability that Y takes on a particular value, such as 4, is not the value of $f(4)$, however. In fact, there are so many other real numbers arbitrarily close to four that the probability of observing Y exactly equal to four is in general 0. We can, however, usefully quantify the probability of observing

[7] **Note for students who have not had integral calculus:** Don't panic! Aside from this section, in which the population mean and variance are characterized for continuous random variables, all that you will need to know about integrals and integration for a course based on this book is that the integral quantifies the area underneath the graph of a function. Understanding exactly what the population mean and variance signify is very important, but you can take that understanding from the previous section (on discrete random variables) with little lost.

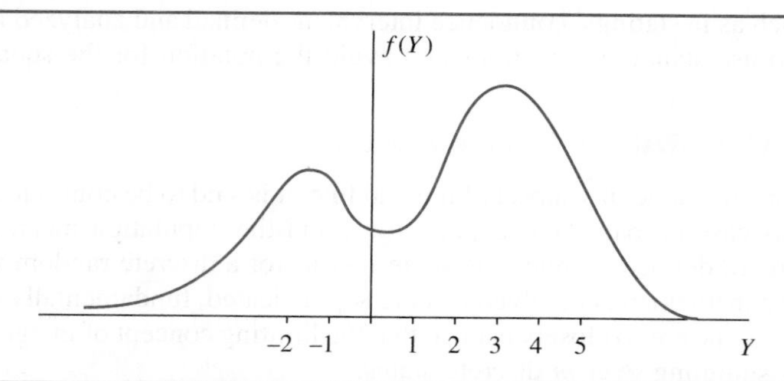

Figure 2-1 A Particular Density Function

Y in an interval of infinitesimal length dY: the probability that an observation on Y will lie in the interval $[4, 4 + dY]$ is equal to $f(4)dY$. Consequently, the probability of observing values of Y in an interval of finite length, such as [4,5], is the area under $f(Y)$ between $y = 4$ and $y = 5$, which is the integral $\int_4^5 f(Y)dY$. Because the probability that y takes on *some* value in the interval $[-\infty, \infty]$ must be one, it follows that the density function $f(Y)$ must be normalized so that $\int_{-\infty}^{\infty} f(Y)dY = 1$. These results are analogous to the observation that for the discrete random variable discussed in the previous section, the probability of drawing a value between c_3 and c_6 equals $p_3 + p_4 + p_5 + p_6$, and that the probability distribution function is normalized so that $\sum_{j=1}^{m} p_j = 1$.

Similarly, supposing that $\varphi(Y)$ is some given function of Y, we can define the expected value of $\varphi(Y)$ as

$$E[\varphi(Y)] = \int_{-\infty}^{\infty} \varphi(Y)f(Y)dY = \lim_{r\to\infty} \int_{-r}^{r} \varphi(Y)f(Y)dY \tag{2-12}$$

and we can (somewhat crudely) interpret this expression as "adding up" all of the various possible values $\varphi(Y)$ can take on, weighting each one by $f(Y)dY$, the probability of observing Y in the interval $[Y, Y + dY]$.

It follows that $E[Y]$, the population mean of Y, is just

$$E[Y] = \mu_Y = \int_{-\infty}^{\infty} Yf(Y)dY \tag{2-13}$$

and that $E[(Y - \mu_Y)^2]$, the population variance of Y, is just

$$E\left[(Y - \mu_Y)^2\right] = \sigma_Y^2 = \int_{-\infty}^{\infty} (Y - \mu_Y)^2 f(Y)dY \tag{2-14}$$

As with the analogous expression for the population mean of a discrete random variable, $E[Y]$ is essentially a weighted sum of the possible values Y can take on, where the density function weights the values by how likely they are to occur; $E[Y]$ can be interpreted as quantifying how large Y is, on average.

Similarly, $E\left[(Y-\mu_Y)^2\right]$, again as with the analogous expression for a discrete random variable, quantifies the dispersion of Y around its mean via its average squared deviation from the mean.

Note that if the allowed range of Y is the interval $[\infty, \infty]$, then the integral defining the expected value of a function $\varphi(Y)$ is itself a limit as the parameter r in the expression defining the expectation becomes arbitrarily large. If the function $\varphi(Y)$ becomes large as $|Y|$ increases faster than the density function $f(Y)$ decreases, then it is possible that this limit does not "exist." For example, consider the integral whose limit corresponds to the expectation which is the variance of Y:

$$E\left[(Y-\mu_Y)^2\right] = \sigma_Y^2 = \int_{-\infty}^{\infty}(Y-\mu_Y)^2 f(Y)dY = \lim_{r\to\infty}\int_{-r}^{r}(Y-\mu_Y)^2 f(Y)dY \tag{2-15}$$

If the tails of the density function $f(Y)$ decay to zero as $|Y|$ becomes very large, but not faster than $(Y-\mu_Y)^2$ is increasing, then the value of the integral from $-r$ to r in this expression just keeps increasing as the parameter r increases. Thus, the variance of a random variable with this density function does not exist. The best way to frame this situation is to think of this expectation – the variance of Y – as unboundedly large in magnitude, and hence not well defined.[8]

2.5 SOME INITIAL RESULTS ON EXPECTATIONS

The two most important things for you to take away from the previous sections are (1) the meaning we attach to the concepts of the population mean and the population variance (as distinct from the sample mean and sample variance) and (2) a precise understanding of how to calculate the expected value of a function of a discrete random variable. The first of these is essential because almost all of the rest of the material in this book is couched in terms of the means and variances of error terms and of parameter estimators in our models. The second of these concepts is essential because we now begin to use this understanding to build the tools which will be used below in analyzing regression models and in doing statistical inference.

In this section we obtain some simple, but highly useful, results on expectations. These results will be generalized later in this chapter to yield the Linearity Property of Expectations.

Let Y be discretely distributed, with given population mean, μ_Y. By definition, then, $E[Y]$ equals μ_Y. Now suppose that b is a fixed constant. (That is, b has the same value regardless of which state the random variable Y is in.) What will be the value of $E[Y-b]$?

$$\begin{aligned} E[(Y-b)] &= \sum_{j=1}^{m}(c_j-b)p_j = \sum_{j=1}^{m}(c_jp_j - b\,p_j) \\ &= \sum_{j=1}^{m}c_jp_j - \sum_{j=1}^{m}b\,p_j \\ &= \sum_{j=1}^{m}c_jp_j - b\sum_{j=1}^{m}p_j \\ &= \mu_Y - b \end{aligned} \tag{2-16}$$

[8] This issue does arise (and in an important way) because some parameter estimators of practical use – e.g., the 2SLS estimator described in Chapter 12 – turn out to have ill-defined sampling variances of precisely this kind in finite samples. This can cause serious problems with the statistical machinery used estimating confidence intervals for (or testing hypotheses about) the model coefficients on such variables.

Thus, subtracting a fixed constant from a random variable lowers its expected value by the amount of that constant. Note that this calculation proceeded in a very similar way to our earlier derivation that the first central moment is always 0; in fact, that derivation is a special case of the present result, where the value of b is μ_Y.[9]

Now suppose that a is a fixed constant – that is, it has the same value regardless of what state occurs – and consider the value of $E[aY]$:

$$E[aY] = \sum_{j=1}^{m} (a\, c_j)p_j = \sum_{j=1}^{m} a\, c_j p_j = a \sum_{j=1}^{m} c_j p_j = a\mu_Y \tag{2-17}$$

Thus, we see that multiplying a random variable by a fixed constant multiplies its expectation by that same constant.[10]

2.6 SOME RESULTS ON VARIANCES

What is the impact on the population variance of Y of subtracting a fixed constant or multiplying by a fixed constant? These results are worth deriving here for two reasons. First, we will need to use these results in Chapter 4 when we "standardize" a parameter estimator to zero mean and unit variance, preparatory to using it for statistical inference. Second, because the coefficient estimates in all of the models considered in this book will be random variables, the calculation of the relevant population variance is a crucial analytic step which will come up over and over again. The precise form of the random variable will differ in each case, but the basic logic of the derivation will always be the same and, in particular, will be practically identical to that of the next two derivations. Consequently, it is a good idea to get this logic straight at the outset, where the algebra is very simple.

First, notice that the variance of the random variable Y is defined to be $E[(Y - E[Y])^2]$, the expected value of the squared deviation of the random variable from its population mean – **regardless of whether Y is a discrete or a continuous random variable.** Therefore, because our derivation is going to begin from this expression, it is no longer going to be necessary to concern ourselves with whether Y is discrete or continuous. Moreover, there is nothing special about the symbol "Y" here: **the variance of *any* random variable is the expected value of its squared deviation from its population mean.**

Now consider the variance of $Y - b$, where b is a fixed constant and Y is a random variable with given population mean μ_Y and given population variance σ_Y^2. From the general definition of the variance of a random variable given above, it must be the case that

$$\text{var}(Y - b) = E\left[([Y - b] - E[Y - b])^2\right] \tag{2-18}$$

It was already shown in the previous section that $E[Y - b] = \mu_Y - b$; it follows that

$$\text{var}(Y - b) = E\left[([Y - b] - [\mu_Y - b])^2\right] \tag{2-19}$$

Next, reflect on what is known about the random variable Y: We know that it has given population variance, σ_Y^2, so it will be all right for our expression for $\text{var}(Y - b)$ to involve σ_Y^2. Moreover, we know that $\sigma_Y^2 \equiv E\left[(Y - \mu_Y)^2\right]$, which clearly involves $(Y - \mu_Y)$. Therefore, it is pretty clearly a

[9] The analogous proof for continuous random variables is essentially identical, but involves integrals instead of sums.

[10] For a continuous random variable, $E[aY] = \int_{-\infty}^{\infty} (aY)f(Y)dY = a\int_{-\infty}^{\infty} Yf(Y)dY = a\mu_Y$.

good idea to get the Y and the μ_Y terms in our expression for var($Y - b$) together. In fact, when we do so, we see that var($Y - b$) can be written simply in terms of σ_Y^2:

$$\begin{aligned} \text{var}(Y-b) &= E\left[([Y-b]-[\mu_Y-b])^2\right] \\ &= E\left[([Y-b-\mu_Y+b])^2\right] \\ &= E\left[(Y-\mu_Y)^2\right] \\ &= \sigma_Y^2 = \text{var}(Y) \end{aligned} \tag{2-20}$$

Finally, whenever it is possible to do so, it is always a good idea to check whether a result makes intuitive sense. Here our result says that subtracting any constant from a random variable leaves its variance unchanged. This makes sense because we already know that subtracting a constant changes the random variable's mean accordingly and that the variance is the expected dispersion *around* the mean.

Finally, consider the variance of aY, where a is a fixed constant and Y is a random variable with given population mean μ_Y and given population variance σ_Y^2. Again using the general definition of the variance of a random variable given above, it must be the case that

$$\text{var}(aY) = E\left[([aY]-E[aY])^2\right] \tag{2-21}$$

We have $E[aY] = a\mu_Y$ from our results in the previous section, so that

$$\text{var}(aY) = E\left[([aY]-a\mu_Y)^2\right] \tag{2-22}$$

And again, because we know that $\text{var}(Y) = \sigma_Y^2 = E\left[(Y-\mu_Y)^2\right]$, it is clearly a good idea to rewrite this expression for var(aY) in terms of $y - \mu_Y$; doing so yields

$$\text{var}(aY) = E\left[(a[Y-\mu_Y])^2\right] = E\left[a^2[Y-\mu_Y]^2\right] \tag{2-23}$$

Now notice that this last term is the expected value of a constant (a^2) times the random variable $(Y-\mu_Y)^2$. Note that our previous result (that $E[aY] = a\,\mu_Y$) actually implies that the expectation of ***any*** constant times ***any*** random variable is equal to that constant times the expected value of the random variable. Consequently, it implies that

$$E\left[a^2[Y-\mu_Y]^2\right] = a^2E\left[[Y-\mu_Y]^2\right] \tag{2-24}$$

Hence,

$$\text{var}(aY) = a^2E\left[[Y-\mu_Y]^2\right] = a^2\text{var}(Y) \tag{2.25}$$

Thus, in general, we find that multiplying a random variable by a constant multiplies its variance by the square of that constant. This result, too, makes intuitive sense: if we double the size of each value of Y – e.g., by halving the units in which we measure Y – then we should expect that the squared dispersion of Y around its mean will quadruple.

2.7 A PAIR OF RANDOM VARIABLES

Next consider a pair of random variables. This is more complicated, but it is absolutely necessary in order to understand the concepts (covariance, correlation, and statistical independence) used to quantify the degree of relatedness between two random variables. So as to simplify the exposition, attention in this section will be restricted to discretely distributed random variables.

Suppose that we simultaneously observe realizations of two distinct random variables, Y and Z, where Y can take on any one of m discrete values and Z can take on any one of n discrete values. Thus, one observation actually corresponds to picking a (Y, Z) pair. For example, you might think of throwing two six-sided dice, one with red dots on its sides and one with blue dots on its sides, letting Y be the number of red dots showing and Z be the number of blue dots showing. (Clearly, $m = n = 6$ in this case.) One observation is now a pair of numbers – the number of red dots showing and the number of blue dots showing. You might further imagine that the two dice are connected by a short rubber band which makes it improbable that the red die will land showing five or six dots when the blue die lands showing one or two dots. Prior to throwing the dice, all that we can know about the values Y and Z will take on is their joint probability distribution, p_{jk}, whose value is the probability that the red die will be observed in its jth state and that the blue die will be observed in its kth state on the same throw:

Distribution of a Pair of Discrete Random Variables

$$
\begin{aligned}
Y &= a_1 \text{ or } a_2 \text{ or} \ldots \text{or } a_m \ (m \text{ possible states}) \\
Z &= b_1 \text{ or } b_2 \text{ or} \ldots \text{or } b_n \ (n \text{ possible states}) \\
p_{jk} &= \text{probability that } Y = a_j \text{ (``}Y \text{ is in state } j\text{'') and that } Z = b_k \text{(``}Z \text{ is in state } k\text{'')}
\end{aligned}
\tag{2-26}
$$

As with the single discrete random variable, the frequentist interpretation of probability implies that $0 \le p_{jk} \le 1$ and that the probabilities must sum to 1, so that $\sum_{j=1}^{m} \sum_{k=1}^{n} p_{jk}$ is equal to 1.[11]

As before, our primary interest is not in the expected values of Y and Z themselves, but in the expected value of some given function that depends on Y and Z; this function might be called $\varphi(Y, Z)$. For example, if we are interested in the total number of dots showing on the two dice mentioned above, then $\varphi(Y, Z)$ equals $Y + Z$. The value of $\varphi(Y, Z)$ is clearly itself a random variable which is discretely distributed over $m \times n$ possible states.[12] Thus, it is reasonable to define the expected value of $\varphi(Y, Z)$ as the weighted sum of the $m \times n$ possible values $\varphi(Y, Z)$ can take on, with the weights being the probability that each of these composite states occurs:

$$
E[\varphi(Y, Z)] \equiv \sum_{j=1}^{m} \sum_{k=1}^{n} \varphi(a_j, b_k) p_{jk} \tag{2-27}
$$

[11] For a pair of continuous random variables, this normalization condition would involve a double integral over the joint density function. This section is couched entirely in terms of discrete random variables primarily so that the discourse is in terms of double sums instead. The Mathematics Review section at the end of the book covers what you need to know about summation notation, including material on double sums.

[12] In contrast, when one observes which states Y and Z are in – i.e., when one obtains a realization of (Y, Z) – then one can calculate a fixed (non-random) realization of $\varphi(Y, Z)$. More explicitly, if the observed realization of (Y, Z) is (a_1, b_2), then the realization of $\varphi(Y, Z)$ is the number $\varphi(a_1, b_2)$.

An explicit example is helpful here. Supposing that $m = 3$, $n = 2$, and that $\varphi(Y, Z) = Y + Z$,

$$E[\varphi(Y,Z)] = (a_1 + b_1)p_{11} + (a_1 + b_2)p_{12} + (a_2 + b_1)p_{21} + (a_2 + b_2)p_{22} + (a_3 + b_1)p_{31} + (a_3 + b_2)p_{32} \tag{2-28}$$

As before, the expected values we are most interested in are the low-order moments. For example, the population mean of Y – the first moment of Y around zero – is still denoted $E[Y]$, but now this expectation is an average over all $m \times n$ possible states:

$$E[Y] \equiv \mu_Y \equiv \sum_{j=1}^{m}\sum_{k=1}^{n} a_j p_{jk} \tag{2-29}$$

and now there is also a population mean for the second random variable, z:

$$E[Z] \equiv \mu_Z \equiv \sum_{j=1}^{m}\sum_{k=1}^{n} b_k p_{jk} \tag{2-30}$$

The population mean $E[Y]$ can sensibly viewed as the value of Y averaged over all of the possible values of both Y and Z – i.e., over all $m \times n$ possible states – and similarly for $E[Z]$. In some circumstances, however, one's interest centers on the expected value of Y given that Z has already been observed to be in a particular state. This expectation is called the "conditional mean of Y given Z" and is usually denoted $E[Y \mid Z = z]$, where z is the particular realization of Z which has been observed. The conditional mean is of some importance because, as we will see in Chapter 5, the Bivariate Regression Model quantifying how the sample variation in one variable depends on that of another can usefully be viewed as parameterizing the conditional mean of the first variable as a linear function of the observed realization of the second variable. We will not actually do very much with the conditional mean, however, so further discussion of it is given in an appendix to this chapter.

With two random variables there are also now two population variances. One, the variance of Y, again characterizes the dispersion of Y around its mean; it is the almost the same as we had before, except that now the expectation is averaging over the $m \times n$ possible states:

$$\operatorname{var}(Y) = E\left[(Y - \mu_Y)^2\right] \equiv \sigma_Y^2 \equiv \sum_{j=1}^{m}\sum_{k=1}^{n} (a_j - \mu_y)^2 p_{jk} \tag{2-31}$$

And there is also a population variance for Z, quantifying its dispersion around its own mean:

$$\operatorname{var}(Z) = E\left[(Z - \mu_z)^2\right] \equiv \sigma_Z^2 \equiv \sum_{j=1}^{m}\sum_{k=1}^{n} (b_k - \mu_z)^2 p_{jk} \tag{2-32}$$

However, we can now define an additional second central moment, the covariance of Y and Z:

$$\text{Covariance of } Y \text{ with } Z = \operatorname{cov}(Y,Z) = E\left[(Y - \mu_y)(Z - \mu_Z)\right] \equiv \sigma_{YZ} \equiv \sum_{j=1}^{m}\sum_{k=1}^{n} (a_j - \mu_y)(b_k - \mu_z)p_{jk} \tag{2-33}$$

If Y and Z are directly related, then observed values of Y will tend to exceed its mean of μ_Y in the same observed (Y, Z) pairs for which Z exceeds μ_Z. And observed values of Y which are less than its mean of μ_Y will similarly tend to usually occur in observed (Y, Z) pairs for which the observed value of Z is also less than μ_Z. Thus, observed values of the random variable $(Y - \mu_Y)(Z - \mu_Z)$ will be positive in either case when Y and Z are directly related. Consequently, if Y and Z are directly related, then one should expect that the product $(Y - \mu_Y)(Z - \mu_z)$ will, on average, be positive; this, of course, is the same thing as saying that one should expect the covariance $\text{cov}(Y, Z)$ or $E[(Y - \mu_Y)(Z - \mu_Z)]$ to be positive. Similarly, if Y and Z are inversely related, then $(Y - \mu_Y)$ and $(Z - \mu_Z)$ will tend to have opposite signs, so that the covariance between Y and Z will be negative.

The sign of the covariance between Y and Z thus indicates whether these two random variables tend to fluctuate together or oppositely. The covariance is a bit awkward as a quantitative measure of how fluctuations in Y are related to fluctuations in Z, however, because it depends on the units in which Y and Z are measured. For example, if Y is height and Z is weight, $\text{cov}(Y, Z)$ will be 12 times larger if height is measured in inches than if height is measured in feet. A better measure of relatedness is $\text{corr}(Y, Z)$, the correlation between Y and Z. The correlation $\text{corr}(Y, Z)$ is a scaled version of the covariance between these two variables:

$$\text{Correlation between } Y \text{ and } Z \equiv \rho_{YZ} \equiv \text{corr}(Y, Z) \equiv \frac{\text{cov}(Y, Z)}{\sqrt{\text{var}(Y)\text{var}(Z)}} \tag{2-34}$$

Clearly, the correlation and covariance are numerically equal for a pair of random variables which both have variance equal to 1. In addition to being invariant to the units in which Y and Z are measured, the correlation ρ_{YZ} can be shown to necessarily lie in the interval $[-1, 1]$; see Exercise 2-9. A correlation of -1 corresponds to an exact linear relationship between Y and Z with a negative slope; a correlation of $+1$ corresponds to an exact linear relationship with a positive slope, as illustrated by the scatterplots in Figures 2-2a and 2-2b.

Intermediate values of ρ_{YZ} correspond to noisy linear relationships between Y and Z, such as we will be modeling in Chapter 5. This situation is illustrated by the scatterplots in Figures 2-2c and 2-2d.

2.8 THE LINEARITY PROPERTY OF EXPECTATIONS

We saw earlier in this chapter that, if a and b are fixed constants, then $E[Y - b] = E[Y] - b$ and $E[aY] = aE[Y]$ for any random variable Y. These results can be combined and generalized into what is called the "Linearity Property of Expectations":

The Linearity Property of Expectations

If $c_1, c_2, \ldots, c_N$ are fixed constants and $Y_1 \ldots Y_N$ are random variables, then

$$E[c_1 Y_1 + c_2 Y_2 + \ldots + c_N Y_N] = c_1 E[Y_1] + c_2 E[Y_2] + \ldots + c_N E[Y_N]$$

or, equivalently,

$$E\left[\sum_{i=1}^{N} c_i Y_i\right] = \sum_{i=1}^{N} c_i E[Y_i] \tag{2-35}$$

In words, the expected value of a weighted sum of random variables is equal to the same weighted sum of the expected values of the random variables. This property will be invoked so frequently below that it will often be referred to as simply the "Linearity Property."

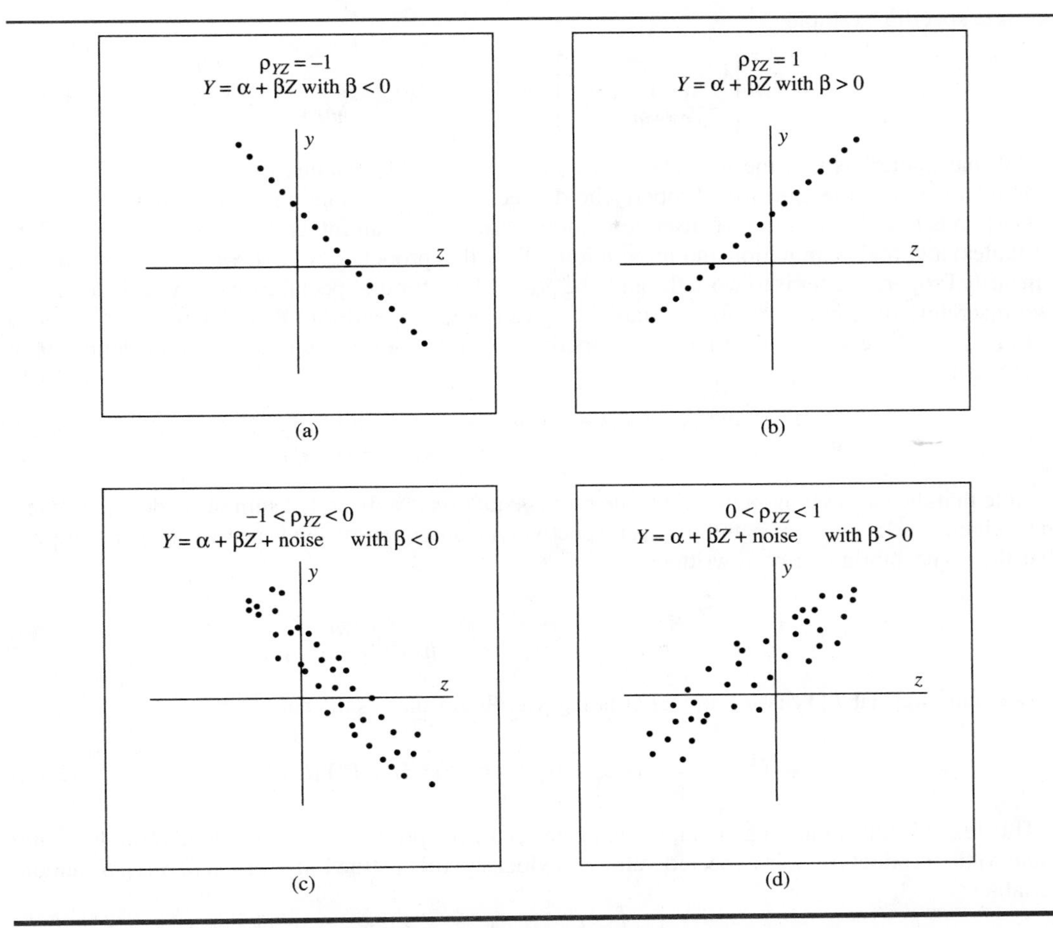

Figure 2-2 Scatterplots Illustrating Different Levels of Correlation

Note carefully that the Linearity Property re-expresses the expected value of a weighted sum of random variables. This is **not** the weighted sum of the particular values that a single, discrete random variable takes on in its different states – indeed, the Linearity Property is equally valid for both continuous and discrete random variables.

The Linearity Property is extremely powerful – it is used frequently in this chapter and in the chapters to come. Much of the reason it is so useful is that it assumes almost nothing about the random variables $Y_1 \dots Y_N$. It doesn't matter whether they are correlated or not. It doesn't even matter if the variables are actually random: for example, if Y_2 is a constant (b, for example) then the Linearity Property implies that $E[c_1 + c_2 b]$ is just $c_1 E[Y_1] + c_2 b$. Even more important, $Y_1 \dots Y_N$ can be functions of random variables. For example, Y_i might be some function R_i that depends on random variables Z_1 and Z_2, in which case the Linearity Property implies that

$$E\left[\sum_{i=1}^{N} c_i R_i(Z_1, Z_2)\right] = \sum_{i=1}^{N} c_i E[R_i(Z_1, Z_2)] \tag{2-36}$$

or, as a specific example,

$$E\left[\sum_{i=1}^{N} c_i (Y_i - \mu)^2\right] = \sum_{i=1}^{N} c_i E\left[(Y_i - \mu)^2\right] \tag{2-37}$$

All that matters is that the weights $c_1 \dots c_N$ must be fixed constants.[13]

Fundamentally, the Linearity Property holds because the expectation of any random variable corresponds to either a sum (for discrete random variables) or an integral (for continuous random variables) and both summation and integration satisfy this property. A good way to understand the Linearity Property better is to work through the proof of it – for the special case of a weighted sum of two discretely distributed random variables – given in an appendix to this chapter.

Let's immediately apply the Linearity Property to obtain a useful result. Consider the definition of cov(Y, Z):

$$\begin{aligned}\operatorname{cov}(Y,Z) &\equiv E[(Y-\mu_Y)(Z-\mu_Z)] \\ &= E[YZ - \mu_Y Z - \mu_Z Y + \mu_Y \mu_Z]\end{aligned} \tag{2-38}$$

Note that the expression on the right side of this equation is a weighted sum of random variables: the weights are 1, $-\mu_Y$, $-\mu_Z$, and $\mu_Y \mu_Z$, respectively. Consequently, the Linearity Property implies that this expectation can be rewritten:

$$\begin{aligned}\operatorname{cov}(Y,Z) &= E[YZ - \mu_Y Z - \mu_Z Z + \mu_Y \mu_Z] \\ &= E[YZ] - \mu_Y E[Z] - \mu_Z E[Y] + \mu_Y\, \mu_Z\end{aligned} \tag{2-39}$$

Recognizing that $E[Y]$ is μ_Y and $E[Z]$ is μ_Z, we obtain the result that

$$\operatorname{cov}(Y,Z) = E[YZ] - \mu_Y \mu_Z = E[YZ] - E[Y]E[Z] \tag{2-40}$$

This result implies that in general, the expectation of the product of two random variables is *not* equal to the product of their expected values – evidently, this is true only for *uncorrelated* random variables:[14]

Multiplicative Property for Uncorrelated Random Variables

$$E[YZ] = E[Y]E[Z] \quad \text{if and only if} \quad \operatorname{corr}(Y,Z) = 0 \tag{2-41}$$

2.9 STATISTICAL INDEPENDENCE

We have just seen that uncorrelated random variables – i.e., random variables with zero covariance – are not *linearly* related and the expectation of their product is equal to the product of their expectations. In contrast, independent random variables are not related in any way at all: linearly or nonlinearly.

We will need to use the concept of independence a number of times later on, so it is important to get clear on what independence means and how it differs from uncorrelatedness.

The joint probability density function or joint probability distribution for a pair of ***independent*** random variables can be expressed as the product of two factors, each of which involves just one of the variables:

[13] The term "fixed constant" has a very simple definition if the random variables are discretely distributed: a fixed constant does not depend on which state any of the random variables might take on.

[14] Recall from the previous section that two random variables are uncorrelated if and only if their covariance is zero.

Statistical Independence

Two random variables, Y and Z, are independently distributed if and only if

a. (continuous case) Their joint probability density function $G(Y,Z)$ is $f_Y(Y)f_Z(Z)$

or

b. (discrete case) Their joint probability distribution p_{jk} is $q_j\, h_k$ (2-42)

where

$$p_{jk} = \text{probability that } Y = a_j \text{ ("}Y\text{ is in state } j\text{") } \textbf{and} \text{ that } Z = b_k \text{ ("}Z\text{ is in state } k\text{")}$$

and

$$q_j = \text{probability that } Y = a_j \text{ ("}Y\text{ is in state } j\text{")}$$
$$h_k = \text{probability that } Z = b_k \text{ ("}Z\text{ is in state } k\text{")}$$

Note that because the density or distribution function factors in this way, the value observed for one variable conveys no information at all about the relative likelihood of observing various values for the other variable. That is what the phrase "independent random variables are not related in any way at all" is intended to convey.

Independence implies a stronger multiplicative property than does uncorrelatedness:

Multiplicative Property for Independent Random Variables

For any functions $g(\cdot)$ and $w(\cdot)$, (2-43)

$$E[g(Y)w(Z)] = E[g(Y)]E[w(Z)] \text{ if } Y \text{ and } Z \text{ are independently distributed}$$

It is instructive to explicitly prove this multiplicative property for the case where Y and Z are independently and discretely distributed:[15]

$$\begin{aligned} E[g(Y)w(Z)] &= \sum_{j=1}^{m}\sum_{k=1}^{n} g(a_j)w(b_k)p_{jk} && \text{definition of expectation} \\ &= \sum_{j=1}^{m}\sum_{k=1}^{n} g(a_j)\, w(b_k)\, q_j h_k && \text{if } Y \text{ and } Z \text{ independent} \\ &= \sum_{j=1}^{m}\sum_{k=1}^{n} g(a_j)q_j\, w(b_k)h_k \\ &= \sum_{j=1}^{m} g(a_j)q_j \sum_{k=1}^{n} w(b_k)h_k && g(a_j)q_j \text{ can come out of sum over } k \\ &= E[g(Y)] \quad E[w(Z)] \end{aligned} \tag{2-44}$$

This proof demonstrates exactly how the factoring of p_{jk} leads to the multiplicative property for independent random variables.

[15] You may find it helpful to write out the step where the double sum is converted into the product of two single sums for the special case where $m = n = 2$; this topic is also addressed in the Mathematics Review section at the end of the book.

An important application of this multiplicative property for independent random variables is to show that independently distributed random variables are necessarily uncorrelated. In particular, if Y and Z are independently distributed, then

$$\begin{aligned} \text{cov}(Y, Z) &= E[[Y - E[Y]][Z - E[Z]]] \\ &= E[[Y - E[Y]]]\, E[[Z - E[Z]]] \quad \text{(because } Y \text{ and } Z \text{ are independent)} \\ &= \quad 0 \qquad\qquad\quad 0 \end{aligned} \tag{2-45}$$

Thus, independence implies uncorrelatedness.

Uncorrelatedness does **not**, however, imply independence; this is because two random variables which are not linearly related might still be related in a nonlinear way. Suppose, for example, that a random variable Q is equal to the square of another random variable, Z, plus some noise, u: i.e., $Q = Z^2 + U$. In that case, a scatterplot plotted from observed (q, z) pairs would look like Figure 2-3:

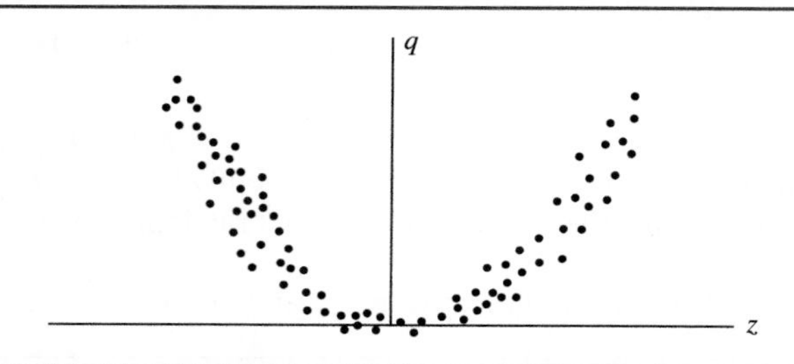

Figure 2-3 Scatterplot of Sample Data from $Q = Z^2 + U$

A glance at this scatterplot makes it clear that Q and Z are rather closely related; thus, they cannot possibly be independently distributed from one another. But if Z is symmetrically distributed around zero – that is, positive and negative values of Z are equally likely – then it can be shown that cov(Q, Z) is 0. (Intuitively, in that case a graph of the best linear approximation to this relationship would be a horizontal straight line, indicative of no linear relationship at all.)

Independence is most commonly asserted for a set of random variables, each of which is to be independently drawn from the same distribution. Such a set of N such variables – which we might denote as $Y_1, Y_2, \ldots Y_N$ – is called a "random sample" from that distribution. Once such a sample is drawn, the actual sample observations (the realizations $y_1, y_2 \ldots y_N$ of the random variables $Y_1, Y_2, \ldots Y_N$) are, of course, fixed numbers. Prior to drawing the sample, however, $Y_1, Y_2, \ldots Y_N$ are "identically and independently distributed" or "IID" random variables, where the term "identically" is referring to the fact that each observation is drawn from exactly the same distribution. Typical notation for a random sample to be drawn from a distribution with population mean μ_Y and population variance σ_Y^2 is thus

$$Y_i \sim \text{IID}\left(\mu_Y, \sigma_Y^2\right) \tag{2-46}$$

Independence is such a strong property that one might well wonder, "How could we ever know that two random variables are independently distributed?" There are basically three ways:

1. {Credible Assertion} A theory whose validity we are maintaining (perhaps so that we can test it) might imply that two random variables are independently distributed. (Or it might be assumed on an exam problem!)
2. {Well-Designed Experiment or Survey} If the data are collected from a well-designed experiment or survey, it is often reasonable to assume that they are independently distributed.

For example, we might collect wage income data from N households using a survey instrument. If the survey is well done, then each wage income observation can be taken as independent from the others. In contrast, suppose that the first $N/2$ households were asked to suggest the names of friends and acquaintances who might like to also participate in the survey. In that case it would be reasonable to suspect that the data from the first half of the sample and the last half of the sample are not independently distributed.

3. {Uncorrelated Normally Distributed Random Variables} Finally, while it is not true in general that uncorrelatedness implies independence, this proposition *is* true for jointly normally distributed random variables. In fact, normality has a number of strong implications for random variables; these are the topic of the next section.

2.10 NORMALLY DISTRIBUTED RANDOM VARIABLES

An overwhelmingly important special case is the normal or "gaussian" distribution.[16] A random variable Y is said to be normally distributed with population mean μ and population variance σ^2 if its probability density function is

$$f^N(Y;\mu,\sigma^2) = \frac{1}{\sqrt{2\pi\sigma^2}} e^{-\frac{(Y-\mu)^2}{2\sigma^2}} \tag{2-47}$$

Note that this density function, which summarizes everything that can be known about Y prior to observing its realization, is completely determined by the values of μ and σ^2; for this reason a normally distributed random variable is often specified using the notation $Y \sim N[\mu, \sigma^2]$.

Looking at this density function, we see that Y itself enters only as $(Y-\mu)^2$; thus, the density is symmetric about its mean. It is also worth noting that the value of this density function decays very rapidly for values of $|Y-\mu|$ larger than four to five times σ. A graph of $f^N(Y;\mu,\sigma^2)$ looks like Figure 2-4:

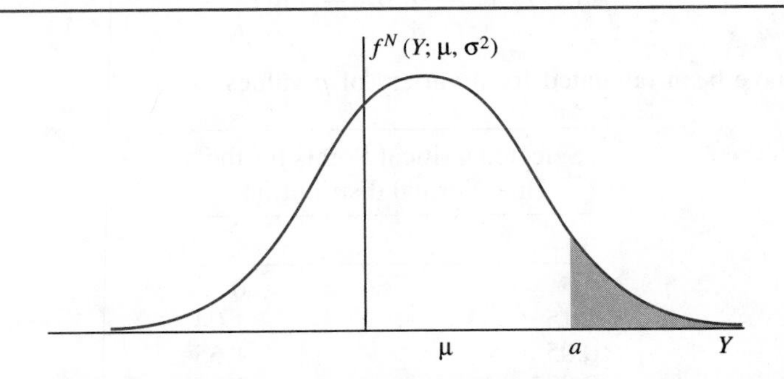

Figure 2-4 Density Function for $Y \sim N(\mu, \sigma^2)$ with Tail Area Illustrated

The shaded area to the right of the point where Y equals the value marked a – often called "the tail area to the right of a" – corresponds to the integral

$$\int_a^{\infty} f^N(Y;\mu,\sigma^2)dy = \int_a^{\infty} \frac{1}{\sqrt{2\pi\sigma^2}} e^{-\frac{(Y-\mu)^2}{2\sigma^2}} dY \tag{2-48}$$

and can be interpreted as the probability of drawing a value of Y greater than or equal to this value. Such integrals in general cannot be evaluated analytically, but tail areas for the "unit normal"

[16] A discussion of related distributions, including the χ^2, F, and Student's distribution, is postponed to Chapter 4.

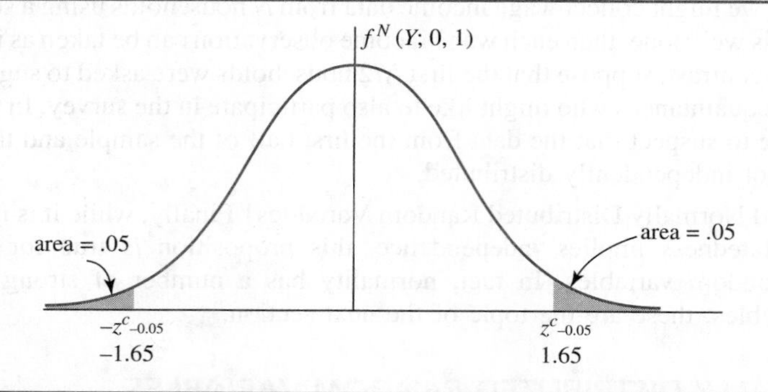

Figure 2-5 Graph of Unit Normal Density Function

distribution, where $\mu = 0$ and $\sigma^2 = 1$, have been extensively tabulated and perfectly adequate numerical approximations are widely available.[17]

For some purposes – notably including the construction of confidence intervals, first covered in Chapter 4 – "critical points" are more convenient. These are most clearly defined with an example: the 5% critical point of the unit normal distribution, $z^c_{0.05}$, is the value such that the probability of drawing a unit normal exceeding this value is .05.[18] In other words, the area under the unit normal density function to the right of $z^c_{.05}$ is .05. Because the density function for the normal distribution is symmetric around 0, this implies that there is also area .05 to the left of $-z^c_{.05}$, as in Figure 2-5.

Thus, the α% critical point of the unit normal distribution is the value z^c_α such that

$$\int_{z^c_\alpha}^{\infty} f^N(Y; \mu = 0, \sigma^2 = 1)\,dY = \alpha \tag{2-49}$$

Values for z^c_α have been tabulated for a variety of p values:

Selected Critical Points for the Unit Normal distribution

α	z^c_α
0.5	0
0.15	1.04
0.05	1.65
0.025	1.96
0.01	2.33
0.005	2.58
0.001	3.08

[17] Most spreadsheet programs and even some scientific hand calculators will compute tail areas for the unit normal distribution. For example, Excel provides a function called "normdist" for this purpose. Or you can program an excellent numerical approximation to this function yourself in just a few lines of code – see Press et al. (1986, p. 164) *Numerical Recipes,* Cambridge University Press. Or you can copy the program "gaustail.exe" – based on the *Numerical Recipes* code – available at www.wiley.com/college/ashley and use it on any Windows-based computer. Active Learning Exercise 2a (at the end of this chapter) allows you to experiment with both of these programs.

[18] Note that this is not the usual convention for defining/notating a critical point: more commonly a 5% critical point is defined as the value such that 5% of the values are smaller than this. That convention relates most clearly to a cumulative distribution function; the definition used here relates most clearly to the tail areas used in statistical inference.

2.11 THREE SPECIAL PROPERTIES OF NORMALLY DISTRIBUTED VARIABLES

Normally distributed random variables have three extremely useful properties. These properties are stated here (without proof) and are used extensively in the following chapters to derive the statistical inference machinery necessary for testing hypotheses and for obtaining confidence intervals:

1. **For normally distributed variables, uncorrelatedness implies independence.**
   Another way of putting this is to say that it is not possible for two jointly normal random variables to be related in a nonlinear fashion: either they are linearly related (i.e., correlated) or they are not related at all (i.e., independent).[19] Recall that all independent random variables are uncorrelated, but that it is not generally true that uncorrelated random variables are independent.
2. **A linear combination (weighted sum) of normally distributed variables is itself a normally distributed variable.**
   This property will turn out to be extremely useful in the following chapters in allowing us to show that parameter estimates, forecasts, and so on (which can be expressed as weighted sums of normally distributed variables) are normally distributed. Note that this property is nearly unique to the normal distribution – in general, it is not the case that weighted sums of random variables from a particular distribution are themselves draws from that same distribution.[20]
3. **A weighted sum involving a large number of random variables is approximately normally distributed.**
   This result motivates much of our interest in normally distributed random variables: because many economic variables can be viewed as weighted sums of a large number of separate influences, it is often reasonable to assume that these variables are approximately normally distributed. In addition, many inherently positive economic variables (e.g., wage rates, firm sizes, etc.) can be viewed as the product of a large number of individual non-negative *factors*. The logarithm of such a variable equals the sum of the logarithms of the individual factors. Thus, for many non-normal economic variables, the logarithm of the variable is approximately normally distributed; this issue is explored in Exercise 2-40.

More formally, the results which lead to this property are called "Central Limit Theorems." The simplest of these theorems (the "Lindeberg–Levy" version) applies to equally weighted sums of identically and independently (IID) random variables with zero mean:

The Central Limit Theorem (Lindeberg–Levy)

If $Y_i \sim IID(\mu, \sigma^2)$, for $i = 1 \ldots N$, then

$$\frac{1}{\sqrt{N}}\sum_{i=1}^{N}(Y_i - \mu) \overset{a}{\sim} N[0, \sigma^2] \tag{2-50}$$

where the symbol "$\overset{a}{\sim}$" stands for "is asymptotically distributed."

Asymptotic or "large sample" theory will be covered in Chapter 11; at this point, "asymptotically distributed" can be taken to mean "approximately distributed, with the approximation becoming arbitrarily accurate as N becomes arbitrarily large."

---

[19] This is proven by observing that the bivariate normal density function factors into two univariate normal density functions (such as Equation 2-47) if, and only if, the covariance parameter is zero.

[20] Most readers should skip this comment, but a more precise statement of this property would state that if the density of a vector of random variables is multivariate normal, then the density of any weighted sum of its components is univariate normal. The possibility that the (marginal) density of each component of a vector is a univariate normal yet the (joint) density of the vector is not multivariate normal cannot be ruled out. In that case, a weighted sum of these components might well not be normally distributed.

Note that the population mean of $Y_i - \mu$ is zero here by construction; remarkably, this turns out to be the key necessary assumption for a version of the Central Limit Theorem to apply, leading to a normal distribution in large samples. In fact, the IID assumption (and hence the equal weighting) is substantially relaxed in other versions of the Central Limit Theorem.[21]

How large does N need to be in order for the Central Limit Theorem to imply that a sum like $(1/\sqrt{N})\sum_{i=1}^{N}(Y_i - \mu)$ is essentially normally distributed? It depends, basically, on two things. First, it depends on just how non-normal the distribution of the Y_i actually is. After all, if the Y_i are normally distributed, then $(1/\sqrt{N})\sum_{i=1}^{N}(Y_i - \mu)$ is exactly normally distributed – even for $N = 1$ – because the second property of normally distributed random variables states that any weighted sum of normally distributed random variables is itself normally distributed. Consequently, one should expect that even small values of N will suffice if the density function for the Y_i is vaguely bell-shaped.

The other crucial issue hinges on exactly what one means by "essentially normal." If one seeks to broadly characterize the shape of the distribution of $(1/\sqrt{N})\sum_{i=1}^{N}(Y_i - \mu)$ over the values which it is most likely to take on, then small values of N (such as 20) will usually suffice, even if the density function for the individual Y_i is not particularly bell-shaped. Unfortunately, for the statistical inference applications in which the Central Limit Theorem is used below, what is usually important is the shape of the *tails* of the distribution of random variables like $(1/\sqrt{N})\sum_{i=1}^{N}(Y_i - \mu)$, and this part of the distribution converges to normality relatively slowly. With values of N greater than 100, however, people generally feel comfortable using the Central Limit Theorem even for the tails of the distribution.[22]

2.12 DISTRIBUTION OF A LINEAR COMBINATION OF NORMALLY DISTRIBUTED RANDOM VARIABLES

Many of the quantities dealt with below (parameter estimators, predictions, and the like) will turn out to be linear combinations (weighted sums) of normally distributed random variables, so it is useful to derive the distribution of such a linear combination here. In this way, the mechanics of the derivation will be familiar when the distribution of this kind of variable is considered later on. To make plain exactly what role the normality assumption plays in the derivation, at the outset the underlying random variables will not be assumed to be normally distributed. Instead, it will only be assumed that these random variables – here called $U_1 \dots U_N$ to correspond with the notation used in Chapter 5 – all have the same mean and variance.

Why is the distribution of a parameter estimator all that important? Foreshadowing some of the results in the chapters to come, the basic motivation is this: When one estimates a parameter in a model using the sample data, all one gets is a number – a single realization of the estimator of that parameter. But we want more. We want to be able to say something about whether or not this is a *good* estimate of the parameter. For that, we need to know whether the distribution of this estimator

[21] For example, a more general form of the Central Limit Theorem is invoked in Appendix 12-1 (Chapter 12), where the asymptotic distribution of the parameter estimator which is the topic of that chapter – and which involves a sum of zero-mean random variables with possibly differing variances – is derived. Also, while it is not an essential issue at this point, but the multiplicative factor $1/\sqrt{N}$ is needed so that the variance of the random variable will tend toward a positive, finite constant (σ^2 here) as the number of terms in the sum grows arbitrarily large.

[22] This issue of how one can determine in practice whether the actual value of N is sufficiently large for asymptotic distributional results to be usefully accurate is readdressed in Section 11.8, where computer-based simulation methods are described.

indicates that the estimator has some of the properties (discussed in Chapter 3) which define and embody the concept of "goodness" in a parameter estimator. And we want to be able to say something about how accurate our estimator is in estimating the parameter. For that, we need to use the distribution of the estimator to construct what is defined (in Chapter 4) as a "confidence interval" for the value of the parameter. And we usually also want to be able to test the validity of hypotheses about this parameter which might be suggested by economic theory. Again, for that we need the distribution of the estimator – and methods discussed in Chapter 4. For these reasons, it turns out to be extraordinarily useful to make some assumptions about certain underlying random variables and then use reasoning essentially identical to that developed in this section to obtain the distribution of the parameter estimator we plan to use.

That motivational preamble complete, let the symbol B – analogous, as we shall see in coming chapters, to the parameter estimator discussed above – stand for a weighted sum of such random variables, where the weights $w_1, w_2, \ldots, w_N$ are fixed constants which will be taken as given here:

$$B \equiv w_1 U_i + w_2 U_i + \ldots + w_N U_i = \sum_{i=1}^{N} w_i U_i \tag{2-51}$$

and let

$$\begin{aligned} E[U_i] &= \mu = \text{mean of } U_i \\ E\left[[U_i - \mu]^2\right] &= \sigma^2 = \text{var}(U_i) = \text{variance of } U_i \\ E\left[[U_i - \mu]\left[U_j - \mu\right]\right] &= \sigma_{ij} = \text{cov}\left(U_i, U_j\right) = \text{covariance of } U_i \text{ and } U_j \end{aligned} \tag{2-52}$$

So as to not clutter the notation, μ and σ^2 are not explicitly labeled with a "U" subscript: it is to be understood from the context that these symbols refer to the population mean and population variance of the random variable U_i rather than to the mean and variance of the random variable B. Note that neither μ nor σ^2 has a subscript "i", this embodies the assumption that $U_1 \ldots U_N$ – while not necessarily identically distributed – all at least have the same mean and variance.

In most of the work in the chapters to come, the underlying random variables will be assumed to be uncorrelated – i.e., corr(U_i, U_j) is assumed to be unequal zero for allvalues of i and j – which implies that the values of σ_{ij} are all 0. But that restriction will not be imposed until the very end of this section.

Finally, the parameters μ, σ^2, and σ_{ij} are taken as given: that is, the intent here is to express the distribution of the random variable B in terms of the values of N, μ, σ^2, and all of the σ_{ij}.

The expectation of B follows directly from a straightforward application of the Linearity Property:

$$E[B] = E\left[\sum_{i=1}^{N} w_i U_i\right] = \sum_{i=1}^{N} w_i E[U_i] = \sum_{i=1}^{N} w_i \mu = \mu \sum_{i=1}^{N} w_i \tag{2-53}$$

Thus, the expectation of a weighted sum of random variables all with mean μ is just μ times the sum of the weights.

As is typical, the calculation of the variance of B is more involved. One always begins by restating the variance in terms of its definition:

$$\text{Var}(B) = E\left[(B - E[B])^2\right] \tag{2-54}$$

and then substituting in an expression for $E[B]$ in terms of given parameter values:

$$\text{Var}(B) = E\left[\left(B - \sum_{i=1}^{N} w_i\mu\right)^2\right] \tag{2-55}$$

The next step is also quite standard: the random variable B is re-expressed in terms of U_1, U_2 , ... U_N, the underlying random variables whose mean, variance, and covariances are known:

$$\text{Var}(B) = E\left[\left(\sum_{i=1}^{N} w_i U_i - \sum_{i=1}^{N} w_i\mu\right)^2\right] \tag{2-56}$$

At this point it is instructive to pause and first consider the special case where $N = 3$:

$$\text{Var}(B) = E\left[([w_1U_1 + w_2U_2 + w_3U_2] - [w_1\mu + w_2\mu + w_3\mu])^2\right] \tag{2-57}$$

The given moments (σ^2 and σ_{ij}, in particular) are defined in terms of expectations involving $U_i - \mu$; consequently, it is useful to combine the two terms in square brackets together:[23]

$$\text{Var}(B) = E\left[(w_1(U_1 - \mu) + w_2(U_2 - \mu) + w_3(U_3 - \mu))^2\right] \tag{2-58}$$

Squaring the term in parentheses yields nine terms, but three of the cross-terms are duplicates, so there are six distinct terms in the expectation:

$$\begin{aligned}\text{Var}(b) = E\Big\{ & w_1^2(U_1 - \mu)^2 + w_2^2(U_2 - \mu)^2 + w_3^2(U_3 - \mu)^2 \\ & + 2\, w_1w_2(U_1 - \mu)(U_2 - \mu) + 2w_1w_3(U_1 - \mu)(U_3 - \mu) \\ & + 2\, w_2w_3(U_2 - \mu)(U_3 - \mu)\}\end{aligned} \tag{2-59}$$

In view of the fact that w_1, w_2, and w_3 are fixed constants, the Linearity Property can be used to simplify this expression:

$$\begin{aligned}\text{Var}(B) &= w_1^2E\left[(U_1 - \mu)^2\right] + w_2^2\, E\left[(U_2 - \mu)^2\right] + w_3^2\left[(U_3 - \mu)^2\right] \\ &\quad + 2\, w_1w_2\, E[(U_1 - \mu)(U_2 - \mu)] + 2\, w_1w_3\, E[(U_1 - \mu)(U_3 - \mu)] \\ &\quad + 2\, w_2w_3\, E[(U_2 - \mu)(U_3 - \mu)] \\ &= w_1^2\, \text{var}(U_1) + w_2^2\, \text{var}(U_2) + w_3^2\, \text{var}(U_3) \\ &\quad + 2\, w_1w_2\, \text{cov}(U_1, U_2) + 2\, w_1w_3\, \text{cov}(U_1, U_3) + 2\, w_2w_3\, \text{cov}(U_2, U_3) \\ &= w_1^2\sigma^2 + w_2^2\sigma^2 + w_3^2\sigma^2 + 2\, w_1w_2\sigma_{12} + 2\, w_1w_3\sigma_{13} + 2\, w_2w_3\sigma_{23}\end{aligned} \tag{2-60}$$

Thus the variance of the weighted sum B is just the variance of the underlying random variables (U_1 ... U_N) times the sum of the squares of the weights, plus some terms involving the covariances of the underlying random variables.

[23] Note also that the entire term in parentheses is going to be squared. It currently has 6 terms in it, which will lead to 36 terms in the square. Surely, it will be more convenient to reduce this to 3 terms, leading to only 9 terms in the square. In general, it is wise to simplify this expression as much as possible prior to squaring it.

After "warming up" on the special case of $N = 3$, we now return to the general expression for the variance of B:

$$\operatorname{Var}(B) = E\left[\left(\sum_{i=1}^{N} w_i U_i - \sum_{i=1}^{N} w_i \mu\right)^2\right] \tag{2-61}$$

and evaluate it for any value of N. This derivation will use summation notation, but its strategy is essentially identical to that used above. Combining these two sums into one,

$$\operatorname{Var}(B) = E\left[\left(\sum_{i=1}^{N} w_i (U_i - \mu)\right)^2\right] \tag{2-62}$$

Replacing the square of the sum by the product of the sum times itself yields

$$\operatorname{Var}(B) = E\left[\left(\sum_{j=1}^{N} w_j (U_j - \mu)\right)\left(\sum_{i=1}^{N} w_i (U_i - \mu)\right)\right] = E\left[H\left(\sum_{i=1}^{N} w_i (U_i - \mu)\right)\right] \tag{2-63}$$

where a different running index is used in each sum so as to keep them distinct. The random variable H is defined so as to emphasize notationally that, while random, the sum $H \equiv \sum_{j=1}^{N} w_j (U_j - \mu)$ can be moved inside the sum over the running index i:

$$\begin{aligned}\operatorname{Var}(B) &= E\left[H \sum_{i=1}^{N} w_i (U_i - \mu)\right] = E\left[\sum_{i=1}^{N} w_i (U_i - \mu) H\right] = E\left[\sum_{i=1}^{N} w_i [(U_i - \mu) H]\right] \\ &= E\left[\sum_{i=1}^{N} w_i \left[(U_i - \mu) \sum_{j=1}^{N} w_j (U_j - \mu)\right]\right]\end{aligned} \tag{2-64}$$

where (having done its work for us) H is replaced by its definition on the last step.

Thus, var(B) is the expected value of a weighted sum of random variables, where the random variables are defined by the expression in the square brackets. This expectation can be rewritten, using the Linearity Property, as the weighted sum of the expected values of these random variables:

$$\begin{aligned}\operatorname{Var}(B) &= \sum_{i=1}^{N} w_i E\left[(U_i - \mu) \sum_{j=1}^{N} w_j (U_j - \mu)\right] \\ &= \sum_{i=1}^{N} w_i E\left[\sum_{j=1}^{N} w_j (U_i - \mu)(U_j - \mu)\right]\end{aligned} \tag{2-65}$$

where the factor $U_i - \mu$ has been moved inside the sum over the running index j. Applying the Linearity Property to the resulting expectation yields

$$\operatorname{Var}(B) = \sum_{i=1}^{N} w_i \left[\sum_{j=1}^{N} w_j E[(U_i - \mu)(U_j - \mu)]\right] \tag{2-66}$$

The expectation in this expression is equal to the variance σ^2 for the terms in the sum over j where j equals i and it is equal to the covariance σ_{ij} for the remaining terms, where j is unequal to i. Thus,

$$\operatorname{Var}(B) = \sum_{i=1}^{N} w_i \left[w_i \sigma^2 + \sum_{\substack{j=1 \\ j \neq i}}^{N} w_j \sigma_{ij}\right] = \sigma^2 \sum_{i=1}^{N} w_i^2 + \sum_{i=1}^{N} \sum_{\substack{j=1 \\ j \neq i}}^{N} w_i w_j \sigma_{ij} \tag{2-67}$$

Thus, for all N, the variance of the weighted sum B is just the variance of the underlying random variables times the sum of the squares of the weights, plus terms involving all of the covariances of the underlying random variables.[24]

If the U_i's are uncorrelated – as will typically be assumed to be the case in the chapters to follow – then $\sigma_{ij} = 0$ for all $i \neq j$. In that case, this result becomes

If

$$B \equiv \sum_{i=1}^{N} w_i U_i$$

with

$$E[U_i] = \mu \quad \text{and} \quad \text{var}(U_i) = \sigma^2 \quad \text{for all } i \text{ in } [1 > 2, \ldots, N]$$

and

$$\text{cov}(U_i, U_j) = 0 \quad \text{for all } i \text{ and } j \text{ in } [1 > 2, \ldots, N]$$

Then

$$E[B] = \mu \sum_{i=1}^{N} w_i \quad \text{and} \quad \text{var}(B) = \sigma^2 \sum_{i=1}^{N} w_i^2$$

(2-68)

If the $U_1 \ldots U_N$ are ***normally distributed*** and uncorrelated, then they are also independent; in that case, the assumptions on the U_i's can be compactly expressed as $U_i \sim \text{NIID}[\mu, \sigma^2]$. Also, because a weighted sum of normally distributed random variables is itself normally distributed, it follows that B is normally distributed. Therefore, if the U_i's are assumed to be normally distributed, then the complete distribution of B is as follows:

If

$$B \equiv \sum_{i=1}^{N} w_i U_i \quad \text{with} \quad U_i \sim \text{NIID}[\mu, \sigma^2]$$

Then

$$B \sim N\left[\mu \sum_{i=1}^{N} w_i,\ \sigma^2 \sum_{i=1}^{N} w_i^2\right]$$

(2-69)

2.13 CONCLUSION

This last derivation, of the distribution of a weighted sum of normally distributed random variables, concludes the chapter and completes your preparation for the material in the chapters to come. In fact, the "hard part" is now over: most of the material from this point on is really just an application of the concepts and techniques you have worked on in this chapter.

---

[24] Alternatively, one could use the result on double sums in the Mathematics Review section at the end of the book to immediately replace the square of $\sum_{i=1}^{N} w_i(U_i - \mu)$ by $\sum_{i=1}^{N}\sum_{j=1}^{N} w_i(U_i - \mu)w_j(U_i - \mu)$ and apply the Linearity Property to the expectation of this double sum.

KEY TERMS

For each term or concept listed below, provide a working definition or explanation:

Expected Value (Population Mean) of a Random Variable
Population Variance of a Random Variable
Covariance of a Pair of Random Variables
Statistical Independence
Normal Distribution
Central Limit Theorem

EXERCISES

2-1. What makes a random variable "random"?

2-2. What is meant by a "discretely distributed" random variable?

2-3. For a discretely distributed random variable with m possible states, what is the value of $\sum_{i=1}^{m} p_i$?

2-4. What is the probability of rolling a number greater than three on a fair die?

2-5.

Realized value of $Y(c_j)$:	5	8	9	11
Probability (p_j):	0.1	0.4	0.2	0.3

What is the value of $E[Y]$? What is the value of var(Y)?

2-6. What is the difference between $E[Y]$, the observed sample mean, $(\bar{y})$, and the sample mean, $(\bar{Y})$?

2-7. Let c_i (the realized value of Y in state i) be equal to the value of i and let $p_1 = p_2 = p_3 = p_4 = 1/8$, $p_5 = p_6 = 0$, and $p_7 = p_8 = 1/4$. What are the values of the population mean and variance of Y?

2-8. Why is the value of $E[Y]$ typically unknown?

2-9. What is the kth central moment about 0? How does this differ from the kth central moment about the mean?

2-10. Let the particular function $g(Y) = Y^3$, $p_1 = p_2 = p_3 = 1/5$, $p_4 = p_5 = p_6 = p_7 = 1/10$, and let c_i (the realized value of Y in state i) be equal to the value of i.

a. What is the value of $E[g(y)]$?

b. What is the value of var$\{g(y)\}$?

2-11. If the random variable Y is continuously distributed on the real line, what values can a particular realization of Y take?

2-12. Suppose $E[Y] = 11.34$. What is the value of $E[Y - 3]$?

2-13. Suppose $E[Y] = 25$. What is the value of $E[3Y]$?

2-14. Suppose var$\{Y\} = 11.34$. What is the value of var$\{Y - 8\}$?

2-15. Suppose var$\{Y\} = 25$. What is the value of var$\{3Y\}$?

2-16. Suppose $E[Y] = 11$ and var$\{Y\} = 3$. Find the values of $E[3Y + 7]$ and var$\{3Y + 7\}$.

2-17. Suppose cov$(Y, Z) < 0$. What does this mean?

2-18. Why is correlation often more useful than covariance?

2-19. What values can the correlation between two random variables take on?

2-20. In the Linearity Property, $E[c_1Y_1 + \ldots + c_NY_N] = c_1E[Y_1] + \ldots + c_N[Y_N]$. What restriction is placed on $c_1 \ldots c_N$?

2-21. Suppose $E[Y] = 4$, $E[Z] = 3$, and $E[YZ] = 13$. What is the value of cov(*Y*, *Z*)?

2-22. Suppose corr(*Y*, *Z*) = 0, $E[Y] = 3$, and $E[Z] = 4$, What is the value of $E[YZ]$?

2-23. In what way are independent random variables related?

2-24. Using the notation of Equation 2-42, suppose that *Y* and *Z* are discretely and independently distributed and that $p_{1,4} = 1/4$. What does this imply about the probability that $Y = a_1$ (regardless of the value that *Z* takes on) and the probability that $Z = b_4$ (regardless of the value that *Y* takes on)?

2-25. Suppose *Y* and *Z* are independent random variables, that *g* (*Y*) and *w* (*Z*) are functions, that $E[g\ (Y)] = 4$, and that $E[g\ (Y)w\ (Z)] = 12$. What is the value of $E[w(Z)]$?

2-26. Suppose *Y* and *Z* are independent random variables. What is the value of cov(*Y*, *Z*)?

2-27. Does cov(*Y*, *Z*) = 0 imply that *Y* and *Z* are independent? Explain your answer.

2-28. When it is asserted that two random variables *Y* and *Z* are "identically and independently distributed," what, exactly, is meant by the term "identically"?

2-29. Suppose that the population mean and variance of a normally distributed variable are given. Does this completely determine the distribution of this random variable? How would your answer differ if the variable were not known to be normally distributed?

2-30. Let $G = \sum_{j=1}^{3} v_i U_i$ with $U_i \sim \text{NIID}[10,\ 4]$ and $v_1 = 3, v_2 = 2, v_3 = 1$. Completely characterize the distribution of *G*.

2-31. Assuming that *a* and *b* are constants and that *X* and *Y* are random variables, show that

$$\text{var}(aX + aY) = a^2\text{var}(X) + 2\,ab\,\text{cov}(X, Y) + b^2\ \text{var}(Y)$$

2-32. Suppose that *Y* is a random variable with mean μ and variance σ_2, and that *Z* is defined

$$Z = 15Y + 3$$

Derive expressions for $E[Z]$ and Var(*Z*) in terms of μ and σ^2.

2-33. Suppose that

$$\begin{aligned} Y &= c + d \quad \text{with probability} \quad P \\ &= d \qquad\ \ \text{with probability} \quad (1 - P) \end{aligned}$$

a. Derive expressions for $E[Y]$ and var(*Y*) in tems of *c*, *d*, and *P*. {Hint: the expression for var (*Y*) is simple: $d^2P\ (1-P)$.}

b. Show that the Var(*Y*) > 0 so long as *d* is not zero and $0 < P < 1$. Briefly interpret this in terms of the meaning attached to the concept of the variance of a random variable.

2-34. This exercise gives you some practice with a discretely distributed random variable:

Probability Distribution of *X*	
probability that $X = 5.0$	0.15
probability that $X = 6.0$	0.25
probability that $X = 7.0$	0.30
probability that $X = 8.0$	0.10
probability that $X = 9.0$	0.20

Four independent sample observations on *X*	
i	x_i
1	6
2	8
3	7
4	7

a. Calculate μ, the population mean of X – i.e., calculate $E[X]$. Is this a realization of a random variable, or is it a fixed constant? What role, if any, do the four sample observations on X play in this calculation?

b. Calculate σ^2, the population variance of X – i.e., calculate $E[(X-\mu)^2]$. Is this a realization of a random variable, or is it a fixed constant? What role, if any, do the four sample observations on X play in this calculation?

c. Calculate $\bar{x}$, the realization of the **sample** mean of X implied by the sample data given above. This realization is a fixed number, as is μ. Are they the same?

d. Calculate the expected value of the square root of X – i.e., $E\left[\sqrt{X}\right]$. {Hint: X is discretely distributed with just five possible values, so your expression should only contain five terms.} How does this compare to the square root of $E[X]$? Think a bit about why these differ in the way they do. {Hint: It has to do with the concavity of the square root function.} Foreshadowing material in Chapter 3, this result implies that if we take the square root of an unbiased estimator of the population variance of a random variable – i.e., the square root of an estimator whose expectation is the correct value for the population variance – we will get an estimator which is not an unbiased estimator of the standard deviation.

2-35. Suppose that $Y_1 \ldots Y_N$ are all uncorrelated – i.e., $\text{cov}(Y_k, Y_s) = 0$ for all unequal values of k and s in $[1, 2, 3, \ldots, N]$. You may also assume that $Y_1 \ldots Y_N$ all have the same population mean, μ, and the same population variance, σ^2. Where the symbols "i" and "j" appear below, assume that both i and j are in $\{1, 2, 3, \ldots, N\}$ and that i is not equal to j; $\overline{Y}$ below denotes the usual sample mean. Derive expressions (involving only μ, σ^2, N, i, and j) for the following:

a. $E\left[Y_i^2\right]$ [Hint: Start from definition of var(Y_i); the answer is $\mu^2 + \sigma^2$.]

b. $E[Y_iY_j]$[Hint: Start from the definition of cov($Y_i Y_j$); the answer is μ^2.]

c. $E\left[Y_i\,\overline{Y}\right]$ [Hint: You might find it easiest to first let i explicitly equal five (with $N > 5$) and then derive an expression for $E\left[Y_5\,\overline{Y}\right]$. That done, you should be able to fairly easily generalize your derivation to any value of i such that $1 \le i \le N$; the answer is $\mu^2 + \sigma^2/N$.]

Use your results in parts a, b, and c above to evaluate the items below. {These results will be used in Chapters 3 and 4 – they are actually meaningful and important results, not just exercises!}

d. $E[\overline{Y}^2]$ [Hint: Replace *one* factor of $\overline{Y}$ by its definition in terms of a sum and use the result obtained in part c.]

e. $\text{Var}\left[\overline{Y}\right]$

f. $\text{cov}\left\{Y_i, \overline{Y}\right\}$

g. $\text{var}\left\{Y_i - \overline{Y}\right\}$

h. $\text{cov}\left\{\left[Y_i - \overline{Y}\right], \overline{Y}\right\}$

i. $\text{cov}\left\{\left[Y_i - \overline{Y}\right], \left[Y_j - \overline{Y}\right]\right\}$

2-36. Assume that $V_1 \ldots V_{50}$ are uncorrelated with mean μ and positive variance σ^2. Define

$$B = \sum_{i=1}^{50} w_i V_i$$

where $w_1 \ldots w_{50}$ are given, fixed constants. Show that $\text{cov}(V_j, B)$ is equal to $w_j\,\sigma^2$ for all j in the interval one to 50 inclusive. Thus, V_3, say, and B are correlated unless w_3 is zero. (Note that V_3 does not actually appear in the expression for B if w_3 does equal zero.)

2-37. Assume that V_i – NIID (μ, σ^2) for all i and define the random variable r as

$$R = \sum_{i=1}^{N} m_i V_i$$

where $m_1 \ldots m_N$ are given, fixed constants. Derive the distribution of R.

2-38. An investor has the opportunity to buy stock in two publicly traded companies, Acme European Security Services and Vulnerable U.S. Business. Acme European Security Services will pay dividends in the amount of Z dollars, where the value of Z, b_k, depends on which of two states of the world occurs. Vulnerable U.S. Business, Inc., will pay dividends in the amount of Y dollars, where the value of Y, a_j, depends on which of two states of the world occurs. Vulnerable U.S. Business will do well if and only if the United State Department of Homeland Security is effective and prevents all terrorist acts in the United States during the year. Acme European Security Services will do well if and only if European security agencies are ineffective, so that they get plenty of business, in Europe and elsewhere. Because the differential impact on the profits of these two firms of possible terrorist activities (in the United States and in Europe), the random variables Z and Y are not independently distributed; in particular, their joint probability distribution is given by

		Acme European Security Services	
		$Z = b_1 = 0$	$Z = b_2 = 10$
Vulnerable U.S. Business	$Y = a_1 = 0$	$p_{11} = .10$	$p_{12} = .40$
	$Y = a_2 = 10$	$p_{21} = .40$	$p_{22} = .10$

Using Equations 2-26 through 2-33:

a. Compute the (population) mean and variance of the dividends which will be paid by Acme European Security Services, Inc., showing your work.

b. Compute the (population) mean and variance of the dividends which will be paid by Vulnerable U. S. Business, Inc., showing your work. Is an investment in shares of Vulnerable U. S. Business, Inc., any riskier than an investment in shares of Acme European Security Services, Inc.?

c. Compute the covariance and the correlation of Y and Z, showing your work. Why, in terms of the probabilities, are these negative?

d. This investor contemplates diversifying his/her portfolio by investing equally in the stock of each of these two firms. Compute the mean and variance of the dividends which would be paid on such a portfolio. Is the diversified portfolio preferable? Briefly explain this result in economic terms.

2-39. Consider two random variables, Y and Z, such that $E[Y]$ and $E[Z]$ are both zero and such that var(Y) and var(Z) are both one. Because both variances are equal to one, ρ_{YZ}, the correlation between Y and Z is in this case numerically equal to cov(Y, Z); your answers to this question can be left in terms of ρ_{YZ}.

a. State expressions for var($Y + Z$) and var($Y - Z$). {Hint: Use the expression for var(B) derived in Exercise 2-31.}

b. How do var($Y + Z$) and var($Y - Z$) differ if $\rho_{YZ} = 0$? Why?

c. What happens to var($Y + Z$) as ρ_{YZ} approaches -1? Why?

d. What happens to var($Y - Z$) as ρ_{YZ} approaches $+1$? Why?

e. What happens to var($Y + Z$) as ρ_{YZ} approaches 1? Why?

f. In view of your answers to parts c and d, is it possible for $|\rho_{yz}|$ to exceed one for these two random variables?

2-40. Wages are observed to vary widely across households, presumably because success and failure in the labor marketplace depend on a large number of genetic, developmental, and environmental factors.

a. Suppose that W_i, the wages of the ith household, equals the sum of k such factors, each of which can be taken to be roughly identically and independently distributed:

$$W_i = X_{i,1} + X_{i,2} + \dots + X_{i,k} = \sum_{j=1}^{k} X_{i,j} \text{ where } X_{i,j} \text{ is approximately i.i.d.}\left(\mu, \sigma^2\right)$$

What does the Central Limit Theorem then imply about the distribution of W_i if k is large? Can this result possibly imply a negative value for observed wages?

b. Suppose that W_i, the wages of the ith household, equals the ***product*** of k such factors, each of which is positive-valued and can be taken to be roughly identically and independently distributed:

$$W_i = Y_{i,1} \times Y_{i,2} \times \dots \times Y_{i,k} \text{ where } Y_{i,j} > 0 \text{ and is approximately i.i.d.}\left(\mu, \sigma^2\right)$$

What does the Central Limit Theorem imply about the distribution of W_i if k is large? What does the Central Limit Theorem imply about the distribution of the *logarithm* of W_i if k is large? Why was it necessary to restrict the multiplicative factors $Y_{i,1} \dots Y_{i,M}$ to be strictly positive? Can this result possibly imply a negative value for observed wages?

2-41. A pair of six-sided dice (one red and one blue) are connected by a short length of rubber band. It has been determined that the joint distribution of the random variables (R, B) is as follows, where R is the number of red dots showing and B is the number of blue dots showing:

		Joint Probability Distribution					
		Number of Dots Showing on Red Die (R)					
Number of Dots Showing on Blue Die (B)		1	2	3	4	5	6
	1	4/60	4/60	0	0	0	0
	2	0	4/60	2/60	3/60	0	0
	3	0	0	3/60	5/60	0	0
	4	0	0	0	6/60	7/60	4/60
	5	0	0	5/60	4/60	0	0
	6	5/60	4/60	0	0	0	0

a. Ignoring the value of B, state the probability distribution for R. (This is the marginal distribution of R.) Compute the value of $E[R]$, the population mean of R.

b. Restricting attention only to those outcomes in which B equals 2 – i.e., in which two dots are showing on the blue die – state the probability distribution for R. This is the conditional distribution of R with $B = 2$. {Hint: Recall that the sum of the probabilities over all of the possible values for R must sum to 1.} Compute the value of $E[R \mid B = 2]$, the mean of R conditional on $B = 2$.

c. Also compute $E[R \mid B = 1]$, $E[R \mid B = 3]$, $E[R \mid B = 4]$, $E[R \mid B = 5]$, and $E[R \mid B = 6]$. What can you conclude about the relationship between B and R based on how the conditional mean of R varies with the observed value of B?

2-42. Suppose that Y and Z are discretely distributed, with joint distribution given by

j	k	$a_j = Y_j$	$b_k = Z_k$	$P_{j,k}$
1	1	2	3	1/27
1	2	2	7	2/27
1	3	2	8	3/27
2	1	4	3	4/27
2	2	4	7	10//27
2	3	4	8	7/27

Keeping three decimal places in all of your calculations,

a. Give an explicit numerical expression for $E(Y)$ and for $E(Z)$.

b. Give an explicit numerical expression for $\text{var}(Y)$ and for $\text{var}(Z)$.

c. Give an explicit numerical expression for $\text{cov}(Y, Z)$.

Active Learning Exercise 2a: The Normal Distribution

The purpose of this exercise is to familiarize you with the normal distribution and to explicitly introduce you to the use of numerical approximations implemented in computer software for evaluating tail areas of distributions. (The latter have largely supplanted the use of printed tables.) In Chapter 4 we will see how these tail areas are used in testing hypotheses about the population mean of a normally distributed variable; in Chapters 7 and 9 similar tail areas are used in testing hypotheses regarding coefficients in regression models.

Instructions:

1. Graph and evaluate the unit normal cumulative distribution and density functions using Excel:

   a. Fill rows 1 to 61 of column A with the values −3.0, −2.9, −2.8 ... 2.8, 2.9, 3.0. The easy way to do this is to enter −3. in cell A1, enter the formula "= a1 +.1" in cell A2, and then fill down to cell A61. Copy this column of data to column C.

   b. Enter "= normdist(A1,0,1,true) "in cell B1 and fill down to cell B61; similarly, enter "= normdist(A1,0,1, false)" in cell D1 and fill down to cell D61. Now column B contains the values of the unit normal cumulative distribution function and column D contains the values of the unit normal density function. Graph the unit normal cumulative distribution function by highlighting cells A1 through B61, selecting the "Insert" tab at the top of this screen, selecting the "Scatter" button, and picking the icon with the smooth curves.
   Repeat for the unit normal density function by instead highlighting cells C1 through D61 and making the same selections. Print out these two plots.

c. What is the probability that a unit normal variable will exceed the value 0.7? This corresponds to 1 minus the height of the cumulative distribution function at value $Z = 0.7$ and also to the area under the density function to the right of 0.7. This area is also equal to the value of the integral

$$\int_{0.7}^{\infty} \frac{1}{\sqrt{2\pi}} e^{-\frac{Z^2}{2}} dZ$$

Note also that, reflecting the fact the unit normal density function is symmetric around its mean of 0, the probability of a unit normal variable exceeding 0 is one-half, so the value of the cumulative distribution function at $Z = 0.0$ is one-half.

2. Calculate unit normal distribution tail areas using the stand-alone program gaustail.exe.
   a. Copy the files "gaustail.exe" and "gaustail.for" (available at www.wiley.com/college/ashley) to a subdirectory on your computer.
   b. Look at the file "gaustail.for" using a word processor or text editor. This file contains the source code for the executable program gaustail.exe. Notice that the program just evaluates a somewhat complicated formula which accurately approximates the required tail areas.
   c. Double click on the file "gaustail.exe" to execute the program.[25] Type in the value ".4" (without the quote marks) and press the Enter key on your keyboard. The program then returns the probability that a unit normal will exceed this value, which should equal .34458, consistent with your Excel result (0.65542) above in cell B35.[26] Thus,

$$\int_{0.4}^{\infty} \frac{1}{\sqrt{2\pi}} e^{-\frac{z^2}{2}} dz = .34458$$

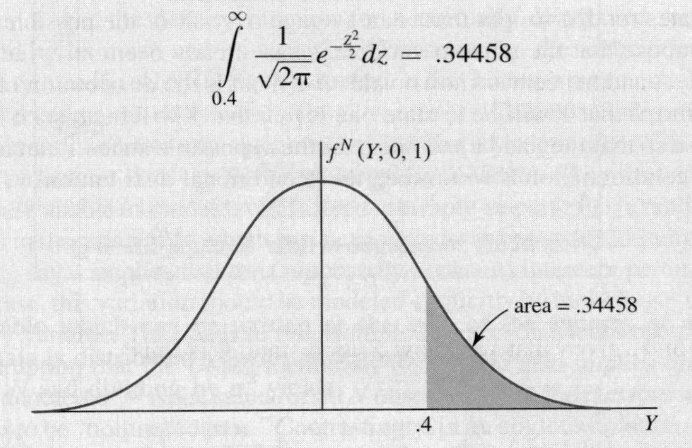

3. Between the nearly omnipresent availability of Excel, ownership of a copy of gaustail.exe, and the fact that typical econometrics software generally evaluates and displays the tail areas relevant to all statistical results obtained anyway, recourse to the statistical tables tabulating tail areas for the unit normal distribution is no longer necessary. This is why you will not find a copy of such a table at the end of this book.

[25] This program executes in the Windows XP and Windows 7 environments, but not in Windows Vista.

[26] Excel will produce nicer-looking and more informative plots if one inserts a line of column labels in the first row; this result will in that case be in cell B36.

APPENDIX 2.1: THE CONDITIONAL MEAN OF A RANDOM VARIABLE

The regression models at the heart of econometrics are often viewed as models for the conditional mean of a variable. Consequently, defining and clarifying the distinction between the marginal and conditional distributions of a random variable is of some importance.

Recall the definition of the distribution of a pair of discrete random variables given earlier in this chapter:

Distribution of a Pair of Discrete Random Variables

$$\begin{aligned} Y &= a_1 \text{ or } a_2 \text{ or} \ldots \text{or } a_m \ (m \text{ possible states}) \\ Z &= b_1 \text{ or } b_2 \text{ or} \ldots \text{or } b_n \ (n \text{ possible states}) \\ p_{jk} &= \text{probability that } Y = a_j \text{ ("}Y\text{ is in state } j\text{") } \textit{and} \text{ that } Z = b_k \text{ ("}Z\text{ is in state } k\text{")} \end{aligned} \tag{A2-1}$$

Note that because a_j does not depend on the running index (k) in the sum over the n possible states Z can be in, $E[Y]$ can also be written as

$$E[Y] \equiv \mu_Y \equiv \sum_{j=1}^{m}\sum_{k=1}^{n} a_j p_{jk} = \sum_{j=1}^{m} a_j \sum_{k=1}^{n} p_{jk} = \sum_{j=1}^{m} a_j \tilde{\ } p_j \tag{A2-2}$$

This expression defines the quantities $\tilde{p}_1 = \sum_{k=1}^{n} p_{1k} \cdots \tilde{p}_m = \sum_{k=1}^{n} p_{mk}$, which are called the "marginal distribution" of Y. Thus, we see that the expected value of Y can equivalently be viewed as its expectation over its marginal distribution. In essence, the marginal distribution assigns each of the m possible states for Y a weight that is an average over all of the possible states Z can take on.

In contrast, suppose that the random variable Z has already been observed to be in a particular state – state 3, say – and hence has known value b_3. What is the distribution of Y in that case? Now the relative likelihood that Y will be in state one is p_{13}, that Y will be in state 2 is p_{23}, and so forth. Normalizing these so that they add up to one over the m possible states Y can take on, we obtain the distribution of Y conditional on $Z = b_3$ – i.e., the "conditional distribution" of Y given that $Z = b_3$:

$$p_1^{Z=b_3} \equiv \frac{p_{13}}{\sum_{s=1}^{m} p_{s3}} \cdots p_m^{Z=b_3} \equiv \frac{p_{m3}}{\sum_{s=1}^{m} p_{s3}} \tag{A2-3}$$

The expectation of Y, given that we know Z is in state 3, is thus

$$E[Y|Z = b_3] \equiv \sum_{j=1}^{m} a_j p_j^{Z=b_3} \tag{A2-4}$$

and is called "the conditional mean of Y, evaluated at $Z = b_3$." The conditional mean is an important concept because it quantifies how Y varies, on average, with Z. That is why we will see in Chapter 5 that it is closely related to the bivariate regression of Y on z.[27]

[27] Exercise 2-41 provides some practice with this concept; see Fruend (1971, p. 133), *Mathematical Statistics*, Prentice-Hall New Jersey: for analogous material on continuous random variables.

APPENDIX 2.2: PROOF OF THE LINEARITY PROPERTY FOR THE EXPECTATION OF A WEIGHTED SUM OF TWO DISCRETELY DISTRIBUTED RANDOM VARIABLES

Suppose that Y and Z are two discretely distributed random variables, with Y taking on values a_1 ... a_m (so that "i" indexes the m possible states for Y) and with Z taking on values b_1 ... b_n, so that "ℓ" indexes the n possible states for Z. The probability of observing Y in state i (i.e., $y = a_i$) and Z in state ℓ (i.e., $z = b_\ell$) is denoted $p_{i\ell}$.

If $f_y(\cdot)$ and $f_z(\cdot)$ are any two specified functions and c_y and c_z are any two (fixed) constants, then the Linearity Property for Expectations states that

$$E\left[c_y f_y(y) + c_z f_z(z)\right] = c_y E\left[f_y(y)\right] + c_z E\left[f_z(z)\right] \tag{A2.5}$$

Proof:

$$\begin{aligned} E\left[c_Y f_Y(Y) + c_Z f_z(Z)\right] &= \sum_{i=1}^{m}\sum_{\ell=1}^{n}\{c_Y f_Y(a_i) + c_Z f_Z(b_\ell)\}p_{i\ell} \\ &= \sum_{i=1}^{m}\sum_{\ell=1}^{n}\{c_Y f_Y(a_i)p_{i\ell} + c_Z f_Z(b_\ell)p_{i\ell}\} \\ &= \sum_{i=1}^{m}\sum_{\ell=1}^{n}\{c_Y f_Y(a_i)p_{i\ell}\} + \sum_{i=1}^{m}\sum_{\ell=1}^{n}\{c_Z f_Z(b_\ell)p_{i\ell}\} \\ &= c_Y\sum_{i=1}^{m}\sum_{\ell=1}^{n}\{f_Y(a_i)p_{i\ell}\} + c_Z\sum_{i=1}^{m}\sum_{\ell=1}^{n}\{f_Z(b_\ell)p_{i\ell}\} \\ &= c_Y E\{f_Y(Y)\} + c_Z E\{f_Z(Z)\} \end{aligned} \tag{A2-6}$$

If the double sums confuse you, try setting the number of states for each of the random variables (m and n) both to two and writing the double sums out explicitly. This proof generalizes easily to a larger number of discretely distributed random variables and to functions which each depend on more than one of the random variables. It also generalizes to continuously distributed random variables, replacing the double sums by double integrals and replacing the probability distribution ($p_{i\ell}$) by a joint density function, $G\,(Y, Z\,)$; in that case one must assume that all of the expectations exist – i.e., are finite.

3

Estimating the Mean of a Normally Distributed Random Variable

3.1 INTRODUCTION

As noted in Chapter 2, the two most important attributes of a random variable are its population mean (μ) and its population variance (σ^2): the first of these quantifies how large it is and the second quantifies how random it is. Indeed, for a normally distributed random variable, these two population quantities completely determine its distribution. Alternatively, we saw that the distribution of a random variable can be used to calculate μ and σ^2.

In practice, however, neither these population quantities (μ and σ^2) nor the distribution are known, and our object is to estimate them using a random sample of N observations on the random variable. This chapter develops the fundamental material on how this can best be accomplished, with particular attention paid to the task of estimating the mean of a normally distributed random variable; the analogous issues involved in estimating the variance are taken up toward the end of Chapter 4, where that material is particularly needed.

It is essential to note that estimating μ (or any parameter in any model, for that matter) is trivially easy if one is unconcerned with the quality of one's estimate. Consequently, the focus here (and throughout this book) is not merely on obtaining a parameter estimate, but rather on obtaining a *good* parameter estimate. Indeed, this chapter is mostly about how this notion of estimator "goodness" can be embodied in a set of properties which an estimator can have or fail to have.

The motivation for covering this material here is twofold. First, the concepts developed in this chapter (such as an estimator's sampling distribution) are also crucial to effectively understanding and using the statistical inference machinery reviewed in Chapter 4. And second, in Chapter 6 we will find that estimating the parameters in a regression model is actually very closely related to estimating the mean of a random variable – so much so that all of the concepts and techniques in this chapter will reappear there. Thus, the idea here is to first describe these concepts and techniques in the simplest and most familiar setting possible.

Suppose, then, that the N random variables $Y_1 \ldots Y_N$ are normally, identically, and independently distributed with population mean μ and population variance σ^2:

$$Y_i \sim \text{NIID}(\mu, \sigma^2) \quad \text{for } i = 1 \ldots N \tag{3-1}$$

How can one use the sample realizations $y_1 \ldots y_N$ of these random variables to estimate μ? The answer to this question might seem intuitively obvious in this simple context: because μ is just the population mean of the Y_i, it is clearly sensible to use the observed sample mean

$$\bar{y} = \left(\frac{1}{N}\right)\sum_{i=1}^{N} y_i \tag{3-2}$$

to estimate μ. This procedure of using a function of sample moments to estimate the analogous function of population moments has a respectable history and is called the "method of moments." But this is not the only choice one could make. In fact, any function depending on some or all of the y_i's and not explicitly depending on any unknown parameters (i.e., on μ or σ^2 in this case) could be used as an estimator of μ. Thus, the sample median[1] (y_{median}), or $\hat{\mu}_{.95} \equiv .95\bar{y}$, or $\tilde{\mu} \equiv 15$ are possible choices also.

How then, might one sensibly choose between $\bar{y}$, y_{median}, $\hat{\mu}_{.95}$, $\tilde{\mu}$, and the multitude of other possible estimators? In the end, as with every other choice in life, the rational selection of an estimator depends on our preferences or values. In econometric work, these values are usually summarized in a handful of properties, the presence of which are taken to characterize "goodness" in an estimator. In this chapter a selection of the most important estimator properties usually considered in econometric analysis is explicitly discussed in the context of estimating μ:

1. Best Fit – the estimator yields a model which fits the sample data well in a particular sense.
2. Unbiased – the estimator is correct on average.
3. Consistent – the estimator is correct for sufficiently large N.
4. Best Linear Unbiased (BLU) – the estimator has the minimum possible sampling error variance out of the class of linear and unbiased estimators.
5. Efficient – the estimator has the minimum possible sampling error variance out of the class of unbiased estimators.
6. Minimum MSE – the estimator has the minimum possible mean squared error.

The "best fit" property is discussed first. This property is intuitively appealing, but it is not fully defined as it stands because the "best fit" estimator depends on what criterion is used for quantifying how well the model fits the sample. In particular, we will find below that the sample mean ($\bar{y}$) yields the best fit on one reasonable criterion, but that the sample median (y_{median}) yields the best fit on another.

The remaining properties are best discussed in terms of an estimator's probability (or "sampling") distribution. Indeed, the concept of an estimator's sampling distribution so thoroughly permeates all econometric analysis that it is essential to carefully review this concept at the outset. Note that the *observed* sample mean ($\bar{y}$ defined earlier) is a fixed number because $y_1 \ldots y_N$ are realizations of the random variables $Y_1 \ldots Y_N$ and therefore are fixed numbers. In contrast, the sample mean itself,

$$\overline{Y} = \left(\frac{1}{N}\right)\sum_{i=1}^{N} Y_i \tag{3-3}$$

is a random variable, because each of $Y_1 \ldots Y_N$ is a random variable distributed NIID(μ, σ^2). Because $\overline{Y}$ is random, its value is characterized by its sampling distribution. This distribution is obtained below using the results derived at the end of Chapter 2 and is then itself used to show that $\overline{Y}$ is an unbiased and consistent estimator for μ.

At that point the specification of an explicit loss function on the estimation errors becomes essential. This function quantifies the costliness of the errors our estimators make – both positive and negative – in

[1] The sample median is the "middle" value; as many of the sample values lie below it as above it.

estimating μ. For one thing, such a specification is necessary in order to say anything meaningful about how desirable unbiasedness in an estimator actually is. Further, by particularizing the loss function to be proportional to the square of the estimation error, it is possible to motivate the last three properties listed above: BLUness, efficiency, and minimum MSE. Interestingly, it turns out that $\overline{Y}$ is BLU and efficient for μ, but it does not have the minimum MSE property.

The discussion continues by considering the first estimator property, "Best Fit."

3.2 ESTIMATING μ BY CURVE FITTING

Because μ, the population mean of the y_i, is effectively a measure of the size of this random variable, fitting a horizontal straight line to the observed data on y_i – i.e., $y_1 \ldots y_N$ – provides an intuitively appealing way to obtain an estimator for μ.

To do this, the y_i observations are plotted against observation number (i) and a horizontal straight line is fit to the data by choosing this line's height so as to minimize some function of the vertical deviations of the y_i data from this line. Letting $\hat{\mu}^{\text{guess}}$ denote our guess as to how high this horizontal line "ought" to be drawn, and letting u_i^{fit} denote the ith of these vertical deviations, or "fitting errors," such a plot might look like Figure 3-1:

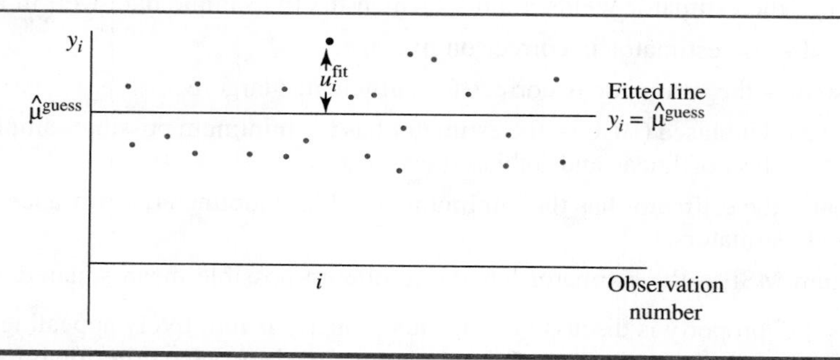

Figure 3-1 Fit of a Horizontal Line to be Sample Data

where u_i^{fit} is defined as $y_i - \hat{\mu}^{\text{guess}}$.

Intuitively, if the object is to fit the line to the sample data, then $\hat{\mu}^{\text{guess}}$ should be chosen so as to minimize the average distance of the plotted points from the line. One way to quantify this "distance" notion is to use the square of the length of the vertical line segment joining the ith plotted observation to the horizontal line; this corresponds to using

$$\left(u_i^{\text{fit}}\right)^2 = \left(y_i - \hat{\mu}^{\text{guess}}\right)^2 \tag{3-4}$$

to measure the distance between y_i and the horizontal line. Note that this choice of a distance measure corresponds to a particular value judgement: it says that we care about positive and negative fitting errors symmetrically and that we care disproportionately about errors that are larger in magnitude.

The sample average of this measure of the vertical distance between the sample observations $\hat{\mu}$ and the horizontal line is thus

$$\frac{1}{N}\sum_{i=1}^{N}\left(u_i^{\text{fit}}\right)^2 = \frac{1}{N}\sum_{i=1}^{N}\left(y_i - \hat{\mu}^{\text{guess}}\right)^2 \equiv \frac{1}{N}\text{SSE}\left(\hat{\mu}^{\text{guess}}\right) \tag{3-5}$$

where the function SSE($\hat{\mu}^{guess}$) defined by this equation is called the "sum of squared fitting errors" or the "sum of squared residuals." The value of $\hat{\mu}^{guess}$ that minimizes this average distance – and hence minimizes SSE($\hat{\mu}^{guess}$) – is called the "least squares" estimator of μ and would typically be denoted $\hat{\mu}_{LS}$. Here it will be called $\hat{\mu}^*_{LS}$ to emphasize that this quantity depends on the fixed realizations, $y_1 \ldots y_N$.[2]

Figure 3-2 plots the function SSE($\hat{\mu}^{guess}$):

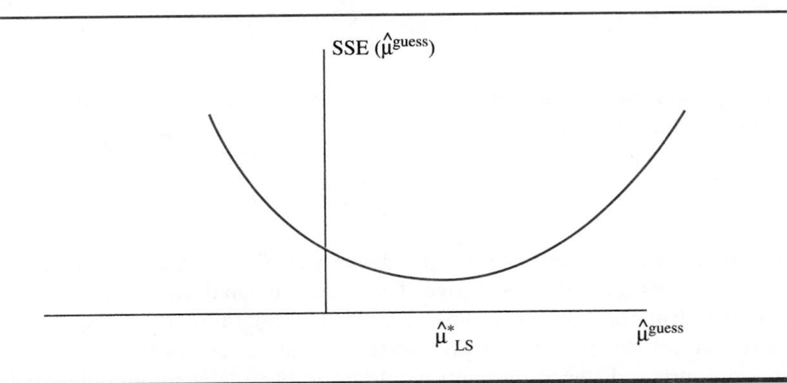

Figure 3-2 Plot of Sum of Squared Fitting Errors Function

The function SSE ($\hat{\mu}^{guess}$) clearly has its minimum at the value of $\hat{\mu}^{guess}$ where a tangent to the curve is a horizontal line – that is, at the value of $\hat{\mu}^{guess}$ for which $\frac{d\,\text{SSE}\left(\hat{\mu}^{guess}\right)}{d\,\hat{\mu}^{guess}} = 0$. Using the fact that the derivative of a sum is equal to the sum of the derivatives of the individual terms,[3]

$$
\begin{aligned}
\frac{d\,\text{SSE}\left(\hat{\mu}^{guess}\right)}{d\hat{\mu}^{guess}} &= \frac{d}{d\hat{\mu}^{guess}}\left\{\sum_{i=1}^{N}\left(y_i - \hat{\mu}^{guess}\right)^2\right\} \\
&= \sum_{i=1}^{N}\frac{d}{d\hat{\mu}^{guess}}\left\{\left(y_i - \hat{\mu}^{guess}\right)^2\right\} \\
&= \sum_{i=1}^{N}(-2)\left(y_i - \hat{\mu}^{guess}\right)
\end{aligned}
\tag{3-6}
$$

Consequently, $\hat{\mu}^*_{LS}$ must satisfy the equation

$$
0 = \sum_{i=1}^{N}(-2)\left(y_i - \hat{\mu}^*_{LS}\right) \tag{3-7}
$$

Note this is $\hat{\mu}^{guess}$ replaced by $\hat{\mu}^*_{LS}$ in this expression because $\hat{\mu}^*_{LS}$ is the value of $\hat{\mu}^{guess}$ for which the derivative of SSE($\hat{\mu}^{guess}$) – the slope of the graph of SSE($\hat{\mu}^{guess}$) versus $\hat{\mu}^{guess}$ – is zero.

[2] The distinction between the random variable $\hat{\mu}_{LS}$ and its sample realization $\hat{\mu}^*_{LS}$ will be developed further later in this chapter. This would also be a good time to refer back to the "Notation" section just prior to Chapter 1.

[3] Write this sum out explicitly for $N = 2$ if the summation notation confuses you; see the Mathematics Review section at the end of the book for a brief calculus review covering differentiation and the chain rule.

Dividing both sides of this last equation by -2 yields

$$0 = \sum_{i=1}^{N}\left(y_i - \hat{\mu}^*_{LS}\right) = \sum_{i=1}^{N} y_i - \sum_{i=1}^{N}\hat{\mu}^*_{LS} = \sum_{i=1}^{N} y_i - N\hat{\mu}^*_{LS} \tag{3-8}$$

Therefore, $\hat{\mu}^*_{LS}$, the value of $\hat{\mu}^{guess}$ which minimizes SSE($\hat{\mu}^{guess}$) for this particular set of sample observations, is

$$\hat{\mu}^*_{LS} = \frac{1}{N}\sum_{1}^{N} y_i = \bar{y} \tag{3-9}$$

Note that $\hat{\mu}^*_{LS}$ is a fixed constant for this particular set of sample observations because $y_1 \ldots y_N$ are fixed constants. In fact, it is a realization of the random variable $\hat{\mu}_{LS}$:

$$\hat{\mu}_{LS} = \frac{1}{N}\sum_{i=1}^{N} Y_i = \overline{Y} \tag{3-10}$$

Thus, the sample mean has at least one nice property as an estimator of μ: it "fits" the sample data best in the least squares sense defined above. The sample mean does *not* have the "best fit" property using alternative distance measures, however. If we care about positive and negative errors symmetrically but we do not care disproportionately about errors that are larger in magnitude, then a more appropriate distance measure would be to use the absolute value of the length of the vertical line segment joining the ith plotted data point to the horizontal line. This value judgement corresponds to using $|y_i - \hat{\mu}^{guess}|$ to measure the distance between y_i and the horizontal line. The sample average of the distance between the y_i and the horizontal line using this distance measure is

$$\frac{1}{N}\sum_{i=1}^{N}|y_i - \hat{\mu}^{guess}| \equiv \frac{1}{N}\text{SAD}(\hat{\mu}^{guess}) \tag{3-11}$$

where the function SAD($\hat{\mu}^{guess}$) defined by this equation is called the "sum of the absolute fitting errors." The value of $\hat{\mu}^{guess}$ that minimizes this average distance – and hence minimizes SAD($\hat{\mu}^{guess}$) – is called the "least absolute deviations" estimator of μ and is denoted $\hat{\mu}^*_{LAD}$. A plot of SAD($\hat{\mu}^{guess}$) versus $\hat{\mu}^{guess}$ is similar in overall appearance to a plot of SSE($\hat{\mu}^{guess}$) except that it is actually not a smooth curve; instead, it is composed of N line segments. Because SAD($\hat{\mu}^{guess}$) is not smooth enough to be conveniently differentiated, characterizing the value of $\hat{\mu}^{guess}$ that minimizes it $\left(\hat{\mu}^*_{LAD}\right)$ is more troublesome than obtaining $\hat{\mu}^*_{LS}$; consequently the derivation is not given here. The result of this derivation, however, is appealingly simple: $\hat{\mu}^*_{LAD}$ is simply y_{median}, the sample median of $y_1 \ldots y_N$.

In practice most econometric analysis is done using least squares rather than least absolute deviation estimators. In large part, this is because least squares estimators like $\hat{\mu}_{LS}$ can be shown to have a number of the desirable properties discussed below, most of which cannot be proven for least absolute deviation estimators like $\hat{\mu}_{LAD}$. Why even mention least absolute deviation curve fitting, then? Fundamentally, the reason for considering least absolute deviation curve fitting here is to make it clear that the "goodness" of least squares curve fitting (and of an estimator's property of yielding the best fit model in this sense) is conditional on a value-laden choice as to how model fitting errors are to be penalized – a reasonable choice, but not the only reasonable choice that could be made.

In fact, sometimes $\hat{\mu}^*_{LAD}$ is clearly preferable to $\hat{\mu}^*_{LS}$ Suppose, for example, that – just due to chance – the third sample observation (i.e., the realization y_3) happens to be quite large compared to all of the other sample observations. In that case, $\hat{\mu}^*_{LS}$ will be unusually large also and (unless N is quite large) will almost certainly notably exceed μ. The sample realization of $\hat{\mu}^*_{LAD}$, in contrast, is completely unaffected by how large the largest sample observation is, because the value of the largest sample observation in general has no impact on the median observation. Thus, with small samples, $\hat{\mu}^*_{LS}$ is sensitive to the occasional unusual observation whereas $\hat{\mu}^*_{LAD}$ is insensitive ("robust") to such outliers.[4]

3.3 THE SAMPLING DISTRIBUTION OF $\overline{Y}$

Viewing the least squares estimator of μ – i.e., $\overline{Y}$ – as a function of the random variables $Y_1 \ldots Y_N$, this estimator is a random variable. Hence, the most that can be known about it, prior to observing the realizations $y_1 \ldots y_N$, is its probability distribution, or "sampling distribution."

The simplest way to obtain the sampling distribution of $\overline{Y}$ is to observe that

$$\overline{Y} = \frac{1}{N}\sum_{i=1}^{N} Y_i = \sum_{i=1}^{N}\frac{1}{N}Y_i \quad \text{with} \quad Y_i \sim \text{NIID}\left[\mu, \sigma^2\right] \tag{3-12}$$

is just a linear combination (weighted sum) of normally distributed random variables. Consequently, its distribution is a special case of the general result obtained at the end of Chapter 2:

If

$$B \equiv \sum_{i=1}^{N} w_i U_i \quad \text{with} \quad U_i \sim \text{NIID}\left[\mu, \sigma^2\right]$$

Then

$$B \sim N\left[\mu\sum_{i=1}^{N} w_i,\; \sigma^2\sum_{i=1}^{N} w_i^2\right] \tag{3-13}$$

Replacing $U_1 \ldots U_N$ by $Y_1 \ldots Y_N$ and setting all of the weights $w_1, w_2 \ldots w_N$ equal to $\frac{1}{N}$, $\overline{Y}$ is clearly equivalent to B. Thus,

$$\begin{aligned}
\overline{Y} &\sim N\left[\mu\sum_{i=1}^{N} w_i,\; \sigma^2\sum_{i=1}^{N} w_i^2\right] \\
&\sim N\left[\mu\sum_{i=1}^{N}\frac{1}{N},\; \sigma^2\sum_{i=1}^{N}\left(\frac{1}{N}\right)^2\right] \\
&\sim N\left[\mu\frac{1}{N}\sum_{i=1}^{N}1,\; \sigma^2\left(\frac{1}{N}\right)^2\sum_{i=1}^{N}1\right] \\
&\sim N\left[\mu,\; \frac{\sigma^2}{N}\right]
\end{aligned} \tag{3-14}$$

because $\sum_{i=1}^{N} 1 = N$.

Alternatively, the same result for this specific case can easily be derived using an alternative approach; doing so turns out to be very instructive. $\overline{Y}$ is a weighted sum of normally distributed random variables, and hence is itself normally distributed. The expected value of $\overline{Y}$ is simply

$$E\left[\overline{Y}\right] = E\left[\frac{1}{N}\sum_{i=1}^{N} Y_i\right] = E\left[\sum_{i=1}^{N}\frac{1}{N}Y_i\right] = \sum_{i=1}^{N}\frac{1}{N}E[Y_i] = \sum_{i=1}^{N}\frac{1}{N}\mu = \mu \tag{3-15}$$

[4] For this reason, parameter estimates based on minimizing the absolute value of the fitting errors are often refered to as "robust" estimators. The reader should be forewarned, however, that this is not the only usage of the adjective "robust" in econometrics.

where the factor of $\frac{1}{N}$ can come inside the sum (because it is a constant) and where the Linearity Property is used to express this expectation of a weighted sum of random variables as the weighted sum of the expectations of the random variables.

Note that averaged over its sampling distribution, $\overline{Y}$ is equal to the population mean it is trying to estimate. This implies that $\overline{Y}$ has the property of unbiasedness or, equivalently, that $\overline{Y}$ is an unbiased estimator of μ. For a general estimator $\hat{\theta}$ which is being used to estimate a population parameter θ,

Bias and the Unbiasedness Property

Bias: If $\hat{\theta}$ is an estimator of θ, $\text{bias}(\hat{\theta}) \equiv E[\hat{\theta}] - \theta$ (3-16)

Unbiasedness: If $\hat{\theta}$ is an estimator of θ, then $\hat{\theta}$ is an unbiased estimator of θ if and only if $\text{bias}(\hat{\theta}) = 0$ or, equivalently, $E[\hat{\theta}] = \theta$

Note that most of the content of the assumption that $Y_i \sim \text{NIID}[\mu, \sigma^2]$ is never actually used in the proof given above that $\overline{Y}$ is an unbiased estimator of μ. In fact, this property for $\overline{Y}$ depends only on the assumption that each observation on Y has the same population mean, μ. Thus, one of the key advantages to understanding the derivation of the unbiasedness of $\overline{Y}$ is the realization that this result is very insensitive to failures of the actual data to conform to our assumptions about it. In particular, the derivation makes it plain that $\overline{Y}$ will still be unbiased for μ even if the observations are not normally distributed, have differing variances, and are not independent of one another!

The issue of how much value should be placed on unbiasedness – how "good" this property really is – is taken up shortly. In the remainder of this section, the variance of the sampling distribution of $\overline{Y}$ – the "sampling variance" of $\overline{Y}$ – is explicitly derived for this specific case. The purpose for doing this is to make it more clear where the result $\text{var}(\overline{Y}) = \frac{\sigma^2}{N}$ comes from and, as in the unbiasedness derivation above, to clarify precisely how this result rests on the validity of the model assumptions.

The derivation begins by re-expressing the variance of $\overline{Y}$ using its definition in terms of the expectations operator; then both $\overline{Y}$ and $E[\overline{Y}]$ are rewritten as sums over the N observation so that $E\left[\left[\overline{Y} - E[\overline{Y}]\right]^2\right]$ can be expressed as the expectation of the square of a single sum:

$$
\begin{aligned}
\text{var}\{\overline{Y}\} = E\left[\left[\overline{Y} - E[\overline{Y}]\right]^2\right] &= E\left[\left[\sum_{i=1}^{N} \frac{1}{N} Y_i - \sum_{i=1}^{N} \frac{1}{N} \mu\right]^2\right] \\
&= E\left[\left[\sum_{i=1}^{N} \left(\frac{1}{N} Y_i - \frac{1}{N} \mu\right)\right]^2\right] \\
&= E\left[\left[\sum_{i=1}^{N} \frac{1}{N} (Y_j - \mu)\right]^2\right] \qquad (3\text{-}17) \\
&= E\left[\left[\sum_{i=1}^{N} \frac{1}{N} (Y_i - \mu)\right]\left[\sum_{j=1}^{N} \frac{1}{N} (Y_j - \mu)\right]\right] \\
&= E\left[\sum_{i=1}^{N} \sum_{j=1}^{N} \frac{1}{N} [Y_i - \mu] \frac{1}{N} [Y_j - \mu]\right]
\end{aligned}
$$

If this last step, replacing the product of two sums by a double sum, seems confusing, try writing out both expressions for the special case where $N = 2$.

Noting that this double sum is just a weighted sum of random variables of the form $[Y_i - \mu]$ times $[Y_j - \mu]$, the Linearity Property allows its expectation to be re-expressed in terms of variances and covariances of Y_i and Y_j. Because $Y_1 \dots Y_N$ are assumed to be independently distributed, these covariances are all 0:

$$
\begin{aligned}
\mathrm{Var}\{\overline{Y}\} &= E\left[\sum_{i=1}^{N}\sum_{j=1}^{N}\frac{1}{N}[Y_i - \mu]\frac{1}{N}[Y_j - \mu]\right] \\
&= E\left[\sum_{i=1}^{N}\sum_{j=1}^{N}\frac{1}{N^2}[Y_i - \mu][Y_j - \mu]\right] \\
&= \sum_{i=1}^{N}\sum_{j=1}^{N}\frac{1}{N^2}E[[Y_i - \mu][Y_j - \mu]] \\
&= \sum_{i=1}^{N}\sum_{\substack{j=1 \\ j\neq i}}^{N}\frac{1}{N^2}E[[Y_i - \mu][Y_j - \mu]] + \sum_{i=1}^{N}\sum_{\substack{j=1 \\ j=i}}^{N}\frac{1}{N^2}E[[Y_i - \mu][Y_j - \mu]] \qquad (3\text{-}18) \\
&= \sum_{i=1}^{N}\sum_{\substack{j=1 \\ j\neq 1}}^{N}\frac{1}{N^2}\mathrm{cov}(Y_i, Y_j) + \sum_{i=1}^{N}\sum_{\substack{j=1 \\ j=i}}^{N}\frac{1}{N^2}\mathrm{var}(Y_i) \\
&= \sum_{i=1}^{N}\sum_{\substack{j=1 \\ j\neq i}}^{N}\frac{1}{N^2}0 + \sigma^2\sum_{i=1}^{N}\frac{1}{N^2} \\
&= \frac{\sigma^2}{N}
\end{aligned}
$$

Note that the derivation of this expression for the variance of $\overline{Y}$ uses quite a bit more of the assumption that $Y_i \sim \mathrm{NIID}[\mu, \sigma^2]$ than did the derivation of $E[\overline{Y}] = \mu$. In fact, we see from this derivation that all N observations must have both the same mean and the same variance in order for this result on $\mathrm{var}(\overline{Y})$ to hold. Moreover, all of the covariances, $\mathrm{cov}(Y_i, Y_j)$, must be 0 – i.e., the observations must be uncorrelated with one another. Notice that it is not necessary for the observations to be normally or independently distributed, however.[5]

This result is typical: demonstrating that model parameter estimates are unbiased usually requires fewer and milder model assumptions than does deriving the usual expressions for the sampling variances of those estimators. In particular, in most of the settings considered in this book we will see that unbiased parameter estimation mainly just requires that the model errors have mean 0, whereas validity of the sampling variance expressions usually requires both constant variances and uncorrelated errors.

These kinds of results are of great practical importance – they put us on notice that approximately unbiased parameter estimators are going to be relatively easy to obtain in real-world settings, but that estimating sampling variances is going to be fundamentally tougher. Moreover, they also forewarn us that any results which hinge on expressions for the sampling variances of our estimators are going to be relatively sensitive to any failures in the model assumptions to hold.

In the sections to come (and in Chapter 4), we will find that the both the optimality of $\overline{Y}$ as an estimator of μ and the validity of all of the usual statistical inference formulas in fact rest on the validity of this expression for the sampling variance. Estimator optimality is a very good thing: in many econometric settings we are short on relevant data, so it is important to make the best use of

[5] Indeed, if you worked Exercise 2-5e, you have already observed this for yourself.

what we have. But the validity of the statistical inference formulas is of even greater practical importance because we use these results to test hypotheses and to quantify the uncertainty in parameter estimates and forecasts.

Note, however, that real-world econometric software blithely plows ahead and utilizes the usual variance formulas based (as above) on a particular set of model assumptions – regardless of whether the model which actually generated the data satisfies those assumptions or not. If the actual data do not at least approximately conform to those assumptions, then the computed results will still be printed out in nicely formatted columns, but these results will range from moderately distorted to completely misleading!

The computer software is fundamentally incapable of either knowing or caring about whether or not the underlying model assumptions are satisfied by the sample data – that is ***our*** job. Thus, in order to have any realistic chance of obtaining useful results from econometric software, it is necessary to be aware of where the key results come from and to understand what modeling assumptions these results are resting upon. The feasibility and importance of using the sample data to check these assumptions will be a recurring theme in this book, a theme which will more explicitly reappear in Chapter 4 and in Chapters 10 through 13.

3.4 CONSISTENCY – A FIRST PASS

In the previous section the assumption that $Y_i \sim \text{NIID}[\mu, \sigma^2]$ was used to show that the sampling distribution of $\overline{Y}$ is

$$\overline{Y} \sim N\left[\mu, \frac{\sigma^2}{N}\right] \tag{3-19}$$

implying that $\hat{\mu}_{LS} = \overline{Y}$ provides an unbiased estimator for the population mean (μ) and that the sampling variance for this estimator is $\frac{\sigma^2}{N}$.

Clearly, then, the sampling variance of $\hat{\mu}_{LS}$ goes to 0 as N, the number of sample observations, becomes large. Because the width of the probability density function for $\hat{\mu}_{LS}$ depends directly on the variance of $\hat{\mu}_{LS}$ and the area under the density function is necessarily one, this result implies that the probability density function for $\hat{\mu}_{LS}$ must be getting taller and skinnier as N increases. Thus, as N becomes arbitrarily large, the probability density function for $\hat{\mu}_{LS}$ becomes arbitrarily tall and arbitrarily concentrated, right on top of μ. In a probablistic sense, then, the value of $\hat{\mu}_{LS}$ is converging to μ as N becomes large. Consequently, the estimator $\hat{\mu}_{LS}$ is said to be a "consistent" estimator for μ.

Consistency is an important estimator property because it embodies the concept that it is possible for us to come to "know" the value of the previously unknown parameter μ if we can just obtain enough sample data on Y. Moreover, there is something fundamentally unappealing about an estimator which does not at least converge to the true population value in this sense as the sample grows. On the other hand, consistency in and of itself is a terribly weak property, because it only speaks to the performance of the estimator with an arbitrarily large sample, whereas our most pressing concern is with the estimator's performance using the amount of sample data actually available to us.

The concept of consistency will be analyzed more thoroughly in Chapter 11, in large part because the more powerful consistency-based results given there allow us to fairly easily analyze parameter estimation in a number of very practical contexts where it is impossible to work out any of the other estimator properties.[6]

[6] The more advanced reader should note that "consistency" is intentionally not being distinguished from "squared-error consistency" at this stage.

3.5 UNBIASEDNESS AND THE OPTIMAL ESTIMATOR

We have seen above that only a small subset of the assumptions made about $Y_1 \ldots Y_N$ are actually necessary in order to show that $\hat{\mu}_{LS}$ is unbiased – i.e., that $E\left[\overline{Y}\right] = \mu$. In particular, all that is needed is that all N observations be drawn from a distribution (or distributions) with the same population mean. So unbiasedness is a relatively easy property to obtain.

But is this property really a good thing? Intuitively, one would think so. Moreover, our work in Chapter 4 will show that unbiasedness is essential for the construction of confidence intervals and the testing of hypotheses. But it is easy to show that unbiased estimators are often not optimal in real-world settings.

The optimal estimator of μ is the estimator with the smallest expected loss, where the loss function quantifies the cost or dis-utility generated by each possible value of $\hat{\mu} - \mu$, the error which estimator $\hat{\mu}$ makes in estimating μ. Suppose, for example that the Congressional Budget Office is estimating the mean real growth rate for the U.S. economy. If they overestimate the real growth rate, then fears of runaway inflation may cause the adoption of contractionary macroeconomic policies and creation of an extremely costly (and unnecessary) recession. In contrast, if they underestimate the real growth rate, then fears of a recession (which are in actuality unfounded) may cause the adoption of expansionary macroeconomic policies which ignite inflation and inflationary expectations. Because value judgements are involved, people will differ as to which of these possibilities is worse. But it is hardly likely that any individual will view these two kinds of outcomes symmetrically. Suppose, for the sake of an explicit example, that an unnecessary recession is deemed more costly than an avoidable bout of inflation. In that case, the Congressional Budget Office's preferences concerning estimation errors can be summarized (modeled) by an asymmetric loss function, Loss $(\hat{\mu} - \mu)$, which might look something like Figure 3-3:

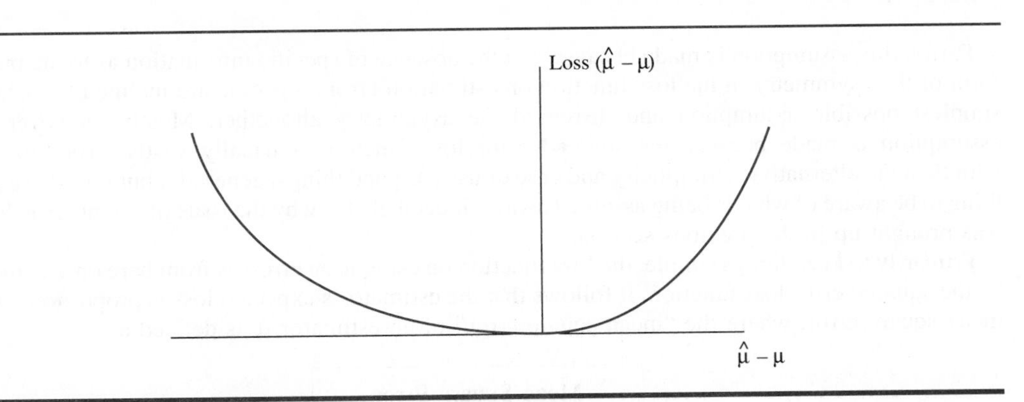

Figure 3-3 An Asymmetric Loss Function on Estimation Errors

Loss $(\hat{\mu} - \mu)$ is the value of the loss associated with using the estimator $\hat{\mu}$. Because $\hat{\mu} - \mu$ is a random variable, Loss $(\hat{\mu} - \mu)$ is a random variable also; hence its actual value is unknown. But the (average) size of the loss can be characterized by $E[\text{Loss}(\hat{\mu} - \mu)]$. This expectation is a fixed constant which could, in principle, be calculated, given the sampling distribution of $\hat{\mu}$ and an explicit functional form for Loss $(\hat{\mu} - \mu)$. The *optimal* estimator is the $\hat{\mu}$ whose sampling distribution makes $E[\text{Loss}(\hat{\mu} - \mu)]$ as small as possible. Calculating and finding the $\hat{\mu}$ whose sampling distribution minimizes $E[\text{Loss}(\hat{\mu} - \mu)]$ might be quite difficult. But it should be intuitively clear that the expected value of the optimal $\hat{\mu}$ in the example laid out in Figure 3-3 will be less than μ: it is clearly optimal to (at least to some degree) systematically underestimate the real growth rate and consequently more frequently err on the side of overstimulating the economy.

In other words, asymmetric preferences over the estimation errors imply that the optimal estimator is biased![7]

3.6 THE SQUARED ERROR LOSS FUNCTION AND THE OPTIMAL ESTIMATOR

As compelling as the argument for asymmetric preferences given in the previous section is, almost all applied work nevertheless either explicitly or implicitly assumes that the underlying loss function on estimation errors is proportional to the square of the error. This loss function, plotted as Figure 3-4, is called the "squared error loss function" and is clearly symmetric:

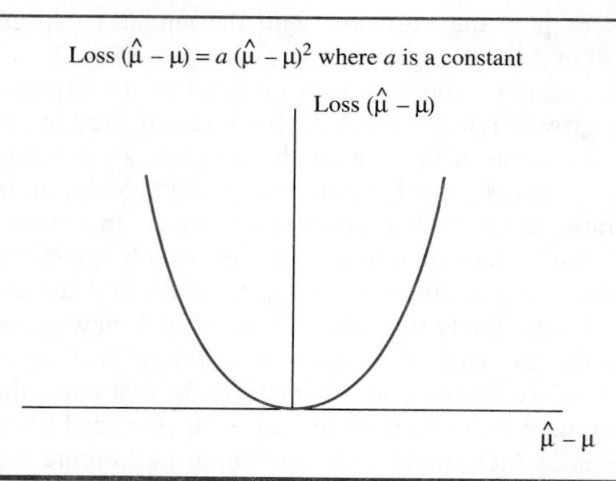

Figure 3-4 Squared Error Loss Function

Partly, this assumption is made because – in the absence of specific information as to the precise form of the asymmetry in the loss function on estimation errors – people are inclined to make the simplest possible assumption and disregard the asymmetry altogether. Mostly, however, this assumption is made because the squared error loss function is usually vastly easier to work with than the alternatives. Simplicity and ease of use are good things, generally, but it is also a good thing to be aware of what is being assumed away – indeed, that is why the issue of asymmetric losses was brought up in the previous section.

Primarily to keep things simple, the loss function on estimation errors is from here on assumed to be the squared error loss function. It follows that the estimator's expected loss is proportional to its mean square error, where the "mean square error" of an estimator $\hat{\mu}$ is defined as

$$\text{Mean Square Error} \quad \text{MSE}(\hat{\mu}) \equiv E[(\hat{\mu} - \mu)^2] \tag{3-20}$$

Thus,

$$E[\text{Loss}(\hat{\mu} - \mu)] = E[a(\hat{\mu} - \mu)^2] = a\,E[(\hat{\mu} - \mu)^2] \propto \text{MSE}(\hat{\mu}) \tag{3-21}$$

Clearly, then, a squared error loss function implies that the optimal estimator is the one with the smallest mean square error.

[7] For a similar argument with a microeconomic flavor, let μ be actual sales for a firm in the coming month. Positive estimation errors will lead to overproduction and excessive inventory holding costs. In contrast, negative estimation errors will lead to underproduction and to customers perhaps permanently lost to the firm's competitors. In this case, the optimal estimate of the mean of future sales is clearly biased upward.

They look rather similar, but the MSE($\hat{\mu}$) and the var($\hat{\mu}$) are identical only for an unbiased estimator:

$$\begin{aligned} \text{MSE}(\hat{\mu}) &= \text{dispersion of } \hat{\mu} \text{ around true value of } \mu = E\left[(\hat{\mu} - \mu)^2\right] \\ \text{var}(\hat{\mu}) &= \text{dispersion of } \hat{\mu} \text{ around its expected value } = E\left[(\hat{\mu} - E[\hat{\mu}])^2\right] \end{aligned} \tag{3-22}$$

There is, however, a simple relationship between the MSE($\hat{\mu}$) and the var($\hat{\mu}$): the mean square error of any estimator equals its sampling variance plus the square of its bias. We will use this result in a number of contexts below, so it is worth proving in general – i.e., not just for the estimator of the population mean of a normally distributed variable. Let $\hat{\mu}$ be an estimator of a parameter μ, then:[8]

$$\begin{aligned} \text{MSE}(\hat{\mu}) &= E\left[(\hat{\mu} - \mu)^2\right] \\ &= E\left[(\hat{\mu} - E[\hat{\mu}] + E[\hat{\mu}] - \mu)^2\right] \\ &= E\left[([\hat{\mu} - E[\hat{\mu}]] + [E[\hat{\mu}] - \mu])^2\right] \\ &= E\left[[\hat{\mu} - E[\hat{\mu}]]^2 + 2[E[\hat{\mu}] - \mu][\hat{\mu} - E[\hat{\mu}]] + [E[\hat{\mu}] - \mu]^2\right] \\ &= E\left[\left([\hat{\mu} - E[\hat{\mu}]]^2 + 2[\text{bias}(\hat{\mu})][\hat{\mu} - E[\hat{\mu}]] + [\text{bias}(\hat{\mu})]\right)^2\right] \\ &= E\left[[\hat{\mu} - E[\hat{\mu}]]^2\right] + 2\text{bias}(\hat{\mu})E[\hat{\mu} - E[\hat{\mu}]] + [\text{bias}(\hat{\mu})]^2 \\ &= E\left[[\hat{\mu} - E[\hat{\mu}]]^2\right] + 2\text{bias}(\hat{\mu})\,0 + [\text{bias}(\hat{\mu})]^2 \\ &= \text{var}(\hat{\mu}) + [\text{bias}(\hat{\mu})]^2 \end{aligned} \tag{3-23}$$

Thus, because the expected loss of $\hat{\mu}$ (due to the errors $\hat{\mu}$ makes in estimating μ) is proportional to MSE($\hat{\mu}$) under a squared error loss function, small sampling variance and small squared bias in $\hat{\mu}$ are both good in the sense of yielding lower expected losses.

What, then, is the optimal ("best") estimator under the squared error loss function assumption? Returning to the simple case of estimating the population mean of a normally distributed variable, suppose that we assume that the optimal estimator of μ is a constant (k) times $\hat{\mu}_{LS} = \overline{Y}$ and calculate the value of k which minimizes the expected losses incurred by this estimator. This is the value of k which minimizes:

$$\begin{aligned} E\left[(k\overline{Y} - \mu)^2\right] = \text{MSE}(k\overline{Y}) &= \text{var}(k\overline{Y}) + \left[\text{bias}(k\overline{Y})\right]^2 \\ &= k^2\text{var}(\overline{Y}) + \left[E\left[k\overline{Y}\right] - \mu\right]^2 \\ &= k^2\left(\frac{\sigma^2}{N}\right) + [k\mu - \mu]^2 \\ &= k^2\left(\frac{\sigma^2}{N}\right) + [k - 1]^2\mu^2 \end{aligned} \tag{3-24}$$

Thus, k^* – the optimal value of k – satisfies

$$\begin{aligned} 0 = \frac{d\text{MSE}(k\overline{Y})}{dk} &= 2k^*\left(\frac{\sigma^2}{N}\right) + 2[k^* - 1]\mu^2 \\ &= 2k^*\left(\frac{\sigma^2}{N} + \mu^2\right) - 2\mu^2 \end{aligned} \tag{3-25}$$

[8] Note that in the following derivation $E[\hat{\mu}]$ is added and subtracted because the sampling variance of $\hat{\mu}$ is the expected value of $(\hat{\mu} - E[\hat{\mu}])^2$. Also note that the bias $(\hat{\mu}) \equiv E[\hat{\mu}] - \mu$ is a fixed (not a random) quantity.

so that k^* is

$$k^* = \frac{\mu^2}{\frac{\sigma^2}{N} + \mu^2} < 1 \tag{3-26}$$

Because k^* is less than one, the optimal estimator of μ is not equal to the unbiased estimator $\overline{Y}$; rather, it is shrunken to some degree toward 0. Evidently, the drop in the sampling variance of $k\overline{Y}$ (produced by multiplying $\overline{Y}$ by a fraction less than one) more than outweighs the resulting increase in the squared bias.

Unfortunately, however, $k^*\overline{Y}$ is not really a proper estimator because its value depends on the unknown ratio μ^2/σ^2. Both of these results are typical: shrinking an unbiased estimator a bit toward 0 always lowers its mean squared error, but the optimal amount to shrink depends on an unknown parameter.[9] Still, it is worth knowing that the optimal estimator is biased, even with a symmetric loss function.

3.7 THE FEASIBLE OPTIMALITY PROPERTIES: EFFICIENCY AND BLUNESS

The unbiasedness of $\hat{\mu}_{LS} = \overline{Y}$ tells us that $\hat{\mu}_{LS}$ is correct on average; the consistency of $\hat{\mu}_{LS}$ tells us that it converges (for sufficiently large samples) to the correct value. It would be nice to be able to show that $\overline{Y}$ is optimal in the sense of minimizing the MSE, but it does not have this property. In fact, in view of the result in the previous section – that the minimum MSE estimator is biased toward 0 – $\overline{Y}$ cannot possibly have this property.

Optimal estimation is thus unfeasible, even in the simple case of a squared error loss function examined in the previous section. Consequently, two weaker optimality concepts, "efficiency" and "Best Linear Unbiasedness" (BLUness), are widely used. These are defined as follows:

Efficiency

An estimator $\hat{\mu}$ is "efficient" for μ if and only if

a. $\hat{\mu}$ is an unbiased estimator of μ

and

b. $\text{var}(\hat{\mu}) \leq \text{var}(\tilde{\mu})$ where $\tilde{\mu}$ is any other unbiased estimator of μ

(3-27)

Best Linear Unbiasedness (BLUness)

An estimator $\hat{\mu}$ is "BLU" for μ if and only if

a. $\hat{\mu}$ is a ***linear*** and unbiased estimator of μ

and

b. $\text{var}(\hat{\mu}) \leq \text{var}(\tilde{\mu})$ where $\tilde{\mu}$ is any other ***linear*** and unbiased estimator of μ

(3-28)

Conceptually, these two properties are almost identical to one another. Both arbitrarily restrict attention to the class of unbiased estimators, but we will see in Chapter 4 that unbiasedness is in any case essential in constructing hypothesis tests and confidence intervals. The only difference between these two properties is that BLUness further restricts attention to the class of estimators which are

[9] Of course, shrinking too much yields an estimator with MSE larger than that of $\overline{Y}$. And replacing μ^2/σ^2 by a sample estimate can easily corrupt k^* with sufficient sampling noise that one is better off with $\overline{Y}$. Nevertheless, simulations in Ashley (1990) "Shrinkage Estimation with General Loss Functions: An Application of Stochastic Dominance Theory," *International Economic Review 31,* 301–314, indicate that .95 $\overline{Y}$ will usually have smaller mean square error than $\overline{Y}$ itself for $|\mu|/\sigma \leq 6$.

linear functions of the sample data. Thus, for example, $\overline{Y}$ is a linear estimator because it is a linear function of $Y_1, Y_2, \ldots Y_N$; in contrast, $\tilde{Y} \equiv \sqrt{Y_1 Y_2}$ is an estimator which is *not* linear. The MSE and the sampling variance are equal for unbiased estimators, so the efficient estimator can be characterized as the estimator which minimizes the MSE over the class of unbiased estimators, and the BLU estimator can be characterized as the estimator which minimizes the MSE over the class of estimators which are both unbiased and linear.

Given that $Y_i \sim \text{NIID}[\mu, \sigma^2]$ it can be shown that $\overline{Y}$ is an efficient estimator for μ, but the proof is beyond the scope of this book.[10] In contrast, the proof that $\overline{Y}$ is BLU is very simple and leads to a good deal of insight into why $\overline{Y}$ has this nice property. In addition, the proof gives insight into which of the assumptions were necessary and which were not. BLUness is also a property we will be able to demonstrate for least squares estimators in some of the more practically useful settings considered in subsequent chapters. Consequently, a proof that $\overline{Y}$ is BLU in this context is given later in this section.

First, however, it is very instructive to consider the bias, sampling variance, and MSE of some simple estimators of μ for the special case where there are only two sample observations – i.e., $N=2$. Five estimators are examined in Table 3-1, under the assumptions that $E[Y_1] = E[Y_2] = \mu$, that $\text{var}(Y_1) = \text{var}(Y_2) = \sigma^2$, and that $\text{cov}(Y_1, Y_2) = 0$:[11]

Table 3-1 Illustrative Estimators of μ for the $N=2$ Case

Estimator	Bias	Variance	MSE
$\hat{\mu}_a = 15$	$15 - \mu$	0	$(15-\mu)^2$
$\hat{\mu}_b = Y_1$	0	σ^2	σ^2
$\hat{\mu}_c = Y_1 + Y_2$	μ	$2\,\sigma^2$	$2\,\sigma^2 + \mu^2$
$\hat{\mu}_d = {}^1/_2\, Y_1 + {}^1/_2 Y_2 = \overline{Y}$	0	$({}^1/_4 + {}^1/_4)\,\sigma^2 = {}^1/_2\,\sigma^2$	${}^1/_2\,\sigma^2$
$\hat{\mu}_e = \gamma Y_1 + (1-\gamma)\, Y_2$	0	$(2\gamma^2 - 2\gamma + 1)\,\sigma^2$	$(2\gamma^2 - 2\gamma + 1)\,\sigma^2$

We have seen that small MSE is a good thing when the squared error loss function is a reasonable representation of one's preferences and that the MSE equals the sampling variance plus the square of the bias. So both sampling variance and bias are "bad."

The estimator $\hat{\mu}_a$ illustrates the fact that it is not hard to find estimators with small sampling variance; in fact, $\hat{\mu}_a$ has no sampling variance at all! The price, of course, is an estimator which is both embarrassing to explain to others and whose level of bias could be quite large in magnitude if μ does not happen to be close to 15.

Next consider $\hat{\mu}_b$. This estimator is unbiased, but it ignores half the sample data and consequently has a sampling variance which is twice as large as that of $\overline{Y}$ leading to a large MSE. Thus, $\hat{\mu}_b$ demonstrates that unbiasedness is not necessarily such a great property, either, if it is accompanied (as in this case) by high sampling variance.

The estimator $\hat{\mu}_c$ illustrates the fact that using all the sample data does not necessarily improve the the estimator's MSE over that of $\hat{\mu}_b$. In this case, the two observations must be entering the estimator with poorly chosen weights.

Multiplying $\hat{\mu}_c$ through by a factor (1/2) – which makes this estimator unbiased – yields the estimator $\hat{\mu}_d$. This estimator, of course, is identical to the sample mean, $\overline{Y}$. It is unbiased and clearly has the smallest MSE and (if we have a squared error loss function) the smallest expected loss – unless μ happens to be close to 15, in which case we are actually better off with $\hat{\mu}_a$.[12]

[10] The proof is not very difficult for this scalar case; a particularly accessible version is given in Theil, H. *Principles of Econometrics*. Wiley: New York, 1971, pp. 384–387.

[11] You might use the result from Exercise 2-1 to compute the mean and variance of each estimator in this table.

[12] Of course, it is difficult to know whether or not μ is in fact close to 15 *a priori* – presumably that is why we want to estimate it in the first place. And, as noted earlier, estimator $\hat{\mu}_a$ is more than a little embarrassing to explain...

There was something a bit arbitrary about how we just obtained the estimator $\hat{\mu}_d$, however. Let's try to do this more systematically. Suppose that we insist that our estimator of μ be unbiased and that, potentially, at least, it uses all of the sample data. So far that doesn't yield an estimator. But if we also restrict our estimator to be a linear function of the sample observations, then it must be of the form given in the table as estimator $\hat{\mu}_e$. Notice that the form of $\hat{\mu}_e$ implies that the sum of the weights equals one – this ensures that $E[\hat{\mu}_e] = \mu$ so that $\hat{\mu}_e$ is unbiased by construction. Because Y_1 and Y_2 are uncorrelated [i.e., $\text{cov}(Y_1, Y_2) = 0$] and both have the same mean and variance, the sampling variance of $\hat{\mu}_e$ is just the variance of Y_i times the sum of the squares of the two weights – i.e., σ^2 times $\gamma^2 + (1-\gamma^2)$, which equals $2\gamma^2 - 2\gamma + 1$.

So let's choose the value of γ to minimize the sampling variance of $\hat{\mu}_e$, thus obtaining the minimum variance estimator out of the class of linear and unbiased estimators of μ. (Of course, that is what is meant by the "best linear unbiased" or "BLU" estimator.) Graphing the sampling variance of $\hat{\mu}_e$ against γ yields Figure 3-5:

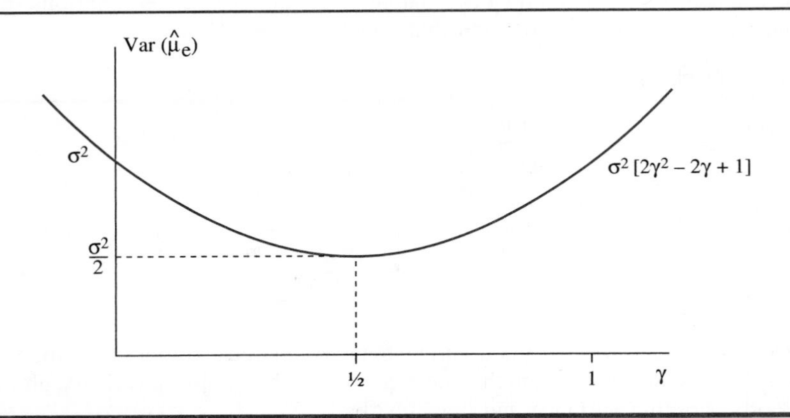

Figure 3-5 Plot of Var ($\hat{\mu}_e$) versus γ

The sampling variance of $\hat{\mu}_e$ is clearly minimized by the value γ^* which satisfies

$$0 = \frac{d}{d\gamma}\left[2\gamma^2 - 2\gamma + 1\right] = 4\gamma^* - 2 \tag{3-29}$$

so that $\gamma^* = 1/2$. Thus, for $N = 2$ at least, these assumptions are sufficient to show that $\overline{Y}$ is the BLU estimator of μ.

Note that this derivation does not use the assumption that Y_1 and Y_2 are normally distributed. Nor is it necessary to assume that Y_1 and Y_2 are independent – it is only necessary to assume that they are uncorrelated. Consequently, this result is insensitive to failures of these two assumptions.

Of course, no one really cares about the special case of just two sample observations. How can we show that the sample mean is the BLU estimator of μ when there are N uncorrelated observations, $Y_1 \ldots Y_N$, each of which has mean μ and variance σ^2? Consider an arbitrary linear estimator for μ, defined by the weights $w_1, w_2, \ldots, w_N$:

$$\hat{\mu}(w_1, w_2, \ldots, w_N) = \sum_{i=1}^{N} w_i Y_i \tag{3-30}$$

and recall the result at the end of Chapter 2 that

> If
> $$\hat{\mu} \equiv \sum_{i=1}^{N} w_i Y_i$$
> with
> $$E[Y_i] = \mu \quad \text{and} \quad \text{var}(Y_i) = \sigma^2 \quad \text{for all } i \in [1, N]$$
> and
> $$\text{cov}(Y_i, Y_j) = 0 \quad \text{for all } i, j \in [1, N] \text{ with } j \neq i$$
> Then
> $$E[\hat{\mu}] = \mu \sum_{i=1}^{N} w_i \quad \text{and} \quad \text{var}(\hat{\mu}) = \sigma^2 \sum_{i=1}^{N} w_i^2$$

(3-31)

where B has been replaced by $\hat{\mu}$ and U_i has been replaced by Y_i. This result implies that $\hat{\mu}(w_1, w_2, \dots, w_N)$ is unbiased for μ if and only if the weights $w_1, w_2, \dots, w_N$ sum to one and that the sampling variance of $\hat{\mu}(w_1, w_2, \dots, w_N)$ is proportional to the sum of the squares of these weights. Thus, the set of weights that make $\hat{\mu}(w_1, w_2, \dots, w_N)$ BLU must satisfy the minimization problem:

$$\text{Choose } w_1, w_2, \dots, w_N \text{ to minimize } \sum_{i=1}^{N} w_i^2 \text{ subject to the constraint } \sum_{i=1}^{N} w_i = 1 \tag{3-32}$$

This constrained minimization problem can be solved for the BLU weights $w_1^*, w_1^*, \dots, w_1^*$ using the method of Lagrangean multipliers. But there is a much simpler way to obtain the solution. Note that w_1, $w_2, \dots, w_N$ enter the minimization problem symmetrically; that is, w_1 affects both the function being minimized and the constraint in exactly the same way as w_{17}, say, does. Consequently, all of the solution values must be equal also. Hence (to satisfy the constraint) each of the w_1^* must be equal to $1/N$. Thus, the sample mean is the BLU estimator of the population mean for uncorrelated observations.

3.8 SUMMARY

Our results on the properties of $\hat{\mu}_{LS}$ as an estimator of μ are summarized in Table 3-2:

Table 3-2 Properties of $\hat{\mu}_{LS} = \overline{Y}$

Property	Required Assumptions
unbiasedness	$E[Y_i] = \mu$ for all i
consistency	$E[Y_i] = \mu$ and $\text{var}(Y_i) = \sigma^2$ and Y_i uncorrelated for all i
minimum MSE	$\hat{\mu}_{LS}$ does not have this property
efficiency	$Y_i \sim \text{NIID}[\mu, \sigma^2]$ for all i
BLUness	$E[Y_i] = \mu$ and $\text{var}(Y_i) = \sigma^2$ and Y_i uncorrelated for all i

Looking at this table, we see that unbiasedness is a relatively easy property to obtain for $\hat{\mu}_{LS}$: the derivation is simple and the property itself does not require much in the way of model assumptions. Consequently, this property is relatively insensitive to failures or inaccuracies in the assumptions made about the sample data. On the other hand, unbiasedness turns out not to be all that great a property unless we care symmetrically about positive and negative estimation errors.

In contrast, optimality – in the sense of minimizing the expected loss – turns out to be an elusive goal, even for a squared error loss function, because we found that the minimum MSE estimator must be biased. Imposing unbiasedness on the optimality concept, we find that $\hat{\mu}_{LS}$ does provide an optimal estimator over the class of unbiased estimators (in the case of efficiency) or over the class of linear and unbiased estimators (in the case of BLUness), but at the cost of assuming quite a bit more about the distribution of the sample data. Because it does not restrict attention to linear estimators, efficiency is a stronger form of optimality than BLUness. But the proof of BLUness is simple and insightful; and efficiency requires the additional assumption that the Y_i are normally distributed. In view of the Central Limit Theorem discussed in Chapter 2, this normality assumption may be innocuous in many real-world settings. Still, it is another assumption whose validity is in question, making efficiency a less credible property than BLUness.[13]

3.9 CONCLUSIONS AND LEAD-IN TO NEXT CHAPTER

It seems obvious that it is far better to obtain good parameter estimators than poor ones. In that context, the material discussed above, by explicitly formulating the properties which embody goodness in an estimator of a population parameter, is crucial. After all, how likely are we to find (and recognize) good parameter estimators without understanding what the concept "good" means?

However, if a particular parameter is so interesting or economically significant as to be all that important to estimate well, it seems ludicrously incomplete to merely provide even a BLU or efficient estimate: what is wanted is a confidence interval explicitly quantifying the uncertainty in our estimate. The relevant ideas and techniques for constructing such intervals (and for testing hypotheses about population quantities) are discussed in Chapter 4. But it is worth noting here that one of the results we will obtain at that point is that it is the optimal (BLU or efficient) estimators which yield the tightest confidence intervals and the sharpest hypothesis tests; at that point a nice empirical example is given.

KEY TERMS

For each term or concept listed below, provide a working definition or explanation:

Unbiased

Consistent

Best Linear Unbiased

Efficient

Minimum MSE

Best Fit

EXERCISES

3-1. If $\hat{\theta}$ is an unbiased estimator of θ, what is the value of $E\left[\hat{\theta}\right]$?

3-2. Consider the observations 2.95, 2.00, 4.30, 3.14, 3.10, 2.60, 3.40, 1.98.
Plot the points and the horizontal line for $\hat{\mu}^{guess}$ equal to 3. Does this appear to be a good estimator? Why, or why not?

3-3. What is meant by the term "least squares estimator"?

[13] On the other hand, the material we will consider in Chapter 4 makes it plain that one must in any case either assume normality or assume that N is very large in order to derive the usual statistical inference machinery.

3-4. Which is more sensitive to outliers: the least squares estimator, or the least absolute deviation estimator?

3-5. Suppose that $\hat{\theta}$ is a biased estimator of θ and that the bias $(\hat{\theta})$ is 7. What is the value of $E[\hat{\theta}]$?

3-6. Why is the assertion that $\overline{Y}$ is an unbiased estimator of the population mean more credible than the assertion that $\text{var}(\overline{Y})$ equals $\text{var}(Y_i)/N$?

3-7. What can an estimator depend on? What can it *not* depend on?

3-8. Explain the difference between the population mean (μ), the sample mean $(\overline{Y})$, and $\bar{y}$, the observed value of the sample mean.

3-9. What value judgment is involved in least squares estimation?

3-10. If $\tilde{\mu}$ is an estimator of μ, what does $E[\tilde{\mu}] - \mu$ represent? Suppose that $\text{var}(\tilde{\mu})$ is 12 and $E[\tilde{\mu}] - \mu$ is -2. What is the value of the mean square error, $\text{MSE}(\tilde{\mu})$?

3-11. In what situations would an optimal estimator be biased?

3-12. If $\tilde{\mu} = \alpha Y_1 + (1-\alpha)Y_2$, in what case is $\tilde{\mu}$ unbiased? Supposing that N is 2, in what case is $\tilde{\mu}$ equal to the sample mean?

3-13. Let $Y_i - \text{NIID}(\mu, \sigma^2)$ for $i = 1,2,3$ and consider the following two estimators of μ:

$$\begin{aligned} \tilde{\mu} &= 1/6Y_1 + 1/2Y_2 + 1/3Y_3 \\ \overline{Y} &= 1/3Y_1 + 1/3Y_2 + 1/3Y_3 \end{aligned}$$

a. Derive the sampling distribution of each estimator.

b. Obtain the bias, sampling variance, and mean square error for each estimator.

c. Is either estimator biased? Can either estimator be BLU or efficient?

3-14. Let $Y_i - \text{NIID}(\mu, \sigma^2)$ for all i in the interval one to N and consider the following two estimators of σ^2:

$$\begin{aligned} \hat{\sigma}^2 &= \frac{1}{N}\sum_{i=1}^{N}\left[Y_i - \overline{Y}\right]^2 \\ S^2 &= \frac{1}{N-1}\sum_{i=1}^{N}\left[Y_i - \overline{Y}\right]^2 \end{aligned}$$

a. Noting that $\hat{\sigma}^2$ is just the fraction $(N-1)/N$ times S^2, show that $\text{var}(\hat{\sigma}^2) < \text{var}(S^2)$.

b. Show that $\text{MSE}(\hat{\sigma}^2) < \text{MSE}(S^2)$. You may use the result that the sampling variance of S^2 is $2\sigma^4/(N-1)$ and also the result (derived in Chapter 4) that S^2 is unbiased under these assumptions about the data.

c. Presuming that one's loss function on estimation errors is proportional to the square of the errors, is the unbiased estimator of σ^2 the estimator which minimizes the expected loss?

3-15. You have observed the following random sample on a normally distributed random variable, Y_i:

i	y_i
1	7.5
2	8.0
3	9.9
4	9.1
5	7.9

a. Compute an efficient estimate of the population mean of this random variable, Y_i, showing your work.
b. Enter these data into the econometric software being used in your course (storing them with variable name "y") and compute the sample mean. In Stata, the command for this would be "summarize *y*."

Active Learning Exercise 3a: Investigating the Consistency of the Sample Mean and Sample Variance Using Computer-Generated Data

Introduction

In this chapter the assumption that the random variables $Y_1 \dots Y_N$ are NIID$[\mu, \sigma^2]$ was used to obtain the result that the sampling distribution of the sample mean is

$$\overline{Y} = \frac{1}{N}\sum_{i=1}^{N} Y_i \sim N\left[\mu, \frac{\sigma^2}{N}\right]$$

This sampling distribution was used to show that $\overline{Y}$ has a number of desirable properties as an estimator of the population mean, μ, including consistency.

Along the way, the derivation itself demonstrates that the normality of $Y_1 \dots Y_N$ is not necessary in order to show that $\overline{Y}$ is a consistent estimator of μ. But the assumptions that $E[Y_i]$ is the same for all N observations and that $\text{cov}(Y_i, Y_j)$ is 0 for all i not equal to j were explicitly used in order to show that the sampling variance of $\overline{Y}$ is σ^2/N, and this result was used to show that $\overline{Y}$ is consistent for μ.[14]

Are these assumptions about $E[Y_i]$ and $\text{cov}(Y_i, Y_j)$ really necessary in order for $\overline{Y}$ to be a consistent estimator of μ? The concept of consistency will be considered more deeply in Chapter 11. There it will be asserted that sample moments provide consistent estimators of the corresponding population moments under fairly broad circumstances. Thus, we should expect that the sample mean $\overline{Y}$ can be a consistent estimator of μ and that the sample variance

$$S^2 = \frac{1}{N-1}\sum_{i=1}^{N}\left(Y_i - \overline{Y}\right)^2$$

can be a consistent estimator of σ^2 even when $Y_1 \dots Y_N$ are not NIID$[\mu, \sigma^2]$.

But how can we confirm this for ourselves? And how can we get any feeling for the relevance of this result in practice, where N might be 30 or even 500 but is not "arbitrarily large"? That is what you will investigate for yourself in this Active Learning Exercise, using computer generated "pseudo-random" data.

[14] Recall that this followed from the observation that $\overline{Y}$ is unbiased and that its sampling variance (σ^2/N) goes to 0 as N becomes large. Thus, the sampling distribution of $\overline{Y}$ becomes a spike, with all of its weight centered right on top of μ, as N becomes arbitrarily large.

The Generation of Pseudo-Random Numbers

Some people – most notably Albert Einstein – have never accepted the proposition that anything in the experiential world is actually random: their view is that variables only appear to be random because we have not mustered the wit (or the data) to model and precisely predict which state of a purportedly random variable will be realized. Professor Einstein was no doubt quite comfortable with the fact that the "random" numbers that we can generate using computers – using algorithms called "linear congruential random number generators" – are not actually random at all: they are what is called "pseudo-random." One big clue to the essential non-randomness of these pseudo-random numbers is that any sequence of such numbers is completely determined by a starting value, called the "initial seed."

"Linear congruentual" is a bit of a mouthful, but the idea behind these random number generators is exceedingly simple. Imagine taking apart an old-style (non-digital) clock, tearing off the hour and second hands and freeing up the minute hand so that it pivots freely. Now imagine that the minute hand points to "3" and that you give it a little nudge. Most likely it will now point to "4" or "5." Give it another little nudge and it will most likely point to "6" or "7." Not a very random-seeming sequence of numbers, right? Instead, imagine giving that minute hand a good shove, so that it spins around and around numerous times. What number will the minute hand point to when it stops spinning? Now it will point to a number between 1 and 12 that is not obviously related to the previous value. Do this repeatedly and you will thereby generate a rather random-seeming sequence of numbers! That is the fundamental secret of random number generation on computers.

This idea is embodied in a numerical algorithm as follows. Let i_1 be a given positive integer – the initial seed referred to above. Then calculate i_2, i_3, and so forth from the recursion formula:

$$i_j = \text{mod}\{ai_{j-1} + b,\ m\}$$

where the value of the "mod" function $\text{mod}\{i, m\}$ is just the remainder from the quotient i/m. (For example, mod{15, 12} equals 3 because there is a remainder of 3 when 1 divides 15 by 12.) An adroit choice of the integer constants a, b, and m will yield an apparently random sequence of integers I_1, I_2, and so on – all of which will lie in the interval $[1, m]$. In that case, the quotient $(I_j - 1)/(m - 1)$ will appear to be a uniformly distributed random variable on the interval [0, 1] if m is large.

A maladroit choice of the parameters a, b, and m, on the other hand, will yield sequences of pseudo-random numbers which, for many initial seeds, do not look random at all. For this reason, there is a good deal of additional analysis (and some art) that goes into choosing these parameters.[15] In practice, high-quality pseudo-random number generators also use a number of additional twists on this theme. A particularly effective maneuver is to "shuffle" the pseudo-random numbers: for example, on the first call to a such a shuffled random number generating routine, 101 random integers ($i_1, \ldots, i_{101}$) are generated as described above. The integers $i_1, \ldots, i_{100}$ are used to fill up a 100-dimensional array; i_{101}, in contrast, is used to create an integer k lying between 1 and 100. Then the kth element of the array is used to calculate $(i_k - 1)/(m - 1)$, which is returned by the routine as the uniform random number from this call, and the value i_{101} is used to replace i_k in the array. In the next call to the routine, the last integer calculated from the recursion (which is now the kth element of the array) is used in the recursion formula to generate a new integer. This new integer is again

[15] See Abramowitz and Stegun (1965) *Handbook of Mathematical Functions*, Dover, New York, pp. 949–50.

used to create an integer k lying between 1 and 100 pointing to which element of the array is to be used to calculate the uniform random variable returned by the routine; as before, that element in the array is then replaced by the new integer. And so forth.

Your Assignment:

1. Copy the program ALE_3a.exe (available at www.wiley.com/ashley) to your hard disk and execute it.[16] The program will prompt you for a sample size, from 2 to 50,000. You should enter "1000" for this value – without the quotation marks, of course.[17] Next the program will ask you to enter an initial seed. You can enter any positive integer you like here (or whatever value your instructor suggests) but note down the value you use so that your work is easily replicable. The program will then generate the specified number of realizations of the random variables you are to work with here and store them on your hard disk in a comma-delimited file named ALE_3a.csv.[18]

   The program generates realizations from five different distributions, each constructed so as to have population mean 0 and population variance 1:

   a. NIID
   b. ASYMMETRIC
   c. FAT-TAILED
   d. NONHOMOGENEOUS_VARIANCE
   e. CORRELATED

   Under the "NIID" heading in the output file are realizations of normally distributed random variables. The "ASYMMETRIC" variates are constructed by squaring normally distributed variates,[19] and the "FAT-TAILED" variates are constructed from Student's t variates with four degrees of freedom.[20] The last two random variables are not identically and independently distributed . The "NONHOMOGENEOUS VARIANCE" variates are constructed so that the even-numbered observations are realizations of NIID(0, $\frac{9}{5}$) variables and the odd-numbered observations are realizations of NIID(0, $\frac{1}{5}$) variables. And the "CORRELATED" variates are constructed so that the correlation between consecutive observations is .70.[21]

---

[17] Program source code is in file ALE_3.for (available at www.wiley.com/college/ashley). Subroutine RAN1 generates a uniform random number between zero and one using a linear congruential random number generator which is a variation on that described above. It is taken from (and documented in) *Numerical Recipes* (Press et al., Cambridge University Press: Cambridge, pp. 195–7.) Pairs of uniform random numbers from RAN1 are used to generate normally distributed variates using the routine GASDEV, from *Numerical Recipes* (p. 202).

[18] Your instructor may ask you to enter a smaller value if the student version of the econometrics software your class is using will not support this many observations. If the program is not compatible with your version of Windows, a sample output file created with initial seed equal to 23 is available at www.wiley.com/college/ashley, labeled "ALE_3.csv".

[19] Or you could generate them yourself – it is very easy. For example, the Excel worksheet function "rand()" inserts a uniformly distributed pseudo-random number into a spreadsheet cell; normdist(rand(),0,1) inserts an NIID(0,1) variate, and (normdist(rand(),0,1))^2 inserts an asymmetrically distributed $\chi^2(1)$ variate. Or, in Stata, the command "drawnorm noise" creates an NIID(0,1) variate with name "noise."

[20] The square of a unit normal variate is a $\chi^2(1)$ variate, which is adjusted to have population mean 0 by subtracting 1 and then dividing by $\sqrt{2}$ so that the population variance is 1. The χ^2 distribution is discussed in Chapter 4.

[21] The Student's t distribution is discussed in Chapter 4; these variates are constructed as $Z/\sqrt{(Z1^2 + Z2^2 + Z3^2 + Z4^2)/4}$ where Z, $Z1$, $Z2$, $Z3$, and $Z4$ are independent unit normals; this variate is then divided by $\sqrt{2}$ so that its population variance is 1.

[22] These are constructed from an AR(1) model: $Y_i = .7Y_{i-1} + U_i$ where $U_i \sim \text{NIID}(0, 1 - .7^2)$ to make its population variance equal to 1. AR(1) processes are discussed in Section 13.4.

2. Read the data you have created into whatever econometrics software your course is using and print out histograms for each variable using all of the data. (In Stata the command "histogram NIID" produces a histogram of the variable named "NIID.") Which of these histograms look obviously unlike what one would expect from normally distributed data?
3. Use the software to compute the sample mean and sample variance for each data series and sample length specified, completing the following table. (In Stata the command "sum if _n<=5, d" computes descriptive statistics for all variables in the data set, using only the first five observations. Round your answers to three decimal places.)

Sample Mean					
N	NIID	ASYMMETRIC	FAT-TAILED	NONHOMOGENEOUS VARIANCE	CORRELATED
5					
50					
250					
1,000					
Seed Used =					

Sample Variance					
N	NIID	ASYMMETRIC	FAT-TAILED	NONHOMOGENEOUS VARIANCE	CORRELATED
5					
50					
250					
1,000					

4. What can you conclude from these results about the consistency of $\overline{Y}$ and S^2 as estimators of μ and σ^2? Does the form of the distribution seem to matter? Does it matter if the data are not identically and independently distributed, at least in the ways examined here? {Important foreshadowing note: This Active Learning Exercise will continue at the end of Chapter 4. There we will find that the validity of our apparatus for testing hypotheses about μ *does* depend crucially on some of the issues examined here; this will primarily be because the result that the sampling variance of $\overline{Y}$ is σ^2/N can become problematic.}

4

Statistical Inference on the Mean of a Normally Distributed Random Variable

4.1 INTRODUCTION

Chapter 3 reviewed the concepts and techniques relevant to estimating μ, the mean of a normally distributed random variable. There $\hat{\mu}_{LS}$, the best fit estimate of μ on a least squares criterion, was shown to be $\bar{y}$, the observed sample mean of the observations. The sampling distribution of the random variable $\overline{Y}$ was then derived and used to show that $\overline{Y}$ is a "good" estimator, in the senses quantified by the concepts of unbiasedness, consistency, BLUness, and efficiency.[1]

However, even an estimator with all of these nice properties is of little practical use unless its uncertainty can be quantified by putting "error bars" around it. This is done by using the sampling distribution of the estimator to construct a confidence interval for the underlying population parameter – an observable interval which contains this population value with a specified probability. Moreover, the point of estimating parameters like μ often rests less on the actual estimate obtained than it does on testing theoretical hypotheses regarding the value of the parameter.

This chapter reviews the statistical inference machinery for constructing confidence intervals and hypothesis tests for the mean of a random variable. The object is to develop these ideas and techniques in the simplest and most familiar context, so that they are fresh in your mind for when they are needed in analyzing regression model parameters in Chapters 7 and 9. The treatment given here emphasizes the basic logic underlying confidence intervals and hypothesis tests and the sense in which their validity rests on the assumptions used in deriving the sampling distribution (and properties) of $\overline{Y}$. Ironically, the process of "diagnostically checking" these assumptions itself involves hypothesis testing of a closely-related sort. Consequently, a preliminary treatment of diagnostic checking is given here by covering techniques for testing hypotheses regarding the equality of the population mean or the population variance across two subsets of the sample data.[2]

Finally, all of this is illustrated using a sample of international real GDP growth rates.

[1] Later on – e.g., in Section 6.2 and henceforth – the word "estimator" will be explicitly reserved for random variables (such as $\overline{Y}$), and the word "estimate" or the phrase "sample estimate" will be used to denote its (fixed) sample realization: $\bar{y}$ or $\hat{\mu}_{LS}$.

[2] A more complete and serious treatment of diagnostic checking is given in Chapters 10, 13, and 14, where diagnostic checking is discussed in the context of the Multiple Regression Model.

4.2 STANDARDIZING THE DISTRIBUTION OF $\overline{Y}$

Presuming that the N sample observations $(y_1, y_2, \ldots, y_N)$ are realizations of a random variable Y_i distributed NIID (μ, σ^2), it was shown in Chapter 3 that the sampling distribution of the sample mean, $\overline{Y} = \frac{1}{N}\sum_{i=1}^{N} Y_i$, is

$$\overline{Y} \sim N\left[\mu, \frac{\sigma^2}{N}\right] \tag{4-1}$$

Recalling from Chapter 2 that for any random variable y and constant b,

$$E[Y - b] = E[Y] - b \quad \text{and} \quad \text{var}(Y - b) = \text{var}(Y) \tag{4-2}$$

it follows that

$$\overline{Y} - \mu \sim N\left[0, \frac{\sigma^2}{N}\right] \tag{4-3}$$

where $\overline{Y}$ is playing the role of Y and μ is playing the role of b. Furthermore, recalling from Chapter 2 that for any random variable Y and constant a,

$$E[a\,Y] = a\,E[Y] \quad \text{and} \quad \text{var}(a\,Y) = a^2\,\text{var}(Y)$$

it follows that

$$Z = \frac{\overline{Y} - \mu}{\sqrt{\frac{\sigma^2}{N}}} \sim N[0, 1] \tag{4-4}$$

Here $\overline{Y} - \mu$ is playing the role of Y and $1/\sqrt{\frac{\sigma^2}{N}}$ is playing the role of a. Transforming a random variable in this way to have 0 mean and unit variance is called "standardization." Note that the form of the distribution is unchanged in this case because weighted sums of normally distributed random variables are still normally distributed.

4.3 CONFIDENCE INTERVALS FOR μ WHEN σ^2 IS KNOWN

For clarity's sake, we begin with the special case where σ^2 is known. In practice, σ^2 is never known. This assumption is only being made so as to first present the material on confidence intervals and hypothesis testing in the simplest setting possible; this assumption is relaxed later in the chapter.

Repeating the essential result of the previous section:

$$Z = \frac{\overline{Y} - \mu}{\sqrt{\frac{\sigma^2}{N}}} \sim N[0, 1] \tag{4-5}$$

This result is used below to derive a 95% confidence interval for μ, an observable interval which contains μ with probability .95.

The critical points of a probability distribution were defined in Chapter 2; in particular, $z^c_{.025} = 1.96$, the 2½% critical point of the unit normal distribution, is defined in such a way that the two shaded areas in Figure 4-1 sum to .050. Consequently, it must be the case that any unit normal variable lies in the interval $[-1.96, 1.96]$ $\left(\text{or}\left[-z^c_{.025}, z^c_{.025}\right]\right)$ with probability .95.

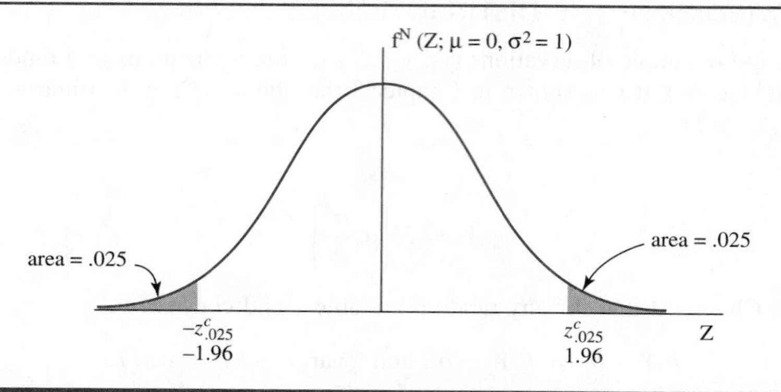

Figure 4-1 The 2½% Critical Point of the Unit Normal Distribution

This implies that

$$-z^c_{.025} \le \frac{\overline{Y} - \mu}{\sqrt{\frac{\sigma^2}{N}}} \le z^c_{.025} \quad \text{with probability .95} \tag{4-6}$$

Multiplying both sides of each of these inequalities by $\sqrt{\sigma^2/N}$ yields

$$-z^c_{.025} \le \overline{Y} - \mu \le z^c_{.025}\sqrt{\frac{\sigma^2}{N}} \quad \text{with probability .95} \tag{4-7}$$

And subtracting $\overline{Y}$ from both sides of each inequality yields

$$-\overline{Y} - z^c_{.025}\sqrt{\frac{\sigma^2}{N}} \le -\mu \le -\overline{Y} + z^c_{.025}\sqrt{\frac{\sigma^2}{N}} \quad \text{with probability .95} \tag{4-8}$$

Finally, multiplying both sides of each inequality by −1 (and therefore flipping the sense of the inequalities from "$\le$" to "$\ge$") yields a 95% confidence interval for μ:

$$\overline{Y} + z^c_{.025}\sqrt{\frac{\sigma^2}{N}} \ge \mu \ge \overline{Y} - z^c_{.025}\sqrt{\frac{\sigma^2}{N}} \quad \text{with probability .95} \tag{4-9}$$

or

$$\overline{Y} + 1.96\sqrt{\frac{\sigma^2}{N}} \ge \mu \ge \overline{Y} - 1.96\sqrt{\frac{\sigma^2}{N}} \quad \text{with probability .95} \tag{4-10}$$

Because σ^2 is known, realizations of the endpoints of this interval can be estimated from the sample data – i.e., from the observed sample mean, $\overline{y}$.

This estimated confidence interval conveys very useful information as to how precisely $\overline{Y}$ estimates μ. Note that this confidence interval does *not* indicate that there is any uncertainty in the value of μ: μ's value is unknown but fixed. What the interval *does* do is quantify how the sampling variability in $\overline{Y}$ impacts our ability to "know" μ using a single realization of $\overline{Y}$. Imagine drawing 10,000 independent samples of $Y_1 \ldots Y_N$, yielding 10,000 realizations of $\overline{Y}$ and hence 10,000 different 95% confidence intervals for μ. We can expect that around 9,500 of these intervals will overlap the true value of μ and that about 500 of them will not.

Of course, there was something a bit arbitrary about the initial choice to obtain an interval containing μ with probability .95. This probability level is quite commonly used, but you will occasionally see .90 or .99 used instead. Clearly, a confidence interval containing μ with a given probability $1 - \alpha$ simply uses the $\alpha/2\%$ critical point instead of the 2½% critical point of the unit normal distribution:

$$\overline{Y} + z^c_{\frac{\alpha}{2}}\sqrt{\frac{\sigma^2}{N}} \geq \mu \geq \overline{Y} - z^c_{\frac{\alpha}{2}}\sqrt{\frac{\sigma^2}{N}} \quad \text{with probability } 1 - \alpha \tag{4-11}$$

These critical points become larger as α becomes smaller – e.g., $z^c_{.005} = 2.57$, whereas $z^c_{.025} = 1.96$. Consequently, a 99% confidence interval for μ will be 31% wider than a 95% interval. Clearly, there is a trade-off here: the 95% confidence interval appears to pin down the value of μ more precisely, but at the cost of a larger risk of failing to actually contain μ's true value. Thus, the choice as to which confidence interval is preferable depends on one's tastes.

Note carefully that the validity of the confidence intervals derived above rests on the validity of the underlying assumption that the Y_i are distributed NIID $[\mu, \sigma^2]$. This assumption was used above in deriving the result that $(\overline{Y} - \mu)/\sqrt{\sigma^2/N}$ is a unit normal. Thus, if any part of this assumption is seriously in error, then the $\alpha\%$ confidence interval given above will not contain μ with probability $1 - \alpha$. The material on hypothesis testing reviewed in the next section will be used at the end of this chapter to show how one can check the assumptions that the population mean and variance are the same for all of the sample observations; methods for testing the assumptions that the observations are normally distributed and uncorrelated are discussed later on, in Chapters 10, 13, and 14.[3]

Note also that the unbiasedness of $\overline{Y}$ played a crucial role in the derivation of the confidence intervals for μ. In particular, it is crucial that the expectation of $\overline{Y}$ is a known function of μ – otherwise it would be impossible to standardize $\overline{Y}$ so as to construct a statistic involving μ which has tabulated critical points. Thus, unbiasedness (or known bias, at least) is necessary in order to use an estimator to construct confidence intervals.

In contrast, the optimality properties (BLUness or efficiency) are *not* necessary for the construction of confidence intervals. But observe that – out of the class of all possible unbiased estimators of μ – it is the *efficient* estimator which yields the *narrowest* $\alpha\%$ confidence interval. (Similarly, out of the class of all estimators of μ which are unbiased and linear, it is the BLU estimator which yields the narrowest $\alpha\%$ confidence interval. Thus, unbiasedness is ordinarily *necessary* in order to use an estimator to construct a confidence interval at all, but optimality is *desirable* in order to be sure that the resulting confidence interval is as narrow as the data will allow.

Of course, the confidence intervals derived in this section are not very practical because σ^2 is almost always unknown. This issue is dealt with later in this chapter by estimating σ^2. First, however, it is useful to see how to test hypotheses about μ in this simple setting where σ^2 is artificially assumed known.

4.4 HYPOTHESIS TESTING WHEN σ^2 IS KNOWN

Often the motivation for estimating μ is primarily to test a theoretical hypothesis about its value. Theory may predict that μ is equal to some particular value (μ_0, say) and the object of estimating μ may revolve entirely around testing whether or not this prediction is consistent with the data – outside of this, the actual value of μ may be of minor interest.

The statement that μ equals this chosen value is called the "null hypothesis":

$$\begin{aligned} H_o: \mu &= \mu_0 \quad \{\text{null hypothesis}\} \\ H_A: \mu &\neq \mu_0 \quad \{\text{alternative hypothesis}\} \end{aligned} \tag{4-12}$$

[3] Recall that the Central Limit Theorem, discussed in Chapter 2, implies that $\overline{Y}$ will typically be approximately normally distributed for large N, but note that the critical points used in the confidence intervals derived above are determined by the shape of the *tails* of the distribution of $\overline{Y}$ and that this is the part of the distribution which converges to normality most slowly.

The observed value of the estimator ($\bar{y}$, in this case) never exactly equals μ_0 so it *always* provides *some* evidence (in the form of $|\bar{y} - \mu_0|$) against the null hypothesis. This sample evidence is weak if $|\bar{y} - \mu_0|$ is small, and strong if $|\bar{y} - \mu_0|$ is large.

The hypothesis testing formalism quantifies the strength of this evidence by considering the question "Assuming that the null hypothesis is actually true, what is the probability that one would have observed a value for the random variable $|\overline{Y} - \mu_0|$ this large or larger, just due to chance?" This probability is called the "*p*-value" for the test.[4] In essence, if H_o is rejected based on this evidence, then the *p*-value is the probability that H_o is being wrongly rejected.[5]

Clearly, a small *p*-value says that the likelihood of obtaining the observed discrepancy $|\bar{y} - \mu_0|$ due to chance is small, suggesting that one should reject the null hypothesis in favor of the alternative hypothesis. By custom, a *p*-value less than .05 – which implies that "H_o can be rejected at the 5% significance level" – is considered adequate grounds for rejecting the null hypothesis. And a *p*-value less than .01 – which says that "H_o can be rejected at the 1% significance level" – is considered "strong" evidence against the null hypothesis. In contrast, a *p*-value in excess of .05 is customarily considered to be no evidence against the null hypothesis at all.

These customary rejection levels are a little arbitrary: it would seem obvious that the appropriate *p*-value threshold for rejecting H_o ought to be critically dependent on the costliness of a false rejection. For example, if μ is the mean number of defective light bulbs in a production batch, it might be quite reasonable to reject a null hypothesis at the 5% level, because the cost of an incorrect rejection is merely that a satisfactory batch of output is discarded. In contrast, if μ is the mean radioactivity level at a foreign nuclear fuel rod reprocessing facility, then it might not be reasonable to reject the null hypothesis H_o: $\mu = 0$ even if we can do so at the 1% level, because an incorrect rejection might well lead to very serious consequences. Instead, it is less arbitrary (and generally more informative) to merely state the *p*-value – the probability that we would be incorrectly rejecting H_o if we do reject it based on this evidence – and then let the reader draw his/her own conclusions. This would seem to be more useful than focusing on whether the null hypothesis can (or cannot) be rejected at the 1% or 5% significance level.[6]

Framed this way, hypothesis testing is straightforward: H_o is assumed to be true and the sampling distribution of the relevant parameter estimator under this assumption is used to calculate the *p*-value for the test.

Thus, in the present context, it is known that

$$\frac{\overline{Y} - \mu}{\sqrt{\frac{\sigma^2}{N}}} \sim N[0, 1] \tag{4-13}$$

if the underlying assumption that the Y_i are distributed NIID $[\mu, \sigma^2]$ is valid. If the null hypothesis is assumed to be true also, then

$$Z_{\text{test}} \equiv \frac{\overline{Y} - \mu_0}{\sqrt{\frac{\sigma^2}{N}}} \sim N[0, 1] \tag{4-14}$$

[4] The *p*-value can also be interpreted as the smallest significance level at which the null hypothesis can be rejected. *p*-values are emphasized here rather than significance levels, in large part because the significance level terminology is a bit misleading: rejection of H_o at a *lower* significance level means that the evidence against H_o is *stronger*.

[5] Wrongly rejecting the null hypothesis is also called a "Type I error."

[6] Therefore, the treatment below focuses on calculating the *p*-values rather than on developing rejection rules based on critical values.

The value of σ^2 is artificially being taken as known in this section, so the sample data $y_1 \ldots y_N$ provide one realization of the test statistic, z_{test}. Clearly, observed values of the random variable Z_{test} which are large in magnitude represent evidence against null hypothesis. The *p*-value for the test is just the probability of observing a unit normal variable larger in magnitude than the observed value of Z_{test}. This probability corresponds to the shaded area in Figure 4-2:

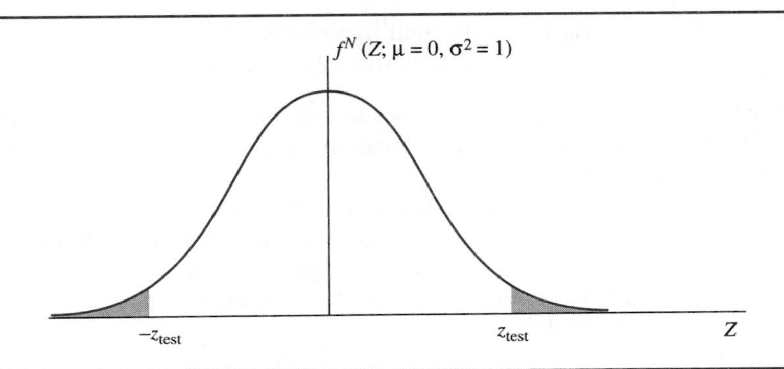

Figure 4-2 *P*-Value for the Two-Tailed Hypothesis Test

This area is easily computed, as described in footnote 17 of Chapter 2, but the calculational details are typically unimportant because modern computer software for computing $\bar{y}$ will typically compute the *p*-value for the test also. What **is** essential is to understand what the test means and how its validity rests on the assumptions underlying the derivation of the sampling distribution of $\overline{Y}$: if these assumptions are invalid, then the calculated *p*-value is *not* the probability that H_o is being wrongly rejected.

Note that construction of this hypothesis test requires an estimator of μ which can be transformed into a test statistic which is (a) computable from the sample data (under the null hypothesis) and which is (b) distributed in such a way that the needed tail areas can be computed. This is clearly impossible if the bias of the estimator of μ is not known; that is one of the main reasons for valuing unbiasedness in an estimator.

Suppose that one used a different estimator for μ – call it $\tilde{Y}$ – which is normally distributed and unbiased, but which does not use the sample data as efficiently as $\overline{Y}$ and consequently has a sampling variance that is twice as large as that of $\overline{Y}$:

$$\tilde{Y} \sim N\left[\mu, \frac{2\sigma^2}{N}\right] \tag{4-15}$$

so that under H_o,

$$\frac{\tilde{Y} - \mu_0}{\sqrt{2}\sqrt{\frac{\sigma^2}{N}}} \sim N[0,\ 1] \tag{4-16}$$

Note that using this less efficient estimator of μ in testing H_o, one would need to observe a discrepancy $|\tilde{y} - \mu_0|$ that was $\sqrt{2} = 1.41$ times larger than $|\bar{y} - \mu_0|$ in order to reject H_o with the same *p*-value. Thus, using $\overline{Y}$, an unbiased estimator with smaller sampling variance, yields a hypothesis test which, on average, will allow one to reject H_o with a smaller *p*-value. It was shown in the previous section that efficiency and BLUness are valuable properties in an estimator because they ensure that the sample estimates are as precise as possible, in the sense of yielding narrow confidence intervals. Here we see that another reason why efficiency and BLUness are valuable properties in an estimator is that in terms of *p*-values, such estimators lead to the sharpest possible hypothesis tests.

The hypothesis test described above is called the "two-tailed" test. If one is somehow able to assume that μ cannot possibly be less that μ_0, then the hypotheses to be tested are really

$$\begin{aligned} H_o &: \mu = \mu_0 \ \{\text{null hypothesis}\} \\ H_A &: \mu > \mu_0 \ \{\text{alternative hypothesis}\} \end{aligned} \tag{4-17}$$

Now the underlying assumptions of the hypothesis test also include the "maintained" assumption that $\mu \geq \mu_0$, in addition to the assumption (used in deriving the sampling distribution of $\overline{Y}$) that the Y_i are distributed NIID $[\mu, \sigma^2]$.

Note that observing a realization $\overline{y} < \mu_0$ still corresponds to evidence against the null hypothesis, but now observing $\overline{y} < \mu_0$ is no longer evidence against the null hypothesis at all.[7] Thus, one will wrongly reject H_o only when realized value $\overline{y}$ sufficiently exceeds μ_0 due to chance; consequently, the *p*-value for this "one-tailed" test is only the area in the rightmost tail of the distribution of the unit normal test statistic, as in Figure 4-3:

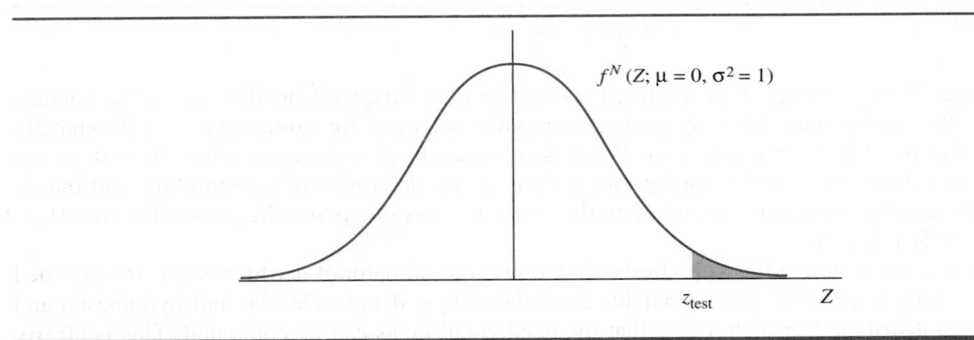

Figure 4-3 *P*-Value for the One-Tailed Hypothesis Test

The information in this additional assumption (that $\mu \geq \mu_0$) makes the inferences sharper in the sense of yielding a smaller *p*-value for a given discrepancy between $\overline{y}$ and μ_0. In fact, the *p*-values are precisely half as large.

A word of warning about one-tailed tests: It is tempting to use one-tailed tests instead of two-tailed tests because they appear to yield stronger results. Indeed, they do appropriately yield stronger results if the additional assumption (that $\mu \geq \mu_0$) is based on results obtained from other data sets and/or is derived from a theory which is not being tested. This makes sense: by combining them with an additional assumption, the N sample observations *ought* to be able to say more about whether or not H_o is true. However, this additional inferential strength is illusory (and it is not appropriate to use the one-tailed test) if the only justification for assuming $\mu \geq \mu_0$ is that the realized value $\overline{y}$ happens to exceed μ_0 for this particular sample. In fact, if one does the one-tailed test with $H_A : \mu > \mu_0$ whenever $\overline{y} > \mu_0$ and does the analogous one-tailed test with $H_A : \mu < \mu_0$ whenever $\overline{y} < \mu_0$, then the true *p*-value – i.e., the actual probability of wrongly rejecting H_o due to chance – will be precisely the *p*-value for the two-tailed test.

[7] Of course, observing a realization of $\overline{Y}$ substantially less than μ_0 might make one wonder about the maintained assumption that $\mu \geq \mu_0$.

4.5 USING S^2 TO ESTIMATE σ^2 (AND INTRODUCING THE CHI-SQUARED DISTRIBUTION)

The population variance (σ^2) is never known in practical circumstances, so the results on confidence intervals and hypothesis testing given above are not yet complete. To make these results complete, σ^2 must be estimated and the fact that this estimator is a random variable with its own sampling distribution must be explicitly taken into account. In particular, it will be shown explicitly in the next section that it suffices to find an estimator of σ^2 which is distributed as a chi-squared variate and is independent of $\overline{Y}$; identifying and analyzing such an estimator is the topic of this section.

If μ were known, finding an estimator of σ^2 and obtaining its sampling distribution would be quite easy. In that case, the natural choice for an estimator of σ^2 would be the sample variance,

$$\hat{\sigma}^2 \equiv \frac{1}{N}\sum_{i=1}^{N}(Y_i - \mu)^2 \tag{4-18}$$

Note that (using the Linearity Property and the definition of σ^2) it is simple to show that $\hat{\sigma}^2$ is unbiased:

$$E[\hat{\sigma}^2] = E\left[\sum_{i=1}^{N}\frac{1}{N}(Y_i - \mu)^2\right] = \sum_{i=1}^{N}\frac{1}{N}E\left[(Y_i - \mu)^2\right] = \sum_{i=1}^{N}\frac{1}{N}\sigma^2 = \sigma^2 \tag{4-19}$$

This estimator of σ^2 also has a simple sampling distribution: $N\hat{\sigma}^2/\sigma^2$ is chi-squared with N degrees of freedom. The chi-squared distribution is most conveniently defined as follows:

Chi-Squared Distribution

If

$$Z_i \sim \text{NIID}\{0,\, 1] \qquad \text{for} \quad i = 1 \ldots m,$$

then

$$Q \equiv \sum_{i=1}^{m} Z_i^2 \sim \chi^2(m) \tag{4-20}$$

"Q is chi-squared with m degrees of freedom"

So any random variable which can be written as the sum of the squares of m independently distributed unit normals is distributed χ^2 with m degrees of freedom.

Multiplying $\hat{\sigma}^2$ by N and dividing by σ^2 yields

$$\frac{N\hat{\sigma}^2}{\sigma^2} = \frac{N}{\sigma^2}\left(\frac{1}{N}\sum_{i=1}^{N}(Y_i - \mu)^2\right) = \sum_{i=1}^{N}\frac{1}{\sigma^2}(Y_i - \mu)^2 = \sum_{i=1}^{N}\left(\frac{Y_i - \mu}{\sigma}\right)^2 \sim \chi^2(N) \tag{4-21}$$

because the $(Y_i - \mu)/\sigma$ are independent unit normal variables when Y_i is distributed NIID $[\mu, \sigma^2]$.

But μ is not known, so $\hat{\sigma}^2$ is not usable as an estimator of σ^2. Instead, it is necessary to replace μ by an estimator $(\overline{Y})$, yielding the unbiased estimator

$$S^2 \equiv \frac{1}{N-1}\sum_{i=1}^{N}(Y_i - \overline{Y})^2 \tag{4-22}$$

It is by no means obvious that S^2 is unbiased. This and several additional key results on S^2 are proven in the remainder of this section using the following intermediate results:

Intermediate Results on Expections of Y_i and $\overline{Y}$

If

$$E[Y_i] = \mu \quad \text{var}(Y_i) = \sigma^2 \quad \text{and} \quad \text{cov}(Y_i, Y_j) = 0 \quad \text{for all } i \text{ and } j$$

then

$$\begin{aligned} E\left[Y_i^2\right] &= \mu^2 + \sigma^2 \\ E\left[Y_i \overline{Y}\right] = E\left[\overline{Y}^2\right] &= \mu^2 + \frac{\sigma^2}{N} \\ \text{var}\left(\frac{Y_i - \overline{Y}}{\sigma}\right) &= 1 - \frac{1}{N} \\ \text{cov}\left(\frac{Y_i - \overline{Y}}{\sigma}, \frac{Y_j - \overline{Y}}{\sigma}\right) &= -\frac{1}{N} \\ \text{cov}\left(Y_i - \overline{Y}, \overline{Y}\right) &= 0 \end{aligned} \tag{4-23}$$

The derivation of these intermediate results was left to the reader as part of the exercises at the end of Chapter 2, Exercise 2-35. These results are used below to show that S^2 is an unbiased estimator and to derive two other results on S^2: its sampling distribution and its independence from $\overline{Y}$. They are then used in the next section to extend the confidence interval/hypothesis testing results on μ to situations where σ^2 is unknown.

Crucial Results on S^2

If

$$Y_i \sim \text{NIID}[\mu, \sigma^2] \quad \text{for } i = 1 \ldots N,$$

then (4-24)

1. $(N-1)S^2/\sigma^2$ approximately $\sim \chi^2(N)$ for large N {proven below}
2. $(N-1)S^2/\sigma^2 \sim \chi^2(N-1)$ {not proven below}
3. $(N-1)S^2/\sigma^2$ is independent of $\overline{Y}$ {proven below}

First, to show that S^2 is unbiased, note that (using the Linearity Property):

$$\begin{aligned} E\left[S^2\right] &= E\left[\frac{1}{N-1}\sum_{i=1}^{N}\left(Y_i - \overline{Y}\right)^2\right] \\ &= \frac{1}{N-1}\sum_{i=1}^{N} E\left[\left(Y_i - \overline{Y}\right)^2\right] \\ &= \frac{1}{N-1}\sum_{i=1}^{N} E\left[Y_i^2 - 2Y_i\overline{Y} + \overline{Y}^2\right] \\ &= \frac{1}{N-1}\sum_{i=1}^{N}\left[E\left[Y_i^2\right] - 2E\left[Y_i\overline{Y}\right] + E\left[\overline{Y}^2\right]\right] \end{aligned} \tag{4-25}$$

Using the intermediate results of Equation 4-23 to evaluate these three expectations,

$$\begin{aligned} E\left[S^2\right] &\equiv \frac{1}{N-1}\sum_{i=1}^{N}\left[E\left[Y_i^2\right] - 2E[Y_i\bar{y}] + E\left[\overline{Y}^2\right]\right] \\ &= \frac{1}{N-1}\sum_{i=1}^{N}\left[\left(\mu^2+\sigma^2\right) - 2\left(\mu^2+\frac{\sigma^2}{N}\right) + \left(\mu^2+\frac{\sigma^2}{N}\right)\right] \\ &= \frac{1}{N-1}\sum_{i=1}^{N}\left[\sigma^2 - 2\frac{\sigma^2}{N} + \frac{\sigma^2}{N}\right] \\ &= \frac{1}{N-1}\sum_{i=1}^{N}\left[(N-2+1)\frac{\sigma^2}{N}\right] = \sigma^2 \end{aligned} \tag{4-26}$$

Thus, using the factor $1/(N-1)$ instead of $1/N$ in the definition of S^2 makes it an unbiased estimator of σ^2. Referring back to the derivation earlier in this section showing that $E\left[\hat{\sigma}^2\right] = \sigma^2$, it is plain that the factor $1/(N-1)$ is needed in the definition of S^2 because the observable estimator $\overline{Y}$ is being substituted for the unknown population mean μ. What is going on here is that the observed deviations $y_1 - \bar{y} \ldots y_N - \bar{y}$ are (on average) a bit smaller in magnitude because these deviations are being calculated from the same $y_1 \ldots y_N$ data used in computing $\bar{y}$; therefore, the sum of the squared deviations in the estimator S^2 must be "blown up" a bit by the $1/(N-1)$ factor to compensate.

In order to derive confidence intervals and hypothesis tests for μ when σ^2 is unknown, it is necessary to show that $(N-1)\,S^2/\sigma^2$ is distributed $\chi^2(N-1)$ independently from $\overline{Y}$. The required independence is easy to show (and is derived later in this section), but the derivation that $(N-1)$ S^2/σ^2 is distributed $\chi^2(N-1)$ requires matrix algebra which is beyond the scope of this book.[8] Consequently, this result is instead motivated here by showing that $(N-1)\,S^2/\sigma^2$ is approximately distributed $\chi^2(N)$ for large N; this turns out to be quite easy.

First, multiply the expression for S^2 by $N-1$ and divide it by σ^2 to yield

$$\frac{(N-1)S^2}{\sigma^2} = \frac{N-1}{\sigma^2}\left(\frac{1}{N-1}\sum_{i=1}^{N}\left(Y_i - \overline{Y}\right)^2\right) = \sum_{i=1}^{N}\frac{1}{\sigma^2}\left(Y_i - \overline{Y}\right)^2 = \sum_{i=1}^{N}\left(\frac{Y_i - \overline{Y}}{\sigma}\right)^2 \tag{4-27}$$

Now note that $\left(Y_i - \overline{Y}\right)/\sigma$ is normally distributed because it is the weighted sum of two normally distributed variables; and it has mean zero because $E\,[Y_i]$ and $E\left[\overline{Y}\right]$ both equal μ. But $\left(Y_i - \overline{Y}\right)$ is not a unit normal because – referring to the "intermediate results" box – its variance is $1 - \frac{1}{N}$ rather than one. For sufficiently large N, however, the variance of $\left(Y_i - \overline{Y}\right)/\sigma$ is arbitrarily close to one. Thus, for large N, $\left(Y_i - \overline{Y}\right)/\sigma$ is essentially a unit normal variable.

Again using the intermediate results of Equation 4-23, the covariance of $\left(Y_i - \overline{Y}\right)/\sigma$ with $\left(Y_j - \overline{Y}\right)/\sigma$ is $-1/N$ for $i \neq j$ – i.e., deviations from the sample mean are somewhat negatively correlated with each other. This negative correlation arises because both deviations are using the same $\overline{Y}$, which is calculated using both Y_i and Y_j. Consequently, $\left(Y_i - \overline{Y}\right)/\sigma$ and $\left(Y_j - \overline{Y}\right)/\sigma$ cannot be independent of one another. But this correlation disappears as N grows, so that the $\left(Y_i - \overline{Y}\right)/\sigma$ terms in the expression for $(N-1)\,S^2/\sigma^2$ become arbitrarily close to being independent as N becomes arbitrarily large. Thus, for sufficiently large N, $(N-1)\,S^2/\sigma^2$ becomes arbitrarily close to being the sum of the squares of N independently distributed unit normals – i.e., for large N, $(N-1)\,S^2/\sigma^2$ is approximately distributed $\chi^2(N)$.

Remarkably – as noted above – a more sophisticated derivation shows that $(N-1)\,S^2/\sigma^2$ is exactly distributed $\chi^2(N-1)$. As N becomes large, of course, the distinction between these two results becomes negligible.

The estimator S^2 has one other crucial property: it is distributed independently from $\overline{Y}$. This follows from the result (quoted in Equation 4-23) that the $\text{cov}\left(Y_i - \overline{Y},\, \overline{Y}\right)$ is zero for all i, which implies that

[8] See Johnston, J., 1984, *Econometric Methods*, McGraw-Hill: New York, pp. 165–7 and 180–2, for a proof.

the sample mean of the observations is uncorrelated with each individual observation's deviation from this sample mean. Both of these random variables are normally distributed; consequently, their uncorrelatedness implies that they are independent – i.e., completely unrelated – even though (because both terms in the covariance involve $\overline{Y}$) they look like they ought to be related. Because $\overline{Y}$ is unrelated to each of the deviations $Y_i - \overline{Y}, \ldots, Y_N - \overline{Y}$, it must be unrelated to their squared values, and to the sum of their squared values, and (hence) to S^2.

It took some effort, but now we have an estimator of σ^2 which is distributed as a chi-squared variable independently from our estimator of μ. These results are used in the next section to obtain confidence intervals and hypothesis tests for μ when, as is typically the case, σ^2 is unknown.

4.6 INFERENCE RESULTS ON μ WHEN σ^2 IS UNKNOWN (AND INTRODUCING THE STUDENT'S t DISTRIBUTION)

In summary, we have now seen that assumption that the Y_i are distributed NIID $[\mu, \sigma^2]$ implies that

$$\frac{\overline{Y} - \mu}{\sqrt{\frac{\sigma^2}{N}}} \sim N[0,\ 1] \tag{4-28}$$

and that

$$\frac{(N-1)\ S^2}{\sigma^2} \sim \chi^2(N-1) \qquad \text{independently from } \overline{Y} \tag{4-29}$$

As shown in earlier sections of this chapter, the unit normal statistic in Equation 4-28 can be used to construct a confidence interval for μ or to test a null hypothesis about μ when σ^2 is given. But those results are not very useful when σ^2 is unknown, because the resulting confidence interval endpoints and hypothesis testing statistics depend explicitly on σ^2. Now that we have an unbiased estimator of σ^2, however, it is natural to consider simply substituting S^2 for σ^2 and making the approximation

$$\frac{\overline{Y} - \mu}{\sqrt{\frac{S^2}{N}}} \approx \frac{\overline{Y} - \mu}{\sqrt{\frac{\sigma^2}{N}}} \tag{4-30}$$

But this new random variable is no longer a unit normal because the estimator S^2 now in its denominator is itself a random variable. Consequently, one might expect the density function for this new random variable to have thicker tails than a unit normal – particularly for small samples, where S^2 will be a fairly "noisy" estimate of σ^2. It is impossible to proceed, however, without knowing the tail areas for the distribution of this new random variable.

Fortunately, because S^2 is a chi-squared variable independent of $\overline{Y}$, this new statistic has a simple and well-known distribution:

Student's *t* Distribution

If

$$Z \sim N(0,\ 1) \text{ and } Q \sim \chi^2(df) \quad \text{independently from } Z$$

then

$$T \equiv \frac{Z}{\sqrt{\frac{Q}{df}}} \sim t(df) \tag{4-31}$$

and

"T is distributed as Student's t with df degrees of freedom"

Letting $(\overline{Y}-\mu)/\sqrt{\sigma^2/N}$ play the role of Z and letting $(N-1)\,S^2/\sigma^2$ play the role of Q,

$$\frac{\dfrac{\overline{Y}-\mu}{\sqrt{\dfrac{\sigma^2}{N}}}}{\sqrt{\dfrac{\dfrac{(N-1)S^2}{\sigma^2}}{N-1}}} = \frac{\dfrac{\overline{Y}-\mu}{\sqrt{\dfrac{\sigma^2}{N}}}}{\sqrt{\dfrac{S^2}{\sigma^2}}} = \left[\frac{\overline{Y}-\mu}{\sqrt{\dfrac{\sigma^2}{N}}}\right]\sqrt{\frac{\sigma^2}{S^2}} = \frac{\overline{Y}-\mu}{\sqrt{\dfrac{\sigma^2}{N}\dfrac{S^2}{\sigma^2}}} = \frac{\overline{Y}-\mu}{\sqrt{\dfrac{S^2}{N}}} \sim t(N-1) \tag{4-32}$$

The shape of the density function for a Student's t variable is very similar to that of a unit normal, except that (as expected) it has thicker tails when the number of degrees of freedom is small. For example, plotting both the unit normal density function and the density function for the Student's t distribution with five degrees of freedom yields Figure 4-4:

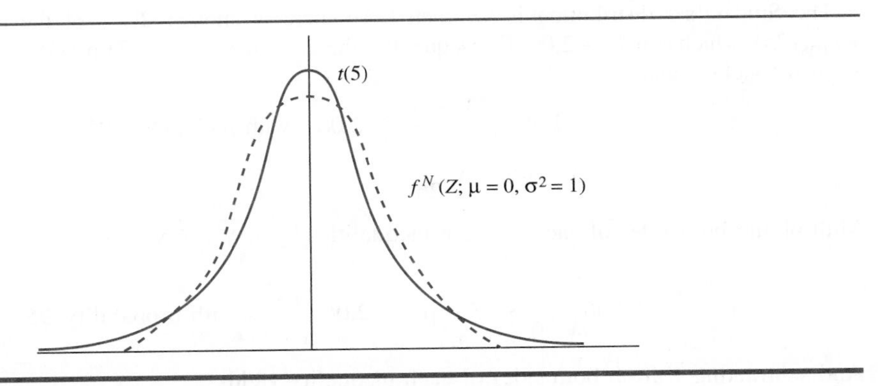

Figure 4-4 Comparison of Student's t with Unit Normal Distribution

Suppose now that there are $N = 26$ sample observations available. In that case, $(\overline{Y}-\mu)/\sqrt{S^2/26}$ is a pick from the Student's t distribution with 25 degrees of freedom. In the known-σ^2 case considered earlier, the analogous statistic – $(\overline{Y}-\mu)/\sqrt{\sigma^2/26}$ – was a unit normal random variable and we constructed confidence intervals for μ and tests of hypotheses concerning μ using critical points and tail areas of the unit normal distribution. To proceed in a a similar fashion here, we need to quantify the shape of the distribution of $(\overline{Y}-\mu)/\sqrt{S^2/26}$ by evaluating critical points and tail areas of the Student's t distribution with 25 degrees of freedom. As with the unit normal distribution considered in Chapter 2, these tail areas cannot be evaluated analytically, but they have been extensively tabulated and accurate numerical approximations for them are widely available.[9] For example, it is known that a random variable which is distributed $t(25)$ will exceed 2.06 with probability .025 – i.e., the area under the $t(25)$ density function to the right of 2.06 is .025 as in Figure 4-5:

[9] In particular, many spreadsheet programs provide functions for computing tail areas for the Student's t distribution – i.e., in Excel this function is called "tdist." Or you can program an excellent numerical approximation to this function yourself in just a few lines of code – see Press et al. (1986, p. 168) *Numerical Recipes,* Cambridge University Press. Or you can copy the program "ttail.exe" (available at www.wiley.com/college/ashley) and use it on any Windows-based computer.

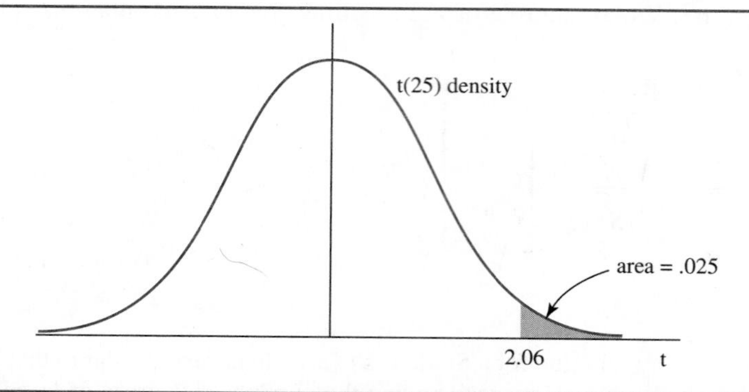

Figure 4-5 Student's t Distribution with 25 Degrees of Freedom, with a Tail Area Illustrated.

This is, of course, equivalent to saying that the 2½% critical point for the Student's t distribution with 25 degrees of freedom is 2.06, or $t^c_{.025}(25) = 2.06$.

The Student's t distribution is symmetric, so there is another 2½% of the area to the left of $-t^c_{.025}(25)$, which equals – 2.06. Consequently, the area in between –2.06 and 2.06 must be .95 and we can conclude that

$$-2.06 \leq \frac{\overline{Y} - \mu}{\sqrt{\frac{S^2}{26}}} \leq 2.06 \quad \text{with probability .95} \tag{4-33}$$

Multiplying both sides of each of these inequalities by $\sqrt{S^2/26}$ yields

$$-2.06\sqrt{\frac{S^2}{26}} \leq \overline{Y} - \mu \leq 2.06\sqrt{\frac{S^2}{26}} \quad \text{with probability .95} \tag{4-34}$$

And subtracting $\overline{Y}$ from both sides of each inequality yields

$$-\overline{Y} - 2.06\sqrt{\frac{S^2}{26}} \leq -\mu \leq -\overline{Y} + 2.06\sqrt{\frac{S^2}{26}} \quad \text{with probability .95} \tag{4-35}$$

Finally, multiplying both sides of each inequality by -1 (and therefore flipping the sense of the inequality from "$\leq$" to "$\geq$") yields a 95% confidence interval for μ:

$$\overline{Y} + 2.06\sqrt{\frac{S^2}{26}} \geq \mu \geq \overline{Y} - 2.06\sqrt{\frac{S^2}{26}} \quad \text{with probability .95} \tag{4-36}$$

This 95% confidence interval is practical because realizations of the random variables $\overline{Y}$ and S^2 can be computed from the sample data $y_1 \ldots y_{26}$.

Note that the resulting interval is a bit wider than the 95% confidence interval based on σ^2,

$$\overline{Y} + 1.96\sqrt{\frac{\sigma^2}{N}} \geq \mu \geq \overline{Y} - 1.96\sqrt{\frac{\sigma^2}{N}} \quad \text{with probability .95} \tag{4-37}$$

because $z^c_{.025} = 1.96$ (the 2½% critical point for the unit normal distribution) is smaller than the 2½% critical point for the Student's t distribution with 25 degrees of freedom. This increase in the width of the confidence interval is the price which must be paid for having to estimate σ^2 using just 26 observations.

As with the case where σ^2 is known, similar reasoning yields a $(1-\alpha)\%$ confidence interval for μ:

$$\overline{Y} + t^c_{\alpha/2}(N{-}1)\sqrt{\frac{S^2}{N}} \geq \mu \geq \overline{Y} - t^c_{\alpha/2}(N{-}1)\sqrt{\frac{S^2}{N}} \quad \text{with probability } 1-\alpha \tag{4-38}$$

where $t^c_{p/2}(N{-}1)$ denotes the $\alpha/2\%$ critical point of the Student's t distribution with $N{-}1$ degree of freedom. Thus, the ½% critical points would be used in order to obtain a 99% confidence interval.

Table 4-1, in which γ stands for the tail probability, summarizes how the ½% and the 2½% critical points of the Student's t distribution vary with the number of degrees of freedom and how they compare to the corresponding critical points of the unit normal distribution:

Table 4-1 Critical Points (½% and 2½%) for the Unit Normal and Student's t Distributions

γ	$N(0,1)$	$t^c_\gamma(120)$	$t^c_\gamma(60)$	$t^c_\gamma(25)$	$t^c_\gamma(15)$	$t^c_\gamma(5)$	$t^c_\gamma(2)$
0.025	1.96	1.98	2.00	2.06	2.13	2.57	4.30
0.005	2.58	2.62	2.66	2.79	2.95	4.03	9.93

Note that the critical points of the Student's t distribution are notably larger than those of the unit normal distribution – leading to wider confidence intervals – where the number of degrees of freedom $(N{-}1)$ is small, so that replacing σ^2 by the sample estimate (s^2) in such cases makes a big difference in the length of the confidence intervals. But the distinction is no longer all that important once one has at least 60 observations available for estimating σ^2.[10]

Again, note carefully that the validity of the confidence intervals derived above depends on the validity of the underlying assumption that the Y_i are distributed NIID $[\mu, \sigma^2]$. This assumption was used in Chapter 3 in deriving the result that $(\overline{Y}-\mu)/\sqrt{\sigma^2/N}$ is a unit normal; it is also used above in showing that $(N{-}1)\, S^2/\sigma^2$ is distributed $\chi^2(N{-}1)$ independently from $\overline{Y}$. Thus, if any part of this assumption is seriously in error, then the confidence intervals given above will not contain μ with the specified probabilities.

The result that, for $Y_1 \ldots Y_N$ distributed NIID $[\mu, \sigma^2]$,

$$\frac{\overline{Y}-\mu}{\sqrt{\frac{S^2}{N}}} \sim t(N{-}1) \tag{4-39}$$

also yields feasible tests of the null hypothesis $H_o: \mu = \mu_0$. This is because (if the null hypothesis is true), then the observable test statistic

$$T_{\text{test}} \equiv \frac{\overline{Y}-\mu_0}{\sqrt{\frac{S^2}{N}}} \tag{4-40}$$

will be a drawing from the $t(N{-}1)$ distribution. Thus, considering the two-tailed alternative hypothesis, $H_A: \mu \neq \mu_o$, the p-value at which H_o can be rejected – i.e., the probability that the null hypothesis is being wrongly rejected – is just the sum of the two tail areas in Figure 4-6, where t_{test} is the sample realization of the random variable T_{test}:

[10] More extensive tabulations of the critical points for the Student's t distribution are available – e.g., see Abramowitz and Stegun (1965) *Handbook of Mathematical Functions*, Dover, p. 990 – but it is usually more convenient to calculate them yourself by repeated use of a computer program such as ttail.exe or the Excel spreadsheet function "tdist," referred to in the previous footnote.

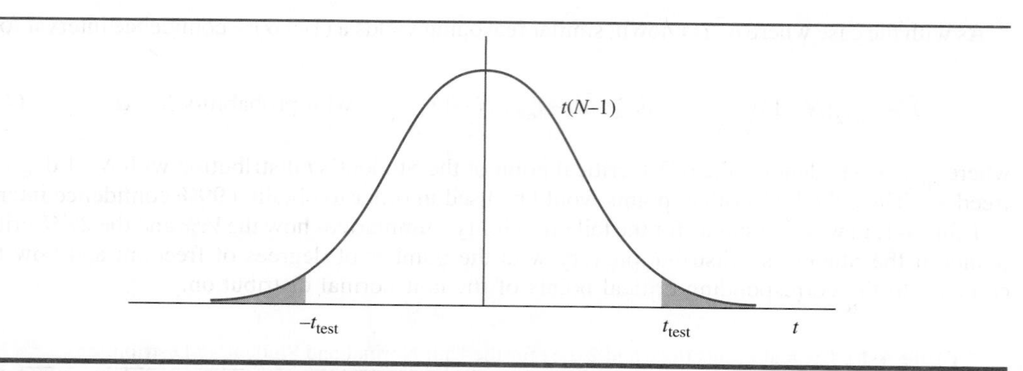

Figure 4-6 Tail Areas for the Two-Tailed Test

4.7 APPLICATION: STATE-LEVEL U.S. UNEMPLOYMENT RATES

Current and historical unemployment rate data can be obtained for each state at the Bureau of Labor Statistics Web site, www.bls.gov/data/home.htm. A histogram of these data for May 2002 is given in Table 4-7.

This histogram does not look exactly like the normal distribution bell-shape, but it is about as close as one ought to expect with only 50 observations.[11] In this section we assume that UR_i, the observed unemployment rate that month for state i, was an independent from a normal distribution with mean μ and variance σ^2 – i.e, we assume that $UR_i \sim \text{NIID}\,[\mu, \sigma^2]$ – and seek to determine what these data allow us to infer about μ, the mean unemployment rate.

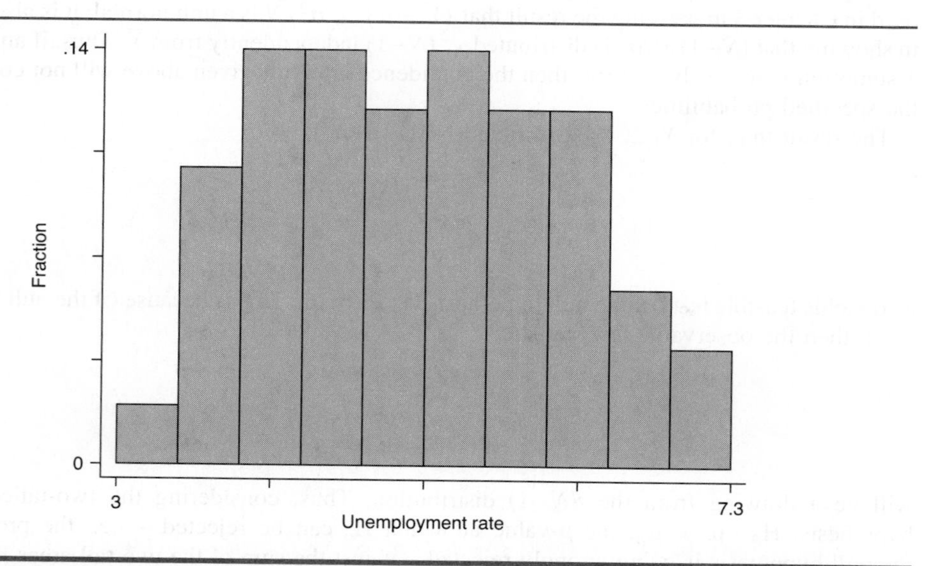

Figure 4-7 Histogram of May, 2002 State-Level U.S. Unemployment Rates

[11] This informal judgement – that these data are normally distributed, to a reasonable approximation – is borne out by the formal normality tests discussed in Section 10.3. In particular, neither the skewness-kurtosis test nor the Shapiro-Wilk test rejects the null hypothesis of normality for these data at the 5% (or even the 30%) level of significance.

If the identities of the 50 particular states corresponding to $UR_1 \ldots UR_{50}$ were unknown, then the assumption that these random variables are identically and independently distributed would be reasonable. Given that we do know these identities, however, it is not so reasonable to suppose that the mean and variance of the distribution from which each state's unemployment rate was drawn were the same for each state.[12] The issue of testing this proposition that μ and σ^2 are the same for all 50 states is taken up in the last two sections of this chapter. Intuitively, however, it does seems likely that μ varies systematically across the states in a manner which it might well be possible to model using observable characteristics of each state. Indeed, the technology for producing and using such models – regression analysis – is the topic of the rest of this book. For the moment, however, μ and σ^2 are assumed to be fixed (although unknown) constants and $UR_1 \ldots UR_{50}$ are taken to be independently distributed.

The observed sample mean and variance for these data are

$$\begin{aligned} \overline{ur} &= \frac{1}{50}\sum_{i=1}^{50} ur_i = 5.104 \\ s_{ur}^2 &= \frac{1}{49}\sum_{i=1}^{50} (ur_i - \overline{ur})^2 = 1.0628 \end{aligned} \tag{4-41}$$

Assuming that $UR_i \sim \text{NIID}\,[\mu, \sigma^2]$,

$$\frac{\overline{UR} - \mu}{\sqrt{\frac{S_{ur}^2}{50}}} \sim t(49) \tag{4-42}$$

so that a 95% confidence interval for μ is

$$\overline{UR} + t_{.025}^c(49)\sqrt{\frac{S_{ur}^2}{N}} \geq \mu \geq \overline{UR} - t_{.025}^c(49)\sqrt{\frac{S_{ur}^2}{N}} \tag{4-43}$$

and the sample realization of this confidence interval is

$$\begin{aligned} 5.104 + t_{.025}^c(49)\,0.146 &\geq \mu \geq 5.104 - t_{.025}^c(49)\,0.146 \\ 5.104 + (2.010)\,0.146 &\geq \mu \geq 5.104 - (2.010)\,0.146 \\ 5.397 &\geq \mu \geq 4.811 \end{aligned} \tag{4-44}$$

Thus, if the UR_i observations are in fact distributed NIID$[\mu, \sigma^2]$, then we can conclude that a 95% confidence interval for μ – the underlying population value of the unemployment rate – is 4.8% to 5.4%.[13]

[12] Equivalently, if the mean value of UR_i is larger for a subset of the states, then the deviations of $UR_1 \ldots UR_{50}$ from any value which is fixed for all 50 states will be correlated with one another, so that the independence assumption becomes untenable.

[13] Note that this result does *not* imply that μ lies in the interval [4.8%, 5.4%] with probability .95: because μ is a fixed number, it either lies in this interval or it doesn't. What this result *does* imply is that the sampling variability in our estimators of the endpoints of this interval is such that 95% of the realizations of these intervals will bracket μ – i.e., if we could draw 10,000 samples (of the 50 unemployment rates) and compute 10,000 realized confidence intervals in this fashion, around 9500 of these confidence intervals would contain μ.

Similarly, to test the null hypothesis $H_o: \mu = 4.80$, say, against the alternative hypothesis $H_o: \mu \neq 4.80$, the appropriate test statistic is

$$\frac{\overline{UR} - 4.80}{\sqrt{\frac{S_{ur}^2}{50}}} \tag{4-45}$$

which is a Student's t variate with 49 degrees of freedom under the assumption that UR_i NIID$[\mu, \sigma^2]$. The realization of this test statistic using our sample data is

$$\frac{\overline{ur} - 4.80}{\sqrt{\frac{s_{ur}^2}{50}}} = \frac{5.104 - 4.800}{.146} = 2.085 \tag{4-46}$$

For the Student's t distribution with 49 degrees of freedom, the sum of the tail area to the left of -2.085 and the tail area to the right of 2.085 – i.e., the probability of observing a t (49) variable whose magnitude exceeds 2.085 – is .042, as illustrated in Figure 4-8:

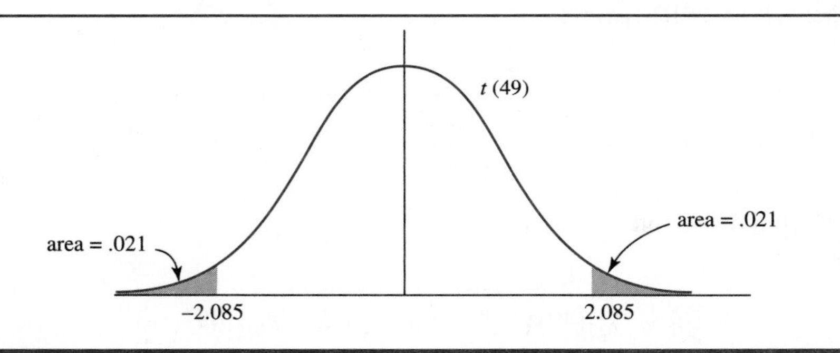

Figure 4-8 Tail Areas for Test of H_o: $\mu = 4.80$

Consequently, this particular null hypothesis can be rejected with p-value .042. Which is to say, if $H_o: \mu = 4.80$ is true, then one would expect to see a realized deviation $|\overline{ur} - 4.80|$ this large or larger just due to chance only 4.2% of the time.[14]

4.8 INTRODUCTION TO DIAGNOSTIC CHECKING: TESTING THE CONSTANCY OF μ ACROSS THE SAMPLE

One of the key assumptions made above is that each observation has the same population mean, i.e., that $E[Y_i] = \mu$ for all i. This assumption is used repeatedly in the derivation of the sampling distribution of $\overline{Y}$, so its violation would invalidate both the derivations of the properties of $\overline{Y}$ (unbiasedness, consistency, BLUness, efficiency) given in Chapter 3 and the derivations of the inference machinery (confidence intervals and hypothesis tests) given earlier in this chapter.

Fortunately – and remarkably – it is often possible to use the sample data itself to check on the validity of this kind of model assumption. This process is called "diagnostic checking." Some

[14] In practice one would typically use econometric software to calculate the statistics $\overline{ur}$ and s^2 and to evaluate the p-value at which the null hypothesis can be rejected. For example, the Stata command "ttest $ur = 4.80$" would perform the calculations described here.

diagnostic checks are very straightforward and informal: as noted in the example of the previous section, simply plotting a histogram of the sample can often give a pretty good indication as to whether or not the assumption that the Y_i are normally distributed is reasonable. Other useful diagnostic checks – such as the one discussed in this section – are themselves formal hypothesis tests.

The assumption that $E[Y_i] = \mu$ for all of the observations in the sample is a case in point. Suppose, continuing with the example of the previous section, that we suspect that the population mean of the distribution from which the unemployment rate is drawn is different for the 11 states constituting the South: Alabama, Arkansas, Florida, Georgia, Louisiana, Mississippi, North Carolina, South Carolina, Tennessee, Texas, and Virginia. We could then partition the 50 observations on state-level unemployment rates for May 2002 into two separate samples and assume that

$$UR_i^s \sim \text{NIID}\left[\mu_s, \sigma^2\right] \text{ for } i = 1, 11 \tag{4-47}$$

and that independently,

$$UR_j^r \sim \text{NIID}\left[\mu_r, \sigma^2\right] \text{ for } j = 1, 39 \tag{4-48}$$

where the superscript or subscript "s" denotes "South" and the subscript "r" denotes "rest."

The question then becomes, is the observed sample mean of the unemployment rates over the 11 southern states $(\overline{ur}_s)$ sufficiently different from the observed sample mean of the unemployment rates over the 39 other states $(\overline{ur}_s)$ that the null hypothesis $\text{H}_o : \mu_s = \mu_r$ can be rejected in favor of the alternative hypothesis $\text{H}_A : \mu_s \neq \mu_r$?

Clearly large values of $|\overline{ur}_s - \overline{ur}_r|$ are evidence against the null hypothesis. In this instance $\overline{ur}_s = 5.58\%$ whereas $\overline{ur}_r = 4.70\%$, which appears to be a substantial difference. But with only 11 observations used in $\overline{ur}_s$, perhaps this is only a sample fluctuation and μ_s actually equals μ_r. To formally test this null hypothesis, the probability of a fluctuation this large or larger due to chance – the p-value for the test – must be quantified using the sampling distribution of the estimator $\overline{UR}_s - \overline{UR}_r$.

The random variable $\overline{UR}_s - \overline{UR}_r$, is normally distributed because it is a weighted sum of two normally distributed random variables. Using the Linearity Principle,

$$E\left[\overline{UR}r_s - \overline{UR}_r\right] = E\left[\overline{UR}_s\right] - E\left[\overline{UR}_r\right] = \mu_s - \mu_r \tag{4-49}$$

Further, using the results on the variance of a linear combination of random variables derived in Chapter 2,

$$\begin{aligned} \text{var}\left(\overline{UR}_s - \overline{UR}_r\right) &= \text{var}\left(\overline{UR}_s\right) - 2\,\text{cov}\left(\overline{UR}_s, \overline{UR}_r\right) + \text{var}\left(\overline{UR}_r\right) \\ &= \frac{\sigma^2}{11} - 0 + \frac{\sigma^2}{39} \end{aligned} \tag{4-50}$$

where $\text{cov}\left(\overline{UR}_s, \overline{UR}_r\right) = 0$ because the two samples are independent.[15] Thus,

$$\overline{UR}_s - \overline{UR}_r \sim N\left[\mu_s - \mu_r, \frac{\sigma^2}{11} + \frac{\sigma^2}{39}\right] \tag{4-51}$$

and

$$\frac{\left(\overline{UR}_s - \overline{UR}_r\right) - \left(\mu_s - \mu_r\right)}{\sqrt{\dfrac{\sigma^2}{11} + \dfrac{\sigma^2}{39}}} \sim N[0, 1] \tag{4-52}$$

Because σ^2, the variance of the distribution from which the unemployment rates are drawn, is assumed to be the same for all states, it can be estimated using a sample variance that "pools" the data

[15] In particular, this is an application of Equation 2-68 from Chapter 2 with $N = 2$ and with w_1 equal to one and w_2 equal to minus one; this result is also a straightforward application of the result which you obtained in working Exercise 2-31.

from both subsamples while taking into account the possibility that μ_s might be unequal to μ_r:

$$\tilde{S}^2 \equiv \frac{1}{48}\left[\sum_{i=1}^{11}\left(UR_i^s - \overline{UR}_s\right)^2 + \sum_{j=1}^{39}\left(UR_j^r - \overline{UR}_r\right)^2\right] \tag{4-53}$$

This estimator is distributed $48\tilde{S}^2/\sigma^2 \sim \chi^2(48)$, independent of $\overline{UR}_s$ and $\overline{UR}_r$.[16] Its sample realization here is

$$\tilde{s}^2 \equiv \frac{1}{48}\left[\sum_{i=1}^{11}\left(ur_i^s - \overline{ur}_s\right)^2 + \sum_{j=1}^{39}\left(ur_j^r - \overline{ur}_r\right)^2\right] = 1.017906 \tag{4-54}$$

It then follows from the definition of the Student's t distribution given above that

$$\frac{\left(\overline{UR}_s - \overline{UR}_r\right) - \left(\mu_s - \mu_r\right)}{\sqrt{\dfrac{\tilde{S}^2}{11} + \dfrac{\tilde{S}^2}{39}}} \sim t(48) \tag{4-55}$$

and, under the null hypothesis $H_o: \mu_s = \mu_r$, that

$$\frac{\overline{UR}_s - \overline{UR}_r}{\sqrt{\dfrac{\tilde{S}^2}{11} + \dfrac{\tilde{S}^2}{39}}} \sim t(48) \tag{4-56}$$

For the data used here, the sample realization of this test statistic is 1.7785. As illustrated in Figure 4-9, the probability of observing a $t(48)$ variable larger than 1.7785 in magnitude (the sum of the two tail areas below) is .082:

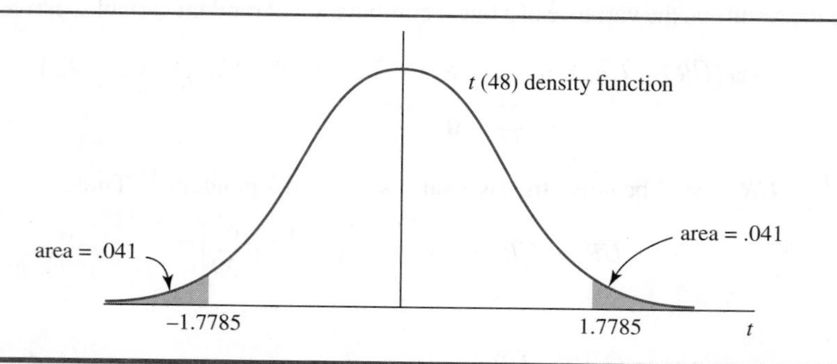

Figure 4-9 Tail Areas for Test of H_o: $\mu_s = \mu_r$

[16] Derivation of this result is omitted because, as with the distribution of S^2 under the assumption of equal population means, the proof requires a good deal of matrix algebra. Intuitively, S^2 is defined with a factor $1/(N-2)$ rather than $1/(N-1)$, and the χ^2 distribution has $N-2$ rather than $N-1$ degrees of freedom, because two population means are being estimated: one for the 11 southern states and one for the rest. This creates two opportunities – one from $\overline{UR}_s$ and one from $\overline{UR}_r$ – to make the deviations of the observed data from the sample mean a bit too small in magnitude because the estimator of the mean is using the same data used in calculating the deviations from the sample means.

Consequently, the p-value for the test is .082 and the null hypothesis $H_o : \mu_s = \mu_r$ can only be rejected at the 8.2% level of significance.[17] We can conclude that the evidence for rejecting the null hypothesis of a distinct mean unemployment rate in the southern states is fairly weak.

4.9 INTRODUCTION TO DIAGNOSTIC CHECKING: TESTING THE CONSTANCY OF σ^2 ACROSS THE SAMPLE

Another assumption made above is that each observation has the same population variance, i.e., that $\text{var}(y_i) = \sigma^2$ for all i. This assumption was still maintained when we tested the constancy of the population mean in the diagnostic check described in the previous section. Using the sample data on U.S. unemployment rates analyzed above, the observed value of the variance of the unemployment rates for the 11 Southern states is $s_s^2 = .7516$, which is notably lower than the sample variance over the remaining states of $s_r^2 = 1.0880$.

But perhaps this discrepancy in the observed sample variances is due to chance. How might we statistically test the null hypothesis, $H_o : \sigma_r^2/\sigma_s^2 = 1$ against the alternative hypothesis, $H_A : \sigma_r^2/\sigma_s^2 \neq 1$? Again assuming that the unemployment rates in the two regions are normally, identically, and independently distributed, but dropping the assumption that the population variance is the same for both regions, we have

$$UR_i^s \sim \text{NIID}\left[\mu_s, \sigma_s^2\right] \quad \text{for } i = 1, 11 \tag{4-57}$$

and, independently,

$$UR_j^r \sim \text{NIID}\left[\mu_r, \sigma_r^2\right] \quad \text{for } j = 1, 39 \tag{4-58}$$

Under these assumptions we know (from the results on the distribution of sample variances obtained earlier in this chapter) that $10S_s^2/\sigma_s^2$ is distributed $\chi^2(10)$ and that $38S_r^2/\sigma_r^2$ is distributed $\chi^2(38)$. These two statistics are independently distributed because each observation used in S_s^2 is independent of each observation used in S_r^2.

It is well known that ratios of chi-squared variables have a simple distribution. In particular:

The F Distribution

If

$$Q_1 \sim \chi^2(df_1) \quad \text{independently from} \quad Q_2 \sim \chi^2(df_2)$$

then

$$F \equiv \frac{\dfrac{Q_1}{df_1}}{\dfrac{Q_2}{df_2}} \sim F(df_1, df_2) \tag{4-59}$$

Consequently,

$$\frac{\dfrac{S_r^2}{\sigma_r^2}}{\dfrac{S_s^2}{\sigma_s^2}} \sim F(38, 10) \tag{4-60}$$

[17] Typical econometric software does all of the arithmetic (and tail area calculations) for us. For example, presuming that the variable "ursouth" contains the 11 unemployment rates for the southern states and that the variable "urrest" contains the rest, then in Stata it would suffice to issue the command "ttest ursouth-urrest, unpaired".

Hence, under the null hypothesis, $H_o : \sigma_r^2/\sigma_s^2 = 1$,

$$\frac{S_r^2}{S_s^2} \sim F(38,\ 10) \tag{4-61}$$

which has a density function which looks like Figure 4-10. Thus, this null hypothesis can be rejected in favor of the alternative hypothesis, $H_A : \sigma_r^2/\sigma_s^2 \neq 1$ with p-value equal to the probability that an $F(38, 10)$ variable differs from one by a larger factor than does the observed variance ratio, $s_r^2/s_s^2 = 1.0880/.7516 = 1.447$. This probability equals .472; it corresponds to the tail area in the $F(38, 10)$ distribution to the right of 1.447 (which is .274) plus the tail area to the left of .691 (the reciprocal of 1.447), which is .198.[18]

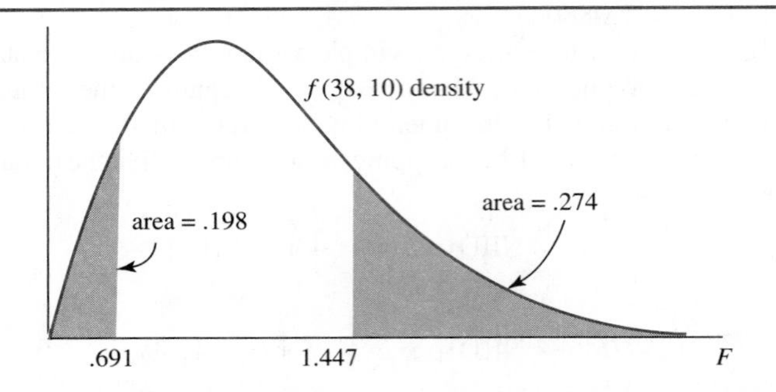

Figure 4-10 Density Function for the $F(38, 10)$ Distribution, Illustrating Tail Areas

These two tail areas are added together to obtain the p-value at which the null hypothesis can be rejected based on this evidence – that the realized sample variance s_r^2 is 1.447 times larger than the sample variance s_s^2. This p-value is the probability that we would have observed evidence against the null hypothesis at least this strong – i.e., one observed sample variance at least 1.447 times bigger than the other – due to chance alone when the two population variances were actually equal.

This p-value (of .472) is so much larger than .05 that we can clearly conclude that the observed sample variance ratio of $s_r^2/s_s^2 = 1.447$ does not provide any evidence against the null hypothesis that the population variance is the same for both the Southern states and the rest of the country.

If this null hypothesis *had* been inconsistent with the sample data, however, then the test of the null hypothesis $H_o : \mu_s = \mu_r$ discussed in the previous section would have been invalid. What would be an appropriate course of action in that case? The best approach is to use the regression methods discussed in the following chapters, but two widely-known approximate tests of $H_o : \mu_s = \mu_r$ which do not assume that $\sigma_s^2 = \sigma_r^2$ are worth mentioning here.

Satterthwaite (1946) and Welch (1947)[19] observe that if

$$UR_i^s \sim \text{NIID}\left[\mu_s, \sigma_s^2\right] \quad \text{for } i = 1,\ n_s \tag{4-62}$$

and, independently,

$$UR_j^r \sim \text{NIID}\left[\mu_r, \sigma_r^2\right] \quad \text{for } j = 1,\ n_r \tag{4-63}$$

[18] These tail areas were calculated using the program "ftest.exe" , available at www.wiley.com/college/ashley; they can also be calculated using the Excel worksheet function "fdist."

[19] F. E. Satterthwaite, "An Approximate Distribution of Variance Components," *Biometrics Bulletin 2(6)*, pp. 110–114, and B. L. Welch, "The Generalization of 'Student's' Problem When Several Different Population Variances Are Involved," *Biometrika 34*, pp. 28–35.

then, under the null hypothesis $H_o : \mu_s = \mu_r$

$$\frac{\overline{UR}_s - \overline{UR}_r}{\sqrt{\frac{S_s^2}{n_s} + \frac{S_r^2}{n_r}}} \tag{4-64}$$

is approximately distributed Student's *t* (*df*) for large values of both n_s and n_r. Satterthwaite and Welch each give a different formula for *df*. Satterthwaite's formula is

$$df = \frac{\left(\frac{s_s^2}{n_s} + \frac{s_r^2}{n_r}\right)^2}{\frac{\left(\frac{s_s^2}{n_s}\right)^2}{n_s - 1} + \frac{\left(\frac{s_r^2}{n_r}\right)^2}{n_r - 1}} \tag{4-65}$$

Welch's formula is similarly opaque, but slightly different.

In either case, the approximation becomes increasingly accurate as σ_s^2 as approaches σ_r^2 and as both sample sizes become large, but of course one can never be certain that n_s and n_r are large enough that the *p*-values based on these approximate distributions are accurate. However, because many computer programs (e.g., Stata) have one or both of these formulas preprogrammed, the additional trouble involved in doing the Satterthwaite and Welch tests is negligible. Indeed, if $H_o : \sigma_r^2/\sigma_s^2 = 1$ can be rejected and both samples are fairly large, then it is sensible to do both the Satterthwaite *and* the Welch test: if they yield similar *p*-values for the test of $H_o : \mu_s = \mu_r$ then it is reasonable to presume that both approximations are tolerably accurate.

4.10 SOME GENERAL COMMENTS ON DIAGNOSTIC CHECKING

The topic of diagnostic checking will covered in greater depth in Chapters 10, 13, and 14, where we will learn how to check the assumptions underlying the Multiple Regression Model. Nevertheless, some general comments are in order at this point:

- **Diagnostic checking is essential.** People who analyze data without checking the model assumptions underlying their work generally produce inferior results.
- **Computer software will not and cannot do the diagnostic checking for us.** The software provides the tools that make doing the diagnostic checks easy, but it also makes it easy to do the calculations ***without*** checking the model assumptions. Basically, the software just evaluates formulas. For example, in the hypothesis testing framework developed earlier in this chapter, the relevant formula is for a *t* statistic ($t = (\bar{y} - \mu_0)/\sqrt{s^2/N}$); but this statistic is a drawing from the Student's *t* distribution with $N-1$ degrees of freedom *only* if the model assumptions ($Y_i \sim \text{NIID}[\mu, \sigma^2]$) are valid. No one evaluates this *t* statistic formula and the tail area for the statistical test based on it by hand – we use computer software for that. However, that is *all* that the software does – it does not check whether the underlying assumptions are remotely consistent with the sample data, it just evaluates the formula for the *t* statistic and calculates the relevant tail area for the Student's *t* distribution with $N-1$ degrees of freedom. But if this *t* statistic is not in fact a drawing from this distribution because the model assumptions are substantially invalid, then this tail area is irrelevant to the actual probability that the null hypothesis is being wrongly rejected. The computer program prints out the resulting *t* statistic and *p*-value just as nicely regardless, but the results are meaningless.
- **Diagnostic checking is not just destructive.** Often a failed diagnostic check guides us toward a better (usually richer) model of the data. For example, finding that unemployment rates are

significantly larger in one area of the country might stimulate us to examine the differences between this area and other states and lead to a regression model (such as those discussed in the following chapters) which actually explains the variation in unemployment rates across the states.

- **Effective diagnostic checking requires data.** Diagnostic checking generally speaking requires at least as much data as does the original inference; diagnostic checks involving hypotheses about population variances generally require considerably more. For example, it may be reasonable to produce a confidence interval for μ with only 20 observations – perhaps because that is all we have – but a test of whether 10 of these observations have a different population variance from the other 10 is unlikely to detect a discrepancy unless it is grotesquely large. This illustrates a hidden problem with really small data sets: such small sample sizes essentially preclude many kinds of diagnostic checking. Thus, one in that case ends up being forced to rely on model assumptions which cannot be effectively checked.
- **Effective diagnostic checking requires engaged, sometimes creative, attention.** The most important diagnostic checks require the analyst to posit something about the *manner* in which the assumptions are (possibly) being violated. This is where our knowledge about the economic context of the problem (and our willingness and/or ability) to connect proactively to what we are doing plays a crucial role in making high-quality results possible.

  For example, in the previous two sections we considered the possibility that the population mean or variance of the data is different for Southern states than for the rest of the United States. Perhaps this was an insightful and relevant choice. Or perhaps it was a silly choice and it would have been far better to partition the 50 states into two groups in some other way. *Some* choice must be made in order to perform the tests at all, and *thoughtful* choices need to be made in order to obtain useful results. If we make a poor choice (or no choice at all) then we may miss detecting serious deficiencies in our model which substantially diminish the meaningfulness of the inferences drawn.

  And there is no shelter in refusing to choose, by instructing a computer to perform every possible test. After all, if we do 100 different hypothesis tests, then chance alone will cause the null hypothesis to be rejected around five times with p-values less than .05.

  Indeed, this is the essential reason why computer software cannot do the diagnostic checking for us: a degree of creativity, judgment, and problem-specific knowledge is necessary in order to reasonably choose which amongst the plethora of possible model deficiencies are the ones which should be tested. This is also, of course, why diagnostic checking cannot be reduced to a set of rules and formulas, although much can (and will) be said later – especially in Chapters 10 through 13 – as to how to proceed.
- **The optimal amount of diagnostic checking is situationally specific.** Because diagnostic checking requires time and creative attention – both of which are scarce resources – the optimal amount of diagnostic checking depends on how difficult the model is to check, on how likely it is that the checking will detect defects that can actually be addressed, and – importantly – on how much time and effort one can afford to spend on improving the results for this particular model.

4.11 CLOSING COMMENTS

This chapter has briefly reviewed all of the statistical inference machinery needed in order to construct confidence intervals and hypothesis tests on the population mean of a normally distributed random variable. The practical applicability of these particular results is quite limited, however, primarily because they necessarily rest on the highly restrictive assumption that $E[Y_i]$ is a constant. In contrast, the point of most econometric analysis is to model the manner in which $E[Y_i]$ varies in response to changes in various observed economic factors; indeed, that is precisely what we are going to do in the coming chapters, using regression analysis.

None of your efforts in tackling the material reviewed in this chapter were wasted, however: we will use almost exactly the same ideas and techniques described here when we turn (in Chapters 7 and 9) to the problem of constructing confidence intervals and hypothesis tests on the coefficients in regression models.

KEY TERMS

For each term or concept listed below, provide a working definition or explanation:

Standardization

Confidence Interval

Null Hypothesis

Alternative Hypothesis

p-Value for Hypothesis Test

Two-tailed Test

One-tailed Test

Chi-Squared Distribution

Student's *t* Distribution

EXERCISES

4-1. When, in practice, is σ^2 known for a set of data? When, in practice, is s^2 known for a set of data?

4-2. What does $z^c_{0.025}$ equal? What does it represent?

4-3. If $\bar{y} = 14$ and $s^2 = 1.02$ using 25 observations on the random variable Y, what is the observed (estimated) 95% confidence interval for the expected value of Y? What must be assumed about $Y_1 \ldots Y_{25}$ in order for this confidence interval to be valid?

4-4. Why do critical points z^c_α become larger as α gets smaller?

4-5. Suppose that $\bar{y} = 46.8$ and $s^2 = 2$ using 16 observations, $y_1 \ldots y_{16}$. At what *p*-value can the null hypothesis $H_o: \mu = 46$ be rejected on the two-tailed test? What must be assumed about $Y_1 \ldots Y_{16}$ in order for this result to be valid? Why would such assumptions about $y_1 \ldots y_{16}$ make no sense?

Sample Data for Questions 4-6 to 4-9			
i	y_i	i	y_i
1	13	6	57
2	45	7	39
3	23	8	42
4	46	9	37
5	32	10	50

4-6. Calculate $\bar{y}$ and s^2 for the above set often observations, showing your work.

4-7. Assuming that the above ten observations are realizations of $Y_1 \ldots Y_{10}$ which are distributed NIID(μ, σ^2), construct a 95% confidence interval for μ.

4-8. Assuming that the above 10 observations are realizations of $Y_1 \ldots Y_{10}$ which are distributed NIID(μ, σ^2), test the null hypothesis $H_o: \mu_0 = 35$ against the alternative hypothesis

$H_A : \mu_0 \neq 35$. Based on the fact that $\bar{y}$ exceeds 35, would it be appropriate to test whether or not μ is significantly greater than 35 by considering the one-tailed test with alternative hypothesis, $H_A : \mu_0 > 35$?

4-9. Again using the above 10 observations, split the sample data into two groups: the first five observations and the last five observations. Calculate the two relevant sample variances, s^2_{first} and s^2_{last}, and test the null hypothesis $H_o : \sigma^2_{first} = \sigma^2_{last}$ against the alternative hypothesis that $H_A : \sigma^2_{first} \neq \sigma^2_{last}$. What must be assumed about $Y_1 \ldots Y_{10}$ in order for this hypothesis test to be valid?

4-10. Assuming that $Y_i \sim \text{NIID}(\mu, 25)$ for all i, show how to test the null hypothesis

$$H_o : \mu = 14$$

against the alternative hypothesis

$$H_A : \mu \neq 14$$

using the sample mean over a normally distributed random sample, using the four observations y_1, y_2, y_3, and y_4. Show your work. Also, derive a 92% confidence interval for μ. You may leave your answer in terms of y_1, y_2, y_3, y_4 and a critical point of the unit normal distribution. Provide a sketch of the unit normal density function which makes clear the meaning of whatever symbol you choose to denote this critical point.

4-11. Let $\tilde{\mu}$ be an estimator of μ with sampling distribution $N\,(\mu + 3, \sigma^2/25)$.

a. Assuming that that σ^2 is given, show how to test obtain the p-value at which the null hypothesis $H_o : \mu = 14$ can be rejected against the alternative hypothesis $H_A : \mu_0 \neq 14$. Show your work.

b. Repeat part a, dropping the assumption that σ^2 is known. Instead, you may assume that an estimator $\hat{\sigma}^2$ is available which is independent of $\tilde{\mu}$ and for which it is known that

$$\frac{38\hat{\sigma}^2}{\sigma^2} \sim \chi^2(16)$$

c. Is $\tilde{\mu}$ a consistent estimator of μ? Is $\tilde{\mu}$ a consistent estimator of $\mu + 3$? (Note that this problem has not specified how many sample observations were used in $\tilde{\mu}$: there could have been 25, 39, 17, or some other number of observations used.)

4-12. As in Exercise 3-15, you have observed the following random sample on a normally distributed variable:

i	y_i
1	7.5
2	8.0
3	9.9
4	9.1
5	7.9

a. Assume that $Y_i \sim \text{NIID}\,(\mu, 4)$ for $i = 1, 2, 3, 4$, and 5. Use the sample mean to test the null hypothesis $H_o : \mu = 7.0$ against the alternative hypothesis $H_A : \mu \neq 7.0$. At what p-value can this null hypothesis be rejected? (You may use the gaustail.exe computer program from the book companion site, www.wiley.com/college/ashley, to compute the relevant tail area of the unit normal density function, or you may use the "normdist" function in

Excel.) Also make a sketch of the unit normal density function to illustrate your answer. Can you reject the null hypothesis at the 1% or 5% levels of significance?

b. Derive a 95% confidence interval for μ.

c. Now drop the artificial assumption that the var (Y_i) is known to be four and instead assume that Y_i is distributed NIID (μ, σ^2) for $i = 1, 2, 3, 4$, and five with σ^2 not known. Again test the null hypothesis $H_o: \mu = 7.0$ against the alternative hypothesis $H_A: \mu \neq 7.0$. At what p-value can this null hypothesis be rejected? (You may use the ttail.exe computer program (available at www.wiley.com/college/ashley) to compute the relevant tail area of the appropriate t distribution density function, or you may use the "tdist" function in Excel.) Also make a sketch of the appropriate t distribution density function to illustrate your answer. Can you reject the null hypothesis at the 1% or 5% levels of significance? Explain why your answer differs from the one you obtained for part a.

d. Again dropping the artificial assumption that the population variance of Y_i is 4, obtain a 95% confidence interval for μ. Explain why your answer differs from the one you obtained for part b in the way that it does.

e. Enter these five observations into the econometric software being used in your course (storing it with variable name "Y") and use the software to test the null hypothesis.[20]

f. Assuming that Y_i is distributed NIID (μ, σ^2) for all five observations, $4s^2/\sigma^2$ is distributed $\chi^2(4)$. Use this result to test the null hypothesis that σ^2 actually does equal 4. (You may use the chisqr.exe computer program (available at www.wiley.com/college/ashley) to compute the relevant tail area of the $\chi^2(4)$ density function, or you may use the "chidist" function in Excel.) Also make a sketch of the $\chi^2(4)$ density function to illustrate your answer. Can you reject the null hypothesis that σ^2 is four at the 1% or 5% levels of significance?[21]

4-13. Now suppose that $Y_i \sim N(\mu, \sigma^2)$ for $i = 1, 2, 3, 4$, and five but that there is good reason to fear that these observations are not independently distributed.

a. Are $\overline{Y}$ and S^2 still unbiased estimators for μ and σ^2?

b. Is the distribution of $4S^2/\sigma^2$ known?

c. Is $4S^2/\sigma^2$ still independent of $\overline{Y}$?

d. Is it still possible to construct hypothesis tests and confidence intervals for μ?

e. Suppose we knew that σ^2 is 4. How would this change your answer to part d? {Hint: because σ^2 is known, the properties of S^2 are irrelevant, but it is still necessary to standardize $\overline{Y}$ to zero mean and unit variance.}

Active Learning Exercise 4a: Investigating the Sensitivity of Hypothesis Test *P*-Values to Departures from the NIID (μ, σ^2) Assumption Using Computer-Generated Data

Introduction

In this chapter the assumption that the random variables $Y_1 \ldots Y_N$ are NIID$[\mu, \sigma^2]$ was used to obtain a p-value for testing the null hypothesis $H_o: \mu = \mu_o$ against the alternative

[20] In Stata, the command for this would be "ttest $Y = 7$."

[21] Using Stata the command for this would be "sdtest $Y = 2$."

hypothesis that $H_A: \mu \neq \mu_0$ for any given value μ_0, based on the result that

$$\frac{\overline{Y} - \mu_0}{\sqrt{\frac{S^2}{N}}} \sim t(N-1)$$

if the null hypothesis is true. It was noted that the normality part of the NIID[μ, σ^2] assumption on Y_1 ... Y_N becomes less and less important as N increases (due to a Central Limit Theorem result) but that (even for large N) the assumptions that Y_1 ... Y_N are uncorrelated and all have the same variance are crucial to the result that the sampling variance of $\overline{Y}$ equals σ^2/N.

You learned how to generate sample data which was in several interesting ways non-NIID in Active Learning Exercise 3a. In that Active Learning Exercise you found that $\overline{Y}$ and S^2 are still consistent estimators of μ and σ^2 regardless of the substantial departures from the NIID assumption considered there. Here you will generate large amounts of sample data on $\overline{Y}/\sqrt{S^2/N}$ and examine the impact of these departures from the NIID assumption on the resulting p-values for testing the null hypothesis $H_o: \mu = 0$ against the alternative hypothesis that $H_A: \mu \neq 0$.

Your Assignment:

1. Copy the program ALE_4a.exe from the companion Web site (www.wiley.com/college/ashley) to your hard disk and execute it. The program will prompt you to enter a value for the sample size (N) to be used in generating realizations (trials) of $\overline{Y}/\sqrt{S^2/N}$. In this Active Learning Exercise you will investigate sample sizes of 30, 100, and 500; you can start with 30. The program will next prompt you to enter a value for the number samples or trials of $\overline{Y}/\sqrt{S^2/N}$ to be generated; you should choose 10000 for this value.[22] Finally, the program will prompt you for a value to use as an initial seed for the random number generator. You can enter any positive integer you like here (or whatever value your instructor suggests) but note down the value you use so that your work is easily replicable.[23] The program will then generate the specified number of realizations of $\overline{Y}/\sqrt{S^2/N}$ for each of the five different underlying distributions for Y_1 ... Y_N considered in Active Learning Exercise 3a and store these realizations on your hard disk in a comma-delimited file named ALE_4.csv; rename this file so that its file name indicates the value of N chosen when you created it using ALE_4a.exe.[24]

   As in Active Learning Exercise 3a, the program generates y_1 ... y_N realizations from five different distributions, each constructed so as to have population mean zero and population variance one:
   a. NIID
   b. ASYMMETRIC

[22] Your instructor may ask you to enter a value less than 10,000 if the student version of the econometrics software your class is using will not support this many observations. In case this program is not compatible with your version of Windows, sample output files created with initial seed equal to 33 are available at www.wiley.com/college/ashley, labeled "ALE_4a_N30.csv", "ALE_4a_N100.csv", and "ALE_4a_N500.csv"; the number of trials implicit in these data files can be reduced using spreadsheet software if a smaller value is necessary. Similar files in Stata format are included, each with extension "dta".

[23] See Active Learning Exercise 3a for a discussion of how pseudo-random number generators work and why they need an initial seed.

[24] Program source code is found in ALE_4a.for (available at www.wiley.com/college/ashley); the code is very similar to that of ALE_3a.for, so the comments in Footnote 3-17 apply here as well.

c. FAT-TAILED
d. NONHOMOGENEOUS_VARIANCE
e. CORRELATED

Under the "NIID" heading in the output file are realizations of $\overline{Y}/\sqrt{S^2/N}$ based on normally identically and independently distributed random variables. The "ASYMMETRIC" $\overline{Y}/\sqrt{S^2/N}$ variates are instead based on squared normally distributed variates;[25] and the "FAT-TAILED" variates are constructed from Student's t variates with four degrees of freedom.[26] The last two random variables used in generating realizations of $\overline{Y}/\sqrt{S^2/N}$ are not identically and independently distributed. The variates used in generating the $\overline{Y}/\sqrt{S^2/N}$ realizations under the "NONHOMOGENEOUS_VARIANCE" heading are constructed so that the even-numbered observations are realizations of NIID(0,9/5) variates and the odd-numbered observations are realizations of NIID(0,1/5) variates. Similarly, the "CORRELATED" variates are constructed so that the correlation between consecutive observations is .70.[27]

2. For each of the three values of N, read the 10,000 simulated values of $\overline{Y}/\sqrt{S^2/N}$ which you have generated into whatever econometrics software your course is using and print out histograms for each of the five variables – i.e., for data generated using each of the five underlying distributions (NIID ... CORRELATED).[28] The Central Limit Theorem implies that all of these histograms should look considerably more like the unit normal density function than did the histograms of the individual observations which you looked at in Active Learning Exercise 3a, especially for the two larger values N. Print out these histograms. Do any of them look obviously unlike what one would expect from a histogram of 10,000 unit normal variates?
3. Use the econometric software to sort the data for each series in turn and use the data browser to observe how many realizations of $\overline{Y}/\sqrt{S^2/N}$ lie outside $\pm t^c_{.025}(N-1)$, the 2½% critical point of the relevant Student's t distribution.[29] The null hypothesis is true here by construction. Consequently, something like 500 (out of 10,000) realizations should exceed $t^c_{.025}(N-1)$ magnitude, just due to chance.[30] In this way, complete the following table:

[25] The square of a unit normal variate is a $\chi^2(1)$ variate, which is adjusted to have population mean zero by subtracting one and then divided by $\sqrt{2}$ so that the population variance is one. The χ^2 distribution is discussed in this chapter; see Equation 4-20.

[26] The Student's t distribution is discussed in this chapter; see Equation 4-31. These variates are constructed as $Z/\sqrt{(Z_1^2+Z_2^2+Z_3^2+Z_4^2)/4}$, where Z, Z_1, Z_2, Z_3, and Z_4 are independent draws from the unit normal distribution; this variate is then divided by $\sqrt{2}$ so that its population variance is one.

[27] These are constructed from an AR(1) model: $Y_i = .7Y_{i-1} + Z_i$ where $Z_i \sim$ NIID $(0,1\text{-}.7^2)$ to make its population variance equal to 1. AR(1) processes are discussed in Section 13.4.

[28] In Stata the command "histogram NIID, normal" produces a histogram of the variable named "NIID" and also plots the unit normal density with population mean and variance equal to the sample mean and sample variance of this variable.

[29] It is convenient to take the absolute value of each variable prior to sorting. In Stata the command "sort NIID" will sort the entire data set in increasing order of the variable "NIID". You can confirm the three critical points given in the table for yourself by using the "ttail.exe" program (available at www.wiley.com/college/ashley).

[30] You should not expect exactly 500 realizations of $\overline{Y}/\sqrt{S^2/N}$ to lie outside $\pm t^c_{.025}(N-1)$, however. In fact, if the true proportion is .05, then the proportion actually observed in 10,000 trials is distributed N (.05, .05*.95/10000) or N (.05, .0022) for large numbers of trials. Thus an estimated 95% confidence interval for this proportion is [.0456, .0544].

Number of $\left|\overline{Y}/\sqrt{S^2/N}\right|$ realizations greater than $t^c_{.025}(N-1)$, out of 10,000 trials						
N	$t^c_{.025}(N-1)$	NIID	ASYMMETRIC	FAT-TAILED	NONHOMOGENEOUS VARIANCE	CORRELATED
30	2.045					
100	1.984					
500	1.965					
Seed Used =						

4. What can you conclude from these results about the importance of the assumption that $Y_1 \ldots Y_N$ are NIID[μ, σ^2] at various sample sizes? Does the form of the distribution seem to matter? Does it matter if the data are not identically and independently distributed, at least in the ways examined here? Is the assumption that the variance is constant across the sample as important as the assumption that the data are uncorrelated?

Part 2

REGRESSION ANALYSIS

Regression modeling is the primary tool that econometrics has to offer for using data to quantify and test economic relationships. The Bivariate Regression Model relates the sample variation in an observed random variable to that of a single explanatory variable; the Multiple Regression model allows the flexibility of multiple explanatory variables. Real-world economic relationships almost always require multiple regression modeling, but a complete analysis of the Multiple Regression model involves a considerable amount of matrix algebra, which is outside the scope of the present treatment. Consequently, this section begins with a thorough treatment of the Bivariate Regression Model; for this model, simple algebra will suffice.

Chapter 5 introduces the Bivariate Regression Model and describes the statistical assumptions underlying the model. This chapter also obtains and interprets the least squares estimates of the model parameters. These model assumptions are used in Chapter 6 to obtain the sampling distributions of the least squares parameter estimators. This chapter then goes on to analyze how the key properties of these parameter estimators – unbiasedness, consistency, and BLUness – depend on the underlying assumptions of the model. The sampling distributions of the least squares estimators are used in Chapter 7 to obtain confidence intervals and derive hypothesis tests for the Bivariate Regression Model parameters; these statistical inference results allow us to quantify the sampling uncertainty in the model parameter estimates and to use the estimated model to test economic hypotheses. You will find that almost everything you learned in Chapters 3 and 4 about estimation and inference with respect to the mean of a random variable is applied afresh in Chapters 6 and 7 to estimation and inference with respect to the key parameter of the Bivariate Regression Model. Finally, Chapter 8 takes up the issue of quantifying how well the model fits the data and discusses how the estimated model can be used to forecast yet-to-be-observed realizations of the random variable being modeled.

The restriction to a single explanatory variable in the Bivariate Regression Model is quite confining with economic data, however. Consequently, these results are extended in Chapter 9 to the Multiple Regression Model, where the sample variation in an observed random variable related to that of a number of explanatory variables. Because matrix algebra is not used here, these extensions are obtained by analogy with the corresponding results in the Bivariate Regression Model rather than by formal derivation.

All of the results of Chapters 5 through 9 hinge on the validity of the statistical assumptions underlying these two forms of regression model, however. In particular, only if these assumptions are satisfied will the least squares estimates of the parameters in these models be high-quality estimates – i.e., unbiased, consistent, and BLU. And only if these assumptions are satisfied will the statistical inference results – i.e., the confidence intervals and hypothesis tests – be meaningfully valid. Chapters 10 through 14 provide methods for using the sample data itself to detect and correct failures of these assumptions – it is these methods that make regression practically useful with real economic data.

5

The Bivariate Regression Model: Introduction, Assumptions, and Parameter Estimates

5.1 INTRODUCTION

The basic statistical analysis reviewed in Part I showed how sample observations on a random variable can be used to estimate its population mean, μ, and to thereby quantitatively characterize its size. More precisely, if the random variables $Y_1 \ldots Y_N$ are normally, identically, and independently distributed – i.e., $Y_i \sim \text{NIID}(\mu, \sigma^2)$ for $i = 1 \ldots N$ – then we saw in Chapters 3 and 4 how to use N sample realizations of these random variables – i.e., $y_1 \ldots y_N$ – to obtain a high-quality estimate of μ, to obtain estimated confidence intervals for μ, and to test hypotheses about μ.

The observed variation in the sample observations $y_1 \ldots y_N$ is just a nuisance in estimating μ, but it is crucial for obtaining confidence intervals for μ and in testing hypotheses about μ because it allows us to estimate the population variance (σ^2) of the random variables $Y_1 \ldots Y_N$. Regression analysis uses this observed sample variation in $y_1 \ldots y_N$ in a different way, to ask and answer a set of deeper and vastly more important questions: *why* do realizations of the random variable Y_i vary in the way that they do? In what manner is the random variable Y_i *related* to other observable variables?

This chapter begins by using an example with real economic data to step through the transition from estimating the population mean of a random variable to estimating the parameters of a simple model in which the sample variation in the observed values $y_1 \ldots y_N$ is modeled as depending (in part) on the sample variation in a single explanatory variable. At that point the statistical assumptions constituting the Bivariate Regression Model are explicitly introduced and used to demonstrate the close relationship between regression modeling and estimation of the mean of a random variable. The statistical assumptions constituting the Bivariate Regression Model are discussed and interpreted at this point because everything we are going to do with this model in subsequent chapters hinges on their validity:

- Showing that our estimators of the model's parameters have desirable properties, such as unbiasedness, consistency, and Best Linear Unbiasedness ("BLU-ness")
- Using our estimators of the model's parameters to obtain confidence intervals containing the population parameters with specified probability
- Using our estimators of the model's parameters to test economically important hypotheses about the population parameters.

It seemed obvious and natural in Chapter 3 to use the sample mean to estimate the population mean of a random variable. In that chapter the surprise was to find that one might, in some circumstances, actually prefer some other estimator, such as the sample median or a shrunken estimator. Equally obvious estimators for the two main parameters of the Bivariate Regression Model do not present themselves, so we next apply the least squares curve fitting concept discussed in Chapter 3 to obtain sample estimates for these parameters.

One of these least squares parameter estimates (the "intercept" estimate) is closely related to the sample mean; the other (the "slope" estimate) is shown to be closely related to the sample analogue of the correlation coefficient discussed in Chapter 2.

Finally, the special case where the explanatory variable is a dummy variable is considered. A dummy variable equals either 1 or 0, depending on whether some condition is satisfied; for example, a gender dummy variable might take on the value 1 for observations corresponding to male respondents and 0 for female respondents. It is shown that the least squares slope estimator is in that case identical to the difference between the sample mean of the male observations and the sample mean of the female observations. The chapter closes with an illustrative example using a college graduation dummy variable to model the impact of education on household income.

5.2 THE TRANSITION FROM MEAN ESTIMATION TO REGRESSION: ANALYZING THE VARIATION OF PER CAPITA REAL OUTPUT ACROSS COUNTRIES

The Penn World Table (PWT) attempts to construct estimates of output, prices, and the like which are reasonably comparable across a large number of countries. In particular, the PWT variable *rgdpl* is an estimate of per capita real GDP – i.e., real output per person – expressed for each of the 125 countries in the sample in terms of 1996 dollars.[1]

Thinking of the observed *rgdpl* value for country *i* in a given year – e.g., 1999 – as an independent drawing from the distribution of an underlying random variable $RGDPL_i$, distributed

$$RGDPL_i \sim \text{IID}\left(\mu_{rgdpl}, \sigma^2_{rgdpl}\right) \tag{5-1}$$

we can use μ_{rgdpl} to characterize the size of per capita real GDP in 1999. Letting $rgdpl_1 \ldots rgdpl_{125}$ stand for the 125 observed $rgdpl_i$ values in the year 1999, a histogram of these $rgdpl_i$ values is shown in Figure 5-1.

Because $RGDPL_1 \ldots RGDPL_{125}$ are assumed to be identically and independently distributed, the results in Chapters 3 and 4 indicate that the sample mean of $RGDPL_i$ is the BLU estimator of its population mean, μ_{rgdpl}, and that the sample variance of $RGDPL_i$ is an unbiased estimator of its population variance, σ^2_{rgdpl}. For these particular sample observations,

$$\overline{rgdpl} = \frac{1}{125}\sum_{i=1}^{125} rgdpl_i = \$8{,}713 \tag{5-2}$$

is the sample realization of this BLU estimator of μ_{rgdpl} and

$$s^2_{rgdpl} = \frac{1}{124}\sum_{i=1}^{125}\left(rgdpl_i - \overline{rgdpl}\right)^2 = 74{,}304{,}400 \tag{5-3}$$

is the sample realization of this unbiased estimator of σ^2_{rgdpl}.

[1] The PWT data are available on the internet in a particularly accessible format. You will explore this site (and the data itself) in Active Learning Exercise 5a.

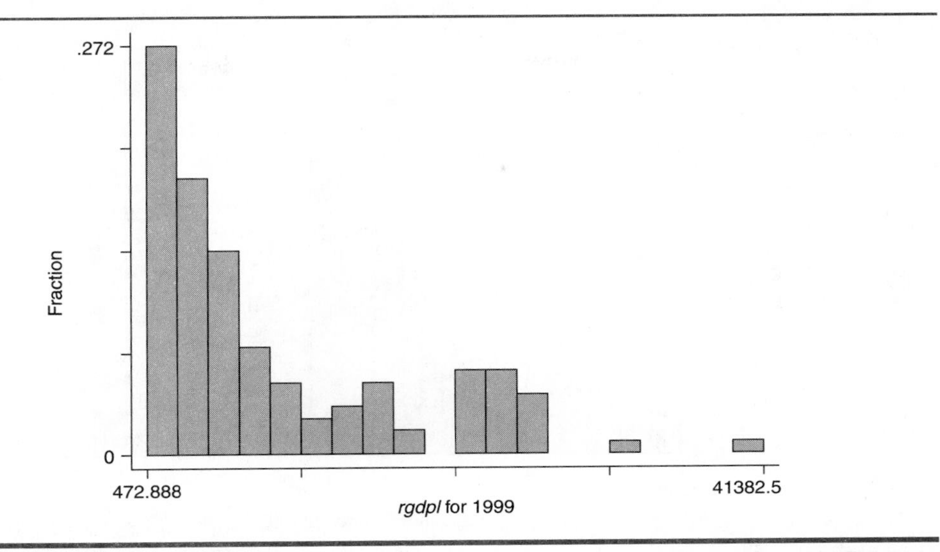

Figure 5-1 Histogram of $rdgpl_i$ Values

It seems evident from the histogram of the $rgdpl_i$ values, however, that these are not drawings from a normal distribution. Thus, the results of Section 4.6 are only approximately applicable and hence

$$\frac{\left(\overline{rgdpl} - \mu_{rgdpl}\right)}{\sqrt{s^2_{rgdpl}/125}} \tag{5-4}$$

is a realization of a random variable which is only approximately distributed Student's t with 124 degrees of freedom. On the other hand, this sample is sufficiently large that confidence intervals based on this Student's t distribution are probably reasonably accurate approximations. Using the Central Limit Theorem results from Exercise 2-40, the shape of this histogram suggests that a histogram of the logarithm of the observed $RGDPL_i$ data might well look more like drawings from a normal distribution, and, indeed, the histogram of $\log(rgdp_i)$ displayed in Figure 5-2 shows that it does.

We will return to the issue of whether it is more appropriate to model the logarithm of $RGDPL_i$ rather than $RGDPL_i$ itself later in this section.

A more pressing problem with these data, however, is that both sample histograms appear to indicate that the distribution of $RGDPL_i$ is bimodal – that is, it has two peaks. This strongly suggests that there are actually two different kinds of country in the sample: underdeveloped countries with real per capita GDP of a few thousand dollars or less, and developed countries with real per capita GDP on the order of \$20,000 or more. If this is the case, then the overall sample mean $\left(\overline{rgdpl} = \$8{,}713\right)$ may be a reasonable estimate of μ_{rgdpl}, but it is a rather poor compromise as a measure of how large the random variable $RGDPL_i$ is, on average. Another way of putting this is to note that the sample mean of $RGDPL_i$ is an unbiased estimator for μ_{rgdpl}, but it is a seriously biased estimator of both $\mu^{underdev}_{rgdpl}$ and μ^{dev}_{rgdpl}, the population mean values of per capita real GDP for the underdeveloped and for the developed countries, respectively.

We could, of course, split the sample into two parts, estimating $\mu^{underdev}_{rgdpl}$ using the observations less than some (slightly arbitrary) cutoff value and estimating μ^{dev}_{rgdpl} using the remaining observations. But this sample separation may not be correct. For example, with any given cutoff value, it may well be the

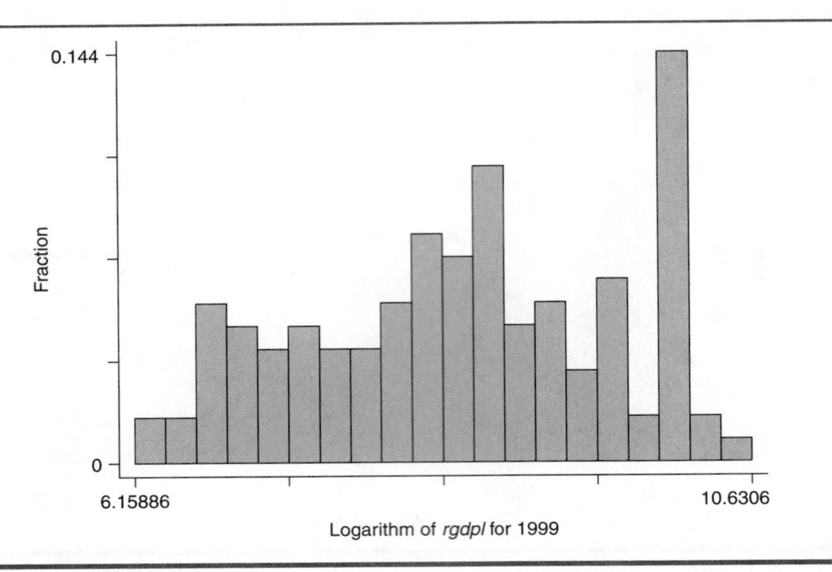

Figure 5-2 Histogram of log(*rgdpl*) Values

case that a country which should be in the developed country sample (i.e., its observed $RGDPL_i$ value is a drawing from the distribution with population mean μ_{rgdpl}^{dev}) will nevertheless wind up in the underdeveloped country sample simply due to chance. Thus, the sample mean of the underdeveloped country observations will actually yield an upwardly biased estimate of $\mu_{rgdpl}^{underdev}$; and the sample mean of the developed country observations will yield an downwardly biased estimate of μ_{rgdpl}^{dev}.

A more graceful approach is to reframe this "problem" in the data as an opportunity to understand it more deeply. In particular, this apparent bimodality of the distribution of $RGDPL_i$ suggests that it might be fruitful to examine a list of the countries in what appears to be an upper peak in the distribution and consider in what other respects these countries stand out from the rest of the countries in the sample. Doing that in this case, it turns out that the countries in the upper peak are mostly the developed economies of Western Europe, plus the United States, Japan, and Australia – all countries with unusually large stocks of physical capital. This result then further suggests that there may be a direct relationship between a country's real output and its stock of real capital. Thus, variations in per capita real capital stocks may explain much of the observed variation in per capita real GDP across these countries and may thereby allow us to more sensibly analyze how the expected value of $RGDPL_i$ varies across countries.

The PWT dataset contains data on past aggregate investment spending for 105 of the 125 countries; these observations can be used to calculate k_i, an estimate of the per capita real capital stock at the beginning of 1999 for country i.[2] (As with $RGDPL_i$ and $rgdpl_i$, we can think of k_i as a realization of a random variable K_i.) A scatterplot of the observed values of $rgdpl_i$ versus k_i is given as Figure 5-3.

[2] More specifically, assuming a 5% annual depreciation rate on physical capital, the observed per capita stock of real capital for country i at the start of year t is $k(t) = .95\ k(t-1) + .01\ ki(t)\ rgdpl(t)$, where $ki(t)$ is a variable in the PWT dataset – the investment share of $rgdpl(t)$, expressed as a percentage. (The "i" in the PWT variable name "$ki(t)$" refers to "investment.") Taking the impact of $k(1959)$ on $k(1999)$ to be negligible, this equation can be iterated for $t = 1960 \ldots 1998$ to obtain $k(1999)$; $k(1999)$ for country i is denoted"k_i," in the text. The depreciation rate could in principle be estimated, but here it is taken as given for simplicity.

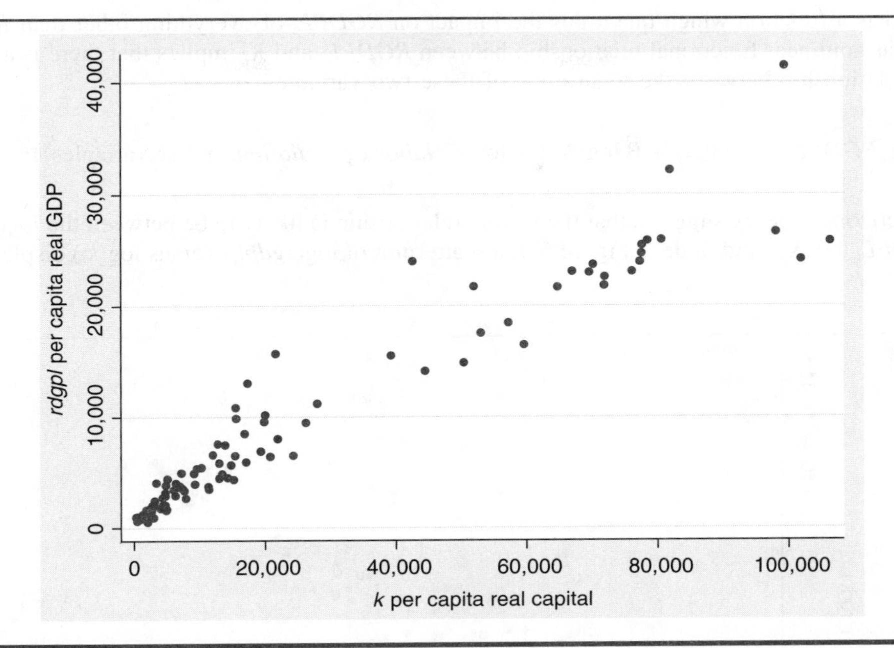

Figure 5-3 Scatterplot of Real Per Capita GDP versus Real Per Capita Capital Stock

This scatterplot confirms our intuition that there is a direct, albeit somewhat noisy, relationship between the observed values of $rgdpl_i$ and k_i. But this relationship does not appear to be very simple. One complication is that the average value of $rgdpl_i$ seems to be less sensitive to k_i when k_i is small than when it is large – i.e., the apparent slope of the data "cloud" seems to be smaller for large values of k_i. A second complication is that the apparent scatter in $rgdpl_i$ – the dispersion of the random variable $RGDPL_i$ around its mean – is clearly larger for the larger values of k_i.

In this case economic theory has an important contribution to make in the analysis. Theory suggests that total real output for country i – which equals per capita real GDP ($RGDPL_i$) times population (POP_i) and is here denoted by Q_i – is determined by an aggregate production function,

$$Q_i = F\left(K_i^{\text{total}}, L_i\right) \tag{5-5}$$

where K_i^{total} (which equals $K_i \times POP_i$) is the total real capital stock for country i, and L_i is the total labor input for country i. A typical simple functional form used for $F\left(K_i^{\text{total}}, L_i\right)$ is the generalized Cobb-Douglas production function:

$$Q_i = A\left(K_i^{\text{total}}\right)^{\beta} L_i^{\lambda} = A(K_i \times POP_i)^{\beta} L_i^{\lambda} \tag{5-6}$$

where A, β, and λ are parameters specifying the technology the countries are using. Thus, assuming Cobb-Douglas production technology, real output per capita (i.e., $RGDPL_i = Q_i / POP_i$) can be written

$$RGDPL_i = A(K_i)^{\beta}\, G(L_i, POP_i, \text{other variables}) \tag{5-7}$$

where G is a function which quantifies the impact on $RGDPL_i$ of everything other than K_i. This particular nonlinear functional relationship between $RGDPL_i$ and K_i implies that there is a simple linear relationship between the logarithms of these two variables:

$$\log(RGDPL_i) = \ln(A) + \beta \log(K_i) + \log(G(labor_i, population_i, \text{other variables})) \tag{5-8}$$

Thus, economic theory suggests that the simple relationship is likely to be between the *logarithms* of $RGDPL_i$ and K_i. And, indeed Figure 5-4, a scatterplot of log($rgdpl_i$) versus log(k_i) displays this:

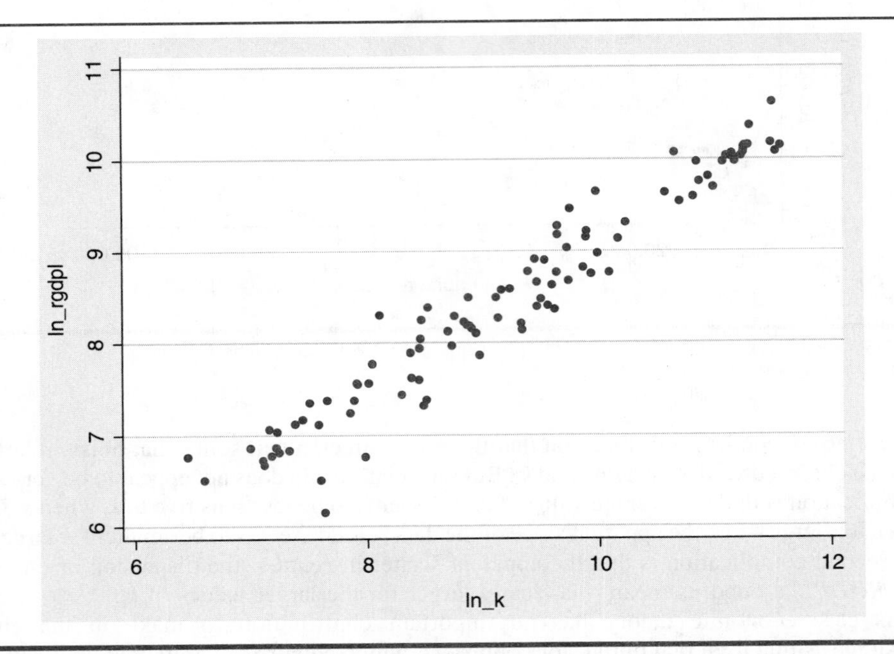

Figure 5-4 Scatterplot of log(Real Per Capita GDP) versus log(Real Per Capital Stock)

This scatterplot now exhibits a roughly constant amount of scatter in the observations and indicates that a linear function of log(k_i) plus some noise (to create the scatter) is a reasonable model for the random variable log($RGDPL_i$).[3] In other words, a reasonable model for these data appears to be

$$\log(RGDPL_i) = \alpha + \beta \log(k_i) + U_i \tag{5-9}$$

where α and β are parameters to be estimated and u_i is a random noise term with constant variance. This equation is a special case of the Bivariate Regression Model, to which we now turn.

[3] For simplicity this scatterplot omits data from four countries (Uganda, Ethiopia, Madagascar, and Mozambique) which have extremely small values of k_i; these observations are reincluded when the nonlinearity in this relationship is examined using the Multiple Regression Model in Chapter 9.

5.3 THE BIVARIATE REGRESSION MODEL – ITS FORM AND THE "FIXED IN REPEATED SAMPLES" CAUSALITY ASSUMPTION

The Bivariate Regression Model is the following set of assumptions:

The Bivariate Regression Model

$$Y_i = \alpha + \beta x_i + U_i \qquad i = 1 \ldots N$$

$x_1 \ldots x_N$ fixed in repeated samples

$$U_i \sim \text{NIID}[0, \sigma^2] \tag{5-10}$$

Equivalently,

Y_i is independently distributed $N[\alpha + \beta x_i, \sigma^2]$ for $i = 1 \ldots N$

The variable Y_i is called the "dependent" variable because its value (strictly, its mean value) is assumed to depend on the "explanatory" variable, x_i. The random variable U_i is usually called the "model error term," because this is the error we would make in using $\alpha + \beta x_i$ to predict the observed value of Y_i – but one can equally well think of U_i as quantifying the impact on Y_i of all of the explanatory variables which have been omitted from this model.

Recalling from Chapter 2 that adding a constant to a random variable increases its mean by that amount and leaves its variance unchanged, the equivalence asserted in the above definition of the Bivariate Regression Model follows from the fact that Y_i is equal to the normally distributed random variable U_i plus the fixed constant, $\alpha + \beta x_i$. (Of course, x_i is a fixed constant only in the sense that it is not random; it obviously varies throughout the sample as i varies.) This equivalence is conceptually important because it clearly highlights the fact that estimating the coefficients in the Bivariate Regression Model is very closely connected to the problem considered in Chapter 3 of estimating the mean of a normally distributed random variable – in fact, the only difference is that here we are parameterizing the mean of Y_i as depending linearly on the explanatory variable x_i.

The assumption that the random variable Y_i depends on the fixed variable x_i rather than on a random variable (X_i), is relaxed in Chapter 11. This assumption is imposed here for two reasons. First, it greatly simplifies the analysis of the model. Second, this asymmetry in the treatment of the dependent versus the explanatory variable reflects an implicit causality assumption which can be quite realistic. For example, one might attempt to explain the variation of reported weekly earnings across households as being due to differences in the respondent's race or gender. Regrettably, race or gender often impacts earnings in real-world societies; arguably, however, weekly earnings do not impact a respondent's race or gender. In this case it is sensible to take the respondent's racial/gender characteristic as fixed and view the βx_i term in the Bivariate Regression Model as merely accounting for racial or gender heterogeneity in the sample. Or one might observe that a time-series variable (such as population) systematically increases over time and choose to use a time trend ($x_i = i$ itself) as an explanatory variable.

This issue is not always quite so straightforward, however. For example, in explaining the sample variation of households' reported weekly earnings as being due to differences in the respondents' education levels, or in explaining the international variation in per capita real output as being due to variations in capital accumulation, it is more graceful to think of both the explanatory variable **and** the dependent variable as random variables. In this case the observed values of the explanatory variable are best viewed as sample realizations of a random variable X_i, and one might most sensibly think of Y_i and X_i as a pair of random variables whose realizations are drawn from a joint distribution.

The distribution of Y_i, given that X_i has already been observed to take on the particular realized value x_i, is called the "conditional distribution of Y_i given X_i." The expected value of Y_i over this distribution is expressed as $E[Y_i \mid X_i = x_i]$ and called "the conditional mean of Y_i given X_i.[4] Where Y_i and X_i are jointly *normally* distributed, it can be shown that $E[Y_i \mid X_i = x_i]$ is in fact a linear function of x_i, so that the expression $\alpha + \beta x_i$ in the Bivariate Regression Model can in this case be sensibly interpreted as the mean of Y_i conditional on having observed this realization of X_i."[5]

Sometimes, however, even this interpretation is inadequate and we are forced to treat the explanatory variable in our regression model explicitly as an "endogenous" random variable, jointly determined with Y_i. This issue is taken up in Chapter 11 (and resolved in Chapter 12); here we will simply assume that the N values which the explanatory variable takes on in the course of the sample can be treated as fixed and therefore denote them as $x_1 \dots x_N$.

This assumption on the explanatory variable is often expressed using the phrase, "$x_1 \dots x_N$ are fixed in repeated samples." This concept is worth exploring a bit because it illustrates a valuable way of thinking about models of this kind and because it will be helpful later on in understanding the meaning of the sampling distribution of the least squares estimator of β. Clearly, we have on hand only one sample, consisting of the $2N$ numbers: $(y_1, x_1) \dots (y_N, x_N)$. But we can imagine a set of, say, 10,000 parallel universes – 10,000 "repeated samples" – in each of which the data we are analyzing is freshly (i.e., independently) generated. In that case, the values of the parameters (α, β, and σ^2) and the explanatory variables ($x_1 \dots x_N$) are assumed to be the same in all 10,000 universes: what differs is that the random model errors ($U_1 \dots U_N$) are realized afresh in each universe, leading to 10,000 distinct realizations of the model errors ($u_1 \dots u_N$) and to 10,000 distinct realizations of the dependent variable: ($y_1 = \alpha + \beta x_1 + u_1$, $y_2 = \alpha + \beta x_2 + u_2$, ... $y_N = \alpha + \beta x_N + u_N$).[6] In this way, $y_1 \dots y_N$ are realizations of random variables (because they differ across the different parallel universes) even though the explanatory variables ($x_1 \dots x_N$) are fixed, in that they are the same set of N numbers for every one of the parallel universes.

Our single sample, then, is thus a set of fixed numbers, $(y_1, x_1) \dots (y_N, x_N)$, where $y_1 \dots y_N$ are the sample data – realizations of the random variables $Y_1 \dots Y_N$ – whose variation over the N observations – the "sample variation in y_i" – we seek to model or explain as depending on the sample variation in $x_1 \dots x_N$. As noted earlier, this is why Y_i is called the "dependent variable" in the model and x_i is called the "explanatory variable." That portion of the sample variation we observe in the y_i which is *not* related to the variation in the x_i is taken to be due to the realization of the additive random error term in the model, U_i. We can take this portion of the observed variation in the y_i as being due to the fact that the parallel universes referred to above are not all identical or, equivalently, we can think of U_i as modeling the impact on y_i of all of the potential explanatory variables (other than x_i) which influence its value.

5.4 THE ASSUMPTIONS ON THE MODEL ERROR TERM, U_i

The Bivariate Regression Model also assumes that the model error term is normally, identically, and independently distributed – i.e., that $U_i \sim \text{NIID}[0, \sigma^2]$.

[4] The concept of a conditional distribution is described in the appendix to Chapter 2 for a pair of discretely distributed random variables. See also Exercise 2-11 for a numerical illustration.

[5] Thus, if Y_i is not normally distributed, then it will usually *not* be appropriate to model Y_i as a linear function of x_i. In such cases it may be possible to find a simple transformation of the dependent variable which appears to be normally distributed; alternatively – as we shall see in Chapter 9 – the additional flexibility of the Multiple Regression Model can be used to model a *nonlinear* relationship between Y_i and x_i.

[6] Note that if each model error were discretely distributed over m possible values – rather than normally distributed, as specified by the Bivariate Regression Model – then the set of random variables ($U_1 \dots U_N$) could take on m^N possible states and one might want to associate one parallel universe with each of these possible states.

This set of assumptions is very similar to the assumption – that Y_i is distributed NIID[μ, σ^2] – made regarding Y_i in Chapter 3, so the discussion in this section will in some ways be quite similar. These assumptions with regard to the U_i are crucial to the derivation, in Chapter 6, of the properties of the least squares estimators of the model parameters α and β and to the construction, in Chapter 7, of hypothesis tests and confidence intervals for these parameters.[7] Moreover, because one portion or another of these assumptions about U_i is frequently violated by real economic data, we will revisit these assumptions in Chapters 10 through 13, when we deal with the practical issues of how to recognize and cope with such violations.[8] The task of the present section, in contrast, is only to expand a bit on what these assumptions with regard to U_i imply.

As in Chapter 3, the normality assumption on U_i is motivated in large part by appealing to the Central Limit Theorem (and its cousins), which imply that roughly equally-weighted sums of large numbers of random variables that are not too far from being identically and independently distributed will be approximately normally distributed. Recalling that U_i quantifies the impact on Y_i of all of the explanatory variables which have been omitted from the model, it is often reasonable to think of U_i as being such a weighted sum of a large number of more or less independent influences on Y_i. Alternatively, as you discovered in working Exercise 2-40, when it is more reasonable to think of U_i as being the *product* of a large number of such influences, then the distribution of its *logarithm* will be approximately normal. In such cases, these considerations suggest that reframing the model in terms of the logarithm of the original dependent variable is more likely to yield a model error term which is at least roughly normal. Either way, the actual validity of this normality assumption is essentially an empirical issue. For example, we will see in Chapter 10 that a histogram of the observed model fitting errors $\left(u_1^{\text{fit}} \ldots u_N^{\text{fit}}\right)$ will typically shed substantial light on the plausibility of this assumption for a particular data set. (These model fitting errors are obtained and discussed later in this chapter; in Chapter 10 they are shown to be reasonable estimates of the model errors, U_1 ... U_N, for large samples.)

We saw in Chapter 2 that the density function for a normally distributed random variable is completely determined by its mean and its variance. Consequently, the assumption that the U_i are identically distributed reduces in this case to an assumption that both the mean and variance of U_i are the same for every observation – in other words, for all values of i. This constant mean can be taken to be 0 at no loss of generality because any such mean value that U_i might otherwise have had can be incorporated into the parameter α of the Bivariate Regression Model. (Any sample variation in the mean of U_i which we are unable to model is considered to simply be part of U_i's random variation.) In contrast, any variation in the mean of U_i which **can** be modeled – as being due to sample variation in an observable variable, z_i, say – implies that the (supposedly constant) intercept parameter α is really a function of z_i; in that case, this variation should be modeled explicitly by including z_i in the model as an additional explanatory variable. This leads to the Multiple Regression Model taken up in Chapter 9.

Similarly, the assumption that the U_i are identically distributed also implies that the population variance of U_i – here denoted σ^2 – is the same for all N observations. Model errors which all have the same variance are said to be "homoscedastic." Contrastingly, in an obvious notation, the failure of this assumption is called "heteroscedasticity," in which case the variance of U_i varies with i: in other words, $\text{var}(U_i) = \sigma_i^2$. By observing where this assumption is used in the next few chapters, it will become apparent that the failure of the homoscedasticity assumption is consequential for both the efficiency of least squares parameter estimation and for the validity of the usual statistical machinery we use for constructing hypothesis tests and confidence intervals on α and β. Moreover – as we already saw in the

[7] For expositional simplicity, attention in Chapter 6 and 7 will mainly focus on the parameter β.

[8] At that point we will need to confront an unfortunate *dis*similarity between the assumptions on Y_i made in Chapter 3 and the assumptions on the model errors (U_i) in the Bivariate Regression Model made here: sample realizations of Y_i are directly observable, whereas sample realizations of U_i are not. In fact, as the "parallel universes" example shows, we would need to know the values of α and β in order to use our sample data (y_i and x_i) to calculate (observe) u_i, a sample realization of U_i.

relationship between $rgdpl_i$ and k_i discussed earlier in this chapter – substantial failures of this assumption can easily occur in modeling actual economic data. Indeed, this example already points to the underlying source of most violations of the homoscedasticity assumption: a failure to correctly specify the functional forms with which the dependent and explanatory variables enter the model.

In that example economic theory supplies functional form guidance which substantially eliminates the heteroscedasticity in the error term of the original model; unhappily, economic theory is usually not that effectively specific. Consequently, it will be essential (in Chapter 10) to learn about practical methods for recognizing and coping with violations of the homoscedasticity assumption. For the present, however, we will simply assume that the homoscedasticity assumption is valid. This is a more reasonable course of action than it might appear at first. For one thing, it allows us to determine which results and techniques actually depend on the homoscedasticity assumption. And, for another, comprehension of the model with homoscedastic errors is vital to understanding the methods for detecting and dealing with heteroscedasticity when we do get to them in Chapter 10.

The assumption that the U_i are all independently distributed is ordinarily an innocuous assumption for cross-sectional data – e.g., where i indexes countries or households – but this assumption is commonly violated to a substantial degree in time-series data, where i indexes the time period in which the observations were made. This assumption is commonly expressed by stating that the model errors are "nonautocorrelated"; and its violation is commonly expressed with the statement that "the model's errors are serially correlated."[9] As with the homoscedasticity assumption, it will become apparent by observing where this assumption is used in the next few chapters that its failure, also, is consequential for both the efficiency of least squares parameter estimation and for the validity of the usual statistical inference machinery. Again, however, it is very useful to simply make this assumption for the present and to use the insights we gain thereby in developing practical techniques (in Chapter 13) for detecting and coping with its failure. In particular, we will find at that point that serial correlation in the model errors of a time-series regression is the natural consequence of a failure to adequately model the ***dynamics*** of the relationship by including explanatory variables involving lagged values of the dependent and explanatory variables; consequently, a failure of the nonautocorrelation assumption is fairly easy to "fix" once it is recognized.

In summary, then, our assumptions on the model errors can be stated as follows:

Bivariate Regression Model Assumptions on U_i

$$U_i \sim \text{NIID}[0,\ \sigma^2]$$

or, equivalently,

$$
\begin{aligned}
&U_i \text{ is normally distributed}\\
&E[U_i] = 0\\
\text{var}(U_i) &= \sigma^2 \text{ \{"homoscedasticity assumption"\}}\\
\text{cov}(U_i,\ U_j) &= 0 \text{ for } i \neq j \text{ \{"nonautocorrelation assumption"\}}
\end{aligned}
\tag{5-11}
$$

and our strategy in the next few chapters will be to examine the consequences of simply assuming that $U_i \sim \text{NIID}[0,\ \sigma^2]$, postponing until Chapters 10 through 13 an inquiry into how one can both check the validity of this assumption empirically and deal with violations should any be detected.

[9] Recall from Chapter 2 that for observations in two distinct time periods t and s, corr(U_t, U_s) must be zero in order for U_t and U_s to be independent, but that zero correlation implies independence only if U_t and U_s are both normally distributed. If the normality assumption is invalid, all that is usually assumed in what remains of the Bivariate Regression Model is that the model errors are uncorrelated.

It is convenient and informative to state the assumptions on the model errors in the forms given above, but this is not the most effective way to express these assumptions for the purpose of deriving the sampling distributions of the least squares estimators of α and β and related results in the next few chapters. For that purpose it is more convenient to restate the homoscedasticity and nonautocorrelation assumptions explicitly in terms of expectations on the model errors. In particular, note that the assumption that $E[U_i]$ is 0 for all values of i and the homoscedasticity assumption together imply that

$$\sigma^2 = \text{var}(U_i) = E\left[[U_i - E[U_i]]^2\right] = E\left[U_1^2\right] \tag{5-12}$$

Similarly, the assumption that $E[U_i]$ is zero for all values of i and the nonautocorrelation assumption together imply that

$$0 = \text{cov}\left(U_i, U_j\right) = E\left[[U_i - E[U_i]]\left[U_j - E\left[U_j\right]\right]\right] = E\left[U_i, U_j\right] \tag{5-13}$$

for all $i \neq j$. Thus, the assumptions constituting the Bivariate Regression Model can alternatively be expressed as

The Bivariate Regression Model
{Alternative Form}

$$\begin{aligned} Y_i &= \alpha + \beta x_i + U_i \quad i = 1 \ldots N \\ &x_1 \ldots x_N \text{ fixed in repeated samples} \\ &U_i \text{ is normally distributed} \\ E[U_i] &= 0 \\ E\left[U_i\, U_j\right] &= \sigma^2 \quad \text{for } i = j \\ &= 0 \quad \text{for } i \neq j \end{aligned} \tag{5-14}$$

In Chapters 6 and 7 we will see that these assumptions are crucial to the derivation of (1) the sampling distributions of the least squares estimators of the parameters α and β, (2) the properties of these estimators, and (3) the statistical inference machinery which allows us to use these estimators to construct confidence intervals and to test hypotheses about α and β. First, however, it is essential to become explicit about where these estimators of the parameters α and β actually come from – i.e., how the sample data (y_1, x_1) ... (y_N, x_N) can be used in practice to estimate the parameters α and β in the Bivariate Regression Model.

5.5 LEAST SQUARES ESTIMATION OF α AND β

It is very useful to begin by viewing the Bivariate Regression Model from a graphical or "curve fitting" perspective. For example, consider again the output versus capital stock scatterplot discussed earlier in this chapter. Letting the logarithm of country i's per capita real GDP in 1999 – i.e., $\log(rgdpl_i)$ – correspond to y_i and letting the country i value of the logarithm of per capita real capital stock at the beginning of 1999 – i.e., $\log(k_i)$ – correspond to x_i, the Bivariate Regression Model in this case becomes

$$\begin{aligned} \log(RGDPL_i) &= \alpha + \beta \log(k_i) + U_i \qquad i = 1 \ldots 105 \\ &\log(k_1) \ldots \log(k_{105}) \text{ fixed in repeated samples} \\ U_i &\sim \text{NIID}[0, \sigma^2] \end{aligned} \tag{5-15}$$

where the parameters α, β, and σ^2 are fixed, but unknown, numbers. If α and β *were* known, then a line with height $\alpha + \beta \ln(k_i)$ could be drawn right on top of the scatterplot – this is called the "population regression line" (shown in Figure 5-5):

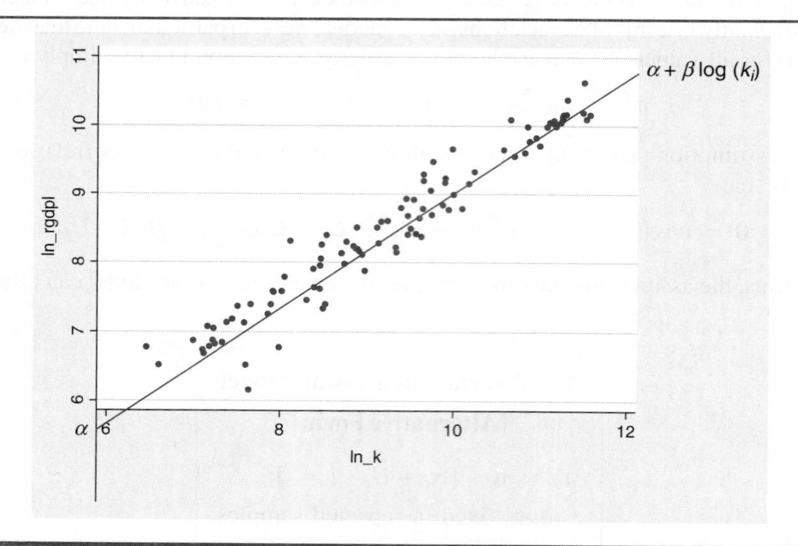

Figure 5-5 Scatterplot with Population Regression Line Drawn In

The parameters α and β in the Bivariate Regression Model are commonly referred to as the "intercept" and "slope" parameters because they correspond to the intercept and slope, respectively, of this population regression line.

Note that u_i the (fixed) realization of the random model error term, U_i, is just the vertical discrepancy between the plotted value of log(*rgdpl*$_i$) for the *i*th country and the height of the population regression line for the corresponding value of log(k_i) for this country – i.e., $\alpha + \beta \ln(k_i)$.

The actual values of the parameters α and β are not known, however, so it is not in practice possible to plot the population regression line on top of the scatterplot or to actually observe the model error realizations, $u_1 \ldots u_{105}$. Thus, the line plotted in Figure 5-5 artificially used the true values for α and β. We can, however, plot a "fitted line" on top of the scatterplot for any given guesses ($\hat{\alpha}^{guess}$ and $\hat{\beta}^{guess}$) of these two parameters. For example, a particular choice of values for $\hat{\alpha}^{guess}$ and $\hat{\beta}^{guess}$ might lead to the fitted line plotted in Figure 5-6.

Clearly, this particular $\hat{\alpha}^{guess}$ choice is considerably too large and this particular $\hat{\beta}^{guess}$ choice is considerably too small, yielding a line which does not fit the sample data very well. In order to choose $\hat{\alpha}^{guess}$ and $\hat{\beta}^{guess}$ so as to ***best*** fit the data, we need a specific and explicit measure of how far away the fitted line is, on average, from the data.

The vertical discrepancy between log(*rgdpl*$_i$), the observed value of the dependent variable for country *i*, and $\hat{\alpha}^{guess} + \hat{\beta}^{guess} \log(k_i)$, the height of the guessed line directly above the value of the explanatory variable for country *i*, is called the "fitting error" or "residual" for the *i*th observation; the symbol "u_i^{fit}" is used here for this quantity. Because there is no reason to care whether the fitting error is positive or negative, we will use the square of its value as our measure of the discrepancy between the *i*th observation on the dependent variable and the fitted line. Thus, for example, this squared discrepancy for the third observation (which, in this data set, corresponds to the country of Mali) is

$$\left(u_3^{fit}\right)^2 = \left(\log(rgdpl_3) - \hat{\alpha}^{guess} - \hat{\beta}^{guess} \log(k_3)\right)^2 \tag{5-16}$$

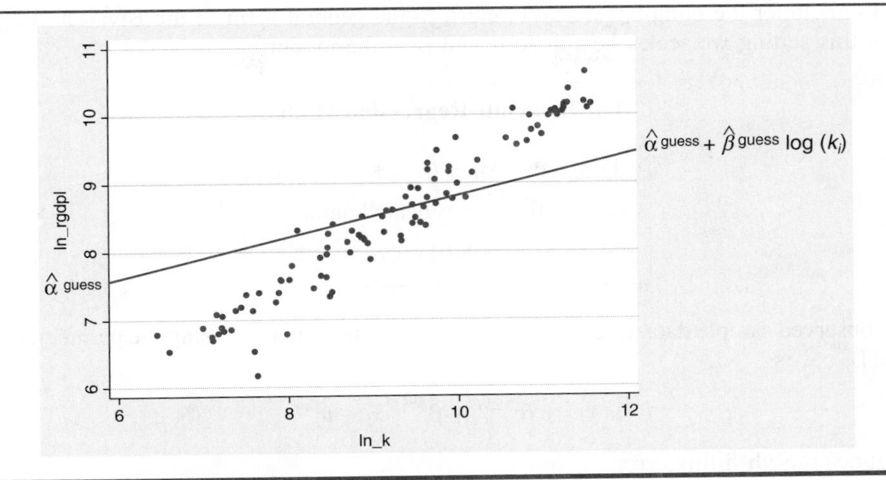

Figure 5-6 Scatterplot with Guessed-At Fitted Line Drawn In

Giving equal weight to the fitting error for each of the 105 sample observations, we choose $\hat{\alpha}^{guess}$ and $\hat{\beta}^{guess}$ so as to minimize

$$\sum_{i=1}^{105}\left(\log(rgdpl_i) - \hat{\alpha}^{guess} - \hat{\beta}^{guess}\log(k_i)\right)^2 \tag{5-17}$$

The resulting values for $\hat{\alpha}^{guess}$ and $\hat{\beta}^{guess}$ are called the "ordinary least squares" or "OLS" estimates of α and β. (By custom, the word "ordinary" is used for the least squares estimator when the model depends linearly on the parameters to be estimated.[10])

This is not, however, the only possible way to measure the discrepancy between the observations on the dependent variable and the height of the fitted line. In particular, one could choose $\hat{\alpha}^{guess}$ and $\hat{\beta}^{guess}$ so as to instead minimize

$$\sum_{i=1}^{105}\left|\log(rgdpl_i) - \hat{\alpha}^{guess} - \hat{\beta}^{guess}\log(k_i)\right| \tag{5-18}$$

leading to what are called the "least absolute deviation (LAD)" or "robust" estimates of α and β. The LAD estimates are actually preferable with sample data containing a few "outliers" – unusually large or small realizations of log($RGDPL_i$). In this chapter the focus will be exclusively on least squares estimation, but LAD estimation will come up again in Chapter 10 as part of the process for diagnostically checking a model for the presence of outliers.[11]

---

[10] To clarify this definition, the model $Y_i = \alpha + \beta x_i^{\delta} + U_i$ is nonlinear in the unknown parameter δ. Hence, least squares estimates of α, β, and δ would not be called OLS estimates.

[11] The pros and cons of LAD estimation are discussed in more detail in the section entitled "Estimating μ by Curve Fitting" in Chapter 3. Modern econometrics software makes robust regression almost as convenient as OLS estimation – e.g., in Stata one can use the "qreg" command to obtain LAD estimates. However, while LAD estimates are relatively insensitive to outliers – i.e., "robust" to outliers – they are generally thought to be otherwise inferior to the OLS estimates in modest samples, because the LAD estimators have only large-sample properties. In contrast, it will be shown in Chapter 6 that the OLS estimators are BLU. For that matter, why make either choice? Why not just draw a straight line through the data in the scatterplot "by eye"? The best answer to this question is that – in exchange for making the assumptions of the Bivariate Regression Model – we can show (in Chapter 6) that the OLS estimators have nice properties (e.g., BLUness) and (in Chapter 7) how to use them in estimating confidence intervals for β and in testing hypotheses about β. Moreover, in Chapters 10, 13, and 14 we will see how one can even, for reasonably large samples, approximately check the validity of these assumptions.

So as to unclutter the notation, we now return to the general form of the Bivariate Regression Model; in this setting we seek to estimate α and β in the model:

The Bivariate Regression Model

$$Y_i = \alpha + \beta x_i + U_i \quad i = 1 \ldots N$$
$$x_1 \ldots x_N \text{ fixed in repeated samples}$$
$$U_i \sim \text{NIID}[0, \sigma^2] \tag{5-19}$$

using the observed sample data, $(y_1, x_1) \ldots (y_N, x_N)$. The fitted equation using the parameter guesses, $\hat{\alpha}^{\text{guess}}$ and $\hat{\beta}^{\text{guess}}$, is

$$y_i = \hat{\alpha}^{\text{guess}} + \hat{\beta}^{\text{guess}} x_i + u_i^{\text{fit}} \tag{5-20}$$

which defines the ith fitting error

$$u_i^{\text{fit}} \equiv y_i - \hat{\alpha}^{\text{guess}} - \hat{\beta}^{\text{guess}} x_i \tag{5-21}$$

for any particular values chosen for $\hat{\alpha}^{\text{guess}}$ and $\hat{\beta}^{\text{guess}}$. Note that $u_1^{\text{fit}} \ldots u_N^{\text{fit}}$ are numbers which can be calculated from the sample data for any given values of $\hat{\alpha}$ and $\hat{\beta}$; they equal $u_1 \ldots u_N$ – the sample realizations of the model errors, $U_1 \ldots U_N$ – if and only if (through accident or divine intervention) $\hat{\alpha}^{\text{guess}}$ happens to equal α and $\hat{\beta}^{\text{guess}}$ happens to equal β.

These chosen values for $\hat{\alpha}$ and $\hat{\beta}$ also imply a fitted line $\hat{\alpha}^{\text{guess}} + \hat{\beta} x_i^{\text{guess}}$ which can be drawn over a scatterplot of the sample data as in Figure 5-7:

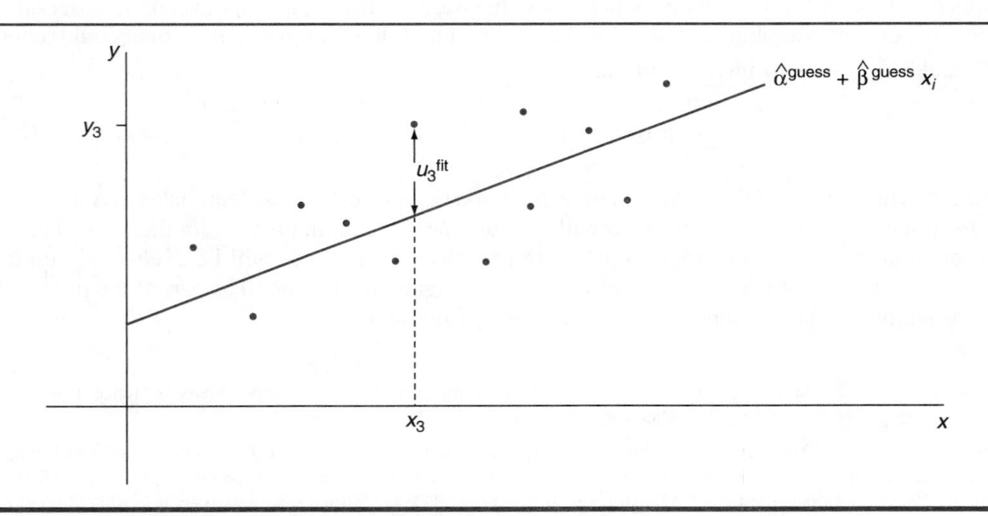

Figure 5-7 Scatterplot Displaying One Fitting Error

where the fitting error for the third observation (u_3^{fit}) is explicitly indicated. The observed fitting errors, $u_i^{\text{fit}} \ldots u_N^{\text{fit}}$, correspond to the "vertical discrepancies" between the sample observations on the dependent variable ($y_1 \ldots y_N$) and the values corresponding to the height of the fitted line for each observation on the explanatory variable: in other words, to $\hat{\alpha}^{\text{guess}} + \hat{\beta}^{\text{guess}} x_1 \ldots \hat{\alpha}^{\text{guess}} + \hat{\beta}^{\text{guess}} x_N$.

Thus, our object is to choose $\hat{\alpha}^{guess}$ and $\hat{\beta}^{guess}$ so as to minimize what is called the "sum of squared fitting errors" function, SSE($\hat{\alpha}$, $\hat{\beta}$):

$$\text{SSE}(\hat{\alpha}^{guess}, \hat{\beta}^{guess}) \equiv \sum_{i=1}^{N} \left(u_i^{fit}\right)^2 = \sum_{i=1}^{N} \left(y_i - \hat{\alpha}^{guess} - \hat{\beta}^{guess} x_i\right)^2 \qquad (5\text{-}22)$$

The function SSE($\hat{\alpha}^{guess}$, $\hat{\beta}^{guess}$) clearly depends not only on $\hat{\alpha}^{guess}$ and $\hat{\beta}^{guess}$ but also on the sample data, $y_1 \dots y_N$ and $x_1 \dots x_N$. This dependence on the sample data is suppressed in the notation so as to focus on how sum of the squared fitting errors depends on the parameter estimates $\hat{\alpha}^{guess}$ and $\hat{\beta}^{guess}$.[12]

Suppose that we fix the value of $\hat{\beta}^{guess}$ at some given value, $\hat{\beta}_o^{guess}$, and examine how SSE ($\hat{\alpha}^{guess}$, $\hat{\beta}_o^{guess}$) depends on $\hat{\alpha}^{guess}$. If $\hat{\alpha}^{guess}$ is very small, then $\hat{\alpha}^{guess} + \hat{\beta}_o^{guess} x_i$ – the height of the fitted line – will lie far below all of the y_i values. This implies that $u_1^{fit} \dots u_N^{fit}$ will all be positive and large, leading to a large value for SSE($\hat{\alpha}^{guess}$, $\hat{\beta}_o^{guess}$). Similarly, if $\hat{\alpha}^{guess}$ is very large, then the fitted line $\hat{\alpha}^{guess} + \hat{\beta}_o^{guess} x_i$ will lie far *above* all of the y_i values, implying that $u_1^{fit} \dots u_N^{fit}$ will all be very negative, and again leading to a large value for SSE($\hat{\alpha}^{guess}$, $\hat{\beta}_o^{guess}$). Somewhere in between – where $\hat{\alpha}^{guess}$ is such that the fitted line is reasonably close to the dots in the scatterplot – some of $u_1^{fit} \dots u_N^{fit}$ values will be negative, some will be positive, and most will be small in magnitude, leading to a relatively small value for SSE($\hat{\alpha}^{guess}$, $\hat{\beta}_o^{guess}$). Thus, a plot of SSE($\hat{\alpha}^{guess}$, $\hat{\beta}_o^{guess}$) versus $\hat{\alpha}^{guess}$ will look like Figure 5-8:

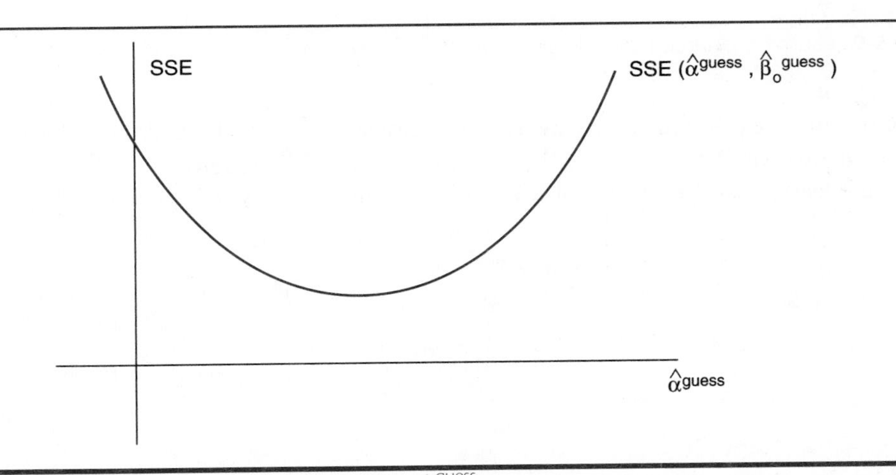

Figure 5-8 Sum of Squared Fitting Errors with $\hat{\beta}^{guess}$ Fixed

The least squares value for $\hat{\alpha}$ based on this particular value for $\hat{\beta}^{guess}$ is the value of $\hat{\alpha}^{guess}$ such that SSE($\hat{\alpha}^{guess}$, $\hat{\beta}_o^{guess}$) is smallest. It is apparent from this diagram that the slope of the SSE ($\hat{\alpha}^{guess}$, $\hat{\beta}_o^{guess}$) curve is negative for values of $\hat{\alpha}^{guess}$ smaller than this and positive for values of

[12] It is preferable to call this function "the sum of squared fitting errors" so as to keep in mind that this function is summing up the observed squared *fitting* errors rather than squared realizations of the model errors, $U_1 \dots U_N$. Thus, "SSFE" would be better notation for this function, but "SSE" is the standard nomenclature.

$\hat{\alpha}^{guess}$ larger than this. Therefore we can characterize the least squares value for $\hat{\alpha}$ as that value of $\hat{\alpha}^{guess}$ at which the derivative of SSE $(\hat{\alpha}^{guess}, \hat{\beta}_o^{guess})$ with respect to $\hat{\alpha}^{guess}$ is zero.

Similarly, if we fix the value of $\hat{\alpha}^{guess}$ at some particular value $\hat{\alpha}_o^{guess}$ and examine how SSE $(\hat{\alpha}_o^{guess}, \hat{\beta}^{guess})$ depends on $\hat{\beta}^{guess}$, we find that the value of SSE$(\hat{\alpha}_o^{guess}, \hat{\beta}^{guess})$ will be large for extreme values of $\hat{\beta}^{guess}$ because these lead to fitted lines whose slopes are so extreme that the fitted line lies near the observed scatter of data only for a few values of the explanatory variable. Thus, a plot of SSE$(\hat{\alpha}_o^{guess}, \hat{\beta}^{guess})$ versus $\hat{\beta}^{guess}$ will look like Figure 5-9:

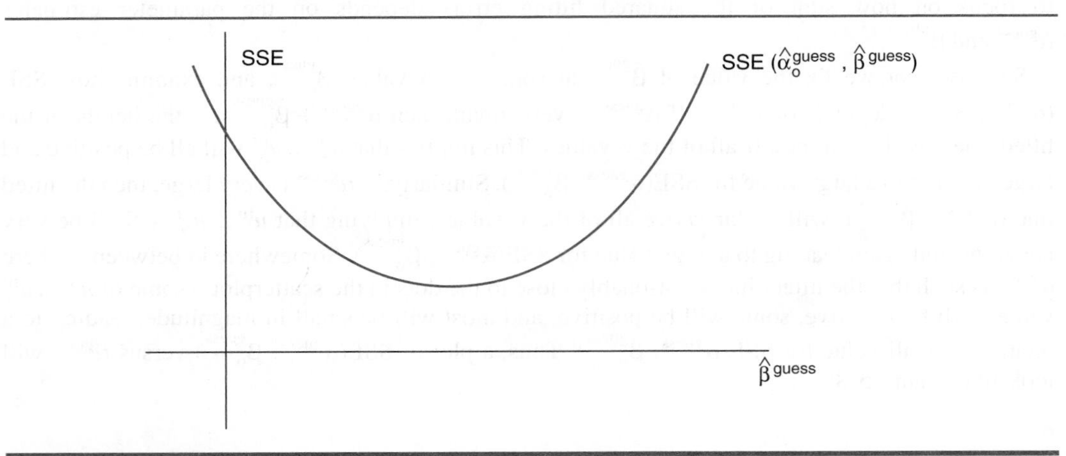

Figure 5-9 Sum of Squared Fitting Errors with $\hat{\alpha}^{guess}$ Fixed

Consequently, we can similarly characterize the least squares value for $\hat{\beta}$ as that value of $\hat{\beta}^{guess}$ at which the derivative of SSE$(\hat{\alpha}_o^{guess}, \hat{\beta}^{guess})$ with respect to $\hat{\beta}^{guess}$ is zero.

Thus, the least squares estimates of α and β must jointly satisfy the conditions

$$
\begin{aligned}
\partial \frac{\text{SSE}(\hat{\alpha}^{guess}, \hat{\beta}^{guess})}{\partial \hat{\alpha}^{guess}} &= 0 \\
\frac{\partial \text{SSE}(\hat{\alpha}^{guess}, \hat{\beta}^{guess})}{\partial \hat{\beta}^{guess}} &= 0
\end{aligned}
\qquad (5\text{-}23)
$$

As noted earlier in this section, these estimates are customarily called the "ordinary least squares" estimates of α and β, or $\hat{\alpha}^*_{ols}$ and $\hat{\beta}^*_{ols}$, where the term "ordinary" merely refers to the fact that the Bivariate Regression Model is linear in the unknown parameters, α and β.[13]

The asterisks on $\hat{\alpha}^*_{ols}$ and $\hat{\beta}^*_{ols}$ are used to notationally reflect the fact that these estimates are fixed numbers determined by the observed sample data: $y_1 \ldots y_N$ and $x_1 \ldots x_N$. Later on (in

[13] This terminology using the word "ordinary" is mentioned and used here only because it is the standard nomenclature. In fact, to unclutter the notation, the "ols" subscript will be dropped altogether in Chapters 6 through 8, where only least squares estimators are considered.

Chapter 6) it will be crucial to distinguish these sample realizations from the least squares estimators ($\hat{\alpha}_{ols}$ and $\hat{\beta}_{ols}$) themselves; there we will see that $\hat{\alpha}_{ols}$ and $\hat{\beta}_{ols}$ are random variables because they depend on the random variables $Y_1 \ldots Y_N$ instead of their sample realizations, $y_1 \ldots y_N$. At that point it will be clear that $\hat{\alpha}^*_{ols}$ and $\hat{\beta}^*_{ols}$ are sample realizations of $\hat{\alpha}_{ols}$ and $\hat{\beta}_{ols}$ in precisely the same way that $\bar{y}$ was a (fixed) sample realization of the (random) estimator $\overline{Y}$ in Chapters 3 and 4.[14]

Considering first the partial derivative of SSE($\hat{\alpha}^{guess}$, $\hat{\beta}^{guess}$) with respect to $\hat{\alpha}^{guess}$, and recalling that it follows from the definitions of the sample means $\bar{x}$ and $\bar{y}$ that $\sum_{i=1}^{N} x_i = N\bar{x}$ and that $\sum_{i=1}^{N} y_i = N\bar{y}$,

$$
\begin{aligned}
\frac{\partial SSE(\hat{\alpha}^{guess}, \hat{\beta}^{guess})}{\partial \hat{\alpha}^{guess}} &= \frac{\partial}{\partial \hat{\alpha}^{guess}} \sum_{i=1}^{N} \left\{ y_i - \hat{\alpha}^{guess} - \hat{\beta}^{guess} x_i \right\}^2 \\
&= \sum_{i=1}^{N} \frac{\partial}{\partial \hat{\alpha}^{guess}} \left\{ y_i - \hat{\alpha}^{guess} - \hat{\beta}^{guess} x_i \right\}^2 \\
&= \sum_{i=1}^{N} -2 \left\{ y_i - \hat{\alpha}^{guess} - \hat{\beta}^{guess} x_i \right\} \\
&= -2 \sum_{i=1}^{N} \left\{ y_i - \hat{\alpha}^{guess} - \hat{\beta}^{guess} x_i \right\} \\
&= -2 \left\{ \sum_{i=1}^{N} y_i - \sum_{i=1}^{N} \hat{\alpha}^{guess} - \hat{\beta}^{guess} \sum_{i=1}^{N} x_i \right\} \\
&= -2 \left\{ N\bar{y} - N\hat{\alpha}^{guess} - \hat{\beta}^{guess} N\bar{x} \right\} \\
&= -2N \left\{ \bar{y} - \hat{\alpha}^{guess} - \hat{\beta}^{guess} \bar{x} \right\}
\end{aligned}
\tag{5-24}
$$

Thus, $\hat{\alpha}^*_{ols}$ and $\hat{\beta}^*_{ols}$ must satisfy the equation

$$
\bar{y} - \hat{\alpha}^*_{ols} - \hat{\beta}^*_{ols}\bar{x} = 0 \tag{5-25}
$$

implying that

$$
\hat{\alpha}^*_{ols} = \bar{y} - \hat{\beta}^*_{ols}\bar{x} \tag{5-26}
$$

[14] As noted in the "Notation" section just prior to Chapter 1, the convention in this book is to use uppercase letters for random variables and lowercase letters for the corresponding sample realizations. The typical practice of denoting regression parameters with lowercase Greek letters is also followed here. Estimators of these parameters are denoted by the addition of a hat ("^") or occasionally a tilde ("~"). However, because many uppercase Greek letters do not at all resemble the corresponding lowercase Greek letter, an asterisk superscript is used throughout the book to distinguish the sample realization of a parameter estimator from the estimator itself.

Next, consider the partial derivative of SSE($\hat{\alpha}$, $\hat{\beta}$), with respect to $\hat{\beta}$,

$$
\begin{aligned}
\frac{\partial \text{SSE}(\hat{\alpha}^{\text{guess}}, \hat{\beta}^{\text{guess}})}{\partial \hat{\beta}^{\text{guess}}} &= \frac{\partial}{\partial \hat{\beta}^{\text{guess}}} \sum_{i=1}^{N} \left\{ y_i - \hat{\alpha}^{\text{guess}} - \hat{\beta}^{\text{guess}} x_i \right\}^2 \\
&= \sum_{i=1}^{N} \frac{\partial}{\partial \hat{\beta}^{\text{guess}}} \left\{ y_i - \hat{\alpha}^{\text{guess}} - \hat{\beta}^{\text{guess}} x_i \right\}^2 \\
&= \sum_{i=1}^{N} -2x_i \left\{ y_i - \hat{\alpha}^{\text{guess}} - \hat{\beta}^{\text{guess}} x_i \right\} \\
&= -2 \sum_{i=1}^{N} x_i \left\{ y_i - \hat{\alpha}^{\text{guess}} - \hat{\beta}^{\text{guess}} x_i \right\} \qquad (5\text{-}27) \\
&= -2 \sum_{i=1}^{N} \left\{ y_i x_i - \hat{\alpha}^{\text{guess}} x_i - \hat{\beta}^{\text{guess}} x_i^2 \right\} \\
&= -2 \left\{ \sum_{i=1}^{N} y_i x_i - \sum_{i=1}^{N} \hat{\alpha}^{\text{guess}} x_i - \hat{\beta}^{\text{guess}} \sum_{i=1}^{N} x_i^2 \right\} \\
&= -2 \left\{ \sum_{i=1}^{N} y_i x_i - \hat{\alpha}^{\text{guess}} N \bar{x} - \hat{\beta}^{\text{guess}} \sum_{i=1}^{N} x_i^2 \right\}
\end{aligned}
$$

Thus, $\hat{\alpha}^*_{\text{ols}}$ and $\hat{\beta}^*_{\text{ols}}$ must also satisfy the equation

$$
0 = \sum_{i=1}^{N} y_i x_i - \hat{\alpha}^*_{\text{ols}} N \bar{x} - \hat{\beta}^*_{\text{ols}} \sum_{i=1}^{N} x_i^2 \qquad (5\text{-}28)
$$

This equation (and its companion, Equation 5-25, obtained from setting $\partial \text{SSE}(\hat{\alpha}^{\text{guess}}, \hat{\beta}^{\text{guess}})/\partial \hat{\beta}^{\text{guess}}$ equal to zero) are often called the Normal Equations. The reader is cautioned, however, that this (common) usage has nothing to do with the normal (gaussian) distribution – indeed, no use at all has been made so far of the assumption that the error term in the model is distributed NIID[0, σ^2].

Note also that $\bar{y}$ and $\bar{x}$ are merely descriptive statistics in this context. That is, you should interpret them only as sample measures of the average size of the observations on Y_i and x_i – not as realizations of estimates of the population means of these two variables. In particular, recall that the Bivariate Regression Model does not even assume that $x_1 \dots x_N$ are realizations of random variables. Moreover, the model implies that, while $y_1 \dots y_N$ are indeed realizations of the random variables $Y_1 \dots Y_N$, these random variables have population means $\alpha + \beta x_1 \dots \alpha + \beta x_N$, respectively, which could each have a different value. Thus $\bar{y}$ is the realization of the random variable $\bar{Y}$, but $\bar{Y}$ cannot be a consistent (or unbiased, or BLU) estimator of "the" population mean of $Y_1 \dots Y_N$, simply because there is no single value of this population mean for $\bar{Y}$ to consistently estimate. Thus, $\bar{y}$ and $\bar{x}$ should not be interpreted as realizations of estimators of anything: they are best thought of either as shorthand for (1/N) times the corresponding sums of $y_1 \dots y_N$ and $x_1 \dots x_N$, respectively, or as descriptive statistics "describing" the observed sizes of the sample observations in these two samples of data.

Substituting our previous expression for $\hat{\alpha}^*_{\text{ols}}$ (Equation 5-25) into Equation 5-28 yields an equation involving only $\hat{\beta}^*_{\text{ols}}$:

$$
0 = \sum_{i=1}^{N} y_i x_i - \left[\bar{y} - \hat{\beta}^*_{\text{ols}} \bar{x} \right] N \bar{x} - \hat{\beta}^*_{\text{ols}} \sum_{i=1}^{N} x_i^2 \qquad (5\text{-}29)
$$

Thus, $\hat{\beta}^*_{ols}$ must satisfy

$$\hat{\beta}^*_{ols}\left[\sum_{i=1}^{N} x_i^2 - N\bar{x}^2\right] = \sum_{i=1}^{N} x_i y_i - N\bar{y}\bar{x} \tag{5-30}$$

This equation can be easily solved for $\hat{\beta}^*_{ols}$ so long as $\sum_{i=1}^{N} x_i^2 - N\bar{x}^2$ is not equal to 0.

Under what circumstances will $\sum_{i=1}^{N} x_i^2 - N\bar{x}^2$ equal 0? At this point it is useful to note that

$$\begin{aligned}\sum_{i=1}^{N}(x_i - \bar{x})^2 &= \sum_{i=1}^{N}(x_i^2 - 2x_i\bar{x} + \bar{x}^2) \\ &= \sum_{i=1}^{N}x_i^2 - 2\sum_{i=1}^{N}x_i\bar{x} + \sum_{i=1}^{N}\bar{x}^2 \\ &= \sum_{i=1}^{N}x_i^2 - 2\bar{x}\left(\sum_{i=1}^{N}x_i\right) + N\bar{x}^2 \\ &= \sum_{i=1}^{N}x_i^2 - 2\bar{x}(N\bar{x}) + N\bar{x}^2 \\ &= \sum_{i=1}^{N}x_i^2 - N\bar{x}^2\end{aligned} \tag{5-31}$$

Thus, the equation for $\hat{\beta}^*_{ols}$ cannot be solved if $\sum_{i=1}^{N}(x_i - \bar{x})^2$ is equal to zero, but this will occur if and only if $x_1 \ldots x_N$ are all equal to one another.

This result makes good sense when you think it through: if all N observations on Y_i are made using the same value for the explanatory variable, x_i, then these data cannot possibly tell us anything about how $E[Y_i]$ varies with changes in the explanatory variable. Alternatively, note that if $x_1 \ldots x_N$ are all equal, then a scatterplot of the sample data must actually look like Figure 5-10. In which case the fitting errors will be unaffected by the value chosen for $\hat{\beta}^{guess}$.

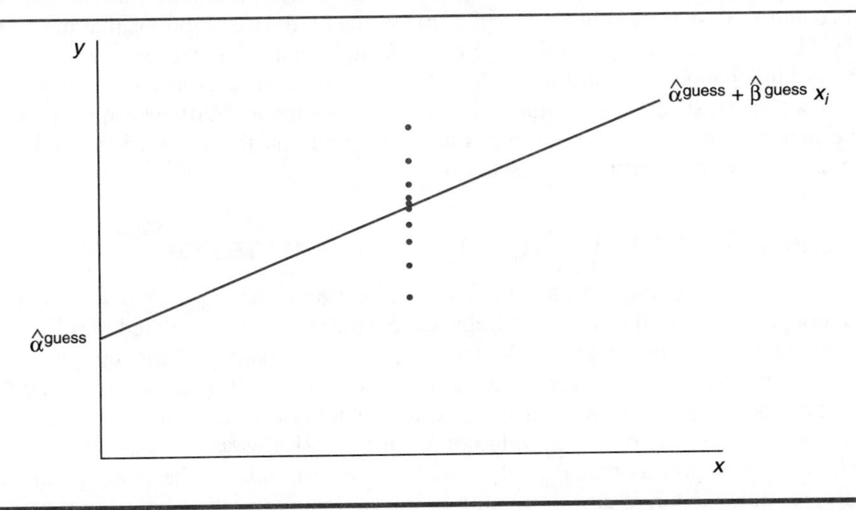

Figure 5-10 Scatterplot and One Possible Fitted Line When the Explanatory Variable Values Are All Equal

Similarly, you will show (in Exercise 5-11) that

$$\sum_{i=1}^{N} y_i x_i - N\bar{y}\bar{x} = \sum_{i=1}^{N}(x_i - \bar{x})(y_i - \bar{y}) \tag{5-32}$$

Thus, assuming that there is at least some sample variation in the x_i values, the least squares slope and intercept estimates are, respectively,

$$\boxed{\begin{aligned}\hat{\beta}^*_{ols} &= \frac{\sum_{i=1}^{N}(x_i - \bar{x})(y_i - \bar{y})}{\sum_{j=1}^{N}(x_j - \bar{x})^2} \\ \hat{\alpha}^*_{ols} &= \bar{y} - \hat{\beta}^*_{ols}\bar{x}\end{aligned}} \tag{5-33}$$

where the running index for the sum in the denominator of $\hat{\beta}^*_{ols}$ has been changed from i to j so as to emphasize that it is distinct from the running index for the sum in the numerator.

For example, using the above formulas the least squares estimates of the intercept and slope coefficients in the regression model for per capita real GDP discussed earlier in this chapter,

$$\log(RGDPL_i) = \alpha + \beta\log(k_i) + U_i \tag{5-34}$$

are

$$\begin{aligned}\log(rgdpl_i) &= \hat{\alpha}^*_{ols} + \hat{\beta}^*_{ols}\log(k_i) + u_i^{fit} \\ &= \underset{(.188)}{1.103} + \underset{(.020)}{.799}\log(k_i) + u_i^{fit}\end{aligned} \tag{5-35}$$

The properties of the estimators ($\hat{\alpha}_{ols}$ and $\hat{\beta}_{ols}$) of which these are sample realizations – i.e., properties such as unbiasedness, consistency, and BLUness – and the meaning/utility of the standard error estimates quoted above (in parentheses, directly below each parameter estimate) are discussed in Chapters 6 and 7. That discussion will explicitly use the model assumptions that the values of the explanatory variable ($\ln(k_i)$) are fixed in repeated samples and that the error term is normally, identically, and independently distributed. Note, however, that those assumptions played no role in the derivation of the least squares parameter estimates given above. Further results, also depending only on the fact that the parameter estimates have been chosen to minimize the sum of squared fitting errors, are developed in the next section.

5.6 INTERPRETING THE LEAST SQUARES ESTIMATES OF α AND β

The first thing to note about the results of the previous section is that $\hat{\alpha}^*_{ols}$, the least squares estimate of the intercept parameter in the Bivariate Regression Model, is closely related to the sample mean of the dependent variable observations. In fact, $\hat{\alpha}^*_{ols}$ clearly equals $\bar{y}$ if the sample mean of the explanatory variable happens to be zero – i.e., if $\bar{x}$ is zero. There is little reason to expect $\bar{x}$ to equal zero in practice, however. Indeed, even if the x_i are realizations of a random variable X_i whose population mean is zero, the observed value of $\bar{x}$ will almost always be nonzero.

The second thing to note is that $\hat{\beta}^*_{ols}$, the least squares estimate of the slope parameter in the Bivariate Regression Model, is closely related to the sample correlation between the explanatory variable and the dependent variable. Now thinking of the x_i as realizations of a random variable, X, the population correlation of X with Y was given in Chapter 2 as

$$\operatorname{corr}(X, Y) \equiv \rho_{XY} \equiv \frac{\operatorname{cov}(X, Y)}{\sqrt{\operatorname{var}(X)\operatorname{var}(Y)}} \tag{5-36}$$

This provides a convenient measure of the strength and kind of association or relationship between these two random variables. Replacing the population covariance and the two population variances in this expression by their analogues using the sample data yields the realized sample correlation, r_{xy}:

$$\begin{aligned} r_{xy} &= \frac{\frac{1}{N}\sum_{i=1}^{N}(x_i-\bar{x})(y_i-\bar{y})}{\sqrt{\left[\frac{1}{N}\sum_{i=1}^{N}(x_i-\bar{x})^2\right]\left[\frac{1}{N}\sum_{i=1}^{N}(y_i-\bar{y})^2\right]}} \\ &= \frac{\sum_{i=1}^{N}(x_i-\bar{x})(y_i-\bar{y})\sqrt{\left[\sum_{i=1}^{N}(x_i-\bar{x})^2\right]}}{\sum_{i=1}^{N}(x_i-\bar{x})^2\sqrt{\left[\sum_{i=1}^{N}(y_i-\bar{y})^2\right]}} \\ &= \hat{\beta}^*_{\text{ols}}\frac{\sqrt{\sum_{i=1}^{N}(x_i-\bar{x})^2}}{\sqrt{\sum_{i=1}^{N}(y_i-\bar{y})^2}} = \hat{\beta}^*_{\text{ols}}\sqrt{\frac{s_x^2}{s_y^2}} \end{aligned} \tag{5-37}$$

where s_x^2 and s_y^2 are the observed sample variances of the observed data on the random variables $X_1 \dots X_N$ and $Y_1 \dots Y_N$, respectively. Thus, $\hat{\beta}^*_{\text{ols}}$ – the estimated coefficient on x_i in a linear model for Y_i – only differs from the sample correlation of X and Y by a positive multiplicative factor. Thus, these two ways of quantifying the sign and strength of the relationship between X and Y are closely related. Indeed, it is this result which motivates the assertion in Chapter 2 that the correlation concept is quantifying the ***linear*** relationship between two random variables.

Note, however, that the correlation concept treats X and Y symmetrically, as two random variables. In contrast, the Bivariate Regression Model assumes that the variations in a random dependent variable (Y_i) are partly caused by variations in its population mean, which is taken to depend on variations in an explanatory variable (x_i) which is itself taken to be nonrandom – i.e., fixed in repeated samples.

Finally, note that the coefficient β in the Bivariate Regression Model can be usefully interpreted as the derivative of the expected value of the dependent variable with respect to the explanatory variable – in other words, as

$$\beta = \frac{dE[Y_i]}{dx_i} \tag{5-38}$$

In interpreting the coefficient estimates from a model like

$$\begin{aligned} \log(rgdpl_i) &= \hat{\alpha}^*_{\text{ols}} + \hat{\beta}^*_{\text{ols}}\log(k_i) + u_i^{\text{fit}} \\ &= \underset{(.188)}{1.103} + \underset{(.020)}{.799}\log(k_i) + u_i^{\text{fit}} \end{aligned} \tag{5-39}$$

in which both the dependent and explanatory variables appear as the logarithms of the original economic quantities, it is further worth noting that $\hat{\beta}^*_{ols}$ can also be interpreted as an estimate of the elasticity of the expected value of $RGDPL_i$ with respect to k_i.[15]

5.7 BIVARIATE REGRESSION WITH A DUMMY VARIABLE: QUANTIFYING THE IMPACT OF COLLEGE GRADUATION ON WEEKLY EARNINGS

The least squares slope estimate has an appealing and useful interpretation when the explanatory variable in the regression model is a qualitative – as opposed to a numeric – variable. A qualitative variable takes on one of several values – usually just the values one or zero – depending on whether or not some particular condition is satisfied. For reasons which are obscure, such variables are almost universally called "dummy" variables, and this common usage will be followed from here on. For example, a gender dummy variable might have value one for males and zero for females. Or, as in the example analyzed in the present section, a dummy variable might be one for survey respondents who have graduated from college and zero otherwise.

Dummy variables tremendously enhance the flexibility with which the Multiple Regression Model (to be introduced in Chapter 9) can productively address the analysis of various economic relationships; they are particularly crucial in addressing (and allowing for) systematic inhomogeneities in the sample data.[16] The usefulness of dummy variables is substantially more limited in the present context because the Bivariate Regression Model allows for only a single explanatory variable. Nevertheless, it is quite illuminating to consider a Bivariate Regression Model in which the explanatory variable is a dummy variable.

For example, consider the model

$$Y_i = \alpha + \beta d_i + U_i \quad U_i \sim \text{NIID}[0, \sigma^2] \tag{5-40}$$

where the index i runs from one to N and where d_i is a dummy variable which is one for the n_{grad} observations in the sample which correspond to college graduates and zero for the $n_{nongrad} = N - n_{grad}$ observations in the sample which correspond to nongraduates. Without loss of generality, it will be assumed that the sample observations have been sorted (renumbered) so that d_i equals one for $i = 1 \ldots n_{grad}$ and d_i equals zero for $i = n_{\text{grad}} + 1 \ldots N$. Because $E[U_i]$ is zero, this model implies that

$$\begin{aligned} E[Y_i] &= \alpha + \beta \quad \text{for college graduates} \\ E[Y_i] &= \alpha \qquad\quad \text{for nongraduates} \end{aligned} \tag{5-41}$$

Thus, the slope parameter β can be interpreted as the difference in the expected value of the dependent variable between the college graduates and the nongraduates. Equivalently, one could interpret β as the expected difference in Y_i between the two groups. Alternatively, because this model is a particular case of the Bivariate Regression Model, this regression model is equivalent to assuming that the Y_i are independently distributed as

$$Y_i \sim N[\alpha + \beta d_i, \sigma^2] \tag{5-42}$$

and we can view the model as allowing for possible inhomogeneity in the population mean of Y_i across the two groups.

Consequently, it should not be surprising that – after some straightforward but extremely tedious algebra, which is relegated to the appendix to this chapter – the least squares estimate of β in this

---

[15] The concept of an elasticity is covered in a microeconomics course. Here it is enough to mention that this particular elasticity estimate of .799 is quantifying the percentage change in the expected value of $RGDPL_i$ per unit percentage change in k_i.

[16] For this reason, dummy variables will come up again in Chapters 9 and 10 and will be crucial in modeling panel data in Chapters 15 and 16.

model turns out to be identical to $\overline{y}_{grade} - \overline{y}_{nongrad}$, the difference between the sample mean of the observed values of Y_i over the college graduates and the analogous sample mean over the observed values of Y_i for the nongraduates.

It is instructive to estimate the parameters in this regression model using actual economic data. In addition to preparing the decennial census, the U.S. Census Bureau collects a great deal of useful survey information at more frequent intervals. In particular, the Census Bureau interviews a large number of households every month for its Current Population Survey (CPS) and publishes the resulting data at www.census.gov. You will learn how to extract and download CPS data to your own computer in Active Learning Exercise 5c (available at www.wiley.com/college/ashley).

Here the data from households surveyed in January of 2002 are used to investigate the impact of college graduation on household earnings. Because this exercise is only intended to illustrate the application of the Bivariate Regression Model, the impact of all of the other relevant CPS variables for which data were collected is pushed into the model error term, U_i, and only 50 sample observations, collected in the Washington D.C.–Baltimore area, are used.

The dependent variable in this model is reported weekly earnings for the *i*th household in the sample. This variable is called *pternwa* in the CPS data set; consequently the dependent variable will be designated $pternwa_i$ instead of Y_i from here on. The explanatory variable – denoted $collegegrad_i$ instead of d_i hereafter – is a dummy variable which takes on the value one for households in which the respondent has graduated from college with at least a bachelor's degree and takes on the value zero otherwise.[17] Data from 25 households with each value of $collegegrad_i$ were chosen at random for use in this example.

The Bivariate Regression Model in this case is thus

$$\begin{gathered} PTERNWA_i = \alpha + \beta\, collegegrad_i + U_i \qquad i = 1 \ldots 50 \\ collegegrad_i \text{ fixed in repeated samples} \\ U_i \sim \text{NIID}[0, \sigma^2] \end{gathered} \tag{5-43}$$

Note that because $collegegrad_i$ is defined so as to be one unit larger for college graduates, the parameter β can also be interpreted as the additional weekly income one might expect a college graduate to earn.[18]

But what is the value of β? Is it even positive? A scatterplot of the sample values of $pternwa_i$ versus the values of $collegegrad_i$ is given in Figure 5-11.

Mean earnings appear to be higher for college graduates – i.e., β seems positive – but it is not clear how much higher.

Moreover, from this scatterplot it seems likely that the variance of U_i – the dispersion of the observations on $PTERNWA_i$ around the (unobservable) population regression line – is pretty different for the two observed values of $collegegrad_i$. This is inconsistent with the assumption that the model errors U_i are all identically distributed.

In addition, using all of the $PTERNWA_i$ observations available in the January, 2002 CPS data set, one obtains the histogram given in Figure 5-12. The asymmetry in this histogram is inconsistent

[17] $Collegegrad_i$ is constructed from the CPS variable peeduca, a categorical variable which takes on values ranging from 31 to 42 for households in which the respondent has not graduated from college and from 43 to 46 for households in which the respondent has graduated from college.

[18] This comment presumes that no relevant explanatory variable which is omitted from the model (because only one explanatory variable is allowed in the Bivariate Regression Model) is correlated with $collegegrad_i$. If there is such an omitted variable, then the college graduation dummy variable will in part be proxying for it. In that case, β is still the expected difference in weekly income between college graduates and nongraduates, but this difference may not actually be due to the additional education – it may be caused, for example, by personal or socioeconomic characteristics which are correlated with college graduation. We will return to this issue of omitted explanatory variables in Chapter 9.

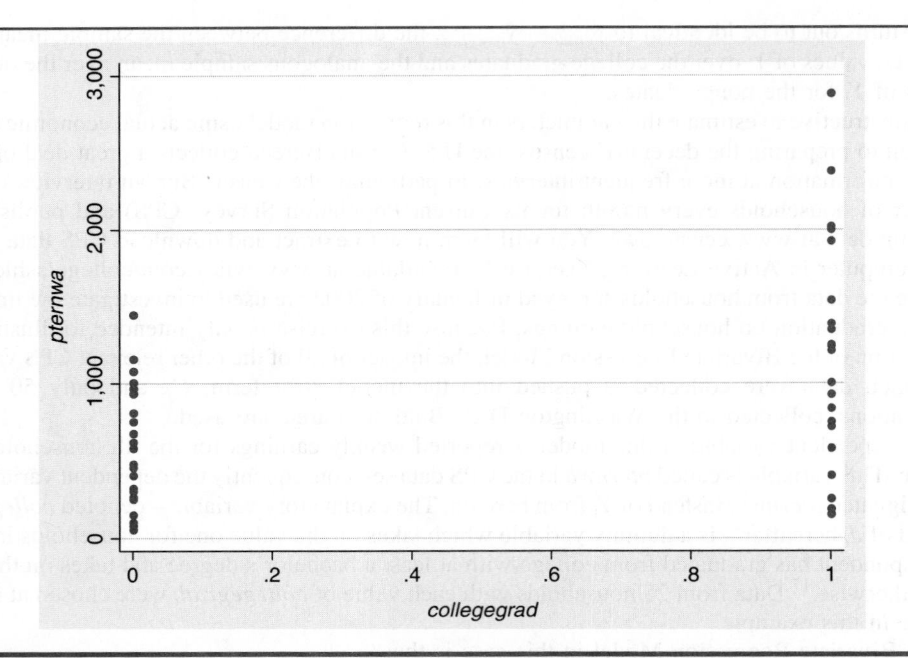

Figure 5-11 Scatterplot of Weekly Income versus the College Graduation Dummy Variable

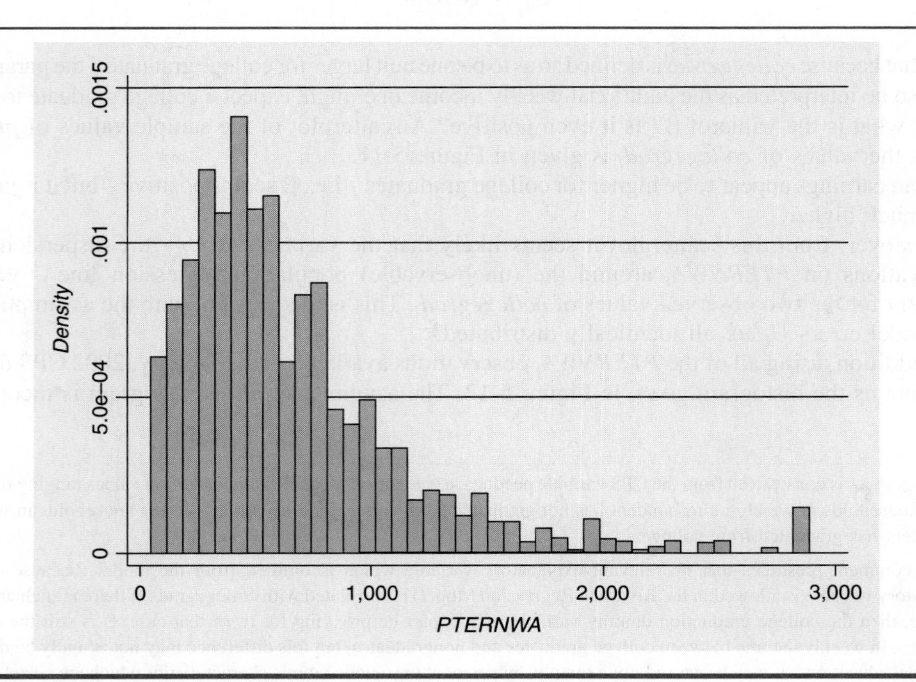

Figure 5-12 Histogram of All Available Observations on Weekly Earnings

with the model assumption that the U_i are normally distributed. Thus, this proposed Bivariate Regression Model for $PTERNWA_i$ is not consistent with the observed properties of the data.

The situation is not hopeless, however. Recalling the results in Exercise 2-40 at the end of Chapter 2 using the Central Limit Theorem, it seems likely that the normal distribution will in this case provide a better approximation to the distribution (for each group) of the *logarithm* of $PTERNWA_i$. A histogram of the sample observations on a new variable ($LOGEARN_i$) defined as log ($pternwa_i$) – Figure 5-13 – indicates that this is indeed the case:

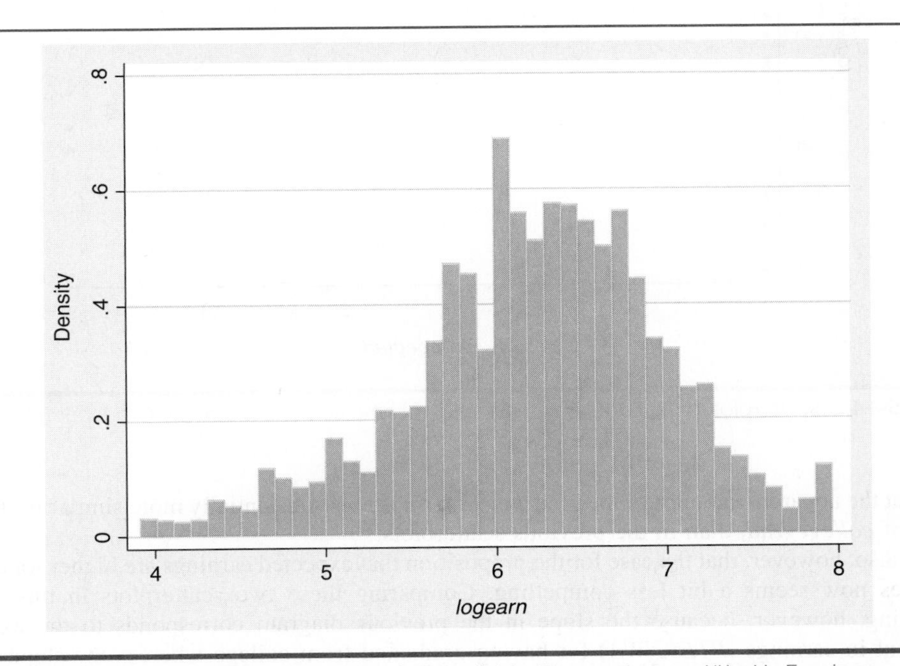

Figure 5-13 Histogram of the Logarithm of All Available Observations on Weekly Earnings

This result suggests that a bivariate model for the dependent variable $LOGEARN_i$ will yield a more reasonable description of the observed data:

$$\boxed{\begin{array}{c} LOGEARN_i = \alpha_1 + \beta_1 collegegrad_i + W_i \quad i = 1 \ldots 50 \\ collegegrad_i \text{ fixed in repeated samples} \\ W_i \sim \text{NIID}[0, \sigma^2] \end{array}} \tag{5-44}$$

Note that the parameters and the error term have been renamed in this model to avoid confusion with those of the previous model. The slope coefficient in this model (β_1) is now the expected increment to the *logarithm* of $PTERNWA_i$ in comparing a college graduate to a nongraduate.

As we shall see hereafter, this model implies that the average *ratio* of earnings for a college graduate to that for a nongraduate is e^{β_1}. Is β_1, the slope coefficient in our new bivariate model, positive? Recalculating the scatterplot using sample observations on this new variable, $LOGEARN_i$, yields Figure 5-14.

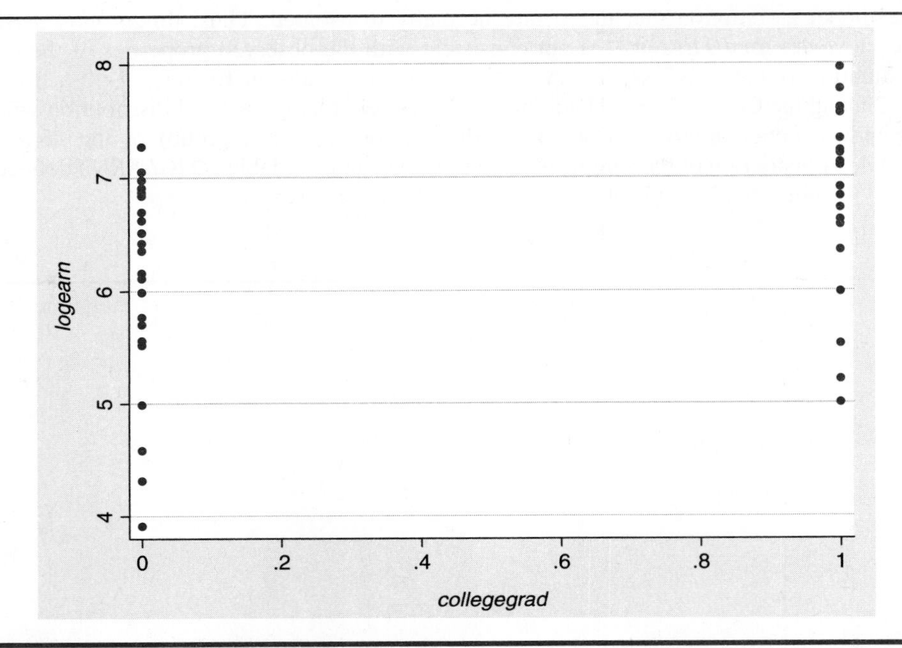

Figure 5-14 Scatterplot of the Logarithm of Weekly Income versus the College Graduation Dummy Variable

Note that the apparent variance of the model error term is now substantially more similar for the two values of $collegegrad_i$ than in the previous scatterplots.[19]

Note also, however, that the case for the proposition that expected earnings are higher for college graduates now seems a bit less compelling. Comparing these two scatterplots in this way is misleading, however, because the slope in the previous diagram corresponds to the expected increment in earnings (*PTERNWA*) for having graduated from college whereas the slope in this diagram corresponds to the expected increment in the *logarithm* of earnings for having graduated from college.

Estimating the parameters α_1 and β_1 in the model for $LOGEARN_i$ using the formulas for the least squares estimates derived earlier in this chapter yields

$$\frac{\sum_{i=1}^{50}\left(collegegrad_i - \overline{collegegrad}\right)\left(logearn_i - \overline{logearn}\right)}{\sum_{i=1}^{50}\left(collegegrad_i - \overline{collegegrad}\right)^2} \tag{5-45}$$

and

$$\overline{logearn} - .873\,\overline{collegegrad} = 6.022 \tag{5-46}$$

[19] Using the F test given at the end of Chapter 2, which assumes that each sample is normally identically and independently distributed, the p-value for rejecting the null hypothesis of equal variances is .57, so this null hypothesis cannot be rejected.

so that the fitted model for $LOGEARN_i$ is

$$logearn_i = 6.022 + 0.873\, collegegrad_i + w_i^{\text{fit}} \tag{5-47}$$

where w_i^{fit} is the least squares fitting error for the ith observation.[20]

In view of the analysis of this model described earlier in this chapter, this estimated model bears two related interpretations. First, the regression model implies that the random variables $LOGEARN_1 \ldots LOGEARN_{50}$ are independently distributed:

$$LOGEARN_i \sim N[\alpha_1 + \beta_1\, collegegrad_i,\, \sigma^2] \tag{5-48}$$

so that

$$LOGEARN_i \sim N[\alpha_1 + \beta_1,\, \sigma^2] \tag{5-49}$$

for the college graduates and

$$LOGEARN_i \sim N[\alpha_1,\, \sigma^2] \tag{5-50}$$

for the nongraduates. Thus, we can view this model as providing an estimate of the mean of the logarithm of reported weekly earnings which allows for an inhomogeneity in the sample due to the fact that both college graduates and nongraduates were surveyed – one could say that this estimate of the mean of $LOGEARN_1$ "controls for" variation in college graduation status.

From this point of view, we might sensibly express these results by stating that our estimate of the mean of the logarithm of reported earnings is 6.895 for the college graduates and 6.022 for the non-graduates. And, from the result on $\hat{\beta}^*_{\text{ols}}$ given in Appendix 5.1, this is exactly what we would observe if we merely calculated the sample mean of the observed $LOGEARN_i$ data separately for each of these groups.

Further, in a second interpretation, we can take .873 (the sample estimate of β_1) as an estimate of the mean difference in the logarithm of reported weekly earnings between college graduates and nongraduates. This difference might be due to the education itself, or it might in part be due to personal qualities – intelligence, determination, good health – which are correlated with having successfully obtained a college degree. To separately estimate the "return" (in terms of the expected value of the logarithm of weekly earnings) to the additional education itself, we would need to control for the variation in these personal qualities by including observed measures of them as additional explanatory variables in the regression model. (Indeed, this sort of generalization is the primary motivation for considering the Multiple Regression Model in Chapter 9.)

The usefulness of this second interpretation is enriched by converting this result into an implication on the expected impact of college graduation on weekly earnings ($PTERNWA_i$) itself. Suppose, to keep the notation explicit and simple, that observation number 7 refers to a college graduate and observation number 33 refers to a nongraduate. Then the model implies that

$$E[LOGEARN_7] = E[LOGEARN_{33}] + \beta_1 \tag{5-51}$$

so that, because $LOGEARN_i$ equals $\ln(PTERNWA_i)$,

$$E[\ln(PTERNWA_7)] = E[\ln(PTERNWA_{33})] + \beta_1 \tag{5-52}$$

[20] The variable name w_i^{fit} is used here rather than u_i^{fit} because the random error term in this model is denoted W_i to distinguish it from the error term in the model for $PTERNWA_i$. This is the fitted model, based on the (fixed) sample realizations, $logearn_i \ldots logearn_N$, so these fitting errors are observed (fixed) numbers; that is why w_i^{fit} is lowercase.

and hence

$$\ln(E[PTERNWA_7]) \cong \ln(E[PTERNWA_{33}]) + \beta_1 \quad (5\text{-}53)$$

where the relationship is now only an approximate equality because the logarithm is a nonlinear function.[21]

Utilizing the fact that $\ln(b) - \ln(c) = \ln(b/c)$ for any values of b and c, this implies that

$$\ln\left(\frac{E[PTERNWA_7]}{E[PTERNWA_{33}]}\right) \cong \beta_1 \quad (5\text{-}54)$$

Applying the exponential function to both sides of this approximate equality and using the fact that the exponential function is the inverse of the logarithm function, so that $e^{\ln(b)}$ equals b for any value of b,

$$\frac{E[PTERNWA_7]}{E[PTERNWA_{33}]} \cong e^{\beta_1} \quad (5\text{-}55)$$

Consequently, this second interpretation of the estimated model also implies an estimate of

$$e^{\hat{\beta}_1} = e^{0.873} = 2.39 \quad (5\text{-}56)$$

for the ratio of expected weekly earnings of a college graduate to those of a nongraduate.

But is the least squares estimate of β_1 a good estimate? And how precise is this estimate of β_1? Can we even reject the null hypothesis that β_i equals zero? Our strategy in the next three chapters will be to defer a consideration of the Multiple Regression Model in favor of learning how to address these kinds of questions in the simpler context of the Bivariate Regression Model. In particular, Chapter 6 takes up the questions

- What are the ***sampling distributions*** of the least squares estimators of α and β?
- How does the ***quality*** of these estimators depend on the assumptions of the model?

Chapter 7 takes up the questions

- How can we use the sample data on $(Y_1, x_1) \dots (Y_N, x_N)$ to obtain ***confidence intervals*** for α and β and to ***test hypotheses*** about α and β?
- How sensitive are these results to the validity of the model assumptions?

Chapter 8 takes up the questions

- How can we ***evaluate the effectiveness of the model*** in fitting the data?
- How can we use the fitted model to ***predict new observations on*** Y_i***?***

The Multiple Regression Model, as noted above, is analyzed in Chapter 9; it is so useful as a tool in checking the assumptions underlying both the Bivariate Regression Model and the Multiple Regression Model itself that we will return to the topic of diagnostically checking these assumptions in Chapters 10, 13, and 14.

[21] The expectation of a nonlinear function of a random variable is not equal to the value of the function evaluated at the expected value of the random variable. Note, however, that much of the error caused by this replacement cancels out because it occurs on both sides of the equation.

KEY TERMS

For each term or concept listed below, provide a working definition or explanation:

Bivariate Regression Model
Dummy Variable
Model Error Term
Conditional Distribution of Y_i Given x_i
Homoscedasticity versus Heteroscedasticity
Nonautocorrelation
SSE
Normal Equations

EXERCISES

5-1. Distinguish between a guessed-at fitted line, the least-squares fitted line, and the population regression line. What is the "intercept" estimate closely related to? The "slope" estimate?

5-2. In the Bivariate Regression Model, what is $E[Y_i]$? What is $\text{var}(Y_i)$?

5-3. What does U_i quantify? What is the distribution of U_i ? Under what circumstance would it be possible to observe $u_1 \ldots u_N$ sample realizations of $U_1 \ldots U_N$?

5-4. What is the assumed distribution of U_i?

5-5. What kind of failure of the Bivariate Regression Model assumptions does each of the following represent?

i. $\text{var}(U_i) \neq \text{var}(U_j)$ for some $i \neq j$

ii. $\text{cov}(U_i, U_j) \neq 0$ for some $i \neq j$

5-6. How does $E\left[U_i^2\right]$ relate to the variance of U_i? Interpret $\text{var}(U_i)$ in words.

5-7. Supposing that $i \neq j$, how does $E[U_i U_j]$ relate to the $\text{cov}(U_i, U_j)$? Interpret the $\text{cov}(U_i, U_j)$ in words.

5-8. Supposing that $\hat{\beta}^{guess}$ is fixed at the value $\hat{\beta}_o^{guess}$, what will a plot of $\text{SSE}(\hat{\alpha}^{guess}, \hat{\beta}_o^{guess})$ versus $\hat{\alpha}^{guess}$ look like? What is happening to the guessed-at line as $\hat{\alpha}^{guess}$ increases? Supposing that $\hat{\alpha}^{guess}$ is fixed at the value $\hat{\beta}_o^{guess}$, what will a plot of $\text{SSE}(\hat{\alpha}_o^{guess}, \hat{\beta}^{guess})$ versus $\hat{\beta}^{guess}$ look like? What is happening to the guessed-at line as $\hat{\beta}^{guess}$ increases?

5-9. The following data have been observed on the dependent variable (Y_i) and on an explanatory variable (x_i):

Observation Number (i)	y_i	x_i
1	22	10
2	38	35
3	16	20
4	39	30
5	55	20

a. Calculate the ordinary least squares (OLS) estimates of the intercept and slope parameters using Equation 5-33.

b. Calculate the sample variance of both variables (s_x^2 and s_y^2) and the sample correlation between x and y (R_{xy}). Confirm that this sample correlation relates to the least squares slope estimate as derived in Section 5.6.

c. Enter this sample data into a regression package (e.g., Stata) and confirm that it yields the same OLS parameter estimates for these data.

5-10. Suppose that the slope of the function SSE($\hat{\alpha}_o$, $\hat{\beta}^{guess}$) is negative for a particular pair of values of $\hat{\alpha}_o$ and $\hat{\beta}^{guess}$. What does this imply about the value of $\hat{\beta}^{guess}$ which minimizes the sum of squared fitting errors for this specified value of $\hat{\alpha}_o$? Illustrate your answer with a sketch of SSE($\hat{\alpha}_o$, $\hat{\beta}^{guess}$) as a function of $\hat{\beta}^{guess}$.

5-11. Show that

$$\sum_{i=1}^{N} y_i x_i - N\overline{y}\overline{x} = \sum_{i=1}^{N} (y_i - \overline{y})(x_i - \overline{x})$$

{Hint: Start with the right-hand side and multiply it out.}

5-12. A least squares regression model explaining the sample variation of $LOGEARN_i$, the logarithm of reported weekly earnings for individual i, yields the estimated Bivariate Regression Model

$$LOGEARN_i = 5.99 + .383\ gender_i + U_i$$

where gender_i is a dummy variable which is, in this case, one for females and zero for males. The issue of how to evaluate the precision of the parameter estimates in a model such as this will be discussed in Chapters 6 and 7; you may ignore these issues in answering this question.

a. What interpretation can be given to this estimated coefficient on the variable gender_i? In particular, what can one say about how the expected value of the logarithm of weekly earnings depends on gender?

b. What can one say about how the expected value of household earnings itself depends on gender?

c. Suppose that it becomes apparent that females are, on average, better educated than males. Presuming that well-educated individuals have a higher marginal product of labor, and hence earn more, than less-educated individuals, what would one expect to happen to the coefficient on $gender_i$ if an education variable were included in the model? Suppose that – due either to inadvertence or to a lack of data – the education variable is omitted from the model. How would the interpretation of the coefficient on $gender_i$ in the above Bivariate Regression Model change in that case?

Active Learning Exercise 5a: Exploring the Penn World Table Data

Instructions:

1. Access the PWT data on the Internet as time-series for individual countries:
   a. Go to the Penn World Tables Web site at datacenter.chass.utoronto.ca/pwt/.
   b. Select the link labelled "PWT 6.1" under the "PWT Previous Editions" heading.[22] Select the "Alphabetical List of Countries" link, then select "Egypt" and "Real GDP per capita (Constant Prices: Laspeyres)" from boxes number one and two. Use the

[22] A newer version, PWT 6.3, is available as of this writing, which updates the data through 2007. This exercise uses version 6.1 to match up with the data used in Section 5.2.

default time period of 1950 to 2000; this is what you will get if you leave both the beginning and ending boxes empty. Leave "topics to be listed" at "columns" and leave the entry in the "format" box at "plain text." Press the "submit" button. What was real GDP per capita in Egypt in 2000?

c. Now repeat step b, changing the "format" selection to "Plot-lines graph." Press the "submit" button and use your browser to print out the plot.

d. In this way, obtain and print out plots of real GDP per capita for several countries of interest – you might look at France, Nigeria, and South Africa, for example. Why do these differ so much?

2. Access the 1999 PWT data on per capital real GDP as a cross-section:

a. These data are available at www.wiley.com/college/ashley in file ALE5a.csv. You should be able to open this file in Excel or in practically any econometric software package which your course might be using. If you are using Stata, you can simply double-click on the file ALE5a.dta.

b. This file contains data on rgdpl_i and k_i (described in the Section 5.2) and their logarithms for each of the 105 countries for which the necessary data on past aggregate investment spending are available. A three-letter country label is provided for each observation – e.g., "UGA" is for Uganda.[23]

c. Reproduce the scatterplot in the text by graphing rgdpl_i against k_i.

d. Now produce the analogous scatterplot using $\ln(\text{rgdpl}_i)$ and $\ln(k_i)$. Notice that this scatterplot looks a bit different from that given in the text. That is because the four observations on Uganda, Ethiopia, Madagascar, and Mozambique are not omitted here. Does the model

$$\text{In}(RGDPL_i) = \alpha + \beta \ln(k_i) + U_\text{i}$$

suggested there still seem reasonable?

e. Estimate α and β in this Bivariate Regression Model anyway. Note that you can expect to precisely reproduce the parameter estimates given in Section 5.5 only if you exclude the first four observations.[24]

f. Now estimate α and β_1 and β_2 in the Multiple Regression Model

$$\ln(RGDPL_i) = \alpha + \beta_1 \ln(k_i) + \beta_2 (\ln(k_i))^2 + V_i$$

This model won't be covered in the text until Chapter 9, but it is easy enough to make the regression software estimate the parameters anyway.[25] Given the shape of the scatterplot you obtained in part d, what sign do you expect for the coefficient β_2?

[23] These country codes are defined in Table A (pp. 13 – 16) of the "PWT 6.1 Data Description" document, a link to which can be found in the "Other Resources" section at the foot of the PWT homepage.

[24] The precise syntax for obtaining these estimates will differ a bit from software package to software package. In Stata the command "regress ln_rgdpl ln_k" estimates α and β using all 105 observations and "regress ln_rgdpl ln_k if _n > 4" instructs the program to omit the first four observations, which happen to be for Uganda, Ethiopia, Madagascar, and Mozambique.

[25] In Stata, for example, you generate the squared variable using the command "generate ln_k_squared = ln_k*ln_k" and estimate the coefficients in the model using the command "regress ln_rgdpl ln_k ln_k_squared".

APPENDIX 5.1: $\hat{\beta}^*_{ols}$ WHEN x_i IS A DUMMY VARIABLE

Section 5.7 considers the Bivariate Regression Model

$$Y_i = \alpha + \beta d_i + U_i \qquad U_i \sim \text{NIID}[0, \sigma^2] \qquad i = 1 \ldots N \tag{A5-1}$$

where d_i is a dummy variable which is one for the n_{grad} observations in the sample which correspond to college graduates and zero for the $n_{nongrad} = N - n_{grad}$ observations in the sample which correspond to nongraduates. It is assumed that the sample observations have been sorted (renumbered) so that d_i equals one for $i = 1 \ldots n_{grad}$ and d_i equals zero for $i = n_{grad} + 1 \ldots N$. It is shown below that $\hat{\beta}^*_{ols}$, the OLS estimate of the slope coefficient in this model, is actually equal to the difference between the sample mean of Y_i for the graduates and the sample mean of Y_i for the nongraduates.

Substituting d_i for x_i in the expression for the OLS slope estimate derived in Section 5.5,

$$\begin{aligned}
\hat{\beta}^*_{ols} &= \frac{\sum_{i=1}^{N}(d_i - \bar{d})(y_i - \bar{y})}{\sum_{j=1}^{N}(d_j - \bar{d})^2} = \frac{\sum_{i=1}^{N} d_i(y_i - \bar{y}) - \sum_{i=1}^{N} \bar{d}(y_i - \bar{y})}{\sum_{j=1}^{N}(d_j - \bar{d})d_j - \sum_{j=1}^{N}(d_j - \bar{d})\bar{d}} \\
&= \frac{\sum_{i=1}^{N}(y_i - \bar{y})d_i - \bar{d}\sum_{i=1}^{N}(y_i - \bar{y})}{\sum_{j=1}^{N}(d_j - \bar{d})d_j - \bar{d}\sum_{j=1}^{N}(d_i - \bar{d})} = \frac{\sum_{i=1}^{N}(y_i - \bar{y})d_i}{\sum_{j=1}^{N}(d_j - \bar{d})} = \frac{\sum_{i=1}^{n_{grad}}(y_i - \bar{y})}{\sum_{j=1}^{n_{grad}}(d_j - \bar{d})}
\end{aligned} \tag{A5-2}$$

Note that $\bar{d}$ can come out of the sum because it does not depend on the running index, and that $\sum_{i=1}^{N}(y_i - \bar{y}) = \sum_{i=1}^{N} y_i - N\bar{y}$, which equals zero from the definition of $\bar{y}$; by the same reasoning, the analogous sum over the deviations of the d_i from their sample mean is also zero.

The variables $\bar{d}$ and $\bar{y}$ are averages over all $N = n_{grad} + n_{nongrad}$ observations; in particular, $\bar{d}$ is just n_{grad}/N and $\bar{y}$ can be rewritten in terms of $\bar{y}_{grad}$ and $\bar{y}_{nongrad}$ as $(n_{grad}\bar{y}_{grad} + n_{nongrad}\bar{y}_{nongrad})/N$. Thus, this expression for $\hat{\beta}^*_{ols}$ can be rewritten

$$\begin{aligned}
\hat{\beta}^*_{ols} &= \frac{\sum_{i=1}^{n_{grad}}(y_i - \bar{y})}{\sum_{j=1}^{n_{grad}}(d_j - \bar{d})} = \frac{n_{grad}\bar{y}_{grad} - n_{grad}\bar{y}}{n_{grad} - n_{grad}\bar{d}} = \frac{y_{grad} - \bar{y}}{1 - \bar{d}} \\
&= \frac{\bar{y}_{grad} - \left[\dfrac{n_{grad}\bar{y}_{grad} + n_{nongrad}\bar{y}_{nongrad}}{N}\right]}{1 - (n_{grad}/N)} = \frac{N\bar{y}_{grad} - n_{grad}\,\bar{y}_{grad} - n_{nongrad}\,\bar{y}_{nongrad}}{N - n_{grad}} \\
&= \frac{(N - n_{grad})\bar{y}_{grad} - (N - n_{grad})\bar{y}_{nongrad}}{N - n_{grad}} = \bar{y}_{grad} - \bar{y}_{nongrad}
\end{aligned} \tag{A5-3}$$

Thus, the least squares slope estimate in a bivariate regression on a dummy variable is simply the difference between the sample mean over the observations for which the dummy variable equals one and the sample mean over the observations for which the dummy variable equals zero.

6

The Bivariate Linear Regression Model: Sampling Distributions and Estimator Properties

6.1 INTRODUCTION

The Bivariate Regression Model, its assumptions, and the observed least squares estimators of its intercept and slope parameters $(\hat{\alpha}_{ols}$ and $\hat{\beta}_{ols})$ were discussed in the previous chapter, along with an empirical example relating weekly household earnings to whether or not the respondent is a college graduate. This empirical example went about as far as it could using only the parameter estimates. In this chapter you will learn how to obtain the sampling distributions of these estimators under the presumption that the sample data satisfy all of the assumptions of the Bivariate Regression Model:

The Bivariate Regression Model
{Alternative Form}

$$
\begin{aligned}
&Y_i = \alpha + \beta x_i + U_i \quad i = 1 \ldots N \\
&x_1 \ldots x_N \text{ fixed in repeated samples} \\
&U_i \text{ is normally distributed} \\
&E[U_i] = 0 \\
&E[U_i U_j] = \sigma^2 \quad \text{for } i = j \\
&\qquad\qquad = 0 \quad \text{for } i \neq j
\end{aligned}
\tag{6-1}
$$

These sampling distributions are then used to show that $\hat{\alpha}_{ols}$ and $\hat{\beta}_{ols}$ have a number of desirable properties. In particular, where all of the assumptions of the Bivariate Regression Model are satisfied, these estimators are shown to be unbiased, consistent, and even optimal in the sense of being best linear unbiased or BLU.[1]

[1] These estimators are also efficient for α and β under the assumptions of the Bivariate Regression Model, but the proof of this is beyond the scope of the present treatment.

6.2 ESTIMATES AND ESTIMATORS

The least squares estimates of α and β derived in Chapter 5 were

$$\hat{\alpha}^* = \bar{y} - \hat{\beta}^* \bar{x} \tag{6-2}$$

and

$$\hat{\beta}^* = \frac{\sum_{i=1}^{N} (x_i - \bar{x})(y_i - \bar{y})}{\sum_{j=1}^{N} (x_j - \bar{x})^2} \tag{6-3}$$

where the "ols" subscripts have now been dropped: from here on $\hat{\alpha}^*$ and $\hat{\beta}^*$ are assumed to be the least squares estimators. Also, recall that the asterisks in these expressions are there to explicitly indicate that these are fixed numbers, determined by the observed sample data, $y_1 \dots y_N$ and $x_1 \dots x_N$.

To proceed, however, it is necessary to recognize that $\hat{\alpha}^*$ and $\hat{\beta}^*$ are actually realizations (picks from the sampling distributions of) the random variables $\hat{\alpha}$ and $\hat{\beta}$, given by

$$\hat{\alpha} = \bar{Y} - \hat{\beta}\,\bar{x} \tag{6-4}$$

and

$$\hat{\beta} = \frac{\sum_{i=1}^{N} (x_i - \bar{x})(Y_i - \bar{Y})}{\sum_{j=1}^{N} (x_j - \bar{x})^2} \tag{6-5}$$

where $\bar{Y}$ is the random variable, $\frac{1}{N}Y_1 + \dots + \frac{1}{N}Y_N$. Note that $Y_1 \dots Y_N$ are random variables because Y_i is the fixed quantity $\alpha + \beta x_i$ plus the (normally distributed) random variable, U_i. Thus, the least squares parameter estimators ($\hat{\alpha}$ and $\hat{\beta}$) are random variables whose randomness arises, fundamentally, from the random character of the model error terms, $U_1 \dots U_N$.

The properties of $\hat{\beta}$ as an estimator of β (and our ability to use a particular realization $\hat{\beta}^*$ to test hypotheses about β and to obtain confidence intervals for β – topics which will be examined in Chapter 7 – both hinge on the sampling distribution of $\hat{\beta}$, so our next task is to derive this sampling distribution. The analogous result for $\hat{\alpha}$ is so similar that you will derive it yourself in Exercise 6-9.

6.3 $\hat{\beta}$ AS A LINEAR ESTIMATOR AND THE LEAST SQUARES WEIGHTS

A simple rewrite of the least squares estimator, $\hat{\beta}$, will save a tremendous amount of tedious algebra and will both simplify and clarify all of our work with this estimator, including the derivation of its sampling distribution. In the previous section we found that $\hat{\beta}$ can be expressed as

$$\hat{\beta} = \frac{\sum_{i=1}^{N} (x_i - \bar{x})(Y_i - \bar{Y})}{\sum_{j=1}^{N} (x_j - \bar{x})^2} \tag{6-6}$$

For convenience, let the symbol φ stand for the sum in the denominator of this expression:

Definition of φ

$$\varphi \equiv \sum_{j=1}^{N} (x_j - \bar{x})^2 \tag{6-7}$$

Then, using the result that

$$\sum_{i=1}^{N} (x_i - \bar{x}) = \sum_{i=1}^{N} x_i - \sum_{i=1}^{N} \bar{x} = \sum_{i=1}^{N} x_i - N\bar{x} = 0 \tag{6-8}$$

$\hat{\beta}$ can be rewritten as a linear function of $Y_1 \dots Y_N$:

$$\begin{aligned}
\hat{\beta} &= \left(\frac{1}{\varphi}\right) \sum_{i=1}^{N} (x_i - \bar{x})(Y_i - \bar{Y}) \\
&= \left(\frac{1}{\varphi}\right) \sum_{i=1}^{N} (x_i - \bar{x}) Y_i - \left(\frac{1}{\varphi}\right) \sum_{i=1}^{N} (x_i - \bar{x}) \bar{Y} \\
&= \sum_{i=1}^{N} \left(\frac{1}{\varphi}\right) (x_i - \bar{x}) Y_i - \left(\frac{\bar{Y}}{\varphi}\right) \sum_{i=1}^{N} (x_i - \bar{x}) \\
&= \sum_{i=1}^{N} \left(\frac{x_i - \bar{x}}{\varphi}\right) Y_i - \left(\frac{\bar{Y}}{\varphi}\right) \sum_{i=1}^{N} (x_i - \bar{x}) \\
&= \sum_{i=1}^{N} \left(\frac{x_i - \bar{x}}{\varphi}\right) Y_i \\
&= \sum_{i=1}^{N} w_i^{\text{ols}} Y_i
\end{aligned} \tag{6-9}$$

This expression for $\hat{\beta}$ defines what are usually called the "the least squares weights," or $w_1^{\text{ols}} \dots w_N^{\text{ols}}$:

$$w_i^{\text{ols}} \equiv \frac{x_i - \bar{x}}{\varphi} = \frac{x_i - \bar{x}}{\sum_{j=1}^{N} (x_j - \bar{x})^2} \quad \text{for } i = 1 \dots N \tag{6-10}$$

Using almost identical arithmetic, $\hat{\beta}^*$ – the sample realization of $\hat{\beta}$ – can be written

$$\hat{\beta}^* = \sum_{i=1}^{N} w_i^{\text{ols}} y_i \tag{6-11}$$

Note that because the w_i^{ols} depend only on the fixed explanatory variables, $x_1 \dots x_N$, these are *fixed* weights. We say, "$\hat{\beta}$ is a linear estimator" because it is a linear function – a weighted sum with fixed weights – of the observations on the dependent variable.[2]

[2] The word "linear" is used a lot in econometrics; unfortunately, its meaning differs from context to context. Here, $\hat{\beta}$ is termed a "linear estimator" because it is a linear function of the observations on the dependent variable. But the Bivariate Regression Model is also typically called a "linear regression model" because it is expressing Y_i as a linear function of the unknown parameters α and β. And, as noted in Chapter 2, expectations are said to satisfy the "linearity property" because the expectation of a linear function of a set of random variables equals that same linear function of the expectations of the random variables.

This result, that

$$\hat{\beta} = \sum_{i=1}^{N} w_i^{ols} Y_i \tag{6-12}$$

implies that the least squares estimator of β is nothing more than a particular weighted sum of the random variables $Y_1 \ldots Y_N$. This is just like $\bar{Y}$, the least squares estimator of the population mean (μ) of a normally distributed random variable, which was analyzed in Chapter 3 under the assumption that $Y_i \sim \text{NIID}[\mu, \sigma^2]$. In fact, the only difference between these two estimators is that Y_i is here instead assumed, under the Bivariate Regression Model, to be independently (but not identically) distributed $N[\alpha + \beta x_i, \sigma^2]$. Consequently, $\hat{\beta}$ is an *unequally* weighted sum of the Y_i, whereas $\bar{Y}$ is an *equally* weighted sum of the Y_i.[3]

What makes the least squares weights so useful – in addition to the fact that they allow us to write $\hat{\beta}$ so simply – is that they have the following three useful properties:

Properties of the Least Squares Weights

$$w_i^{ols} = \frac{x_i - \bar{x}}{\varphi} = \frac{x_i - \bar{x}}{\sum_{j=1}^{N}(x_j - \bar{x})^2} \quad \text{for } i = 1 \ldots N$$

$$(1) \quad \sum_{i=1}^{N} w_i^{ols} = 0$$

$$(2) \quad \sum_{i=1}^{N} w_i^{ols} x_i = 1 \tag{6-13}$$

$$(3) \quad \sum_{i=1}^{N} \left(w_i^{ols}\right)^2 = \frac{1}{\varphi} = \frac{1}{\sum_{j=1}^{N}(x_j - \bar{x})^2}$$

These three properties are very simple to derive. For example, because (as shown in Equation 6-8) $\sum_{i=1}^{N}(x_i - \bar{x})$ is zero, it follows that

$$\sum_{i=1}^{N} w_i^{ols} = \sum_{i=1}^{N} \frac{x_i - \bar{x}}{\varphi} = \frac{1}{\varphi}\sum_{i=1}^{N}(x_i - \bar{x}) = 0 \tag{6-14}$$

You will derive the remaining two properties in Exercise 6-8.

6.4 THE SAMPLING DISTRIBUTION OF $\hat{\beta}$

At this point the Bivariate Regression Model assumption that the model errors ($U_1 \ldots U_N$) are distributed NIID[0, σ^2] becomes essential. Recall, from Equations 5-14 and 6-1, that this

[3] Similarly, you will show in Exercise 6-9 that $\hat{\alpha}$, the least squares estimator of α, is also a linear estimator. It, too, is an unequally weighted sum of $Y_1 \ldots Y_N$, except in the special case where the sum of the N explanatory variable values is zero (so that $\bar{x} = 0$), in which case $\hat{\alpha} = \bar{Y}$.

assumption implies the alternative form of the model used here:

The Bivariate Regression Model
{Alternative Form}

$$
\begin{aligned}
&Y_i = \alpha + \beta x_i + U_i \quad i = 1 \ldots N \\
&x_1 \ldots x_N \text{ fixed in repeated samples} \\
&U_i \text{ is normally distributed} \\
&E[U_i] = 0 \\
&E[U_i U_j] = \sigma^2 \quad \text{for } i = j \\
&\qquad\qquad = 0 \quad \text{for } i \neq j
\end{aligned}
\tag{6-15}
$$

Substituting this expression for Y_i into $\hat{\beta} = \sum_{i=1}^{N} w_i^{\text{ols}} Y_i$ yields a simple equation relating $\hat{\beta}$ to the population coefficient (β) and the model errors, $U_1 \ldots U_N$:

$$
\begin{aligned}
\hat{\beta} = \sum_{i=1}^{N} w_i^{\text{ols}} Y_i &= \sum_{i=1}^{N} w_i^{\text{ols}} \{\alpha + \beta x_i + U_i\} \\
&= \sum_{i=1}^{N} \{w_i^{\text{ols}}\, \alpha + w_i^{\text{ols}}\, \beta x_i + w_i^{\text{ols}} U_i\} \\
&= \alpha \sum_{i=1}^{N} w_i^{\text{ols}} + \beta \sum_{i=1}^{N} w_i^{\text{ols}} x_i + \sum_{i=1}^{N} w_i^{\text{ols}} U_i \\
&= \alpha 0 + \beta 1 + \sum_{i=1}^{N} w_i^{\text{ols}} U_i \\
&= \beta + \sum_{i=1}^{N} w_i^{\text{ols}} U_i
\end{aligned}
\tag{6-16}
$$

This expression for $\hat{\beta}$ is very useful because the distribution of the model errors is specified by the assumptions of the Bivariate Regression Model. In particular, because $U_1 \ldots U_N$ are assumed to be normally distributed, we see that $\hat{\beta}$ can be written as a weighted sum of normally distributed variates. Thus, $\hat{\beta}$ is itself normally distributed.[4] Consequently, its sampling distribution is completely characterized by its mean and variance:

$$\hat{\beta} \sim N\left[E[\hat{\beta}],\, \text{var}(\hat{\beta})\right] \tag{6-17}$$

Evaluating first the mean of $\hat{\beta}$,

$$E[\hat{\beta}] = E\left[\beta + \sum_{i=1}^{N} w_i^{\text{ols}} U_i\right] = \beta + \sum_{i=1}^{N} w_i^{\text{ols}} E[U_i] = \beta \tag{6-18}$$

This result implies that

$\hat{\beta}$ is an unbiased estimator for β

[4] Recall that, as noted in Chapter 2, even unequally weighted sums of random variables like the U_i are approximately normally distributed if the weights are not too unequal and if N is sufficiently large. Thus, this result – as a good approximation – is not very sensitive to departures of the U_i from normality if the sample is large.

This is an important result because we saw in Chapter 4 that unbiasedness is crucial to the construction of hypothesis tests and confidence intervals.[5] Note also that this is an extremely robust property: all that is actually used in obtaining it is the observation that $\hat{\beta}$ is the least squares estimator of β in the model $Y_i = \alpha + \beta x_i + U_i$ with the x_i fixed in repeated samples and $E[U_i] = 0$.

Noting that $E[U_i] = 0$ follows from the fact that the model contains an intercept, α, this result yields an insight of great practical significance: ***it is almost always a good idea to include an intercept in any regression model you estimate, because doing so goes a long way toward ensuring that your least squares parameter estimators are at least unbiased.*** Indeed, we will find later on (in Chapter 9) that this insight holds also for the Multiple Regression Model, in which multiple explanatory variables are allowed.[6]

Next consider the sampling variance of $\hat{\beta}$ – i.e., the population variance of the random variable $\hat{\beta}$. Because the result derived above implies that $\hat{\beta} - \beta = \sum_{i=1}^{N} w_i^{ols} U_i$, one way to derive this variance is to note that

$$\text{var}(\hat{\beta}) = \text{var}(\hat{\beta} - \beta) = \text{var}\left(\sum_{i=1}^{N} w_i^{ols} U_i\right) \tag{6-19}$$

which equals $\sigma^2 \sum_{i=1}^{N} \left(w_i^{ols}\right)^2$ using the result on the variance of a weighted sum of uncorrelated random variables derived at the end of Chapter 2.[7] This result is so important, however, that it is worth deriving it afresh here.

Substituting the results that $E\left[\hat{\beta}\right] = \beta$ and that $\hat{\beta} - \beta = \sum_{i=1}^{N} w_i^{ols} U_i$ into the definition of the population variance of $\hat{\beta}$ yields

$$\begin{aligned}
\text{var}(\hat{\beta}) &= E\left[\left[\hat{\beta} - E\left[\hat{\beta}\right]\right]^2\right] \\
&= E\left[\left[\hat{\beta} - \beta\right]^2\right] \\
&= E\left[\left[\sum_{i=1}^{N} w_i^{ols} U_i\right]^2\right] \\
&= E\left[\sum_{j=1}^{N} w_j^{ols} U_j \sum_{i=1}^{N} w_i^{ols} U_i\right] \\
&= E\left[H\left[\sum_{i=1}^{N} w_i^{ols} U_i\right]\right]
\end{aligned} \tag{6-20}$$

[5] More precisely, known bias is necessary. In practice, however, estimator bias is typically only known in those cases for which it can be shown to be zero – i.e., for unbiased estimators.

[6] A note of caution is in order here: While this result does guarantee that $E\left[\hat{\beta}\right] = \beta$, it will not be fully appropriate to interpret β as $\partial E[Y_i]/\partial x_i$ if the model has inadvertently omitted an additional explanatory variable which is correlated in its sample movements with x_i. This is because, in that case, x_i will in part be acting as a proxy for this omitted variable and β will thus be modeling the impact on $E[Y_i]$ of both variables. In this instance one should either include this additional explanatory variable in the regression equation (yielding the Multiple Regression Model we will study in Chapter 9) or one should appropriately modify how one interprets the coefficient β.

[7] There the symbol "B" plays the role of "$\hat{\beta} - \beta$", "w_i" plays the role of w_i^{ols}, and $E[U_i]$ is μ, which here is zero.

where H stands for the random variable $\sum_{j=1}^{N} w_j^{ols} U_j$. Bringing the factor of H inside the sum over the running index i,

$$\begin{aligned}\text{var}(\hat{\beta}) &= E\left[\sum_{i=1}^{N} H\, w_i^{ols} U_i\right] \\ &= E\left[\sum_{i=1}^{N} w_i^{ols}(U_i H)\right] \\ &= \sum_{i=1}^{N} w_i^{ols} E[U_i H]\end{aligned} \tag{6-21}$$

where the last step uses the Linearity Property of Chapter 2. Evaluating this expectation,

$$\begin{aligned}E[U_i H] &= E\left[U_i \sum_{j=1}^{N} w_j^{ols} U_j\right] \\ &= E\left[\sum_{j=1}^{N} w_j^{ols} U_i U_j\right] \\ &= \sum_{j=1}^{N} w_j^{ols} E[U_i U_j] \quad \text{using the Linearity Property} \\ &= w_i^{ols}\,\sigma^2\end{aligned} \tag{6-22}$$

where the last step follows because $E[U_i U_j]$ is zero when i is unequal to j (due to the non-autocorrelation assumption) and because $E[U_i U_j] = E[U_i^2]$ is σ^2 when i is equal to j, due to the homoscedasticity assumption.

Substituting this expression for $E[U_i H]$ into the expression for $\text{var}(\hat{\beta})$,

$$\begin{aligned}\text{var}(\hat{\beta}) &= \sum_{i=1}^{N} w_i^{ols} E[U_i H] \\ &= \sum_{i=1}^{N} w_i^{ols}\left(w_i^{ols}\,\sigma^2\right) = \sigma^2 \sum_{i=1}^{N}\left(w_i^{ols}\right)^2\end{aligned} \tag{6-23}$$

so that, using the third property of the least squares weights,

$$\begin{aligned}\text{var}(\hat{\beta}) &= \sigma^2 \sum_{i=1}^{N}\left(w_i^{ols}\right)^2 \\ &= \sigma^2 \frac{1}{\varphi} \\ &= \sigma^2 \frac{1}{\sum_{j=1}^{N}(x_j - \bar{x})^2} = \frac{\sigma^2}{\sum_{j=1}^{N}(x_j - \bar{x})^2}\end{aligned} \tag{6-24}$$

Thus, the complete sampling distribution of $\hat{\beta}$ is

Sampling Distribution of $\hat{\beta}$

$$\hat{\beta} \sim N\left[\beta\,,\ \frac{\sigma^2}{\sum_{j=1}^{N}\left(x_j - \bar{x}\right)^2}\right] \tag{6-25}$$

Both the numerator and the denominator of the expression for the sampling variance of $\hat{\beta}$ in Equation 6-25 make intuitive sense. For example, the numerator shows that the variance of $\hat{\beta}$ will be small – indicating that $\hat{\beta}$ yields a very precise estimate of β – whenever σ^2, the variance of the model errors (U_i), is small. This makes sense because the vertical deviations of the sample observations from the population regression line are realizations of U_1 ... U_N; thus, observed data which clusters tightly around the population regression line corresponds to a small value for σ^2.

Turning next to the denominator of the expression for var($\hat{\beta}$), the sum $\sum_{j=1}^{N}\left(x_j - \bar{x}\right)^2$ measures the amount of sample dispersion in the observed values of the explanatory variable: it is large if Y_i is observed for a variety of quite different values of the explanatory variable, and it is close to zero if Y_i is always observed for pretty much the same value of the explanatory variable. In the latter case, $x_1 \approx x_2 \approx \ldots \approx x_N$, so each of these is approximately equal to $\bar{x}$; hence, $\left(x_j - \bar{x}\right)^2$ is very small for all values of i. Thus, the sampling variance of $\hat{\beta}$ becomes large – indicating that $\hat{\beta}$ is a very imprecise estimate of β – when there is little sample variation in the explanatory variable. This makes sense because β quantifies the sensitivity of $E[Y_i]$ to x_i. After all, how can one accurately estimate how $E[Y_i]$ varies with x_i unless Y_i is observed for substantially differing values of x_i?

This point can also be approached graphically. Consider the scatterplot for the extreme case where there is almost no sample variation in the explanatory variable:

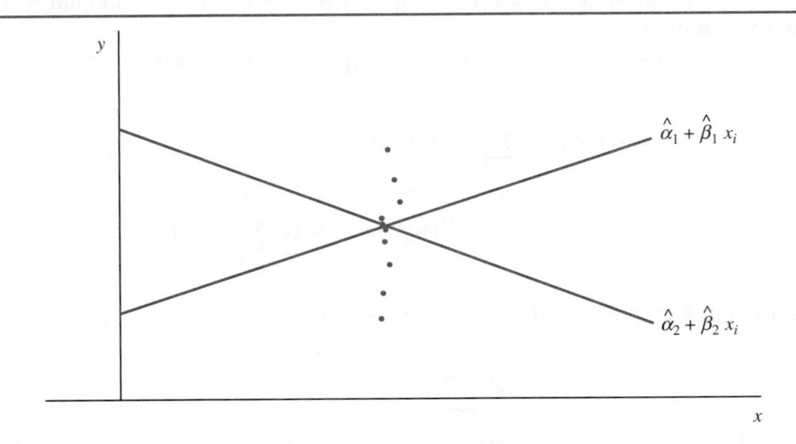

Figure 6-1 Two Fitted Lines When There Is Almost No Explanatory Variable Variation

Note that positively and negatively sloped lines all yield essentially the same set of fitting errors, reflecting the fact that sample data observed with little x_i variation has little to say about the value of β. Thus, the inverse dependence of the sampling variance of the least squares slope estimator on $\sum_{j=1}^{N}\left(x_j - \bar{x}\right)^2$ makes sense intuitively: we get a precise estimate of the slope coefficient in the model only when there is enough sample variation in the explanatory variable that lines with notably different slopes fit the data notably differently.[8]

Suppose instead that we are free to choose the values $x_1 \ldots x_N$ for which the realizations of $Y_1 \ldots Y_N$ are observed, subject only to the constraint that each value of the explanatory variable must lie in the given interval $[x_{min}, x_{max}]$. For example, we might have funding to make a social experiment in N otherwise equivalent locales, in each of which we can set the minimum wage (in the interval $[x_{min}, x_{max}]$) and observe the resulting value of local employment, Y_i. What values should we choose for $x_1 \ldots x_N$ so as to minimize the sampling variance of the resulting estimate of β, the slope of the relationship between employment and the local minimum wage? Clearly, we should in this case set the minimum wage equal to x_{min} for half our N locales and equal to x_{max} for the remaining locales. This choice does yield the smallest value for the sampling variance of $\hat{\beta}$; it leads to a scatterplot and fitted line plotted in Figure 6-2.

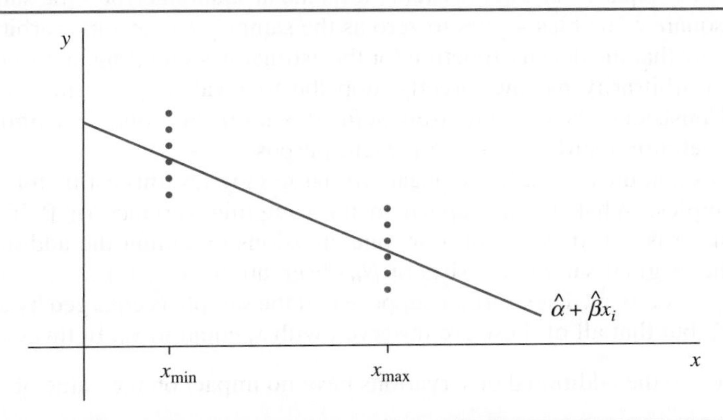

Figure 6-2 Scatterplot with Explantory Data Chosen to Minimize Variance of $\hat{\beta}$

There is a substantial risk associated with this choice, however. Suppose that – in violation of the Bivariate Regression Model assumption – local employment (Y_i) is related in a *nonlinear* fashion to x_i, the local minimum wage, so that Y_i actually equals $\alpha_o + \beta_o x_i + \gamma_o (x_i)^2 + U_i$ with γ_o positive. In that case, a plot of the data and of the fitted regression line, $Y_i = \hat{\alpha}_o + \hat{\beta}_o x_i + \hat{\gamma}_o x_i^2$, would look like Figure 6-3.

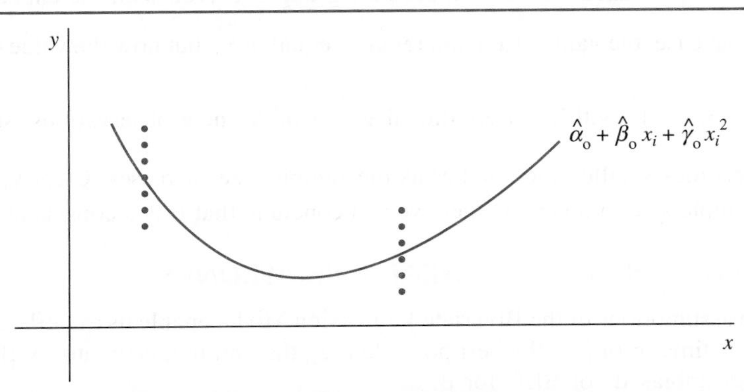

Figure 6-3 The Problem with Choosing the Explanatory Data to Minimize the Variance of $\hat{\beta}$

[8] Recall also, from Equation 5-30 in Section 5.5, that $\sum_{j=1}^{N} (x_j - \bar{x})^2$ must be nonzero in order to solve for the least squares estimator of β.

Note that fitted lines $\left(\hat{\alpha} + \hat{\beta}_o x_i + \hat{\gamma}_o x_i^2\right)$ with differing – and even quite negative – values for $\hat{\gamma}_o$ will all have exactly the same fitting errors for sample data with the x_i values chosen in this way. Thus, choosing to split the x_i values between the smallest and largest possible values yields the most precise estimate of the slope if the relationship is really linear, but costs us the ability to check on this linearity assumption by estimating γ_o – for that we need observations on Y_i for intermediate values of x_i.

6.5 PROPERTIES OF $\hat{\beta}$: CONSISTENCY

The unbiasedness of $\hat{\beta}$ followed directly from the sampling distribution of $\hat{\beta}$. In Chapter 3 it was informally noted that $\bar{Y}$ is "consistent" as an estimator of $\mu = E[Y_i]$ because it is unbiased and its sampling variance goes to zero as the sample size becomes arbitrarily large. More formally, an estimator is said to be "squared error consistent" if its mean squared error – the sum of its sampling variance and the square of its bias – goes to zero as the sample size becomes arbitrarily large. One could in that case say that the density function for the estimator's sampling distribution is becoming arbitrarily tall and arbitrarily narrow directly atop the true value (β) as the sample size grows arbitrarily large. Consistency is more precisely defined in terms of probability limits in Chapter 11, but this informal definition suffices for the present purpose.

Here it is obvious that the bias in $\hat{\beta}$ disappears for large samples: this estimator has no bias at all, even in small samples. What would happen to the sampling variance of $\hat{\beta}$ if more data were available? This, it turns out, depends on how one envisions obtaining the additional data.

Suppose that the original sample consists of N_o observations, $(y_1, x_1) \ldots (y_{N_o}, x_{N_o})$, and that the sample mean of $x_1 \ldots x_{N_o}$ is $\bar{x}_o$. Then further suppose that the sample is enlarged by adding additional observations on Y_i, but that all of these are observed with x_i equal to $\bar{x}_o$. In this case the value of $\bar{x}$ remains equal to $\bar{x}_o$, so the additional observations have no impact on the value of $\sum_{j=1}^{N} (x_j - \bar{x})^2$ and hence no impact at all on the sampling variance of $\hat{\beta}$. Clearly, $\hat{\beta}$ is not a consistent estimator if we imagine increasing the amount of sample data in this way.

Instead, suppose that the sample is enlarged by adding additional observations on Y_i which are observed for a similar mix of x_i values to that of our existing sample. For example, we might suppose that observations on Y_i are added to the sample in groups of N_o new observations – one observed with the explanatory variable equal to x_1, one with the explanatory variable equal to x_2, and so forth, with the last additional realization of Y_i in the new group observed with the explanatory variable equal to x_{No}. In that case, the value of $\bar{x}$ again remains equal to $\bar{x}_o$, but now the value of $\sum_{j=1}^{N} (x_j - \bar{x})^2$ increases by $\sum_{j=1}^{N_o} (x_j - \bar{x})^2$ with each additional group of N_o new observations, so the sampling variance of $\hat{\beta}$ becomes smaller and smaller as the sample size increases. Clearly, if we envision increasing the sample size in this way, then we can conclude that $\hat{\beta}$ is a consistent estimator of β.

6.6 PROPERTIES OF $\hat{\beta}$: BEST LINEAR UNBIASEDNESS

Remarkably, the assumptions of the Bivariate Regression Model enable us to fairly easily show that the least squares estimator of β is the best possible (i.e., the optimal) estimator of β in the sense of being "best linear unbiased" or BLU for β.

BLUness was defined in Chapter 3 as follows: an estimator is BLU if it has the smallest possible sampling variance out of the class of all unbiased estimators which are linear functions of the sample data. There it was shown that the sample mean is the BLU estimator for the population mean if the sample observations are uncorrelated and have identical means and variances.

Normality was not necessary for BLUness, but it was asserted that the sample mean has the stronger optimality property of "efficiency" if the sample observations are further assumed to be normally distributed. Recall that an estimator is efficient if it has the smallest sampling variance out of the class of all unbiased estimators, linear or not. The proof that the sample mean is the efficient estimator of the population mean was not given in Chapter 3 because it is beyond the scope of this book, but it is worth noting that efficiency is a stronger (better) optimality property than BLUness because it rules out the possibility that there is some *nonlinear* unbiased estimator which has a smaller sampling variance than the estimator under consideration.

A similar set of results is obtained here for $\hat{\beta}$. In particular, it is shown below that $\hat{\beta}$ is a BLU estimator for β. This result uses all of the Bivariate Regression Model assumptions except for the assumption that the model errors are normally distributed. It can further be shown (but is not shown here) that the additional assumption that the model errors are normally distributed allows one to conclude that $\hat{\beta}$ is also efficient for β.

First, observe that $\hat{\beta}$ is linear, because we saw that it can be written as a linear function of Y_1 ... Y_N:

$$\hat{\beta} = \sum_{i=1}^{N} w_i^{\text{ols}} Y_i \tag{6-26}$$

And $\hat{\beta}$ is unbiased, because we found that $E\left[\hat{\beta}\right] = \beta$. $\hat{\beta}$ is BLU if it is a linear and unbiased estimator of β and *if there is no other linear and unbiased estimator of β which has a smaller sampling variance.*

Using the procedure given in Chapter 5, it is quite possible to calculate the sampling variance of any particular estimator of β which is a linear function of Y_1 ... Y_N and compare it to that of $\hat{\beta}$. But how can we do this for *every possible* linear (and unbiased) estimator of β?

Surprisingly, this turns out to be fairly easy. Consider $\tilde{\beta}$, an arbitrary linear estimator of β:

$$\tilde{\beta} = \sum_{i=1}^{N} \left\{ w_i^{\text{ols}} + g_i \right\} Y_i \tag{6-27}$$

where $w_1^{\text{ols}} \ldots w_N^{\text{ols}}$ are the least squares weights defined in Equation 6-10 and g_1 ... g_N are a set of arbitrary fixed numbers. Here "fixed" means that none of the g_i depends on any of the random variables Y_1 ... Y_N. Thus, because g_1 ... g_N can be any numbers at all, any possible linear estimator of β can be expressed as $\tilde{\beta}$. Our strategy, then, is to determine what restrictions unbiasedness places on the g_1 ... g_N weights and then calculate the sampling variance of $\tilde{\beta}$ under these restrictions. We will find that the resulting expression for var($\tilde{\beta}$) makes it plain that the sampling variance of $\tilde{\beta}$ can never be smaller than that of $\tilde{\beta}$, which proves the result that $\tilde{\beta}$ is BLU.

As a first step, it is helpful to re-express $\tilde{\beta}$ in terms of the model errors, U_1 ... U_N:

$$\begin{aligned}
\tilde{\beta} &= \sum_{i=1}^{N} \left\{ w_i^{\text{ols}} + g_i \right\} Y_i \\
&= \sum_{i=1}^{N} \left\{ w_i^{\text{ols}} + g_i \right\} [\alpha + \beta x_i + U_i] \\
&= \sum_{i=1}^{N} \left\{ w_i^{\text{ols}} + g_i \right\} \alpha + \sum_{i=1}^{N} \left\{ w_i^{\text{ols}} + g_i \right\} \beta x_i + \sum_{i=1}^{N} \left\{ w_i^{\text{ols}} + g_i \right\} U_i \\
&= \alpha \sum_{i=1}^{N} \left\{ w_i^{\text{ols}} + g_i \right\} + \beta \sum_{i=1}^{N} \left\{ w_i^{\text{ols}} + g_i \right\} x_i + \sum_{i=1}^{N} \left\{ w_i^{\text{ols}} + g_i \right\} U_i \\
&= \alpha \sum_{i=1}^{N} w_i^{\text{ols}} + \alpha \sum_{i=1}^{N} g_i + \beta \sum_{i=1}^{N} w_i^{\text{ols}} x_i + \beta \sum_{i=1}^{N} g_i x_i + \sum_{i=1}^{N} \left\{ w_i^{\text{ols}} + g_i \right\} U_i \\
&= \alpha 0 + \alpha \sum_{i=1}^{N} g_i + \beta 1 + \beta \sum_{i=1}^{N} g_i x_i + \sum_{i=1}^{N} \left\{ w_i^{\text{ols}} + g_i \right\} U_i \\
&= \alpha \sum_{i=1}^{N} g_i + \beta + \beta \sum_{i=1}^{N} g_i x_i + \sum_{i=1}^{N} \left\{ w_i^{\text{ols}} + g_i \right\} U_i
\end{aligned} \tag{6-28}$$

We are only interested in estimators which are unbiased for β, regardless of the actual values of α and β. This requirement that $E[\tilde{\beta}] = \beta$ places an important restriction on the otherwise arbitrary weights, $g_1 \dots g_N$:

$$
\begin{aligned}
E[\tilde{\beta}] &= E\left[\alpha\sum_{i=1}^{N} g_i + \beta + \beta\sum_{i=1}^{N} g_i x_i + \sum_{i=1}^{N}\{w_i^{\text{ols}} + g_i\}U_i\right] \\
&= \beta + \alpha\sum_{i=1}^{N} g_i + \beta\sum_{i=1}^{N} g_i x_i + E\left[\sum_{i=1}^{N}\{w_i^{\text{ols}} + g_i\}U_i\right] \\
&= \beta + \alpha\sum_{i=1}^{N} g_i + \beta\sum_{i=1}^{N} g_i x_i + \sum_{i=1}^{N}\{w_i^{\text{ols}} + g_i\}E[U_i] \\
&= \beta + \alpha\sum_{i=1}^{N} g_i + \beta\sum_{i=1}^{N} g_i x_i + \sum_{i=1}^{N}\{w_i^{\text{ols}} + g_i\}0 \\
&= \beta + \alpha\sum_{i=1}^{N} g_i + \beta\sum_{i=1}^{N} g_i x_i
\end{aligned}
\tag{6-29}
$$

so that

$$
\tilde{\beta} - E[\tilde{\beta}] = \sum_{i=1}^{N}\{w_i^{\text{ols}} + g_i\}U_i \tag{6-30}
$$

and $\tilde{\beta}$ is unbiased for β – regardless of the actual values of α and β – if and only if the weights $g_1 \dots g_N$ satisfy the conditions $\sum_{i=1}^{N} g_i = \sum_{i=1}^{N} g_i x_i = 0$.

We seek to show that the variance of $\tilde{\beta}$ – this linear and unbiased (but otherwise arbitrary) estimator of β – can never be smaller than that of the least squares estimator. The derivation of the sampling variance of $\tilde{\beta}$ is essentially identical to that of $\hat{\beta}$, so it is abbreviated here:

$$
\begin{aligned}
\text{var}(\tilde{\beta}) &= E\left[[\tilde{\beta} - E[\tilde{\beta}]]^2\right] \\
&= E\left[\left[\sum_{i=1}^{N}(w_i^{\text{ols}} + g_i)U_i\right]^2\right] \\
&= E\left[\sum_{j=1}^{N}(w_j^{\text{ols}} + g_j)U_j \sum_{i=1}^{N}(w_i^{\text{ols}} + g_i)U_i\right] \\
&= \sigma^2\sum_{i=1}^{N}(w_i^{\text{ols}} + g_i)^2
\end{aligned}
\tag{6-31}
$$

This last step follows from exactly the same reasoning used in deriving $\hat{\beta}$ earlier in this chapter – the only difference being that "w_i^{ols}" and "w_j^{ols}" are replaced by "$w_i^{\text{ols}} + g_i$" and "$w_j^{\text{ols}} + g_j$". Thus, the variance of $\tilde{\beta}$ can be written

$$
\begin{aligned}
\operatorname{var}(\tilde{\beta}) &= \sigma^2 \sum_{i=1}^{N} \left[w_i^{\text{ols}} + g_i\right]^2 \\
&= \sigma^2 \sum_{i=1}^{N} \left[\left(w_i^{\text{ols}}\right)^2 + 2w_i^{\text{ols}} g_i + g_i^2\right] \\
&= \sigma^2 \sum_{i=1}^{N} \left(w_i^{\text{ols}}\right)^2 + 2\sigma^2 \sum_{i=1}^{N} w_i^{\text{ols}} g_i + \sigma^2 \sum_{i=1}^{N} g_i^2 \\
&= \operatorname{var}(\hat{\beta}) + 2\sigma^2 \sum_{i=1}^{N} \left[\frac{x_i - \bar{x}}{\varphi}\right] g_i + \sigma^2 \sum_{i=1}^{N} g_i^2 \qquad (6\text{-}32) \\
&= \operatorname{var}(\hat{\beta}) + \frac{2\sigma^2}{\varphi} \sum_{i=1}^{N} [x_i - \bar{x}] g_i + \sigma^2 \sum_{i=1}^{N} g_i^2 \\
&= \operatorname{var}(\hat{\beta}) + \frac{2\sigma^2}{\varphi} \sum_{i=1}^{N} g_i x_i - \frac{2\sigma^2 \bar{x}}{\varphi} \sum_{i=1}^{N} g_i + \sigma^2 \sum_{i=1}^{N} g_i^2 \\
&= \operatorname{var}(\hat{\beta}) + 0 + 0 + \sigma^2 \sum_{i=1}^{N} g_i^2
\end{aligned}
$$

where the two zeros in the above expression arise from the two unbiasedness conditions on the g_i weights, that $\sum_{i=1}^{N} g_i = \sum_{i=1}^{N} g_i x_i = 0$. Because each of the g_i^2 terms in $\sum_{i=1}^{N} g_i^2$ is necessarily non-negative, it follows that the arbitrary linear and unbiased estimator, $\tilde{\beta}$, cannot possibly have a smaller sampling variance than the least squares estimator, $\hat{\beta}$. Because $\hat{\beta}$ is linear and unbiased and no other linear and unbiased estimator can have a smaller sampling variance than it does, $\hat{\beta}$ is the best linear unbiased (BLU) estimator for β.[9]

A similar derivation yields the result that the least squares intercept estimator is BLU also; you will show this yourself in Exercise 6-10. It is worth emphasizing that both of these results (and the derivation of the sampling variance of each estimator) explicitly utilized the nonautocorrelation and homoscedasticity (but not the normality) assumptions of the Bivariate Regression Model, so we can expect these results to be sensitive to failures of those assumptions.

6.7 SUMMARY

In this chapter we have derived the sampling distributions of the least squares estimators of $\hat{\alpha}$ and $\hat{\beta}$. We found that $\hat{\beta}$ is a ***good*** estimator of β in the sense that it is unbiased, consistent, and BLU, so long as the Bivariate Regression Model assumptions are satisfied.

---

[9] Indeed, this proof shows that $\tilde{\beta}$ must have a strictly larger variance than $\hat{\beta}$, because the variances of the two estimators are equal only if all of the g_i are zero, in which case $\tilde{\beta}$ is identical to $\hat{\beta}$. As noted above, this proof did not utilize the assumption that the U_i are normally distributed. Additionally, as noted in the text, assuming normality allows one to prove a stronger result: that $\hat{\beta}$ is efficient for β. Efficiency implies that there is no other unbiased estimator of β – linear or not – with smaller sampling variance than $\hat{\beta}$. The proof that $\hat{\beta}$ is efficient is beyond the scope of this book, however.

Thus, returning to the household earnings model from the end of Chapter 5,

$$LOGEARN_i = \alpha_1 + \beta_1 collegegrad_i + N_i \qquad i = 1 \ldots 50$$
$$collegegrad_i \text{ fixed in repeated samples} \qquad (6\text{-}33)$$
$$N_i \sim NIID[0, \sigma^2]$$

we can now conclude that our least squares estimate of 0.873 for β_1 – the impact of college graduation on the expected logarithm of household earnings – is a *good* estimate in that the estimator used to obtain it (being BLU) has the smallest possible mean square error of any linear unbiased estimator for this parameter.

That is very useful. This estimate of β_1 is essentially uninterpretable, however, unless we can quantify how imprecise it is by constructing confidence intervals for β_1 based on it or unless we can use it to test hypotheses about β_1. That is the topic of the next chapter.

KEY TERMS

For each term or concept listed below, provide a working definition or explanation:

Least Squares Weights

Sampling Distribution of an Estimator

Unbiasedness

Squared Error Consistency

Best Linear Unbiasedness

Efficiency

EXERCISES

6-1. Explain the distinction between $\hat{\beta}^*$ and $\hat{\beta}$.

6-2. Which assumptions of the Bivariate Regression Model are needed in order to show that $\hat{\beta}$ is unbiased? Why is it important that $\hat{\beta}$ is unbiased? Under what circumstances would one prefer a *biased* estimator of β?

6-3. Which assumptions of the Bivariate Regression Model are needed in order to derive the expression for the sampling variance of $\hat{\beta}$?

6-4. How should one select the values for $x_1, x_2, \ldots, x_N$ so as to minimize sampling variance of $\hat{\beta}$ if the only constraint on the x_i is that they all lie in the interval from $x_{\min}$ and $x_{\max}$? What is the risk associated with choosing x_i's in this fashion?

6-5. Explain how different ways of envisioning adding more observations affects whether or not $\hat{\beta}$ is a consistent estimator of β.

6-6. Why is efficiency a stronger optimality property than BLUness?

6-7. Which assumption of the Bivariate Regression model allows one to conclude that $\hat{\beta}$ is an efficient, as well as BLU, estimator of β?

6-8. Derive the three properties of the least squares weights, $w_1^{ols} \ldots w_N^{ols}$, as stated in Equation 6-13.

6-9. Consider the sampling distribution of the ordinary least squares estimator of the intercept parameter, α.

a. Use the result that $\hat{\alpha} = \bar{Y} - \hat{\beta}\bar{x}$ to show that

$$\hat{\alpha} = \sum_{i=1}^{N} \left(\frac{1}{N} - \bar{x} w_i^{\text{ols}} \right) Y_i$$

b. Use the properties of the least squares weights to show that

$$\hat{\alpha} = \alpha + \sum_{i=1}^{N} \left(\frac{1}{N} - \bar{x} w_i^{\text{ols}} \right) U_i$$

c. Use the result of part b (and the assumptions of the Bivariate Regression Model) to show that

$$\hat{\alpha} \sim N\left[\alpha, \frac{\sigma^2}{N}\left(1 + \frac{N\bar{x}^2}{\varphi}\right)\right]$$

d. Use the result of part b (and the assumptions of the Bivariate Regression Model) to show that $\text{cov}(\hat{\alpha}, \hat{\beta}) = -\sigma^2 \bar{x}/\varphi$.

e. Sketch a scatterplot of data $(y_1, x_1) \ldots (y_{20}, x_{20})$ in which α and β are both positive and for which $\bar{x}$ is negative, and use it to rationalize the sign of your result for $\text{cov}(\hat{\alpha}, \hat{\beta})$ in part d.

6-10. Using your result in Exercise 6-9, show that $\hat{\alpha}$, the OLS estimator of α in the Bivariate Regression Model, is consistent and BLU.

6-11. Consider the no-intercept regression model:

$$Y_i = \beta x_i + U_i \quad U_i \sim NIID(0, \sigma^2)$$

with the x_i fixed in repeated samples. This model is not suitable for use with real data, because – since it does not contain an intercept – the assumption that $E[U_i]$ equals zero could easily fail, leading to a biased ordinary least squares parameter estimator for β. It is suitable for use in exercises such as this one, however, because it is both a little different from what is done in the text itself and involves less algebra.

a. Sketch how a scatterplot of, say, 10 observations on (Y_i, x_i) might look if there is a direct, only somewhat noisy, relationship between Y_i and x_i. Include the population regression line (based on β) and a fitted line (based on the estimate $\hat{\beta}$). Note that the fitted line for this model is constrained to run through the origin. Explicitly indicate the model error and fitting error for one particular observation.

b. Derive an expression for the sum of squared fitting errors, $\text{SSE}(\hat{\beta}^{\text{guess}})$ for this model and explicitly minimize it to obtain an expression for the (realized) least squares estimator of β, $\hat{\beta}^*$.

c. Show that $\hat{\beta}^*$ is a linear estimator, obtain the least squares weights and their properties, and derive the relationship between $\hat{\beta}$, β, and $U_1 \ldots U_N$.

d. Derive the sampling distribution of $\hat{\beta}$, showing that $\hat{\beta}$ is unbiased so long as $E[U_i]$ equals zero for all observations. Is this expectation necessarily zero for this model? Which of the model assumptions were *not* needed in order to show that $\hat{\beta}$ is unbiased? Which of the model assumptions were *not* needed in order to calculate the sampling variance of $\hat{\beta}$?

e. Show that $\hat{\beta}$ is consistent so long as a mixture of new x_i values are used as the sample length is increased.

f. Show that $\hat{\beta}$ is BLU. Which of the model assumptions were *not* needed for this result?

6-12. Suppose that there are four sample observations on y_i and x_i:

y	x
3.5	1.0
−3.2	−1.0
−.3	0
.3	0

and that you are willing to assume (as in Exercise 6-11) that

$$Y_i = \beta x_i + U_i \quad U_i \sim \text{NIID}(0, \sigma^2)$$

a. Sketch a scatterplot for these data.

b. State the OLS estimator, $\hat{\beta}$, explicitly as a weighted sum of Y_1, Y_2, Y_3, and Y_4, exhibiting the numerical values for the weights.

c. Substitute in the observed values for Y_1, Y_2, Y_3, and Y_4 – i.e., y_1, y_2, y_3, and y_4 – so as to obtain a numerical value for $\hat{\beta}^*$. {Hint: $\hat{\beta}^*$ equals 3.35.}

d. Calculate the fitting errors $u_1^{\text{fit}} \ldots u_4^{\text{fit}}$ and SSE(b) for $b = 3.60$, 3.35, and 3.00, completing the table below. {Here "b" is used to denote a value for the estimator of β which is not necessarily the OLS estimator. Thus, $u_i^{\text{fit}} = y_i - bx_i$.}

e. Are your results on SSE(b) in this table consistent with $\hat{\beta}^*$ equaling 3.35?

b	u_1^{fit}	u_2^{fit}	u_3^{fit}	u_4^{fit}	SSE(b)
3.60					
3.35					
3.00					

f. Do you notice anything a bit strange about the values you obtain for u_3^{fit} and u_4^{fit}? What does this result imply about the impact of the observations y_3 and y_4 on $\hat{\beta}^*$? Are the values you obtained in part b for w_3^{ols} and w_4^{ols} consistent with this implication?

g. Check your calculations by entering the data into Excel (or whatever econometric software is being used in your course) and estimating a model with no intercept.[10]

[10] In Excel, check the "constant is zero" box. In Stata, type the data into the cells of the data editor and estimate the regression equation using the command "reg *y x*, noconstant".

Active Learning Exercise 6a: Outliers and Other Perhaps Overly Influential Observations: Investigating the Sensitivity of $\hat{\beta}$ to an Outlier Using Computer-Generated Data

Introduction

In this exercise you will first use least squares fitting to estimate the parameter β in the Bivariate Regression Model:

$$Y_i = \alpha + \beta x_i + U_i \quad U_i \sim \text{NIID}[0, \sigma^2]$$

using data generated from this model with α set to zero and β set to one. Then you will modify these data to have an outlier in the 22nd observation by substantially decreasing the value of y_{22}, observing how the scatterplot and the least squares estimate of β change as a result. You will also examine how the impact of an outlier of given size declines as the sample size increases. Finally, you will examine how the impact of such an outlier is dramatically mitigated by using an alternative regression procedure, which minimizes the sample sum of the absolute values of the fitting errors rather than minimizing the sample sum of the squared fitting errors.

This alternative regression technique is referred to in the text as "least absolute deviation" or "LAD" regression, but it goes by many names: "least absolute value regression," "robust regression," "median regression," and "minimum L1-norm regression." As you will demonstrate for yourself in this exercise, LAD regression estimates are relatively robust to outliers. But they have several disadvantages. For one thing, the LAD parameter estimates have no small-sample optimality properties: they are neither efficient nor BLU. For another, their sampling distributions are only known for large samples, so the hypothesis testing and confidence interval results we will obtain in Chapter 7 for the OLS estimates will not be available for the LAD estimates, except in large samples.

The detection and treatment of outliers will be discussed further in Chapter 10, as part of the diagnostic checking of the Multiple Regression Model. Two points are worth mentioning here, however:

a. The best "treatment" for an apparent outlier is to figure out why it is present. Was there an error in measuring or entering this observation, (y_i, x_i)? Does this outlier represent an interesting or important anomaly in the sample? For example, some years ago the author was modeling the inflation rate, as measured by the monthly growth rate in the Consumer Price Index, and observed an obvious outlier in the series in the early 1970s. No data entry error was found but, on investigation, it turned out that this was the month in which President Nixon ended price controls on food products. Thus, the appropriate treatment in this case was clearly to model the fact that the intercept in the regression would be expected to shift upward for that month, rather than to ameliorate the symptom of the outlier using LAD regression.[11]

b. If there appear to be several outliers in a particular sample, it is usually *not* a good idea to model them – in such instances the apparent "outliers" are usually the ordinary result of a

[11] Indeed, in this (and several examples in Chapter 10) modeling such an intercept shift can provide the most economically interesting result of the analysis.

model error term whose distribution has "fat tails" compared to those of the gaussian distribution.

Your Assignment:

1. Copy the data file ALE6a.csv (available at www.wiley.com/college/ashley) to your hard disk and read it in to Excel or whatever econometrics software your course is using. If you are using Stata, you can use ALE6a.dta.
2. Using 25, 50, 100, and 500 of the observations on Y and x in this data set, make scatterplots and estimate β in the Bivariate Regression Model.[12] Enter the resulting values of $\hat{\beta}^{OLS}$ (to three decimal places) in the column of the table below which is labeled "$y_{22} = 1.998$."
3. Now use your econometrics software to generate two new dependent variables ("ymodestoutlier" and "ybigoutlier") which are equal to y except that observation number 22 is decreased to -2.0 and -10.0, respectively.[13] Again make scatterplots for all four sample sizes, but now print out all eight scatterplots. Does the 22nd observation now stand out as odd in the scatterplots?
4. Next estimate β again using ymodestoutlier and ybigoutlier instead of y for all four sample sizes, entering the resulting $\hat{\beta}^{OLS}$ values into the appropriate column of the table. Is the value of $\hat{\beta}^{OLS}$ noticeably affected by these outliers?
5. What happens to the impact of the outlier on $\hat{\beta}^{OLS}$ as the sample length increases to 500?
6. Finally – if the econometric software you are using supports it – re-estimate β in each case using Least Absolute Deviations estimation and complete the rest of the table.[14] What impact does the outlier in y_i have on $\hat{\beta}^{LAD}$?

N	$y_{22} = 1.998$		$y_{22} = -2.000$		$y_{22} = -10.000$	
	$\hat{\beta}^{OLS}$	$\hat{\beta}^{LAD}$	$\hat{\beta}^{OLS}$	$\hat{\beta}^{LAD}$	$\hat{\beta}^{OLS}$	$\hat{\beta}^{LAD}$
25						
50						
100						
500						

Epilogue on outliers and other perhaps overly influential observations

Ultimately, what's unfortunate about an outlier is that such an observation makes $\hat{\beta}^{OLS}$ inordinately sensitive to a single sample observation – (y_{22}, x_{22}), say. In contrast, the βx_i term in the Bivariate Regression Model bespeaks of a stable statistical regularity in how fluctuations in the explanatory variable impact Y_i over the *entire* sample, support for which

[12] In Stata the relevant commands for using the first 50 observations would be "scatter y x if _n<=50" and "reg y x if _n<=50", respectively.

[13] This could be done in Stata using the commands, "gen ymodestoutlier = y" and replace ymodestoutlier = –2. if _n == 22".

[14] In Stata this amounts to replacing "reg" by "qreg" in the regression command. Note that qreg is still very fast, but that the LAD coefficient estimators are neither BLU nor even unbiased: they are only consistent. Thus, using qreg with only 25 or 50 observations is problematic – certainly, the LAD coefficient standard error estimates are not reliable for samples this small. Notably, Stata (and similar programs) give no warning of this.

should therefore be more or less evident *throughout* the sample. Put differently, we ideally want what you might call a "broad consensus" from the data set as to the value of β, rather than a $\hat{\beta}^*$ mostly determined by an extreme "opinion" from a single observation.

Recall that

$$\hat{\beta}^* = \sum_{i=1}^{N} w_i^{ols} y_i \quad \text{where} \quad w_i^{ols} = \frac{x_i - \bar{x}}{\sum_{i=1}^{N} (x_i - \bar{x})^2}$$

Thus, $\hat{\beta}^*$ will depend inordinately on, for example, the 22nd observation if and only if the magnitude of the $w_{22}^{ols} y_{22}$ term in this sum is large compared to the rest of the sum.

Looked at this way, it is then obvious why the impact of a single outlier dwindles as N increases. Aside from that, however, this result also makes it plain that there are actually ***two*** ways that the 22nd observation can be exceptionally influential: $|w_{22}^{ols} y_{22}|$ can be overwhelmingly large if either

$$\text{(a)} \quad |y_{22}| \gg 0$$

or

$$\text{(b)} \quad |x_{22} - \bar{x}| \gg 0$$

This Active Learning Exercise has explored the consequence of a very large value for y_{22}. This is what we ordinarily term "an outlier." And this is what we usually seek to detect, explain, remove, or ameliorate the impact of, as being due to a transcription error or a unique historical incident. The second source of this kind of sensitivity of $\hat{\beta}^*$ to the single observation (y_{22}, x_{22}) – a particularly large value for $|x_{22} - \bar{x}|$ – is more benign, but still awkward.

The upshot of this second source is that observations on the dependent variable made based on a value for the explanatory variable well away from its sample mean are simply more influential in determining the value of $\hat{\beta}^*$. Indeed, a realization of Y_i observed with x_i equal to $\bar{x}$ has no impact on $\hat{\beta}^*$ at all.[15]

This result is in accordance with common sense: Since β quantifies the sensitivity of $E[Y_i]$ to changes in x_i, of course we learn more about β from observations on Y_i made with more extreme values of x_i. Indeed, recall that this is why the precision with which we can estimate β, as quantified by the sampling variance of $\hat{\beta}$, depends inversely on the degree of sample variation in $x_1 \ldots x_N$. It is also why – as seen in the text immediately prior to this exercise – one obtains the smallest sampling variance by choosing to sample Y_i using the most extreme values possible for $x_1 \ldots x_N$. In an important and meaningful sense, sampling the random variable Y_i for a large value of $|x_i - \bar{x}|$ corresponds to observing the outcome of a particularly well-designed and informative experiment.

Still, it is simply not wise to base one's estimate of β primarily on a single (y_i, x_i) observation. For this reason, it is a good idea to make a histogram of the x_i data and to be concerned if there are one or two values of $|x_i - \bar{x}|$ which are inordinately large.

[15] Evidently, such y_i observations are irrelevant to our enterprise, except insofar as their observed fitting errors provide data useful for estimating σ^2, the variance of the model error term. In Chapter 7 we will see that estimation of σ^2 is essential in practice for obtaining confidence intervals for β and for testing hypotheses about β.

7

The Bivariate Linear Regression Model: Inference on β

7.1 INTRODUCTION

The last two chapters concentrated on the estimation of the slope parameter β in the Bivariate Regression Model and on using the assumptions of the model to derive the sampling distribution of $\hat{\beta}$, the least squares estimator of β. This sampling distribution was then used to show that $\hat{\beta}$ is unbiased, consistent, and BLU. In this chapter, the sampling distribution of $\hat{\beta}$ is used to derive confidence intervals and hypothesis tests for β. (You will obtain analogous inference results for the intercept parameter, α, in Exercise 7-9.)

Most frequently, the main point of estimating regression model parameters is to test hypotheses about them, hypotheses which correspond to the predictions of either formal or informal economic theories. For example, it is apparent from the scatterplot Dollar and Kraay obtained in the World Bank study described in Chapter 1 that there is a direct relationship between "*meangrow*," the growth rate in a country's real GDP per capita, and "*poorgrow*," the corresponding growth rate in real GDP per capita going to the poorest 20% of the country's population as in Figure 7-1.

But the most interesting question which Dollar and Kraay's work raises about this relationship is whether or not the slope of this relationship is or is not one: if the slope is one, then the poor share equally in economic growth, and growth can be taken to be "income distribution neutral." This economic question corresponds to a specific hypothesis about the coefficient β in the particular Bivariate Regression Model,

$$POORGROW_i = \alpha + \beta\, meangrow_i + U_i \tag{7-1}$$

Using the most recent observations on the 92 countries in Dollar and Kraay's sample, the least squares estimate of β in this model is 1.31. This estimate noticeably exceeds one, indicating that the poor actually benefit disproportionately from economic growth. For example, this result implies that the poor in a country whose per capita real growth rate rises 3% (from, say, 1.0% to 4.0%) will, on average, experience a 3.9% rise in their per capita real growth rate. If it is real, this result is clearly economically significant.

But the meaningfulness of this result depends crucially on the accuracy of the estimate of β on which it is based. After all, with only 92 observations – and quite a bit of apparent noise in the scatterplot – one might legitimately wonder whether the difference between one and this sample estimate of β is just an artifact of the noise in the individual observations. In other words, there is

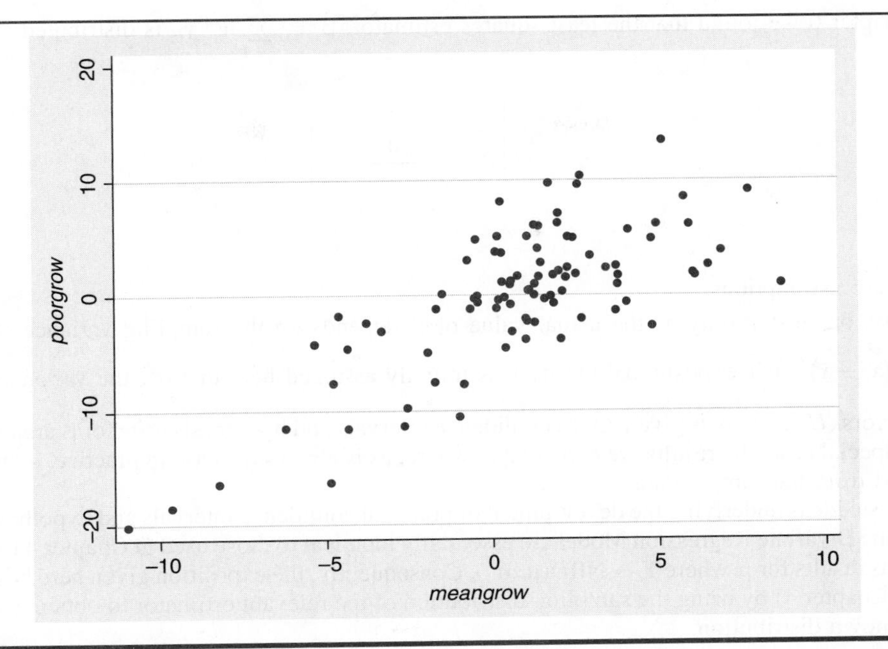

Figure 7-1 Stata Scatterplot of $poorgrow_i$ versus $meangrow_i$ Data.

considerable room to doubt whether or not the difference between the sample estimate of 1.31 and one is *statistically* significant.

Addressing that doubt – by showing how to explicitly test the null hypothesis that β equals one – is one of the key topics of the present chapter. The other key topic of this chapter – showing how to quantify the uncertainty as to the true value of β via an estimated confidence interval for β – effectively addresses the issue of economic significance by exhibiting the degree to which an estimated confidence interval for β includes a range of values which differ from one in their *economic* significance.

The assumptions of the Bivariate Regression Model, discussed in Chapter 5, can be summarized as follows:

The Bivariate Regression Model

$$Y_i = \alpha + \beta x_i + U_i \quad i = 1 \dots N$$

Assumptions:

x_i fixed in repeated samples

and (7-2)

$$U_i \sim \text{NIID}[0, \sigma^2] \text{ or } \begin{bmatrix} U_i \text{ normally distributed} \\ E[U_i] = 0 \\ E[U_i^2] = \sigma^2 \\ E[U_i U_j] = 0 \quad \text{if } i \neq j \end{bmatrix}$$

In Chapter 6 we found that the least squares estimator, $\hat{\beta} = \sum_{i=1}^{N} w_i^{ols} y_i$, is distributed

$$\hat{\beta} \sim N\left[\beta, \frac{\sigma^2}{\sum_{j=1}^{N}(x_j - \bar{x})^2}\right] \tag{7-3}$$

under these assumptions.

Clearly, our uncertainty as the actual value of β depends on the sampling variance of $\hat{\beta}$, or $\sigma^2 / \sum_{j=1}^{N}(x_j - \bar{x})^2$. For expositional clarity it is initially assumed here that σ^2, the variance of the model errors (U_1 ... U_N), is given. Once confidence intervals and hypothesis tests for β are obtained for this special case, the results are extended to where, as is always the case in practice, σ^2 must be estimated from the sample data.

The basic ideas underlying the development of practical confidence intervals and hypothesis tests for β in the Bivariate Regression Model are essentially identical to those used in Chapter 4 to obtain analogous results for μ where $Y_i \sim \text{NIID}(\mu, \sigma^2)$. Consequently, the exposition given here begins (as it did in Chapter 4) by using the sampling distribution of the relevant estimator to obtain a statistic with a known distribution.

7.2 A STATISTIC FOR β WITH A KNOWN DISTRIBUTION

Here, the relevant estimator, of course, is $\hat{\beta}$. The expression for its sampling distribution given above proved very useful in Chapter 6 for deriving the properties of $\hat{\beta}$, but it is more convenient to work with the unit normal distribution for inference purposes. Subtracting the mean of $\hat{\beta}$ and dividing by the square root of its variance standardizes $\hat{\beta}$ to zero mean and unit variance, yielding

$$\frac{\hat{\beta} - \beta}{\sqrt{\sigma^2 / \sum_{j=1}^{N}(x_j - \bar{x})^2}} \sim N[0, 1] \tag{7-4}$$

7.3 A 95% CONFIDENCE INTERVAL FOR β WITH σ^2 GIVEN

Recall from Chapter 2 that by definition, a unit normal variate exceeds its 2½% critical point ($z^c_{.025}$, or 1.96) with probability .025 and is also less than its 97½% critical point ($z^c_{.975}$, or −1.96) with probability 1 − .975 or .025. Thus, a unit normal variate lies in between these two critical points with probability .95, as illustrated in Figure 7-2.

Therefore, with probability .95,

$$z^c_{.975} \leq \frac{\hat{\beta} - \beta}{\sqrt{\sigma^2 / \sum_{j=1}^{N}(x_j - \bar{x})^2}} \leq z^c_{.025} \tag{7-5}$$

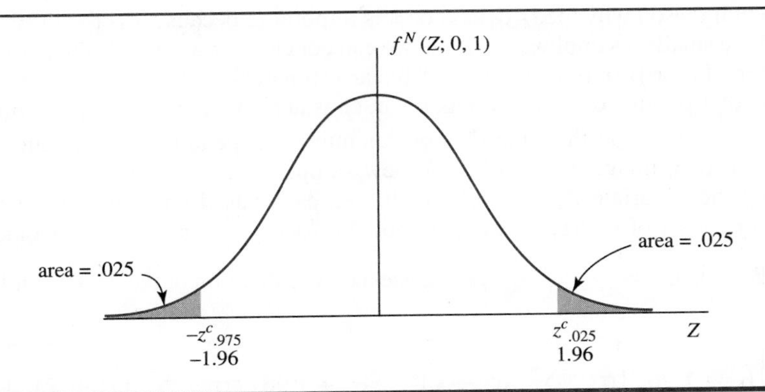

Figure 7-2 Unit Normal Density Function with Critical Points Illustrated

or, equivalently,

$$-1.96 \leq \frac{\hat{\beta} - \beta}{\sqrt{\sigma^2 / \sum_{j=1}^{N} (x_j - \bar{x})^2}} \leq 1.96 \tag{7-6}$$

It follows that, also with probability .95,

$$-1.96\sqrt{\sigma^2/\sum_{j=1}^{N}(x_j - \bar{x})^2} \;\leq\; \hat{\beta} - \beta \;\leq\; 1.96\sqrt{\sigma^2/\sum_{j=1}^{N}(xX_j - \bar{x})^2}$$

$$-\hat{\beta} - 1.96\sqrt{\sigma^2/\sum_{j=1}^{N}(x_j - \bar{x})^2} \;\leq\; -\beta \;\leq\; -\hat{\beta} + 1.96\sqrt{\sigma^2/\sum_{j=1}^{N}(x_j - \bar{x})^2} \tag{7-7}$$

$$\hat{\beta} + 1.96\sqrt{\sigma^2/\sum_{j=1}^{N}(x_j - \bar{x})^2} \;\geq\; \beta \;\geq\; \hat{\beta} - 1.96\sqrt{\sigma^2/\sum_{j=1}^{N}(x_j - \bar{x})^2}$$

so that the interval

$$\left[\hat{\beta} - 1.96\sqrt{\sigma^2/\sum_{j=1}^{N}(x_j - \bar{x})^2},\quad \hat{\beta} + 1.96\sqrt{\sigma^2/\sum_{j=1}^{N}(x_j - \bar{x})^2}\right] \tag{7-8}$$

contains β with probability .95 – i.e., it is a 95% confidence interval for β. Of course, if any of the assumptions of the Bivariate Regression Model are invalid – i.e., the x_i are not fixed or the U_i are not distributed NIID[0, σ^2] – then this interval will *not* in general contain β with probability .95.

The derivation of a 99% confidence interval is essentially identical, only using the ½% critical point, $z^c_{.005}$, or 2.57, instead of $z^c_{.025}$. Clearly, this interval must be wider – by a factor of 2.57/1.96 – so as to contain β with the specified higher probability.

Note also, that the unbiasedness of $\hat{\beta}$ was necessary in order to standardize $\hat{\beta}$ to zero mean in Section 7.2, and that the derivation given above makes it plain that the width of any confidence interval for β based on $\hat{\beta}$ is proportional to the square root of the sampling variance of $\hat{\beta}$. Indeed, this is the fundamental reason why the BLUness of $\hat{\beta}$ is important: because it is the linear and unbiased estimator with the smallest sampling variance, we can conclude that $\hat{\beta}$ yields the narrowest possible confidence intervals for β out of the class of linear estimators.

Finally, note that β is a fixed, though unknown, constant. The .95 or .99 "probability" involved here stems from the fact that the endpoints of this interval depend on the random variable $\hat{\beta}$. To better understand this, imagine that a billion new samples (y_1 ... y_N) were to be obtained, each generated using the Bivariate Regression Model: i.e., each based on combining the same values x_1 ... x_N with a new set of realizations of the model errors. Each such sample would yield a new realization of $\hat{\beta}$ – i.e., $\hat{\beta}^* = \sum_{i=1}^{N} w_i^{ols} y_i$ – and hence a new realization of the 95% confidence interval:

$$\left[\hat{\beta}^* - 1.96\sqrt{\sigma^2 / \sum_{j=1}^{N} (x_j - \bar{x})^2},\quad \hat{\beta}^* + 1.96\sqrt{\sigma^2 / \sum_{j=1}^{N} (x_j - \bar{x})^2}\right] \tag{7-9}$$

Then we could expect that close to 95% of these billion realized confidence intervals would contain β, but that 5% of the $\hat{\beta}^*$ realizations would be so unusually large or small that the resulting confidence interval would fail to contain the (fixed) value β.

7.4 ESTIMATES VERSUS ESTIMATORS AND THE ROLE OF THE MODEL ASSUMPTIONS

Because it is so crucial to understanding the meaning of the 95% confidence interval for β derived in the previous section, it is well at this point to re-emphasize and expand a bit on the distinction between the least squares estimator of β, which is the random variable:

$$\hat{\beta} = \sum_{i=1}^{N} w_i^{ols} Y_i \sim N\left[\beta, \frac{\sigma^2}{\sum_{j=1}^{N} (x_j - \bar{x})^2}\right] \tag{7-10}$$

and its sample realization, the parameter estimate:

$$\hat{\beta}^* = \sum_{i=1}^{N} w_i^{ols} y_i = \frac{\sum_{i=1}^{N} (x_i - \bar{x})(y_i - \bar{y})}{\sum_{j=1}^{N} (x_j - \bar{x})^2} \tag{7-11}$$

The estimate $\hat{\beta}^*$ is a fixed number which can be explicitly calculated from the observed sample data, (y_1, x_1) ... (y_N, x_N), using the above formula.[1] It was obtained in Chapter 5 by fitting a straight line to the observed sample data so as to minimize the sum of squared fitting errors. Recall that the derivation of this formula made no use of any of the Bivariate Regression Model assumptions except for the restriction that the expectation of the dependent variable is a linear function of observed values of the explanatory variable, x_i.

This formula for $\hat{\beta}^*$ and the numerical result of applying it to the sample data thus have nothing to do with the assumption that the x_i are fixed in repeated samples nor with the assumption that the

[1] In contrast, the estimator $\hat{\beta}$ is a random variable, because it depends on the variables Y_1 ... Y_N, which the model specifies as depending on the normally distributed model errors, U_1 ... U_N.

model errors are distributed NIID(0, σ^2). We are consequently free to substitute the observed sample data into this formula – either by hand or using computer software – with no regard for whether or not these assumptions are remotely valid approximations to the way in which the data were generated.

However, what we get in that case is a sample estimate of β with only one property: it corresponds to the slope of the straight line which best fits the sample data. We know nothing additional in that case about quality of this estimate; nor can we say anything quantitatively meaningful about how accurate or inaccurate this estimate is; nor can we use this estimate to draw any meaningful inferences about whether or not β equals any specified value.

In sharp contrast, if we are willing (and sensibly able) to make the additional assumptions constituting the Bivariate Regression Model – i.e., that the x_i are fixed in repeated samples and that the model errors are distributed NIID(0, σ^2) – then we saw in Chapter 6 that this sample estimate $\hat{\beta}^*$ is a realization of the random variable $\hat{\beta}$, with the particular distribution given above. In that case we can meaningfully assert that $\hat{\beta}^*$ represents a good – indeed, in the sense of being BLU, an optimal – use of the sample data. Moreover, it has just been shown that we can in that case further use $\hat{\beta}^*$ to compute a 95% confidence interval which meaningfully quantifies the uncertainty with which $\hat{\beta}^*$ estimates β, and (shortly) we will additionally see how to use $\hat{\beta}^*$ to meaningfully test specific hypotheses about the value of β.

Note that the formula for the endpoints of the 95% confidence interval is still just an algebraic expression,

$$\hat{\beta}^* \pm 1.96\sqrt{\sigma^2 / \sum_{j=1}^{N} (x_j - \bar{x})^2} \tag{7-12}$$

which (with σ^2, for the moment, artificially given) can be easily evaluated using a computer program – **regardless of whether the assumptions underlying the derivation of our interpretation of it are valid or not**. Thus, the confidence interval endpoints can (and will!) be computed by the software regardless – the only problem is that the computed interval will not in fact contain β with the specified probability unless the model assumptions are satisfied. The econometric software is inherently oblivious to this issue – a sensitivity to the likely validity (or otherwise) of the model assumptions is **our** responsibility.

As we have just seen in the previous section, then, reliance on the model assumptions allows us to generalize from our particular sample data to make statements (such as the assertion that $\hat{\beta}$ is BLU or that a confidence interval based on $\hat{\beta}^*$ will contain β with specified probability) pertaining to what *would* happen were we able to observe additional samples of N observations. But of what practical use is this if we do not know whether the model assumptions are valid?

The simple, honest answer is: it *isn't* of all that much use in tiny samples. If N is very small, then the validity of the optimality and inference results developed above rests crucially on assumptions which can only be taken on faith. If N is not so small, however, most of the model assumptions can be at least approximately checked using the sample data itself; moreover, we can usually in that case at least approximately fix whatever deviations from the assumptions that we find.

This topic of using the sample data to both check the model assumptions and to respecify the model, if necessary, so that these assumptions are reasonably consistent with the observed data is taken up in detail in Chapters 10 and 13, under the heading of diagnostically checking a regression model. Feel free to skip ahead to that material now if you like; here, however, it is more appropriate to continue developing the practical results implied by the Bivariate Regression Model assumptions. In particular, it is now time to explicitly consider how to use $\hat{\beta}^*$ to test specific hypotheses about the value of β; then it will be necessary to deal with the fact that σ^2 is not known.

7.5 TESTING A HYPOTHESIS ABOUT β WITH σ^2 GIVEN

A particular null hypothesis about β, such as $H_o : \beta = 3$, can be tested against the alternative hypothesis, $H_A : \beta \neq 3$, using the result that the assumptions of the Bivariate Regression Model imply that the test statistic

$$\frac{\hat{\beta} - 3}{\sqrt{\sigma^2 / \sum_{j=1}^{N} (x_j - \bar{x})^2}} \sim N[0, 1] \tag{7-13}$$

under this null hypothesis. This test statistic is therefore a unit normal if and only if the null hypothesis is true. Recalling that σ^2 is (for the moment) given, a realization of this test statistic,

$$\frac{\hat{\beta}^* - 3}{\sqrt{\sigma^2 / \sum_{j=1}^{N} (x_j - \bar{x})^2}} \tag{7-14}$$

can be computed from the sample data and compared to the density function of the unit normal distribution.

The magnitude of this observed test statistic clearly depends on the size of the discrepancy between the sample realization of the unbiased estimator of β – i.e., $\hat{\beta}^*$ – and the claimed value of β under the null hypothesis. If the magnitude of the realized value of this unit normal test statistic is observed to be larger than five, for example, then it is pretty obvious that something is wrong; the chance of drawing a realization from the unit normal distribution greater than five in magnitude is only about one in a million. Clearly, in such a case either (a) at least one of the assumptions of the Bivariate Regression Model is not valid for these sample data or (b) the null hypothesis is false. Maintaining the assumptions of the model, one would thus in that case reject the null hypothesis and accept the alternative hypothesis, that $\beta \neq 3$.

For a less extreme discrepancy between $\hat{\beta}^*$ and the claimed value of β under the null hypothesis, it is informative to compute the "*p*-value" – the probability that a discrepancy of this magnitude (or larger) could arise due to chance, even though the null hypothesis (and the maintained assumptions of the Bivariate Regression Model) are all correct. The *p*-value can also be interpreted as the probability that one would wrongly reject the null hypothesis, were one to decide to reject the null hypothesis whenever the sample evidence against it is at least this strong.

For the unit normal test statistic given at the beginning of this section, this *p*-value is just the probability of observing a unit normal random variable larger in magnitude than the magnitude of the observed test statistic:

$$\left| \frac{\hat{\beta}^* - 3}{\sqrt{\sigma^2 / \sum_{j=1}^{N} (x_j - \bar{x})^2}} \right| \tag{7-15}$$

Suppose, for example, that this test statistic is observed to be 1.8. The tail area of the unit normal distribution to the right of 1.8 is .036; because the gaussian distribution is symmetric around its mean, this implies that the tail area to the left of -1.8 is also .036, as illustrated in Figure 7-3.

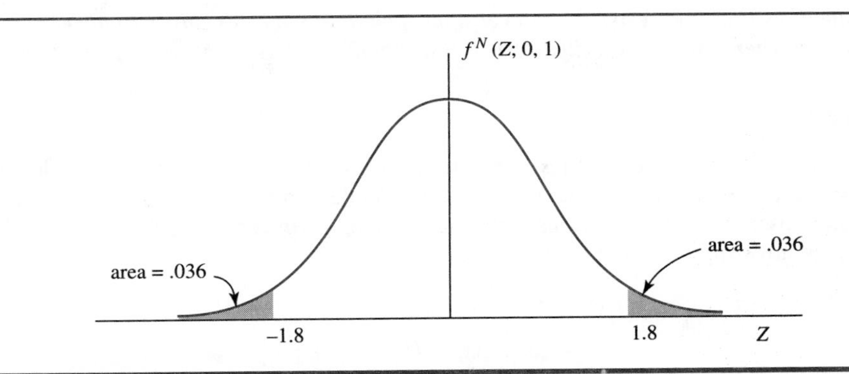

Figure 7-3 Unit Normal Density with Tail Areas Illustrated

Thus, the null hypothesis can in this instance be rejected with p-value .072 or "at the 7% level of significance." If the null hypothesis is rejected, there is a 7% chance that $H_o : \beta = 3$ is actually true and that this hypothesis is being wrongly rejected due to the fact that the observed value of $\hat{\beta}^*$ leading to this test statistic value is an unusual realization of the random variable $\hat{\beta}$.

It is customary to reject the null hypothesis only when the implied p-value is less than .05. This custom has the advantage of eliminating the need to compute tail areas for the unit normal distribution – one simply rejects the null hypothesis ("at the 5% level") whenever the unit normal test statistic exceeds the 2½% critical point ($z^c_{.025}$, or 1.96). Many years ago the computations involved in computing adequate approximations for the tail areas under the unit normal density function were substantial, so this was a real advantage. With modern computing equipment, however, that is no longer the case. Moreover, this custom is more than a little arbitrary: in some circumstances a 5% chance of wrongly rejecting the null hypothesis is an acceptable risk, in others it is not. Consequently it is certainly more informative and usually preferable to quote the p-value for the test. Moreover, in view of the fact that modern econometric software typically computes the p-values for us in any case, it is usually not even any more trouble.

The hypothesis testing procedure just described is called the "two-tailed" test, because the computation of the p-value includes both tails of the distribution, allowing for the possibility of wrongly rejecting the null due to either a positive or a negative (chance) deviation of $\hat{\beta}^*$ from the value for β specified in the null hypothesis. Occasionally a one-tailed test is appropriate. Suppose that the economic theory one is testing rules out the possibility that β is less than 3. It is appropriate in that case to augment the Bivariate Regression Model assumptions with the parameter restriction $\beta \geq 3$ and test the null hypothesis $H_o : \beta = 3$ against the alternative hypothesis, $H_A : \beta > 3$. The null hypothesis (and the distribution of the test statistic given at the beginning of this section) are unchanged, so this test statistic is still distributed as a unit normal under the null hypothesis. One can expect, therefore, that $\hat{\beta}^* - 3$ will be negative about half of the time if the null hypothesis is true. But such deviations are no longer evidence against the null hypothesis and should never yield a rejection of it – rather, the null hypothesis will be rejected only when $\hat{\beta}^* - 3$ is sufficiently positive. Consequently, in this instance, the p-value – the probability of wrongly rejecting the null hypothesis – will consist only of the tail area to the right of the observed value of the test statistic. In effect, the p-value is halved in exchange for increasing the content of the model assumptions.

Note, however, that a policy of testing the alternative assumption $H_A : \beta > 3$ when $\hat{\beta}^*$ exceeds 3 and testing the alternative assumption $H_A : \beta < 3$ when $\hat{\beta}^*$ is less than 3 is equivalent to doing the two-tailed test; in that case the p-value must include the area in both tails if it is to correctly quantify the probability of wrongly rejecting the null hypothesis. ***This issue often arises when the null***

hypothesis specifies that β is zero – it is never appropriate in such instances to observe that $\hat{\beta}^*$ is positive, say, and then use a one-tailed test to test whether "$\hat{\beta}^*$ is significantly positive"!

7.6 ESTIMATING σ^2

When – as is ordinarily the case – σ^2 is unknown, it must be estimated from the sample data. But how can $\sigma^2 = \text{var}(U_i)$ be estimated when the regression model errors, $U_1 \ldots U_N$, are not observable? The U_i's are not observed, but realizations of the least squares fitting errors, $U_1^{\text{fit}} \ldots U_N^{\text{fit}}$, are. Note that the fitting errors are simply related to the model errors:

$$
\begin{aligned}
U_i^{\text{fit}} &= Y_i - [\hat{\alpha} + \hat{\beta} x_i] \\
&= [\alpha + \beta x_i + U_i] - [\hat{\alpha} + \hat{\beta} x_i] \\
&= U_i - [\hat{\alpha} - \alpha] - [\hat{\beta} x_i - \beta x_i] \\
&= U_i - [\hat{\alpha} - \alpha] - x_i[\hat{\beta} - \beta]
\end{aligned} \tag{7-16}
$$

Recall from Chapter 6 that $\hat{\alpha}$ and $\hat{\beta}$ are consistent estimators of α and β, respectively. This followed from the fact that each estimator is unbiased and has sampling variance that disappears as the sample size grows large. Consequently, for sufficiently large N, the sampling errors $\hat{\alpha} - \alpha$ and $\hat{\beta} - \beta$ are almost always negligible. The fitting errors, $U_1^{\text{fit}} \ldots U_N^{\text{fit}}$, thus become extremely good approximations for the regression errors ($U_1 \ldots U_N$) as N becomes very large.[2]

Therefore, defining

$$S^2 \equiv \frac{1}{N-2} \sum_{i=1}^{N} \left(U_i^{\text{fit}}\right)^2 \tag{7-17}$$

it follows that for large N,

$$S^2 \approx \frac{1}{N-2} \sum_{i=1}^{N} U_i^2 \tag{7-18}$$

Hence, the expected value of S^2 is

$$
\begin{aligned}
E[S^2] &\approx E\left[\frac{1}{N-2} \sum_{i=1}^{N} U_i^2\right] \\
&\approx \frac{1}{N-2} \sum_{i=1}^{N} E\left[U_i^2\right] \\
&\approx \frac{1}{N-2} \sum_{i=1}^{N} \sigma^2 \\
&\approx \frac{N}{N-2} \sigma^2 \approx \sigma^2
\end{aligned} \tag{7-19}
$$

[2] The consistency of $\hat{\alpha}$ is shown in Exercise 6-10; a more formal treatment of consistency is given in Chapter 14. Note that the observed (realized) fitting errors, $u_1^{\text{fit}} \ldots u_N^{\text{fit}}$, given by

$$u_i^{\text{fit}} = Y_i - [\hat{\alpha}^* + \hat{\beta}^* x_i]$$

are essentially equivalent to sample realizations of $U_1 \ldots U_N$ if the sample is sufficiently large. This result on the observed fitting errors also plays a crucial role in diagnostically checking the model assumption that $U_i \sim \text{NIID}(0, \sigma^2)$ in Chapters 10 and 13.

for large N. Thus, S^2 is an unbiased estimator for σ^2 in large samples. Because of the "$1/(N-2)$" factor in its definition, S^2 is an unbiased estimator for σ^2 in small samples also, but the derivation of this is relegated to Exercise 7-10 because it involves a good deal of algebra.

7.7 PROPERTIES OF S^2

The unbiasedness of S^2 as an estimator of σ^2 is not actually its most important property, however. The most important properties of S^2 are as follows:

Properties of S^2

1. S^2 is independent of $\hat{\alpha}$ and $\hat{\beta}$
2. $\dfrac{(N-2)S^2}{\sigma^2} \sim \chi^2(N-2)$

(7-20)

These two properties are crucial because they allow us to show (in the next section) that substituting S^2 for the unknown value σ^2 in the statistic

$$\frac{\hat{\beta} - \beta}{\sqrt{\sigma^2 / \sum_{j=1}^{N} (x_j - \bar{x})^2}} \sim N[0, 1] \tag{7-21}$$

yields an observable statistic with a known distribution.

The result that S^2 is independently distributed from both $\hat{\alpha}$ and $\hat{\beta}$ follows from the fact that (under the assumptions of the Bivariate Regression Model) $\text{cov}(U_j^{\text{fit}}, \hat{\alpha})$ and $\text{cov}(U_j^{\text{fit}}, \hat{\beta})$ are both zero for all values of j from 1 to N. The evaluation of $\text{cov}(U_j^{\text{fit}}, \hat{\beta})$ is straightforward, but tedious, so the algebra is relegated to an appendix to this chapter; the analogous result for $\hat{\alpha}$ is left for Exercise 7-11. Because $U_1^{\text{fit}} \ldots U_N^{\text{fit}}$, $\hat{\alpha}$ and $\hat{\beta}$ are all normally distributed – and because uncorrelated normally distributed variables are independently distributed – it follows that both $\hat{\alpha}$ and $\hat{\beta}$ are independent of $U_1^{\text{fit}} \ldots U_N^{\text{fit}}$, and hence of S^2.

A proof that $(N-2)\,S^2/\sigma^2$ is distributed $\chi^2\,(N-2)$ is beyond the scope of this book, but it is simple and illuminating to derive this result approximately for large samples, where $U_i^{\text{fit}} \approx U_i$.

In that case,

$$\frac{(N-2)S^2}{\sigma^2} = \frac{1}{\sigma^2}\sum_{i=1}^{N}\left(U_i^{\text{fit}}\right)^2 = \sum_{i=1}^{N}\left(\frac{U_i^{\text{fit}}}{\sigma}\right)^2 \approx \sum_{i=1}^{N}\left(\frac{U_i}{\sigma}\right)^2 \tag{7-22}$$

Because $U_i \sim \text{NIID}[0, \sigma^2]$, the U_i/σ whose squares are being added up in this last sum are all independent unit normals. Thus, from the definition of the chi squared distribution given in Chapter 4, $(N-2)\,S^2/\sigma^2$ is approximately distributed $\chi^2(N)$ for large N.[3]

[3] A more sophisticated derivation – using a good deal of matrix algebra – shows that the distribution of $(N-2)\,S^2/\sigma^2$ is exactly $\chi^2\,(N-2)$ for all N greater than two. For example, see J. Johnston and J. DiNardo (1997, 4th edition, pp. 493–95), *Econometric Methods*, McGraw-Hill, New York.

7.8 A STATISTIC FOR β NOT INVOLVING σ^2

A Student's t variate with k degrees for freedom was defined in Equation 4-31 as

$$t = \frac{Z}{\sqrt{\frac{Q}{k}}} \sim t(k) \tag{7-23}$$

where $Z \sim N\,[0,1]$ independent of $Q \sim \chi^2\,(k)$. The results in the previous section show that

$$\frac{\hat{\beta} - \beta}{\sqrt{\sigma^2 / \sum_{j=1}^{N} (x_j - \bar{x})^2}} \sim N[0, 1] \tag{7-24}$$

independent of

$$\frac{(N-2)\,S^2}{\sigma^2} \sim \chi^2(N-2) \tag{7-25}$$

Consequently,

$$\frac{\left\{\frac{\hat{\beta} - \beta}{\sqrt{\sigma^2 / \sum_{j=1}^{N} (x_j - \bar{x})^2}}\right\}}{\sqrt{\frac{\left\{\frac{(N-2)\,S^2}{\sigma^2}\right\}}{N-2}}} \sim t(N-2) \tag{7-26}$$

which is equivalent, after a bit of cancellation and rearrangement, to

$$\frac{\hat{\beta} - \beta}{\sqrt{S^2 / \sum_{j=1}^{N} (x_j - \bar{x})^2}} \sim t(N-2) \tag{7-27}$$

Thus, the net effect of replacing σ^2 by S^2 is to change the distribution of the test statistic from a unit normal to a Student's t variate with $N-2$ degrees of freedom.

7.9 A 95% CONFIDENCE INTERVAL FOR β WITH σ^2 UNKNOWN

By definition, a random variable which is distributed as Student's t with $N-2$ degrees of freedom exceeds its 2½% critical point $\left(t^c_{.025}(N-2)\right)$ with probability .025 and is less than its 97½% critical point $\left(t^c_{.975}(N-2)\right)$ with probability 1 − .975 or .025. Thus, a Student's t variate with $N-2$ degrees of freedom lies in between these two critical points with probability .95, as illustrated in Figure 7-4, so that

$$t^c_{.975}(N-2) \leq \frac{\hat{\beta} - \beta}{\sqrt{S^2 / \sum_{j=1}^{N} (x_j - \bar{x})^2}} \leq t^c_{.025}(N-2) \tag{7-28}$$

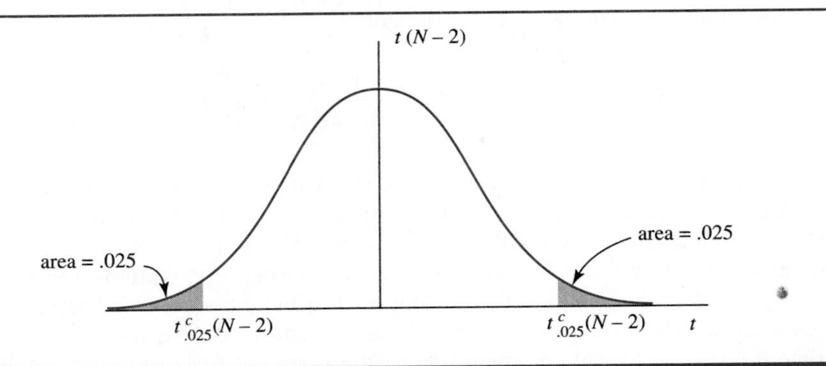

Figure 7-4 Student's *t* Density Function with Critical Points Illustrated

with probability .95. Like the unit normal distribution – which it resembles, except for having a sharper peak and thicker tails – the Student's *t* distribution is symmetric around zero; consequently, $t^c_{.975}(N-2) = -t^c_{.025}(N-2)$, so that

$$-t^c_{.025}(N-2) \le \frac{\hat{\beta}-\beta}{\sqrt{S^2/\sum_{j=1}^{N}(x_j-\bar{x})^2}} \le t^c_{.025}(N-2) \tag{7-29}$$

with probability .95. Consequently, also with probability .95,

$$\begin{aligned}
-t^c_{.025}(N-2)\sqrt{S^2/\sum_{j=1}^{N}(x_j-\bar{x})^2} &\le \hat{\beta}-\beta \le t^c_{.025}(N-2)\sqrt{S^2/\sum_{j=1}^{N}(x_j-\bar{x})^2} \\
-\hat{\beta}-t^c_{.025}(N-2)\sqrt{S^2/\sum_{j=1}^{N}(x_j-\bar{x})^2} &\le -\beta \le -\hat{\beta}+t^c_{.025}(N-2)\sqrt{S^2/\sum_{j=1}^{N}(x_j-\bar{x})^2} \\
\hat{\beta}+t^c_{.025}(N-2)\sqrt{S^2/\sum_{j=1}^{N}(x_j-\bar{x})^2} &\ge \beta \ge \hat{\beta}-t^c_{.025}(N-2)\sqrt{S^2/\sum_{j=1}^{N}(x_j-\bar{x})^2}
\end{aligned} \tag{7-30}$$

so that

$$\beta = \hat{\beta} \pm t^c_{.025}(N-2)\sqrt{S^2/\sum_{j=1}^{N}(x_j-\bar{x})^2} \tag{7-31}$$

with probability .95. A sample realization of this confidence interval is thus

$$\beta = \hat{\beta}^* \pm t^c_{.025}(N-2)\sqrt{s^2/\sum_{j=1}^{N}(x_j-\bar{x})^2} \tag{7-32}$$

where s^2 is the sample realization of the estimator S^2:

$$S^2 \equiv \frac{1}{N-2}\sum_{i=1}^{N}\left(U_i^{\text{fit}}\right)^2 = \frac{1}{N-2}\sum_{i=1}^{N}\left(Y_i - \hat{\alpha} - \hat{\beta}x_i\right)^2 \tag{7-33}$$

and, if we could obtain many realizations of this interval, 95% of them would contain β.

Note that the line of reasoning given above is virtually identical to that used earlier in this chapter (where σ^2 was taken as given) except that the unknown value of σ^2 is replaced by the estimator S^2 and (consequently) the 2½% critical point of the unit normal distribution (1.96) is replaced by $t^c_{.025}(N-2)$, the 2½% critical point of the Student's t distribution with $N-2$ degrees of freedom. Of course – as with the 95% confidence interval based on known σ^2 – if any of the assumptions of the Bivariate Regression Model are invalid – i.e., the x_i are not fixed or the U_i are not distributed NIID[0, σ^2] – then this interval will ***not*** in general contain β with probability .95.

Clearly, one would instead use the ½% critical point of the Student's t distribution in order to obtain a 99% confidence interval for β. The following table, in which γ stands for the tail probability, summarizes how the ½% and the 2½% critical points of the Student's t distribution vary with the number of degrees of freedom and how they compare to the corresponding critical points of the unit normal distribution:[4]

Critical Points (½% and 2½%) for the Unit Normal and Student's t Distributions						
γ	$N(0,1)$	$t^c_\gamma(60)$	$t^c_\gamma(25)$	$t^c_\gamma(15)$	$t^c_\gamma(5)$	$t^c_\gamma(2)$
0.025	1.96	2.00	2.06	2.13	2.57	4.3
0.005	2.58	2.66	2.79	2.95	4.03	9.93

Note that the critical points of the Student's t distribution are notably larger than those of the unit normal distribution – leading to wider confidence intervals – where the number of degrees of freedom ($N-2$) is small. Thus, replacing σ^2 by the sample estimate (s^2) makes a big difference when there are few sample observations available for use in s^2, but that the distinction is no longer all that important once one has substantially more than 60 observations available for estimating σ^2.

7.10 TESTING A HYPOTHESIS ABOUT β WITH σ^2 UNKNOWN

Similarly, testing a hypothesis about β when σ^2 is unknown is virtually identical to the case discussed earlier in this chapter where σ^2 was given; again, the only difference in the result is that the test statistic now involves S^2 instead of σ^2 and this statistic is distributed Student's t with $N-2$ degrees of freedom under the null hypothesis rather than as a unit normal.

For example, the null hypothesis $H_o : \beta = 3$ can be tested against the alternative hypothesis, $H_A : \beta \neq 3$ using the fact that

$$\frac{\hat{\beta} - 3}{\sqrt{S^2 / \sum_{j=1}^{N}(x_j - \bar{x})^2}} \sim t(N-2) \tag{7-34}$$

[4] This table is, of course, identical to the one given in Chapter 4.

if the assumptions of the Bivariate Model are valid and the null hypothesis is true. One simply computes the sample realization of this test statistic:

$$\frac{\hat{\beta}^* - 3}{\sqrt{s^2 / \sum_{j=1}^{N} (x_j - \bar{x})^2}} \tag{7-35}$$

and compares it to the density function for the Student's t distribution with $N-2$ degrees of freedom.

As earlier in this chapter – when σ^2 was assumed given – the magnitude of this test statistic clearly depends on how large the discrepancy is between $\hat{\beta}^*$ (the sample realization of the unbiased estimator of β) and the value for β asserted by the null hypothesis. Again, if the magnitude of this Student's t test statistic is observed to be large, then it is pretty obvious that something is wrong: either (a) at least one of the assumptions of the Bivariate Regression Model is invalid for these data or (b) the null hypothesis is false. Maintaining the assumptions of the model, one would thus in that case reject the null hypothesis.

Also as before, for a less extreme discrepancy between $\hat{\beta}$ and its claimed value under the null hypothesis, it is informative to compute the "p-value" – the probability that a discrepancy of this magnitude (or larger) could arise due to chance, even though both the maintained assumptions of the model and the null hypothesis are correct. The p-value can also be interpreted as the probability that one is wrongly rejecting the null hypothesis, if one does reject it based on evidence of this strength. For the test statistic given at the beginning of this section, the p-value is just the probability of observing a Student's t variate with $N-2$ degrees of freedom larger in magnitude than the observed magnitude of the test statistic. Suppose, for example, that the test statistic is observed to be 1.8 with a sample size of N equal to 41. The tail area of the Student's t distribution (with 39 degrees of freedom) to the right of 1.8 is .040; because the Student's t distribution is symmetric around its mean, this implies that the tail area to the left of -1.8 is also .040 as illustrated in Figure 7-5.

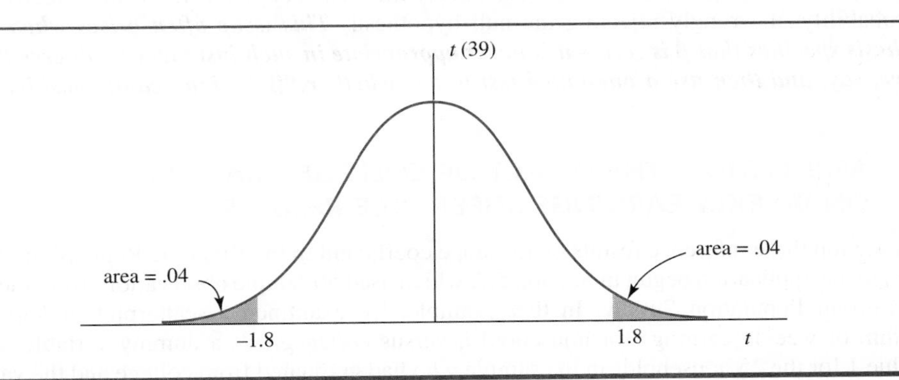

Figure 7-5 Student's *t* Density Function with Tail Areas Illustrated

Thus, the null hypothesis can in this instance be rejected with p-value .080 or "at the 8% level of significance." If the null hypothesis is rejected, there is an 8% chance that it is actually true and it is being wrongly rejected.

As noted earlier in this chapter, it is customary to reject the null hypothesis only when the implied p-value is less than .05. Here, this custom has the advantage of eliminating the need to compute tail areas for the Student's t distribution – one simply rejects the null hypothesis ("at the 5% level") whenever the test statistic exceeds $t^c_{.025}(N-2)$, the 2½% critical point of the Student's t distribution with $N-2$ degrees of freedom. As noted earlier with regard to the unit normal distribution, many years ago the computations involved in computing adequate approximations for the tail areas of the Student's t distribution were substantial, so this was a real advantage. With modern computing equipment, however, that is no longer the case.[5]

Moreover – as noted earlier for the test assuming σ^2 is given – this custom is more than a little arbitrary: in some circumstances a 5% chance of wrongly rejecting the null hypothesis is an acceptable risk, in others it is not. Consequently – because modern econometric software typically computes the p-values in any case – it is more informative and usually preferable to quote the p-value for the test.

Also as before, the hypothesis testing procedure just described is called the "two-tailed" test, because the computation of the p-value includes both tails of the distribution, allowing for the possibility of wrongly rejecting the null due to either a positive or a negative (chance) deviation of $\hat{\beta}$ from the value for of β specified in the null hypothesis.[6]

Occasionally a one-tailed test is appropriate. Suppose that the economic theory one is testing rules out the possibility that β is less than 3. It is appropriate in that case to augment the Bivariate Regression Model assumptions with the parameter restriction $\beta \geq 3$ and test the null hypothesis $H_o : \beta = 3$ against the alternative hypothesis, $H_A : \beta > 3$. The null hypothesis (and the distribution of the test statistic given at the beginning of this section) are unchanged, so this test statistic is still distributed Student's t with $N-2$ degrees of freedom under the null hypothesis. Consequently, one can expect that $\hat{\beta} - 3$ will be negative about half of the time if the null hypothesis is true. But such deviations are no longer evidence against the null hypothesis and should never yield a rejection of it – rather, the null hypothesis will be rejected only when $\hat{\beta} - 3$ is sufficiently positive. Consequently, in this instance the p-value – the probability of wrongly rejecting the null hypothesis – will consist only of the tail area to the right of the observed value of the test statistic. In effect, the p-value is halved in exchange for increasing the amount assumed.

Note, however, that a policy of testing the alternative assumption $H_A : \beta > 3$ when $\hat{\beta}^*$ exceeds 3 and testing the alternative assumption $H_A : \beta < 3$ when $\hat{\beta}^*$ is less than 3 is equivalent to doing the two-tailed test; in that case the p-value must include the area in both tails if it is to correctly quantify the probability of wrongly rejecting the null hypothesis. ***This issue often arises when the null hypothesis specifies that β is zero – it is never appropriate in such instances to observe that $\hat{\beta}^*$ is positive, say, and then use a one-tailed test to test whether "$\hat{\beta}^*$ is significantly positive"!***

7.11 APPLICATION: THE IMPACT OF COLLEGE GRADUATION ON WEEKLY EARNINGS (INFERENCE RESULTS)

In this section these inference results on the slope coefficient in the Bivariate Regression Model are applied to the application begun in Section 5.7, which used 50 sample observations from the January 2002 Current Population Survey. In that example, we examined a scatterplot of $logearn_i$, the logarithm of weekly earnings for household i, versus $collegegrad_i$, a dummy variable taking on the value 1 for the 25 households in the sample who had graduated from college and the value 0 for the 25 households who had not graduated from college college, as in Figure 7-6.

[5] In particular, many spreadsheet programs provide worksheet functions for computing tail areas for the Student's t distribution – i.e., in Excel this function is called "tdist." Or you can program an excellent numerical approximation to this function yourself in just a few lines of code – see Press et al. (1986, p. 168), *Numerical Recipes*, Cambridge University Press. Or you can copy the program "ttail.exe" (available at www.wiley.com/college/ashley) and use it on any Windows-based computer.

[6] The alert reader will note that the text following is almost identical to that ending the section on hypothesis testing with σ^2 given. That is intentional: the ideas are the same regardless of which test statistic one is able to use.

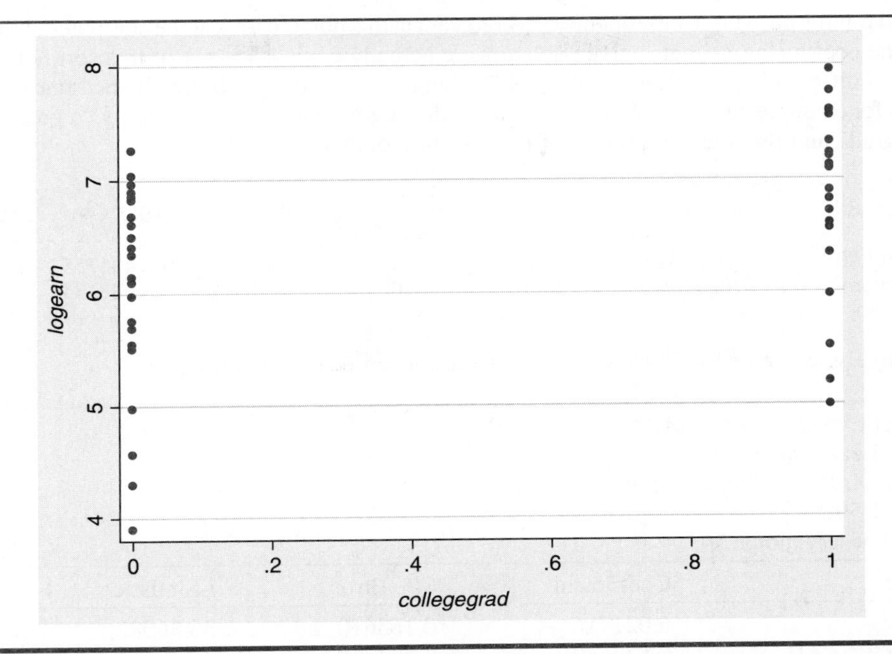

Figure 7-6 Scatterplot of the Logarithm of Weekly Income versus College Graduation Dummy Variable

and used the formulas derived in Chapter 5 for the least squares estimators of α_1 and β_1 in the model:

$$\begin{array}{c} LOGEARN_i = \alpha_1 + \beta_1\, collegegrad_i + W_i \quad i = 1 \ldots 50 \\ collegegrad_i \text{ fixed in repeated samples} \\ W_i \sim \text{NIID}[0, \sigma^2] \end{array} \tag{7-36}$$

to obtain the following estimated model:

$$\begin{aligned} logearn_i &= \hat{\alpha}_1^* + \hat{\beta}_1^*\, collegegrad_i + w_i^{\text{fit}} \\ &= 6.022 + 0.873\, collegegrad_i + w_i^{\text{fit}} \end{aligned} \tag{7-37}$$

Thus, $logearn_1$ ... $logearn_{50}$, this particular set of sample realizations of $LOGEARN_1$ ... $LOGEARN_{50}$, yields $\hat{\beta}_1^*$ and $\hat{\alpha}_1^*$, the sample realizations of the estimators $\hat{\beta}_1$ and $\hat{\alpha}_1$, through the formulas

$$\hat{\alpha}_1^* = \overline{logearn} - .873\, \overline{collegegrad} = 6.022 \tag{7-38}$$

and

$$\hat{\beta}_1^* = \frac{\sum_{i=1}^{50} (collegegrad_i - \overline{collegegrad})\,(logearn_i - \overline{logearn})}{\sum_{j=1}^{50} (collegegrad_j - \overline{collegegrad})^2} = 0.873 \tag{7-39}$$

Well, in principle these formulas were used. In practice, parameter estimates like these are almost always obtained using commercially-available software (Stata, EViews, SAS, Minitab, etc.)

designed for this purpose. Consequently, it is relevant at this point to look at the computer output from which the coefficient estimates given above were actually copied. Output of this sort is formatted somewhat differently by each software package, but it always conveys basically the same estimates. In Stata, for example, the command for estimating this regression equation is simply "regress *logearn* collegegrad" and the relevant portion of the resulting output is:

```
-------------------------------------------------------------------------------
     LOGEARN |      Coef.     Std. Err.      t     P>|t|    [95% Conf. Interval]
-------------+-----------------------------------------------------------------
 COLLEGEGRAD |   .8726619    .2342079      3.73    0.001     .4017553  1.343569
       _cons |   6.021716    .16561       36.36    0.000     5.688735  6.354698
-------------------------------------------------------------------------------
```

Alternatively, estimated in EViews, the relevant portion of the output is

Dependent Variable: *LOGEARN*
Method: Least Squares
Date: 04/14/04 Time: 16:19
Sample: 1 50
Included observations: 50

Variable	Coefficient	Std. Error	*t*-Statistic	Prob.
C	6.021716	0.165610	36.36082	0.0000
COLLEGEGRAD	0.872662	0.234208	3.726014	0.0005

and similarly for the other programs.

Focusing on the estimates relating to β_1, we have already seen the formula yielding $\hat{\beta}_1^*$ equal to .872662. The sampling variance of $\hat{\beta}_1$ is

$$\frac{\sigma^2}{\sum_{j=1}^{50} (collegegrad_j - \overline{collegegrad})^2} \tag{7-40}$$

for which we have the unbiased estimator

$$\frac{S^2}{\sum_{j=1}^{50} (collegegrad_j - \overline{collegegrad})^2} \tag{7-41}$$

which is a random variable – recall that $(50 - 2)S^2/\sigma^2$ is distributed $\chi^2(50 - 2)$ under the assumptions of the model – whose sample realization here is

$$\frac{s^2}{\sum_{j=1}^{50} (collegegrad_j - \overline{collegegrad})^2} = (.234208)^2 \tag{7-42}$$

where s^2 is obtained from

$$s^2 = \frac{1}{50-2}\sum_{i=1}^{50} (logearn_i - 6.02172 - .872662\, collegegrad_i)^2 \tag{7-43}$$

We can conclude that the "estimated standard error" for $\hat{\beta}_1$ is .234.

Given the probable sampling errors in this estimated standard error, there is certainly no need to quote this estimate with any greater precision than .234. Similarly, given that $\hat{\beta}_1$ has an estimated standard error of .234, there is no reason to quote very many decimal places for $\hat{\beta}_1$ itself, either. Indeed, under the model assumptions given above,

$$\frac{\hat{\beta}_1 - \beta_1}{\sqrt{S^2 / \sum_{j=1}^{50} (collegegrad_j - \overline{collegegrad})^2}} \sim t(50-2) \tag{7-44}$$

so that a (realized) 95% confidence interval for β_1 is

$$\begin{aligned} \beta_1^* &= \hat{\beta}_1 \pm t^c_{.025}(48)\sqrt{s^2 / \sum_{j=1}^{50} (collegegrad_j - \overline{collegegrad})^2} \\ &= \hat{\beta}_1^* \pm 2.011\sqrt{s^2 / \sum_{j=1}^{50} (collegegrad_j - \overline{collegegrad})^2} \end{aligned} \tag{7-45}$$

where $t^c_{.025}(48)$ can either be read off from the relevant table (if you can find it when you need it) or obtained iteratively from a program that computes tail areas for the Student's t distribution.[7] Thus, the realized value of this 95% confidence interval using these data is

$$\begin{aligned} \beta_1 &= 0.873 \pm 2.011(.234) \\ &= [.402, 1.344] \end{aligned} \tag{7-46}$$

which is identical to the 95% confidence interval quoted in the Stata output.

Presuming that the model assumptions are valid, we can conclude from this result that the actual impact of college graduation on the logarithm of expected earnings lies within the interval [.402, 1.344] with probability .95. Note that this also implies that the *factor* by which earnings, on average, are larger for a household which has graduated college lies within the interval $[e^{.402}, e^{1.344}]$ = [1.49, 3.83] with probability .95. Clearly, this estimate of β_1 is rather imprecise; but then again this regression equation was estimated using only 50 sample observations.[8]

Stata and EViews, like all such computer programs, assume in their standard output that we are interested in testing the null hypothesis $H_o: \beta_1 = 0$, so they compute and display the statistic

$$\frac{\hat{\beta}_1^* - 0}{\sqrt{s^2 / \sum_{j=1}^{50} (collegegrad_j - \overline{collegegrad})^2}} = \frac{0.873 - 0}{.234} = 3.73 \tag{7-47}$$

under the "t" heading and also compute for us the p-value with which this null hypothesis can be rejected based on these sample estimates – which is to say, the probability that a Student's t variable with 48 degrees of freedom will exceed 3.73 in magnitude. Here this probability is .0005; note that this figure is rounded up to .001 in the Stata output. Therefore, we can conclude that the null hypothesis that college graduation has no impact on expected earnings can be rejected with a

---

[7] See Footnote 7-5.

[8] In fact, it is rather remarkable that we can conclude as much as we have using such a small data set. Note, however, that the worst limitation on our results imposed by having only 50 observations may not actually be the resulting estimation imprecision observed above. Rather, the worst limitation may well be the fact that this very small sample size makes it very difficult to check the Bivariate Regression Model assumptions using the methods covered in Chapters 10 and 13.

p-value of .0005 or, equivalently, at the .05% significance level, presuming that the model assumptions are all valid.

Thus, the expected increment in the logarithm of earnings is not only economically significant – corresponding to an expected factor of $e^{.873} = 2.39$ – but also statistically significant. Note that "economic significance" depends on how large the estimate of β_1 is, whereas "statistical significance" hinges on how large the estimate of β_1 is compared to its estimated standard error.

Other null hypotheses are not so easily rejected using these estimates. Suppose, for example, that one wanted to test the null hypothesis $H_o : \beta_1 = .402$ against the alternative hypothesis $H_A : \beta_1 \neq .402$. This null hypothesis corresponds to college graduates earning a factor $e^{.402}$ or 1.49 times more, on average, than nongraduates. The appropriate statistic for testing this null hypothesis is

$$\frac{\hat{\beta}_1^* - .402}{\sqrt{s^2 / \sum_{j=1}^{50} \left(collegegrad_j - \overline{collegegrad}\right)^2}} = \frac{0.873 - .402}{.234} = 2.01 \qquad (7\text{-}48)$$

The econometric software does not automatically calculate the p-value at which this null hypothesis can be rejected, because it has no way of knowing what value of β_1 we are specifying under the null hypothesis. We can use tables or stand-alone software to calculate the probability that a Student's t variable with 48 degrees of freedom will exceed 2.01 in magnitude or – usually much more conveniently – ask the software to do the test.[9] Either way, the p-value comes out .05 in this instance, so that this null hypothesis can just barely be rejected at the 5% level.[10]

7.12 APPLICATION: IS GROWTH GOOD FOR THE POOR?

Returning to the Dollar and Kraay data set considered at that outset of this chapter, it is instructive at this point to explicitly consider the computer output from which the quoted estimate of 1.31 for β in the regression model was obtained:

```
------------------------------------------------------------------------------
poorgrow |      Coef.    Std. Err.      t     P>|t|     [95% Conf. Interval]
------------------------------------------------------------------------------
meangrow |   1.312503     .122821     10.69   0.000      1.068498   1.556509
   _cons |  -1.250916     .4421076    -2.83   0.006     -2.12924    -.3725924
------------------------------------------------------------------------------
```

In this case our primary interest is in testing the null hypothesis, $H_o : \beta = 1$, against the alternative hypothesis, $H_A : \beta \neq 1$, based on the model assumptions that

$$\boxed{\begin{gathered} POORGROW_i = \alpha + \beta\, meangrow_i + U_i \quad i = 1 \ldots 92 \\ meangrow_i \text{ fixed in repeated samples} \\ U_i \sim \text{NIID}[0, \sigma^2] \end{gathered}} \qquad (7\text{-}49)$$

Note that the one-tailed test of the alternative hypothesis $H_A : \beta > 1$ would be inappropriate here because, had the realized value of $\hat{\beta}$ been less than one, our interest would no doubt have centered on

[9] See Footnote 7-5 regarding such stand-alone software. In Stata, the appropriate command would simply be "test collegegrad=.402"; other programs would have similar commands.

[10] Note that it is not accidental that the p-value for which a null hypothesis specifying a value right on the edge of the 95% confidence interval can be rejected turns out to be .05.

the opposite alternative hypothesis, $H_A : \beta < 1$. Under these model assumptions,

$$\frac{1.313 - 1.00}{.123} = \frac{.31}{.123} = 2.55 \tag{7-50}$$

is a realization of a Student's t random variable with $N - 2 = 90$ degrees of freedom if H_o is true. A Student's t variable with this many degrees of freedom will exceed 2.55 in magnitude with probability .013, so we can reject this null hypothesis at the 2%, but not the 1%, level of significance.

As usual, the meaningfulness of this result hinges on the validity of the model assumptions. We will return to the topic of checking these assumptions in Chapters 10 and 13, once we have the Multiple Regression Model at our disposal for use in that endeavor.

7.13 SUMMARY

In this chapter we have seen how to use the estimated Bivariate Regression Model to construct confidence intervals for the parameter β in the model and how to test hypotheses about this slope parameter. ***Because these results were derived using the assumptions of the Bivariate Regression Model, their validity rests on the validity of these assumptions***. Are these assumptions reasonable for the data at hand? How can one tell? Checking these assumptions requires the use of the Multiple Regression Model, which is covered in Chapter 9, so this topic will be taken up in earnest in Chapters 10 and 13.

In the meantime, the next chapter completes the analysis of the Bivariate Regression Model, tackling the practical problems of quantifying how well a regression model fits the data and of using an estimated model for prediction.

KEY TERMS

For each term or concept listed below, provide a working definition or explanation:

Economic vs. Statistical Significance

Confidence Interval

Hypothesis Test

One-Tailed vs. Two-Tailed Hypothesis Test

S^2 and its distribution

EXERCISES

7-1. Under what circumstance can one conclude that a particular estimator yields the narrowest possible confidence interval out of the class of linear estimators?

7-2. Explain the difference between $\hat{\beta}$ and $\hat{\beta}^*$.

7-3. For a particular sample of 25 observations $\varphi = \sum_{j=1}^{N} (x_j - \bar{x})^2$ is 8966.7, the observed value of $\hat{\beta}^*$ is 2.98, and the value of s^2 is 12.3.

   a. State the realized value of an appropriate statistic for testing the null hypothesis, $H_o : \beta = 3$, against the alternative hypothesis, $H_A : \beta \neq 3$.

   b. What distribution is this statistic drawn from if the null hypothesis is true? What other assumptions are necessary?

   c. At what p-value can H_o be rejected? Given this result, would you reject H_o?

7-4. For a particular sample of 2,500 observations $\varphi = \sum_{j=1}^{N} (x_j - \bar{x})^2$ is 8966.7, the observed value of $\hat{\beta}^*$ is 2.98, and the value of s^2 is 12.3.

a. State the realized value of an appropriate statistic for testing the null hypothesis, $H_o : \beta = 3$ against the alternative hypothesis, $H_A : \beta \neq 3$.

b. What distribution is this statistic drawn from if the null hypothesis is true? What other assumptions are necessary?

c. At what p-value can H_o be rejected? Given this result, would you reject H_o?

7-5. For a particular sample of 25 observations $\varphi = \sum_{j=1}^{N} (x_j - \bar{x})^2$ is 225,000, the observed value of $\hat{\beta}^*$ is 3.02, and the value of s^2 is 13.

a. State the realized value of an appropriate statistic for testing the null hypothesis, $H_o : \beta = 3$ against the alternative hypothesis, $H_A : \beta \neq 3$.

b. What distribution is this statistic drawn from if the null hypothesis is true? What other assumptions are necessary?

c. At what p-value can H_o be rejected? Given this result, would you reject H_o?

7-6. Describe a situation in which rejecting if the p-value is 0.05 is an acceptable risk, and a situation in which it is not.

7-7. When is a one-tailed test appropriate for testing a hypothesis on a parameter β? When is it not appropriate? What difference does it make?

7-8. Calculate the following, using the Bivariate Regression Model and the following data:

Year	y_i	x_i
1995	250	1
1996	387	3
1997	500	6
1998	590	7
1999	820	10
2000	540	8
2001	309	2
2002	498	4
2003	1034	12
2004	650	9

a. $\bar{y}$, $\bar{x}$, $\sum_{i=1}^{10} (x_i - \bar{y})(x_i - \bar{x})$, and $\sum_{i=1}^{10} (x_i - \bar{x})$

b. $\hat{\beta}^*$

c. s^2

d. A 95% confidence interval for the slope parameter – why is this confidence interval so wide?

For the null hypothesis, $H_o : \beta = 75$, in parts e through g compute:

e. An appropriate statistic for testing H_o

f. What distribution is this statistic drawn from if the null hypothesis is true? What other assumptions are necessary?

g. At what p-value can H_o be rejected – given this result, would you reject H_o?

7-9. Use the sampling distribution derived in Exercise 6-9 for $\hat{\alpha}$, the OLS estimator of α in the Bivariate Regression Model to do the following:

a. Derive a theoretical expression for a 95% confidence interval for α.

b. Show how to test the null hypothesis $H_o : \alpha = 4$ versus the alternative hypothesis that $H_A : \alpha \neq 4$. You may initially assume that σ^2 is known; then repeat your analysis dropping this assumption.

7-10. Show that S^2 is an unbiased estimator of σ^2 under the assumptions of the Bivariate Regression Model.

7-11. Show that S^2 is independent of $\hat{\alpha}$ under the assumptions of the Bivariate Regression Model.

7-12. Continuing Exercise 6-11, again consider the simpler regression model

$$Y_i = \beta x_i + U_i \qquad U_i \sim \text{NIID}(0, \sigma^2)$$

where the x_i are assumed to be fixed in repeated samples. As before, this model is not suitable for use with real data because the absence of an intercept in the model implies that the assumption that $E[U_i] = 0$ could fail, leading to a biased least squares estimate of β. It is, however, quite suitable for use in exercises such as this one because it is a little different from what is done in the text itself and because it involves less algebra.

a. Derive the relationship between the fitting errors (U_i^{fit}) and the model errors (U_i).

b. Show that $S^2 \equiv \frac{1}{N-1}\sum_{i=1}^{N}\left(U_i^{\text{fit}}\right)^2$ is unbiased for σ^2 and independent of $\hat{\beta}$.

c. Motivate the result that $(N-1)S^2/\sigma^2 \sim \chi^2(N-1)$ by showing that $(N-1)S^2/\sigma^2$ is approximately distributed $\chi^2(N)$ for large N.

d. First assuming that σ^2 is known and then dropping this assumption, use the sampling distribution for $\hat{\beta}$ derived in Exercise 6-11 to:

i. Derive a 95% confidence interval for β.

ii. Show how to test the null hypothesis $H_o : \beta = 10$ versus the alternative hypothesis that $H_A : \beta \neq 10$.

7-13. Continuing Exercise 6-12, again suppose that you have four sample observations (y_1, x_1) ... (y_4, x_4):

y	x
3.5	1.0
−3.2	−1.0
−.3	0
.3	0

and are willing to assume that

$$Y_i = \beta x_i + U_i \qquad U_i \sim \text{NIID}(0, \sigma^2)$$

where the x_i are assumed to be fixed in repeated samples.

a. Use the realized OLS estimator $\hat{\beta}^*$, and the observed fitting errors $u_1^{\text{fit}} \dots u_4^{\text{fit}}$ (which you calculated in Exercise 6-12) to obtain s^2, the realized value of the unbiased estimator of σ^2. {Note that because y_3 and y_4 affect the values of u_3^{fit} and u_4^{fit}, these observations do have an impact on s^2, even though they have no impact on $\hat{\beta}^*$.}

b. Calculate $s^2/(x_1^2+x_2^2+x_3^2+x_4^2)$, which is an unbiased estimate of the sampling variance of $\hat{\beta}$ for this model. The square root of this estimator is a consistent estimate of the standard deviation of $\hat{\beta}$ the "estimated standard error" for $\hat{\beta}$.

c. Using your results from Exercise 7-12, then,

$$\frac{\hat{\beta}-\beta}{\sqrt{S^2/(x_1^2+x_2^2+x_3^2+x_4^2)}} \sim t(3)$$

Use this result to derive and compute a 95% confidence interval for β. {Hint: the 2½% critical point of the $t(3)$ distribution is 3.18.}

d. Test the null hypothesis that $\beta = 4$ against the alternative hypothesis that $\beta \neq 4$. Calculate the p-value for the test using ttail.exe (available at www.wiley.com/college/ashley) or the "tdist" function in Excel; also produce an appropriate sketch. Briefly, what does this p-value mean?

e. As in Exercise 6-12e, check your calculations by inputting the data into Excel (or the econometric software being used in your course) and estimating a model with no intercept. {In Stata this model would be estimated using the command "regress y x, noconstant". The Stata command "test $x = 4$" allows you to check the p-value you obtained in part d. above.[11]}

Active Learning Exercise 7a: Investigating the Sensitivity of Slope Coefficient Inference to Departures from the $U_i \sim \text{NIID}(0, \sigma^2)$ Assumption Using Computer-Generated Data

Introduction

In this chapter the assumptions of the Bivariate Regression Model, that

$$Y_i = \alpha + \beta x_i + U_i \qquad U_i \sim \text{NIID}[0, \sigma^2]$$

with $x_1 \dots x_N$ fixed in repeated samples, were used to obtain a p-value for testing the null hypothesis $H_o : \beta = \beta_o$ against the alternative hypothesis that $H_A : \beta \neq \beta_o$ for any given value β_o, based on the result that

$$\frac{\hat{\beta}-\beta_o}{\sqrt{\dfrac{S^2}{\sum_{i=1}^{N}(x_i-\bar{x})^2}}} \sim t(N-2)$$

[11] It follows directly from the definitions given in Chapter 4 that the square of a unit normal variate is a $\chi^2(1)$ variate; consequently, the square of a $t(N-1)$ variate is distributed $F(1, N-1)$. Because Stata actually computes the square of the t statistic you calculated here, the test statistic it quotes is distributed $F(1, N-1)$ under the null hypothesis that $\beta = 4$.

if the null hypothesis is true, where $\hat{\beta}$ is the least squares estimator of β. It was noted that the normality part of the assumption that $U_i \sim \text{NIID}[0, \sigma^2]$ becomes less and less important as N increases (due to the Central Limit Theorem result), but that the assumptions that $U_1 \ldots U_N$ are uncorrelated and all have the same variance are crucial to the result that the sampling variance of $\hat{\beta}$ equals $\sigma^2 / \sum_{i=1}^{N} (x_i - \bar{x})^2$, even for large N.

In Active Learning Exercise 6b (available at www.wiley.com/college/ashley) you learned how to generate sample data on (y_i, x_i) from the Bivariate Regression Model in which the assumption that $U_i \sim \text{NIID}[0, \sigma^2]$ is violated in several interesting ways. In that exercise you found that $\hat{\beta}$ is still a consistent estimator of β, regardless of the substantial departures from the NIID assumption considered there. In this Active Learning Exercise you will generate 10,000 realizations of the random variable

$$t_{\hat{\beta}} = \frac{\hat{\beta} - \beta}{\sqrt{S^2 / \sum_{i=1}^{N} (x_i - \bar{x})^2}}$$

from the Bivariate Regression Model with β set equal to one. You will use these realizations to examine the impact of the departures from the $U_i \sim \text{NIID}(0, \sigma^2)$ assumption studied in Active Learning Exercise 6b on the resulting p-values for testing the null hypothesis $H_o : \beta = 1$ against the alternative hypothesis that $H_A : \beta \neq 1$.[12]

Your Assignment:

1. You are to copy the program ALE7a.exe available at www.wiley.com/college/ashley to your hard disk and execute it.[13] The program will prompt you to enter a value for the sample size (N) to be used in generating realizations of $t_{\hat{\beta}}$. In this exercise you will investigate sample sizes of 30, 100, and 500; you can start with N equal to 30. The program will next prompt you to enter a value for the number of realizations (or "trials") of $t_{\hat{\beta}}$ to be generated; you should choose *10000* for this value.[14] Finally, the program will prompt you for a value to use as an initial seed for the random number generator. You can enter any positive integer you like here (or whatever value your instructor suggests), but note down the value you use so that your work is easily replicable.[15]

[12] Note that this Active Learning Exercise is very similar to Active Learning Exercise 4a. That is not an accident! It necessarily follows from the fact that one can fruitfully view a regression model as a parameterization of the conditional mean of the dependent variable. Consequently, estimation and inference for the slope parameter in a regression model is actually closely related to estimation and inference on a population mean.

[13] Program source code is available at www.wiley.com/college/ashley as file ALE_7a.for. Subroutine RAN1 generates a uniform random number between zero and one using a linear congruential random number generator which is a variation on that described above. It is taken from (and documented in) *Numerical Recipes* (Press et al. Cambridge University Press: Cambridge, pp. 195–97). Pairs of uniform random numbers from RAN1 are used to generate normally distributed variates using the routine GASDEV, from *Numerical Recipes* (p. 202).

[14] Your instructor may ask you to enter a value less than 10000 if the student version of the econometrics software your class is using will not support this many observations. In case the program is not compatible with your version of Windows, output files created with initial seed equal to 23 are available at www.wiley.com/college/ashley, labeled "ALE_7a_N30.csv," "ALE_7a_N100.csv," and "ALE_7a_N500.csv"; For Stata users, similar "*.dta" files are provided. The number of trials implicit in these comma delimited (csv) files can be reduced using spreadsheet software if a smaller value is necessary.

[15] See Active Learning Exercise 3a or Active Learning Exercise 6b for a discussion of how pseudo-random number generators work and why they need an initial seed.

2. The program then generates N values of the explanatory variable, $x_1 \ldots x_N$. These are generated once only and then used repeatedly for all 10,000 of the trials. These values are generated as independent draws from a unit normal distribution and adjusted to have sample mean zero and

$$\sum_{i=1}^{N} (x_i - \bar{x})^2 = \sum_{i=1}^{N} x_i^2 = N$$

3. As in Active Learning Exercise 6b, realizations of the dependent variables ($Y_1 \ldots Y_N$) are then generated from the population regression equation, $Y_i = x_i + U_i$. (Clearly, the parameters α and β in the Bivariate Regression Model have the values zero and one, respectively, in these simulations.) The program generates realizations of the model error terms, $U_1 \ldots U_N$ as drawings from the same five different distributions considered in Active Learning Exercise 6b (available at www.wiley.com/college/ashley):
   a. NIID
   b. ASYMMETRIC
   c. FAT-TAILED
   d. HETEROSCEDASTIC
   e. AUTOCORRELATED

   The program then stores the resulting 10,000 realizations of $t_{\hat{\beta}}$ for each of these five cases in the comma delimited file ALE7a.csv. (It is advisable to rename this file so as to explicitly indicate the sample length used in the simulations: e.g., "ALE7a_N100.csv" where N was set to 100 when the program ALE7a.exe was run.) Under the "NIID" heading in this file are realizations of $t_{\hat{\beta}}$ based on normally identically and independently distributed model error terms. The realizations of $t_{\hat{\beta}}$ under the "ASYMMETRIC" heading are based on model error terms which are constructed by squaring normally distributed variates;[16] the "FAT-TAILED" error terms are analogously generated using model errors which are realizations of Student's t variates with four degrees of freedom.[17] The model error terms used in generating the realizations of $t_{\hat{\beta}}$ under the last two headings are not identically and independently distributed. The "HETEROSCEDASTIC" error terms are constructed so that U_i are independently distributed, but with variance proportional to x_i^2. Similarly, the model error terms used in generating the realizations of $t_{\hat{\beta}}$ under the "AUTOCORRELATED" heading are constructed so that the correlation between consecutive values of the model error term is .70.[18]

4. For each of the three values of N – i.e., 30, 100, and 500 – enter the 10,000 realizations of $t_{\hat{\beta}}$ test statistic which you have generated – one for each of the five different model error term distributions – into whatever econometrics software your course is using and print out histograms for each variable using all 10,000 realizations of the test statistic.[19] The derivation that this statistic is distributed Student's t with (N–2) degrees

[16] The square of a unit normal variate is a χ^2 (1) variate, which is adjusted to have population mean zero by subtracting one and then divided by the square root of two that the population variance is one. The χ^2 distribution is discussed in Chapter 4.

[17] The Student's t distribution is discussed in Chapter 4; these variates are constructed as $Z/\sqrt{(Z1^2 + Z2^2 + Z3^2 + Z4^2)/4}$, where $Z, Z1, Z2, Z3$, and $Z4$ are independent unit normals; this variate is then divided by $\sqrt{2}$ so that its population variance is one.

[18] These are constructed from an AR(1) model: $U_i = .7U_{i-1} + V_i$ where $V_i \sim \text{NIID}(0,1-.7^2)$ to make its population variance equal to one. AR(1) processes are discussed in Section 13.4.

[19] In Stata the command "histogram NIID, normal" produces a histogram of the variable named "NIID" and also plots the unit normal density with population mean and variance equal to the sample mean and sample variance of this variable.

of freedom used the assumption that the model errors are NIID(0, σ^2), so you should not expect these histograms to quite match up to the unit normal density function. (Except for the "NIID" case, of course. Note that a histogram of the $t(28)$ density function is already not visually distinguishable from that of the $N(0,1)$ density function.) Do any of these histograms look obviously unlike what one would expect from normally distributed data? Do the discrepancies disappear as the sample length becomes larger?

5. Use the econometric software to sort the data for each variable in turn and observe how many realizations of $t_{\hat{\beta}}$ lie outside $\pm\, t^c_{.025}\,(N-2)$, the relevant critical point for testing the null hypothesis that β equals zero.[20] The null hypothesis is true here by construction; consequently, something like 500 out of the 10,000 realizations of $t_{\hat{\beta}}$ should exceed $t^c_{.025}\,(N-2)$ in magnitude, just due to chance.[21] In this way complete the following table:

Number of realizations greater in magnitude than $t^c_{.025}\,(N-2)$, out of 10,000 trials						
N	$t^c_{.025}\,(N-2)$	NIID	ASYMMETRIC	FAT-TAILED	HETERO-SCEDASTIC	AUTO-CORRELATED
30	2.048					
100	1.984					
500	1.965					
Seed Used =						

6. What can you conclude from these results about the importance of the assumption that $U_1 \ldots U_N$ are NIID[0, σ^2] at various sample sizes? Does the form of the model error distribution seem to matter? Does it matter if the model errors are not identically and independently distributed, at least in the ways examined here? Do these problems caused by serially correlated and/or heteroscedastic model errors disappear for larger samples?

7. Is the assumption that the models errors are uncorrelated as important in this particular example as the assumption that the errors all have the same variance? The "no" which should be your answer to this question is actually a misleading artifact. It is caused by the fact that the values chosen for $x_1 \ldots x_N$ in this example had no pattern with respect to the observation number – they are independently distributed – whereas the "AUTOCORRELATED" model errors did: the model error for each observation was generated so as to be correlated with the model error from the immediately "previous" observation – i.e., from the datum with observation number smaller by one. This issue is addressed in Active Learning Exercise 7b located at the book companion site: www.wiley.com/college/ashley.

---

[20] It is convenient to take the absolute value of each variable prior to sorting. In Stata the command "sort NIID" will sort the entire data set in increasing order of the variable NIID. You can confirm the three critical points given in the table for yourself by using the "ttail.exe" program available at www.wiley.com/college/ashley.

[21] You should not expect exactly 500 realizations of $t_{\hat{\beta}}$ to lie outside $\pm\, t^c_{.025}\,(N-2)$, however. In fact, if the true proportion is .05, then the proportion actually observed in 10,000 trials is distributed N (.05, .05*.95/10000) or N (.05, .0022) for large numbers of trials. Thus a two-standard-error interval would be [456, 544].

Epilogue

Your work in Active Learning Exercise 6b demonstrated that the slope parameter β in the Bivariate Regression Model can be consistently estimated regardless of whether the model errors are normally, identically, and independently distributed. In contrast, however, if one wants to either test hypotheses about β and obtain meaningful p-values to make confidence intervals for β which actually contain the true value of β with the specified probability, then it is essential that both the homoscedasticity assumption (that the variance of the model error U_i is constant across the sample and the nonautocorrelation assumption (that $\text{corr}(U_i, U_j)$ is zero for i not equal to j) are satisfied. Fairly simple methods for detecting and approximately correcting for such deviations from the homoscedasticity and nonautocorrelation assumptions are developed in Chapters 10, 13, and 14; these methods are reasonably effective if sufficient sample data are available.

APPENDIX 7.1: PROOF THAT S^2 IS INDEPENDENT OF $\hat{\beta}$

To show that S^2 is independent of $\hat{\beta}$, consider the covariance of $\hat{\beta}$ with the jth fitting error, U_j^{fit}. Because $E\left[U_j^{\text{fit}}\right]$ is zero[22] and $\hat{\beta}$ is unbiased, this covariance is

$$
\begin{aligned}
\text{cov}(U_j^{\text{fit}}, \hat{\beta}) &= E\left[\left[U_j^{\text{fit}} - E\left[U_j^{\text{fit}}\right]\right]\left[\hat{\beta} - E\left[\hat{\beta}\right]\right]\right] \\
&= E\left[U_j^{\text{fit}}\left[\hat{\beta} - \beta\right]\right] \\
&= E\left[\left(U_j - [\hat{\alpha} - \alpha] - x_j\left[\hat{\beta} - \beta\right]\right)\left[\hat{\beta} - \beta\right]\right] \\
&= E\left[\left[U_j\left[\hat{\beta} - \beta\right]\right]\right] - E\left[[\hat{\alpha} - \alpha]\left[\hat{\beta} - \beta\right]\right] - x_j E\left[\left[\hat{\beta} - \beta\right]^2\right] \\
&= E\left[U_j\left[\hat{\beta} - \beta\right]\right] - \text{cov}(\hat{\alpha}, \hat{\beta}) - x_j \text{var}(\hat{\beta})
\end{aligned}
$$

The variance of $\hat{\beta}$ was shown in Chapter 6 to equal σ^2/φ, where $\varphi = \sum_{i=1}^{N}(x_i - \bar{x})^2$; from Exercise 6-9, $\text{cov}(\hat{\alpha}, \hat{\beta}) = -\sigma^2\bar{x}/\varphi$. Consequently, $\text{cov}(U_j^{\text{fit}}, \hat{\beta})$ equals

$$
\begin{aligned}
\text{cov}(U_j^{\text{fit}}, \hat{\beta}) &= E\left[U_j\left[\hat{\beta} - \beta\right]\right] + \sigma^2\bar{x}/\varphi - x_j\sigma^2/\varphi \\
&= E\left[U_j\left[\sum_{i=1}^{N} w_i^{\text{ols}} U_i\right]\right] - (x_j - \bar{x})\sigma^2/\varphi \\
&= E\left[\sum_{i=1}^{N} w_i^{\text{ols}} U_i U_j\right] - \sigma^2 w_j^{\text{ols}} \\
&= \sum_{i=1}^{N} w_i^{\text{ols}} E\left[U_i U_j\right] - \sigma^2 w_j^{\text{ols}}
\end{aligned}
$$

Because U_i has constant variance, the expectation $E\left[U_i U_j\right]$ is equal to σ^2 whenever $i = j$; and because the regression errors are uncorrelated, this expectation is equal to zero otherwise. Hence,

$$
\begin{aligned}
\text{cov}(U_j^{\text{fit}}, \hat{\beta}) &= \sum_{i=1}^{N} w_i^{\text{ols}} E\left[U_i U_j\right] - \sigma^2 w_j^{\text{ols}} \\
&= w_i^{\text{ols}}\sigma^2 - \sigma^2 w_j^{\text{ols}} = 0
\end{aligned}
$$

Thus, the each of the fitting errors, $U_1^{\text{fit}} \ldots U_N^{\text{fit}}$, is uncorrelated with $\hat{\beta}$. The estimator $\hat{\beta}$ is gaussian. And because each of the three terms in $U_j^{\text{fit}} = U_j - [\hat{\alpha} - \alpha] - x_j[\hat{\beta} - \beta]$ is normally distributed, U_j^{fit} is normally distributed also. Uncorrelated jointly normal variates are independent, so this implies that $\hat{\beta}$ is independent of $U_1^{\text{fit}} \ldots U_N^{\text{fit}}$. Hence $\hat{\beta}$ is independent of any function of $U_1^{\text{fit}} \ldots U_N^{\text{fit}}$, such as S^2.[23]

[22] $E\left[U_j^{\text{fit}}\right] = E\left[U_j\right] - E[\hat{\alpha} - \alpha] - x_i E[\hat{\beta} - \beta] = 0.$

[23] "Uncorrelated jointly normal" specifically means that $(U_1 \ldots U_N)$ is distributed as a multivariate normal with a diagonal variance-covariance matrix; dependent variates can be transformed so as to have normal marginal distributions, but that is not what is intended here.

8

The Bivariate Regression Model: R^2 and Prediction

8.1 INTRODUCTION

In Chapters 5 and 6 we saw how to estimate the parameters of the Bivariate Regression Model using least squares fitting, we used the assumptions of the model to derive the sampling distributions of these parameter estimates, and we used these sampling distributions to show that the least squares estimates are *good* parameter estimates in the sense of having the desirable properties of unbiasedness, consistencey, and BLUness. In Chapter 7 we saw how to do something really practical with an estimated Bivariate Regression Model, by using the sampling distribution of $\hat{\beta}$ to derive confidence intervals and hypothesis tests for the slope parameter, β.

In this chapter we continue and complete our analysis of the Bivariate Regression Model in this practical vein, tackling the following questions:

- Does the model fit the sample data well? How well does sample variation in x_i "explain" the sample variation in the random variable Y_i?
- Is the model able to predict sample data on Y_i not used in estimating the model? How can the Bivariate Regression Model be used to provide confidence intervals for predicted values of Y_i?

As examined here, both of these topics primarily address the essential model validation issue: "Is this regression model we have just estimated any good?"

The first part of the chapter introduces – and criticizes – the oft-quoted goodness-of-fit measure called R^2. A discussion of goodness-of-fit measures which do a better job of measuring the overall effectiveness of regression model cannot be completed until the Multiple Regression Model is described in Chapter 9, however.

Where the data are in time order – as in aggregate macroeconomic time-series data or as in microeconomic sales data – predicting unobserved (future) realizations of Y_i is a highly important end unto itself. Indeed, one of the main practical uses of econometric models is to make such forecasts of time-ordered dependent variables using data on one or more currently observed explanatory variables, so much so that Chapters 17 and 18 are primarily devoted to this topic. Even where the data are not in time order, however, prediction can still play an important role in model validation. Consequently, this chapter begins the discussion of prediction in regression modeling.

Such predictions of Y_i are indispensable guides to setting policy (in the context of macroeconomic forecasting) and to scheduling production (in the context of microeconomic sales forecasting). The relevant x_i value might actually be known at the time the Y_i prediction needs to be made. Or x_i might be unknown, because (for example) it is a policy variable (such as a target interest rate) whose value is still under consideration. In that case, Y_i forecasts conditional on various likely choices for x_i often form whatever rational basis there can be for the analysis of policy. In either case, it is essential to be able to place error bars around whatever predictions are made.

Each of these topics is now considered in turn.

8.2 QUANTIFYING HOW WELL THE MODEL FITS THE DATA

In view of the fact that the estimates of the parameters α and β in the Bivariate Model are chosen so as to best fit a straight line to the sample data, it is clearly relevant to quantify how well the resulting estimated model actually does fit the data. In principle, such a measure will be useful both in assessing the value of a particular model and in comparing one proposed model for the data to another.

The most common goodness-of-fit measure is called R^2. This nomenclature derives from the result (obtained below) that this measure is numerically equal to the square of the sample correlation between the data on the explanatory and the dependent variables in the Bivariate Regression Model; this goodness-of-fit measure bears several other, probably more useful, interpretations as well, however.

On the other hand, it is fair to say that people pay far too much attention to R^2. For one thing, R^2 turns out to not be very useful for comparing regression models with differing numbers of explanatory variables; consequently, we will need to return to this topic in Chapter 9. Beyond that – as will become apparent below – the interpretation of R^2 is both subjective and problematic. Still, some form of R^2 is quoted for almost every estimated regression model. For example, the estimated model for the application analyzed in the previous chapters would ordinarily have been expressed

$$\underset{}{logearn_i} = \underset{(.166)}{6.022} + \underset{(.234)}{0.873}\ collegegrad_i + w_i^{\text{fit}} \qquad \begin{aligned} R^2 &= .224 \\ s^2 &= .686 \end{aligned} \tag{8-1}$$

Consequently, it is important to understand how R^2 is calculated and what it does (and doesn't) mean.

Fundamentally, we seek to model the variation in $y_1 \dots y_N$, the realized values of the dependent variable, across the sample. R^2 quantifies the proportion of this sample variation in Y_i that is "captured" by the $\hat{\alpha} + \hat{\beta}x_i$ part of the fitted Bivariate Regression Model. This portion of the fitted model is an estimate of the mean of Y_i, conditional on the observed value of x_i:

$$Y_i = \alpha + \beta x_i + U_i = E[Y_i|x_i] + U_i \tag{8-2}$$

because the presence of the intercept term (α) implies that $E[U_i] = 0$. The sample variation in the realizations $y_1 \dots y_N$ thus arises from two sources, corresponding to the two terms on the right-hand side of this equation. More explicitly, the y_i observations vary across the sample because:

1. The x_i vary with i, causing $E[Y_i|x_i] = \alpha + \beta x_i$ to vary.
2. The U_i are random variables, so that Y_i is not actually equal to $E[Y_i|x_i]$.

The amount of sample variation in the y_i can be measured by

$$\text{SST} = \text{sum of squares total} \equiv \sum_{i=1}^{N} (y_i - \bar{y})^2 \tag{8-3}$$

SST *looks* like a sample realization of $(N-1)$ times an estimator of the population variance of Y_i. But it really isn't, because the Y_i are not identically distributed: $E[Y_i] = \alpha + \beta x_i$ is different for each different value of x_i, whereas this estimator is taking $E[Y_i]$ to be a constant which could reasonably be estimated by the estimator $\overline{Y}$. SST can still, however, be sensibly used as a *descriptive statistic* summarizing how unequal to one another the $y_1 \dots y_N$ are.

If we quantify the sample variation in the y_i using SST and estimate β using the least squares estimator, then the sample variation in the y_i splits neatly into two parts, one corresponding to each of the two sources listed above. To see this, first recall from Chapter 5 that the least squares estimators $\hat{\alpha}^*$ and $\hat{\beta}^*$ must satisfy the equations

$$\sum_{i=1}^{N}\left\{y_i - \hat{\alpha}^* - \hat{\beta}^* x_i\right\} = \sum_{i=1}^{N} u_i^{\text{fit}} = N\bar{y} - N\hat{\alpha}^* - N\hat{\beta}^*\bar{x} = 0 \tag{8-4}$$

$$\sum_{i=1}^{N} x_i\left\{u_i - \hat{\alpha}^* - \hat{\beta}^* x_i\right\} = \sum_{i=1}^{N} x_i u_i^{\text{fit}} = 0 \tag{8-5}$$

in order to make the partial derivatives of SSE $(\hat{\alpha}^{\text{guess}}, \hat{\beta}^{\text{guess}})$ with respect to both $\hat{\alpha}^{\text{guess}}$ and $\hat{\beta}^{\text{guess}}$ equal to zero. The first of these two equations implies that $\bar{y} - \hat{\alpha}^* - \hat{\beta}^*\bar{x} = 0$; substituting this and the equation for the fitted model $\left(y_i = \hat{\alpha}^* + \hat{\beta}^* x_i + u_i^{\text{fit}}\right)$ into the definition of SST given above yields

$$\begin{aligned} \text{SST} &= \sum_{i=1}^{N}(y_i - \bar{y})^2 \\ &= \sum_{i=1}^{N}\left\{\left(\hat{\alpha}^* + \hat{\beta}^* x_i + u_i^{\text{fit}}\right) - \left(\hat{\alpha}^* + \hat{\beta}^*\bar{x}\right)\right\}^2 \\ &= \sum_{i=1}^{N}\left\{\hat{\beta}^*[x_i - \bar{x}] + u_i^{\text{fit}}\right\}^2 \\ &= \sum_{i=1}^{N}\left\{\left(\hat{\beta}^*\right)^2[x_i - \bar{x}]^2 + 2\hat{\beta}^*[x_i - \bar{x}]u_i^{\text{fit}} + \left(u_i^{\text{fit}}\right)^2\right\} \end{aligned} \tag{8-6}$$

so that

$$\begin{aligned} \text{SST} &= \sum_{i=1}^{N}\left\{\left(\hat{\beta}^*\right)^2[x_i - \bar{x}]^2 + 2\hat{\beta}^*[x_i - \bar{x}]u_i^{\text{fit}} + \left(u_i^{\text{fit}}\right)^2\right\} \\ &= \sum_{i=1}^{N}\left(\hat{\beta}^*\right)^2[x_i - \bar{x}]^2 + 2\hat{\beta}^*\sum_{i=1}^{N}x_i u_i^{\text{fit}} - 2\hat{\beta}^*\bar{x}\sum_{i=1}^{N}u_i^{\text{fit}} + \sum_{i=1}^{N}\left(u_i^{\text{fit}}\right)^2 \\ &= \left(\hat{\beta}^*\right)^2\sum_{i=1}^{N}[x_i - \bar{x}]^2 + 0 + 0 + \text{SSE}(\hat{\alpha}^*, \hat{\beta}^*) \end{aligned} \tag{8-7}$$

Thus, using the two conditions characterizing $\hat{\alpha}^{\text{guess}}$ and $\hat{\beta}^{\text{guess}}$ as minimizing SSE$(\hat{\alpha}^{\text{guess}}, \hat{\beta}^{\text{guess}})$, SST splits cleanly into a part – SSE$(\hat{\alpha}^*, \hat{\beta}^*)$ – which is clearly due to the imperfect fit of the model to the sample data and a part – $\left(\hat{\beta}^*\right)^2 \sum_{i=1}^{N} [x_i - \bar{x}]^2$ – which is clearly due to the size of $\hat{\beta}^*$ and to the degree to which x_i varies across the sample. Because SSE$(\hat{\alpha}^*, \hat{\beta}^*)$ is the portion of SST which the sample variation in $\hat{\alpha}^* - \hat{\beta}^* x_i$ does *not* reproduce, $\left(\hat{\beta}^*\right)^2 \sum_{i=1}^{N} [x_i - \bar{x}]^2$ must evidently be the portion of SST which the sample variation in $\hat{\alpha}^* - \hat{\beta}^* x_i$ *does* reproduce.[1]

Therefore R^2 is defined as

$$R^2 \equiv \frac{\left(\hat{\beta}^*\right)^2 \sum_{i=1}^{N} [x_i - \bar{x}]^2}{\sum_{i=1}^{N} (y_i - \bar{y})^2} = \frac{\left(\hat{\beta}^*\right)^2 \sum_{i=1}^{N} [x_i - \bar{x}]^2}{\text{SST}} \tag{8-8}$$

and interpreted as the fraction of the sample variation in the dependent variable which is "explained" by the fitted model. Viewing SST/$(N-1)$ as the sample variance of $y_1 \ldots y_N$ – i.e., ignoring the fact (noted above) that this statistic is really characterizing the dispersion of $y_1 \ldots y_N$ around $\bar{y}$ rather than around an estimate (e.g., $\hat{\alpha}^* + \hat{\beta}^* x_i$) of their actual means – this interpretation is often verbally expressed by identifying R^2 as "the fraction of the variance of y_i explained by the fitted model."

Next, note that the expression for R^2 in Equation 8-8 is identical to the square of the expression for r_{xy}, the sample correlation between the data on the explanatory variable ($x_1 \ldots x_N$) and the observed realizations of the dependent variable ($y_1 \ldots y_N$), obtained in Section 5.6. Thus, R^2 also equals the square of the sample correlation between y_i and any linear function of x_i, such as $\hat{\alpha}^*_{\text{OLS}} + \hat{\beta}^*_{\text{OLS}} x_i$. Hence R^2 bears a second interpretation as a consistent estimate of the squared correlation between the dependent variable in the regression model and the model's predicted value for Y_i, as defined and analyzed in Section 8.4. And this, of course, is the motivation for calling this statistic "R^2" in the first place.

R^2 has a third useful interpretation as a goodness-of-fit measure. Substituting SST – SSE$(\hat{\alpha}^*, \hat{\beta}^*)$ for $\left(\hat{\beta}^*\right)^2 \sum_{i=1}^{N} [x_i - \bar{x}]^2$ in the above expression yields

$$R^2 = \frac{\left(\hat{\beta}^*\right)^2 \sum_{i=1}^{N} [x_i - \bar{x}]^2}{\text{SST}} = \frac{\text{SST} - \text{SSE}(\hat{\alpha}^*, \hat{\beta}^*)}{\text{SST}} = 1 - \frac{\text{SSE}(\hat{\alpha}^*, \hat{\beta}^*)}{\text{SST}} \tag{8-9}$$

What can this set of equations tell us about the size of R^2? If $(\hat{\beta}^*)^2$ is close to zero, then the estimated model is a poor fit to the data – the sample variation in x_i is apparently irrelevant to the sample variation in y_i – and R^2 is close to zero. In contrast, a model which fits the data very well (and hence for which SSE$(\hat{\alpha}^*, \hat{\beta}^*)$ is very small) will have R^2 close to one. Thus R^2 lies in the interval [0, 1] and it is reasonable to interpret it as a goodness-of-fit measure.

At this point, however, a good deal of subjectiveness creeps into the discourse – how high does R^2 need to be in order to characterize the fit as "good"? In practice, this depends on both the context and on one's tastes. Generally speaking, household survey data contains so much noise in each observation that most analysts are quite happy with an R^2 value of around .20. In contrast, most people would consider a regression equation involving aggregated (e.g., macroeconomic) data to be a poor fit to the data with an R^2 less than, say, .50.

It must also be pointed out that it is not always a good idea to use R^2 to quantify the degree of relationship between two time-series variables. For example, suppose that Y_t and x_t are two unrelated time-series, each of whose sample behavior is dominated by an upward time trend – e.g., aggregate annual U.S. consumption spending and the population of Madagascar. An estimated

[1] Note that the assumptions about the model error term played no role here; this decomposition of the sample variation in $y_1 \ldots y_N$ is just a consequence of the fact that $\hat{\beta}$ is the least squares estimator of β.

regression model relating these two variables will have an R^2 very close to one, simply because all variables dominated by an upward time trend vary in much the same way – they rise each period.[2]

And a low R^2 may merely imply that the form of the regression equation has been grievously misspecified, not that the two variables are unrelated. For example suppose that a scatterplot of the (y_i, x_i) data looks like Figure 8-1, because Y_i is nonlinearly related to x_i. In this case, the best-fit straight line to the data will have $\hat{\beta}^2$ (and hence R^2) close to zero – accurately reflecting the fact the linear model does fit the data poorly – even though there is in fact a close (nonlinear) relationship between Y_i and x_i^2:

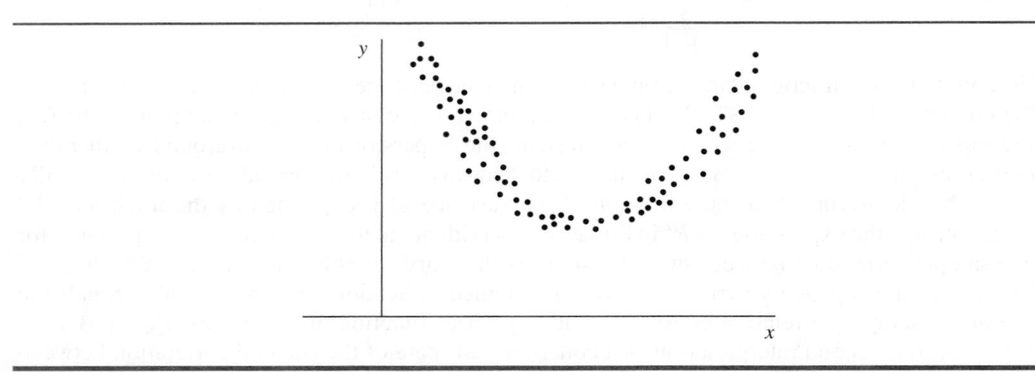

Figure 8-1 Scatterplot where Y is nonlinearly related to x.

In Chapter 9 we will return to the topic of R^2 in the context of the Multiple Regression Model, in which there may be more than one explanatory variable in the regression equation. There we will find that R^2 always rises as one adds additional explanatory variables to the model. Consequently, while one could sensibly use R^2 to compare two different bivariate regression models for y_i, it is not a good idea to use R^2 as a "figure of merit" for comparing two regression models with differing numbers of explanatory variables: more sophisticated measures (discussed in Section 9.6) are needed in such cases.

8.3 PREDICTION AS A TOOL FOR MODEL VALIDATION

Sometimes the underlying motivation behind our effort to estimate the Bivariate Regression Model is not to use the $(y_1, x_1) \ldots (y_N, x_N)$ data to estimate a confidence interval for β or to test hypotheses about β, but rather to predict the value of the random variable Y_{N+1}, conditional on a particular given value for x_{N+1}.

Most commonly this situation arises with time-series data. In that context, the ith observation on the random variable Y is its observed value in period i, so predicting y_{N+1} corresponds to forecasting a future value of Y_i – its realized value in the time period immediately following the last available observation on the dependent variable. This is called "postsample" forecasting and, as noted in the first section of this chapter, is clearly of substantial practical value in many circumstances. However, prediction of Y_{N+1} is also possible for cross-sectional data, where the index i might refer to the ith country in an international data set or to the ith household in a survey. In such an instance y_{N+1} would be the observed value for Y_i in a country or household whose data were not used in estimating

[2] This estimated model will also grotesquely violate the Bivariate Regression Model nonautocorrelation assumption that $\text{cov}(U_i, U_j) = 0$. Trended time-series can be readily detected by simply plotting them against time; we will learn how to detect and deal with violations of the nonautocorrelation assumption in Chapter 13.

the model coefficients. To allow for both possibilities, one can describe the predicted value of Y_{N+1} as an "out-of-sample" rather than as a "postsample" prediction.

It is fairly obvious why one might want to predict future values of Y_i, but out-of-sample prediction in addition has a crucial role to play in *validating* models, regardless of whether they are based on time-series data or on cross-sectional data.

Suppose, as is commonly the case, that a number of bivariate models for Y_i have been considered (and estimated), using a number of different explanatory variables. These alternative models might correspond to different theoretical frameworks, as when one group of economists models the quarterly growth rate in GDP using the previous quarter's money supply growth rate as the explanatory variable, whereas another group of economists uses last quarter's budget deficit as its explanatory variable. Or these alternative models might correspond to differing practical modeling choices on which economic theory is silent – as when we first consider using the growth rate in the money supply in the immediately previous quarter as our explanatory variable and then consider the possibility that perhaps what is important is the growth rate in the money supply lagged two quarters. Or we might at first model a person's earnings as depending on whether the person graduated from college, but consider alternative models for earnings based on whether the person graduated from high school, or on the person's total number of years of schooling, or on the square of the person's total number of years of schooling, etc. – the list of possibilities goes on and on.

Note that, if we try enough possible definitions for the explanatory variable x_i, sooner or later we are going to find one yielding a good fit to the data – i.e., an estimated model with a high R^2. In fact, this is still the case even if we use a computer program to generate a large number of $x_1 \dots x_N$ data sets at random in such a way that x_i does not relate to Y_i at all! Moreover, notice that the high R^2 of the resulting estimated regression equation implies that the value of $\hat{\beta}^2$ is large also, so that the magnitude of the t statistic we would use to test the null hypothesis H_o: $\beta = 0$ against the alternative hypothesis that H_A: $\beta \neq 0$ will be large also, leading us to incorrectly reject H_o. Thus, the degree to which a high R^2 value (and rejection of the null hypothesis that $\beta = 0$ with a small p-value) "proves" that this particular choice for x_i is closely related to (actually causes a substantial amount of the sample variation in) Y_i in fact depends crucially on how hard we tried – i.e., it depends on how many different models we considered in order to obtain this high R^2 and low p-value.

In essence, if you formulate and estimate a sufficiently large number of models for Y_i, a high R^2 and rejection of H_o: $\beta = 0$ with a small p-value is inevitable – *even if Y_i is actually unrelated to all of the explanatory variables used in these models.* In fact, the observed p-value for rejecting H_o: $\beta = 0$ should come out less than .01 for about 1% of these estimated models. This problem is called "spurious regression due to data mining."

What can we do to avoid being "snookered" by this kind of spurious regression? First, we need to recognize that some degree of data mining is usually unavoidable: economic theory is never sufficiently explicit about the form of the relationship as to totally eliminate a need to consider alternative model specifications. Second, we need to interpret the meaningfulness of the R^2 we obtain for our final model (and the p-value with which we reject H_o: $\beta = 0$) in the light of our knowledge as to how intense a specification search was utilized in order to produce them. As we shall see in Chapter 9, one way to do this is to estimate a Multiple Regression Model including in the model all of the explanatory variables we have considered. Third (and also covered in Chapter 9) we can use multiple regression modeling to test whether the key coefficients in our estimated model are stable across subsets of our sample data – spurious regressions generally have unstable coefficients.

Finally, we can evaluate the degree to which the relationship we have quantified in our model is "real" by holding out some of the sample data for out-of-sample model validation. For example, if you have observations on log(wages) for 3,000 households, you might use only the first 2,500 observations for estimating models. Then, once you have produced one or two models that you think are pretty good using only these first 2,500 observations, you can ask "how well does each of these estimated models predict the sample variation in log(wages) for the remaining 500 observations?" If one of your estimated models is a spurious regression, which appeared to be satisfactory only because of data mining, then it is very unlikely that it will be able to predict the variation in log(wages) outside of the sample over which it was formulated and estimated.

For this reason – and, of course, because prediction is often the reason we modeled Y_i in the first place – we now turn our attention to the task of using an estimated regression model based on the sample data $(y_1, x_1) \dots (y_N, x_N)$ to predict the value of Y_{N+1} given x_{N+1}.

8.4 PREDICTING Y_{N+1} GIVEN x_{N+1}

Assume that the Bivariate Regression Model also holds for period (observation number) $N+1$, thus:

$$Y_{N+1} = \alpha + \beta x_{N+1} + U_{N+1} \tag{8-10}$$

so that $U_{N+1} \sim N[0, \sigma^2]$ independently of $U_1 \dots U_N$. And assume that the sample data (y_i, x_i, $i = 1 \dots N$) are available with which to estimate α and β; x_{N+1} is assumed known also, but not Y_{N+1} or y_{N+1}. Then the predictor,

$$\hat{Y}_{N+1} = \hat{\alpha} + \hat{\beta} x_{N+1} \tag{8-11}$$

with sample realization

$$\hat{y}_{N+1} = \hat{\alpha}^* + \hat{\beta}^* x_{N+1} \tag{8-12}$$

provides a sensible way to predict the value of the random variable Y_{N+1} conditional on knowing x_{N+1}. The error this predictor makes in forecasting Y_{N+1} is the random variable $Y_{N+1} - \hat{Y}_{N+1}$; this error can be written

$$\begin{aligned} Y_{N+1} - \hat{Y}_{N+1} &= (\alpha + \beta x_{N+1} + U_{N+1}) - (\hat{\alpha} + \hat{\beta} x_{N+1}) \\ &= U_{N+1} - (\hat{\alpha} - \alpha) - (\hat{\beta} - \beta) x_{N+1} \end{aligned} \tag{8-13}$$

This prediction error can thus be decomposed into two parts: U_{N+1} and $-(\hat{\alpha} - \alpha) - (\hat{\beta} - \beta)x_{N+1}$. The first part ($U_{N+1}$) is inherent in the random character of Y_{N+1}; indeed, this model error term is the source of the randomness in Y_{N+1}. This error term is essentially unpredictable because it is assumed to be independent of $U_1 \dots U_N$; consequently, it is independent of all of the previous observations on the dependent variable.

The second part of the prediction error $\left\{-(\hat{\alpha} - \alpha) - (\hat{\beta} - \beta)x_{N+1}\right\}$ is clearly due to our inability to perfectly estimate the population parameters α and β using only the N observations $(y_1, x_1) \dots (y_N, x_N)$. We know from the results in Chapter 6 that $\hat{\alpha}$ and $\hat{\beta}$ are consistent estimators of α and β; consequently, the sampling errors $(\hat{\alpha} - \alpha)$ and $(\hat{\beta} - \beta)$ in this portion of the expression for the prediction error must become negligible for large N.

Note that the sampling error in $\hat{\beta}$ enters the prediction error expression multiplied by x_{N+1}. This reflects the fact that errors in estimating β matter only when x_{N+1} is sizeable: only then is the prediction relying heavily on our estimate of how the conditional mean of Y_i depends on the value of x_i.

It follows from this expression (Exercise 8-1) that the prediction error, $Y_{N+1} - \hat{Y}_{N+1}$, is distributed

$$\hat{Y}_{N+1} - Y_{N+1} \sim N\left[0, \sigma^2\left(1 + \frac{1}{N} + \frac{(x_{N+1} - \bar{x})^2}{\sum_{j=1}^{N}(x_j - \bar{x})^2}\right)\right] \tag{8-14}$$

if all of the assumptions underlying the Bivariate Regression Model are satisfied.

Evidently, $\hat{Y}_{N+1}$ is an unbiased predictor for Y_{N+1} – i.e., correct on average. In parameter estimation, unbiasedness is usually considered a desirable property. Indeed, it was shown in Chapter 7 that unbiasedness (or, at least, known bias) is essential to the construction of hypothesis tests and confidence intervals. But unbiasedness is not necessarily a good property in a predictor. For example, if a central bank acts on an overprediction of future inflation, sharply cuts the growth rate of the money supply, and plunges the economy into an otherwise avoidable recession, then the costs to society would likely be much larger than if the central bank acts on an underprediction of similar magnitude, fails to cut the money growth rate, and allows a higher than expected inflation rate to ensue. If so, then it would be rational (expected loss minimizing) for the central bank to use a predictor of the future inflation rate which is biased downward. Similarly, a firm basing its production plans on a prediction of future sales will typically incur quite different costs from an overprediction than from an underprediction. The costs associated with overpredicting sales depend on overtime wage rates and inventory holding costs, whereas the costs associated with underpredicting sales by the same amount hinge on whether such an error will lead to a stock-out and on the amount of sales that will be permanently lost should a stock-out occur. Because these two kinds of costs are hardly likely to be symmetric, it follows that such a firm will want to act on a biased forecast of future sales.[3]

Nevertheless, this unbiased predictor is very commonly used. And, in any case, it provides a sensible starting point, even if one is going to depart from it in practice for the kinds of reasons given earlier.

As with the prediction error itself, the variance of the prediction error again splits into two components. The first part (σ^2) is due to U_{N+1}, the unforecastable random component of Y_{N+1}, whereas the second part,

$$\sigma^2\left(\frac{1}{N} + \frac{(x_{N+1} - \bar{x})^2}{\sum_{j=1}^{N} (x_j - \bar{x})^2}\right) \tag{8-15}$$

basically arises from the sampling errors in and $\hat{\alpha}$ and $\hat{\beta}$.

Because σ^2 is not known, it is estimated, using

$$\begin{aligned} S^2 &= \left[\frac{1}{N-2}\right]\sum_{i=1}^{N}\left(U_i^{\text{fit}}\right)^2 \\ &= \left[\frac{1}{N-2}\right]\sum_{i=1}^{N}\left(Y_i - \hat{\alpha} - \hat{\beta}x_i\right)^2 \end{aligned} \tag{8-16}$$

in order to obtain a practical confidence interval for the expected value of Y_{N+1}.

Note from the above expression that S^2 does not involve Y_{N+1}; consequently, it is independent of U_{N+1}. From our results in Chapter 7,

$$\frac{(N-2)S^2}{\sigma^2} \sim \chi^2(N-2) \tag{8-17}$$

independently of $\hat{\alpha}$ and $\hat{\beta}$ if all of the assumptions of the Bivariate Model are satisfied. Looking at the expression for $Y_{N+1} - \hat{Y}_{N+1}$,

$$\begin{aligned} Y_{N+1} - \hat{Y}_{N+1} &= (\alpha + \beta x_{N+1} + U_{N+1}) - (\hat{\alpha} + \hat{\beta}x_{N+1}) \\ &= U_{N+1} - (\hat{\alpha} - \alpha) - (\hat{\beta} - \beta)x_{N+1} \end{aligned} \tag{8-18}$$

[3] Forecasting – unbiased and otherwise – will be considered again, more deeply, in Section 17.2.

we see, then, that S^2 is actually independent of every term in this expression. Thus S^2 and $Y_{N+1} - \hat{Y}_{N+1}$ are independent, so we can use $(N-2)S^2/\sigma^2 \sim \chi^2(N-2)$ and

$$\frac{\hat{Y}_{N+1} - Y_{N+1}}{\sqrt{\sigma^2\left(1 + \frac{1}{N} + \frac{(x_{N+1} - \bar{x})^2}{\sum_{j=1}^{N}(x_j - \bar{x})^2}\right)}} \sim N[0, 1] \tag{8-19}$$

to construct a t statistic:

$$\frac{\dfrac{\hat{Y}_{N+1} - Y_{N+1}}{\sqrt{\sigma^2\left(1 + \frac{1}{N} + \frac{(x_{N+1} - \bar{x})^2}{\sum_{j=1}^{N}(x_j - \bar{x})^2}\right)}}}{\sqrt{\dfrac{\frac{(N-2)S^2}{\sigma^2}}{N-2}}} \sim t(N-2) \tag{8-20}$$

From the definition given in Equation 4-31, this statistic is distributed $t(N-2)$ because it is of the form

$$\frac{Z}{\sqrt{\dfrac{Q}{N-2}}} \tag{8-21}$$

where Z is a unit normal variable independent of Q, which is a chi-squared variable with $N-2$ degrees of freedom. This expression simplifies to yield

$$\frac{\hat{Y}_{N+1} - Y_{N+1}}{\sqrt{S^2\left(1 + \frac{1}{N} + \frac{(x_{N+1} - \bar{x})^2}{\sum_{j=1}^{N}(x_j - \bar{x})^2}\right)}} \sim t(N-2) \tag{8-22}$$

from which it follows that an estimated 95% confidence interval for Y_{N+1} is

$$\hat{y}_{N+1} \pm t^c_{.025}\sqrt{s^2\left(1 + \frac{1}{N} + \frac{(x_{N+1} - \bar{x})^2}{\sum_{j=1}^{N}(x_j - \bar{x})^2}\right)} \tag{8-23}$$

where $t^c_{.025}$ is the 2½% critical point of the Student's t distribution with $N-2$ degrees of freedom.

Looking at this expression for the 95% confidence interval for Y_{N+1}, it is evident that the width of the confidence interval is smallest if x_{N+1} is close to its sample mean and grows as the magnitude of $x_{N+1} - \bar{x}$ increases. An earnest word of caution is in order at this point. This widening of the confidence interval as $|x_{N+1} - \bar{x}|$ increases correctly quantifies the increased uncertainty in our forecast of Y_{N+1} as we start relying more and more heavily on the accuracy of $\hat{\beta}$. *However, the validity of this confidence interval hinges on all of the assumptions of the Bivariate Regression Model being satisfied – notably including the assumption that the mean of* Y_i *is a linear function of* x_i. *This assumption may be quite a good approximation over the range of x values observed in the available sample data, but it may fail miserably for* x_{N+1} *values notably outside of this range.*

Figure 8-2 illustrates this point. Here the true model for Y_i correctly describes $E[Y_i \mid X_i]$ as a quadratic function of x_i, but our linear Bivariate Regression Model is a perfectly adequate approximation over the limited range of values for x_i observed in the sample. This error in specifying the model causes no serious problem unless and until one is so foolhardy as to use the model to forecast Y_{N+1} for a value of x_{N+1} well outside the observed range:

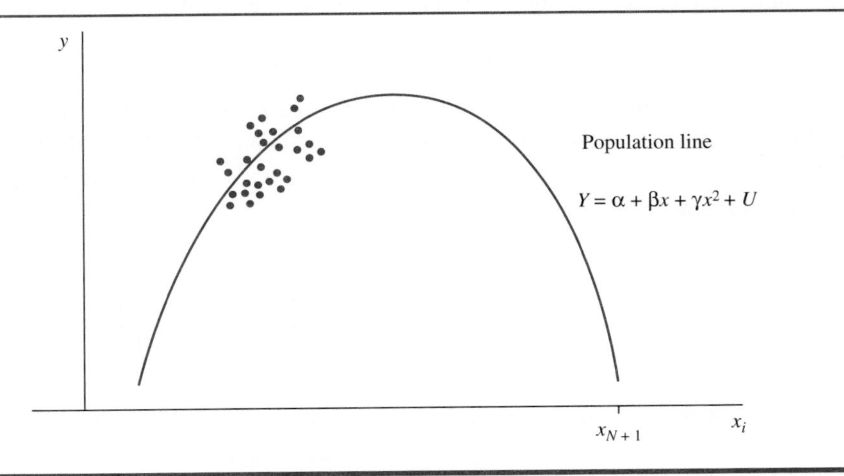

Figure 8-2 Illustration of a Disastrous Forecast from a Linear Regression Model

Clearly, even a small number of observations on Y_i based on x_i values similar to x_{N+1} would at least alert us to this problem. If such data are simply not available, however, the best you can do is to be very, very wary of relying on the predictor $\hat{Y}_{N+1}$ in this circumstance.

We have now reached the end of the issues which are most gracefully discussed in the context of the Bivariate Regression Model. In order to make further progress in understanding how to analyze data using regression analysis we must at this point move on to consider the Multiple Regression Model, which allows for multiple explanatory variables in the regression equation. That is the topic of the next chapter.

KEY TERMS

For each term or concept listed below, provide a working definition or explanation:

Fitting Error vs. Prediction Error

SST vs. SSR vs. SSE

R^2

Spurious Regression due to Data Mining

EXERCISES

8-1. Using the expression for the forecast error $(Y_{N+1} - \hat{Y}_{N+1})$ given in Equation 8-14, show that it is distributed

$$\hat{Y}_{N+1} - Y_{N+1} \sim N\left[0, \sigma^2\left(1 + \frac{1}{N} + \frac{(x_{N+1} - \bar{x})^2}{\sum_{j=1}^{N}(x_j - \bar{x})^2}\right)\right]$$

if all the assumptions underlying the Bivariate Regression Model (Equation 5-14) are satisfied. {Hint: you will need to use the results obtained in Chapter 6 (and in Exercise 6-9) on the sampling variances of $\hat{\alpha}$ and $\hat{\beta}$ and on $\text{cov}(\hat{\alpha}, \hat{\beta})$. Note that because U_{N+1} is independent of $U_1 \ldots U_N$, $E[u_{N+1}\, u_i]$ is zero for all i in the interval $[1, N]$.

8-2. Continuing Exercises 6-11 and 7-12, again consider the simpler regression model

$$Y_i = \beta x_i + U_i \quad U_i \sim \text{NIID}(0, \sigma^2)$$

now assuming that this model is valid for observations $i = 1 \ldots N+1$ and that x_{N+1} is known but that y_{N+1} is not, so that a realization of $\hat{Y}_{N+1} = \hat{\beta}x_{N+1}$ will be used to forecast Y_{N+1}.

a. Derive an expression for the forecast error $(\hat{Y}_{N+1} - Y_{N+1})$ involving U_{N+1} and $\hat{\beta} - \beta$.

b. Show that the forecast errors are distributed:

$$\hat{Y}_{N+1} - Y_{N+1} \sim N\left[0, \sigma^2\left(1 + \frac{x_{N+1}^2}{\sum_{j=1}^{N} x_j^2}\right)\right]$$

c. Using your results from Exercise 7-12, show that a 95% confidence interval for Y_{N+1} is

$$\hat{Y}_{N+1} \pm t^c_{.025}\sqrt{S^2\left(1 + \frac{x_{N+1}^2}{\sum_{j=1}^{N} x_j^2}\right)}$$

where $t^c_{.025}$ is the 2½% critical point of the Student's t distribution with $N-1$ degrees of freedom.

8-3. Continuing Exercises 6-12 and 7-13 – and using your results from Exercise 8-2 – suppose that $x_5 = .5$:

a. Calculate the predicted value of Y_5.

b. State the estimated distribution of the errors made by the prediction $\hat{Y}_5$.

c. Use your answer for part b to calculate an estimated 95% confidence interval for Y_5. What happens to the width of this interval as x_5^2 increases? Why does this make sense? What else should you be wary of as x_5^2 increases?

d. As in Exercises 6-12 and 7-13, check your calculations by inputting the data into the econometric software being used in your course and estimating a model with no intercept. {In Stata this model would be estimated using the command "reg y x, noconstant". The Stata command "predict yhat" stores the predicted values $\{\hat{y}_i = \hat{\beta}x_i \text{ for } i = 1 \ldots 5\}$ as Stata variable "yhat" and the command "predict stderror, stdp" stores the estimated standard errors for these predictions as Stata variable "stderror."}

Active Learning Exercise 8a: On the Folly of Trying Too Hard: A Simple Example of "Data Mining"

Introduction

Not really trying is a recipe for failure in most parts of life. Strangely, in many of the most important endeavors in life, trying too hard is not a great idea, either. Finding the regression model that fits the sample data best may (or may not) be the most important endeavor in your life at some point in the future. But it turns out that such search activity is in fact one of those endeavors in which you want to be careful about trying too hard. This Active Learning Exercise illustrates that fact.

In this exercise you will generate *N* observations on a dependent variable (*Y*) and on a number of unrelated explanatory variables, here labeled "x1" ... "x100." By estimating various bivariate regression models for these data, you will demonstrate that one can easily find an explanatory variable which appears to be statistically significant just due to chance. However, re-estimating this model separately over the first and the second halves of the sample, you will very likely observe that such bogus models do not usually represent a stable relationship over the entire sample.

Your Assignment:

1. Copy the program ALE8a.exe (available at www.wiley.com/college/ashley) to your hard disk and execute it.[4] The program will prompt you to enter a sample length; 100 observations will work fine. Then it will prompt you to enter a value to use as the initial seed for the random number generator. You can enter any positive integer you like here (or whatever value your instructor suggests) but write down the value you use so that your work is easily replicable.[5]
2. The program then generates 100 observations for the dependent variable, *Y*, and for each of the possible explanatory variables, x1 ... x100.[6] All observations on all variables are normally identically and independently distributed, so all of the possible bivariate regression models – *Y* versus x1, *Y* versus x2, ... , *Y* versus x100 – satisfy all of the assumptions of the Bivariate Regression Model. Of course, the true values of alpha and beta are in every case precisely zero.
3. Estimate all of these bivariate models looking for the one whose estimated *t* ratio on $\hat{\beta}$ is largest in magnitude. This is also, of course, the model with the highest value for R^2 and the smallest *p*-value for rejecting the null hypothesis H_o: $\beta = 0$ against the alternative hypothesis H_A: $\beta \neq 0$.[7]

[4] Program source code is available at www.wiley.com/college/ashley as file ALE8a.for. Subroutine RAN1 generates a uniform random number between zero and one using a linear congruential random number generator which is a variation on that described above. It is taken from (and documented in) *Numerical Recipes* (Press et al., Cambridge University Press: Cambridge, pp. 195–97.) Pairs of uniform random numbers from RAN1 are used to generate normally distributed variates using the routine GASDEV, from *Numerical Recipes* (p. 202). In case the program is not compatible with your version of Windows, a sample output file created with 100 observations on each series and initial seed equal to 23 is available at www.wiley.com/college/ashley, labeled "ALE8a.csv".

[5] See Active Learning Exercise 3a and Active Learning Exercise 6b (available at www.wiley.com/college/ashley) for a discussion of how pseudo-random number generators work and why they need an initial seed.

[6] One hundred explanatory variables are generated regardless of what sample size you enter.

[7] You can save yourself some drudgery by first running multiple regression models in which you regress realizations of *Y* against, say, 20 of the explanatory variables at a time.

a. How many models do you expect to find with a p-value smaller than .05?
b. How many models do you expect to find with a p-value smaller than .01?
c. How many such models – with a p-value smaller than 0.05 for rejecting H_o: $\beta = 0$ – *do* you find? Report the regression output for these models.
d. What is the smallest p-value that you find?

4. Re-estimate your best-looking model separately over the first and the second halves of the sample and report the regression output for these two models. Does the slope coefficient in the original model appear to be stable over both halves of the sample?[8]

[8] Supposing that x5 is the best explanatory variable, the Stata commands for this would be "reg y x5 if _$n \Leftarrow 50$" and "reg y x5 if _$n > 50$". More formal tests for parameter stability are discussed in Chapters 9 and 10.

9

The Multiple Regression Model

9.1 INTRODUCTION

Our coverage of the basic Bivariate Model is now complete. Analysis of this model allowed us to examine regression parameter estimation and inference in the simplest possible setting. But the modeling of real-world economic data sets – and even, as we saw in Chapter 8, beginning to check the assumptions of the Bivariate Model – requires that we broaden the modeling framework to include multiple explanatory variables in the regression model. This broader framework is called the Multiple Regression Model and is the topic of this chapter.

None of our work on the Bivariate Model will go to waste, however. In particular, because a complete analysis of multiple regression requires a background in matrix algebra which is beyond the scope of this book, many of the results on the Multiple Regression Model – for example, the BLUness of the least squares parameter estimates – will merely be stated here and motivated by reference to the analogous results for the Bivariate Regression Model. And you will find that a number of other derivations in this chapter – those, for example, of the sampling distributions of the parameter estimates and of the inference results based on these estimates – are quite similar to the analogous derivations in the context of the Bivariate Regression Model.

Other issues arise here which could not occur in the context of the Bivariate Regression Model. We must now deal with the issues associated with overelaborate and underelaborate models. Also unique to the Multiple Regression Model is the problem of multicollinearity, where the sample variation in one explanatory variable is uncomfortably similar to that of another.

The Multiple Regression Model is vastly more powerful than the Bivariate Regression Model; this chapter closes with several examples illustrating its applicability.

9.2 THE MULTIPLE REGRESSION MODEL

The Multiple Regression Model is a straightforward generalization of the Bivariate Model to include multiple explanatory variables:

The Multiple Regression Model

$$
\begin{gathered}
Y_i = \beta_1 x_{i,1} + \beta_2 x_{i,2} + \beta_3 x_{i,3} + \cdots + \beta_k x_{i,k} + U_i \qquad i = 1 \dots N \\
x_{i,1} = 1 \quad \text{for} \quad i = 1 \dots N \\
x_{i,j} \text{ is "fixed in repeated samples" for } i = 1 \dots N \text{ and for } j = 2 \dots k \\
U_i \sim \text{NIID}[0, \sigma^2]
\end{gathered}
\tag{9-1}
$$

Equivalently,

Y_i is independently (but not identically) distributed

$N[\beta_1 x_{i,1} \dots \beta_k x_{i,k}, \sigma^2]$

Indeed, the Multiple Regression Model reduces to the Bivariate Regression Model for the special case where k equals two. Note that the Multiple Regression Model implies that each observed y_i value is a realization of a random variable (Y_i) which is normally and independently distributed. However, as with the Bivariate Regression Model, Y_i is not identically distributed, because its population mean is taken to depend linearly on the ith value of each of k explanatory variables, $x_{i,1}, x_{i,2}, \dots, x_{i,k}$.

It is common to include a constant (an "intercept") in the model by setting the value of one of the explanatory variables equal to one for every observation; here – as is typical – the first explanatory variable is used for this purpose. Inclusion of an intercept in the model is desirable here for the same reason that an intercept is useful in the Bivariate Regression Model: the presence of this term allows us to assume that $E[U_i]$ is zero with no loss of generality, and we will see that this is sufficient to make the least squares estimators of $\beta_1 \dots \beta_k$ unbiased.

The interpretation and nomenclature for all of the other assumptions of the Multiple Regression Model are essentially identical to those given for the Bivariate Regression Model in Chapter 5, so little more needs to be said about them here.

9.3 WHY THE MULTIPLE REGRESSION MODEL IS NECESSARY AND IMPORTANT

First of all, the multiple regression model is necessary where the sample variation in the dependent variable is caused by sample variation in more than one observed explanatory variable. This situation is, of course, extremely common with economic data. For example, fluctuations in the growth rate of aggregate consumption spending may primarily depend on fluctuations in the growth rate of aggregate disposable income, but are also known to depend on changes in the interest rate. Similarly, in a household earnings equation, education levels are of primary importance, but demographic characteristics such as age, gender, and race must also be considered.

Multiple regression is also generally necessary for modeling nonlinearities in economic relationships. For example, sample variation in the logarithm of an individual's earnings might well depend nonlinearly on the individual's education level. Where "edu_i" is the number of years of schooling for the ith individual, a simple way to model this is with the model,

$$LOGEARN_i = \beta_1 + \beta_2\, edu_i + \beta_3 edu_i^2 + U_i \tag{9-2}$$

Note that the null hypothesis $H_o: \beta_3 = 0$ corresponds to a linear relationship in this instance and that this model implies that the expected return to an additional year of education is a linear function of education level, rising with years of schooling if the parameter β_3 is positive:[1]

$$\left(\frac{\partial E[LOGEARN_i]}{\partial edu_i}\right) = \beta_2 + 2\beta_3 edu_i \tag{9-3}$$

Quite often there are also inhomogeneities in economic data sets which correspond to observable variables; the Multiple Regression Model enables us to both quantify the significance of such inhomogeneities and to allow for them so that they do not distort our estimates of the coefficients on other explanatory variables. For example, in the previous model there might be earnings data for both male and female individuals in our sample; we could allow for a gender-related systematic discrepancy in $E[LOGEARN_i]$ by including a gender dummy variable in the model:

$$LOGEARN_i = \beta_1 + \beta_2\, edu_i + \beta_3\, edu_i^2 + \beta_4\, gender_i + U_i \tag{9-4}$$

[1] The fact that edu_i generally takes on only integer values is glossed over here. Also, note that the partial derivative ("∂" rather than "d") notation is unnecessary in Equation 9-3, as $E[LOGEARN_i]$ is actually a function of only a single variable, edu_i.

where $gender_i$ equals zero for females and one for males. The gender dummy variable in this model shifts the constant in the regression model upward by an amount β_4 for males. Presuming that the individuals in the sample are otherwise similar except for education level and gender, the parameter β_4 in this model allows us to quantify and test for the earnings impact of gender-based labor market discrimination while allowing for ("controlling for") the fact that the individuals in the sample might have systematically different educational histories. Similarly, the parameters β_2 and β_3 in this model allow us to quantify and test for a (possibly nonlinear) impact of education on earnings while controlling for the possibility that the women in the sample might, for example, on average be more highly educated but discriminated against.

Note that, if β_4 in the previous regression model is nonzero, then the intercept in Equation 9-4 in essence has one value for the male individuals in the sample and another value for the female individuals in the model. Clearly, it is not possible in that case for any single estimator of the intercept to be either unbiased or consistent for both of these values. We could, however, interpret our least squares estimator of the intercept in that instance as an unbiased and consistent estimate of a gender-averaged value for this constant.

Finally, the Multiple Regression Model allows us to test for (and allow for) model parameter instability across the sample. Suppose that one has formulated the model

$$LOGEARN_i = \beta_1 + \beta_2\, edu_i + U_i \tag{9-5}$$

for quantifying the impact of education on earnings, but one is concerned that the impact of an additional year of education (β_2) may differ for men and women. The model

$$LOGEARN_i = \beta_1 + \beta_2 edu_i + \beta_3\, gender_i \times edu_i + U_i \tag{9-6}$$

explicitly allows for this possibility: β_2 is the impact of an additional year of education on the logarithm of earnings for a household with $gender_i$ equal to zero, whereas $\beta_2 + \beta_3$ is the impact of an additional year of education on the logarithm of earnings for a household with $gender_i$ equal to one. Consequently, one can test for this possibility – which amounts to instability across the sample in the slope coefficient of the previous regression model – by simply testing the null hypothesis H_o: $\beta_3 = 0$.

9.4 MULTIPLE REGRESSION PARAMETER ESTIMATES VIA LEAST SQUARES FITTING

In the context of the Bivariate Model it was natural to motivate least squares parameter estimation by appealing to the "fit" of a straight line to a scatterplot of the sample data (y_1, x_1) ... (y_N, x_N). This approach becomes awkward once there are two explanatory variables because the scatterplot is now a three-dimensional cloud of data points. And the scatterplot approach is almost useless for models with three or more explanatory variables, because it is virtually impossible to visualize even higher-dimensional clouds of data points.

It is still easy to define fitting errors for the model, however:

$$u_i^{\text{fit}} \equiv y_i - \hat{\beta}_1^{\text{guess}} x_{i1} - \cdots - \hat{\beta}_k^{\text{guess}} x_{ik} \tag{9-7}$$

where $\hat{\beta}_1^{\text{guess}} \ldots \hat{\beta}_k^{\text{guess}}$ are estimates of the parameters $\beta_1 \ldots \beta_k$. Based on these guessed estimates, $u_1^{\text{fit}} \ldots u_N^{\text{fit}}$ are the observed errors the fitted model makes in reproducing y_1 ... y_N. Consequently – as with the Bivariate Regression Model – it makes sense to choose $\hat{\beta}_1^{\text{guess}} \ldots \hat{\beta}_k^{\text{guess}}$ so as to minimize

$$\text{SSE}\left[\hat{\beta}_1^{\text{guess}} \ldots \hat{\beta}_k^{\text{guess}}\right] = \sum_{i=1}^{N} \left(u_i^{\text{fit}}\right)^2 = \sum_{i=1}^{N} \left[y_i - \hat{\beta}_1^{\text{guess}} x_{i1} - \cdots - \hat{\beta}_k^{\text{guess}} x_{ik}\right]^2 \tag{9-8}$$

The remainder of this section is devoted to characterizing and obtaining the least squares estimates, $\hat{\beta}_{\text{ols},1}^{*} \ldots \hat{\beta}_{\text{ols},k}^{*}$, which together constitute the solution to this minimization problem. As before, with the coefficient estimates for the Bivariate Regression Model, the asterisk in this notation is used to explicitly indicate that these are the (fixed) realizations of the least squares estimators, $\hat{\beta}_{ols,1} \dots \hat{\beta}_{ols,k}$. These least squares estimators are random variables whose sampling distributions will be characterized (later in this chapter) and used to derive the properties of these estimators and the statistical inference results which are used for estimating confidence intervals for $\beta_1 \dots \beta_k$ and for testing hypotheses about $\beta_1 \dots \beta_k$.

How can we characterize the k parameter estimates $\hat{\beta}^*_{ols,1} \dots \hat{\beta}^*_{ols,k}$? For the sake of definiteness, let's assume that k is greater than or equal to 3 and focus on the estimator of a typical one of these coefficients: $\hat{\beta}^*_{ols,3}$, the estimate of β_3. What condition characterizes the value of $\hat{\beta}_3^{guess}$ which minimizes the sum of squared fitting errors, assuming that we have somehow already obtained the other $k-1$ least squares parameter estimates, $\hat{\beta}^*_{ols,1}$, $\hat{\beta}^*_{ols,2}$, $\hat{\beta}^*_{ols,4}$, ..., $\hat{\beta}^*_{ols,k}$? Holding $\hat{\beta}_1^{guess}$, $\hat{\beta}_2^{guess}$ and $\hat{\beta}_4^{guess} \dots \hat{\beta}_k^{guess}$ constant at these optimal values, $SSE\left\{\hat{\beta}_1^{guess} \dots \hat{\beta}_k^{guess}\right\}$ becomes $SSE\left(\hat{\beta}^*_{ols,1}, \hat{\beta}^*_{ols,2}, \hat{\beta}_3^{guess}, \hat{\beta}^*_{ols,4}, \dots, \hat{\beta}^*_{ols,k}\right)$, a function of $\hat{\beta}_3^{guess}$ alone. Graphing this function against $\hat{\beta}_3^{guess}$ yields Figure 9-1.

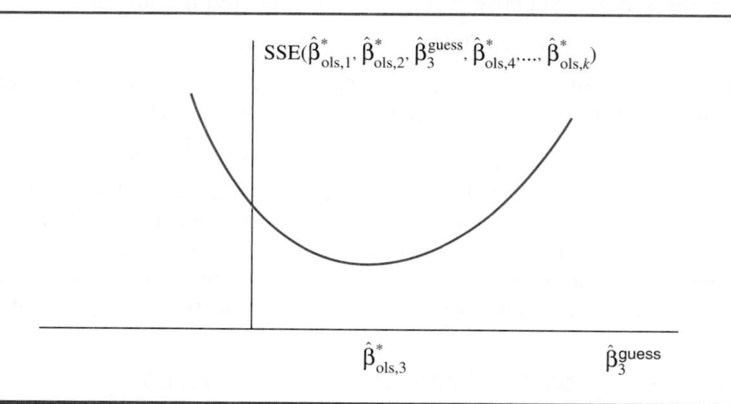

Figure 9-1 The OLS Estimate of β_3

Clearly, $\hat{\beta}^*_{ols,3}$ – the optimal value of $\hat{\beta}_3^{guess}$ – is the value of $\hat{\beta}_3^{guess}$ for which the slope of a line tangent to this curve is horizontal. Thus, $\hat{\beta}^*_{ols,3}$ must satisfy the condition

$$\frac{\partial SSE\left[\hat{\beta}_1^{guess} \dots \hat{\beta}_k^{guess}\right]}{\partial \hat{\beta}_3^{guess}} = 0 \tag{9-9}$$

where this partial derivative is evaluated at $\hat{\beta}_1^{guess} = \hat{\beta}^*_{ols,1} \dots \hat{\beta}_k^{guess} = \hat{\beta}^*_{ols,k}$. There was nothing special about the third parameter estimate, so we can conclude that $\hat{\beta}^*_{ols,1} \dots \hat{\beta}^*_{ols,k}$, the values of $\hat{\beta}_1^{guess} \dots \hat{\beta}_k^{guess}$ which jointly minimize $SSE\left[\hat{\beta}_1^{guess} \dots \hat{\beta}_k^{guess}\right]$, must satisfy the k equations,

$$\left\{\begin{array}{c} \dfrac{\partial SSE\left[\hat{\beta}_1^{guess} \dots \hat{\beta}_k^{guess}\right]}{\partial \hat{\beta}_1^{guess}} = 0 \\ \dots \\ \dfrac{\partial SSE\left[\hat{\beta}_1^{guess} \dots \hat{\beta}_k^{guess}\right]}{\partial \hat{\beta}_k^{guess}} = 0 \end{array}\right\} \tag{9-10}$$

evaluated at $\hat{\beta}_1^{guess} = \hat{\beta}^*_{ols,1}$ through $\hat{\beta}_k^{guess} = \hat{\beta}^*_{ols,k}$.

Each of these k conditions is just a linear equation in the k unknowns $\hat{\beta}^*_{ols,1} \ldots \hat{\beta}^*_{ols,k}$. For example, the third of these conditions is

$$
\begin{aligned}
0 = \frac{\partial \text{SSE}\left[\hat{\beta}_1^{guess} \ldots \hat{\beta}_k^{guess}\right]}{\partial \hat{\beta}_3^{guess}} = \frac{\partial \sum_{i=1}^{N} \left(u_i^{fit}\right)^2}{\partial \hat{\beta}_3^{guess}} &= \frac{\partial \sum_{i=1}^{N} \left[y_i - \hat{\beta}_1^{guess} x_{i1} - \hat{\beta}_2^{guess} x_{i2} - \hat{\beta}_3^{guess} x_{i3} - \cdots - \hat{\beta}_k^{guess} x_{ik}\right]^2}{\partial \hat{\beta}_3^{guess}} \\
&= \sum_{i=1}^{N} \frac{\partial \left[y_i - \hat{\beta}_1^{guess} x_{i1} - \hat{\beta}_2^{guess} x_{i2} - \hat{\beta}_3^{guess} x_{i3} - \cdots - \hat{\beta}_k^{guess} x_{ik}\right]^2}{\partial \hat{\beta}_3^{guess}} \\
&= \sum_{i=1}^{N} (-2x_{i3}) \left[y_i - \hat{\beta}^*_{ols,1} x_{i1} - \hat{\beta}^*_2 x_{i2} - \hat{\beta}^*_3 x_{i3} - \cdots - \hat{\beta}^*_{ols,k} x_{ik}\right] \\
&= -2 \sum_{i=1}^{N} \left[y_i x_{i3} - \hat{\beta}^*_{ols,1} x_{i1} x_{i3} - \hat{\beta}^*_{ols,2} x_{i2} x_{i3} - \hat{\beta}^*_{ols,3} x_{i3}^2 - \cdots - \hat{\beta}^*_{ols,k} x_{ik} x_{i3}\right]
\end{aligned}
\tag{9-11}
$$

Note that $\hat{\beta}_1^{guess} \ldots \hat{\beta}_k^{guess}$ in the equations above are, after a point, replaced by $\hat{\beta}^*_{ols,1} \ldots \hat{\beta}^*_{ols,k}$ to reflect the fact that the equality of this partial derivative to zero (along with the other $k-1$ analogous equalities) characterizes the (realized) least squares estimates, $\hat{\beta}^*_{ols,1} \ldots \hat{\beta}^*_{ols,k}$. (Note that, as in Section 6.2, the asterisks indicate explicitly that these are the realizations of the estimators, $\hat{\beta}_{ols,1} \ldots \hat{\beta}_{ols,k}$).

Multiplying this expression through by $-1/2$ and collecting the terms into separate sums,

$$
\begin{aligned}
0 &= \sum_{i=1}^{N} \left[y_i x_{i3} - \hat{\beta}^*_{ols,1} x_{i1} x_{i3} - \hat{\beta}^*_{ols,2} x_{i2} x_{i3} - \hat{\beta}^*_{ols,3} x_{i3}^2 - \cdots - \hat{\beta}^*_{ols,k} x_{ik} x_{i3}\right] \\
&= \sum_{i=1}^{N} y_i x_{i3} - \hat{\beta}^*_{ols,1} \sum_{i=1}^{N} x_{i1} x_{i3} - \hat{\beta}^*_{ols,2} \sum_{i=1}^{N} x_{i2} x_{i3} - \hat{\beta}^*_{ols,3} \sum_{i=1}^{N} x_{i3}^2 - \cdots - \hat{\beta}^*_{ols,k} \sum_{i=1}^{N} x_{ik} x_{i3}
\end{aligned}
\tag{9-12}
$$

All of these sums can be easily calculated using the sample data; thus, the partial derivative condition characterizing the minimization of $\text{SSE}\left\{\hat{\beta}_1^{guess} \ldots \hat{\beta}_k^{guess}\right\}$ over $\hat{\beta}_3^{guess}$ yields one linear equation in the k unknowns, $\hat{\beta}^*_{ols,1} \ldots \hat{\beta}^*_{ols,k}$.

Each of the other $k-1$ conditions for minimizing $\text{SSE}\left\{\hat{\beta}_1^{guess} \ldots \hat{\beta}_k^{guess}\right\}$ yields a similar linear equation which $\hat{\beta}^*_{ols,1} \ldots \hat{\beta}^*_{ols,k}$ must satisfy, for a total of k linear equations in k unknowns. By custom, these are called the "normal equations," even though they have nothing to do with normally distributed random variables – indeed, note that none of the assumptions on $U_1 \ldots U_N$ were used in their derivation.

So long as none of these k equations is redundant (e.g., a linear multiple of one of the other equations) nor inconsistent with one of the other equations, these equations can in principle be numerically solved for $\hat{\beta}^*_{ols,1} \ldots \hat{\beta}^*_{ols,k}$. In practice, however, economic data frequently yields a set of k normal equations which are numerically challenging to solve, due to a buildup of rounding errors in intermediate calculations. High-quality econometrics computer software effectively eliminates this problem by using sophisticated matrix algebra routines to solve these equations. For this reason, however, you should be wary of using less-specialized software (such as Excel) to estimate the coefficients in multiple regression models.

9.5 PROPERTIES AND SAMPLING DISTRIBUTION OF $\hat{\beta}_{ols,1} \ldots \hat{\beta}_{ols,k}$

The Multiple Regression Model can be analyzed to obtain the sampling distribution of the least squares parameter estimates and their properties as estimators in much the same way that we analyzed the Bivariate Regression Model in Chapter 6. This is not surprising, in view of the fact that the Bivariate Regression Model is simply a special case of the Multiple Regression Model, with k equal to two. Because the results are essentially identical to those obtained for the Bivariate Regression Model and because their derivation requires matrix algebra that is beyond the scope of this book, the analogous results for $\hat{\beta}_{ols,1} \dots \hat{\beta}_{ols,k}$ are mostly summarized, rather than derived, below.

First, when one solves the k normal equations for $\hat{\beta}^*_{ols,1} \dots \hat{\beta}^*_{ols,k}$ it turns out that each of these k solutions is still a linear function of $y_1 \dots y_N$, the observed realizations of the dependent variables, $Y_1 \dots Y_N$. In particular, for the jth parameter this fixed estimate can be written

$$\hat{\beta}^*_{ols,j} = \sum_{i=1}^{N} w^{ols}_{ji} y_i = \hat{\beta}^*_j \tag{9-13}$$

which is the sample realization of the estimator

$$\hat{\beta}_{ols,j} = \sum_{i=1}^{N} w^{ols}_{ji} Y_i = \hat{\beta}_j \tag{9-14}$$

where the "ols" subscript is dropped at this point so as to make the notation less cluttered: it is to be understood from here on that $\hat{\beta}_1 \dots \hat{\beta}_k$ and $\hat{\beta}^*_1 \dots \hat{\beta}^*_k$ are the least squares estimators and their corresponding sample realizations.

The weights $w^{ols}_{j1} \dots w^{ols}_{jN}$ in the estimator $\hat{\beta}_j$ will again be called "the least squares weights." These are fixed (nonrandom) constants which depend only – but in a complicated way – on the explanatory variable data, $(x_{11} \dots x_{1k}) \dots (x_{N1} \dots x_{Nk})$. Note that the w^{ols}_{ji} are now indexed with an additional subscript to allow for the fact that the least squares weights defining $\hat{\beta}_1$ – i.e., $w^{ols}_{11} \dots w^{ols}_{1N}$ – will in general differ from the weights $w^{ols}_{21} \dots w^{ols}_{2N}$ defining $\hat{\beta}_2$, and so forth.

Just as the fact that the Bivariate Regression Model least squares weights had the properties $\sum_{i=1}^{N} w^{ols}_i = 0$ and $\sum_{i=1}^{N} w^{ols}_i x_i = 1$ (which led to the result that $\hat{\beta} = \beta + \sum_{i=1}^{N} w^{ols}_i U_i$), the least squares weights here satisfy a number of analogous properties. In particular, the weighted sum $\sum_{i=1}^{N} w^{ols}_{ji} x_{i\ell}$ equals one for ℓ equal to j and equals zero otherwise.[2] These properties ensure that $\hat{\beta}_j$ can be written as

$$\hat{\beta}_j = \sum_{i=1}^{N} w^{ols}_{ji} Y_i = \beta_j + \sum_{i=1}^{N} w^{ols}_{ji} U_i \tag{9-15}$$

Thus, each of the least squares estimators can again be written as the parameter it is intended to estimate plus a simple weighted sum of the model errors. The derivation of these properties of the least squares weights and of this result on $\hat{\beta}_j$ are omitted here because they require matrix algebra. But an explicit example with k equal to 3 – i.e., with an intercept plus two explanatory variables in the model – will clarify what these results mean.

Suppose, then, that

$$Y_i = \beta_1 x_{i,1} + \beta_2 x_{i,2} + \beta_3 x_{i,3} + U_i \tag{9-16}$$

where $x_{i,1}$ is set to one for all N values of i and that, to keep the expressions simpler, the data on each of the two remaining explanatory variables has been expressed as a deviation from its sample mean

[2] The advanced reader who is aware that the Multiple Regression Model can be rewritten compactly in matrix notation as $Y = X\beta + U$ might find it useful to note that $w^{ols}_{j1} \dots w^{ols}_{jN}$ are the N components of the jth row of the $(k \times N)$ dimensional $(X^tX)^{-1}X^t$ matrix and that these properties follow from the fact that $(X^tX)^{-1}X^tX$ is clearly just the k dimensional identity matrix.

so that the sums $\sum_{i=1}^{N} x_{i2}$ and $\sum_{i=1}^{N} x_{i3}$ are both zero by construction. In that case, after a good deal of tedious (but straightforward) algebra, it can be shown that

$$
\begin{aligned}
w_{1i}^{\text{ols}} &= \frac{1}{N} \\
w_{2i}^{\text{ols}} &= \frac{x_{i2}\sum_{m=1}^{N} x_{m3}^2 - x_{i3}\sum_{m=1}^{N} x_{m2}x_{m3}}{\sum_{m=1}^{N} x_{m2}^2 \sum_{m=1}^{N} x_{m3}^2 - \left(\sum_{m=1}^{N} x_{m2}x_{m3}\right)^2} \\
w_{3i}^{\text{ols}} &= \frac{x_{i3}\sum_{m=1}^{N} x_{m2}^2 - x_{i2}\sum_{m=1}^{N} x_{m2}x_{m3}}{\sum_{m=1}^{N} x_{m2}^2 \sum_{m=1}^{N} x_{m3}^2 - \left(\sum_{m=1}^{N} x_{m2}x_{m3}\right)^2}
\end{aligned}
\tag{9-17}
$$

For a multiple regression model with three or more explanatory variables, explicit formulas like these for the least squares weights would become even more unwieldy, but are no different in character: they are just messy expressions involving the (fixed) data on the explanatory variables.[3] In practice, of course, the k linear equations for $\hat{\beta}_1^* \ldots \hat{\beta}_k^*$, the sample realizations of $\hat{\beta}_1 \ldots \hat{\beta}_k$, are solved numerically, so explicit formulas for the least squares weights are not needed.

Returning to the general expression relating the least squares estimator of β_j to the model errors, $U_1 \ldots U_N$,

$$
\hat{\beta}_j = \sum_{i=1}^{N} w_{ji}^{\text{ols}} Y_i = \beta_j + \sum_{i=1}^{N} w_{ji}^{\text{ols}} U_i \tag{9-18}
$$

it is evident that $\hat{\beta}_j$ is just a weighted sum of the model errors. Consequently, $\hat{\beta}_j$ is distributed normally if $U_1 \ldots U_N$ are. (Through the generalizations of the Central Limit Theorem alluded to in Chapter 2, $\hat{\beta}_j$ is approximately normally distributed for large N even if $U_1 \ldots U_N$ are not normally distributed.) Thus, the sampling distribution of $\hat{\beta}_j$ is completely characterized by its mean and variance.

Considering first the mean of $\hat{\beta}_j$ and evaluating the expected value of the expression given above for $\hat{\beta}_j$,

$$
E[\hat{\beta}_j] = E\left[\beta_j + \sum_{i=1}^{N} w_{ji}^{\text{ols}} U_i\right] = \beta_j + \sum_{i=1}^{N} w_{ji}^{\text{ols}} E[U_i] = \beta_j \tag{9-19}
$$

Thus, as with the Bivariate Regression Model, forcing $E[U_i]$ to equal zero by including an intercept in the model essentially implies that the least squares parameter estimates will be unbiased.[4]

[3] Expressed in terms of matrix algebra, in contrast, the expressions for the least squares estimators and the least squares weights are fairly simple and essentially unchanged for any value of k. Note also that, as mentioned earlier in this chapter, well-designed econometric software solves the k normal equations numerically using sophisticated matrix inversion routines rather than by obtaining and evaluating formulas like these to compute $\hat{\beta}_1^* \ldots \hat{\beta}_k^*$. One way to see why sophisticated numerical matrix inversion routines are necessary is to note that if the two terms in the denominators of the expressions given above are almost equal, then the denominator itself will be difficult to calculate with any precision. This is frequently the case with economic data, also yielding the multicollinearity problem discussed later in this chapter.

[4] This result also rests on the assumption that the form of the model is correct. We will see later on in this chapter that wrongly omitting an explanatory variable from the model can cause the estimated coefficients on the other explanatory variables to be biased. The assumption is also being made here that the explanatory variables are fixed (i.e., not random); this assumption will need to be relaxed in Chapter 11 when we consider the special problems posed in estimating an equation which is part of a simultaneous equation system.

Turning to the sampling variance of $\hat{\beta}_j$,

$$
\begin{aligned}
\text{var}(\hat{\beta}_j) &= E\left[\left[\hat{\beta}_j - E\left[\hat{\beta}_j\right]\right]^2\right] \\
&= E\left[\left[\hat{\beta}_j - \beta_j\right]^2\right] \\
&= E\left[\left[\sum_{i=1}^{N} w_{ji}^{\text{ols}}\, U_i\right]^2\right] \\
&= E\left[\sum_{m=1}^{N} w_{jm}^{\text{ols}}\, U_m \sum_{i=1}^{N} w_{ji}^{\text{ols}}\, U_i\right] \\
&= E\left[H \sum_{i=1}^{N} w_{ji}^{\text{ols}}\, U_i\right]
\end{aligned}
\tag{9-20}
$$

where H stands for the random variable $\sum_{m=1}^{N} w_{jm}^{\text{ols}}\, U_m$. Bringing the factor of H inside the sum over the running index i,

$$
\begin{aligned}
\text{var}(\hat{\beta}_j) &= E\left[H \sum_{i=1}^{N} w_{ji}^{\text{ols}} U_i\right] \\
&= E\left[\sum_{i=1}^{N} w_{ji}^{\text{ols}} (U_i H)\right] \\
&= \sum_{i=1}^{N} w_{ji}^{\text{ols}} E[U_i H]
\end{aligned}
\tag{9-21}
$$

where the last step uses the Linearity Property of Chapter 2. Evaluating this expectation,

$$
\begin{aligned}
E[U_i H] &= E\left[U_i \sum_{m=1}^{N} w_{jm}^{\text{ols}}\, U_m\right] \\
&= E\left[\sum_{m=1}^{N} w_{jm}^{\text{ols}}\, U_i\, U_m\right] \\
&= \sum_{m=1}^{N} w_{jm}^{\text{ols}}\, E[U_i\, U_m] \quad \text{using the Linearity Property} \\
&= w_{ji}^{\text{ols}}\, \sigma^2
\end{aligned}
\tag{9-22}
$$

where the last step follows because (using the nonautocorrelation and homoscedasticity assumptions on the model error term)

$$
\begin{aligned}
E[U_i U_m] &= \sigma^2 \text{ for } \quad i = m \\
&= 0 \quad \text{for} \quad i \neq m
\end{aligned}
\tag{9-23}
$$

Consequently, the only term in the sum over m which needs to be retained is the one for which m equals i.

Substituting this expression for $E[U_i H]$ into the expression for $\text{var}(\hat{\beta}_j)$,[5]

$$\begin{aligned} \text{var}(\hat{\beta}_j) &= \sum_{i=1}^{N} w_{ji}^{\text{ols}} E[U_i H] \\ &= \sum_{i=1}^{N} w_{ji}^{\text{ols}} \left(w_{ji}^{\text{ols}} \sigma^2 \right) = \sigma^2 \sum_{i=1}^{N} \left(w_{ji}^{\text{ols}} \right)^2 \end{aligned} \tag{9-24}$$

The sampling distribution of $\hat{\beta}_j$ is thus

$$\hat{\beta}_j \sim N\left[\beta_j, \; \sigma^2 \sum_{i=1}^{N} \left(w_{ji}^{\text{ols}} \right)^2 \right] \tag{9-25}$$

which implies that

$$\frac{\hat{\beta}_j - \beta_j}{\sqrt{\sigma^2 \sum_{i=1}^{N} \left(w_{ji}^{\text{ols}} \right)^2}} \sim N[0, 1] \tag{9-26}$$

Note how the assumptions that the regression errors are uncorrelated and that each has the same variance are again crucial to the derivation of the expression for the variance of the estimator and hence to the result that this latter statistic is a unit normal.

We have already seen that $\hat{\beta}_j$ is an unbiased estimator for β_j. The sampling distribution of $\hat{\beta}_j$ makes it possible to show that this estimator has all the other nice properties which we found for $\hat{\beta}$ in the Bivariate Regression Model:

1. $\hat{\beta}_j$ is consistent for β_j.
2. $\hat{\beta}_j$ is BLU for β_j – that is, there is no other linear and unbiased estimator of β_j with sampling variance smaller than the $\text{var}(\hat{\beta}_j)$.
3. $\hat{\beta}_j$ is efficient for β_j – that is, there is no other unbiased estimator of β_j (linear or not) with sampling variance smaller than the $\text{var}(\hat{\beta}_j)$.

The derivation of these properties, requiring matrix algebra, is beyond the scope of this book. Indeed, the main reason for analyzing the Bivariate Regression Model in such detail in Chapters 6 and 7 was to obtain these sorts of results in a setting where the derivations *are* sufficiently simple as to be feasible here.

As with the results on $\hat{\beta}$ in the Bivariate Regression Model, the proof that $\hat{\beta}_j$ is efficient for β_j requires that $U_j \sim \text{NIID}[0, \sigma^2]$; for BLUness, in contrast, we need only assume that $E[U_i] = 0$, that $E[U_i U_m] = 0$ (for $i \neq m$), and that $E[U_i^2] = \sigma^2$. As in the Bivariate Regression Model, with the x_{ij} fixed, $\hat{\beta}_j$ is consistent for β_j so long as we imagine additional observations on the dependent variable being added to the sample with sensible concomitant values for $x_{i1} \ldots x_{ik}$; the consistency of $\hat{\beta}_j$ where the explanatory variable values are not fixed is discussed in Chapter 11.

The assumptions of the Multiple Regression Model also imply that

$$S^2 \equiv \left(\frac{1}{N-k} \right) \sum_{i=1}^{N} \left(U_i^{\text{fit}} \right)^2 \tag{9-27}$$

[5] Note that this is our usual result (from Equation 2-68) on the variance of a weighted sum of uncorrelated random variables which all have the same mean and variance: the variance of the weighted sum equals the variance of the underlying random variables times the sum of the squares of the weights.

is an unbiased estimator of σ^2 which is independent of $\hat{\beta}_1 \dots \hat{\beta}_k$ and distributed chi squared with, in this case, $N-k$ degrees of freedom:

$$\frac{(N-k)S^2}{\sigma^2} \sim \chi^2(N-k) \quad \text{independent of} \quad \hat{\beta}_1 \dots \hat{\beta}_k \tag{9-28}$$

Thus, using the definition of a Student's t variate given in Equation 4-31,

$$\frac{\left\{ \dfrac{\hat{\beta}_j - \beta_j}{\sqrt{\sigma^2 \sum_{i=1}^{N} \left(w_{ji}^{\text{ols}}\right)^2}} \right\}}{\sqrt{\dfrac{\frac{(N-k)S^2}{\sigma^2}}{N-k}}} \sim t(N-k) \tag{9-29}$$

which is equivalent, after a bit of cancellation and rearrangement, to

$$\frac{\hat{\beta}_j - \beta_j}{\sqrt{S^2 \sum_{i=1}^{N} \left(w_{ji}^{\text{ols}}\right)^2}} \sim t(N-k) \tag{9-30}$$

The denominator of this expression is called the "standard error" of the estimator $\hat{\beta}_j$.

This result yields hypothesis tests and confidence intervals for β_j in exactly the same way that the analogous results were obtained in Chapter 7 for $\hat{\beta}$ in the Bivariate Model. For example, a 95% confidence interval for β_j is

$$\beta_j = \hat{\beta}_j \pm t^c_{.025}(N-k)\sqrt{S^2 \sum_{i=1}^{N} \left(w_{ji}^{\text{ols}}\right)^2} \tag{9-31}$$

Finally, it is often extremely useful in practice to be able to test null hypotheses involving linear restrictions on $\beta_1 \dots \beta_k$. For example, in a regression model explaining the logarithm of the ith individual's wages, x_{i2} might be the individual's education level and x_{i3} might be the square of the individual's education level. In that case, the t statistic derived above could be used to test H_o: $\beta_3 = 0$, corresponding to the proposition that education level enters the equation linearly, but the proposition that education level does not enter the equation at all corresponds to testing H_o: $\beta_2 = 0$ *and* $\beta_3 = 0$.

Also, sometimes theory suggests a need to test whether or not a particular linear relationship holds between the coefficients $\beta_1 \dots \beta_k$. For example, suppose that we have collected sample data on output (y_i), capital stock ($capital_i$), and labor used ($labor_i$) for N firms in an industry and that we are willing to assume that all of the firms use the same (generalized Cobb-Douglas) technology. In that case the regression model

$$Y_i = A\ capital_i^{\beta_2}\ labor_i^{\beta_3}\ e^{U_i} \qquad U_i \sim \text{NIID}(0, \sigma^2) \tag{9-32}$$

would be appropriate, where A is a constant. (Note that, by using a multiplicative error term of this form, even a highly negative drawing of U_i does not yield a negative value for output.) Taking the logarithm of both sides of this equation yields an instance of the Multiple Regression Model:

$$\ln(Y_i) = \beta_1 + \beta_2 \ln(capital_i) + \beta_3 \ln(labor_i) + U_i \qquad U_i \sim \text{NIID}(0, \sigma^2) \tag{9-33}$$

wherein the null hypothesis H_o: $\beta_2 + \beta_3 = 1$ corresponds to the economic hypothesis that the technology that these firms are using exhibits constant returns to scale.

Testing single or multiple linear restrictions on $\beta_1 \ldots \beta_k$ turns out to be quite easy using the following result. Suppose that you want to test the validity of r distinct linear restrictions on $\beta_1 \ldots \beta_k$, where r is some integer in the interval $[1, k]$. Let "URSS" stand for the sum of the squared fitting errors (SSE) from estimating $\beta_1 \ldots \beta_k$ in the usual way; here "URSS" is short for "unrestricted sum of squares." Now re-estimate the equation, imposing the linear restrictions to be tested. In the production function example given above, the null hypothesis consists of just one restriction, that $\beta_2 + \beta_3 = 1$; thus, r equals one in this instance. Imposing this restriction corresponds to estimating β_1 and β_2 in the regression model:

$$\begin{aligned} \ln(Y_i) &= \beta_1 + \beta_2 \ln(capital_i) + (1 - \beta_2)\ln(labor_i) + U_i \\ \ln(Y_i) - \ln(labor_i) &= \beta_1 + \beta_2\{\ln(capital_i) - \ln(labor_i)\} + U_i \\ \ln(Y_i / labor_i) &= \beta_1 + \beta_2 \ln(capital_i / labor_i) + U_i \end{aligned} \tag{9-34}$$

Letting the sum of squared fitting errors (SSE) from this "restricted" regression equation be called "RSS" – where "RSS" is short for "restricted sum of squares" – then the assumptions of the Multiple Regression Model imply that

$$\hat{F} \equiv \frac{(\text{RSS} - \text{URSS})/r}{\text{URSS}/(N-k)} \sim F(r, N-k) \tag{9-35}$$

under the null hypothesis that all r linear restrictions are true.[6] Thus, H_o can be rejected with p-value – illustrated in Figure 9-2 – equal to the probability that an $F(r, N-k)$ variate exceeds $\hat{F}$:

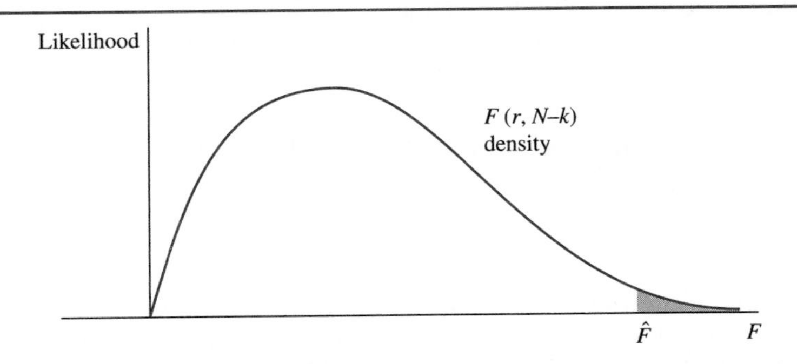

Figure 9-2 *F* Distribution Density Function

In practice, one hardly ever needs to explicitly calculate sample realizations of RSS and URSS and substitute them into Equation 9-35 – as we shall see in the applications at the end of this chapter, modern computer software does the arithmetic for us. For that matter, in practice one hardly ever solves the normal equations by hand to obtain the least squares weights $w_{11}^{ols} \ldots w_{1N}^{ols} \ldots w_{k1}^{ols} \ldots w_{kN}^{ols}$, the least squares parameter estimates $(\hat{\beta}_1^* \ldots \hat{\beta}_k^*)$, and so forth – this arithmetic, too, is almost invariably done using computer programs designed for this task.[7]

[6] The proof of this proposition is beyond the scope of the present treatment, as it requires matrix algebra.

[7] For example, if the data were stored as variables named *lny*, *lncapital*, and *lnlabor* then in Stata the appropriate commands would be "reg lny lncapital lnlabor" to estimate the model and then "test lncapital + lnlabor = 1" to evaluate the appropriate F statistic and p-value.

It is always prudent, however, to have a pretty good idea of what a computer program is doing. Moreover, in clarifying what the software does – solve linear equations, evaluate formulas, and compute tail areas of distributions – we are reminded of what the software does not (and cannot) do: it does not and cannot check whether these are the right equations to solve, whether these are appropriate formulas to evaluate, or whether these are the right tail areas to be computing. That is *our* job.

Why might these equations, formulas, and tail areas be inappropriate? Their relevance rests on the validity of the assumptions of the Multiple Regression Model, because these assumptions were used in their derivation. The computer software doesn't know or care about these assumptions. But ***we*** can and should care about the validity of these assumptions: indeed, the point of this section is that the least squares parameter estimators ($\hat{\beta}_1 \ldots \hat{\beta}_k$) have "good" properties and the inferences based on them are meaningful if and only if these assumptions are valid.

The assumption in Equation 9.1 that the model errors are NIID(0, σ^2) can actually be checked if there is a reasonably large amount of sample data; and the material in Section 9.3 has already shown how one can use multiple regression itself to test both the linearity of the model specification and the stability of the model coefficients across the sample. Chapters 10 and 13 develop this topic of "diagnostic checking" in detail; they further address the practical issue of how to proceed when one's model fails some of these checks.[8]

The next two sections of the present chapter deal with a different aspect of the model specification: what if the regression model specified in Equation 9.1 inadvertently includes an extraneous explanatory variable or inadvertently omits a pertinent one?[9]

9.6 OVERELABORATE MULTIPLE REGRESSION MODELS

Fundamentally, there are only two ways to err in choosing the set of explanatory variables in the Multiple Regression Model: one can include extraneous explanatory variables which do not belong in the model, or one can wrongly omit explanatory variables which do belong in the model. The first of these possibilities is considered in this section.

Suppose that the expected value of Y_i depends on x_{i2}, but we mistakenly estimate a multiple regression model additionally including an extraneous explanatory variable, x_{i3}:

Extraneous Variable Included in Model

$$\begin{aligned} &\text{True Model:} & Y_i &= \beta_i + \beta_2 x_{i2} + V_i \\ &\text{Estimated Model:} & Y_i &= \beta_i + \beta_2 x_{i2} + \beta_3 x_{i3} + U_i \end{aligned} \tag{9-36}$$

If the true model satisfies the assumptions of the Multiple Regression Model (and x_{i3} is fixed), then so does the estimated model – it's just that the value of β_3 is zero. Consequently, the OLS coefficient estimators, $\hat{\beta}_1$, $\hat{\beta}_2$, and $\hat{\beta}_3$ are unbiased and consistent. These parameter estimates are not BLU or efficient, however, because one could obtain unbiased estimates of these coefficients with somewhat smaller sampling variances by estimating the true model. This estimation inefficiency is inconsequential, however, unless the value of $N-k$ is small, where k is the number of parameters estimated.

[8] Recall that Sections 4.8 and 4.9 addressed diagnostic checking in the context of the "univariate regression" model, wherein one is simply estimating the population mean of a random variable. Tests were developed there for the constancy of this mean across two parts of the sample (corresponding to a test of parameter stability) and for the constancy of the variable's population variance across two parts of the sample. (The latter corresponds to a test for homoscedasticity in the regression model errors here.) These two sections were intended primarily as a "warmup," and to introduce the idea of diagnostic checking promptly. Chapters 10 and 13 are able to go much further, in large part because multiple regression is now available to us as a tool.

[9] The assumption that the explanatory variables are "fixed in repeated samples" is taken up in Chapter 11.

The usual results for the sampling distributions of $\hat{\beta}_1$, $\hat{\beta}_2$, and $\hat{\beta}_3$ are valid because the estimated regression equation satisfies all of the assumptions of the Multiple Regression Model. Thus, in the notation of the previous section, the statistic

$$\frac{\hat{\beta}_3}{\sqrt{S^2 / \sum_{i=1}^{N} \left(w_{3i}^{\text{ols}}\right)^2}} \tag{9-37}$$

is distributed $t(N-3)$ under the null hypothesis H_0: $\beta_3 = 0$ and provides a valid test of this null hypothesis. In particular, the magnitude of this statistic will exceed the .005 (.5%) critical point of the t distribution with $N-3$ degrees of freedom only 1% of the time. Consequently, this t test will ordinarily alert us to the fact that $|\hat{\beta}_3|$ is so small that x_{i3} is most likely irrelevant.

On the other hand (about 1% of the time!) the magnitude of this t statistic will – just due to chance – exceed the .5% critical point of the t distribution and fool us into thinking that the mean of Y_i depends on x_{i3}, that x_{i3} will be helpful in predicting Y_i, and so forth. That is unavoidable and should be tolerably inconsequential unless the inclusion of x_{i3} in the model was part of a pattern of specification search activity on our part which included "trying out" a substantial number of possible explanatory variables. Clearly, if we estimate a substantial number of regression models using a different choice for x_{i3} each time, then the chance that we will wrongly reject the null hypothesis H_o: $\beta_3 = 0$ on this 1% hypothesis test will climb substantially above 1%. This, of course, is the "spurious regression due to data mining" problem discussed in Chapter 8.

Note that the problem is dramatically ameliorated if all of the explanatory variables under consideration are included at once; the Multiple Regression Model allows us to conveniently do this. For example, if 12 possible explanatory variables (in addition to x_{i2}) are included in the model, then the 12 coefficients $\beta_3 \ldots \beta_{14}$ would be estimated and we could appropriately test whether any of these explanatory variables is relevant by simply testing the joint null hypothesis H_o: $\beta_3 = \beta_4 = \cdots = \beta_{13} = \beta_{14} = 0$ using the F statistic given in the previous section. In this case URSS would simply be the value of SSE for the regression including all 13 explanatory variables and RSS would be the value of SSE for a regression equation including only x_{i1} and x_{i2}. The distribution of the F statistic used in the test now explicitly adjusts for the fact that we are "trying out" 12 possible explanatory variables.

Alternatively (as suggested in Chapter 8), we could observe that – if β_3 is zero, but $|\hat{\beta}_3|$ is large due to a sample fluctuation – then it is quite unlikely that $|\hat{\beta}_3|$ will be sizeable over most subsets of the sample data. This is because a spurious coefficient estimate typically arises from the confluence of a handful of unusual observations concentrated in one part of the sample. In other words, "spurious" coefficient estimates – ones which appear to be significantly different from zero only due to bad luck or data mining – are generally unstable across the sample.

Such instability can easily be checked: Define a dummy variable x_{i4} equal to x_{i3} for all values of i in the first half of the sample and equal to zero for the remaining observations. Then estimate the regression equation

$$Y_i = \beta_1 + \beta_2 x_{i2} + \beta_3 x_{i3} + \beta_4 x_{i4} + U_i \tag{9-38}$$

and test the null hypothesis H_o: $\beta_4 = 0$ using the estimated t statistic on $\hat{\beta}_4$. Because β_4 is the difference between the value of the coefficient on x_{i3} in the two halves of the sample, this null hypothesis corresponds to the hypothesis that the coefficient on x_{i3} is stable across both halves of the sample.[10]

[10] This test is usually known as the "Chow test," after the econometrician who first suggested it.

Out-of-sample prediction effectiveness provides another potent tool for detecting spurious regression coefficients. In this example, the regression model including the extraneous explanatory variable x_{i3} will provide inferior out-of-sample predictions (on average) because zero is a better estimate of β_3 than is $\hat{\beta}_3$. Indeed, when $|\hat{\beta}_3|$ is, by chance, sizeable, then the out-of-sample predictions based on it will be substantially inferior. The out-of-sample prediction errors for the Multiple Regression Model and their sampling distribution are discussed in the appendix to this chapter; model prediction is taken up in greater depth in Chapters 17 and 18.

Reasons why one might care differently about positive than about negative prediction errors are discussed in Section 8.4 (where analogous results are derived for out-of-sample prediction in the Bivariate Regression Model) and again in Section 17.2, where optimal forecasting from a time-series analysis perspective is discussed. Presuming nevertheless – as is commonly done, for simplicity – that the costs associated with prediction errors are symmetric, it is sensible to quantify the size of the prediction error by their average squared value over the out-of-sample observations. Formal tests for whether this out-of-sample mean square error (MSE) is significantly larger for one model than another are beyond the scope of this section; they will be described in Section 18.5. It is worth noting here, however, that Ashley and Ye (2010) review this literature and Ashley (2003)[11] provides simulation results indicating that fairly large out-of-sample data sets are necessary – e.g., over 100 out-of-sample observations are typically needed in order for an MSE reduction of 20% to be statistically significant at the 5% level. On the other hand, the Multiple Regression Model evaluation issue is usually not one of whether or not inclusion of x_{i3} significantly improves the model's out-of-sample predictions – if $\hat{\beta}_3$ spuriously appears to be significant due to data mining, then the inclusion of x_{i3} in the model will usually *increase* the out-of-sample MSE rather than decrease it.

It is worth noting, however, that a very simple test for assessing the ability of a model to predict a particular set of m out-of-sample observations can be obtained by merely regressing the actual out-of-sample data on the model predictions of these data $\hat{y}_{N+1} \dots \hat{y}_{N+m}$:

$$Y_i = \lambda_o + \lambda_1 \hat{y}_i + V_i \qquad i = N+1 \dots N+m \tag{9-39}$$

and testing the null hypothesis that λ_o is zero and that λ_1 is one. Overelaborate models will typically fail this test.

It should also be noted that an over-reliance on R^2 as a "figure of merit" for an estimated model is an invitation to the production of overelaborate models. By analogy with the expression for R^2 in the Bivariate Regression Model given in Chapter 8, R^2 for the Multiple Regression Model is defined as

$$R^2 \equiv 1 - \frac{\sum_{i=1}^{N} \left(u_i^{\text{fit}}\right)^2}{\sum_{i=1}^{N} (y_i - \bar{y})^2} \tag{9-40}$$

where $u_1^{\text{fit}} \dots u_N^{\text{fit}}$ are, as before, the observed least squares fitting errors. As in Chapter 8, R^2 lies between zero and one and can be interpreted as both a "goodness of fit" measure and as the fraction of the sample variation in y_i "explained" by sample variation in the explanatory variables included in the model. Note, however, that including a $(k+1)$st explanatory variable in the regression model will

[11] Ashley, R., and H. Ye (2011) "On the Granger Causality between Median Inflation and Price Dispersion" *Applied Economics* (in press). Available at ashleymac.econ.vt.edu/working_papers/price_dispersion_causality.pdf. Ashley, R. (2003) "Statistically Significant Forecasting Improvements: How Much Out-of-Sample Data Is Likely Necessary?" *International Journal of Forecasting 19,* pp. 229–39.

necessarily lower $\sum_{i=1}^{N}\left(u_i^{\text{fit}}\right)^2$ and therefore raise R^2 – regardless of how small $\left|\hat{\beta}_{k+1}\right|$ is – unless $\hat{\beta}_{k+1}$ is precisely zero.

For this reason most people prefer to use a modified version of R^2 which is called "adjusted R^2" or "R_c^2." It is defined as

$$R_c^2 \equiv 1 - \frac{\frac{1}{N-k}\sum_{i=1}^{N}\left(u_i^{\text{fit}}\right)^2}{\frac{1}{N-1}\sum_{i=1}^{N}\left(y_i-\bar{y}\right)^2} = 1 - \frac{s^2}{\frac{1}{N-1}\sum_{i=1}^{N}\left(y_i-\bar{y}\right)^2} \tag{9-41}$$

Adjusted R^2 is sometimes called "R^2 corrected for degrees of freedom" because the $(N-k)^{-1}$ term appearing in the numerator makes R_c^2 smaller compared to ordinary R^2 as the number of explanatory variables increases. This particular "degrees of freedom" correction is initially appealing because, under the assumptions of the Multiple Regression Model, s^2 is the sample realization of an unbiased estimator of σ^2.[12]

Adjusted R^2 has a couple of drawbacks of its own, however. For one thing, it is no longer guaranteed to be non-negative, but this of little consequence since negative values of adjusted R^2 will only occur for fairly terrible models. A more significant problem with adjusted R^2 is that it can be shown to always rise whenever an additional explanatory variable enters the equation with an estimated t ratio exceeding one in magnitude. Thus, adjusted R^2 is clearly under-correcting for the additional degree of freedom "lost" when an additional explanatory variable is added.

Consequently, several alternative regression equation criteria have been devised, each of which penalizes additional explanatory variables more heavily than does adjusted R^2:

$$\begin{aligned}
\text{FPE} &= \text{Final Prediction Error Criterion} &&= \frac{N+k}{N-k}\sum_{i=1}^{N}\left(u_i^{\text{fit}}\right)^2 = (N+k)s^2 \\
\text{SC} &= \text{Schwarz Criterion (BIC)} &&= \ln\left(\frac{1}{N}\sum_{i=1}^{N}\left(u_i^{\text{fit}}\right)^2\right) + \frac{k\ln(N)}{N} \\
\text{AIC} &= \text{Akaike Information Criterion} &&= \ln\left(\frac{1}{N}\sum_{i=1}^{N}\left(u_i^{\text{fit}}\right)^2\right) + \frac{2k}{N}
\end{aligned} \tag{9-42}$$

In contrast to adjusted R_c^2 for these criteria a smaller value is preferred. All three of these criteria are in use, but the SC (or BIC) and AIC criteria are now more commonly used than is the FPE.[13]

9.7 UNDERELABORATE MULTIPLE REGRESSION MODELS

The other way to err in choosing the set of explanatory variables in a regression model is to fail to include an explanatory variable which *does* belong in the model. Suppose that the expected value of Y_i depends on x_{i2} and on x_{i3}, but we mistakenly estimate a multiple regression model

[12] Note, however, that the sample variance of the dependent variable in the denominator term is not an unbiased estimator of the population variance of Y_i because $\overline{Y}$ cannot possibly be an unbiased estimator of $E[Y_i]$, a quantity which the Multiple Regression Model implies is different for each value of i.

[13] It should be noted that while all three of these criteria (and s^2, for that matter) yield equivalent results when N is very large, the AIC criterion tends to yield overly complicated models; most analysts therefore prefer the SC criterion. Stata automatically displays adjusted R^2 in the output from the "regress" command; following this with the command "estat ic" will cause Stata to compute and display the Schwarz Criterion (BIC) and the AIC statistic.

omitting x_{i3}:

Variable Wrongly Omitted from Model

$$\text{True Model:} \quad Y_i = \beta_1 + \beta_2 x_{i2} + \beta_3 x_{i3} + U_i \tag{9-43}$$
$$\text{Estimated Model:} \quad Y_i = \gamma_1 + \gamma_2 x_{i2} + V_i$$

Here the coefficients in the estimated model are given different symbols because, as we shall see below, they are not necessarily identical to the analogous coefficients in the true model.

Supposing that the true model satisfies all the assumptions of the Multiple Regression Model, what properties will $\hat{\gamma}_2$ from the estimated model have? Because the true model satisfies all the assumptions of the Multiple Regression Model, the model actually estimated also satisfies all the assumptions of the Multiple Regression Model. Consequently, $\hat{\gamma}_2$ is an unbiased and consistent estimate of γ_2.[14]

The problem is that $\hat{\gamma}_2$ may be an *in*consistent estimator of β_2. What's the difference? We can interpret β_2 as the partial derivative of the expected value of Y_i with respect to x_{i2}, holding x_{i3} fixed – i.e., "controlling for x_{i3}." In contrast, γ_2 is the derivative of the expected value of Y_i with respect to x_{i2}, averaged over whatever values x_{i3} took on during the course of the sample.

These are not necessarily the same thing! For example, suppose that Y_i is the logarithm of earnings for household i in Slobbovia and x_{i2} is a measure of household i's educational level. And suppose further that households residing in Upper Slobbovia ($x_{i3} = 1$) are more highly educated (on average) than households residing in Lower Slobbovia ($x_{i3} = 0$), but that wages are lower (on average) in Upper Slobbovia because firms in Upper Slobbovia have less capital stock. Then γ_2 might be close to zero even though β_2 is quite large, simply because the more highly educated households in the sample tend to live in Upper Slobbovia where wages are low. In essence, the education level variable (x_{i2}) in the estimated model is partly modeling the impact of education on wages and partly acting as a substitute (a "proxy") for the omitted geographical variable (x_{i3}), causing the coefficient on x_{i2} in the estimated model to be an unbiased and consistent estimate of some mixture of β_2 and β_3.

The following example makes this issue clearer.

9.8 APPLICATION: THE CURIOUS RELATIONSHIP BETWEEN MARRIAGE AND DEATH

The scatterplot in Figure 9-3 displays U.S. Census Bureau data from 49 states (excluding Nevada) on the number of deaths and the number of marriages taking place in each state during the year 1980.[15]

Two things are immediately apparent from this scatterplot. First, there is evidently a failure here of the homoscedasticity assumption, which specifies that the variance of the model error term is the same for all 49 observations. Consequently, this example will be taken up again in Chapter 10, where tests for (and model respecification inspired by) failure of the homoscedasticity assumption are discussed. Second, these data appear to provide strong evidence for a strong, direct relationship between marriage and death. Unsurprisingly, this is echoed in an estimated multiple regression

[14] This is not quite accurate. The error term in the estimated model (V_i) equals $\beta_3 x_{i3} + U_i$, which is not normally distributed with a constant mean if x_{i3} is fixed (i.e., nonrandom); instead, its mean varies with i. It can still be shown, however, that $\hat{\gamma}_2$ is unbiased and consistent for γ_2 if x_{i3} is treated as random; this is dealt with in Chapter 11.

[15] The observations on Nevada are excluded, for specific reasons which you can probably guess. These reasons are discussed in Section 10.3.

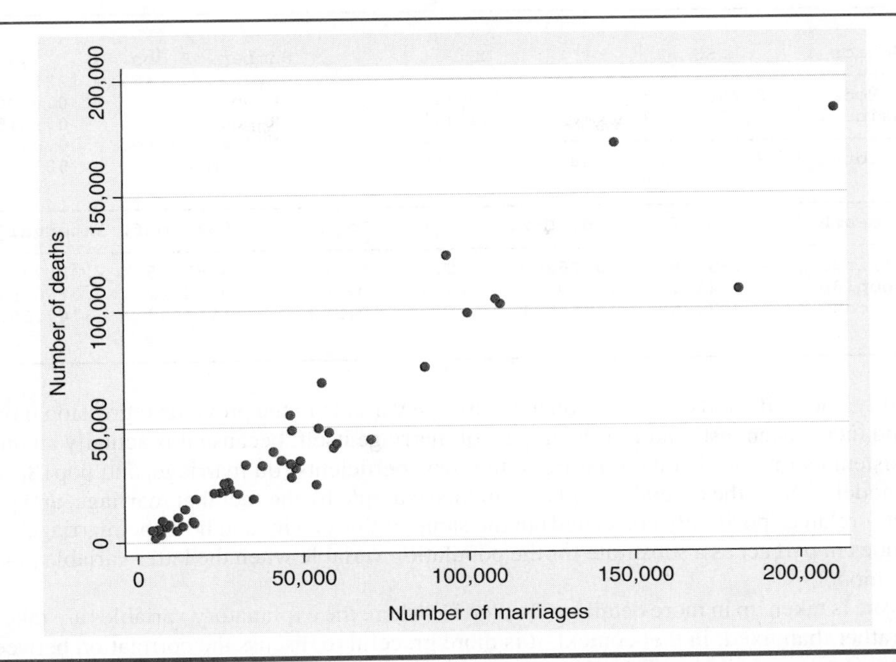

Figure 9-3 Scatterplot of Number of Deaths versus Number of Marriages (State-Level, 1980)

model based on these data, which yields an estimate of .888 for the coefficient on the number of marriages.[16]

```
      Source |       SS       df       MS              Number of obs =      49
-------------+------------------------------           F(  1,    47) =  390.91
       Model |  7.5185e+10     1  7.5185e+10           Prob > F      =  0.0000
    Residual |  9.0398e+09    47   192335400           R-squared     =  0.8927
-------------+------------------------------           Adj R-squared =  0.8904
       Total |  8.4225e+10    48  1.7547e+09           Root MSE      =   13869

------------------------------------------------------------------------------
       death |      Coef.   Std. Err.      t    P>|t|     [95% Conf. Interval]
-------------+----------------------------------------------------------------
    marriage |   .8883568   .0449314    19.77   0.000     .7979665    .9787472
       _cons |  -1007.422    2874.15    -0.35   0.728    -6789.466    4774.622
------------------------------------------------------------------------------
```

Marriage is not a recognized mortality risk, so what is going on here? Evidently, the number of marriages is proxying in this model for an omitted explanatory variable: the population of the state, with which it is highly correlated. And indeed, when pop18p, the Census Bureau's measure of the 18+ year old population is included in the regression model, the estimated coefficient on the number of marriages is no longer positive:

[16] The estimated standard error and confidence interval for this coefficient are not to be taken seriously, of course, in view of the heteroscedasticity alluded to above, which invalidates the derivations of the formulas used to calculate these inference results.

```
      Source |       SS       df       MS              Number of obs =      49
-------------+------------------------------           F(  2,    46) = 1221.38
       Model |  8.2668e+10     2  4.1334e+10           Prob > F      =  0.0000
    Residual |  1.5567e+09    46    33842177           R-squared     =  0.9815
-------------+------------------------------           Adj R-squared =  0.9807
       Total |  8.4225e+10    48  1.7547e+09           Root MSE      =  5817.4

------------------------------------------------------------------------------
       death |      Coef.   Std. Err.      t    P>|t|     [95% Conf. Interval]
-------------+----------------------------------------------------------------
    marriage |  -.1699764   .0736258    -2.31   0.026    -.3181775   -.0217753
      pop18p |   .0141611   .0009523    14.87   0.000     .0122442    .0160781
       _cons |   1302.368   1215.581     1.07   0.290     -1144.47    3749.206
```

Evidently, the estimated coefficient on the marriage variable in the previous regression model is a biased and inconsistent estimator of the impact of marriage itself, because it is actually an unbiased and consistent estimator of some mixture of the two coefficients (on marriage_i and pop18p_i) in the present model.[17] Note the crucial role played in this example by the fact that marriage_i and pop18p_i are directly related (positively correlated) in the sample: this is why and how the marriage variable can and does in part act as a substitute for the population variable when the latter variable is omitted from the model.

This issue is taken up in more detail in Chapter 11, where the explanatory variables are taken to be random rather than fixed; in that context, it is more graceful to discuss the correlation between two of these explanatory variables. There it is shown that the inconsistency of the OLS estimator of β_2 in a model like Equation 9.1 is proportional to β_3 times the correlation between the second and third explanatory variables. Thus, the OLS estimator of β_2 is inconsistent if and only if x_{i3} was wrongly omitted (i.e., $\beta_3 \neq 0$) and x_{i3} is linearly related to the included explanatory variable, x_{i2}.

We can conclude that wrongly omitting an explanatory variable from the model is problematic if and only if the omitted variable varies across the sample in a similar way as do explanatory variables which are included in the model. Even then, the least squares estimates of the coefficients on the included variables are unbiased and consistent – it is just that one must be careful in interpreting what these estimators are unbiased and consistent for, because the included explanatory variables will in part be proxying for the wrongly omitted variable.

9.9 MULTICOLLINEARITY

With typical economic data, it is quite common for the sample variation in one explanatory variable to be rather similar to that of another. This situation is called "multicollinearity" and arises because economic data is usually obtained from surveys rather than from well-designed experiments.

Where the data for one explanatory variable is an exact multiple of the data on another – the case of "perfect multicollinearity" – it is impossible to solve the normal equations for the least squares estimators, $\hat{\beta}_1 \ldots \hat{\beta}_k$, simply because no unique solution exists. After all, if $x_{i2} = \alpha x_{i3}$, then a model with weight on $\hat{\beta}_2$ will fit the data in precisely the same way as a model with weight on $\hat{\beta}_3$.

[17] When this example is considered again in Chapter 10 we will find that the estimated standard errors and confidence intervals for this model are still invalid due to heteroscedasticity in the error term. In particular, applying the diagnostic checking methods described there, it will turn out that the variance of the error term in this model depends directly on the value of pop18p_i, suggesting that a model relating per capita death rates to per capita marriage rates is more likely to satisfy the homoscedasticity assumption.

The same thing happens if any weighted sum of the data on several explanatory variables exactly reproduces the sample data on another variable. This occurs quite frequently when beginners work with dummy variables. For example, suppose that x_{i2} is a dummy variable for gender which is one for male respondents and zero for female respondents and suppose that x_{i3} is a similar dummy variable which instead takes on the value one only for female respondents. In this case $x_{i2}+x_{i3}$ is one for every value of i, so increasing the intercept coefficient ($\hat{\beta}_1$) has the same effect on the fitting errors as does an equal increase in $\hat{\beta}_2$ and $\hat{\beta}_3$; consequently, there is no unique way to choose $\hat{\beta}_1$, $\hat{\beta}_2$, and $\hat{\beta}_3$ so as to minimize the sum of the squares of the fitting errors. In this case, one must either drop the intercept term or drop one of the two dummy variables. (It doesn't matter which, but it will be slightly more convenient to test whether gender impacts the intercept if one of the dummy variables is dropped.)

More commonly the multicollinearity is imperfect – e.g, $x_{i2} \approx \alpha x_{i3}$. In this case the normal equations can still be solved for the least squares estimators, but high-quality numerical routines are required or else round-off error will yield extremely imprecise solutions. This is why one should be wary of using the multiple regression option in spreadsheet software, as noted in Section 9.4.

Imperfect (but severe) multicollinearity has no impact on the properties of $\hat{\beta}_1 \ldots \hat{\beta}_k$: they are still unbiased, consistent, BLU, and efficient. The estimators can, however, become quite sensitive to minor changes in the data. It is instructive, for example, to examine the explicit expressions given for $\hat{\beta}_2^{ols}$ in the special case considered earlier in this chapter. In that case,

$$\hat{\beta}_2 = w_{2,1}^{ols} Y_1 + w_{2,2}^{ols} Y_2 + \cdots + w_{2,N}^{ols} Y_N \tag{9-44}$$

and its sample realization is

$$\hat{\beta}_2^* = w_{2,1}^{ols} y_1 + w_{2,2}^{ols} y_2 + \cdots + w_{2,N}^{ols} y_N \tag{9-45}$$

where the least squares weights for the estimates of β_2, $w_{2,1}^{ols} \ldots w_{2,N}^{ols}$, are given by the expression

$$w_{2,i}^{ols} = \frac{X_{i2} \sum\limits_{m=1}^{N} X_{m3}^2 - X_{i3} \sum\limits_{m=1}^{N} X_{m2} X_{m3}}{\sum\limits_{m=1}^{N} X_{m2}^2 \sum\limits_{m=1}^{N} X_{m3}^2 - \left(\sum\limits_{m=1}^{N} X_{m2} X_{m3} \right)^2} \qquad i = 1 \ldots N \tag{9-46}$$

Note that the denominator in this expression for $w_{2,i}^{ols}$ gets closer and closer to zero as x_{m2} becomes closer and closer to αx_{m3}. (Try substituting αx_{m3} for x_{m2} and you see that the denominator becomes precisely zero.) Consequently, as the multicollinearity becomes more and more severe, the values of $w_{2,1}^{ols} \ldots w_{2,N}^{ols}$ become quite large, so that minor changes in $y_1 \ldots y_N$ have a major impact on the value of $\hat{\beta}_2^* = \sum\limits_{i=1}^{N} w_{2,i}^{ols} y_i$. When you consider that the regression is poised between placing value on $\hat{\beta}_2^*$ versus placing value on $\hat{\beta}_3^*$, this result makes a lot of sense.

Severe multicollinearity also tends to yield large estimates for the sampling variances of the parameter estimates. In particular, recall that (particularizing the expression for $j=2$) it was found earlier in this chapter that

$$\hat{\beta}_2 \sim N\left[\beta_2, \sigma^2 \sum_{i=1}^{N} \left(w_{2,i}^{ols}\right)^2\right] \tag{9-47}$$

Thus, as the least squares weights $w_{2,1}^{ols} \ldots w_{2,N}^{ols}$ become large due to the multicollinearity, the sampling variance of $\hat{\beta}_2$ balloons. This is the regression machinery telling us that our estimate of β_2

is very imprecisely determined. And it *is* imprecisely determined: due to the fact that x_{i2} varies in much the same way as does x_{i3}, these sample data have little to say about whether the weight should be on $\hat{\beta}_2$ or whether it should be on $\hat{\beta}_3$.[18]

These large sampling variances for the estimated coefficients translate into small estimated t statistics which can often make it impossible to reject either H_o: $\beta_2 = 0$ **or** H_o: $\beta_3 = 0$, even though the regression fits well (R_c^2 is close to one), and one can easily reject the joint null hypothesis H_o: $\beta_2 = \beta_3 = 0$.

What can be done about multicollinearity? Unfortunately, the only real cure is to obtain a better data set in which there is a larger amount of independent variation in the explanatory variables. Palliatives exist, but the reader is cautioned that these only make the estimated regression equation *look* better and can actually worsen the quality of the results.

One such palliative measure is to drop one of the explanatory variables from the equation. This will yield an estimated equation that fits almost as well and has small sampling variance estimates on each estimated coefficient. But note that this is precisely the circumstance where omitting an explanatory variable causes the least squares coefficient estimates on the remaining explanatory variables to become biased and inconsistent. And they are. In the example given above, dropping x_{i3} from the model will cause x_{i2} to proxy for the effects of x_{i3}, so that $\hat{\beta}_2$ is now a consistent estimator not for $\beta_2 = \partial E[Y_i]/\partial x_{i2}$ but for some mixture of β_2 and of $\beta_3 = \partial E[Y_i]/\partial x_{i3}$. Of course, if one is willing to more or less explicitly reinterpret the coefficient on x_{i2} as modeling both the impact of x_{i2} and x_{i3} on the expected value of Y_i, then this is all right.

Other palliative methods (such as "ridge regression") alleviate the symptoms of the multicollinearity, but cannot resolve the basic problem, which is that the sample data do not contain the information necessary in order to precisely estimate the individual coefficients. Overall, it would seem preferable to either live with the large sampling variance estimates or to drop variables and explicitly reinterpret the coefficient estimates than to use methods which induce a spurious appearance of precision into the estimates.[19]

9.10 APPLICATION: THE IMPACT OF COLLEGE GRADUATION AND GENDER ON WEEKLY EARNINGS

Data from 50 households chosen from the Census Bureau's January 2002 Current Population Survey data set were analyzed in Chapters 5, 6, and 7. There the (observed) dependent variable was "*lnearn*$_i$," the logarithm of the respondent's weekly earnings as reported in that survey.[20] The single explanatory variable in the Bivariate Regression Model estimated in Chapter 6 was "*collegrad*$_i$," a dummy variable taking on the value one for the 25 respondents in the sample who had graduated from college and zero for the 25 respondents who had not finished college. Here an additional explanatory variable from the Current Population Survey is used. The additional explanatory variable is "*pesex*$_i$," which is a gender dummy variable taking on the value one for male respondents and two for female respondents.

[18] Another model way to see this is to note that $\hat{\beta}_2 = \beta_2 + \sum_{i=1}^{N} w_{2,i}^{ols} U_i$, so that multicollinearity makes $\hat{\beta}_2$ very sensitive to the regression model errors, $U_1 \ldots U_N$.

[19] Where forecasting (rather than parameter inference) is the principal goal, ridge regression can be advantageous. In that context one might also consider dropping variables so as to make several distinct models and averaging the resulting forecasts. These issues are considered in Section 18.7.

[20] Recall that the logarithm of earnings was used because a histogram of the data on earnings indicated that this transformation would make the assumption of a gaussian error term more plausible, so we are already starting to formulate our regression model with a view toward at least approximately ensuring the validity of the model assumptions.

The model to be estimated is now

$$LOGEARN_i = \beta_1 + \beta_2\, collegegrad_i + \beta_3\, pesex_i + U_i \tag{9-48}$$

The Stata syntax for estimating β_1, β_2, and β_3 is "regress logearn collegegrad pesex," which produces the output

```
      Source |       SS       df       MS              Number of obs =      50
-------------+------------------------------           F(  2,    47) =   10.31
       Model |  12.9399187     2  6.46995934           Prob > F      =  0.0002
    Residual |  29.4913289    47  .627475082           R-squared     =  0.3050
-------------+------------------------------           Adj R-squared =  0.2754
       Total |  42.4312475    49  .865943827           Root MSE      =  .79213

------------------------------------------------------------------------------
     logearn |      Coef.   Std. Err.      t    P>|t|     [95% Conf. Interval]
-------------+----------------------------------------------------------------
 collegegrad |   .8517204   .2242286     3.80   0.000     .4006307     1.30281
       pesex |  -.5235391   .2242286    -2.33   0.024    -.9746288   -.0724494
       _cons |   6.817496   .3758488    18.14   0.000     6.061385    7.573606
------------------------------------------------------------------------------
```

All this output has been covered in the previous sections of this chapter – here what is needed is just to link it all up. Let's begin the row marked "pesex." The estimated coefficient on $pesex_i$ is

$$\hat{\beta}_3^* = \sum_{i=1}^{50} w_{3,i}^{ols}\, logearn_i = -.5235391 \tag{9-49}$$

with estimated standard error (the square root of its estimated sampling variance) equal to

$$\sqrt{s^2 / \sum_{i=1}^{50} \left(w_{3,i}^{ols}\right)^2} = .2242286 \tag{9-50}$$

and estimated t ratio (under H_o: $\beta_3 = 0$) equal to

$$\frac{\hat{\beta}_3}{\sqrt{s^2 / \sum_{i=1}^{50} \left(w_{3,i}^{ols}\right)^2}} = \frac{-.5235391}{.2242286} = -2.33 \sim t(50-3) \tag{9-51}$$

The tail area in the Student's t distribution with 47 degrees of freedom to the right of 2.33 is .012 so that H_o: $\beta_3 = 0$ can be rejected in favor of H_A: $\beta_3 \neq 0$ with p-value of .024. Presuming that this model passes the diagnostic checks to be covered in the next chapter, so that the assumptions of the Multiple Regression Model can be taken to be reasonably close to valid, we can thus conclude that gender impacts household earnings at the 3% level of significance.

Similarly, a 95% confidence interval for β_3 is

$$\hat{\beta}_3 \pm t_{.025}^{c}(47) \sqrt{s^2 \sum_{i=1}^{50} \left(w_{3,i}^{ols}\right)^2} \tag{9-52}$$

whose sample realization here is [−.975, −.072]; this interval is only worth quoting to a couple of decimal places in view of the evident imprecision with which β_3 and σ^2 are being estimated here with only 50 sample observations.

The row marked "collegegrad" gives the analogous results for $\hat{\beta}_2$ and the row marked "_cons" gives the results for $\hat{\beta}_1$.

Turning to the upper left hand portion of the output, "SS" is short for "sum of squares" and "MS" is this quantity divided by 47, the number of "degrees of freedom" here. Thus, from the row marked "Residual,"

$$\text{SSE}\left[\hat{\beta}_1^* \ldots \hat{\beta}_3^*\right] = \sum_{i=1}^{50} \left\{u_i^{\text{fit}}\right\}^2 = 29.4913289 \tag{9-53}$$

and

$$s^2 = \left(\frac{1}{50-3}\right) \sum_{i=1}^{50} \left\{u_i^{\text{fit}}\right\}^2 = .627475082 \tag{9-54}$$

Stata also computes the square root of this ($\sqrt{.627475082} = .79213$), labeling it "Root MSE." And from the row marked "Total",

$$\text{SST} = \text{Sum of Squares Total} = \sum_{i=1}^{50} \left(logearn_i - \overline{logearn}\right)^2 = 42.4312475 \tag{9-55}$$

and the sample variance of the dependent variable is SST/(N−1) = .865943827.

Stata (in common with many programs) automatically computes the F statistic for testing the null hypothesis that all of the coefficients except the intercept are zero. In this case there are $r=2$ restrictions, URSS = SSE = 29.4913289, and RSS = SST = 42.4312475, so that the F statistic is

$$\frac{\dfrac{42.4312475 - 29.4913289}{2}}{\dfrac{29.4913289}{47}} = \frac{6.4699593}{.627475082} = 10.31 \sim F(2, 47) \tag{9-56}$$

and the tail area to the right of 10.31 {the probability that an $F(2, 47)$ variate exceeds 10.31} is .0002. Frankly, this test is not all that informative: R_c^2 conveys the same information in a more interpretable form. This test is covered here because almost every regression program prints out this test statistic and because it serves as a useful example of how to test a multiple parameter restriction.

Finally, R^2 and adjusted R^2 are calculated as defined earlier:

$$\begin{aligned} R^2 &\equiv 1 - \frac{\sum_{i=1}^{50} \left\{u_i^{\text{fit}}\right\}^2}{\sum_{i=1}^{50} \left(logearn_i - \overline{logearn}\right)^2} = 1 - \frac{29.4913289}{42.4312475} = .3050 \\ R_c^2 &\equiv 1 - \frac{\frac{1}{47}\sum_{i=1}^{50} \left\{u_i^{\text{fit}}\right\}^2}{\frac{1}{50}\sum_{i=1}^{50} \left(logearn_i - \overline{logearn}\right)^2} = 1 - \frac{.627475082}{.865943827} = .2754 \end{aligned} \tag{9-57}$$

indicating that this regression equation "explains" about 28% of the sample variation in $logearn_i$.

Presuming that the assumptions of the Multiple Regression Model are reasonably valid here, both gender and graduation from college have a statistically significant impact on the logarithm of household earnings. But they have opposite signs. One might wonder, "Does the positive impact of graduating college outweigh the negative impact of gender discrimination?" This question corresponds to testing the null hypothesis H_o: $\beta_2 + \beta_3 = 0$ against the alternative hypothesis H_A: $\beta_2 + \beta_3 \neq 0$. Note that the two-tailed alternative is appropriate here because we probably would have tested the opposite one-tailed alternative had β_3 happened to be positive instead of negative. This test can be done by estimating obtaining RSS as the sum of squared fitting errors from the restricted regression imposing the constraint that $\beta_2 + \beta_3 = 0$. (This amounts to regressing $logearn_i$ on a new explanatory variable defined as $collegegrad_i - pesex_i$.) One then computes the test statistic

$$\frac{\dfrac{\text{RSS} - 29.4913289}{1}}{\dfrac{29.4913289}{47}} \tag{9-58}$$

which is a drawing from the $F(1, 47)$ distribution if the null hypothesis $\{H_o: \beta_2 + \beta_3 = 0\}$ is true. Here this is unnecessary, however, because Stata (like most modern econometric software) will do the arithmetic and tail area calculations for us. In Stata the command for doing this is simply:

```
test collegegrad + pesex = 0                                    (9-59)
```

and yields the output:

```
. test collegegrad + pesex = 0

(1) collegegrad + pesex = 0                                      (9-60)

F( 1 ,   47) = 1.03
Prob > F = 0.3154
```

indicating that the null hypothesis can be rejected only at the 31.5% level. Thus, it can be concluded – again assuming that the model's assumptions are reasonably valid – that the two parameter estimates are sufficiently noisy with 50 observations used that the null hypothesis that the two coefficients sum to zero cannot be rejected.

It is also worth noting that including the gender dummy variable in the model makes very little difference in the estimated coefficient on $collegegrad_i$ – this estimate fell from .873 to .852, a drop which is not large compared to the estimated standard error in the estimate of .224. Apparently either the gender ratio of college graduates is similar to that of non-graduates or there is only a weak correlation between gender and college graduation.

In essence, the coefficient β_2 is quantifying the return to education. Is the estimate we have obtained *economically* credible? $\hat{\beta}_2 = .852$ corresponds to mean weekly earnings being larger for college graduates by a factor of $e^{.852}$ or 2.34, which seems rather high. The estimated 95% confidence interval for $\hat{\beta}_2$ implies a 95% confidence interval for the earnings factor of $[e^{.401}, e^{1.30}]$ or [1.49, 3.67]. This confidence interval estimate looks a bit more reasonable, at least on the low end. Re-estimating the equation using the entire data set of 491 households living in the Baltimore–Washington area yields an estimated 95% confidence interval for the earnings factor of $[e^{.560}, e^{.835}]$

or [1.75, 2.31]. This still seems rather large. Even aside from the fact that this model has not been subjected to diagnostic tests to check the validity of the model assumptions – e.g., the assumption of an error term with constant variance – it seems likely that this model needs considerable additional work in order to meaningfully quantify the impact of a college degree on weekly earnings. For example, one would no doubt want to model the respondent's education in more detail with a set of dummy variables for different education levels, and it is almost certainly necessary to consider the impact of additional explanatory variables which would allow one to control for age and race.[21]

9.11 APPLICATION: VOTE FRAUD IN PHILADELPHIA SENATORIAL ELECTIONS

This example illustrates the fact that sometimes the reason we need to quantify a relationship is to demonstrate that a particular observation breaks that pattern. The pattern at issue in this case is an historical relationship between voting outcomes based on machine counts versus outcomes in the same elections based on absentee balloting.

According to an article in the *New York Times* (April 11, 1994) a special election was held in Philadelphia in November 1993 to fill a vacant seat in District 2 of the Pennsylvania State Senate. The balloting results were as follows:

Candidate	Machine count	Absentee ballot count	Total
William Stinson (Democrat)	19,127	1,396	20,523
Bruce Marks (Republican)	19,691	371	20,062
Dem.–Rep. margin of victory	−564	1,025	461

resulting in Mr. Stinson being seated in January of 1994, giving each party exactly half of the seats in the Pennsylvania State Senate. The Republican candidate, Marks, charged that the Democrats (who at the time controlled the Philadelphia County Board of Elections) had fraudulently manipulated the absentee balloting so as to favor Mr. Stinson. Judge Clarence Newcomer of the Federal District Court in Philadelphia agreed, throwing out all of the absentee ballots and declaring Mr. Marks the winner. Mr. Stinson appealed this decision and, on March 12, the Federal Appellate Court ruled that Judge Newcomer was correct in voiding the result of the election, but ordered him to consider calling a new election instead of seating Mr. Marks.

As part of Judge Newcomer's deliberations on this matter, a Princeton University economist, Professor Orley Ashenfelter, was called in. He obtained data on 21 previous contests in this senatorial district and plotted the machine count Democratic margin of victory in each election against the corresponding Democratic margin of victory on the absentee balloting. Thanks to Professor Ashenfelter's kindness in providing the data, this scatterplot is reproduced as Figure 9-4.

[21] For example, see Cawley, J., J. Heckman, and E. Vytlacil, "Three Observations on Wages and Measured Cognitive Ability," *Labour Economics 8*, pp. 419–42 for a more state-of-the-art model of this sort.

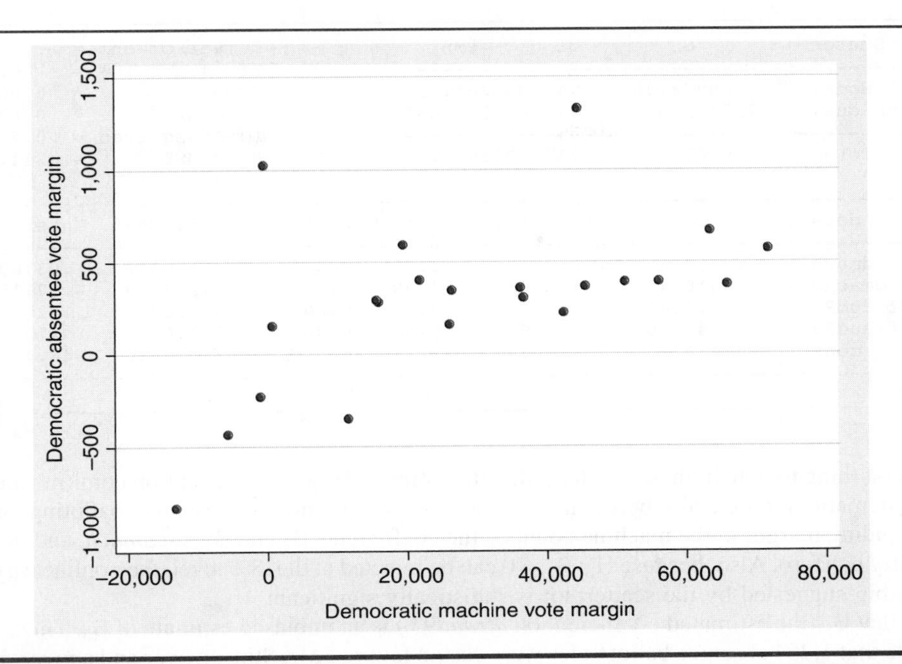

Figure 9-4 Scatterplot of Historical Philadelphia State Senate Election Results: Democractic Victory Margin on Absentee Ballots versus on Machine Count

Looking at this scatterplot it seems evident that – except for two elections which stand out as unusual – there is a systematic direct relationship between the Democratic victory margin on the absentee balloting and that on the machine count, although perhaps not quite a linear relationship. The two "unusual" observations correspond to the 1993 Marks-Stinson contest and a 1992 race conducted by the same Board of Elections; the 1993 election corresponds to the leftmost unusual observation. This suggests the following regression model

$$DABS_i = \beta_1 + \beta_2 dmach_i + \beta_3 dmach2_i + \beta_4 dfraud92_i + \beta_5 dfraud93_i + U_i \tag{9-61}$$

where, for the ith election in the data set,

$dabs_i$ = Democratic vote margin on the absentee balloting, realized value.
$dmach_i$ = Democratic vote margin on the machine count.
$dmach2_i = (dmach_i)^2$
$dfraud92_i$ = Dummy variable: 1 for unusual 1992 election; otherwise 0.
$dfraud93_i$ = Dummy variable: 1 for Marks-Stinson contest; otherwise 0.

Here we will blithely presume that the assumptions of the Multiple Regression Model – e.g., that $u_i \sim \text{NIID}[0, \sigma^2]$ – are satisfied; the issue of how to check these assumptions will be taken up in Chapters 10 and 13. The Stata syntax for estimating $\beta_1 \dots \beta_5$ is:

```
regress dabs dmach dmach 2 dfraud 92 dfraud 93
```
(9-62)

which produces the following output:

```
      Source |       SS       df       MS              Number of obs =      22
-------------+------------------------------           F(  4,    17) =   20.92
       Model |  3729072.48     4  932268.121           Prob > F      =  0.0000
    Residual |  757405.517    17  44553.2657           R-squared     =  0.8312
-------------+------------------------------           Adj R-squared =  0.7915
       Total |  4486478.00    21   213641.81           Root MSE      =  211.08

------------------------------------------------------------------------------
        dabs |      Coef.   Std. Err.      t    P>|t|     [95% Conf. Interval]
-------------+----------------------------------------------------------------
       dmach |   .0260669   .0052276     4.99   0.000     .0150377    .0370961
      dmach2 |  -.2410147   .0805093    -2.99   0.008    -.4108745   -.0711549
    dfraud92 |   861.1181   220.4078     3.91   0.001     396.0982    1326.138
    dfraud93 |   1254.256   225.8891     5.55   0.000     777.6715     1730.84
       _cons |  -214.4774   78.70074    -2.73   0.014    -380.5215   -48.43338
------------------------------------------------------------------------------
```

The first thing to note in these results is that the estimated regression equation confirms that there is a systematic relationship between the Democratic margin on absentee balloting and the corresponding margin in the machine counts – the coefficients β_2 and β_3 (on $dmach_i$ and $dmach2_i$) are clearly nonzero. Also, because H_o: $\beta_3 = 0$ can be rejected at the .8% level, the nonlinearity in the relationship suggested by the scatterplot is statistically significant.

Note that $\hat{\beta}_5$ (the estimated coefficient on $dfraud93_i$) is an unbiased estimate of β_5. Thus, we can conclude that 1,254 absentee ballot votes were cast in favor of Mr. Stinson over and above what one might expect based on the historical relationship between machine counts and absentee ballot counts. So far, however, this says nothing about whether or not the Democrats cheated, because 1,254 votes could, in principle, be a trivial amount compared to the statistical imprecision (noisiness) of this historical relationship. In other words, any conclusion as to whether or not the Democrats cheated on the absentee balloting hinges on whether or not $\hat{\beta}_5$ sufficiently exceeds its estimated standard deviation that the null hypothesis H_o: $\beta_5 = 0$ can be rejected.

Presuming, as noted above, that the assumptions of the Multiple Regression Model are satisfied, the test statistic

$$\frac{\hat{\beta}_5^* - \beta_5}{\sqrt{s^2 \Big/ \sum_{i=1}^{22} w_{5i}^2}} = \frac{1254 - \beta_5}{225.9} \tag{9-63}$$

is a realization of a $t(17)$ variate. Thus, the null hypothesis H_o: $\beta_5 = 0$ can in fact be rejected in favor of the alternative hypothesis H_A: $\beta_5 \neq 0$, with p-value equal to the probability that the magnitude of a $t(17)$ variate will exceed $1254/225.9 = 5.55$. From the Stata output, this probability is less than .0005. Note that a two-tailed test is appropriate here, because if the null hypothesis is true then it is equally likely that we would (due to chance) have observed a negative value for $\hat{\beta}_5$, in which case we might well have been testing whether this negative value for $\hat{\beta}_5$ is significantly below zero.[22]

Of course, this result begs the question: the real issue is not whether the Board of Elections cheated, but rather whether they did or did not cheat by a sufficient amount to affect the outcome of the election. This corresponds to testing H_o: $\beta_5 = 460$ against the one-tailed alternative hypothesis,

[22] And one could test the proposition that the Board of Elections did not cheat in either the 1992 *or* the 1993 election by testing the null hypothesis that $\beta_4 = 0$ and $\beta_5 = 0$. This joint hypothesis could be tested using the F statistic given earlier in the chapter with RSS being the sum of squared fitting errors from fitting a regression model omitting both $dfraud92_i$ and $dfraud93_i$. Alternatively – because computer programs like Stata are designed to make this sort of test easy – one could merely use the Stata command "test dfraud92 defraud93."

H_A: $\beta_5 < 460$.[23] If the assumptions of the Multiple Regression Model are valid and if this null hypothesis is true, then

$$\frac{\hat{\beta}_5^* - \beta_5}{\sqrt{s^2 / \sum_{i=1}^{22} \{w_{5i}^{ols}\}^2}} = \frac{1254.26 - 460}{225.89} = 3.52 \tag{9-64}$$

is a realization from the $t(17)$ distribution. A $t(17)$ variate will exceed 3.51 only .13% of the time, so this null hypothesis can be rejected with a p-value of .0013 or .13%. Alternatively, one could make Stata do the arithmetic and the (two-tailed) area calculation by asking it to test the linear restriction that $\beta_5 - 460 = 0$. The Stata syntax for this test is:

```
test  dfraud93 - 460
```
(9-65)

which yields the output for the analogous two-tailed test:

```
F(1,17)  = 12.36
Prob > F = 0.0026
```
(9-66)

Noting (from their definitions in Chapter 2) that an F variate with one degree of freedom in the numerator is the square of the analogous t variate – and that $\sqrt{12.36}$ is 3.52 – the essential equivalence of these two ways of testing this null hypothesis is apparent. Either way, this result can be interpreted as follows: if the Democrats only cheated on enough absentee ballots as to make the election a squeaker for Marks, then we would expect to see the 1993 dot in the scatterplot stick out above the normal historical pattern by this much (or more) with probability only .13%.

The reader may be interested to know that Mr. Marks held onto his Senate seat, but not for long:

> ... *in the regular election in November 1994, Bruce Marks lost by 393 votes to Christina Tartaglione, the daughter of the chair of the board of elections, one of the people allegedly involved in the suspected fraud. This time, both candidates agreed that the election had been conducted fairly.*[24]

KEY TERMS

For each term or concept listed below, provide a working definition or explanation:

Multiple Regression Model vs. Bivariate Regression Model

Nonlinearity in Model

Model Parameter Instability

Least Squares Weights: w_{ji}^{ols} vs. w_i^{ols}

Unbiasedness vs. Consistency vs. BLUness vs. Efficiency

Over-elaborate vs. Under-elaborate Model

R^2 vs. Adjusted R^2 vs. Schwarz Criterion (SC or BIC)

---

[23] A one-tailed test is appropriate here because (presuming that β_5 does equal 460, so that the cheating was only sufficient in and of itself to *almost* cause Stinson to win the election) only a positive sampling fluctuation in $\hat{\beta}_5^{ols} - \beta_5$ will cause us to wrongly reject the null hypothesis that the cheating did not affect the election outcome. Note carefully, however, that a canny attorney would surely use the two-tailed test anyway, so that he or she could explain to Judge Newcomer that "there are two ways to do the test, but this way gives the other side the benefit of the doubt." Sometimes obtaining the sharpest result is not the best move!

[24] Jessica M. Utts, *Seeing Through Statistics* (2nd edition, 1999, p. 400) Duxbury Press: Pacific Grove, CA.

EXERCISES

9-1. Suppose that

$$Y_i = \alpha_o + \beta_o x_i + \gamma_o z_i + V_i \qquad V_i \sim \text{NIID}[0, \sigma^2]$$

where the x_t and z_t are fixed in repeated samples with $\bar{x} = \bar{z} = 0$, but that you mistakenly estimate

$$Y_i = \alpha + \beta x_i + U_i$$

so that $U_i = \gamma_o z_i + V_i$.

a. Show that

$$E\left[\hat{\beta}\right] = \beta_o + \gamma_o \left[\frac{\sum_{i=1}^{N} z_i x_i}{\sum_{i=1}^{N} x_i^2}\right]$$

so that $\hat{\beta}$ is biased unless either γ_o or the sample correlation of x with z is zero. Why does this result make sense?

b. Is $\hat{\beta}$ a consistent estimator for β? Is $\hat{\beta}$ a consistent estimator for β_o? {Note that you could interpret β_o as the partial derivative $\partial E[Y]/\partial x$, holding z constant – i.e., "controlling for z." In contrast, you could interpret β as the total derivative, $dE[Y]/dx$, in which the indirect effect of x on $E[Y]$ (through its impact on z) is also being included.}

9-2. Suppose that you have sample data on production (q_i), capital (k_i), and labor (l_i) for N firms, each of which uses the same, generalized Cobb-Douglas, technology. Thus, your model for Q_i is

$$Q_i = A\, k_i^{\beta}\, l_i^{\gamma}\, e^{U_i} \qquad U_i \sim \text{NIID}[0, \sigma^2]$$

Note that modeling the error term in this multiplicative fashion ensures that the model can never yield a negative realized value for Q_i: an extremely negative realization of U_i merely makes the factor e^{U_i} a small positive number.

a. How could the parameters β and γ be estimated using OLS? {Hint: Consider taking the natural logarithm of both sides of the equation for Q_i.}

b. How could these parameter estimates be used to test the theoretical prediction that the technology these firms use exhibits constant returns to scale?

9-3. Consider again the 1993 Panel Study on Income Dynamics data on *v30810*$_i$ (month born), *v30821*$_i$ (1992 labor income), and *v30820*$_i$ (highest grade completed), which you worked with in Active Learning Exercise 4b (available at www.wiley.com/college/ashley).

a. Utilize the econometric software being used in your course to generate 12 dummy variables, one for each value *v30810*$_i$ takes on. Thus, for example, *jandum*$_i$ would be set to one for each respondent for which *v30810*$_i$ equals 1 and set to zero otherwise; similarly, *febdum*$_i$ would be set to one for each respondent for which *v30810*$_i$ equals 2 and set to zero otherwise, and so forth. {The Stata commands for generating these birth month dummy variables are "gen jandum = (V30810==1)" and "gen febdum = (V30810==2)".}

b. Estimate a multiple regression model assuming that the logarithm of labor income is linearly related to years of schooling, but that the intercept in the relationship might differ for respondents born in different months of the year. (In Exercise 4-14, you generated a new variable – $lnincome_i$ – as the natural logarithm of $v30821_i$.) Is it feasible to estimate the coefficients in this regression model? Why not? {Hint: The sample data for the sum of the 12 birth month dummy variables is one for every observation.}

c. Re-estimate the model from part b, dropping the $jandum_i$ explanatory variable. What interpretation can you give to the estimated coefficient on $maydum_i$? How would your interpretation of the dummy variable coefficients differ if you had instead included all 12 of them, but dropped the intercept from the regression equation? (These two models would fit the data identically and yield the same estimate for the coefficient on $v30820_i$, but one would be more convenient for visualizing the variation in E[$lnincome_i$] across birth months, whereas the other would be more convenient for testing whether respondents born in May on average earn more than respondents born in January.)

d. If the assumptions of the Multiple Regression Model are valid for these data, at what significance level can the null hypothesis that education level (highest grade completed) has no impact on income be rejected? Is this a one-tailed or two-tailed test? What is the estimated impact of an additional year of schooling on the logarithm of expected income? What is the estimated impact of an additional year of schooling on expected income itself? Is this impact statistically significant? Is this impact *economically* significant? {Hint: $e^{.01088}$ equals 1.0109.}

e. Controlling (as is done in this regression model) for education level, do people who were born in May on average have different income than people who were born in January? If the assumptions of the Multiple Regression Model are valid for these data, at what significance level can the null hypothesis that the true (population) value of the coefficient on $maydum_i$ is zero be rejected? Is this a one-tailed or two-tailed test?

f. Make a scatterplot of the relationship between $lnincome_i$ and $v30820_i$, ignoring the birth month dummy variables. Also make a histogram of $v30820_i$. Do you detect something odd in these results? Is the Multiple Regression Model assumption that the model errors are gaussian credible here? (Do you really think that there is a group of households who have completed 99 years of schooling? Doesn't the Constitution outlaw cruel and unusual punishment? What do you think is going on here with these observations?)

g. Generate a new education level variable (edu_i) which omits the observations for which $v30820_i$ equals 99 and repeat your regression analysis, substituting edu for $v30820_i$. {In Stata, the command for creating this new explanatory variable would be "gen edu = $v30820_i$ if v30820<99".}

i. Based on the adjusted R^2 value, does the model using edu fit_i the $lnincome_i$ data better?

ii. If the assumptions of the Multiple Regression Model are now all valid for these data, at what significance level can the null hypothesis that the true (population) value of the coefficient on $maydum_i$ is zero be rejected? What can you conclude about the inference result you obtained in part e?

This exercise will be reconsidered at the end of Chapters 10 through 13, after the coverage of how to diagnostically check the assumptions of the Multiple Regression Model is more complete.

9-4. An epidemiologist carefully specifies and estimates a model for the risk of breast cancer in 2,151 adult (female) nurses whose mothers were surveyed (years previously) as to the dietary consumption habits of these nurses when they were three to five years old. This survey queried the mothers with respect to the little girls' consumption of 30 different foods: whole milk, oranges, eggs, broccoli, french fries, ground beef, hot dogs, etc. The epidemiologist finds that the coefficient on consumption of french fries in the model for adult risk of breast cancer is 3.6

estimated standard errors away from what would correspond, in the Multiple Regression Model, to a coefficient value of zero; none of the other 29 coefficients was statistically significant. Assuming that everything else about the way this study was conducted is correct and appropriate, why is it likely a bad idea to conclude, based on this evidence, that eating french fries as a child has anything to do with cancer risk later in life? What reasonably straightforward hypothesis test would help sort this issue out?[25]

Active Learning Exercise 9a: A Statistical Examination of the Florida Voting in the November 2000 Presidential Election – Did Mistaken Votes for Pat Buchanan Swing the Election from Gore to Bush?

Introduction

It was alleged in November 2000 that the design of the ballots used in the Florida county of Palm Beach was such that it was very easy for a voter to mistakenly cast a ballot for Pat Buchanan when intending to vote for Al Gore. Presuming that the relative popularity of these two candidates was stable across counties of comparable sizes, this suggests that it might be fruitful to look at a scatterplot relating the number of votes cast for Buchanan in a given county ("$buchanan_i$") to "$total_i$", the total number of votes cast in that county for the major candidates in the race – Bush, Gore, Nader, and Buchanan:

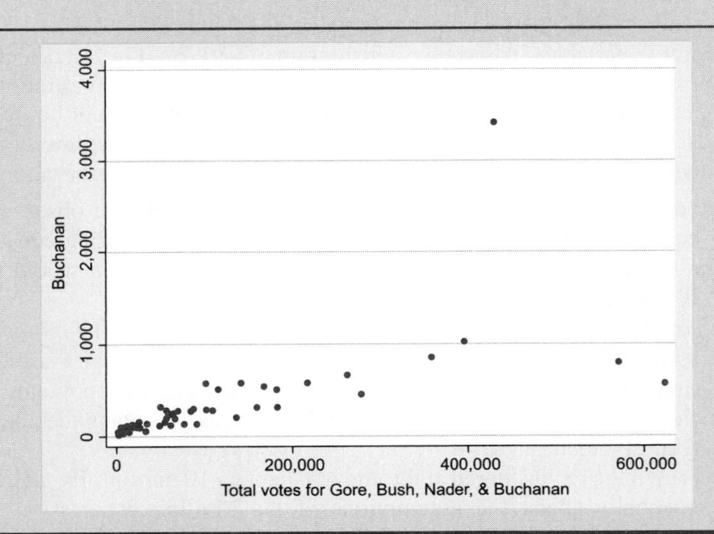

Figure 9-5 Scatterplot of Votes for Buchanan versus Total Votes, U.S. Presidential Election of 2000 (Florida Counties Only)

[25] This example is not fictional, although the model estimated was not exactly the Multiple Regression Model as defined here. See Michels, K. B., B. A. Rosner, W. Chumlea, G. Colditz, and W. C. Willett (2006) "Preschool Diet and Adult Risk of Cancer," *International Journal of Cancer 118*, pp. 749–54.

Two features immediately stand out in this scatterplot. First, there is an obvious outlier which, on examination, is for the county of Palm Beach. Second, there does appear to be a distinct relationship between the total votes cast and the number cast for Buchanan, but there is some reason to suspect that the relationship is not linear.

Your Assignment:

1. Copy file ALE9a.csv (available at www.wiley.com/college/ashley) to your hard disk and read it into whatever econometrics software is in use in your course.
2. Make a scatterplot of your own, relating $buchanan_i$ to $total_i$ for the 67 Florida counties.
3. Generate a dummy variable ("$palmb_i$"), which is one for Palm Beach County and zero otherwise.[26] Verify that this variable was correctly generated by examining or listing its values.
4. Estimate a regression model relating $buchanan_i$ to $total_i$ and $palmb_i$. What is the meaning of a population value of zero for the coefficient on $palmb_i$? Assuming that the assumptions of the Multiple Regression Model are all satisfied, what is an estimated 95% confidence interval for the coefficient on $palmb_i$?[27] What is the econometric interpretation of this estimated confidence interval? Given that the election hinged on only a few hundred votes in Florida, provide an interpretation of your result from the perspective of a partisan Gore supporter and an alternative interpretation from the perspective of a partisan Bush supporter.
5. The tools for checking the assumptions of this Multiple Regression Model will be covered in Chapter 10.[28] Here, check the assumption made by this particular model that the relationship between $buchanan_i$ and $total_i$ is linear by generating a new variable which is the square of $total_i$ and including it in the model. At what p-value can you reject the null hypothesis that the coefficient on this squared variable is zero? Does this improvement in the model notably change the estimated 95% confidence interval for coefficient on the Palm Beach dummy variable?
6. Generate new variables which are the logarithms of $buchanan_i$ and $total_i$. In what ways does the scatterplot of $\log(buchanan_i)$ versus $\log(total_i)$ look more attractive than that of $buchanan_i$ versus $total_i$ in terms of our model assumptions? {Hint: You will find it helpful to produce a scatterplot of $\log(buchanan_i)$ versus $\log(total_i)$ which omits the Palm Beach County observation.[29]}
7. Estimate a regression model relating $\log(buchanan_i)$ to $\log(total_i)$ and $palmb_i$. What is the meaning of a population value of zero for the coefficient on $palmb_i$? Assuming that the assumptions of the Multiple Regression Model are all satisfied, at what p-value can the null hypothesis that the coefficient on the Palm Beach county dummy is zero be rejected? What is an estimated 95% confidence interval for the coefficient on this dummy variable? What is the econometric interpretation of this estimated confidence interval? Provide an interpretation of your result from the perspective of a partisan Bush supporter and an alternative interpretation from the perspective of a partisan Gore supporter.

[26] In Stata the command "gen palmb = (_n == 50)" creates the required dummy variable since Palm Beach County is the 50th observation in the data set.

[27] A long glance at the scatterplot indicates that the model error homoscedasticity assumption is suspect for this model, however. The model in logarithms, suggested in part 6, is much more promising in this regard.

[28] Foreshadowing, in the present instance the auxiliary regression of the squared fitting errors versus $total_i$ is informative, although one must note that a sample length of only 67 is a bit skimpy for using the fitting errors as proxies for the model errors.

[29] In Stata the command "scatter buchanan total if _n != 50" would do this.

APPENDIX 9.1: PREDICTION USING THE MULTIPLE REGRESSION MODEL

This appendix provides more detail on the discussion of out-of-sample prediction given in Section 9.6. Out-of-sample prediction is not fundamentally any different using an estimated Multiple Regression Model than it is using an estimated Bivariate Regression Model: there is just more algebra involved. Consequently, because all of the important ideas were covered in some detail when this topic was developed in Section 8.4, the analogous results for prediction using an estimated Multiple Regression Model are merely summarized here. The topic of post-sample forecasting, from the perspective of time-series analysis, is taken up in more depth in Chapter 17.

Assuming that the Multiple Regression Model assumptions hold for observation number $N+1$ as well as for the initial N observations, and that values are available for all k explanatory variables corresponding to observation Y_{N+1}, the usual predictor of Y_{N+1} is the random variable

$$\hat{Y}_{N+1} \equiv \hat{\beta}_1 x_{N+1,1} + \hat{\beta}_2 x_{N+1,2} + \cdots + \hat{\beta}_k x_{N+1,k} \tag{A9-1}$$

So that the resulting prediction error is

$$Y_{N+1} - \hat{Y}_{N+1} \equiv U_{N+1} - (\hat{\beta}_1 - \beta_1)x_{N+1,1} - (\hat{\beta}_2 - \beta_2)x_{N+1,2} - \cdots - (\hat{\beta}_k - \beta_k)x_{N+1,k} \tag{A9-2}$$

and we see that $\hat{Y}_{N+1}$ is an unbiased predictor for Y_{N+1} because $E[U_{N+1}]$ is zero by assumption and the OLS estimators $\hat{\beta}_1 \ldots \hat{\beta}_k$ are themselves unbiased.

From

$$\hat{\beta}_j = \beta_j + \sum_{i=1}^{N} w_{ji}^{\text{ols}}\, U_i \tag{A9-3}$$

and the derivation of $\text{var}(\hat{\beta}_j)$ given earlier in this chapter, it is evident that $\text{var}(\hat{\beta}_1) \ldots \text{var}(\hat{\beta}_k)$ and each of the covariances $\text{cov}(\hat{\beta}_j,\ \hat{\beta}_\ell)$ – for $j \neq \ell$, of course – is just σ^2 times a messy function of all of the data on the k explanatory variables. It follows that the sampling variance of the prediction error can also be expressed as σ^2 times a messy function of all of the data on the k explanatory variables:

$$\begin{aligned}\text{var}(Y_{N+1} - \hat{Y}_{N+1}) &= \sigma^2 + \sum_{j=1}^{k} x_{N+1,j}^2\, \text{var}(\hat{\beta}_j) \\ &\quad + \sum_{j=1}^{k}\sum_{\ell=1}^{j-1} x_{N+1,j}x_{N+1,\ell}\, \text{cov}(\hat{\beta}_j,\ \hat{\beta}_\ell) \\ &= \sigma^2 \Omega(\tilde{x})\end{aligned} \tag{A9-4}$$

Here the symbol $\Omega(\tilde{x})$ is used to denote the indicated (complicated) function of all of the data on the k explanatory variables. Thus,

$$\frac{Y_{N+1} - \hat{Y}_{N+1}}{\sqrt{\sigma^2 \Omega(\tilde{x})}} \sim N[0, 1] \tag{A9-5}$$

Because $(N-k)S^2/\sigma^2$ is distributed $\sigma^2(N-k)$ independently of $\hat{\beta}_1,\ \hat{\beta}_2 \ldots \hat{\beta}_k$ under the assumptions of the Multiple Regression Model, $(N-k)S^2/\sigma^2$ is also independent of $Y_{N+1} - \hat{Y}_{N+1}$. Consequently,

$$\frac{\dfrac{Y_{N+1} - \hat{Y}_{N+1}}{\sqrt{\sigma^2 \Omega(\tilde{x})}}}{\sqrt{\dfrac{(N-k)S^2/\sigma^2}{N-k}}} = \frac{Y_{N+1} - \hat{Y}_{N+1}}{\sqrt{S^2 \Omega(\tilde{x})}} \sim t(N-k) \tag{A9-6}$$

so that a 95% confidence interval for y_{N+1} is just

$$\left[\hat{y}_{N+1} - t^c_{.025}\sqrt{S^2\Omega(\tilde{x})}, \hat{y}_{N+1} + t^c_{.025}\sqrt{S^2\Omega(\tilde{x})}\right] \tag{A9-7}$$

where $t^c_{.025}$ is the 2½% critical point of the Student's t distribution with $N-k$ degrees of freedom.

These expressions look a bit more complicated, but they are essentially identical to the analogous results for the Bivariate Regression Model derived in Section 8.4. Computer software does all the arithmetic of computing $\hat{Y}_{N+1}$ and $\sqrt{S^2\Omega(\tilde{x})}$ – that is why there was no real need here to write out an explicit expression for $\Omega(\tilde{x})$. It is *our* responsibility, on the other hand, to make sure that the assumptions of the Multiple Regression Model underlying the validity of these formulas are reasonably satisfied: that is the purpose of the diagnostic checking techniques described in the next chapter.[30]

[30] It is also worth repeating the warning developed in the analogous discussion in Chapter 8 to the effect that the prediction $\hat{Y}_{N+1}$ can easily become wildly inaccurate – with no warning from its estimated standard error, $\sqrt{S^2\Omega(\tilde{x})}$ – if Y_i is not actually a linear function of x_{i1} ... x_{ik} and one bases $\hat{Y}_{N+1}$ on $x_{N+1,1}$ ... $x_{N+1,k}$ values notably outside the ranges observed for these variables in the sample.

10

Diagnostically Checking and Respecifying the Multiple Regression Model: Dealing with Potential Outliers and Heteroscedasticity in the Cross-Sectional Data Case

10.1 INTRODUCTION

The previous chapters have shown how the parameters of the Bivariate Regression Model and the Multivariate Regression Model can be estimated by minimizing the sum of the squared fitting errors. *If* the assumptions underlying these models are satisfied, then these parameter estimates have been shown to have desirable properties: unbiasedness, consistency, and BLUness. Further, we have seen how – under these assumptions – one can use these estimates to test economic hypotheses and to estimate confidence intervals containing the true (population) parameter values with some specified probability.

These are very useful results. All of them, however, hinge on the validity of the model assumptions. Econometric software (Stata, SAS, EViews, etc.) makes it quite easy to estimate regression model parameters, test hypotheses about them, and obtain estimates of the abovementioned confidence intervals. But these computer programs only evaluate formulas – such as those derived in Chapters 5 through 9 – using the input sample data. The programs neither know nor care about the validity (or otherwise) of the underlying model assumptions which make these formulas relevant and meaningful: detecting and dealing with failures of these assumptions is called "diagnostically checking the model" and is the human analyst's job.[1]

The role of this chapter is to provide the reader with the tools for doing that job in the context of a regression model using cross-sectional data and exogenous – "fixed in repeated samples" – explanatory variables. A description of additional tools, appropriate to models using time-series data and to models with non-exogenous ("endogenous") explanatory variables, requires the additional material on probability limits and consistency covered in Chapter 11; the estimation and diagnostic checking of such models will be described in Chapters 12 through 14.

[1] See also the initial introduction to diagnostic checking – regarding estimation and inference with respect to the mean of a normally distributed variate – developed at the end of Chapter 4.

The diagnostic checking tools described here are reasonably straightforward, but it should be noted at the outset that the application of these tools is not completely mechanical: it requires some focused effort, aided by a bit of common sense and, at times, some insight into the economic problem being analyzed. It should also be noted that successful application of these tools requires a nontrivial amount of sample data: an analyst with less than, say, 40 sample observations is not in a position to effectively check most of the model assumptions – in that situation one is pretty much forced to just make the assumptions and hope for the best. Finally, even with fairly large samples, one might as well recognize at the outset that absolute certainty is not available in this part of one's life: one is not going to end up certain that one's regression model satisfies all of the assumptions. One can, however, end up moderately confident that one's regression model is reasonably consistent with the assumptions of the Multiple Regression Model. This requires (as noted above) some effort, some insight, and the tools described here – but yields much better results than ignoring the possibility that the model assumptions are substantially violated.

Each of the model assumptions falls into one of two fundamental categories:

- Assumptions about the *form* of the model – that is, the assumption that Y_i equals $\beta_1 x_{i1} + \ldots + \beta_k x_{ik}$ plus a random error term U_i, and
- *Statistical* assumptions about this error term – that is, the assumption that $U_i \sim \text{NIID}(0, \sigma^2)$.

Regarding the first of these categories, Chapter 9 already discussed both "over-elaborate" models (where one or more extraneous explanatory variables are included in the model) and "under-elaborate" models, where one or more explanatory variables are wrongly omitted from the model – due to either data unavailability or to inadvertence. We saw there that over-elaboration was of minor significance, so long as plenty of sample observations are available. Omission of an important explanatory variable, in contrast, was seen to be potentially disastrous if the sample variation in an omitted variable is related to that of an included variable, unless one is aware of the omission and able to appropriately reinterpret the meaning of the coefficients $\beta_1 \ldots \beta_k$.[2]

The linearity of the model specification is the assumption that the expected value of Y_i (conditional on the fixed values of $x_{i1} \ldots x_{ik}$) is a *linear* function of $x_{i1} \ldots x_{ik}$. As noted at the beginning of Chapter 9, this assumption is readily checked, in a crude sort of way, by tentatively including simple nonlinear terms, such as $(x_{i1})^2$ or $x_{i2}x_{i3}$, in the model specification. It is also worth noting that the intent of the model often more or less dictates a nonlinear form for an explanatory variable. For example, if the point of the model is to obtain an estimate of the derivative of the expected value of dependent variable with respect to *percentage* changes in, say, household income then it is simplest to use the *logarithm* of household income (rather than household income itself) as the explanatory variable, so that the coefficient on the income variable corresponds to this particular derivative.[3]

A sensible and relevant final diagnostic check on one's specification of the form of a regression is to test it for parameter stability. This topic was initially discussed in Section 9.3, where it was explicitly noted that allowing for quadratic nonlinearity in a relationship – in that case, between an

[2] Recall that the appropriate interpretation of β_3, say, is as the partial derivative of $E[Y_i]$ with respect to x_{i3}, holding the values of the remaining $k-1$ explanatory variables fixed – and averaging over all other influences on Y_i. Wrongly omitting an explanatory variable which is unrelated to the k explanatory variables included in the model turns out to be of no great significance, except that the model will fit the data less well. In contrast, wrongly omitting an explanatory variable whose sample variation is substantially similar to that of one of the k explanatory variables included in the model – x_{i3}, say – is quite problematic. Fundamentally this is because x_{i3} will in that case "proxy" for the omitted variable and β_3 will in that case be some mixture of the partial derivative of $E[Y_i]$ with respect to x_{i3} and the partial derivative of $E[Y_i]$ with respect to the omitted variable.

[3] Suppose, for example, that x_i in the Bivariate Regression Model is actually the logarithm of income$_i$, so that $E[Y_i] = \alpha + \beta \ln(income_i)$. Then $d\{E[Y_i]\} = \beta d\{\ln(income_i)\} = \beta d\{income_i\}/income_i$, so that $\beta/100$ is the rate of change of $E[Y_i]$ with respect to *percentage* changes in *income*$_i$. Similarly, if Y_i is actually the logarithm of, say, consumption, then β can be interpreted as the *elasticity* of consumption with respect to income – see Active Learning Exercise 10c (available at www.wiley.com/college/ashley) for an illustrative example.

earnings variable and the number of years of schooling – is essentially equivalent to specifying that the coefficient on education is actually itself a linear function of educational level. Thus, if the linear model wrongly omits the squared-education term then the coefficient on education level is not a constant, but rather a (linear) function of education level.

A number of sophisticated tests for parameter *in*stability have been proposed in the econometrics literature. These tests are usually formulated for time-series regression models, because time itself provides a natural ordering (time-order) in this context. These tests are commonly referred to as tests for "structural change." A currently popular such test, which one might therefore hope to find conveniently implemented in a typical econometric software package, is due to Bai and Perron (1998).[4] The Bai-Perron test assumes that the coefficients on all $k-1$ non-intercept explanatory variables abruptly change their values at each of j time periods, each of which is called a "breakpoint." It tests both the value of j – i.e., $j = 0$, 1, 2, etc. – and the statistical significance of the parameter instability, against a null hypothesis that the parameters are all stable across the sample. One could equally well apply the Bai-Perron test to the Bivariate Regression Model, however, by simply reordering (sorting) the data on both the dependent and the explanatory variable according to the value of the explanatory variable.[5]

The Bai-Perron test is not appropriate in a cross-sectional data context with $k-1 > 1$ non-intercept explanatory variables, however, because there is no reason in this setting to think that all of these $k-1$ coefficients change at the same value of the single explanatory variable on which one sorted the data set. It makes better sense in this setting to sort the data set on the explanatory variable for which the coefficient-stability assumption is most suspect, create ℓ dummy variables (each of which is one over a specific subset of the observed values of this explanatory variable, and zero for all other observations), and estimate a Multiple Regression Model replacing this explanatory variable by the ℓ variables obtained from the product of this explanatory variable with each of these dummy variables.

For example, suppose that the model has three explanatory variables – $x_{i,1}$, x_{i2}, and x_{i3} – and that it is the stability of β_3 (across the different observed values of x_{i3}) which is at issue. Letting ℓ be equal to four allows β_3 to take on four different values across the sample. After sorting the data set on x_{i3}, one might define D_{i1} (the first of the four dummy variables) to equal one for the first quarter of the data set – i.e., for observation number one up through the integer nearest to $N/4$ – and zero otherwise. Similarly, D_{i2} is defined equal to one for the second quarter of the data set and set equal to zero for all of the other observations; D_{i3} is set equal to one for the third quarter of the data set; and D_{i4} equal to one for the last quarter of the data set. Then one could test for this particular form of parameter instability by estimating the regression model

$$Y_i = \gamma_1 x_{i,1} + \gamma_2 x_{i,2} + \gamma_3 x_{i,3} D_{i,1} + \gamma_4 x_{i,3} D_{i,2} + \gamma_5 x_{i,3} D_{i,3} + \gamma_6 x_{i,3} D_{i,4} + U_i \qquad (10\text{-}1)$$

and testing the null hypothesis that $\gamma_3 = \gamma_4 = \gamma_5 = \gamma_6$. Moreover, the sample estimates of γ_3, γ_4, γ_5, and γ_6 – and especially the estimated confidence intervals for them – provide an estimated "picture" of how β_3 varies with increasing values of x_{i3}.[6] This picture clearly becomes more detailed as one increases the value of ℓ; the cost of such increases is that the precision with which the additional parameters can be estimated (and the likelihood of correctly rejecting the null hypothesis when it is false) both drop off. Note also that, if the manner in which β_3 varies with x_{i3} is smooth rather than

[4] Bai, Jushan, and Pierre Perron (1998) "Estimating and Testing Linear Models with Multiple Structural Changes," *Econometrica 66(1)*, 47–78.

[5] Econometric software generally makes such sorting very easy. In Stata, for example, the command "sort varname" sorts the entire data set (all of the variables) so that the observations on the variable "varname" are in nondecreasing order.

[6] One could alternatively create the ℓ variables to each correspond to a range of values for x_{i3} rather than to one-fourth of the sorted sample.

abrupt, then one might do better to model β_3 as varying linearly with x_{i3}, in which case one is right back at including $(x_{i3})^2$ in the model.[7]

The assumption that the explanatory variables are "fixed in repeated samples" was discussed in Section 5.3. This assumption is unfortunately not so easily checked; nor are violations of it so easily dealt with. But dealt with they can be, using an econometric technique known as "instrumental variables estimation." A useful consideration of this very important topic must be delayed until Chapter 12, however, because it requires the additional material on probability theory covered in Chapter 11.[8]

Finally, the last piece of the *form* of the model specification is a choice as to the form with which the dependent variable enters the model. For example, will Y_i be the average income for the ith country in the sample, or would the dependent variable in the model be more appropriately specified as the logarithm of the ith country's income, or perhaps as per capita income for the ith country? This choice turns out to interact strongly with a consideration of the *statistical* assumptions on the error term – in particular on the assumptions that the model error term, U_i, is normally distributed and homoscedastic. The remainder of this chapter focuses on precisely these two assumptions: how to sensibly test whether or not they are (to a reasonable degree) satisfied and how to respond to sample indications that they are seriously violated.[9]

10.2 THE FITTING ERRORS AS LARGE-SAMPLE ESTIMATES OF THE MODEL ERRORS, $U_1 \dots U_N$

There is a simple relationship between the fitting errors and the model errors in the Bivariate Regression Model; in that model the fitting errors are

$$\begin{aligned} U_i^{\text{fit}} &= Y_i - [\hat{\alpha} + \hat{\beta} x_i] \\ &= [\alpha + \beta x_i + U_i] - [\hat{\alpha} + \hat{\beta} x_i] \\ &= U_i - [\hat{\alpha} - \alpha] - [\hat{\beta} x_i + \beta x_i] \\ &= U_i - [\hat{\alpha} - \alpha] - x_i\,[\hat{\beta} + \beta] \end{aligned} \tag{10-2}$$

where the model has been substituted in for Y_i and the terms rearranged.[10] Recall from Equation 6-16 that

$$\hat{\beta} = \beta + \sum_{i=1}^{N} w_i^{\text{ols}} U_i \tag{10-3}$$

[7] With time-series data, where the data set is ordinarily sorted in increasing time-order and the usual issue is whether (and in what way) a coefficient such as β_3 varies over time, many different specifications have been proposed for the time-evolution of a regression parameter. The simplest of these are the abrupt-change specifications discussed above; another is to assume that β_3 is a linear or quadratic function of time (observation number) – this suggests an alternative specification examined in Exercise 10-1. Ashley (1984, *Economic Inquiry XXII*, 253–67) examined these (and a number of substantially more sophisticated alternatives) and found that one is usually just as well off using the straightforward dummy-variable approach described above.

[8] See also the discussion of this topic at the end of Active Learning Exercise 10b (available at www.wiley.com/college/ashley).

[9] The material in Chapters 5 and 9 showed that inclusion of an intercept in the regression model automatically implies that $E[U_i]$ is zero – and takes one a considerable way toward unbiased parameter estimates. Thus, in general no sensible person will omit the intercept; consequently, this portion of the assumptions on the model error ordinarily need not be checked at all. The non-autocorrelation assumption – that corr(U_i, U_j) equals zero for all $i \neq j$ – is frequently quite problematic for models using time-series data, but the analysis of these models requires the additional probability theory material to be covered in Chapter 11. Consequently, coverage of diagnostic checking of this portion of the assumptions on the model errors is delayed until Chapters 13 and 14.

[10] This relationship was previously derived in the "Estimating σ^2" section of Chapter 7. The relationship is almost as simple in the Multiple Regression Model – see Exercise 10-3.

and that, from Exercise 6-9,

$$\hat{\alpha} = \sum_{i=1}^{N} \left(\frac{1}{N} - \bar{x} w_i^{\text{ols}} \right) Y_i = \alpha + \sum_{i=1}^{N} \left(\frac{1}{N} - \bar{x} w_i^{\text{ols}} \right) U_i \tag{10-4}$$

Thus, both $\hat{\alpha} - \alpha$ and $\hat{\beta} - \beta$ are just weighted sums of $U_1 \dots U_N$, and hence are normally distributed if $U_1 \dots U_N$ are. The model fitting errors U_i^{fit} are normally distributed if and only if the model errors are normally distributed, so we can check the assumption that the model errors (which are not directly observed) are normally distributed by checking whether or not the observed fitting errors are normally distributed.

Note, however, that homoscedasticity (constant variance for all observations) in the model errors does not imply that this assumption also holds for the model fitting errors – at least, not in small samples. In fact, recall from Equation 6-10 that w_i^{ols}, the OLS weight for the ith observation, is

$$w_i^{\text{ols}} = \frac{x_i - \bar{x}}{\varphi} = \frac{x_i - \bar{x}}{\sum_{j=1}^{N} \left(x_j - \bar{x} \right)^2} \tag{10-5}$$

so that the weights on $U_1 \dots U_N$ in $\hat{\alpha} - \alpha$ and $\hat{\beta} - \beta$ clearly depend on $x_1 \dots x_N$. Thus, the variance of the ith fitting error – $\text{var}\left(U_1^{\text{fit}}\right)$ – depends on $x_1 \dots x_N$ even if $\text{var}(U_i)$ is a constant for all values of i.

However, since the OLS parameter estimates $\left(\hat{\alpha} \text{ and } \hat{\beta}\right)$ are consistent estimators of α and β, the estimation errors $\left(\hat{\alpha} - \alpha \text{ and } \hat{\beta} - \beta\right)$ are negligible for large samples. Thus, for sufficiently large N, the model fitting errors – $U_1^{\text{fit}} \dots U_N^{\text{fit}}$ – are essentially equivalent to $U_1 \dots U_N$, the actual model errors and – for large samples, at least – one can thus check the assumption of homoscedastic model errors by checking the homoscedasticity of the model fitting errors.[11]

How large a sample is "sufficiently large" for this equivalence to be an adequate approximation? Ultimately, the sense of this question depends on exactly what use one is making of the approximation – and its answer is almost never known in practice. On the other hand – as a "cultural norm" – it is reasonable to state that most econometricians and applied economists would feel comfortable using the fitting errors as proxies for the actual errors for sample sizes in excess of 100 and would (or probably should) feel uncomfortable with this substitution for sample lengths much smaller than 40. Thus, the comment in the first section of this chapter – to the effect that "an analyst with less than, say, 40 sample observations is not in a position to effectively check most of the model assumptions" – is based on this norm.

10.3 REASONS FOR CHECKING THE NORMALITY OF THE MODEL ERRORS, $U_1 \dots U_N$

The reasons for caring about (and checking) the normality of the model errors fall into two categories: the reasons which initially appear to be important and those which are not so obvious, but which are actually crucially important.

At the outset, it would appear that the most important reasons for checking normality are that a number of the key results obtained in Chapters 5 and 9 depend on this assumption about the model errors. In the first place, the derivation that the least squares parameter estimates are normally distributed followed directly from the observation that these estimators could be written as weighted sums of $U_1 \dots U_N$ – e.g., see equations 10-3 and 10-4 – and this distributional result on the parameter estimates is necessary in order for the hypothesis testing and confidence interval estimation results to be valid. On the other hand, the parameter estimators are known to be approximately normally

[11] The same argument holds with respect to checking the non-autocorrelation assumption, which topic is taken up in Chapters 13 and 14.

distributed for large samples in any case, by application of the Central Limit Theorem; this result is derived in Chapter 11. Thus, all of these statistical inference results are still valid for large samples, even if the model errors are not normally distributed.

Secondly, while normality of the model errors was not used in showing that the parameter estimators are BLU, it was asserted in Chapter 5 and in Chapter 9 that these estimators have the stronger optimality property of *efficiency* if the model errors are normally distributed. Recall that a BLU estimator of a parameter has the smallest sampling variance of any unbiased estimator for this parameter which is a linear function of $Y_1 \ldots Y_N$. In contrast, an efficient estimator has the smallest sampling variance of any unbiased estimator of the parameter, regardless of whether it is a linear function of $Y_1 \ldots Y_N$ or not. Thus, if the model errors are not normally distributed, then there could be a (presumably nonlinear) unbiased estimator for this parameter which has a smaller sampling variance than does the least squares estimator. On the other hand, if the sample is large, then the sampling variance of the BLU parameter estimates is likely small enough that this distinction between BLU and efficient estimation is not a major concern – in any case, it is completely unclear how to obtain this better nonlinear estimator.

Thus – for reasonably large samples, at least – neither of these reasons for worrying about the normality of the model errors seems all that important. (And the usual statistical tests for normality are only valid for large samples anyway.[12]) Why care about checking it, then?

First, the errors in a regression model can be highly non-normal – leading to substantial estimation inefficiency – where the dependent variable is in the form of a proportion and hence is inherently restricted to the interval [0, 1]. Where none of the actual observations $y_1 \ldots y_N$ is close to either limit, then one might consider transforming the dependent variable so that the error term is more sensibly normally distributed. Monotonic functions of the ratio $Y_i/(1 - Y_i)$, such as $\ln[Y_i/(1 - Y_i)]$ or $Y_i/(1 - Y_i)$ itself, are worth considering in that context. Such transformations are not appropriate, however, where some (or even many) observations are close to (or at) the limiting values of the interval; this topic is discussed in Chapter 16.

There is also a second good reason for checking on the normality of the model errors, which will be emphasized at this point: the simple, graphical methods for assessing the normality of the model errors are crucial to identifying the presence of any *influential outliers* in the data set. An *outlier* (or *outlying observation*) is any observation (on either the dependent variable or on any of the explanatory variables) which is sufficiently idiosyncratic as to imply a model error which is unusually large in magnitude.[13]

Of course, the model errors are not observed, but – as shown earlier in this chapter – the observed fitting errors will approximate them well for reasonably large samples. In that case, for example, if the U_i are distributed $N(0, \sigma^2)$, then an observed U_i^{fit} value around 2.6σ in magnitude will naturally occur about once in every 100 observations and would hardly merit the adjective "unusual" in a sample of several hundred. In contrast, a fitting error larger than 3.9σ will naturally occur only about once in every 10,000 observations and thus might reasonably be termed an "outlier" in a sample of only several hundred observations.[14]

[12] Examples include the skewness-kurtosis test and the Shapiro-Wilks test. The Stata commands for invoking these two tests are "sktest *varname*" and "swilks *varname*" – respectively – where "*varname*" is the name of the variable to be tested.

[13] See also Active Learning Exercise 6a.

[14] At least, this is reasonable if the model errors are, in fact, normally distributed. Because model errors can be thought of as the sum of a large number of unmodeled (at least approximately independent) influences on the value of the dependent variable, the Central Limit Theorem (Section 2.11) suggests that the normality assumption will usually be reasonable. And it ordinarily is. The most common exception one observes in practice is for financial return time-series, such as the return to holding a share of common stock in a typical corporation: the distribution of such returns (and of errors in models for them) typically has "thicker tails" than the normal distribution. The fitting errors from models for such financial returns series thus typically exhibit notably more "outliers" than one would expect were these data normally distributed.

Outliers in the model fitting errors are not in themselves usually of any great concern, except insofar as they inflate the estimate of the variance of the model errors, leading to (perhaps unrealistically) wide confidence intervals. Recall that the unbiased estimator of var(U_i) is

$$S^2 = \frac{1}{N-k}\sum_{i=1}^{N}\left(U_i^{\text{fit}}\right)^2 \tag{10-6}$$

whose value is relatively sensitive to a few extreme values in $U_1^{\text{fit}} \dots U_N^{\text{fit}}$ because of the squaring. Outliers are also of some concern if the number of sample observations is small enough that the validity of the normality assumption itself seems consequential.

What *does* make an outlier in the model fitting errors of great concern, in contrast, is if it corresponds to what is called an *influential* observation. An influential observation is simply an observation that *matters* because one or more of the model parameter estimates is unusually sensitive to its value. This is most easily understood in the context of the Bivariate Regression Model, where the slope estimator is

$$\hat{\beta} = \sum_{i=1}^{N} w_i^{\text{ols}} Y_i \tag{10-7}$$

with least squares weights given by[15]

$$w_i^{\text{ols}} = \frac{x_i - \bar{x}}{\varphi} = \frac{x_i - \bar{x}}{\sum_{\ell=1}^{N}(x_\ell - \bar{x})^2} \quad \text{for } i = 1 \dots N \tag{10-8}$$

Clearly, any value of i for which w_i^{ols} is large in magnitude is an influential observation – and corresponds to an observation for which $|x_i - \bar{x}|$ is large. Thus, what is problematic is an unusually large model error (an outlier) which happens to occur in an observation which is influential because the value of the explanatory variable for this observation is unusually large (or small) compared with the sample average of the explanatory variable values. Roughly speaking, the same argument applies for outliers in the Multiple Regression Model.[16]

This algebra underlying the OLS slope estimator in the Bivariate Regression Model explains the point about influential outlying observations in theory. In practice, however, a few plots – easily produced using typical econometric software – are what is needed.

First, as noted in previous chapters, one can easily produce histograms – plots of the relative frequency with which various size ranges appear in the sample – for both the dependent variable and

[15] The alert reader will note that ℓ is being used here and below in instances where j was used in Chapters 5 through 8. That is because, now that we have dealt with the Multiple Regression Model, j is usually going to be reserved to specify a particular explanatory variable in the model.

[16] In the Multiple Regression Model what is at issue for the influentiality of the ith model error with respect to the OLS estimate of the jth coefficient (β_j) is the magnitude of OLS weight on Y_i: w_{ji}^{ols}, defined in Section 9.5. These weights are given there explicitly for the special case of two explanatory variables. With more than two explanatory variables, however, an analysis of influentiality requires matrix algebra because the expressions for the OLS weights otherwise become impracticably unwieldly. In particular, in that case the OLS weight on Y_i – i.e., w_{ji}^{ols} – is most gracefully defined as the (i, j)th element of the $k \times N$ matrix $(X^tX)^{-1}X^t$, with X as usually defined. The influentiality of the ith model error on the OLS estimate of the jth coefficient (β_j) is then quantified by the magnitude of w_{ji}^{ols} relative to the sizes of the other elements in the jth row of this matrix.

the model fitting errors.[17] Outlying observations are easily noted in such plots, and specifically identified by explicitly listing, say, all of the sample observations for which the magnitude of the fitting error exceeds four times the realized value of S.[18]

For example, consider again the U.S. Census Bureau data (for each state, in 1980) on the number of deaths which took place ($death_i$), the number of marriages performed ($marriage_i$), and the population of age at least 18 years old ($pop18p_i$). These data were analyzed in Section 9.8 to illustrate the disastrous consequences of omitting an explanatory variable ($pop18p_i$, in that case) from a regression model (for $death_i$) when the sample variation in this omitted variable is very similar to that of an included variable – $marriage_i$, in that case. Here, instead suppose that one were using this particular Census Bureau data set to construct a regression model explaining the sample variation in the *per capita* marriage rate,

$$marriage\_rate_i = \frac{marriage_i}{pop18p_i} \tag{10-9}$$

Once the data on $marriage_i$ and $pop18p_i$ are entered into an econometric package, it is easy enough to compute $marriage\_rate_i$ and to display a histogram (Figure 10-1) of its values for the 50 states:[19]

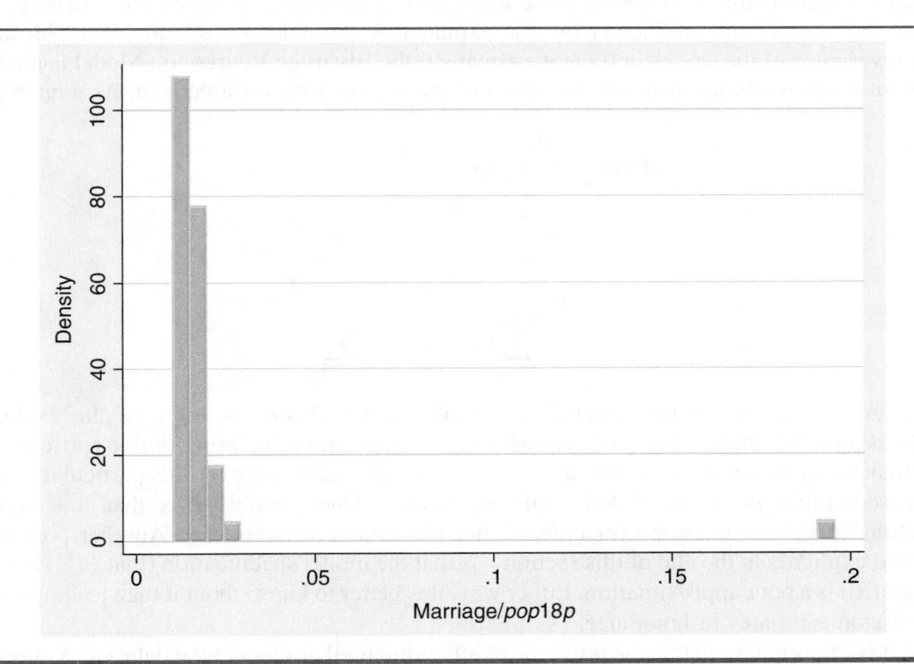

Figure 10-1 Histogram of Per Capita State-Level Marriage Rates

[17] In Stata, for example, if the dependent variable is called *y* and the fitting errors have been saved using the "predict resids, *r*" command, then one could use the commands "histogram *y*, normal" and "histogram resids, normal". The option "normal" causes Stata to additionally plot the frequency distribution of the corresponding normal variate with population mean and variance equal to the sample mean and variance of the specified variable, facilitating comparison.

[18] For example, if the fitting errors are called "*resids*" and *s* equals 1.5, one could use the Stata "list" command with a logical clause: "list y resids if abs(resids) > 6".

[19] The required Stata commands, for example, are "gen marriage_rate = marriage/pop18p" and "histogram marriage_rate, bin(40)". The option "bin(40)" forces Stata to break the range of *marriage_rate* into 40 equal intervals.

As is commonly the case, sophisticated statistical analysis of the data is actually not necessary: one glance at this histogram is sufficient to make it obvious that the 1980 value of $marriage\_rate_i$ for one state – Nevada, in this case – is substantially different from all the rest. As is also often the case, the cause of the outlier is plain once one has taken the trouble to observe its existence: in this case, the cause is that bridal chapels are a uniquely substantial business in Nevada.

If $marriage\_rate_i$ is the dependent variable in a regression model, then, one would certainly want to allow for the fact that this one state is so different from the others. One way to do this would be to simply omit this observation from the data set used. Another, usually preferable, approach is to include a dummy variable for this observation as an additional explanatory variable in the model; this allows the model intercept to be different for the particular observation for which the dummy variable equals one.[20] The dummy variable approach is preferable because it both exhibits the fact that this observation was treated as distinct and also – through the estimated coefficient on the dummy variable – quantifies the degree to which this observation is, in fact, different.[21]

In contrast, if $marriage\_rate_i$ is an explanatory variable in a regression model, then the issues with regard to the outlying (Nevada) observation are notably different. Per the previous discussion, an observation for which one of the explanatory variable takes on an unusually large – or small – value, as a deviation from its sample mean, is an *influential* observation. But this is potentially a *good* thing: after all, it is precisely this kind of sample variation in the explanatory variables which helps us obtain a precise estimate of the coefficient on this explanatory variable. Recall, for example, that the sampling variance of the slope coefficient estimate in the Bivariate Regression Model is an inverse function of the magnitudes of these deviations of the explanatory variable from its sample mean:

$$
\begin{aligned}
\text{var}(\hat{\beta}) &= \sigma^2 \sum_{\ell=1}^{N} \left(w_\ell^{\text{ols}}\right)^2 \\
&= \sigma^2 \frac{1}{\varphi} \\
&= \sigma^2 \frac{1}{\sum_{i=1}^{N}(x_i - \bar{x})^2} = \frac{\sigma^2}{\sum_{i=1}^{N}(x_i - \bar{x})^2}
\end{aligned}
\tag{10-10}
$$

Thus, an observation on the dependent variable for which one or more of the explanatory variables is an influential outlier – i.e., for which $|x_i - \bar{x}|$ is unusually large for this particular value of i – can actually be good and useful, unless $|x_i - \bar{x}|$ is unusually large for this particular value of i because something is wrong. What could be wrong? One possibility is that this particular observation on x_i was measured (or entered into the data set) incorrectly. Another possibility – considered explicitly at the end of this section – is that the model specification (that $E(Y_i)$ is a *linear* function of x_i) is a poor approximation. Either way, it is better to know about it than to simply accept the regression estimates in ignorance.

Thus, it is important to detect the presence of any influential outliers in the data set. A simple and fairly effective way to do this in practice is to make a scatterplot of the dependent variable

[20] Thus, an outlier in the dependent variable could be viewed as the consequence of wrongly omitting this particular explanatory variable.

[21] Supposing that Nevada is observation number 7, say, in the data set, then the Stata command for estimating a model relating marriage_rate$_i$ to a variable z$_i$ would be "regress marriage_rate z". The analogous command, omitting Nevada, would be "regress marriage_rate z if _n != 7". The Stata command for creating the requisite dummy variable would be "gen nevada_dummy = (_n == 7)", so that the command for estimating the model in which the intercept shifts for Nevada would be "regress marriage_rate z nevada_dummy". (The operator "==" corresponds to equality and the operator "!=" corresponds to non-equality in Stata logical clauses.)

observations versus each of the explanatory variables and look for outliers (observed values which are well away from the "cloud" of plotted points) that are likely to be influential. In other words, in the context of the *j*th explanatory variable in the Multiple Regression Model, one should look for points in the scatterplot of y_i versus x_{ji} for which the magnitude of the deviation of this explanatory variable from its sample mean $\left(|x_{j,i} - \bar{x}_j|\right)$ is large.[22]

Consider, for example, the scatterplot displayed in Figure 10-2, made using artificially generated data. Fifty of the observations were generated from the Bivariate Regression model, $Y_i = 1.0 + .3x_i + U_i$; in addition, three outliers (labeled A, B, and C) are included in the data set:

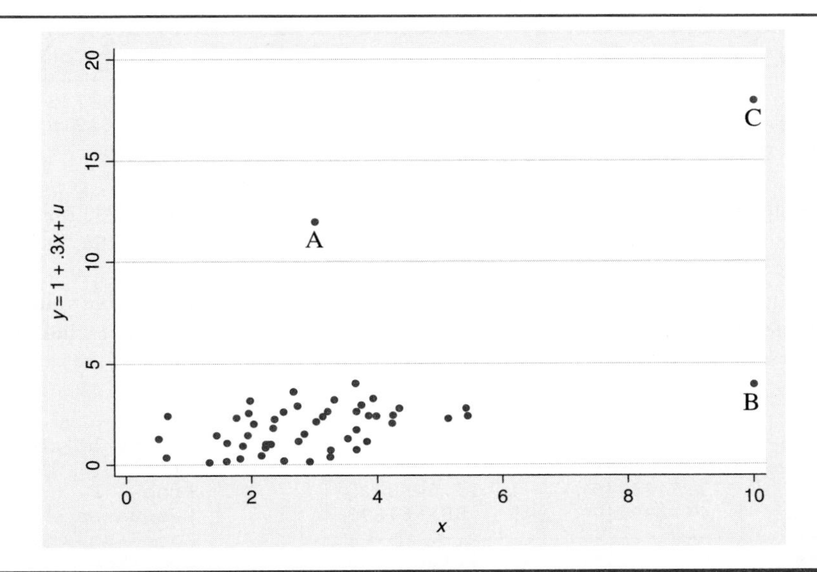

Figure 10-2 Scatterplot Illustrating Influential (and Non-Influential) Outliers

Not including any of points A, B, and C in the sample, OLS regression output for this model is:

```
      Source |       SS       df       MS              Number of obs =      50
-------------+------------------------------           F(  1,    48) =    9.97
       Model |  8.9709521      1   8.9709521           Prob > F      =  0.0027
    Residual |  43.1791434    48  .899565488           R-squared     =  0.1720
-------------+------------------------------           Adj R-squared =  0.1548
       Total |  52.1500955    49  1.06428766           Root MSE      =  .94845

------------------------------------------------------------------------------
           y |      Coef.   Std. Err.      t    P>|t|     [95% Conf. Interval]
-------------+----------------------------------------------------------------
           x |   .3701387   .1172092     3.16   0.003     .1344738    .6058035
       _cons |   .7652904   .3572221     2.14   0.037     .0470474    1.483533
------------------------------------------------------------------------------
```

reflecting a reasonable estimate ($.37 \pm .12$) for the slope coefficient.

[22] **Important Note:** Do *not* use such a plot to graphically assess the size or sign of the multiple regression coefficient β_j: as we saw in Chapter 9, such a scatterplot can be very misleading with regard to the value of the coefficient β_j. Fundamentally, this is because a scatterplot is inherently limited to quantifying the *bivariate* relationship between the dependent variable and this particular explanatory variable, averaging over all of the other explanatory variable values. The multiple regression coefficient β_j, in contrast, quantifies the relationship between the dependent variable and this explanatory variable while implicitly holding the values of all of the other explanatory variables constant.

If one were to neglect to notice (and therefore fail to either eliminate or "dummy out") point A – the non-influential outlier – this regression output would become:

```
      Source |       SS       df       MS              Number of obs =      51
-------------+------------------------------           F(  1,    49) =    3.52
       Model |  10.3091819     1  10.3091819           Prob > F      =  0.0667
    Residual |  143.624431    49  2.93111084           R-squared     =  0.0670
-------------+------------------------------           Adj R-squared =  0.0479
       Total |  153.933613    50  3.07867226           Root MSE      =   1.712

------------------------------------------------------------------------------
           y |      Coef.   Std. Err.      t    P>|t|     [95% Conf. Interval]
-------------+----------------------------------------------------------------
           x |   .3966956   .2115249     1.88   0.067    -.0283795    .8217708
       _cons |   .8886986   .6444746     1.38   0.174    -.4064215    2.183819
------------------------------------------------------------------------------
```

Note that the slope estimate is still reasonable in size, but is now (at $.40 \pm .21$) quite imprecisely estimated. This is because the outlier is inflating s^2, the realized value of the estimator of the variance of the model errors.[23]

The observation labeled "B" is both influential (because the explanatory variable value is well away from its sample mean) and "in line" with the actual relationship. Thus, including this (very informative) observation in the data set, leads to a much more precise estimate of the slope coefficient:

```
      Source |       SS       df       MS              Number of obs =      51
-------------+------------------------------           F(  1,    49) =   15.33
       Model |  13.5488745     1  13.5488745           Prob > F      =  0.0003
    Residual |   43.299717    49  .883667693           R-squared     =  0.2383
-------------+------------------------------           Adj R-squared =  0.2228
       Total |  56.8485915    50  1.13697183           Root MSE      =  .94004

------------------------------------------------------------------------------
           y |      Coef.   Std. Err.      t    P>|t|     [95% Conf. Interval]
-------------+----------------------------------------------------------------
           x |   .3418271    .087297     3.92   0.000     .1663972    .5172569
       _cons |   .8400956    .290416     2.89   0.006     .2564828    1.423708
------------------------------------------------------------------------------
```

In contrast, including – i.e., failing to notice and eliminate – point C, the influential (but "wrong") outlier, yields regression results which are quite misleading:

```
      Source |       SS       df       MS              Number of obs =      51
-------------+------------------------------           F(  1,    49) =   55.76
       Model |  164.523504     1  164.523504           Prob > F      =  0.0000
    Residual |  144.576816    49  2.95054727           R-squared     =  0.5323
-------------+------------------------------           Adj R-squared =  0.5227
       Total |  309.100321    50  6.18200641           Root MSE      =  1.7177

------------------------------------------------------------------------------
           y |      Coef.   Std. Err.      t    P>|t|     [95% Conf. Interval]
-------------+----------------------------------------------------------------
           x |   1.191156   .1595167     7.47   0.000     .8705957    1.511717
       _cons |  -1.404009   .5306734    -2.65   0.011    -2.470437   -.3375808
------------------------------------------------------------------------------
```

[23] Stata reports the square root of s^2 as "Root MSE"; so s^2 has essentially tripled from $(.94845)^2 = .900$ to $(1.712)^2 = 2.93$.

Thus, observing any of these three outliers in the scatterplot, one would be well advised to look into why it is appearing in the data set. If, upon examination, there is a sensible reason for treating this observation as special and different, then including in the regression a dummy variable which allows the intercept to differ for this observation is appropriate. If not, then the best that one can honestly do is to, one way or another, let one's readers know about this sensitivity in one's results to this single observation.

Two last points should be made concerning the data set including point C. First, note that much of the reason that the OLS parameter estimates for this data set are unduly influenced by this single observation is that least squares estimation is relatively sensitive to outliers. It is very easy nowadays to also estimate the model using the LAD (or "robust regression") method discussed in Section 5.5, wherein the parameter estimates are chosen to minimize the sum of the absolute values of the fitting errors rather than the sum of their squared values. If the LAD parameter estimates differ substantially from the OLS estimates, this one might well suspect that there is a problem with outliers and look into that. Using Stata, the command to estimate this model using robust regression is simply "qreg *y x*, quantile(.50)" and (including all three outliers) yields the output:

```
------------------------------------------------------------------------------
           y |      Coef.   Std. Err.      t    P>|t|     [95% Conf. Interval]
-------------+----------------------------------------------------------------
           x |   .3841711   .1262031     3.04   0.004     .1308078    .6375344
       _cons |   .7395647   .4525136     1.63   0.108    -.1688942    1.648024
------------------------------------------------------------------------------
```

Note that the slope estimate is very similar to that obtained using OLS on the data set excluding the outliers.[24]

Second, the model which generated the data is known in this example, but that would obviously not be the case in practice. Suppose instead that the generating model was not known. Point C could in that case be extremely valuable sample evidence that the posited linear relationship between $E[Y_i]$ and x_i is a good approximation only over the limited range $0 \leq x_i \leq 6$ and that the relationship is substantially nonlinear for larger values of x_i. The data set including point C would allow one to estimate a Multiple Regression Model including a term in $(x_i)^2$ – and to test whether or not the coefficient on this term is significantly different from zero – but one would want to keep in mind that the coefficient estimate on $(x_i)^2$ is basically resting on this single observation.

Finally, how useful are such scatterplots with actual data? On this point, consider again the U.S. Census Bureau data (for each state, in 1980) on the number of deaths which took place ($death_i$), the number of marriages performed ($marriage_i$), and the population of age at least 18 years old ($pop18p_i$). As noted earlier in this section, these data were analyzed in Chapter 9 – dropping the Nevada observation – to illustrate the disastrous consequences of omitting an explanatory variable ($pop18p_i$, in that case) from a regression model (for $death_i$) when the sample variation in this omitted variable is very similar to that of the included variable, $marriage_i$. Here, let us revisit that model, no longer assuming that it is obvious that the Nevada observation is so different as to require special

[24] A major disadvantage of robust regression, however, is that the estimated standard errors are valid only for large samples, so it would not be a good idea to take the estimated standard error of the coefficient on the variable x in this model very seriously with only 53 observations. Standard error estimates for the parameter estimates in this model can be easily obtained using 1,000 bootstrap simulations via the Stata command "bsqreg *y x*, quantile(.50) reps(1000)", but it should be noted that the bootstrap itself is only justified for large samples, so 53 observations still seems a bit skimpy. Bootstrap simulation methods are covered in Section 11.8.

treatment. In that case, the relevant scatterplot is Figure 10-3, which plots the number of deaths recorded in state i ($death_i$) versus the number of marriages recorded in state i ($marriage_i$):

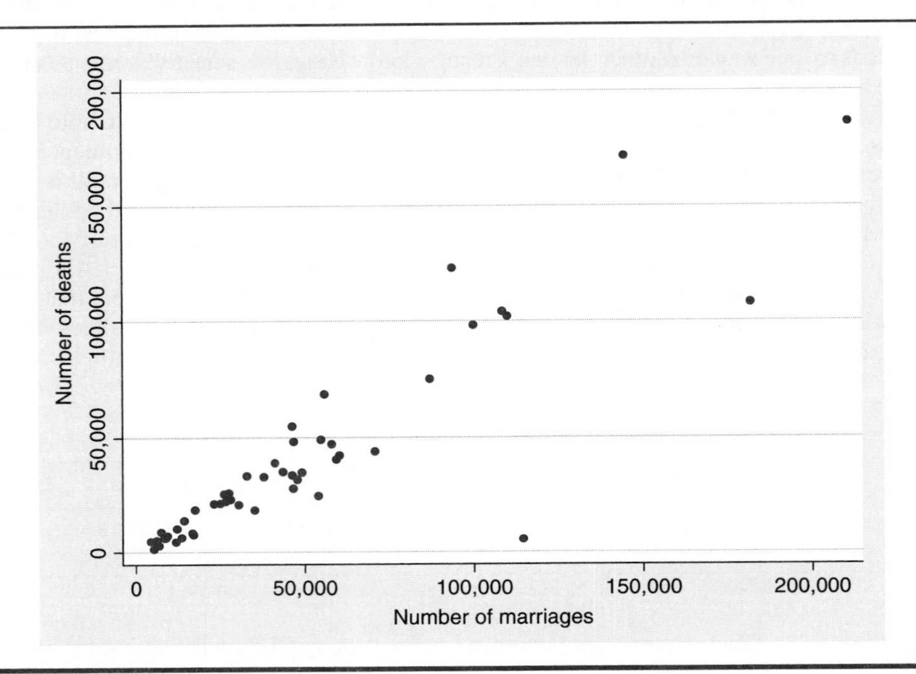

Figure 10-3 Scatterplot of Deaths versus Marriages (State-Level, 1980) Including Nevada.

Clearly, there is an outlier in this data set which, upon examination, is for Nevada – the number of deaths recorded for this state is obviously lower than one might expect, given the number of marriages recorded. Reference to the histogram of the *marriage_rate* variable displayed earlier in this section (and to the analogous histogram of deaths-per-capita, not displayed) makes it plain that the problem here is one of an outlier in the $marriage_i$ variable, and a moment's thought makes it obvious that this is due to the bridal chapel industry in Nevada.

Is this outlier in the explanatory variable ($marriage_i$) also influential? The sample average of $marriage_i$ in 1980 was 47,000, so the observation on Nevada (of 114,333) does appear to be notably above the sample mean, indicating that this outlier is in fact fairly influential. Using Stata to re-estimate a model for the variable "death," respecified to include a dummy variable allowing the intercept to differ for the Nevada observation, yields the output:

```
      Source |       SS       df       MS              Number of obs =      50
-------------+------------------------------           F(  2,    47) =  198.45
       Model |  7.6339e+10     2  3.8169e+10           Prob > F      =  0.0000
    Residual |  9.0398e+09    47   192335400           R-squared     =  0.8941
-------------+------------------------------           Adj R-squared =  0.8896
       Total |  8.5379e+10    49  1.7424e+09           Root MSE      =   13869

------------------------------------------------------------------------------
       death |      Coef.   Std. Err.      t    P>|t|     [95% Conf. Interval]
-------------+----------------------------------------------------------------
    marriage |   .8883568   .0449314    19.77   0.000     .7979665    .9787472
nevada_dummy |  -94709.08   14338.53    -6.61   0.000    -123554.5   -65863.68
       _cons |  -1007.422    2874.15    -0.35   0.728    -6789.466    4774.622
------------------------------------------------------------------------------
```

whereas the analogous output for the model ignoring the oddness of the Nevada observation is:

```
      Source |       SS       df       MS              Number of obs =      50
-------------+------------------------------           F(  1,     48) =  187.11
       Model |  6.7948e+10     1  6.7948e+10           Prob > F      =  0.0000
    Residual |  1.7431e+10    48   363148832           R-squared     =  0.7958
-------------+------------------------------           Adj R-squared =  0.7916
       Total |  8.5379e+10    49  1.7424e+09           Root MSE      =   19056

------------------------------------------------------------------------------
       death |      Coef.   Std. Err.      t    P>|t|     [95% Conf. Interval]
-------------+----------------------------------------------------------------
    marriage |   .8251248   .0603219    13.68   0.000     .7038395    .9464101
       _cons |   114.6514   3942.414     0.03   0.977    -7812.103    8041.406
------------------------------------------------------------------------------
```

Thus, the Nevada outlier in essence "pulled" the OLS coefficient estimate down from .89 to .82. Is this difference meaningful? First, note that it was evident from the discussion of this model in Chapter 9 that the "real" impact of $marriage_i$ on $death_i$ is not captured by this model at all in the first place: the variable $marriage_i$ is in fact mostly proxying for population (e.g., $pop18p_i$) here. Second – even if we were take this coefficient seriously – note that the amount of "scatter" in the plot is much larger for the observations with larger values of $marriage_i$: evidently, the homoscedasticity assumption is severely violated in both of these model specifications. Consequently – as shown in the next section – the reported standard error estimates for the estimated coefficients on $marriage_i$ in these two models (computed using formulas based on the validity of the homoscedasticity assumption) are invalid, and probably to a substantial degree. Thus, it is not clear whether the difference between these two estimates (of the coefficient on $marriage_i$) is statistically significant or not.

The issues involved in recognizing and dealing with a failure of the homoscedasticity assumption are taken up in the remainder of this chapter.

10.4 HETEROSCEDASTICITY AND ITS CONSEQUENCES

The homoscedasticity assumption is the assumption that the variance of the model error term is a constant across the sample: i.e., that $\text{var}(U_i) = \sigma^2$. The violation of this assumption – called *heteroscedasticity* – thus amounts to assuming that the variance of the model error term varies across the sample: i.e., that $\text{var}(U_i) = \sigma_i^2$, where at least one of $\sigma_1^2 \cdots \sigma_N^2$ differs from the rest. Because practically everything about the homoscedasticity assumption (and its violation) is the same in both the Bivariate Regression Model and the Multiple Regression Model, the discussion here will be couched in terms of the (simpler) Bivariate Regression Model.

The homoscedasticity assumption actually played no role in showing that the OLS slope estimator ($\hat{\beta}$) in the Bivariate Regression Model is unbiased and consistent. But it was crucial to the calculation of the sampling variance of $\hat{\beta}$ and hence to the demonstration that $\hat{\beta}$ is BLU and to the derivation of all of the machinery for using $\hat{\beta}$ for statistical inference – i.e., to the construction of hypothesis tests and confidence intervals for β. Thus, the analysis of heteroscedasticity begins by revising the (Chapter 6) derivation of $\text{var}(\hat{\beta})$ – the sampling variance of the slope estimator in the Bivariate Regression Model – replacing the homoscedasticity assumption by an alternative assumption of heteroscedasticity: $\text{var}(U_i) = \sigma_i^2$.

The derivation of $\text{var}(\hat{\beta})$ starts out in the same way as in Chapter 6, where it was assumed the model errors are homoscedastic. Substituting the results that $E[\hat{\beta}] = \beta$ and that $\hat{\beta} - \beta = \sum_{i=1}^{N} w_i^{\text{ols}} U_i$ into the definition of the population variance of $\hat{\beta}$ yields

$$
\begin{aligned}
\operatorname{var}(\hat{\beta}) &= E\left[\left[\hat{\beta} - E[\hat{\beta}]\right]^2\right] \\
&= E\left[\left[\hat{\beta} - \beta\right]^2\right] \\
&= E\left[\left[\sum_{i=1}^{N} w_i^{\text{ols}} U_i\right]^2\right] \\
&= E\left[\sum_{\ell=1}^{N} w_\ell^{\text{ols}} U_\ell \sum_{i=1}^{N} w_i^{\text{ols}} U_i\right] \\
&= E\left[H \sum_{i=1}^{N} w_i^{\text{ols}} U_i\right]
\end{aligned}
\tag{10-11}
$$

where H stands for the random variable $\sum_{\ell=1}^{N} w_\ell^{\text{ols}} U_\ell$. Bringing the factor of H inside the sum over the running index i,

$$
\begin{aligned}
\operatorname{var}(\hat{\beta}) &= E\left[\sum_{i=1}^{N} H w_i^{\text{ols}} U_i\right] \\
&= E\left[\sum_{i=1}^{N} w_i^{\text{ols}} (U_i H)\right] \\
&= \sum_{i=1}^{N} w_i^{\text{ols}} E[U_i H]
\end{aligned}
\tag{10-12}
$$

where the last step uses the Linearity Property of Chapter 2. Evaluating this expectation,

$$
\begin{aligned}
E[U_i H] &= E\left[U_i \sum_{\ell=1}^{N} w_\ell^{\text{ols}} U_\ell\right] \\
&= E\left[\sum_{\ell=1}^{N} w_\ell^{\text{ols}} U_i U_\ell\right] \\
&= \sum_{\ell=1}^{N} w_\ell^{\text{ols}} E[U_i U_\ell] \\
&= w_i^{\text{ols}} E\left[U_i^2\right] \\
&= w_i^{\text{ols}} \sigma_i^2
\end{aligned}
\tag{10-13}
$$

where the third-to-last step again uses the Linearity Property and the second-to-last step follows because $E[U_i U_\ell]$ is zero when i is unequal to ℓ, due to the nonautocorrelation assumption. The final step in the sequence of equations above is where the failure of the homoscedasticity assumption plays its role: now $E[U_i^2]$ equals σ_i^2 (rather than the constant, σ^2) when i is equal to ℓ, due to the heteroscedasticity.

Substituting this expression for $E[U_i H]$ into the expression for $\text{var}(\hat{\beta})$,

$$\begin{aligned}\text{var}(\hat{\beta}) &= \sum_{i=1}^{N} w_i^{\text{ols}} E[U_i H] \\ &= \sum_{i=1}^{N} w_i^{\text{ols}} \left(w_i^{\text{ols}} \sigma_i^2\right) = \sum_{i=1}^{N} \sigma_i^2 \left(w_i^{\text{ols}}\right)^2\end{aligned} \tag{10-14}$$

Note that since σ_i^2 now depends on the running index, it cannot come out of this sum. Thus, $\text{var}(\hat{\beta})$ is no longer proportional to

$$\sum_{i=1}^{N} \left(w_i^{\text{ols}}\right)^2 = \frac{1}{\varphi} = \frac{1}{\sum_{j=1}^{N} \left(x_j - \bar{x}\right)^2} \tag{10-15}$$

Thus, all the results which depended on this proportionality – including the derivation that $\hat{\beta}$ is the best linear unbiased (BLU) estimator of β – are no longer valid. In particular, the usual formulas implemented in econometric software for calculating estimated standard errors, estimated t ratios, estimated confidence intervals, and p-values for hypothesis tests are all based on this proportionality. Consequently, when the model errors are actually heteroscedastic, these computed results are simply wrong.

The next few sections address the issues involved in testing for (and dealing with) the presence of heteroscedasticity in the model errors.

10.5 TESTING FOR HETEROSCEDASTICITY

Because of the potentially dire consequences of heteroscedasticity – especially with respect to statistical inference – the econometrics literature has paid a good deal of attention to developing tests to detect it. This section will not review all of that literature. Instead, it will describe two straightforward ways to examine an estimated regression model for the presence of heteroscedasticity in the model errors – one graphical, and another based on what is called an "auxiliary regression." Both of these methods presume that one knows (or at least suspects) *something* about the form of the heteroscedasticity – i.e., something about how and why the value of $\text{var}(U_i)$ varies across the sample. Both methods also presume that the sample is sufficiently large that the fitting errors are a reasonable approximation to the model errors. Along the way, each of these testing methods will be illustrated using the "death versus marriage" example of the previous section.

Suppose – per that example – that the dependent variable (Y_i) is the number of deaths in state i in the year 1980 and the explanatory variable is the corresponding number of marriages. Looking again at the relevant scatterplot – repeated as Figure 10-4 – it is (perhaps) obvious that $U_1 \dots U_N$, the vertical deviations of $Y_1 \dots Y_N$ from the population regression line, are hardly likely to be random variables which all have the same variance, σ^2.

But pairwise scatterplots such as this become problematic when there is more than one explanatory variable. Instead, it is better to base a graphical approach on the fitting errors themselves, which are equally available in the Multiple Regression Model setting.

In this case one might sensibly fear that $\text{var}(U_i)$ is larger for the more populous states in the sample – i.e., for those with larger values of $pop18p_i$, the population 18 (or more) years old. Presuming that the sample is large enough that the observed fitting error realizations $\left(u_1^{\text{fit}} \dots u_N^{\text{fit}}\right)$ are good proxies for the (unobserved) model error realizations $(u_1 \dots u_N)$, one could confirm (or dispel)

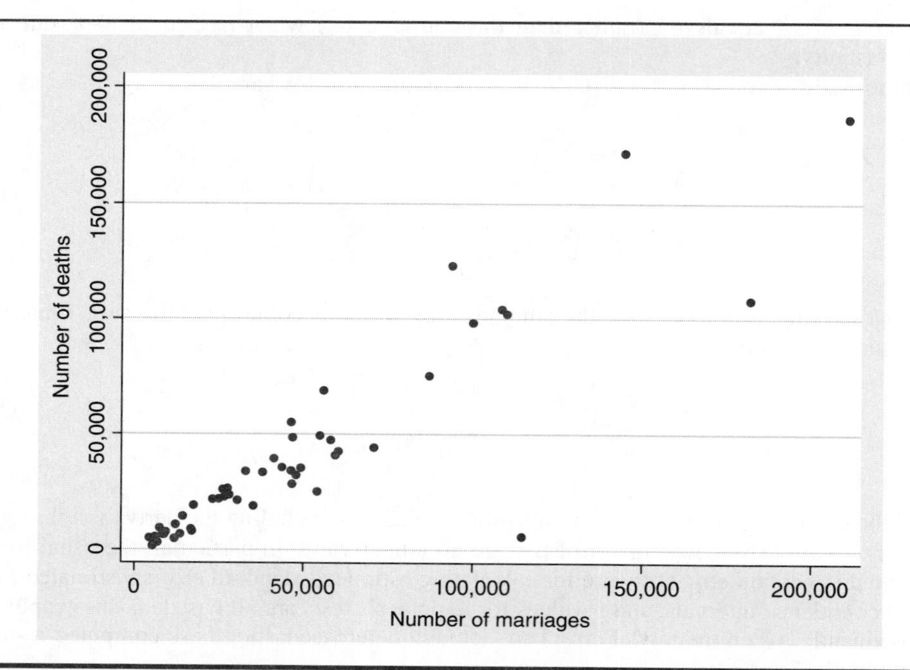

Figure 10-4 Scatterplot of Deaths versus Marriages (State-Level, 1980) Including Nevada

this fear by sorting the observations in increasing order of $pop18p_i$, graphing u_i^{fit} against observation number, and looking to see whether or not the apparent "scatter" in u_i^{fit} is larger for the larger values of $pop18p_i$. In Stata, for example, the commands to estimate the regression model, save the fitting errors as the variable named "*resids*", generate an variable ("*obsnum*") whose value is the observation number, and make the plot are:

```
regress death marriage nevada_dummy
predict resids , r
sort pop18p
generate obsnum = _n
scatter resids obsnum
```

These commands yield Figure 10-5. While 50 observations is a bit skimpy for using the observed fitting errors as proxies for model errors, note that this plot clearly confirms the suspicion that var(U_i) depends directly on $pop18p_i$.

The "auxiliary regression" approach to testing for heteroscedasticity is a bit more formal than this graphical approach, but has the advantage that it allows one to simultaneously evaluate (and compare) the sample evidence for several hypotheses as to the source of any heteroscedasticity in the model errors. It also produces a more clear-cut answer with regard to whether the homoscedasticity assumption is valid.

The auxiliary regression approach works as follows. Suppose that one suspects that, if var(U_i) is not a constant, then it is most likely a function of a known group of m observed variables, $z_{i1} \ldots z_{im}$. These might (or might not) include some of the explanatory variables in the model. In the "death versus marriage" model, for example, m might be one and one might specify z_{i1} equal to $pop18p_i$. Or in a model for the wages of the ith household, one might worry that perhaps the model fits

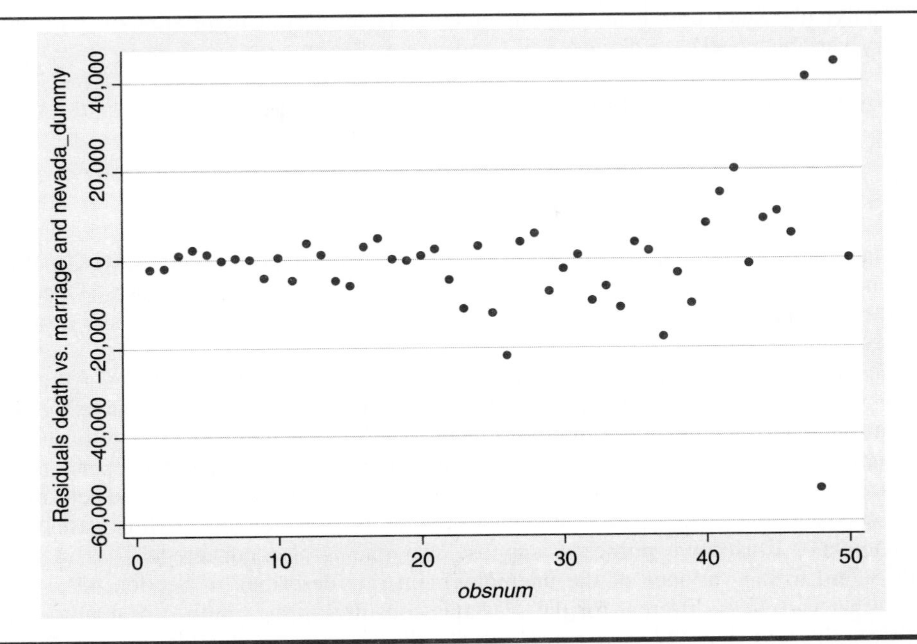

Figure 10-5 Plot of Sorted Fitting Errors

differently – has a different value for var(U_i) – for observations corresponding to a male head of household than for a female head of household and/or for observations in which the household resides in one area of the country. In that case the sensible value for m is two, z_{i1} being a gender dummy variable and z_{i2} being a dummy variable which is one for households in the possibly different region and zero otherwise.[25]

Having specified which observable variables are the likely determinants of variation in var(U_i) across the sample, one can then easily test for heteroscedasticity of this form by noting that for large samples, var(U_i) is approximately equivalent to $\text{var}\left(U_i^{\text{fit}}\right)$, which, in turn, is equal (on average) to $\left(U_i^{\text{fit}}\right)^2$. Thus, for large samples, one can model how var(U_i) varies with $z_{i1} \ldots z_{im}$ by estimating an *auxiliary regression model* with $\left(U_i^{\text{fit}}\right)^2$ as the dependent variable and $z_{i1} \ldots z_{im}$ as the explanatory variables:

$$\left(U_i^{\text{fit}}\right)^2 = \gamma_o + \gamma_1 z_{i1} + \gamma_2 z_{i2} + \ldots + \gamma_m z_{im} + V_i \tag{10-16}$$

Testing the null hypothesis of homoscedasticity then corresponds to testing the multiple null hypothesis H_o: $\gamma_1 = \gamma_2 = \ldots = \gamma_m = 0$ against the alternative hypothesis that at least one of these coefficients is unequal to zero. A nice feature of this test is that the estimates of $\gamma_1 \ldots \gamma_m$ (and their estimated standard errors) allow one to fairly easily determine which of $z_{i1} \ldots z_{im}$ are significant sources of heteroscedasticity in the errors for the original model and which are not.[26]

[25] Note that this example subsumes the situation analyzed in Section 4.9; that situation corresponds to a regression model which has no explanatory variables, only an intercept.

[26] This test for heteroscedasticity is based on a formal test due to Breusch, T. S., and A. R. Pagan (1979) *Econometrica 47(5)*, 1287–94.

Specifically, the Stata commands to implement this test for a regression model with three explanatory variables ("$x1$", "$x2$", and "$x3$") and m equal to two are:

```
regress y x1 x2 x3
predict resids , r
generate residsqr = resids * resids
regress residsqr z1 z2
test z1 z2
```

where the last command computes the p-value for testing the null hypothesis that var(U_i) in the model for Y_i is homoscedastic, at least in that it does not vary appreciably with either z_{i1} or z_{i2}. Of course, this functionality is not unique to Stata; one could easily implement this procedure in any econometric software package.

Applying this heteroscedasticity test to the "death versus marriage" example of the previous section, one would first estimate the model for *death*$_i$ (including the dummy variable for Nevada), save the fitting errors, and generate a new variable ("*residsqr*") which is the square of these fitting errors. Finally, one would estimate the auxiliary regression model, in which the dependent variable is the squared fitting error and the explanatory variable or variables are the proposed determinants of the heteroscedasticity, $z_{i1} \ldots z_{im}$. As noted earlier, an obvious choice in this case would be $z_{i1} = pop18p_i$. For illustrative purposes, suppose that one is also concerned – as in the crude test with regard to the variance of the unemployment rate described in Section 4.9; – with the possibility that var(U_i) is different for the 11 states constituting the South – Alabama, Arkansas, Florida, Georgia, Louisiana, Mississippi, North Carolina, South Carolina, Tennessee, Texas, and Virginia – and that "south_dummy$_i$" has been generated as a dummy variable which is one for each of these states and zero otherwise. Then the Stata output for the auxiliary regression is:

```
      Source |       SS       df       MS              Number of obs =      50
-------------+------------------------------           F(  2,     47) =   10.64
       Model |  4.1405e+18     2  2.0702e+18           Prob > F      =  0.0002
    Residual |  9.1478e+18    47  1.9463e+17           R-squared     =  0.3116
-------------+------------------------------           Adj R-squared =  0.2823
       Total |  1.3288e+19    49  2.7119e+17           Root MSE      = 4.4e+08

------------------------------------------------------------------------------
resid_squared|      Coef.   Std. Err.      t    P>|t|     [95% Conf. Interval]
-------------+----------------------------------------------------------------
      pop18p |   80.54254   18.48929     4.36   0.000      43.34688    117.7382
 south_dummy |   1.54e+08   1.52e+08     1.02   0.315     -1.51e+08    4.59e+08
       _cons |  -1.15e+08   9.03e+07    -1.27   0.211     -2.96e+08    6.72e+07
------------------------------------------------------------------------------
```

Note that the null hypothesis that the coefficient in the auxiliary regression on $pop18p_i$ is zero can be rejected with p-value no larger than .0005 and that the analogous null hypothesis with respect to the coefficient on *south_dummy*$_i$ can only be rejected with a p-value substantially larger than .05. Thus, one can conclude that var(U_i) does depend (directly) on the population of state i, but that it is not different for the states of the South.[27]

[27] In general one should base one's decision as to whether or not heteroscedasticity is present on the test of the joint hypothesis that the coefficients on both explanatory variables are zero. In this way, as noted in the "Overelaborate Multiple Regression Models" section of Chapter 9, the test p-value accounts for the fact that two possible sources of heteroscedasticity were tested. The p-value for the test of this joint hypothesis is still less than .0005 for this particular regression model. Also, note that the coefficient estimate on "south_dummy$_i$" is rather large in magnitude. This is because the squaring operation exaggerates the size (large or small) of the fitting errors and can be avoided by taking the trouble to use $\left(U_i^{\text{fit}}\right)^2/s$ as the dependent variable instead of $\left(U_i^{\text{fit}}\right)^2$. This scaling is worth doing if the coefficient estimates are very small – less than .0001, say – so as to eliminate potential numerical problems from round-off errors.

10.6 CORRECTING FOR HETEROSCEDASTICITY OF KNOWN FORM

In view of the potentially severe consequences of heteroscedasticity with respect to statistical inference, what can be done about it? If one knows something about the form of the heteroscedasticity – i.e., about the manner in which var(U_i) varies across the sample – then the model can generally be respecified so as to (approximately) eliminate the problem. Estimation of this respecified model then yields statistical inferences which are (approximately) valid. It also yields parameter estimates which are (approximately) BLU.[28]

It is instructive to first examine the case where the form of the heteroscedasticity is completely and exactly known. Thus, consider the usual Multiple Regression Model, but where the assumption of homoscedasticity – that the variances of U_i is the constant, σ^2 – has been replaced by the assumption that U_i is *heteroscedastic*, where $\text{var}(U_i) = \sigma^2\omega_i^2$, with the values of $\omega_1^2 \ldots \omega_N^2$ known. (It will shortly become clear why these N constants are specified in "squared" form.) The regression model is now

$$
\begin{gathered}
Y_i = \beta_1 x_{i,1} + \beta_2 x_{i,2} + \beta_3 x_{i,3} + \ldots + \beta_k x_{i,k} + U_i \quad i = 1 \ldots N \\
x_{i,1} = 1 \text{ for } i = 1 \ldots N \\
x_{i,j} \text{ fixed in repeated samples for } i = 1 \ldots N \text{ and for } j = 2 \ldots k \\
U_i \sim \text{NIID}[0, \sigma^2\omega_i^2]
\end{gathered}
\tag{10-17}
$$

Next, divide this regression equation through on both sides by the constant ω_i, yielding

$$
\begin{gathered}
\frac{Y_i}{\omega_i} = \beta_1 \frac{x_{i,1}}{\omega_i} + \beta_2 \frac{x_{i,2}}{\omega_i} + \beta_3 \frac{x_{i,3}}{\omega_i} + \ldots + \beta_k \frac{x_{i,k}}{\omega_i} + V_i \quad i = 1 \ldots N \\
x_{i,1} = 1 \text{ for } i = 1 \ldots N \\
\frac{x_{i,j}}{\omega_i} \text{ fixed in repeated samples for } i = 1 \ldots N \text{ and for } j = 2 \ldots k \\
V_i \sim \text{NIID}[0, \sigma^2]
\end{gathered}
\tag{10-18}
$$

where V_i is just U_i/ω_i, and hence (by construction) has constant variance $\text{var}(V_i) = \sigma^2$. This modified regression model has the same unknown parameters ($\beta_1 \ldots \beta_k$ and σ^2) as the original model, but now – using Y_i/ω_i as the dependent and $x_{i,1}/\omega_i \ldots x_{i,k}/\omega_i$ as the explanatory variables – it satisfies all of the assumptions of the Multiple Regression Model. Thus, if the weights $\omega_1^2 \ldots \omega_N^2$ were known, it very easy to obtain BLU estimates of (and valid inferences regarding) the model parameters $\beta_1 \ldots \beta_k$.

Of course, in practice, the weights $\omega_1^2 \ldots \omega_N^2$ are not known. But they can themselves be estimated if one knows something about the form of the heteroscedasticity. Suppose, for example, that one is estimating a model for household wages and fears that var(U_i) is higher for households with a male head of household than for households with a female head of household. One could in that case estimate the model for household wages separately for the two kinds of households and estimate the weight ω_i^2 as equal to 1.0 for the observations with a male head of household and as equal to $(s^2)_{female}/(s^2)_{male}$ for the observations with a female head of household, where $(s^2)_{female}$ is the observed value of S^2 for the regression using only the female head of household data, and

[28] Where the form of the heteroscedasticity is not known at all but the sample is large, it is still possible to obtain consistent estimates of the standard errors of the coefficient estimates, yielding valid statistical inferences. The specification of the form of model itself – and the efficiency of the coefficient estimates – is not thereby improved, however. This topic is taken up in the next section.

similarly for $(s^2)_{male}$. This procedure will work well as long as there are a sufficiently large number of observations for both kinds of households that $(s^2)_{female}/(s^2)_{male}$ is a reasonably precise estimate of the actual (population) ratio of these two variances.[29]

The "death versus marriage" example of the previous section provides another example. Here the auxiliary regression has indicated that $\text{var}(U_i)$ is apparently a direct function of the ith state's population, $pop18p_i$. One might then guess that ω_i^2 is proportional to $(pop18p_i)^2$; that is $Var(U_i) = \sigma^2 (pop18p_i)^2$. The transformed regression model which one would then estimate is

$$\frac{marriage_i}{pop18p_i} = \beta_1 + \beta_2 \frac{death_i}{pop18p_i} + \beta_3\, nevada\_dummy_i + V_i \tag{10-19}$$

Notice that the new regression model – "cured" of heteroscedasticity – here corresponds to a model respecification in which per capita variables have been substituted for the "raw" variables. In this case an informed and sensible reaction to the observed heteroscedasticity in the original model errors has led to what, in retrospect, is a clearly more reasonable model specification. One could generalize that heteroscedasticity (if one has the wit to seek it out, as a possibility) is Mother Nature's way of pointing an analyst at the need for a better model specification – one for which least squares estimation yields BLU parameter estimates and valid statistical inferences.[30]

Re-estimating the model for state-level death rates, again using the 1980 Census data, but now re-expressing both $death_i$ and $marriage_i$ in per capita form, yields the estimated model:

```
      Source |       SS       df       MS              Number of obs =      50
-------------+------------------------------           F(  2,    47) =    4.82
       Model |  .000023819     2  .000011909           Prob > F      =  0.0125
    Residual |  .000116216    47  2.4727e-06           R-squared     =  0.1701
-------------+------------------------------           Adj R-squared =  0.1348
       Total |  .000140035    49  2.8579e-06           Root MSE      =  .00157

------------------------------------------------------------------------------
  death_rate |      Coef.   Std. Err.      t    P>|t|     [95% Conf. Interval]
-------------+----------------------------------------------------------------
marriage_rate|  -.1968441   .0684956    -2.87   0.006    -.3346394   -.0590488
nevada_dummy |   .0336634   .0124633     2.70   0.010     .0085904    .0587363
       _cons |   .0148368   .0010564    14.05   0.000     .0127117    .0169619
------------------------------------------------------------------------------
```

Observe that the sign of the estimated coefficient on the state-level marriage rate is now negative – and significantly so, at the 1% level using the two-tailed hypothesis test result Stata reports. Is this result credible and meaningful?

The first thing to note is that this large shift in the coefficient estimate on the marriage-related variable is not directly due to the elimination of the heteroscedasticity. It is actually due to the fact that the coefficient estimate in the original model – even after the impact of the Nevada outlier was eliminated – was grossly distorted by the omission of an explanatory variable to control for the size of the state. Recall that what makes an omitted explanatory variable consequential is how similar its sample variation is to that of the included variables. The omitted variable in this case – something akin to $pop18p_i$ – varies across the states in much the same way as $marriage_i$, so the coefficient on $marriage_i$ was in fact mostly quantifying how $death_i$ varies with population. The new regression

[29] Procedures like this are known under the acronym "FGLS," standing for "feasible generalized least squares." These procedures are usually an improvement over simply ignoring the heteroscedasticity if (and only if) one has more than 40 to 50 observations.

[30] Equation 10-19 illustrates the fact that an adroit analyst would not mechanically put every explanatory variable in per capita form – just the ones for which it makes sense. And one could easily tell whether or not one has "underdone" it in this respect by checking the resulting model's fitting errors for heteroscedasticity – as one ought, in any case.

model – explaining sample variation in the per capita death rate in terms of the per capita marriage rate – still does not include a state-size variable (such as $pop18p_i$) as an explanatory variable. Perhaps a variable such as $pop18p_i$ *should* be included in the model, but its omission (if wrongful) is not likely to be very consequential because the sample variation in the (included) per capita marriage variable most likely is not particularly similar to that of $pop18p_i$.

Note that fixing (or greatly ameliorating) one problem – heteroscedasticity, in this case – greatly helped in this case with another – coefficient bias due to an omitted variable. That is typical. Note also that thinking about it suggested the investigation of yet another possible improvement in the model – inclusion of an explanatory variable to control for state-size. That is typical also.[31]

Are the results of this model now econometrically credible and meaningful? That is, does the model now conform reasonably well to the assumptions of the Multiple Regression Model?

Having worked on "fixing" the heteroscedasticity problem, one might well check that it is now resolved. Estimating an auxiliary regression relating the squared fitting errors from the respecified model to the $marriage\_rate_i$ explanatory variable yields:

```
      Source |       SS       df       MS              Number of obs =      50
-------------+------------------------------           F(  1,    48) =    1.42
       Model |  2.9259e-11     1  2.9259e-11           Prob > F      =  0.2389
    Residual |  9.8761e-10    48  2.0575e-11           R-squared     =  0.0288
-------------+------------------------------           Adj R-squared =  0.0085
       Total |  1.0169e-09    49  2.0752e-11           Root MSE      = 4.5e-06

------------------------------------------------------------------------------
resids_sqared|      Coef.   Std. Err.      t    P>|t|     [95% Conf. Interval]
-------------+----------------------------------------------------------------
      pop18p |  -2.25e-13   1.89e-13    -1.19   0.239    -6.05e-13    1.55e-13
       _cons |   3.06e-06   8.87e-07     3.44   0.001     1.27e-06    4.84e-06
------------------------------------------------------------------------------
```

Thus, there is no evidence that var(V_i) varies with $pop18p_i$; this auxiliary regression does not, of course, rule out other possible forms of heteroscedasticity.

A histogram of the fitting errors and a scatterplot of the fitting errors versus observation number (with the data set now sorted in order of increasing values of $marriage\_rate_i$) are plotted in Figures 10-6 and 10-7.

Both of these plots indicate that two of the fitting errors (which turn out to correspond to Alaska and Hawaii) are unusually small. Should these be considered outliers? That is debatable. But it might be fruitful to think about *why* the relationship might be different for these two states.

Next, considering the possibility of non-normal errors due to outliers, it is useful to again consider the kind of scatterplots recommended earlier for investigating that issue; here, by plotting, in Figure 10-8, the dependent variable ($death\_rate_i$) against the key explanatory variable in the model, $marriage\_rate_i$. The scatterplot in Figure 10-8 is essentially unusable, due to the (now even more marked) outlier for Nevada. Dropping this observation from the scatterplot yields Figure 10-9.

[31] And further thought about possibly important omitted explanatory variables is also likely a fruitful exercise, if one is to take this modeling exercise seriously. For example, one might wonder whether a negative coefficient on $marriage\_rate_i$ is due to this variable proxying for some feature of the age distribution in state i. Or one might well want to specify a model for the per capita death rate from fundamental considerations (based on biological or sociological theories) rather than by starting – as here – from a purely empirical approach. Certainly most economists would start from a theory-based specification for modeling the sample behavior of economic dependent variables.

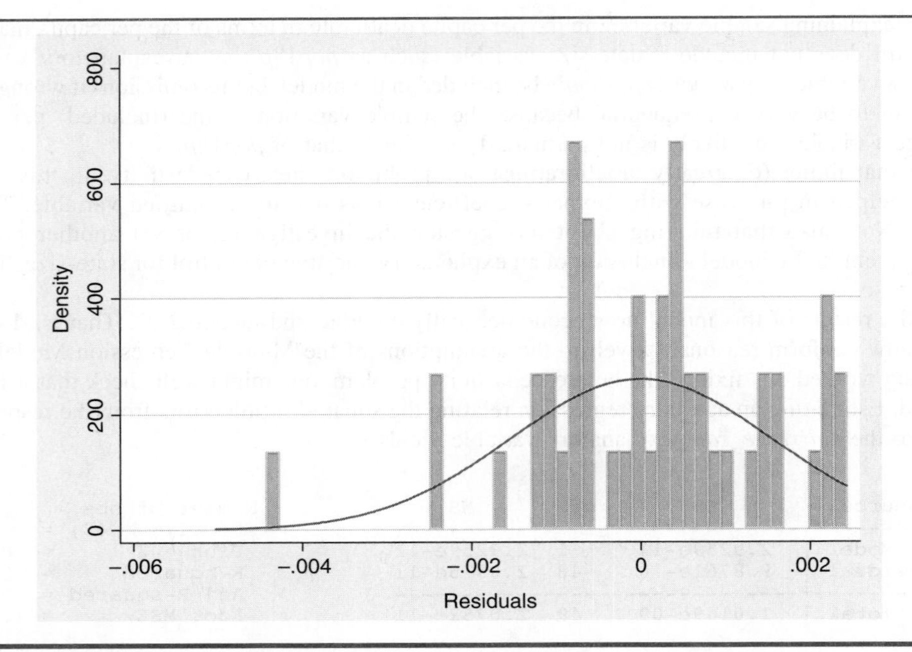

Figure 10-6 Histogram of Fitting Errors from Model for $marriage\_rate_i$

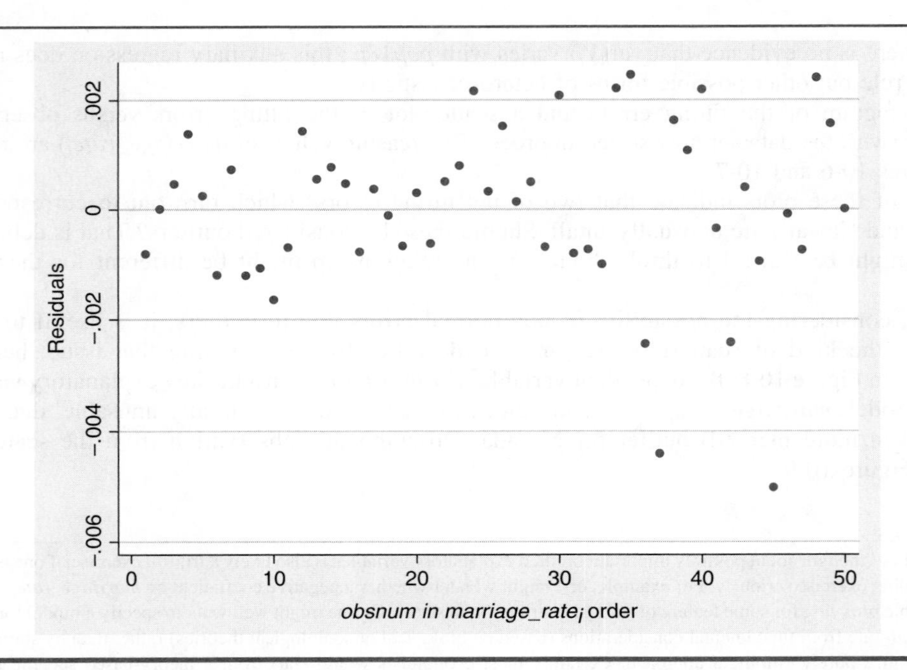

Figure 10-7 Plot of Fitting Errors from Model for $marriage\_rate_i$ versus Observation Number

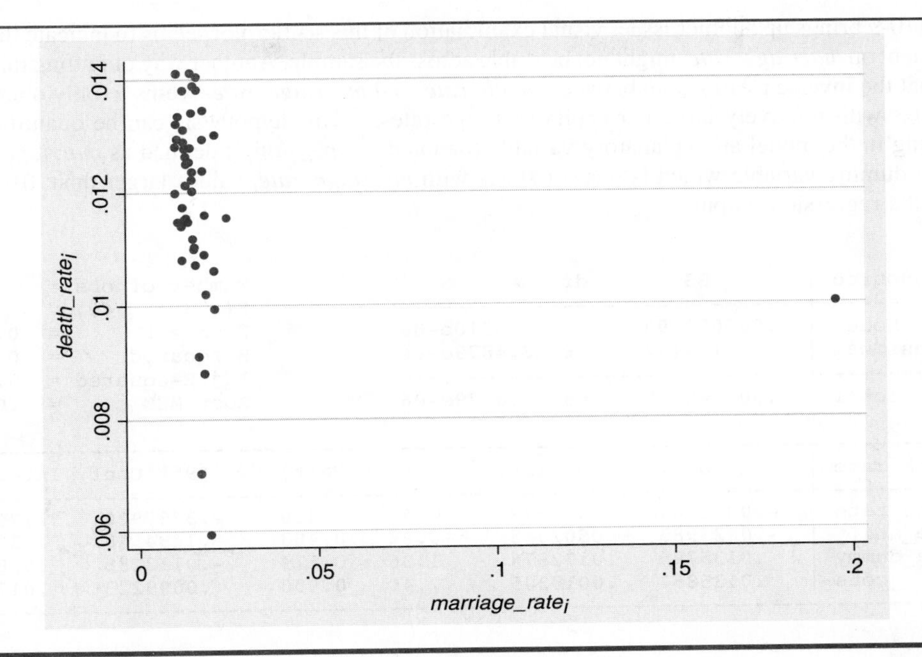

Figure 10-8 Scatterplot of $death\_rate_i$ versus $marriage\_rate_i$

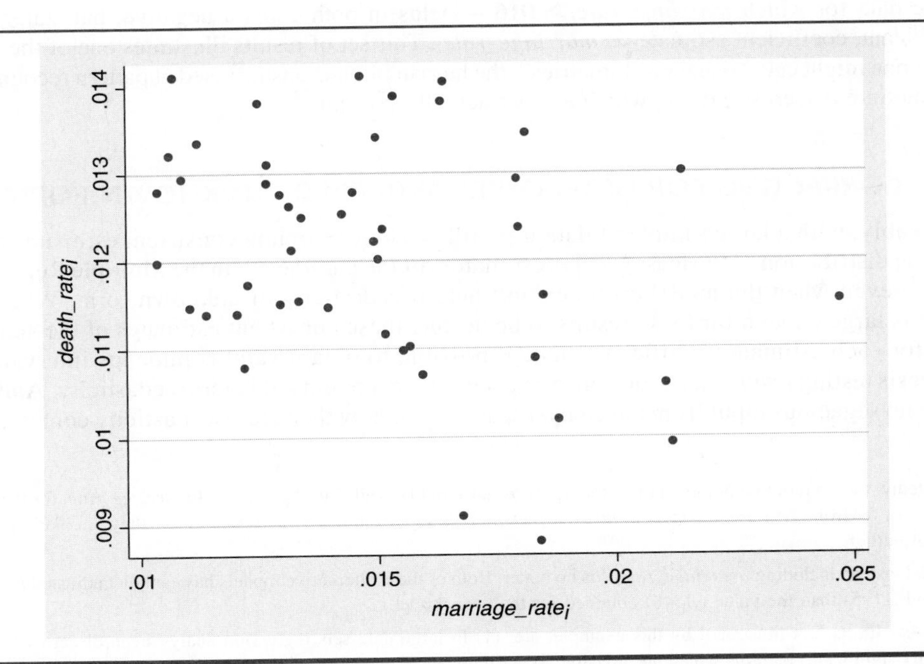

Figure 10-9 Scatterplot of $death\_rate_i$ versus $marriage\_rate_i$, Omitting Nevada

Figure 10-9 brings up another issue: visual examination of this scatterplot seems to indicate that the coefficient on $marriage\_rate_i$ might not be stable across the sample. Another way of putting this is to note that the inverse relationship between $death\_rate_i$ and $marriage\_rate_i$ seems to only obtain for the states with relatively large per capita marriage rates.[32] This hypothesis can be quantified by including in the model an explanatory variable (denoted "$slope\_shift_i$") defined as $marriage\_rate_i$ times a dummy variable which is one for states with $marriage\_rate_i$ values larger than .016; this yields the regression output:

```
      Source |       SS       df       MS              Number of obs =      50
-------------+------------------------------           F(  3,    46) =    3.43
       Model |  .000025593     3  8.5310e-06           Prob > F      =  0.0246
    Residual |  .000114442    46  2.4879e-06           R-squared     =  0.1828
-------------+------------------------------           Adj R-squared =  0.1295
       Total |  .000140035    49  2.8579e-06           Root MSE      =  .00158

------------------------------------------------------------------------------
  death_rate |      Coef.   Std. Err.      t    P>|t|     [95% Conf. Interval]
-------------+----------------------------------------------------------------
mariage_rate |  -.0964843   .1372692    -0.70   0.486    -.3727928    .1798241
 slope_shift |  -.0423983   .0502045    -0.84   0.403    -.1434548    .0586581
nevada_dummy |   .0235795   .0172876     1.36   0.179    -.0112186    .0583777
       _cons |   .0135867   .0018205     7.46   0.000     .0099223    .0172511
------------------------------------------------------------------------------
```

The estimated coefficient on "slope_shift" is negative, as expected from the scatterplot, but note that it is decidedly not statistically different from zero. Evidently, the apparent nonlinearity in the scatterplot is not supported by the data itself.[33] In fact, estimating the model separately for both portions of the data set – i.e., first using just the data for which $marriage\_rate_i < .016$ and then using just the data for which $marriage\_rate_i \geq .016$ – yields in both cases a negative, but statistically insignificant, coefficient estimate on $marriage\_rate_i$. This set of results illustrates one of the limits of what one might call "visual econometrics": the human brain is unsurpassed at pattern recognition, but sometime discerns patterns which are not actually present.[34]

10.7 CORRECTING FOR HETEROSCEDASTICITY OF UNKNOWN FORM

Remarkably, with a large sample of data it is still possible to obtain consistent estimates of the sampling distribution of the least squares estimators of the parameters in the Multiple Regression Model – even when the model errors exhibit heteroscedasticity of unknown form. Where the sample is large enough for these results to be usable, these consistent estimates of the standard errors for each estimated coefficient make it possible to obtain valid confidence intervals and hypothesis testing results in the presence of even severe amounts of heteroscedasticity. And they require no sagacious input from the analyst as to why or how the heteroscedasticity comes about.

[32] Admittedly, the bottom two points in this plot are for Alaska and Hawaii. But the values of $marriage\_rate_i$ for these two states are not far from the sample mean of $marriage\_rate_i$ (.019) so – even if they *are* "outliers" – they are likely not very influential outliers.

[33] A model instead including $(marriage\_rate_i)^2$ is no better. Both of these alternative models have smaller adjusted R^2 values (.1295 and .1195) than the value (.1348) obtained for the base model.

[34] Two other limits, not illustrated by this example, are: (1) in large data sets regression analysis can discern weak (but statistically significant) patterns which are invisible to the human eye and (2) the human brain is not equipped to consider scatterplots in more than two or three dimensions.

On the other hand, these results yield no guidance as to how one might respecify one's model so as to obtain a better model or more efficient (closer to BLU) parameter estimates: the results described below only "fix" the standard error estimates, which heteroscedasticity otherwise distorts. It is also well to emphasize at the outset that these "robust" standard error estimates – called "robust" because they are robust to the presence of heteroscedasticity – are only valid for large samples.[35]

In practice, robust standard error estimates are very easy to obtain: all econometric software packages worthy of the name will compute these standard error estimates (at the user's option) with no fuss at all. In Stata, for example, the command:

```
regress y x1 x2 x3
```

computes the parameter estimates, a standard error estimate for each parameter estimate, and so forth for a regression model with dependent variable "y" and explanatory variables "$x1$", "$x2$", and "$x3$". The command for estimating this regression model and instead computing the robust standard error estimates is simply:

```
regress y x1 x2 x3 , robust
```

The formulas which the econometric software uses for computing the robust standard errors are straightforward, also. For example, the robust standard error estimator for $\hat{\beta}$ (the OLS slope estimator in the Bivariate Regression Model), is computed as the square root of the variance estimator:

$$\left[\operatorname{var}(\hat{\beta})\right]^{\text{robust}} = \sum_{i=1}^{N} \left(w_i^{\text{ols}}\right)^2 \left(u_i^{\text{fit}}\right)^2 \tag{10-20}$$

which leads to the robust standard error estimate

$$\sqrt{\left[\operatorname{var}(\hat{\beta})\right]^{\text{robust}}} = \sqrt{\sum_{i=1}^{N} (w_i^{\text{ols}})^2 (u_i^{\text{fit}})^2} \tag{10-21}$$

where w_i^{ols} is the usual OLS weight for the ith term in the expression for $\hat{\beta}$ and u_i^{fit} is the observed fitting error for the ith observation. These standard error estimates are usually nowadays called "White-Eicker standard errors" after White (1980) and Eicker (1963), who first proposed them.

Where do Equation 10-20 – and analogous results for computing robust standard errors for coefficient estimates from the Multiple Regression Model – come from? The remainder of this section provides a simple demonstration that the expression given in Equation 10-20 is an unbiased estimator for the actual sampling variance of $\hat{\beta}$, at least to the extent that the sample is sufficiently large that the fitting errors can be substituted for the model errors. In fact, this demonstration requires only a minor amendment to the end of the derivation of the sampling variance of $\hat{\beta}$ (in the presence of heteroscedastic errors) given in equations 10-11 through 10-14.

[35] How large is large enough? Absent a simulation study for the particular data set under consideration, one can never be certain. (And the bootstrap simulation method described in Section 11.8 is, as noted there, specifically not appropriate for a model with heteroscedastic errors.) Generally speaking, experienced analysts are usually dubious about using these results with less than around 40 observations and casually confident about using them when the sample substantially exceeds 100 observations.

This amended derivation begins in precisely the same way, so equations 10-11 and 10-12 are simply repeated here:

$$\begin{aligned}
\text{var}(\hat{\beta}) &= E\left[\left[\hat{\beta} - E\left[\hat{\beta}\right]\right]^2\right] \\
&= E\left[\left[\hat{\beta} - \beta\right]^2\right] \\
&= E\left[\left[\sum_{i=1}^{N} w_i^{\text{ols}} U_i\right]^2\right] \\
&= E\left[\sum_{\ell=1}^{N} w_\ell^{\text{ols}} U_\ell \sum_{i=1}^{N} w_i^{\text{ols}} U_i\right] \\
&= E\left[H \sum_{i=1}^{N} w_i^{\text{ols}} U_i\right]
\end{aligned} \tag{10-11}$$

where H stands for the random variable $\sum_{\ell=1}^{N} w_\ell^{\text{ols}} U_j$. Bringing the factor of H inside the sum over the running index i,

$$\begin{aligned}
\text{var}(\hat{\beta}) &= E\left[\sum_{i=1}^{N} H w_i^{\text{ols}} U_i\right] \\
&= E\left[\sum_{i=1}^{N} w_i^{\text{ols}} (U_i H)\right] \\
&= \sum_{i=1}^{N} w_i^{\text{ols}} E[U_i H]
\end{aligned} \tag{10-12}$$

where the last step uses the Linearity Property of Chapter 2.

Here is where the derivation begins to differ. Evaluating the expectation in Equation 10-12,

$$\begin{aligned}
E[U_i H] &= E\left[U_i \sum_{\ell=1}^{N} w_\ell^{\text{ols}} U_\ell\right] \\
&= E\left[\sum_{\ell=1}^{N} w_\ell^{\text{ols}} U_i U_\ell\right] \\
&= \sum_{\ell=1}^{N} w_\ell^{\text{ols}} E[U_i U_\ell] \\
&= w_i^{\text{ols}} E\left[U_i^2\right] \\
&\approx w_i^{\text{ols}} E\left[\left(U_i^{\text{fit}}\right)^2\right]
\end{aligned} \tag{10-22}$$

where (as in Equation 10-13) the third-to-last step again uses the Linearity Property and the second-to-last step follows because $E[U_i U_\ell]$ is zero when i is unequal to ℓ, due to the nonautocorrelation assumption. The final step in the sequence of equations above is now different, however. Here, instead of evaluating $E[U_i^2]$ as σ_i^2, we instead recognize that – for sufficiently large samples – the fitting error U_i^{fit} is a good approximation to the model error, U_i.

Substituting this expression for $E[U_iH]$ from Equation 10-22 into the previous expression – Equation 10-12 – for $\text{var}(\hat{\beta})$ yields

$$\begin{aligned}\text{var}(\hat{\beta}) &= \sum_{i=1}^{N} w_i^{\text{ols}} E[U_iH] \\ &= \sum_{i=1}^{N} w_i^{\text{ols}} \left(w_i^{\text{ols}} E\left[\left(U_i^{\text{fit}} \right)^2 \right] \right) \\ &= \sum_{i=1}^{N} \left(w_i^{\text{ols}} \right)^2 E\left[\left(U_i^{\text{fit}} \right)^2 \right]\end{aligned} \tag{10-23}$$

Taking the expected value of both sides of Equation 10-20 yields

$$E\left[\left[\text{var}(\hat{\beta}) \right]^{\text{robust}} \right] = E\left[\sum_{i=1}^{N} \left(w_i^{\text{ols}} \right)^2 \left(U_i^{\text{fit}} \right)^2 \right] = \sum_{i=1}^{N} \left(w_i^{\text{ols}} \right)^2 E\left[\left(U_i^{\text{fit}} \right)^2 \right] \tag{10-24}$$

which has the same right-hand side as Equation 10-23. Thus,

$$E\left[\left[\text{var}(\hat{\beta}) \right]^{\text{robust}} \right] = \text{var}(\hat{\beta}) \tag{10-25}$$

and the robust estimator of $\text{var}(\hat{\beta})$ given in Equation 10-20 is an unbiased estimator when the sample size is sufficiently large that the model errors can be replaced by the fitting errors.

This unbiasedness result is nice, but what's really wanted is a proof that the robust standard error estimate – the square root of Equation 10-20 – provides an at least consistent estimator of the actual standard errors of $\hat{\beta}$ – i.e. of $\sqrt{\text{var}(\hat{\beta})}$. This is not difficult to do, but requires the sharper statistical tools covered in Chapter 11.[36]

For samples sufficiently large that their use is justified, the robust standard error estimates discussed in this section completely resolve the problems with hypothesis testing and confidence interval construction posed by heteroscedastic model errors. Nevertheless, it is still a good idea to test for heteroscedasticity in the fashion described in the previous section, so as to give the data a chance to point one toward a better model specification.[37]

---

[36] That derivation constitutes Exercise 11-7.

[37] For large samples with heteroscedasticity of unknown form – and where it has proven infeasible to improve the model specification so as to eliminate the heteroscedasticity – the best estimation technique to use is Generalized Method of Moments (GMM) estimation. GMM is covered in Section 19.4. In this context GMM essentially implements the FGLS estimator discussed above (immediately below Equations 10-17 and 10-18), by using the squared fitting errors from the OLS regression – $(u_1^{\text{fit}})^2 \ldots (u_N^{\text{fit}})^2$ – to "estimate" the weights $\omega_1^2 \ldots \omega_N^2$ and then using these weights (as in Equation 10-18) to respecify the model so that the error term is (asymptotically) homoscedastic. The alert reader will recognize this latter substitution as the same "trick" used in the White-Eicker robust standard error estimator. The advantage of GMM, where it is conveniently implemented in the software one is using, is that it provides asymptotically efficient parameter estimates as well as consistent standard error estimates. As with the robust standard error estimates, its disadvantages are that it is only asymptotically justified and that it encourages one to view heteroscedasticity as a minor problem which is easily fixed, rather than as a symptom of model misspecification which merits further analysis.

10.8 APPLICATION: IS GROWTH GOOD FOR THE POOR? DIAGNOSTICALLY CHECKING THE DOLLAR-KRAAY MODEL

Chapter 1 discussed a 2002 journal article by Dollar and Kraay at the World Bank,[38] which addressed the issue of whether or not the real growth induced by globalization in the 1980s and 1990s was good for the world's poor. Dollar and Kraay used data on each of 92 countries to model the relationship between its per capita real GDP growth rate – "$meangrow_1$" ... "$meangrow_{92}$" – during this period and the corresponding growth rate in per capita real GDP received by the poorest 20% of its population, "$poorgrow_1$" ... "$poorgrow_{92}$". As described in Chapter 1, the key issue in this model is whether the coefficient on $poorgrow_i$ in this model is equal to one – indicating that growth has no impact on the distribution of income in a country – or whether this coefficient is less than one, indicating that growth increases income inequality.

The Dollar and Kraay data were reanalyzed in Ashley (2008), using only the most recent observation for each country, typically a five-year growth rate from the late 1990s.[39] These data yielded the estimated model:

Source	SS	df	MS
Model	1940.42707	1	1940.42707
Residual	1529.2702	90	16.9918911
Total	3469.69727	91	38.1285415

Number of obs	= 92
F(1, 90)	= 114.20
Prob > F	= 0.0000
R-squared	= 0.5592
Adj R-squared	= 0.5544
Root MSE	= 4.1221

poorgrow	Coef.	Std. Err.	t	P>|t|	[95% Conf.	Interval]
meangrow	1.312503	.122821	10.69	0.000	1.068498	1.556509
_cons	-1.250916	.4421076	-2.83	0.006	-2.12924	-.3725924

which apparently indicates that the coefficient on $meangrow_i$ is, if anything, greater than one. Prior to taking these coefficient (and standard error) estimates seriously, however, it is appropriate to apply the methods described in this chapter to diagnostically check the model.

One might first examine a scatterplot of the data on $poorgrow_i$ versus the data on $meangrow_i$ (Figure 10-10) and a histogram of the fitting errors (Figure 10-11). These plots appear to be reasonably consistent with a model in which the random variable $POORGROW_i$ is a linear function of $meangrow_i$, plus a model error term U_i distributed NIID(0, σ^2).[40] In particular, there are no obvious outliers in the scatterplot, nor is there any persuasive evidence that the relationship is nonlinear.

[38] Dollar, David, and Aart Kraay (2002) "Growth Is Good for the Poor," *Journal of Economic Growth 7,* pp. 195–225; a working paper version and their data can be found at www.worldbank.org/research/growth.

[39] See Ashley (2008) "Growth May Be Good for the Poor, but Decline Is Disastrous: On the Non-Robustness of the Dollar-Kraay Result," *International Review of Economics and Finance 17,* 333–38. There it is noted that much of Dollar and Kraay's panel data set is sampled at quite unequal time intervals, rendering the panel-data methods covered in Chapters 15 and 16 problematic. Consequently, only the most recent growth rate data for each country are used here and these data are analyzed as a cross-section model.

[40] This histogram was specified to resolve the fitting errors into eight equal ranges (using the Stata "bin(8)" option; the comparison plot of the corresponding normal density function with mean and variance equal to the corresponding sample values was generated by including the Stata "normal" option. The histogram appears more ragged (and less normal) when a larger number of ranges is specified.

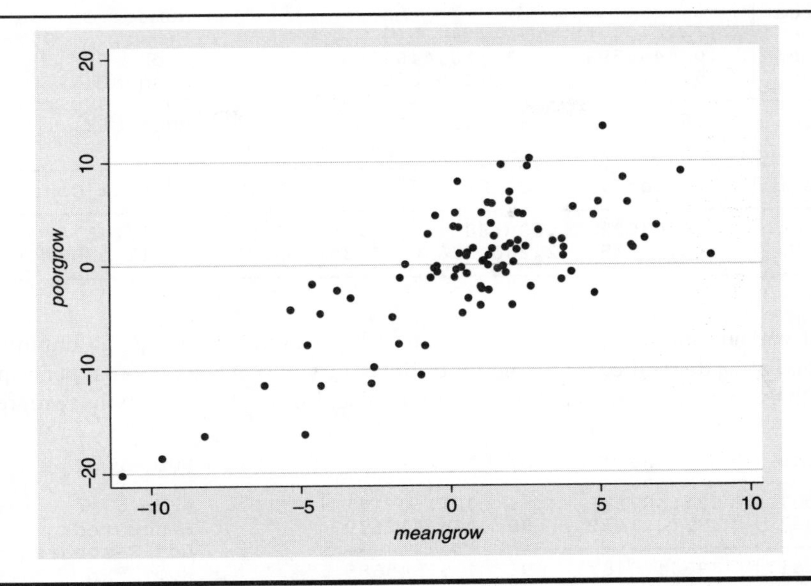

Figure 10-10 Scatterplot for Dollar-Kraay Data

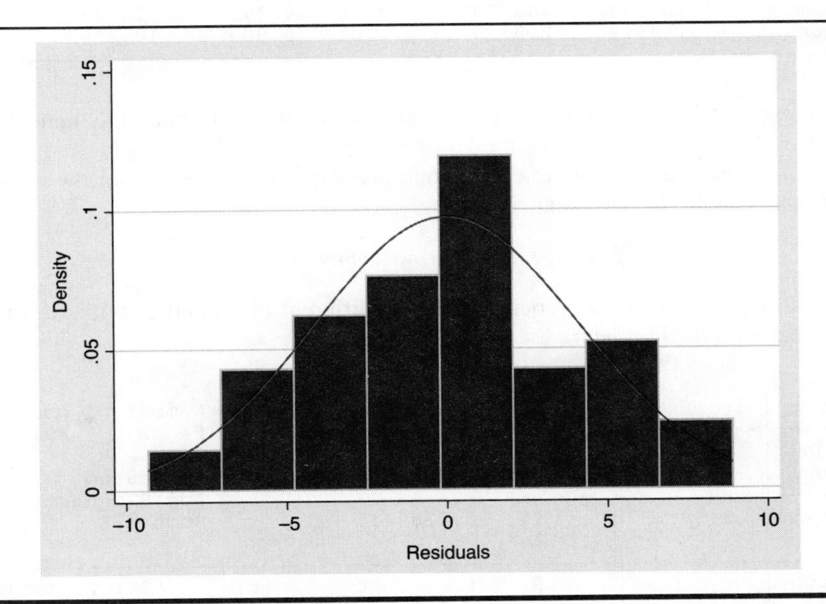

Figure 10-11 Histogram of Fitting Errors for the Estimated Dollar-Kraay Model

One might, however, wonder whether the homoscedasticity assumption is valid, since there appears to be less scatter in the scatterplot for the smaller values of $poorgrow_i$ and $meangrow_i$. Regressing the squared fitting errors against $meangrow_i$ yields the estimated auxiliary equation:

```
      Source |       SS       df       MS              Number of obs =      92
-------------+------------------------------           F(  1,    90) =    0.02
       Model |  10.4464598     1  10.4464598           Prob > F      =  0.8779
    Residual |  39624.2018    90  440.268909           R-squared     =  0.0003
-------------+------------------------------           Adj R-squared = -0.0108
       Total |  39634.6482    91  435.545585           Root MSE      =  20.983

------------------------------------------------------------------------------
    residsqr |      Coef.   Std. Err.      t    P>|t|     [95% Conf. Interval]
-------------+----------------------------------------------------------------
    meangrow |   .0963022   .6251882     0.15   0.878    -1.145743    1.338348
       _cons |   16.54115   2.250433     7.35   0.000     12.07027    21.01203
------------------------------------------------------------------------------
```

An alternative auxiliary regression can also be estimated using a dummy variable ("$neggrowdummy_i$") defined equal to one for each country with a negative real per-capita growth rate (i.e., with $meangrow_i < 0$) and set to zero otherwise. Results for this auxiliary regression are:

```
      Source |       SS       df       MS              Number of obs =      92
-------------+------------------------------           F(  1,    90) =    0.74
       Model |  321.507121     1  321.507121           Prob > F      =  0.3932
    Residual |  39313.1411    90  436.812679           R-squared     =  0.0081
-------------+------------------------------           Adj R-squared = -0.0029
       Total |  39634.6482    91  435.545585           Root MSE      =    20.9

------------------------------------------------------------------------------
    residsqr |      Coef.   Std. Err.      t    P>|t|     [95% Conf. Interval]
-------------+----------------------------------------------------------------
neggrowdummy|   4.151744   4.839304     0.86   0.393    -5.462377    13.76587
       _cons |   15.44918    2.57262     6.01   0.000     10.33822    20.56014
------------------------------------------------------------------------------
```

Neither of these auxiliary regressions gives any reason to doubt that the homoscedasticity assumption is reasonably valid for this model of $poorgrow_i$.

This model fails miserably, however, when one investigates whether or not the relationship is stable across the sample. In particular, including

$$meangrowneg_i \equiv neggrowdummy_i \times meangrow_i \tag{10-25}$$

in the model allows the $meangrow_i$ coefficient to be different for countries with negative growth rates; the estimated model is then:

```
      Source |       SS       df       MS              Number of obs =      92
-------------+------------------------------           F(  2,    89) =   72.94
       Model |  2155.01007     2  1077.50504           Prob > F      =  0.0000
    Residual |   1314.6872    89  14.7717663           R-squared     =  0.6211
-------------+------------------------------           Adj R-squared =  0.6126
       Total |  3469.69727    91  38.1285415           Root MSE      =  3.8434

------------------------------------------------------------------------------
    poorgrow |      Coef.   Std. Err.      t    P>|t|     [95% Conf. Interval]
-------------+----------------------------------------------------------------
    meangrow |   .6395362   .2104527     3.04   0.003     .2213711    1.057701
 meangrowneg |   1.309921   .3436874     3.81   0.000     .6270213     1.99282
       _cons |   .5592576   .6288791     0.89   0.376    -.6903118    1.808827
------------------------------------------------------------------------------
```

Evidently, the slope coefficient in the model for $poorgrow_i$ is significantly larger for the countries in which $meangrow_i$ is negative!

The coefficient on $meangrow_i$ – now, in essence, based only on the data from the countries with nonnegative growth rates – is less than one; this result would appear to indicate that growth in fact ordinarily has a negative impact on the income distribution. Note, however, that the p-value at which the null hypothesis that the coefficient on $meangrow_i$ equals one can be rejected on the two-tailed test is .090, so one cannot conclude that the coefficient on $meangrow_i$ is significantly different from one at the 5% level of significance for the countries with nonnegative growth rates.[41]

The foregoing regression model is particularly graceful for testing whether or not the coefficient on $meangrow_i$ is stable across the sample. An essentially equivalent model which more clearly displays the parameter variation across the two groups of countries is obtained from defining

$$meangrowpos_i \equiv (1 - neggrowdummy_i) \times meangrow_i \tag{10-26}$$

Replacing $meangrow_i$ in the model by $meangrowpos_i$ and $meangrowneg_i$ yields separate estimates of the coefficient on $meangrow_i$ for the countries with positive and negative growth rates:

```
      Source |       SS       df       MS              Number of obs =      92
-------------+------------------------------           F(  2,    89) =   72.94
       Model |  2155.01007     2  1077.50504           Prob > F      =  0.0000
    Residual |   1314.6872    89  14.7717663           R-squared     =  0.6211
-------------+------------------------------           Adj R-squared =  0.6126
       Total |  3469.69727    91  38.1285415           Root MSE      =  3.8434

------------------------------------------------------------------------------
    poorgrow |      Coef.   Std. Err.      t    P>|t|     [95% Conf. Interval]
-------------+----------------------------------------------------------------
 meangrowpos |   .6395362   .2104527     3.04   0.003     .2213711    1.057701
 meangrowneg |   1.949457   .2025904     9.62   0.000     1.546914       2.352
       _cons |   .5592576   .6288791     0.89   0.376    -.6903118    1.808827
------------------------------------------------------------------------------
```

This estimated model more clearly displays the parameter variation. The coefficient on $meangrowpos_i$ is obviously positive: one can read off the p-value at which the null hypothesis that this coefficient equals zero (on the two-tailed test) as .003. But that is irrelevant: the hypothesis of interest is whether or not these coefficients differ from one. The null hypothesis that the coefficient on $meangrowpos_i$ equals one can again be rejected, but only with p-value .090. (This result is the same as before because these last two regression models are essentially identical.) The null hypothesis that the coefficient on $meangrowneg_i$ equals one, in contrast, can be rejected – again on the two-tailed test – with p-value less than .00005. Evidently, positive growth may (or may not) be good for the poor, but negative growth is clearly very bad for the poor.

KEY TERMS

For each term or concept listed below, provide a working definition or explanation:

Diagnostic Checking

Linear Function

Parameter Instability

Fixed in Repeated Samples

Model Errors vs. Fitting Errors

[41] In Stata this two-tailed p-value is obtained using the command "test meangrow = 1." Note that the one-tailed test – which would yield a p-value for rejection of the null hypothesis only half as large – is inappropriate here. That is because one would likely have tested whether or not this coefficient was significantly *larger* than one if the parameter estimate had exceeded one.

Outlier
Influential Observation
Homoscedasticity vs. Heteroscedasticity
Robust Standard Error Estimates

EXERCISES

10-1. Detail how one could use the Multiple Regression Model to test (and allow for) sample variation in the slope coefficient in the Bivariate Regression model under the following specific circumstances:

a. The slope coefficient is different for males than for females, where the observed dummy variable d_i is zero for males and one for females.

b. The slope coefficient is itself a linear function of the explanatory variable, x_i.

10-2. Continuing Exercise 6-12, suppose again that there are four sample observations on y_i and x_i:

y	x
3.5	1.0
−3.2	−1.0
−.3	0
.3	0

and that you are willing to assume that

$$Y_i = \beta x_i + U_i \quad U_i \sim \text{NIID}(0, \sigma^2)$$

Expand on your answers to parts a, b, and f of Exercise 6-12 to comment on the influentiality of each of these four observations.

10-3. Derive the relationship between the fitting errors and the model errors for the Multiple Regression Model. (This result was obtained as Equation 10-2 for the Bivariate Regression Model.)

10-4. List the important (and the unimportant) reasons for checking the validity of the assumption that the model errors are normally distributed. List several ways to check this assumption.

10-5. Discuss the distinction between an outlier in the model errors of the Bivariate Regression model and an outlier in the explanatory variable. Can the same observation pair be both? In which cases is the outlier influential with respect to the slope estimate? Illustrate your discussion with a scatterplot.

10-6. Why is a scatterplot relating the observations on the dependent variable to those on an explanatory variable potentially misleading in the context of the Multiple Regression Model? In what way are such plots still valuable?

10-7. It is hypothesized that the variance of the model errors in a model of the real growth rate of country *i* may be a function of population (pop_i) and/or of distance from the equator ($latitude_i$).

a. If this is the case, what impact would it have on the quality (e.g., unbiasedness, consistency, BLUness) of the OLS parameter estimates in this model? What impact would it have on the statistical inference results – hypothesis tests and parameter confidence intervals – based on the OLS parameter estimates?

b. How could one test for such heteroscedasticity using graphical methods?

c. How could one test for such heteroscedasticity using an auxiliary regression? What advantages (and disadvantages) does this approach have, relative to the graphical methods?

d. Supposing that the variance of the model errors appears to be proportional to the square of pop_i, what model respecification is suggested? What if the variance of the model errors appears to be proportional to $latitude_i$?

e. Presuming that you found heteroscedasticity and were able to respecify the model so as to more or less eliminate it, what are the advantages (and disadvantages, if any) of respecifying the model rather than either (i) ignoring the heteroscedasticity or (ii) using robust standard error estimates?

Active Learning Exercise 10a: The Fitting Errors as Approximations for the Model Errors

Introduction

In this exercise you will use data generated from the particular Bivariate Regression Model

$$Y_i = 1 + 2x_i + U_i \quad U_i \sim \text{NIID}(0, 1)$$

to examine how well the OLS fitting errors approximate the actual model errors for various sample sizes.

Your Assignment:

1. Copy the data file ALE10a.csv (available at www.wiley.com/college/ashley) to your hard disk and read it into the econometrics software your course is using. (Or ALE10a.dta if you are using Stata.) This file contains 500 values of x_i and 500 realizations of the random variables U_i and Y_i.[42]
2. Estimate the regression model and save the fitting errors as $uhat500_1$ ... $uhat500_{500}$.
   a. Plot and print out a scatterplot relating the values of u_1 ... u_{500} to the values of $uhat500_1$ ... $uhat500_{500}$.[43] To the extent that the fitting errors are a good approximation the model errors, the points on this scatterplot will lie on a straight line through the origin with slope one.
   b. Compute the square of the sample correlation between the model errors and the fitting errors.[44] You can interpret this squared correlation as the fraction of the variation in the model error "captured" by the fitting errors. Note that, per Section 8.2, one can obtain the same figure as the (unadjusted) R^2 of a bivariate regression for U_i using $uhat500_i$ as the explanatory variable.
   c. Based on these results, do the fitting errors from a regression model estimated using 500 observations appear to be a good approximation to the model errors?

---

[42] The values of the x_i in this file are realizations of independent unit normals. In Stata, these data can be generated using the statements:

```
drawnorm u, n(500) seed(23)
drawnorm x, n(500) seed(13)
generate y = 1 + 2*x + u
```

[43] The commands for doing this in Stata are "regress y x", "predict uhat, r", and "scatter u uhat".

[44] The command for calculating the correlation is "corr u uhat" in Stata.

3. Repeat step 2 – including the scatterplot – using only the first $N = 25$, 50, 100, and 250 observations to estimate the model.[45] Denote the fitting errors you obtain using 25, 50, 100, and 250 observations as "*uhat*25", "*uhat*50", "*uhat*100", and "*uhat*250". Comment on the quality of the approximation as the sample size becomes smaller. (Why is the squared sample correlation actually larger for fitting errors from a regression with $N = 50$ than for fitting errors from a regression with $N = 100$?)

N	$\{\text{sample corr}(u_i, u_i^{\text{fit}})\}^2$
25	
50	
100	
250	
500	

4. Looking at Equation 10-2, it is obvious that the model fitting errors are heteroscedastic, even if the model errors are homoscedastic, with $\text{var}(U_i^{\text{fit}})$ clearly depending on the value of x_i. But this heteroscedasticity in the fitting errors should become negligible as the sample length increases. Investigate that issue here by regressing the squared values of *uhat*25$_i$, *uhat*50$_i$, *uhat*100$_i$, *uhat*250$_i$, and *uhat*500$_i$ on the square of the explanatory variable – i.e., on $(x_i)^2$. (Don't forget to limit the sample used in your auxiliary regression to just the observations used in the model estimated to obtain this set of fitting errors.)[46] Enter the estimated t ratio (and the p-value for rejecting the null hypothesis that the coefficient on $(x_i)^2$ in the model for the squared fitting errors is zero) for each sample length in the table below. Do these auxiliary regressions indicate that this heteroscedasticity induced in the fitting errors is important in extent?

N	t ratio	p-value
25		
50		
100		
250		
500		

[45] In Stata, this is most easily achieved by using "if _n ≤ 250" in the regression command. Re-estimate the model for each sample size.

[46] Setting the fitting errors to "missing" outside the actual sample period – using, for example, "replace uhat250 = . if _n > 250" in Stata immediately after generating the fitting errors using the "predict uhat250, r" statement – is a good way to prevent errors in this regard. It is also a good idea to immediately label fitting errors (using the data editor or the "label variable" command); one otherwise tends to forget which fitting error variable is which.

11

Stochastic Regressors and Endogeneity

11.1 INTRODUCTION

The exposition up to this point has shown how to estimate a regression model using cross-sectional (as opposed to time-series) data so as to obtain reasonably high-quality parameter estimates and statistical inferences – under the assumption that the explanatory variables are "fixed in repeated samples." In particular, the material on diagnostic checking and model respecification in Chapter 10 showed how a quantity of sample data can be used *either* to reassure the analyst as to the approximate validity of the other assumptions crucial to the quality of the estimators and the validity of the statistical inference machinery in a cross-section data setting *or* to suggest model respecifications leading to a formulation for which such reassurance might be forthcoming.

That is a substantial accomplishment, but it is not enough – fundamentally because, in economic modeling, the assumption that the explanatory variables are all fixed in repeated samples is frequently unreasonable. This assumption – hereafter referred to simply as the assumption of "fixed-regressors" – must therefore often be dropped, in favor of allowing for explanatory variables which are specified as random variables – i.e., "stochastic regressors."[1] The problem is that almost all of our previous results – on the quality (properties) of the least squares parameter estimates and on the statistical inference machinery used to create hypothesis tests and confidence intervals – rest on sampling distribution derivations which depend on the fixed-regressors assumption.

Thus, violations of this assumption are potentially very consequential. The first sections of this chapter develop the theoretical tools for understanding this consequentiality. Here at the outset, however, it is well to first discuss why this assumption is so frequently violated to a substantial degree.

For one thing, a good deal of relevant economic data is observed sequentially over time. Quarterly real GDP and the monthly unemployment rate are familiar examples of such "time-series." The Penn World Table (PWT) – which was introduced in Active Learning Exercise 5a – provides a good example of a "panel" data set; this is simply a collection of such time-series over a number of similar entities. For example, in version 6.1 of the PWT, one can find observations on real per capita GDP as an annual time-series (1950 to 2000) for each of 168 countries.[2] The analysis of data such as these will be taken up in Chapters 13 and 14. Such data have not been considered here so far because adequately modeling it usually requires the specification of a dynamic regression model, in which lagged values of the dependent variable appear on the right-hand side of the regression model equation as explanatory variables. It does not make sense to assume that a lagged value of the dependent variable is fixed in repeated samples, because each new ("repeated") sample is

[1] The words "stochastic" and "random" are essentially synonymous and will be used interchangeably in this chapter.

[2] See the version 6.1 PWT Web site: at datacenter.chass.utoronto.ca/pwt61/.

characterized by a new sequence of model errors, leading to a new sequence of dependent variable observations and hence to a new sequence of lagged values of the dependent variable.

Moreover, even if we were willing to restrict our attention to purely cross-sectional data – all observed for the same time period – in *economic* settings the crucially relevant explanatory variables are quite often *endogenous*: that is, statistically related to the model error term. Indeed, many econometricians would argue that it is primarily this aspect of economic data which makes econometrics distinct from ordinary statistics. Foreshadowing the results to come – in Section 11.4 – it is endogenous stochastic regressors that cause the worst problem: biased and inconsistent OLS parameter estimates. In contrast, we will find that the other problems caused by stochastic regressors all dwindle to insignificance as the amount of sample data available becomes large.

It was useful – indeed, necessary – to begin our study of regression analysis by first coming to understand OLS regression under the fixed-regressors assumption. However, continuing to make the fixed-regressors assumption when one or more of the explanatory variables is actually an endogenous stochastic regressor is not an effective approach: the endogeneity still makes our actual parameter estimates biased and inconsistent even if we have assumed it away!

Why is endogeneity so common in regression models with economic data? Endogeneity arises from three distinct sources:

- Omitted variables
- Measurement error
- Joint determination (simultaneity)

Each of these sources is described at some length in its own section later on in this chapter, but a brief mention of each is worthwhile right now. The problem with omitted explanatory variables (and, in particular, omitted explanatory variables which are related to included explanatory variables) has already been discussed in Chapter 9. Here, this problem is recast in terms of the fact that omitted explanatory variables are necessarily subsumed in the model error term. Consequently, any omitted explanatory variable which is related to an included explanatory variable induces a relationship between this included explanatory variable and the model error term – i.e., endogeneity. Similarly, explanatory variables whose observed values are corrupted by measurement error become endogenous because the measurement error itself becomes part of the model error term. Finally, an explanatory variable will be endogenous if it is jointly determined with the dependent variable by a set of simultaneous equations. Such joint determination is common in economic systems. Indeed, it is an essential characteristic of many theoretical economic models: aggregate consumption and income provide a typical example from macroeconomic analysis; price and quantity observations which are jointly determined by market equilibrium provide a typical example from microeconomic analysis.

The first task in investigating the consequentiality of dropping the fixed-regressors assumption is to determine what needs to be assumed about stochastic regressors in order to still obtain even the simplest property for OLS parameter estimators: unbiasedness. The analysis of this issue – and all of the rest, really – actually hinges solely on the stochastic nature of the explanatory variables, not on their multiplicity. Consequently – for simplicity – all of the explicit analysis will focus on estimation of the slope coefficient in the Bivariate Regression Model. Section 11.2 shows that with a stochastic regressor, the OLS slope estimator is still unbiased only if each observation on the explanatory variable is statistically independent of – that is, completely unrelated to – every observation on the model error term. Such a regressor is called "exogenous."

Further progress in analyzing the Bivariate Regression Model – i.e., in investigating the properties of the OLS slope estimator and deriving inference machinery for testing hypotheses and estimating confidence intervals – is only possible under an assumption that the sample is large. Most of the necessary "large-sample" or "asymptotic" concepts – e.g., limiting distributions and the property of consistency – have been already been foreshadowed in previous chapters; these ideas are developed here (in Section 11.3) in greater depth.[3] These sharper tools are then used in Section 11.4 to obtain the key requirement for the OLS parameter estimator to at least be a consistent estimator of the true slope coefficient: the explanatory variable in the model must, at least for large samples, be uncorrelated with the model error term. The following sections detail how this requirement fails to hold for explanatory variables which are endogenous due to the problems cited above: omitted variables, measurement error, and joint determination. The large-sample concepts developed in this chapter are then applied to the practical problems of dealing with endogenous explanatory variables (in Chapter 12) and of dealing with dynamic regression models (in Chapters 13 and 14).

The last section in this chapter describes simulation methods which can be used to estimate the impact of stochastic regressors on the quality of the OLS regression parameter estimators for any given sample size – and, in particular, how this impact varies with sample size. These methods are worth introducing for two reasons. First, with reasonably large samples, they provide a feasible (albeit computationally intensive) alternative to statistical inference based on asymptotic theory in any particular case. Second, they can be used occasionally to address the perennial worry, "Is the actually-available sample large enough for the concepts developed here and the techniques described in subsequent chapters to be useful?"

11.2 UNBIASEDNESS OF THE OLS SLOPE ESTIMATOR WITH A STOCHASTIC REGRESSOR INDEPENDENT OF THE MODEL ERRORS

Dropping the fixed-regressors model assumption, there is still one result which is easily obtainable on OLS regression parameter estimation without getting involved with asymptotic theory. It is worth describing here because it both delineates how the (now) stochastic nature of the explanatory variable destroys most of our previous results and also because it indicates how strong an assumption we would need to make in order to restore those previous results. Deriving this result also provides a good opportunity to discuss the ways in which the model needs to be modified so as to accommodate a stochastic explanatory variable and is, in any case, necessary in order to set up the algebra needed for the analysis.

Dropping the fixed-regressors assumption, then, the Bivariate Regression Model of Chapter 5 becomes

The Bivariate Regression Model

(Stochastic Regressor Case)

$$
\begin{gathered}
Y_i = \alpha + \beta X_i + U_i \quad i = 1 \ldots N \\
U_i \sim \text{IID}[0, \sigma_u^2] \\
X_i \sim \text{IID}[0, \sigma_x^2] \quad \sigma_u^2 > 0 \\
\text{Cov}(X_i, U_i) = \sigma_{xu} \\
\text{Cov}(X_i^2, U_i^2) = 0
\end{gathered}
\tag{11-1}
$$

Note that the explanatory variable in Equation 11-1 is now denoted with a capital letter (X_i) – rather than the lowercase letter (x_i) used in Chapters 5 through 8 – so as to explicitly express the fact that this regressor is now a random variable. Now, however, specific assumptions must be made about the manner in which $X_1 \ldots X_N$ are distributed. In this chapter it is assumed that these random variables

[3] The terms "large-sample" and "asymptotic" will be used interchangeably below. Similarly, the terms "limiting distribution" and "asymptotic distribution" are synonymous and will, after a few repetitions, also be used interchangeably.

are identically and independently distributed, with mean zero and positive variance, σ_x^2; in Chapter 13 this assumption is relaxed to allow for an explanatory variable which is a time-series, whose current value might well be correlated with its value for previous periods. The zero-mean assumption can be made at no loss of generality because of the presence of an intercept in the model. And it would make no sense to allow σ_x^2 to be zero since, in that case X_i would be zero for every observation, clearly precluding any possibility of estimating the coefficient β. The assumption that the X_i are identically distributed – while often reasonable – is a real assumption, however. It is made here – and in almost every treatment of regression with stochastic regressors – so as to keep the analysis tractable.

Further, it is not necessary to assume that either the X_i or the model errors (U_i) are normally distributed. This is because the normality of the (asymptotic) sampling distribution of $\hat{\beta}^{OLS}$, the least squares estimator of β for this model, will follow – in Appendix 11.2 – from a Central Limit Theorem argument rather than relying, as it did in the fixed-regressor model, on an assumption that the model errors are themselves normally distributed.[4] On the other hand, the application of the Central Limit Theorem requires independent – not just uncorrelated – model errors.

It is worth noting at the outset, however, that the derivation of the asymptotic sampling distribution of $\hat{\beta}^{OLS}$ requires the additional assumptions that both $\text{cov}(X_i, U_i)$ and $\text{cov}(X_i^2, U_i^2)$ are equal to zero. It should be evident from the initial discussion of endogeneity in Section 11.1 that this assumption on $\text{cov}(X_i, U_i)$ is often of dubious validity in actual empirical settings; and it will become clear later in this chapter (in Section 11.4) that this assumption is also essentially necessary in order for the least squares estimator of β to even be consistent.[5] (Fixing this problem is the work of Chapter 12!)

Turning to the second condition, it is useful to re-express this covariance using its definition in terms of expectations:

$$\text{cov}\left(X_i^2, U_i^2\right) = E\left[\left(X_i^2 - \sigma_x^2\right), \left(U_i^2 - \sigma_u^2\right)\right] \tag{11-2}$$

Setting this covariance to zero thus amounts to assuming that the (squared) magnitudes of the explanatory variable fluctuations are uncorrelated with the magnitudes of the model error fluctuations. Thus, these two conditions could together be interpreted as requiring that neither the level nor the magnitude of the fluctuations in the explanatory variable is correlated with the corresponding level or magnitude of the model error term. Roughly speaking, while somewhat "wild" values of both the explanatory variable and the model error can occur, it is being assumed that there is no systematic tendency for such wildness to occur (or to not occur) in the explanatory variable for the same observations in which it happens to occur in the model error term. We could instead assume that X_i and U_i are independently distributed, but this is stronger than necessary.[6]

The sample data are still the set of observed realizations: $(y_1, x_1) \ldots (y_N, x_N)$. Thus, the actually-observed least squares estimate of β is the same as was derived in Chapter 5:

$$\hat{\beta}^*_{\text{ols}} = \frac{\sum_{i=1}^{N} (y_i - \bar{y})}{\sum_{\ell=1}^{N} (x_\ell - \bar{x})^2} = \sum_{i=1}^{N} w_i^{\text{ols}} y_i \tag{11-3a}$$

[4] Recall from Chapter 10 that the actual value of diagnostically checking the normality assumption lies in the way it induces the analyst to look more carefully at the data for outliers, etc.

[5] Actually, we will find that $\hat{\beta}^{OLS}$ is consistent for β so long as $\text{cov}(X_i, U_i)$ goes to zero for sufficiently large N; this distinction is suppressed here for clarity.

[6] For example, such an independence assumption would be further assuming that *every* function of X_i is uncorrelated with *every* function of U_i. Note also that – even though this assumption is clearly distinct from the assumption that the U_i are homoscedastic – the derivation in Appendix 11.2 shows that the formulas for computing White-Eicker (heteroscedasticity-robust) standard error estimates in practice provide a convenient large-sample correction for any violations of this assumption.

where the "least squares weights" $w_1^{ols} \dots w_N^{ols}$ are, as before, defined as

$$w_i^{ols} = \frac{(x_i - \bar{x})}{\sum\limits_{\ell=i}^{N} (x_\ell - \bar{x})^2} \tag{11-3b}$$

for $i = 1 \dots N$.

Also as before, further progress compels us to regard this (fixed) estimate of β as the sample realization of the random variable, $\hat{\beta}^{OLS}$, but the ith OLS weight is now written a bit differently, as

$$W_i^{ols} = \frac{X_i - \overline{X}}{\sum\limits_{\ell=1}^{N} (X_\ell - \overline{X})^2} \tag{11-4}$$

The difference is that $W_1^{ols} \dots W_N^{ols}$ are now random variables, and are hence denoted with capital letters:

$$\hat{\beta}^{OLS} = \sum_{i=1}^{N} W_i^{ols} Y_i \tag{11-5}$$

Is $\hat{\beta}^{OLS}$ still an unbiased estimator of the parameter β? It is useful to first rewrite Equation 11-5 in terms of the model errors:

$$\begin{aligned} \hat{\beta}^{OLS} &= \sum_{i=1}^{N} W_i^{ols} Y_i = \sum_{i=1}^{N} W_i^{ols} (\alpha + \beta X_i + U_i) \\ &= \alpha \sum_{i=1}^{N} W_i^{ols} + \beta \sum_{i=1}^{N} W_i^{ols} X_i + \sum_{i=1}^{N} W_i^{ols} U_i \\ &= \beta + \sum_{i=1}^{N} W_i^{ols} U_i \end{aligned} \tag{11-6}$$

Note that the last step in Equation 11-6 uses the fact that, even though $W_1^{ols} \dots W_N^{ols}$ are random variables, $\sum\limits_{i=1}^{N} W_i^{ols}$ and $\sum\limits_{i=1}^{N} W_i^{ols} X_i$ are not – as shown in Exercise 11-1, these two sums are equal to zero and one, respectively.

Taking the expected value of both sides of Equation 11-6 yields

$$\begin{aligned} E\left[\hat{\beta}^{OLS}\right] &= E\left[\beta + \sum_{i=1}^{N} W_i^{ols} U_i\right] \\ &= \beta + \sum_{i=1}^{N} E\left[W_i^{ols} U_i\right] \end{aligned} \tag{11-7}$$

Thus, $\hat{\beta}^{OLS}$ is still an unbiased estimator of the parameter β if and only if the expected value of the product of W_i^{ols} and U_i equals zero for all N values of i. The expected value of U_i is assumed to be zero in Equation 11-1, but this does not imply that the expectation of the *product* of W_i^{ols} and U_i is equal to zero. The expectation of the product of W_i^{ols} and U_i is equal to the product of the expectations of W_i^{ols} and U_i if and only if these two random variables are *uncorrelated*, which there is no reason to believe is the case.[7]

[7] Recall from Chapter 2 that, for any pair of random variables Y and Z, $\text{cov}(YZ) = E[YZ] - E[Y]E[Z]$. So the expected value of their product equals the product of their expectations if and only if their covariance is zero, in which case they are uncorrelated.

In fact, the only circumstance in which $E\left[W_i^{ols} U_i\right]$ will clearly equal zero is if every one of the N random variables $X_1 \ldots X_N$ is independently distributed from U_i. Only in that case is W_i^{ols} – which is a function of $X_1 \ldots X_N$ – independently distributed from U_i, and hence uncorrelated with it. Thus, the only circumstance under which we can be sure that $\hat{\beta}^{OLS}$ is still an unbiased estimator of β is if the explanatory variable for every one of the N observations is independently distributed from (i.e., completely unrelated to) all N model errors.

Obviously, then, $\hat{\beta}^{OLS}$ is not in general going to be an unbiased estimator of β if the explanatory variable is a stochastic, rather than a fixed, regressor. Thus, $\hat{\beta}^{OLS}$ is clearly not going to be BLU or efficient either, because those properties require unbiasedness. Moreover, recall that all of the hypothesis testing and confidence interval results in Chapters 7 and 9 rest on the unbiasedness of $\hat{\beta}^{OLS}$ also.[8]

Yikes! It would seem that we have just lost everything! But that conclusion is not warranted. The concepts and results developed in the next two sections will make it clear that $\hat{\beta}^{OLS}$ is still at least a consistent estimator of β under a much weaker assumption on the relationship between X_i and U_i: the assumption that X_i and U_i are, at least for sufficiently large samples, uncorrelated. And (if $\hat{\beta}^{OLS}$ is consistent) then it will be possible to obtain a useful approximation to its actual sampling distribution that is arbitrarily accurate for sufficiently large samples – what is called a "limiting" or "asymptotic" sampling distribution for $\hat{\beta}^{OLS}$. This approximate sampling distribution will allow us to still test null hypotheses regarding β and to still calculate confidence intervals for β – at least for large samples. These results, however, require that we deepen our understanding of asymptotic theory beyond the intuitive definition of consistency given in Chapters 3 and 6. That is the work of the next section.

11.3 A BRIEF INTRODUCTION TO ASYMPTOTIC THEORY

At the end of Chapter 2 we obtained expressions for the mean and variance of a weighted sum of N uncorrelated random variables, given that each one is a drawing from a (possibly quite distinct) distribution, but assuming that each of these distributions has the same mean (μ) and variance (σ^2):

If

$$B \equiv \sum_{i=1}^{N} w_i U_i$$

with

$$E[U_i] = \mu \text{ and } \operatorname{var}(U_i) = \sigma^2 \quad \text{for all } i \text{ in } \{1,,2,\ldots,N\}$$

and

$$\operatorname{cov}(U_i,\ U_j) = 0 \quad \text{for all } i \text{ and } j \text{ in } \{1,,2,\ldots,N\}$$

Then

$$E[B] = \mu \sum_{i=1}^{N} w_i \quad \text{and} \quad \operatorname{var}(B) = \sigma^2 \sum_{i=1}^{N} w_i^2 \tag{11-8}$$

At this point it is useful to consider the special case of this result where each of the weights ($w_1 \ldots w_N$) is set equal to $1/N$. Replacing the symbols $U_1 \ldots U_N$ for the random variables in Equation 11-8 by $V_1 \ldots$

[8] Actually, these inference results only require an estimator with known bias. In practice, however, that virtually always requires an unbiased estimator.

V_N – because $U_1 \ldots U_N$ are in use in the present chapter as the model errors of Equation 11-1 – and notationally recognizing that the random variable B is now actually the sample mean of $V_1 \ldots V_N$, yields the result

$$\text{If} \quad \overline{V} \equiv \frac{1}{N}\sum_{i=1}^{N} V_i$$
$$\text{with}$$
$$E[V_i] = \mu \quad \text{and} \quad \text{var}(V_i) = \sigma^2 \quad \text{for all } i \text{ in } \{1,,2,\ldots,N\}$$
$$\text{and}$$
$$\text{cov}(V_i, V_j) = 0 \quad \text{for all } i \neq j \text{ in } \{1,,2,\ldots,N\}$$
$$\text{Then}$$
$$E[\overline{V}] = \mu \quad \text{and} \quad \text{var}(\overline{V}) = \frac{\sigma^2}{N}. \tag{11-9}$$

Thus, for data such as these – which are uncorrelated and all share the same population mean and variance, but which are not necessarily drawn from the same distribution – the sample mean is an unbiased estimator of the population mean and has sampling variance σ^2/N.

Note that the variance of $\overline{V}$ goes to zero as N, the amount of sample data available for estimating μ, grows arbitrarily large. Consequently, the density function for the sampling distribution of $\overline{V}$ must in some sense be converging, so as to more and more closely resemble a "spike" with an arbitrarily small width (because the variance of $\overline{V}$ is going to zero), an arbitrarily large height (because the total area under the density function must equal one), and a location arbitrarily close to μ, because the expected value of $\overline{V}$ is μ. Thus, using an actual sample of data with N sufficiently large, one could be essentially certain that $\overline{v}$, the observed realization of $\overline{V}$, is arbitrarily close to the actual value of μ.

Now for some vocabulary: The formal name for this kind of convergence is "convergence in probability." This would typically be expressed by stating that "the probability limit of $\overline{V}$ is μ" or, equivalently, that "$\overline{V}$ converges in probability to the non-stochastic limit μ" or – again equivalently – by merely stating that "plim($\overline{V}$) equals μ." There is also a standard name for this kind of result – in which some set of assumptions about the underlying data yields a conclusion as to the probability limit of a sample moment. Generically, such a result is called a "Law of Large Numbers" or "LLN." An extremely typical example is the LLN for identically and independently distributed data:

The Law of Large Numbers (LLN) {IID Case}

$$V_i \sim \text{IID}(\mu, \sigma^2) \Rightarrow \text{plim}\left(\frac{1}{N}\sum_{i=1}^{N} V_i\right) = \mu \tag{11-10}$$

Note that Equation 11-10 is not really "the" Law of Large Numbers: it is one of many possible LLNs for $\overline{V}$, each corresponding to a different set of assumptions on the individual V_i's. For example, in a particular setting where heteroscedasticity is an issue, one might need to use an LLN which relaxes the assumption that the V_i all share the same population variance. Or in a setting (such as we will encounter in Chapters 13 and 14) where the V_i are actually time-series data, one might need to use an LLN which allows for a specific degree of serial correlation in the observations from period to period. Indeed, the intuitive discussion leading up to the Equation 11-10 suggests that this LLN is actually unnecessarily restrictive in its assumption. In particular, the convergence of $\overline{V}$ does not in fact appear to require that the V_i's be identically distributed – it apparently suffices that their means and variances are the same. Nor is independence clearly necessary, as uncorrelatedness sufficed in order to derive the needed result on the sampling variance of $\overline{V}$.

A great deal of work has been done proving LLNs for various different variations on the IID assumption. This work has also led to a set of "algebraic" results on probability limits which make them extremely easy to manipulate and evaluate. Appendix 11.1 lists a useful selection of these results, all of which have been proven for the case where the underlying data is identically and independently distributed.[9] Looking at these results, one can see that it is a simple matter to evaluate the probability limit of a sum, product, or quotient of two estimators. Appendix 11.1 also gives a result – the "Slutsky Theorem" – which states that the probability limit of a continuous function of an estimator equals that function of probability limit of the estimator. Thus, for example, if one knows the probability limit of an estimator of a population variance, then the probability limit of the standard deviation is just the square root of this, since the square root is a continuous function.[10] Note also that the restatement of the LLN in Appendix 11.1 is more powerful than it might at first appear, as the V_i can be any random variable (or function of several multiple random variables) whose expectation is finite. Thus, for example, this result implies that the probability limit of a sample variance or covariance is equal to the corresponding population variance or covariance.

The net effect of these results is to make it fairly easy to express the probability limit of practically any estimator in terms of the combination of population moments which might correspond to what the estimator is attempting to estimate. This ability to manipulate probability limits motivates the formal definition of the property of consistency for an estimator of some population quantity (or model parameter) μ:

Consistency of Estimator $\hat{V}$

$$\text{plim}(\hat{V}) = \mu \quad \Longleftrightarrow \quad \hat{V} \text{ in a consistent estimator of } \mu \tag{11-11}$$

Thus, it is often feasible to evaluate the probability limit of a regression model parameter estimator and say something cogent as to the circumstances under which it is (or is not) consistent. Indeed, this is exactly what we will do with respect to $\hat{\beta}^{OLS}$ in the next section.

Most analysts regard consistency as an essential quality in an estimator, to the point where an estimator which is not at least consistent is pretty much regarded as junk. In principle that is not really justified: one can imagine an estimator which is slightly inconsistent, but which is quite useful because it has a small mean square error for modest sample sizes.[11] And a consistent estimator is not necessarily a good estimator. For example, per Exercise 11-2, if $\hat{V}$ is a consistent estimator of μ, then so is $\hat{V} + \left[10^{1000}/N^{.001}\right]$. At least one of this pair of estimators is incredibly terrible! Still, the actual estimators which we find to be consistent in the context of regression models in practice appear to be fairly useful, at least in reasonably large samples. And – as noted above – most people simply have no use for estimators which are not at least consistent.

[9] Hamilton (1994, Chapter 7) provides a more detailed treatment of these results, including both proofs and extensions of these same results to sequences of random variables for which the underlying observations V_1 ... V_N are a serially correlated time-series rather than independently distributed observations. An extension of this sort is needed in order to apply these results to the autoregressive models considered in Chapter 13. James D. Hamilton (1994, Chapter 7) *Time-Series Analysis*, Princeton University Press: Princeton.

[10] Note that the operation of taking the expected value of a random variable does not have this property! Thus, the square root of an unbiased variance estimator is not an unbiased estimator of the standard deviation.

[11] Recall from Chapter 3 that the minimum-MSE estimator of the mean of a random variable is biased toward zero, so biased estimation is actually a good thing, even when one's loss function on estimation errors is symmetric. The optimal amount of bias in the minimum-MSE shrinkage estimator disappears as the sample size becomes arbitrarily large, however, so this particular biased estimator is still consistent. See Exercise 11-4.

Once one has a consistent estimator, however, its main use is in inference on the unknown parameter: μ here, or the regression equation slope parameter in the next section. Typically one wants to either estimate a confidence interval for this parameter or to test a hypothesis about it. To that end, it is crucial to extend this probabilistic convergence notion to what is called "convergence in distribution" or "convergence to a stochastic probability limit." This amounts to multiplying the deviation of an estimator from its probability limit by an appropriate function of the sample size so that the result converges in probability to a random variable with finite variance as the sample size becomes arbitrarily large.

For most estimators this function is just the square root of the sample size. For example, if $V_1 \ldots V_N$ are specified as in Equation 11-9, then $\sqrt{N}\left[\overline{V} - \text{plim}(\overline{V})\right] = \sqrt{N}\left[\overline{V} - \mu\right]$ is a random variable with finite variance (σ^2) for any value of N, so in this particular case no actual "convergence" is even necessary. The fact of the matter, however, is that $\sqrt{N}\left[\tilde{V} - \mu\right]$ typically converges to a random variable with a finite variance for any estimator $\tilde{V}$ which is a consistent estimator of μ.

Let G denote the distribution of this random variable which $\sqrt{N}\left[\tilde{V} - \mu\right]$ tends to – in the same way that we use the symbol "N" in $N[\mu, \sigma^2]$ to denote a normal distribution, except that here the distribution is (at this point) unknown. The variance of $\sqrt{N}\left[\tilde{V} - \mu\right]$ then will be denoted σ_g^2. In that case we could say that $\sqrt{N}\left[\tilde{V} - \mu\right]$ "converges in distribution to a random variable with asymptotic distribution $G[0, \sigma_g^2]$" and identify this random variable as the probability limit of $\sqrt{N}\left[\tilde{V} - \mu\right]$. This is what is meant by the phrase "$\sqrt{N}\left[\tilde{V} - \mu\right]$ converges to a stochastic probability limit." This convergence can, equivalently, be expressed as either

$$\text{plim}\left(\sqrt{N}\left[\tilde{V} - \mu\right]\right) = G\left[0, \sigma_g^2\right] \quad \text{or} \quad \sqrt{N}\left[\tilde{V} - \mu\right] \xrightarrow{d} G\left[0, \sigma_g^2\right] \tag{11-12}$$

In Equation 11-12 the symbol $\xrightarrow{d}$ stands for "tends in distribution to" or, equivalently, "is asymptotically distributed as" and one would say that the "asymptotic variance" of $\sqrt{N}\left[\tilde{V} - \mu\right]$ is σ_g^2 or, more commonly, that the asymptotic variance of $\tilde{V}$ itself is σ_g^2/N.[12]

It is awkward, however, that the shape of the G distribution is, at this point, unknown. If we *did* know the shape of this distribution – and had access to a consistent estimator of σ_g^2 – then we could (at least for large samples) use a single realization of $\tilde{V}$ to do inference on μ.

For example, suppose that we have collected $N = 812$ observations on V_i, for which we are willing to assume that Equation 11-9 holds. (I.e., we are willing to assume that the V_i are uncorrelated draws from distributions which might differ from each other in shape – due to sampling difficulties, say – but all have same mean μ and the same variance σ_g^2.) Thus, from the reasoning at the beginning of this section, the sample mean, $\overline{V}$, is a consistent estimator of μ. Now suppose that the realized sample mean – i.e., the average of our 812 actual observations: $v_1 \ldots v_{812}$ – is 3.2 and that the empirical issue is whether or not this sample result constitutes persuasive evidence against our economic theory, which (for the purpose of this example) predicts a value of 3.0 for μ. Thus, our intent is to test the null hypothesis H_o: $\mu = 3.0$ against the alternative hypothesis H_A: $\mu \neq 3.0$. Further, suppose that we have obtained 6.14 as the realized value of $\tilde{\sigma}_g^2$, a consistent estimator of σ_g^2.[13] Finally, we explicitly suppose that the value of N used in this example (812) is sufficiently large that it reasonable to think that the asymptotic distribution of $\sqrt{N}\left[\overline{V} - \mu\right]$ is a reasonable approximation to its actual distribution – i.e., the convergence in

[12] Another common notation for the asymptotic variance of $\hat{\theta}$ is "avar($\hat{\theta}$)." For example, the large-sample optimality concept of "asymptotic efficiency" is defined in terms of asymptotic variances: $\hat{\theta}$ is asymptotically efficient if and only if it is consistent for θ and there is no other consistent estimator of θ, $\tilde{\theta}$ for which $\text{avar}(\tilde{\theta}) < \text{avar}(\hat{\theta})$. The topic of asymptotic efficiency will arise in Chapter 17, in the context of maximum likelihood estimation. See Exercise 11-6 for more material on (and some practice with) the concept of asymptotic variance.

[13] If the V_i were IID with finite variance, then the LLN in Appendix 11.1 would imply that the sample variance of the V_i is a consistent estimator of σ_g^2, but that assumption has not been made about the V_i in this example – yet. Instead, only Equation 11-9 has been assumed. Thus, the consistency of the variance estimator in this example is, at this point, simply being assumed.

distribution discussed here has, to a reasonable extent, occurred – and that N is also large enough that the realized value (6.14) of the variance estimator $\tilde{\sigma}_g^2$ is a reasonably good estimate of σ_g^2.

Given all that, then the reasonable statistic for testing the null hypothesis H_o: $\mu = 3.0$ is

$$G_{test} = \left|\sqrt{812}(\overline{V} - 3.0)\right| \xrightarrow{d} G\left[0,\ \sigma_g^2\right] \tag{11-13}$$

for which we have a single realization,

$$g_{test} = \left|\sqrt{812}(3.20 - 3.0)\right| = 5.70 \tag{11-14}$$

The fact that g_{test} differs from zero is evidence against the null hypothesis. But is it *strong* evidence? If we believe that 6.14, our estimate of σ_g^2, is accurate, then g_{test} is $5.70/\sqrt{6.14} = 2.30$ estimated standard deviations away from its expected value (of zero) under the null hypothesis. So the null hypothesis is neither clearly consistent with our sample estimate of μ, nor clearly false. In fact, it might be possible to reject the null hypothesis with a rather small p-value – or it might not: the answer depends on just how little area there is under the density function for $\sqrt{N}\left[\overline{V} - \mu\right]$ to the right of 5.70 and to the left of -5.70. And we can't calculate that are without knowing more about the asymptotic sampling distribution of $\sqrt{N}\left[\overline{V} - \mu\right]$ than just its mean and variance.

That is where the Central Limit Theorem (or "CLT") comes into play: it specifies the rest of the shape of the asymptotic distribution of $\sqrt{N}\left[\overline{V} - \mu\right]$. As with the Law of Large Numbers, there are many versions of the CLT, each of which is specific to a particular set of assumptions about the underlying data, $V_1 \ldots V_N$. Our work here, however, will only require the most basic version of the CLT, which assumes that the V_i are identically and independently distributed with finite variance:[14]

The Central Limit Theorem {**Lindeberg-Lévy**}

$$V_i \sim \text{IID}(\mu,\ \sigma_v^2) \text{ implies that}$$

$$\text{plim}\left[\frac{1}{\sqrt{N}}\sum_{i=1}^{N} V_i\right] = \text{plim}\left[\sqrt{N}\,\overline{V}\right] = N\left[\mu,\ \sigma_v^2\right] \tag{11-15}$$

Recall that only the weaker assumptions of Equation 11-9 – that the V_i are uncorrelated and all have the same mean and variance – were needed in order to show that $\overline{V}$ is consistent for μ, but we then ended up not knowing enough about the asymptotic sampling distribution of $\sqrt{N}\left[\overline{V} - \mu\right]$ to actually complete our inference example. By assuming just a bit more – that the V_i are independent and identically distributed – we get the rest of the asymptotic sampling distribution: it is normal!

Now the example can be completed: If the V_i are assumed to be IID(μ, σ_v^2), then the CLT implies that $\sqrt{N}\left[\overline{V} - \mu\right]$ is (for this large sample) essentially normally distributed. Since g_{test} is $5.70/\sqrt{6.14} = 2.30$ estimated standard deviations away from its expected value (of zero) under the null hypothesis H_o: $\mu = 3.0$ this null hypothesis can be rejected with a p-value of .021. Additionally, an (asymptotically valid) 95% confidence interval for μ is $3.20 \pm 1.96\sqrt{6.14/812}$ or [3.03, 3.37].

Obtaining the asymptotic distribution of an estimator, such as $\hat{\beta}^{OLS}$, then consists of two parts. First one shows that the estimator is consistent (or not!) by computing its probability limit. This task

[14] See Mood and Graybill (1963, Section 7.6) for a proof of this version of the CLT using a moment generating function approach. The CLT assumptions can be weakened in many ways: the V_i need not all have the same variance, and substantial amounts of dependence among the V_i can be handled. Some parts cannot be weakened, however: CLT results obtain only for estimators which can be written as sums of zero-mean random variables with finite variance. Mood, A. M., and F. A. Graybill (1963), *Introduction to the Theory of Statistics*, McGraw-Hill: New York.

involves using the "algebraic" results in Appendix 11.1 to rewrite the estimator in terms of the probability limits of sample moments; then the LLN result is used to rewrite this expression in terms of population moments. That result generally makes it plain whether or not the estimator is consistent. For a consistent estimator, one then rewrites the estimator in a form such that the CLT can be employed. This is all done for $\hat{\beta}^{OLS}$, the slope estimator in the Bivariate Regression Model of Equation 11-1, in the next section. Unfortunately, the news on consistency for $\hat{\beta}^{OLS}$ is not good: it is quite easy for $\hat{\beta}^{OLS}$ to be inconsistent due to endogeneity in X_i. The sections which follow examine this issue.

11.4 ASYMPTOTIC RESULTS FOR THE OLS SLOPE ESTIMATOR WITH A STOCHASTIC REGRESSOR

In this section the asymptotic concepts introduced in Section 11.3 are applied to $\hat{\beta}^{OLS}$, the OLS estimator of the slope parameter in the Bivariate Regression Model of Equation 11-1. Using the result (from Exercise 11-1) that $\sum_{i=1}^{N} W_i^{ols}$ is zero, Equation 11-6, $\hat{\beta}$ can now be written as

$$
\begin{aligned}
\hat{\beta}^{OLS} &= \beta + \sum_{i=1}^{N} W_i^{ols} U_i - \overline{U} \sum_{i=1}^{N} W_i^{ols} \\
&= \beta + \sum_{i=1}^{N} W_i^{ols} (U_i - \overline{U}) \\
&= \beta + \sum_{i=1}^{N} \frac{X_i - \overline{X}}{\sum_{\ell=1}^{N} (X_\ell - \overline{X})^2} (U_i - \overline{U})
\end{aligned}
\tag{11-16}
$$

where the last step follows from substituting in the definition of W_i^{ols} from Equation 11-4. Letting Φ stand for the sum $\sum_{\ell=1}^{N} (X_\ell^2 - \overline{X})^2$, this becomes

$$
\begin{aligned}
\hat{\beta} &= \beta + \sum_{i=1}^{N} \left[\frac{X_i - \overline{X}}{\Phi} \right] (U_i - \overline{U}) \\
&= \beta + \frac{1}{\Phi} \sum_{i=1}^{N} (X_i - \overline{X})(U_i - \overline{U}) \\
&= \beta + \frac{\sum_{i=1}^{N} (X_i - \overline{X})(U_i - \overline{U})}{\Phi} \\
&= \beta + \frac{\sum_{i=1}^{N} (X_i - \overline{X})(U_i - \overline{U})}{\sum_{\ell=1}^{N} (X_\ell - \overline{X})^2} \\
&= \beta + \frac{\frac{1}{N} \sum_{i=1}^{N} (X_i - \overline{X})(U_i - \overline{U})}{\frac{1}{N} \sum_{\ell=1}^{N} (X_\ell - \overline{X})^2} \\
&= \beta + \frac{\widehat{\text{cov}}(X, U)}{\widehat{\text{var}}(X)}
\end{aligned}
\tag{11-17}
$$

Thus, taking the probability limit of both sides of Equation 11-17 and applying the results from Appendix 11.1,

$$
\begin{aligned}
\text{plim}(\hat{\beta}) &= \text{plim}\left(\beta + \frac{\widehat{\text{cov}}(X,U)}{\widehat{\text{var}}(X)}\right) \\
&= \text{plim}(\beta) + \text{plim}\left(\frac{\widehat{\text{cov}}(X,U)}{\widehat{\text{var}}(X)}\right) \\
&= \lim_{N\to\infty}(\beta) + \text{plim}\left(\frac{\widehat{\text{cov}}(X,U)}{\widehat{\text{var}}(X)}\right) \\
&= \beta + \frac{\text{plim}(\widehat{\text{cov}}(X,U))}{\text{plim}(\widehat{\text{var}}(X))} \\
&= \beta + \frac{\text{plim}(\widehat{\text{cov}}(X,U))}{\sigma_x^2} \\
&= \beta + \frac{\sigma_{xu}}{\sigma_x^2}
\end{aligned}
\tag{11-18}
$$

where the second step in Equation 11-18 uses the "Linearity" property (with $a = b = 1$), the third step uses the "Reduction to Ordinary Limit" property (since β is not random), and the fourth step uses the "Division" property.[15] Finally, the last two steps in this equation use the Law of Large Numbers property to evaluate the probability limits of the sample covariance of X_i with U_i and the sample variance of X_i.

Equation 11-18 implies that $\hat{\beta}^{OLS}$ will be a consistent estimator of β if the probability limit of the sample covariance of X_i with U_i is zero – i.e., if the explanatory variable is uncorrelated with the model errors and that $\hat{\beta}^{OLS}$ will be an ***in***consistent estimator of β if the explanatory variable *is* correlated with the model errors – i.e, if X_i is endogenous. Consequently, most of the remaining sections of this chapter will focus on the likely sources of such endogeneity.

Prior to that, however, this section closes with two additional comments on Equation 11-18 and by describing the results on the asymptotic sampling distribution of $\hat{\beta}^{OLS}$ derived in Appendix 11.2.

First, it is not quite correct to state that $\hat{\beta}^{OLS}$ is an inconsistent estimator of β whenever σ_{xu} is non-zero, as a careful examination of the second to last equation in Equation 11-18 shows that $\hat{\beta}^{OLS}$ is in fact consistent so long as $\text{plim}(\widehat{\text{cov}}(X,U))$ is zero, which actually only requires that any correlation between the explanatory variable and the model errors disappears as the sample size becomes large. This condition is called "asymptotic uncorrelatedness." This distinction between uncorrelatedness and asymptotic uncorrelatedness is not important for the economic sources of endogeneity discussed below, but it does turn out to be crucial for the consistency of the "two-stage least squares" estimator introduced in Chapter 12; this estimator can allow us to still obtain consistent parameter estimates despite serious endogeneity problems and is consequently widely used in empirical econometric work.

Second, in some settings the result in Equation 11-18 can yield very useful information on the *sign* of the inconsistency in $\hat{\beta}^{OLS}$. In particular, it implies that $\hat{\beta}^{OLS}$ will converge, for large samples, to a value which is larger than β if X is positively correlated with the model error term and that $\hat{\beta}^{OLS}$ will converge to a value which is smaller than β if X is negatively correlated with the model error term. Sometimes, as (for example) in the case of endogeneity induced by measurement error

[15] Note that the division property requires that the probability limit in what will become the denominator is not zero; and recall that $\sigma_x^2 > 0$ was assumed in Equation 11-1, because – if the population variance of X were zero – then all of the realizations of $X_1 \dots X_N$ would be the same value, precluding any possibility of estimating β.

considered in Section 11-6, it is possible to infer the sign of this correlation and use this result to predict the direction of the inconsistency.

The asymptotic distribution of $\hat{\beta}^{OLS}$ is derived in Appendix 11.2 using the Central Limit Theorem:

$$\sqrt{N}\left(\hat{\beta}^{OLS} - \beta\right) \xrightarrow{d} N\left[0, \frac{\sigma_u^2}{\sigma_x^2}\right] \tag{11-19}$$

Thus, the asymptotic variance of $\hat{\beta}^{OLS}$ is

$$\text{avar}\left(\hat{\beta}^{OLS}\right) = \frac{1}{N}\frac{\sigma_u^2}{\sigma_x^2} \tag{11-20}$$

which can be consistently estimated by

$$\widehat{\text{avar}}\left(\hat{\beta}^{OLS}\right) = \frac{1}{N}\frac{S_u^2}{S_x^2} \tag{11-21}$$

where S_u^2 and S_x^2 are the sample variances of the fitting errors and X_i,

$$S_u^2 \equiv \frac{1}{N}\sum_{i=1}^{N}\left(U_i^{\text{fit}}\right)^2 \quad \text{and} \quad S_x^2 \equiv \frac{1}{N}\sum_{i=1}^{N} X_i^2 \tag{11-22}$$

Therefore

$$\left[\hat{\beta}^* - 1.96\sqrt{\frac{1}{N}\frac{s_u^2}{s_x^2}},\ \hat{\beta}^* + 1.96\sqrt{\frac{1}{N}\frac{s_u^2}{s_x^2}}\right] \tag{11-23}$$

provides an asymptotically valid 95% confidence interval for β, where $\hat{\beta}^*$ is the realized value of $\hat{\beta}^{OLS}$, s_u^2 is the realized value of the sample variance of the fitting errors, and s_x^2 is the realized value of the sample variance of the X_i.

These expressions are all essentially identical to the analogous results for the model whose explanatory variable is fixed in repeated samples. Thus, if $\hat{\beta}^{OLS}$ is consistent – and presuming that the sample is sufficiently large as to make the use of the asymptotic sampling distribution for $\hat{\beta}^{OLS}$ reasonable – the computing formulas based on the fixed-regressor model (which are what is implemented econometric software) are still applicable in the stochastic regressors case.[16] Moreover, although the derivation in this section was based on the Bivariate Regression Model, all of the results obtained here in broad terms carry over to the Multiple Regression Model.

In either model, however, the OLS parameter estimates are consistent if and only if the stochastic regressors are at least asymptotically uncorrelated with the model error term. The next few sections will explore several modeling circumstances which induce endogeneity in an explanatory variable such that this asymptotic non-correlation condition fails. Chapter 12, however, will derive a technique – instrumental variables estimation – which can nevertheless provide consistent parameter estimates despite such endogeneity in an explanatory variable.

[16] With a large sample – which is the only setting in which the asymptotic sampling distribution of $\hat{\beta}^{OLS}$ is relevant anyhow – the prudent analyst would specify the computation of White-Eicker (heteroscedasticity robust) standard errors, however. This would ensure consistent standard error estimation in the face of violations of either the homoscedasticity assumption or of the assumption that $\text{cov}(X_i^2, U_i^2)$ equals zero.

11.5 ENDOGENOUS REGRESSORS: OMITTED VARIABLES

One way that a stochastic regressor can become endogenous is if another potential explanatory variable which is correlated with it has been wrongly omitted from the model. Suppose, for example, that the model to be estimated is specified as

$$\begin{aligned} Y_i &= \alpha + \beta X_i + U_i \quad i = 1 \dots N \\ U_i &\sim \text{NIID}[0, \sigma_u^2] \end{aligned} \tag{11-24}$$

whereas it is the regression model

$$\begin{aligned} Y_i &= \alpha + \beta X_i + \gamma Z_i + V_i \quad i = 1 \dots N \\ V_i &\sim \text{NIID}[0, \sigma_v^2] \end{aligned} \tag{11-25}$$

which is well-specified, in the sense that the error term V_i subsumes all of the influences on Y_i which are separate from (unrelated to, and hence independent from) the zero-mean variables, X_i and Z_i. In particular, this independence implies that V_i is uncorrelated (not linearly related to) X_i, so that cov (V_i, X_i) is zero.

Note that these two models – Equations 11-24 and 11-25 – together imply that

$$U_i = \gamma Z_i + V_i \tag{11-26}$$

Multiplying both sides of Equation 11-26 by X_i and taking expectations yields

$$\begin{aligned} E[U_i X_i] &= E[(\gamma Z_i + V_i) X_i] \\ &= \gamma E[Z_i X_i] + E[V_i X_i] \end{aligned} \tag{11-27}$$

which implies that[17]

$$\begin{aligned} \text{cov}(U_i X_i) &= \gamma \,\text{cov}(Z_i X_i) + \text{cov}(V_i X_i) \\ &= \gamma \,\text{cov}(Z_i X_i) \end{aligned} \tag{11-28}$$

The covariance of X_i with V_i, the model error in the equation including both variables, is zero because Equation 11-25 is assumed to be well-specified, as discussed above. Equation 11-28 thus specifies the circumstances in which the omission of Z_i from the regression model induces correlation between the still-included explanatory variable (X_i) and the U_i, the resulting model error in Equation 11-24. X_i is correlated with U_i – and this correlation does not disappear as the sample size increases – if and only if Z_i was wrongly omitted (so that $\gamma \neq 0$) *and* Z_i is correlated with X_i. This combination of circumstances, by the result in Equation 11-18, renders X_i endogenous and makes the OLS parameter estimator $\hat{\beta}$ (in Equation 11-24) inconsistent, as an estimator of β in Equation 11-25.

Note that this is basically the same result as was obtained in Section 9.7, the "Underelaborate Multiple Regression Models" section of Chapter 9. As there, the inconsistency in the least squares estimator is fundamentally arising because X_i is "proxying" (in Equation 11-24) for the omitted variable, Z_i. Thus, in a sense, $\hat{\beta}$ is not an inconsistent estimator in Equation 11-24: it is merely consistent for a different parameter – some mixture of the partial derivative of $E[Y_i]$ with respect to X_i (β in Equation 11-25) and of the partial derivative of $E[Y_i]$ with respect to Z_i (γ in Equation 11-25). This is still problematic, however, if what one needs for policy purposes – or, worse, believes that one is obtaining – is a consistent estimate of the first of these two partial derivatives.[18]

---

[17] Recall from Chapter 2 that cov(U_i, X_i), for example, equals $E[U_i X_i] - E[U_i]E[X_i]$ and that $E[X_i]$ is assumed to equal zero here.

[18] Alternatively, note that β means one thing (the partial derivative of $E[Y_i]$ holding both X_i and Z_i constant) in Equation 11-25, whereas β has a different meaning (the partial derivative of $E[Y_i]$ holding only X_i constant and averaging over Z_i) in Equation 11-24. Thus, it is no wonder that the two parameter estimates converge to different probability limits.

11.6 ENDOGENOUS REGRESSORS: MEASUREMENT ERROR

Another way that a stochastic regressor can become endogenous is if its observed values are corrupted by measurement error. Suppose, for example, that the true relationship to be estimated is

$$\begin{aligned} Y_i &= \alpha + \beta X_i^{\text{true}} + U_i \quad i = 1 \dots N \\ U_i &\sim \text{NIID}[0, \sigma_u^2] \end{aligned} \tag{11-29}$$

so that, if this model is well-specified, then the error term U_i must be independent of X_i^{true} – because it is subsuming all of the influences on Y_i other than X_i^{true}. Thus, U_i must be uncorrelated with X_i^{true}; hence, $\text{cov}(U_i, X_i^{\text{true}})$ and $E[U_i X_i^{\text{true}}]$ are both zero.

However, due to measurement errors, the actually-available observations on this explanatory variable are realizations of the corrupted variable, X_i. Letting M_i denote the measurement error corrupting these available observations,

$$X_i \equiv X_i^{\text{true}} + M_i \tag{11-30}$$

It will be assumed here that these measurement errors are identically and independently distributed with mean zero and variance σ_m^2. It will also be assumed that these measurement errors are uncorrelated with both the true values of the explanatory variable (X_i^{true}) and with U_i, the error term in the model for Y_i. Thus, $\text{cov}(M_i, X_i^{\text{true}})$ and $\text{cov}(M_i, U_i)$ are both zero, implying that $E[M_i X_i^{\text{true}}]$ and $E[M_i U_i]$ are both zero also.

Because the uncorrupted data – i.e., realizations of $X_1 \dots X_N$ – are unavailable, the regression model actually estimated is

$$\begin{aligned} Y_i &= \alpha + \beta X_i + V_i \\ &= \alpha + \beta\left(X_i^{\text{true}} + M_i\right) + V_i \end{aligned} \tag{11-31}$$

which, comparing Equations 11-29 and 11-31, implies that $V_i = U_i - \beta M_i$. Thus, Equation 11-31 can be rewritten as

$$Y_i = \alpha + \beta\left(X_i^{\text{true}} + M_i\right) + \left(U_i - \beta M_i\right) \tag{11-32}$$

The covariance between the explanatory variable in the model actually estimated and the error term in this model is therefore

$$\begin{aligned} \text{cov}\left[\left(X_i^{\text{true}} + M_i\right), \left(U_i - \beta M_i\right)\right] &= E\left[\left(X_i^{\text{true}} + M_i\right)\left(U_i - \beta M_i\right)\right] \\ &= E\left[X_i^{\text{true}} U_i - \beta X_i^{\text{true}} M_i + M_i U_i - \beta M_i^2\right] \\ &= E\left[X_i^{\text{true}} U_i\right] - \beta E\left[X_i^{\text{true}} M_i\right] + E[M_i U_i] - \beta E\left[M_i^2\right] \\ &= -\beta E\left[M_i^2\right] \\ &= -\beta \sigma_m^2 < 0 \end{aligned} \tag{11-33}$$

Thus, the measurement error in the (corrupted) explanatory variable actually used in the estimation model induces a correlation between this explanatory variable and the model error. This correlation will not change – and hence will not disappear – as the sample size becomes large, so Equation 11-18 implies that the OLS estimator $\hat{\beta}$ in Equation 11-31 is an inconsistent estimator of β.

Remarkably, Equation 11-18 allows the sign of this inconsistency to be predicted: if β is positive, then $\hat{\beta}$ will converge, for large samples, to a value which is too small; if β is negative, then $\hat{\beta}$ will converge, for large samples, to a value which is too large. This result can be very useful. Suppose that our theory predicts a positive value for β and that (using a fairly large sample) the OLS estimate of $\hat{\beta}$ is in fact positive, so much so that the null hypothesis H_o: $\beta = 0$ could be rejected using the estimated asymptotic distribution of $\hat{\beta}$ if $\hat{\beta}$ were credibly a consistent estimator of β. But $\hat{\beta}$ is clearly not a consistent estimator because measurement error in X_i is known to be a substantial problem. However, since Equation 11-30 implies that our OLS estimate is actually converging to a value *lower* than β, we can infer that, were the inconsistency in $\hat{\beta}$ removed, then this null hypothesis would be rejected with an even smaller *p*-value.

11.7 ENDOGENOUS REGRESSORS: JOINT DETERMINATION – INTRODUCTION TO SIMULTANEOUS EQUATION MACROECONOMIC AND MICROECONOMIC MODELS

Another source of endogeneity in explanatory variables is where the regressor is jointly determined with the dependent variable because the equation being estimated is part of a set of simultaneous equations. Endogeneity of this sort is so common in applied economic work as to be practically endemic.

One way to see why this is the case is to note that this kind of endogeneity is often alternatively described as being due to "reverse causation." This terminology arises because the essential source of this endogeneity is the breakdown of the causality assumption embodied in the usual regression model with fixed-regressors. In that model the sample fluctuations in the dependent variable are taken to be caused by fluctuations in the explanatory variable, but not vice-versa. (The sample variation in the explanatory variable – because it is "fixed in repeated samples" – cannot be caused by fluctuations in the dependent variable.)

Consider then, as an example, the consumption function in a simple macroeconomic model. This consumption function might explain sample variation in C_i (aggregate consumption expenditures) as being due to sample variation in aggregate income, Y_i:

$$C_i = \beta_1 + \beta_2 Y_i + U_i \tag{11-34}$$

But it is clearly untenable to assume that the causality runs only from aggregate income to aggregate consumption expenditures when (per the GDP identity) aggregate consumption expenditures form the bulk of aggregate income. In fact, it is a rarity to find an interesting explanatory variable in an economic model whose sample variation cannot, to one extent or another, be ascribed to variation in the dependent variable.

Why and how does this joint determination of dependent and explanatory variable cause endogeneity – and consequent inconsistency in the OLS parameter estimator?

Consider the quintessential microeconomic model, where the price fetched and the quantity traded of some good – athletic shoes, say – are determined by supply and demand in *N* similar markets and the *N* sample observations are the consequent market equilibrium values of price and quantity.

In this framework one would model the quantity of shoes demanded in the *i*th market as having been determined by utility maximization subject to a budget constraint. In the simplest possible setting, this yields a demand relationship like

$$Q_i^d = aP_i + bR_i + U_i \qquad U_i \sim \text{IID}(0, \sigma_u^2) \tag{11-35}$$

Q_i^d in this equation is the quantity of shoes demanded and R_i is some measurable, fixed, characteristic of the potential shoe customers in market *i*, such as average income or a taste parameter. In any practical setting there would be many such exogenous characteristics, but only one is specified here – and the intercept is dropped – just to keep the equations as simple as possible.[19] P_i is the price of a shoe;

[19] "Exogenous" means "determined outside the model," and hence taken as "fixed in repeated samples." Clearly, it is the opposite of "endogenous."

this is taken as fixed in the utility maximization "calculation" which the shoe customers implicitly perform. However, as will become apparent below, P_i is actually a random variable from the analyst's perspective, because of the two random error terms in the model: U_i, subsuming all of the other (unmodeled) characteristics of the customers in this market, and V_i, which will be the model error term in the supply relationship, to be specified shortly.

Equation 11-35 is the solution to the optimization problem of the customers in market i. It takes account of all of the customers' relevant characteristics – R_i and all of the rest, subsumed in U_i – and also takes as given the only market information the customers need: P_i. Thus, the parameters characterizing this equation – a, b, and σ_u^2 – do depend on the tastes and other characteristics of the customers, but not on anything else. In particular, these parameters do not depend on any characteristics of the shoe-producing firms. Equation 11-35 is called a "structural equation" and these parameters are called "structural parameters" because they speak to the underlying structure of the economic optimization problem faced by the customers – e.g., to their tastes with regard to shoes versus other goods. If this optimization problem has been well and gracefully posed, then it should be possible to use estimates of these parameters to say something specific and useful about this underlying economic structure. Importantly, these structural parameters might (indeed, should) depend on changes in the customers' tastes and circumstances – due to, say, shoe advertising, or to a change in the income tax rate. But – because they only depend on the customer characteristics and circumstances – these structural parameters are unaffected by changes in the shoe producers' circumstances, such as fluctuations in leather prices.

Similarly, in a basic version of this framework one would model Q_i^s, the quantity of shoes supplied in the ith market, as having been determined by profit maximization on the part of the shoe-producing firms in this market. In the simplest possible setting, this yields a supply relationship like

$$Q_i^s = cP_i + dM_i + V_i \qquad V_i \sim \text{IID}(0, \sigma_v^2) \tag{11-36}$$

In this equation M_i is some measurable, fixed, characteristic of the environment faced by the shoe-producing firms in market i, such as the cost of leather or a corporate tax rate.[20] Again, in any practical setting there would be many such exogenous characteristics, but here – to keep things as simple as possible – only one is specified and the intercept is dropped. The model error, V_i, subsumes all of the other, unmodeled characteristics and factors affecting the firms' profit maximization problem. P_i is again the price of a shoe; as with the demand function, P_i is taken as fixed in the profit maximization "calculation" which the shoe producers implicitly perform, but P_i is actually a random variable from the analyst's perspective.

Equation 11-36, again, is a structural equation: as the solution to the optimization problem of the producers in market i, it takes account of all of the producers' relevant characteristics – M_i and all of the rest, subsumed in V_i – and also takes as given the only market information the firms need: P_i. Thus, the parameters characterizing this equation – c, d, and σ_v^2 – do depend on the costs, technology (i.e., production function), and other characteristics of the shoe producers, but not on anything else – in particular, not on the characteristics and circumstances of the shoe customers. Again, Equation 11-36 is called a "structural equation" and these parameters are called "structural parameters" because they speak to the underlying structure of the economic optimization problem faced, in this case, by the shoe producers – for example, these structural parameters would depend on the production technology available to them. And, as with the demand relationship, if this optimization problem has been well posed, then it should be possible to use estimates of these parameters to say something specific and useful about this underlying economic structure. Importantly, these structural parameters might

[20] Numerous possible complications are being glossed over in this example, to keep it simple and clear. For example, this list could have included the wage rate shoe producers pay. But if R_i is household income and many households work for shoe producers, then this choice for M_i is not completely distinct from R_i – and so forth.

depend on changes in the producers' costs and circumstances – due to, say, a change in the cost of raw materials or a change in the interest rate on business loans – but (because they only depend on the producers' characteristics and circumstances) these parameters are – by construction – unaffected by changes in the tastes or incomes of potential shoe customers.

Thus, it is the structural parameters which need to be estimated here. These are the model parameters which are closely related to the economic structures – utility functions, production functions, and the like – which are of theoretical interest. And these are the parameters which are likely of the greatest interest for policy analysis, because a policy shift affecting, say, the technology used by the shoe producers should have an identifiable impact on the supply function parameters, while having no impact on the parameters in the demand function.

At first glance, there would appear to be no great difficulty in estimating the structural parameters in, say, Equation 11-35 – i.e., a, b, and σ_u^2. Presuming that one has obtained sample observations $(q_1^d, p_1, r_1) \ldots (q_N^d, p_N, r_N)$ – i.e., realizations of the random variables $(Q_1^d, P_1, R_1) \ldots (Q_N^d, P_N, R_N)$ – one can simply use the OLS estimators covered in Chapter 9.

The problem with this approach is that the resulting OLS parameter estimators yield inconsistent estimates of the structural parameters a and b. This inconsistency arises because – while (Q_i^d, P_i) are in fact observed – the values of these random variables are jointly determined as the equilibrium quantity and price in the ith market. That is, the variable P_i – which will be observed as p_i – has adjusted to make the values of quantity demand (Q_i^d) and quantity supplied (Q_i^s) equal. This equilibration makes one of the explanatory variables (P_i) in both regression equations endogenous – i.e., correlated with the model error. Consequently, from the results on the Bivariate Regression Model earlier in this chapter – Equation 11-18 – the OLS parameter estimators of all four parameters – a, b, c and d – are not consistent.

To see this explicitly, equate Q_i^d and Q_i^s in Equations 11-35 and 11-36 and solve for P_i:

$$aP_i + bR_i + U_i = cP_i + dM_i + V_i \tag{11-37}$$

so that

$$(a-c)P_i = dM_i - bR_i + V_i - U_i \tag{11-38}$$

Quantity demanded will ordinarily be an inverse function of price and quantity supplied will ordinarily be a direct function of price, so it is safe to assume that $a \neq c$, and divide both sides of Equation 11-38 by $a - c$.

This yields an equation expressing P_i in terms of the two exogenous variables and the two structural error terms:

$$P_i = \frac{d}{a-c}M_i - \frac{b}{a-c}R_i + \frac{1}{a-c}V_i - \frac{1}{a-c}U_i \tag{11-39}$$

Note that P_i depends linearly on both U_i and V_i! Thus, in general, P_i is correlated with the error terms in both Equation 11-35 and 11-36 and these correlations will not disappear (or even change) with larger sample sizes. Consequently, the OLS parameter estimates of a, b, c and d from using OLS to estimate Equations 11-35 and 11-36 are all inconsistent.[21]

Recall that because what is observed are the equilibrium market outcomes, P_i has adjusted to make Q_i^d equal Q_i^s. Thus, denoting both of these by Q_i and substituting Equation 11-39 into either Equation 11-35 or 11-36 yields the same equation for Q_i:

$$Q_i = \frac{ad}{a-c}M_i - \frac{cb}{a-c}R_i + \frac{a}{a-c}V_i - \frac{a}{a-c}U_i \tag{11-40}$$

[21] In fact, in Exercise 11-12 you will calculate $\text{cov}(P_i, U_i)$ and $\text{cov}(P_i, V_i)$ explicitly and show that they cannot both be zero unless U_i and V_i are perfectly correlated.

Two features are noteworthy about Equations 11-39 and 11-40. First, each of these equations can be treated as a regression model in its own right, by simply selecting a (capitalized!) symbol for the weighted sum of V_i and U_i. Thus, these two equations can be rewritten as

$$\begin{aligned} P_i &= \beta_{PM} M_i + \beta_{PR} R_i + D_i^P \qquad D_i^P \sim \text{IID}\left[0, \sigma_{DP}^2\right] \\ Q_i &= \beta_{QM} M_i + \beta_{QR} R_i + D_i^Q \qquad D_i^Q \sim \text{IID}\left[0, \sigma_{DQ}^2\right] \end{aligned} \tag{11-41}$$

where σ_{DP}^2 and σ_{DQ}^2 can be can be fairly easily expressed in terms of a, c, σ_u^2, and σ_v^2.[22] These are called the "reduced form" equations for P_i and Q_i. Note that – in contrast to the structural form equations, Equations 11-35 and 11-36 – one can use OLS to consistently estimate the coefficients β_{PM}, β_{PR}, β_{QM}, and β_{QR}. This follows because both M_i and R_i are exogenous and hence can be taken as "fixed in repeated samples." (Or, at worst, they can be taken to be random variables which are uncorrelated with both of the structural errors, U_i and V_i, and hence uncorrelated with the reduced form equation errors, D_i^P and D_i^Q.)

But these consistently estimated reduced form coefficients are not really what is wanted: what is wanted are estimates of the structural coefficients: a, b, c, and d. Why care about the difference? The reduced form coefficients are fine for estimating the impact of a change in, say, M_i on the expected value of the equilibrium price or quantity – those impacts are just what is quantified by β_{PM} and β_{QM}, respectively. However, because each reduced form coefficient is a mixture of structural coefficients from both the demand and supply structural equations, the reduced form coefficients do not relate clearly to either the tastes (utility function) implicitly underlying the demand relation or the technology (production function) implicitly underlying the supply relation – they depend on both. Because of this, from a policy evaluation perspective, a policy change which impacts only supply (e.g., in this case, a tax on leather) can be expected to change the values of all four reduced form coefficients; similarly, a policy change (such as an advertising campaign) which impacts only demand will also effect all four reduced form coefficients. In contrast, each such policy change would have affected only the relevant pair of the structural coefficients. So the reduced form coefficients are consistently estimatable using OLS, but they are not as useful.

What can be done? The most generally effective technique for dealing with endogenous stochastic regressors is the instrumental variables method described in Chapter 12. At this point, however, it is well worth noting that the example given in this section is itself so very simple that one can get consistent estimates of the structural coefficients using a much simpler approach, called "indirect least squares" or "ILS."

The ILS estimation method is applicable here because there is a clear one-to-one relationship in this case between the reduced form coefficients and the structural coefficients. Comparing Equations 11-39 and 11-40 to Equation 11-41, it is evident that

$$\begin{aligned} \beta_{PM} &= \frac{d}{a-c} \\ \beta_{PR} &= -\frac{b}{a-c} \\ \beta_{QM} &= \frac{ad}{a-c} \\ \beta_{QR} &= \frac{cb}{a-c} \end{aligned} \tag{11-42}$$

[22] But there is no pressing need to do so.

which implies, after a bit of algebra – in Exercise 11-13 – that

$$
\begin{aligned}
a &= \frac{\beta_{QM}}{\beta_{PM}} \\
b &= -\left(\frac{\beta_{QM}}{\beta_{PM}} - \frac{\beta_{QR}}{\beta_{PR}}\right)\beta_{PR} \\
c &= \frac{\beta_{QR}}{\beta_{PR}} \\
d &= \left(\frac{\beta_{QM}}{\beta_{PM}} - \frac{\beta_{QR}}{\beta_{PR}}\right)\beta_{PM}
\end{aligned}
\tag{11-43}
$$

The ILS estimators of a, b, c, and d are then

$$
\begin{aligned}
\hat{a}_{\text{ILS}} &= \frac{\hat{\beta}_{QM}}{\hat{\beta}_{PM}} \\
\hat{b}_{\text{ILS}} &= -\left(\frac{\hat{\beta}_{QM}}{\hat{\beta}_{PM}} - \frac{\hat{\beta}_{QR}}{\hat{\beta}_{PR}}\right)\hat{\beta}_{PR} \\
\hat{c}_{\text{ILS}} &= \frac{\hat{\beta}_{QR}}{\hat{\beta}_{PR}} \\
\hat{d}_{\text{ILS}} &= \left(\frac{\hat{\beta}_{QM}}{\hat{\beta}_{PM}} - \frac{\hat{\beta}_{QR}}{\hat{\beta}_{PR}}\right)\hat{\beta}_{PM}
\end{aligned}
\tag{11-44}
$$

where $\hat{\beta}_{PM}$, $\hat{\beta}_{PR}$, $\hat{\beta}_{QM}$, and $\hat{\beta}_{QR}$ are the OLS parameter estimates of β_{PM}, β_{PR}, β_{QM}, and β_{QR} in Equation 11-41. Using Property #5 (the Slutsky theorem) from Appendix 11.1, these continuous functions of $\hat{\beta}_{PM}$, $\hat{\beta}_{PR}$, $\hat{\beta}_{QM}$, and $\hat{\beta}_{QR}$ are thus consistent estimators of the corresponding functions β_{PM}, β_{PR}, β_{QM}, and β_{QR} and hence are consistent estimators of a, b, c, and d.

That is very nice, but notice that it rested upon our ability to solve for each of the structural coefficients as a unique function of the reduced form coefficients. That is feasible if and only if each structural equation is what is known as "exactly identified." Exact identification is by no means always – or even typically – the case in practice. When there is a multiplicity of solutions for the coefficients of a particular structural equation in terms of the reduced form coefficients, the equation is said to be "overidentified" and estimation via the indirect least squares method is not possible.[23] In such cases, however, the instrumental variables method described in Chapter 12 can be used.

11.8 HOW LARGE A SAMPLE IS "LARGE ENOUGH"? THE SIMULATION ALTERNATIVE

It should now be evident that in many real world settings, asymptotic properties – most commonly, just consistency – are the best that we can hope for. Construction of confidence intervals and testing of hypotheses then proceeds using the asymptotic distribution of the estimators. But our sample

[23] Conditions have been derived which enable one to determine the identification status of a particular structural equation fairly easily, but these will not be covered here. See, for example, J. Kmenta (1986, "Elements of Econometrics," MacMillan Publishing Company: New York, Chapter 13) for a fairly accessible treatment. It *is* worth noting, however, that the two structural equations in this model are exactly identified because each one of them excludes one of the exogenous variables.

sizes are plainly not "arbitrarily large." Any reasonable person would find this state of affairs troubling.

Fortunately, however, there is an alternative: simulation methods. These methods are computationally intensive, but that is usually not a big obstacle nowadays: instead of getting a practically instantaneous answer, one might need to go get a cup of coffee while the computation runs.[24] There are, however, several other serious problems with these methods and these are well to mention at the outset. First, simulation methods are just beginning to be implemented in available econometric software. Consequently, it is sometimes necessary to do a bit of custom programming in order to get exactly what one wants. Second, simulation methods still require that the data satisfy certain assumptions. In fact – as will be described below – these assumptions are in a sense even stronger than those of the Multiple Regression Model. Finally, in a sense also to be clarified below, these simulation methods themselves are only asymptotically justified. This last point is not as bad as it sounds, however: it merely means that one has to think carefully about the meaningfulness of what one is doing if the actual sample is less than, say, 40 observations – a wise practice in any case.

Simulation methods come in three distinct flavors: the "jackknife," "monte carlo simulation," and "bootstrap."[25] The bootstrap is more widely used in econometric work – and more widely implemented in econometric software – so it is emphasized here, with the other two approaches mentioned only in passing.

All three of these methods basically work the same way; here this will be explained in the context of estimating the slope parameter (β) in the Bivariate Regression Model. All three methods proceed by generating M "new" data sets, each of length N^*; the methods differ only in how this data generation is done, which will be described presently. M is commonly set to a fairly large number, such as 1,000 or 10,000; the idea is to set M large enough so that the results of interest are insensitive to the choice.[26] The value chosen for N^* may be equal to the original sample size (N) or not – indeed, the ability to examine how the inference results vary with the value chosen for N^* can be the principal point of the exercise.

The usual least-squares estimate of slope parameter (β) is then obtained using each of these M data sets, yielding M realizations from an approximation to the sampling distribution of $\hat{\beta}$. In particular, the sampling variance of $\hat{\beta}$ is estimated by the "sample" variance of these M realizations of $\hat{\beta}$ and the simulation-based estimated standard error for $\hat{\beta}$ is then obtained as the square root of this sample variance. In many implementations of these methods the sampling distribution is at this point taken to be gaussian, with mean equal to the true value of β and variance equal to this sample variance; hypothesis testing and the estimation of confidence intervals for β then proceeds in exactly the same way as was described in Sections 7.3 and 7.5.[27]

---

[24] Indeed, in practice the computation time is usually only an issue when one makes a mistake and needs to rerun it.

[25] Some authors refer to these last two methods as the "parametric bootstrap" and the "nonparametric bootstrap," respectively.

[26] And so that the results are also insensitive to the value of the "seed" used to initialize the random number generator. Larger values of M are necessary in order to effectively simulate the "tails" of a sampling distribution: e.g., with M equal to 1,000, the largest 1% of the simulated samples comprises only 10 simulated values. Generally speaking, a value of M equal to 10,000 is considered acceptable.

[27] Some implementations – notably including that in Stata, described in some detail in the next section – also provide an option to use the "percentile method" for constructing confidence intervals. Using this option, a 95% confidence interval for β (for example) is estimated as running from the 2½% quantile to the 97½% quantile of the sample of M values for $\hat{\beta}$, where the 2½% quantile is the value such that 2½% of the M values are less than this and the 97½% quantile is the value such that 97½% of the M values are less than this. Generally speaking, the percentile method requires larger values for M in order for the estimated confidence interval to stabilize – i.e., not change appreciably if the calculation is repeated with a different seed for the random number generator. More explicitly, most econometricians would expect that a value for M of 1,000 replications would suffice under the normal approximation, whereas many would want 10,000 replications when using the percentile method to estimate confidence intervals; especially, when using the percentile method, a 99% confidence interval requires a larger value for M than does a 95% confidence interval.

In the "jackknife" method each of the M new data sets is obtained by simply dropping one of the original sample observations. Clearly, in this method the value of N^* will most gracefully equal $N - 1$ and, there being at most N ways to drop an observation from the sample, the value of M cannot exceed N. The jackknife is less widely used because of these limitations.

In the "monte carlo" method, the parameters of the model (α, β, and σ^2, in the case of the Bivariate Regression Model) are first estimated using the actual sample data. Then it is assumed that these estimates are equal to the true values of the parameters and each new sample on $Y_1 \dots Y_{N^*}$ is obtained by using a random number generator to draw independent realizations from the distributions $N(\alpha + \beta x_1, \sigma^2) \dots N(\alpha + \beta x_{N^*}, \sigma^2)$. If the basic model (with $x_1 \dots x_N$ "fixed in repeated samples") is being simulated, then the same values for $x_1 \dots x_{N^*}$ are used in generating all M new samples on $Y_1 \dots Y_{N^*}$. This process is straightforward so long as N^* is no larger than N; where N^* exceeds N, then a typical implementation begins reusing the x_i – that is, x_1 is used for x_{N+1}, x_2 is used for x_{N+2}, and so forth. If the Bivariate Regression Model with a stochastic regressor (Equation 11-1) is being simulated, then the distribution of the X_i is estimated (using the N actual sample observations) and a new set of realizations for $x_1 \dots x_{N^*}$ is drawn from this estimated distribution for each of the M simulated new data sets. (If X_i appears to be continuously distributed, it is usually assumed to normally distributed for this purpose; if X_i is a dummy variable, then it is usually assumed to be generated by a binomial distribution.)

Note that in either case, the implied model error terms are identically and independently distributed for each of the N^* observations in each of the M new samples, so this assumption is being imposed on all of the generated data. If this assumption was not valid for the mechanism that generated the actual sample data, then the monte carlo simulated data can yield misleading results.[28] Note also that monte carlo simulation does not in any way alleviate the parameter estimation inconsistency which arises if X_i is endogenous. (Monte carlo simulation methods can, however, be applied to the instrumental variables estimator which will be covered in Chapter 12, and which *does* address this problem.) Finally, note that the monte carlo simulation approach is itself only justified for large samples, simply because the relevant parameters in the distributions used for drawing the monte carlo samples are necessarily estimated using the N original sample observations.

Many of these same issues arise for the "bootstrap" simulation method also, but it avoids the distributional assumptions necessary for the monte carlo method; the bootstrap is also easier to program into a statistical package for general use.

The application of bootstrap simulation to the fixed-regressor case of the Bivariate Regression Model will be described first. Here the intercept and slope parameters of the model (α and β, respectively) are still first estimated using the actual sample data and these two estimates are still taken as equal to the true values of these parameters, so that N values of the model error term ($U_1 \dots U_N$) are available: $y_1 - \alpha - \beta x_1 \dots y_N - \alpha - \beta x_N$. But σ^2 no longer needs to be estimated, and it is no longer assumed that U_i is normally distributed. Instead, the distribution of the model error term is approximated by the so-called "empirical distribution," which is a discrete probability distribution which assigns probability $\frac{1}{N}$ to each of the "observed" values $U_1 \dots U_N$. (The reason that "observed" is in quotation marks is that these values are observed only because α and β have been set equal to the sample estimates; of course, what is actually being done here includes approximating the model errors by the fitting errors obtained using the original sample data.) For sufficiently large values of N, this empirical distribution can be

[28] Thus, it makes no sense to apply monte carlo simulation methods to a regression model for which one wants or needs to use robust standard error estimates because one suspects the presence of heteroscedasticity in the model errors: one must first specify the model in such a way as to eliminate any heteroscedasticity in the model errors. Similarly – foreshadowing results to be obtained in Chapter 13 – it makes no sense to apply monte carlo simulation methods to a regression model for which one wants or needs to use Newey-West standard error estimates because one suspects the presence of serial correlation in the model errors: one must first specify sufficient dynamics in the model so that the model errors are credibly non-autocorrelated.

shown to be an arbitrarily good approximation to the actual distribution of the model errors – this is what is called the "bootstrap approximation." One can then obtain N^* approximations to draw from the actual distribution of the model errors by drawing N^* realizations from this empirical distribution.

This process of making new draws from the empirical distribution of the (fitting) errors is called "resampling" or sometimes just "bootstrapping." It proceeds by simply using a random number generator to draw N^* integers from the interval [1, N]. For example, if the first such integer drawn is 33, then the realized value of U_1 in this bootstrap sample is the 33rd of the fitting errors from the estimated model based on the actual data and y_1 is $\alpha + \beta x_1 + u_{33}^{fit}$; if the second such integer drawn is 8, then the value of U_2 in this bootstrap sample is the eighth of the fitting errors from the originally estimated model and y_2 is $\alpha + \beta x_1 + u_8^{fit}$. And so forth.

As in the monte carlo simulations, this is fine for the Bivarate Regression Model with a fixed-regressor and for which $N^* \leq N$ – in which case values for $x_1 \ldots x_{N^*}$ are available and the same values $x_1 \ldots x_{N^*}$ are used in generating all M new samples. But it needs to be modified (by reusing the observed values $x_1 \ldots x_N$) whenever N^* exceeds N. Bootstrapping a new set of data pairs – $(y_1, x_1) \ldots (y_{N^*}, x_{N^*})$ – from the Bivarate Regression Model with a stochastic regressor is even easier: one simply picks N^* integers at random from the interval [1, N] and uses these to specify which data pairs from the original sample are used in the new sample. For example, suppose (as before) that the first such integer drawn is 33; in that case the first bootstrap observation is (y_{33}, x_{33}). And if the second such integer drawn is 8, then the second bootstrap observation is (y_8, x_8). And so forth, until all N^* observations in the first bootstrap sample are selected. Then the process is repeated in order to obtain all M samples.

As with the monte carlo simulations, note that (for either the fixed-regressors or stochastic regressors case), the bootstrapped model error terms are – by construction – identically and independently distributed for each of the N^* observations in each of the M new samples. Thus, this assumption is being imposed on all of the generated data. Again, if this assumption is not valid for the mechanism that generated the actual sample data, then the bootstrap-simulated data can yield misleading results.[29] And note also that – as with monte carlo simulation – bootstrap simulation does not in any way alleviate the parameter estimation inconsistency which arises if X_i is endogenous.[30]

[29] Thus, as with the monte carlo simulated data, it makes no sense to apply basic bootstrap simulation methods to a regression model for which one wants or needs to use robust standard error estimates because one suspects the presence of heteroscedasticity in the model errors: one must first specify the model in such a way as to eliminate any heteroscedasticity in the model errors. Similarly – foreshadowing results to be obtained in Chapter 13 – it makes no sense to apply basic bootstrap simulation methods to a regression model for which one wants or needs to use Newey-West standard error estimates because one suspects the presence of serial correlation in the model errors: one must first specify sufficient dynamics in the model so that the model errors are credibly non-autocorrelated. In contrast to monte carlo methods, however, variations on the basic bootstrap can handle models with non-IID errors. For serially dependent data, one can use the "block bootstrap" – e.g., as described in Politis and Romano (1994) – whereas, for heteroscedastic model errors, one can use the "wild bootstrap" e.g., as described in Goncalves et al. (2004). One will usually have to program these oneself, however. Politis, D. N., and J. P. Romano, (1994). The Stationary Bootstrap. *J. Amer. Statist. Assoc., 89:1303–13*; and Goncalves, S., and L. Kilian (2004). "Bootstrapping Autoregressions with Conditional Heteroskedasticity of Unknown Form." *Journal of Econometrics 123*, 89–120.

[30] In principle, the bootstrap (and related simulation methods) can be applied to the instrumental variables estimation method to be covered in Chapter 12, which *does* address the endogeneity problem. In practice, however, the bootstrap does not work well with instrumental variables estimators. This is because the sampling distributions of these estimators are relatively fat-tailed, basically because many of the higher-order moments of their sampling distributions are not bounded. In contrast, the bootstrap-simulated variables are inherently discretely distributed draws from an approximating distribution with at most N possible values – clearly, the tails of this approximating distribution cut off sharply.

Finally, note that the bootstrap simulation approach is itself only justified for large samples. In the fixed-regressor model this is because the empirical distribution of the fitting errors from the original model is a good approximation to the actual distribution of the model errors only for large samples. In the stochastic regressor model this is because the empirical distribution of (Y_i, X_i) – placing equal weight on each of the N pairs (y_1, x_1) ... (y_N, x_N) – is a good approximation to the actual distribution of these pairs of random variables only for large values of N. Thus, the bootstrap simulation approach is not reasonable if the original sample size (N) is tiny – e.g., 10. On the other hand, the bootstrap, in particular, is known to usually yield good approximations to the sampling distributions of the resulting regression parameter estimators even for rather modest sample lengths – on the order of 40 to 50; see Active Learning Exercise 11b (available at www .wiley.com/college/ashley) for an example (and a qualification) of this. At the least, one can use the bootstrap with varying values of N^* to get a quantitative feel for how the regression inference results – hypothesis test p-values and confidence interval estimates – vary with the sample size. One can thereby more or less answer the question posed at the outset of this section, "How large a sample is 'large enough'?"[31]

11.9 AN EXAMPLE: BOOTSTRAPPING THE ANGRIST-KRUEGER (1991) MODEL

A number of econometric packages – e.g., Stata – have recently begun implementing bootstrap simulation methods in a relatively easy-to-use fashion.[32] An application of bootstrap simulation to a well-known study from the labor economics literature – Angrist and Krueger (1991) – provides a nice illustrative example of both the usefulness and the limitations of the Stata bootstrap implementation. Angrist and Krueger use a sample of observations on the logarithm of weekly wages and on the educational level (in years of schooling) of 329,509 U.S. men to estimate the impact of schooling on wages. Their model also includes year-of-birth dummy variables to allow for the fact that these men were born in years 1930 through 1939. The sample size here is obviously quite large but – as Angrist and Krueger were well aware – the usual least squares parameter estimators are inconsistent in this case because the education variable is endogenous. Consequently, this model will be reanalyzed in Chapter 12 as an example of the usefulness of instrumental variables estimation method introduced there to provide consistent parameter estimation despite such endogeneity in an explanatory variable. This endogeneity will be ignored here, however, so as to focus on using the Angrist-Krueger model and data set as an illustration of the bootstrap simulation method.

[31] See Ashley (1998) for an application – to testing the mean square forecast error from competing models in a short postsample period – in which a "double bootstrap" is used to approximately quantify the degree to which the bootstrap approximation itself is problematic because the sample is small. Bootstrap simulation methods are also used in situations where asymptotic results are unavailable or infeasible, such as where it is only possible to solve for the fitting errors (as a function of the parameter estimates) numerically because the model is too complicated for an analytic solution to be obtained. Ashley, R., 1998. A new technique for postsample model selection and validation. *Journal of Economic Dynamics and Control 22*, 647–665.

[32] In fact, Stata now implements the jackknife and monte carlo methods also, but these implementations are not as flexible as is the implementation of the bootstrap and will not be discussed here.

First estimating the Angrist-Krueger model using OLS, the relevant Stata command is:

```
regress lwklywge edu yr1 yr2 yr3 yr4 yr5 yr6 yr7 yr8 yr9
```

where *lwklywge* is the logarithm of weekly wages, *edu* is the number of years of schooling, and *yr*1 through *yr*9 are dummy variables which allow the intercept to shift for men born in years 1931 through 1939, respectively. After only a very brief pause, this command yields the regression output:

```
      Source |       SS       df       MS              Number of obs =  329509
-------------+------------------------------           F( 10,329498) = 4397.45
       Model |  17878.1592     10  1787.81592          Prob > F      =  0.0000
    Residual |  133959.716329498  .406556993           R-squared     =  0.1177
-------------+------------------------------           Adj R-squared =  0.1177
       Total |  151837.875329508  .460801788           Root MSE      =  .63762

------------------------------------------------------------------------------
    lwklywge |      Coef.   Std. Err.      t    P>|t|     [95% Conf. Interval]
-------------+----------------------------------------------------------------
         edu |    .071081    .000339   209.67   0.000     .0704166    .0717455
         yr1 |  -.0063875   .0050393    -1.27   0.205    -.0162644    .0034895
         yr2 |  -.0148384   .0049724    -2.98   0.003    -.0245841   -.0050927
         yr3 |  -.0175832   .0050325    -3.49   0.000    -.0274468   -.0077195
         yr4 |  -.0209993   .0049845    -4.21   0.000    -.0307688   -.0112297
         yr5 |  -.0328947   .0049515    -6.64   0.000    -.0425994     -.02319
         yr6 |  -.0317808   .0049557    -6.41   0.000    -.0414937   -.0220678
         yr7 |  -.0367121   .0049082    -7.48   0.000    -.0463321   -.0270921
         yr8 |  -.0368905   .0048656    -7.58   0.000     -.046427   -.0273539
         yr9 |  -.0481636   .0048468    -9.94   0.000    -.0576633    -.038664
       _cons |   5.017348   .0054706   917.14   0.000     5.006626    5.028071
------------------------------------------------------------------------------
```

Were it reasonable to assume that the education variable is fixed in repeated samples – or that it is stochastic but asymptotically uncorrelated with the model error term – then the estimated coefficient on edu_i in this regression model would be consistent. Because the sample is so large, this estimate is quite precise: estimated coefficient on edu_i is $.071081 \pm .000339$, yielding an estimated 95% confidence interval of [.07042, .07175].

These assumptions about edu_i are in doubt but, that is not the point here. This section examines the questions: How can one make Stata produce bootstrapped estimation results for this model? Will a bootstrapped estimate of this coefficient, its estimated standard error, and the resulting 95% confidence interval yield notably different results? Finally, having seen how to obtain bootstrapped results, which allow one to conveniently modify the sample size, how much data of this quality is actually necessary in order to reject the null hypothesis that this coefficient is zero at the 5% level – i.e., in order for the 95% confidence interval for the coefficient on edu_i to be sufficiently short as to not include the value zero?

In view of the fact that simple bootstrap simulation is inappropriate for a model with a heteroscedastic error term, it is useful to first re-estimate this model with robust standard error estimates. The Stata command for this is:

```
regress lwklywge edu yr1 yr2 yr3 yr4 yr5 yr6 yr7 yr8 yr9, robust
```

which yields output,

```
Linear regression                                      Number of obs =   329509
                                                       F( 10,329498) = 3482.92
                                                       Prob > F      =   0.0000
                                                       R-squared     =   0.1177
                                                       Root MSE      =   .63762

------------------------------------------------------------------------------
             |               Robust
    lwklywge |      Coef.   Std. Err.      t    P>|t|     [95% Conf. Interval]
-------------+----------------------------------------------------------------
         edu |    .071081   .0003815   186.34   0.000     .0703334    .0718287
         yr1 |  -.0063875   .0051236    -1.25   0.213    -.0164295    .0036546
         yr2 |  -.0148384   .0050521    -2.94   0.003    -.0247403   -.0049364
         yr3 |  -.0175832   .0050685    -3.47   0.001    -.0275172   -.0076491
         yr4 |  -.0209993   .0050622    -4.15   0.000    -.0309209   -.0110776
         yr5 |  -.0328947   .0050395    -6.53   0.000    -.0427719   -.0230174
         yr6 |  -.0317808   .0049703    -6.39   0.000    -.0415224   -.0220392
         yr7 |  -.0367121   .0048945    -7.50   0.000    -.0463052   -.0271191
         yr8 |  -.0368905   .0048564    -7.60   0.000    -.0464089    -.027372
         yr9 |  -.0481636   .0048334    -9.96   0.000    -.0576369   -.0386904
       _cons |   5.017348   .0060187   833.63   0.000     5.005552    5.029145
------------------------------------------------------------------------------
```

Thus, using a standard error estimator which is robust to heteroscedastic model errors, the estimate of the coefficient on edu_i is $.071081 \pm .000382$, yielding a 95% confidence interval of [.07033, .07182]. In view of the fact that the robust standard error estimate differs little from the usual estimates, it would appear that – while regressor endogeneity will turn out (in Chapter 12) to be a problem in this model – heteroscedasticity in the model errors is not.[33]

Thus, it is not unreasonable to use the bootstrap to obtain an alternative set of standard error estimates and confidence interval estimates for this model coefficient. This will first be done while continuing to maintain the same sample size in the bootstrapped samples as in Angrist and Krueger's actual sample. Ideally it would be possible to choose whether to bootstrap based on an assumption that the regressors are fixed in repeated samples or based on an assumption that the regressors are stochastic. Under the fixed-regressor assumption each of the M new data sets is obtained using bootstrap resampling to obtain 329,509 new fitting errors; this is done by picking these at random from among the 329,509 fitting errors from the OLS-estimated model. The ith new value for the dependent variable ($lwklywge_i$) is then obtained by adding to the ith new fitting error first the OLS intercept estimate (5.017348) and then the weighted sum of the ten explanatory variables (edu_i, $\text{yr}1_i, \ldots, \text{yr}9_i$) from the original sample, where the weights are the OLS parameter estimates: $.071081, -.0063875, -.0148384, \ldots, -.0481636$. In contrast, assuming stochastic regressors, the ith observation in a bootstrap replication is obtained by choosing a random integer ℓ (between 1 and 329509) and then setting $lwklywge_i$ in the bootstrap replication equal to $lwklywge_\ell$, the ℓth observation on $lwklywge$ in the original sample; setting edu_i equal to edu_ℓ, the ℓth observation on edu in the original sample; setting $yr1_i$ equal to $yr1_\ell$, the ℓth observation on the dummy variable $yr1$ in the original sample, and so forth. It is the latter (stochastic regressor) form of bootstrap simulation which is implemented in Stata; the Stata command for doing this is:

[33] Note that obtaining standard error estimates (for the OLS parameter estimates) which are robust to heteroscedastic errors is not the same thing as estimating the parameter estimates via LAD ("robust") regression. The latter is estimating the regression coefficients so as to minimize the sum of the absolute values of the fitting errors rather than the squared values of the fitting errors, yielding parameter estimates which are "robust" with respect to outlying observations. Re-estimating the Angrist-Krueger model using robust regression – for which the Stata command is "qreg *lwklywge edu yr1 yr2 yr3 yr4 yr5 yr6 yr7 yr8 yr9* , quantile(.50)" – yields an estimated edu_i coefficient of $.0656 \pm .0001$. This estimate differs from the OLS estimate of $.0711 \pm .0003$ by .0055, which would appear to be statistically significant. Thus, one might suspect the presence of a few influential outliers in the Angrist-Krueger data set and, indeed, looking at the relevant scatterplot (Figure 11-2 later in this chapter), it does look like there are a couple of suspect observations with only one or two years of schooling.

```
bootstrap , reps(1000) size(329509) seed(345) saving(c:\stataboot ,
  replace) : regress lwklywge edu yr1 yr2 yr3 yr4 yr5 yr6 yr7 yr8 yr9
```

or, equivalently:

```
regress lwklywge edu yr1 yr2 yr3 yr4 yr5 yr6 yr7 yr8 yr9 ,
  vce(boot , reps(1000) size(329509) seed(345) saving(c:\stataboot))
```

This command specifies that M equal to 1,000 bootstrap replications will be performed; the default value is 50 replications had the "reps" option been omitted. Similarly, this command explicitly sets the value of N^* to 329509, which here equals N. Stata would have defaulted to setting N^* equal to N if the "size" option been omitted; it is included here so that it will be clear how to change it later on. Unfortunately, another limitation in the Stata implementation is that it is not possible to set N^* greater than N. This command also specifies an initial "seed" for the random number generator, so that Stata will generate exactly the same sequence of random integers – and consequently yield the same set of M new bootstrapped data sets – each time this command is executed. Omitting the seed option causes Stata to generate a new sequence (and different estimation results) every time this command is issued. Each different value specified for the initial seed will yield slightly different results also, with the difference becoming negligible as the number of bootstrap replications increases. In fact, one can determine that the value chosen for the number of replications is sufficiently large by observing whether or not the bootstrap results differ appreciably for different seed values. The "saving" portion of the command specifies a location and filename – in this case specified as "stataboot.dta" in the root directory of the c: drive – which will contain the 1,000 replicated values of each model coefficient estimate; these will be labeled "_b_edu", "_b_yr1", ... , _b_yr9" in the resulting Stata file. This option is useful if one wants to compute summary statistics or a histogram, as illustrated below.[34] Finally, note that it is possible to specify the "robust" standard error estimation option for the regress command in the first of these two command formats, but this is not correct: one should not be using the bootstrap at all if the errors are heteroscedastic, as this violates an assumption (that the data are identically distributed) which underlies the bootstrap simulations.[35]

Using the Angrist-Krueger data set, this command takes about 30 minutes to execute on a reasonably fast Windows computer and yields the following output:

```
Linear regression                          Number of obs    =     329509
                                           Replications     =       1000
                                           Wald chi2(10)    =   36269.46
                                           Prob > chi2      =     0.0000
                                           R-squared        =     0.1177
                                           Adj R-squared    =     0.1177
                                           Root MSE         =     0.6376
```

[34] It is a good idea to specify descriptive file names, or else you will lose track of these files quickly. Stata gives the filename its standard extension, "dta" and format so that this saved file is easily opened in Stata. Note that the "vce(·)" form of the command does not accept a "replace" option, so it is necessary in that case to ensure that there is no file with this name and location prior to attempting to execute the command.

[35] Instead, one should be respecifying the form of the variables in the model – usually the dependent variable, in particular – so that the implied model error term is homoscedastic; or one could use the "wild bootstrap" – see Footnote 11-29. Similarly – foreshadowing results in Chapter 13 – bootstrap simulation is inappropriate for a time-series regression unless sufficient dynamics have been included in the model specification so that the model errors are non-autocorrelated. Thus, it would not be appropriate to bootstrap a model for which there was any need to compute the Newey-West standard errors covered in Section 13.7.

lwklywge	Observed Coef.	Bootstrap Std. Err.	z	P>|z|	Normal-based [95% Conf. Interval]	
edu	.071081	.0003748	189.64	0.000	.0703464	.0718157
yr1	-.0063875	.0051074	-1.25	0.211	-.0163977	.0036228
yr2	-.0148384	.0050178	-2.96	0.003	-.0246731	-.0050036
yr3	-.0175832	.0051043	-3.44	0.001	-.0275874	-.007579
yr4	-.0209993	.0050108	-4.19	0.000	-.0308202	-.0111783
yr5	-.0328947	.0052241	-6.30	0.000	-.0431337	-.0226556
yr6	-.0317808	.0050821	-6.25	0.000	-.0417416	-.02182
yr7	-.0367121	.0047276	-7.77	0.000	-.0459781	-.0274461
yr8	-.0368905	.0048962	-7.53	0.000	-.0464868	-.0272941
yr9	-.0481636	.0049453	-9.74	0.000	-.0578562	-.0384711
_cons	5.017348	.0059003	850.35	0.000	5.005784	5.028913

The routine reports the estimated coefficient on the education variable (*edu*) from the original regression; it reports the sample standard deviation of the 1,000 bootstrap estimates as the "Bootstrap Std. Err." To obtain the sample mean of the 1,000 values of _b_edu, simply open the file stataboot.dta (or whatever file you specified in the "saving" option) and use the summarize command:

```
summarize _b_edu
```

which reports the sample mean of _b_edu as .0710904 and the sample standard deviation of _b_edu as .0003748. It is quite typical that there is little difference between the original (OLS) estimate of the coefficient and the sample mean of the bootstrap estimates; this is why the sample mean of the bootstrap estimates is not ordinarily reported. Note that the bootstrapped standard error estimate on the *edu* coefficient (.0003748) does not differ very much from the OLS estimate of .000339; this suggests (as one might expect with a sample this huge) that the asymptotic distribution of the OLS parameter estimators is a good approximation to the actual sampling distribution – except for the (likely) parameter estimator inconsistency here due to endogeneity in the education variable, which will also occur in each bootstrap sample. While this file is open in Stata, it is instructive to make a histogram of the 1,000 bootstrap estimates, using the command "histogram _b_edu"; see Figure 11-1.

The bootstrap parameter estimates appear to be close to normally distributed. This is often the case; consequently, the reported bootstrap confidence interval for the education coefficient – [.07035, .071827] – is based on the assumption that the bootstrap coefficient estimates are normally distributed around their sample mean, with standard deviation equal to their sample standard deviation. A "percentile-based" confidence interval, as described in Footnote 11-27, is sometimes preferable because it does not rely on this normality assumption, but it requires more bootstrap replications than are needed to just obtain a bootstrapped standard error estimate. The summarize command does not output the two quantiles one would want for a 95% confidence interval, but they are easily obtained by sorting the data set on the values of _b_edu (using the Stata command "sort _b_edu") and browsing the data set to obtain the 25th and 975th sorted values, respectively.[36] The percentile-based confidence interval coefficient – [.07036, .07186] – is virtually identical in this case and both are very similar to the OLS confidence interval estimate of [.07042, .07175]. Percentile-based confidence intervals will turn out to be essential, however, in dealing with estimators (such as the two-stage least squares estimator introduced in Chapter 12) which have thick-tailed sampling distributions in finite samples.

[36] Or, more conveniently, one can follow the bootstrap estimation command by the "estat bootstrap , percentile" command, which calculates and displays percentile confidence intervals for each estimated coefficient. (This works substantially better than using the more sophisticated Stata "centile _b_edu , level(95)" command. It is also worth mentioning that the "test" and "testnl" Stata commands can be used after a bootstrap estimation to calculate p-values for testing linear and nonlinear null hypotheses involving the model coefficients; the use of the "test" command was illustrated in the applications of Sections 9.9 and 9.10.

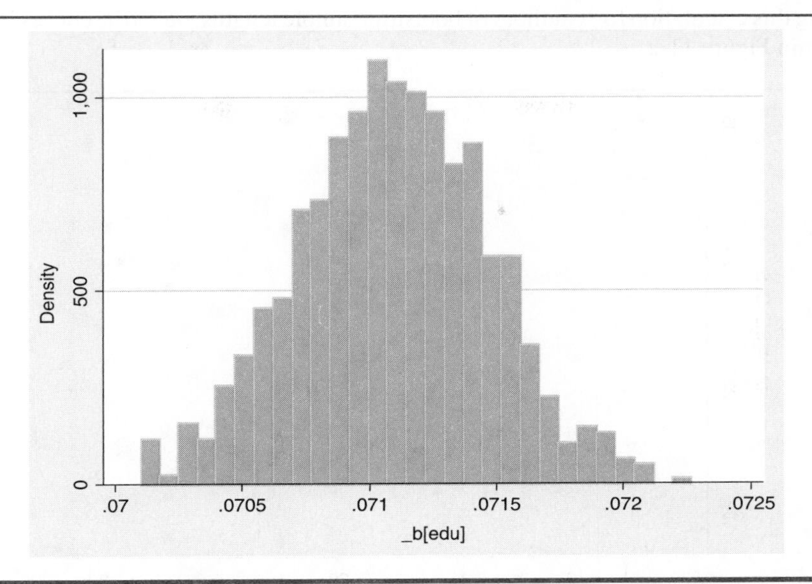

Figure 11-1 Histogram of Booststrapped OLS Slope Estimates for the Angrist-Krueger Model

Evidently it is a bit time-consuming, but not all that difficult (using Stata, at least) to produce bootstrapped regression estimation results. But in choosing to bootstrap one is losing the option of computing standard error estimates which are still consistent in the presence of heteroscedasticity: the bootstrapped standard error estimates are inconsistent unless one has specified the model well enough that (to a reasonable approximation) it has identically and independently distributed errors. Moreover – as we just saw with the Angrist-Krueger model – in large samples the bootstrap results are not all that different from the OLS results. One might expect the bootstrapped standard error estimates and estimated confidence intervals to differ more from (and be preferable to) the OLS results with smaller samples – e.g., less than a couple of hundred observations – where the asymptotic theory underlying the OLS results might well be breaking down. Of course, in truly small samples – e.g., less than, say, 40 observations – one should not expect the bootstrap approximation (replacing an actual distribution by an empirical distribution placing equal weight on each sample observation) to remain valid either.

Finally – since it is convenient to do so using bootstrap simulation – it is informative to examine how the bootstrapped standard error estimates and 95% confidence interval estimates change as the sample length is varied. The Stata implementation of the bootstrap does not allow the sample length to be increased, but it is already quite large in the Angrist-Krueger example.[37] Thus, the interest here is in obtaining analogous results with samples which are substantially smaller, but not so small as to make the bootstrap approximation itself suspect. The Stata command for calculating bootstrap estimates with new samples of (for example) 500 observations each is hardly different:[38]

```
bootstrap, reps(10000) size(500) seed(345) saving(c:\stataboot,
  replace): regress lwklywge edu yr1 yr2 yr3 yr4 yr5 yr6 yr7 yr8 yr9
```

[37] This, along with the absence of an option to keep the regressors fixed in repeated samples, is an instance of where one might still need to do some custom programming in order to get the simulation results one wants to have.

[38] Note that the regression output from this command will, in Stata version 10.1 at least, incorrectly indicate that the sample size is still 329,509.

Repeating this calculation for a number of bootstrap sample lengths yields the entries in Table 11-1 and the plot in Figure 11-2:

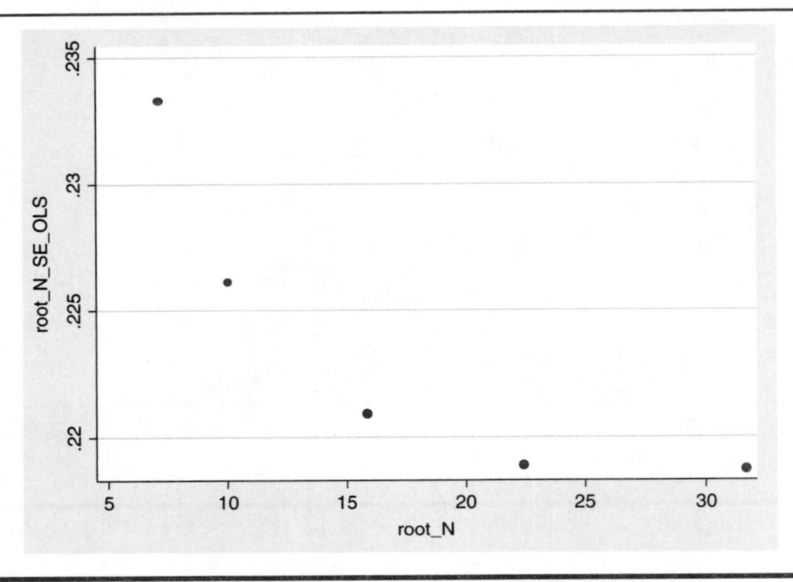

Figure 11-2 Plot of $\sqrt{N}$ Times the Square Root of the Bootstrap $\text{var}(\hat{\beta}_{edu})$ versus $\sqrt{N}$

Two conclusions emerge from these calculations. Note first that, since asymptotic variances are of the form {constant}/N, the bootstrap estimate of the sampling distribution of $\hat{\beta}_{edu}$ has essentially converged to the asymptotic sampling distribution when the quantity plotted in Figure 11-2 has converged to this constant. Looking at the corresponding column of Table 11-1 or at the plot in Figure 11-2, it is evident that the bootstrap estimate of the sampling variance of $\hat{\beta}_{edu}$ has essentially converged once one has well over 250 observations, but that a sample length less than around 100 observations is skimpy.[39]

Table 11-1 Bootstrap Confidence Intervals on the Angrist-Krueger Education Variable Coefficient

N^*	95% Confidence Interval	Estimated Standard Error	$\sqrt{N^*}$	$\sqrt{N^*}$ (Estimated Standard Error)
50	[.006, .137]	.0337	7.07	.2333
100	[.027, .115]	.0226	10.00	.2261
250	[.044, .098]	.0140	15.81	.2209
500	[.052, .090]	.0098	22.36	.2189

[39] It would be nice to be able to indicate that one can always use simulation methods to ascertain in this way how large a sample is needed in order for asymptotic variances to be reliable. Unfortunately – in all honesty – that is not the case. This is because some parameter estimators – notably including the two-stage least squares instrumental variable estimators discussed in Chapter 12 – have nice asymptotic sampling distributions, but disturbingly pathological finite-sample sampling distributions. In particular, only the lowest-order moments of the sampling distributions of such instrumental variables estimators are even bounded in finite samples. For this reason, a plot entirely analogous to Figure 11-2, but in which the two-stage least squares estimator of β is calculated for each bootstrapped sample instead of the OLS estimator, does not decline nicely at all as either N or $\sqrt{N}$ increases. Looking at the simulated values of such estimators, it is apparent that what is going on is that the estimator is usually fine, but occasionally (and not sufficiently rarely) it is way off. Consequently, bootstrap simulation does not always provide a resolution of our uncertainty as to how large a value of N is "large enough." On the other hand it does work well in many contexts (other than instrumental variables estimation) and – when it does work – a plot analogous to Figure 11-2 makes it plain that it is doing so.

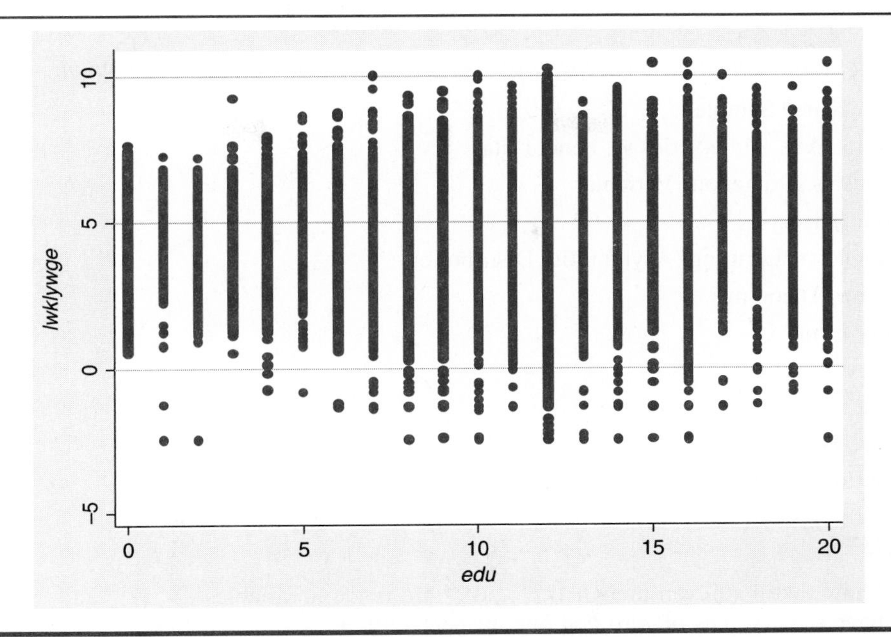

Figure 11-3 Scatterplot of the Logarithm of Weekly Wages ($lwklywge_i$) versus Years of Schooling (edu_i)

Second, note that the Angrist-Krueger estimate of the coefficient on years of schooling is significantly different from zero even for a bootstrap sample of 100, which is probably as small as is reasonable to use in this case.

On the other hand, it is unreasonable to expect this education variable to be uncorrelated with the model errors, so $\hat{\beta}_{edu}$ is most likely an inconsistent estimator of β_{edu}, which invalidates these inference results. This issue is taken up – and, in reasonable measure, resolved – in the next chapter, using instrumental variables estimation.

Finally, it is important to make one last point with the Angrist-Krueger model: While the estimated coefficient on β_{edu}, is *statistically* significant, that is not the same thing as *economically* significant. In fact, their estimate of the return to education – while positive and significantly different from zero at the 5% level even using just a couple of hundred bootstrap samples – is actually quite small, especially compared to the individual variation in the logarithm of weekly wages. The underwhelming slope in the scatterplot of $lwklywge_i$ versus edu_i (Figure 11-3) makes this plain.[40]

[40] The vertical striping in Figure 11-3 is due to the fact that the years-of-schooling variable is integer-valued. Also, recall that it is easy to misinterpret the slope in a scatterplot when there are multiple explanatory variables in the model. This is because the scatterplot implicitly averages over the values of all of the other explanatory variables in the model, whereas the remarkable strength of multiple regression is that it allows us to obtain an estimate of the partial derivative of the expected value of this dependent variable with respect to schooling. That partial derivative implicitly holds the values of the other explanatory variables constant – "conditions on them" – rather than averaging over them. However, since the other explanatory variables in the Angrist-Krueger model are just birth-year dummies, it seems likely that the scatterplot is not particularly misleading in this case.

KEY TERMS

For each term or concept listed below, provide a working definition or explanation:

Fixed in Repeated Samples
Cross-sectional vs. Time-series vs. Panel Data
Endogenous vs. Exogenous Variable
Asymptotic Theory
Finite Sample vs. Limiting (Asymptotic) Distribution
Central Limit Theorem
Probability Limit
Consistency
Asymptotic Variance
Asymptotic Efficiency
Structural Equation vs. Reduced Form Equation

EXERCISES

11-1. Show that that, even though $W_1^{ols} \ldots W_N^{ols}$ are random variables, $\sum_{i=1}^{N} W_i^{ols}$ and $\sum_{i=1}^{N} W_i^{ols} X_i$ have fixed values of zero and one, respectively.

11-2. Show that, if $\hat{V}$ is a consistent estimator for some parameter, then so is $\hat{V} + \frac{10^{1000}}{N^{.001}}$.

11-3. Show that, if $\hat{V}_N$ is an asymptotically efficient estimator for some parameter, then so is $\hat{V}_N + \frac{10^{1000}}{N^{\alpha}}$ for all values of α greater than one. An asymptotically efficient estimator is asymptotically unbiased and no other asymptotically unbiased estimator has a smaller asymptotic variance. Thus, asymptotic efficiency is the large-sample analogue of the efficiency property, defined in Equation 3-27. The asymptotic bias is simply the limit of the ordinary bias as N becomes unboundedly large. (See Footnote 11-12; a useful expression for the asymptotic variance of an estimator is given in Exercise 11-6.)

11-4. Referring back to Section 3.6, for $V_i \sim \text{iid}(\mu, \sigma^2)$ the estimator of μ of form $k\overline{V}$ with minimum mean square error has

$$k^* = \frac{\mu^2}{\frac{\sigma^2}{N} + \mu^2} < 1$$

Show that this estimator, while biased for any finite value of N, is still a consistent estimator of μ.

11-5. A space probe is launched to collect data on the Martian atmosphere with the intent of estimating a parameter θ characterizing the prevalence of oxygen. The probe will radio back atmospheric data – one observation per day – which will be used to calculate $\hat{\theta}$, an estimator of θ which is known to be consistent and even asymptotically efficient. The asymptotic variance of $\hat{\theta}$ is known to be $30/N$, where N is the number of observations.

Scenario 1: The probe lands safely.

Scenario 2: The probe's primary battery is damaged on landing and the first 20 days of data are lost while engineers figure out how to turn on the backup battery.

Scenario 3: The probe's radio antenna is damaged on landing resulting in a permanently weak signal, such that the data reaches Earth only 80% of the time.

a. Effectively, what is the asymptotic distribution of $\hat{\theta}$ under each scenario?

b. At any given time during the mission, the actual sampling variance of $\hat{\theta}$ is whatever it is, based on how much data have been received on Earth. If this analysis were done prior to launch, however, do the large-sample results speak to the question of allocating engineering resources between antenna design and battery reconfiguration software design?

11-6. Suppose that $\hat{\theta}$ is a consistent and asymptotically efficient estimator of θ. In each case answer the question if possible or state why an answer is infeasible. Hint: The asymptotic variance of any estimator $\tilde{\theta}$ can be obtained from

$$\text{avar}(\tilde{\theta}) \equiv \left(\frac{1}{N}\right)\lim\left(NE\left[\left\{\tilde{\theta} - \text{plim}(\tilde{\theta})\right\}^2\right]\right)$$

where the indicated limit is taken as N becomes unboundedly large. See Exercise 11-3 for a definition of asymptotic efficiency.

a. Calculate the plim$(\tilde{\theta} + 2)$ and the asymptotic variance of $\tilde{\theta} + 2$. Is this estimator consistent for θ? Is it asymptotically efficient for θ?

b. Calculate the plim$(.7\tilde{\theta})$ and the asymptotic variance of $.7\tilde{\theta}$. Is this estimator consistent for θ? Is it asymptotically efficient for θ?

c. Calculate the plim$(\sqrt{\hat{\theta}})$ and the asymptotic variance of $\sqrt{\hat{\theta}}$. Is this estimator consistent for $\sqrt{\theta}$? Is it asymptotically efficient for $\sqrt{\theta}$?

11-7. Suppose that S^2 is an unbiased and consistent estimator of σ^2, the variance of the error term, U_i, in a regression equation.

a. Is S an unbiased estimator of the standard deviation of u_i – i.e., for the square root of its variance?

b. Is S a consistent estimator of the standard deviation of u_i – i.e., for the square root of its variance?

11-8. Show that the sample correlation between two random variables is a consistent estimator of the corresponding population correlation.

11-9. Consider two estimators of the variance of the model error, U_i, in the Multiple Regression Model of Chapter 9, where N is the sample size and k is the number of explanatory variables (including the intercept) in the model

$$S^2 = \frac{1}{N-k}\sum_{i=1}^{N}\left(U_i^{\text{fit}}\right)^2$$

$$\hat{\sigma}^2 = \frac{1}{N}\sum_{i=1}^{N}\left(U_i^{\text{fit}}\right)^2 = \frac{N-k}{N}S^2$$

The observed fitting errors for the model are $u_1^{\text{fit}} \dots u_N^{\text{fit}}$, the realizations of the random variables, $U_1^{\text{fit}} \dots U_N^{\text{fit}}$. Under the assumptions of this model, S^2 is an unbiased and consistent estimator of σ^2, the variance of U_i.

a. Calculate the bias in $\hat{\sigma}^2$. Is this estimator always biased? Does the bias disappear as N becomes arbitrarily large?

b. Compare plim$(\hat{\sigma}^2)$ and plim(S^2). Is $\hat{\sigma}^2$ a consistent estimator of σ^2?

c. Show that var$(\hat{\sigma}^2) <$ var(S^2).

11-10. Use the asymptotic distribution of $\hat{\beta}$ given in Equation 11-19 – and the realized values of s_u^2 and s_x^2 – to test the null hypothesis H_o: $\beta = 4$ against the alternative hypothesis H_o: $\beta \neq 4$.

11-11. In an influential article in the *American Economic Review*[41] Acemoglu and coauthors analyzed the role that the quality of a country's institutions play in its economic growth. Using data on a cross-section of 64 countries, they found that the logarithm of 1995 per capita output for the *i*th country (Y_i) is directly related to R_i, an index that measures protection against arbitrary expropriation afforded by the *i*th country's legal institutions.[42] In particular, using OLS, their estimated regression model is

$$\log y_i = \underset{(0.41)}{4.66} + \underset{(0.06)}{0.52}\, R_i + n_i \qquad \overline{R}^2 = .533$$

where the figures in parentheses are estimated standard errors and $\overline{R}^2$ is R^2 adjusted for degrees of freedom. The coefficient on R_i would appear to be statistically significant and positive, but Acemoglu et al. worry that this OLS parameter estimate is the realization of an inconsistent estimator because R_i is a very noisy measurement of an underlying "true" index of institution quality. Presuming this to be the case, would a regression equation estimated using this "true" index be likely to produce a smaller or a larger estimate of the coefficient on R_i?

11-12. Using the pair of regression models given by Equations 11-35 and 11-36, let σ_{uv} denote $\text{cov}(U_i, V_i)$ and let ρ_{uv} denote $\text{corr}(U_i, V_i)$. Assume that the variables M_i and R_i are exogenous – that is, uncorrelated with the structural errors U_i and V_i.

a. Show that the reduced form equation for P_i is

$$P_i = \frac{d}{a-c}M_i - \frac{b}{a-c}R_i + \frac{1}{a-c}V - \frac{1}{a-c}U_i$$

as given in Equation 11-39. Why is it obvious that $a - c < 0$?

b. Show that the covariance between P_i and the model error in the demand relation is

$$\text{cov}(P_i, U_i) = \frac{\sigma_u \sigma_v}{a-c}\left(\rho_{uv} - \frac{\sigma_u}{\sigma_v}\right)$$

where ρ_{uv} is the correlation between U_i and V_i. Clearly, P_i is in general correlated with U_i. Consequently, OLS does not in general provide consistent estimators of the structural coefficients *a* and *b*.

c. Show that the covariance between P_i and the model error in the supply relation is

$$\text{cov}(P_i, V_i) = \frac{\sigma_u \sigma_v}{a-c}\left(\frac{\sigma_v}{\sigma_u} - \rho_{uv}\right)$$

Clearly, P_i is in general correlated with V_i. Consequently, OLS does not in general provide consistent estimators of the structural coefficients *c* and *d*.

d. Combine these results to show that the only way OLS estimation of both structural equations can yield consistent estimates is if U_i and V_i are perfectly correlated, in which case there is an exact linear relationship between them and hence really only one random error term in this two-equation system.

---

[41] Acemoglu, D., S. Johnson, and J. A. Robinson (2001) "The Colonial Origins of Comparative Development: An Empirical investigation." *American Economic Review 91(5)*, 1369–1401; this article is available on the web at www.jstor.org/sici?sici=0002-8282%28200112%2991%3A5%3C1369%3ATCOOCD%3E2.0.CO%3B2-9&cookieSet=1. In particular, see the "Base Sample" column of Table 2. You will work with their data in Active Learning Exercise 12a at the end of the next chapter.

[42] R_i varies over a range from zero to 10; for example, R_i is 10.00 for the U.S., 9.32 for Singapore, 8.27 for India, 6.27 for Ghana, and 4.00 for Mali. See Acemoglu et al. (2001, pp. 1377–78) for more details.

11-13. Using Equation 11-42, solve for Equation 11-44, the consistent Indirect Least Squares (ILS) estimators of the structural coefficients: a, b, c, and d.

Active Learning Exercise 11a: Central Limit Theorem Convergence for $\hat{\beta}^{OLS}$ in the Bivariate Regression Model

Introduction

With a stochastic regressor, it is clear from Equation 11-6,

$$\hat{\beta}^{OLS} = \beta + \sum_{i=1}^{N} W_i^{ols} U_i \quad \text{(ALE11a-1)}$$

that an assumption that the model errors (U_i) of the Bivariate Regression Model are normally distributed is no longer sufficient to imply that the slope estimator $\hat{\beta}^{OLS}$ is normally distributed. This is because the OLS weights (Equation 11-4) are now themselves random variables:

$$W_i^{ols} = \frac{X_i - \overline{X}}{\sum_{\ell=1}^{N} \left(X_\ell - \overline{X}\right)^2} \quad \text{(ALE11a-2)}$$

and $X_1 \dots X_N$ are now taken to be random variables.

Instead, the sampling distribution of $\hat{\beta}^{OLS}$ – including both its form and its variance – is now obtained asymptotically, using the Central Limit Theorem derivation detailed in Appendix 11.2, yielding the result,

$$\sqrt{N}\left(\hat{\beta}^{OLS} - \beta\right) \xrightarrow{d} N\left[0, \frac{\sigma_u^2}{\sigma_x^2}\right] \quad \text{(ALE11a-3)}$$

where σ_u^2 is the variance of U_i and σ_x^2 is the variance of X_i.

This asymptotic result is based instead on an assumption that U_i and X_i are each identically and independently distributed – and additional assumptions given in Equation 11-1. These assumptions together ensure that

$$V_i = \frac{X_i U_i}{\sigma_x^2} \sim \text{IID}\left(0, \frac{\sigma_u^2}{\sigma_x^2}\right) \quad \text{(ALE11a-4)}$$

The details of the derivation are given in Appendix 11.2, but the result for the asymptotic sampling distribution of $\sqrt{N}\left(\hat{\beta}^{OLS} - \beta\right)$ basically follows from applying the Lindeberg-Lévy form of the Central Limit Theorem, which can here be restated as

$$V_i \sim \text{IID}(0, \sigma_v^2) \Rightarrow \sqrt{N}\,\overline{V} \xrightarrow{d} N\left[0, \sigma_v^2\right] \quad \text{(ALE11a-5)}$$

It is well known that this convergence in distribution implied by the Central Limit Theorem does not usually require very large values of N for adequate convergence near the mean of $\sqrt{N}\,\overline{V}$. The purpose of this Active Learning Exercise is to investigate the convergence of this asymptotic approximation to the sampling distribution of $\sqrt{N}\overline{V} =$

$\sqrt{N}\left(\hat{\beta}^{OLS} - \beta\right)$ – i.e., Equation ALE11a-3 – in its *tails*, which are what is relevant for inference on β.

In particular, you will use X_i data that are generated from several distributions which are qualitatively relevant to applied economic analysis. To that end, while U_i will be assumed NIID(0,1), three separate assumptions – each corresponding to a kind of explanatory variable one might encounter in practice – will be made as to the distribution of the explanatory variable, X_i. First, it will be assumed that the X_i are uniformly distributed – this is intended to correspond to an explanatory variable whose values are well-scattered, but not normally distributed. Second, it will be assumed that the X_i are non-normally distributed in the opposite way, by drawing them from the Student's t distribution with four degrees of freedom, whose density function is bell-shaped, but with substantially fatter tails than the normal distribution density function. Finally, it will be assumed that the X_i are binomially distributed, taking on one value with probability P equal to 0.30 and the other value with probability P equal to 0.70. This latter specification corresponds to a dummy variable separating the sample observations into two groups, corresponding to different genders (in household data) or to different levels of development (in international data).

In each case you will use one of the three computer programs supplied with this exercise (ALE11a_uniform_X.exe, ALE11a_students_tee_X.exe, and ALE11a_binomial_X.exe) to generate a large number (M) of data sets – $(y_1, x_1) \ldots (y_N, x_N)$ – from the Bivariate Regression Model,

$$Y_i = 1.0 + 2.0X_i + U_i \qquad U_i \sim \text{NIID}(0, 1) \tag{ALE11a-6}$$

Each of these M data sets will constitute one "replication" or "trial." These three programs then estimate the slope coefficient in this model using OLS and compute M realizations of

$$\frac{\sqrt{N}\left(\hat{\beta}^{OLS} - \beta\right)}{\sqrt{\sigma_u^2/\sigma_x^2}} \quad \text{and} \quad \frac{\sqrt{N}\left(\hat{\beta}^{OLS} - \beta\right)}{\sqrt{s_u^2/s_x^2}} \tag{ALE11a-7}$$

Note that one of these statistics depends on knowing σ_u^2 and σ_x^2, the population variances of U_i and X_i, but the other statistic is completely computable from the sample data set for each trial, at least for given β. From the Central Limit Theorem, each of these statistics should approximately be a drawing from the unit normal distribution if N is large. Hence 99% of these realizations should lie in the interval [−2.576, 2.576] if the Central Limit Theorem has "converged" this far out in the tails of the sampling distribution of $\hat{\beta}^{OLS}$. Your task will be to investigate the extent to which this convergence actually occurs (for several values of N) under these three different assumptions on the distribution of $X_1 \ldots X_N$.

Your Assignment:

1. Copy the program files ALE11a_uniform_X.exe, ALE11a_students_tee_X.exe, and ALE11a_binomial_X.exe (available at www.wiley.com/college/ashley) to your hard disk.
2. Begin by executing ALE11a_uniform_X.exe; this program generates X_i as a random variable uniformly distributed on the interval [0.0, 1.0].[43] The program will prompt you to enter a value for N, the number of observations on (Y_i, X_i) to generate on each trial. Simply

[43] The programs for this exercise execute properly in Windows XP and Windows 7 – or emulators of same – but do not work in all versions of Windows Vista.

type in a number in the interval [2, 5,000] and press the "Enter" key. Looking at part 4, it is reasonable to begin with a value of 1,000 observations for N. If you mistype an entry at this (or any later point), just kill the window by mouse-clicking on the × in the upper right-hand corner of the window, or press the "Ctrl" and "Break" keys on the keyboard.

The program will then prompt you to enter a value for M, the number of trials to be generated. Set this to a small number the first time you run the program – e.g., 5 – so that you will see some kind of result promptly, but M will routinely be set to 100,000 trials for the calculations you will do to fill in Table ALE11a. The program will then prompt you to enter a value for "alpha" (the population value of the model intercept) and "beta" (the population value of the model slope parameter). These can be set to '1.0' and '2.0' here – their values are actually immaterial to the results you will be obtaining in this exercise. Finally, the program will prompt you to enter an initial 'seed' integer to initialize the random number generator used in producing the realizations of X_i and U_i.[44] The program will then execute for a bit, perhaps for several minutes if you choose larger values of N and M. Then it will write two files to your hard disk and close up its window.

3. The first file generated is named "ALE11a_uniform_first_trial.csv." It is a text file containing the observations (y_1, x_1) ... (y_N, x_N) generated for the first trial, in a comma delimited form which can be read in by any spreadsheet or statistical program. Read this file into the econometrics software your course is using, estimate the regression of the variable y on the variable x, and turn in a printout of your results. With $N = 5{,}000$, the parameter estimates should closely echo the values you specified. Also produce and print out a histogram of the generated data on X_i: The shape of this histogram should be consistent with X_i being uniformly distributed on the interval [0.0, 1.0]. Note down the slope estimate and its estimated standard error.
4. The second file generated is named "ALE11a_uniform.csv." It is a text file containing the M calculated realizations of the two statistics given in Equation ALE11a-7, again in comma delimited format, so that it is easily read by any spreadsheet or statistical program. Print out and turn in the first few rows of this file. Confirm that the first entry under the "zee_squared_used" heading equals the quotient obtained by dividing the deviation of your $\hat{\beta}^{OLS}$ estimate (obtained above) from the value of β you entered (2.0, if you followed the directions in part 2), divided by the estimated standard error you obtained above for your estimate.[45]
5. Now repeat this calculation specifying N equal to 10 and M equal to 100,000. If the statistical software you are using will accommodate it, read the resulting

[44] This seed can be any positive integer you choose; if you make note of the seed you specify, then your results can be precisely duplicated. See Active Learning Exercise 3a for a description of how uniformly distributed random numbers are generated on a computer. Source code for each of the programs used in this exercise is found at www.wiley.com/college/ashley in files with extension "for". Subroutine RAN1 generates a uniform random number between zero and one using a linear congruential random number generator which is a variation on that described in Active Learning Exercise 3a. It is taken from (and documented in) *Numerical Recipes* (Press et al. Cambridge University Press: Cambridge, pp. 195–97.) Pairs of uniform random numbers from RAN1 are used to generate normally distributed variates using the routine GASDEV, from *Numerical Recipes* (p. 202).

[45] The agreement will be close, but not exact, because the simulation software computes the unbiased estimator of the variance of X_i, which divides the sum of the squared deviations of the x_i by $(N-1)$, whereas the regression software effectively divides by N.

"ALE11a_uniform.csv" file into it; if your software will not deal with this large a file, you will need to complete the assignment using a spreadsheet.[46]

a. Make a histogram of both variables; if your statistical software allows for this, have it overlay on this histogram plot the normal density with population mean and variance corresponding to the sample mean and variance of the data.[47] Do you notice a minor discrepancy between the normal density and the histogram of one of these variables at N equal to 10?

b. Next complete one entry in Table ALE11a by computing the fraction of each of these 100,000 realizations whose magnitude exceeds 2.576, the ½% critical point of the unit normal distribution. For the variable zee_ssquared_used, this is effectively an estimate of the coverage of the corresponding 99% confidence interval given as Equation 11-23.[48] Quote your figures to three decimal places.[49]

6. Repeat the calculations from Part 5b, so as to complete the "$X_i \sim$ uniform [0, 1]" section of Table ALE11a for $N = 25$, 50, and 100.

7. Repeat the calculations for Part 3 and Part 5b, now using the program "ALE11a_students_tee_X.exe." This program generates the X_i values as draws from the Student's t distribution with four degrees of freedom.[50] When you repeat Part 3, you will observe from the histogram of $x_1 \dots x_{1000}$ that this distribution is bell-shaped, but has a sharper central peak and fatter tails than does the unit normal distribution. As in Parts 5b and 6, now complete the "$X_i \sim$ Student's $t(4)$" section of Table ALE11a for $N = 10$, 25, 50, and 100.

8. Finally, repeat the calculations for Part 3 and Part 5b, now using the program "ALE11a_binomial_X.exe." This program generates the X_i values as draws from the Binomial distribution, in which X_i takes on the value 0.0 with probability .3 and the value 1.0 with probability 0.7.[51] When you repeat Part 3, you will observe from the histogram of $x_1 \dots x_{1000}$ that this distribution is totally unlike the unit normal distribution, but it is very relevant to consider here, as data on an explanatory variable which is a dummy variable

---

[46] Or set a much smaller value for M and obtain substantially less clarifying results – check with your instructor on this point.

[47] In Stata, for example, the command "histogram zee_sigma_used , normal" does this.

[48] In a spreadsheet, you might sort each column and observe the row numbers for which the statistic first exceeds −2.576 and then exceeds 2.576. In Stata it is easier to execute the command, "sum zee_ssquared_used if zee_ssquared_used <= 2.576 & zee_ssquared_used >= -2.576" and divide the resulting number of observations used by 100,000.

[49] With $M = 100{,}000$ trials, each entry in Table ALE11a will vary a bit with the seed chosen; these figures are themselves asymptotically distributed $N[c, c(1-c)/M]$, where c is the actual confidence interval coverage. The value of 1.960 times the square root of (0.01)(0.99)/100000. is 0.00062. Thus, an estimated 95% confidence interval quantifying the uncertainty of the estimates in this table is the value given, plus or minus .00062. That is why it is pointless to record these entries to more than three decimal places; it is also why the value of M was set so high in this exercise.

[50] These are generated in ALE11a_students_tee_X.exe directly using the characterization of the Student's t distribution given in Equation 7-23 of Section 7.8, which references the characterization of the χ^2 distribution given in Equation 4-20 of Section 4.5. First, a $\chi^2(4)$ variate (Q) is created, by generating four independent unit normal variates and adding up their squared values. Then the $t(4)$ variate is created by generating another independent unit normal and dividing it by the square root of (Q/4).

[51] These variates are generated in ALE11a_binomial_X.exe by generating a variate which is uniformly distributed on the interval [0, 1] and setting x_i equal to zero when this uniform variate is less than 0.3 and equal to one otherwise. This procedure is apt to occasionally produce generated explanatory variable data sets $x_1 \dots x_N$ which are entirely equal to one or zero if the value of N is not large. In such cases, βx_i is not distinguishable from the intercept term – and hence β is impossible to estimate – so $x_1 \dots x_N$ were simply redrawn in each such instance. (Yes, that implies that $X_1 \dots X_N$ are not precisely independent of one another.)

would typically look just like this. As in Parts 5b and 6, now complete the "$X_i \sim$ Binomial ($P = .3$)" section of Table ALE11a for $N = 10, 25, 50$, and 100.

9. Examining the results you have collected in Table ALE11a, what conclusion can you draw as to the convergence of the Central Limit Theorem this far out into the tails of the sampling distribution? (Note that X_i – while markedly non-normally distributed – is, throughout this exercise, generated independently from U_i. Thus, the results obtained here are for the case where endogeneity in X_i is not an issue.)

Table ALE11a Empirical Coverage of Asymptotic 99% Confidence Intervals

	$N = 10$	$N = 25$	$N = 50$	$N = 100$
$X_i \sim$ uniform [0, 1]				
Using σ_x^2 and σ_u^2				
Using s_x^2 and s_u^2				
$X_i \sim$ Student's $t(4)$				
Using σ_x^2 and σ_u^2				
Using s_x^2 and s_u^2				
$X_i \sim$ Binomial ($P = .3$)				
Using σ_x^2 and σ_u^2				
Using s_x^2 and s_u^2				

CONCLUSIONS

One lesson to learn from this exercise is that modern econometric software makes it quite easy to obtain standard error estimates – and consequent parameter inferences and confidence intervals – from the bootstrap. On the other hand, another lesson to take away from this exercise is that the bootstrap is itself only justified for large samples – and a sample of 40 to 120 observations is a large sample in some settings, but not in others. In particular, one might want to be wary of using the bootstrap in such sample lengths with a dummy variable which only equals zero for a handful of the sample observations.

APPENDIX 11.1: THE ALGEBRA OF PROBABILITY LIMITS

Let $\hat{V}$ and $\hat{V}$ be two estimators, each of which is defined in such a way that its probability limit is finite and each of which is based on observations $V_1 \ldots V_N$, which are assumed to all be identically and independently distributed.[52] Then it can be shown that the following results all hold:

1. (Linearity) Assuming that a and b are fixed constants,

$$\text{plim}(a\hat{V} + b\tilde{V}) = a\,\text{plim}(\hat{V}) + b\,\text{plim}(\tilde{V}) \tag{A11-1}$$

2. (Multiplication)

$$\text{plim}(\hat{V} \times \tilde{V}) = \text{plim}(\hat{V}) + \text{plim}(\tilde{V}) \tag{A11-2}$$

3. (Division) Assuming that $\text{plim}(\tilde{V}) \neq 0$,

$$\text{plim}\left(\frac{\hat{V}}{\tilde{V}}\right) = \frac{\text{plim}(\hat{V})}{\text{plim}(\tilde{V})} \tag{A11-3}$$

4. (Reduction to Ordinary Limit) Assuming that F_N is a nonstochastic function of N,

$$\text{plim}(F_N) = \lim_{N\to\infty} [F_N] \tag{A11-4}$$

5. (Slutsky Theorem) For any continuous function $F\{\cdot\}$,[53]

$$\text{plim}(F\{\hat{V}\}) = F\{\text{plim}(\hat{V})\} \tag{A11-5}$$

6. (Law of Large Numbers) Assuming that $E[V_i]$ is finite,

$$\text{plim}\left(\frac{1}{N}\sum_{i=1}^{N} V_i\right) = E[V_i] \tag{A11-6}$$

7. (Central Limit Theorem – Lindeberg-Lévy)

$$V_i \sim \text{IID}(\mu, \sigma_v^2) \Rightarrow \text{plim}\left[\frac{1}{\sqrt{N}}\sum_{i=1}^{N} V_i\right] = \text{plim}\left[\sqrt{N}\,\overline{V}\right] = N\left[\mu, \sigma_v^2\right] \tag{A11-7}$$

8. (Asymptotic Equivalence)

If $\text{plim}(\hat{V}) = \text{plim}(\hat{V})$, then their limiting distributions are the same. (A11-8)

[52] Strictly speaking, $\hat{V}$ and $\tilde{V}$ are two sequences of estimators such that the probability limit of each is either a finite number or a random variable with finite variance. Hamilton (1994, Chapter 7) provides a more detailed treatment and proofs, including extensions of these same results to sequences for which the underlying observations are a serially dependent time-series rather than independently distributed observations. These extensions are used in Chapter 13. James D. Hamilton (1994), *Time Series Analysis*, Princeton University Press: Princeton, NJ.

[53] A function $F\{z\}$ is continuous if and only if the limit of $F\{z\}$ as z approaches z_o is $F\{z_o\}$ for all values of z_o – i.e., the function has no sudden jumps.

APPENDIX 11.2: DERIVATION OF THE ASYMPTOTIC SAMPLING DISTRIBUTION OF THE OLS SLOPE ESTIMATOR

The asymptotic distribution of $\hat{\beta}^{OLS}$, the OLS estimator of β in the Bivariate Regression Model of Equation 11-1, is

$$\sqrt{N}\left(\hat{\beta}^{OLS} - \beta\right) \xrightarrow{d} N\left[0,\ \frac{\sigma_u^2}{\sigma_x^2}\right] \tag{A11-9}$$

where it is assumed for all values of i that $\text{cov}(X_i, U_i)$ is zero, so that $\hat{\beta}^{OLS}$ is a consistent estimator of β. This result is proven below using the Lindeberg-Lévy form of the Central Limit Theorem, as stated in either Equation 11-15 or Equation A11-7, with μ set to zero:

$$V_i \sim \text{IID}(0, \sigma_v^2) \Rightarrow \text{plim}\left[\frac{1}{\sqrt{N}}\sum_{i=1}^{N} V_i\right] = \text{plim}\left[\sqrt{N}\,\overline{V}\right] = N\left[0, \sigma_v^2\right] \tag{A11-10}$$

and using Equations 11-4 and 11-6, which express $\hat{\beta}^{OLS}$ in terms of the model errors, $U_1 \ldots U_N$:

$$\hat{\beta}^{OLS} = \beta + \sum_{i=1}^{N} W_i^{ols} U_i \quad \text{where} \quad W_i^{ols} \equiv \frac{X_i - \overline{X}}{\sum\limits_{\ell=1}^{N} \left(X_\ell - \overline{X}\right)^2} \tag{A11-11}$$

Recall that the Bivariate Regression Model of Equation 11-1 also assumes that $U_i \sim \text{IID}(0, \sigma_u^2)$ and that $\text{cov}(X_i^2, U_i^2)$ is zero. Equation 11-1 in addition assumes that $X_i \sim \text{IID}(0, \sigma_x^2)$, but the expected value of X_i will be denoted as μ_x below – i.e., $X_i \sim \text{IID}(\mu_x, \sigma_x^2)$ – even though the value of μ_x is actually zero. This notation makes the expressions obtained below a bit longer but – hopefully – a bit more clear.

The strategy of the proof is to rewrite $\text{plim}\left[\sqrt{N}\left(\hat{\beta}^{OLS} - \beta\right)\right]$ as the probability limit of $\sqrt{N}$ times the sample mean of a zero-mean random variable – which will be called "V_i" – and proceed to show that V_i is identically and independently distributed. The $\text{plim}\left[\sqrt{N}\left(\hat{\beta}^{OLS} - \beta\right)\right]$ – i.e., the asymptotic distribution of $\sqrt{N}\left(\hat{\beta}^{OLS} - \beta\right)$ – then follows directly from the Central Limit Theorem, as stated in Equation A11-7.

This process seems lengthy because a good many lines are needed when each algebraic step in this rewriting process is explicitly displayed, but almost every step is either an ordinary algebraic rearrangement, or a simple substitution (using Equation A11-11, for example), or is an application of one of the algebraic properties of the probability limit, as given in Appendix 11.1. Rewriting $\text{plim}\left[\sqrt{N}\left(\hat{\beta}^{OLS} - \beta\right)\right]$, then, yields

$$\begin{aligned}
\text{plim}\left[\sqrt{N}\left(\hat{\beta}^{OLS} - \beta\right)\right] &= \text{plim}\left[\sqrt{N}\sum_{i=1}^{N} W_i^{OLS} U_i\right] \\
&= \text{plim}\left[\sqrt{N}\sum_{i=1}^{N}\left(\frac{X_i - \overline{X}}{\sum\limits_{\ell=1}^{N}\left(X_\ell - \overline{X}\right)^2}\right) U_i\right]
\end{aligned}$$

$$= \text{plim}\left[\sqrt{N}\sum_{i=1}^{N}\left(\frac{X_i - \overline{X}}{N\widehat{\text{var}}(X)}\right)U_i\right]$$

$$= \text{plim}\left[\frac{1}{\widehat{\text{var}}(X)}\sqrt{N}\sum_{i=1}^{N}\frac{1}{N}\left(X_i - \overline{X}\right)U_i\right]$$

$$= \text{plim}\left[\frac{1}{\widehat{\text{var}}(X)}\right]\text{plim}\left[\sqrt{N}\sum_{i=1}^{N}\frac{1}{N}\left(X_i - \overline{X}\right)U_i\right]$$

$$= \frac{1}{\sigma_x^2}\,\text{plim}\left[\sqrt{N}\sum_{i=1}^{N}\frac{1}{N}\left(X_i - \overline{X}\right)U_i\right] \qquad \text{(A11-12)}$$

Note that the validity of this last step rests on the indicated probability limit existing – that is, in this case, corresponding to the probability limit of a random variable with finite variance. That this is not a problem becomes clear later in the derivation.

In the next step μ_x, the population mean of X_i, is both added and subtracted in the expression. This leads to an additional term in the expression which, after a few more steps, is shown to have probability limit zero and then disappears from the remainder of the derivation. The reason why this apparent detour is necessary is that it effectively replaces $\overline{X}$ by μ_x in our eventual result, the zero-mean variable which we will call "V_i." This replacement is crucial in showing that the V_i are independently distributed because $\overline{X}$ depends on all of $X_1 \ldots X_N$ whereas μ_x is a fixed constant. Proceeding along these lines, then,

$$\text{plim}\left[\sqrt{N}\left(\hat{\beta}^{\text{OLS}} - \beta\right)\right] = \frac{1}{\sigma_x^2}\text{plim}\left[\sqrt{N}\sum_{i=1}^{N}\frac{1}{N}\left(X_i - \overline{X}\right)U_i\right]$$

$$= \frac{1}{\sigma_x^2}\text{plim}\left[\sqrt{N}\sum_{i=1}^{N}\frac{1}{N}\left(X_i - \mu_x + \mu_x - \overline{X}\right)U_i\right]$$

$$= \frac{1}{\sigma_x^2}\text{plim}\left[\sqrt{N}\sum_{i=1}^{N}\frac{1}{N}(X_i - \mu_x)U_i + \sqrt{N}\sum_{i=1}^{N}\frac{1}{N}\left(\mu_i - \overline{X}\right)U_i\right]$$

$$= \frac{1}{\sigma_x^2}\text{plim}\left[\sqrt{N}\sum_{i=1}^{N}\frac{1}{N}(X_i - \mu_x)U_i\right] + \frac{1}{\sigma_x^2}\text{plim}\left[\sqrt{N}\sum_{i=1}^{N}\frac{1}{N}\left(\mu_i - \overline{X}\right)U_i\right]$$

$$= \frac{1}{\sigma_x^2}\text{plim}\left[\sqrt{N}\sum_{i=1}^{N}\frac{1}{N}(X_i - \mu_x)U_i\right] + \frac{1}{\sigma_x^2}\text{plim}\left[\left(\mu_i - \overline{X}\right)\sqrt{N}\,\overline{U}\right]$$

$$= \frac{1}{\sigma_x^2}\text{plim}\left[\sqrt{N}\sum_{i=1}^{N}\frac{1}{N}(X_i - \mu_x)U_i\right] + \frac{1}{\sigma_x^2}\text{plim}\left[\left(\mu_i - \overline{X}\right)\right]\text{plim}\left[\sqrt{N}\,\overline{U}\right]$$

$$= \frac{1}{\sigma_x^2}\text{plim}\left[\sqrt{N}\sum_{i=1}^{N}\frac{1}{N}(X_i - \mu_x)U_i\right]$$

$$
\begin{aligned}
&= \text{plim}\left[\sqrt{N}\sum_{i=1}^{N}\frac{1}{N}\left(\frac{1}{\sigma_x^2}(X_i - \mu_x)U_i\right)\right] \\
&= \text{plim}\left[\sqrt{N}\frac{1}{N}\sum_{i=1}^{N}\left(\frac{1}{\sigma_x^2}(X_i - \mu_x)U_i\right)\right] \\
&= \text{plim}\left[\sqrt{N}\,\overline{V}\right]
\end{aligned} \tag{A11-13}
$$

where V_i is thus defined as $\frac{1}{\sigma_x^2}(X_i - \mu_x)U_i$.[54]

Thus, by defining V_i in this way, we see that $\text{plim}\left[\sqrt{N}\left(\hat{\beta}^{OLS} - \beta\right)\right]$ can be re-expressed as the probability limit of $\sqrt{N}$ times the sample mean of $V_1 \ldots V_N$. In order to use the CLT – Equation A11-7 – to conclude from this result that $\sqrt{N}\left(\hat{\beta}^{OLS} - \beta\right)$ is asymptotically normal with mean 0 and variance $\text{var}(V_i)$, we must now show that V_i has mean zero, is independently distributed, and has a well-defined variance. Note that because $E(U_i)$ is zero, $E(V_i)$ is actually proportional to $\text{cov}(X_i, U_i)$:

$$
E(V_i) = \frac{1}{\sigma_x^2}\text{cov}(X_i, U_i) \tag{A11-14}
$$

Thus, $E(V_i)$ equals zero so long as X_i is not endogenous.[55] Because X_i and U_i are each independently distributed for each value of i, it follows that the V_i are independently distributed also.[56] Since $E(V_i)$ is zero, the variance of V_i is just $E(V_i^2)$; so the variance of V_i can be expressed as

$$
\begin{aligned}
\text{var}(V_i) &= E\left(V_i^2\right) \\
&= E\left(\frac{1}{\sigma_x^4}[X_i - \mu_x]^2 U_i^2\right) \\
&= \frac{1}{\sigma_x^4}E\left([X_i - \mu_x]^2 U_i^2\right) \\
&= \frac{1}{\sigma_x^4}E\left([X_i - \mu_x]^2\right)E\left(U_i^2\right) \\
&= \frac{1}{\sigma_x^4}\sigma_x^2\sigma_u^2 = \frac{\sigma_u^2}{\sigma_x^2}
\end{aligned} \tag{A11-15}
$$

Note that the expected value of the product $[X_i - \mu_x]^2 U_i^2$ equals the product of the expected values of these two factors because of the assumption in Equation 11-1 that $\text{cov}(X_i^2, U_i^2)$ is zero. This completes the proof.

[54] Note that, per the first footnote in Appendix 11.1, Equation A11-2 can be applied to re-express the probability limit of the product of $\mu_x - \overline{X}$ and $\sqrt{N}\,\overline{U}$ as the product of the probability limit of $\mu_x - \overline{X}$ times the probability limit of $\sqrt{N}\,\overline{U}$ only because both of these factors have well-defined probability limits. In this case $U_i \sim \text{IID}(0, \sigma_u^2)$ implies that $\text{plim}\left[\sqrt{N}\overline{U}\right]$ is a normally distributed variate with variance equal to σ_u^2, using the Central Limit Theorem; and $X_i \sim \text{IID}(\mu_x, \sigma_u^2)$ implies that $\text{plim}\left[\mu_x - \overline{X}\right]$ equals zero.

[55] Note that the application of the Central Limit Theorem requires that $\text{cov}(X_i, U_i)$ equals zero. This is a stronger assumption than requiring that $\text{plim}[\widehat{\text{cov}}(X_i, U_i)]$ equals zero, which is all that is necessary (in Equation 11-18) to show that $\hat{\beta}^{OLS}$ is consistent.

[56] This would not have been the case for $\left(1/\sigma_x^2\right)\left(X_i - \overline{X}\right)U_i$ because $\overline{X}$ depends on all N observations.

Two additional comments are worthwhile at this point. First, this proof can be easily extended to a generalization of the model in Equation 11-1 in which the homoscedasticity assumption – $\text{var}(U_i) = \sigma_u^2$ – is replaced by $\text{var}(U_i) = \sigma_{u,i}^2$. This extension requires the use of a more general form of the Central Limit Theorem than Equation A11-10; this more general version instead assumes that $V_i \sim \text{IID}[0, \sigma_{v,i}^2]$ and replaces σ_v^2 in the right-hand side by the large-sample limit of the average value $\sigma_{v,i}^2$ over the sample – e.g., see Davidson and MacKinnon (2004, p. 149).[57] The extension is not difficult; it ends a few steps earlier than the present development, at the point in Equation A11-15 where

$$\text{var}(V_i)\frac{1}{\sigma_x^4}E\left([Xi - \mu_x]^2 U_i^2\right) \tag{A11-16}$$

so that the final result is

$$\sqrt{N}\left(\hat{\beta}^{OLS} - \beta\right) \xrightarrow{d} N\left[0, \frac{E\left([X_i - \mu_x]^2 U_i^2\right)}{\sigma_x^4}\right] \tag{A11-17}$$

and the expectation on the right-hand side is in practice replaced by the analogous sample average, which consistently estimates it. The resulting asymptotic standard error estimates for $\hat{\beta}^{OLS}$ are identical to the White-Eicker "robust" standard error estimates discussed in Section 10.7 and readily available in most econometric packages.[58]

Second, it is also worth noting that – were one unwilling to make the assumption that $\text{cov}\left(X_i^2, U_i^2\right)$ is zero – one could still reach the result given as Equation A11-17 and use this for inference. Implementing this result amounts to simply using the White-Eicker robust standard errors even though the homoscedasticity assumption is being maintained. Asymptotically, this makes no difference, but – in more modest samples – one would expect to obtain more accurate standard error estimates using the A11-9 result.

[57] Davidson, R., and J. G. MacKinnon (1993), *Econometric Theory and Methods*, Oxford University Press.

[58] For example, in Stata, simply add the "robust" option to the "regress" command.

12

Instrumental Variables Estimation

12.1 INTRODUCTION – WHY IT IS CHALLENGING TO TEST FOR ENDOGENEITY

Under the assumption that the explanatory variables are exogenous – i.e., "fixed in repeated samples" – we have so far seen how to estimate *and* diagnostically check a regression model using cross-sectional (as opposed to time-series) data, and to thereby obtain reasonably high-quality parameter estimates and statistical inferences. In Chapter 11, however, it became clear that consequential violations of this "fixed-regressors" assumption – due to omitted variables, measurement error, and joint determination (simultaneity) – must be quite common.

Unfortunately, it is essentially impossible to directly test for endogeneity.[1] The reason for this becomes clear from an examination of the Bivariate Regression Model, as amended in Chapter 11 to include a stochastic regressor:

The Bivariate Regression Model
(Stochastic Regressor Case)

$$
\begin{aligned}
Y_i &= \alpha + \beta X_i + U_i \qquad i = 1 \ldots N \\
U_i &\sim \text{IID}\left[0,\ \sigma_u^2\right] \\
X_i &\sim \text{IID}\left[0, \sigma_x^2\right] \ \sigma_x^2 > 0 \\
\text{Cov}(X_i, U_i) &= \sigma_{xu} \\
\text{Cov}\left(X_i^2, U_i^2\right) &= 0
\end{aligned}
\tag{12-1}
$$

Recall that the key result in Chapter 11 was that $\hat{\beta}^{\text{OLS}}$ is a consistent estimator of β if and only if X_i is asymptotically uncorrelated with U_i – that is, if and only if σ_{xu} approaches zero for sufficiently large samples. (In fact, $\sigma_{xu} \neq 0$ is, in essence, what is meant by the term, "endogenous regressor.")

Consequently, for large samples, it would seem to be straightforward to test for endogeneity simply estimate σ_{xu} using the sample covariance of X_i with the OLS fitting errors:

$$
\hat{\sigma}_{xu} = \frac{1}{N}\sum_{i=1}^{N} X_i U_i^{\text{fit}} \tag{12-2}
$$

[1] Indirect testing is possible, however, by comparing the OLS estimates to those obtained using the instrumental variables method described in this chapter; this will be discussed later.

exploiting the fact that

$$
\begin{aligned}
U_i^{\text{fit}} &= Y_i - \left[\hat{\beta} X_i\right] \\
&= \left[\beta X_i + U_i\right] - \left[\hat{\beta} X_i\right] \\
&= U_i - \left[\hat{\beta} X_i - \beta X_i\right] \\
&= U_i - X_i\left[\hat{\beta} - \beta\right]
\end{aligned}
\tag{12-3}
$$

so that – if $\hat{\beta}$ is a consistent estimator of β – U_i^{fit} is equivalent to U_i for sufficiently large samples. The problem is that – if σ_{xu} does not disappear in large samples – then $\hat{\beta}^{\text{OLS}}$ is *not* a consistent estimator of β, so $U_{li}^{\text{fit}} \ldots U_N^{\text{fit}}$ are not asymptotically equivalent to $U_{li} \ldots U_N$. Consequently, $\hat{\sigma}_{xu}$ does not provide a consistent estimator of σ_{xu}.

Alternatively, recall – from the development of the least-squares fitting of the Bivariate Regression Model in Chapter 5 – that

$$
\begin{aligned}
\frac{\partial \text{SSE}\left(\hat{\beta}^{\text{guess}}\right)}{\partial \hat{\beta}^{\text{guess}}} &= \frac{\partial}{\partial \hat{\beta}^{\text{guess}}} \sum_{i=1}^{N} \left\{ y_i - \hat{\alpha}^{\text{guess}} - \hat{\beta}^{\text{guess}} x_i \right\}^2 \\
&= \sum_{i=1}^{N} \frac{\partial}{\partial \hat{\beta}^{\text{guess}}} \left\{ y_i - \hat{\alpha}^{\text{guess}} - \hat{\beta}^{\text{guess}} x_i \right\}^2 \\
&= \sum_{i=1}^{N} -2x_i \left\{ y_i - \hat{\alpha}^{\text{guess}} - \hat{\beta}^{\text{guess}} x_i \right\} \\
&= -2\sum_{i=1}^{N} x_i \left\{ y_i - \hat{\alpha}^{\text{guess}} - \hat{\beta}^{\text{guess}} x_i \right\}
\end{aligned}
\tag{5-27}
$$

The OLS (least-squares) value of $\hat{\beta}^{\text{guess}}$ – i.e., that which minimizes $\text{SSE}\left(\hat{\beta}^{\text{guess}}\right)$ – makes this partial derivative zero, and hence must satisfy

$$
\begin{aligned}
0 = \frac{\partial \text{SSE}\left(\hat{\beta}^{\text{guess}}\right)}{\partial \hat{\beta}^{\text{guess}}} &= -2\sum_{i=1}^{N} x_i \left\{ y_i - \hat{\alpha}^{\text{guess}} - \hat{\beta}^{\text{guess}} x_i \right\} \\
&= -2\sum_{i=1}^{N} x_i \left\{ u_i^{\text{fit}} \right\}
\end{aligned}
\tag{12-4}
$$

Consequently, the OLS estimator $\hat{\beta}^{\text{OLS}}$ must *by construction* yield fitting errors which exactly satisfy

$$
\hat{\sigma}_{xu} = \frac{1}{N} \sum_{i=1}^{N} x_i u_i^{\text{fit}} = 0 \tag{12-5}
$$

Thus, using the least squares parameter estimates, the sample estimate of the covariance between X_j and the fitting errors $(\hat{\sigma}_{xu})$ is inherently zero.

Consequently, $\hat{\sigma}_{xu}$ cannot possibly provide a useful estimate of σ_{xu}, the population covariance between X_i and U_i. Indeed, the fact that the OLS estimator forces this sample covariance to equal zero when (in the case where X_i is endogenous) the corresponding population covariance is non-zero is another way of understanding why and how the OLS parameter estimate must be inconsistent in this circumstance.

How, then, can one determine whether or not endogeneity in the explanatory variables is a serious problem or not? The foregoing discussion clarifies why it is not possible to directly test this proposition. Consequently, in practice, careful analysts argue this point using *theory* – informal or formal – to decide whether or not endogeneity (due to measurement error, omitted variables, or joint determination) is important or not.[2]

Sometimes – as in the Acemoglu (2001) study, which is the subject of Active Learning Exercise 12a – the authors identify measurement error as the source of the endogeneity in an explanatory variable. (The way in which measurement error induces a correlation between an explanatory variable (as measured) and the model error term is discussed in Section 11.6.) More typically, however, the endogeneity discussion hinges on the possibility of omitted variables which are correlated with the explanatory variables or on the possibility of correlation between an explanatory variable and the model error term due to either "reverse causation" between the dependent variable and an explanatory variable or due to "joint determination," where the dependent variable and an explanatory are jointly determined by a set of simultaneous equations. The ways in which these two situations result in endogeneity are described at some length in Sections 11.5 and 11.7; the discussion here elaborates on the "reverse causality" issue.

A regression model inherently posits a causal relationship in which fluctuations in the explanatory variables cause part of the observed fluctuations in the dependent variable, with the remainder of these observed fluctuations attributed to other causal influences which are subsumed in the model error term. We say that there is "reverse causation" if the sample fluctuations in an explanatory variable not only help cause the sample fluctuations in the dependent variable (which is why this explanatory variable is included in the model) but are also themselves caused by the fluctuations in the dependent variable. In other words, there is reverse causation if the causal connection between these two variables runs both ways.[3]

This reverse causality issue comes up very frequently in applied economic work; the two feasible approaches for disentangling it are both introduced in the next section. One of these approaches ("Granger-causality") inherently applies only to time-series data – data, such as the monthly Consumer Price Index, which are ordered in time. An extended exposition of this (and other) topics in time-series analysis is given in Chapter 17 and 18, so Granger-causality is only briefly introduced here. The rest of the next section introduces the primary econometric tool for dealing with reverse causality and, indeed, for dealing with all forms of explanatory variable endogeneity: the instrumental variables estimation technique. This estimation approach is so important that the remainder of the chapter is devoted to it.

12.2 CORRELATION VERSUS CAUSATION – TWO WAYS TO UNTIE THE KNOT

It is frequently observed that two random variables are correlated without being causally related. For example, fluctuations in the flow rate of the river running through a town and fluctuations in umbrella usage by the town's residents are likely to be positively correlated, yet neither of these variables is causally related to the other: they are both driven by fluctuations in the rainfall rate. Similarly, in a cross-sectional sample of different countries, the growth rate of real output and the quality of the educational system might well be positively correlated, but this correlation does not

[2] In new research, Ashley and Parmeter (2011) show how one can at least estimate the sensitivity of one's inferential conclusions – e.g. the *p*-value at which one can reject some particular null hypothesis – to likely posited amounts of endogeneity in the regressors. In particular, this paper shows how to calculate the maximum values of $|\text{corr}(X_{il}, U_i)| \ldots |\text{corr}(X_{ik}, U_i)|$ in the Multiple Regression Model such that the rejection of a particular null hypothesis remains significant at, say, the 5% level. If these maximum correlations are quite low (e.g., less than .05), then one can conclude that the inference is "fragile" with respect to likely endogeneity problems; if these maximum values are high, then the inference is "robust" to likely levels of endogeneity in the explanatory variables. This paper also provides a detailed review of the literature in this area. Ashley, R., and C. Parmeter (2011), "Sensitivity Analysis of GMM Inference" Mimeo at ashleymac.econ.vt.edu/working_papers/Ashley_Panneter_Credible_GMM.pdf.

[3] This is called "feedback" in the time-series literature – see Chapter 17.

necessarily imply that education causes growth: it might be that a wealthier country can simply afford better schools.

Philosophers have argued for many centuries over the nature and appropriate definition of "causality." Econometricians have largely ignored this debate and come up with two techniques for operationally defining "causality" and for, in favorable circumstances, untying the knot and actually distinguishing a causal relationship from a mere correlation.

One of these two approaches is available to us if we have time-series data, such as the real growth rate (Y_t) and educational quality (E_t) in a particular country for year t. In that case we can leverage the fact that – whatever one might reasonably mean by the words "cause" and "effect" – it would hardly make sense for the "effect" to precede the "cause" in time and it *would* make sense for the "cause" to precede the "effect" in time. Thus, if fluctuations in E_t "cause" fluctuations in Y_t, then one might expect that knowledge of past fluctuations in E_t from previous years would be uniquely helpful in forecasting this year's fluctuation in Y_t. Conversely, if knowledge of past fluctuations in E_t is *not* helpful in forecasting current fluctuations in Y_t, then it is unreasonable to think that fluctuations in E_t "cause" fluctuations in Y_t, unless the causal influence takes its entire effect within a year.

This way of conceptualizing the word "cause" is called "Granger-causality" after Granger (1969), in which it was first proposed.[4] Completion of the program of operationalizing this definition of causality will described in more detail when this topic reappears in Section 18.5. Three points are crucial here.

First, every example in which the Granger-causality concept fails to be reasonable corresponds to the omission of a third (or fourth, or fifth ...) variable from the analytic framework – a variable which (in this example) actually Granger-causes both Y_t and E_t, but with different lags. The discussion here tacitly assumes that enough other past variables were included in both the forecasting model for Y_t which includes past E_t fluctuations and in the forecasting model for Y_t which omits these past E_t fluctuations, so that one is not omitting an important variable from both forecasting models.

That said, the second crucial point is to note that if the forecasting model for Y_t including past E_t fluctuations does do a better job of forecasting the current fluctuations in Y_t than does the forecasting model for Y_t excluding past E_t fluctuations, then one can conclude that fluctuations in E_t Granger-cause fluctuations in Y_t. Moreover, it is in that case reasonable to infer that past fluctuations in E_t "cause" current fluctuations in Y_t – regardless of whether E_t is contemporaneously correlated with Y_t or not. Thus, in this instance, an observed contemporaneous correlation (if there is one) is consistent with causality. In contrast, if past fluctuations in E_t do *not* Granger-cause current fluctuations in Y_t, then an observation of contemporaneous correlation between E_t and Y_t is not interpretable in causal terms: fluctuations in E_t might, in this instance, be causing fluctuations in Y_t, or vice-versa, or both. This situation could easily arise if the causal relationship between these two variables operates on a monthly time scale, whereas the data are only observed quarterly.

Now, for the final point, presume that Y_t is the dependent variable in a proposed regression model and that E_t is one of the explanatory variables. The "fixed in repeated samples" assumption in the original Multiple Regression Model is then unreasonable if the fluctuations in the dependent variable (Y_t) Granger-cause fluctuations in the explanatory variable E_t, regardless of whether Y_t is contemporaneously correlated with E_t or not. (Of course, it is only where these two variables are contemporaneously correlated that one might have thought E_t, as distinct from E_{t-1}, useful as an explanatory variable in a regression model for Y_t in the first place.) In that case – where Y_t Granger-causes fluctuations in the explanatory variable E_t and these two variables are also contemporaneously correlated – one can expect E_t to be correlated with the regression model error (leading to inconsistent OLS parameter estimates) and can clearly interpret this inconsistency as being due to

[4] See Granger, C. W. J. (1969), "Investigating Causal Relations by Econometric Models and Cross-Spectral Methods" *Econometrica 37*, 424–38, and Ashley, R., C. W. J. Granger, and R. Schraalensee (1980), "Advertising and Aggregate Consumption: An Analysis of Causality" *Econometrica 48*, 1149–68.

"reverse causality." Granger-causality in the "wrong" direction (i.e., from dependent variable to explanatory variable) thus makes the single-equation regression model inappropriate: it indicates that one ought to be considering a set of simultaneous equations jointly determining E_t and Y_t. Note, however, that endogeneity due to reverse causality (and the resulting parameter estimation inconsistency) can occur even in the absence of Granger-causality in the wrong direction: the reverse causation may be occurring within a single time period, so that the Granger-causality formalism cannot detect it. Thus, the Granger-causality approach can potentially alert one to endogeneity-inducing reverse causation, but it can also miss it.

The Granger-causality formalism is uniquely useful in its potential to identify the direction of causation between two variables without relying on theory. (Presuming that one has a sufficiently complete set of time-series data, measured at sufficiently frequent intervals.) Granger-causality can thereby potentially alert us to endogeneity-inducing reverse causation. On the other hand, it does not address or detect other sources of endogeneity – e.g., omitted variables and measurement error – and it is applicable only to time-series data. Moreover, it provides no help in obtaining consistent regression parameter estimates; at best it detects the problem.

For this reason we now turn to the primary econometric approach for both dealing with endogenous explanatory variables in regression models *and* (in that context) legitimately identifying causal relations between correlated variables. This approach is called "instrumental variables estimation." It is broadly useful, regardless of whether the data are time-ordered (or not) and regardless of the source of the endogeneity in the explanatory variables. For sufficiently large samples – and where its additional assumptions are satisfied – instrumental variables estimation yields consistent regression model parameter estimates and yields useful asymptotically valid statistical inferences (i.e., hypothesis tests and confidence intervals) for the model coefficients. If E_i, say, is then statistically significant as an explanatory variable in such a model for Y_i (and if no relevant explanatory variable, correlated with E_i, has been inadvertently omitted from the model), then one can legitimately conclude that sample fluctuations in E_i cause at least a portion of the sample fluctuations in Y_i.[5]

As one might expect, however, there is a "catch." The "catch" is in those additional assumptions. Instrumental variables estimation requires additional observed data series – called "instruments" – which must satisfy certain assumptions in order to be "valid" instruments and yield both consistent parameter estimates and asymptotically valid statistical inferences.

In order to even compute the instrumental variables parameter estimator, one must have sample observations on at least as many instruments as there are endogenous variables in the model.[6] For simplicity, the exposition given here will be for the stochastic regressor case of the Bivariate Regression Model – i.e., Equation 12-1. This model has a single endogenous variable (X_i, with $\sigma_{xu} \neq 0$), so that a single instrument – which will be called Z_i – will suffice. But the

[5] Note that the subscripts just switched from t to i – emphasizing the fact that the instrumental variables approach is equally applicable to a cross-sectional data set, where the observations on (Y_i, E_i) refer to different countries rather than to different time periods.

[6] A model with just as many instruments as endogenous explanatory variables is called "exactly identified." A model with more instruments than endogenous explanatory variables is called "overidentified" and will be considered in Section 12.5, where the Two-Stage Least Squares ("2SLS") method is discussed. For technical completeness, a bit more needs to be said (and a concept from linear algebra used) where the model has more than one endogenous explanatory variable. In that case it is no longer sufficient to just require that the number of instruments at least equals the number of endogenous explanatory variables. In addition, the rank of the matrix whose columns are the data on the instruments must equal the number of endogenous explanatory variables (for exact identification) or exceed this number (for overidentification). Crudely put, the rank of this matrix is the number of instruments which are distinct, in the sense of not being exactly expressible as a weighted sum of the other instruments. Expositions of instrumental variables estimation in the context of the Multiple Regression Model, using linear algebra extensively, can be found in many places – e.g. Johnston and Dinardo (1997) *Econometric Methods* McGraw-Hill: New York, Kmenta (1986) *Elements of Econometrics* MacMillan: New York, and Angrist and Pischke (2008) *Mostly Harmless Econometrics: An Empiricist's Companion* Princeton University Press: Princeton.

number of instruments is generally not the problem. The *problem* is typically with the instrument validity assumptions: a "valid" instrument is an observed variable characterized by two properties:

- A valid instrument is *correlated* with at least one of the endogenous explanatory variables.
- A valid instrument is *uncorrelated*, at least asymptotically, with the model error term.

There is no difficulty in verifying the first of these conditions, at least for large samples, because (per Exercise 11-8) the sample correlations between a proposed instrument and the explanatory variables provide consistent estimates of the population correlations.

The second condition is problematic, however. In fact, this condition cannot, in practice, actually be tested at all.[7] The reason for this is exactly the same as the reason why it is not possible to directly test for endogeneity: the model errors (U_i) are not observable, even for large samples, unless one has consistent estimates of the model parameters. And, of course, consistent parameter estimates are exactly what one *doesn't* have if some of the explanatory variables are endogenous and the validity of the instruments is in doubt. Consequently, the specification of a credibly valid instrument requires some creative thought.

Indeed, applied econometric work quite often hinges on the creative specification of an ostensibly valid instrument for an endogenous explanatory variable. And the critiques of such work quite often consist of arguments against the supposed non-correlation of this clever instrument with the model error term. A couple of examples from the applied econometrics literature will give the reader an idea of what is meant by a "clever instrument."

Acemoglu, Johnson, and Robinson (2001) estimate a cross-sectional model relating the real growth rate in a country to an index of the quality of its legal–political institutions, but recognize that the institutional index they use – which actually measures the political risk of government appropriation of privately held assets – is a noisy measure of the actual quality of the country's institutions, and is hence endogenous. Acemoglu et al.'s clever idea is to restrict their sample to countries which were once European colonies and to note that the (available) disease mortality rate among the original European settlers of such colonies is correlated with the current quality of the legal–political institutions in a former colony, but credibly *un*correlated with the errors which the government appropriation risk index makes in measuring the current quality of a country's legal–political institutions. Their argument is that, where the climate was such that the European settlers had a high disease mortality rate, the colonizing country governed from afar and did not export its people (and institutional values) to the colony. Their claim is that this mortality rate is uncorrelated with the (current) measurement errors in the political risk index, and hence uncorrelated with the model error term.[8] Consequently, they claim that this settler mortality rate is a valid instrument for the true value of the institution quality in such a former colony.[9]

A second example is provided by a classic study in the labor economics literature by Angrist and Krueger (1991).[10] This study was already examined in Section 11.9, where it was used – ignoring

[7] It is possible to test the validity of overidentifying conditions. (This is particularly graceful to do when instrumental variables estimation is implemented using Generalized Method of Moments (GMM) – GMM estimation is described in Section 19.4.) But all such tests presume the existence of a sufficient number of valid instruments.

[8] Recall – from Section 11.6 – that the reason measurement error in an explanatory variable induces endogeneity is that the measurement error ends up forming part of the model error term. Thus, a variable which is uncorrelated with the measurement error will be uncorrelated with the model error term.

[9] Active Learning Exercise 12a involves replicating their results. For details, see Acemoglu, D., S. Johnson, and J. Robinson (2001) "The Colonial Origins of Comparative Development: An Empirical Investigation" *American Economic Review 91(5)*, 1369–1401.

[10] Angrist, J., and A. Krueger (1991), "Does Compulsory School Attendance Affect Schooling and Earnings?" *Quarterly Journal of Economics 106(4)*, 979–1014.

the endogeneity in their key explanatory variable – to illustrate the usefulness of the bootstrap in quantifying how estimated inference results vary with the size of the sample.

Why is endogeneity an issue in the Angrist-Krueger study, and what is their clever idea for obtaining a valid instrument? The Angrist-Krueger model is typical of many in applied labor economics in using an education measure to help explain cross-sectional variation in household or individual earnings. In their case the sample variation in the logarithm of weekly earnings for 329,509 U.S. men born between 1930 and 1939 is modeled using observations on each individual's number of years of schooling and on a set of nine dummy variables allowing the intercept to vary depending on the individual's year of birth; the data are drawn from the 1980 Census. The endogeneity problem in their model arises because both earnings and education are partly driven by unobservable (or, at least, unobserved) individual ability and taste variables. Because they are unobserved, these variables are necessarily omitted from the model and consequently end up forming part of the model error term. And because these ability and taste variables are correlated with education, their presence in the model error term induces a correlation between the model errors and this explanatory variable; this correlation renders the education variable endogenous.[11] Thus, the OLS parameter estimates – e.g. those obtained in Section 11.9, whether bootstrapped or not – are inconsistent.

Angrist and Krueger's clever idea is to note that men born earlier in the calendar year – in the first quarter of the year, for example – reach the minimum school-leaving age at an earlier grade level and thus tend to have somewhat less education than men born later in the year. So birth-quarter is correlated with an individual's education level. Angrist and Krueger posit, however, that birth-quarter is *not* correlated with the unobserved taste and ability factors which make the years-of-schooling explanatory variable endogenous. Consequently, they claim that birth-quarter dummy variables provide valid instruments for years-of-schooling in their wage equation.

Angrist and Krueger's work has been criticized on several grounds. For one thing, later authors – e.g., Gormaker, Kagan, Caspi, and Silva (1997) and Polizzi, Matting, and Dombrowski (2007) – find evidence that birth-quarter is actually correlated with shyness and other psychological attributes. Hence, the birth-quarter variable is itself endogenous in an earnings regression, although perhaps less so than the schooling variables.

On the other hand, it is likely that almost every potential instrument is to some degree itself endogenous.[12] Ashley and Parmeter (2011) have proposed an empirically feasible instrument-quality measure: the sensitivity of the model's most important inference results to likely flaws in the instrument.[13] We find, for example, that only a minor amount of posited correlation (e.g., 0.02) between Angrist and Krueger's instruments and the model error term is sufficient to eliminate their principal conclusion, that the coefficient on schooling in their earnings equation is statistically significant at the 1% level. Thus, their statistical inference is what one might call "fragile" with respect to possible violations of their instrument validity assumption. In contrast, Acemoglu et al.'s principal conclusion – that the coefficient on the quality of a country's legal–political institutions in a model for real output is statistically significant at the 5% level – turns out to be highly robust, even

[11] See Section 11.5.

[12] Exceptions might include age (for a person) and the land area or average latitude (for a country).

[13] This sensitivity analysis is closely related to that described in Footnote 12-2 – and also in Ashley and Parmeter (2011) – except that here the sensitivity of the inferential conclusion is being evaluated relative to likely (posited) flaws in j of the instruments rather than to the possibility of endogeneity in one or more explanatory variables. In particular, Ashley and Parmeter (2011) shows how to calculate the maximum values of $|\text{corr}(Z_{il}, U_i)| \ldots |\text{corr}(Z_{ij}, U_i)|$ for these j instruments such that the rejection of this particular null hypothesis remains significant at, say, the 1% level. GMM estimation and inference in general, with an application to the Angrist-Krueger model in particular, are discussed in Section 19.4; the role of sensitivity analysis is explored in Chapter 20.

to fairly substantial posited correlations between their colonial settler mortality instrument and the model error term.

Another possible criticism of the Angrist and Krueger model is also worth mentioning, more because this issue is so prominent in all discussions of instrumental variables estimation than because it is a valid criticism of the Angrist and Krueger instruments. This issue is usually referred to as the "weak instruments" problem. Angrist and Krueger actually used 30 instruments: all of the feasible products of the four possible birth-quarter dummy variables and the 10 possible birth-year dummy variables.[14] But none of these instruments is very correlated with the endogenous schooling variable; in fact, the largest sample correlation is less than .03 in magnitude. The usual impact of nearly violating the condition that the instrument must be correlated with the endogenous explanatory variable is that the estimated standard errors of the instrumental variables parameter estimates balloon upwards to the point where the estimates are useless for hypothesis testing. In this instance, however, Angrist and Krueger are still able to obtain a quite precise estimate of this schooling coefficient –.089, with an estimated standard error of .016 – despite the weakness of their instruments. In small part this is because they use so many instruments; in large part it is because their sample is so very large.

There is a theoretical concern, however, associated with using large numbers of weak instruments: it has been shown that the asymptotic sampling distributions of the instrumental variables estimators become ill-behaved when one simultaneously allows the instruments to become weaker (but more numerous) as the sample size becomes unboundedly large.[15] There is thus reason to fear that the usual standard error estimates provided by instrumental variables estimation will become unreliable in such a limit. Much attention has been given to the "weak instruments" problem in general, but this is not the appropriate limit to consider for the Angrist-Krueger study: in their model the number of instruments sensibly remains fixed (at 30) as the number of men surveyed increases. Nevertheless, the "weak instruments" literature strongly suggests that one should be quite cautious in claiming to excuse weakness in one's instruments on the grounds that they are numerous.

In summary, then, the first instrument validity assumption – that the instrument is correlated with the endogenous explanatory variable – is easily checked, but only occasionally problematic if the sample is sufficiently large. In contrast, the second instrument validity assumption (that the instrument is asymptotically uncorrelated with the model error) is not empirically testable, although it is now possible to at least check whether or not violations of it of reasonable size are empirically consequential – e.g., see footnote 12-13. This second instrument validity assumption is typically at least somewhat problematic and some creative thought is usually required in order to even get close to satisfying it.

Still, the instrumental variables estimation approach is very widely used in applied econometrics, simply because it is the only approach available for estimating a regression model with one or more endogenous explanatory variables and still obtaining consistent parameter estimates and asymptotically valid statistical inference results. This consistency result is derived (for the Bivariate Regression Model with a single instrument) in the next section. The asymptotic sampling

[14] They had to leave out 10 of these products so that no weighted sum of the instruments equals one for every observation; see Exercise 12-3. The formal algebra associated with this restriction is not covered here – as it requires a treatment of instrumental variables estimation making extensive use of linear algebra – but the discussion of multicollinearity in Section 9.8 conveys much of the essence of this issue.

[15] Stock J., J. Wright, and M. Yogo (2002), "A Survey of Weak Instruments and Weak Identification in Generalized Method of Moments," *Journal of Business and Economic Statistics 20(4)*, 518–29, and Dufour, J.-M (2003), "Identification, Weak Instruments and Statistical Inference in Econometrics," *Canadian Journal of Economics 36(4)*, 767–808 are primary references on the "weak instruments" problem. Bound, J., D. Jaeger, and R. Baker (1995), "Problems with Instrumental Variables Estimation When the Correlation between the Instruments and the Endogenous Explanatory Variable Is Weak," *Journal of the American Statistical Association 90(430)*, 443–50 suggest that weak instruments are likely to lead to the "fragile" inferences discussed in Ashley and Parmeter (2011) and referred to in Footnote 12-13.

distribution of this estimator, and its use in testing hypotheses and constructing confidence intervals, is covered in the immediately following section. Practical implementation aspects, such as the extension to models with more instruments and/or more endogenous explanatory variables and a worked example (the Angrist-Krueger model) using a typical econometrics program, are described in the remainder of the chapter.

12.3 THE INSTRUMENTAL VARIABLES SLOPE ESTIMATOR (AND PROOF OF ITS CONSISTENCY) IN THE BIVARIATE REGRESSION MODEL

The last portion of the previous section introduced the instrumental variable estimation method – and the concept of a valid instrument – but did not actually specify how one can use a valid instrument to obtain consistent estimates of regression model parameters in the presence of explanatory variable endogeneity. This section does precisely that, in the simplest possible setting, that of the Bivariate Regression Model with no intercept and a single, valid instrument:

The Bivariate Regression Model

Endogenous Regressor Case
With a Single, Valid Instrument

$$
\begin{aligned}
Y_i &= \alpha + \beta X_i + U_i \qquad i = 1 \ldots N \\
U_i &\sim \text{IID}\left[0,\ \sigma_u^2\right] \\
X_i &\sim \text{IID}\left[0, \sigma_x^2\right]\ \sigma_x^2 > 0 \\
\text{Cov}(X_i, U_i) &= \sigma_{xu} \neq 0 \quad (X_i \text{ endogenous})
\end{aligned}
\tag{12-6}
$$

with one valid instrument, Z_i :

$$
\begin{aligned}
Z_i &\sim \text{IID}\left[0, \sigma_z^2\right] \quad \sigma_z^2 > 0 \\
\text{Cov}(Z_i, X_i) &= \sigma_{zx} \neq 0
\end{aligned}
$$

$$
\text{plim}\left[\frac{1}{N}\sum_{i=1}^{N}(Z_i - \overline{Z})\left(U_i - \overline{U}\right)\right] = \text{plim}[\widehat{\text{cov}}(Z_i, U_i)] = 0
$$

and

$$
\text{Cov}\left(Z_i^2, U_i^2\right) = 0
$$

It should be noted at the outset that the results obtained here do not require that U_i (or X_i or Z_i) are normally distributed. Unfortunately, this is because all of the results which can be obtained for this model, as in Chapter 11, are only asymptotic – i.e., they are valid only for large samples. On the other hand, even the distributional assumptions that *are* made in Equation 12-6 – that these random variables are identically and independently distributed (IID) – can actually be substantially weakened.[16]

The last assumption in Equation 12-6 – to the effect that

$$
\text{cov}\left(Z_i^2, U_i^2\right) = E\left[\left(Z_i^2 - \sigma_z^2\right)\left(U_i^2 - \sigma_u^2\right)\right] \tag{12-7}
$$

[16] In particular, the asymptotic sampling distribution for the instrumental variables estimator of β can still be derived (and consistently estimated) for heteroscedastic U_i and for X_i and Z_i which are serially correlated time-series. These issues are touched upon in Appendices 12.1 and 13.1, respectively.

is zero – is equivalent to assuming that the (squared) magnitudes of the fluctuations in the instrument Z_i are uncorrelated with the magnitudes of the model error fluctuations. This assumption is not necessary for the derivation of $\hat{\beta}^{IV}$, the consistent instrumental variables estimator of β, which is given below. But it is required in the derivation of the asymptotic sampling distribution of $\hat{\beta}^{IV}$, so it is included in Equation 12-6.[17]

The derivation of $\hat{\beta}^{IV}$ (and the proof that it is a consistent estimator of β) begins with the multiplication of both sides of the model equation in Equation 12-6 by the deviation of the instrument, Z_i, from its sample mean:

$$(Z_i - \overline{Z})Y_i = (Z_i - \overline{Z})\beta X_i + (Z_i - \overline{Z})U_i \tag{12-8}$$

Summing both sides of this equation and dividing by N,

$$\begin{aligned}
\frac{1}{N}\sum_{i=1}^{N}(Z_i - \overline{Z})Y_i &= \frac{1}{N}\sum_{i=1}^{N}[\beta(Z_i - \overline{Z})X_i + (Z_i - \overline{Z})U_i] \\
&= \beta\frac{1}{N}\sum_{i=1}^{N}(Z_i - \overline{Z})X_i + \frac{1}{N}\sum_{i=1}^{N}(Z_i - \overline{Z})U_i \\
&= \beta\frac{1}{N}\sum_{i=1}^{N}(Z_i - \overline{Z})X_i + \frac{1}{N}\sum_{i=1}^{N}(Z_i - \overline{Z})U_i \\
&\quad - \beta\frac{1}{N}\sum_{i=1}^{N}(Z_i - \overline{Z})\overline{X} - \frac{1}{N}\sum_{i=1}^{N}(Z_i - \overline{Z})\overline{U} \\
&= \beta\frac{1}{N}\sum_{i=1}^{N}(Z_i - \overline{Z})(X_i - \overline{X}) + \frac{1}{N}\sum_{i=1}^{N}(Z_i - \overline{Z})(U_i - \overline{U}) \\
&= \beta\,\widehat{\text{cov}}(Z_i, X_i) + \widehat{\text{cov}}(Z_i, U_i)
\end{aligned} \tag{12-9}$$

where the two sums subtracted in the third line of Equation 12-9 are both zero.[18] Note that (for the same reason) the sum $\frac{1}{N}\sum_{i=1}^{N}(Z_i - \overline{Z})\overline{Y}$ is zero also; so the left-hand side of Equation 12-9 can be rewritten as

$$\begin{aligned}
\frac{1}{N}\sum_{i=1}^{N}(Z_i - \overline{Z})Y_i &= \frac{1}{N}\sum_{i=1}^{N}(Z_i - \overline{Z})Y_i - \frac{1}{N}\sum_{i=1}^{N}(Z_i - \overline{Z})\overline{Y} \\
&= \frac{1}{N}\sum_{i=1}^{N}(Z_i - \overline{Z})(Y_i - \overline{Y}) \\
&= \widehat{\text{cov}}(Z_i, Y_i)
\end{aligned} \tag{12-10}$$

Thus, Equation 12-9 can be re-expressed more simply as

$$\widehat{\text{cov}}(Z_i, Y_i) = \beta\,\widehat{\text{cov}}(Z_i, X_i) + \widehat{\text{cov}}(Z_i, U_i) \tag{12-11}$$

[17] Note that this condition replaces the assumption that $\text{Cov}(X_i^2, U_i^2) = 0$ in Equation 11-1. This is neither an accident nor a mistake. Once the reader has digested the material in this chapter it will be both feasible and useful to note that the OLS slope estimator analyzed in Chapter 11 corresponds to choosing $Z_i = X_i$ – i.e., to using X_i, as an instrument for itself.

[18] See Exercise 12-1.

Taking the probability limit of both sides of the Equation 12-11 and using the "Linearity" property from Appendix 11.1,

$$\begin{aligned} \text{plim}[\widehat{\text{cov}}(Z_i, Y_i)] &= \text{plim}[\beta\, \widehat{\text{cov}}(Z_i, X_i) \;+ \widehat{\text{cov}}(Z_i, U_i)] \\ &= \beta\, \text{plim}[\widehat{\text{cov}}(Z_i, X_i)] + \text{plim}[\widehat{\text{cov}}(Z_i, U_i)] \\ &= \beta\, \text{plim}[\widehat{\text{cov}}(Z_i, X_i)] + \qquad 0 \\ &= \beta\, \text{plim}[\widehat{\text{cov}}(Z_i, X_i)] \end{aligned} \tag{12-12}$$

where the last step in Equation 12-12 uses the "Law of Large Numbers" property from Appendix 11.1 and the fact that $\text{plim}[\widehat{\text{cov}}(Z_i, U_i)]$ must be zero if Z_i is a valid instrument.

Noting that $\sigma_{zx} = \text{cov}(Z_i, X_i)$ is assumed to be non-zero, it must be – using the "Law of Large Numbers" property from Appendix 11.1 – that $\text{plim}[\widehat{\text{cov}}(Z_i, X_i)]$ in the right-hand side of the last line of Equation 12-12 is non-zero. Dividing both sides of Equation 12-12 by this non-zero quantity – and using the "Division" property from Appendix 11.1 – it then follows that

$$\frac{\text{plim}[\widehat{\text{cov}}(Z_i, Y_i)]}{\text{plim}[\widehat{\text{cov}}(Z_i, X_i)]} = \text{plim}\left[\frac{\widehat{\text{cov}}(Z_i, Y_i)}{\widehat{\text{cov}}(Z_i, X_i)}\right] = \beta \tag{12-13}$$

Thus, defining the instrumental variables estimator of β as

$$\hat{\beta}^{\text{IV}} \equiv \frac{\widehat{\text{cov}}(Z_i, Y_i)}{\widehat{\text{cov}}(Z_i, X_i)} \tag{12-14}$$

we see that $\hat{\beta}^{\text{IV}}$ is a consistent estimator of β if Z_i is a valid instrument for X_i – that is, if $\text{plim}[\widehat{\text{cov}}(Z_i, U_i)]$ is zero and $\text{cov}(Z_i, X_i)$ is non-zero.

Note that it is not necessary to assume that the instrument (Z_i) is uncorrelated with the model error (U_i): all that is necessary in order to obtain consistency for $\hat{\beta}^{\text{IV}}$ is that

$$\text{plim}\left[\frac{1}{N}\sum_{i=1}^{N}(Z_i - \overline{Z})(U_i - \overline{U})\right] = \text{plim}[\widehat{\text{cov}}(Z_i, U_i)] = 0 \tag{12-15}$$

The assumption embodied in Equation 12-15 is usually called "asymptotic uncorrelatedness" because it implies that the correlation between the instrument (Z_i) and the model error (U_i) becomes negligible for sufficiently large samples; this concept was first defined in Chapter 11. This distinction between "uncorrelatedness" and "asymptotic uncorrelatedness" looks like an unimportant detail at the moment. But in Section 12.5 this weaker condition will be crucial in obtaining a consistent parameter estimator – the "Two-Stage Least Squares" estimator – for over-identified models, where one is fortunate enough to have available more than the minimally necessary number of instruments.

12.4 INFERENCE USING THE INSTRUMENTAL VARIABLES SLOPE ESTIMATOR

As with the estimators in previous chapters, inference requires a sampling distribution for $\hat{\beta}^{\text{IV}}$; here what is needed is the limiting or asymptotic distribution defined in Chapter 11. As before, it is helpful to re-express $\hat{\beta}^{\text{IV}}$ as a weighted sum of the model errors.

To that end, it is useful to abbreviate the notation for the sample covariance between Z_i and X_i;

$$\hat{\sigma}_{zx} \equiv \frac{1}{N}\sum_{i=1}^{N}(Z_i - \overline{Z})(X_i - \overline{X}) = \widehat{\text{cov}}(Z_i, X_i) \tag{12-16}$$

and to rewrite $\hat{\beta}^{\text{IV}}$ from Equation 12-14 as an explicitly linear estimator:

$$
\begin{aligned}
\hat{\beta}^{\text{IV}} &= \frac{\widehat{\text{cov}}(Z_i, Y_i)}{\widehat{\text{cov}}(Z_i, X_i)} = \frac{\widehat{\text{cov}}(Z_i, Y_i)}{\hat{\sigma}_{zx}} = \frac{1}{\hat{\sigma}_{zx}}\widehat{\text{cov}}(Z_i, Y_i) \\
&= \frac{1}{\hat{\sigma}_{zx}}\frac{1}{N}\sum_{i=1}^{N}(Z_i - \overline{Z})(Y_i - \overline{Y}) \\
&= \frac{1}{\hat{\sigma}_{zx}}\frac{1}{N}\sum_{i=1}^{N}(Z_i - \overline{Z})Y_i - \frac{1}{\hat{\sigma}_{zx}}\frac{1}{N}\sum_{i=1}^{N}(Z_i - \overline{Z})\overline{Y} \\
&= \frac{1}{\hat{\sigma}_{zx}}\frac{1}{N}\sum_{i=1}^{N}(Z_i - \overline{Z})Y_i - \frac{1}{\hat{\sigma}_{zx}}\frac{1}{N}\overline{Y}\sum_{i=1}^{N}(Z_i - \overline{Z}) \\
&= \frac{1}{\hat{\sigma}_{zx}}\frac{1}{N}\sum_{i=1}^{N}(Z_i - \overline{Z})Y_i \\
&= \sum_{i=1}^{N}\left[\frac{Z_i - \overline{Z}}{N\hat{\sigma}_{zx}}\right]Y_i \\
&= \sum_{i=1}^{N}W_i^{\text{IV}}Y_i
\end{aligned}
\tag{12-17}
$$

which last line defines the "IV regression weights," W_i^{IV},

$$
W_i^{\text{IV}} \equiv \frac{Z_i - \overline{Z}}{N\,\hat{\sigma}_{zx}} \tag{12-18}
$$

It follows (Exercise 12-2) from this definition that

$$
\sum_{i=1}^{N}W_i^{\text{IV}} = 0 \quad \text{and} \quad \sum_{i=1}^{N}W_i^{\text{IV}}X_i = 1 \tag{12-19}
$$

Substituting the model equation for Y_i from Equation 12-6 into Equation 12-18 and using the results on W_i^{IV} from Equation 12-19,

$$
\begin{aligned}
\hat{\beta}^{\text{IV}} &= \sum_{i=1}^{N}W_i^{\text{IV}}Y_i \\
&= \sum_{i=1}^{N}W_i^{\text{IV}}[\alpha + \beta X_i + U_i] \\
&= \alpha\sum_{i=1}^{N}W_i^{\text{IV}} + \beta\sum_{i=1}^{N}W_i^{\text{IV}}X_i + \sum_{i=1}^{N}W_i^{\text{IV}}U_i \\
&= \beta + \sum_{i=1}^{N}W_i^{\text{IV}}U_i
\end{aligned}
\tag{12-20}
$$

Thus $\hat{\beta}^{\text{IV}}$, like the estimators of β obtained in previous chapters, is still just a weighted sum of the model error terms, $U_i \ldots U_N$. As in Chapter 11, however, the weights $\left(W_I^{\text{IV}} \ldots W_N^{\text{IV}}\right)$ are themselves random variables – and the model errors are no longer assumed to be normally distributed – so the derivation of the (asymptotic) sampling distribution of $\hat{\beta}^{\text{IV}}$ is technically more challenging than the analogous derivation for the sampling distribution of $\hat{\beta}^{\text{OLS}}$ in the fixed-regressor model of Chapter 5; this derivation is therefore relegated to Appendix 12.1. The result itself, however, is very simple:

$$\sqrt{N}\left(\hat{\beta}^{\text{IV}} - \beta\right) \xrightarrow{d} N\left[0, \frac{\sigma_z^2 \sigma_u^2}{\left(\sigma_{zx}\right)^2}\right] \tag{12-21}$$

or, equivalently,

$$\hat{\beta}^{\text{IV}} \overset{d}{\sim} N\left[\beta, \frac{1}{N} \frac{\sigma_z^2 \sigma_u^2}{\left(\sigma_{zx}\right)^2}\right] \tag{12-22}$$

Thus, if σ_z^2, σ_{zx}, and σ_u^2 were known, then an (asymptotically) appropriate statistic for inference on β would be

$$\frac{\sqrt{N}\left(\hat{\beta}^{\text{IV}} - \beta\right)}{\dfrac{\sigma_z \sigma_u}{\sigma_{zx}}} \xrightarrow{d} N[0,\ 1] \tag{12-23}$$

The values of σ_z, σ_{zx}, and σ_u are not known, but – because all of this is for large samples – they can be replaced by the consistent sample estimates s_z, s_{zx}, and s_u, obtained (using the observed data) from the estimators,[19]

$$\begin{aligned} S_z^2 &= \frac{1}{N-1}\sum_{i=1}^{N}\left(Z_i - \overline{Z}\right)^2 \\ S_{zx} &= \frac{1}{N-1}\sum_{i=1}^{N}\left(Z_i - \overline{Z}\right)\left(X_i - \overline{X}\right) \\ S_u^2 &= \frac{1}{N-1}\sum_{i=1}^{N}\left(Y_i - \hat{\alpha}^{\text{IV}} - \hat{\beta}^{\text{IV}} X_i\right)^2 \end{aligned} \tag{12-24}$$

The consistency of S_z^2 and S_{zx} for the corresponding population moments follows from the "Law of Large Numbers" property in Appendix 11.1; the consistency of S_u^2 is proven in Exercise 12-5.[20] Because the square root is a continuous function, the "Slutsky Theorem" property in Appendix 11.1 then implies that S_z and S_u are consistent estimators of the square roots of σ_z^2 and σ_u^2, respectively. Thus, Equation 12-23 can in practice be replaced by the (asymptotically equivalent) result,

$$\frac{\sqrt{N}\left(\hat{\beta}^{\text{IV}} - \beta\right)}{\dfrac{s_z s_u}{s_{zx}}} \xrightarrow{d} N[0,\ 1] \tag{12-25}$$

One might wonder about the validity of simply replacing $\sigma_z \sigma_u / \sigma_{zx}$ in Equation 12-24 by this quotient of estimators, $s_z s_u / s_{zx}$. Most analysts would not worry much about this, however, as one is

[19] The focus in this chapter is on consistent estimation of the slope parameter, β, but it is easy to show that $\hat{\alpha}^{\text{IV}} \equiv \overline{Y} - \hat{\beta}^{\text{IV}}\overline{X}$ provides a consistent estimator for α – see Exercise 12-4.

[20] This derivation makes it plain that it makes no difference, asymptotically, whether one divides by N or by N–1; thus, S_{zx} and $\hat{\sigma}_{zx}$ are essentially equivalent. In fact, if using N–1 instead of N in any of these estimators makes any notable difference in one's inference results, then N is most likely too small for it to be appropriate to use an asymptotic sampling distribution.

already assuming that the sample is large in using the asymptotic distribution of $\hat{\beta}^{IV}$ in the first place. Note that a similar issue came up in Section 4.6, where the estimated confidence intervals for μ, the mean of a normally distributed variate, became larger when σ^2 was replaced by the sample estimate s^2 and the relevant critical point of the unit normal distribution was therefore replaced by a critical point of the Student's t distribution. Comparing the critical points of these two distributions, however, it was clear that this substitution makes little difference for samples in excess of 60 observations. The substitution here is more extensive, but these results suggest that it is not a problem for samples well in excess of, say, 100 observations.

An asymptotically appropriate statistic for testing the null hypothesis $H_o : \beta = \beta_o$ against the two-sided alternative hypothesis $H_A : \beta \neq \beta_o$, then, is

$$\frac{\sqrt{N}\left(\hat{\beta}^{IV} - \beta_o\right)}{\dfrac{s_z s_u}{s_{zx}}} \xrightarrow{d} N[0,\ 1] \tag{12-26}$$

Therefore – using essentially identical reasoning as for the analogous results in Chapters 4, 7, and 9 – Equation 12-26 implies that the (now only asymptotically valid) p-value at which H_o can be rejected is just double the tail area of the unit normal density to the right of the observed test statistic value,

$$\left| \frac{\sqrt{N}\left(\left\{\hat{\beta}^{IV}\right\}^* - \beta_o\right)}{\dfrac{s_z s_u}{s_{zx}}} \right| \tag{12-27}$$

where $\left\{\hat{\beta}^{IV}\right\}^*$ is the realized value of the estimator $\hat{\beta}^{IV}$. Similarly, Equation 12-26 implies that

$$\left\{\hat{\beta}^{IV}\right\}^* \pm 1.96 \frac{s_z s_u}{\sqrt{N} s_{zx}} \tag{12-28}$$

is an (asymptotically valid) estimate of a 95% confidence interval for β.

Returning to Equation 12-22, the asymptotic variance of $\hat{\beta}^{IV}$ can be rewritten in several ways which are worth considering. First, noting that $\left(\rho_{zx}\right)^2 = \left(\sigma_{zx}\right)^2 / \left(\sigma_z^2 \sigma_x^2\right)$ is the square of the correlation between the instrument (Z_i) and the endogenous variable (X_i),

$$\text{avar}\left(\hat{\beta}^{IV}\right) = \frac{1}{N} \frac{\sigma_z^2 \sigma_u^2}{\left(\sigma_{zx}\right)^2} = \frac{1}{N} \frac{\sigma_u^2}{\rho_{zx}^2 \sigma_x^2} \tag{12-29}$$

This result suggests a useful way to think about the sampling variance of $\hat{\beta}^{IV}$: it depends inversely on the amount of sample variation there is in the explanatory variable $\left(\sigma_x^2\right)$ and – crucially – also inversely on the magnitude of the correlation of the instrument with this explanatory variable. In fact, looking back at Equation 11-20, the expression for the asymptotic sampling distribution of the OLS estimator of β,

$$\text{avar}\left(\hat{\beta}^{OLS}\right) = \frac{1}{N} \frac{\sigma_u^2}{\sigma_x^2} \tag{12-30}$$

we see that (for large samples) the sampling variance of $\hat{\beta}^{IV}$ always exceeds that of $\hat{\beta}^{OLS}$. The asymptotic sampling variance of $\hat{\beta}^{IV}$ is clearly only a little bit larger if the instrument is highly correlated with the explanatory variable, but Equation 12-29 shows that it will be substantially larger if this correlation is not so high. Of course, $\hat{\beta}^{IV}$ is consistent, whereas $\hat{\beta}^{OLS}$ is not. Evidently, the *kind* of price we pay for consistency is in higher sampling variance for our slope estimator – and, consequently, in wider confidence intervals and in larger hypothesis test p-values. And the *size* of the price we pay depends crucially on the *quality* of the instrument – i.e., on how correlated it is with the endogenous explanatory variable.

Finally, recall (from Section 12.1) that it not possible to estimate the correlation between the instrument Z_i and the model errors (U_i) – fundamentally because the model errors are not observed. (And because the U_i cannot even be consistently estimated unless we have consistent estimates of the parameters α and β, consistent estimation of which requires an instrument Z_i which is uncorrelated with the model errors.)

But we *can* estimate the squared correlation $(\rho_{zx})^2$ that figures in Equation 12-29 and quantifies the price we pay for having to use an instrument for X_i : $(\rho_{zx})^2$ is just equal to $(\sigma_{zx})^2/(\sigma_z^2\sigma_x^2)$, each term in which can be consistently estimated using the sample data on X_i and Z_i. It turns out to be more useful, however, to instead estimate a regression equation in which X_i is the dependent variable and Z_i is the explanatory variable. Recall from Section 8.2 that the observed R^2 of any bivariate regression equation estimated using OLS is closely related to the square of the sample correlation between the dependent variable and the explanatory variable. Thus, ρ_{zx}^2 in Equation 12-29 is closely related to the R^2 of such a regression model, in which X_i is the dependent variable and Z_i is the explanatory variable. In fact, exactly such a regression model will be called the "first-stage" regression in the discussion of Two-Stage Least Squares estimation in the next section; consequently, it is convenient to call this R^2 value "R^2_{first}" here. It can be shown (Exercise 12-9) that

$$\text{plim}\left(R^2_{\text{first}}\right) = \frac{(\sigma_{zx})^2}{\sigma_z^2\sigma_x^2} \tag{12-31}$$

Substituting this result into Equation 12-29 yields

$$\text{avar}\left(\hat{\beta}^{\text{IV}}\right) = \frac{1}{N}\frac{\sigma_z^2\sigma_u^2}{(\sigma_{zx})^2} = \frac{1}{N}\frac{\sigma_u^2}{\left[\text{plim}\left(R^2_{\text{first}}\right)\right]\sigma_x^2} \tag{12-32}$$

Thus, the asymptotic variance of $\hat{\beta}^{\text{IV}}$ can also be viewed as depending inversely on how well a ("first-stage") regression model using data on the instrument as an explanatory variable fits the data on the endogenous variable, X_i.

12.5 THE TWO-STAGE LEAST SQUARES ESTIMATOR FOR THE OVERIDENTIFIED CASE

The analysis up to this point has focused on a very simple case – the exactly identified Bivariate Regression Model, with a single endogenous explanatory variable (X_i) and a single instrument (Z_i). The idea was to provide, in this very simple setting, as clear and thorough an account as possible of the key results on the instrumental variables estimator: its consistency and its asymptotic sampling distribution.

More commonly, however, the number of instruments exceeds the number of endogenous variables. For example, in the Angrist and Krueger model for the logarithm of U.S. men's weekly wages described in Section 12.2, there is one endogenous explanatory variable (years of schooling) and 30 instruments – all of the feasible combinations of birth-quarter and birth-year. This situation is called "overidentification."

Overidentification turns out to be very beneficial. So long as all of the instruments are valid – i.e., correlated with the endogenous explanatory variables and asymptotically *un*correlated with the model error term – these additional instruments can be used to improve the precision with which the model parameters can be estimated, leading to sharper inferences and narrower estimated confidence intervals.

But overidentification clearly also complicates matters. In the Angrist-Krueger model, for example, $\hat{\beta}^{IV}$ can be computed in a great many different ways: using each of these instruments, one at a time, or in any combination. But it makes better sense to find some more or less optimal way to use all 30 instruments at once, so as to obtain a single – best – estimator of the coefficient on education in the weekly wages model. The "Two-Stage Least Squares" (or "2SLS") estimator does precisely that, by using a preliminary ("first-stage") regression to aggregate the 30 instruments into a single, composite instrument. This composite instrument is then used as an instrument for the endogenous explanatory variable in a final ("second stage") regression.[21]

It is also not uncommon for more than one explanatory model in an actual empirical model to be endogenous.

The Two-Stage Least Squares estimator effectively addresses both of these issues. For clarity, it is described here for the simplest possible overidentified model with more than one endogenous variable: a Multiple Regression Model, (as in Equation 9-1), but with $k \geq 3$ stochastic explanatory variables – two of which ($X_{i,2}$ and X_{i3}) are endogenous – and with three valid instruments (Z_{i1}, Z_{i2}, and Z_{i3}) available:

Multiple Regression Model

Stochastic Regressors Case

with two endogenous explanatory variables and three instruments

(all for $i = 1 \ldots N$)

$$
\begin{aligned}
Y_i &= \beta_1 X_{i,1} + \beta_2 X_{i,2} + \beta_3 X_{i,3} + \ldots + \beta_k X_{i,k} + U_i \\
U_i &\sim \text{IID}\left[0, \sigma_u^2\right] \\
X_{i,1} &= 1 \\
X_{i,j} &\sim \text{IID}\left[0, \sigma_{xj}^2\right] \text{ with } \sigma_{xj}^2 > 0 \ \& \ \text{cov}\left(X_{i,j}, U_i\right) \neq 0 \text{ for } j = 2 \text{ and } 3 \\
X_{i,j} &\sim \text{IID}\left[0, \sigma_{xj}^2\right] \text{ with } \sigma_{xj}^2 > 0 \ \& \ \text{cov}\left(X_{i,j}, U_i\right) = 0 \text{ for } j \geq 4
\end{aligned}
\tag{12-33}
$$

With three valid instruments (Z_{i1}, Z_{i2}, and Z_{i3}) such that (for $\ell = 1, 2$, and 3)

$$
\begin{aligned}
Z_{i\ell} &\sim \text{IID}\left[0, \sigma_\ell^2\right] \text{ with } \sigma_{z\ell}^2 > 0 \\
\text{Cov}\left(Z_{i\ell}, X_{ij}\right) &\neq 0 \text{ for } j = 2, \text{ and } 3 \\
\text{plim}\left[\frac{1}{N}\sum_{i=1}^{N} Z_{i\ell} U_i\right] &= \text{plim}\left[\widehat{\text{cov}}(Z_{i\ell}, U_i)\right] = 0
\end{aligned}
$$

and also

$$
\text{cov}\left(Z_{i\ell}^2, U_i^2\right) = 0
$$

Note that $\sigma_{x2}^2, \ldots, \sigma_{xk}^2$ are all assumed to be strictly positive (so that there is some sample variation in each explanatory variable) and that the second and third explanatory variables are endogenous

[21] Two-Stage Least Squares is not the only way of obtaining consistent estimates for an overidentified model. Especially where the homoscedasticity and/or non-autocorrelation assumptions with regard to the model errors are suspect or where one wants to test the validity of the overidentifying restricitions, the generalized method of moments (GMM) estimation approach is preferable – see Section 19.4.

because they are correlated with the model error term. The remaining $k-3$ explanatory variables are stochastic, but not endogenous, because they are assumed to be uncorrelated with the model error term. The three instruments – just enough so that the model is overidentified – are valid because they are correlated with the two endogenous explanatory variables and themselves (at least asymptotically) uncorrelated with the model error term.[22]

The last assumption, as in Equation 12-6 for the Bivariate Regression Model, in essence broadens the instrument validity assumption to also require that the squared value of each instrument is uncorrelated with the squared value of the model error. As in the Bivariate Regression Model, this additional assumption is not needed for estimator consistency, but is necessary in order to derive the asymptotic sampling distribution of the Two-Stage Least Squares estimator.

The proof of the consistency of the Two-Stage Least Squares estimator is only sketched here and the derivation of an explicit formula for its asymptotic sampling distribution is omitted altogether, as these results require a good deal of matrix algebra and are not qualitatively different from the analogous results just derived and discussed for the special case of the instrumental variables estimator of the coefficient on the (single) endogenous variable in a just-identified Bivariate Regression Model. Indeed, the fundamental motivation for the detailed consideration of this simpler model in Section 12.4 is to enable the reader to understand the essential ideas and considerations underlying the Two-Stage Least Squares estimator in the simplest possible context.

The remainder of this section does three things. First, it describes in more detail how the two-stage least squares estimator is defined, in the specific context of the Equation 12-33 model, and how this estimator sensibly combines the three available instruments into two composite instruments – one for each of the two endogenous variables in the model. Second, it motivates the assertion that the Two-Stage Least Squares estimators for this model are consistent, by explicitly showing that the first of these composite instruments is asymptotically uncorrelated with the model error; the corresponding proof for the second composite instrument is very similar and is relegated to Exercise 12-11. Finally, the section closes with a description of the (very easy) mechanics of applying Two-Stage Least Squares estimation in practice, using the command syntax for a typical computer package (Stata) as an illustrative example.

Each of the two first-stage regressions is just a Multiple Regression Model whose dependent variable is one of the endogenous explanatory variables and whose explanatory variables are the three instruments (Z_{i1}, Z_{i2}, and Z_{i3}) and the $k-3$ non-endogenous explanatory variables $(X_{i,4} \ldots X_{i,k})$. The two first-stage regressions for the model of Equation 12-33 are thus

$$X_{i,2} = \gamma_{1,1}Z_{i,1} + \gamma_{2,1}Z_{i,2} + \gamma_{3,1}Z_{i,3} + \gamma_{4,1}X_{i,4} + \gamma_{5,1}X_{i,5} + \ldots + \gamma_{k+3,1}X_{i,k} + V_{i1} \tag{12-34}$$

$$X_{i,3} = \gamma_{1,2}Z_{i,1} + \gamma_{2,2}Z_{i,2} + \gamma_{3,2}Z_{i,3} + \gamma_{4,2}X_{i,4} + \gamma_{5,2}X_{i,5} + \ldots + \gamma_{k+3,2}X_{i,k} + V_{i2} \tag{12-35}$$

Had there been 30 instead of three instruments, all 30 of these instruments would have been included in both of these first-stage regression equations. And if there had been five instead of two endogenous explanatory variables, then there would have been five instead of two first-stage equations, one for each. The error terms in these two first-stage regression models ($V_{i,1}$ and $V_{i,2}$) are both identically and independently distributed with mean zero because, under the assumptions of Equation 12-32, the dependent variables and all of the explanatory variables in both first-stage

[22] Normality need not be assumed for any of these random variables, since only asymptotic results will be available for instrumental variables estimator anyway. Also note that – while not emphasized here, because linear algebra is not being used – correlations between the $k-1$ stochastic explanatory variables are not being ruled out, nor are correlations between the three instruments. Finally, note that it is not strictly necessary to assume – as is done in Equation 12-33 – that all three instruments are correlated with both endogenous explanatory variables; this assumption was made here for simplicity.

equations are identically and independently distributed with mean zero. It was thus unnecessary to include an intercept in these equations, so these two intercept coefficients are omitted here to minimize the algebra. One would, however, routinely include an intercept in the first-stage regression equations in practice.

Each of these two first-stage regression equations is estimated using OLS, exactly as described in Chapter 9. The analysis here will now focus solely on Equation 12-34; the analogous development for Equation 12-35 is very similar and is relegated to Exercise 12-11. The estimated form of Equation 12-34 is

$$X_{i,2} = \hat{\gamma}_{1,1}^{\text{OLS}} Z_{i,1} + \hat{\gamma}_{2,1}^{\text{OLS}} Z_{i,2} + \hat{\gamma}_{3,1}^{\text{OLS}} Z_{i,3} + \hat{\gamma}_{4,1}^{\text{OLS}} X_{i,4} + \hat{\gamma}_{5,1}^{\text{OLS}} X_{i,5} + \ldots + \hat{\gamma}_{k+3,1}^{\text{OLS}} X_{i,k} + V_{i1}^{\text{fit}} \quad \text{(12-36)}$$

which leads to $\hat{X}_{i,2}$, the composite instrument for $X_{i,2}$:

$$\hat{X}_{i,2} = \hat{\gamma}_{1,1}^{\text{OLS}} Z_{i,1} + \hat{\gamma}_{2,1}^{\text{OLS}} Z_{i,2} + \hat{\gamma}_{3,1}^{\text{OLS}} Z_{i,3} + \hat{\gamma}_{4,1}^{\text{OLS}} X_{i,4} + \hat{\gamma}_{5,1}^{\text{OLS}} X_{i,5} + \ldots + \hat{\gamma}_{k+3,1}^{\text{OLS}} X_{i,k} \quad \text{(12-37)}$$

Is $\hat{X}_{i,2}$ a valid instrument for $X_{i,2}$? In order to be a valid instrument, $\hat{X}_{i,2}$ must be both correlated with $X_{i,2}$ and asymptotically uncorrelated with the model error term, U_i. The instrument $\hat{X}_{i,2}$ will be correlated with $X_{i,2}$ to some degree so long as Equation 12-36 has a non-zero value for R^2. Indeed, squared magnitude of $\text{corr}(\hat{X}_{i,2}, X_{i,2})$ is essentially equal to the first-stage equation R^2 for large samples. The Equation 12-32 result for the simple bivariate model suggests – and it is broadly true – that the asymptotic variances of the Two-Stage Least Squares estimators will be inversely related to the first-stage R^2 values.

Demonstrating that $\hat{X}_{i,2}$ is asymptotically uncorrelated with U_i is not at all difficult, but it does require a bit of algebra, so this proof is given in Appendix 12.2. The result hinges on the fact that all of the OLS parameter estimators in Equation 12-36 converge in probability to fixed numbers. Thus, $\hat{X}_{i,2}$ is asymptotically equivalent to a weighted sum of the instruments $(Z_{i1}, Z_{i2}, \text{ and } Z_{i3})$ and the non-endogenous explanatory variables $(X_{i,4} \ldots X_{i,k})$, all of which are assumed to be uncorrelated with U_i. The Two-Stage Least Squares composite instrument for $X_{i,2}$ is therefore a valid instrument if and only if none of $(Z_{i1}, Z_{i2}, Z_{i3}, X_{i,4}, \ldots, X_{i,k})$ is asymptotically correlated with U_i and at least one of $(Z_{i1}, Z_{i2}, Z_{i3}, X_{i4}, \ldots, X_{i,k})$ is asymptotically correlated with $X_{i,2}$, so that the first-stage equation R^2 does not go to zero.

One can then use $\hat{X}_{i,2}$ and $\hat{X}_{i,3}$ as instruments for the endogenous regressors $X_{i,2}$ and $X_{i,3}$ and derive consistent instrumental variables estimators for $\beta_1 \ldots \beta_k$ in Equation 12-33 via reasoning essentially identical to that used Section 12.3 – but couched in matrix algebra, so as to account for the multiplicity of instruments and explanatory variables. These estimators are then called $\hat{\beta}_1^{\text{2SLS}} \ \ldots \ \hat{\beta}_k^{\text{2SLS}}$. This is, of course, beyond the scope of the present treatment.

Alternatively, but less formally, one can simply substitute these two composite instruments $(\hat{X}_{i,2} \text{ and } \hat{X}_{i,3})$ into Equation 12-33 as substitutes for $X_{i,2}$ and $X_{i,3}$:

$$Y_i = \beta_1 + \beta_2 \hat{X}_{i,2} + \beta_3 \hat{X}_{i,3} + \beta_4 X_{i,4} + \ldots + \beta_k X_{i,k} + U_i \quad \text{(12-38)}$$

and estimate the resulting model using OLS; the resulting parameter estimates are numerically equivalent to $\hat{\beta}_1^{\text{2SLS}} \ \ldots \ \hat{\beta}_k^{\text{2SLS}}$.

Typical econometric software makes Two-Stage Least Squares estimation very easy in practice. For example, supposing that k equals five, the Stata command for estimating Equation 12-33 would be:

```
ivregress 2sls y (x2 x3 = z1 z2 z3) x4 x5
```
(12-39)

If one wants Stata to also display the regression output for the two first-stage regression equations, one could specify this using the command:

```
ivregress 2sls y (x2 x3 = z1 z2 z3) x4 x5, first
```
(12-40)

This option is useful because it allows one to confirm that each of the (in this instance) two first-stage regression models fits reasonably well, by examining its corrected R^2. Also, an examination of the estimated t statistics on the first-stage coefficient estimates gives valuable insight into which of the variables are most useful as instruments for each of the two endogenous variables in this example.

If one in addition wants Stata to compute the White-Eicker standard error estimates for $\hat{\beta}_1^{2SLS} \ldots \hat{\beta}_k^{2SLS}$, which are consistent estimates even if there heteroscedasticity of unknown form in U_i, the Stata command syntax is simply:[23]

```
ivregress 2sls y (x2 x3 = z1 z2 z3) x4 x5, first robust
```
(12-41)

12.6 APPLICATION: THE RELATIONSHIP BETWEEN EDUCATION AND WAGES (ANGRIST AND KRUEGER, 1991)

The Angrist-Krueger (1991) model uses data from the 1980 Census to relate the logarithm of weekly wages ($lwklywge_i$) for a large sample of U.S. men to their education level (measured as years of schooling, edu_i) and nine birth-year dummy variables ($yr1 \ldots yr9$); these latter nine explanatory variables allow the intercept to adjust for the fact that the men in the sample were born in years 1930 through 1939.

The OLS coefficient estimates (on edu_i, and *yrl ... year9*) for this model were obtained in Section 11.8. The likely endogeneity in the education variable was explicitly ignored there, so as to instead demonstrate how bootstrapped standard error estimates could be obtained. These estimated standard errors were then used to evaluate the degree to which the asymptotic sampling distribution of $\hat{\beta}_{edu}^{OLS}$ had "converged" for simulated data sets of various sizes.

Dealing with this likely endogeneity in edu_i was a principal feature of Angrist and Krueger's paper, however, and the clever instrument proposed by Angrist and Krueger was described in Section 12.1. As noted there, the Angrist-Krueger instruments for edu_i are the thirty possible combinations of combinations of birth-quarter dummy variables and the ten birth-year dummy variables (*yr0 ... yr9*). These instruments are named *qtr220*, *qtr221*, *qtr222*, *qtr223 ... qtr229*, *qtr320*, *qtr321*, *qtr323 ... qtr329*, *qtr420*, *qtr421*, *qtr422*, *qtr423 ... qtr429* in the Angrist-Krueger data set, so the same notation is used here.[24]

---

[23] See Section 10.7. As noted there, the use of robust standard error estimates is a poor substitute for specifying the model in such a way that it has homoscedastic errors in the first place, but this is not always feasible. Also, per Footnote 10-42, GMM-based instrumental variables estimation will provide asymptotically efficient parameter estimates in the presence of heteroscedasticity as well as consistent standard error estimates, so it is really the method of choice in that situation. GMM is discussed in Section 19.4.

[24] The variable *qtr423* is the product of a dummy variable which is 1 for men born in the fourth quarter of the year times a dummy variable which is one for men born in 1933. It is not obvious why there is a "2" in the middle of each variable name; perhaps it somehow stands for "times." The other 10 possible instruments – which would no doubt have been called *qtr20* through *qtr29* – must be omitted so that there is no weighted sum of the instruments which precisely duplicates an intercept variable, such as $X_{i1} = 1$ in Equation 12-33.

The OLS estimates displayed in Section 11.8 are the result of the Stata command:

```
regress lwklywge edu yr1 yr2 yr3 yr4 yr5 yr6 yr7 yr8 yr9
```
(12-42)

and produces the following output:

```
      Source |       SS       df       MS              Number of obs =  329509
-------------+------------------------------           F( 10,329498) = 4397.45
       Model |  17878.1592    10  1787.81592           Prob > F      =  0.0000
    Residual |  133959.716329498  .406556993           R-squared     =  0.1177
-------------+------------------------------           Adj R-squared =  0.1177
       Total |  151837.875329508  .460801788           Root MSE      =  .63762

------------------------------------------------------------------------------
    lwklywge |      Coef.   Std. Err.      t    P>|t|     [95% Conf. Interval]
-------------+----------------------------------------------------------------
         edu |    .071081    .000339   209.67   0.000     .0704166    .0717455
         yr1 |  -.0063875   .0050393    -1.27   0.205    -.0162644    .0034895
         yr2 |  -.0148384   .0049724    -2.98   0.003    -.0245841   -.0050927
         yr3 |  -.0175832   .0050325    -3.49   0.000    -.0274468   -.0077195
         yr4 |  -.0209993   .0049845    -4.21   0.000    -.0307688   -.0112297
         yr5 |  -.0328947   .0049515    -6.64   0.000    -.0425994     -.02319
         yr6 |  -.0317808   .0049557    -6.41   0.000    -.0414937   -.0220678
         yr7 |  -.0367121   .0049082    -7.48   0.000    -.0463321   -.0270921
         yr8 |  -.0368905   .0048656    -7.58   0.000     -.046427   -.0273539
         yr9 |  -.0481636   .0048468    -9.94   0.000    -.0576633    -.038664
       _cons |   5.017348   .0054706   917.14   0.000     5.006626    5.028071
------------------------------------------------------------------------------
```

whereas, using the Stata syntax for obtaining the Two-Stage Least Squares estimates, as described in Equation 12-39, the command:

```
ivregress 2sls lwklywge (edu = qtr220 qtr221 qtr222 qtr223 qtr224 qtr225 qtr226
  qtr227 qtr228 qtr229 qtr320 qtr321 qtr322 qtr323 qtr324 qtr325 qtr326 qtr327
  qtr328 qtr329 qtr420 qtr421 qtr422 qtr423 qtr424 qtr425 qtr426 qtr427
  qtr428 qtr429) yr1 yr2 yr3 yr4 yr5 yr6 yr7 yr8 yr9
```
(12-43)

produces the Two-Stage Least Squares estimates:[25]

```
      Source |       SS       df       MS              Number of obs =  329509
-------------+------------------------------           F( 10,329498) =    4.17
       Model |  16727.6008    10  1672.76008           Prob > F      =  0.0000
    Residual |  135110.275329498  .410048846           R-squared     =  0.1102
-------------+------------------------------           Adj R-squared =  0.1101
       Total |  151837.875329508  .460801788           Root MSE      =  .64035

------------------------------------------------------------------------------
    lwklywge |      Coef.   Std. Err.      t    P>|t|     [95% Conf. Interval]
-------------+----------------------------------------------------------------
         edu |   .0891155   .0161101     5.53   0.000     .0575401    .1206908
         yr1 |  -.0088813   .0055293    -1.61   0.108    -.0197187    .0019561
         yr2 |  -.0180303   .0057501    -3.14   0.002    -.0293003   -.0067603
         yr3 |  -.0217955   .0063006    -3.46   0.001    -.0341444   -.0094466
```

[25] These estimates replicate the first two columns of Table V in Angrist and Krueger (1991).

```
         yr4 |  -.0257878    .006584    -3.92   0.000    -.0386922   -.0128834
         yr5 |  -.0388275   .0072665    -5.34   0.000    -.0530696   -.0245853
         yr6 |  -.0387617   .0079775    -4.86   0.000    -.0543973   -.0231261
         yr7 |  -.0448175   .0087578    -5.12   0.000    -.0619825   -.0276524
         yr8 |  -.0465455   .0099112    -4.70   0.000    -.0659711   -.0271198
         yr9 |  -.0585271   .0104575    -5.60   0.000    -.0790235   -.0380307
       _cons |   4.792727    .200684    23.88   0.000     4.399392    5.186062
------------------------------------------------------------------------------
Instrumented:  edu
Instruments:   yr1 yr2 yr3 yr4 yr5 yr6 yr7 yr8 yr9 qtr220 qtr221 qtr222 qtr223
               qtr224 qtr225 qtr226 qtr227 qtr228 qtr229 qtr320 qtr321 qtr322
               qtr323 qtr324 qtr325 qtr326 qtr327 qtr328 qtr329 qtr420 qtr421
               qtr422 qtr423 qtr424 qtr425 qtr426 qtr427 qtr428 qtr429
------------------------------------------------------------------------------
```

Notice that the Two-Stage Least Square estimates are considerably less precise: the estimated standard error on edu_i has risen from .0003 (for the OLS estimate) to .0161 for the 2SLS estimate. This is because the instruments are quite weakly correlated with edu_i: the R^2 for the first-stage regression is only .003.[26] At this point it is useful to refer back to the result in Equation 12-32, obtained using the simple Bivariate Regression Model of Equation 12-6 with only one endogenous explanatory variable and one instrument. This result shows that the asymptotic variance of the instrumental variables slope estimator depends inversely on the magnitude of the correlation of the instrument with the endogenous variable; hence this asymptotic variance depends inversely on the R^2 value for the first-stage regression. Thus, with such a weak first-stage regression, Angrist and Krueger actually needed their very large sample in order to obtain a sufficiently precise estimator of the coefficient on edu_i as to be able to draw any conclusions.

It is noteworthy that the OLS estimate of the coefficient on edu_i (of .071) is not all that different from the 2SLS estimate of .089. Is this difference statistically significant? The 2SLS estimate is so imprecise that its estimated 95% confidence interval ([.057, 126]) clearly includes the value .089. On the other hand, if any endogeneity in edu_i is really negligible (so that the OLS results are valid), then the 2SLS estimate of .089 is clearly well outside the 95% confidence interval ([.070, .072]) from the OLS estimation.

Neither of these informal tests is appropriate, however, because they neglect the fact these estimates are both realizations of random variables – and correlated ones, at that. The first econometric test of the null hypothesis that the OLS parameter estimates differ so little from the 2SLS ones that edu_i can be taken as exogenous (and the OLS results used) is due to Hausman (1978).[27] However, as originally implemented – e.g., in the Stata "hausman" command – this test has unfortunate properties in finite samples (even quite large ones), so it has been supplanted by what is called the "omitted variables" or "OV" version of the Hausman test. Because it requires matrix algebra, the derivation of the OV Hausman test is beyond the scope of the present treatment,[28] but the idea behind it (and its implementation) are both very simple. The OV Hausman test assumes that the sample is large and that the instruments used are valid; it then tests the null hypothesis that the actual model errors U_i are uncorrelated with edu_i – i.e., it tests the null hypothesis that edu_i is *not* appreciably endogenous. If that is the case, then the OLS coefficient estimates are consistent, leading to OLS fitting errors which are (asymptotically) equivalent to the model errors. But if the instruments are valid, then they (and hence, the predicted value of edu_i from the first-stage regression) are asymptotically uncorrelated with the model errors. Thus, there should be no sample variation in the OLS fitting errors for the predicted value of edu_i from the first-stage regression to "explain," so this predicted value should enter the original model with coefficient zero. Thus, the test

[26] This R^2 value was read off of output which was obtained by specifying the "first" option, as in Equation 12-40.

[27] Hausman, J. A. (1978), "Specification Tests in Econometrics," *Econometrica 46*, 1251–71.

[28] See Kennedy (2008, pp. 153–54) for an exposition. Kennedy, P. 2008. *A Guide to Econometrics*. Wiley-Blackwell.

is very simple to implement: simply add the instruments to the model as additional explantory variables, re-estimate using OLS, and test the null hypothesis that the coefficients on the additional coefficients are all zero. There is effectively only one instrument in the present case – the predicted value of edu_i from the first-stage 2SLS regression – so this is added to the original equation and the significance of its coefficient assessed using the usual t test.

If the OV Hausman test null hypothesis is rejected, then the 2SLS results are significantly different from the OLS ones, and a strong case can be made for using them instead of the OLS results.[29] If the null hypothesis is not rejected, then the case for preferring the 2SLS results based on this particular set of instruments is weakened – as the test is indicating that they are either invalid or unnecessary – and it will not be easy to convince others of the validity of the 2SLS inference results if they substantively disagree with the OLS ones. On the other hand, such disagreement is extremely unlikely because the reason the test did not reject is precisely because the difference between the OLS and 2SLS results is not statistically significant. In essence, then, if the OV Hausman test does reject the null hypothesis, then one should use the 2SLS results; if the test does not reject the null hypothesis, then one must do the analysis both ways and hope – usually successfully – that one's inference results are qualitatively similar either way.

The Angrist-Krueger model falls in this latter category. The predicted values of edu_i from the first-stage regression are obtained by regressing edu_i on the instruments ($qtr220i$ ... $qtr429_i$) and on the exogenous explanatory variables ($yr1_i \dots yr9_i$). This variable is then added as an additional explanatory variable to Equation 12-42, but its estimated coefficient is not statistically significant – the null hypothesis that it is zero can be rejected only with a p-value of .261. Thus, the empirical evidence for preferring the 2SLS estimates for the Angrist-Krueger model as it stands is actually quite weak. On the other hand, the theoretical arguments for the endogeneity of edu_i and for the validity (if not the strength) of the quarter-of-birth instruments are both appealing. The validity of the OV Hausman test also rests on the validity of the instruments and on the validity of the other model assumptions, so diagnostically checking the model is the next task.

Recalling the argument given at some length in Section 12.1, the instrument validity issue cannot be empirically checked. This is because checking it requires consistent estimates of U_1 ... U_N, which can be obtained only if one has consistent estimates of $\beta_{edu}, \beta_{yr1}, \beta_{yr2}, \dots,$ and β_{yr9}. But consistent estimates of these model parameters are exactly what one does *not* have if some of the instruments are not valid.[30] Assuming that the instruments are valid, however, the other aspects of the model specification can be checked using the techniques described in Chapter 10.

For example, using the Stata commands:

```
predict twoslsresids, r
histogram twoslsresids, normal
```
(12-44)

to save the 2SLS fitting errors (under the name "*twoslsresids*") and make a histogram of them, with a plot of the density of a normal distribution (with mean and variance equal to the sample values for the fitting errors) yields Figure 12-1.

[29] Of course, the validity of this test also hinges on the validity of the other model assumptions – i.e, with regard to outliers, nonlinearity, and the homoscedasticity/nonautocorrelation of the model errors. The latter assumptions will be diagnostically checked, using the methods described in Chapter 10, shortly. And note that the validity of the test also hinges on the validity of the underlying instruments ($qtr220_i$ ... $qtr429_i$) and the exogeneity of the other explanatory variables (yrl_i ... $yr9_i$); these assumptions can only be theoretically justified: their validity can only be empirically tested if we have valid instruments for *them*. Finally, recall that any hypothesis test will falsely reject the null hypothesis with some non-zero probability due to chance – indeed, that probability is precisely the p-value for the test rejection.

[30] As noted in sections 12.1 and 12.2, the best one can do is examine the sensitivity of key model inference results to instrument flaws of likely magnitudes. Ashley and Parmeter (2011) do find – perhaps because the Angrist-Krueger instruments are so weak – that the inference results on β_{edu} are very sensitive to even minor flaws in these instruments.

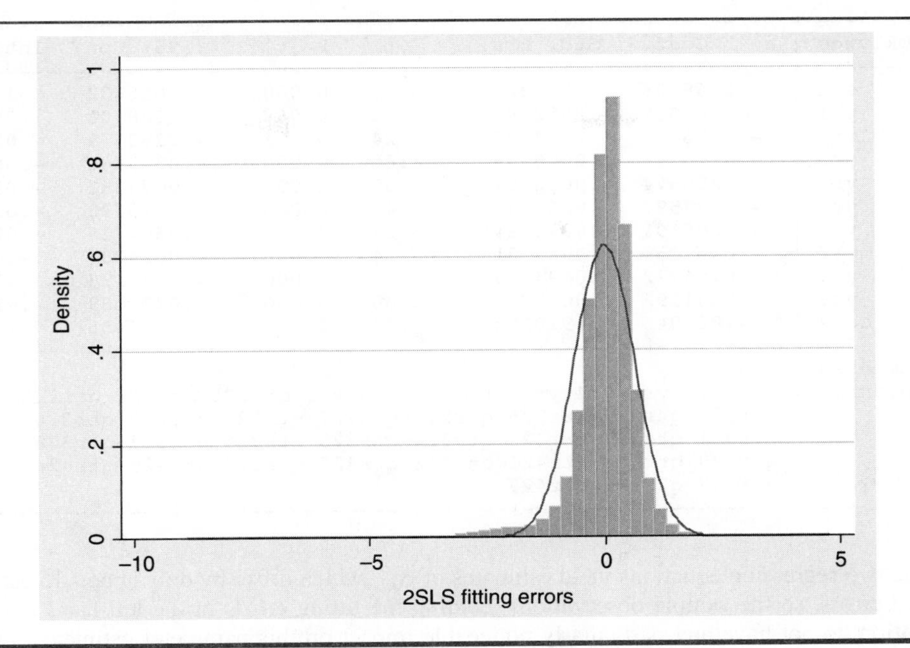

Figure 12-1 Histogram of 2SLS Fitting Errors for the Angrist-Krueger Model

Note that the fitting errors appear to be somewhat asymmetric and substantially "leptokurtic." Leptokurtic simply means that the distribution has more weight on values which are either very small or very large in magnitude than does the normal distribution – for this reason, leptokurtic distributions are sometimes characterized as "fat-tailed." Here the number of fitting errors which are less than -5.0 is 687 out of 329,509 observations.[31] This number is not really comparable to the number one would expect from a gaussian variate because of the asymmetry. But it is easy to check whether or not dropping these observations materially changes the regression results.

The Stata statement:

```
ivregress 2sls lwklywge (edu = qtr220 qtr221 gtr 222 gtr 223
  qtr 224 qtr 225 qtr 226 qtr 227 qtr 228 qtr 229 qtr 320 qtr 321
  qtr 322 qtr 323 qtr 324 qtr 325 qtr 326 qtr 327 qtr 328 qtr 329 qtr 420
  qtr 421 qtr 422 qtr 423 qtr 424 qtr 425 qtr 426 qtr 427 qtr 428 qtr 429)
  yr 1 yr 2 yr 3 yr 4 yr 5 yr 6 yr 7 yr 8 yr 9 if twoslsresids >- 5
```
(12-45)

drops these observations, yielding the regression output:

```
Instrumental variables (2SLS) regression

      Source |       SS       df       MS              Number of obs =  329207
-------------+------------------------------           F( 10,329196) =    4.49
       Model |  16887.0128    10  1688.70128           Prob > F      =  0.0000
    Residual |  122396.515329196  .371804382           R-squared     =  0.1212
-------------+------------------------------           Adj R-squared =  0.1212
       Total |  139283.528329206  .423089276           Root MSE      =  .60976
```

[31] This figure was obtained by simply sorting the fitting errors in increasing order and browsing the data.

```
------------------------------------------------------------------------------
    lwklywge |      Coef.   Std. Err.      t    P>|t|     [95% Conf. Interval]
-------------+----------------------------------------------------------------
         edu |   .0868838   .0153328     5.67   0.000      .056832    .1169355
         yr1 |   -.009582   .0052597    -1.82   0.068    -.0198908    .0007268
         yr2 |  -.0176751   .0054597    -3.24   0.001    -.0283759   -.0069743
         yr3 |  -.0216012   .0059985    -3.60   0.000    -.0333581   -.0098443
         yr4 |  -.0250674   .0062607    -4.00   0.000    -.0373382   -.0127966
         yr5 |  -.0377597   .0069148    -5.46   0.000    -.0513125   -.0242069
         yr6 |  -.0396101   .0075824    -5.22   0.000    -.0544714   -.0247489
         yr7 |  -.0461159   .0083231    -5.54   0.000    -.0624289    -.029803
         yr8 |  -.0464172   .0094364    -4.92   0.000    -.0649123    -.027922
         yr9 |  -.0581192   .0099235    -5.86   0.000    -.0775689   -.0386694
       _cons |   4.827045   .1910193    25.27   0.000     4.452653    5.201437
------------------------------------------------------------------------------
Instrumented:  edu
Instruments:   yr1 yr2 yr3 yr4 yr5 yr6 yr7 yr8 yr9 qtr220 qtr221 qtr222
               qtr223 qtr224 qtr225 qtr226 qtr227 qtr228 qtr229 qtr320
               qtr321 qtr322 qtr323 qtr324 qtr325 qtr326 qtr327 qtr328
               qtr329 qtr420 qtr421 qtr422 qtr423 qtr424 qtr425 qtr426
               qtr427 qtr428 qtr429
------------------------------------------------------------------------------
```

These two regression equations yield estimates of β_{edu} which differ by only about .15 estimated standard errors, so the sample observations yielding the fitting errors in the left-hand tail of the distribution do not have any particularly noticeable impact on this parameter estimate.

Another reasonable diagnostic check is to make a scatterplot of the sample values of $lwklywge_i$ versus edu_i using the Stata command:

```
scatter lwklywge edu
```
(12-46)

which yields Figure 12-2.

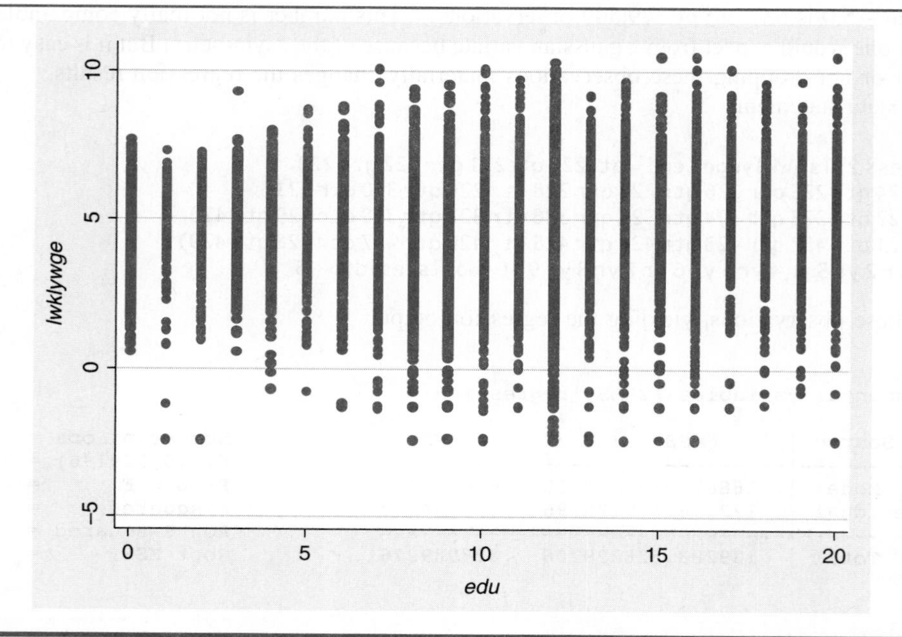

Figure 12-2 Scatterplot of Logarithm of Weekly Wages versus Years of Schooling

The vertical striping in this scatterplot is due to the fact that the number of years of schooling takes on integer values. Allowing for this, the scatterplot seems unexceptional, except that one might be a bit surprised – dismayed, even – to observe that there is no marked upward slope in this scatterplot. Evidently, while $\hat{\beta}_{edu}^{2SLS}$ is statistically different from zero in this large sample, it is not really very large at all.[32] In any case, there is no evidence in this scatterplot of major outliers, nor of major heteroscedasticity problems.

As noted in Chapter 10, the homoscedasticity assumption can be checked further in several ways. One approach is to regress the squared fitting errors on variables which one posits might be related to any systematic variation in var(U_i) across the sample. Estimating such a regression model using the educational variable and the birth-year dummy variables as explanatory variable yields what initially seems like a very significant result:

```
      Source |       SS       df       MS              Number of obs =  329509
-------------+------------------------------           F( 10,329498) =   13.84
       Model |  424.080022      10  42.4080022           Prob > F      =  0.0000
    Residual |     1009793329498  3.06464076           R-squared     =  0.0004
-------------+------------------------------           Adj R-squared =  0.0004
       Total |  1010217.08329508  3.06583476           Root MSE      =  1.7506

------------------------------------------------------------------------------
    residsqr |      Coef.   Std. Err.      t    P>|t|     [95% Conf. Interval]
-------------+----------------------------------------------------------------
         edu |   -.009983   .0009308   -10.73   0.000    -.0118073   -.0081588
         yr1 |   .0013083   .0138358     0.09   0.925    -.0258093     .028426
         yr2 |   .0016585   .0136519     0.12   0.903    -.0250988    .0284158
         yr3 |  -.0141625   .0138171    -1.03   0.305    -.0412436    .0129185
         yr4 |   .0004069   .0136853     0.03   0.976    -.0264159    .0272296
         yr5 |   .0028874   .0135944     0.21   0.832    -.0237574    .0295321
         yr6 |  -.0192142    .013606    -1.41   0.158    -.0458815    .0074531
         yr7 |  -.0286022   .0134758    -2.12   0.034    -.0550144   -.0021899
         yr8 |  -.0299924   .0133589    -2.25   0.025    -.0561754   -.0038095
         yr9 |  -.0259433   .0133072    -1.95   0.051    -.0520251    .0001385
       _cons |   .5491081   .0150199    36.56   0.000     .5196696    .5785466
------------------------------------------------------------------------------
```

But the significance of the coefficient on edu_i in this model disappears once one allows for the endogeneity in edu_i by estimating the equation using Two-Stage Least Squares:

```
Instrumental variables (2SLS) regression

      Source |       SS       df       MS              Number of obs =  329509
-------------+------------------------------           F( 10,329498) =    2.41
       Model | -2626.79166      10 -262.679166           Prob > F      =  0.0074
    Residual |  1012843.87329498  3.07389991           R-squared     =       .
-------------+------------------------------           Adj R-squared =       .
       Total |  1010217.08329508  3.06583476           Root MSE      =  1.7533
```

[32] Recall – as noted for a similar scatterplot at the end of Chapter 11 – that it is easy to misinterpret the slope in a scatterplot when there are multiple explanatory variables in the model. This is because the scatterplot implicitly averages over the values of all of the other explanatory variables in the model, whereas the remarkable strength of multiple regression is that it allows us to obtain an estimate of the partial derivative of (in this case) the expected value of weekly wages with respect to schooling. That partial derivative implicitly holds the values of the other explanatory variables constant – "conditions on them" – rather than averaging over them. However, since the other explanatory variables in the Angrist-Krueger model are just birth-year dummies, it seems likely that the scatterplot is not terribly misleading in this case. The expected impact of an additional year of education on wages later in life is statistically significant – and, corresponding to a factor of $e^{.087}$ (which equals 1.091 on wages themselves) is economically significant – but that does not lead to a scatterplot slope which looks very sizable compared to the noise in the observations on individuals in the sample.

```
------------------------------------------------------------------------------
    residsqr |      Coef.   Std. Err.      t    P>|t|     [95% Conf. Interval]
-------------+----------------------------------------------------------------
         edu |   -.03935   .0441088    -0.89   0.372    -.1258019    .0471019
         yr1 |  .0053693   .0151391     0.35   0.723     -.024303    .0350416
         yr2 |  .0068563   .0157435     0.44   0.663    -.0240006    .0377131
         yr3 | -.0073031   .0172507    -0.42   0.672     -.041114    .0265077
         yr4 |  .0082044   .0180266     0.46   0.649    -.0271272    .0435361
         yr5 |  .0125482   .0198954     0.63   0.528    -.0264462    .0515426
         yr6 | -.0078466    .021842    -0.36   0.719    -.0506563     .034963
         yr7 | -.0154035   .0239785    -0.64   0.521    -.0624007    .0315936
         yr8 | -.0142704   .0271364    -0.53   0.599     -.067457    .0389163
         yr9 | -.0090676   .0286322    -0.32   0.751    -.0651859    .0470507
       _cons |  .9148785   .5494647     1.67   0.096    -.1620566    1.991814
------------------------------------------------------------------------------
Instrumented:  edu
Instruments:   yr1 yr2 yr3 yr4 yr5 yr6 yr7 yr8 yr9 qtr220 qtr221 qtr222
               qtr223 qtr224 qtr225 qtr226 qtr227 qtr228 qtr229 qtr320
               qtr321 qtr322 qtr323 qtr324 qtr325 qtr326 qtr327 qtr328
               qtr329 qtr420 qtr421 qtr422 qtr423 qtr424 qtr425 qtr426
               qtr427 qtr428 qtr429
------------------------------------------------------------------------------
```

In view of the scatterplot plot results – which appear to be fairly benign with respect to heteroscedasticity in the errors of the weekly wages equation itself – it seems reasonable to ignore the OLS results on the squared-error regression model in favor of the 2SLS results in this case. But first one would surely want to check whether an estimated standard error estimate for $\hat{\beta}_{edu}^{2SLS}$ which is robust to heteroscedasticity of unspecified form yields notably different results, using the Stata command:

```
ivregress 2sls lwklywge (edu = gtr220 qtr221 qtr222 qtr223 qtr224 qtr225
  qtr226 qtr227 qtr228 qtr229 qtr320 qtr321 qtr322 qtr323 qtr324
  qtr325 qtr326 qtr327 qtr328 qtr329 qtr420 qtr421 qtr422 qtr423
  qtr424 qtr425 qtr426 qtr427 qtr428 qtr429) yr1 yr2 yr3 yr4 yr5 yr6
  yr7 yr8 yr9,  robust
```
(12-47)

This yields the following regression output:

```
Instrumental variables (2SLS) regression               Number of obs =  329509
                                                       F( 10,329498) =    4.10
                                                       Prob > F      =  0.0000
                                                       R-squared     =  0.1102
                                                       Root MSE      =  .64035

------------------------------------------------------------------------------
             |               Robust
    lwklywge |      Coef.   Std. Err.      t    P>|t|     [95% Conf. Interval]
-------------+----------------------------------------------------------------
         edu |   .0891155   .0162123     5.50   0.000     .0573398    .1208911
         yr1 |  -.0088813   .0056154    -1.58   0.114    -.0198873    .0021247
         yr2 |  -.0180303   .0058058    -3.11   0.002    -.0294095   -.0066511
         yr3 |  -.0217955   .0063396    -3.44   0.001     -.034221     -.00937
```

```
         yr4 |  -.0257878   .0066637    -3.87   0.000     -.0388484   -.0127271
         yr5 |  -.0388275   .0073567    -5.28   0.000     -.0532464   -.0244085
         yr6 |  -.0387617    .008038    -4.82   0.000     -.0545159   -.0230074
         yr7 |  -.0448175   .0088089    -5.09   0.000     -.0620826   -.0275524
         yr8 |  -.0465455   .0099434    -4.68   0.000     -.0660343   -.0270566
         yr9 |  -.0585271   .0105171    -5.56   0.000     -.0791403   -.0379139
       _cons |   4.792727   .2019671    23.73   0.000      4.396877    5.188577
------------------------------------------------------------------------------
Instrumented:  edu
Instruments:   yr1 yr2 yr3 yr4 yr5 yr6 yr7 yr8 yr9 qtr220 qtr221 qtr222
               qtr223 qtr224 qtr225 qtr226 qtr227 qtr228 qtr229 qtr320
               qtr321 qtr322 qtr323 qtr324 qtr325 qtr326 qtr327 qtr328
               qtr329 qtr420 qtr421 qtr422 qtr423 qtr424 qtr425 qtr426
               qtr427 qtr428 qtr429
------------------------------------------------------------------------------
```

The robust standard error estimate for $\hat{\beta}_{edu}^{2SLS}$ (of .0162) is essentially identical to the ordinary estimate (of .0161), so this approach, too, indicates that heteroscedasticity is not a problem for the Angrist-Krueger model.

The last diagnostic check is to examine whether the key coefficient estimate – $\hat{\beta}_{edu}^{2SLS}$, in this case – is stable across the sample when the sample is split in meaningful ways. Angrist and Krueger display (in their Table V) Two-Stage Least Squares estimation results on $\hat{\beta}_{edu}^{2SLS}$ for several models, including additional explanatory variables, such as race, residence in a city (SMSA), marital status, region, age and the square of age, none of which materially alter their results. Note however, that these variations on the model in effect only allow the intercept to vary with race, city residence, and so forth: it does not address the issue of the degree to which the coefficient β_{edu} varies with these variables. The issue of the degree to which β_{edu} varies with, say, age could addressed – and modeled, if necessary – by including in the model a variable which is the product of age times years of schooling and testing whether or not the coefficient on this product variable is statistically significant.

In summary, then, the Angrist-Krueger 2SLS model basically passes its diagnostic checks, thus – conditional on the validity of the Angrist-Krueger instruments – it is reasonable to take the OV Hausman test results seriously and conclude that the 2SLS is not demonstrably superior to a simple OLS regression which ignores the likely endogeneity in the education variable.

What was the point of fussing with the 2SLS estimation then? For one thing, the OLS parameter estimate is basically just reporting the fact that (allowing for the variation in the birth-year dummy variables) weekly wages are correlated with years of schooling. We know, however, that correlation does not imply causation: a positive value for β_{edu} could just as easily arise from sample variation in weekly and in years of schooling both being driven by an (unobserved) personal ability variable as from individuals obtaining a positive return to education in the form of higher wages later on. In sharp contrast, insofar as one believes that the Angrist-Krueger birth-quarter instruments are valid instruments, $\hat{\beta}_{edu}^{2SLS}$ can be given a *causal* interpretation as quantifying the degree to which sample variation in years of schooling *causes* sample variation in weekly wages. Thus, a 95% confidence interval for β_{edu} obtained using the sampling distribution of $\hat{\beta}_{edu}^{2SLS}$ may be substantially wider than that provided by $\hat{\beta}_{edu}^{OLS}$, but it is more meaningfully interpretable than the anologous OLS result.

Also, notably, the 2SLS edu_i parameter estimate yields the same qualitative conclusion as the OLS result – i.e., that education has a positive impact on wages later on. Moreover, the two estimates of the coefficient on edu_i – .089 from 2SLS and .071 from OLS – are even quantitatively very similar.[33]

[33] Since $e^{.071}$ equals 1.074 and $e^{.089}$ equals 1.093, one could more easily interpret the *economic* significance of these two estimates (and the distinction between them) by noting that the OLS estimate implies an eventual 7.4% increase in wages per additional year of education, whereas the 2SLS estimate implies an eventual 9.3% increase in wages per additional year of education.

Indeed, the failure of the OV Hausman test to reject its null hypothesis is actually due to the fact that this difference between $\hat{\beta}_{edu}^{2SLS}$ and $\hat{\beta}_{edu}^{OLS}$ is small. So one could conclude that the *economic* result that education matters to future wages is robust to whatever amount of estimation inconsistency results from the endogeneity in the education variable, a result which one could only have been obtained by using instrumental variables methods to estimate the education parameter consistently.

On the other hand, the near-agreement of the OLS and 2SLS estimates could merely reflect the fact that the Angrist-Krueger instrument idea, while clever, may not be all that good. We have already seen that because these instruments are in fact only weakly correlated with edu_i, the resulting first-stage regression model fits the education data very poorly. That is why it takes such a huge sample in order to obtain a sufficiently precise 2SLS estimator as to be statistically significant, and this very imprecision contributes to the failure of the OV Hausman test to reject the null hypothesis that $\hat{\beta}_{edu}^{OLS}$ is inconsistent. And this imprecision also implies that the near-agreement of the two estimates could easily itself be due to chance – after all, the estimated 95% confidence interval for $\hat{\beta}_{edu}^{2SLS}$ is accordingly fairly wide: from .058 to .121 using the Equation 12-43 results. This result indicates that $\hat{\beta}_{edu}^{2SLS}$ could easily have yielded a notably different realization. Moreover, the later work by Gortnaker et al. (1997) and Polizzi et al. (2007) already cited in Section 12.2 suggests that the Angrist-Krueger instruments are not even so clearly uncorrelated with the model errors – due to apparent correlations between birth-quarter and personal psychological characteristics – so that $\hat{\beta}_{edu}^{2SLS}$ may still be an inconsistent estimator. Finally, the recent sensitivity results of Ashley and Parmeter (2011) indicate that inferences on $\hat{\beta}_{edu}^{2SLS}$ are quite sensitive to even minor flaws in the instruments. Still, even with all those caveats, $\hat{\beta}_{edu}^{2SLS}$ is probably closer to being a consistent estimator of β_{edu} than is $\hat{\beta}_{edu}^{OLS}$. And, in any case, our insight into the impact of education on wages has most likely been considerably enhanced by a consideration of Angrist-Krueger's model.

KEY TERMS

For each term or concept listed below, provide a working definition or explanation:

Endogenous vs. Exogenous Explanatory Variable

Reverse Causality

Granger-Causality

Correlation vs. Causation

Valid vs. Invalid Instrument

Asymptotic Correlation

Overidentified vs. Exactly Identified model

Two-Stage Least Squares (2SLS) Estimator

EXERCISES

12-1. Show that

a. $\sum_{i=1}^{N}(Z_i - \overline{Z}) = 0$ for any set of random variables $Z_1 \ldots Z_N$.

b. Use your result in part a to show that $Q\sum_{i=1}^{N}(Z_i - \overline{Z}) = \sum_{i=1}^{N}(Z_i - \overline{Z})Q = 0$ for any random variable Q.

c. Use your result in part b to show that

$$\sum_{i=1}^{N}(Z_i - \overline{Z})\overline{X} = \sum_{i=1}^{N}(Z_i - \overline{Z})\overline{U} = \sum_{i=1}^{N}(Z_i - \overline{Z})\overline{Y} = 0$$

justifying the substitutions made in, and immediately following, Equation 12-9.

12-2. Use the definition of W_i^{IV} in Equation 12-18 to show that

$$\sum_{i=1}^{N} W_i^{\mathrm{IV}} = 0 \text{ and } \sum_{i=1}^{N} W_i^{\mathrm{IV}} X_i = 1$$

12-3. Suppose that Angrist and Krueger's data set had contained data on men born in just two years – e.g., 1930 and 1931 – so that there are eight possible products of birth-quarter and birth-year dummy variables. Show that it is possible to find weighted sums of these eight variables which are collinear with the explanatory variable associated with an intercept coefficient – i.e., equal to one for every observation – unless two of these eight variables are dropped.

12-4. Using the model given in Equation 12-6 – and presuming that $\hat{\beta}^{\mathrm{IV}}$ is a consistent estimator of β – show that $\hat{\alpha}^{\mathrm{IV}} \equiv \overline{Y} - \hat{\beta}^{\mathrm{IV}}\overline{X}$ provides a consistent estimator of α. {Hint: Sum both sides of the model equation and divide by N; then add and subtract $\hat{\beta}^{\mathrm{IV}}\overline{X}$ and solve for $\hat{\alpha}^{\mathrm{IV}}$.}

12-5. Using the model given in Equation 12-6 – and presuming that both $\hat{\alpha}^{\mathrm{IV}}$ and $\hat{\beta}^{\mathrm{IV}}$ are consistent estimators – show that

$$\tilde{S}_u^2 \equiv \frac{1}{N-\lambda}\sum_{i=1}^{N}\left(Y_i - \hat{\alpha}^{\mathrm{IV}}X_i\right)^2$$

is a consistent estimator of σ_u^2, where λ is any finite constant.[34]

12-6. Starting with Equation 12-26, show how to calculate an asymptotically valid p-value at which the null hypothesis, $\mathrm{H_o} : \beta = \beta_o$ can be rejected, in favor of the two-sided alternative hypothesis, $\mathrm{H_A} : \beta \neq \beta_o$.

12-7. Starting with Equation 12-23, derive an asymptotically valid estimate of a 99% confidence interval for β.

12-8. Suppose that $g(\cdot)$ and $h(\cdot)$ are functions of the data such that $\mathrm{plim}[g(\cdot)]$ equals the fixed constant c and $\mathrm{plim}[h(\cdot)]$ equals the fixed constant d. Presuming that the limiting distribution of the estimator $\hat{\theta}$ is a unit normal, show that

$$\frac{g(\cdot)\left(\hat{\theta} + h(\cdot) - d\right)}{c} \xrightarrow{d} N[0,\ 1]$$

[34] In fact, $\tilde{S}^2$ is a consistent estimator of σ_u^2 for any λ which increases less quickly than N – i.e., for any λ proportional to $N^{1-\gamma}$ with $\gamma > 0$.

12-9. Consider a Bivariate Regression Model in which the dependent variable is X_i, the explanatory variable is Z_i, and the slope coefficient is called γ. Use the Chapter 8 definitions of R^2, SSR, and SST to show that R^2 for this regression equation can be written as

$$R^2 = \frac{\text{SSR}}{\text{SST}} = \frac{\left(\hat{\gamma}^{OLS}\right)^2 \sum_{i=1}^{N} \left(Z_i - \overline{Z}\right)^2}{\sum_{i=1}^{N} \left(X_i - \overline{X}\right)^2}$$

Use this expression (and Equations 11-4 and 11-5, suitably modified to reflect that the dependent variable is X_i here) to show that the probability limit of R^2 is

$$\text{plim}\left(R^2\right) = \frac{\left(\sigma_{zx}\right)^2}{\sigma_z^2 \sigma_x^2}$$

This result is used in Equations 12-31 and 12-32.

12-10. Show explicitly that for any random variables $R_1 \ldots R_N$ and $Q_1 \ldots Q_N$, their sample covariance can be re-expressed as

$$\begin{aligned}
\widehat{\text{cov}}(R_i, Q_i) &= \frac{1}{N}\sum_{i=1}^{N}\left(R_i - \overline{R}\right)\left(Q_i - \overline{Q}\right) \\
&= \frac{1}{N}\sum_{i=1}^{N} R_i Q_i - \frac{1}{N}\sum_{i=1}^{N} R_i \frac{1}{N}\sum_{i=1}^{N} Q_i \\
&= \frac{1}{N}\sum_{i=1}^{N} R_i Q_i - \overline{R}\overline{Q}
\end{aligned}$$

This result is used in Appendix 12.2.

12-11. Use similar reasoning to that employed in Appendix 12.2 to show that the Two-Stage Least Squares composite instrument for $X_{i,3}$ based on the first-stage regression model defined in Equation 12-35 is asymptotically uncorrelated with U_i if and only if the three underlying instruments (Z_{i1}, Z_{i2}, and Z_{i3}) are themselves asymptotically uncorrelated with U_i.

Active Learning Exercise 12a: The Role of Institutions ("Rule of Law") in Economic Growth

Introduction

In an influential application of Two-Stage Least Squares estimation, Acemoglu, Johnson, and Robinson (AJR, 2001)[35] examine the role that the quality of a country's institutions play

[35] Uses data from Acemoglu, D., S. Johnson, and J. A. Robinson (2001), "The Colonial Origins of Comparative Development," *The American Economic Review 91(5)*, 1369–1401.

in its economic development. In particular, AJR model the variation in real per capita GDP across a sample of countries using an index of the political risk of firms' assets being expropriated by the local government. This index, $Risk_i$, varies from 0 (for countries in which this risk is high) to 10 (for countries in which this risk is low). For example, the average value of this index over the period 1985 to 1995 (used by AJR) is 3.50 for Zaire and 9.73 for Canada. One could reasonably take this index as a measure of the effectiveness of the "rule of law" in a given country. AJR posit that instrumental variables estimation is necessary in this case because this index of political risk is a very noisy measure of the actual effective quality of the institutional arrangements in a country, as they affect economic development. In particular, they note:

> In reality the set of institutions that matter for economic performance is very complex, and any single measure is bound to capture only part of the "true institutions," creating a typical measurement error problem. Moreover, what matters for current income is presumably not only institutions today, but also institutions in the past. Our measure of institutions which refers to 1985–1995 will not be perfectly correlated with these.
>
> [AJR (2001, p. 1385–86)]

The outstanding feature of the AJR paper is their creative choice of an instrument for the true level of the quality of a country's institutions. AJR restrict their sample to countries which were once European colonies and use historical figures on the mortality rate of the early European settlers as their instrument for actual institutional quality. Their idea is that European colonizers exported their (presumably high-quality) political/social institutions only to those of their colonies in which the climate was hospitable to settlement by Europeans, such as Canada and what would become the United States. More tropical colonies (e.g., Nigeria) in which the local diseases made actual settlement by European colonists hazardous were ruled by proxy from afar. This led to a lower transmission of European values/culture/institutions to these colonies. AJR express it this way:

1. There were different types of colonization policies which created different sets of institutions. At one extreme, European powers set up "extractive states," exemplified by the Belgian colonization of the Congo. These institutions did not introduce much protection for private property, nor did they provide checks and balances against government appropriation. In fact, the main purpose of the extractive state was to transfer as much of the resources of the colony to the colonizer.

   At the other extreme, many Europeans migrated and settled in a number of colonies, creating what the historian Alfred Crosby (1986) calls "Neo-Europes." The settlers tried to replicate European institutions, with strong emphasis on private property and checks against government power. Primary examples of this include Australia, New Zealand, Canada, and the United States.
2. The colonization strategy was influenced by the feasibility of settlements. In places where the disease environment was not favorable to European settlement, the cards were stacked against the creation of Neo-Europes, and the formation of the extractive state was more likely.
3. The colonial state and institutions persisted even after independence.

[AJR (2001, p. 1370)]

Using a sample of 64 countries which were at one time European colonies, AJR obtained the OLS model estimates

$$\begin{aligned} Y_i &= \underset{(0.41)}{4.66} + \underset{(0.06)}{0.52}\ Risk_i + U_i \qquad R_c^2 = .533 \end{aligned} \tag{ALE12a-1}$$

where Y_i is the logarithm of 1995 per capita GDP for country i and $Risk_i$ is the "protection from risk of expropriation" index described above, averaged over the period 1985–95, and the figures in parentheses are (OLS) estimated standard errors.[36]

Their first-stage regression for the risk index is

$$Risk_i = \underset{(0.61)}{9.34} - \underset{(0.127)}{0.61}\ mortality_i + V_i \qquad R_c^2 = .258 \tag{ALE12a-2}$$

so there is no problem here with the instrument being insufficiently correlated with $Risk_i$. And their second-stage estimates for the Y_i model are[37]

$$Y_i = \underset{(1.02)}{1.91} + \underset{(0.16)}{0.94}\ Risk_i + W_i \qquad R_c^2 = .174 \tag{ALE12a-3}$$

In this Active Learning Exercise you will replicate these results and diagnostically check their model.

Your Assignment:

1. Copy the data file ALE_12a.csv (available at www.wiley.com/college.ashley) to your hard disk and read it into the econometrics software your course is using. (Or ALE_12a.dta if you are using Stata.) This file contains observations on

country	Country name
y	Logarithm of real GDP per capita 1995 (PPP basis, "logpgp95" in AJR)
risk	Risk of expropriation ("avexpr" in AJR)
mortality	Mortality rate for European settlers ("extmort4" in AJR)
latitude	Absolute value of latitude of country's capital (over 90, "lat_abst" in AJR) for each of the 64 countries used by AJR.

2. First replicate (and print the output for) AJR's estimated OLS regression model. Then re-estimate the model using Two-Stage Least Squares and the "mortality" instrument.[38]
   a. Compare the two estimates (and the associated estimated t-ratios) for the coefficient on the political risk index.
   b. At what p-value can the null hypothesis that the coefficient on $Risk_i$ is zero be rejected?
3. Assuming that $mortality_i$ is valid instrument for $Risk_i$ – which seems reasonable because of the time-ordering and the substantial first-stage regression R_c^2 – and assuming that the other model assumptions are reasonably valid (which will be checked below), then both of these coefficient estimates are consistent for the underlying coefficient on the quality of country i's institutions if this "quality" is measured by $Risk_i$ with negligible

[36] From column 2 of Table 2 in (AJR, 2001).

[37] From column 1 of Table 4 in (AJR, 2001).

[38] The Stata syntax is "ivregress 2sls y (risk = mortality), first".

measurement error. (In that case the 2SLS estimator is notably less efficient, so one should prefer to use the OLS estimate.) In contrast, if $Risk_i$ is endogenous due to this kind of measurement error, then only the 2SLS estimator is consistent for the underlying coefficient on institutional quality, so the two estimates should (on average) differ. The OV Hausman test, described in Section 12.6, tests whether or not the realized values of the OLS and 2SLS estimators actually do differ significantly, and hence tests whether or not endogeneity in $Risk_i$ is sufficiently severe that it is better to use the noisier (but consistent) 2SLS estimator. To implement the OV Hausman test, simply obtain the predicted value of $Risk_i$ from the first-stage regression and include it as an additional regressor in the original OLS model: the null hypothesis that the OLS and 2SLS are actually the same (so that endogeneity is not important) corresponds to this additional regressor entering the model with coefficient zero. Perform this test for the AJR model. Is endogeneity important here?

4. Diagnostically check the estimated Two-Stage Least Squares model:
   a. Save the fitting errors with the name "residuals _2SLS" and make a histogram of them. Do they appear to be normally distributed? Are there any evident outliers?
   b. Print a scatterplot of y_i versus $risk_i$. Are there any evident outliers? Is there evident heteroscedasticity?
   c. Check for heteroscedasticity by estimating the auxiliary regression relating the squared fitting errors to $Risk_i$, $mortality_i$, and $latitude_i$. Also try estimating White-Eicker standard errors to see if they differ substantially from the OLS standard error estimates.
   d. Check for nonlinearity in the relationship by including the square of $risk_i$ in the model and also including the square of $mortality_i$ as an additional instrument.
   e. Check for instability in the intercept and slope coefficients with respect to the "latitude" variable. (Since the $latitude_i \times Risk_i$ interaction variable is presumably endogenous also, you will need to also include a "$latitude_i \times mortality_i$" instrument.)

Conclusions:

The AJR Two-Stage Least Squares results seem reasonably well-founded, although the scatterplot does indicate that perhaps there may be two groups of countries to be modeled.[39] The fact that the 2SLS coefficient is larger than the OLS coefficient is consistent with the OLS coefficient being biased toward zero by measurement error.[40]

[39] Even if there are, however, the scatterplot suggests that only the intercept will be affected.

[40] Active Learning Exercise 12d (available at www.wiley.com/college/ashley) examines the quantitative impact of measurement error on OLS parameter estimates.

APPENDIX 12.1: DERIVATION OF THE ASYMPTOTIC SAMPLING DISTRIBUTION OF THE INSTRUMENTAL VARIABLES SLOPE ESTIMATOR

The asymptotic distribution of $\hat{\beta}^{IV}$, the instrumental variables estimator of β in the Bivariate Regression Model of Equation 12-6, is

$$\sqrt{N}\left(\hat{\beta}^{IV} - \beta\right) \xrightarrow{d} N\left[0, \frac{\sigma_z^2 \sigma_u^2}{(\sigma_{zx})^2}\right] \tag{A12-1}$$

where it is assumed for all values of i that $\text{cov}(Z_i, U_i)$ is zero, so that $\hat{\beta}^{IV}$ is a consistent estimator of β. This result is proven below using the Lindeberg-Lévy form of the Central Limit Theorem, as stated in either Equation 11-15 or Equation A11-7, with μ set to zero:

$$V_i \sim \text{IID}\left(0, \sigma_v^2\right) \Rightarrow \text{plim}\left[\frac{1}{\sqrt{N}}\sum_{i=1}^{N} V_i\right] = \text{plim}\left[\sqrt{N}\,\overline{V}\right] = N\left[0, \sigma_v^2\right] \tag{A12-2}$$

and using Equations 12-18 and 12-20, which express $\hat{\beta}^{IV}$ in terms of the model errors, $U_1 \ldots U_N$:

$$\hat{\beta}^{IV} = \beta + \sum_{i=1}^{N} W_i^{IV} U_i \quad \text{where} \quad W_i^{IV} \equiv \frac{Z_i - \overline{Z}}{N\hat{\sigma}_{zx}} \tag{A12-3}$$

Recall that the Bivariate Regression Model of Equation 12-6 also assumes that $X_i \sim \text{IID}\left(0, \sigma_x^2\right)$, that $U_i \sim \text{IID}\left(0, \sigma_u^2\right)$, that $\sigma_{zx} = \text{cov}(Z_i, X_i)$ is zero, and that $\text{cov}\left(Z_i^2, U_i^2\right)$ is zero.

The strategy of the proof is to rewrite $\text{plim}\left[\sqrt{N}\left(\hat{\beta}^{IV} - \beta\right)\right]$ as the probability limit of $\sqrt{N}$ times the sample mean of a zero-mean random variable – which will be called "V_i" – and proceed to show that V_i is identically and independently distributed. The $\text{plim}\left[\sqrt{N}\left(\hat{\beta}^{IV} - \beta\right)\right]$ – i.e., the asymptotic distribution of $\sqrt{N}\left(\hat{\beta}^{IV} - \beta\right)$ – then follows directly from the CLT, as stated in Equation A12-2.

This process seems lengthy because a good many lines are needed when each algebraic step in this rewriting process is explicitly displayed, but almost every step is either an ordinary algebraic rearrangement or a simple substitution (using Equation A11-1, for example), or is an application of one of the algebraic properties of the probability limit, as given in Appendix 11.1. Rewriting $\text{plim}\left[\sqrt{N}\left(\hat{\beta}^{IV} - \beta\right)\right]$, then, yields

$$\begin{aligned}
\text{plim}\left[\sqrt{N}\left(\hat{\beta}^{IV} - \beta\right)\right] &= \text{plim}\left[\sqrt{N}\sum_{i=1}^{N} W_i^{IV} U_i\right] \\
&= \text{plim}\left[\sqrt{N}\sum_{i=1}^{N}\left(\frac{Z_i - \overline{Z}}{N\hat{\sigma}_{zx}}\right) U_i\right] \\
&= \text{plim}\left[\frac{1}{\hat{\sigma}_{zx}}\sqrt{N}\sum_{i=1}^{N}\frac{1}{N}\left(Z_i - \overline{Z}\right) U_i\right] \\
&= \text{plim}\left[\frac{1}{\hat{\sigma}_{zx}}\right]\text{plim}\left[\sqrt{N}\sum_{i=1}^{N}\frac{1}{N}\left(Z_i - \overline{Z}\right) U_i\right] \\
&= \frac{1}{\sigma_{zx}}\text{plim}\left[\sqrt{N}\sum_{i=1}^{N}\frac{1}{N}\left(Z_i - \overline{Z}\right) U_i\right]
\end{aligned} \tag{A12-4}$$

Note that the validity of this last step rests on the indicated probability limit existing – that is, in this case, corresponding to a random variable with finite variance. That this is not a problem becomes clear later in the derivation.

In the next step μ_z, the population mean of Z_i, is both added and subtracted in the expression. This leads to an additional term in the expression which, after a few more steps, is shown to have probability limit zero and then disappears from the remainder of the derivation. The reason why this apparent detour is necessary is that it effectively replaces $\overline{Z}$ by μ_z, in our eventual result, the zero-mean variable which we will call "V_i." This replacement is crucial in showing that the V_i are independently distributed because $\overline{Z}$ depends on all of $Z_1 \ldots Z_N$ whereas μ_z is a fixed constant. Proceeding along these lines, then,

$$
\begin{aligned}
\text{plim}\left[\sqrt{N}\left(\hat{\beta}^{\text{IV}} - \beta\right)\right] &= \frac{1}{\sigma_{zx}}\text{plim}\left[\sqrt{N}\sum_{i=1}^{N}\frac{1}{N}\left(Z_i - \overline{Z}\right)U_i\right] \\
&= \frac{1}{\sigma_{zx}}\text{plim}\left[\sqrt{N}\sum_{i=1}^{N}\frac{1}{N}\left(Z_i - \mu_z + \mu_z - \overline{Z}\right)U_i\right] \\
&= \frac{1}{\sigma_{zx}}\text{plim}\left[\sqrt{N}\sum_{i=1}^{N}\frac{1}{N}\left(Z_i - \mu_z\right)U_i + \sqrt{N}\sum_{i=1}^{N}\frac{1}{N}\left(\mu_z - \overline{Z}\right)U_i\right] \\
&= \frac{1}{\sigma_{zx}}\text{plim}\left[\sqrt{N}\sum_{i=1}^{N}\frac{1}{N}\left(Z_i - \mu_z\right)U_i\right] + \frac{1}{\sigma_{zx}}\text{plim}\left[\sqrt{N}\sum_{i=1}^{N}\frac{1}{N}\left(\mu_z - \overline{Z}\right)U_i\right] \\
&= \frac{1}{\sigma_{zx}}\text{plim}\left[\sqrt{N}\sum_{i=1}^{N}\frac{1}{N}\left(Z_i - \mu_z\right)U_i\right] + \frac{1}{\sigma_{zx}}\text{plim}\left[\left(\mu_z - \overline{Z}\right)\sqrt{N}\,\overline{U}\right] \\
&= \frac{1}{\sigma_{zx}}\text{plim}\left[\sqrt{N}\sum_{i=1}^{N}\frac{1}{N}\left(Z_i - \mu_z\right)U_i\right] + \frac{1}{\sigma_{zx}}\text{plim}\left[\left(\mu_z - \overline{Z}\right)\right]\text{plim}\left[\sqrt{N}\,\overline{U}\right] \\
&= \frac{1}{\sigma_{zx}}\text{plim}\left[\sqrt{N}\sum_{i=1}^{N}\frac{1}{N}\left(Z_i - \mu_z\right)U_i\right] \\
&= \text{plim}\left[\sqrt{N}\sum_{i=1}^{N}\frac{1}{N}\left(\frac{1}{\sigma_{zx}}\left(Z_i - \mu_z\right)U_i\right)\right] \\
&= \text{plim}\left[\sqrt{N}\frac{1}{N}\sum_{i=1}^{N}\left(\frac{1}{\sigma_{zx}}\left(Z_i - \mu_z\right)U_i\right)\right] \\
&= \text{plim}\left[\sqrt{N}\,\overline{V}\right]
\end{aligned}
\tag{A12-5}
$$

where V_i is thus defined as $\frac{1}{\sigma_{zx}}\left(Z_i - \mu_z\right)U_i$.[41]

[41] Note that, per the first footnote in Appendix 11.1, Equation A11-2 can be applied to re-express the probability limit of the product of $\mu_z - Z$ and $\sqrt{N}\,\overline{U}$ as the product of the probability limit of $\mu_z - Z$ times the probability limit of $\sqrt{N}\,\overline{U}$ only because both of these factors have well-defined probability limits. In this case $U_i \sim \text{IID}(0, \sigma_u^2)$ implies that $\text{plim}\left[\sqrt{N}\,\overline{U}\right]$ is a normally distributed variate with variance equal to σ_u^2, using the Central Limit Theorem.

Thus, by defining V_i in this way, we see that $\text{plim}\left[\sqrt{N}\left(\hat{\beta}^{IV} - \beta\right)\right]$ can be re-expressed as the probability limit of $\sqrt{N}$ times the sample mean of $V_1 \ldots V_N$. In order to use the CLT – i.e., Equation A12-2 – to conclude from this result that $\sqrt{N}\left(\hat{\beta}^{IV} - \beta\right)$ is asymptotically normal with mean zero and variance $\text{var}(V_i)$, we must now show that V_i has mean zero, is independently distributed, and has a well-defined variance. Note that because $E[U_i]$ is zero, $E[V_i]$ is actually proportional to $\text{cov}(Z_i, U_i)$:

$$E[V_i] = \frac{1}{\sigma_{zx}} \text{cov}(Z_i, U_i) \tag{A12-6}$$

Thus, $E[V_i]$ equals zero so long as Z_i is uncorrelated with the model errors.[42] Because Z_i and U_i are each independently distributed for each value of i, it follows that the V_i are independently distributed also.[43] Since $E[V_i]$ is zero, the variance of V_i is just $E\left[V_i^2\right]$; so the variance of V_i can be expressed as

$$\begin{aligned} \text{var}(V_i) &= E\left[V_i^2\right] \\ &= E\left[\frac{1}{(\sigma_{zx})^2}\left[Z_i - \mu_z\right]^2 U_i^2\right] \\ &= \frac{1}{(\sigma_{zx})^2} E\left[\left[Z_i - \mu_z\right]^2 U_i^2\right] \\ &= \frac{1}{(\sigma_{zx})^2} E\left[\left[Z_i - \mu_z\right]^2\right] E\left[U_i^2\right] \\ &= \frac{1}{(\sigma_{zx})^2} \sigma_z^2 \sigma_u^2 = \frac{\sigma_z^2 \sigma_u^2}{(\sigma_{zx})^2} \end{aligned} \tag{A12-7}$$

Note that the expected value of the product $\left[Z_i - \mu_z\right]^2 U_i^2$ equals the product of the expected values of these two factors in the fourth line of Equation A12-7 because of the assumption in Equation 12-6 that $\text{cov}\left(Z_i^2, U_i^2\right)$ is zero. This completes the proof.

Three additional comments are worthwhile at this point, the first two of which are essentially identical to those made at the end of Appendix 11.1. First, this proof can be easily extended to a generalization of the model in Equation 12-6, in which the homoscedasticity assumption – $\text{var}(U_i) = \sigma_u^2$ – is replaced by $\text{var}(U_i) = \sigma_{ui}^2$. This extension requires the use of a more general form of the Central Limit Theorem than Equation A11-10; this more general version instead assumes that $V_i \sim \text{IID}\left[0, \sigma_{vi}^2\right]$ and replaces σ_v^2 in the right-hand side by the large-sample limit of the average value σ_{vi}^2 over the sample – e.g., see Davidson and MacKinnon (2004, p. 149).[44] The extension is not difficult; it ends a few steps earlier than the present development, at the point in Equation A12-7 where

$$\text{var}(V_i) = \frac{1}{(\sigma_{zx})^2} E\left[\left[Z_i - \mu_z\right]^2 U_i^2\right] \tag{A12-8}$$

[42] Note that the application of the Central Limit Theorem requires that $\text{cov}(Z_i, U_i)$ equals zero. This is a stronger assumption than requiring that $\text{plim}[\widehat{\text{cov}}(Z_i, U_i)]$ equals zero, which is all that is necessary (in Equation 12-12) to show that $\hat{\beta}^{IV}$ is consistent. Of course, were $\text{cov}(Z_i, U_i)$ equal to a non-zero constant, γ, then this derivation would be identical, except that one would instead derive the probability limit of $\sqrt{N}\left(\hat{\beta}^{IV} - \beta - \gamma\right)$.

[43] This would not have been the case for $(1/\sigma_{zx})(Z_i - \overline{Z})U_i$, because $\overline{Z}$ depends on all N observations.

[44] Davidson, R., and J. G. MacKinnon, (1993), *Econometric Theory and Methods*, Oxford University Press.

so that the final result is

$$\sqrt{N}\left(\hat{\beta}^{\text{IV}} - \beta\right) \xrightarrow{d} N\left[0, \frac{E\left[\left[Z_i - \mu_z\right]^2 U_i^2\right]}{(\sigma_{zx})^2}\right] \tag{A12-9}$$

and the expectation on the right-hand side is in practice replaced by the analogous sample average, which consistently estimates it. The resulting asymptotic standard error estimates for $\hat{\beta}^{\text{IV}}$ are identical to the White-Eicker "robust" standard error estimates discussed in Section 10.7 for $\hat{\beta}^{\text{IV}}$ and readily available in many econometric packages.[45]

Second, it is also worth noting that – were one unwilling to make the assumption that $\text{cov}\left(Z_i^2, U_i^2\right)$ is zero – one could still reach the result given as Equation A12-8 and use this for inference. Implementing this result amounts to simply using the White-Eicker robust standard errors even though the homoscedasticity assumption is being maintained. Asymptotically, this makes no difference, but – in more modest samples – one would expect to obtain more accurate standard error estimates using the A12-1 result.

Finally, it is worth pointing out that it is not accidental that the foregoing derivation and results are quite similar to those of Appendix 11.1, as $\hat{\beta}^{\text{OLS}}$ can be considered to be a special case of the instrumental variables estimator – where the original explanatory variable (X_i) is used as an instrument for itself.

[45] For example, in Stata, simply add the "robust" option to the "ivregress 2sls" command.

APPENDIX 12.2: PROOF THAT THE 2SLS COMPOSITE INSTRUMENT IS ASYMPTOTICALLY UNCORRELATED WITH THE MODEL ERROR TERM

The Two-Stage Least Squares composite instrument for the endogenous regressor $X_{i,2}$ in the Multiple Regression Model (Equation 12-33) is $\hat{X}_{i,2}$, which is given in Equation 12-37 as

$$\hat{X}_{i,2} = \hat{\gamma}_{l,1}^{OLS} Z_{i,1} + \hat{\gamma}_{2,1}^{OLS} Z_{i,2} + \hat{\gamma}_{3,1}^{OLS} Z_{i,3} + \hat{\gamma}_{4,1}^{OLS} X_{i,4} + \hat{\gamma}_{5,1}^{OLS} X_{i,5} + \ldots + \hat{\gamma}_{k+3,1}^{OLS} X_{i,k} \qquad \text{(A12-10)}$$

where the estimators $\hat{\gamma}_{l,1}^{OLS} \ldots \hat{\gamma}_{k+3,1}^{OLS}$ are obtained from OLS estimation of the first-stage regression equation, Equation 12-34. The purpose of this section is to show that $\hat{X}_{i,2}$ is asymptotically uncorrelated with U_i, the model error term in Equation 12-33, so long as the non-endogenous variables in the model $(X_{i,4} \ldots X_{i,k})$ and the three instruments $(Z_{i,1},\ Z_{i,2},\ \text{and}\ Z_{i,3})$ are all asymptotically uncorrelated with U_i.[46]

$\hat{X}_{i,2}$ is asymptotically uncorrelated with U_i if $\text{plim}\{\widehat{\text{cov}}(\hat{X}_{i,2}, U_i)\}$ is zero. From the definition of a sample covariance – and letting $\overline{X}_{\text{hat},2}$ stand for the sample mean of $\hat{X}_{i,2}$ – this is equivalent to requiring that

$$\begin{aligned}
\text{plim}\{\widehat{\text{cov}}(\hat{X}_{i,2}, U_i)\} &= \text{plim}\left\{\frac{1}{N}\sum_{i=1}^{N}\left[\left(\hat{X}_{i,2} - \overline{X}_{\text{hat},2}\right)\left(U_i - \overline{U}\right)\right]\right\} \\
&= \text{plim}\left\{\frac{1}{N}\sum_{i=1}^{N}\left[\hat{X}_{i,2}U_i\right] - \overline{X}_{\text{hat},2}\overline{U}\right\} \\
&= \text{plim}\left\{\frac{1}{N}\sum_{i=1}^{N}\left[\hat{X}_{i,2}U_i\right]\right\} - \text{plim}\{\overline{X}_{\text{hat},2}\}\text{plim}\{\overline{U}\} \\
&= \text{plim}\left\{\frac{1}{N}\sum_{i=1}^{N}\left[\hat{X}_{i,2}U_i\right]\right\}
\end{aligned} \qquad \text{(A12-11)}$$

The second equality in Equation A12-11 follows from the result obtained in Exercise 12-10; the third equality follows from the addition and multiplication properties given in Appendix 11.1. The probability limit of $\overline{U}$ is equal to the population mean of $\overline{U}$ from the Law of Large Numbers given in Appendix 11.1; this population mean is zero because (due to the inclusion of an intercept in the model) each of the U_i has mean zero.

Substituting into Equation A12-11 the definition of $\hat{X}_{i,2}$, the Two-Stage Least Squares composite instrument for the endogenous regressor $X_{i,2}$, from Equation 12-37, yields

$$\begin{aligned}
&\text{plim}\{\widehat{\text{cov}}(\hat{X}_{i,2}, U_1)\} \\
&= \text{plim}\left\{\frac{1}{N}\sum_{i=1}^{N}\left[\left(\hat{\gamma}_{i,1}^{OLS} Z_{i,1} + \hat{\gamma}_{2,1}^{OLS} Z_{i,2} + \hat{\gamma}_{3,1}^{OLS} Z_{i,3} + \hat{\gamma}_{4,1}^{OLS} X_{i,4} + \hat{\gamma}_{5,1}^{OLS} X_{i,5} + \ldots + \hat{\gamma}_{k+3,1}^{OLS} X_{i,k}\right) U_i\right]\right\} \\
&= \text{plim}\left\{\frac{1}{N}\sum_{i=1}^{N}\left(\hat{\gamma}_{i,1}^{OLS} Z_{i,1}U_i + \hat{\gamma}_{2,1}^{OLS} Z_{i,2}U_i + \hat{\gamma}_{3,1}^{OLS} Z_{i,3}U_i + \hat{\gamma}_{4,1}^{OLS} X_{i,4}U_i + \hat{\gamma}_{5,1}^{OLS} X_{i,5}U_i\right.\right. \\
&\qquad \left.\left. + \ldots + \hat{\gamma}_{k+3,1}^{OLS} X_{i,k}U_i\right)\right\}
\end{aligned}$$

[46] The analogous demonstration for $\hat{X}_{i,3}$, the composite instrument for $X_{i,3}$ (the second endogenous variable in the model of Equation 12-33), is Exercise 12-11.

$$
\begin{aligned}
&= \text{plim}\Big\{\hat{\gamma}_{i,1}^{OLS}\widehat{\text{cov}}(Z_{i,1}, U_i) + \hat{\gamma}_{2,1}^{OLS}\widehat{\text{cov}}(Z_{i,2}, U_i) + \hat{\gamma}_{3,1}^{OLS}\widehat{\text{cov}}(Z_{i,3}, U_i) + \hat{\gamma}_{4,1}^{OLS}\widehat{\text{cov}}(X_{i,4}, U_i) \\
&\qquad + \hat{\gamma}_{5,1}^{OLS}\widehat{\text{cov}}(X_{i,5}, U_i) + \ldots + \hat{\gamma}_{k+3,1}^{OLS}\widehat{\text{cov}}(X_{i,k}, U_i)\Big\} \\
&= \text{plim}\Big\{\hat{\gamma}_{1,1}^{OLS}\Big\}\text{plim}\big\{\widehat{\text{cov}}(Z_{i,1}, U_i)\big\} + \text{plim}\Big\{\hat{\gamma}_{2,1}^{OLS}\Big\}\text{plim}\big\{\widehat{\text{cov}}(Z_{i,2}, U_i)\big\} \\
&\qquad + \text{plim}\Big\{\hat{\gamma}_{3,1}^{OLS}\Big\}\text{plim}\big\{\widehat{\text{cov}}(Z_{i,3}, U_i)\big\} \\
&\quad + \text{plim}\Big\{\hat{\gamma}_{4,1}^{OLS}\Big\}\text{plim}\big\{\widehat{\text{cov}}(X_{i,4}, U_i)\big\} + \text{plim}\Big\{\hat{\gamma}_{5,1}^{OLS}\Big\}\text{plim}\big\{\widehat{\text{cov}}(X_{i,5}, U_i)\big\} \\
&\qquad + \ldots + \text{plim}\Big\{\hat{\gamma}_{k+3,1}^{OLS}\Big\}\text{plim}\big\{\widehat{\text{cov}}(X_{i,k}, U_i)\big\}
\end{aligned}
\tag{A12-12}
$$

where the result of Exercise 12-10 is used to convert terms like $\frac{1}{N}\sum_{i=1}^{N} Z_{i,1}\, U_i$ into $\widehat{\text{cov}}(Z_{i,1}\, U_i)$.[47] Finally, note that each term in the right-hand side of the last part of Equation A12-16 contains a factor which is the probability limit of the sample covariance of either one of the three instruments $(Z_{i,1},\, Z_{i,2},\text{ and } Z_{i,3})$ or of one of the non-endogenous variables in the model $(X_{i,4} \ldots X_{i,k})$ with the model error (U_i). Consequently, if each of these variables is asymptotically uncorrelated with the model error, then the composite instrument $\hat{X}_{i,2}$ is asymptotically uncorrelated with U_i, the model error term.

[47] Since the probability limit is going to be taken, the term in $\overline{U}$ can be ignored.

13

Diagnostically Checking and Respecifying the Multiple Regression Model: The Time-Series Data Case (Part A)

13.1 AN INTRODUCTION TO TIME-SERIES DATA, WITH A "ROAD MAP" FOR THIS CHAPTER

First, a brief review of the development so far. Under the assumption that the explanatory variables are "fixed in repeated samples" we have seen how to estimate *and* diagnostically check a regression model using cross-sectional (as opposed to time-series) data, and to thereby obtain good parameter estimates and reasonably valid inference results based on OLS model fitting. In particular, under the fixed-regressors assumption – and where the other assumptions, such as homoscedastic and non-autocorrelated model errors – are valid, the OLS slope estimator in the Bivariate Regression Model was shown (in Chapter 6) to be Best Linear Unbiased (BLU) and (in Chapter 7) to yield inference results – hypothesis tests and confidence intervals – which are valid even in small samples. Chapter 9 extended these results to the Multiple Regression Model. Then Chapter 10 showed how, with a reasonably large sample, one could check all of the model assumptions (except the ones regarding fixed-regressors and non-autocorrelated model errors) and deal with the problems which arise.

Recognizing that the assumption of fixed-regressors is quite restrictive, this assumption was relaxed in Chapter 11. For essentially exogenous stochastic regressors – i.e., for explanatory variables which are at least asymptotically uncorrelated with the model error term – it was shown that the OLS slope estimator in a simple Bivariate Regression Model is still consistent and that useful inference results can still be obtained (at least for large samples) using estimates of its asymptotic sampling distribution. These results all extend to the Multiple Regression Model.[1] The development in Chapter 11 also showed that the endogeneity in explanatory variables which is frequently encountered in econometric work – due to reverse causality, measurement errors, or joint determination – leads to inconsistent OLS parameter estimates and, consequently, to invalid inference results. But Chapter 12 showed how to use instrumental variables (Two-Stage Least

[1] Using matrix algebra, which was not done here.

Squares or 2SLS) estimation to eliminate – or at least substantially reduce – these endogeneity-related problems.[2]

In this chapter the asymptotic theory concepts covered in Chapter 11 – probability limits and asymptotic sampling distributions – are used to extend the diagnostic checking (and model respecification) methods described in Chapter 10 to models based on time-series data, wherein the validity of the non-autocorrelation assumption on the model errors becomes a crucial issue.

A time-series data set consists of observations which are ordered in time, usually observed at equally spaced time intervals.[3] Here attention will be restricted to such "equispaced" time-series and time will be routinely indexed by a variable t which takes on consecutive integer values from 1 to T.

Time-series data are widely available in applied macroeconomic (and other) settings. For example, the Penn World Table[4] includes a variety of annual macroeconomic time-series from 1950 to 2004 on 188 countries. Figure 13-1, for instance, plots PWT data on real per capita GDP for Morocco.

A good source of macroeconomic time-series data on the United States is the FRED database maintained by the St. Louis Federal Reserve Bank. For example, Figure 13-2 plots FRED quarterly data from 1948I to 2009II on the change in U.S. real net exports of goods and services.[5]

Monthly macroeconomic time-series data is a bit less common, but a good deal of it is available on consumer prices, unemployment rates, interest rates, indices of industrial production, etc.[6] For example, Figure 13-3 plots FRED monthly data on U.S. capacity utilization over the period from January 1967 to July 2009, at "seasonally adjusted at annual rates," or "SAAR." This means that the monthly growth rate has been seasonally adjusted (using an estimate of its seasonal pattern) and then expressed as an annualized growth rate were 12 such monthly growth rates to occur in sequence. Seasonal adjustment makes most monthly data substantially more interpretable, but the seasonal pattern for each time-series must be estimated – and it is always changing. The Department of Commerce has a complicated method for continuously updating estimates of the seasonal pattern

---

[2] The material in Chapter 12 also showed that it is not possible to actually test for explanatory variable endogeneity (or to diagnostically check for instrumental flaws) because consistent parameter estimates are needed in order to consistently estimate the model errors which are necessary for such checks. The most that can be done in this direction is to use the results in Ashley and Parmeter (2011), cited in Footnote 12-2, to assess the degree to which a particular inference of interest is sensitive to likely amounts of endogeneity or instrumental flaws.

[3] Time-series data observed at unequally spaced intervals most frequently arises when an occasional observation is omitted from an otherwise equally spaced data set. In some contexts these omitted data can be worked around; in other contexts they are best estimated, by interpolation using observed adjacent values. (E.g., see the Stata routine "impute.") The data set created by Dollar and Kraay (2002) and discussed in Sections 1.1 and 10.8 is unusual in that it suffers from this problem to a marked degree. Indeed, because of this they were unable to include appropriate dynamics (lagged explanatory variables) in their time-series models, since the gap between one observation and another in their data set ranged from 5 to 23 years in length. Consequently, as detailed in Ashley (2008), Dollar and Kraay neglected to include a lagged dependent variable in one of their key models, which omission so skewed their inference results that they failed to detect the fact that their key coefficient is substantially different for countries with negative versus positive growth rates. A description of a practical, straightforward method for recognizing (and eliminating) wrongly omitted model dynamics is the essential topic of this chapter.

[4] See Section 5.1 and Active Learning Exercise 5a and their Web site at pwt.econ.upenn.edu/php_site/pwt_index.php.

[5] Source: research.stlouisfed.org/fred2/. These data were downloaded as a comma delimited file and imported into Stata. A numeric quarter variable was created using the command "generate quarter = _n". The Stata command "tsset quarter" then caused Stata to generate the annualized quarterly change in the "net_exports" variable, using the command "generate change_net_exports = 4*(net_exports – L1.net_exports". (The "tsset" command informed Stata that these data are a time-series, ordered by the value of the variable "quarter"; the "L1." syntax directed Stata to use the time-series lagged one period; and the factor of four put the change on an annualized basis.) The command "scatter change_net_exports quarter" then produced the scatterplot.

[6] For example, see the Bureau of Labor Statistics Consumer Price Index Web site at www.bls.gov/cpi/.

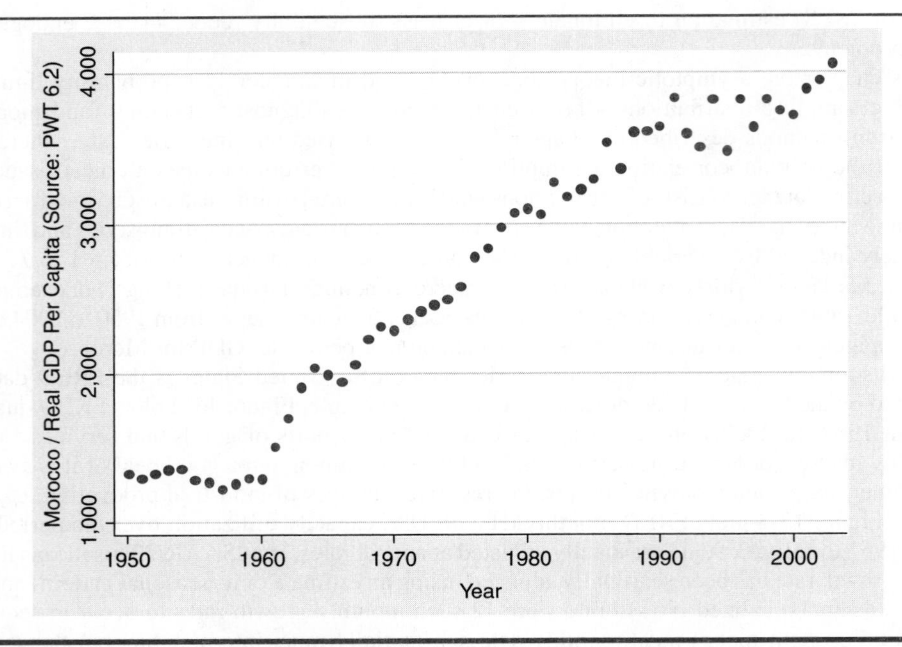

Figure 13-1 Real Per Capita GDP for Morocco

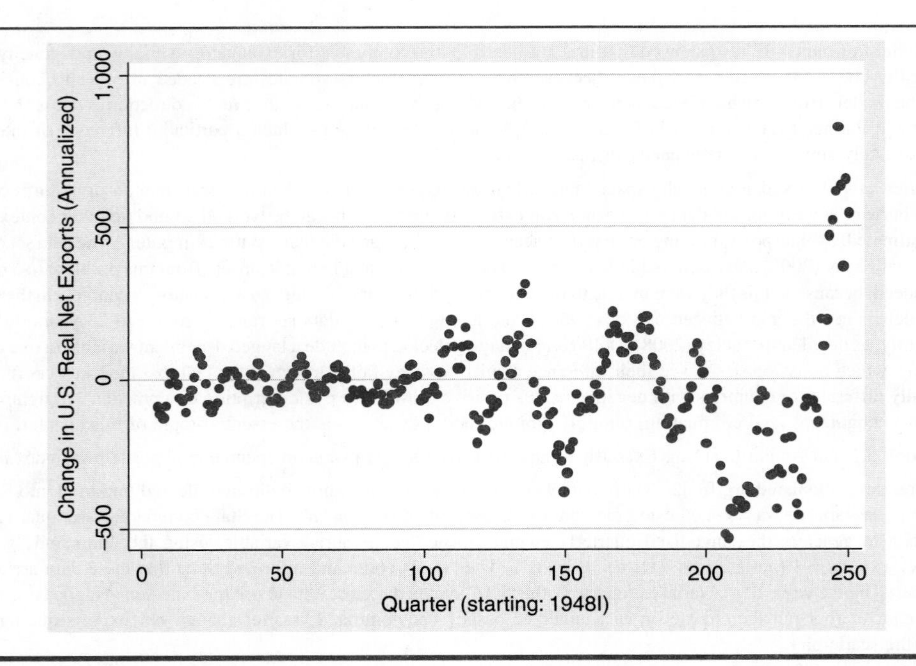

Figure 13-2 Annualized Quarterly Change in U.S. Real Net Exports

in each SAAR series it produces; the Box-Jenkins (ARMA) method covered in Section 18.3 provides a simpler and more transparent way to seasonally adjust a time-series:[7]

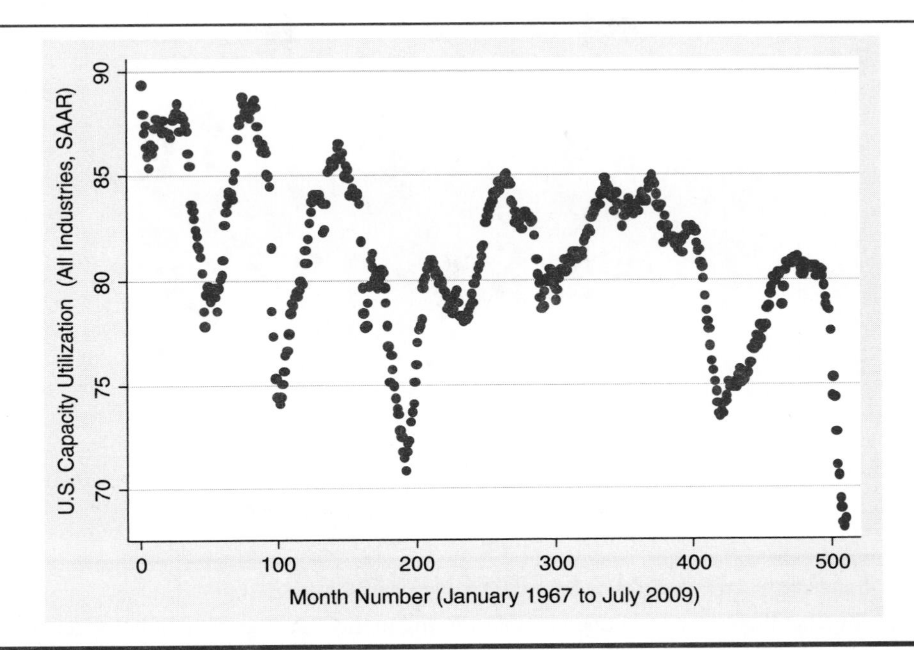

Figure 13-3 Monthly U.S. Capacity Utilization

Daily (and even more frequent) data are available on financial variables, such as exchange rates, interest rates, and stock prices. For example, the daily returns to holding shares in all corporations publicly traded on U.S. stock exchanges are commercially available from the Center for Research in Security Prices (CRSP) at the Graduate School of Business at the University of Chicago; this daily return is computed as $\log(p_t/p_{t-1})$, where p_t is the price of the stock at the close of the market day.[8] Figure 13-4, for instance, plots the daily returns to holding shares in Ford Motor Company over a sample of 2,258 consecutive trading days from January 2, 1998, to December 29, 2006.

The econometric analysis of time-series data differs from that of cross-sectional data in four major (albeit interrelated) respects.

First of all, the examples given above surely make it plain that there is a uniquely useful way to display time-series data: as a scatterplot of the observed values versus the time variable, t. Such a scatterplot is routinely called a "time plot" (or a "timeplot" or a "t-plot") of the data. This feature of time-series data is even more important than it at first appears. For example, even a cursory examination of such timeplots immediately suggests the possibility that trend variables (functions of t itself) and dynamical variables (lagged values of the observed variable) may prove useful (or even necessary) as explanatory variables in modeling the time-series.

[7] It is worth noting that measured monthly growth rates in macroeconomic data are usually so noisy that extrapolating them out for a whole year is quite often misleading. Thus, when interpreting monthly data on the Consumer Price Index, for example, most experienced analysts prefer to look at the change in this index over this same month in the previous year. (This data transformation is called a "seasonal difference"; in Stata the command for generating such a difference in a monthly variable named "cpi" is simply "generate cpi_seasonal_dif = cpi – L12.cpi". This practice not only averages out a good deal of the measurement error in the monthly changes, but also eliminates the need to seasonally adjust the data.

[8] These reported returns are also adjusted for dividends paid.

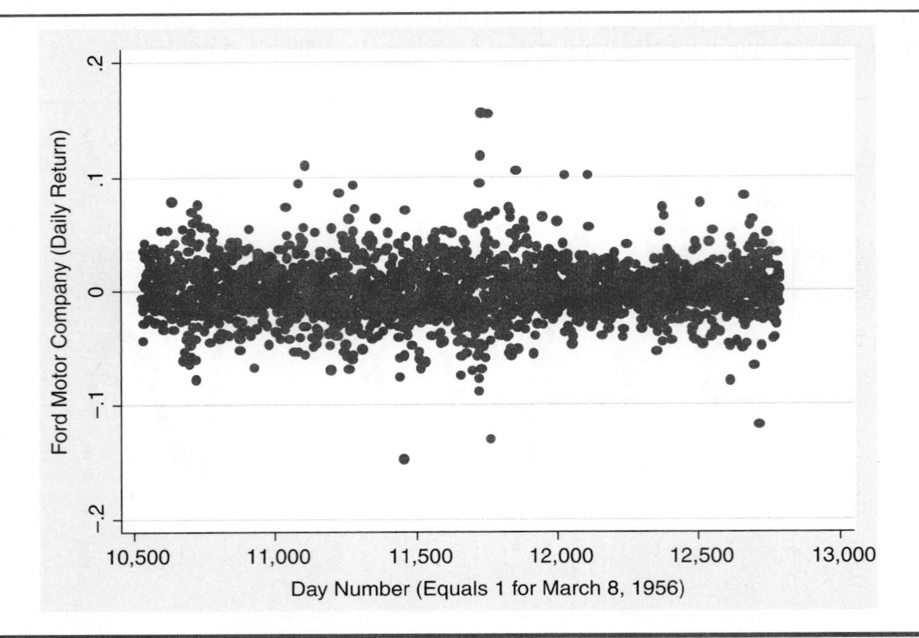

Figure 13-4 Daily Returns to Ford Motor Company Stock

Second, now that there is at least one natural ordering to the data, the issue of homogeneity across the sample immediately becomes both more obtrusive and more accessible. A glance at Figure 13-3, for example, makes it plain that the mean value of real per capita output in Morocco is not a constant, but rather has been trending upward. Similarly, even a cursory inspection of Figure 13-2 reveals that the nature of the process generating changes in U.S. net exports – most obviously including its variance – shifted in the early 1970s; clearly, model error heteroscedasticity is likely going to be an important potential issue in modeling these data. For Moroccan output, one's model must clearly deal with the changing mean; for U.S. net exports, one might instead choose to forego modeling the earlier data.[9] In either case, the time plot has brought into focus a feature of the data which would likely be disastrous for a regression model to ignore. Similarly, it is always essential to consider the possibility of model slope coefficients varying across the sample: the cross-sectional data example in Section 10.8 using the Dollar-Kraay data surely attests to that. But, with time-series data, parameter variation in the parameters across time itself becomes a salient issue. In this context it is useful to think of smooth, slow time variation in model parameters (intercept and/or slopes) as "trendlike" behavior, whereas relatively sudden changes are best thought of as "structural breaks."[10]

[9] Unless, of course, the intent of the analysis is to obtain deeper understanding of the economic and/or political forces underlying this shift.

[10] The issue of diagnostic checking for parameter instability has already appeared (in the context of models using cross-sectional data) in Section 10.1, which included a brief description of the Bai-Perron (1998) framework for testing against structural breaks. More broadly, the issues raised in this paragraph – of the homogeneity across time of the mean, variance, and autocovariances of a time-series – are collectively termed "covariance stationarity." Covariance stationarity will be dealt with fully in Section 17.3, where it constitutes the fundamental assumption underlying linear time-series analysis. Whether conceptually or empirically, distinguishing deterministic from stochastic trendlike behavior – perhaps because it *is* so fundamental – turns out to be a much more challenging issue than it might at first appear; Ashley and Patterson (2010) provides an accessible and illustrative example using long-term climate data. Ashley, R., and D. M. Patterson (2010), "Apparent Long Memory in Time Series as an Artifact of a Time-Varying Mean: Considering Alternatives to the Fractionally Integrated Model", *Macroeconomic Dynamics, 14*:59–87. ashleymac.econ.vt.edu/working_papers/long_memory.pdf.

Third, the assumption that the model error term is independently distributed for each observation is usually innocuous in a model based on cross-sectional data.[11] With time-series data, in contrast, this assumption is routinely violated to a degree that substantially invalidates the statistical inference machinery programmed into econometrics software, which uses computing formulas based on the assumption that the model errors are all uncorrelated. Thus, substantially incorrect *p*-values for rejecting null hypotheses with regard to model coefficients and 95% confidence intervals whose actual coverage is nothing like 95% are commonplace in time-series regression models for which this assumption has not been adequately diagnostically checked. Indeed, exhibiting the consequentiality of substantive failures of the non-autocorrelation regression model assumption and describing straightforward, practical methods for detecting and dealing with them is one of the main points of the present chapter.

Finally, the fourth major way in which the econometric analysis of time-series data differs from that of cross-sectional data is – like the first way – a very positive one. While the consequences of an "untreated" failure of the non-autocorrelation assumption can be quite serious for the validity of statistical inference based on an estimated regression model, the cure is relatively simple. That is because – as will become apparent in Section 13.7 – serially correlated model errors are the natural consequence of missing *dynamics* in the model. Consequently, the problem can almost always be eliminated by simply including the necessary dynamics – usually in the form of lagged variables in the existing data set – in the model specification.[12] In contrast, it is quite often not so clear how to appropriately respecify a model based on cross-sectional data so as to eliminate a failure of the homoscedasticity regression model assumption.

Moreover, once these missing dynamics are properly included, the resulting dynamic econometric model can be quite useful in generating short-term forecasts of the dependent variable. Thus, dealing with the problem of serially correlated model errors – a problem which naturally arises with time-series data and which, undealt with, substantially undermines our ability to validly test hypotheses and estimate meaningful confidence intervals – yields a wonderful opportunity to do something very useful (and highly prized): predict the future. Such predictions can be useful for analyzing the likely effects of a planned policy, or they can be quite valuable in simply forecasting the near-term future environment in which a firm (or an economy) will operate.

The issues and methods associated with how to use time-series data to make good forecasting models – and, for that matter, sensibly confronting the issue of what constitutes a "good" forecast – require the extended treatment accorded them in Chapters 17 and 18. The remainder of the present chapter proceeds as follows:

- In Section 13.2 the analysis of the Bivariate Regression Model (as it was defined in Chapter 6, with an explanatory variable which is fixed in repeated samples) is extended, dropping the assumption of non-autocorrelated model errors. This section shows that the OLS slope estimator $\left(\hat{\beta}^{OLS}\right)$ is still unbiased – albeit no longer BLU – but that serial correlation in the model errors invalidates the usual expression for the sampling variance of $\left(\hat{\beta}^{OLS}\right)$ and hence invalidates the usual inference results programmed into econometric software.
- Section 13.3 demonstrates how dramatically the OLS inference results can mislead in the presence of severe serial correlation in the model errors, using a real-world macroeconomic

[11] Regression models based on cross-sectional data with important *spatial* interrelationships are exceptional in this regard. For example, one might expect correlations between model errors in geographically adjacent counties or countries.

[12] Serially correlated errors can also arise from missing dynamics in the form of omitted explanatory variables or, occasionally, from misspecified functional forms. Including more linear dynamics – i.e., lags in the dependent and explanatory variables – can eliminate serial correlation in the model errors yet leave one with model errors which are not serially independent and, crucially, fail to model the actual dynamics in the relationship if these dynamics are substantially nonlinear. Nonlinear dynamic models are described in Chapter 18.

example with trended data, as seen in the section on the consumption function in almost every textbook used to teach a first-year undergraduate course in macroeconomics. A closely related example – using data which are not trended, but highly correlated with their own recent past – is also considered, yielding inference results which are almost as misleading.[13]

- Section 13.4 introduces the simplest model for serial correlation in a time-series – the autoregressive model of order one or "AR(1) Model"; Section 13.5 analyzes the estimation of the key parameter in this model, showing that OLS can provide a consistent estimator of it.
- Section 13.6 extends the analysis of the Bivariate Regression Model – as it was reformulated in Equation 11.1 with a stochastic regressor – to allow for serially correlated model errors. If this stochastic regressor is uncorrelated with the model errors, then the slope coefficient estimate $(\hat{\beta}^{OLS})$ is still consistent, but its asymptotic sampling distribution (Equation 11–19) is no longer valid because its derivation (in Appendix 11.2) relied on the assumption that the model errors are serially independent, which is no longer the case. Consequently – as with the fixed-regressor case in Section 13.2 – any serial correlation in the model errors invalidates the usual expression for the sampling variance of $(\hat{\beta}^{OLS})$ and hence invalidates the usual inference results programmed into econometric software. Section 13.6 illustrates this point by showing that the model errors in the consumption function fitted in Section 13.3 to detrended U.S. data are serially correlated to a significant degree, explaining why the model yielded clearly incorrect inferences.
- At this point it is quite evident that something must be done about serial correlation in regression model errors or else the OLS parameter estimates, while consistent, will be worse than useless for parameter inference purposes. Section 13.7 show how to deal with such serial correlation in the model errors so as to both obtain valid inferences and a better dynamic formulation of the way in which the dependent variable is related to the explanatory variable or variables in a regression model. This methodology is applied to the Section 13.3 model for detrended U.S. consumption spending, yielding – at last – reasonable inference results for this simple model.

Chapter 14 extends this discussion to the multivariate models we must usually deal with in practice.

13.2 THE BIVARIATE TIME-SERIES REGRESSION MODEL WITH FIXED-REGRESSORS BUT SERIALLY CORRELATED MODEL ERRORS, $U_1 \ldots U_T$

This model is specified explicitly in Equation 13-1:

The Time-Series Regression Model with Fixed-Regressors but Serially Correlated Model Errors

$$
\begin{aligned}
Y_t &= \alpha + \beta x_t + U_t \qquad t = 1 \ldots T \\
&x_1 \ldots x_T \text{ fixed in repeated samples} \\
&U_t \text{ is normally distributed} \\
E[U_t] &= 0 \\
E[U_t U_{t-\ell}] &= \sigma^2 = \gamma_o \quad \text{for } \ell = 0 \\
&= \gamma_\ell \qquad \text{for } \ell \neq 0
\end{aligned}
\tag{13-1}
$$

[13] This second example in fact uses exactly the same aggregate U.S. consumption spending and disposable income data as does the first, but in the form of deviations of the time-series from their (log-linear) trends.

The first thing to note about this model is that it is identical to the Bivariate Regression model specified as Equation 6-1, except that the observations are now indexed by t instead of i, the sample length is denoted by T rather than N, and the non-autocorrelation assumption with regard to the model errors is no longer being made.

In particular, recall that Equation 6-1 assumed that $E[U_iU_j]$ – which equals $\text{cov}(U_i, U_j)$, since $E[U_i]$ is zero – is zero for any pair of observations for which i is not equal to j. In contrast, with time-series data it is essential to explicitly recognize that U_t might be correlated with itself lagged one or several periods. Consequently it is worth setting out the standard notation for describing and specifying such serial correlations and autocovariances:

Autocovariance and Autocorrelation of a Mean-Zero Time-Series, Z_t

$$\text{Autocovariance of } Z_t \text{ at lag } \ell \equiv \text{cov}(Z_t, Z_{t-\ell}) \equiv E[Z_t Z_{t-\ell}] \equiv \gamma_\ell$$
$$\text{Autocorrelation of } Z_t \text{ at lag } \ell \equiv \text{cov}(Z_t, Z_{t-\ell})/\text{var}(Z_t) \equiv \gamma_\ell/\gamma_0 \equiv \rho_\ell \tag{13-2}$$

The generic variable name Z is used above because these definitions will later on be applied to all sorts of random variables – dependent variables and explanatory variables – as well as to model error terms; their primary application in this chapter, however, is to the model error term, U_t.[14]

The assumptions in Equation 13-1 are stated in terms of autocovariances because these are easier to work with – in terms of deriving an expression for the sampling variance of $\hat{\beta}^{OLS}$, for example. But both autocovariances and autocorrelations are defined in Equation 13-2 because autocorrelations are more interpretable.[15] Finally, note that the definitions in Equation 13-2 implicitly assume that $E[Z_t]$, $\text{var}(Z_t)$, ρ_ℓ, and γ_ℓ are all constants which do not depend on time, an assumption which is collectively called "covariance stationarity." The plotted figures earlier in Section 5.1 make it abundantly clear that many economic time-series are not themselves covariance stationarity; note, however, that this property is being assumed in Equation 13-1 only for the model error term.[16]

Thus, the only essential difference between the time-series Bivariate Regression Model with fixed-regressors and the original version of the model (Equation 6-1) is that the time-series version of the model explicitly allows for the possibility that some or all of the autocovariances $\gamma_1, \gamma_2, \gamma_3, \ldots, \gamma_{t-1}$ might be non-zero.

Modifying Equations 6-10, 6-12, 6-13, and 6-16 only insofar as the observations are now indexed by t instead of i and the sample length is now denoted by T rather than N, the OLS estimator of the slope parameter $\left(\hat{\beta}^{OLS}\right)$ can be written as

$$\hat{\beta}^{OLS} = \sum_{t=1}^{T} w_t^{ols} Y_t = \beta + \sum_{t=1}^{T} w_t^{ols} U_t \tag{13-3}$$

[14] The lag length ℓ is more typically denoted using the letters j or k; script ℓ is used here so as to reserve these other letters for use in notating the Multiple Regression Model.

[15] Recall, from Chapter 2, that the correlation of two random variables is a measure of the strength of linear relationship between them and that the magnitude of the maximum correlation possible between any two random variables is one, with this limit being approached as the two variables become exactly linearly related.

[16] Covariance stationarity plays a central role in the material on time-series analysis and forecasting covered in Chapter 17. Consequently, further discussion of the issues and techniques involved in ensuring, where necessary, that the data being used are reasonably covariance stationary is deferred for now.

where the OLS weights are now denoted

$$w_t^{\text{ols}} = \frac{x_t - \bar{x}}{\varphi} = \frac{x_t - \bar{x}}{\sum_{\ell=1}^{T} (x_\ell - \bar{x})^2} \quad \text{for } t = 1 \ldots T \tag{13-4}$$

with the following properties:

Properties of the Least Square Weights

$$\begin{aligned} &(1) \quad \sum_{t=1}^{T} w_t^{\text{ols}} = 0 \\ &(2) \quad \sum_{t=1}^{T} w_t^{\text{ols}}\, x_t = 1 \\ &(3) \quad \sum_{t=1}^{T} \left(w_t^{\text{ols}}\right)^2 = \frac{1}{\varphi} = \frac{1}{\sum_{\ell=1}^{T} (x_\ell - \bar{x})^2} \end{aligned} \tag{13-5}$$

Thus, taking the expectation of both sides of Equation 13-3, $\hat{\beta}^{\text{OLS}}$ is clearly still an unbiased estimator of β. But the good news ends there: the remainder of this section will show that the sampling distribution of $\hat{\beta}^{\text{OLS}}$ given in Equation 6-25 is no longer valid if any of the model error autocovariances $(\gamma_1, \gamma_2, \gamma_3, \ldots, \gamma_{T-1})$ is non-zero or (equivalently) if any of the model error autocorrelations $(\rho_1, \rho_2, \rho_3, \ldots, \rho_{T-1})$ is non-zero. The normality of $\hat{\beta}^{\text{OLS}}$ still follows from the result (Equation 13-3) that $\hat{\beta}^{\text{OLS}}$ is a weighted sum of the normally distributed error terms, $U_1 \ldots U_T$; the problem arises in the derivation of the sampling variance of $\hat{\beta}^{\text{OLS}}$.

The first few steps in the derivation of $\text{var}(\hat{\beta})^{\text{OLS}}$ are the same as in Equations 6-20 and 6-21. In particular, substituting the results that $E\left[\hat{\beta}^{\text{OLS}}\right] = \beta$ and that $\hat{\beta}^{\text{OLS}} - \beta = \sum_{t=1}^{T} w_t^{\text{ols}}\, U_t$ (from taking the expectation of Equation 13-3) into the definition of the population variance of $\hat{\beta}^{\text{OLS}}$ still yields

$$\begin{aligned} \text{var}\left(\hat{\beta}^{\text{OLS}}\right) &= E\left[\left(\hat{\beta} - E[\hat{\beta}]\right)^2\right] \\ &= E\left[\left(\hat{\beta} - \beta\right)^2\right] \\ &= E\left[\left(\sum_{t=1}^{T} w_t^{\text{ols}} U_t\right)^2\right] \\ &= E\left[\sum_{s=1}^{T} w_s^{\text{ols}} U_s \sum_{t=1}^{T} w_t^{\text{ols}} U_t\right] \\ &= E\left[H \sum_{t=1}^{T} w_t^{\text{ols}} U_t\right] \end{aligned} \tag{13-6}$$

where H is used to temporarily replace the random variable $\sum_{s=1}^{T} w_s^{ols} U_s$. And, as in Equation 6-21, bringing the factor of H inside the sum over the running index t,

$$\begin{aligned} \text{var}\left(\hat{\beta}^{OLS}\right) &= E\left[\sum_{t=1}^{T} H w_t^{ols} U_t\right] \\ &= E\left[\sum_{t=1}^{T} w_t^{ols} (U_t H)\right] \\ &= \sum_{t=1}^{T} w_t^{ols} E[U_t H] \end{aligned} \tag{13-7}$$

where the last step uses the Linearity Property of Expectations of Chapter 2.

Here, however is where the non-zero model error covariances begin to make a difference in the derivation. Evaluating the expectation $E[U_t H]$,

$$\begin{aligned} E[U_t H] &= E\left[U_t \sum_{s=1}^{T} w_s^{ols} U_s\right] \\ &= E\left[\sum_{s=1}^{T} w_s^{ols} U_t U_s\right] \\ &= \sum_{s=1}^{T} w_s^{ols} E[U_t U_s] \\ &= \sum_{s=1}^{T} w_s^{ols} \gamma_{t-s} \end{aligned} \tag{13-8}$$

where the last step uses the definition of an autocovariance given in Equation 13-2, here applied to the model errors.[17]

Substituting this expression for $E[U_t H]$ into the expression for Equation 13-7, the result for $\text{var}(\hat{\beta})$ is

$$\begin{aligned} \text{var}\left(\hat{\beta}^{OLS}\right) &= \sum_{t=1}^{T} w_t^{ols} E[U_t H] \\ &= \sum_{t=1}^{T} w_t^{ols} \left(\sum_{s=1}^{T} w_s^{ols} \gamma_{t-s}\right) \\ &= \sum_{t=1}^{T} \sum_{s=1}^{T} \left(w_t^{ols} w_s^{ols} \gamma_{t-s}\right) \\ &= \sum_{t=1}^{T} \sum_{s=1}^{T} \left(w_t^{ols} w_s^{ols} \sigma^2 \rho_{t-s}\right) \\ &= \sigma^2 \sum_{t=1}^{T} \left(w_t^{ols}\right)^2 \text{ plus terms in } \rho_1 \ldots \rho_{T-1} \end{aligned} \tag{13-9}$$

[17] Note that this definition implies that γ_ℓ equals $\gamma_{-\ell}$. It also implies that γ_0 equals $\text{var}(U_t)$ – i.e., σ^2 – so that ρ_0 is inherently equal to one.

For example, in the special case of T equal to four, this result for the sampling variance of $\hat{\beta}$ is[18]

$$\begin{aligned}
\text{var}(\hat{\beta}) &= \sigma^2 \sum_{t=1}^{4}\sum_{s=1}^{4}\left(w_t^{\text{ols}} w_s^{\text{ols}} \rho_{t-s}\right) \\
&= \sigma^2\left[\left(w_1^{\text{ols}}\right)^2 + \left(w_2^{\text{ols}}\right)^2 + \left(w_3^{\text{ols}}\right)^2 + \left(w_4^{\text{ols}}\right)^2\right] \\
&\quad + 2\rho_1\sigma^2\left[w_1^{\text{ols}}w_2^{\text{ols}} + w_2^{\text{ols}}w_3^{\text{ols}} + w_3^{\text{ols}}w_4^{\text{ols}}\right] \\
&\quad + 2\rho_2\sigma^2\left[w_1^{\text{ols}}w_3^{\text{ols}} + w_2^{\text{ols}}w_4^{\text{ols}}\right] \\
&\quad + 2\rho_3\sigma^2 w_1^{\text{ols}}w_4^{\text{ols}}
\end{aligned} \tag{13-10}$$

Thus, while OLS still yields an unbiased estimate of β, the usual expression for the sampling variance of $\hat{\beta}^{OLS}$ – given as part of Equation 6-25 – is correct only when all of the error term autocorrelations (ρ_1 ... ρ_{T-1}) are zero. When the non-autocorrelation assumption on the model errors is violated by the process which generated the sample data incorrect, then the usual expression for the sampling variance of $\hat{\beta}^{OLS}$ is incorrect. This result therefore invalidates both the Chapter 6 proof that $\hat{\beta}^{OLS}$ is BLU and all of the inference machinery results (on hypothesis testing and confidence intervals) developed in Chapter 7.

There is no reason to think that the analogous results in Chapter 9 for the Multiple Regression Model are any more robust to failures of this assumption. But these are formulas programmed into all econometrics software! Evidently, even in the most favorable circumstance imaginable for estimating regression coefficients using time-series data – where the regressors are all fixed in repeated samples – the regression software will compute hypothesis test rejection p-value estimates and confidence interval estimates which are simply wrong when the non-autocorrelation assumption is violated.

Clearly, minor departures from the assumption – where $\rho_1, \rho_2, \rho_3, \ldots, \rho_{T-1}$ are non-zero, but very small in magnitude – will only make the inference results a little bit wrong. But are the actual violations one might well see with real-world time-series data that small? Or can they be serious enough to turn the inference results based on the formulas ignoring serial correlation into meaningless twaddle?

The next section investigates this question with an empirical example based on U.S. macroeconomic data. While not typical of most professional applied econometric work, it *is* fair to say that this example is based on what is quite likely the most frequently looked at scatterplot in the world, as this scatterplot appears in print in virtually every textbook used in teaching undergraduate introductory macroeconomics courses. The results are not encouraging for the practice of ignoring violations of the non-autocorrelation model assumption. Fortunately, the remainder of this chapter lays out how to detect and deal with such violations in a straightforward and reasonably effective manner.

[18] It is instructive – and the object of Exercise 13-1 – to also write out Equation 13-9 oneself for the special case of T equal to five and compare it to the result given here as Equation 13-10. It should quickly become evident that the discrepancy between these results and an expression for $\text{var}\left(\hat{\beta}^{OLS}\right)$ based on assuming that $\rho_1, \rho_2, \rho_3, \ldots, \rho_{T-1}$ are all zero does not disappear as T grows.

13.3 DISASTROUS PARAMETER INFERENCE WITH CORRELATED MODEL ERRORS: TWO CAUTIONARY EXAMPLES BASED ON U.S. CONSUMPTION EXPENDITURES DATA

The analysis in Section 13.2 makes it clear that serial correlation in regression model errors invalidates the usual formulas for the sampling variance of the OLS slope estimators, potentially distorting any inference results – hypothesis test *p*-values or confidence intervals – based on them. The computing formulas implemented in econometric software are in fact based on such formulas – extended to the Multiple Regression Model setting, but still assuming that the non-autocorrelation assumption on the model errors is valid. Consequently, this is potentially a quite serious issue.

This section uses several examples to address the question of whether this potential for substantial inferential distortions is a real and present danger in analyzing actual economic time-series data. Foreshadowing the results, the answer to this question is: "Yes, the danger is quite real." On the other hand, these examples themselves already yield simple insights into how to avoid the most serious pitfalls. And the material in the remaining sections of this chapter provides straightforward tools which (with reasonably large samples) enable one to detect and largely eliminate such inferential distortions in working with time-series data.

The first example is based on a scatterplot used in virtually every undergraduate introductory macroeconomics textbook to motivate the aggregate consumption function relationship. The data specifications and sample periods used vary somewhat from textbook to textbook, but the scatterplot is always basically the same: a plot of real personal consumption expenditures versus real disposable income. And it always looks like Figure 13-5, which uses annual U.S. data from 1947–2008 obtained from the U.S. Bureau of Economic Analysis Web site:

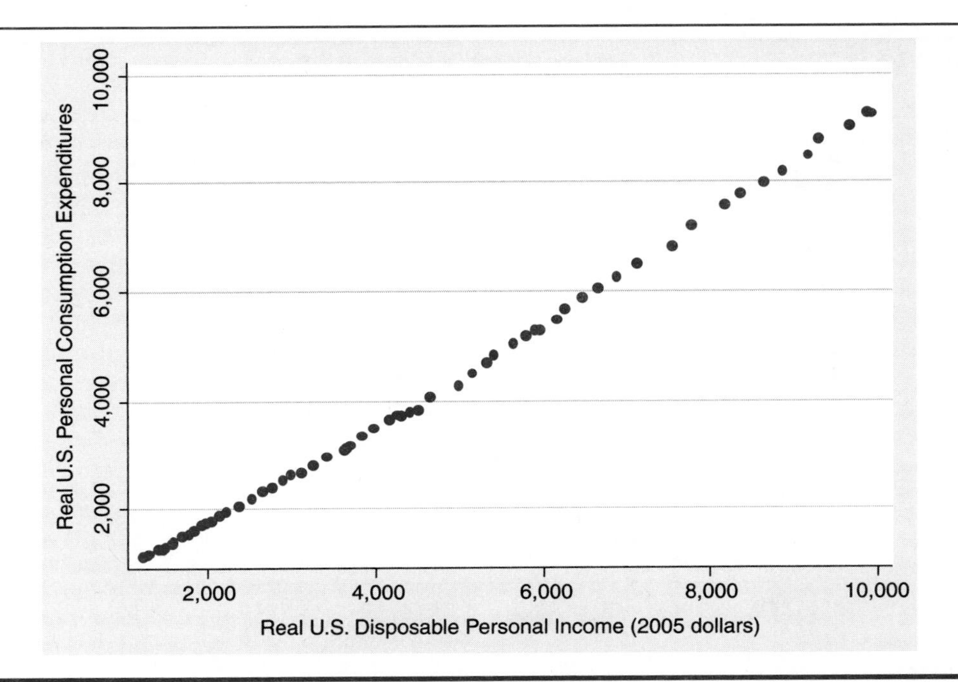

Figure 13-5 U.S. Personal Consumption Expenditures vs. Disposable Income

This scatterplot would appear at first glance to provide strong evidence for a direct relationship between U.S. aggregate personal consumption expenditures and disposable personal income over the sample period. In fact, however, it provides no evidence whatsoever with regard to this relationship: it reflects only the fact that all strongly trended time-series are closely related to the passage of time. In particular, time plots of these two time-series are displayed in Figures 13-6a and 13-6b. Note that both of these time-series vary in much the same way every year – they rise! No wonder that they appear to be closely related.

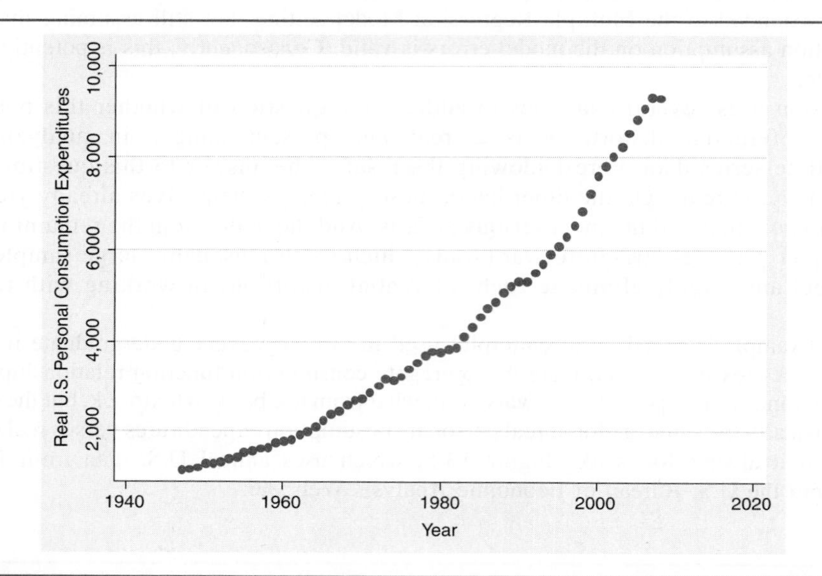

Figure 13-6a Time Plot of U.S. Real Personal Consumption

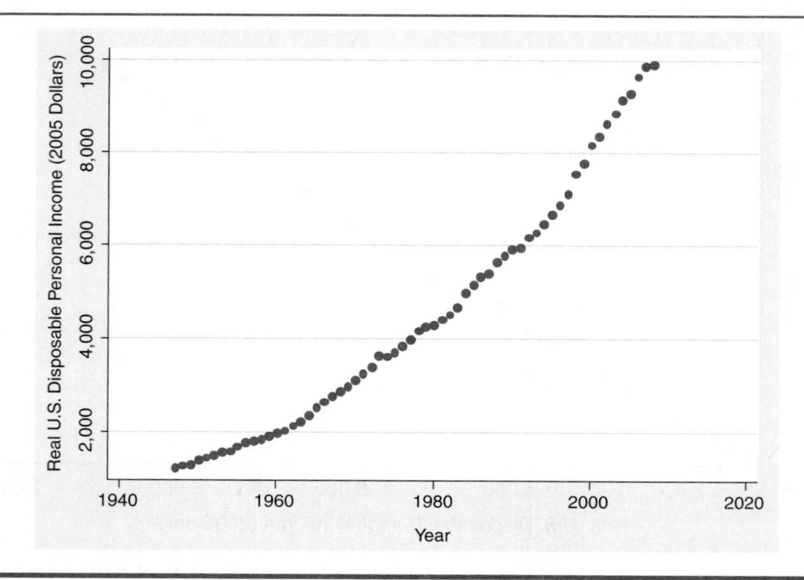

Figure 13-6b Time Plot of U.S. Real Disposable Income

Estimating a Bivariate Regression Model for personal consumption expenditures (PCE_t) using disposable personal income (di_t) as the explanatory variable yields the Stata output:[19]

```
      Source |       SS       df       MS              Number of obs =      62
-------------+------------------------------           F(  1,    60) =33771.13
       Model |  364816095     1  364816095             Prob > F      =  0.0000
    Residual |  648156.22    60  10802.6037            R-squared     =  0.9982
-------------+------------------------------           Adj R-squared =  0.9982
       Total |  365464251    61  5991217.23            Root MSE      =  103.94

------------------------------------------------------------------------------
pce          |      Coef.   Std. Err.      t    P>|t|     [95% Conf. Interval]
-------------+----------------------------------------------------------------
di           |   .9395469   .0051126   183.77   0.000     .9293201    .9497738
       _cons |  -140.8404   26.62211    -5.29   0.000    -194.0926   -87.58825
------------------------------------------------------------------------------
```

This regression output strongly echoes the message from the scatterplot: these two time-series appear to be closely related, with a regression R^2 of .998 and an estimated 95% confidence interval for the slope coefficient – at this point interpreted by the textbook author as the U.S. marginal propensity to consume (mpc) – of [.929, .950].

Plotting the fitting errors from this estimated model against time yields Figure 13-7:

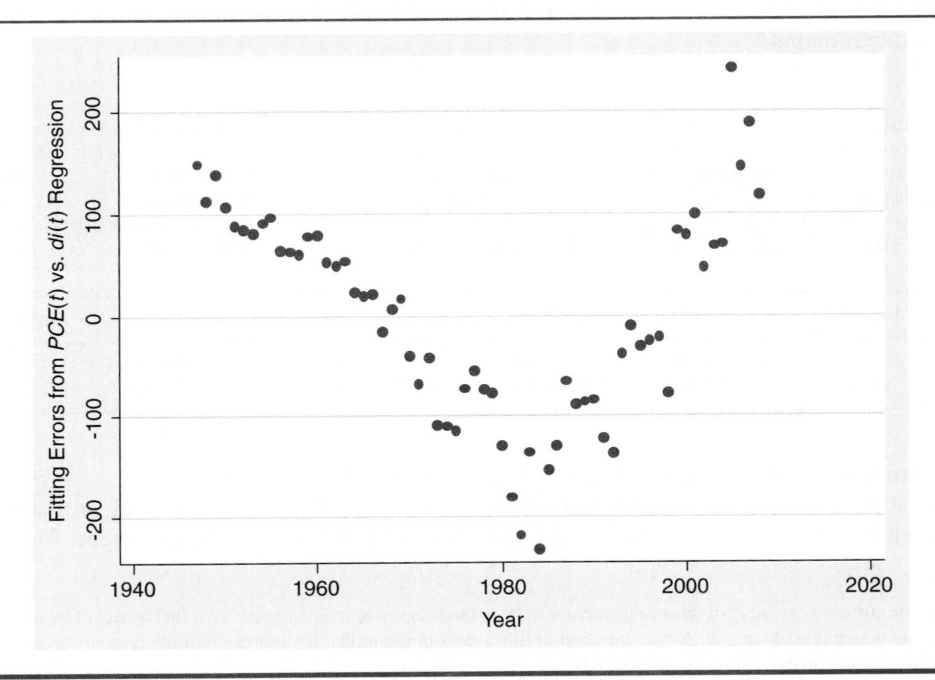

Figure 13-7 Time Plot of Fitting Errors from Regression of U.S. Personal Consumption Expenditures on U.S. Disposable Income

[19] The variable di_t is expressed in lowercase because it is being taken as fixed in repeated samples here; time-series regression models with stochastic regressors will be analyzed in Section 13.4.

Note that the deviation of these fitting errors from their sample mean (of zero) has the same sign in consecutive years for almost every year in the sample. Thus, it is not surprising that the sample autocorrelation at lag one for these fitting errors (.885) is quite high. This time plot and autocorrelation estimate both make it plain that the nonautocorrelation assumption is grotesquely violated by this regression model. Thus, the estimated standard error for the coefficient on di_t (and the confidence interval for the marginal propensity to consume based on it) are completely without foundation.

However, since it turns out to be interesting and useful to improve on this model, it is worth noting that this sample estimate of the autocorrelation of the fitting errors at lag one – which is just the sample covariance of the fitting errors with themselves lagged one period divided by their sample variance – is not a consistent estimate of ρ_1. It cannot be, because a close look at Figure 13-7 indicates that the population variance of the fitting errors increased substantially after around 1970; the sample variance can hardly be a consistent estimator of both the earlier and the later values of the population variance. This heteroscedasticity is very easy to eliminate in the present case by simply respecifying the model so as to relate the *logarithm* of PCE_t to the *logarithm* of di_t. (This logarithmic transformation also turns the nonlinear time trends in these two time-series – Figure 13-6a,b – into linear trends, which will be simpler to remove when it is time to do so, a bit later in this section.) Note, however, that the coefficient on $\log(di_t)$ in a model for $\log(PCE_t)$ is now the expected value of the *elasticity* of consumption spending with respect to disposable income – i.e., the expected percentage change in consumption per unit percentage change in disposable income – which is not same thing as the marginal propensity to consume.[20]

Defining ln_pce_t and ln_di_t as the logarithms of consumption spending and disposable income, respectively, and estimating a bivariate regression model instead using these two time-series yields the regression output:

```
      Source |       SS       df       MS              Number of obs =      62
-------------+------------------------------           F(  1,    60) =43217.51
       Model |  24.4628091     1  24.4628091           Prob > F      =  0.0000
    Residual |  .033962356    60  .000566039           R-squared     =  0.9986
-------------+------------------------------           Adj R-squared =  0.9986
       Total |  24.4967715    61  .401586418           Root MSE      =  .02379

------------------------------------------------------------------------------
      ln_pce|      Coef.   Std. Err.      t    P>|t|     [95% Conf. Interval]
-------------+----------------------------------------------------------------
       ln_di |   1.008717   .0048522   207.89   0.000     .9990116    1.018423
       _cons |    -.17438   .0400784    -4.35   0.000    -.2545487   -.0942113
------------------------------------------------------------------------------
```

The fitting errors for this estimated model are plotted in Figure 13-8.

This estimated regression model again echoes the message of the scatterplot and, at first glance, looks even better than the one in the original variables: the R^2 of .999 is even a bit higher (indicating

[20] Taking the current-year value of disposable income to be a fixed-regressor in this model is another aspect of this regression specification which is problematic. A consideration of this aspect of the model is suppressed in the present section so as to focus the discussion on the degree to which trends and serial correlation invalidate the usual inference results. The previous-year value of disposable income could have been used as the explanatory variable instead, but that would weaken the connection between the analysis here and the familiar scatterplot we all see in those introductory macroeconomics textbooks. Alternatively, a model based on the general approach advocated later on this chapter (which eliminates the serial correlation via respecification to include appropriate dynamics in the model) could be estimated as it stands using 2SLS or GMM; GMM is introduced in Section 19.4. In contrast, since detrending is very much to the point here – and the straightforward way to detrend these data also eliminates the heteroscedasticity – it does seem worthwhile to immediately point out the heteroscedasticity in the fitting errors.

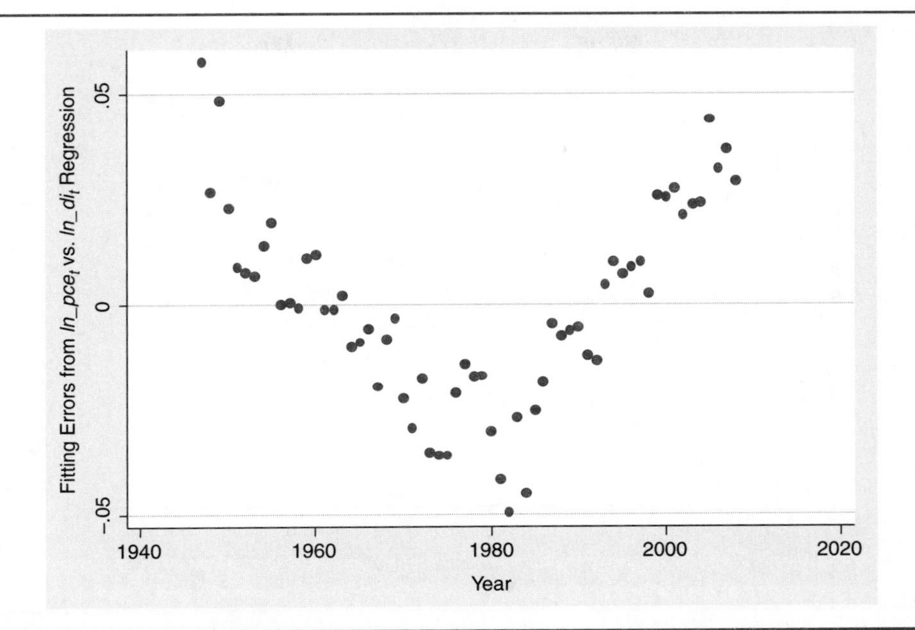

Figure 13-8 Time Plot of Fitting Errors from Regression of Logarithm of U.S. Real Personal Consumption Expenditures on the Logarithm of U.S. Real Disposable Income

a better fit to the data) and an estimated 95% confidence interval for the slope coefficient – now to be interpreted as the expected elasticity of consumption spending with respect to disposable income – is now even narrower, at [.999, 1.018].[21] Moreover, the time plot of the fitting errors in Figure 13-8 now seems have a reasonably constant variance across the sample. The serial correlation in the fitting errors is still grotesquely large, however. In particular, the sample estimate of the autocorrelation of these fitting errors at lag one – which is likely to be a reasonable estimate of ρ_1 now that the heteroscedasticity problem is resolved – is still very high, at .872.[22]

Still, this elasticity estimate ought to be unbiased – unless we have inadvertently omitted an explanatory variable which is correlated with ln_di_t – and it is surely plausible that this elasticity should be close to one.[23] So what's the problem? The problem is that – even though it may well be the case that this elasticity actually is substantially positive – neither the scatterplot nor these regression inference results actually provide any evidence at all in support of the proposition that disposable income is related to consumption spending.

To demonstrate this, consider the following alternative explanatory variable. It is constructed so as to have the same linear time trend as ln_di_t and so as to fluctuate around this trend with the same (sample) variance and autocovariances as does ln_di_t. The only difference is that these fluctuations

[21] Note that while a marginal propensity to consume of one is theoretically awkward, an elasticity of one merely says that a small percentage change in disposable income causes an equal percentage aggregate consumption spending.

[22] Estimating autocorrelation coefficients at various lags will be discussed at some length in Chapter 17. The estimate quoted here is consistent, but note that the sample length (62 yearly observations) is skimpy; moreover, the fitting errors are only consistent estimates of the model errors themselves. The true value of ρ_1 is probably even closer to one than this.

[23] Plausible to a Keynesian macroeconomist, anyway. Others might wonder whether the current increase in real disposable income is caused by a cut in net taxes which rational households will expect to eventually have to repay in the form of future taxes or seigniorage (due to inflation); such a household would save most of its disposable income increase.

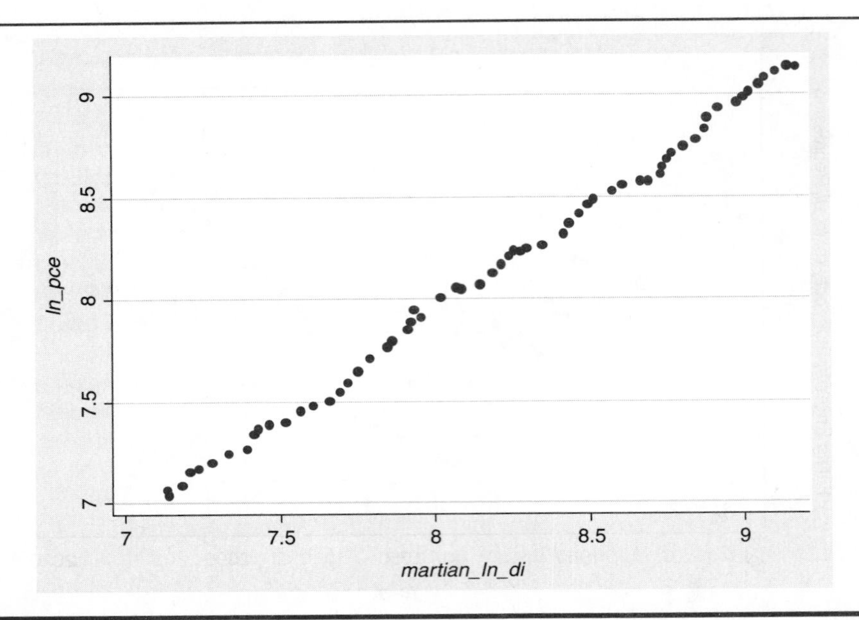

Figure 13-9 Logarithm of U.S. Personal Consumption Expenditures versus Martian Logarithm of Disposable Income

are drawn from a random number generator and have nothing whatever to do with the U.S. economy. To emphasize this latter aspect, this time-series will be referred to below as "Martian logarithm disposable income" or "$martian\_ln\_di_t$."[24]

Figure 13-9 plots a scatterplot relating the logarithm of U.S. consumption expenditures (ln_pce_t) to Martian disposable income.

And estimating a bivariate regression model for ln_pce_t, but now using $martian\_ln\_di_t$ as the explanatory variable, yields the regression output:

```
      Source |       SS       df       MS              Number of obs =      62
-------------+------------------------------           F(  1,    60) =19520.73
       Model |  24.4217076     1  24.4217076           Prob > F      =  0.0000
    Residual |  .075063926    60  .001251065           R-squared     =  0.9969
-------------+------------------------------           Adj R-squared =  0.9969
       Total |  24.4967715    61  .401586418           Root MSE      =  .03537

------------------------------------------------------------------------------
      ln_PCE |      Coef.   Std. Err.      t    P>|t|     [95% Conf. Interval]
-------------+----------------------------------------------------------------
martian_ln_di|   1.035843   .0074139   139.72   0.000     1.021013    1.050673
       _cons |  -.3452634   .0608531    -5.67   0.000    -.4669878   -.223539
------------------------------------------------------------------------------
```

[24] "*Alpha_centaurian_ln_di*$_t$" might be a more appropriate variable name as – if Martian macroeconomies actually existed – they might be slightly correlated with U.S. macroeconomic fluctuations via the common factor of exposure to the same solar wind; relativistic considerations preclude such an effect (on an annual basis) for macroeconomies more than one light-year distant. Less whimsically, it should be noted that the $martian\ ln\_di_t$ data were generated by estimating an AR(p) model ($p = 1$ was sufficient) for the deviations of U.S. ln_di_t from its estimated linear trend and simulating this estimated model using NIID model errors generated to have population variance equal to the estimated variance of the AR(1) model fitting errors. The AR(1) model is defined in Section 13.4; using the notation defined there, the sample estimate of φ_1 is .945. Anyone who prefers to instead refer to these generated data as $Z_t^{generated}$ is certainly free to do so.

And the fitting errors for this estimated model are plotted in Figure 13-10:

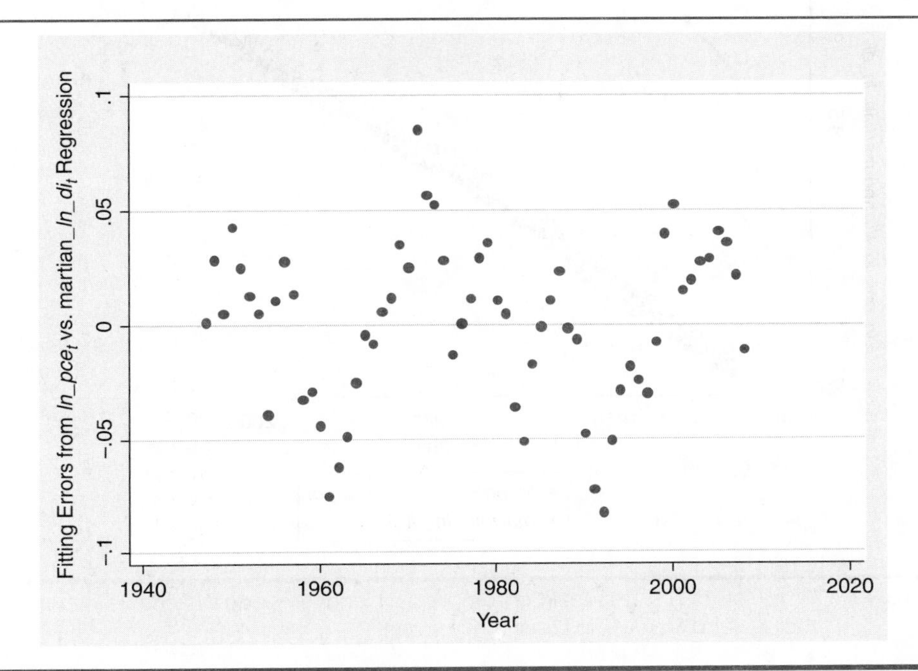

Figure 13-10 Time Plot of Fitting Errors from Regression of Logarithm of U.S. Personal Consumption Expenditures on Martian Logarithm Disposable Income

This estimated regression model again echoes the message of the scatterplot (Figure 13-9) and actually looks just as good as the regression model using the logarithm of U.S. disposable income: the R^2 still very high (at .997) and the 95% confidence interval for the expected elasticity of U.S. consumption spending with respect to Martian logarithm disposable income is still quite narrow, at [1.021, 1.051]. The sample estimate of the correlation of these fitting errors with themselves lagged one year (.763) is still quite high, however, consistent with the time plot in Figure 13-10, which, again, displays fitting errors which keep the same sign for years at a time.

Thus, if you believe that the scatterplot of Figure 13-5 – and the regression results based on the logarithms of those data – provide any actual evidence for a direct relationship between U.S. consumption expenditures and U.S. disposable income, then you must admit that the evidence is equally good for a direct relationship between U.S. consumption expenditures and Martian logarithm disposable income.

What has gone wrong here? Figure 13-11 provides a big hint: it plots the sample data on all three time-series – ln_pce_t, ln_di_t, and $martian\_ln\_di_t$ – against time.

Clearly, all three of these time-series are closely related to one another, simply because each one of them behaves in much the same way during the course of the sample: in each case the time-series' sample behavior is dominated by a trend. The strong serial correlation in both regression's fitting errors renders completely invalid the usual formulas used to compute the standard error estimates for both slope coefficient estimates; that is why the estimated confidence intervals are so narrow.

This failure of the non-autocorrelation assumption in the two regression models is overwhelmed here, however, by a worse problem: each of these regression equations is omitting an explanatory

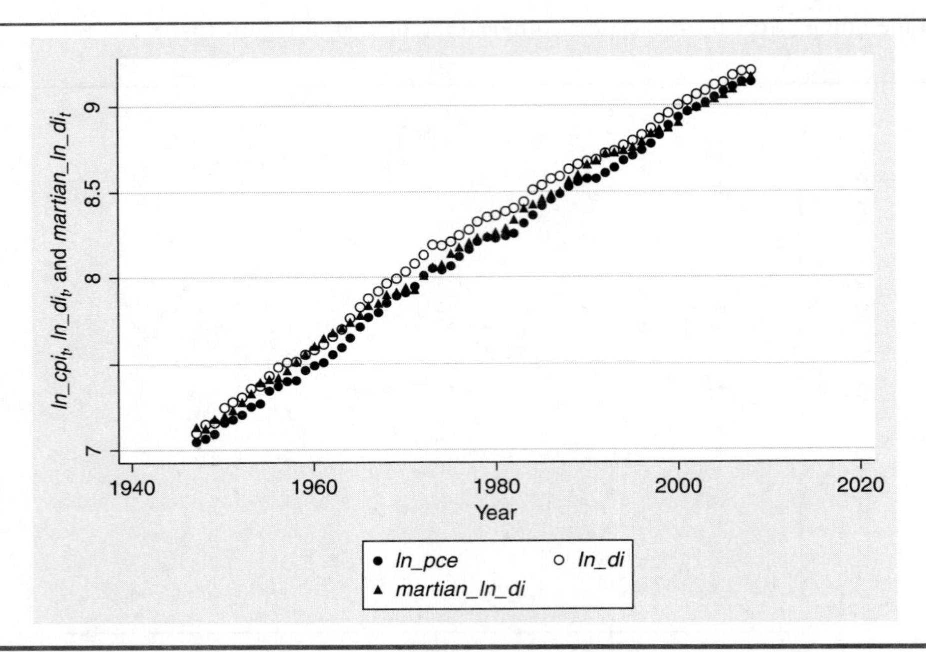

Figure 13-11 Time Plots of U.S. Personal Consumption Expenditures and Disposable Income for Both the U.S. and Mars (All in Logarithmic Form)

variable (time itself) which is highly correlated with the included explanatory variable. Thus, the trend in Martian logarithm disposable income is able to proxy for the trend in U.S. consumption spending just as well as does the trend in U.S. disposable income. This yields biased OLS estimates and, consequently, in each regression an estimated confidence interval which is centered on the ratio of the two trend slopes rather than on a value which has anything to do with a consumption-income relationship.

This realization immediately suggests that all would be well if one simply first removes the trend from each of these time-series prior to making scatterplots or estimating regression equations. Let's try that with these data, by estimating a regression model for the logarithm of each of the three variables, using time itself as the explanatory variable and denoting the three resulting fitting error time-series as $PCEDETRENDED_t$, $di\_detrended_t$, and $martian\_di\_detrended_t$.[25]

Scatterplots for this detrended data are given in Figures 13-12a and 13-12b.

At first glance, this seems to have worked: the scatterplot evidence for a direct relationship– in this instance, a positive elasticity – between U.S. disposable income and U.S. consumption expenditures now seems noisier and less compelling, but at least the evidence is now clearly stronger for a relationship with U.S. disposable income than for a relationship with Martian disposable income.

On the other hand, the Bivariate Regression Model estimated using the data plotted in Figure 13-12b seems to clearly indicate that there is a direct relationship between deviations of the logarithm of U.S.

[25] The logarithmic transformation is necessary so that the trend to be estimated is linear, but the "ln" in each variable name is, for simplicity, dropped at this point. The two detrended variables which are going to be used as explanatory variables are in lowercase because they are going to be treated as fixed in repeated samples.

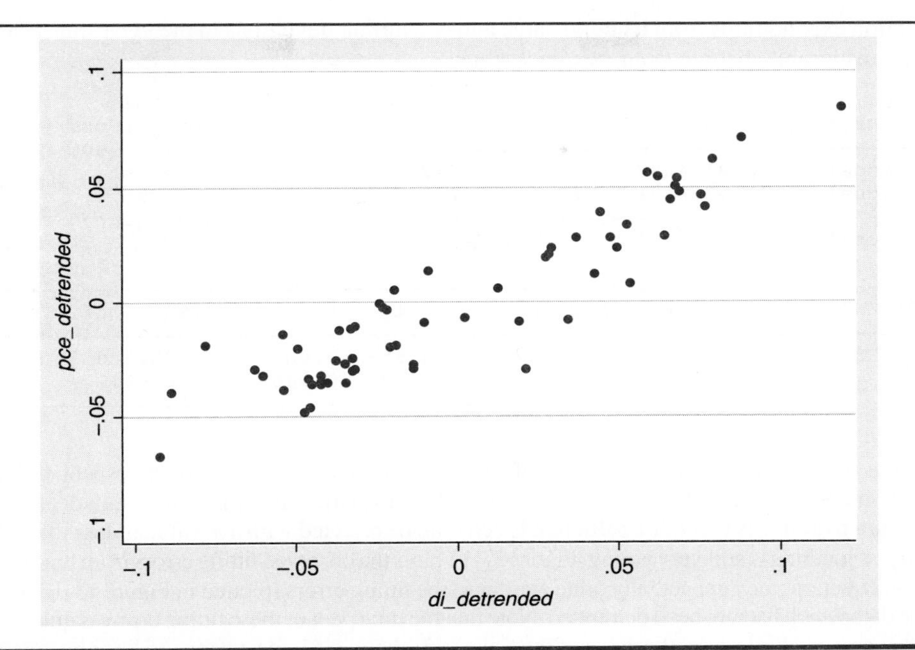

Figure 13-12a Detrended Logarithm of U.S. Real Personal Consumption Expenditures versus Detrended Logarithm of U.S. Real Disposable Income

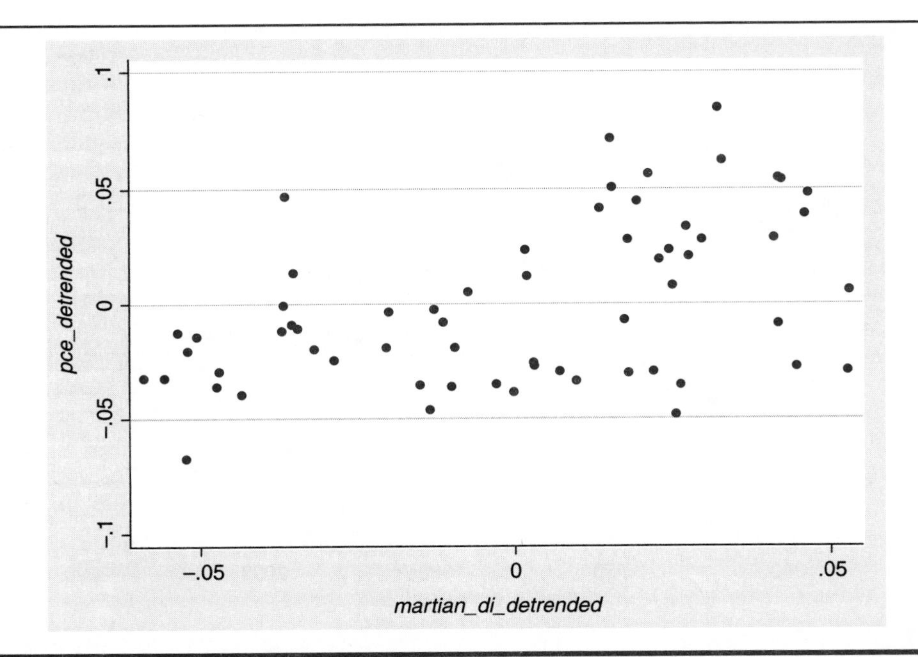

Figure 13-12b Detrended Logarithm of U.S. Real Personal Consumption Expenditures versus Detrended Logarithm of Martian Disposable Income

consumption expenditures from its trend value and concurrent deviations in the logarithm of Martian logarithm disposable income from *its* trend value:

```
      Source |       SS       df       MS              Number of obs =      62
-------------+------------------------------           F(  1,    60) =   20.73
       Model |  .019134283     1  .019134283           Prob > F      =  0.0000
    Residual |  .055388191    60  .000923137           R-squared     =  0.2568
-------------+------------------------------           Adj R-squared =  0.2444
       Total |  .074522474    61   .00122168           Root MSE      =  .03038

------------------------------------------------------------------------------
PCE_DETRENDED |      Coef.   Std. Err.      t    P>|t|     [95% Conf. Interval]
-------------+----------------------------------------------------------------
MARS_DETRENDED|   .5498348     .12077     4.55   0.000     .3082588    .7914108
        _cons| -.0002922   .0038592    -0.08   0.940    -.0080117    .0074273
------------------------------------------------------------------------------
```

Indeed, the estimated expected elasticity of U.S. consumption spending with respect to Martian disposable income ($.550 \pm .121$) is both economically substantial and apparently statistically significant: the null hypothesis that this coefficient is zero can be rejected with a *p*-value of less than .00005!

Clearly, something is still very wrong. Figure 13-13 plots the observed fitting errors from this estimated regression equation; they are actually quite similar to the fitting errors (plotted in Figure 13-10) obtained using the data which had not been detrended. Note that the time path of these fitting errors is quite smooth: while its average value is zero, the value of the time-series has a distinct tendency to lie either above zero for a number of consecutive years or to lie below zero for similarly lengthy contiguous periods. Indeed, the sample correlation between a fitting error from this regression equation and its value for the previous year is .817. The sample length here (62 annual observations) is a bit small for placing much faith in the

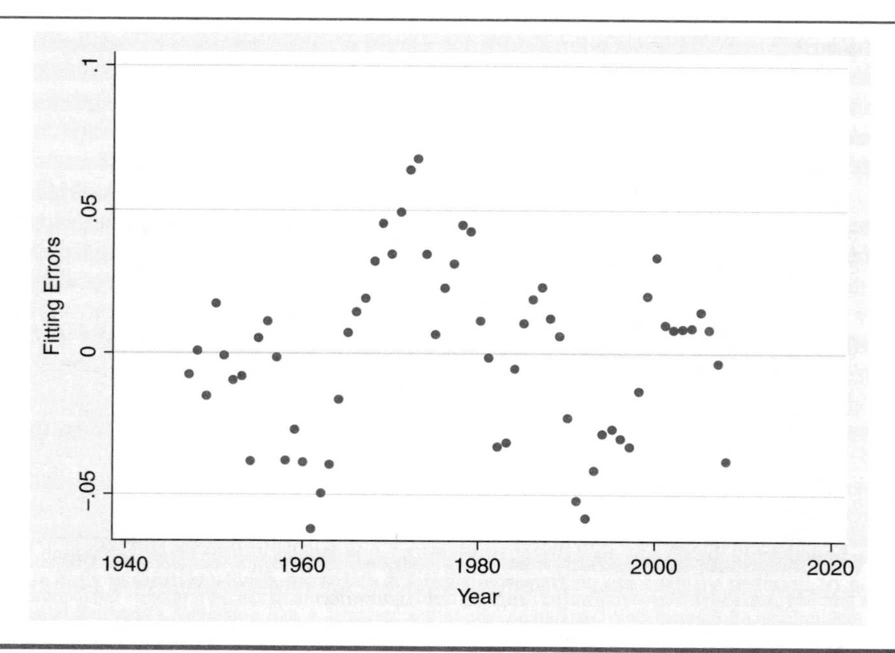

Figure 13-13 Time Plot of Fitting Errors from the Regression of the Detrended Logarithm of U.S. Real Personal Consumption Expenditures

precision of this sample estimate of ρ_1. Nevertheless, it is reasonably safe to conclude from it that the population autocorrelation of the model errors in this regression equation at lag one is substantially positive.[26]

Equation 13-9 shows that the actual sampling variance of the OLS slope estimator in the time-series version of the Bivariate Regression Model with Fixed-Regressors (Equation 13-1) depends on ρ_1 – and on $\rho_2, \rho_3, \ldots, \rho_{61}$ as well, for that matter. But the computing formula used by the econometrics software to estimate the standard error of the sampling distribution from which the estimated slope coefficient (.550) obtained in the regression purports to be a typical sample realization is based on the assumption that these model error autocorrelations are all zero. Thus, the standard error estimate (of .122, in this case) on the $martian\_di\_detrended_t$ coefficient estimate is not a consistent estimate of the actual standard deviation of the sampling distribution from which the estimate of the coefficient on Martian disposable income is a sample realization. In this case – as is typical with positively correlated model errors – the estimated standard error is too small, leading to a spurious rejection of the null hypothesis that the coefficient on the detrended Martian disposable income coefficient is zero.[27]

Thus, regressing one trended time-series on another and expecting to obtain sensible inference results is pretty clearly a bad idea. And even first detrending the two time-series does not really eliminate the problem. Indeed, perhaps the most important point to draw from this section is that – even without trends in the data – serial correlation in actual time-series regression model errors can easily be sufficiently severe as to yield substantially incorrect – i.e., outright wrong – inferences on the statistical significance of regression coefficients.

But the detrended data example does suggest how to proceed: in order to obtain reliable statistical inference results using time-series data, we need to learn how to model, detect, and deal with the likely presence of serial correlation in regression model errors.

13.4 THE AR(1) MODEL FOR SERIAL DEPENDENCE IN A TIME-SERIES

The reality is that economic time-series – regardless of whether they make their appearance in our models as dependent variables, or as explanatory variables, or as error terms – quite often exhibit substantial amounts of serial correlation. The most effective way to begin dealing with this fact of life is to start with a simple linear model for this serial dependence, the Autoregressive Model of Order One or "AR(1)" model:[28]

The Autoregressive Model of Order One or AR(1) Model

$$
\begin{aligned}
Y_t &= \varphi_0 + \varphi_1 Y_{t-1} + U_t \qquad t = 2 \ldots T \\
|\varphi_1| &< 1 \\
U_t &\sim \mathrm{IID}\left[0, \sigma_u^2\right]
\end{aligned}
\tag{13-11}
$$

[26] As will be discussed in Chapter 17, sample autocorrelations are only consistent estimates of the corresponding population autocorrelations, but this estimator is also known to be biased downward, so ρ_1 is probably, if anything, larger than .817 in this instance.

[27] Strictly speaking, Equation 13-1 is not a very appropriate model for the regression of the detrended U.S. consumption expenditures data on the detrended Martian disposable income data, because it is a bit awkward to assume that detrended disposable income is fixed in repeated samples. However, recalling the results of Section 11.4 (and foreshadowing the results of Section 13.4), the same computing formulas for the standard error estimators still result when the regressor is allowed to stochastic; the only difference is that their validity is then justified only in large samples. Of course, one could fuss over the degree to which the 62 years of data used here constitute a large sample, but that would be to miss the point of the example.

[28] Recall from Chapter 2 that correlation is a good and reasonable measure of the degree of *linear* relationship between two random variables, but is frequently misleading when the actual relationship is nonlinear. Because nonlinear serial dependence can be an important feature of economic time-series data, nonlinear models for serial dependence will be discussed later on, in Section 18.6.

The name for this model arises because it expresses Y_t in the form of a regression equation, with itself lagged one period as the sole explanatory variable. An "AR(2)" model for Y_t would include Y_{t-2} as an additional explanatory variable, with coefficient φ_2; an "AR(3)" model for Y_t would include Y_{t-3}, with coefficient φ_3, and so forth.

Low-order autoregressive models have been in use since the 1920s, yet – because of their simplicity and usefulness – they continue to inspire new and interesting research to the present day.[29] Higher-order autoregressive models (and a number of other models for serial dependence, which will be introduced in Chapter 17) can be very useful in analyzing economic data, especially for forecasting purposes. The focus in this section, however, is on thoroughly understanding the AR(1) model. That understanding will shortly make it clear both how to detect serial correlation problems in regression model errors and how to then appropriately respecify the model so as to eliminate these problems, thereby obtaining reasonably valid statistical hypothesis test results and estimated parameter confidence intervals.

The first thing to notice about the AR(1) Model as defined in Equation 13-11 is that it is essentially a special case of the Bivariate Regression Model with a stochastic regressor – Equation 11-1 – analyzed in some detail in Sections 11.2 and 11.4. Several of the differences are just notational. For example, as noted earlier it is more natural with time-series data to use the symbol t instead of i in the variable subscripting and to similarly use T instead of N for the sample length. And the slope parameter in the AR(1) model, as noted above, is called φ_1 instead of β so as to facilitate the generalization to higher-order AR models.

Several other differences between the AR(1) Model and the Bivariate Regression Model with a stochastic regressor require more comment. The explanatory variable is now specified to be the dependent variable lagged one period. Consequently, its variance is clearly positive. Thus, in contrast to Equation 11-1, this does not need to be explicitly assumed. Similarly, because the current model error (U_t) is assumed to be independent of all prior model errors, it is independent of all past values of the dependent variable – i.e., U_t is independent of Y_{t-1}, Y_{t-2}, and so forth. Any function of U_t is thus uncorrelated with any function of Y_{t-1}; this implies that $\text{cov}\left(Y_{t-1}^2, U_t^2\right)$ is zero so, in contrast to Equation 11-1, this does not need to be assumed either. Moreover, this result also implies that $\text{cov}(Y_{t-1}, U_t)$ is zero also, so that Y_{t-1} is not endogenous.[30] This uncorrelatedness of Y_{t-1} with U_t is crucial to showing – in Section 13.5 – that $\hat{\varphi}_1^{OLS}$, the least squares estimator of φ_1, is a consistent estimator.[31]

On the other hand, because the AR(1) Model implies that the explanatory variable Y_t is correlated with its own recent past, it is clearly no longer appropriate to make the Equation 11-1 assumption that the explanatory variable in the model is independently distributed for each observation. Fortunately, the structure of the AR(1) Model allows us to still nevertheless show that $\hat{\varphi}_1^{OLS}$ is a consistent estimator and that its asymptotic sampling distribution is identical (except for the restriction of its validity to large samples) to the sampling distribution of $\hat{\beta}^{OLS}$ in the Bivariate Regression Model with a fixed-regressor.[32]

---

[29] See, for example, Yule (1927) for an early empirical application of the AR(2) model or Bao (2007) for recent new results on the small-sample properties of $\hat{\varphi}_1^{OLS}$ in the AR(1) model with non-normal errors. G. Udny Yule (1927), "On a Method of Investigating Periodicities in Disturbed Series, with Special Reference to Wolfer's Sunspot Numbers." *Philosophical Transactions of the Royal Society of London, Ser. A, Vol. 226*, pp. 267–98, available at rsta.royalsocietypublishing.org/content/226/636-646. Bao, Y. (2007), "The Approximate Moments of the Least Squares Estimator for the Stationary Autoregressive Model Under a General Error Distribution." *Econometric Theory 23*, 1013–21.

[30] Exercise 13-4 provides more detail on these results.

[31] Unless the model is misspecified and Y_t is really generated by some other mechanism, such as an AR(2) or AR(3) model; this issue is explored in Exercise 13-3.

[32] In particular, the consistency result on $\hat{\varphi}_1^{OLS}$ (Equation 13-25) requires a Law of Large Numbers allowing for the fact that Y_t and $Y_{t-1}U_t$ are no longer serially independent and the derivation of the asymptotic sampling distribution of $\hat{\varphi}_1^{OLS}$ in Appendix 13.1 will in addition use a different Central Limit Theorem reflecting the non-independence of the $Y_{t-1}U_t$.

It is very useful – and not difficult – to re-express the AR(1) Model in what is called "moving average" form. This amounts to rewriting Y_t as a weighted sum of current and past model errors; this is convenient because the model errors are assumed to be distributed IID$[0, \sigma_u^2]$. The explanatory variable Y_{t-1} can itself be written in terms of its own past, using Equation 13-11:

$$Y_{t-1} = \varphi_0 + \varphi_1 Y_{t-2} + U_{t-1} \tag{13-12}$$

Substituting Equation 13-12 into the right-hand side of Equation 13-11 yields

$$\begin{aligned} Y_t &= \varphi_0 + \varphi_1[\varphi_0 + \varphi_1 Y_{t-2} + U_{t-1}] + U_t \\ &= \varphi_0(1+\varphi_1) + (U_t + \varphi_1 U_{t-1}) + \varphi_1^2 Y_{t-2} \end{aligned} \tag{13-13}$$

Now using Equation 13-11 to express Y_{t-2} in terms of its own past,

$$Y_{t-2} = \varphi_0 + \varphi_1 Y_{t-3} + U_{t-2} \tag{13-14}$$

and substituting this expression for Y_{t-2} into Equation 13-13 yields

$$\begin{aligned} Y_t &= \varphi_0(1+\varphi_1) + (U_t + \varphi_1 U_{t-1}) + \varphi_1^2[\varphi_0 + \varphi_1 Y_{t-3} + U_{t-2}] \\ &= \varphi_0\left(1+\varphi_1+\varphi_1^2\right) + \left(U_t + \varphi_1 U_{t-1} + \varphi_1^2 U_{t-2}\right) + \varphi_1^3 Y_{t-3} \end{aligned} \tag{13-15}$$

Evidently, after τ such substitutions,

$$\begin{aligned} Y_t &= \varphi_0\left(1+\varphi_1+\varphi_1^2+\cdots+\varphi_1^\tau\right) + \left(U_t + \varphi_1\, U_{t-1} + \varphi_1^2\, U_{t-2} + \cdots + \varphi_1^\tau\, U_{t-\tau}\right) + \varphi_1^{\tau+1} Y_{t-\tau-1} \\ &= \frac{\varphi_0\left(1-\varphi_1^{\tau+1}\right)}{1-\varphi_1} + \sum_{\ell=0}^{\tau}(\varphi_1)^\ell\, U_{t-\ell} + \varphi_1^{\tau+1}\, Y_{t-\tau-1} \end{aligned} \tag{13-16}$$

Thus, letting τ become arbitrarily large,

$$Y_t = \frac{\varphi_0}{1-\varphi_1} + \sum_{\ell=0}^{\infty}(\varphi_1)^\ell\, U_{t-\ell} \tag{13-17}$$

since $|\varphi_1|$ is assumed to be less than one. Equation 13-18 is called the "MA(∞)" form of the AR(1) Model, since it re-expresses Y_t as a moving average of an infinite number of lagged values of the model error term. Note that this expression implicitly assumes that the model's assumptions can also be applied to time periods long prior to the beginning of the actual sample period, which begins with an observation for Y_1.

Using the MA(∞) form of the model to re-express Y_{t-1} makes it plain that Y_{t-1} depends only on $U_{t-1}, U_{t-2}, U_{t-3}$, and so forth, so it is actually independent of the model error term, U_t. Thus – as noted above – the AR(1) Model automatically satisfies the two "other" assumptions of the Equation 11-1; that is why they did not need to be included in Equation 13-11. The MA(∞) form of the model also makes it very easy to derive useful expressions for the mean, variance, autocovariances, and autocorrelations of Y_t.

For example, the expected value of Y_t is

$$\begin{aligned} E[Y_t] &= E\left[\frac{\varphi_0}{1-\varphi_1} + \sum_{\ell=0}^{\infty}(\varphi_1)^\ell U_{t-\ell}\right] \\ &= \frac{\varphi_0}{1-\varphi_1} + \sum_{\ell=0}^{\infty}(\varphi_1)^\ell E[U_{t-\ell}] \\ &= \frac{\varphi_0}{1-\varphi_1} \end{aligned} \tag{13-18}$$

And the variance of Y_t is

$$
\begin{aligned}
\mathrm{var}(Y_t) = \sigma_y^2 &= E\left[\left(Y_t - \frac{\varphi_0}{1-\varphi_1}\right)^2\right] \\
&= E\left[\left(\sum_{\ell=0}^{\infty}(\varphi_1)^{\ell}U_{t-\ell}\right)^2\right] \\
&= E\left[\left(\sum_{\ell=0}^{\infty}(\varphi_1)^{\ell}U_{t-\ell}\right)\left(\sum_{s=0}^{\infty}(\varphi_1)^{s}U_{t-s}\right)\right] \\
&= E\left[\sum_{\ell=0}^{\infty}\sum_{s=0}^{\infty}(\varphi_1)^{\ell}U_{t-\ell}(\varphi_1)^{s}U_{t-s}\right] \\
&= E\left[\sum_{\ell=0}^{\infty}\sum_{s=0}^{\infty}(\varphi_1)^{\ell}(\varphi_1)^{s}U_{t-\ell}\,U_{t-s}\right] \\
&= \sum_{\ell=0}^{\infty}\sum_{s=0}^{\infty}(\varphi_1)^{\ell}(\varphi_1)^{s}E[U_{t-\ell}\,U_{t-s}] \\
&= \sum_{\ell=0}^{\infty}(\varphi_1)^{2\ell}E\left[U_{t-\ell}^2\right] \\
&= \sigma_u^2\sum_{\ell=0}^{\infty}(\varphi_1)^{2\ell} = \frac{\sigma_u^2}{1-\varphi_1^2}
\end{aligned}
\tag{13-19}
$$

where the next to last step uses the fact that the U_t are serially independent and hence serially uncorrelated, which implies that $E[U_{t-\ell}\,U_{t-s}]$ is equal to zero unless ℓ is equal to s.

A similar derivation (in Exercise 13-5) shows that

$$
\gamma_j = \mathrm{cov}(Y_t,\, Y_{t-j}) = E\left[\left(Y_t - \frac{\varphi_0}{1-\varphi_1}\right)\left(Y_{t-j} - \frac{\varphi_0}{1-\varphi_1}\right)\right] = \varphi_1^j\,\mathrm{var}(Y_t) \tag{13-20}
$$

so that the autocorrelations of Y_t are

$$
\rho_j = \mathrm{corr}(Y_t,\, Y_{t-j}) = \frac{\mathrm{cov}(Y_t,\, Y_{t-j})}{\sqrt{\mathrm{var}(Y_t)\mathrm{var}(Y_{t-j})}} = \frac{\mathrm{cov}(Y_t,\, Y_{t-j})}{\mathrm{var}(Y_t)} = \varphi_1^j \tag{13-21}
$$

Thus, data generated by the AR(1) Model are serially correlated. Note that the parameter φ_1 turns out to be numerically equal to ρ_1, the correlation between the current value of Y_t and its immediately previous value, Y_{t-1}. But ρ_j, the correlation of Y_t with itself j periods previous, decays geometrically as the relative lag j increases. Consequently, if φ_1 is positive – which is typically the case with economic time-series – then a positive fluctuation of Y_t away from its mean tends to be followed by additional positive deviations from the mean; whereas a negative deviation from the mean tends to be followed by subsequent negative deviations. An AR(1) model with φ_1 positive consequently generates Y_t time-series data which are smoother than one would expect from independently distributed data – just like the regression fitting errors we observed in Figures 13-10 and 13-13 earlier in this chapter.

Returning to Equations 13-18 and 13-19, for the mean and variance of Y_t, note that the restriction in Equation 13-11 that $|\varphi_1|$ must be strictly less than one is clearly important: both the mean and the variance of Y_t blow up as φ_1 approaches one! A model such as this, with φ_1 equal to one, is not really an AR(1) Model as defined here – it is called a "random walk." More precisely, such a model with $\varphi_0 \neq 0$ is called a "random walk with drift" because it can be shown that (for a given value of Y_0) the mean of Y_t increases as $\varphi_0 t$ and its variance as $\sigma_u^2 t$. Thus, its mean value trends ("drifts") with slope φ_0 and its variance increases over time without bound. In an alternative nomenclature, Y_t is said to be "generated by a process which is integrated of order one" or "$Y_t \sim$ I(1)." And – in yet another alternative nomenclature, but one which is quite common in econometrics and applied economics – the model for Y_t is said, in this circumstance, to have what is called a "unit root."

Economic time-series with unit roots do occur – and can cause major problems with inference when they appear as explanatory variables in regression models – so we will return to this concept later on in this chapter and again in Chapter 18. At this point, however, the first order of business is to show that the AR(1) Model parameter φ_1 can be consistently estimated using OLS. Then, in the following two sections – Section 13.6 and Section 13.7 – what we have learned about the AR(1) Model will be applied to the detection and elimination of violations of the non-autocorrelation assumption in the Bivariate Regression Model and in the Multiple Regression Model.

13.5 THE CONSISTENCY OF $\hat{\varphi}_1^{OLS}$ AS AN ESTIMATOR OF φ_1 IN THE AR(1) MODEL AND ITS ASYMPTOTIC DISTRIBUTION

Because the AR(1) Model is almost just a special case of Bivariate Regression Model with a stochastic regressor (Equation 11-1), the proof that $\hat{\varphi}_1^{OLS}$ is a consistent estimator of φ_1 is very similar to that given in Section 11.4. The asymptotic sampling distribution of $\hat{\varphi}_1^{OLS}$ is essentially identical to what one would expect – replacing the variance of X_t by the variance of Y_{t-1} – but its derivation requires some care since Y_{t-1} is not serially independent, as was assumed for X_t. This derivation is detailed in Appendix 13.1; the demonstration that $\hat{\varphi}_1^{OLS}$ is a consistent estimator of φ_1 is given here.

Substituting Y_{t-1} for X_i in Equation 11-3b of Section 11.2, the OLS weights for $\hat{\varphi}_1^{OLS}$ are

$$W_i^{ols} = \frac{X_i - \overline{X}}{\sum\limits_{\ell=1}^{N} \left(X_\ell - \overline{X}\right)^2} \quad \Rightarrow \quad W_t^{ols} = \frac{Y_{t-1} - \overline{Y}}{\sum\limits_{\ell=2}^{N} \left(Y_{\ell-1} - \overline{Y}\right)^2} \tag{13-22}$$

Note that the sum in the denominator of W_t^{ols} begins in period two, since Y_0 will not be available in the sample data. Thus, only $T-1$ sample observations are actually available for estimating φ_1, and $\overline{Y}$ in Equation 13-22 accordingly uses only the last $T-1$ observations on Y_t. Because only asymptotic results are possible for $\hat{\varphi}_1^{OLS}$, this "loss" of one observation is not an important concern.

Proceeding as in Equation 11-6, then,

$$\begin{aligned}
\hat{\varphi}_1^{OLS} &= \sum_{t=2}^{T} W_t^{ols}\, Y_t = \sum_{t=2}^{T} W_t^{ols} (\varphi_0 + \varphi_1\, Y_{t-1} + U_t) \\
&= \varphi_0 \sum_{t=2}^{T} W_t^{ols} + \varphi_1 \sum_{t=2}^{T} W_t^{ols} Y_{t-1} + \sum_{t=2}^{T} W_t^{ols} U_t \\
&= \varphi_1 + \sum_{t=2}^{T} W_i^{ols} U_t
\end{aligned} \tag{13-23}$$

which uses the results (from Exercise 13-6) that $\sum\limits_{t=2}^{N} W_t^{ols}$ equals zero and that $\sum\limits_{t=2}^{N} W_t^{ols} Y_{t-1}$ equals one.

Equation 11-6 from Section 11.4 can now be written as

$$
\begin{aligned}
\hat{\varphi}_1^{\mathrm{OLS}} &= \varphi_1 + \sum_{t=2}^{T} W_t^{\mathrm{ols}} U_t - \overline{U} \sum_{t=2}^{T} W_t^{\mathrm{ols}} \\
&= \varphi_1 + \sum_{t=2}^{T} W_t^{\mathrm{ols}} \left(U_t - \overline{U} \right) \\
&= \varphi_1 + \sum_{t=2}^{T} \left[\frac{Y_{t-1} - \overline{Y}}{\sum_{\ell=2}^{T} \left(Y_{\ell-1} - \overline{Y} \right)^2} \right] \left(U_t - \overline{U} \right)
\end{aligned}
\tag{13-24}
$$

Letting G now stand for the sum $\sum_{\ell=2}^{T} \left(Y_{\ell-1} - \overline{Y} \right)$, this becomes

$$
\begin{aligned}
\hat{\varphi}_1^{\mathrm{OLS}} &= \varphi_1 + \sum_{t=2}^{T} \left[\frac{Y_{t-1} - \overline{Y}}{G} \right] \left(U_t - \overline{U} \right) \\
&= \varphi_1 + \frac{1}{G} \sum_{t=2}^{T} \left(Y_{t-1} - \overline{Y} \right) \left(U_t - \overline{U} \right) \\
&= \varphi_1 + \frac{\sum_{t=2}^{T} \left(Y_{t-1} - \overline{Y} \right) \left(U_t - \overline{U} \right)}{G} \\
&= \varphi_1 + \frac{\sum_{t=2}^{T} \left(Y_{t-1} - \overline{Y} \right) \left(U_t - \overline{U} \right)}{\sum_{\ell=2}^{N} \left(Y_{\ell-1} - \overline{Y} \right)^2} \\
&= \varphi_1 + \frac{\frac{1}{T-1} \sum_{t=2}^{T} \left(Y_{t-1} - \overline{Y} \right) \left(U_t - \overline{U} \right)}{\frac{1}{T-1} \sum_{\ell=2}^{N} \left(Y_{\ell-1} - \overline{Y} \right)^2} \\
&= \varphi_1 + \frac{\widehat{\mathrm{cov}}\left(Y_{t-1},\, U_t \right)}{\widehat{\mathrm{var}}\left(Y_{t-1} \right)}
\end{aligned}
\tag{13-25}
$$

Taking the probability limit of both sides of Equation 13-25 and applying the results from Appendix 11.1,[33]

[33] The results on probability limits given in Appendix 11.1 assumed that the relevant random variables are independently distributed, whereas that is plainly not the case for the serially dependent time-series $Y_2 \dots Y_T$. Also, the time-series $Y_1 U_2 \dots Y_{T-1} U_T$ – although serially uncorrelated – is not serially independent, either. It can be shown, however – e.g., in Hamilton (1994, Chapter 7) – that all of the Appendix 11.1 results follow for both of these serially dependent series because both of these time-series are covariance stationary and because for each the sum of the magnitudes of its autocovariances is bounded. (See Exercises 13-4d and 13-5.) The derivation of Equation 13-27, the asymptotic sampling distribution for $\hat{\varphi}_1^{\mathrm{OLS}}$, however, must apply a Central Limit Theorem with regard to sequences of sample means of $Y_{t-1} U_t$, which requires something closer to serial independence (a "martingale difference") on the part of $Y_{t-1} U_t$; this is discussed in Appendix 13.1.

$$\begin{aligned}
\text{plim}\left(\hat{\varphi}_1^{\text{OLS}}\right) &= \text{plim}\left(\varphi_1 + \frac{\widehat{\text{cov}}(Y_{t-1},\, U_t)}{\widehat{\text{var}}(Y_{t-1})}\right) \\
&= \text{plim}(\varphi_1) + \text{plim}\left(\frac{\widehat{\text{cov}}(Y_{t-1},\, U_t)}{\widehat{\text{var}}(Y_{t-1})}\right) \\
&= \lim_{N\to\infty}(\varphi_1) + \text{plim}\left(\frac{\widehat{\text{cov}}(Y_{t-1},\, U_t)}{\widehat{\text{var}}(Y_{t-1})}\right) \\
&= \varphi_1 + \frac{\text{plim}(\widehat{\text{cov}}(Y_{t-1},\, U_t))}{\text{plim}(\widehat{\text{var}}(Y_{t-1}))} \\
&= \varphi_1 + \frac{\text{cov}(Y_{t-1},\, U_t)}{\text{var}(Y_{t-1})} \\
&= \varphi_1
\end{aligned} \tag{13-26}$$

where the second step in Equation 13-26 uses the "Linearity" property (with $a = b = 1$), the third step uses the "Reduction to Ordinary Limit" property (since φ_1 is not random), and the fourth step uses the "Division" property.[34] Finally, the last two steps in this equation use the Law of Large Numbers property to evaluate the probability limits of the sample covariance of Y_{t-1} with U_t and the sample variance of Y_{t-1}. The covariance of Y_{t-1} with U_t is zero because the MA(∞) form of the model in Equation 13-17 implies that Y_{t-1} does not depend on the current value of the model error – see Exercise 13-4.

Thus, $\hat{\varphi}_1^{\text{OLS}}$ is consistent for φ_1, albeit biased. The asymptotic sampling distribution for $\hat{\varphi}_1^{\text{OLS}}$ is derived in Appendix 13.1; the result is

$$\sqrt{T-1}\left(\hat{\varphi}_1^{\text{OLS}} - \varphi_1\right) \xrightarrow{d} N\left[0, \frac{\sigma_u^2}{\text{var}(Y_{t-1})}\right] = N\left[0, 1 - \varphi_1^2\right] \tag{13-27}$$

where the second part of Equation 13-27 recognizes that variance of Y_{t-1} is identical to the variance of Y_t itself; the result from Equation 13-19 is substituted in on the right-hand side of this equation.[35]

Consequently – just as in Section 11.4 – the asymptotic sampling distribution of $\hat{\varphi}_1^{\text{OLS}}$ yields essentially the same computing formulas (for standard errors, confidence intervals, hypothesis test rejection p-values, etc.) as does the Bivariate Regression Model with a fixed-regressor. Therefore – so long as Y_t really is generated by the AR(1) model, and so long as the sample length T is sufficiently large that the asymptotic distribution $\hat{\varphi}_1^{\text{OLS}}$ is a reasonable approximation to its actual sampling distribution – the results from the usual OLS computer output can be interpreted as if the explanatory variable were fixed in repeated samples.

Broadly speaking, this aspect of the asymptotic results obtained here in the specific setting of the AR(1) Model carries over to the Multiple Regression Model, including explanatory variables in addition to Y_{t-1}: the results from the usual OLS computer output can be interpreted as if the explanatory variable were fixed in repeated samples *if* the sample is large enough for the asymptotic sampling distribution of the parameter estimators to be relevant and *if* the model is well specified in terms of error term homoscedasticity, omitted variables, and endogeneity issues.

---

[34] Note that the division property requires that the probability limit in what will become the denominator is not zero; this is not an issue here, because it is obvious that the variance of Y_{t-1} is strictly positive.

[35] Of course, per Exercise 13-3, if the true generating mechanism for Y_t is actually some other model – such as a higher-order AR model, or one of the nonlinear models discussed in Section 18.6 – then Equation 13-11 is omitting explanatory variables, one or more of which might be correlated with Y_{t-1}. In that case $\hat{\varphi}_1^{\text{OLS}}$ is no longer a consistent estimator of φ_1 and Equation 13-27 is not the asymptotic sampling distribution for $\hat{\varphi}_1^{\text{OLS}}$.

As noted at the outset, adding more lags in Y_t to the AR(1) model yields the AR(2) model, the AR(3) model, etc. Chapter 17 will analyze such higher-order autoregressive models. It will also discuss another simple approach to modeling linear serial dependence, based on moving average models of finite order q; these are essentially identical to the MA(∞) model of Equation 13-17, only with just q lags in U_t included in the model. A systematic approach to choosing the lag lengths for both AR(p) and MA(q) models will be presented at that point; this approach turns out to yield surprisingly good models for use in short-term forecasting.

Or this extension to the Multiple Regression Model might go beyond additional lags in the dependent variable to include dynamics in other explanatory variables; that topic is taken up in Section 13.8 and all of the issues involved in specifying and diagnostically checking such a model are described in the sections following it. First, however, more needs to be said about the Bivariate Regression Model in the time-series context by returning to the simple empirical example introduced in Section 13.3.

13.6 APPLICATION OF THE AR(1) MODEL TO THE ERRORS OF THE (DETRENDED) U.S. CONSUMPTION FUNCTION – AND A STRAIGHTFORWARD TEST FOR SERIALLY CORRELATED REGRESSION ERRORS

Recall, from Equation 13-21, that one implication of the AR(1) Model is that ρ_j, the correlation of Y_t with itself lagged j periods, equals φ_1^j, and hence decays geometrically as j increases. Thus, with positive values of φ_1, the AR(1) Model implies decaying, but positive, low-order autocorrelations. These are qualitatively consistent with the relatively "smooth" time patterns often observed in economic data: any deviation in the time-series away from its mean tends to persist for a number of periods.

In particular, this is exactly the pattern observed in the fitting errors for the two models for the logarithm of U.S. real personal consumption expenditures in Section 13.3 and plotted in Figures 13-10 and 13-13.[36] Briefly reviewing the results of that section, two points were made there.

First, it was demonstrated there that both the scatterplot and the estimated regression model supposedly displaying/quantifying the relationship between U.S. consumption spending and disposable income are virtually meaningless because the sample behavior of both of these time-series is completely dominated by a linear trend. This demonstration was implemented by creating an artificially generated analogue of the logarithm of U.S. real disposable income which similarly varies around a linear time trend but which is – by construction – completely unrelated to U.S. consumption spending. This artificially generated time-series was, somewhat whimsically, dubbed "Martian logarithm disposable income" or "*martian_ln_di$_t$*" so as to emphasize its complete unrelatedness to the U.S. consumption spending time-series. Both the scatterplot (Figure 13-9) and the estimated regression model supposedly displaying/quantifying the relationship between U.S. consumption spending and disposable income on Mars yielded equally strong evidence for a close relationship as did the scatterplot (Figure 13-5) and the estimated regression model using U.S. disposable income data.

Second – noting that the trends in U.S consumption spending and Martian disposable income were likely driving the spurious appearance of a strong relationship between these two time-series – Section 13.3 then went on to similarly consider scatterplots (Figures 13-12a and 13-12b) and estimated regression models supposedly displaying/quantifying the relationship between *detrended* U.S. consumption spending and *detrended* disposable income – again using either the U.S. or the "Martian" income data. The scatterplots in Figures 13-12a and 13-12b at least now had the good grace to indicate a stronger direct relationship between detrended U.S. consumption spending and detrended U.S. disposable income than between detrended U.S. consumption spending and detrended Martian

[36] Recall that the logarithms of both real consumption spending and real disposable income were analyzed so that the trends in these two time-series were linear functions of time. For clarity of exposition, explicit references to this logarithmic transformation will usually be omitted in this section, as it is to be understood as having been applied to the original data.

disposable income. But the estimated regression model for detrended U.S. consumption spending using the detrended Martian disposable income data as the explanatory variable still clearly indicated the existence of a strong link between U.S. consumption spending (now detrended) and happenings on Mars. In particular, looking back at the computer output for this estimated regression equation – quoted at the end of Section 13.3 – the estimated coefficient on detrended Martian disposable income is $.550 \pm .121$. So the estimated t ratio one would use for a test of the null hypothesis of no relationship between detrended U.S. consumption spending and detrended Martian disposable income is over 4.5; thus, this null hypothesis can be rejected with p-value less than .0005.

However, looking back at Figure 13-13 – a time plot of the fitting errors for this regression model – the marked tendency of these fitting errors to remain above (or below) their mean value for years at a time clearly indicated that the fitting errors in this estimated model are serially correlated. Presuming that the slope parameter in the model for detrended U.S. consumption spending has at least been consistently estimated, these fitting errors are asymptotically equivalent to the model errors, so it is evident that the model errors for this regression model seriously violate the assumption that the model errors are independently distributed – the "non-autocorrelation" assumption, loosely speaking.[37] In contrast, the estimated standard error (.121) for the sampling distribution of the slope estimator in this model is computed by the software using formulas based on an asymptotic sampling distribution result – essentially Equation 11-19 – which rests on an assumption that the model errors are independently distributed.[38] Consequently, this standard error estimate is a sample realization from an inconsistent estimator, so it is not surprising that it is inaccurate. What *is* surprising is that this estimate is so *far* off: since we know that the population coefficient on detrended Martian disposable income is actually zero, this standard error must (unless our coefficient estimate of .550 is quite an unlucky one) be at least something like .3 to .4 – i.e., at least around four times larger than the estimated value.

Simply pointing out the smoothness in a time plot, such as Figure 13-13, is a rather subjective way to evaluate the plausibility (or otherwise) of the non-autocorrelation assumption. It is instead both more convenient and more objective to model the serial correlation in regression model fitting errors using the autoregressive framework introduced/analyzed in Sections 13.4 and 13.5. Then one can simply test the null hypothesis that the AR(1) Model parameter φ_1 is equal to zero. Implementing that idea is the topic of the remainder of this section. Foreshadowing, this approach further suggests a straightforward procedure for eliminating the violations of the nonautocorrelation assumption; that procedure is described (and applied to the model for detrended U.S. annual consumption spending) in Section 13.7.

At that point – as in Chapter 9 with the fixed-regressor model – it will be time to heuristically extend these bivariate regression insights and results to the real-world setting of a dynamic model involving more complicated dynamics and multiple explanatory variables. That extension is made in Chapter 14 and applied to a more realistic model of U.S. consumption spending in the remainder of that chapter.

Returning, for now, to the topic of testing for a failure of the nonautocorrelation assumption in the Bivariate Regression Model of Equation 11-1, the model itself must first be modified to allow for the possibility of serial correlated model errors. Equation 13-28 respecifies this model to allow for model errors which are themselves generated by the AR(1) Model of Equation 13-11, with its notation suitably amended so that this is now a model for the regression errors, U_t. In particular, the

[37] Recall that the non-autocorrelation assumption had to be strengthened in Equation 11-1 (for the Bivariate Regression Model with a stochastic regressor) to an assumption that the model errors are serially independent so as show that $\hat{\beta}^{OLS}$ is consistent for β and so as to apply a Central Limit Theorem to obtain the usual result for the asymptotic sampling distribution of $\hat{\beta}^{OLS}$. For continuity with the earlier chapters, however, it is convenient – and common practice – to continue calling this the "non-autocorrelation" assumption without further comment.

[38] Thus, the computing formula for this estimated standard error is essentially equivalent to the square root of $(1/62)\hat{\text{var}}(u_t^{\text{fit}})/\hat{\text{var}}(x_t)$ where the $u_1^{\text{fit}} \dots u_{62}^{\text{fit}}$ are the T observed fitting errors and $x_1 \dots x_{62}$ are the T observed values of detrended Martian disposable income.

intercept (φ_0) in the AR(1) Model is now dropped, because the inclusion of an intercept (α) in the regression model makes it redundant. Also, since the observations on both the dependent and the explanatory variable are now ordered in time, the observation subscripts in the regression model have been replaced by t and the sample size by T. More substantively, note that – since the focus here is on testing for serial correlation in the model errors rather than on possible endogeneity in the explanatory variable – the value of $\text{plim}(\widehat{\text{cov}}(X_t, U_t))$ is now assumed to be zero. Thus, $\hat{\alpha}^{\text{OLS}}$ and $\hat{\beta}^{\text{OLS}}$ are consistent estimators of α and β. For this setting the Bivariate Regression Model is thus

The Bivariate Regression Model with AR(1) Errors

$$\begin{aligned} Y_t &= \alpha + \beta X_t + U_t \qquad t = 1 \ldots T \\ U_t &= \varphi_0 + \varphi_1 U_{t-1} + V_t \quad |\varphi_1| < 1 \\ V_t &\sim \text{IID}\left[0, \sigma_v^2\right] \\ X_t &\sim \text{IID}\left[0, \sigma_x^2\right] \quad \sigma_x^2 > 0 \\ \text{plim}(\widehat{\text{cov}}(X_t, U_t)) &= 0 \\ \text{Cov}\left(X_t^2, U_t^2\right) &= 0 \end{aligned} \tag{13-28}$$

The consistency of $\hat{\alpha}^{\text{OLS}}$ and $\hat{\beta}^{\text{OLS}}$ implies that $\text{plim}[U_t^{\text{fit}}]$ is equal to $\text{plim}[U_t]$:

$$\begin{aligned} \text{plim}\left[U_t^{\text{fit}}\right] &= \text{plim}\left[Y_t - \left\{\hat{\alpha}^{\text{OLS}} + \hat{\beta}^{\text{OLS}} X_t\right\}\right] \\ &= \text{plim}\left[\{\alpha + \beta X_t + U_t\} - \left\{\hat{\alpha}^{\text{OLS}} + \hat{\beta}^{\text{OLS}} X_t\right\}\right] \\ &= \text{plim}\left[U_t + \left\{\alpha - \hat{\alpha}^{\text{OLS}}\right\} - \left\{\hat{\beta}^{\text{OLS}} - \beta\right\} X_t\right] \\ &= \text{plim}[U_t] - \text{plim}\left[\hat{\alpha}^{\text{OLS}} - \alpha\right] - \text{plim}\left[\hat{\beta}^{\text{OLS}} - \beta\right] \text{plim}[X_t] \\ &= \text{plim}[U_t] \end{aligned} \tag{13-29}$$

Thus, since they have the same probability limit, the random variables U_t^{fit} and U_t are asymptotically equivalent. Therefore, for large samples, the parameter φ_1 in the AR(1) Model for U_t specified in Equation 13-28 can be estimated using sample realizations of the observable time-series $U_t^{\text{fit}} \ldots U_t^{\text{fit}}$.[39] Testing for a failure of the non-autocorrelation assumption is then straightforward: simply estimate the AR(1) Model for the model fitting errors and test the null hypothesis H_o: $\varphi_1 = 0$ against the alternative hypothesis H_A: $\varphi_1 \neq 0$.[40]

[39] All that the derivation in Equation 13-29 uses is the definition of the fitting errors and the assumption that the model parameters are consistently estimated. Thus, the fitting errors are aymptotically equivalent to the model errors for any regression model whose parameters are consistently estimated; this includes regression models with multiple explanatory variables and, if instrumental variables estimates based on valid instruments are used, regression models with endogenous explanatory variables.

[40] This is by no means the only way to test for AR(1) serial correlation in regression model errors, but it is certainly the simplest – and all of the alternative tests are asymptotically equivalent to it. Another well-known test is the Durbin-Watson test. This test claims to be valid in small samples. That is formally true, although perhaps of rather limited value in a world rife with stochastic regressors. But the Durbin-Watson test is not applicable if there are lagged dependent variables already included in the model. Moreover, it can easily fail to provide a definite answer as to whether one can reject H_o: $\varphi_1 = 0$ at, say, the 5% level or not, which is an unpalatable property. And, in any case, anything one would contemplate *doing* about a rejection of this null hypothesis is only asymptotically justified. One can consult Madalla (1977), Kmenta (1986), or Davidson and MacKinnon (2004) for more detail on the Durbin-Watson and related tests for AR(1) serial correlation. Madalla, G. S. (1977), *Econometrics*, McGraw-Hill: New York. Kmenta, J. (1986), *Elements of Econometrics*, Macmillan: New York. Davidson, R., and J. G. MacKinnon (2004), *Econometric Theory and Practice*, Oxford University Press: Oxford.

Applying this result to the regression model for detrended U.S. consumption spending using the detrended Martian disposable income data as the explanatory variable – and making the slightly heroic assumption that 62 observations constitutes a sufficiently large sample – it is very easy to estimate the coefficient φ_1 in the AR(1) model for the model errors (U_t) using the observed fitting errors, u_2^{fit} ... u_{62}^{fit} plotted in Figure 13-13:[41]

```
      Source |       SS       df       MS              Number of obs =      61
-------------+------------------------------           F(  1,    59) =   82.21
       Model |  .043700492     1  .043700492           Prob > F      =  0.0000
    Residual |  .031362281    59  .000531564           R-squared     =  0.5822
-------------+------------------------------           Adj R-squared =  0.5751
       Total |  .075062773    60  .001251046           Root MSE      =  .02306

------------------------------------------------------------------------------
resids_mars  |      Coef.   Std. Err.      t    P>|t|     [95% Conf. Interval]
-------------+----------------------------------------------------------------
resids_mars  |
         L1. |   .7636119   .0842185     9.07   0.000     .5950912    .9321327
       _cons |  -.0001531    .002952    -0.05   0.959     -.00606     .0057539
------------------------------------------------------------------------------
```

Once one has estimated this AR(1) model for the fitting errors, estimating an AR(2) model is extremely quick and easy:[42]

```
      Source |       SS       df       MS              Number of obs =      60
-------------+------------------------------           F(  2,    57) =   43.19
       Model |  .044739732     2  .022369866           Prob > F      =  0.0000
    Residual |  .029524194    57  .000517968           R-squared     =  0.6024
-------------+------------------------------           Adj R-squared =  0.5885
       Total |  .074263926    59  .001258711           Root MSE      =  .02276

------------------------------------------------------------------------------
resids_mars  |      Coef.   Std. Err.      t    P>|t|     [95% Conf. Interval]
-------------+----------------------------------------------------------------
resids_mars  |
         L1. |   .9075371   .1300596     6.98   0.000     .6470972    1.167977
         L2. |  -.1881466   .1304533    -1.44   0.155    -.4493749    .0730817
       _cons |  -.0006651   .0029385    -0.23   0.822    -.0065493     .005219
------------------------------------------------------------------------------
```

Is this extension to an AR(2) model an improvement? At first glance, it seems clear that the AR(1) model is better, since the observed realization of the estimator $\hat{\varphi}_2^{OLS}$ (equal to $-.1881466$ here) is only 1.44 times larger in magnitude than its estimated standard error. Thus, the null hypothesis that φ_2 is zero cannot be rejected at the 5% level; the p-value for this test is .155.

However, at second glance, note that the estimated AR(2) model actually fits the data better than the AR(1) model, yielding an adjusted R^2 value of .5885, which is larger than the value of .5751 for the AR(1) model.[43] As noted in Section 9.5, however, adjusted R^2 is known to

[41] Where t is the observation number and *resids_mars* are the fitting errors for the model relating the detrended logarithm of U.S. consumption spending to the detrended logarithm of Martian disposable income, the Stata commands for estimating this regression model are "tsset t" and then "regress resids_mars L1.resids_mars".

[42] In Stata, the command for generating this regression output is just "regress resids_mars L1.resids_mars L2.resids_mars".

[43] One might suspect from this result that the standard error estimate on $\hat{\varphi}_2^{OLS}$ is a bit inflated by multicollinearity, caused by the fact that $resids\_mars_t$ is so highly autocorrelated that the sample variation in $resids\_mars_{t-1}$ fairly closely resembles that of $resids\_mars_{t-2}$. This makes it difficult for the regression inference machinery to distinguish between these two explanatory variables. See Section 9.8 for a discussion of multicollinearity.

undercorrect for model complexity; the Schwarz Criterion defined in Section 9.5 provides a better way to compare these two fitted models. The Schwarz Criterion (SC) value is larger for the AR(2) model, so the better fit of this model to the sample data is not sufficient to compensate for the additional parameter estimated.[44] We can thus reasonably conclude that the AR(1) model is probably better. Still, the sample is not all that large here, whereas all of this analysis (the asymptotic equivalence of the fitting errors to the actual errors, the consistency of $\hat{\varphi}_2^{OLS}$, and the use of the SC criterion) is only asymptotically justified. Moreover, it will be very easy to reconsider this decision later on in the modeling process, when the dynamics of the regression model for the detrended logarithm of U.S. consumption spending are respecified in the next section.

For now, however, it is reasonable to conclude – based on these results – that there is very strong evidence that the non-autocorrelation assumption is seriously violated in the model relating detrended U.S. consumption spending to the detrended Martian disposable income time-series. Consequently, there is good reason to doubt the validity of the hypothesis test rejecting the null hypothesis that the population value of the coefficient on Martian disposable income is really zero.

Evidently, it is very easy to test whether the non-autocorrelation assumption is valid or not: simply save the fitting errors and estimate a few low-order autoregressive models for their serial dependence. But what is an analyst to do if the test indicates that the non-autocorrelation assumption is violated? That is the topic of the next section.

13.7 DYNAMIC MODEL RESPECIFICATION: AN EFFECTIVE RESPONSE TO SERIALLY CORRELATED REGRESSION MODEL ERRORS, WITH AN APPLICATION TO THE (DETRENDED) U.S. CONSUMPTION FUNCTION

Suppose, then, that the Bivariate Regression Model with AR(1) Errors – as laid out in Equation 13-28 – is the correct specification of the relationship between Y_t and X_t, with a non-zero value for φ_1, so that serial correlation is actually present in the model errors. We now know that $\hat{\beta}^{OLS}$ is a consistent (albeit biased) estimator of β in this model, but that the Equation 11-19 result for the asymptotic distribution of $\hat{\beta}^{OLS}$ – which is actually implemented in econometric software – is incorrect for non-zero φ_1, leading to inference results which are potentially quite misleading. Moreover, we have seen in the consumption function example examined here that this potential for achieving substantially misleading inference results is easily achieved using actual economic data.

There are two basic approaches for dealing with this situation. One approach is to use the estimated value (the sample realization) of $\hat{\varphi}_1^{OLS}$ to "correct" the estimation procedure for the presence of serial correlation in the model errors. The most widely used algorithm for doing this is based on the Generalized Least Squares ("GLS") estimator originally proposed by Aitken (1934); this approach is usually called "Feasible Generalized Least Squares" or "FGLS."[45] The FGLS approach will be described later in this section. The other approach – which is advocated here – is to observe that the serial correlation in the error term is actually just a symptom of missing dynamics in the model specification: appropriately respecify the model to include those dynamics and the serial

[44] The SC statistic equals ln(SSE/T) + $k$ln(T)/T, which is ln(0.031362/61) + 2ln(61)/61 or −7.438 for the AR(1) model (with $k = 2$) versus ln(0.029524/60) + 3ln(60)/60 or −7.412 for the AR(2) model (with $k = 3$). Note that SC depends directly on both the sum of squared fitting errors (SSE) and on the number of parameters estimated (k), so a better model will have a smaller value for the SC. The Stata post-estimation command "estat ic" will compute and display the SC (or BIC) statistic; if one is using a different program, it is easy enough to create a little spreadsheet that does the calculation and save it for when one needs it.

[45] Aitken, A. C. (1934) "On the Least-Squares and Linear Combinations of Observations," *Proc. Royal Soc. 55*, 42–48.

correlation in the model errors disappears. As an added bonus, the respecified model more properly describes the dynamics of the actual process which generated the sample data.[46]

The first (and most essential) steps in describing either approach – FGLS or model re-specification – are identical, and actually quite simple. Begin with the regression model equation for Y_t from Equation 13-27:

$$Y_t = \alpha + \beta X_t + U_t \tag{13-30}$$

Now rewrite Equation 13-30 for the previous period:

$$Y_{t-1} = \alpha + \beta X_{t-1} + U_{t-1} \tag{13-31}$$

Then multiply Equation 13-31 by φ_1 and subtract the resulting equation from Equation 13-30, to yield

$$\begin{aligned} Y_t - \varphi_1 Y_{t-1} &= [\alpha + \beta X_t + U_t] - \varphi_1[\alpha + \beta X_{t-1} + U_{t-1}] \\ &= \alpha(1 - \varphi_1) + \beta(X_t - \varphi_1 X_{t-1}) + (U_t - \varphi_1 U_{t-1}) \end{aligned} \tag{13-32}$$

Now observe that if the U_t really are generated by the AR(1) Model in Equation 13-28, then $U_t - \varphi_1 U_{t-1}$ is actually the independently distributed time-series V_t, so that

$$Y_t - \varphi_1 Y_{t-1} = \alpha(1 - \varphi_1) + \beta(X_t - \varphi_1 X_{t-1}) + V_t \qquad V_t \sim \text{IID}\left[0, \sigma_v^2\right] \tag{13-33}$$

Thus, if the errors in the original model are generated by an AR(1) process, then any regression model based on Equation 13-33 has an error term (V_t) which satisfies the non-autocorrelation assumption.

From this point the development can go in two alternative directions. In the various implementations of the GLS/Aitken FGLS "correction" procedures, one estimates φ_1 and then applies OLS to Equation 13-33, rewritten as

$$Y_t^* = \tilde{\alpha} + \beta X_t^* + V_t \tag{13-34a}$$

where $\tilde{\alpha}$ is a new intercept term and where Y_t^* and X_t^* are defined by

$$\begin{aligned} Y_t^* &\equiv Y_t - \hat{\varphi}_1 Y_{t-1} \\ X_t^* &\equiv X_t - \hat{\varphi}_1 X_{t-1} \end{aligned} \tag{13-34b}$$

for $t = 2 \ldots T$.

In the "Hildreth-Lu" implementation of FGLS, φ_1 is estimated via a what is called a "grid search." In this grid search $\hat{\varphi}_1$ is varied from -0.9 to 0.9 in increments of 0.1 and the value of $\hat{\varphi}_1$ yielding the largest R^2 value for Equation 13-34a is noted; then $\hat{\varphi}_1$ is varied over a finer grid (in increments of .01) centered on this value of $\hat{\varphi}_1$. The FGLS estimates of α and β are then taken from the regression based on the $\hat{\varphi}_1$ estimate yielding the best fit to the sample data.

Alternatively, in the "Cochrane-Orcutt" implementation of FGLS, OLS is used to estimate the parameters α and β in the original equation ($Y_t = \alpha + \beta X_t + U_t$) and thereby obtain a first estimate

[46] The Generalized Method of Moments ("GMM") provides a third approach to dealing with serial correlation in regression model errors. GMM is covered in Section 19.4. However, it is worth noting – even at this point – however, that (like FGLS) GMM only "corrects" for serial correlation in the errors: unlike the procedure described here, it does not lead to a better-specified regression model.

of the fitting errors $u_1^{\rm fit} \ldots u_T^{\rm fit}$. A first estimate of φ_1 is then obtained by applying OLS to the AR(1) model on these fitting errors – i.e., to $u_t^{\rm fit} = \varphi_1 u_{t-1}^{\rm fit} + v_t$.[47] Then the parameters α and β are re-estimated by using this first estimate of φ_1 in Equations 13-34a and 13-34b. These estimates of α and β yield a second estimate of the fitting errors, a second estimate of φ_1, and – again using Equations 13-34a and 13-34b – a new estimate of α and β. And so forth, until the estimated values of α and β settle down. The resulting Cochrane-Orcutt estimator can be shown to be asymptotically equivalent to the Hildreth-Lu estimator, but they differ a bit in modest samples.[48]

A better approach, however, results from rearranging Equation 13-33 by adding $\varphi_1 Y_{t-1}$ to both sides:

$$\begin{aligned} Y_t &= \varphi_1 Y_{t-1} + \alpha(1-\varphi_1) + \beta(X_t - \varphi_1 X_{t-1}) + V_t \\ V_t &\sim \text{IID}\left[0, \sigma_v^2\right] \end{aligned} \tag{13-34c}$$

and noting that this implies that

$$\begin{aligned} Y_t &= \alpha(1-\varphi_1) + \varphi_1 Y_{t-1} + \beta(X_t - \varphi_1 X_{t-1}) + V_t \\ &= (\alpha - \alpha\varphi_1) + \varphi_1 Y_{t-1} + \beta X_t - \beta\varphi_1 X_{t-1} + V_t \end{aligned} \tag{13-35}$$

where V_t is still IID$[0, \sigma_v^2]$. This model could be rewritten as

$$Y_t = \gamma_0 + \gamma_1 Y_{t-1} + \gamma_2 X_t + \gamma_3 X_{t-1} + V_t \tag{13-36}$$

and the parameters $\gamma_0 \ldots \gamma_3$ estimated using OLS. The estimator $\hat{\gamma}_2^{\rm OLS}$ then provides a consistent estimator of β and – since the model errors V_t are, by construction, IID$[0, \sigma_v^2]$ – the usual regression statistical inference results and computing formals are all valid, at least for large samples.

Thus, the AR(1) serial correlation in the model errors for the original model is really just indicating that these lagged terms in Y_t and X_t need to be included in the model specification! Include them, and then there will be no need for FGLS autocorrelation corrections.

Suppose that an AR(2) model is necessary in order to model the serial dependence in U_t, the original model errors – i.e., in order to yield a serially independent error term in the autoregressive model for U_t. Using the same reasoning, in that case *two* lags in Y_t and X_t need to be included in the model specification. And so forth – see Exercise 13-7.

This respecification approach is much simpler. And it leads to a fundamentally better model than does the FGLS "correction" approach. Why not just do this, then, and respecify the model to include the relevant dynamics instead of bothering with FGLS? In the main, the answer to this question is that there usually *is* no good reason for pursuing the "correction" strategy rather than respecifying the model to include the necessary dynamics.

But "usually" is not the same as "always": there are situations where including the necessary dynamics in the model specification is not a good idea. For one thing, note that the respecification approach requires the estimation of more parameters – substantially more parameters if the number of explanatory variables and/or the order of the AR(p) model used becomes sizeable. So one could imagine a situation where there are sufficient data for an asymptotically justified

[47] Since these estimates of α and β are consistent, $u_t^{\rm fit}$ is a sample realization of a random variable ($U_t^{\rm fit}$) which is asymptotically equivalent to U_t; consequently $\hat{\varphi}_1^{\rm OLS}$ obtained in this way is at least a consistent estimator of φ_1.

[48] Simulation work indicates that the Hildreth-Lu estimator is not clearly better (or worse) than the Cochrane-Orcutt estimator in small samples. Note, however, that the first observation (Y_1, X_1) is "lost" in making the transformation in Equation 13-34b. It can be shown to be a slight improvement to define Y_1^* equal to $Y_1\sqrt{1-\hat{\varphi}_1^2}$ and X_1^* equal to $X_1\sqrt{1-\hat{\varphi}_1^2}$; this still yields $V_t \sim$ IID$[0, \sigma_v^2]$, but fully utilizes all T sample observations. See Exercise 13-6.

procedure like FGLS to be reasonable, but insufficient data for it to be reasonable to estimate the respecified model.[49]

In other modeling situations the respecification of the model to include dynamics can destroy the point of the enterprise. Active Learning Exercise 13b (available at www.wiley.com/college/ashley) provides a good example of this situation. The point of this exercise is to empirically examine the stability over time of a particular kind of macroeconomic monetary policy called the "Taylor Rule." The sample data clearly indicate that the implied model error term in this model for how the U.S. central bank sets the short term interest rate is serially correlated to a significant degree and in a manner which changes over the various sub-periods considered. The serial correlation can be modeled by including different dynamics in each model, but the models for the various sub-periods would then no longer be comparable with each other and none would correspond to the "Taylor Rule" itself as it is commonly understood.

The most graceful approach in this circumstance is to leave the model specification itself alone and to compute what are called "Newey-West" standard errors for the model coefficient estimates and use these in the inference work. Newey-West standard error estimates are the "serial correlation" analogue to the White-Eicker ("robust") standard error estimates discussed in Section 10.7 in connection with heteroscedastic model errors. Like the White-Eicker standard error estimates, they are only asymptotically justified – and hence are only appropriate to use in large samples – and induce no improvement (or even any change) in the parameter estimates. But they do provide consistent estimates of the parameter estimator standard errors, so that one can still construct asymptotically valid confidence intervals and hypothesis tests, even though the model errors are serially correlated. Unlike the White-Eicker estimates – which required no specification at all with regard to the form of the heteroscedasticity – the Newey-West standard error estimates require that one at least specify a maximum lag, beyond which the model errors are assumed to be serially uncorrelated.

The idea underlying the Newey-West standard error estimates is otherwise so similar to that underlying the White-Eicker estimates that the simplest way to describe it is to just repeat the formula given in Chapter 10 for the White-Eicker robust standard error estimator for $\hat{\beta}$, the OLS slope estimator in the Bivariate Regression Model and then restate it as the corresponding Newey-West estimator. From Equation 10-20, the White-Eicker (robust) standard error estimate is

$$\sqrt{\left[\text{var}(\hat{\beta})\right]^{\text{robust}}} = \sqrt{\sum_{i=1}^{N}\left(w_i^{\text{ols}}\right)^2\left(u_i^{\text{fit}}\right)^2} \tag{10-21}$$

where w_i^{ols} is the usual OLS weight for the ith term in the expression for $\hat{\beta}$ and u_i^{fit} is the observed fitting error for the ith observation. The corresponding Newey-West estimator, allowing for serial correlation out to (for example) one lag is

$$\sqrt{\left[\text{var}(\hat{\beta})\right]^{\text{Newey-West}}} = \sqrt{\sum_{i=1}^{N}\left(w_i^{\text{ols}}\right)^2\left(u_i^{\text{fit}}\right)^2 + \sum_{i=2}^{N}\left(w_i^{\text{ols}}w_{i-1}^{\text{ols}}\right)\left(u_i^{\text{fit}}u_{i-1}^{\text{fit}}\right)} \tag{13-37}$$

Note that the Newey-West estimator subsumes the White-Eicker terms, so it is also robust against heteroscedasticity in the model errors.[50]

[49] In that circumstance – with model parameters $\beta_0 \ldots \beta_k$ and AR model parameters $\varphi_0 \ldots \varphi_p$ – one might estimate the parameters in the equation analogous to Equation 13-35 directly by minimizing the sum of squared fitting errors with respect to these $k+p+2$ parameters. Since the model is now a nonlinear function of the parameters, this procedure is called "nonlinear least squares" rather than "ordinary least squares" and is numerically more challenging because it involves a numerical minimization of a function of $k+p+2$ variables rather than just solving linear equations. This minimization is essentially identical to the analogous Hildreth-Lu FGLS procedure described in the body of the text. Many econometrics programs provide a facility for estimating regression models using nonlinear least squares – e.g., the "nl" command in Stata.

[50] Equation 13-37 is correct but a bit misleading, as the additional terms which would be added so as to account for serial correlation at larger lags will enter with diminished weights. This down-weighting is necessary so as to ensure that the Newey-West variance estimate is always positive – e.g., see Davidson and MacKinnon (1993, p. 611).

Newey-West standard errors are easy enough to calculate in practice: in Stata, for example, one merely replaces the OLS "regress" (or "reg") command by the word "newey" and one must add an option specifying the maximum lag at which serial correlation in the model errors is contemplated. Choosing a larger value for this maximum allowed lag is safer, but makes a larger demand on the length of the sample. In fact, the Newey-West standard error estimates will still be inconsistent (like the OLS estimates) if this lag is chosen too small; and they will be nonsense if the lag is chosen too large for the sample length available. (As a rule of thumb, even one lag is probably "too much" with substantially less than 80 observations.)

Thus, one is usually better off with the model respecification approach: it both provides consistent standard error estimates and produces a fundamentally better model for the data. It is worth noting, however, that adding dynamics in a sloppy way can leave one worse off than not adding them at all. Simply estimating the original model at least provides a consistent estimate of β: the problem is that the accompanying estimated standard errors, confidence intervals, and hypothesis test rejection *p*-values are then frequently quite distorted. Thus, this consistent estimator is almost impossible to interpret in any non-misleading way. But even this consistency property for $\hat{\beta}^{OLS}$ is lost if one respecifies the model based on an assumption that the U_t is generated by an AR(p) model when one should have assumed that it is generated by an AR($p+1$) model. Suppose, for example, that one assumes that U_t is generated by an AR(1) model when, in reality, U_t is generated by an AR(2) model. In that case one will have included Y_{t-1} and X_{t-1} in the model specification but (incorrectly) failed to include Y_{t-2} and X_{t-2}. These two incorrectly omitted variables are then part of the model error term. And this omission will make the estimator $\hat{\gamma}_2^{OLS}$ in Equation 13-36 an inconsistent estimator of β to the extent that Y_{t-2} and/or X_{t-2} is correlated with X_t. This is a serious concern, but the moral here is that it is essential to include *sufficient* dynamics in the equation – not that one should forgo modeling the dynamics altogether, as one does by either ignoring the serial correlation in the original model, by "correcting" it by using the FGLS approach, or by just using Newey-West standard error estimates.

How does this all work in practice? Let's return now to the simple consumption function considered in Section 13.3, which spuriously indicated that the relationship between detrended data on U.S. consumption spending ($PCE\_DETRENDED_t$) and the artificially generated data on detrended Martian disposable income ($mars\_detrended_t$) is both economically and statistically significant. (The Martian variable name is denoted in lowercase because this variable was taken to be fixed in repeated in samples in Section 13.3; this assumption is relaxed shortly.) To review, the OLS estimated model obtained in that section was:

```
      Source |       SS       df       MS              Number of obs =      62
-------------+------------------------------           F(  1,     60) =   20.73
       Model |  .019134283     1  .019134283           Prob > F      =  0.0000
    Residual |  .055388191    60  .000923137           R-squared     =  0.2568
-------------+------------------------------           Adj R-squared =  0.2444
       Total |  .074522474    61   .00122168           Root MSE      =  .03038

------------------------------------------------------------------------------
PCE_DETRENDED |     Coef.   Std. Err.      t    P>|t|     [95% Conf. Interval]
-------------+----------------------------------------------------------------
MARS_DETRENDED|  .5498348     .12077     4.55   0.000     .3082588    .7914108
        _cons| -.0002922   .0038592    -0.08   0.940    -.0080117    .0074273
------------------------------------------------------------------------------
```

Thus, the realized value of $\hat{\beta}^{OLS}$, the estimated elasticity of detrended U.S. consumption with respect to detrended Martian disposable income, is $.55 \pm .12$, which appears to be significantly different from zero (*p*-value for rejecting H_o: $\beta = 0$ is less than .0005) and which yields an estimated 95% confidence interval for β of [.31, .79].

In Section 13.6, $\hat{\varphi}_1^{OLS}$ from an AR(1) model for these fitting errors strongly indicated that φ_1 is non-zero in an AR(1) model for the actual model errors. Thus, while the elasticity estimate of .55 is consistent, there is good reason to think that the standard error estimate (.12) – and all of the inference results based on it – may be quite misleading. The estimated models for the fitting errors in Section 13.6 also provided some evidence for the possibility that U_t might instead be generated by an AR(2) model; this possibility warrants further investigation below. For the moment, however, it is reasonable to provisionally proceed on the assumption that the AR(1) formulation for the model errors is appropriate.

Reframing the model for $PCE\_DETRENDED_t$ in the context of Equation 13-28 – the Bivariate Regression Model with a stochastic regressor and AR(1) model errors – and, of course, substituting $PCE\_DETRENDED_t$ for Y_t and $MARTIAN\ DI\_DETRENDED_t$ for X_t, yields the model

$$
\begin{aligned}
PCE\_DETRENDED_t &= \alpha + \beta MARTIAN\_DI\_DETRENDED + U_t \\
U_t &= \varphi_0 + \varphi_1 U_{t-1} + V_t \qquad |\varphi_1| < 1 \\
V_t &\sim \text{IID}\left[0, \sigma_v^2\right] \\
MARTIAN\_DI\_DETRENDED &\sim \text{IID}\left[0, \sigma_{\text{mars}}^2\right] \qquad \sigma_{\text{mars}}^2 > 0 \\
\text{plim}(\widehat{\text{cov}}(MARTIAN\_DI\_DETRENDED, U_t)) &= 0 \\
\text{Cov}(MARTIAN\_DI\_DETRENDED^2, U_t^2) &= 0
\end{aligned}
\tag{13-38}
$$

Thus, the respecified model is

$$
\begin{aligned}
PCE\_DETRENDED_t = {} & \gamma_0 + \gamma_1\, PCE\_DETRENDED_{t-1} + \gamma_2\, MARTIAN\_DETRENDED_t \\
& + \gamma_3\, MARTIAN\_DI\_DETRENDED_{t-1} + V_t
\end{aligned}
\tag{13-39}
$$

Estimating Equation 13-39 using OLS yields the output:[51]

```
      Source |       SS       df       MS              Number of obs =      61
-------------+------------------------------           F(  3,    57) =   70.63
       Model |  .058443471     3  .019481157           Prob > F      =  0.0000
    Residual |  .015721211    57  .000275811           R-squared     =  0.7880
-------------+------------------------------           Adj R-squared =  0.7769
       Total |  .074164682    60  .001236078           Root MSE      =  .01661

------------------------------------------------------------------------------
PCE_DETRENDED|      Coef.   Std. Err.      t    P>|t|     [95% Conf. Interval]
-------------+----------------------------------------------------------------
PCE_DETRENDED|
         L1. |   .8449276    .070451    11.99   0.000     .7038519    .9860032
MARTIAN_DI_DETRENDED
         --. |   .1733659   .1166826     1.49   0.143     -.060287    .4070187
         L1. |  -.0203751   .1219756    -0.17   0.868    -.2646269    .2238768
       _cons |  -.0006564   .0021282    -0.31   0.759     -.004918    .0036053
------------------------------------------------------------------------------
```

Now that appropriate dynamics have been included in the model specification, the estimated coefficient on $MARTIAN\_DI\_DETRENDED_t$ is $.173 \pm .117$, the null hypothesis that this coefficient is non-zero can be rejected only with a large p-value (.143), and the estimated 95% confidence interval for this coefficient ([−.060, .407]) clearly includes zero. Thus, there is

[51] This output was doctored slightly so as to display the full name of the explanatory variable.

no longer any serious evidence that β, the coefficient on detrended logarithm of Martian disposable income, is not zero.

Figure 13-14 plots the fitting errors for this estimated regression model:

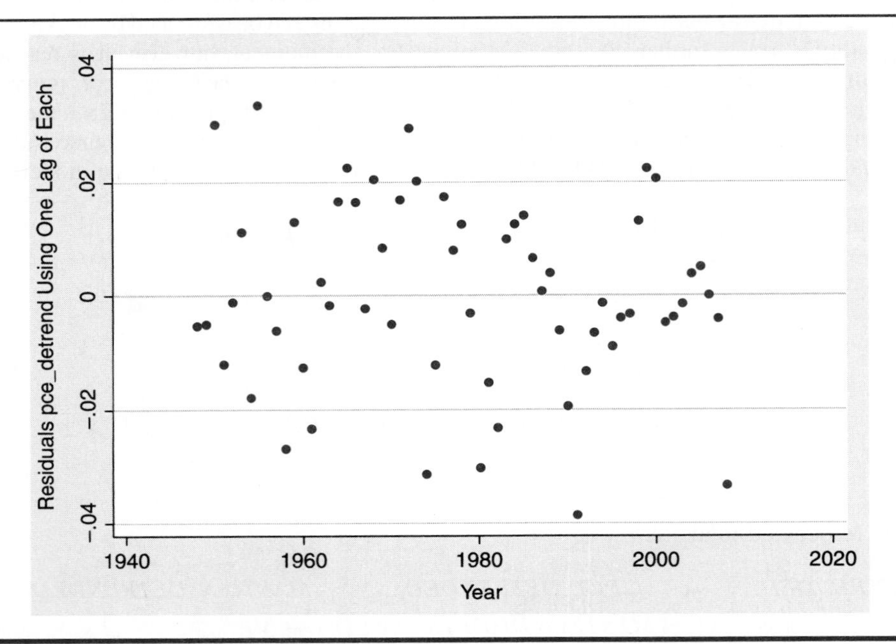

Figure 13-14 Time Plot of Fitting Errors from the Respecified Regression of the Detrended Logarithm of U.S. Real Personal Consumption Expenditures on the Detrended Logarithm of Martian Disposable Income

And an estimated AR(1) model for these fitting errors yields:

```
      Source |       SS       df       MS              Number of obs =      60
-------------+------------------------------           F(  1,     58) =    3.19
       Model |  .000817969     1  .000817969           Prob > F      =  0.0793
    Residual |   .01487372    58  .000256443           R-squared     =  0.0521
-------------+------------------------------           Adj R-squared =  0.0358
       Total |  .015691689    59  .000265961           Root MSE      =  .01601

------------------------------------------------------------------------------
resids_ar1_respec| Coef.    Std. Err.      t    P>|t|     [95% Conf. Interval]
-------------+----------------------------------------------------------------
resids_ar1_respec|
         L1. |   .2367405   .1325561     1.79   0.079    -.0285994    .5020804
       _cons |  -.0000415   .0020687    -0.02   0.984    -.0041825    .0040994
------------------------------------------------------------------------------
```

Thus, there is neither visual nor statistical evidence for serial correlation in the fitting errors of the respecified model.

Recall from the discussion in Section 13.6 that an AR(2) model for the fitting errors of the original regression model looked almost as good as did an AR(1) model. This result suggests that it might be prudent to also entertain the possibility that U_t in Equation 13-38 is generated by an AR(2) model. One should therefore also consider a respecified model which in addition includes $PCE\_DETRENDED_{t-2}$ and $MARTIAN\_DI\_DETRENDED_{t-2}$ as explanatory variables. Estimating this additional model takes only a few seconds, and yields the output:

```
      Source |       SS       df       MS              Number of obs =      60
-------------+------------------------------           F(  5,    54) =   44.12
       Model |  .058741612     5  .011748322           Prob > F      =  0.0000
    Residual |  .014379974    54  .000266296           R-squared     =  0.8033
-------------+------------------------------           Adj R-squared =  0.7851
       Total |  .073121586    59  .001239349           Root MSE      =  .01632

------------------------------------------------------------------------------
PCE_DETRENDED|      Coef.   Std. Err.      t    P>|t|     [95% Conf. Interval]
-------------+----------------------------------------------------------------
PCE_DETRENDED|
         L1. |   1.081318   .1383292     7.82   0.000     .8039847    1.358651
         L2. |  -.2842264   .1368179    -2.08   0.043    -.5585298   -.0099231
MARTIAN_DI_DETRENDED
         --. |   .2162485   .1401779     1.54   0.129    -.0647913    .4972884
         L1. |  -.0432085   .1821446    -0.24   0.813    -.4083864    .3219695
         L2. |   .0043891   .1354839     0.03   0.974    -.2672398     .276018
       _cons |  -.0005836   .0021129    -0.28   0.783    -.0048197    .0036526
------------------------------------------------------------------------------
```

This model fits the sample data a bit better, in that it has a slightly higher adjusted R^2, but it has a larger (worse) value for the Schwarz Criterion (SC), which does a better job of correcting for model complexity than does adjusted R^2.[52] Thus, it would be reasonable to choose the model with one lag in each variable in this case. There is actually no need to choose between these two models, however, as both yield the same conclusion: once appropriate dynamics have been included in the model specification, there is no evidence for rejecting the null hypothesis that the coefficients on detrended Martian disposable income are all zero.

This modeling exercise – here and in Section 13.6 – has hopefully made it clear that neither the scatterplot reproduced earlier in this chapter as Figure 13-5 (and also in a very *large* number of introductory macroeconomics textbooks) nor the estimated regression equation based on it actually provide any empirical evidence whatsoever for a direct relationship between U.S. consumption spending and U.S. disposable income: there is equally strong evidence of this kind for a relationship between U.S. consumption spending and Martian disposable income. Moreover, detrending both time-series – as we have just seen in this section – still yields "strong" evidence for a totally spurious relationship between these two time-series, but only if one fails to deal with the serial correlation in the model errors – e.g., by including the necessary dynamics in the model.

The results of this section suggest that it would be useful to next respecify the relationship between (trended) U.S. consumption spending and (trended) *U.S.* disposable income to incorporate the dynamics which are no doubt necessary in order for this model to satisfy the non-autocorrelation assumption. Such a model would be of some interest, since it corresponds closely to the scatterplot found in so many introductory macroeconomics textbooks. On the other hand, outside of this textbook scatterplot, it is not common practice to use annual data to quantify a macroeconomic relationship of this sort when quarterly and monthly data are available. Moreover, the model

[52] The Schwarz Criterion (SC, defined in Section 9.5) equals $\ln(SSE/T) + k\ln(T)/T$, which is $\ln(0.015721/61) + 4\ln(61)/61$ or -7.994 for the model with one lag in each variable and versus $\ln(0.014380/60) + 6\ln(60)/60$ or -7.927 for the model with two lags in each variable. Note that SC depends directly on both the sum of squared fitting errors (SSE) and on the number of parameters estimated (k), so a better model will have a smaller value for the SC.

considered up to this point looked at a contemporaneous relationship between consumption spending and disposable income – so as to be consistent with the textbook scatterplot – but there is every reason to expect current disposable income to be an endogenous explanatory variable in such a model, due to the well-known joint determination of these two macroeconomic quantities.

Consequently, it makes better sense at this point to abandon the annual U.S. consumption spending data analyzed in the examples so far and to instead turn our attention to a related, but different (and richer), example: the construction of a model for the dynamic relationship between current *monthly* U.S. consumption spending and concomitant *lagged* values of both U.S. disposable income and a short-term interest rate in the immediately previous months. This relationship is of substantial macroeconomic interest. Moreover, this modeling project makes a very good example, illustrating both the model specification ideas and the diagnostic checking techniques described in both Chapter 10 and in the present chapter.

On the other hand, it obvious that this enterprise requires that we also abandon the Bivariate Regression Model framework of Equations 11-1, 13-11, and 13-28 in favor of a dynamic generalization of Equation 9-1, the Multiple Regression Model. In particular, this generalization must not only allow for stochastic explanatory variables but also explicitly allow for both multiple lagged values of the dependent variable and multiple lags (dynamics) in the explanatory variables.[53] This generalization of our results is the topic of the next chapter.

KEY TERMS

For each term or concept listed below, provide a working definition or explanation:

Autocorrelated Regression Model Error Term
Autocorrelated Errors in Model with Fixed-Regressors
Autocorrelated Errors in Model with Stochastic Regressors
Covariance Stationary Time-Series
AR(1) Time-Series

EXERCISES

13-1. For the special case of T equal to five, explicitly write out the expression (Equation 13-9) for the sampling variance of the OLS slope estimator in the Bivariate Regression Model with a fixed-regressor. Is the dependence of this sampling variance on the autocorrelations of the model errors at low lags (e.g., ρ_1, ρ_2, and ρ_3) likely to become negligible for larger values of T?

13-2. Using the definition of W_t^{ols} given in Equation 13-22, show that that $\sum_{t=2}^{N} W_t^{\text{ols}}$ equals zero and that $\sum_{t=2}^{N} W_t^{\text{ols}} Y_{t-1}$ equals one.

13-3. Suppose that Y_t is actually generated by the AR(3) model

$$Y_t = \tilde{\varphi}_0 + \tilde{\varphi}_1 Y_{t-1} + \tilde{\varphi}_2 Y_{t-2} + \tilde{\varphi}_3 Y_{t-3} + V_t \tag{13-40}$$

where it is assumed that $V_t \sim \text{IID}\left[0, \sigma_v^2\right]$ and that V_t is uncorrelated with Y_{t-1}, Y_{t-2}, and Y_{t-3}. It is safe to assume, based on this model, that Y_t is not uncorrelated with both Y_{t-1} and Y_{t-2}. Show that a (misspecified) AR(1) model for Y_t – defined as in Equation 13-11 – corresponds to the Bivariate Regression Model of Equation 11-1 with an endogenous regressor. In other words, show that $\text{cov}(Y_{t-1}, U_t)$ is non-zero so long as either $\tilde{\varphi}_2$ or $\tilde{\varphi}_3$ is

[53] Note that Equations 13-35 and 13-38 already depart in this direction.

non-zero, but that the endogeneity disappears if $\tilde{\varphi}_2$ and $\tilde{\varphi}_3$ are both zero. {Hint: Observe that U_t equals $\tilde{\varphi}_2 Y_{t-2} + \tilde{\varphi}_3 Y_{t-3} + V_t$}. Thus, even though it is not necessary to assume that $\text{cov}(Y_{t-1}, U_t)$ is zero in order for $\tilde{\varphi}_1^{OLS}$ to be a consistent estimator of φ_1 in a correctly-specified AR(1) model, this endogeneity causes $\tilde{\varphi}_1^{OLS}$ to be an inconsistent estimator of φ_1 in the AR(1) if Y_t is actually generated by a higher-order AR model.[54]

13-4. Use the MA(∞) form of the AR(1) Model – Equation 13-17 – to show that

a. U_t is independent of $Y_{t-\ell}$ for all strictly positive values of ℓ.

b. $\text{Cov}(Y_{t-1}^2, U_t^2)$ is zero, which is equivalent to the assumption that $\text{Cov}(X_i^2, U_i^2)$ is zero, made in the Bivariate Regression Model of Equation 11-1.

c. $\text{Cov}(Y_{t-1}, U_t)$ is zero, which is equivalent to assuming that $\text{Cov}(X_i, U_i)$ is zero in the Bivariate Regression Model of Equation 11-1, and which implies that Y_{t-1} is not an endogenous explanatory variable in this model.

d. $\text{Cov}(Y_{t-1}U_t, Y_{t-1-j}U_{t-j})$ is zero for all strictly positive values of j. Thus, the sum of the magnitudes of the autocovariances of $Y_{t-1}U_t$ is clearly bounded, because all of these autocovariances are zero for non-zero values of j. From Hamilton (1994, p. 188) this implies that $\text{plim}(\widehat{\text{cov}}(Y_{t-1}, U_t))$ equals $\text{cov}(Y_{t-1}, U_t)$, which is needed (in Equation 13-25) to show that $\hat{\varphi}_1^{OLS}$ is a consistent estimator of φ_1.

13-5. Use the MA(∞) form of the AR(1) Model – Equation 13-17 – to show that

$$\gamma_j = \text{cov}(Y_t, Y_{t-j}) = E\left[\left(Y_t - \frac{\varphi_o}{1-\varphi_1}\right)\left(Y_{t-j} - \frac{\varphi_o}{1-\varphi_1}\right)\right] = \varphi_1^j \text{var}(Y_t) \qquad (13\text{-}41)$$

and that

$$\rho_j = \text{corr}(Y_t, Y_{t-j}) = \varphi_1^j \qquad (13\text{-}42)$$

Equation 13-41 shows that $\sum_{j=0}^{\infty} |\gamma_j|$ is bounded for the AR(1) model, which implies that a Law of Large Numbers (Equation A11-6) still applies to the sample mean and sample variance of Y_t, even though Y_t is not identically and independently distributed. {See Hamilton (1994, p. 188).}

13-6. Show that defining Y_1^* equal to $Y_1\sqrt{1-\varphi_1^2}$ and X_1^* equal to $X_1\sqrt{1-\varphi_1^2}$ in Equations 13-34a and 13-34b – the transformed versions of Equation 13-30, based on the "Bivariate Regression Model with AR(1) Errors" given as Equation 13-28 – still yields $V_t \sim \text{IID}[0, \sigma_v^2]$. The transformed regression model now uses all T observations, which yields noticeably more efficient parameter estimation in very small samples. This increase in estimation efficiency is of modest practical relevance, however, since (at best) only consistent estimates of φ_1 are available.

13-7. Suppose that U_t, the model errors in Equation 13-28, are instead generated by an AR(3) Model – i.e., the model for U_t now also includes terms in U_{t-2} and U_{t-3}. Show that including three lags of both Y_t and X_t in the model specification yields a regression model with independently distributed errors. How would the respecified model differ if there were four explanatory variables in the original model instead of just one? In what way could this prove problematic?

[54] Note that to estimate an AR(1) model for Y_t when a higher-order AR model specification is appropriate is to wrongly omit explanatory variables which are correlated with the included variable, Y_{t-1}. Thus, as usual when such explanatory variables are wrongly omitted, the OLS estimator of the coefficient on the included explanatory variable – Y_{t-1} in this case – becomes inconsistent because this included variable proxies for the omitted variables.

APPENDIX 13.1: DERIVATION OF THE ASYMPTOTIC SAMPLING DISTRIBUTION OF $\hat{\varphi}_1^{OLS}$ IN THE AR(1) MODEL

The asymptotic sampling distribution of $\hat{\varphi}_1^{OLS}$, the OLS estimator of φ_1 in the AR(1) Model (Equation 13-11), is given in Equation 13-27 as

$$\sqrt{T-1}\left(\hat{\varphi}_1^{OLS} - \varphi_1\right) \xrightarrow{d} N\left[0, \frac{\sigma_u^2}{\text{var}(Y_{t-1})}\right] \tag{A13-1}$$

where, because $\text{cov}(Y_{t-1}, U_t)$ is zero for all values of t, $\hat{\varphi}_1^{OLS}$ is a consistent estimator of φ_1. This result is proven below.

The derivation of this result is essentially identical to that used in Appendix 11.2, with two differences. First, the notation used is modified so as to reflect the fact that the observations are now indexed using the symbol t – now running from 2 to T – and the sample size is now denoted $T-1$ instead of N. The observation for which t is one must be dropped because Y_{t-1} for that observation is not observed. The distinction between T and $T-1$ clearly does not matter asymptotically, but it seems clearer to be consistent about defining sample quantities – such as the sample variance of Y_{t-1} – using the number of sample observations of the relevant quantity divided by the actual number of such observations, which here is $T-1$.

The second difference is much less visible in the derivation, but is more important. Recast in this modified notation, the Lindeberg-Lévy form of the Central Limit Theorem states that

$$V_t \sim \text{IID}(0, \sigma_v^2) \quad \Rightarrow \quad \text{plim}\left[\frac{1}{\sqrt{T-1}}\sum_{t=2}^{T} V_t\right] = \text{plim}\left[\sqrt{T-1}\;\overline{V}\right] = N\left[0, \sigma_v^2\right] \tag{A13-2}$$

This is still true, but it is no longer relevant to the problem at hand, because – analogous to the result obtained in (and just after) Equation A11-13, and derived below – V_t here corresponds to $\frac{1}{\sigma_y^2}(Y_{t-1} - \mu_y)U_t$, which is not serially independent. The fact that U_t is serially independent suffices to imply that $\frac{1}{\sigma_y^2}(Y_{t-1} - \mu_y)U_t$ is serially uncorrelated, but serial uncorrelatedness is not sufficient in order for a Central Limit Theorem to apply.[55] More specifically, serial uncorrelatedness says that this random variable $\frac{1}{\sigma_y^2}(Y_{t-1} - \mu_y)U_t$ is not linearly related to its own past, but asymptotic normality requires a stronger degree of unrelatedness than this. On the other hand, asymptotic normality does not require that this random variable be serially independent; it only requires that it be what is called a "martingale difference sequence."

A time-series Z_t is a martingale difference sequence if $E[Z_t f(Z_{t-1}, Z_{t-2}, Z_{t-3}, \ldots)]$ is zero for all functions $f(Z_{t-1}, Z_{t-2}, Z_{t-3}, \ldots)$: that is, if Z_t is not in any way forecastable from its own past, linearly or nonlinearly. This is a much stronger statement about Z_t's relationship to its past values than to say that Z_t is serially uncorrelated, because such non-autocorrelation only implies that Z_t is not *linearly* forecastable from its own past. But it is a considerably weaker statement about Z_t than asserting that Z_t is serially independent, in that serial independence implies that any *function* of Z_t – e.g., Z_t^2 – is not in any way forecastable from past values of Z_t. Thus, if Z_t is serially independent, then

[55] This serial uncorrelatedness is proven in Exercise 13-4d; it follows from the fact that U_t is independent of $(Y_{t-1} - \mu_y)(Y_{t-1-j} - \mu_y)U_{t-j}$ for all positive values of j, since the latter factor involves only U_{t-j}, U_{t-j-1}, U_{t-j-2}, etc.

$E[g(Z_t)\, f(Z_{t-1}, Z_{t-2}, Z_{t-3}, \ldots)]$ is zero for all functions $f(Z_{t-1}, Z_{t-2}, Z_{t-3}, \ldots)$ and also for all functions $g(Z_t)$. Thus, for example, if Z_t is a martingale difference sequence, then its variance could be forecastable from its own past, whereas this would not be possible if Z_t is serially independent.

This distinction is relevant here because the assumption – made in the AR(1) Model – that the model error term U_t is serially independent *is* sufficient to imply that random variables of the form $U_t U_{t-j}$ are martingale difference sequences for all positive values of j, even though such random variables are not serially independent.[56] Since the MA(∞) form of the AR(1) Model – Equation 13-17 – expresses Y_{t-1} as a linear function of U_{t-1}, U_{t-2}, etc., it follows from the assumption that U_t is serially independent that $\frac{1}{\sigma_y^2}\left(Y_{t-1} - \mu_y\right)U_t$ is a martingale difference sequence. Therefore, it is possible to apply below what one might call the Martingale Difference form of the Central Limit Theorem:

$$
\begin{aligned}
V_t &\sim \mathrm{MD}(0, \sigma_v^2) \\
&\geq \operatorname{plim}\left[\frac{1}{\sqrt{T-1}}\sum_{t=2}^{T} V_t\right] = \operatorname{plim}\left[\sqrt{T-1}\,\overline{V}\right] = N(0, \sigma_v^2)
\end{aligned}
\tag{A13-3}
$$

where the notation "$V_t \sim \mathrm{MD}(0, \sigma_v^2)$" says that V_t is a martingale difference sequence with bounded variance σ_v^2.[57]

The remainder of the derivation of Equation A13-1 is essentially identical to that of Equation A11-9 given in Appendix 11.2, except for the notational differences noted above and for the fact that, as noted below, several assumptions made in Appendix 11.2 are no longer necessary because they follow from the form of the AR(1) Model.

In particular, using Equation 13-23, which expresses $\hat{\varphi}_1^{\mathrm{OLS}}$ in terms of the model errors, $U_1 \ldots U_T$,

$$
\hat{\varphi}_1^{\mathrm{OLS}} = \varphi_1 + \sum_{t=2}^{T} W_t^{\mathrm{ols}} U_t \qquad \text{where} \quad W_t^{\mathrm{ols}} \equiv \frac{Y_{t-1} - \overline{Y}}{\sum\limits_{\ell=2}^{T}\left(Y_{\ell-} - \overline{Y}\right)^2}
\tag{A13-4}
$$

Recall that the AR(1) Model of Equation 13-11 in addition assumes that $U_t \sim \mathrm{IID}(0, \sigma_u^2)$ and that $|\varphi_1| < 1$. Also, note that Equation 13-17, the MA(∞) form of the model, implies that U_t is independent of Y_{t-1}; this result implies that both $\operatorname{cov}(Y_{t-1}, U_t)$ and $\operatorname{cov}(Y_{t-1}^2, U_t^2)$ are zero, which hence no longer need to be assumed.[58]

The strategy of the proof is to rewrite $\operatorname{plim}\left[\sqrt{T-1}\left(\hat{\varphi}_1^{\mathrm{OLS}} - \varphi_1\right)\right]$ as the probability limit of $\sqrt{T-1}$ times the sample mean of a zero-mean random variable – to be called V_t – which is a martingale difference sequence because U_t is assumed serially independent in the AR(1) Model.

---

[56] For example, see Hamilton (1994, p. 190).

[57] For example, see Hamilton (1994, p. 193) for a statement – and White (1984, p. 130) for a proof – of a somewhat more general result than this, which allows for the variance of V_t to vary over time. This form of the Central Limit Theorem also requires that $E[|V_t|^r]$ is bounded for some value of r larger than two; this additional condition will be assumed in the present case without further comment. This statement of the Central Limit Theorem also incorporates the result in Hamilton (1994, Equation 7.2.14) with k set to zero. White, H. (1984) *Asymptotic Theory for Econometricians*. Academic Press: Orlando.

[58] Recall that Equation 11-1 and, in particular, the derivation of the asymptotic sampling distribution of $\sqrt{N}\left(\hat{\beta}^{\mathrm{OLS}} - \beta\right)$ in Appendix 11.1 required an assumption that $\operatorname{cov}(X_i^2, U_i^2)$ is zero. Here the analogue of this assumption follows from the structure of the model, as does the zero value of $\operatorname{cov}(Y_{t-1}, U_t)$, which is the analogue here of the Equation 11-1 assumption that $\operatorname{cov}(X_i, U_i)$ is zero.

The $\text{plim}\left[\sqrt{T-1}\left(\hat{\varphi}_1^{OLS}-\varphi_1\right)\right]$ – i.e., the asymptotic distribution of $\sqrt{T-1}\left(\hat{\varphi}_1^{OLS}-\varphi_1\right)$ – then follows directly from the Central Limit Theorem, as stated in Equation A13-3.

As in Appendix 11.2, this process seems lengthy because a good many lines are needed when each algebraic step in this rewriting process is explicitly displayed, but almost every step is either an ordinary algebraic rearrangement, or is a simple substitution (using Equation A13-11, for example), or is an application of one of the algebraic properties of the probability limit, as given in Appendix 11.1.[59] Rewriting $\text{plim}\left[\sqrt{T-1}\left(\hat{\varphi}_1^{OLS}-\varphi_1\right)\right]$, then, yields

$$\begin{aligned}
\text{plim}\left[\sqrt{T-1}\left(\hat{\varphi}_1^{OLS}-\varphi\right)\right] &= \text{plim}\left[\sqrt{T-1}\sum_{t=2}^{T} W_t^{OLS} U_t\right] \\
&= \text{plim}\left[\sqrt{T-1}\sum_{t=2}^{T}\left(\frac{Y_{t-1}-\overline{Y}}{\sum_{\ell=2}^{T}\left(Y_{\ell-1}-\overline{Y}\right)^2}\right)U_t\right] \\
&= \text{plim}\left[\sqrt{T-1}\sum_{t=2}^{T}\frac{Y_{t-1}-\overline{Y}}{(T-1)\widehat{\text{var}}(Y)}U_t\right] \\
&= \text{plim}\left[\frac{1}{\widehat{\text{var}}(Y)}\sqrt{T-1}\sum_{t=2}^{T}\frac{1}{(T-1)}\left(Y_{t-1}-\overline{Y}\right)U_t\right] \\
&= \text{plim}\left[\frac{1}{\widehat{\text{var}}(Y)}\right]\text{plim}\left[\sqrt{T-1}\sum_{t=2}^{T}\frac{1}{(T-1)}\left(Y_{t-1}-\overline{Y}\right)U_t\right] \\
&= \frac{1}{\sigma_y^2}\text{plim}\left[\sqrt{T-1}\sum_{t=2}^{T}\frac{1}{T-1}\left(Y_{t-1}-\overline{Y}\right)U_t\right]
\end{aligned} \tag{A13-5}$$

Note that the validity of the last step rests on both of the indicated probability limits existing. Here, of course $\widehat{\text{var}}(Y)$ is denoting the sample variance of Y_{t-1} over its $T-1$ sample values; its probability limit equals σ_y^2 so long as the variance of Y_t (and hence the variance of Y_{t-1}) is finite which – from Equation 13-19 – is the case if (and only if) $|\varphi_1|$ is less than one.[60] That the probability limit of the right-hand factor is finite becomes clear later in the derivation.

In the next step μ_y, the population mean of Y_{t-1}, is both added and subtracted in the expression. This leads to an additional term in the expression which, after a few more steps, is shown to have probability limit zero and then disappears from the remainder of the derivation. The reason why this apparent detour is necessary is that it effectively replaces $\overline{Y}$ by μ_y in the eventual result, the zero-mean variable which will be called V_t. This replacement is crucial in showing that the V_t are a martingale difference sequence because $\overline{Y}$ depends on all of $Y_2 \ldots Y_T$ whereas μ_y is a fixed constant.

[59] Except for the Central Limit Theorem itself, these algebraic properties are all still justified because the relevant random variables are either a martingale difference sequences (in the case of $(Y_{t-1}-\mu_y)U_t$) or a covariance stationary time-series for which the sum of the magnitudes of the autocovariances is bounded (in the case of Y_t) – see Hamilton (1994, Chapter 7).

[60] Thus, for example, this derivation becomes invalid in the "unit root" case, where the process generating Y_t is a random walk – i.e. $Y_t = Y_{t-1} + \nu_t$ with $\nu_t \sim \text{IID}[0, \sigma_\nu^2]$. In that case the variance of Y_t (and of Y_{t-1}) does not have a well-defined, finite value – see the discussion following Equation 13-21.

Proceeding along these lines, then,

$$
\begin{aligned}
\text{plim}\left[\sqrt{T-1}\left(\hat{\beta}^{\text{OLS}}-\beta\right)\right] &= \frac{1}{\sigma_y^2}\text{plim}\left[\sqrt{T-1}\sum_{t=2}^{T-1}\frac{1}{T-1}\left(Y_{t-1}-\overline{Y}\right)U_t\right] \\
&= \frac{1}{\sigma_y^2}\text{plim}\left[\sqrt{T-1}\sum_{t=2}^{T-1}\frac{1}{T-1}\left(Y_{t-1}-\mu_y+\mu_y-\overline{Y}\right)U_t\right] \\
&= \frac{1}{\sigma_y^2}\text{plim}\left[\sqrt{T-1}\sum_{t=2}^{T-1}\frac{1}{T-1}\left(Y_{t-1}-\mu_y\right)U_t+\sqrt{T-1}\sum_{t=2}^{T-1}\frac{1}{T-1}\left(\mu_y-\overline{Y}\right)U_t\right] \\
&= \frac{1}{\sigma_y^2}\text{plim}\left[\sqrt{T-1}\sum_{t=2}^{T-1}\frac{1}{T-1}\left(Y_{t-1}-\mu_y\right)U_t\right]+\frac{1}{\sigma_y^2}\text{plim}\left[\sqrt{T-1}\sum_{i=2}^{T-1}\frac{1}{T-1}\left(\mu_y-\overline{Y}\right)U_t\right] \\
&= \frac{1}{\sigma_y^2}\text{plim}\left[\sqrt{T-1}\sum_{t=2}^{T-1}\frac{1}{T-1}\left(Y_{t-1}-\mu_y\right)U_t\right]+\frac{1}{\sigma_y^2}\text{plim}\left[\left(\mu_y-\overline{Y}\right)\sqrt{T-1}\,\overline{U}\right] \\
&= \frac{1}{\sigma_y^2}\text{plim}\left[\sqrt{T-1}\sum_{t=2}^{T-1}\frac{1}{T-1}\left(Y_{t-1}-\mu_y\right)U_t\right]+\frac{1}{\sigma_y^2}\text{plim}\left[\left(\mu_y-\overline{Y}\right)\right]\text{plim}\left[\sqrt{T-1}\,\overline{U}\right] \\
&= \frac{1}{\sigma_y^2}\text{plim}\left[\sqrt{T-1}\sum_{t=2}^{T-1}\frac{1}{T-1}\left(Y_{t-1}-\mu_y\right)U_t\right] \qquad \text{(A13-6)} \\
&= \text{plim}\left[\sqrt{T-1}\sum_{t=2}^{T-1}\frac{1}{T-1}\left(\frac{1}{\sigma_y^2}\left(Y_{t-1}-\mu_y\right)U_t\right)\right] \\
&= \text{plim}\left[\sqrt{T-1}\frac{1}{T-1}\sum_{t=2}^{T-1}\left(\frac{1}{\sigma_y^2}\left(Y_{t-1}-\mu_y\right)U_t\right)\right] \\
&= \text{plim}\left[\sqrt{T-1}\,\overline{V}\right]
\end{aligned}
$$

where V_t is defined as $\frac{1}{\sigma_y^2}\left(Y_{t-1}-\mu_y\right)U_t$.[61]

Thus, by defining V_t in this way, $\text{plim}\left[\sqrt{T-1}\left(\hat{\varphi}_1^{\text{OLS}}-\varphi_1\right)\right]$ can be re-expressed as the probability limit of $\sqrt{T-1}$ times the sample mean of $V_2 \ldots V_{T-1}$, where V_t is a martingale difference sequence with mean zero, and which is assumed to have bounded variance, σ_v^2.

Therefore, applying the Central Limit Theorem – Equation A13-3 – it can be concluded that $\text{plim}\left[\sqrt{T-1}\left(\hat{\varphi}_1^{\text{OLS}}-\varphi_1\right)\right]$ is asymptotically normal with mean zero and asymptotic variance equal to $\text{var}(V_t)$.

[61] Note that Equation A11-2 can be applied to re-express the probability limit of the product of $\mu_y-\overline{Y}$ and $\sqrt{T-1}\,\overline{U}$ as the product of the probability limit of $\mu_y-\overline{Y}$ times the probability limit of $\sqrt{T-1}\,\overline{U}$ only because both of these factors have well-defined probability limits. (Equation A11-2 extends to this case, where the Y_t are not independently distributed, because (as noted in the previous footnote) the AR(1) Model implies that the Y_t are covariance stationary with autocovariances the sum of the magnitudes of which is bounded.) Note that, as in Appendix 11.2, $U_t \sim \text{IID}(0, \sigma_u^2)$ implies that $\text{plim}\left[\sqrt{T-1}\,\overline{U}\right]$ is a normally distributed variate with variance equal to σ_u^2, using the Lindeberg-Lévy form of the Central Limit Theorem.

Utilizing the fact that the AR(1) Model implies that U_t is independent of Y_{t-1},

$$\begin{aligned}
\text{var}(V_t) &= E\left[\frac{1}{\sigma_y^4}\left(Y_{t-1} - \mu_y\right)^2 U_t^2\right] \\
&= \frac{1}{\sigma_y^4} E\left[\left(Y_{t-1} - \mu_y\right)^2\right] E\left[U_t^2\right] \\
&= \frac{1}{\sigma_y^4}\, \sigma_y^2\, \sigma_u^2 \\
&= \frac{\sigma_u^2}{\sigma_y^2}
\end{aligned} \tag{A13-7}$$

which completes the derivation of Equation A13-1.

14

Diagnostically Checking and Respecifying the Multiple Regression Model: The Time-Series Data Case (Part B)

14.1 INTRODUCTION: GENERALIZING THE RESULTS TO MULTIPLE TIME-SERIES

The results on time-series econometrics developed in Chapter 13 are based on very simple regression models which (as with the bivariate fixed-regressor models treated in Chapters 5 through 8) could be analyzed using scalar arithmetic – i.e., using summation notation instead of matrix algebra. As in Chapter 9 (which covered the Multiple Regression Model with fixed-regressors) and as in Chapter 10 (which extended this analysis to multiple regression models with stochastic regressors but serially independent model errors), there comes a point where all of the insights gained and techniques developed using these simple models must be heuristically extended to the more complex formulations needed in real-world modeling situations.

That is the topic of Section 14.2, where the analogous results for estimating the fully dynamic Multiple Regression Model – and using it for inference purposes – are described. One of these real-world complications is that in practice, a good many time-series used as explanatory variables in econometric models are so highly autocorrelated as to no longer have the bounded variance needed for the validity of the asymptotic inference machinery; this topic is explored in Section 14.3.[1]

Sections 14.4, 14.5, and 14.6 illustrate the usefulness of this material by formulating several models of monthly U.S. consumption spending, each based on disposable income and interest rate data from previous months. Three kinds of models are formulated: one in the changes of the variables, one on a mixture of changes and levels in the variables, and one in the levels only; Section 14.6 focuses on how to diagnostically check a model as part of the model-building process. Finally, Section 14.7

[1] The issue of integrated time-series ("unit roots") first arose in Section 13.4 in connection with the variance of an AR(1) time-series and surfaced again in the derivation of the asymptotic sampling distribution of the OLS estimator of the key parameter in the AR(1) Model, in Section 13.4, and Appendix 13.1. It is first fully articulated, however, in Section 14.3. Foreshadowing, the detection and modeling of cointegration is discussed in Section 14.5, whereas the issues regarding modeling and inference in "levels" models are addressed in Section 14.6, using a simple variation on the "Lag-Augmented VAR" approach of Yamamoto and Toda (1995).

concludes the chapter with a discussion of the relative advantages and disadvantages of these three modeling approaches.

14.2 THE DYNAMIC MULTIPLE REGRESSION MODEL

The premise of this book is that the best way to understand multivariate regression models is to first thoroughly analyze the simple bivariate regression model. Thus, under the initial assumption of explanatory variables which could be taken as fixed in repeated samples, the first step (in Chapters 5 through 8) was to completely analyze the Bivariate Regression Model – with a single, fixed-regressor. We saw how to estimate β, the slope parameter in this model using the OLS estimator, $\hat{\beta}^{OLS}$. And we saw exactly what assumptions were needed in order to obtain the sampling distribution of $\hat{\beta}^{OLS}$, how to use this sampling distribution to show that $\hat{\beta}^{OLS}$ is a good estimator (unbiased, consistent, and BLU), and how to use the sampling distribution of $\hat{\beta}^{OLS}$ for inference (hypothesis tests and confidence interval estimation).

All of these results were completely developed using only scalar arithmetic – i.e., summation notation – rather than using linear algebra. Scalar arithmetic can only go so far, however, so these results had to be heuristically extended (in Chapter 9) to encompass the Multiple Regression Model. A few additional concepts – the impact of omitted variables, better measures for use in model evaluation (adjusted R^2 and the Schwarz Criterion), and the problem of overly-similar explanatory variables (multicollinearity) – had to await the Multiple Regression Model in order to make sense. More limitingly, explicit formulas for the OLS parameter estimates and their sampling variances could not be derived using scalar arithmetic, so these formulas for the Multiple Regression Model with fixed-regressors – which formulas are what is actually implemented in econometric software – were basically "pointed at" rather than derived (or even fully stated), by analogy to what was completely derived in the context of the Bivariate Regression Model.

In this section the two bivariate regression models with stochastic regressors and serially independent model errors introduced so far are generalized and folded together into the Dynamic Multiple Regression Model. These two dynamic bivariate regression models are Equation 11-1 from Chapter 11:

The Bivariate Regression Model
(Stochastic Regressor Case)

$$
\begin{aligned}
Y_i &= \alpha + \beta X_i + U_i \quad i = 1 \ldots N \\
U_i &\sim \text{IID}[0, \sigma_u^2] \\
X_i &\sim \text{IID}[0, \sigma_x^2] \quad \sigma_x^2 > 0 \\
\text{Cov}(X_i, U_i) &= \sigma_{xu} \\
\text{Cov}(X_i^2, U_i^2) &= 0
\end{aligned}
\tag{14-1}
$$

and Equation 13-11 from the previous chapter:

The Autoregressive Model of Order One or AR(1) Model

$$
\begin{aligned}
Y_t &= \varphi_0 + \varphi_1 Y_{t-1} + U_t \quad t = 2 \ldots T \\
|\varphi_1| &< 1 \\
U_t &\sim \text{IID}[0, \sigma_u^2]
\end{aligned}
\tag{14-2}
$$

The Dynamic Multiple Regression Model allows for both multiple lags in the dependent variable (a generalization of the AR(1) Model, Equation 13-11) and multiple lags (dynamic structure) in multiple stochastic explanatory variables (a generalization of Equation 11-1). For simplicity, the Dynamic Multiple Regression Model is written out below, as Equation 14-3, for the special case of just three explanatory variables. This yields a model which is sufficiently general as to both subsume the empirical example (Sections 13-10 and 13-11) and to also make it quite clear how more extensive models would be analogously formulated. Of course, because of the restriction in the present treatment to scalar (non-matrix) algebra, the computing formulas for the OLS parameter estimators and their asymptotic sampling distribution will not be explicitly obtained here: the idea of the present treatment is to derive these formulas explicitly for the two bivariate special cases (Equations 11-1 and 13-11), to understand the assumptions making up the more general model, and to thereby obtain a heuristic understanding of the results for the general model. To that end, a few general comments are in order before specifically describing each of the assumptions of the Dynamic Multiple Regression Model of Equation 14-3.

Perhaps the most important comment to make is that these assumptions are intended to comprise the weakest intelligible set of assumptions which must be appended to the model equation in Equation 14-3 so as to still obtain the two key results which were explicitly derived for these two restricted (bivariate) regression models with stochastic regressors:

(a) *OLS yields consistent parameter estimators* – absent explanatory variable endogeneity issues (which can still be handled using two stage least squares with valid instruments, per the development in Chapter 12) and assuming, as in the previous models, that any important explanatory variables which have been omitted from the model are either uncorrelated with the included variables or are allowed for in the interpretation of the coefficients on the included variables.[2]

And:

(b) *The usual regression computer output is still valid if the sample is sufficiently large,* because the asymptotic sampling distribution of the OLS parameter estimators – obtained from an application of a suitable Central Limit Theorem – is identical in form to the analogous result obtained treating the regressors as fixed in repeated samples, and programmed into econometric software.

The set of assumptions given in Equation 14-3 is sufficient to this purpose, but there is no guarantee that these are the very weakest set yielding these two results.

Each of the remaining two general observations is an insight, gleaned from our analysis of the simple Bivariate Regression Model with a fixed-regressor earlier in the book, which is still quite useful in the present context.

First, in Chapter 5 we found that simply including an intercept parameter in the model (plus not omitting a significant explanatory variable correlated with the included one) sufficed to imply that the OLS slope estimator was unbiased. Unbiasedness is no longer an issue here – with stochastic regressors, our estimators are at best consistent. Moreover, consistency does not in fact require

[2] Recall, from the discussion in Chapter 9, that the problem with an omitted variable which is correlated with an included one is that the included variable "proxies" for the omitted one, yielding OLS parameter estimators which are consistent estimates of parameters corresponding to different partial derivatives of the expected value of the dependent variable than we intended: the partial derivatives actually (consistently) estimated are a mixture of the partial derivative with respect to the explanatory variable included and the partial derivatives with respect to the explanatory variable (or variables) omitted. Unrecognized, this problem can be disastrous; recognized, it can at least be allowed for in the interpretation of the results. (This interpretation is, of course, more problematic if the omitted variable is correlated with more than one included variable.) Note also that such omitted variables are much less of an issue if, as is common for the Dynamic Multiple Regression Model, the purpose of the model is as a forecasting tool rather than as a means for testing theory via parameter inference. Indeed, in the forecasting context, this "proxying" is an advantage when the requisite data on an important explanatory variable are unavailable.

the zero-mean error term which inclusion of an intercept in the regression equation ensures. However, the argument leading to the asymptotic sampling distribution for the OLS parameter estimators in the models with stochastic regressors *does* require a zero-mean error term. In particular, reviewing all three of these derivations – comprising Appendices 11.2, 12.1, and 13.1 – these derivations are all of the same form: Some specific assumption is made about the dependence of V_t, a zero-mean random variable with variance σ^2. Then a version of the Central Limit Theorem implies that $\sqrt{T}V$ is asymptotically distributed $N[0, \sigma^2]$; this is tantamount to obtaining the asymptotic sampling distribution of the OLS parameter estimator. Different versions of the Central Limit Theorem make different assumptions about the dependence of the V_t variable – different assumptions about its *lack* of dependence, actually – and different assumptions about how homogeneous its variance is across the sample, but *all* versions of the Central Limit Theorem assume that V_t has mean zero. The exact form of the variable V_t varies from model to model: in the model of Equation 11-1, V_i was proportional to $(X_i - \mu_x)U_i$; in the model of Equation 13-11, V_t was proportional to $Y_{t-1}U_t$; in the Dynamic Multiple Regression Model, V_t is a vector with components like each of these, with U_t multiplying a lagged value of either the dependent variable or one of the explanatory variables. In all of these cases, however, $E[V_t]$ requires that the model error U_t has mean zero – which we get from including an intercept in the model equation. Thus, the general conclusion from the earlier chapters – that including an intercept in the model is almost always a good idea – still holds.

A second general observation – this time from Chapter 6 – also still holds: the purpose of most of the model assumptions is to allow us to derive a sampling distribution for the OLS parameter estimates and to thereby enable us to do the kinds of statistical inference work – the construction of hypothesis tests and the estimation of confidence intervals – originally described in Chapter 7. The validity of this inference work thus rests on the validity of these assumptions; consequently, it behooves us to diagnostically check these assumptions insofar as we can. Some of the model assumptions in Equation 14-3 are more amenable to such checking – and to "fixing" via model re-specification – than others; the empirical example worked out in Sections 14.4, 14.5, and 14.6 illustrates how this is done.

That said, the Dynamic Multiple Regression Model can be written out as

The Dynamic Multiple Regression Model

(Three Regressor Case $t = 1 \ldots T$)

$$
\begin{aligned}
Y_t &= \alpha + \sum_{\ell=1}^{L_o} \varphi_\ell Y_{t-\ell} + \sum_{\ell=0}^{L_1} \beta_{\ell,1} X_{t-\ell,1} + \sum_{\ell=0}^{L_2} \beta_{\ell,2} X_{t-\ell,2} + \sum_{\ell=0}^{L_3} \beta_{\ell,3} X_{t-\ell,3} + U_t \\
U_t &\sim \mathrm{IID}[0, \sigma_u^2] \\
\mathrm{Cov}(X_{t-\ell,j}, U_t) &= 0 \text{ for } j = 1, 2, 3 \text{ and } \ell = 0 \ldots L_j \\
\mathrm{Cov}(X_{t-\ell,i} X_{t-k,j}, U_t^2) &= 0 \text{ for all } (X_{t-\ell,i}, X_{t-k,j}) \text{ included in the model} \\
\mathrm{Var}(Y_t) &\text{ bounded unless } L_o = 0 \\
\mathrm{Var}(X_{t,j}) &> 0 \text{ and bounded for } j = 1, 2, \text{ and } 3
\end{aligned}
\tag{14-3}
$$

Most, but not all, of these assumptions are familiar from the previous models. Some (but not all) of them are essential from an empirical implementation point of view – i.e., essential to consider and deal with, via diagnostic checking and/or consequent model respecification. In any case, Equation 14-3 states both the model equation for the Dynamic Multiple Regression Model and also essentially all of the assumptions needed.[3] Here – per the discussion earlier in this section – the term "needed" means "needed in order for the OLS estimators of its parameters to be consistent estimators with an asymptotic sampling distribution which is equivalent, for sufficiently large samples, to the results obtained for the Multiple Regression Model with fixed-regressors." Since it is these fixed-regressor results which are programmed up in all econometric software, one could equally well interpret "needed" to mean "needed in order for the regression results we obtain from the econometric software to be, at least for large samples, valid." The remainder of this section discusses these assumptions: what they mean, which are important (and why), and what (if anything) to do about violations of them.

The first assumption to discuss is the model equation itself. Note that, per the discussion earlier in this section, it contains – as recommended – an intercept term, allowing it to be assumed that $E[U_t]$ is zero with no loss of generality. Also, note that three explanatory variables are explicitly included in the model. Additional explanatory variables could be easily included (in an obvious notation), but this choice matches up with the empirical examples which follow; clearly, one could alternatively eliminate, say, $X_{t,3}$ from the model by simply setting L_3 to zero.[4]

The second assumption is that U_t is identically and independently distributed in each time period. As detailed in Section 13.6 earlier in this chapter, violations of this assumption in the form of serial *correlation* can be detected using an auxiliary AR(p) regression on the fitting errors. And – per the development in Section 13.7 – serial correlation in the model errors can be eliminated by simply adding more dynamics to the model specification via increasing the values of the maximum lags included in the model – L_o, L_1, L_2, and L_3. Thus, presuming that L_o, L_1, L_2, and L_3 have been specified to be adequately large, it follows that U_t is serially uncorrelated. Such non-autocorrelation is all that is required with regard to model error serial non-dependence for regression models with explanatory variables which are fixed in repeated samples.

Models with stochastic explanatory variables require the stronger serial non-dependence assumption that the model errors are serially independent, however. This is because all such models rely on a Central Limit Theorem to obtain a (now only asymptotic) sampling distribution for the OLS parameter estimators, and the application of a Central Limit Theorem requires serially

[3] The phrase "essentially all" is necessary because Equation 14-3 actually omits a few assumptions; hopefully, a major gain in clarity compensates for the loss in formal completeness these omissions create. For example, the assumption on the explanatory variables which rules out perfect multicollinearity is omitted because a proper statement of it involves the rank of a matrix which is not being specified here. In a similar vein, the Central Limit Theorem applied in order to derive the asymptotic sampling distribution of the OLS parameter estimators for Equation 14-3 is a multivariate version of the theorem stated in Equation A13-3. This theorem requires a moment boundedness condition analogous to that specified in the footnote immediately following Equation A13-3 and it also requires that the random variables $(X_{t,1} - \mu_{x,1})U_t$, $(X_{t,2} - \mu_{x,2})U_t$, and $(X_{t,3} - \mu_{x,3})U_t$ are jointly a martingale difference sequence – which is to say that

$$E\big[[(X_{t,j} - \mu_{xj})U_t]\, g\,\{\text{lagged values of } (X_{t,1} - \mu_{x1})U_t, (X_{t,2} - \mu_{x2})U_t, (X_{t,3} - \mu_{x3})U_t\}\big]$$

equals

$$E[(X_{t,j} - \mu_{xj})U_t]\, E[g\{\text{lagged values of } (X_{t,1} - \mu_{x1})U_t, (X_{t,2} - \mu_{x2})U_t, (X_{t,3} - \mu_{x3})U_t\}]$$

for all functions $g\{\cdot\}$ and $j = 1, 2$, or 3. This assumption was not necessary for the model of Equation 11-1 because the X_i were independently distributed, whereas the three explanatory variables in the Dynamic Multiple Regression Model can be serially correlated.

[4] If the lag lengths L_o, L_1, L_2, and L_3 are all equal, then the Dynamic Multiple Regression Model can be construed as one equation of a four-equation system which jointly models the four time-series (Y_t, $X_{t,1}$, $X_{t,2}$, and $X_{t,3}$) in terms of their past values. Such sytem is called the Vector Autoregressive (or "VAR") Model; this is a generalization of the AR(p) Model and is considered in Section 17.6.

independent model errors.[5] This assumption is stronger than the assumption of serially uncorrelated model errors: serially uncorrelated model errors are not *linearly* related to their own past; serially independent model errors cannot be related to their own past in *any* way. This stronger assumption is ruling out any unmodeled nonlinearity in the model specification.

Statistical tests are described in Chapter 18 which allow one to test the null hypothesis that the model errors are serially independent, but these tests do not give much guidance as to exactly how one should respecify the form of the model if this null hypothesis is rejected. Consequently, in practice one's options are to either include some squared terms in the model – e.g., $X_{t,3}$ might actually be the square of $X_{t,2}$ – or to instead radically reframe the model specification using one of the nonlinear formulations discussed in Section 18.6. If the latter option is taken, then one can compare the postsample forecasting performance of the resulting model to that of a model based on Equation 14-3; specific methods for doing this are described in Section 18.5.

The assumption that U_t is identically distributed implies that the variance of U_t is a constant. This is the homoscedasticity assumption discussed at length in Chapters 5 and 10. The methods for detecting and dealing with heteroscedasticity in Chapter 10 apply equally well to the Dynamic Multiple Regression Model, so they need not be repeated here. It is worth noting, however, that the Central Limit Theorem used to obtain the asymptotic sampling distribution of the OLS parameter estimators does assume homoscedasticity so, as with the fixed-regressor models, heteroscedasticity which is not dealt with will yield invalid inferences in the present context as well. On the other hand – as noted in Appendices 11.2 and 13.1 – versions of the Central Limit Theorem explicitly allowing for heteroscedastic model errors are available, and yield asymptotic sampling distribution results equivalent to using the White-Eicker robust standard error estimates discussed in Chapter 10. Thus, this portion of the assumptions in Equation 14-3 can be easily relaxed by instructing the software to compute these robust standard error estimates.

The next assumption listed in Equation 14-3 specifies that the explanatory variables are all uncorrelated with the model errors; this assumption is ruling out endogeneity in the explanatory variables. As in the model of Equation 11-1 – and the extended discussion of this issue in Chapter 12 – such endogeneity could arise from omitted variables, from measurement error in one of the included explanatory variables, or from Y_t and one (or more) of the explanatory variables being jointly determined. Joint determination – where Y_t is simultaneously determined with one or more of the explanatory variables – is a potential source of endogeneity only if the contemporaneous terms ($X_{t,1}$, $X_{t,2}$, and $X_{t,3}$) are included in the model. These terms are quite often omitted from the specification of a model like Equation 14-3 for this reason.

As in the bivariate model explicitly considered in Chapter 12, violations of this non-endogeneity assumption result in inconsistent OLS paramater estimators and, of course, invalid inference results. As noted in Chapter 12, this assumption cannot be diagnostically checked: the best that can be done is to examine the degree to which the most important inference results are sensitive to likely violations.[6] On the other hand, if this assumption is not valid, then consistent parameter estimates (and asymptotically valid inferences) can still be obtained by using instrumental variables estimation – e.g., the two-stage least squares estimators – exactly as described in Chapter 12. This, of course, requires one to have valid instruments available for use in the first-stage regression equations.[7]

[5] The random variable V_t for which the Central Limit Theorem makes a statement (regarding the asymptotic distribution of $\sqrt{T}V$) does not need to be serially independent – e.g. in Appendix 13.1, V_t needs only to be a martingale difference sequence. However, the derivation in Appendix 13.1 illustrates how it is generally necessary to assume that the model errors are serial independent in order to show that V_t is a martingale difference sequence.

[6] See Ashley and Parmeter (2011).

[7] Lagged variables not included in the model as explanatory variables often make useful instruments for estimating the Dynamic Multiple Regression Model – unless the endogeneity is due to omitted variables, in which case these lagged variables are often themselves correlated with U_t.

The next assumption listed in Equation 14-3 is a generalization of the Model 11-1 assumption that $\text{cov}(X_t^2, U_t^2)$ equals zero. This assumption is not necessary for the application of the Central Limit Theorem. Reference to the derivation in Appendix 11.2, however, shows that it *is* necessary in order for the usual OLS formula for the sampling variance of the parameter estimators to still apply, but that it is not necessary if one is computing White-Eicker standard error estimates.[8]

Finally, the last two assumptions in Equation 14-3 essentially require that each of the explanatory variables – including the lagged values of Y_t – has a well-defined, bounded population variance.[9] This requirement seems innocuous enough on the face of it, but it turns out to be empirically important – and frequently problematic in practice. The reason that bounded variance matters is actually simple enough: The Central Limit Theorem used to show that the OLS estimators of the parameters in the Dynamic Multiple Regression Model are asymptotically normal requires that all of the explanatory variables in the model – the relevant lagged values of Y_t and all of the specified current or lagged values of $X_{t,1}$, $X_{t,2}$, and $X_{t,3}$ – have bounded variances. If this requirement is not met, then the Central Limit Theorem is inapplicable and the asymptotic sampling distributions for the OLS parameter estimators it provides – which are what is programmed into econometric software – can be a poor approximation to the actual sampling distributions, even for very large samples. This can lead to seriously distorted *p*-values for rejecting null hypotheses regarding the model parameters.

But how could something as seemingly arcane as an explanatory variable with unbounded variance actually come up in practice? That is the topic of the next section.

14.3 I(1) OR "RANDOM WALK" TIME-SERIES

The Dynamic Multiple Regression Model of Equation 14-3 explicitly assumes that all of the explanatory variables in the model have bounded (finite) variance. As noted earlier, the reason for this assumption is that it allows the application of a Central Limit Theorem, so as to obtain an asymptotic sampling distribution for the OLS parameter estimators which is gaussian and, in fact, (asymptotically) equivalent to the usual OLS result for a regression model with fixed-regressors. That result is exceedingly convenient because this usual distributional result is programmed into econometric software packages. But why bother to make this bounded variance assumption? Isn't it obvious that any economic time-series we might use as an explanatory variable in a regression model would have a population variance which is at least bounded? What would "unbounded variance" in a time-series mean, anyway? It turns out that a particularly severe form of serial dependence – one which is actually quite common in economic time-series – actually does imply unbounded variance in the series; consequently these questions are examined in this section.

Consider again the AR(1) Model of Equation 13-11, but now calling the time-series "Z_t" instead of Y_t, so as to notationally reflect the fact that this time-series might be either a lagged value of the dependent variable or one of the other explanatory variables in Equation 14-3. Also, at this point it is

[8] The advanced reader might wonder why no mention is made here of the Newey-West standard error estimates discussed in Section 13.7. These are rendered unnecessary by the inclusion of sufficient dynamics in the model, so that the model errors are consequently not serially correlated.

[9] The positive variance requirement on the other explanatory variables should be self-evident: if $\text{var}(X_{t,j})$ is zero, then there will be no sampling variation in this explanatory variable; in that case estimation of coefficients on current or lagged values of $X_{t,j}$ is plainly infeasible.

more convenient to drop the intercept from the model and instead specify a mean value for the model error term:

The AR(1) Model

$$\begin{aligned} Z_t &= \varphi_1 Z_{t-1} + U_t \\ |\varphi_1| &< 1 \\ U_t &\sim \mathrm{IID}[\mu_u, \sigma_u^2] \end{aligned} \tag{14-4}$$

Taking the expected value of both sides of Equation 14-4,

$$E(Z_t) = \varphi_1 E(Z_{t-1}) + \mu_u \tag{14-5}$$

so that

$$Z_t - E(Z_t) = \varphi_1[Z_{t-1} - E(Z_{t-1})] + [U_t - \mu_u] \tag{14-6}$$

By repeated substitutions (essentially identical to Equations 13-12 through 13-17), this implies that the deviations of Z_t from its mean can be written in MA(∞) form as

$$\begin{aligned} Z_t - E(Z_t) &= \varphi_1^{\tau+1}[Z_{t-\tau-1} - E(Z_{t-\tau-1})] + \sum_{\ell=0}^{\tau}(\varphi_1)^{\ell}[U_{t-\ell} - \mu_u] \\ &= \sum_{\ell=0}^{\infty}(\varphi_1)^{\ell}[U_{t-\ell} - \mu_u] \end{aligned} \tag{14-7}$$

Thus, as in Equation 13-19, the variance of Z_t is

$$\begin{aligned} \mathrm{var}(Z_t) &= \sigma_u^2 \sum_{\ell=0}^{\infty}(\varphi_1)^{2\ell} \\ &= \sigma_u^2[1 + \varphi_1^2 + \varphi_1^4 + \varphi_1^6 + \varphi_1^8 + \ldots] \\ &= \frac{\sigma_u^2}{1 - \varphi_1^2} \end{aligned} \tag{14-8}$$

Consider now what happens to the variance of Z_t as the parameter φ_1 approaches one: it blows up! Moreover, Equation 14-8 makes it plain just how and why this happens: as φ_1 approaches one, Z_t becomes arbitrarily close to being an equally weighted sum of an infinite number of random variables: $U_t - \mu_u$, $U_{t-1} - \mu_u$, $U_{t-2} - \mu_u$, and so forth. Since these variables are independently distributed, they are uncorrelated; consequently, the variance of their sum is just the sum of their individual variances.[10] Thus, the variance of Z_t necessarily becomes arbitrarily large as φ_1 approaches one.

In the limit as φ_1 goes to one, Z_t is said to be "integrated of order one" or – more compactly – "$Z_t \sim \mathrm{I}(1)$." This is just nomenclature, but it is a somewhat natural choice, since an integral in ordinary calculus is also defined as a limit of a sum.[11] The "order one" part of this nomenclature

[10] Recall from Chapter 2 that $\mathrm{var}(aU_1 + bU_2) = a^2\,\mathrm{var}(U_1) + 2ab\mathrm{cov}(U_1, U_2) + b^2\mathrm{var}(U_2)$, where a and b are any fixed constants.

[11] The analogy is not to be pushed very far, however, as the limit in calculus is over the number of terms in the sum, whereas the limit here is taken as φ_1 goes to one.

refers to the fact that differencing Z_t once – i.e., considering $Z_t - Z_{t-1}$, the period-to-period change in Z_t – transforms Z_t into a covariance stationary time-series with a well-defined, finite variance. Thus, in this notation, $Z_t \sim \text{I}(1)$ implies that $Z_t - Z_{t-1} \sim \text{I}(0)$.[12]

An essentially synonymous verbalism for an I(1) time-series is to say that it has "a unit root" or that it is "a random walk." The "unit root" nomenclature will be explained in Chapters 17 and 18, where we take a deeper look at lag structures, autoregressive models, and moving average models. But a brief introduction to the concept of a random walk is immediately helpful.

The usual metaphor for a random walk is to imagine a (presumably drunken) individual – the "walker" – whose movement is constrained to a straight line, and who takes one "step" in each time period. Letting Z_t denote the position of the walker on the line at the beginning of period t, Z_t is called a "random" walk because the size of the step which the walker takes in period t is assumed to be a random variable $U_t \sim \text{IID}(\mu_u, \sigma_u^2)$. Thus, if U_t is positive, then the walker moves to the right in period t; whereas the walker moves to the left if U_t is negative. Clearly, then $Z_t - Z_{t-1}$ equals U_t and $Z_t = Z_{t-1} + U_t$. Thus, the position of the walker at time t would correspond precisely to the value of Z_t in the AR(1) Model of Equation 13-11 with φ_1 equal to one, had this value for φ_1 not been explicitly ruled out for the AR(1) Model.

If the position of the walker at the beginning of some particular period – which one could denote as period zero – were a known (fixed) value, Z_o, then it is easy to show (Exercise 14-1) that

$$E(Z_t) = Z_o + \mu_u t \tag{14-9}$$

and

$$\text{var}(Z_t) = \sigma_u^2 t \tag{14-10}$$

Therefore, Z_t has a linear time trend if μ_u is non-zero, and its population variance increases linearly with the number of time periods which have elapsed since the particular point in time at which the value of the time-series was known with certainty. If one pushes this particular period farther and farther back in time, then the current variance of Z_t around its linear trend value becomes larger and larger. Thus, in the limit where this period is pushed arbitrarily far back, the variance of Z_t is arbitrarily large. This is another way to conceptualize the statement "the variance of Z_t is unbounded."

The time path of data generated by an AR(1) Model with a large value of φ_1 is very smooth compared to that which one would observe for serially uncorrelated noise. This characteristic follows from the Equation 13-21 result for the AR(1) Model which, recast in the notation of Equation 14-4, implies that

$$\rho_j = \text{corr}(Z_t, Z_{t-j}) = \frac{\text{cov}(Z_t, Z_{t-j})}{\sqrt{\text{var}(Z_t)\,\text{var}(Z_{t-j})}} = \frac{\text{cov}(Z_t, Z_{t-j})}{\text{var}(Z_t)} = \varphi_1^j \tag{14-11}$$

Thus, if φ_1 is close to one, then ρ_1, ρ_2, ρ_3, etc. are all close to one; and these population quantities all become even closer and closer to one as φ_1 approaches one. Of course, these autocorrelations are all

[12] Recall that a covariance stationary time-series is a series for which the mean, the variance, and the autocovariances at all lags are well-defined constants – that is, these population quantities are bounded and do not vary over time. An I(2) time-series is defined analogously: such a time-series needs to be differenced twice in order to yield a covariance stationary series. I(2) time-series are quite uncommon in applied economic analysis, however. Covariance stationarity is discussed in more detail in Section 17.3.

ill-defined in the I(1) limit – where φ_1 equals one – because the variances in the denominators of the quotients in Equation 14-11 are no longer well defined.

Another way to see this, which is still valid in the limit as φ_1 goes to one, is to take the expected value of Equation 14-7, yielding

$$E(Z_t - E(Z_t)) = \varphi_1 E(Z_{t-1} - E(Z_{t-1})) \tag{14-12}$$

which shows that for φ_1 close to (or equal to) one, the expected deviation of Z_t from its mean is almost the same in each period as it was in the previous period. In other words, Z_t varies very smoothly over time.

Now consider again the first part of Equation 14-7:

$$Z_t - E(Z_t) = \varphi_1^{\tau+1}[Z_{t-\tau-1} - E(Z_{t-\tau-1})] + \sum_{\ell=0}^{\tau} (\varphi_1)^{\ell}[U_{t-\ell} - \mu_u] \tag{14-13}$$

In essence, this result says that the current deviation of Z_t from its mean value is equal to $(\varphi_1)^{\tau}$ times its deviation from the mean τ periods ago, plus some zero-mean noise. Thus, fluctuations of Z_t away from its mean will tend to persist if φ_1 is positive. These fluctuations are *quite* persistent if φ_1 is large, but still – in the end – fluctuations in Z_t eventually (on average) decay away, so that Z_t reverts to fluctuating around its mean $\left(\text{of } \mu_u/[1-\varphi_1]\right)$ with a (finite) variance of $\sigma_u^2/[1-\varphi_1^2]$. This property of I(0) time-series is called "mean reversion."

By way of contrast, in the I(1) limit such fluctuations do not revert to the mean: they are permanent. The failure of I(1) time-series to exhibit this mean reversion behavior is intuitively evident from the "random walk" description of an I(1) series: the walker at particular position (Z_{t-1}) at the end of period $t-1$ will step forward by an amount U_t in period t – or backward, if the realized value of U_t is negative. And the amount by which the walker moves is an independent drawing from the distribution of U_t, *irrespective* of the value of Z_{t-1}. Thus, the fact that Z_{t-1} might be substantially larger or smaller than $E(Z_t)$ is completely irrelevant to what the walker will do in period t. Consequently, Z_t has no systematic tendency to return to any particular value: it will wander around at random and hence $|Z_t - E(Z_t)|$ will eventually become arbitrarily large. That, of course, is consistent with the variance of Z_t being unboundedly large in the I(1) case.

Let's see how these concepts play out in the context of an actual economic time-series. Consider, for example, the logarithm of the daily closing value of the Standard & Poor's "S&P 500" index of corporate stock prices, over a sample consisting of the 15,031 days in the period from January 3, 1950 through September 28, 2009.[13] There is fairly strong evidence – which we will examine shortly – supporting the proposition that these data are I(1).

Denoting this time-series as "*log(SP500$_t$)*," Figure 14-1 displays a time plot of *log(SP500$_t$)* over this sample period is as follows:

[13] This index tracks the stock prices of 500 large corporations whose shares are actively traded in the U. S. stock markets. For more detail on Standard & Poor's (and their stock market indices), see their Wikipedia entry at en.wikipedia.org/wiki/Standard_and_Poors. The logarithm is taken, as usual, to convert a nonlinear time trend into the linear trend you observe in Figure 14-1. This transformation is particularly graceful – to financial economists – because the change in *log(SP500$_t$)* equals the daily yield on holding this market portfolio; multiplying this daily yield by 100 times the number of days in a year would convert this into the annual percentage yield.

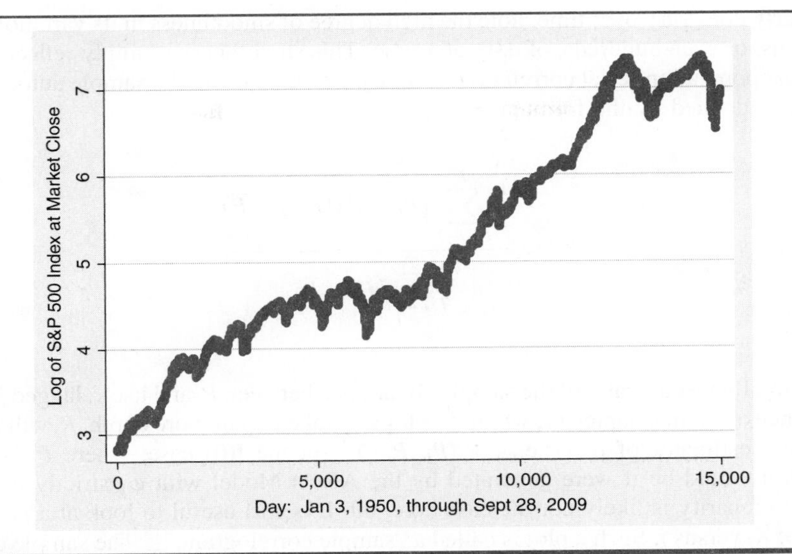

Figure 14-1 Time Plot of Logarithm of S&P 500 Stock Market Index

This time-series is obviously dominated by a linear time trend, which is not in itself relevant to the question at hand, so Figure 14-2 replots these data – which we will now simply denote as "P_t" – after removal of the trend:[14]

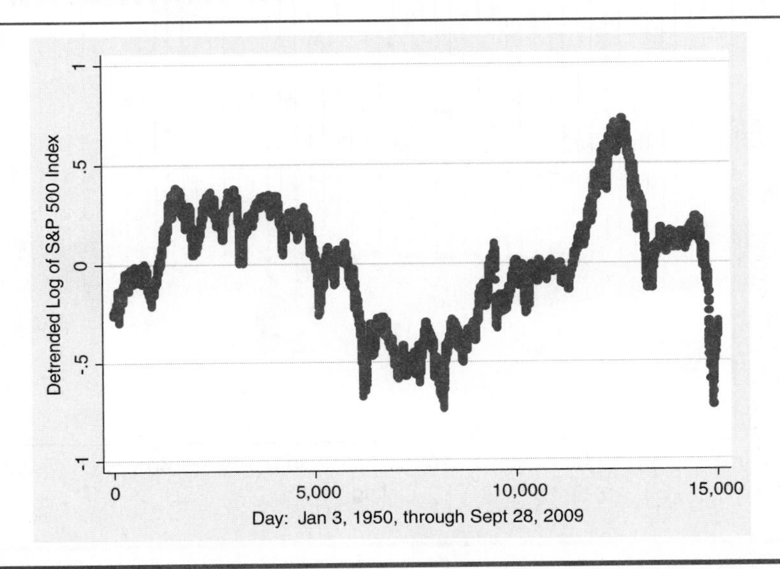

Figure 14-2 Time Plot of P_t, the Detrended Logarithm of S&P 500 Stock Market Index

[14] Clearly, per Section 13.3, these are the fitting errors from a regression equation of this time-series versus observation number. The time trend itself can, if necessary, be included in a regression model (along with $log(SP500_t)$; the important issue (considered in Sections 14.4 through 14.7) is whether or not the deviations of $log(SP500_t)$ from its trend are I(1) or, instead, are a covariance stationary AR(1) time-series with φ_1 large.

While P_t clearly does vary over time, note the high degree of smoothness in its variation, on a time-scale of dozens, or even hundreds, of days at a time. This smoothness is amply reflected in sample estimates of its population serial correlations – ρ_1, ρ_2, ρ_3, etc. – using the sample autocorrelations – r_1, r_2, r_3, etc. – defined by the formula

$$R_j = \frac{\frac{1}{T}\sum_{t=j+1}^{T}\left(P_t - \overline{P}\right)\left(P_{t-j} - \overline{P}\right)}{\frac{1}{T}\sum_{t=1}^{T}\left(P_t - \overline{P}\right)^2} \tag{14-14}$$

which is essentially just the ratio of the sample covariance between P_t and itself, lagged j days, to the sample variance of P_t. In Chapter 17, where this topic is taken up in more depth, R_j will be shown to be a consistent estimator of ρ_j – i.e., corr(P_t, P_{t-j}) – in the I(0) case, where P_t is covariance stationary, as it would be if were generated by the AR(1) Model with φ_1 strictly less than one. Covariance stationarity is likely not the case here, but it is still useful to look at a plot of sample realizations of R_j versus j. Such a plot is called a "sample correlogram."[15] The sample correlogram of P_t is displayed in Figure 14-3.

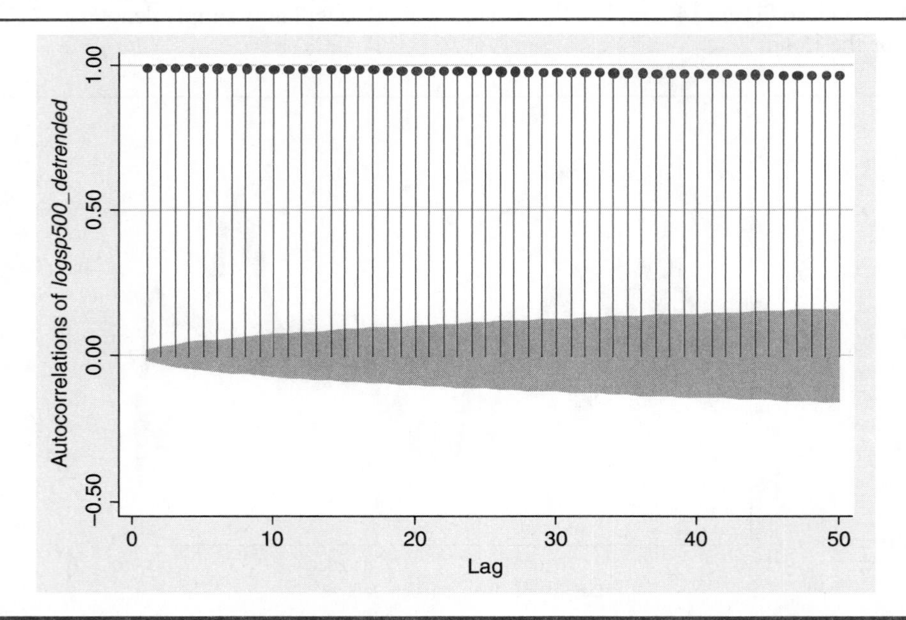

Figure 14-3 Sample Correlogram of P_t, the Detrended Logarithm of the S&P 500 Stock Market Index

[15] Most econometric software is set up to produce sample correlograms very easily. In Stata one must first let the program know that this is time-series data, using the "tsset tee" command, where "tee" is an observation number variable. Then the command "ac logsp500_dterended, lags(50)" yields the sample correlogram plot displayed here. The shaded portion of this plot is described in Chapter 17; it can be ignored here.

This is the typical sample correlogram pattern one would observe with data generated to be an I(1) random walk: the observed autocorrelation at lag one, r_1, is almost (but not quite) one and r_j decays very, very slowly as j increases, reflecting the fact that P_t is basically equal to P_{t-1} plus a little bit of noise each period. Consequently the sample autocorrelation between P_t and itself lagged 50 (or, indeed, several hundreds) of days previous is still close to one.

Because the positive serial dependence in P_t is so strong, sample fluctuations in this time-series (which, recall, represent deviations of $log(SP500_t)$ from its linear trend line) have a strong tendency to persist for a substantial number of days; this leads to the succession of slowly varying "local trends" which are apparent in the time plots of both $log(SP500_t)$ and P_t.

Note that Equation 14-13 implies that a fluctuation in an AR(1) time-series away from its mean will be persistent if φ_1 is sizeable, but it will (on average) eventually decay away over time; a fluctuation in an I(1) time-series, in contrast, is permanent. This property of I(0) time-series is called "mean reversion." Mean reversion in this instance says that P_t (on average) decays to its mean of zero – this corresponds to $log(SP500_t)$ decaying (on average) back to its trend line.

Is P_t an AR(1) time-series with a fairly large value of φ_1 or is it an I(1) time-series with unbounded variance? The sample correlogram in Figure 14-3 suggests that P_t is I(1), since the sample autocorrelations are very close to one and decay very slowly as the relative lag increases. The visual evidence from the time plot of P_t in Figure 14-2 is more mixed, however. The time variation in P_t does appear to consist of very smooth local trends, leading to highly persistent, seemingly random departures from the mean of zero. But these departures from the mean do not appear to be permanent: the time-series did return to its mean several times. On the other hand, that was during the course of a sample of over 15,000 days! Note also that the plotted P_t values are the deviations from a linear trend estimated using these very observations: had $log(SP500_t)$ wandered off in either direction at either the beginning or at the end of the sample period – and maybe it did! – this would have impacted the estimated trend line. The magnitude of the excursions of P_t may have increased during the course of the sample – indicative of a random walk, wandering off to positive or negative infinity – but not convincingly so.[16]

Several formal statistical tests have been developed to test the null hypothesis that a time-series is I(1), perhaps around a linear time trend, against the alternative that it is a covariance stationary – i.e., I(0) – series, albeit perhaps highly autocorrelated. The most practical (and popular) of these is called the "Augmented Dickey-Fuller" or "ADF" test. It is described here by applying it to the $log(SP500_t)$ data.

The ADF test statistic is obtained by using OLS to estimate the parameters in a model for $\Delta log(SP500_t)$ – the daily change in $log(SP500_t)$ – using the level of $log(SP500_{t-1})$ as an explanatory variable and including in the regression model (as necessary) an intercept, a time trend, and lags in $\Delta log(SP500_t)$. In fact, the ADF test statistic is simply the estimated t ratio on the lagged level series: $log(SP500_{t-1})$, in this case. If the null hypothesis is true – and $log(SP500_t)$ is an I(1) random walk – then the coefficient on $log(SP500_{t-1})$ in this regression model should be zero. If the null hypothesis is false – and $log(SP500_t)$ is really an I(0) AR(1) series with φ_1 less than one – then the coefficient on $log(SP500_{t-1})$ in this regression model should be negative.[17]

[16] This observation suggests that there might be some sort of "restoring force" operating which causes P_t to become mean-reverting, but is only apparent when $|P_t|$ is large. Nonlinear models, such as the Threshold Autoregression Model discussed in Chapter 17, can be useful in modeling such behavior. In such a model, P_t can be a random walk for small-to-medium sized values of $|P_{t-1}|$, but shifts over to an AR(1) Model with φ_1 less than one whenever $|P_{t-1}|$ exceeds a threshold value. Another way such mean reversion can occur is in the error-correction model of a cointegrated multivariate relationship. In a cointegrated relationship the change in the time-series depends inversely on the deviation of the level of the series from that specified by a long-term relationship, effectively inducing mean reversion. Such a cointegrated relationship is explored at the end of Section 14-5, in the context of a model for the growth rate of U.S. consumption expenditures.

[17] See Exercise 14-2. Also, see Active Learning Exercise 14b (available at www.wiley.com/college/ashley) for another empirical example.

The only complication is that under the null hypothesis, the explanatory variable $log(SP500_{t-1})$ does not have bounded variance, so the distribution of the statistic on the OLS estimator of the coefficient on $log(SP500_{t-1})$ is not a drawing from the Student's t distribution. The test is still practical, however, because the necessary critical points for the distribution from which this estimated t statistic *is* a drawing have been calculated using simulation methods. For example, Davidson and MacKinnon (1993, p. 708) quote the following asymptotic critical points from their own simulations:[18]

Table 14-1 Critical Points for One-Tailed ADF Test

Test Statistic	1%	5%	10%
no intercept	−2.56	−1.94	−1.62
intercept only	−3.43	−2.86	−2.57
intercept and time trend	−3.96	−3.41	−3.13

Thus, in a regression of the change in the time-series against its level, including an intercept, a linear time trend, and enough lags in the change of the time-series to eliminate any serial correlation in the fitting errors, one can reject the null hypothesis of an I(1) generating mechanism for the level of the time-series at the 5% level of significance if the estimated t ratio on the level of the series is smaller than −3.41. Thus, in that case, the p-value for the rejection of the null hypothesis is less than .05. Note that *negative* values of the coefficient on the level are evidence *against* the null hypothesis; thus, one needs to observe a test statistic which is more negative than this – i.e., less than −3.96 – in order to reject the null hypothesis of an I(1) series at the 1% level.

Applying the ADF test to the data on $log(SP500_t)$, a bit of experimentation makes it plain that two lags in $\Delta log(SP500_t)$ are needed, and that both the intercept and a time trend are needed. The resulting OLS regression output is:

```
      Source |       SS       df       MS              Number of obs =   15028
-------------+------------------------------           F(  4, 15023) =   16.42
       Model |  .006139561     4  .00153489            Prob > F      =  0.0000
    Residual |  1.40464151 15023  .000093499           R-squared     =  0.0044
-------------+------------------------------           Adj R-squared =  0.0041
       Total |  1.41078107 15027  .000093883           Root MSE      =  .00967

------------------------------------------------------------------------------
chg_logsp500 |      Coef.   Std. Err.      t    P>|t|     [95% Conf. Interval]
-------------+----------------------------------------------------------------
      daynum |   1.31e-07   7.74e-08     1.70   0.089    -2.02e-08    2.83e-07
    logsp500 |
         L1. |  -.0005236    .000269    -1.95   0.052    -.0010509    3.74e-06
chg_logsp500 |
         L1. |   .0394845   .0081487     4.85   0.000     .0235119     .055457
         L2. |  -.0514046   .0081487    -6.31   0.000    -.0673769   -.0354322
       _cons |   .0020009   .0008419     2.38   0.017     .0003506    .0036511
------------------------------------------------------------------------------
```

for which the estimated t statistic on $log(SP500_t)$ is −1.95, which is not smaller than −3.13, so one cannot reject the null hypothesis that $log(SP500_t) \sim$ I(1) at even the 10% level.

[18] These are valid for large samples, assuming that enough lags in the lagged "change series" have been included so as to eliminate any serial correlation in the errors. Davidson, R., and J. G. MacKinnon (1993), *Estimation and Inference in Econometrics*, Oxford University Press: Oxford.

Thus, the ADF test provides no empirical basis for rejecting the null hypothesis that $log(SP500_t)$ is integrated of order one. Had the test rejected this null hypothesis at, say, the 5% level, then it would be reasonable to assume that the $log(SP500_t)$ has bounded variance. This would justify including $log(SP500_t)$ in a regression model (e.g., Equation 14-3) as an explanatory variable, expecting that the usual asymptotic sampling distribution for the OLS estimator of its coefficient is reasonably valid. It would also be reasonable to use $log(SP500_t)$ as the dependent variable in such a regression model. This is called "modeling in levels."

But the test did not reject this null hypothesis. It didn't even come close. One would think that it could therefore be concluded that the null hypothesis – to the effect that $log(SP500_t)$ is an I(1) time-series, which needs to be differenced in order to have a bounded variance – is true. In that case, one should instead be using $\Delta log(SP500_t)$ in one's regression models. This is called "modeling in changes."

That conclusion would be wholly unwarranted, however, on two grounds. First, Perron (1989) has shown that a structural break in a time-series (i.e., a sudden and permanent shift in its mean) will cause the ADF test to substantially underreject the I(1) null hypothesis.[19] Second, and more importantly, the fact that one cannot reject the null hypothesis does not at all imply that the alternative hypothesis is true. It only implies that we did not have sufficiently strong evidence against the null hypothesis in order to reject it. This point is particularly important in the present instance, because the ADF test in fact has extremely low power to reject the null hypothesis for data which is almost I(1) – say, because it was actually generated by an AR(1) Model with φ_1 close to, albeit strictly less than, one. In other words, for data of this kind, the ADF test will almost never reject the null hypothesis – even though it is false, and the time-series is really I(0) and thus does not need to be differenced. Thus, the formal test is very unlikely to reject the null hypothesis (when it is actually false) in precisely the same circumstance in which we most need help in making up our minds: where the smoothness of the time plot and form of the sample correlogram are already telling us that the data are very highly autocorrelated, but we are just not sure whether or not φ_1 is actually equal to one.[20]

As noted at the end of the previous section, since a time-series Z_t which is I(1) does not have a bounded variance, the usual Central Limit Theorem no longer applies when such a Z_t is used as an explanatory variable in a regression model like Equation 14-3. And it is this Central Limit Theorem which ensures that the OLS parameter estimators are asymptotically normal and which provides the expressions for the asymptotic variances of the estimators that are programmed into econometric software. It is possible to derive the asymptotic sampling distribution of the OLS parameter estimators for the I(1) case (corresponding to $\varphi_1 = 1$) and also for the case where φ_1 is slightly exceeds one, but these results are well beyond the scope of the present treatment.[21] In neither case, however, is the asymptotic distribution of the OLS parameter estimators even close to a normal distribution. (Except, remarkably enough, in one special – but not altogether uncommon – circumstance: where Z_t is "cointegrated" with one or more other I(1) time-series. Cointegration will be defined and illustrated later in this chapter, in Section 14.5.) In general, however, the usual computing formulas for the estimated standard errors of the OLS parameter estimators (and the

[19] P. Perron (1989), "The Great Crash, Title Oil Price Shock, and the Unit Root Hypothesis" *Econometrica 57,* 1361–1401.

[20] Recall that the rejection of a null hypothesis with a reasonably low *p*-value allows meaningful conclusions to be drawn; a failure to reject the null hypothesis does not really mean anything at all. The ADF-GLS test proposed by Elliott, Rothenberg, and Stock (1996) has higher power to reject the I(1) null hypothesis than the standard ADF test, but not sufficiently higher as to substantially vitiate the conclusions given in the text. Elliott, G. T., T. J. Rothenberg, and J. H. Stock (1996), "Efficient tests for an Autoregressive Unit Root," *Econometrica 64,* 813–836.

[21] For example, see Phillips, Magdalinos, and Giraitis (2008) for recent work on this topic. Phillips, Peter C. B., T. Magdalinos, and L. Giraitis (2008), "Smoothing Local-to-Moderate Unit Root Theory," Cowles Foundation Discussion Paper #1659 available at cowles.econ.yale.edu/P/cd/d16b/dl659.pdf.

consequent confidence intervals and hypothesis test p-values) are all invalid – and typically substantially distorted – for an explanatory variable which is I(1).[22]

What is an analyst to do, then: model in "levels" – using variables analogous to Z_t as dependent and explanatory variables – or model in "changes" by, in essence, first differencing the model equation, so that the dependent and explanatory variables are analogous to $Z_t - Z_{t-1}$? The first point to make is this: the prudent person will pursue *both* modeling strategies and hope that the most relevant conclusions drawn will be insensitive to the choice. This chapter itself exemplifies this good and prudent behavior by working the illustrative empirical example – an analysis of monthly U.S. consumption expenditures in terms of lagged disposable income and a short-term interest rate – first in "changes" (Sections 14.4 and 14.5) and then in "levels" (Section 14.6). The second point to make is that for data which are substantially autocorrelated, there are advantages – and downside risks – to either approach. As is often the case in life, the advantages are most efficiently reaped and the downside risks most adroitly avoided by the person who is most clearly aware of their existence. Thus, the strategy here is to work the example both ways and, armed by those experiences, to return to this question in Section 14.7, at the very end of the chapter.

14.4 CAPSTONE EXAMPLE PART 1: MODELING MONTHLY U.S. CONSUMPTION EXPENDITURES IN GROWTH RATES

The first question that arises in any modeling exercise is what data to use. Context and purpose drive many of these choices; econometric considerations, as we have already seen, also have a role to play, as does data availability.

If the purpose of the exercise is to confront a particular theory with the data, then the theory itself should play the major role in the variable selection decision. Still, the decision as to whether to use a logarithmic (or some other) transformation is more reasonably addressed from homoscedasticity considerations. Analogously, if the purpose of a time-series model is to obtain good short-term forecasts, then modeling the dynamics is paramount, but – as we have seen – doing so is also essential in meeting the non-autocorrelation assumption, so as to obtain valid inferences. And if the model is intended to be useful for medium-term or long-term forecasting, it had better include the relevant explanatory variables – and ones whose future values are forecastable, as well. Moreover, obviously, a model intended to be useful for policy analysis – i.e., for forecasting variables of interest, conditional on different assumptions as to the future time paths of policy variables – had better include those policy variables as explanatory variables. Not so obviously, a *failure* to include additional explanatory variables which are relevant to the sample behavior of the dependent variable and whose sample behavior happens to resemble that of one of these included policy variables can lead to inconsistent parameter estimates, and to both inferences and policy predictions which are substantially misleading.

This is a good moment at which to recall – from the discussion in Chapter 9 – that another way to frame this "omitted variable" issue is to note that the parameter inconsistency alluded to immediately above fundamentally arises because the other explanatory variables "try" to proxy for the omitted variable – insofar as they can do so, because they are correlated with it. From a forecasting point of view, this is desirable; sometimes we don't have data on some of the explanatory variables which would be helpful. From a policy analysis or a statistical inference point of view, in contrast, such "proxying" can be disastrous, especially when the analyst is unaware of it.

Yet another useful way to frame this issue is to note that omitting a (possibly important) explanatory variable may be necessary – because we do not have the requisite sample data – but it has the effect of changing what the coefficients on the other explanatory variables *mean*: if

---

[22] See Exercise 13-11.

explanatory variables X and Z are included in a model for Y but Q is omitted, then the population coefficient on X is now the partial derivative of the expected value of Y with respect to X holding Z constant *and averaging over the possible values of* Q; whereas, if Q is included in the model also, then the population coefficient on X is the partial derivative of the expected value of Y with respect to X, holding both Z and Q constant. Another way of putting this is to note that the coefficient on X in a model also including both Z and Q as explanatory variables quantifies how one would expect the results of a new "experimental" outcome on Y to turn out with a new value set for X as one unit larger, controlling for (i.e., holding constant in the experiment) both Z and Q. Whereas, the coefficient on X in a model omitting Q as an explanatory variable quantifies how one would expect the results of a new experimental outcome on Y to turn out with a new value set for X as one unit larger, controlling for (i.e., holding constant) only Z and averaging over the impact of differing values for Q which might occur.

Usually – but not always – what we want to estimate is the impact of a unit change in X on the expected value of the dependent variable Y while controlling for all other variables which impact Y. The miracle of multiple regression is that we can *statistically* control for variation in these other variables even when we cannot do so in the data collection process – but we need to at least collect the data on these other variables whose sample behavior we could not experimentally control. If we can and do collect these data, then we can compare the estimated regression model including the experimentally uncontrolled variables to an estimated model omitting them and also estimate the degree to which these omitted variables are correlated, in the sample data, to the included variables. Often, however, we cannot do this because the requisite data collection was infeasible. Our statistical analysis of the data is then necessarily averaging over the values of, rather than controlling for, these other variables. In general, it is better to be aware that we are doing this, so that we can assign appropriate meaning to the coefficients we can and do estimate. On the other hand, human nature is such that people often prefer denial ...

There are a number of available choices for specifying the form of the dependent variable, Y_t, in the Dynamic Multiple Regression Model of Equation 14-3; and similar considerations apply to the explanatory variables – e.g., in this case, to $X_{t-\ell,1}, X_{t-\ell,2}$, and $X_{t-\ell,3}$, for the various values of the lag, ℓ. One can model Y_t itself. Or, if Y_t is always positive, then one can model its logarithm, $\log(Y_t)$. Alternatively, if one of these has a linear trend, then one might model its deviation from trend. These choices are generally fairly easy to make, because one choice typically leads to a variable which has a more stable mean and variance during the course of the sample period; or one choice leads to a variable with a reasonably linear trend (or, better, no trend at all) and the other does not.[23] Any of these choices corresponds to modeling Y_t "in levels."

Alternatively, one can choose to model Y_t "in changes." Again, within this context, there are several different formulations. In particular, one can model ΔY_t (which is $Y_t - Y_{t-1}$, the change in Y_t) or – for variables which are always positive – one can choose to model its growth rate, $\Delta\ln(Y_t)$, which is $\ln(Y_t) - \ln(Y_{t-1})$.[24] Again, it is usually not difficult to choose between ΔY_t and $\Delta\ln(Y_t)$,

[23] The logarithm is not the only possible choice for a variance-stabilizing transformation – e.g., see Box and Cox (1964) – but it is the simplest, and the most commonly used. G. E. P. Box and D. R. Cox (1964), "An Analysis of Transformations," *Journal of the Royal Statistical Society B 26*, 211–243.

[24] Note that $\Delta\ln(Y_t) = \ln(Y_t) - \ln(Y_{t-1}) = \ln(Y_t/Y_{t-1})$ and is often multiplied by 100 to put it into "percentage" terms, or by s100 (where "s" is the number of periods in a year), to "annualize" the growth rate. But the actual percentage change in Y_t is $100\Delta Y_t/Y_{t-1}$; this "percentage change" way of defining/calculating a growth rate is inferior to using $100\Delta\ln(Y_t)$ because growth rates based on the change in the logarithm decompose gracefully. For example, suppose that P_tQ_t equals Y_t – as in the GDP deflator times real GDP equaling nominal GDP. Then $100\Delta\ln(P_t) + 100\Delta\ln(Q_t)$ precisely equals $100\Delta\ln(Y_t)$, whereas an analogous equality does not hold between percentage growth rates and is not even a good approximation if any of the growth rates is sizeable.

since the logarithm is only defined for positive values of Y_t and since one of these two choices typically has a more stable variance during the course of the sample period.[25]

The "model in changes" versus "model in levels" decision is not so straightforward, however. Section 14.3 has just examined one of the key issues in this choice: are the levels of the dependent and explanatory variables covariance stationary – i.e., I(0) – time-series or are they "random walk" – i.e. I(1) – time-series with unbounded variances? Settling this issue for a particular time-series – as we have just seen – is itself not easy when the series is strongly autocorrelated. Recent simulation work by Ashley and Verbrugge (2009)[26] has shed some light on the matter, indicating that both approaches have value. Consequently, as noted above, both kinds of modeling will be illustrated here, but the present section begins the exposition by focusing on a model "in changes." The analogous model in "levels" is constructed in Section 14.6; and, as noted above, the two approaches are compared and discussed in Section 14.7.

In particular, the remainder of this section considers a specific example, in which monthly data on real U.S. personal consumption expenditures (C_t) is modeled using data on real disposable income (Y_t) and on a short-term interest rate (R_t), the yield on 30-day Treasury Bills.[27]

The next few sections yield several models using these data, any of which can be used to forecast U.S. consumption spending – either its level *or* its change – a few months ahead of time.[28] They certainly each provide a vastly more valid test of the Keynesian "marginal propensity to consume" idea than one can obtain from the bogus scatterplots typically found in textbooks, which motivated the empirical example in Section 13.3 above. The inclusion of the interest rate in the models makes them also potentially useful for assessing the impact of monetary policy on this portion of the macroeconomy. And, from a scientific perspective, this inclusion makes it feasible to test for the "Pigou effect" – an inverse impact of interest rates on consumption spending – predicted by some macroeconomic theories. Of course, if one is really serious about testing macroeconomic theory, one would likely do better to begin from a much more carefully delineated theory, which would no doubt suggest additional explanatory variables – e.g., exports, an index of consumer sentiment, and/or government expenditures – monthly data on some of which might well be available. Here, however, these models are being constructed primarily for illustrative purposes, so we will just consider models using these two explanatory variables.

As noted above, the model in the present section is developed in "changes" format – that is, as a model relating changes in C_t (or its monthly growth rate, 100 times the change in its logarithm) to changes in Y_t (or its growth rate) and to changes in R_t (or its growth rate), with the alternative model in "levels" format to be considered in Section 14.6. The data are available on a monthly basis beginning in February 1959; reserving the last 81 observations currently available (from January 2003 through July 2009) as a "postsample period" or "holdout sample" for testing the model, leaves

[25] Sometimes either choice – using the logarithmic transformation or not – seems equally good. One might in that case choose on the basis of which variable one actually prefers to forecast (if this is the dependent variable) or on the basis of which choice yields results which are most easily communicated to one's intended audience. The choice is still consequential for forecasting far into the future, but discomfort with regard to this consequentiality should serve as a reminder that projecting that far into the future may not be a good idea: e.g., see the scatterplots at the end of Section 8.4.

[26] Ashley, R., and R. Verbrugge (2009), "To Difference or Not to Difference: A Monte Carlo Investigation of Inference in Vector Autoregression Models." *International Journal of Data Analysis Techniques and Strategies 1(3)*: 242–74, available at ashleymac.econ.vt.edu/working_papers/varsim.pdf.

[27] These data were downloaded from the FRED data base at the St. Louis Federal Reserve Bank, available at research .stlouisfed.org/fred2/; this Web site is very well designed – it is not difficult.

[28] Chapters 17 and 18 describe forecasting concepts in depth, but it is worth noting here that either kind of model can provide either kind of forecast. If the last sample period is period T, then the forecast of Y_{T+1} from the "changes" model (for ΔY_t) is simply the known value of Y_T plus the forecast of ΔY_{t+1}. Similarly, the forecast of ΔY_{t+1} from the "levels" model is just the forecast of Y_{T+1} less the known value of Y_T.

a sample of 527 observations.[29] Section 18.5 will describe how postsample forecasting effectiveness can be used to assess the value of a model such as this one.

Plotting the sample period data for both the monthly change and the monthly growth rate for all three variables yields Figures 14-4, 14-5, and 14-6.[30] These time plots make it plain that the variance of the monthly growth rate time-series is notably more stable over the sample period than is the monthly change for each of the three variables. On the other hand, the subperiod during which the variance of the monthly change in the interest is apparently elevated roughly corresponds to the term (August 1979 to August 1987) of Paul Volcker as chairman of the Federal Reserve, during which period a notably idiosyncratic approach to monetary policy was applied. Consequently, it actually makes better sense to use the change in the interest rate instead of its growth rate and – because there was no concomitant increase in the variance of the growth rate of consumption spending during the Volcker subperiod – to allow for the possibility that the coefficients on the interest rate variables were different during these months. This nicely illustrates how institutional information can trump simply looking at the data.[31]

Note that the data here – as is typically the case – do not in any case appear to have constant variance in either change or growth rate format over the entire period. The growth rate in consumption spending, for example, seems to have lower variance in at least part of the latter portion of the sample. It is both tempting and (usually) appropriate to drop a modest amount of data whose covariance stationarity – constancy in mean, variance, and autocorrelations – is clearly suspect when the stationarity is pretty clearly failing in a very early portion of the sample. In that case the sample length lost is more than compensated for by the higher degree of homogeneity in the sample (and accompanying larger likelihood of identifying a model with stable parameters); and one can also reasonably claim that the least recent data is the least relevant for both scientific and for short-term forecasting purposes.

This tactic is clearly impractical, however, when the "different-looking" data is not in the very earliest portion of the sample period. Where there is a sensible reason for the apparent failure of covariance stationarity in a subperiod – as with the higher variance in the interest rate changes during the Volcker subperiod alluded to above – one can account for an apparent inhomogeneity in the data (as will be done below for the Volcker subperiod) in the modeling process itself. Otherwise, one is faced with either truncating the sample in an unappealing way or with tolerating some degree of inhomogeneity in the sample data. There is almost always some problem of this sort in some portion of the data set, so a practical analyst must simply get used to that. One can always,

[29] The original data are SAAR – "seasonally adjusted at annual rates" – so, to be fully consistent with this, one would multiply both the monthly changes and the monthly growth rates by 12; that was not done here. Ideally, one would want to use seasonally unadjusted data and adjust it for seasonal patterns oneself, using the methods given in Chapter 18, because the seasonal adjustment procedure used by the Bureau of Economic Analysis involves a moving two-sided filter which can distort dynamics to some degree. It is also common for the BEA seasonal adjustment procedure to induce small, but artifactual, negative serial correlations correlations in the data at the seasonal lag. These should be ignored for scientific purposes; they could be of help in forecasting, but are usually not strong enough to be worth modeling for that purpose either. Seasonally unadjusted data are more trouble to model (since one has to deal with the seasonal dependencies oneself) and, as in the present example, are usually much more difficult – often impossible – to obtain.

[30] The postsample data are not plotted – but they were briefly looked at. The only noteworthy feature to these data is that the monthly growth rate in the interest rate fluctuates wildly – with values ranging from -184% to $+146\%$ in the period September 2008 to January 2009 – which will provide a postsample challenge to any model using the growth rate of the interest rate as an explanatory variable.

[31] Were r_chg_t the dependent variable in the model, then one would expect to find heteroscedasticity in the model errors and it would be appropriate to use standard error estimates which are robust to such heteroscedasticity – i.e., the White-Eicker estimates – from the outset. In the present context it is not apparent at the outset that heteroscedasticity in the model errors is a problem, although this will become apparent during the course of the diagnostic checking of the model. Note that it is a homoscedastic model error term which is really desired: heteroscedasticity in the dependent variable which is driven by heteroscedasticity in the explanatory variables is quite all right.

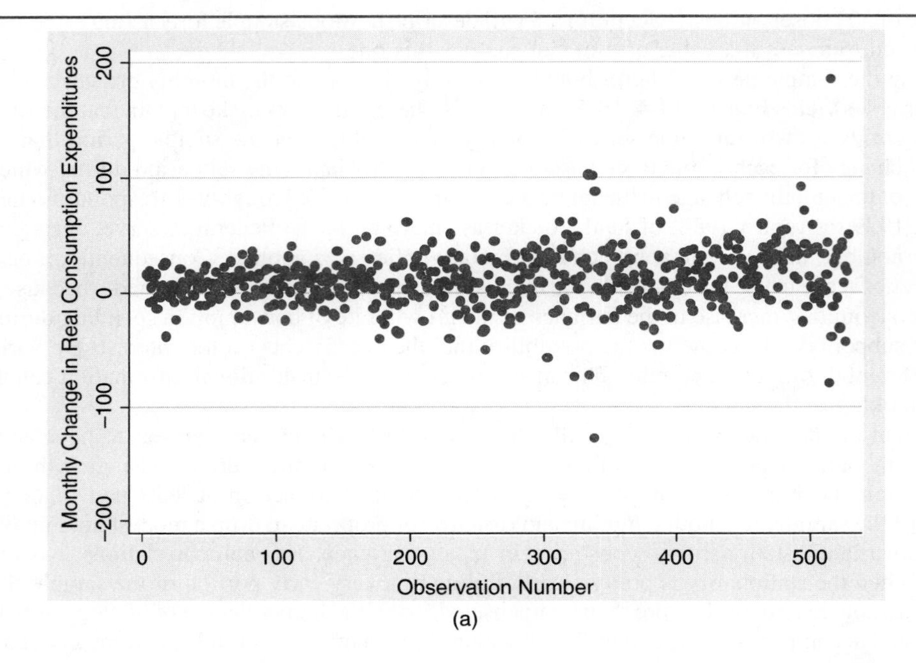

(a)

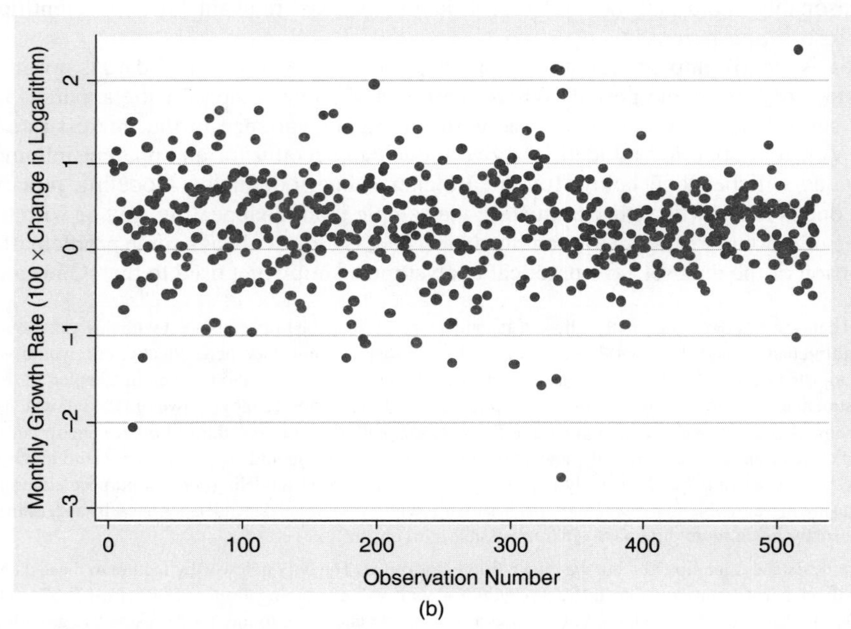

(b)

Figure 14-4 Time Plots of Monthly Change and Monthly Growth Rate of U.S. Real Personal Consumption Expenditures (February, 1959 to December, 2002)

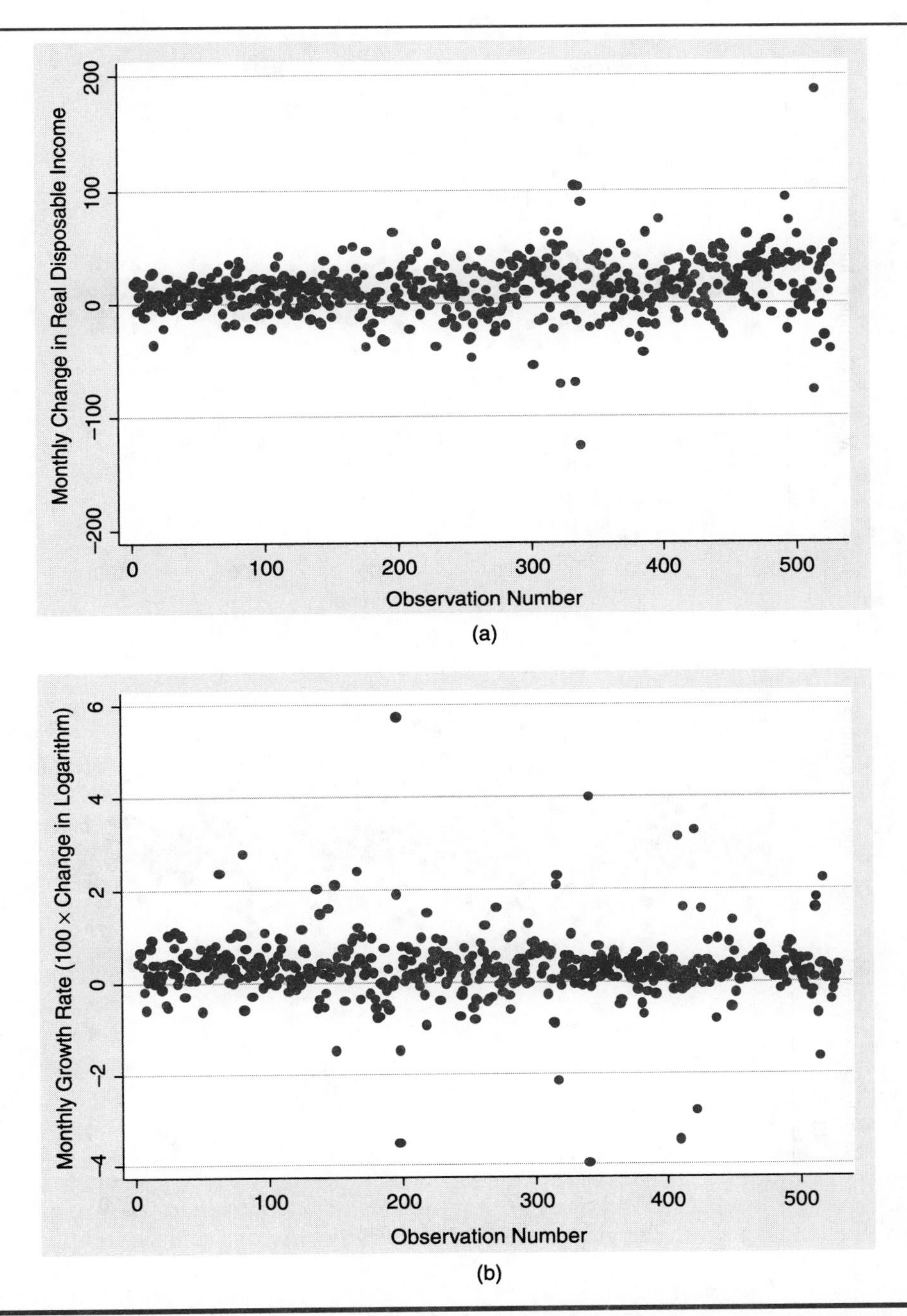

Figure 14-5 Time Plots of Monthly Change and Monthly Growth Rate of U.S. Real Disposable Income (February, 1959 to December, 2002)

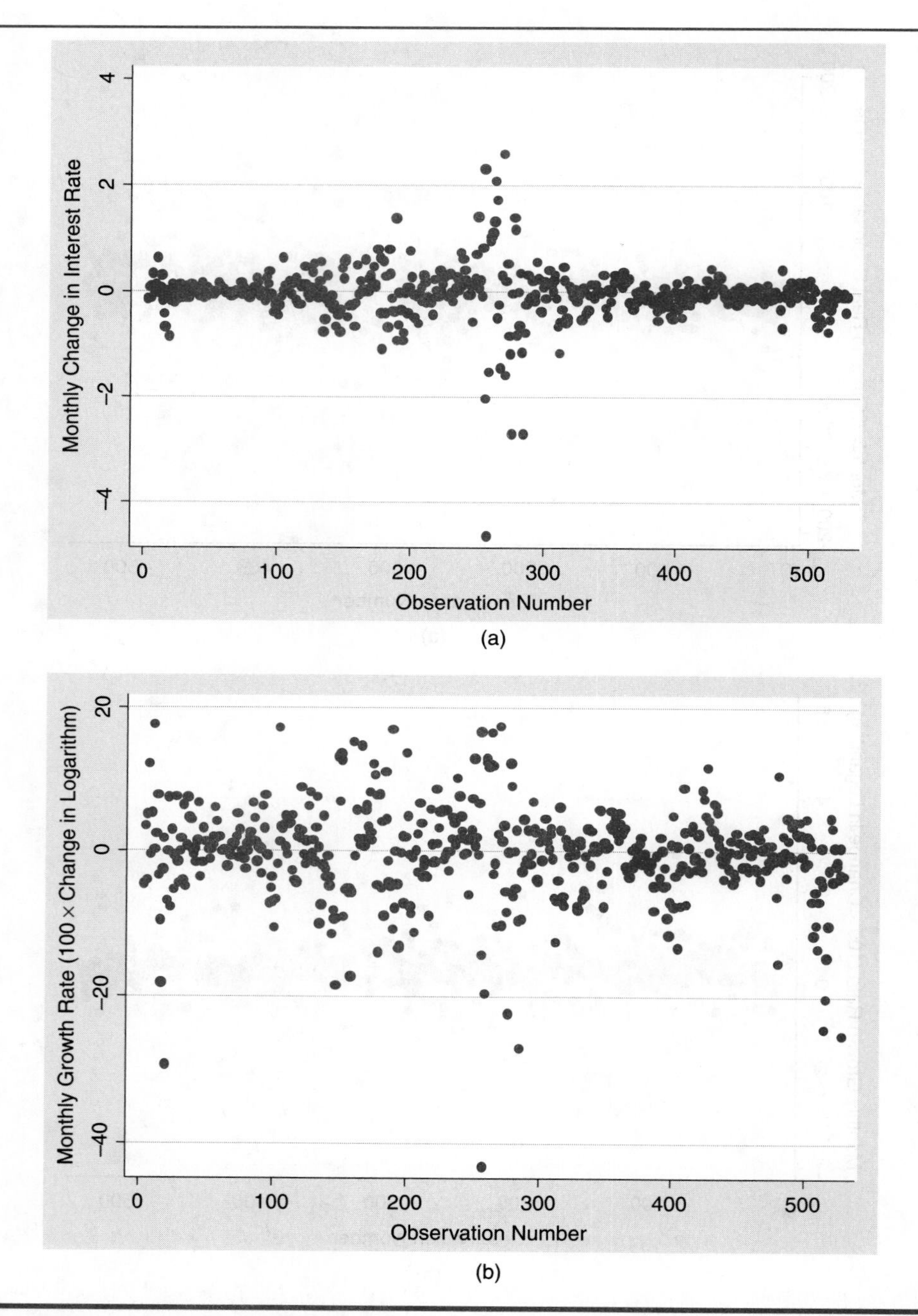

Figure 14-6 Time Plots of Monthly Change and Monthly Growth Rate of Yield on U.S. 3-Month Treasury Bills (February, 1959 to December, 2002)

however – to the degree to which time is available – analyze and compare separate models using either subsets of the data or different choices with regard to the logarithm transformation. And one should routinely diagnostically check one's "final" model for parameter stability: if the model passes this test, then the underlying assumptions of the present nature were probably all right; if not, then these choices need to be revisited.

Here we will simply proceed with a model for the growth rate of consumption spending – "c_grow_t" defined equal to $100[\log(C_t) - \log(C_{t-1})]$ – in terms of the growth rate of disposable income – "y_grow_t," defined equal to $100[\log(Y_t) - \log(Y_{t-1})]$ – and in terms of the change in the interest rate – "r_chg_t," defined equal to $[R_t - R_{t-1}]$. As indicated in the discussion earlier, the model also includes an interaction variable, $volcker\_rchg_t$, defined as the product of r_chg_t and a dummy variable ($volcker_t$), which is one for each month during the period August 1979 to August 1987 and zero otherwise; this variable will allow for the possibility that the coefficients on lagged values of r_chg_t are different in the Volcker period. In particular, per the material in Section 9.2, each estimated coefficient on a lagged value of $volcker\_rchg_t$ can be interpreted as an estimate of the amount by which the analogous coefficient on r_chg_t was larger during the Volcker subperiod.

Next, even though scatterplots are known to be potentially misleading in a multivariate context, consider Figure 14-7 – a scatterplot of c_grow_t versus y_grow_{t-1} – if only to see if there are any obvious outliers in the relationship:

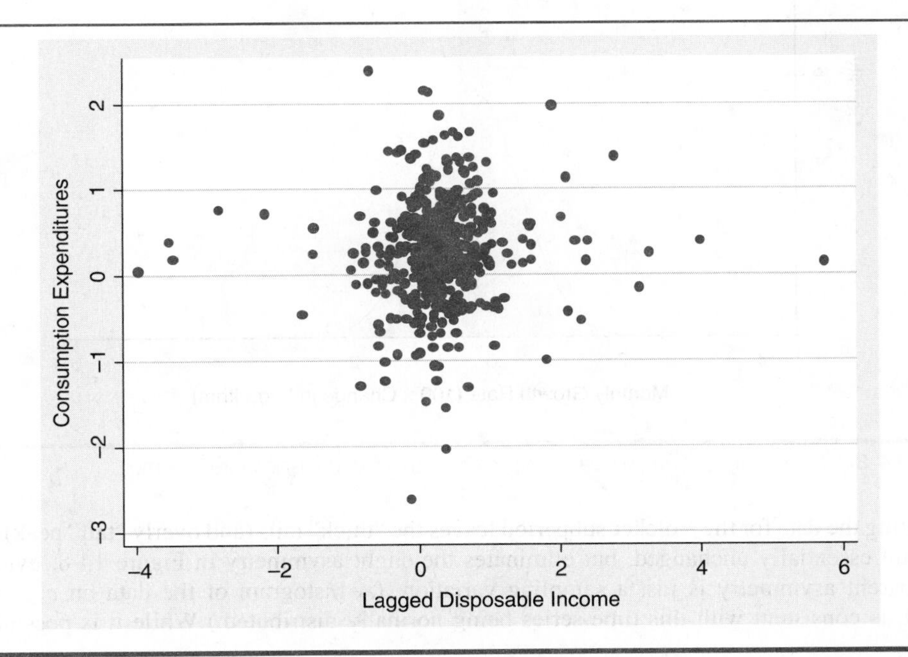

Figure 14-7 Scatterplot of Growth Rate in Consumption Spending versus Lagged Growth Rate in Disposable Income

Two features stand out in this scatterplot. The first feature to note is that there is little evidence here of a relationship between these two variables which is based solely on just one or two outlying observations. In fact, there is little evidence of any relationship at all! Moreover, this scatterplot looks much the same if one either drops the data from the Volcker subperiod or uses only the data from the Volcker subperiod. It will become evident shortly that this result is primarily an artifact of the inadequacy of the scatterplot technique in this context: multivariate regression modeling will yield strong evidence of a relationship, albeit not one that is quite as strong as one might expect or hope for; this relationship will be "spread" over a number of lags in y_grow_t, however, so it is not apparent in this scatterplot. Models in the "changes" format are, in any case, usually much weaker in terms of the fit to the sample data than are models in the "levels" format. This is a natural consequence of the fact that a change or growth rate in a time-series emphasizes the noise in the period-to-period variation in the series.

Before moving on from this scatterplot, however, a second feature is worth noting: Regardless of whether the data from the Volker subperiod are included or not, there appear to be quite a few more observations on y_grow_{t-1} in this scatterplot which are larger in magnitude than one might expect if y_grow_t were normally distributed. A histogram of the sample data on y_grow_t, including a plot of the gaussian density with matching mean and variance, in Figure 14-8 confirms this.[32]

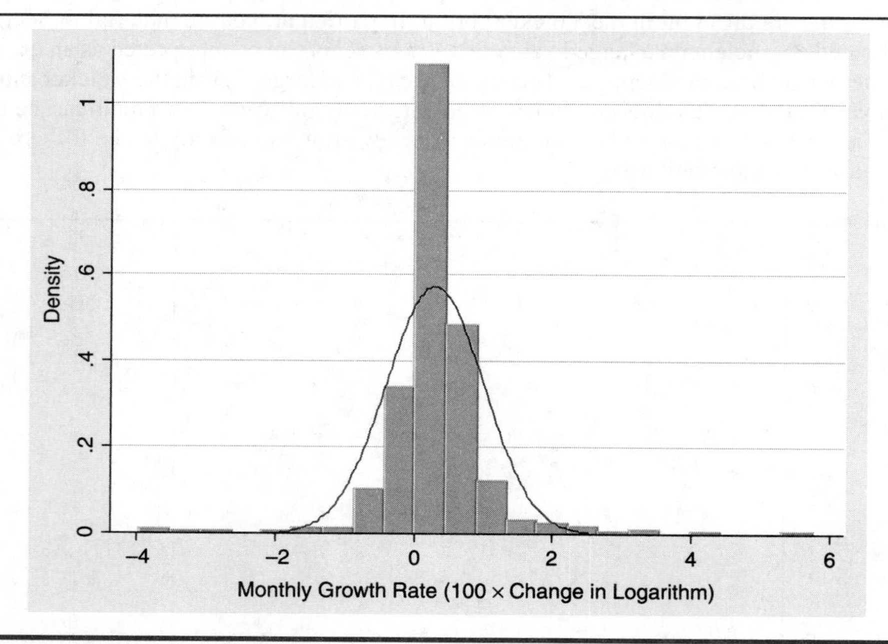

Figure 14-8 Histogram of Sample Data on the Growth Rate in Disposable Income

Omitting the data for the Volcker subperiod leaves the "thick" tails (and overly "tall" peak) in this histogram essentially unchanged, but eliminates the slight asymmetry in Figure 14-8; evidently, this apparent asymmetry is just a sampling variation. (A histogram of the data on c_grow_t, in contrast, is consistent with this time-series being normally distributed.) While it is possible that

[32] Formal testing is not necessarily so useful (or necessary) in this setting, but the most appropriate test in the present context is the "skewness-kurtosis" normality test, which – as its name suggests – tests for deviations from normality in terms of both asymmetry around the mean ("skewness") and non-gaussian tail behavior ("kurtosis"). Skewness is quantified using the sample third moment around the mean; kurtosis is quantified using the sample fourth moment around the mean. The estimated kurtosis will exceed that expected for gaussian data if the data are either "fat-tailed," or overly-clustered around the mean, or (as in the case of y_grow_t) both. The command for this test in Stata is "sktest *y_grow*". For y_grow_t the null hypothesis of normality is rejected (looking at either just the estimated skewness, just the estimated kurtosis, or both) with *p*-value less than .0005. These results illustrate the problem with formal tests of normality: they are only valid for large samples, but even then they are of rather limited value because in that setting they tend to reject at the usually considered significance levels even for modest departures from normality (as in the skewness here) which are not necessarily of great interest.

y_grow_t is generated as a weighted sum of non-gaussian shocks, it is much more likely that this noticeable non-normality in y_grow_t is due to nonlinear serial dependence in this time-series. (The detection and modeling of nonlinear serial dependence in a time-series is described in Section 18.6.) This result suggests that the relationship between c_grow_t and lagged y_grow_t might be usefully modeled within one of the nonlinear frameworks also described in Chapter 18. Thus, the model developed in the remainder of this section, which expresses c_grow_t as a linear function of past values of y_grow_t, is only a linear approximation to a relationship which is perhaps nonlinear to a substantial degree.[33] Further consideration of these issues can wait until Chapter 18, where we will find that nonlinear modeling is substantially more challenging than the basically linear modeling undertaken in the present section; still, it does suggest that we might want to at least consider including some squared explanatory variables in the present model.

Continuing on with a linear specification for the relationship between c_grow_t and lagged values of y_grow_t, r_chg_t, and $volcker\_rchg_t$, there are two different approaches to formulating a model. One can either begin with a small model and add additional lagged variables – "as needed" – or one can begin with the most complicated model one is willing to envision estimating and then pare away lagged variables whose coefficients are statistically insignificant.

The "begin small" approach is sometimes called the "textbook" method – usually by someone criticizing it! – because econometrics textbooks in the early days of the discipline (i.e., the 1950s and 1960s) emphasized obtaining the model specification almost entirely from economic theory and using FGLS (Section 13.7) to "correct" the parameter estimates, if need be, for any heteroscedasticity or serial correlation found in the model fitting errors. Maintaining a strong connection between the statistical model being estimated and a theoretical model – the testing of which was typically the object of the exercise – seemed absolutely essential. And econometric data sets – usually based on annual data – were typically quite small in those days, so it was not feasible to estimate very complicated models. The strong connection to a theoretical model *is* essential if testing this theory is the main point of the analysis. (And, quite typically, it still *is* the main point of the analysis.) The problem with this theory-driven "begin small" approach, however, is that the "data mining" inherent in then attempting to improve the model (by "trying out" additional variables and lags) invalidates the p-values reported for the relevant hypothesis tests with regard to parameters in the final model. For example, if 20 alternative models are considered, it is hardly surprising to find one of them a statistical improvement at the 5% level of significance, just due to chance. Many estimated relationships of dubious validity were obtained based on this way of formulating models, eventually eroding the profession's confidence in this approach.

Larger data sets (often quarterly or monthly) were becoming available at that point in time; it was becoming well known that large macroeconometric models based on the "textbook" specification approach were failing to outperform simple extrapolative models at forecasting, and people were, in

[33] Of course, that makes the OLS parameter estimates inconsistent as estimators of the parameters in this underlying nonlinear formulation, but they would still be consistent as estimators of the parameters in the linear approximating model specified here, if these parameters were constants. The advanced reader might note that all of the results obtained in Chapter 11 using the model of Equation 11.1– i.e., the consistency of $\hat{\beta}^{OLS}$, the asymptotic sampling distribution for $\hat{\beta}^{OLS}$, and the analogous results for multivariate extensions of the model – are still valid when X_i, and U_i are time-series which are not serially independent. Instead, it is sufficient to assume only that X_t and U_t are both covariance stationary – i.e., their means, variances, and autocovariances (γ_j) do not vary over time, that (for both series) the sum of $|\gamma_j|$ over all possible values of j (from one to infinity) is bounded, and that the product X_tU_t is a martingale difference. (The relationship between the martingale difference property and serial independence is explained in Appendix 13.1.) Those assumptions are frequently not unreasonable. The problem is that since the linear approximating model is misspecified, its parameters vary over time. Consequently, $\hat{\beta}^{OLS}$ cannot possibly be a consistent estimator for β, since β does not have a unique value to estimate. Thus, this hint that the relationship between y_grow_t and its own past may be significantly nonlinear suggests that the standard error estimates for the OLS coefficient estimates on lagged y_grow_t in the linear approximating model should be used with a dollop of caution.

any case, becoming less confident of the ability of economic theory to provide trustworthy model specifications.[34] In this context, the "begin large" approach – prominently advocated by David Hendry (1995) at the London School of Economics and consequently often called the "LSE" approach – began to dominate.[35] If sufficient data are available to make it feasible, this approach has a strong advantage: providing that the starting model is "large enough," at least one's first set of hypothesis tests is valid. The problem with this approach – even for fairly large data sets, such as the one used in this section – is that a model which is too badly overparameterized may yield results which are so washed-out as to provide poor guidance as to which explanatory variables to remove so as to improve it. This topic is further discussed in Section 18.4.

The approach used here will be to begin by estimating a model which includes 12 lags (a full year) in each of the three explanatory variables – i.e., lags in y_grow_t, r_chg_t, and $volcker\_rchg_t$ – plus 12 lags in the dependent variable (i.e., lags in c_grow_t). That yields a model with 49 parameters to estimate. That seems like a lot of parameters; on the other hand, there are 528 months of sample data available for estimating them.[36] This corresponds to the LSE approach, in that it seems rather unlikely that more 12 lags are relevant – chances are that we will simply be eliminating clearly insignificant coefficients from this model at the longer lags. On the other hand, it is easy and feasible to estimate a few more complicated models as a diagnostic check on this formulation; and it seems prudent to at least consider a few such models, increasing the maximum lag length to 24 for each variable, one at a time.

Estimation of a model for c_grow_t based on 12 lags in each variable, then, yields the regression output shown on the next page.

It seems evident that this model was sufficiently parameterized at the outset: apparently, at most nine lags in c_grow_t and five lags in y_grow_t are needed; adding additional, lags (out to lag 24) – first in c_grow_t, then in y_grow_t, and then in r_chg_t – confirms this conclusion.[37]

The case for including any lags at all in r_chg_t and $volcker\_rchg_t$ seems initially dubious, but a test of the null hypothesis that all 24 of these coefficients are zero is rejected with a p-value of .0007; apparently, the model is simply so overparameterized with regard to these variables that the

[34] See Granger and Newbold (1977, Section 8.4) on the dismal forecasting performance of large-scale macroeconometric forecasting models in that era (compared to that provided by simple AR(p)-type models) and Ashley (1988) for an indictment of their forecasting performance relative to an absolute standard of forecasting effectiveness. Granger, C. W. J., and P. Newbold (1997), *Forecasting Economic Time Series*, Academic Press: New York and Ashley, R. 1988, "On the Relative Worth of Recent Macroeconomic Forecasts." *International Journal of Forecasting 4*:363–76.

[35] See Hendry, D. (1995) for a detailed exposition of LSE approach. Hendry, D. (1995), *Dynamic Econometrics*, Oxford University Press: Oxford.

[36] With quarterly data one would have only one-third as many observations per year. But including a year or two of lags in the model requires estimation of only one-third as many parameters. Also, the available U.S. quarterly data usually begins in 1947, so there are more years. On the other hand, some of the U.S. data prior to 1952 or so can look a bit "wild," causing one to strongly doubt the value of including it in the sample period. In the end, a prudent analyst using quarterly data ends up in much the same place: one starts out using at least a year or so of lags in each variable – a bit more if the model is relatively uncomplicated and the sample reasonably long; a bit less otherwise. In view of the fact that only asymptotic results are available on the OLS parameter estimates, time-series modeling using annual data is inherently more problematic. Available sample lengths will increase in the next 50 to 100 years – if we are willing to wait! – but the assumption that the earlier data is still relevant may become increasing untenable.

[37] In all of those additional terms, two were individually significant: one on c_grow_{t-20} ($t = 3.28$) and another on c_grow_{t-24} ($t = -2.77$). An isolated significant coefficient at an oddball lag, such as the one on c_grow_{t-20}, is ordinarily just random sampling variation and should be ignored. In the present instance, however, it appears that the sequence of coefficients on the lagged values of c_grow_t forms a pattern in which the coefficient is oscillating as it decays. (Such a lag structure can be modeled with just a few parameters using ratios of polynomials in the lag operator, as described in Chapters 17 and 18. For now the lag structure on c_grow_t is simply truncated at lag nine.) The term at lag 24 is most likely an artifact of the seasonal adjustment procedure used by the Bureau of Economic Analysis. This procedure quite commonly induces weak negative serial correlations in data at small multiples of the seasonal lag; these correlations are usually not worthwhile to model.

Source	SS	df	MS
Model	35.2388143	48	.734141965
Residual	134.479509	466	.288582637
Total	169.718323	514	.33019129

Number of obs =	515
F(48, 466) =	2.54
Prob > F =	0.0000
R-squared =	0.2076
Adj R-squared =	0.1260
Root MSE =	.5372

c_grow		Coef.	Std. Err.	t	P>|t|	[95% Conf.	Interval]
c_grow							
	L1	-.3254225	.0479728	-6.78	0.000	-.4196923	-.2311527
	L2	-.1724936	.0505228	-3.41	0.001	-.2717744	-.0732128
	L3	-.0795301	.0516535	-1.54	0.124	-.1810327	.0219724
	L4	-.0982419	.0529826	-1.85	0.064	-.2023562	.0058724
	L5	-.0235434	.0521272	-0.45	0.652	-.125977	.0788901
	L6	.1148642	.0512364	2.24	0.025	.0141812	.2155471
	L7	.1398423	.0510301	2.74	0.006	.0395647	.24012
	L8	.1449776	.0512086	2.83	0.005	.0443493	.2456059
	L9	.075668	.0511924	1.48	0.140	-.0249285	.1762644
	L10	-.0035463	.0506397	-0.07	0.944	-.1030567	.0959641
	L11	.0467011	.0495364	0.94	0.346	-.0506412	.1440435
	L12	.0388466	.0477497	0.81	0.416	-.0549848	.132678
y_grow							
	L1	.1617686	.039599	4.09	0.000	.0839539	.2395832
	L2	.1673299	.0409729	4.08	0.000	.0868153	.2478445
	L3	.1321844	.0420691	3.14	0.002	.0495158	.2148529
	L4	.0956325	.0429271	2.23	0.026	.0112778	.1799872
	L5	.0862266	.0429137	2.01	0.045	.0018983	.1705548
	L6	-.0361619	.0425009	-0.85	0.395	-.1196791	.0473553
	L7	.0141757	.0423496	0.33	0.738	-.0690441	.0973955
	L8	-.0013968	.0423016	-0.03	0.974	-.0845224	.0817287
	L9	.001453	.0422474	0.03	0.973	-.0815661	.0844721
	L10	.03579	.040719	0.88	0.380	-.0442256	.1158057
	L11	.0564022	.0395901	1.42	0.155	-.0213951	.1341995
	L12	.0097253	.0386242	0.25	0.801	-.0661739	.0856245
r_chg							
	L1	-.1363226	.1047072	-1.30	0.194	-.3420794	.0694342
	L2	.0022989	.1063253	0.02	0.983	-.2066376	.2112354
	L3	-.1858133	.1059035	-1.75	0.080	-.3939209	.0222942
	L4	.0122903	.1061717	0.12	0.908	-.1963443	.2209249
	L5	-.0214293	.1054394	-0.20	0.839	-.2286249	.1857664
	L6	.0674108	.1054961	0.64	0.523	-.1398961	.2747177
	L7	-.1446276	.1058222	-1.37	0.172	-.3525754	.0633201
	L8	-.0770182	.1056623	-0.73	0.466	-.2846517	.1306153
	L9	.1080712	.1049051	1.03	0.303	-.0980744	.3142168
	L10	-.1291465	.1059655	-1.22	0.224	-.3373759	.0790829
	L11	-.1680876	.1066282	-1.58	0.116	-.3776193	.041444
	L12	.0065654	.1049906	0.06	0.950	-.1997483	.212879
volcker_rchg							
	L1	.1651639	.1259358	1.31	0.190	-.0823085	.4126363
	L2	-.2539252	.1317826	-1.93	0.055	-.5128869	.0050366
	L3	.244036	.1334595	1.83	0.068	-.0182209	.5062928
	L4	-.1826113	.1336658	-1.37	0.173	-.4452735	.080051
	L5	-.1135601	.1344678	-0.84	0.399	-.3777985	.1506783
	L6	-.2861106	.1353094	-2.11	0.035	-.5520027	-.0202186
	L7	.2479958	.1356752	1.83	0.068	-.0186152	.5146067
	L8	-.2188745	.1346226	-1.63	0.105	-.483417	.045668
	L9	-.0434931	.1323421	-0.33	0.743	-.3035543	.2165681
	L10	-.0148227	.1330084	-0.11	0.911	-.2761932	.2465477
	L11	.1291315	.1315656	0.98	0.327	-.1294039	.3876669
	L12	-.1618452	.1273001	-1.27	0.204	-.4119985	.088308
_cons		.1226217	.0566422	2.16	0.031	.0113159	.2339275

individual coefficient estimates are uninformative. Therefore the model is next pared down to include only nine lags in c_grow_t and five lags in y_grow_t, and then the pair of variables (r_chg_{t-j} and $volcker\_rchg_{t-j}$) is eliminated – one at a time, beginning with the term at lag j equal to 12 – so long as the estimated coefficients on r_chg_{t-j} and $volcker\_rchg_{t-j}$ are both statististically insignificant. This process is continued, arriving at the model:

Source	SS	df	MS
Model	21.4225258	20	1.07112629
Residual	148.577328	497	.298948346
Total	169.999854	517	.328819833

Number of obs =	518
F(20, 497) =	3.58
Prob > F =	0.0000
R-squared =	0.1260
Adj R-squared =	0.0908
Root MSE =	.54676

c_grow		Coef.	Std. Err.	t	P>|t|	[95% Conf.	Interval]
c_grow							
	L1	-.2922741	.0465113	-6.28	0.000	-.383657	-.2008912
	L2	-.1266041	.0479901	-2.64	0.009	-.2208925	-.0323157
	L3	-.0303269	.0479641	-0.63	0.527	-.1245642	.0639105
	L4	-.0497808	.0481637	-1.03	0.302	-.1444102	.0448487
	L5	.0057589	.0475099	0.12	0.904	-.0875861	.0991039
	L6	.1050301	.0448718	2.34	0.020	.0168684	.1931918
	L7	.1327759	.0449813	2.95	0.003	.0443991	.2211528
	L8	.1368333	.0451722	3.03	0.003	.0480813	.2255854
	L9	.0687069	.0442243	1.55	0.121	-.0181827	.1555966
y_grow							
	L1	.1489547	.0382919	3.89	0.000	.0737208	.2241886
	L2	.1361307	.0397831	3.42	0.001	.0579668	.2142945
	L3	.1134861	.0400446	2.83	0.005	.0348085	.1921637
	L4	.0806661	.0397354	2.03	0.043	.0025961	.1587361
	L5	.0661788	.0387562	1.71	0.088	-.0099674	.1423251
r_chg							
	L1	-.082388	.1007761	-0.82	0.414	-.2803877	.1156116
	L2	-.0182862	.1031351	-0.18	0.859	-.2209209	.1843484
	L3	-.2358475	.0998981	-2.36	0.019	-.4321222	-.0395729
volcker_rchg							
	L1	.118236	.1198693	0.99	0.324	-.117277	.3537491
	L2	-.1274158	.1235207	-1.03	0.303	-.3701028	.1152713
	L3	.2110932	.1193554	1.77	0.078	-.0234102	.4455966
_cons		.1506739	.0511208	2.95	0.003	.0502343	.2511134

At this point the null hypothesis that the coefficients on all three lags of $volcker\_rchg_t$ are zero is tested again; the p-value for this test is .269, so these variables are eliminated from the model: while there is evidence for a "Pigou" effect at a lag of three months, there is apparently no evidence that this relationship was any different during the Volcker subperiod. This yields the estimated model:

Source	SS	df	MS
Model	20.243817	17	1.19081276
Residual	149.756037	500	.299512074
Total	169.999854	517	.328819833

Number of obs =	518
F(17, 500) =	3.98
Prob > F =	0.0000
R-squared =	0.1191
Adj R-squared =	0.0891
Root MSE =	.54728

c_grow		Coef.	Std. Err.	t	P>|t|	[95% Conf.	Interval]
c_grow							
	L1	-.2937912	.0464578	-6.32	0.000	-.3850677	-.2025147
	L2	-.122496	.0478798	-2.56	0.011	-.2165664	-.0284257
	L3	-.0268547	.0478948	-0.56	0.575	-.1209545	.0672451
	L4	-.0500547	.0480436	-1.04	0.298	-.1444468	.0443375

		Coef.	Std. Err.	t	P>|t|	[95% Conf.	Interval]
	L5	.0102145	.047291	0.22	0.829	-.0826991	.103128
	L6	.0985473	.0444787	2.22	0.027	.0111592	.1859354
	L7	.1249201	.0445253	2.81	0.005	.0374403	.2123998
	L8	.1312677	.0447459	2.93	0.004	.0433545	.2191808
	L9	.060856	.0438212	1.39	0.166	-.0252404	.1469525
y_grow							
	L1	.1507502	.0382546	3.94	0.000	.0755906	.2259098
	L2	.1316127	.0397227	3.31	0.001	.0535687	.2096567
	L3	.1140775	.0400135	2.85	0.005	.0354622	.1926929
	L4	.0783296	.0397123	1.97	0.049	.000306	.1563532
	L5	.0611537	.0385985	1.58	0.114	-.0146814	.1369889
r_chg							
	L1	-.018162	.0554657	-0.33	0.743	-.1271365	.0908126
	L2	-.0942309	.0574788	-1.64	0.102	-.2071607	.0186988
	L3	-.0972686	.055388	-1.76	0.080	-.2060904	.0115533
_cons		.157918	.0504608	3.13	0.002	.0587767	.2570593

The coefficients on c_grow_{t-9} and y_grow_{t-5} are not significantly different from zero, but note that each one appears to be a sensible part of a decaying lag structure; thus, in each case the OLS estimate is probably better than setting the coefficient to zero.

The Pigou effect – an impact of the interest rate on consumption spending – seems to have disappeared, but this is not so: the null hypothesis that the coefficients on all three lags of r_chg_t are zero can be rejected with p-value equal to 0.0241. It is almost always a very poor idea to eliminate individual lagged variables from an otherwise-significant lag structure because the individual coefficient is not statistically significant. In the present case, however, it would appear that the impact of a change in the interest rate does not begin to significantly impact the growth rate in consumption spending until several months have passed, so it seems sensible to eliminate r_chg_{t-1} and r_chg_{t-2} from the model and see if this improves matters. It clearly does, yielding a tentative model which is worth submitting to diagnostic checking, even though the terms in c_grow_{t-9} and y_grow_{t-5} are still very marginal:

Source	SS	df	MS
Model	19.1394941	15	1.27596627
Residual	150.86036	502	.300518645
Total	169.999854	517	.328819833

Number of obs =	518
F(15, 502) =	4.25
Prob > F =	0.0000
R-squared =	0.1126
Adj R-squared =	0.0861
Root MSE =	.5482

c_grow		Coef.	Std. Err.	t	P>|t|	[95% Conf.	Interval]
c_grow							
	L1	-.2930271	.0465069	-6.30	0.000	-.3843992	-.2016549
	L2	-.1276048	.0477198	-2.67	0.008	-.2213599	-.0338497
	L3	-.0374102	.047	-0.80	0.426	-.1297512	.0549307
	L4	-.0637138	.0475874	-1.34	0.181	-.1572089	.0297812
	L5	.0099941	.0472671	0.21	0.833	-.0828716	.1028598
	L6	.0976214	.0445474	2.19	0.029	.0100992	.1851437
	L7	.1271779	.0445705	2.85	0.005	.0396102	.2147456
	L8	.1300299	.0448161	2.90	0.004	.0419796	.2180802
	L9	.0605728	.0436087	1.39	0.165	-.0251052	.1462509
y_grow							
	L1	.1488007	.0382772	3.89	0.000	.0735974	.2240039
	L2	.1293168	.0397584	3.25	0.001	.0512034	.2074301
	L3	.1106822	.0399541	2.77	0.006	.0321843	.1891801
	L4	.0721	.039646	1.82	0.070	-.0057925	.1499925
	L5	.059974	.0386277	1.55	0.121	-.015918	.135866
r_chg							
	L3	-.1238923	.0514408	-2.41	0.016	-.224958	-.0228266
_cons		.1711933	.049849	3.43	0.001	.073255	.2691316

Before proceeding with that, however, it is worth reviewing the process so far. It began with a model thought likely to be somewhat, but not absurdly, more complex than necessary. Statistically insignificant terms (or groups of terms) at the largest lags were then successively dropped; only at the last step was it recognized that a lag structure might not begin at lag one. Some analysts might instead prefer to simply search over possible specifications and choose the one that minimizes the Schwarz Criterion or BIC. Such a search procedure has the advantage of appearing to be more objective than the one used here. On the other hand, by treating all terms symmetrically, it places no premium on a feature that "real" lag structures usually exhibit: they are smooth. Thus, actual lag structures usually begin at some minimum lag – typically, but not always, a lag of one period – and continue on to larger lags, until they either end or decay away. (Again, this topic of search procedures is further discussed in Section 18.4.)

Consequently, if $\hat{\beta}_{1,j} \ldots \hat{\beta}_{4,j}$ form a reasonable-looking lag structure, with $\hat{\beta}_{4,j}$ significant and if both $\hat{\beta}_{5,j} \ldots \hat{\beta}_{7,j}$ and $\hat{\beta}_{9,j} \ldots \hat{\beta}_{11,j}$ are all small and insignificant, then an apparently significant $\hat{\beta}_{8,j}$ estimate is very likely just due to sampling error – even though including $X_{t-8,j}$ in the model lowers the value of the BIC.[38] Conversely, if $\hat{\beta}_{4,j}$ and $\hat{\beta}_{6,j}$ are both significant, then the OLS estimator of $\beta_{5,j}$ is probably a better estimate of $\beta_{5,j}$ than is zero – even if $|\hat{\beta}_{5,j}|$ is so small as to be insignificant, and even if the inclusion of $X_{t-5,j}$ in the model raises the value of the BIC.

Including $X_{t-5,j}$ in the model in the previous instance yields a less "parsimonious" model, in that almost the same fit to the data (i.e., the same sum of squared fitting errors) could be achieved in a model which omits this explanatory variable, and which thereby requires the estimation of one less parameter. Parsimony is a very important feature in any model to be estimated using a small sample, because the OLS parameter estimators are not BLU or efficient in a model which includes unnecessary explanatory variables: the price one pays for estimating irrelevant parameters is unnecessarily higher OLS sampling variances. Hence, model parsimony is always a consideration. On the other hand, in the present modeling context the sample needs to be sufficiently large as to justify the use of asymptotic theory, so that consistency is a property worth caring about and so that it is reasonable to use the asymptotic sampling distribution provided by the Central Limit Theorem for inference. In that context, a bit of estimation inefficiency due to the estimation of a few – possibly – unnecessary parameters in the middle of a lag structure is simply not worth worrying about.

Still – all else equal – a parsimonious model is a better model; consequently, it is worth foreshadowing at this point that the "intervention analysis" modeling technique described in Section 18.4 has the potential to smoothly model the decaying lag structures in the present model with just a couple of parameters rather than the present 14.

Returning to the present model, the first diagnostic check is to look at a time plot and histogram of the fitting errors for evidence of any obvious outliers, heteroscedasticity, or serial correlation.[39]

These plots (comprising Figure 14-9) both look basically all right, except – possibly – for a smaller error variance in the period 1992 to 1998, which here corresponds to observations number 397 to 480.

Since this relationship is multivariate, scatterplots are often misleading as to the size and stability of the various relationships embodied in the model. They are still useful in looking for possible influential outliers, however. A scatterplot of c_grow_t versus y_grow_{t-1} (Figure 14-7)

[38] In contrast, an apparently significant, but isolated, term at the seasonal lag – i.e., $\hat{\beta}_{12,j}$ – probably deserves to be taken seriously. This is usually not an issue with seasonally adjusted data, except for the common occurrence of a small (but statistically significant) negative coefficient on the dependent variable at the seasonal lag. When present, such a coefficient is actually just an artifact of the procedure the Bureau of Economic Analysis uses for seasonally adjusting data and is generally not worth modeling.

[39] See Table 14-3 in Section 14.6 for a concise summary of diagnostic checking.

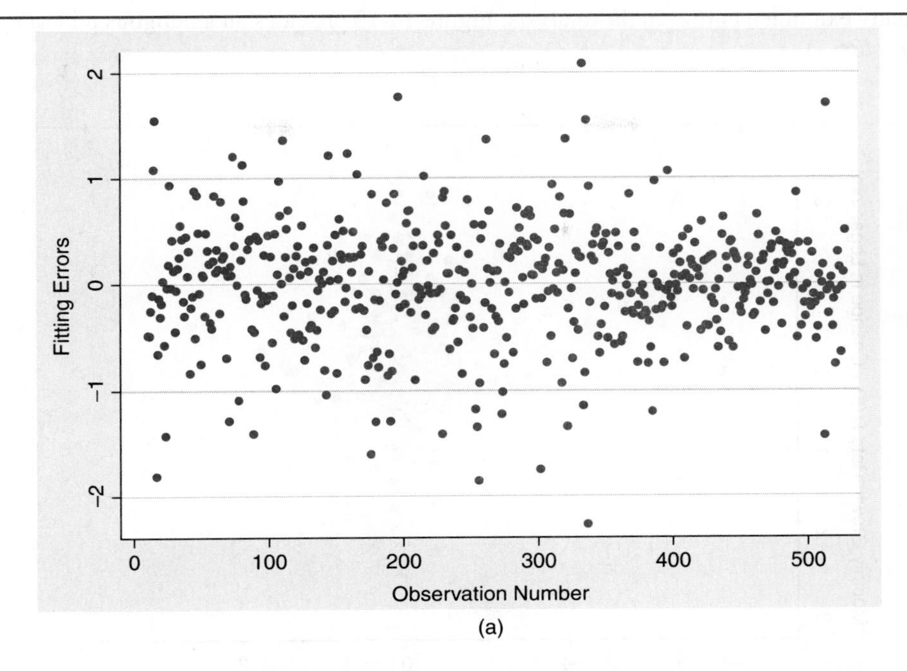

(a)

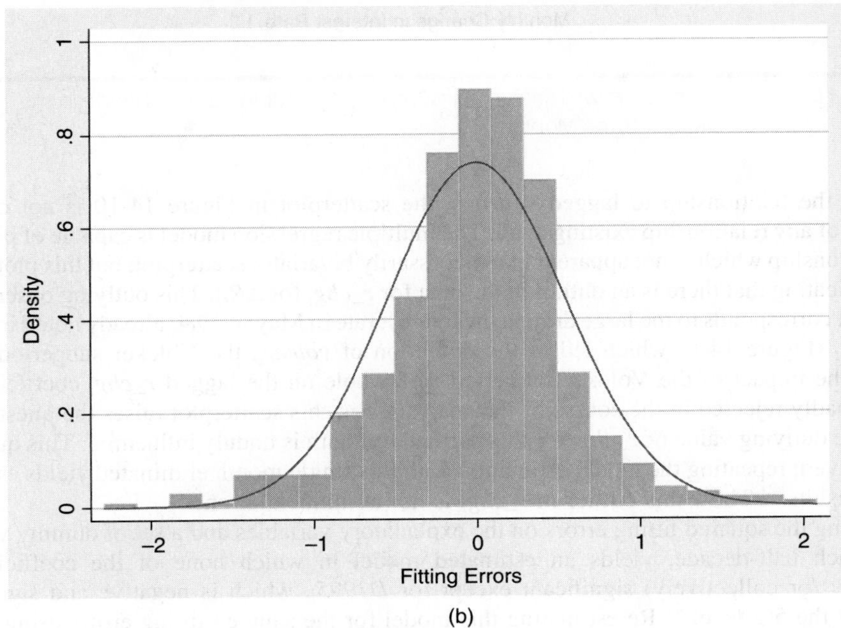

(b)

Figure 14-9 Time Plot and Histogram of Fitting Errors from the Regression of the Monthly Growth Rate of U.S. Real Personal Consumption Expenditures on the Growth Rate of U.S. Disposable Income and the Change in the Interest Rate

was already examined earlier in the analysis; Figure 14-10 provides an analogous plot of c_grow_t versus r_chg_{t-3}:

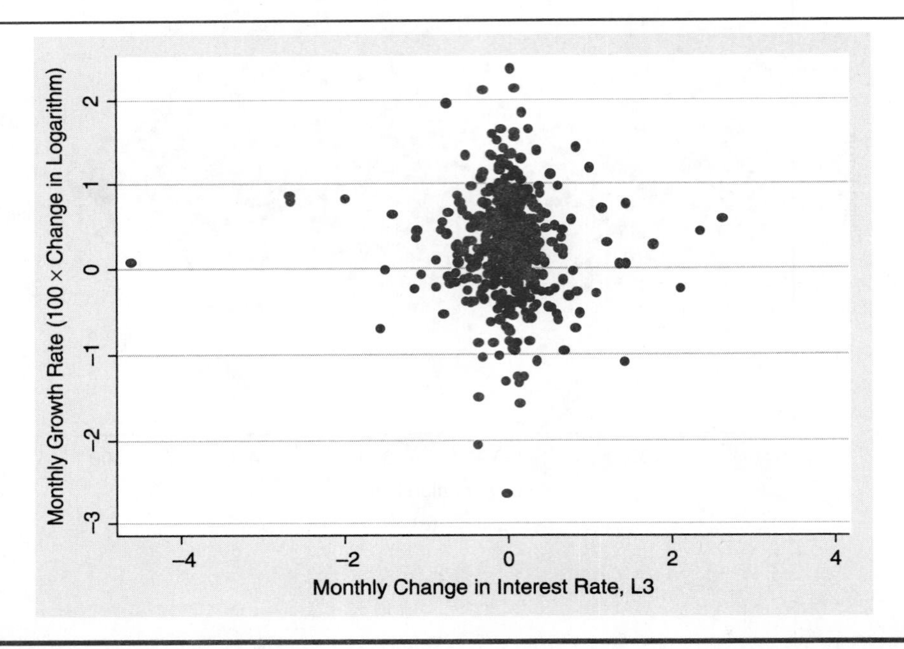

Figure 14-10 Scatterplot of Growth Rate in Consumption Spending versus Change in the Interest Rate, Lagged Three Months

As with the relationship to lagged y_grow_t, the scatterplot in Figure 14-10 is not obviously supportive of any relationship existing at all. The multiple regression model is capable of picking up a real relationship which is not apparent in a (necessarily bivariate) scatterplot, but this plot is pretty clearly indicating that there is an outlier in the data for r_chg_t (or ΔR_t). This outlying observation is not news: it corresponds to the large drop in the interest rate in May of 1980 already noted in the time plot of ΔR_t (Figure 14-6) which led to the definition of $volker_t$, the Volcker subperiod dummy variable. The impact of the Volcker subperiod as a whole on the lagged r_chg_t coefficients was already broadly rejected in the course of the analysis. But this scatterplot raises the question as to whether the outlying value of r_chg_t for this particular month is unduly influential. This question is easily resolved: repeating the model estimation with this single month eliminated yields essentially identical results.[40] Thus, this outlier in r_chg_t is not an influential one.

Regressing the squared fitting errors on the explanatory variables and a set of dummy variables, one for each half-decade, yields an estimated model in which none of the coefficients are individually (or collectively) significant except for $D1995_t$, which is negative and significantly non-zero at the 5% level.[41] Re-estimating this model for the squared fitting errors using only the half-decade dummy variables yields the estimated model:

[40] The most convenient way to do this is to append the if statement "if L3.r_chg >−4" to the regression command.

[41] $D1965_t$ is one for the period January 1965 through December 1969, and so forth. An easy way to make dummy variables in Stata is to generate a variable equal to the value of a logical expression: e.g., "generate *D1965* = (_n >= 73 & _n <133)".

Source	SS	df	MS
Model	5.94772445	7	.849674921
Residual	163.031409	510	.31966943
Total	168.979134	517	.32684552

Number of obs	=	518
F(7, 510)	=	2.66
Prob > F	=	0.0104
R-squared	=	0.0352
Adj R-squared	=	0.0220
Root MSE	=	.56539

residsqr	Coef.	Std. Err.	t	P>|t|	[95% Conf.	Interval]
D1965	.0096047	.0926809	0.10	0.918	-.1724788	.1916881
D1970	.0753126	.0926809	0.81	0.417	-.1067708	.257396
D1975	-.0336514	.0926809	-0.36	0.717	-.2157348	.148432
D1980	.1055026	.0926809	1.14	0.256	-.0765808	.2875861
D1985	.1597278	.0926809	1.72	0.085	-.0223556	.3418113
D1990	-.1401021	.0926809	-1.51	0.131	-.3221855	.0419813
D1995	-.1896843	.0926809	-2.05	0.041	-.3717678	-.0076009
_cons	.2927756	.0571133	5.13	0.000	.1805692	.404982

The null hypothesis that the coefficients on all seven of these half-decade dummy variables are zero can be rejected with *p*-value .010, so there does appear to be a bit of heteroscedasticity in the model errors, just as their time plot indicated. Re-estimating the model for c_grow_t, then, this time computing robust (White-Eicker) standard error estimates for the coefficient estimates yields:[42]

Regression with robust standard errors

Number of obs	=	518
F(15, 502)	=	3.35
Prob > F	=	0.0000
R-squared	=	0.1126
Root MSE	=	.5482

c_grow		Coef.	Robust Std. Err.	t	P>|t|	[95% Conf.	Interval]
c_grow							
	L1	-.2930271	.0659261	-4.44	0.000	-.4225521	-.1635021
	L2	-.1276048	.0557165	-2.29	0.022	-.237071	-.0181386
	L3	-.0374102	.0517974	-0.72	0.470	-.1391766	.0643561
	L4	-.0637138	.0550264	-1.16	0.247	-.1718243	.0443967
	L5	.0099941	.0479708	0.21	0.835	-.0842541	.1042423
	L6	.0976214	.0487665	2.00	0.046	.0018098	.1934331
	L7	.1271779	.0510635	2.49	0.013	.0268533	.2275024
	L8	.1300299	.0472495	2.75	0.006	.0371988	.222861
	L9	.0605728	.04147	1.46	0.145	-.0209032	.1420489
y_grow							
	L1	.1488007	.039306	3.79	0.000	.0715762	.2260251
	L2	.1293168	.0399617	3.24	0.001	.050804	.2078296
	L3	.1106822	.0400296	2.77	0.006	.032036	.1893284
	L4	.0721	.0385626	1.87	0.062	-.003664	.1478639
	L5	.059974	.0335877	1.79	0.075	-.0060158	.1259638
r_chg							
	L3	-.1238923	.0505184	-2.45	0.015	-.2231458	-.0246389
_cons		.1711933	.0548384	3.12	0.002	.0634523	.2789343

[42] Recall that specifying the "robust" option for the Stata "regress" command will direct the program to compute White-Eicker standard error estimates.

These standard error estimates are not much different from the usual OLS standard error estimates, but – due to the evidence of heteroscedasticity in the present model, they are probably preferable.

Given the care already taken to include sufficient dynamics, it would be surprising to find any substantial evidence of serial correlation in the fitting errors from this model. But it is easy to check for this by simply estimating an AR(p) model for the fitting errors; this yields nothing remotely significant for any value of p less than or equal to 12.

Next it is worthwhile to check the model specification for possible nonlinearities. As noted in Section 9.3, a very simple – albeit crude – test for such nonlinearities is to include squared terms in the model specification and observe whether or not their estimated coefficients are significantly different from zero. This was done in the present instance – including $(y\_grow_{t-1})^2$ ... $(y\_grow_{t-5})^2$ and $(r\_chg_{t-3})^2$ in the model – but none of these terms entered with significant coefficients.[43]

Finally, it is important to check the model for parameter stability. The first (and simplest) way to check this is to include the half-decade dummy variables in the model; this checks for whether or not the intercept estimate is stable over the sample period. This estimated regression equation yielded no evidence of parameter instability. Another diagnostic check is to include interaction terms ($D1965_t \times r\_chg_{t-3}$ ... $D1995_t \times r\_chg_{t-3}$) to test for possible time variation in the coefficient on r_chg_{t-3}.[44] An estimated model checking for both of these possibilities is:

```
Regression with robust standard errors                 Number of obs =      518
                                                       F( 29,    488) =     2.37
                                                       Prob > F      =   0.0001
                                                       R-squared     =   0.1384
                                                       Root MSE      =   .54786

------------------------------------------------------------------------------
             |               Robust
c_grow       |      Coef.   Std. Err.      t    P>|t|     [95% Conf. Interval]
-------------+----------------------------------------------------------------
c_grow       |
          L1 |  -.3114314    .067953    -4.58   0.000     -.444948   -.1779148
          L2 |  -.1445325   .0548774    -2.63   0.009    -.2523577   -.0367073
          L3 |  -.0628448   .0519759    -1.21   0.227    -.1649689    .0392794

          L4 |  -.0851213   .0555865    -1.53   0.126    -.1943398    .0240971
          L5 |   .0016021   .0476627     0.03   0.973    -.0920474    .0952515
          L6 |   .1029805     .04761     2.16   0.031     .0094346    .1965265
          L7 |   .1247304   .0518031     2.41   0.016     .0229458     .226515
          L8 |   .1257397   .0469839     2.68   0.008     .0334239    .2180555
          L9 |   .0637804    .043117     1.48   0.140    -.0209374    .1484983
y_grow       |
          L1 |   .1582409   .0394074     4.02   0.000     .0808117    .2356701
```

[43] One can also consider mixed nonlinear terms, such as $y\_grow_{t-1} \times y\_grow_{t-2}$ or $y\_grow_{t-1} \times r\_chg_{t-3}$. Tests and models for nonlinear dynamics are described in Section 18.6.

[44] The Bai-Perron (1998) procedure (described in Section 10.1) provides a more thorough check for structural shifts in that it considers the possibility of a shift in every model coefficient in every period. However, it is not widely implemented in econometric packages – e.g., it is not yet implemented in Stata. That could, of course, change in a future version. See also the (related) sup-Wald test of Andrews (1993, 2003). The straightforward dummy variable checks advocated here are well founded under the null hypothesis (of stable coefficients) and easy to do; rejection on such simple tests might motivate the application of these more detailed tests to further identify and localize problematic instabilities. Bai, Jushan, and Pierre Perron (1998), "Estimating and Testing Linear Models with Multiple Structural Changes," *Econometrica 66(1),* 47–78; Andrews, D. W. K. (1993), "Tests for Parameter Instability and Structural Change with Unknown Change Point," *Econometrica 61,* 821–56; and Andrews, D.W. K. (2003), "Tests for Parameter Instability and Structural Change with Unknown Change Point: A Corrigendum," *Econometrica 71,* 395–97.

	L2	.1374273	.0393705	3.49	0.001	.0600706	.214784
	L3	.1059041	.0395301	2.68	0.008	.0282339	.1835743
	L4	.0731014	.0383375	1.91	0.057	-.0022255	.1484282
	L5	.0746871	.0354575	2.11	0.036	.005019	.1443552
r_chg							
	L3	.1325775	.2414168	0.55	0.583	-.3417672	.6069223
D1965		.0922728	.0904433	1.02	0.308	-.0854336	.2699792
D1970		-.054803	.0975963	-0.56	0.575	-.2465637	.1369578
D1975		.1191815	.086671	1.38	0.170	-.0511129	.2894758
D1980		-.0210099	.1021443	-0.21	0.837	-.2217067	.1796869
D1985		.0507581	.1018098	0.50	0.618	-.1492815	.2507977
D1990		-.0274832	.0765242	-0.36	0.720	-.1778408	.1228744
D1995		.1042299	.0698085	1.49	0.136	-.0329325	.2413922
D1965_rchg3		-.3800615	.4214017	-0.90	0.368	-1.208047	.4479241
D1970_rchg3		-.3656826	.3048844	-1.20	0.231	-.9647307	.2333655
D1975_rchg3		-.7141473	.3322406	-2.15	0.032	-1.366946	-.0613486
D1980_rchg3		-.192239	.2469475	-0.78	0.437	-.6774506	.2929726
D1985_rchg3		-.5214925	.3396583	-1.54	0.125	-1.188866	.1458808
D1990_rchg3		-.3846809	.3490856	-1.10	0.271	-1.070577	.3012154
D1995_rchg3		-.4492475	.4153229	-1.08	0.280	-1.265289	.3667943
_cons		.160837	.0787828	2.04	0.042	.0060416	.3156325

Note that one of these interaction term coefficients is significantly different from zero at the 3% level, but one expects some such estimates due to chance: the null hypothesis that all seven interaction coefficients are zero can only be rejected with a *p*-value of .233, which is to say that it cannot be rejected at all. This diagnostic check provides additional evidence that unmodeled nonlinearity in this relationship is not a problem, as – if it *were* a problem – then the model coefficients would be unstable over time.[45]

With the exception of a minor heteroscedasticity problem, then, this model passes all of its diagnostic checks. Thus, it is reasonable to use this model – redropping the dummy variables – for inference. In particular, based on the White-Eicker standard error estimates, the null hypothesis that all five of the coefficients on the lagged values of *y_grow* are zero can be rejected with *p*-value .002 and the null hypothesis that the coefficient on r_chg_{t-3} is zero can be rejected with *p*-value .015.[46] It can therefore be concluded that the monthly growth rate of U.S. consumption spending is indeed directly related to recent growth rates in disposable income and inversely related to the 30-day yield on Treasury Bills, lagged three months.

This model is not exactly stellar in terms of sample fit: without all the dummy variables, its adjusted R^2 is only .113. Thus, the model is only able to "explain" around 11% of the sample variation in the monthly growth rate of consumption spending. This result is actually fairly reasonable, however: it reflects the fact that there is a lot of more-or-less-inexplicable noise in the monthly data. Is this model able to forecast future values of the growth rate of consumption spending in the ensuing 81 months of postsample data (from January 2003 through July 2009) currently available as this is being written? Methods for investigating this issue will be described in Section 18.5, after forecasting has been treated in more depth.

In the meantime, the next two sections of this chapter address two alternative approaches for modeling these monthly consumption expenditures data, both of which utilize the "levels" in the model, explanatory variables. The first of these approaches, explored in Section 14.5, utilizes the levels data in combination with the changes data, in a model which is still for the growth rate

[45] There is some evidence of a nonlinear generating mechanism for y_grow_t; this is reflected in the non-normality apparent in its histogram, Figure 14-8. But there is no strong evidence for nonlinearity in the relationship between c_grow_t and past values of y_grow_t.

[46] The Stata command for the inference on the lagged y_grow_t coefficients is simply "test L1.*y_grow* L2.*y_grow* L3.*y_grow* L4.*y_grow* LS.*y_grow*".

dependent variable: $\Delta log(C_t)$ or c_grow_t. The second approach, in Section 14.6, develops a model for the level time-series, $log(C_t)$.

14.5 CAPSTONE EXAMPLE PART 2: MODELING MONTHLY U.S. CONSUMPTION EXPENDITURES IN GROWTH RATES AND LEVELS (COINTEGRATED MODEL)

This section defines the concept of "cointegrated" time-series and develops a potentially richer model – the "Vector Error-Correction Model" or "VECM" – for the variable in "changes," $\Delta log(C_t)$ or c_grow_t in the present example.

Before going on to that model, however, it is worth noting that the "changes" model considered in the previous section at first glance seems most appropriate where $log(C_t)$ is an I(1) time-series, as described in Section 14.3. Recall that an I(1) time-series is essentially a "random walk" – and needs to be first differenced in order to be covariance stationary, or even to have a bounded variance. Based on the sample data, is this a reasonable characterization of $log(C_t)$?

The Augmented Dickey-Fuller (ADF) test described in Section 14.3 certainly provides no evidence against the null hypothesis that $log(C_t)$ is an I(1) time-series. The relevant estimated ADF regression equation, which turns out to require only one lag in $\Delta log(C_t)$, is:

```
      Source |       SS       df       MS              Number of obs =     526
-------------+------------------------------           F(  3,   522) =    7.47
       Model |  7.14536705     3  2.38178902           Prob > F      =  0.0001
    Residual |  166.460783   522  .318890389           R-squared     =  0.0412
-------------+------------------------------           Adj R-squared =  0.0356
       Total |   173.60615   525  .330678381           Root MSE      =   .5647

------------------------------------------------------------------------------
      c_grow |      Coef.   Std. Err.      t    P>|t|     [95% Conf. Interval]
-------------+----------------------------------------------------------------
         tee |   .0039074   .0020518     1.90   0.057    -.0001234    .0079382
       log_c |
         L1. |  -1.413424   .7129234    -1.98   0.048    -2.813975    -.012872
      c_grow |
         L1. |  -.1757317   .0429298    -4.09   0.000    -.2600682   -.0913952
       _cons |   10.97046   5.337132     2.06   0.040     .4855608    21.45535
------------------------------------------------------------------------------
```

The ADF test statistic is the estimated t-ratio on $log(C_{t-1})$, which is -1.98. This statistic is not sufficiently negative as to allow rejection of the I(1) null hypothesis at even the 10% level. In fact, referring to the table of ADF test critical points in Section 14.3, rejection at even the 10% level would have required a test statistic smaller than -3.13, so the ADF test is not even close to rejecting the null hypothesis that $log(C_t)$ is an I(1) time-series.

On the other hand, looking at Figure 14-11, the time path of the deviations of $log(C_t)$ from its estimated linear trend – while very smooth – do not at all appear to be wandering off to values which are larger and larger in magnitude over time. Quite the reverse: these deviations appear to be confined somehow over time – as if there were a kind of long-run "restoring force" influencing the mean value of the growth rate of consumption spending – the expected value of the change in $log(C_t)$ – whenever $log(C_t)$ departed too much from its trend line value.

It was for precisely this kind of situation that Engle and Granger (1987) proposed the concept of "cointegration." Their idea was that even though $log(C_t)$ and $log(Y_t)$ are each individually I(1), there might be a weighted sum of them which is I(0). This I(0) weighted sum might thus be appropriate to include as an explanatory variable in the model for $\Delta ln(C_t)$, so as to provide exactly this kind of

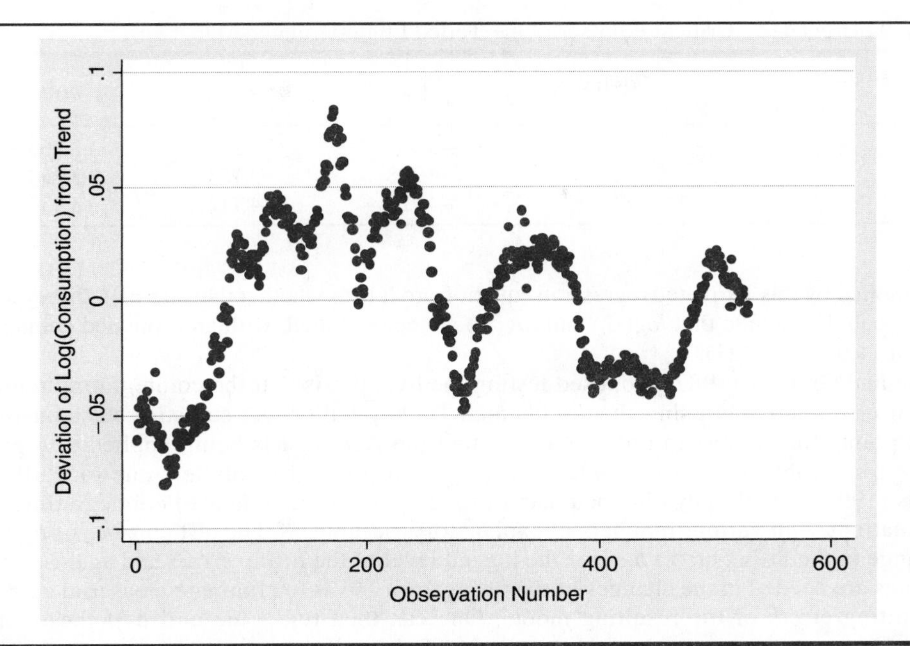

Figure 14-11 Time Plot of Deviations of Log(C_t) from Its Estimated Linear Trend

long-run "restoring force." They called the resulting model for $\Delta ln(C_t)$ the "Vector Error-Correction Model" or "VECM" and denoted this set of weights as the "cointegrating vector" for these two time-series.

To examine this idea in the present context, one might estimate what is called a "cointegrating" regression model for $log(C_t)$, using $log(Y_t)$ as the explanatory variable, and then examine the resulting fitting errors to see whether or not there is evidence against these fitting errors constituting an I(1) time-series. If there is strong evidence against these fitting errors being I(1), then it would be reasonable to infer that they are I(0) and, hence, that cointegration is present. The output from estimating such a regression equation is:

```
      Source |       SS       df       MS              Number of obs =     528
-------------+------------------------------           F(  1,   526) =       .
       Model |  101.435296     1  101.435296           Prob > F      =  0.0000
    Residual |  .213780303   526  .000406426           R-squared     =  0.9979
-------------+------------------------------           Adj R-squared =  0.9979
       Total |  101.649077   527  .192882498           Root MSE      =  .02016

------------------------------------------------------------------------------
       log_c |      Coef.   Std. Err.      t    P>|t|     [95% Conf. Interval]
-------------+----------------------------------------------------------------
       log_y |   1.020826   .0020434   499.58   0.000     1.016812     1.02484
       _cons |  -.2854491   .0171052   -16.69   0.000    -.319052   -.2518462
------------------------------------------------------------------------------
```

The standard error estimates in this regression equation are, of course, not to be taken seriously – nor does anyone worry about the likely endogeneity in $log(Y_t)$: the issue is whether or not the fitting

Table 14-2 Critical Points for One-Tailed Engle-Granger ADF Test

Number of Explanatory Variables in Cointegration Model	1%	5%	10%
1	−3.962	−3.365	−3.066
2	−4.308	−3.768	−3.450
3	−4.733	−4.112	−3.833

errors implied by this estimated regression equation are I(1) or whether they are I(0). If they are I(0), then one could conclude that $log(C_t)$ and $log(Y_t)$ are cointegrated, with an estimated cointegrating vector of (1.000, −1.021).[47]

Engle and Granger (1987) proposed testing the hypothesis that the cointegrating regression equation errors are I(1) using the Augmented Dickey-Fuller test statistic, but adjusting the critical points for the test to reflect the fact that the ADF test is being applied to regression fitting errors. Table 14-2 lists a selection of critical points for this test due to Phillips and Ouliaris (1990), which they obtained using fitting errors from simulated cointegrating regression equations with various numbers of explanatory variables.[48] The test consists of regressing the change in the fitting errors against the lagged level of the fitting errors and against however many lags are needed in the changes of the fitting errors so as to eliminate any serial correlation in the fitting errors of the resulting model. One can then reject the null hypothesis that the cointegrating equation errors are I(1) at, say, the 5% level if the estimated *t*-ratio on the lagged-level term in this regression equation is smaller than (i.e., more negative than) the 5% critical point listed in Table 14-2.

Note that the "natural" null hypothesis to test in this circumstance would be that the errors are I(0). But that is not how the Engle-Granger ADF test is set up: the null hypothesis is that the fitting errors in the cointegrating regression model are I(1). Thus, what is really being tested is the null hypothesis that the time-series are *not* cointegrated. Consequently, rejection of the null hypothesis at, say, the 5% level implies that one can conclude that there *is* cointegration, with only a 5% chance that this conclusion is false. Failure to reject the I(1) null hypothesis *suggests* that the null hypothesis is true – and that the time-series in the cointegrating regression model are actually not cointegrated, but it does not actually *prove* anything: this failure to reject the null might merely mean that the test simply failed to detect the cointegration.[49]

The relevant Engle-Granger ADF test regression for "$coint_t$," the fitting errors from the cointegrating regression model relating $\log(C_t)$ to $\log(Y_t)$, quoted above, is:

[47] This is not the only way to estimate a cointegrating vector; Stock and Watson suggest including both lags and leads of changes in the right-hand-side variable in the cointegration regression model. Stock, J. H., and M. W. Watson (1993), "A Simple Estimator of Cointegrating Vectors in Higher-Order Integrated Systems," *Econometrica 61(4),* 783–820.

[48] The number of explanatory variables in the present instance is just one. These critical points are taken directly from Table IIb of Phillips and Ouliaris (1990); these authors also provide critical points for several additional significance levels, for up to five explanatory variables, and for ADF test regressions either omitting the intercept or including a linear time trend. Phillips, P.C.B., and S. Ouliaris (1990), "Asymptotic Properties of Residual Based Tests for Cointegration," *Econometrica 58(1),* 165–94.

[49] Note that unmodeled structural breaks in a time-series "look like" I(1) behavior to ADF-type tests, yielding a bias toward not rejecting the I(1) null hypothesis. Thus, the presence of such structural breaks in the cointegrating regression fitting errors would bias the test toward failing to detect cointegration when it was really present. This observation suggests that one might want to check for obvious structural breaks – e.g., with a time plot – when the Engle-Granger ADF test does not reject the I(1) null hypothesis.

```
      Source |       SS       df       MS              Number of obs =     523
-------------+------------------------------           F(  5,   517) =   19.00
       Model |  .005293466     5  .001058693           Prob > F      =  0.0000
    Residual |  .028815026   517  .000055735           R-squared     =  0.1552
-------------+------------------------------           Adj R-squared =  0.1470
       Total |  .034108492   522  .000065342           Root MSE      =  .00747

------------------------------------------------------------------------------
  chg_coint |      Coef.   Std. Err.      t    P>|t|     [95% Conf. Interval]
-------------+----------------------------------------------------------------
       coint |
         L1. |  -.0386253   .0171375    -2.25   0.025    -.0722929   -.0049576
   chg_coint |
         L1. |  -.2957369   .0453642    -6.52   0.000    -.3848577   -.2066161
         L2. |  -.2391226   .0451069    -5.30   0.000     -.327738   -.1505072
         L3. |  -.2725643    .044655    -6.10   0.000    -.3602918   -.1848367
         L4. |  -.0693742   .0438077    -1.58   0.114    -.1554372    .0166889
       _cons |  -2.45e-06   .0003265    -0.01   0.994    -.0006438    .0006389
------------------------------------------------------------------------------
```

Thus, the ADF test statistic here is −2.25, which is not less than even the 10% critical point (−3.066) in the first line of Table 14-2, so one cannot reject the null hypothesis that these errors are I(1). As noted above, this suggests that $log(C_t)$ and $log(Y_t)$ are not cointegrated. A time plot of the cointegrating model fitting errors (Figure 14-12) shows that the fitting errors $coint_t$ are quite a mess, however:

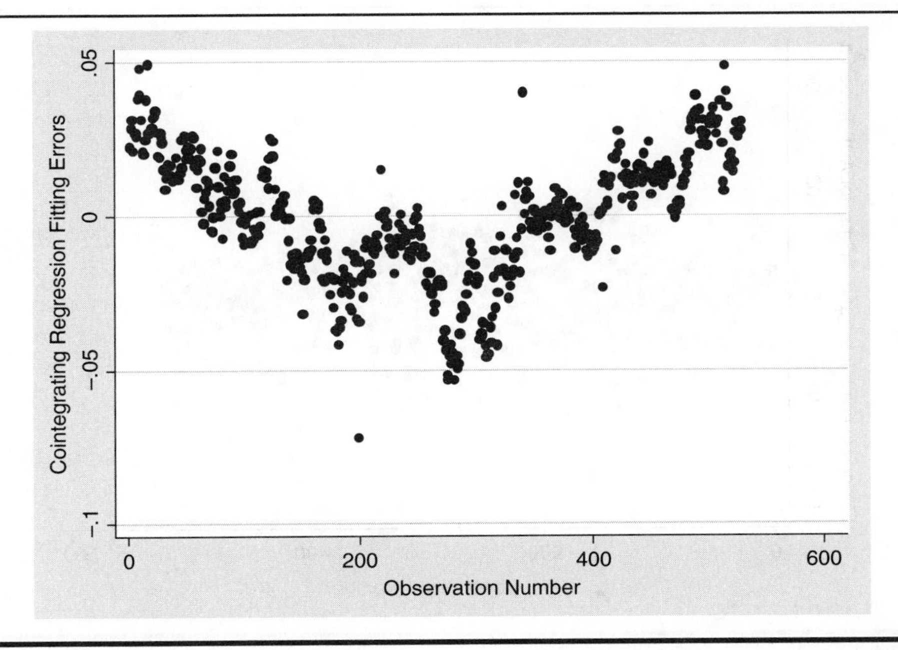

Figure 14-12 Time Plot of Fitting Errors from the Cointegrating Regression Model for $\log(C_t)$ Using $\log(Y_t)$

This time plot certainly indicates that the fitting errors are not covariance stationary I(0) noise, as the cointegrated model requires: they look more like I(1) noise superimposed on a nonlinear time trend.

Suppose instead that one considers the possibility that the levels in all three of the model variables – $log(C_t)$, $log(Y_t)$, and R_t – are cointegrated. In that case, the cointegrating regression model is:

```
      Source |       SS       df       MS              Number of obs =     528
-------------+------------------------------           F(  2,    525) =       .
       Model |  101.529197     2  50.7645987           Prob > F      =  0.0000
    Residual |  .119879043   525  .000228341           R-squared     =  0.9988
-------------+------------------------------           Adj R-squared =  0.9988
       Total |  101.649077   527  .192882498           Root MSE      =  .01511

------------------------------------------------------------------------------
       log_c |      Coef.   Std. Err.      t    P>|t|     [95% Conf. Interval]
-------------+----------------------------------------------------------------
       log_y |    1.02573   .0015506   661.51   0.000     1.022684    1.028776
           R |  -.0050635   .0002497   -20.28   0.000     -.005554   -.004573
       _cons |   -.297251   .0128344   -23.16   0.000    -.3224641   -.2720379
------------------------------------------------------------------------------
```

A time plot of the fitting errors from this cointegrating regression equation is actually fairly consistent with these errors being covariance stationary (albeit likely non-gaussian) I(0) noise:

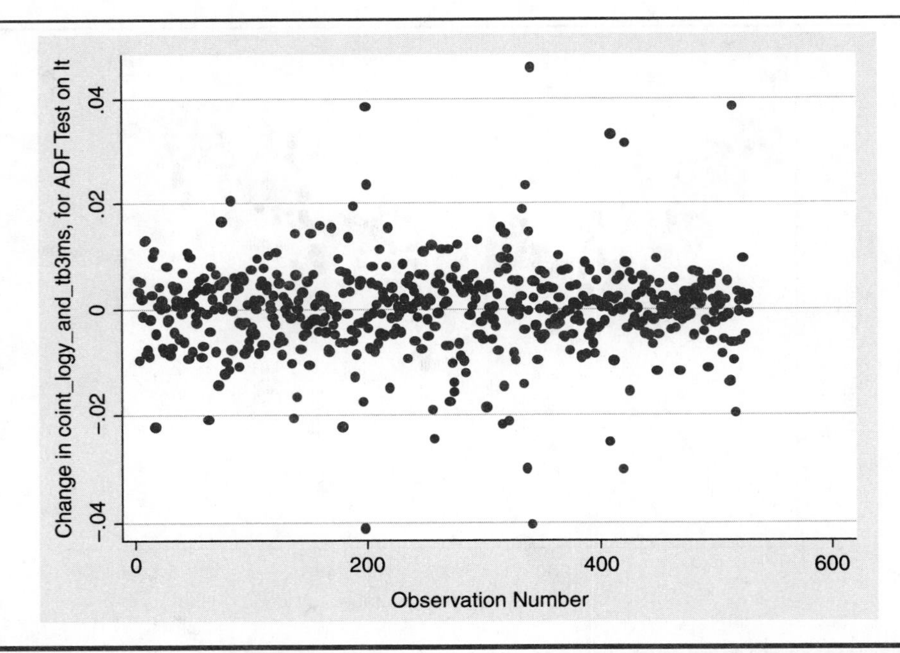

Figure 14-13 Time Plot of Fitting Errors from the Cointegrating Regression Model for $\log(C_t)$ Using $\log(Y_t)$ and R_t

And the estimated Engle-Granger ADF test regression model obtained using the fitting errors – again called "coint_t" – from this cointegrating regression model is:

Source	SS	df	MS
Model	.005673387	4	.001418347
Residual	.031950486	519	.000061562
Total	.037623873	523	.000071939

Number of obs	=	524
F(4, 519)	=	23.04
Prob > F	=	0.0000
R-squared	=	0.1508
Adj R-squared	=	0.1442
Root MSE	=	.00785

chg_coint	Coef.	Std. Err.	t	P>|t|	[95% Conf.	Interval]
coint						
L1.	-.096222	.0249325	-3.86	0.000	-.1452031	-.047241
chg_coint						
L1.	-.2029439	.0446796	-4.54	0.000	-.290719	-.1151688
L2.	-.1837483	.043891	-4.19	0.000	-.269974	-.0975225
L3.	-.2233371	.0426831	-5.23	0.000	-.30719	-.1394842
_cons	-.0000405	.0003428	-0.12	0.906	-.0007139	.0006329

The ADF test statistic here is -3.86, which is less than the 5% critical point (-3.768) in the second line of Table 14-2, so one can reject the null hypothesis that these cointegration equation fitting errors are I(1) at the 5% (although not the 1%) level of significance.[50] Thus, if one rejects the null hypothesis that the cointegrating regression fitting errors are I(1) – and hence accepts the hypothesis that $log(C_t)$, $log(Y_t)$, and R_t are cointegrated – then there is only a 5% chance that this conclusion is simply an artifact of sampling error in the Engle-Granger ADF test regression.

The estimated cointegrating regression model thus indicates that "$coint_t$," defined by the equation:

$$coint_t \equiv log(C_t) - 1.02573\, log(Y_t) + .00506R_t + .29725 \tag{14-15}$$

is an I(0) time-series with zero mean. Equation 14-15 can therefore be interpreted as an estimated long-run relationship between these three time-series. Importantly, the existence of this long-run relationship explains why the time plot in Figure 14-11 shows that $log(C_t)$ does not wander off at random from its trend value: were $log(C_t)$ to do so, then it would depart overmuch from the expected value for it implied by Equation 14-15.

The estimated long-run relationship implied by the cointegration of these three time-series strongly suggests that $coint_{t-1}$, the lagged fitting errors from the cointegration regression model, "belongs" as an explanatory variable in the model for the changes in $log(C_t)$; explanatory variables such as $coint_{t-1}$ are called "error-correction terms." In fact, this interpretation of these fitting errors predicts that $coint_{t-1}$ will enter the model for $\Delta log(C_t)$ with a *negative* coefficient. In this way a value of $log(C_t)$ which is larger than is consistent with the long-run relationship pushes the expected value of $\Delta log(C_t)$ down, tending to bring $log(C_t)$ back in consonance with the long-run relationship. Similarly, a negative coefficient on $coint_{t-1}$ implies that a value of $log(C_t)$ which is smaller than is consistent with the long-run relationship pushes the expected value of $\Delta log(C_t)$ up, again tending to bring $log(C_t)$ back toward the long-run relationship.

Adding $coint_{t-1}$, obtained by lagging Equation 14-15 one month, to the model for $\Delta log(C_t)$ from Section 14.4 yields what is called the "Vector Error-Correction Model" or "VECM" for $\Delta log(C_t)$:

[50] The critical points from the second line of Table 14-2 are appropriate because there are now two variables in the cointegratiag regression model.

```
Linear regression                                   Number of obs =     518
                                                    F( 16,   501) =    4.12
                                                    Prob > F      =  0.0000
                                                    R-squared     =  0.1426
                                                    Root MSE      =  .53939

------------------------------------------------------------------------------
             |               Robust
      c_grow |      Coef.   Std. Err.      t    P>|t|     [95% Conf. Interval]
-------------+----------------------------------------------------------------
      c_grow |
         L1. |  -.2604713   .0645094    -4.04   0.000    -.3872136   -.1337289
         L2. |  -.1056023     .05369    -1.97   0.050    -.2110875   -.0001171
         L3. |   -.018975   .0509884    -0.37   0.710    -.1191525    .0812025
         L4. |  -.0555133   .0550116    -1.01   0.313    -.1635952    .0525686
         L5. |   .0104419   .0475021     0.22   0.826     -.082886    .1037699
         L6. |   .0986703   .0477765     2.07   0.039     .0048033    .1925372
         L7. |   .1321548   .0496522     2.66   0.008     .0346027    .2297069
         L8. |   .1430348   .0460314     3.11   0.002     .0525965    .2334731
         L9. |   .0701342   .0407758     1.72   0.086    -.0099784    .1502467
      y_grow |
         L1. |    .096314   .0409721     2.35   0.019     .0158157    .1768123
         L2. |   .0889683   .0410793     2.17   0.031     .0082595    .1696771
         L3. |   .0825818   .0404227     2.04   0.042     .0031628    .1620008
         L4. |   .0547276     .03912     1.40   0.162    -.0221319    .1315871
         L5. |   .0457399    .032041     1.43   0.154    -.0172113    .1086911
       r_chg |
         L3. |  -.0788944   .0497268    -1.59   0.113    -.1765933    .0188044
       coint |
         L1. |  -7.270745   1.875028    -3.88   0.000    -10.95463   -3.586859
       _cons |   .1804055   .0538372     3.35   0.001      .074631      .28618
------------------------------------------------------------------------------
```

Notice that $coint_{t-1}$ does in fact enter the estimated VECM equation with the expected negative coefficient estimate and that this estimate is significantly different from zero with p-value less than .0005, based on the estimated t ratio of -3.88. As one might expect from the addition of a quite significant additional explanatory variable, R^2 is also a bit larger than for the original model (rising from .113 to .143), but it is still not terribly large.

Interestingly, the addition of the error-correction term involving the lagged level of the short-term interest rate makes the contribution of ΔR_{t-3} notably less significant; one might even drop this explanatory variable from the model. The terms in $\Delta log(C_{t-9})$, $\Delta log(Y_{t-4})$, and $\Delta log(Y_{t-5})$ are probably worth retaining, as these appear to be sensible portions of decaying lag structures. Material in Chapters 17 and 18 on ratios of polynomials in the lag operator will provide ways to model such lag structures with a smaller number of coefficients.

These last two sections – developing two models for the change in $log(C_t)$ – provide both a (minor) modeling triumph and a disturbing warning.

Section 14.4 identified, estimated, and diagnostically checked a model for $\Delta log(C_t)$ which exploits the dynamic relationship between this growth rate and past values of $\Delta log(C_t)$, $\Delta log(Y_t)$, and ΔR_t; this is called the model "in changes." Arguably – at first glance – this model satisfies the assumptions of the Dynamic Multiple Regression Model (Equation 14-3) sufficiently well that the OLS model parameter estimates are, to a reasonable approximation, consistent. Similarly, at first glance, this model satisfies the assumptions of the Dynamic Multiple Regression Model sufficiently well that the asymptotic inference machinery provided by the Central Limit Theorem – analogous to the results obtained explicitly for simple models in Appendices 10.2 and 13.1 – ought to be reasonably valid for large samples. That validity is of practical value because these results are programmed into the usual econometric software.

Note, however, that this model "in changes" is based on an information set consisting of the past values of $\Delta log(C_t)$, $\Delta log(Y_t)$, and ΔR_t. Thus, the consistently estimated coefficients in it are to be interpreted as partial derivatives of the expected value of $\Delta log(C_t)$, holding the past values of $\Delta log(C_t)$, $\Delta log(Y_t)$, and ΔR_t constant and averaging over everything else.

The results in the present section have yielded an alternative model for $\Delta log(C_t)$, in which the inclusion of an error-correction term – based on the realization that $log(C_t)$, $log(Y_t)$, and R_t are in fact cointegrated – provides an improved model for $\Delta log(C_t)$. This model is both statistically and economically richer than the model of Section 14.4. Note, however, that the coefficient estimates in this model are a bit different, and also suggest that the term in ΔR_{t-3} may not even belong in the relationship.

It is not unreasonable that these coefficient estimates in the VECM model are different: they bear a somewhat different interpretation than do those of the Section 14.4 model for $\Delta log(C_t)$: they are still partial derivatives of the expected value of $\Delta log(C_t)$ with respect to the various explanatory variables, but these partial derivatives are now also holding the values of the lagged *levels* variables – $log(C_{t-1})$, $log(Y_{t-1})$, and R_{t-1} – constant. In practice, however, if one knows (i.e., can condition upon) the past values of $\Delta log(C_t)$, $\Delta log(Y_t)$, and R_t, then one would no doubt also know the values of $log(C_{t-1})$, $log(Y_{t-1})$, and R_{t-1} as well, but (in any case) it is now this wider set of variables which is empirically relevant.

It is the set of estimates produced in the present section which are consistent for the coefficients of real interest. One could therefore conclude that the Section 14.4 "changes" model for $\Delta log(C_t)$, which failed to include the error-correction term, is misspecified with respect to the empirically relevant (wider) set of variables and hence yielded inconsistent estimates of the parameters we actually care about. Put another way: while the Section 14.4 model apparently satisfied the assumptions of the Dynamic Multiple Regression Model, it in fact did *not* satisfy the model equation portion of Equation 14-3, because it wrongly omitted the error-correction term. Thus, while the VECM model for $\Delta log(C_t)$ developed in the present section represents progress toward a better, richer description of the mechanism generating $\Delta log(C_t)$, it also provides the sobering insight that the model developed and estimated in Section 14.4 was actually inadequate.

The next section examines a third (and final!) strategy for modeling the monthly data on U.S. consumption expenditures using past data on disposable income and a short-term interest rate. This time the model will be "in levels": the level $log(C_t)$ will be modeled in terms of past values of the levels of $log(C_t)$, $log(Y_t)$, and R_t.

14.6 CAPSTONE EXAMPLE PART 3: MODELING THE LEVEL OF MONTHLY U.S. CONSUMPTION EXPENDITURES

One of the lessons of Sections 14.4 and 14.5 is that, once the set of explanatory variables – in this case, past values of $log(C_t)$, $log(Y_t)$, and R_t – is decided upon, modeling the change in the logarithm of consumption expenditures is reasonably straightforward. Certainly, it is not all that difficult to include enough past values of the changes in the explanatory variables – i.e., $\Delta log(C_t)$, $\Delta log(Y_t)$, and ΔR_t – in the model, nor is it that difficult to (at least approximately) diagnostically check the model with respect to possible heteroscedasticity, nonlinearities, and structural shifts. Broadening the model, in Section 14.5, to account for possible cointegration posed a few additional challenges – one could clearly choose the wrong form of cointegration if one failed to plot the error-correction term and appropriately test for cointegration – but the modeling process still seems feasible enough.

Moreover, it is intuitively appealing to formulate all of the non-dummy variables in a model as I(0) time-series if one is modeling the sample behavior of a dependent variable as a linear function of past values of explanatory variables (plus an error term) and estimating the model coefficients by minimizing the sum of the squared fitting errors. In particular, since the sum of squared fitting errors is proportional to the sample variance of the fitting errors, it seems appropriate that all the other terms in the equation should have well-defined (bounded) population variances, which would not be the case for I(1) time-series.

That all argues for modeling $\Delta log(C_t)$ – i.e., for modeling "in changes," perhaps with a cointegration-based error-correction term. That would seem to be preferable to modeling "in levels," in which case the dependent variable $log(C_t)$ would be expressed solely in terms of level variables, such as past values of $log(C_t)$, $log(Y_t)$, and R_t.

On the other hand, looking closely at Equation 14-3, it is apparent that the model "in levels" actually subsumes both the model "in changes" and the Vector Error-Correction Model (VECM) as special cases. For example, the particular model

$$\Delta log(C_t) = .3\Delta log(C_{t-1}) + .2\Delta log(Y_{t-1}) + .1[log(C_{t-1}) - .8\, log(Y_{t-1})] + U_t \tag{14-16}$$

is actually equivalent to the model

$$\begin{aligned} log(C_t) &= 1.3\, log(C_{t-1}) - .3\, log(C_{t-2}) + .2\, log(Y_{t-1}) - .2\, log(Y_{t-2}) \\ &\quad + .1[log(C_{t-1}) - .8\, log(Y_{t-1})] + U_t \\ &= 1.4\, log(C_{t-1}) - .3\, log(C_{t-2}) + .12\, log(Y_{t-1}) - .2\, log(Y_{t-2}) + U_t \end{aligned} \tag{14-17}$$

Thus, using the "levels" model, one does not need to worry about the existence or form of cointegration. Nor, in using the "levels" model, need one be concerned that $log(C_t)$ might already be I(0), so that $\Delta log(C_t)$ is an "overdifference": so long as sufficient lags are included in the "levels" model, the coefficient estimation procedure itself allows the fit to the data to determine all of the necessary dynamics.

The danger of overdifferencing the dependent variable deserves a bit more comment. The discussion of the Augmented Dickey Fuller (ADF) test in Section 14.3 already made it clear that there is a substantial risk that the ADF test will wrongly fail to reject the I(1) null hypothesis for any time-series which is highly autocorrelated. The result is that one can easily be misled into overdifferencing a dependent variable.

It will shortly become apparent that the change in a covariance stationary time-series – an "overdifferenced time-series" – has awkward statistical properties. But it is still covariance stationary, with a well-defined, bounded variance.[51] For example, consider the time-series Z_t which would result from overdifferencing Y_t, a zero-mean, covariance stationary time-series generated by an AR(1) Model:

$$\begin{gathered} Z_t \equiv Y_t - Y_{t-1} \\ Y_t = \varphi_1 Y_{t-1} + U_t \qquad |\varphi_1| < 1 \qquad U_t \sim \mathrm{IID}[0,\, \sigma_u^2] \end{gathered} \tag{14-18}$$

Using the MA(∞) expression for Y_t (Equation 13-17) it is not difficult to express Z_t in MA(∞) form – as a weighted sum of the current and past values of the error series, U_t, with declining weights on error terms farther and farther in the past:

$$\begin{aligned} Z_t &= U_t + (\varphi_1 - 1)U_{t-1} + (\varphi_1 - 1)\varphi_1 U_{t-2} + (\varphi_1 - 1)(\varphi_1)^2 U_{t-3} \\ &\quad + (\varphi_1 - 1)(\varphi_1)^3 U_{t-4} + (\varphi_1 - 1)(\varphi_1)^4 U_{t-5} \ldots \end{aligned} \tag{14-19}$$

[51] Recall that a covariance stationary time-series X_t has a mean, variance, and autocovariances which are bounded and do not vary over time. Hence, covariance stationarity implies that a time-series is I(0). The converse is not true, however: X_t could be I(0) – i.e., not require differencing in order to have a bounded variance – yet X_t still might not be covariance stationary, because one or more of its mean, variance, or autocovariances varies over time. These aspects of covariance stationarity are emphasized when this concept is discussed in Section 17.3.

This result (derived in Exercise 14-9) implies that the variance of Z_t in this case equals $2\sigma_u^2(1 + \varphi_1)$, which is clearly bounded.

However, if Z_t is overdifferenced – as it is, by construction, in Equation 14-18 – it is no longer possible to sensibly express Z_t in terms of its own past, as an autoregressive model with eventually declining weights on values of Z_t farther and farther in the past. The algebra for converting Equation 14-19 into an autoregressive representation for Z_t is actually quite easy, but will not be covered until Section 17.4, so this result is only quoted here:

$$Z_t = (\varphi_1 - 1)Z_{t-1} + (\varphi_1 - 1)Z_{t-2} + (\varphi_1 - 1)Z_{t-3} + (\varphi_1 - 1)Z_{t-4} + \ldots + U_t \qquad (14\text{-}20)$$

Note that, because the coefficient on Z_{t-j} in Equation 14-20 does not eventually decay in magnitude as the lag j increases, a times series Z_t generated by Equation 14-18 cannot be approximated by an AR(p) Model for any finite value of p. Thus, effectively, the expected value of an overdifferenced time-series like Z_t cannot be predicted from its own past.[52]

Of course, if an inadvertently overdifferenced time-series (such as Z_t above) is the dependent variable in a Dynamic Multiple Regression Model, then one will not *have* to forecast it solely from its own past: even if prediction (as well as parameter inference) is a modeling objective, then the estimated Dynamic Multiple Regression Model will be used for this purpose. But it is reasonable to expect that such a dependent variable might well lead to a problematic Dynamic Multiple Regression Model also.[53] Moreover, one might well want to compare the performance of this model to that of a simple autoregressive model for Z_t, which we have just seen is problematic if Z_t is an overdifferenced time-series. Also, if an overdifferenced variable like Z_t is an explanatory variable in the Dynamic Multiple Regression Model, then one might need to forecast its future values using an autoregressive model in order to utilize the Dynamic Multiple Regression Model to project more than one period into the future. Thus, if the model "in changes" has inadvertently overdifferenced either the dependent or explanatory variables, then – while the resulting time-series are still covariance stationary and still have bounded variances – their dynamics are distorted in a way which is, at best, disturbing.

In summary, then, the model "in levels" has the important advantage that it subsumes both the model "in changes" and the Vector Error-Correction Model as special cases. Thus, in particular, it

[52] One can still estimate AR(p) models for Z_t, but these are all badly misspecified, in view of Equation 14-20. Consequently, the OLS parameter estimators in such models cannot be consistent and one can hardly recommend that anyone knowingly do this. (Overdifferenced panel-data models are routinely estimated, however; this topic is discussed in Section 16.2. In that context, a transformation due to Arellano and Bover (1995, equations 24 and 25) effectively eliminates the non-invertible serial correlation induced by the overdifference. This approach is clearly appropriate in the panel-data context, where the time-series are short; its usefulness in the context of the time-series models discussed in the present chapter – e.g., for Z_t in Equation 14-18 – is a research topic under current investigation.) The MA(∞) representation of Z_t – Equation 14-19 – is awkward also, even though it does have eventually declining weights; such moving average models are called "non-invertible" and will be discussed in Section 17.5. The advanced reader – who has already read Chapter 17! – might note that Z_t equals $(1 - B)(1 - \varphi_1 B)^{-1} U_t$, where B is the lag operator. (That is, $B^j X_t = X_{t-j}$.) Thus, formally, $(1 - B)^{-1}(1 - \varphi_1 B)Z_t$ equals U_t, which yields the formal AR(∞) representation of Z_t given in Equation 14-20. But even though it is easily confirmed that $(1-B)$ times $(1 + B + B^2 + B^3 + \ldots)$ equals one, the lag structure $(1 + B + B^2 + B^3 + \ldots)$ does not provide an actual inverse for $(1-B)$, because it does not have weights on B^j which eventually decline in magnitude.

[53] And it does. This topic will (almost) recur in Section 18.4 when "vector autoregressive" (VAR) models are briefly discussed, as such models are frequently analyzed in terms of their the impulse response functions. (The impulse response function is essentially an MA(∞) form of the model.) Simulations reported in Ashley and Verbrugge (2009) show that estimated impulse response functions for overdifferenced bivariate VAR models are highly distorted, even for very large samples. Might this be correctable using the Arellano/Bover GLS transformation alluded to in the previous footnote? The answer to that question, as noted in the previous footnote, is not yet known. Ashley, R., and R. Verbrugge (2009) "To Difference or Not to Difference: A Monte Carlo Investigation of Inference in Vector Autoregression Models." *International Journal of Data Analysis Techniques and Strategies (13):* 242-274, available at ashleymac.econ.vt.edu/working_papers/varsim.pdf.

eliminates the danger of failing to correctly specify a cointegrating error-correction term. Moreover, it also eliminates the possibility of having overdifferenced the model.

The model "in levels" does have one major defect, however: the explanatory variables in this model are usually I(1) time-series. But such I(1) time-series have unbounded variances, which violates a crucial assumption of Equation 14-3, which defines the Dynamic Multiple Regression Model. Consequently, while the OLS parameter estimators for the model are still consistent, they are not, in general, asymptotically normally distributed. Moreover, the asymptotic standard error results provided for these parameter estimators by the Central Limit Theorem – and implemented in econometric software – are not valid either. Since valid statistical inference on the model coefficients is a major – in many cases, the sole – reason for constructing the model, this would seem to be an overwhelming defect for the model "in levels."

This drawback of the "levels" model can be overcome, however. Sims, Stock, and Watson (1990) showed that there are two circumstances in which the usual asymptotic sampling distribution result for an OLS-estimated coefficient in a model like the Dynamic Multiple Regression Model is still valid, even when some or all of the explanatory variables are I(1) series.[54]

The first circumstance is when the coefficient multiplies an explanatory variable which is also part of a cointegrating relationship. Thus, in the U.S. monthly consumption model used as an example in the previous two sections, the Sims-Stock-Watson (1990) result indicates that the usual asymptotic sampling distribution results still obtain for the OLS coefficient estimators in the "levels" model, even though the lagged values of $log(C_t)$, $log(Y_t)$, and R_t are all I(1) series, because each of these variables appears in the cointegrating relationship, Equation 14-15. That result is potentially useful for this particular model, if one cares to rely on the validity of the cointegration finding. But it is not useful in general. For one thing, it is not typically the case that all of the explanatory variables in the "levels" model appear in a cointegrating relationship. Moreover, part of the appeal of the "levels" model is that it avoids the problem of determining which (if any) of the variables are cointegrated, along with the attendant possibility of erring in this determination.

The second circumstance seems unimportant at first glance, but it actually yields a reasonably general solution to the problem. The Sims-Stock-Watson (1990) result also indicates that the usual asymptotic sampling distribution results still obtain for the OLS estimators of coefficients on any explanatory variables which are I(0). This result initially appears irrelevant, since the entire problem is that some or all of the explanatory variables in the "levels" model are I(1) series. However, a simple rearrangement of the "levels" model – first suggested by Toda and Yamamoto (1995)[55] – can be used to *create* I(0) explanatory variables, whose estimated coefficients can then be used to test hypotheses with regard to the parameters on the original explanatory variables. The cost is that one additional coefficient must be estimated for each lag structure in the model, slightly increasing the parameter sampling variances and thus reducing the efficiency of the OLS estimators somewhat. This efficiency reduction ought to be negligible, however, if the sample is sufficiently large for it to be reasonable to be using an asymptotic sampling distribution in the first place.

The Toda-Yamamoto rearrangement yields what they call a "lag-augmented" model. Their rearrangement is explained below using a simple example, then this example will be used to illustrate

[54] Sims, C. A., J. H. Stock, and M. W. Watson (1990), "Inference in Linear Times Series Models with Some Unit Roots" *Econometrica 58(1),* 113–44.

[55] Yamada and Toda (1998, pp. 58–59) provide a clearer exposition. Toda and Yamamoto proposed their method for application to "Vector Autoregression" or VAR models, which are a bit different from the Dynamic Multiple Regression Model considered here – see Section 18.4. But the essential idea is the same, so it will nevertheless be referred to here as the "lag augmented" model here. Toda, H. Y., and T. Yamamoto (1995), "Statistical Inference in Vector Autoregressions with Possibly Integrated Processes," *J. Econometrics 66,* 225–50. Yamada, H., and H. Y. Toda (1998), "Inference in Possibly Integrated Vector Autoregressive Models: Some Finite Sample Evidence." *Journal of Econometrics 86,* 55–95.

the even simpler way that this idea will be applied here. Consider the following special case of the Dynamic Multiple Regression Model, where the second subscript on the coefficients and on the explanatory variable has been omitted because there is only one explanatory variable in this model:

$$Y_t = \beta_1 X_{t-1} + \beta_2 X_{t-2} + \beta_3 X_{t-3} + U_t \tag{14-21}$$

And suppose that X_t is an I(1) time-series, so that $\Delta X_t = X_t - X_{t-1}$ is an I(0) series. Now note that Equation 14-21 can be re-expressed as

$$Y_t = \beta_1 \Delta X_{t-1} + (\beta_1 + \beta_2)\Delta X_{t-2} + (\beta_1 + \beta_2 + \beta_3)\Delta X_{t-3} + (\beta_1 + \beta_2 + \beta_3)X_{t-4} + U_t \tag{14-22}$$

since, on substituting $\Delta X_{t-1} = X_{t-1} - X_{t-2}, \Delta X_{t-2} = X_{t-2} - X_{t-3}$, and $\Delta X_{t-3} = X_{t-3} - X_{t-4}$ into Equation 14-22, everything cancels except for the terms in Equation 14-21. Thus, if one estimates $\lambda_1, \lambda_2, \lambda_3,$ and λ_4 in the model,

$$Y_t = \lambda_1 \Delta X_{t-1} + \lambda_2 \Delta X_{t-2} + \lambda_3 \Delta X_{t-3} + \lambda_4 X_{t-4} + U_t \tag{14-23}$$

then $\hat{\lambda}_1^{ols}, \hat{\lambda}_2^{ols}, \hat{\lambda}_3^{ols}$, and $\hat{\lambda}_4^{ols}$ are consistent estimators of $\beta_1, \beta_1 + \beta_2, \beta_1 + \beta_2 + \beta_3$, and $\beta_1 + \beta_2 + \beta_3$, respectively. Moreover, since λ_1, λ_2, and λ_3 are – by construction – coefficients on I(0) variables, the Sims-Stock-Watson (1990) result implies that the usual asymptotic sampling distribution results apply to the estimators $\hat{\lambda}_1^{ols}, \hat{\lambda}_2^{ols}$, and $\hat{\lambda}_3^{ols}$.

Thus, if one wanted to test whether or not the β_3 in Equation 14-21 is zero, one could estimate the "lag augmented" model of Equation 14-23 and use the usual regression results to test the null hypothesis that $\lambda_3 - \lambda_2$ is zero.[56]

Alternatively – and equivalently – one could replace only X_{t-3} in Equation 14-21 (by ΔX_{t-3} and X_{t-4}) and simply test the null hypothesis that the coefficient on ΔX_{t-3} is zero. This is the way the "lag augmented" regression idea is used below.[57]

Returning, then, to the example of modeling the monthly U.S. consumption data, one's initial "levels" model – using the "begin large" (LSE) approach described in Section 14.4 – might consist of a model for $log(C_t)$ which uses one through 12 lags in each explanatory variable: $log(C_t)$, $log(Y_t)$, R_t, and $(volcker_t R_t)$, where the lags in $(volcker_t R_t)$ are included so as to allow at the outset for the possibility that each coefficient on the interest rate is different for the Volcker period. Since each of these explanatory variables is likely I(1), the term at lag 12 is replaced by the corresponding term in the change of the variable at lag 12 plus an additional term in the level of the variable at lag 13. For example, the explanatory variable $log(Y_{t-12})$ is replaced by the pair of explanatory variables, $\Delta log(Y_{t-12})$ and $log(Y_{t-13})$; the significance of the coefficient on $log(Y_{t-12})$ is then obtained from a hypothesis test with respect to the coefficient on I(0) variable, $\Delta log(Y_{t-12})$. In addition, since the levels variables might be trended, a linear time trend is included in the model. Note that estimation of this model requires estimation of just five additional coefficients: one at the end of each lag structure and the coefficient on the time trend.[58]

Because heteroscedastic errors would seem likely to be an issue – due to the change in the apparent variance of ΔR_t in the Volcker subperiod – the model is estimated both with and

[56] For example, in Stata, the syntax for this would merely be "test chg_x3 – chg_x2 = 0", where chg_x3 is the name for ΔX_{t-3} and chg_x2 is the name for ΔX_{t-2}.

[57] See Exercise 14-10.

[58] In addition, of course, one loses one observation at the beginning of the sample, since the lag structures now go back one more month because of the lag-augmentation. If the loss of six degrees of freedom is an important issue, then the sample is not large enough for the use of asymptotic standard error estimates in the first place.

without White-Eicker robust standard error estimates.[59] The coefficient on each of the four explanatory variables at lag 12 is then tested for statistical significance, using the estimated t-ratio on the "change" variable at that lag. None turns out to be significantly different from zero, so the analogous model with 11 lags is estimated and the coefficient on each "change" variable at lag 11 is similarly tested. And so forth. In this way, the model specification is successively "pared down."

With the exception of a single, isolated coefficient – on the change in the interest rate in the model with 10 lags – it quickly becomes apparent that almost all of these coefficients at larger lags are insignificant: i.e., the original model specification was overly complex. Such over-parameterization is not problematic for the models "in changes" because the sample variation in the changes of the various explanatory variables is very distinct. For these "levels" models, in contrast, the explanatory variables (the time trend, lags in $log(C_t)$ and $log(Y_t)$, and lags in R_t and $volcker\_R_t$) all tend to be somewhat similar in their sample variation, yielding a degree of the "multicollinearity" problem described in Section 9.8. Recall that symptoms of multicollinearity frequently include standard error estimates on individual coefficients which are at least somewhat inflated and also often include a relatively high sensitivity of the coefficient estimates to minor changes in either the list of explanatory variables included or in the sample period. (The latter is relevant because inclusion of an additional lag in the model causes the sample period to begin one period later.) Because of this tendency toward multicollinearity problems, regression estimation simply does not "work" as well for the (very serially dependent) explanatory variables in the "levels" formulation as it does for the variables in the "changes" formulation, particularly in overly complex models. This problem improves as one drops variables and/or pares the number of lags down, but it is an inherent difficulty in applying the LSE approach to the model in "levels" form.

An argument could be made for simply comparing the Schwarz Criterion (BIC) value for the model with 11 lags to that of the model with 12 lags – and so forth.[60] The t statistics (and the p-values based on them) for the individual coefficients at the largest lags are more informative, however, because they are specific to each lag structure, rather than evaluating the model as a whole. BIC comparisons are most useful once one has already narrowed the field substantially, in helping one decide between two particular model specifications. This is especially the case where the two models being compared are "non-nested" – that is, where neither model is a special case of the other because each model includes an explanatory variable not used in the other. Indeed, in that case there is no simple hypothesis to test which distinguishes between the two models.

Note, however, that while the BIC statistic explicitly accounts for the number of coefficients estimated in each model, it makes no allowance for the fact that a real lag structure is unlikely to have a gap in it. That is, if lags two through four and lags seven through nine are in a lag structure, it is hardly likely that the coefficients corresponding to lags five and six are actually zero, even if they are small in magnitude.[61] Also, importantly, the BIC statistic makes no allowance for the number other models previously looked at in whatever specification search has yielded each model. Postsample forecasting effectiveness comparisons are more informative in this regard, but must be used sparingly; such postsample comparisons are discussed in Section 18.5.

Returning to the particular model at hand, the specification search process described above ended with a model including just two lags in $log(C_t)$ and one lag in $log(Y_t)$:

---

[59] It is so quick and easy to do the estimation both ways in Stata – by merely appending the "robust" option – that one need not be highly motivated to do so. Robust standard error estimates are reported later.

[60] The Schwarz Criterion (SC or BIC, defined in Section 9.5) equals $\ln(SSE/T) + k\ \ln(T)/T$, where k is the number of parameters estimated, so a smaller value indicates a better model; Stata computes the BIC statistic if one specifies the "estat ic" postestimation command.

[61] This reasoning would not apply if the gap was between, say, the term at lag nine and the term at lag 12, since (with monthly data) the term at lag 12 has a separate interpretation as a seasonal (annual) relationship.

```
Linear regression                               Number of obs =      525
                                                F(  6,    518) =        .
                                                Prob > F      =   0.0000
                                                R-squared     =   0.9998
                                                Root MSE      =   .00561
```

log_c	Coef.	Robust Std. Err.	t	P>|t|	[95% Conf.	Interval]
obsnum	.0000473	.0000199	2.37	0.018	8.10e-06	.0000864
log_c L1.	.7663471	.0644582	11.89	0.000	.6397154	.8929787
log_c_chg L2.	.1619228	.0687926	2.35	0.019	.026776	.2970697
log_c L3.	.194716	.0630622	3.09	0.002	.0708268	.3186051
log_y_chg L1.	.0991781	.0355907	2.79	0.006	.0292583	.1690979
log_y L2.	.0225737	.0130544	1.73	0.084	-.0030724	.0482197
_cons	.1233198	.0519722	2.37	0.018	.0212176	.225422

Note that the notation $L1.log\_c_t$ stands for $\log(C_{t-1})$ and that $L2.log\_c\_chg$ stands for $\Delta log(C_{t-2})$ or, equivalently, $log(C_{t-2}) - log(C_{t-3})$. Clearly, $100\Delta log(C_{t-2})$ is equivalent to the lagged growth. rate, c_grow_{t-2}, used in Section 14.4. Similarly, $L1.log\_y_t$ stands for $log(Y_{t-1})$ and $L1.log\_y\_chg_t$ stands for $\Delta log(Y_{t-1})$, which equals $log(Y_{t-1}) - log(Y_{t-2})$.

Per the "lag augmentation" argument of Equations 14-21 through 14-23, the population coefficients on $L2.log\_c\_chg_t$ and $L3.log\_c_t\_chg_t$ in this model should be equal to each other.[62] Because $\Delta log(C_{t-2})$ is arguably an I(0) time-series, the estimated standard error for the estimator of the coefficient on it (i.e., on $L2.log\_c\_chg_t$) in the estimated regression model quoted above – and the consequent t ratio, p-value, and 95% confidence intervals – are all asymptotically valid. In contrast, the analogous estimates with regard to $L3.log\_c_t$ – or with regard to $L2.log\_c_t$ in a model without lag augmentation – would all be distorted by the fact that these lagged values of $log(C_t)$ are all I(1) time-series. Note that the coefficient estimators on $L2.log\_c\_chg_t$ and $L3.log\_c_t$ are both consistent estimators and their sample realizations here (.1619228 and .194716) are essentially equivalent, given that the (asymptotically valid) estimated standard error on the $L2.log\_c\_chg_t$ coefficient estimate is .069.

At first glance, this model appears to be worth diagnostically checking. In view of the significance of ΔR_{t-3} in the model "in changes," however, it seems prudent to first consider reintroducing a few terms in lagged R_t and $volcker_t R_t$ into the model, now that the model specification with regard to lags in $log(C_t)$ and $log(Y_t)$ has stabilized. Therefore, R_{t-j} and $volcker_{t-j}R_{t-j}$ are next reincluded in the model: first for lag j equal to one, then for j equal to one and two, then for j equal to one through three, and then for j equal to one through four. The coefficient on ΔR_{t-j} is significantly different from zero in none of the resulting estimated lag-augmented models. Dropping the term in $\Delta volcker_t R_t$ from the process and repeating this sequence of model estimations yields similar results. However, because the final specification of the model "in changes" had omitted both ΔR_t at lags one and two and included only ΔR_{t-3}, two additional lag-augmented models are next considered: one including ΔR_{t-3} (and R_{t-4}) and another including both of these variables and

[62] And both of these population coefficients should be equal to the sum of the coefficients on $L1.log\_c_t$ and $L2.log\_c_t$ in a model using only these two variables, and which does not use lag augmentation.

also both $\Delta(volcker_{t-3}R_{t-3})$ and $volcker_{t-4}R_{t-4}$. The coefficient on $\Delta(volcker_{t-3}R_{t-3})$ in the latter model is tiny and not statistically significant, but the model including ΔR_{t-3} and R_{t-4} appears to be an improvement:

```
Linear regression                                   Number of obs =        524
                                                    F(  8,   515) =          .
                                                    Prob > F      =     0.0000
                                                    R-squared     =     0.9998
                                                    Root MSE      =     .00545

------------------------------------------------------------------------------
             |               Robust
       log_c |      Coef.   Std. Err.      t    P>|t|     [95% Conf. Interval]
-------------+----------------------------------------------------------------
      obsnum |   .0000423   .0000196     2.16   0.031     3.80e-06    .0000808
       log_c |
         L1. |   .6936218   .0643856    10.77   0.000     .5671312    .8201124
   log_c_chg |
         L2. |   .1426901   .0662827     2.15   0.032     .0124723    .2729078
       log_c |
         L3. |   .2042749   .0602092     3.39   0.001      .085989    .3225609
   log_y_chg |
         L1. |   .1242831   .0384584     3.23   0.001     .0487285    .1998378
       log_y |
         L2. |   .0895051   .0190183     4.71   0.000     .0521421     .126868
       r_chg |
         L3. |  -.0009263   .0004645    -1.99   0.047    -.0018389   -.0000137
     r_level |
         L4. |   -.000734     .00014    -5.24   0.000    -.0010091   -.0004589
       _cons |   .0906091   .0523089     1.73   0.084    -.0121558    .1933741
------------------------------------------------------------------------------
```

In particular, note that the estimated coefficient on $L3.r\_chg_t$ (i.e., on ΔR_{t-3}) is negative and that the null hypothesis that this coefficient is zero can be rejected with a p-value of .047. This estimated regression equation also has a smaller Schwarz Criterion (BIC) value than the model omitting ΔR_{t-3} and R_{t-4}. Thus, this model appears to be worth diagnostically checking. Note, however, that this interest rate term – corresponding to the "Pigou" effect" in macroeconomic theory – would most likely have been missed altogether, were it not for the fact that the model "in changes" had suggested that the interest rate affects consumption with a three-month lag.[63]

Table 14-3 summarizes the diagnostic checking of a model such as this. There is nothing really new in this summary. In fact, the alert reader will recognize these steps as essentially identical to what was done for the model "in changes" at the end of Section 14.4 and in Section 14.5, the main difference being that one does not need to either search or test for possible cointegration in the specification of a model "in levels."

The remainder of this section runs through these diagnostic checks for the model developed above for $\log(C_t)$. It is probably worth noting explicitly at this point that none of these diagnostic checks needs to be lengthy or difficult. How much time and attention is optimal or reasonable to devote to the analysis of each depends partly on how well (or poorly) the checks turn out. It also depends quite a bit on how important optimizing the quality of this particular model is and, concomitantly, how much time and energy are available for the task. Without a doubt, the worst possible approach is to

[63] The estimated coefficients on $L3.r\_chg_t$ and $L4.r\_level_t$ are – as one should expect, from the lag augmentation setup – not significantly different from each other, using the (asymptotically valid) standard error estimate on the $L3.r\_chg_t$ coefficient.

Table 14-3 Summary of Diagnostic Checking for a Time-Series Model "in Levels"[64]

Object	Technique	Notes
1. Normality	Histogram of u_t^{fit}	For outlier detection also; alternatively, compare the OLS and robust (LAD) regression results.
2. Outliers	Time Plot of u_t^{fit}	Can detect outliers, heteroscedasticity, and parameter instability.
	Scatterplots on Key Bivariate Relationships	Beware of using these for anything beyond outlier detection in multivariate contexts!
	LAD or "Robust" Regression	See Sections 5.5 and 10.3.
3. Homoscedasticity	Time Plot of u_t^{fit}	Can detect outliers and parameter instability also.
	$(u_t^{fit})^2$ Regression	Detects heteroscedasticity and can suggest model respecification.
	Robust Standard Errors	"Fixes" standard error estimates.
4. Non-Autocorrelation	AR(p) Model for u_t^{fit}	Can suggest model dynamics respecification.
5. Nonlinearity	Include Squared Terms	Simple approach; roughly allows for nonlinearity also.
	Test for nonlinear serial dependence	These tests and a selection of non-linear models are discussed in Chapter 18.
6. Parameter Stability	Dummy Variables on Intercept Dummy Variables on Key Coefficients	Simple, albeit low-resolution approach; allows for parameter instability also.
7. Out-of-sample Forecasting	Use estimated model to forecast in post-sample period.	Forecast theory and its use in model evaluation is covered in Chapter 18.

build the diagnostic checking up into an insurmountable task and then abandon it altogether: a happy medium that one is willing to actually do (and think about constructively) is the optimum.

That said, the first step is always to save the model fitting errors under some name that one will recognize more than a few minutes later. The fitting errors from the model developed above for log (C_t) using two lags in $\log(C_t)$, one lag in $\log(Y_t)$, and a term in R_{t-3} are denoted "$logc\_resids_t$" below.[65]

[64] A model "in changes" would need to also consider the issue of whether the level of the dependent variable is really I(1) and the possibility of cointegration – see Sections 14.3 and 14.5. In diagnostic check #7, the out-of-sample data used in checking a cross-sectional model would be called a "hold-out" sample rather than a "post-sample period," but the idea – and the utility – of the diagnostic check are essentially identical.

[65] The estimation model quoted above also includes terms in $log(C_{t-3})$, $log(Y_{t-2})$, and R_{t-4} because of the "lag-augmentation" maneuver.

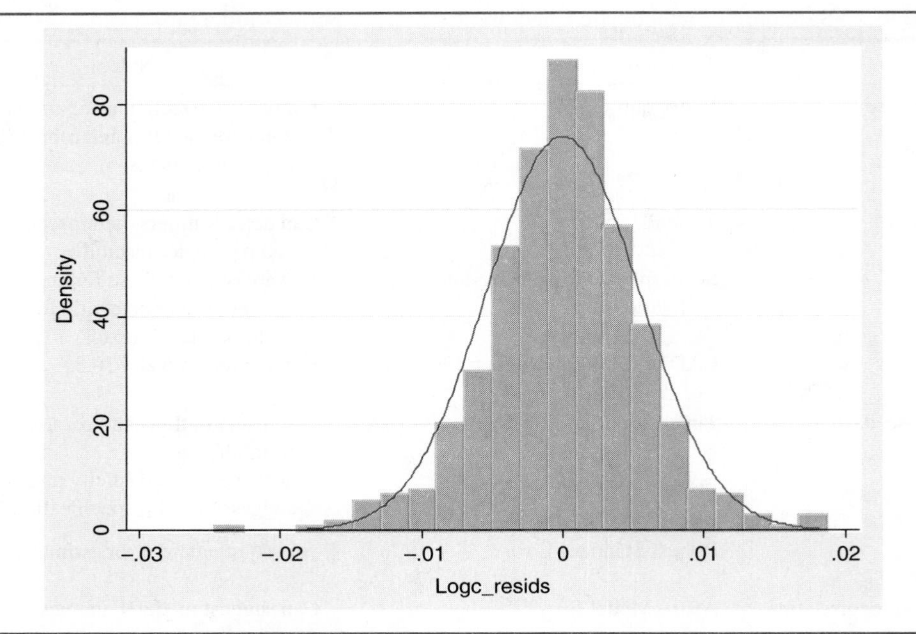

Figure 14-14 Histogram of Log(C_t) Model Fitting Errors

Every econometrics program makes it easy to save regression model fitting errors, although each has a different syntax for doing so.[66]

The first diagnostic check in Table 14-3 is to make the histogram, plotted in Figure 14-14, of these fitting errors. This histogram is produced in Stata using the command "histogram logc_resids, normal" in which the "normal" option specifies that the gaussian density function with population mean and variance equaling the sample mean and variance of $logc\_resids_t$ is plotted also. The distribution of the fitting errors appears to be slightly skewed, with tails a bit thicker than one would expect from perfectly gaussian errors. But these deviations do not appear to be very serious. Recall that the Central Limit Theorem implies that the limiting distributions of the estimator sampling distributions will be gaussian even for substantially non-gaussian model errors, so the modest deviations observed here would be inconsequential even for substantially smaller sample lengths than that available here. Evidence of dramatic departures from normality would have cast doubt on the functional forms chosen – logarithms, here – or might suggest an omitted variable.[67] An outlier in the model errors would have shown up in the histogram also.

Figure 14-15 plots the model fitting errors versus observation number. This plot does not reveal any problem with outliers. Had it done so, one could assess their importance by

[66] In Stata, the command "predict logc_resids$_t$, r" saves the fitting errors, u_t^{fit}, as variable *logc_rez*. Be aware, however, that this variable will be defined for every observation in the data set. The sample period in the present example corresponds to observations number 1 through 528, with the subsequent 80 observations reserved for postsample forecasting. So as to avoid a lot of repeated – and possibly error-prone – "if" statements in subsequent operations, it is therefore efficient and prudent to reset all of these postsample observations on $logc\_resids_t$ to "missing" immediately after this variable is created, using the command "replace logc__resids = . if obsnum > 528".

[67] A bimodal error distribution, for example, could be caused by a failure to account for some sample inhomogeneity – a structural shift in a time-series model such as this, or the presence of two distinct subpopulations in a cross-sectional model.

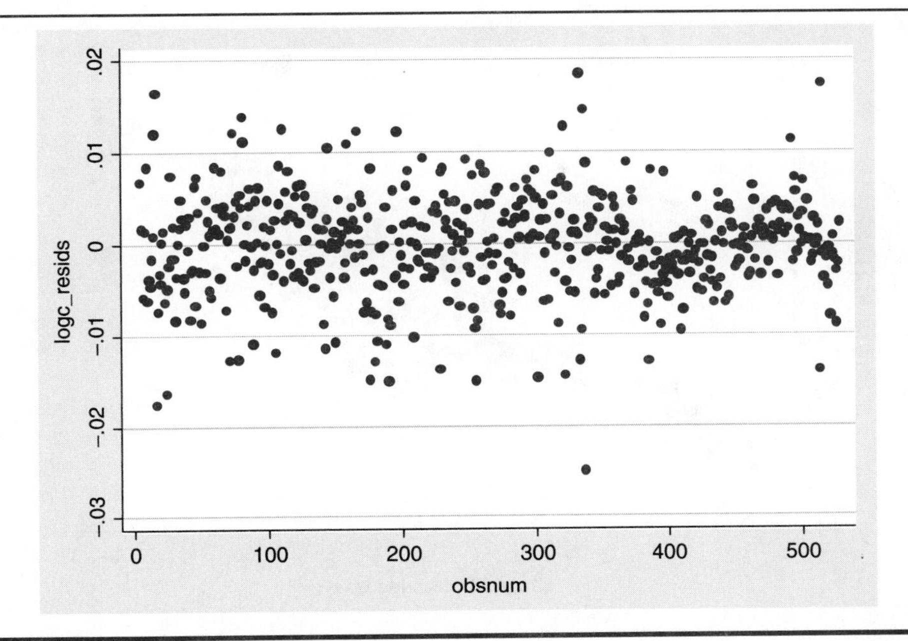

Figure 14-15 Time Plot of Log(C_t) Model Fitting Errors

re-estimating the model using the LAD ("robust regression") method discussed in Section 5.5. Recall that LAD regression minimizes the sum of the absolute values of the fitting errors rather than their squares and hence is less sensitive to outlying observations. LAD estimation is simple and easy using modern econometric software – see the example given in the Section 10.3 discussion of outliers.[68]

But Figure 14-15 does indicate that some heteroscedasticity is likely present in the model errors: the variance of u_t^{fit} appears to be noticeably smaller for observations in the range $400 \leq$ obsnum ≤ 480 or so. Evidently, it is a good idea in this instance to have used the White-Eicker robust standard error estimates in the modeling leading up to this point, even though this period of (apparently) reduced error variance roughly corresponds to the years 1992 to 1998, rather than to the Volcker subperiod which motivated the choice.[69]

Had the time plot become notably smoother {i.e., positively autocorrelated) over some sub-period, then this would point toward a serious instability in the parameters, most likely especially in the parameters $\varphi_1 \ldots \varphi_{Lo}$ on the lagged values of the dependent variable. There is no evidence of that here.

The key economic parameter in this model is clearly the one on $log(Y_{t-1})$, which is estimated in this lag-augmented model as the coefficient on $log\_y\_chg_{t-1}$, $\Delta log(Y_{t-1})$. Recalling that scatterplots can be highly misleading in multivariate contexts such as this one, such a plot is still useful in screening for possible outliers.[70] Plotting $log(C_t)$ against $\Delta log(Y_{t-1})$ is pointless in this setting, because the coefficient on $\Delta log(Y_{t-1})$ makes sense here only if $log(Y_{t-2})$ is being controlled for. And

[68] In Stata, for example, one simply uses the "qreg" command, with the "quantile(.50)" option, instead of the "regress" command.

[69] The Volcker subperiod comprised observations number 248 to 344, which period corresponds to August 1979 to August 1987.

[70] In a multivariate context a change in another explanatory variable can cause the slope of a (necessarily bivariate) scatterplots to shift around; thus, scatterplot are not useful for estimating or assessing the stability of multiple regression coefficients.

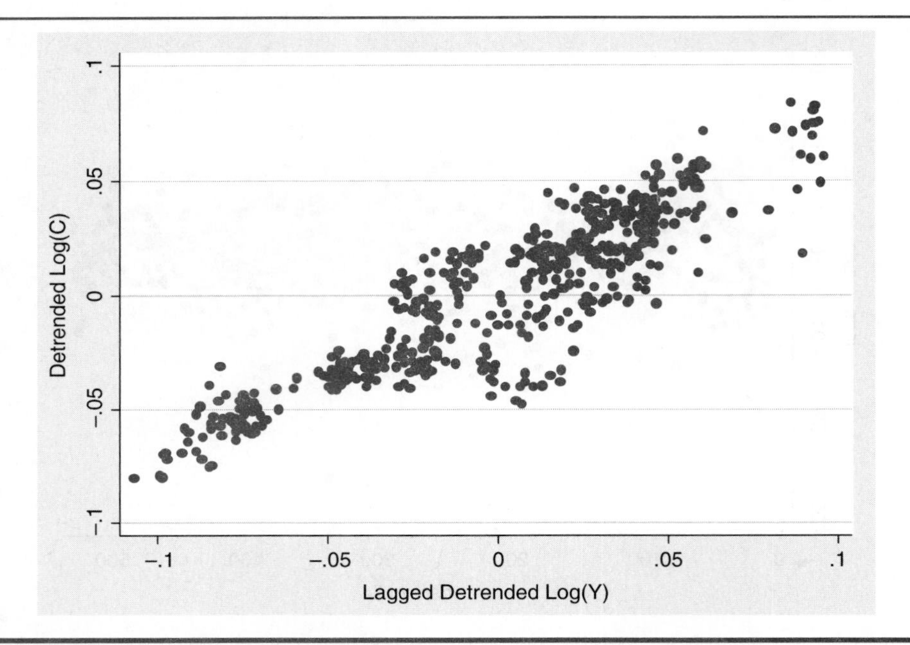

Figure 14-16 Scatterplot of Detrended Log(C_t) versus Detrended Log(Y_{t-1})

a plot of $log(C_t)$ against $log(Y_{t-1})$ is completely dominated by the linear time trends in these two series. One can, however, detrend each of these time-series by fitting it to a linear time trend and sensibly plot the resulting fitting errors from these two trend regressions against each other. As with the time plot of the model fitting errors, such a plot indicates that mild heteroscedasticity might be present, but that there is no reason to think that the significant regression relationship found between $\log(C_t)$ and $\log(Y_{t-1})$ is an artifact due to outliers.

Referring back to Table 14-3, the next aspect of the model to diagnostically check is the homoscedasticity assumption. None of the non-intercept coefficients is significant in a model regressing the squared fitting errors on the explanatory variables in the model. One can also regress the squared fitting errors against the eight dummy variables for each half-decade in the sample period, as in Section 14.4. In this regression equation (as one would expect from Figure 14-15, the time plot of the fitting errors) the coefficients on the dummy variables for the first and second half of the 1990s are both negative and significantly different from zero.[71] White-Eicker heteroscedasticity-robust standard error estimates have already been routinely employed in this particular analysis because of *a priori* concerns about this issue; consequently, this heteroscedasticity in the model errors has already been addressed. In any case, the ordinary standard error estimates in general are not substantially different from the robust standard error estimates for these models.

Because additional lags in all of the variables have already been examined for inclusion in the model, it would seem to be unlikely that there is substantial serial correlation in the model error term. Nevertheless, it is a good idea to check this, by estimating an AR(p) model for the fitting errors. Here a value of p equal to 12 seems clearly sufficient, yielding the estimated model:

[71] See Footnote 14-41 for the definitions of these dummy variables.

```
Linear regression                                      Number of obs =      512
                                                       F( 12,   499) =     1.91
                                                       Prob > F      =   0.0313
                                                       R-squared     =   0.0477
                                                       Root MSE      =   .00528

------------------------------------------------------------------------------
             |               Robust
logc_resids  |      Coef.   Std. Err.      t    P>|t|     [95% Conf. Interval]
-------------+----------------------------------------------------------------
logc_resids  |
         L1. |  -.0436068   .0594682    -0.73   0.464    -.1604457    .0732322
         L2. |  -.0169034    .050796    -0.33   0.739    -.1167038     .082897
         L3. |  -.0005277   .0510501    -0.01   0.992    -.1008273     .099772
         L4. |  -.0357877   .0513793    -0.70   0.486    -.1367341    .0651587
         L5. |   .0505023   .0401246     1.26   0.209    -.0283318    .1293363
         L6. |   .1094025     .04283     2.55   0.011     .0252533    .1935518
         L7. |   .1044651   .0486683     2.15   0.032      .008845    .2000852
         L8. |   .1134613     .04895     2.32   0.021     .0172878    .2096348
         L9. |   .0442289   .0413131     1.07   0.285    -.0369401     .125398
        L10. |  -.0070974   .0416713    -0.17   0.865    -.0889703    .0747755
        L11. |   .0703758   .0497873     1.41   0.158    -.0274429    .1681944
        L12. |   .0095037   .0469482     0.20   0.840    -.0827369    .1017443
       _cons |  -.0000647   .0002334    -0.28   0.782    -.0005233    .0003938
------------------------------------------------------------------------------
```

which, at first glance, appears to have significant terms at lags six, seven, and eight. Testing the null hypothesis that all 12 autoregressive coefficients are zero, this null hypothesis can be rejected with *p*-value equal to .031.[72] Increasing the length of the lag structure in $\log(C_t)$ incrementally out to lag eight does eliminate this feature in the AR(*p*) model of the fitting errors, but it does not appear to yield a better model for $\log(C_t)$ as each of the additional coefficient estimates is statistically insignificant. Thus, the apparently significant coefficients in the AR(*p*) model for the fitting errors do not in this case seem to be meaningful indications of missing linear dynamics in the model for $\log(C_t)$. A result such as this can be caused by nonlinear dynamics which have been incorrectly omitted from the model specification or it can be caused by instability in the intercept or slope parameters – these issues are addressed in the next diagnostic checks. In the present case, however, they are probably just artifacts due to the fact that the model for log (C_t) involves dependent and explanatory variables which are so highly serially dependent.

Referring again to Table 14-3, the next part of the model to check is the assumption that the expected value of $log(C_t)$ is a linear function $log(Y_{t-1})$ and of R_{t-3}. Including the squares of these variables in the model – in a lag-augmented fashion – yields the estimated model:

```
Linear regression                                      Number of obs =      524
                                                       F( 12,   511) =        .
                                                       Prob > F      =   0.0000
                                                       R-squared     =   0.9998
                                                       Root MSE      =   .00543

------------------------------------------------------------------------------
             |               Robust
       log_c |      Coef.   Std. Err.      t    P>|t|     [95% Conf. Interval]
-------------+----------------------------------------------------------------
      obsnum |   .0000433   .0000255     1.70   0.090    -6.75e-06    .0000933
       log_c |
         L1. |   .6735023   .0662151    10.17   0.000      .543415    .8035897
   log_c_chg |
```

[72] One can either test this set of 12 linear restrictions using the Stata "test" command or, equivalently, use the *F* test quoted with the regression results.

L2.	.1465353	.067633	2.17	0.031	.0136624	.2794083
log_c						
L3.	.2096587	.0614266	3.41	0.001	.088979	.3303384
log_y_chg						
L1.	1.758332	.9903075	1.78	0.076	-.1872434	3.703907
log_y						
L2.	.0483704	.0373641	1.29	0.196	-.0250356	.1217765
r_chg						
L3.	-.0011654	.0017039	-0.68	0.494	-.0045129	.0021821
r_level						
L4.	.0000829	.0004161	0.20	0.842	-.0007347	.0009004
chg_sqr_log_y						
L1.	-.0964882	.0580733	-1.66	0.097	-.2105801	.0176036
sqr_log_y						
L2.	.0033755	.0029659	1.14	0.256	-.0024514	.0092023
chg_sqr_r						
L3.	7.54e-06	.0000802	0.09	0.925	-.0001501	.0001652
sqr_r						
L4.	-.000049	.0000251	-1.96	0.051	-.0000983	2.33e-07
_cons	.3164958	.1795915	1.76	0.079	-.0363327	.6693244

Here $L1.chg\_sqr\_log\_y_t$ is the variable name given to $[log(Y_{t-1})]^2 - [log(Y_{t-2})]^2$ and $L2.sqr\_log\_y_t$ is the variable name given to $[log(Y_{t-2})]^2$. Per the argument for lag augmentation given earlier in this section, when $[log(Y_{t-1})]^2$ – i.e., *L1.sqr_log_y* – is replaced in the model by $L1.chg\_sqr\_log\_y_t$ and $L2.sqr\_log\_y_t$, their population coefficients are equal to each other and to the population coefficient on $[log(Y_{t-1})]^2$ in the original (pre-replacement) model. This is useful because $[log(Y_{t-1})]^2 - [\log(Y_{t-2})]^2$ is likely an I(0) variable, whereas $[log(Y_{t-1})]^2$ is likely an I(1) variable. Thus, the asymptotic distribution of the OLS estimator of the coefficient on $[log(Y_{t-1})]^2 - [log(Y_{t-2})]^2$ – i.e., the coefficient on $L1.chg\_sqr\_log\_y_t$ in the lag-augmented model, is much more likely to be a reasonable approximation to the actual estimator sampling distribution than if this coefficient had been directly estimated. Similarly, the lag-augmented model includes both $L4.sqr\_r_t$ (which is $[R_{t-4}]^2$) and $L3.chg\_sqr\_r_t$ (which is $[R_{t-3}]^2 - [R_{t-4}]^2$), so that the usual asymptotic sampling distribution estimate for the coefficient on $L3.chg\_sqr\_r_t$ is valid even though $(R_t)^2$ is likely an I(1) variable. The coefficients on $L1.chg\_sqr\_log\_y_t$ and on $L3.chg\_sqr\_r_t$ are not significantly different from zero, so there is no evidence of nonlinearity in these two relationships. Section 18.6 will discuss more sensitive and sophisticated ways to check for missing nonlinear dynamics in the model and surveys some potentially superior frameworks for modeling such dynamics if they are present.

Again referring to Table 14-3, the next aspect of the model to diagnostically check is the stability of the parameters. This is most simply checked by first including in the model the seven half-decade dummy variables – $D1965_t$, $D1970_t$, ... , and $D1995_t$ – defined in Section 14.4 and used there to check the model "in changes" for parameter stability. The inclusion of these dummy variables in the model effectively allows the model intercept to vary over time.[73] The null hypothesis that the coefficients on all seven of these dummy variables are zero can be rejected with a *p*-value of .0001, so there is strong evidence that the intercept in the

[73] For example, per Footnote 14-41, $D1965_t$ is defined to be one for the period January 1995 through December 1969 and zero otherwise; the other six dummy variables are defined analogously. The coefficient on $D1965_t$ is thus the expected difference between the intercept in this period and its value in the first portion of the sample period, which consists of the months January 1959 through December 1964. See Footnote 14-44 for references to more sophisticated tests for parameter instability.

model is in fact not stable over time and these dummy variables are included in the next set of models.[74]

These half-decade dummy variables are next interacted with R_{t-3} and with $log(Y_{t-1})$ – in two separate regression models – so as to assess the stability of the coefficients on these two variables. Since each of these variables is I(1), the inferences on the interaction coefficients must be done using a lag augmented model; each of these regressions models thus requires the inclusion of 14 additional variables. For example, the regression model testing the stability of the coefficient on R_{t-3} includes $\Delta[D1965_{t-3}R_{t-3}]$ and $D1965_{t-4}R_{t-4}$, $\Delta[D1970_{t-3}R_{t-3}]$ and $D1970_{t-4}R_{t-4}$, ... $\Delta[D1995_{t-3}R_{t-3}]$ and $D1995_{t-4}R_{t-4}$. The null hypothesis that the coefficients on the seven additional change variables – i.e., $\Delta[D1965_{t-3}R_{t-3}]$ ... $\Delta[D1995_{t-3}R_{t-3}]$ – are all zero can be rejected only with *p*-value equal to .301, so this coefficient passes its stability test.

The analogous stability test with respect to the coefficient on $\log(Y_{t-1})$, in contrast, indicates that this coefficient is significantly larger in the 1965 to 1980 subperiods. In fact, the null hypothesis that the coefficients on all seven additional change variables included in this model – i.e., on $\Delta[D1965_{t-1}\,log(Y_{t-1})]$ ... $\Delta[D1995_{t-1}log(Y_{t-1})]$ – are zero can be rejected only with *p*-value less than .00005. However, the seven intercept-shift coefficients are no longer individually or jointly significant once these interactions with the $log(Y_{t-1}])$ variable are included; the *p*-value for the rejection of the null hypothesis that these seven coefficients are all zero is now .177. The intercept dummy variables are therefore dropped from the model, allowing for time variation in the coefficient on $log(Y_{t-1})$.

That leaves two candidate models: one which allows the intercept to vary over time and one which instead allows the coefficient on $log(Y_{t-1})$ to vary. So as to more clearly compare them, the key estimation results for each of these models are summarized in Table 14-4. Although both of these models yield similar coefficient estimates for the trend and for the lagged values of $log(C_t)$ and R_t, they are clearly different in their implications as to the coefficient on $log(Y_{t-1})$ – i.e., as to the estimated expected elasticity of consumption spending with respect to disposable income.[75] It is not exactly obvious which model is preferable, however, since the varying-intercept model fits better in terms of the BIC measure, whereas the model in which the coefficient on $log(Y_{t-1})$ varies both fits better in terms of s^2 and leads to a rejection of the key null hypothesis (of stable coefficients) with a notably smaller *p*-value.

The BIC goodness-of-fit measure is usually preferable to s^2, the unbiased estimate of the model error variance, because it can be shown that s^2 falls whenever a variable added to a regression model enters with an estimated coefficient with a *t*-ratio larger than one in magnitude; yet a coefficient with a *t*-ratio less than two in magnitude is not statistically significant at the usual (5%) level of significance.[76] Thus, s^2 must be underpenalizing model complication. Ordinarily, the BIC statistic is better-behaved in this respect, but it may be *over*penalizing model complication in the model in which the coefficient on $log(Y_{t-1})$ varies. This is because the lag-augmentation maneuver causes one to add *two* explanatory variable to the model for each slope dummy variable added. For example, in order to estimate an asymptotically valid standard error for the estimated coefficient on $D1965_{t-1}Y_{t-1}$, one must actually include both $\Delta(D1965_{t-1}Y_{t-1})$ and $D1965_{t-2}Y_{t-2}$ in the regression model and use the estimation results on the $\Delta(D1965_{t-1}Y_{t-1})$ coefficient.

Overall, the model in which the coefficient on $log(Y_{t-1})$ varies therefore seems preferable. But the case for choosing it over the varying-intercept model is hardly compelling. This dilemma leads to the last diagnostic check listed in Table 14-4, which is to use the postsample period – here, the

[74] The BIC statistic is actually larger for the model including these dummy variables, even though they are highly significant as a group and it hardly makes sense to pick and choose which ones to include. This illustrates the folly of choosing a model specification by mechanically minimizing a criterion like the BIC.

[75] This elasticity estimate is listed in Table 14-4 as .123 for the model which allows for time-variation in coefficient on $\log(Y_{t-1})$ – which is quite similar to the analogous estimate (.120) in the model allowing for time-variation in the intercept. Note, however, that this is just the estimate for the initial (1959–1964) subperiod: this elasticity rises substantially in subsequent subperiods.

[76] The discussion of R_c^2, as defined in Section 9.5, is not relevant here: because $log(C_t)$ is trended, R_c^2 is equal to .9999 for all of the models considered, and hence is not even quoted. But R_c^2 is an inverse function of s^2, so that is what enters the discussion at this point.

Table 14-4 Summary of the Two Models for $Log(C_t)$[77]

	Model					
	Intercept varies			$Log(Y_{t-1})$ coefficient varies		
Variable	Coefficient	$\lvert t \rvert$	*P*-value	Coefficient	$\lvert t \rvert$	*P*-value
$Log(C_{t-1})$	.654	10.12	<.0005	.649	9.96	<.0005
$Log(C_{t-2})$	.138	2.55	.011	.130	2.40	.017
$Log(Y_{t-1})$)	.120	3.28	.001	.123	3.37	.001
R_{t-3} ($\times 10^3$)	−.993	1.96	.051	−1.032	2.05	.041
Time trend ($\times 10^3$)	−.108	2.00	.046	.097	1.73	.084
Shift Coefficient ($\times 10^3$)						
1965–1969	3.364	2.15	.032	1.466	2.27	.024
1970–1974	0.915	0.45	.653	1.599	1.94	.052
1975–1979	2.541	1.44	.152	2.185	2.43	.015
1980–1984	1.570	0.84	.400	1.137	1.24	.215
1985–1989	1.620	1.14	.253	1.005	1.16	.248
1990–1994	−2.337	2.04	.042	0.144	0.19	.850
1995–2002	0.370	0.30	.762	−0.569	0.99	.320
Summary Statistics						
s^2 ($\times 10^5$)	2.884			2.841		
BIC	−10.295			−10.238		
p-value for joint test on shift coefficients	.0001			<.00005		

81 months from January 2003 through July 2009 – to check on whether the estimated model is able to forecast outside of the sample period used in constructing it. It is not unusual to wind up with several models which are tough to choose between. Here there are four:

- The model "in changes" for $\Delta log(C_t)$, specified and estimated in Section 14.4.
- The cointegrated model for $\Delta log(C_t)$, specified and estimated in Section 14.5.
- The model "in levels" for $log(C_t)$ with a time-varying intercept.
- The model "in levels" for $log(C_t)$ with a time-varying coefficient on $log(Y_{t-1})$.

Each of these estimated models can be used to predict the values of the 81 postsample values of $\Delta log(C_t)$, yielding an estimate of the mean squared forecasting error (MSE) of the model, but that was not actually done here.[78] Postsample forecasting is discussed further in Section 18.5.

[77] An intercept was estimated for each model, but not listed; inference results are based on White-Eicker standard errors from suitably lag-augmented models. Lag augmentation was used for all variables except the time trend and the intercept dummies; the standard error, *t* ratio, and *p*-value for the $log(C_{t-1})$ coefficient estimate are based on a lag-augmented model using both $\Delta log(C_{t-1})$ and $\Delta log(C_{t-2})$, as in Equations 13-55 to 13-57. *P*-values for individual coefficients are for the two-tailed test of the null hypothesis that the coefficient is zero; the *p*-value for the joint test is in each case for rejecting the null hypothesis that all seven shift coefficients are zero.

[78] Letting *T* denote the last sample period used in estimating the model, a model for $log(C_t)$ yields a forecast of $log(C_{T+1})$, but also provides a forecast of $\Delta log(C_{T+1})$: the value of this forecast of $log(C_{T+1})$ minus the last sample value of $log(C_t)$. Similarly, a model for $\Delta log(C_t)$ can also be used to make a forecast of $log(C_{T+1})$, but the average size of the postsample errors in forecasting $log(C_t)$ are problematic to assess because they are likely to be I(1), in which case their variance (and MSE) are not well defined. In forecasting using the model for $log(C_t)$ with a time-varying intercept, one would need to assume that the intercept remains constant in the postsample period, presumably at its value for the 1995–2002 subperiod. Similarly, using the model for $log(C_t)$ with a time-varying $log(Y_{t-1})$ coefficient, one would need to assume that this coefficient remains constant in the postsample period, again presumably at its value for the 1995–2002 subperiod.

14.7 WHICH IS BETTER: TO MODEL IN LEVELS OR TO MODEL IN CHANGES?

In terms of qualitative conclusions, all four models agree: (1) there is a good deal of momentum in the dynamics, so that lags in consumption spending are an important determinant of current consumption spending, (2) there is a significant direct relationship between current consumption spending and disposable income in the previous month, and (3) there is a significant inverse relationship between current consumption spending and the short-term interest rate, with a lag of three months. Forecasting will be taken up in Chapter 18, but one would expect that the postsample forecasting performance of the models is similar also. From a modeling perspective, however, another set of issues comes to the fore.

The development in Section 14.6 makes it fairly clear that properly modeling "in levels" is simply awkward. For one thing, because the explanatory variables in such a model are typically I(1), one must continually fuss with lag-augmentation terms in order to obtain valid inferences. Furthermore, because the "levels" explanatory variables are so highly autocorrelated, their variation across the sample all tends to be fairly similar – much more so than the "changes" variables. Consequently, regressions in levels tend to exhibit symptoms of multicollinearity: individual coefficients tend to be less precisely estimated and changes to one part of the specification (e.g., omitting R_{t-1} and R_{t-2}) can affect the significance of another part (e.g., the coefficient on R_{t-3}). Indeed, the estimated levels models identify notably less of the lagged dependent variable dynamics (e.g., the terms at lags three to nine months) which are evident in the models "in changes" and it is arguable that the R_{t-3} term in the levels model would likely have been missed altogether had it not been for guidance from the models in changes.[79]

The model "in changes" presents problematic features of its own, although some of these "problems" could be reframed as "opportunities." For example, outliers and heteroscedasticity each tend to be more prominently displayed in variables "in changes" than in variables "in levels." That is a nuisance, but it is also an opportunity to better understand (and deal with) what is actually occurring in the data. Another example is that in order to properly specify a model "in changes," one is obligated to uncover a cointegrating relationship (if there is one) and include it as an error-correction term in the model. The model "in levels," in contrast, automatically subsumes any cointegration: one cannot get this wrong. On the other hand, the levels formulation precludes the descriptive/analytic richness of the Vector Error-Correction Model, if one does manage to correctly specify it.

The one unalloyed problematic feature to the model "in changes" is that it can involve an over-difference of the dependent variable. Per the discussion of this topic in the context of Equations 14-18 to 14-20, such overdifferencing does not affect the consistency of parameter estimation or the validity of the parameter inferences in the model "in changes," but it does suggest a distortion in at least some of the dynamics implied by this model.[80] Such over-differencing will occur whenever one incorrectly fails to reject the null hypothesis – that the time-series is I(1) – on a "unit roots" test, wrongly concludes that the time-series is I(1), and thus differences it. But such "incorrect failures to reject" are commonplace with unit roots tests – and particularly in those very situations where one is wondering whether to model "in changes" or "in levels" – simply because unit roots tests have little power to distinguish between a highly autocorrelated time-series and a time-series with a unit root.

The monthly consumption model examined here provides a good example of this problem. So as to focus on just the $log(C_t)$ dynamics, let Z_t stand for all of the other terms in the model: the intercept,

[79] On the other hand, the coefficient on ΔR_{t-3} in the model in changes is actually less clearly significant than the coefficient on R_{t-3} in the levels models, once the form of the lag structure was identified.

[80] See Footnote 14-53.

the term in $log(Y_{t-1})$, the term in R_{t-3}, and the terms involving the dummy variables. The estimated model from Table 14-4 in which the coefficient on $log(Y_{t-1})$ is allowed to vary over time can then be written simply as

$$log(C_t) = .649\,log(C_{t-1}) + .130\,log(C_{t-1}) + Z_t + U_t \tag{14-24}$$

It is useful at this point to define what is known as the "lag operator." This operator – usually denoted by either the symbol "B" or the symbol "L" – simply lags a time-series by one period. That is, B times X_t is X_{t-1}. Similarly, B^2X_t is X_{t-2}, B^3X_t is X_{t-3}, and so forth. In this notation the Equation 14-24 model for $log(C_t)$ can be written as

$$(1 - .649B - .130B^2)\,log(C_t) = Z_t + U_t \tag{14-25}$$

Factoring this quadratic polynomial into the product of two first-order polynomials yields[81]

$$(1 - .810B)(1 + .161B)\,log(C_t) = Z_t + U_t \tag{14-26}$$

If $log(C_t)$ were really I(1) – so that it is appropriate to model $\Delta log(C_t) = (1-B)\text{log}(C_t)$ – then one would expect to see a factor considerably closer to $(1-B)$ than the factor $(1 - .810B)$ observed here.[82] But the relevant Augmented Dickey-Fuller (ADF) test results clearly indicates that the null hypothesis of a unit root in $log(C_t)$ cannot be rejected at even the 10% level of significance.[83] The failure of a hypothesis test to reject the null hypothesis does not imply that the null hypothesis is false: it only implies that there is insufficient evidence upon which to confidently reject it. Still, a sensible person paying attention to this ADF test result would probably not reject the null hypothesis in this case and therefore proceed with a model "in changes" – which might well, then, be over-differenced. Thus, the risk of over-differencing is surely present in using the model "in changes."

It should be evident at this point that each of these approaches – modeling "in levels" or modeling "in changes" – has its strengths and weaknesses. Consequently, a really careful and complete analysis would approach the data *both* ways, as was done here in Sections 14.4 through 14.6. Still, one might note that when the author needed to construct an example for Section 15.3, he chose to model the relationship between time-series which were differenced so as to be clearly I(0). This reflects an underlying aesthetic that least-squares estimation of linear relationships is fundamentally most appropriately conducted using variables with clearly well-defined variances and covariances.

---

[81] See Exercise 14-11 as to how this factorization is done. Alternatively, simply multiply out the two linear factors in Equation 14-26 to confirm that their product equals the quadratic polynomial in Equation 14-25.

[82] Foreshadowing material from Chapters 17 and 18, it can be shown – e.g., Box and Jenkins (1976, p. 58) – that one of these factors equals $(1-B)$ if the sum of the coefficients on $log(C_{t-1})$ and on $log(C_{t-2})$ equals one. This equality is very easy to test here since the population coefficient on $\Delta log(C_{t-2})$ in the lag-augmented model including $\Delta log(C_{t-1})$, $\Delta log(C_{t-2})$, and $log(C_{t-3})$ is precisely this sum. Estimating this model (including an intercept, a time trend, the term in $log(Y_{t-1})$, the term in R_{t-3}, and the $log(Y_{t-1})$ coefficient shift dummy variables, as in Table 14-4) yields an estimated coefficient on $\Delta log(C_{t-2})$ of $.779 \pm .054$; the null hypothesis that the population value of this coefficient is one can be rejected with p-value $< .00005$. Box, G. E, P., and G. M. Jenkins (1976), *Time Series Analysis: Forecasting and Control*, Holden-Day, New York.

[83] The ADF test is discussed in Section 14.3.

KEY TERMS

For each term or concept listed below, provide a working definition or explanation:

I(0) Time-Series
I(1) Time-Series
Augmented Dickey-Fuller (ADF) Test
Schwarz Criterion or BIC
Cointegrated Time-Series
Cointegrating Regression Model
Error-Correction Term
Engle-Granger ADF Test
Vector Error-Correction Model
Over-Differenced Time-Series
Inference Using Lag-Augmented Models (both ways)
Modeling "in Changes" vs. Modeling "in Levels"

EXERCISES

14-1. Assume that Z_t is a random walk, generated by

$$Z_t = Z_{t-1} + U_t \qquad U_t \sim \text{IID}[0, \sigma_u^2] \tag{14-27}$$

For the special case where Z_0 is fixed and given, derive and interpret expressions for the time evolution of $E(Z_t)$ and $\text{var}(Z_t)$. Noting that the time period in which Z_t is given could be any particular period, what does this result imply that one should expect for the values of $|Z_t|$ in the long-term future?

14-2. Assuming that Z_t is generated by the AR(1) Model, as given in Equation 14-4, show that the regression equation for the Augmented Dickey-Fuller (ADF) test will yield a negative coefficient on Z_{t-1}. Use your result to explain why it is appropriate that the ADF test rejection p-value is computed on the basis of a one-tailed test.

14-3. Suppose that the impact of using an I(1) explanatory variable is to make the actual asymptotic sampling distribution of a parameter estimator thick-tailed, by comparison with the (normal) asymptotic distribution which the Central Limit Theorem would have otherwise provided. Assuming (correctly) that the sample length is sufficiently large and (incorrectly) that the usual asymptotic results are valid, will the resulting p-values for rejecting null hypotheses about the model coefficients be distorted upward or downward? What will this imply, with respect to the likelihood of an analyst wrongly rejecting such null hypotheses?

14-4. The estimated regression equation for a particular implementation of the Augmented Dickey-Fuller (ADF) test is

$$\Delta Y_t = \underset{(2.50)}{3.0} + \underset{(3.80)}{.02t} - \underset{(-3.50)}{1.20 Y_{t-1}} + \underset{(4.20)}{3.0 Z_t} + U_t \tag{14-28}$$

with estimated t ratios in parentheses and a large sample; you can presume that the inclusion of Y_{t-1} in this model is sufficient to yield apparently non-autocorrelated fitting errors and that Y_t appears to be linearly trended.

a. At what significance level can the null hypothesis that $Y_t \sim I(1)$ be rejected? How would your answer change if the estimated coefficient on Y_{t-1} had instead been the positive value, 1.20?

b. Suppose that one had obtained the same estimated t ratio on Y_{t-1} in an ADF regression model for these data which does not include the time trend. In what way would this change the rejection significance level? Why would doing this be inappropriate?

c. Suppose that this regression model has been estimated as part of an Engle-Granger test for cointegration between a variable Z_t and both X_t and a time trend, t. In that case the Y_t observations are actually the fitting errors from regressing Z_t on X_t and t. At what significance level can the null hypothesis – that these errors in the cointegrating relationship are I(1) – be rejected? (Recall that, if the I(1) null hypothesis *is* rejected, then the validity of the cointegrating relationship is *not* rejected.)

14-5. Suppose that

$$\Delta Y_t = 3.0 + 2.5\Delta X_{t-1} + U_t \tag{14-29}$$

State two specific models in the levels of Y_t, Y_{t-1}, X_t, and X_{t-1-1} which yield this model "in changes." {Hint: Think about different values for the intercept in the model "in levels."}

14-6. Suppose that

$$\Delta Y_t = 3.0 + 2.5\Delta X_{t-1} + 0.3(Y_{t-1} - 1.2X_{t-1}) + U_t \tag{14-30}$$

a. What is nonsensical about this Vector Error-Correction Model?

b. Fixing the evident mistake in how Equation 14-30 was written out, state a specific model in the levels of Y_t, Y_{t-1}, X_t, and X_{t-1} which is equivalent to this model. In what way is this model "in levels" less restrictive than the equation above, which appears to be a Vector Error-Correction Model?

14-7. Can every model "in changes" (or every Vector Error-Correction Model) be rewritten as a model "in levels"?

14-8. Does every model "in levels" correspond to a model "in changes"?

14-9. Suppose that a time-series Z_t is the first difference of the covariance stationary time-series Y_t given by the AR(1) Model of Equation 13-11. Thus, $Z_t = Y_t - Y_{t-1}$ and is "overdifferenced." You may assume that the parameter φ_0 is zero so as to simplify the algebra.

a. Use Equation 13-17, the MA(∞) representation of Y_t, to show that the MA(∞) representation of Z_t is

$$\begin{aligned} Z_t = \; & U_t + (\varphi_1 - 1)U_{t-1} + (\varphi_1 - 1)\varphi_1 U_{t-2} - (\varphi_1 - 1)(\varphi_1)^2 U_{t-3} \\ & + (\varphi_1 - 1)(\varphi_1)^3 U_{t-4} + (\varphi_1 - 1)(\varphi_1)^4 U_{t-5} \ldots \end{aligned} \tag{14-31}$$

which has weights which decline in magnitude, thus deriving Equation 14-19.

b. Use the result in part a to show that the var(Z_t) equals $2\sigma_u^2/(1+\varphi_1)$, which is bounded.

14-10. Consider the Dynamic Multiple Regression Model of Equation 14-3 with $L_0 = 2$, $L_1 = 1$, $L_2 = 2$, and $L_3 = 0$, and assume that $X_{t,1}$, $X_{t,2}$, and $X_{t,3}$ are all I(1) time-series. Show how to test a null hypothesis about the parameter $\beta_{2,2}$ by re-formulating the model in lag-augmented form. How many additional coefficients would need to be estimated?

14-11. Factor the polynomial $(1 - .649B - .130B^2)$ into $(1 - .810B)(1 + .161B)$. {Hint: This is done by multiplying out $(1 - \lambda_1 B)(1 - \lambda_2 B)$, which yields two equations in the two unknowns, λ_1 and λ_2.}

Active Learning Exercise 14a: Analyzing the Food Price Sub-Index of the Monthly U.S. Consumer Price Index

Introduction

This Active Learning Exercise provides an illustration of how one can model a typical monthly macroeconomic time-series variable using just its own past. Such models are surprisingly useful for short-term forecasting purposes. The issues involved in constructing such models (and using them in forecasting) will be examined in some detail in Chapter 17. The focus here is on how to specify and estimate a simple such model in a careful way.

Your Assignment:

1. Copy the data file ALE_14a.csv (available at www.wiley.com/college/ashley) to your hard disk and read it in to the econometrics software your course is using. (Or copy ALE_14a.dta if you are using Stata.) This file contains 453 observations (from January 1972 to September 2009) on "cpi_food_sa$_t$," – the seasonally adjusted food sub-index of the U.S. Consumer Price Index (CPI). These data were downloaded from the Bureau of Labor Statistics Web site at www.bls.gov/data/.
2. Because there is a natural ordering to time-series data, the first step in analyzing it is always to plot the data against time, so as to check whether the data are covariance stationary – i.e., to check whether an assumption that the mean, variance, and autocovariances of the data are constants is reasonable.[84] Usually, it is necessary to transform the data.
   a. Generate an observation number variable ($obsnum_t$) and a variable ($log\_cpi\_food_t$) which is the logarithm of $cpi\_food\_sa_t$ and plot both food price index time-series against $obsnum_t$. Is the mean of either of these time-series constant over time?
   b. Generate the monthly change ($chg\_foodcpi_t$) and the annualized monthly percentage growth rate ($cpi\_food\_grow_t$) and plot these against time. Is it reasonable to assume that the mean and variance of either of these time-series are constant over time?[85]
   c. Make a histogram of the data on $chg\_foodcpi_t$. Do the time plot and histogram of this time-series suggest that there may be an outlier in this time-series? Find out more about this particular observation by listing the values of the variables $month_t$, $year_t$, and $chg\_foodcpi_t$ for which $chg\_foodcpi_t$ exceeds 1.5.[86]

[84] See Footnote 14-12 and Section 17.3.

[85] The monthly change in cpi_food_sa$_t$ can be conveniently generated in Stata using "cpi_food_sa - L1.cpi_food_sa" and the annualized monthly growth rate in cpi_food_sa$_t$ can be conveniently generated in Stata using "1200*(log_cpi_food - L1.log_cpi_food" after obsnum$_t$ is specified as the time index variable, using the "xtset obsnum" command.

[86] It is noteworthy that President Nixon lifted price controls on food on July 18, 1973; the full text of the speech in which he announced this can be found at "www.presidency.ucsb.edu/ws/index.php?pid=3905&st=&st1=; there is no mention of this event, however available at en.wikipedia.org/wiki/1973.

d. Compare the deviation of the value of the August 1973 value of $chg\_foodcpi_t$ (from its sample mean) to its sample standard deviation. Were this random variable normally distributed, would one expect to see a deviation this large in a sample of 452 observations? (Note that this is merely an informal assessment rather than a statistically credible test. For one thing, an assumption that the distribution of $chg\_foodcpi_t$ is adequately approximated by a normal distribution in its tails is suspect; the Central Limit Theorem only motivates a normality assumption for the density more or less near the mean. Also, the sample variance is a consistent estimator of the population variance only if the observations are uncorrelated with one another; the serial dependence of $chg\_foodcpi_t$ is investigated in the next question.)

3. Estimate an AR(12) model for $chg\_foodcpi_t$. Then include a dummy variable shifting the intercept for the August, 1973 observation. Estimate a "final" model including just the dummy variable and lags 1, 2, 3, and 12 in the dependent variable.
   a. Is the dummy variable statistically significant?
   b. What interpretation is warranted for the seasonal term in the model?
   c. What interpretation can be given to the adjusted R^2 for the model? Would it likely be a good idea – in terms of forecasting effectiveness – to use dummy variables to eliminate some of the other, not-quite-so-large values of $chg\_foodcpi_t$? How might one test this notion?

4. Each month the announcement of the CPI figures for the previous month is big news. Given the noise in the monthly figures, is such attention warranted?
   a. Investigate this by computing the ratio of a typical value for $chg\_foodcpi_t$ – e.g., its sample mean of .4 – to its sample standard deviation. What can you conclude?
   b. The sample variance of the time-series used in part a of this question is an unbiased estimator of the population variance, however, only if the time-series is serially uncorrelated; consequently, the estimated standard deviation is a consistent estimator of the population standard deviation only in that case. Use your final model for $chg\_foodcpi_t$ to examine this issue.
      i. First, test the null hypothesis that all four lagged term coefficients in the final model are zero.
      ii. But is the estimated serial correlation implied by this model sufficiently strong as to cause a substantial amount of inconsistency in the standard deviation estimator? There is a simple formula for the variance of a time-series generated by an AR(p) model which can be easily applied to address this issue, assuming that the sample is sufficiently large that one can sensibly use the estimated model coefficients, error variance, and sample autocorrelations as good approximations to the analogous population quantities: $\varphi_1, \varphi_2, \varphi_3, \varphi_{12}, \sigma_u^2, \rho_1, \rho_2, \rho_3$, and ρ_{12}:[87]

$$\text{var}(\text{chg\_foodcpi}_t) = \frac{\sigma_u^2}{1 - \rho_1\varphi_1 - \rho_2\varphi_2 - \rho_3\varphi_3 - \rho_4\varphi_4 - \ldots - \rho_{12}\varphi_{12}} \qquad \text{(ALE14a-1)}$$

Consistent sample estimates of ρ_1, ρ_2, ρ_3, and ρ_{12} can be obtained from the Stata command "corrgram chg_foodcpi if obsnum !=20, lags(12)"; σ_u^2 can be consistently estimated by s^2 (which is $.37342^2$ here); and the model coefficient estimates provide consistent estimates of $\varphi_1, \varphi_2, \varphi_3$, and φ_{12}. Use this formula to obtain a

[87] This formula can be found in Box and Jenkins (1976, Equation 3.2.8). A straightforward procedure for numerically inverting a lag operator is developed in Section 17-4 which clarifies and simplifies this kind of calculation.

consistent estimate of the standard deviation of $chg\_foodcpi_t$. With the amount of serial correlation observed here, is the distortion in the ordinary sample estimate of the standard deviation of $chg\_foodcpi_t$ substantial?

Concluding Comments:

It is clearly not very difficult to model a monthly time-series like $cpi\_food\_sa_t$ in terms of just its own past. Surprisingly, one can thereby obtain a model – in this case for the monthly change in the price index – which is likely to reduce the one-month-ahead forecast error variance by perhaps 10-15% over a 'naive' forecast not using the information in the recent past of this time-series.

Along the way, this example illustrates the usefulness of plotting the data.[88] The results also strongly suggest that, while it might be useful to forecast such monthly data, it is probably not a good idea to pay much attention to individual monthly observations – such as the one for the current month! – because it is mostly just noise. A better use for the current observation on a monthly macroeconomic time-series is probably to compute either the change or the growth rate in the series over its value for the same month in the previous year.

[88] This topic is taken up in deeper and more complete fashion in Section 17.3.

Part 3

ADDITIONAL TOPICS IN REGRESSION ANALYSIS

The purpose of Parts I and II was to describe the theory and practice of basic regression modeling – for both cross-sectional and time-series data – in as much depth as possible using scalar algebra. Part III is different. Here the idea is to introduce, in a simple way, a selection of additional areas of econometrics which are characteristic and important. Brevity is an issue in such a survey, so the coverage of these areas is by no means comprehensive for each of these areas. Sufficient detail is provided in each chapter, however, so as to both convey the essence of each area and to enable the reader to sensibly begin applying the key techniques of that area to real data. Four topics have been chosen for inclusion here:[1]

- Panel data methods
- Time-series analysis
- Maximum Likelihood (MLE) Estimation – with an application to Binary Choice Models
- Generalized Method of Moments (GMM) Estimation – with an application to IV regression models in which the model errors are heteroscedastic

Panel data – the topic of Chapters 15 and 16 – is a hybrid combination of cross-sectional and time-series data. In a panel data set, a (typically quite short) time-series is obtained for each of a (typically quite large) number of "units," where a "unit" is usually an individual respondent or a country, depending on the context. Such hybrid data sets yield the large samples needed for effective estimation, diagnostic checking, and inference. But they require specialized methods in order to deal with the likely heterogeneity of the sample across the different units.

Time-series analysis – the topic of Chapters 17 and 18 – is an area distinct from the "time-series econometrics" covered in Chapters 13 and 14, although the distinction has diminished somewhat in recent years as a number of ideas from time-series analysis – such as unit roots – have become a part of mainstream econometrics. Generally speaking, "time-series analysis" has focused on forecasting and on relatively small models – usually involving only one (or just a few) time-series – where the model specification is cheerfully mined from the sample data. In contrast, "time-series econometrics" has focused on parameter estimation/inference, on models typically involving a number (in

[1] Many other important and interesting topics have, for a number of reasons, been omitted from this edition. These topics include: nonparametric regression, quantile regression, censored regression, spectral analysis, and Bayesian methods.

some cases quite a large number) of time-series, and on settings where the model specification can be primarily generated using economic theory. The reader might note that the "capstone example" in Sections 14.4 through 14.6 actually illustrates both of these approaches to the modeling of time-series data. The model for monthly consumption spending developed there is small, and the model specification is largely derived from the sample data itself rather than relying on economic theory. But the emphasis throughout Chapters 13 and 14 was on estimation and inference rather than on forecasting.

In contrast, Chapters 17 and 18 adopt the "time-series analysis" perspective and consider model forecasting as an end in itself. Chapter 17 begins by focusing on the crucial topic of defining what one means by a "good" or "optimal" forecast. It then goes on to describe practical methods for obtaining a forecasting model for a time-series using just a linear function of its own past. Chapter 18 extends this survey of time-series analysis to multivariate – but still small – linear models (for forecasting several time-series in terms of their joint past) and to techniques for detecting and exploiting nonlinear serial dependence in a time-series.[2]

Chapter 19 provides an introduction to two additional approaches for estimating the parameters of a regression model: Maximum Likelihood Estimation (MLE) and the Generalized Method of Moments (GMM). The previous chapters have all focused on the least-squares estimation of the coefficients in a linear parameterization of the conditional mean of the dependent variable. As drawn out in Chapters 5 and 9, it is fruitful to view this estimation approach in terms of fitting a curve – a straight line, in the case of the Bivariate Regression Model – to the sample data, so as to minimize the sum of the squared deviations of the sample data from the fitted line. This is an entirely satisfactory way to generate high-quality regression model parameter estimators in many circumstances. But least-squares estimation is not suitable – indeed, it is not even feasible – in some empirically important settings.

The first part of Chapter 19 describes a different approach to parameter estimation, in which the parameters estimates are chosen so as to maximize the likelihood that one would have observed the sample data. This approach is ideally suited to estimating econometric models with unobserved ("latent") variables, such as the Binary-Choice Model of Equation 19-10. This variation on multiple regression analysis explicitly recognizes the fact that, in a number of important settings, the observed dependent variable is not a number (such as the logarithm of wages or the growth rate of consumption spending) but is instead the outcome of a decision. For example, an individual has decided to enter the labor force – or not. Or an individual has defaulted on his/her credit card debts – or not.

It is clearly useful to be able to model choices such as these and to test whether, and to what degree, various explanatory variables are relevant to an individual's decisions. It is easy enough to convert the observed choices into numbers, by simply defining a dummy variable which assigns a value of zero to one of the choice outcomes and a value of one to the other. But there is still a problem: A linear regression model does not gracefully yield zeros and ones as predicted values. Thus, it is more appropriate in this case to construct a linear regression model for an unobserved ('latent') dependent variable – which one might call a "propensity to choose" – and to model this propensity as a linear function of observed explanatory variables. The individual's observed choice is then taken to depend on whether or not the value of this propensity exceeds some threshold value.

The only problem with this approach is that there are no observed (sample) values for this "propensity to choose," even though it is the dependent variable in the regression model whose coefficients are to be estimated: all that is actually available is a sample of observations on the dummy variable specifying the binary outcome of the decision. One could, of course, simply substitute this dummy variable value for the unobserved dependent variable and estimate the

[2] The role of out-of-sample prediction in regression model validation is discussed in Section 8.3. And the mechanics of such prediction is covered in Section 8.4 and Appendix 9.1 – for the bivariate and multiple regression models, respectively. That material is important, but it is developed in a context where forecasting *per se* is a secondary activity.

regression model parameters using OLS. But the resulting OLS parameter estimators are not consistent estimators of the actual parameter values characterizing how (and whether) an individual's decision depends on the observable explanatory variables. Remarkably, however, it is still possible to obtain consistent parameter estimators and asymptotically valid inferences in settings such as these using Maximum Likelihood Estimation.

The remaining half of Chapter 19 introduces and applies a third approach to regression parameter estimation, the "Generalized Method of Moments" or "GMM." In the GMM approach, the regression model parameters are estimated based on the degree to which the estimated model reproduces a set of posited "population moment conditions." Where these moment conditions are implications of, say, a rational expectations theoretical model, GMM is often the only way that the model parameters can be estimated. Where these moment conditions are the necessary conditions for instrument validity in an IV regression model with endogenous explanatory variables, then GMM can provide asymptotically efficient parameter estimation in cases where two-stage least squares estimation (2SLS) is only consistent. GMM is also of theoretical interest, because it actually subsumes both the OLS and 2SLS estimators as special cases. For all of these reasons, GMM is an important tool in modern empirical analysis.

Chapter 20 then concludes the book with some overall comments on econometric modeling using the methods described herein.

15

Regression Modeling with Panel Data (Part A)

15.1 INTRODUCTION: A SOURCE OF LARGE (BUT LIKELY HETEROGENEOUS) DATA SETS

A panel data set is a hybrid of cross-sectional and time-series data, in which a time-series of length T is collected on each of M "units." In a microeconomic setting, a unit might be an individual survey respondent; in a growth/development setting, a unit might be a particular country.[1] The time-series in a panel data set are typically very short – e.g., T might only be five to ten periods, but the number of units is typically quite large: M might be in the hundreds, or even in the thousands.[2] Thus, in practice, panel data sets are a rich source of large data sets in applied economics.

In fact several of the data sets used in examples or Active Learning Exercises in earlier chapters are actually panel data sets. The reader might usefully browse the Web sites for several of these at this point:

- Panel Study of Income Dynamics (PSID)
  psidonline.isr.umich.edu/
- Penn World Table (PWT)
  pwt.econ.upenn.edu/php_site/pwt_index.php

and

- National Longitudinal Surveys of Labor Market Experience (NLS)
  www.bis.gov/nls/

Large samples are a practical necessity as soon as one is forced to abandon the assumption that the regression explanatory variables are fixed in repeated samples: the parameter estimates are typically then (at best) consistent, and inference must then be based on asymptotic sampling distributions derived from Central Limit Theorem arguments. This retreat from the assumption of fixed-regressors

[1] Thus, the text below refers to "M respondents," or "M countries," or "M states," depending on the context. Also, note that this defines a "balanced" panel; a panel data set is "unbalanced" if the number of observations is not equal for all of the units. Where more data are available for some units, its omission reduces parameter estimation precision; its inclusion, on the other hand, risks an overemphasis on these units. Inclusion is usually the better option, because significant distortion due to such overemphasis can be detected in diagnostically checking the model. Because the analysis in this chapter is typically not restricted to balanced panels, the sample length for unit i will typically be denoted "T_i".

[2] In fact, in an effort to keep the topic manageable, this chapter will focus solely on panel methods designed for the small-T and large-M case. Thus, no (further) mention will be made of partial FGLS methods, as implemented (for example) in the Stata routines xtpcse and xtgls.

may be due to endogeneity implied by economic theory, leading to the use of instrumental variables estimation. Or it may be due to the necessary specification of dynamics in the model – including the addition of lags in the dependent variable to the model specification – so as to eliminate serial correlation in the model errors. Large samples are also needed if heteroscedasticity in the model errors mandates the use of White-Eicker (robust) standard error estimates, as these are only asymptotically justified. Moreover, large samples are in any case usually necessary in order to obtain usefully precise parameter estimates and meaningfully sharp hypothesis tests. This is especially the case with individual-level data, where the variance of the model error term is often substantial compared to the amount of dependent variable variation modeled by the economic explanatory variables.[3]

Thus, the large sample length of $M \times T$ observations provided by a panel with M units and T observations is very welcome – indeed, it is often absolutely necessary. The larger sample length provided by a panel data set comes at a cost, however: one must deal with the fact that a panel data set can be non-homogeneous across either the units, or the time periods, or both. That turns out to present challenges which are still, in some respects, a frontier area of research in econometrics: this (and the next) chapter survey the current status of methods used for coping with this heterogeneity.

15.2 REVISITING THE CHAPTER 5 ILLUSTRATIVE EXAMPLE USING DATA FROM THE PENN WORLD TABLE

Consider again the model for a country's real per capita GDP used in Sections 5.2 and 5.5 to first introduce the Bivariate Regression Model. That example started from an examination of the mean of what we will now call $RGDPL_{i,1999}$ – the random variable observed as the Penn World Table (PWT) Version 6.1 datum on real per capita GDP for country i in year 1999, $rgdpl_{i,1999}$. It then proceeded to a scatterplot relating $rgdpl_{i,1999}$ to what we will now call $K_{i,1999}$ – the real per capita capital stock of country i in year 1999. Notably, the subscript "1999" in the above variables is now necessary: Version 6.1 of the PWT is actually a panel data set, with observations on each country beginning in various years – from 1950 to 1994 – and ending in the year 2000.[4]

This led to our first example of the Bivariate Regression Model, restated here as

$$
\begin{aligned}
\log\left(RGDPL_{i,1999}\right) &= \alpha + \beta \log\left(k_{i,1999}\right) + U_{i,1999} \qquad i = 1 \ldots 105 \\
\log\left(k_{1,1999}\right) &\ldots \log\left(k_{105,1999}\right) \text{ fixed in repeated samples} \\
U_{i,1999} &\sim \text{NIID}\left[0, \sigma_u^2\right]
\end{aligned}
\tag{15-1}
$$

and yielding the OLS estimated model

$$
\begin{aligned}
\log\left(rgdpl_{i,1999}\right) &= \hat{\alpha}^*_{\text{ols}} + \hat{\beta}^*_{\text{ols}} \log\left(k_{i,1999}\right) + u^{\text{fit}}_{i,1999} \\
&= \underset{(.188)}{1.103} + \underset{(.020)}{.799} \log\left(k_{i,1999}\right) + u^{\text{fit}}_{i,1999}
\end{aligned}
\tag{15-2}
$$

This cross-sectional model assumes that the model parameters $\left(\alpha, \beta, \text{ and } \sigma_u^2\right)$ are all fixed constants which, in particular, are the same for all 105 countries in the year 1999. This equation thus models

[3] Recall that estimator sampling variances generally decline with sample size more or less proportionately to the reciprocal of the sample length. Coefficient estimator standard errors therefore approximately decline as the reciprocal of the square root of the sample length. Thus, for example, a doubling of the estimation precision requires a quadrupling of the sample length.

[4] Note that, per Footnote 15-1, the PWT Version 6.1 is clearly an unbalanced data set.

all of the observed 1999 variation in log($rgdpl_{i,\,1999}$) across the 105 countries as being due to either variation in the country's capital stock – $\log(k_{i,1999})$ – or due to variations in the plethora of other variables subsumed in the model error term, $\log(U_{i,1999})$.

Suppose, however, that the parameters α, β, and σ_u^2 are also the same (i.e., homogeneous) for the other years in the PWT sample. Then these parameters could be estimated from the entire data set, which has well over 40 times more observations and would thus yield estimated coefficient standard errors which one would expect to be roughly *six times* smaller.

This model utilizing the entire data set is called the "pooled model" because all of the data have been pooled together:

$$
\begin{aligned}
\log(RGDPL_{i,t}) &= \alpha + \beta \log(k_{i,t}) + U_{i,t} \\
\log(k_{1,t}) \ldots &\log(k_{105,t}) \text{ fixed in repeated samples} \\
U_{i,t} &\sim \text{NIID}\left[0, \sigma_u^2\right] \\
i = 1 \ldots 105 & \qquad t = 1950 \ldots 2000
\end{aligned}
\tag{15-3}
$$

where, as noted above, the data for a number of countries begins well after 1950, so not all (i,t) combinations exist in the data set. The interpretation of the model parameters $(\alpha,\ \beta,\ \text{and}\ \sigma_u^2)$ in Equation 15-3 is unchanged. In particular, β is still the partial derivative of the expected value of the logarithm of real per capita GDP in country i with respect to this country's real per capita capital stock – it is just more precisely estimated because the sample is much larger.

On the other hand, the assumption that the parameters α, β, and σ_u^2 are identical over all of those countries and all of those years seems hardly credible – and the violation of this homogeneity assumption will cause OLS estimation of the pooled model to yield inconsistent estimators for both the model parameters and for the standard errors of their sampling distributions. Indeed, the point of this chapter is to describe how one can, with reasonable effectiveness, allow for such heterogeneity.

In view of the developments subsequent to Chapter 5, the regression model of Equations 15-1 and 15-3 should at this point seem so restricted as to no longer make an interesting example. In particular, it is now clear (from Chapter 9) how to include multiple explanatory variables in the model.

In addition, from Chapter 11, it is now evident that the assumption of regressors "fixed in repeated samples" is probably untenable here. In particular, $\log(K_{i,t})$ is quite likely jointly determined with $\log(RGDPL_{i,t})$, implying that it is correlated with $U_{i,t}$ – i.e., it is a stochastic and endogenous explanatory variable. Even in the most favorable circumstance – where the correlation between $\log(K_{i,t})$ and $U_{i,t}$ is small in magnitude, so that the endogeneity is negligible – the untenability of this "fixed-regressors" assumption still implies that $\hat{\beta}^{OLS}$ is only a consistent estimator of β, and that its estimated standard error is only asymptotically valid. Thus, the larger sample in the pooled model is probably necessary as well as welcome. More likely, however, the endogeneity in $\log(K_{i,t})$ is not credibly negligible. Therefore, if only in order to determine whether or not the key results are artifacts of endogeneity-induced estimation inconsistency, one or more instruments must be found (per Chapter 12) for $\log(K_{i,t})$, in order to obtain a consistent estimate of β and to make valid inferences concerning it.

Moreover – even putting the endogeneity issue aside until Sections 16.1 and 16.2 – while it is reasonable enough to assume that the model errors in Equation 15-1 are independently distributed across the 105 countries in this cross-sectional sample, it is hardly tenable to assume that the country i model errors in the pooled panel data model of Equation 15-3 are independently distributed across the time periods. Indeed, the development in Chapter 14 strongly suggests that, for any given value of i, $U_{i,t}$ is probably very strongly autocorrelated, because a time-series like log($RGDPL_{i,t}$) is likely to be I(1) – i.e., to be so substantially correlated with its own recent past that it has a unit root. The regression model should in that case be analyzed in differenced form.

Thus, while this illustrative example from Chapter 5 (here recast as Equation 15-1) did provide a useful transition at that point from the estimation of a population mean to the formulation of a bivariate regression model, a new illustrative model is introduced below, in Section 15.3. It is couched in terms of "changes" rather than "levels," so that it is reasonable to assume that the model error errors are I(0) and to (at least initially) assume that they are serially uncorrelated. This new example also explicitly allows for multiple explanatory variables. In particular, it models the growth rate in the PWT real output per capita datum for country i and year t as depending on the growth rate in country i's volume of trade (as a fraction of real output) in year t and also on the growth rates in the proportions of real output which country i allocates to consumption, investment, and government spending in year t. This example also uses the most recent version of the PWT data – Version 6.3 – which includes data up through the year 2007 and on a larger number of countries.[5]

This model is used in Sections 15.4 and 15.5 to illustrate how the central issue of panel data analysis – the likely heterogeneity of the underlying relationships across the countries and the time periods – is addressed using two of the three dominant approaches to panel data estimation: the Fixed Effects Model and the Random Effects Model. Section 15.5 closes with a reasonably practical method for choosing between these two models in practice. The chosen model – which happens to be the Random Effects Model in this instance – is then (in Section 15.6) diagnostically checked, using methods very similar to those already covered in Chapters 10 and 14.

The Fixed Effects Model and the Random Effects Model are introduced and analyzed (in Sections 15.4 and 15.5, respectively) under an assumption – detailed below – that the explanatory variables are "strictly exogenous." This means that the value of each explanatory variable in any given time period is assumed to be uncorrelated with the model error term in *all* periods – current, past, and future. This strict exogeneity assumption will be partially relaxed in Section 16.1 of the next chapter, so as to introduce dynamics into the model; these dynamics will enter the model in the form of an explanatory variable which is the dependent variable lagged one period. Finally, when some of the explanatory variables are endogenous – for any of the several reasons discussed at length in Chapter 11 – the strict exogeneity assumption must be dropped altogether. This motivates the introduction, in Section 16.2, of a third commonly used model for obtaining consistent parameter estimation with panel data: the First-Differences model.

15.3 A MULTIVARIATE EMPIRICAL EXAMPLE

As noted in the previous section, the pooled model directly applies OLS to all of the data, ignoring its structure as a panel data set. Compared to a cross-sectional regression for a single time period, the pooled model provides a far larger sample, but it can easily yield inconsistent parameter estimates and asymptotically invalid inference results if – as is likely – not all of the model parameters are homogeneous across all of the units and all of the time periods.

This section introduces an empirical example which will be used in the remainder of the chapter to describe and illustrate the econometric methods which are used to allow for such heterogeneity – either in the model intercept (Section 15.4) or via a separate component in the model error term (Section 15.5). Heterogeneity in the variance of the model error (i.e., heteroscedasticity) will be tested for (and allowed for) almost from the outset. So as to facilitate the exposition, however, failures in the other model assumptions – e.g. the assumptions of non-autocorrelation in the model

[5] At least, the PWT Version 6.3 was the most current version as of this writing; a newer version is no doubt currently available by now.

errors, homogeneity in the slope coefficients, and explanatory variable exogeneity – are addressed later in the chapter. The analysis of this empirical example is illustrated explicitly using Stata commands and output; but similar functionality is available in other programs, as the techniques described here are quite standard.

The empirical model introduced in this section is loosely based on the economic model implicitly considered by Summers and Heston (1991), in which they initially described the Penn World Table data set.[6] As formulated here, the model relates $Y_{i,t}$ – the growth rate in $RGDPL_{i,t}$, real per capita GDP in country i and year t – to the contemporaneous growth rate in real trade openness, here expressed as the ratio of the sum of exports plus imports to $RGDPL_{i,t}$. Additional explanatory variables in the model are the annual changes in consumption spending $(C_{i,t})$, investment spending $(I_{i,t})$, and government spending $(G_{i,t})$, all expressed as shares of $RGDPL_{i,t}$. More explicitly:

$$Y_{i,t} = 100\log\left[\frac{RGDPL_{i,t}}{RGDPL_{i,t-1}}\right] \tag{15-4}$$

$$OPEN_{i,t} = 100\log\left[\frac{\dfrac{EXPORTS_{i,t}+IMPORTS_{i,t}}{RGDPL_{i,t}}}{\dfrac{EXPORTS_{i,t-1}+IMPORTS_{i,t-1}}{RGDPL_{i,t-1}}}\right] \tag{15-5}$$

$$CSHARE_{i,t} = \left[\frac{C_{i,t}}{RGDPL_{i,t}}\right] - \left[\frac{C_{i,t-1}}{RGDPL_{i,t-1}}\right] \tag{15-6}$$

$$ISHARE_{i,t} = \left[\frac{I_{i,t}}{RGDPL_{i,t}}\right] - \left[\frac{I_{i,t-1}}{RGDPL_{i,t-1}}\right] \tag{15-7}$$

$$GSHARE_{i,t} = \left[\frac{G_{i,t}}{RGDPL_{i,t}}\right] - \left[\frac{G_{i,t-1}}{RGDPL_{i,t-1}}\right] \tag{15-8}$$

$RGDPL_{i,t}$, $EXPORTS_{i,t}$, $IMPORTS_{i,t}$, and the three "share" variables used in the right-hand sides of Equations 15-6 to 15-8 are all very highly autocorrelated. It is consequently evident that these data must either be modeled in differenced form ("in changes") or that it will be necessary to include lagged dependent variables in the models. As discussed in Chapter 14 for non-panel time-series, with strongly autocorrelated time-series data the choice between modeling "in levels" versus modeling "in changes" corresponds to deciding whether or not the dependent variable does or does not have a unit root – and this can sometimes be a tough call. A notable literature on testing for such a unit root in the context of a panel data set has developed in recent years. This enterprise suffers,

[6] Summers, R., and A. Heston (1991), "The Penn World Table (Mark 5): An Expanded Set of International Comparisons, 1950–1988," *Quarterly Journal of Economics 106,* 327–68. This data set was created so as to make the observations on the various countries as comparable as possible. The data used here are from PWT Version 6.3, which is available at Web site pwt.econ.upenn.edu/php_site/pwt_index.php; the construction of the variables is documented at pwt.econ.upenn.edu/Documentation/append61.pdf. All of the data on the specified variables are used, with the following exceptions: Serbia and Timor-Leste are dropped from the sample because data on these two countries are available only for a single year. And, per the recommendation in the "What is New in PWT 6.3" link, the (official) "China Version 1" data are dropped in favor of the (non-official) "China Version 2" figures, based on results in Maddison and Wu (2007). The Maddison and Wu (2007) article is posted at pwt.econ.upenn.edu/papers/Maddison-Wu%20(Harry's%20draft%20version%2029%20Jan%2007).pdf.

however, from the same problems noted in Chapter 14 for unit root testing in nonpanel data models, and from other difficulties as well; consequently, it will not be emphasized here.[7]

The choice to model "in changes" is clearly indicated for the data set considered here, however, as it is fairly obvious that the "levels" variables – $RGDPL_{i,t}$, $EXPORTS_{i,t}$, $IMPORTS_{i,t}$, etc. – are most likely all I(1) time-series. Furthermore, the diagnostic checking in Section 15.6 with respect to serial correlation in the errors of models based on the differenced data – i.e., using $Y_{i,t}$,$OPEN_{i,t}$, $CSHARE_{i,t}$, etc. – clearly indicates that the model "in changes" developed below is not overdifferenced.

Growth rates – i.e., changes in the logarithms of the time-series – are used in defining the variables for real output and trade openness (Equations 15-4 and 15-5) because the changes in $RGDPL_{i,t}$ and in $(EXPORTS_{i,t} + IMPORTS_{i,t})/RGDPL_{i,t}$ appear to be log-normally distributed; that is, the logarithm transformation is both necessary and sufficient in order to make the histograms of the sample data on these "change" variables at least roughly consistent with an assumption of normality. Simple changes (without a logarithmic transformation) are used for the consumption, investment, and government shares of output (Equations 15-6 to 15-8) because these share variables are basically fractions and their changes do not appear to be log-normally distributed. Also, investment spending is occasionally negative, so the logarithmic transformation would in any case be awkward.

Thus, the pooled regression model for this revised and expanded illustrative example can be written

$$\begin{aligned} Y_{i,t} &= \alpha + \beta_{open} OPEN_{i,t} + \beta_{cshare} CSHARE_{i,t} + \beta_{ishare} ISHARE_{i,t} \\ &\quad + \beta_{gshare} GSHARE_{i,t} + U_{i,t} \end{aligned} \tag{15-9}$$

where (for the moment) the parameters $(\alpha,\ \beta_{open},\ \beta_{cshare},\ \beta_{ishare},\ \beta_{gshare},\ \text{and}\ \sigma_u^2)$ are assumed constant across the entire sample and $U_{i,t}$ is assumed to be both $\text{IID}(0,\ \sigma_u^2)$ and uncorrelated with all of the explanatory variables. OLS yields consistent parameter estimators under these assumptions, but they are hardly likely to be satisfied for these data or for typical panel data sets.[8] In particular, the assumption that α is constant over all 187 countries is highly problematic; indeed, the noncredibility of this assumption is precisely why this pooled regression model is only a prelude for the models actually used, below, to analyze panel data.

---

[7] See Cameron and Trivedi (2009, pp. 272–73) for a more nuanced discussion of such tests. The latest iteration of Stata at this writing (Version 11) implements a number of these tests; evidently, other people are more enthusiastic about such testing. Also, note that it will become clear later on (in Chapter 16) that the inclusion of lagged dependent variables – which would surely figure prominently as explanatory variables in any model "in levels" – is inherently awkward in most panel data settings because a lagged dependent variable cannot be strictly exogenous. This suggests that it is optimal to lean more toward the model in "in changes" with panel data. Finally, foreshadowing material in Section 16.2, note that first-differencing – i.e., modeling "in changes" – can itself eliminate hetereogeneity in the intercept of a panel data regression model across the units. In fact, such first-differencing is central to the current best-practice approach for dealing with such heterogeneity in the presence of endogenous explanatory variables. But there is no guarantee that first-differencing is sufficient to eliminate this inter-unit heterogeneity. Indeed, the first-differencing used here in the definitions of $Y_{i,t}$, $OPEN_{i,t}$, etc. certainly does not do so: the results from the Baltagi and Li (1990) test discussed at the end of Section 15.5 make this very plain. Cameron, A. C., and P. K. Trivedi (2009), "Microeconomics Using Stata," Stata Press: College Station.

[8] This model is actually making all of the assumptions of the Dynamic Multiple Regression Model (Equation 13-40) which were required in order for OLS to provide consistent parameter estimators, but with no lagged dependent variables ($L_o = 0$) and four (instead of three) explanatory variables; these assumptions are, for simplicity, not all being listed here. If $U_{i,t}$ is not uncorrelated with an explanatory variable such as $CSHARE_{i,t}$, then $CSHARE_{i,t}$ is endogenous; consequently – per Chapter 11 – one would not expect OLS estimators to be consistent in that case. Instrumental variable methods for dealing with endogeneity induced in an explanatory variable such as $CSHARE_{i,t}$ by the usual sources – e.g., joint determination – are described in Section 16.2. In addition, however, there is also the distinct possibility in the pooled model above that a variable like $CSHARE_{i,t}$ is correlated with the country-specific component of $U_{i,t}$, denoted v_i below. The OLS estimators for Equation 15-9 will be inconsistent in that case also. Foreshadowing, endogeneity of this sort will also lead to inconsistent estimation in the Random Effects Model introduced in Section 15.5; that is why such correlations must be explicitly ruled out by Equation 15-18 in order for the Random Effects Model to be appropriate.

The sample runs from year 1951 (54 countries) through year 2007 (187 countries); so T_i – the number of years of data on $Y_{i,t}$, $OPEN_{i,t}$, $CSHARE_{i,t}$, $ISHARE_{i,t}$, and $GSHARE_{i,t}$ available for country i – varies, in this case from 13 to 57. Using this sample, the Stata output from OLS estimation of Equation 15-9 is:

```
. reg y  open  cshare ishare gshare

      Source |       SS       df       MS              Number of obs =    8180
-------------+------------------------------           F(  4,  8175) =  239.70
       Model |  47725.6454     4  11931.4113           Prob > F      =  0.0000
    Residual |  406923.491  8175  49.7765739           R-squared     =  0.1050
-------------+------------------------------           Adj R-squared =  0.1045
       Total |  454649.137  8179  55.5873746           Root MSE      =  7.0553

------------------------------------------------------------------------------
           y |      Coef.   Std. Err.      t    P>|t|     [95% Conf. Interval]
-------------+----------------------------------------------------------------
        open |  -.0212227   .0064558    -3.29   0.001    -.0338777   -.0085676
      cshare |  -.3494399   .0136229   -25.65   0.000    -.3761442   -.3227355
      ishare |   .0426341   .0197555     2.16   0.031     .0039082    .0813599
      gshare |  -.4156622   .0291995   -14.24   0.000    -.4729008   -.3584237
       _cons |   1.932431   .0785912    24.59   0.000     1.778372     2.08649
------------------------------------------------------------------------------
```

Before taking these estimates at all seriously, however, it is well to immediately relax the homogeneity assumption to the effect that $\text{var}(U_{i,t})$ is the same for all observations; this is just the usual homoscedasticity assumption discussed in Chapter 10. As in Section 10.7, this homoscedasticity assumption can be easily relaxed – at least with regard to obtaining consistent estimates of the standard errors of the sampling distributions of $\hat{\alpha}^{OLS}$, $\hat{\beta}^{OLS}_{OPEN}$, $\hat{\beta}^{OLS}_{CSHARE}$, $\hat{\beta}^{OLS}_{ISHARE}$, and $\hat{\beta}^{OLS}_{GSHARE}$ – by simply using the "vce(robust)" option to specify the estimation of White-Eicker standard errors.[9] Specifying this option yields the Stata output:

```
regress y  open  cshare ishare gshare , vce(robust)

Linear regression                                      Number of obs =    8180
                                                       F(  4,  8175) =   33.94
                                                       Prob > F      =  0.0000
                                                       R-squared     =  0.1050
                                                       Root MSE      =  7.0553

------------------------------------------------------------------------------
             |               Robust
           y |      Coef.   Std. Err.      t    P>|t|     [95% Conf. Interval]
-------------+----------------------------------------------------------------
        open |  -.0212227   .0169413    -1.25   0.210    -.0544319    .0119866
      cshare |  -.3494399   .0366281    -9.54   0.000    -.4212403   -.2776394
      ishare |   .0426341   .0479602     0.89   0.374    -.0513802    .1366483
      gshare |  -.4156622   .0765595    -5.43   0.000    -.5657383   -.2655861
       _cons |   1.932431   .0831218    23.25   0.000     1.769491    2.095371
------------------------------------------------------------------------------
```

[9] Per the discussion in Section 10.7, the White-Eicker standard error estimates correct for the inconsistency in the OLS standard error estimators when the model errors are heteroscedastic. The OLS parameter estimators themselves are consistent despite the heteroscedasticity; but they are no longer BLU or efficient, even asymptotically. The White-Eicker standard error estimates do not ameliorate this inefficiency, as they do not affect the parameter estimators at all. Generalized Method of Moments (GMM) estimation provides parameter estimators which are asymptotically more efficient than the OLS estimators when the model errors are heteroscedastic; GMM is introduced in Section 19.4.

Note that the robust standard error estimates are substantially different from the OLS standard error estimates. It is reasonable to conclude from this result that heteroscedasticity is a major problem in the pooled model for this particular data set and that it is consequently appropriate to concentrate solely on the results with robust standard error estimates.[10] These results will be referred to as the "pooled estimation results."

Pending diagnostic checking (in Section 15.6), it seems reasonable to at least temporarily assume that the slope coefficients $(\beta_{open}, \beta_{cshare}, \beta_{ishare}, \text{and } \beta_{gshare})$ are fixed constants which are also stable across the sample. In other words, β_{open}, β_{cshare}, β_{ishare}, and β_{gshare} are not only assumed to be fixed in repeated samples, but are also taken to be the same for all countries and years. This is not a reasonable assumption to make regarding the intercept coefficient, α, however – even temporarily. Indeed, the relaxation of this assumption is the defining characteristic of the "panel data methods" which are the topic of this chapter.

To accommodate the relaxation of this assumption, the model error is decomposed into three components:

$$
\begin{aligned}
U_{i,t} &= v_i + \lambda_t + \varepsilon_{i,t} \\
\varepsilon_{i,t} &\sim \text{IID}(0, \sigma_\varepsilon^2) \qquad i = 1 \ldots M \qquad t = 1 \ldots T_i
\end{aligned}
\tag{15-10}
$$

Here v_i is a country-specific component and λ_t is a year-specific component. The remaining component $(\varepsilon_{i,t})$ is called the "idiosyncratic shock."[11]

One could hope that this decomposition would leave $\varepsilon_{i,t}$ homoscedastic, as implied by the second line of Equation 15-10, but this is usually not the case. And, in fact, it is not the case in the present example. In such instances the variance of $\varepsilon_{i,t}$ depends – in many settings, systematically – on country and year, so that $\varepsilon_{i,t}$ is only independently (but not identically) distributed. The parameter σ_ε^2 should thus be denoted something like $(\sigma_\varepsilon^2)_{i,t}$; this notational complication will generally be suppressed below for expositional simplicity.

The variability (across repeated samples) of $\varepsilon_{i,t}$ is thus allowed to be country- and/or year-specific, but the expected value of $\varepsilon_{i,t}$ is still assumed to be the same – i.e., zero – for all countries and years. Again, pending diagnostic checking (in Section 15.6), $\varepsilon_{i,t}$ will be taken to be independently distributed for all values of i and t, so – notationally ignoring the heteroscedasticity in $\varepsilon_{i,t}$ – the mode] for $Y_{i,t}$ becomes

$$
\begin{aligned}
Y_{i,t} &= \alpha + \beta_{open} OPEN_{i,t} + \beta_{cshare} CSHARE_{i,t} + \beta_{ishare} ISHARE_{i,t} \\
&\quad + \beta_{gshare} GSHARE_{i,t} + v_i + \lambda_t + \varepsilon_{i,t} \varepsilon_{i,t} \sim \text{IID}(0, \sigma_\varepsilon^2)
\end{aligned}
\tag{15-11}
$$

Note that Equation 15-10 specifies nothing with respect to the distributions of the (possibly) random variables v_i and λ_t. In fact, λ_t is usually taken to be fixed in repeated samples – that is, it is assumed to not be random at all. In that case, Equation 15-11 is simply allowing the intercept to vary across the years in

[10] Autocorrelation in the $U_{i,t}$ of the pooled model is usually a problem also, but is not being emphasized at this particular point in the exposition. In fact, you will show in Exercise 15-5 that $U_{i,t}$ is inherently autocorrelated whenever the country-specific component of $U_{i,t}$, is taken to be random – as in Section 15.5. Fundamentally, this is because every error $U_{i,t}$ for country i shares the same country-specific component; this shared component induces a correlation across all of the time periods among the $U_{i,t}$, for any particular country. Foreshadowing material covered in Section 15.4, the presence of such autocorrelation (and heteroscedasticity as well) can be easily dealt with by computing "cluster-robust" standard error estimates; indeed, the use of such estimates is now standard in estimating panel data models. Cluster-robust standard error estimates are specified in Stata by simply specifying "vce(cluster countrynum)" instead of "vce(robust)" in the list of options for the regress command, where "countrynum" is a numeric variable which indexes each country in the sample. The cluster-robust standard error estimates are 30% to 40% larger than the White-Eicker estimates in the present instance; thus, autocorrelation is a non-trivial problem in this particular pooled model also, in addition to heteroscedasticity.

[11] Equation 15-10 embodies a fairly standard nomenclature for this decomposition, so the usual convention in this book of denoting a (random) model error term using an uppercase letter and denoting its realization with the corresponding lowercase letter is suspended here. A realization of $\varepsilon_{i,t}$ could be denoted $\varepsilon_{i,t}^*$.

the sample. Here, as noted earlier, T_i – the number of observations available for country i – varies from 13 to 57. As is typically the case, the maximum value of T_i is small here, compared to the 8,180 sample observations available. Consequently, the variation in λ_t can be captured by simply including 56 appropriately-defined dummy variables $(D1952_{i,t} \ldots D2007_{i,t})$ in the model specification. ($D1952_{i,t}$ is set to one for all observations from year 1952 and to zero otherwise; the other dummy variables are similarly defined.[12])

One could instead specify a linear or quadratic time trend which is assumed to be identical across countries; that way of specifying the time variation adds only one or two additional parameters to be estimated, instead of 56. On the other hand, either a linear or quadratic trend specification choice risks incorrectly specifying the form of the time-dependence.[13] Moreover, either of these two specific trend specifications saves a notable number of degrees of freedom only when the number of time periods of data available is sizeable, which is where this risk is largest. Specifying a linear or quadratic trend does, however, facilitate diagnostically checking whether the pattern of time-dependence in fact does differ across several groups of countries in the sample.

Overall, the dummy variable approach is usually preferable; it is certainly necessary in the present instance, where – as will be apparent in the estimated model quoted in the next section – the estimated coefficients on $D1952_{i,t} \ldots D2007_{i,t}$ are statistically significant and do not vary in a manner which could have been captured by a simple polynomial. In the author's view it is practical and prudent to routinely include dummy variables of this nature, thereby allowing for time-heterogeneity in the intercept, from the very outset: if the coefficients modeling the time variation are not, as a group, statistically significant, then they can be dropped from the model specification at a later stage in the modeling process.[14]

Note, however, that all of these formulations for λ_t are implicitly assuming that the time-dependence of the intercept is homogeneous across the M countries. The possibility that the coefficients on the dummy variables modeling the time variation in λ_t themselves vary across the countries is not ruled out, it is simply not being considered at this point in the modeling process: one can (and, to a reasonable extent, generally should) routinely investigate the across-country "stability" of all of the model coefficients – including those on linear trend variables or on these time-variation dummy variables – as part of the diagnostic checking process. Similarly, it is useful to check whether coefficients such as β_{open}, β_{cshare}, etc. are stable across the time periods. In either case, finding a deficiency in the model specification opens up the opportunity to either look for a richer economic specification (leading to a model with coefficients which are more stable across

[12] $D1951_{i,t}$ can be included in the model also, but only if the intercept (α) is dropped from the model specification. This is, of course, statistically equivalent; the choice is a matter of convenience. The coefficients on the 57 dummy variables model in that case model the time pattern itself, rather than its increment with respect to the first sample period; this pattern is often more easily interpreted. On the other hand, one must then explicitly drop the intercept in every regression estimation command issued, as intercept estimation is (for good reason!) the usual default option in most computer programs. Also, the null hypothesis of time-homogeneity in that case corresponds to 56 parameter equality restrictions rather than to 56 coefficient zero restrictions, which typically involves more keystrokes – and hence more opportunities for typographical errors. It is worth noting that, in Stata, a sequence of variables such as *D1952* through *D2007* can be abbreviated as "D1952-D2007" in regression commands. This abbreviation is not allowed in the hypothesis testing ("test") command, however, because it would be difficult to distinguish it from a reference to the difference between the coefficients on the two variables $D1952_{i,t}$ and $D2007_{i,t}$.

[13] Foreshadowing, it will be shown in Section 16.2 that the First-Differences Model is implicitly assuming a linear time trend with a slope which is homogeneous across the countries.

[14] The reader is advised that this is not the most conventional approach; that is why the phrase "in the author's view" appears in the text. More typically, models allowing only for heterogeneity across units ("one-way" models) are discussed first and models additionally allowing for heterogeneity across time ("two-way" models) are developed subsequently. The heterogeneity across time in two-way models is sometimes modeled with dummy variables (as here) and sometimes modeled in a "random effects" manner. (The "random effects" approach is described in Section 15.5 below, where it is used to model heterogeneity in the intercept across countries.) The dummy variable approach is most graceful in cases where the ratio of the average number of periods per unit to the number of units is relatively small; this ratio would actually be substantially smaller in a typical panel data set than it is in the particular example used here.

periods and countries) or to at least use appropriate interaction terms to adjust for such heterogeneity, so that it cannot distort one's estimates and inferences with regard to crucial coefficients.

Turning now to the v_i term in Equations 15-10 and 15-11, the best way to interpret this variable is to view it as modeling that portion of the variation in the expected value of $Y_{i,t}$ across the M countries which is not "explained" by the across-country variation in the explanatory variables: $OPEN_{i,t}$, $CSHARE_{i,t}$, $ISHARE_{i,t}$, and $GSHARE_{i,t}$. One approach is to treat the values $v_1 \ldots v_M$ as "fixed in repeated samples" – just as was done with the time components, $\lambda_1 \ldots \lambda_{57}$ – and, in effect, model their variation using dummy variables. This choice corresponds to what is called the "Fixed Effects Model," discussed in the next section, Section 15.4. Alternatively, v_i can be specified as a random variable, which is equivalent to assuming that it is *not* "fixed in repeated samples." This choice corresponds to the "Random Effects Model," discussed in Section 15.5.

But repeated samples are not available: we only have one data set! Surprisingly, it is nevertheless frequently possible to distinguish empirically which of these two models is appropriate for the data set at hand. This is because, as will be seen in the next two sections, OLS yields consistent estimators of the parameters in Equation 15-11 for the Fixed Effects Model, whereas consistent OLS parameter estimation in the Random Effects Model requires an additional assumption: Equation 15-18, which is discussed in Section 15.5. Consequently, the two models will, for sufficiently large samples, yield observably distinct parameter estimates if this additional assumption is false for the data set being analyzed. Thus, if the parameter estimates from the two models differ significantly, then the Random Effects Model is inappropriate.

Because the estimation of both the Fixed Effects Model and the Random Effects Model is usually quite feasible, both have been conveniently implemented in current econometric software. Consequently, both models are in common use – indeed, one often estimates both of them. Each of these models has been extensively analyzed in the econometrics literature and each has its advantages and disadvantages; these are explored below, in Sections 15.4 and 15.5.

In particular – foreshadowing these results – the Random Effects Model estimators of coefficients like β_{open}, β_{cshare}, β_{ishare}, and β_{gshare} are more efficient than the analogous Fixed Effects Model estimators, *if* the additional assumption alluded to above (Equation 15-18) is satisfied. As noted above, the validity of this additional assumption implies that the coefficient estimates from the two models are not significantly different from one another in large samples; consequently, the Random Effects Model coefficient estimates will be preferable in that case, because they are more precise. But if the coefficient estimates from the two models *do* differ significantly from one another, then the Fixed Effects Model coefficient estimates are preferable, because the Random Effects Model coefficient estimates are inconsistent in that case.

On the other hand, coefficients on explanatory variables which do not vary over time – such as an individual's race or a country's land area – simply cannot be estimated in a Fixed Effects Model; in that case the choice will be between two other approaches described below: the "Between Effects Model" (described in Section 15.4, along with the Fixed Effects Model) and the "Hausman-Taylor estimator," described at the end of Section 15.5, immediately after the description of the Random Effects Model.[15] Sections 15.4 and 15.5 describe all of these models – and their issues – in turn; the topic of diagnostic checking is taken up in Section 15.6, since it is similar across all of these modeling approaches.

Finally, almost all of these techniques become problematic once dynamics (in the form of lagged values of the dependent variable) and/or endogeneity (in the form of correlations between explanatory variables and the idiosyncratic error term, $\varepsilon_{i,t}$) are included in the model specification. These are often important features of the economic problem at hand; the econometric complications they induce are discussed in Sections 16.1 and 16.2, respectively. In particular, the "First-Differences Model" is introduced in Section 16.2 to provide a practical solution to the problems of parameter estimation and inference in both of these settings, at least where the sample is sufficiently large.

[15] Hausman, J. A., and W. E. Taylor (1981), "Panel Data and Unobservable Individual Effects." *Econometrica 49*,1377–98.

15.4 THE FIXED EFFECTS AND THE BETWEEN EFFECTS MODELS

In the Fixed Effects Model, the values of $\nu_1 \ldots \nu_M$ from the decomposition of $U_{i,t}$ in Equation 15-10 are taken to be a set of M fixed constants, effectively shifting the intercept for each of the M countries in this example. Thus, a straightforward solution to the problem of estimating β_{open}, β_{cshare}, β_{ishare}, and β_{gshare} – while allowing for these shifts in the intercept – is to simply replace the intercept (α) in Equation 15-11 by a weighted sum of M dummy variables (one for each country), in much the same way that the heterogeneity across time is modeled.

This country-dummy variable approach is usually computationally feasible, but it is a bit awkward when M is sizeable. For example, there are 187 countries in the Penn World Table data set used here, so this way of estimating the Fixed Effects Model would appear to require that one do quite a bit of tedious (and error-prone) typing in order to generate the 187 necessary dummy variables.[16]

Fortunately, it is not necessary to estimate these M country-specific dummy variable coefficients: it turns out to be completely equivalent to apply OLS to a transformed version of Equation 15-11. This transformation is called the "within" (or sometimes the "within-group") transformation and it is very straightforward: the "within" transformed value of a variable or error component is just its original value minus its sample mean over all of the sample data for that particular country.

Having replaced λ_t in Equation 15-11 by the dummy variables $D1952_{i,t} \ldots D2007_{i,t}$, the "within" transformed variables and components – now labeled with superscript "FE" – are:

$$
\begin{aligned}
Y_{i,t}^{FF} &= Y_{i,t} - \overline{Y_i} && \text{where} \quad \overline{Y_i} \equiv \frac{1}{T_i}\sum_{s=1}^{T_i} Y_{i,s} \\
OPEN_{i,t}^{FE} &= OPEN_{i,t} - \overline{OPEN_i} && \text{where} \quad \overline{OPEN_i} \equiv \frac{1}{T_i}\sum_{s=1}^{T_i} OPEN_{i,s} \\
CSHARE_{i,t}^{FE} &= CSHARE_{i,t} - \overline{CSHARE_i} && \text{where} \quad \overline{CSHARE_i} \equiv \frac{1}{T_i}\sum_{s=1}^{T_i} CSHARE_{i,s} \\
ISHARE_{i,t}^{FE} &= ISHARE_{i,t} - \overline{ISHARE_i} && \text{where} \quad \overline{ISHARE_i} \equiv \frac{1}{T_i}\sum_{s=1}^{T_i} ISHARE_{i,s} \\
GSHARE_{i,t}^{FE} &= GSHARE_{i,t} - \overline{GSHARE_i} && \text{where} \quad \overline{GSHARE_i} \equiv \frac{1}{T_i}\sum_{s=1}^{T_i} GSHARE_{i,s} \qquad (15\text{-}12) \\
D1952_{i,t}^{FE} &= D1952_{i,t} - \overline{D1952_i} && \text{where} \quad \overline{D1952_i} \equiv \frac{1}{T_i}\sum_{s=1}^{T_i} D1952_{i,s} \\
&\ldots \\
D2007_{i,t}^{FE} &= D2007_{i,t} - \overline{D2007_i} && \text{where} \quad \overline{D2007_i} \equiv \frac{1}{T_i}\sum_{s=1}^{T_i} D2007_{i,s} \\
\nu_i^{FE} &= \nu_i - \overline{\nu_i} = 0 && \text{where} \quad \overline{\nu_i} \equiv \frac{1}{T_i}\sum_{s=1}^{T_i} \nu_i \\
\varepsilon_{i,t}^{FE} &= \varepsilon_{i,t} - \overline{\varepsilon_i} && \text{where} \quad \overline{\varepsilon_i} \equiv \frac{1}{T_i}\sum_{s=1}^{T_i} \varepsilon_{i,s}
\end{aligned}
$$

[16] This approach also uses a lot of computer memory, but memory is cheap and plentiful. The analyst's time – and the risk of typographical errors – are more important considerations. There is also a formal theoretical problem in that the number of dummy variable coefficients estimated increases with M; this is awkward because the asymptotic distribution of the OLS estimators is defined in terms of a probability limit as M becomes arbitrarily large. Note that the intercept is retained here, so that only 156 dummy variables are needed.

The Fixed Effects Model estimators of β_{open}, β_{cshare}, β_{ishare}, β_{gshare}, and $\lambda_{1952} \ldots \lambda_{2007}$ can then be obtained by simply applying OLS estimation to the transformed model,

$$
\begin{aligned}
Y_{i,t}^{FE} &= \beta_{open} OPEN_{i,t}^{FE} + \beta_{cshare} CSHARE_{i,t}^{FE} + \beta_{ishare} ISHARE_{i,t}^{FE} + \beta_{gshare} GSHARE_{i,t}^{FE} \\
&\quad + \lambda_{1952} D1952_{i,t}^{FE} + \ldots + \lambda_{2007} D2007_{i,t}^{FE} + \varepsilon_{i,t}^{FE}
\end{aligned}
\tag{15-13}
$$

It can be shown that OLS applied to the "within" transformed data is equivalent to including the M country-specific dummy variables; this derivation requires a good bit of linear algebra, so that is not done here.[17] This result is intuitively appealing, however, in view of the fact that the "within" transformation has eliminated v_i from the model altogether: since v_i is the same for each of the T_i observations on country i, v_i is necessarily equal to its country-mean, $\overline{v}_i$. Consequently, v_i^{FE}, the "within" transformation of v_i, is exactly zero.

Recall also that the analysis of the Bivariate Regression Model example in Section 5.7 and Appendix 5.1 showed that there is a close relationship between the OLS estimate of the coefficient on a dummy variable and an estimated mean over a portion of the sample. In that model – consisting of only an intercept and a single dummy variable – Appendix 5.1 provides the algebra showing that the OLS estimate of the coefficient on the dummy variable is numerically equal to the difference between the sample mean of the dependent variable observations for which the dummy variable is one and the sample mean of the dependent variable observations for which the dummy variable is zero. Thus, in that simple context, including the dummy variable in the model is equivalent to adjusting the data on the dependent variable so that both parts of the sample have the same sample mean.

It is also worth noting explicitly that the intercept (α) in Equation 15-11 has been eliminated from Equation 15-13; this elimination occurs because the variable (equal to one for each observation) which produces the intercept in the Multiple Regression Model is reduced to zero by the "within" transformation. This result, too, is consistent with the notion at the beginning of this section that α was to be replaced by the M country-specific dummy variables. Unfortunately, the "within" transformation also eliminates any other explanatory variable which does not vary over time: such variables only impact $v_1 \ldots v_M$ in the context of the Fixed Effects Model, so the coefficients on such explanatory variables cannot be estimated in this framework.

Exercise 15-1 illustrates both of these points explicitly using a tiny data set in which the variable $OPEN_{i,t}$ is taken to be constant over time for the two countries considered. Exercises 15-2 and 15-3 explicitly illustrate the "within" transformation on two data sets with time-varying explanatory variables, but which are so small that one can easily see exactly what the transformation is doing. Understanding the "within" transformation thoroughly is important because variations on the Fixed Effects Model (including the Random Effects Model discussed in the next section) are widely used in empirical work, and because modern econometric software usually just performs the transformation – at our bidding, but out of sight.[18]

Two further points must be made before turning to an explicit empirical illustration based on the PWT data set. First, it is essential to note that the 'within' transformation "mixes up" the time-observations on each variable to which it is applied. For example, the value of $OPEN_{7,2}^{FE}$, the transformed observation on $OPEN_{i,t}$ for the second year in the sample for the seventh country, clearly depends on $\overline{OPEN_7}$. But $\overline{OPEN_7}$, is the sample mean of $OPEN_{7,t}$ over all T_7 of the years of data

[17] For example, see Arellano (2003, p. 16) for a derivation. Arellano, M. (2003), *Panel Data Econometrics*, Oxford University Press.

[18] Also, standard econometric software (e.g., Stata) does not always do exactly what one needs, so it is occasionally necessary to program parts of the calculations oneself. An example of this is provided by the generalized Hausman test discussed in the next section and implemented in a Stata *do* file in Appendix 15.1; implementation of this test requires explicit programming of both the "within" transformation and the related transformation for the Random Effects Model, described in the next section.

available for the seventh country. Thus, $OPEN^{FE}_{7,2}$ in fact depends on *all* of the available observations on $OPEN_{7,t}$. This is consequential because the consistency of the OLS estimators of the parameters in Equation 15-13 – per the assumptions of the Dynamic Multiple Regression Model (Equation 14-3) – requires that the explanatory variables (such as $OPEN^{FE}_{i,t}$) are all exogenous: that is, uncorrelated with the model error term in this regression equation, the transformed variable, $\varepsilon^{FE}_{i,t}$.

But are they? So far we have only assumed that the original explanatory variables ($OPEN_{i,t}$, $CSHARE_{i,t}$, $CISHARE_{i,t}$, and $GSHARE_{i,t}$) are exogenous – that is, uncorrelated with the model error term, $U_{i,t}$. Here the model error components v_i and λ_t defined in Equation 15-10 have been assumed to be fixed, so this amounts to assuming that these original explanatory variables are all uncorrelated with the idiosyncratic component, $\varepsilon_{i,t}$. This may or may not be a reasonable assumption; that issue is dealt with in Section 16.2, using the First-Differences Model and instrumental variables estimation. However, even assuming that an original explanatory variable (e.g., $OPEN_{i,t}$) is exogenous, it is by no means clear that the corresponding transformed variable (e.g., $OPEN^{FE}_{i,2}$) is still exogenous.

And, in fact, the "within" transformed variables are *not* exogenous, unless a stronger exogeneity assumption is made regarding the original variables. The standard such exogeneity assumption made for panel data models is that explanatory variables like $OPEN_{i,t}$ are what is called "strictly" exogenous

Strict Exogeneity Assumption

$$\begin{aligned} \text{corr}\left(OPEN_{i,\tau},\ \varepsilon_{i,t}\right) &= 0 \\ \text{corr}\left(CSHARE_{i,\tau},\ \varepsilon_{i,t}\right) &= 0 \\ \text{corr}\left(ISHARE_{i,\tau},\ \varepsilon_{i,t}\right) &= 0 \\ \text{corr}\left(GSHARE_{i,\tau}\ \varepsilon_{i,t}\right) &= 0 \end{aligned} \tag{15-14}$$

for **all** values of τ and t

Thus, strict exogeneity of $OPEN_{i,t}$ requires that $OPEN_{i,t}$ is uncorrelated with $\varepsilon_{i,\tau}$ for *all* values of τ, not just for τ equal to t. An assumption of strict exogeneity for $OPEN_{i,t}$, $CSHARE_{i,t}$, $CISHARE_{i,t}$, and $GSHARE_{i,t}$ is exactly what is needed in order to ensure that the transformed variables – $OPEN^{FE}_{i,t}$, $CSHARE^{FE}_{i,t}$, $ISHARE^{FE}_{i,t}$, and $GSHARE^{FE}_{i,t}$ – are all uncorrelated with $\varepsilon^{FE}_{i,t}$. OLS estimation of Equation 15-13 hence yields consistent estimators if – and only if – all of the explanatory variables in the model are strictly exogenous.

Strict exogeneity is quite a strong assumption, however. If $OPEN_{i,t}$, for example, is strictly exogenous, then $OPEN_{i,t}$ is uncorrelated with the idiosyncratic error component $\left(\varepsilon_{i,t}\right)$ at *all* relative lags. This rules out a lot more than the contemporaneous correlation arising from the endogeneity sources discussed in Chapter 11, such as joint determination with $Y_{i,t}$ and measurement error in $OPEN_{i,t}$: it further rules out the possibility that either past or future values of $OPEN_{i,t}$ are correlated with the current value of $\varepsilon_{i,t}$.

One could ensure that past values of $OPEN_{i,t}$ are uncorrelated with the current value of $\varepsilon_{i,t}$ by simply including a sufficient number of lagged values of $OPEN_{i,t}$ as additional explanatory variables in the model specification. The terms in $OPEN_{t-1}$, $OPEN_{t-2}$, etc. in the respecified model would then eliminate any linear dependence on these variables in the newly implied model error term. Thus, failure of this part of strict exogeneity can be interpreted as an "omitted variables" problem; one has failed to include sufficient dynamics in the model in the form of lags in the explanatory variables.

An explanatory variable whose lagged values are uncorrelated with the current values of $\varepsilon_{i,t}$ is called "predetermined." Note that this is equivalent to saying that the current value of a predetermined explanatory variable is uncorrelated with future values of $\varepsilon_{i,t}$. Indeed, this way of expressing the definition motivates the terminology: a predetermined variable can be thought of as being observed – "determined" – prior to the drawing of a realization of $\varepsilon_{i,t}$.

In contrast, it is not generally possible to ensure that *future* values of $OPEN_{i,t}$ are uncorrelated with the current value of $\varepsilon_{i,t}$. In particular, if there is "feedback" in the relationship between $Y_{i,t}$ and $OPEN_{i,t}$, then a current fluctuation of $Y_{i,t}$ away from its mean – i.e., a non-zero realization of $\varepsilon_{i,t}$ – has an impact on future values of $OPEN_{i,t}$, implying that future values of $OPEN_{i,t}$ are necessarily correlated with the current value of $\varepsilon_{i,t}$. Hence $OPEN_{i,t}$ cannot possibly be strictly exogenous in that case.[19]

An explanatory variable which is uncorrelated with the current value of $\varepsilon_{i,t}$, but which is correlated with either its past or future values, is said to be "weakly exogenous." The term "exogenous variable," as used in previous chapters, thus only excludes endogeneity: it is inexplicit with regard to whether the variable is strictly exogenous (uncorrelated with any values of $\varepsilon_{i,t}$: past, present, or future), predetermined (uncorrelated with current and future values $\varepsilon_{i,t}$), or only weakly exogenous (uncorrelated with the current value of $\varepsilon_{i,t}$, but quite possibly correlated with past and/or future values). Thus, "weak exogeneity" is similar to "exogeneity," but with an implicit implication that strict exogeneity does not necessarily hold.

Strict exogeneity is clearly a notably stronger assumption than was needed in Chapters 11 and 12. The "within" transformation induces a contemporaneous correlation between the transformed values of such a weakly exogenous variable and the (transformed) model error term. Thus, OLS applied to the "within" transformed regression model (Equation 15-13) leads to inconsistent parameter estimates if any of the explanatory variables is only weakly exogenous: strict exogeneity is a necessary condition for consistent parameter estimation in the context of the Fixed Effects Model. Sections 16.1 and 16.2 will explicitly consider how to proceed when an assumption of strict exogeneity is not viable, as when the model includes explanatory variables which are lagged values of the dependent variable or when an explanatory variable is endogenous – e.g., due to joint determination.

Second, before getting on with actually estimating the Fixed Effects Model, it is worth noting that – because the sample mean for the data on country i involves all of the observations on that country – the "within" transformation applied to $\varepsilon_{i,t}$ induces a degree of serial correlation in $\varepsilon_{i,t}^{\mathrm{FE}}$. In particular, it is easy to show (Exercise 15-4) that the serial independence assumed for $\varepsilon_{i,t}$ implies that

$$\operatorname{corr}\left(\varepsilon_{i,t}^{FE}, \varepsilon_{i,\tau}^{FE}\right) = \frac{-1}{T_i - 1} \tag{15-15}$$

for all $t \neq \tau$. Since this serial correlation renders both the usual OLS standard error estimators and the White-Eicker ("robust") standard error estimators inconsistent, it is nowadays customary to instead estimate what are called "cluster-robust" standard, error estimates for the Fixed Effects Model parameter estimators.[20]

The cluster-robust standard errors are the logical extension to the present context –where $\varepsilon_{i,t}^{\mathrm{FE}}$ are serially correlated, but still independently distributed across the different countries – of the White-Eicker notion for obtaining heteroscedasticity-robust estimators of the variance of the asymptotic sampling distribution of the OLS parameter estimators. Like the White-Eicker estimators, the cluster-robust standard error estimators are only asymptotically justified, but they do not assume any particular structure (such as Equation 15-15, induced by the "within" transformation) on

[19] One could clearly eliminate these correlations by including future values of $OPEN_{i,t}$ as explanatory variables in the model. Many people find such specifications intuitively unappealing, but they naturally arise in models based on rational expectations theory. Also, note that including such future values provides a straightforward way to test the validity of the strict exogeneity assumption.

[20] Note that "nowadays customary" means that recent versions of Stata now automatically compute cluster-robust standard errors – see Footnote 15-22. As described in Footnote 15-9 – in the context of noting the heteroscedasticity in the errors for the pooled model for these data – it is also nowadays common to use GMM estimation to allow for this serial correlation induced in $\varepsilon_{i,t}^{\mathrm{FE}}$, also thereby producing more efficient parameter estimators.

the intracountry correlations of the model errors. The cluster-robust standard error estimators thus allow for the possibility that the underlying idiosyncratic model error $(\varepsilon_{i,t})$ might itself be serially correlated. The cluster-robust standard error estimators also allow for heteroscedasticity of arbitrary form in the model errors. Thus, the cluster-robust standard error estimators allow for the possibility that the model errors for country i might be both heteroscedastic and correlated with the other errors for country i: all that they rule out is any correlation between the model errors in one country and those in another country.

The White-Eicker standard error estimators were discussed and motivated in Chapter 10, in the context of the Bivariate Regression Model; so it is sensible to motivate the cluster-robust standard error estimator by beginning in that context. In particular, it was shown in Section 10.7 that if the sample is sufficiently large that the fitting errors $(U_l^{\text{fit}} \ldots U_N^{\text{fit}})$ are a good approximation to the actual model errors $(U_i \ldots U_N)$, then

$$\left[\text{var}(\hat{\beta})\right]^{\text{robust}} = \sum_{i=1}^{N} \left(w_i^{\text{ols}}\right)^2 \left(U_i^{\text{fit}}\right)^2 \tag{10-20}$$

is an unbiased estimator of the sampling variance of the OLS slope estimator $(\hat{\beta})$, even when the variance of U_i is not a constant for all N observations. (In Equation 10-20 $w_1^{\text{ols}} \ldots w_N^{\text{ols}}$ are the Bivariate Regression Model OLS weights from Equation 6-10.) The cluster-robust estimator simply extends this idea to a panel data setting, allowing ε_{it}^{FE} to be both heteroscedastic *and* correlated with its value for this same country in other time periods. The cluster-robust estimator still assumes that ε_{it}^{FE} is uncorrelated with all values of $\varepsilon_{j\tau}^{FE}$, the idiosyncratic component of the model error for a *different* country (j) in any year τ. Thus, the value of $E\left[\varepsilon_{it}^{FE}\,\varepsilon_{i\tau}^{FE}\right]$ is unrestricted for all of the possible values of τ (from one to T_i), but $E\left[\varepsilon_{it}^{FE}\,\varepsilon_{j\tau}^{FE}\right]$ is assumed to be zero for all values of t and τ when i is not equal to j.

For notational simplicity, attention is again restricted to a bivariate model, with just one explanatory variable ($OPEN_{i,t}$, say) and hence just one slope coefficient, β_{open}.[21] Focusing on just the terms arising from the observations on the first country in the sample, the cluster-robust estimator analogous to the expression in Equation 10-20 is then

$$\begin{aligned}\left[\text{var}(\hat{\beta}_{open})\right]^{cluster-robust} &= \sum_{\tau_1=1}^{T_1}\sum_{\tau_2=1}^{T_1} w_{\tau_1}^{\text{ols}} w_{\tau_2}^{\text{ols}} \varepsilon_{1,\tau_1}^{FE,\text{fit}} \varepsilon_{1,\tau_2}^{FE,\text{fit}} \\ &\quad + \text{similar terms for countries } 2,\ 3,\ 4, \ldots, M\end{aligned} \tag{15-16}$$

where "$\varepsilon_{1,t}^{FE,\text{ fit}}$" is the fitting error from the (now bivariate) Fixed Effects Model regression for country 1 in period t. Note that the terms in Equation 15-16 with τ_1 equal to τ_2 are exactly equivalent to the terms in the White-Eicker variance estimator, whereas the terms with τ_1 unequal to τ_2 allow for the serial correlation of the idiosyncratic component of the model error within the T_i observations for country i.[22]

Actually obtaining the OLS estimates for the Fixed Effects Model of Equation 15-13 – and cluster-robust standard error estimates – is very easy in practice, because this is such a standard

[21] One could easily modify this expression for the fall model of Equation 15-13 replacing the Bivariate Regression Model OLS weights with the appropriate Multiple Regression Model OLS weights (defined in Equation 9-13) for the slope coefficient at issue.

[22] To be a bit more explicit, the Bivariate Regression Model OLS weights (w_t^{OLS}) in Equation 15-16 would be calculated by substituting the $N = 8180$ sample values of $OPEN_{i,t}^{FE}$ in for $x_l \ldots x_N$ in the expression, given for w_i^{OLS} in Equation 6-10. The idea underlying the cluster-robust standard error estimates is exactly the same for the full model; this restriction to the bivariate setting is imposed only so as to parallel the development used in Chapter 10 to justify the White-Eicker estimates and so as to leverage the full derivation of the bivariate OLS estimator weights given in Chapter 6.

technique that it is preprogrammed into most econometrics software. In Stata, for example, it only requires two lines:

```
xtset countrynum year
xtreg y open cshare gshare ishare d1952-d2007, vce(robust) fe
```

Here *countrynum* is a numeric variable which is defined so as to have a single, distinct value for each country; the "xtset" command specifies that this variable indexes the units (countries, in the present example) and that the variable *year* indexes time. The "xtreg" command – with the option "fe" – directs Stata to perform the "within" transformation on all of the variables and to estimate the resulting regression model (Equation 15-13) using OLS.[23]

This command produces the output:

```
Fixed-effects (within) regression               Number of obs      =      8180
Group variable: countrynum                      Number of groups   =       187

R-sq:  within  = 0.1436                         Obs per group: min =        13
       between = 0.1883                                        avg =      43.7
       overall = 0.1407                                        max =        57

                                                F(60,186)          =     11.84
corr(u_i, Xb)  = 0.0224                         Prob > F           =    0.0000

                         (Std. Err. adjusted for 187 clusters in countrynum)
------------------------------------------------------------------------------
             |               Robust
           y |      Coef.   Std. Err.      t    P>|t|     [95% Conf. Interval]
-------------+----------------------------------------------------------------
        open |   -.031497   .0170318    -1.85   0.066    -.0650973    .0021032
      cshare |  -.3367431   .0452489    -7.44   0.000    -.4260102   -.2474761
      ishare |   .0234417   .0678222     0.35   0.730    -.1103579    .1572413
      gshare |  -.3997391   .0912954    -4.38   0.000    -.5798467   -.2196315
       d1952 |  -2.447967   .9970184    -2.46   0.015    -4.414885   -.4810485
       d1953 |  -2.003874   1.065327    -1.88   0.062    -4.105552    .0978045
       d1954 |   -1.22653   .9584061    -1.28   0.202    -3.117274    .6642134
       d1955 |  -1.062603   .7719517    -1.38   0.170    -2.585509    .4603035
       d1956 |  -1.059915    .951751    -1.11   0.267    -2.937529    .8176999
       d1957 |   -1.31065   .8116349    -1.61   0.108    -2.911844    .2905431
       d1958 |  -3.306192   .9440756    -3.50   0.001    -5.168664   -1.443719
       d1959 |  -1.918447   .9821972    -1.95   0.052    -3.856126     .019232
```

[23] One might naturally suppose that the "vce(robust)" option is directing Stata to compute White-Eicker standard error estimates here. This is no longer the case, as of Stata 9.1. In fact, based on results in Stock and Watson (2008), the "xtreg" routine now computes the cluster-robust standard error estimates discussed above when the "fe vce(robust)" option is specified. (As of version 11, this is also the case when "xtreg" is used to estimate the Random Effects Model discussed in Section 15.5.) Absent specifying the use of version 9.0 (using the Stata "version" command) or computing the "within" transform oneself (e.g., using a do file such as that given in Appendix 15.1), then, one is going to get standard error estimates that are also robust to within-country autocorrelation whether one wants that or not. Of course, per Equation 15-15, one probably *should* want the cluster robust standard error estimates, because the "within" transformation in any case induces a degree of serial correlation into $\varepsilon_{i,t}^{FE}$. On the other hand, one might also expect that the cluster-robust estimators will yield less precise standard error estimates where the serial correlation is weak, as when T_i is sizeable. Stock and Watson's theoretical and simulation results indicate that the latter is not the case, however: the cluster-robust standard error estimator is generally preferable to the White-Eicker estimator under the "within" transform, even for larger values of T_i. Fundamentally, the problem is that the number of $\overline{X}_i$ estimates used in computing the 'within' transform rises with the sample length, distorting the asymptotic distributions; the cluster-robust standard error estimators happen to be notably less affected by this distortion than are the White-Eicker estimators. Stock, J. H., and M. W. Watson (2008), "Heteroskedacity-Robust Standard Errors for Fixed Effects Panel Data Regression," *Econometrica 76(1)*, 155–74.

```
[Lines for d1960 through d1990 omitted.]

       d1991 | -3.920854   1.215374    -3.23   0.001    -6.318544   -1.523163
       d1992 | -4.794247   1.027376    -4.67   0.000    -6.821055   -2.767439
       d1993 | -3.407247   1.048094    -3.25   0.001    -5.474927   -1.339567
       d1994 | -4.498506   1.037416    -4.34   0.000     -6.54512   -2.451892
       d1995 | -1.629996   .9682794    -1.68   0.094    -3.540218    .2802256
       d1996 | -.8757428   .9748571    -0.90   0.370    -2.798941    1.047455
       d1997 | -.8328124   1.038618    -0.80   0.424    -2.881799    1.216174
       d1998 | -2.066323   .9177331    -2.25   0.026    -3.876827   -.2558191
       d1999 | -2.190439   .9463825    -2.31   0.022    -4.057462   -.3234153
       d2000 | -1.313824   .9260424    -1.42   0.158    -3.140721    .5130721
       d2001 | -2.231524   .9101172    -2.45   0.015    -4.027003   -.4360445
       d2002 |  -1.85112   .9275075    -2.00   0.047    -3.680907    -.021333
       d2003 | -1.625902   .9141909    -1.78   0.077    -3.429418    .1776139
       d2004 |   .664636   .9084773     0.73   0.465    -1.127608     2.45688
       d2005 | -.1066762   .8244071    -0.13   0.897    -1.733067    1.519714
       d2006 |    .32892   .8395718     0.39   0.696    -1.327387    1.985227
       d2007 |  .1516318   .8584427     0.18   0.860    -1.541904    1.845168
       _cons |  3.699413   .8032905     4.61   0.000     2.114681    5.284144
-------------+----------------------------------------------------------------
     sigma_u | 1.8469114
     sigma_e |  6.806955
         rho | .06857035   (fraction of variance due to u_i)
------------------------------------------------------------------------------
```

Here some of the regression results on the dummy variables $d1952_{i,t} \ldots d2007_{i,t}$ in the Stata output have been reproduced (so as to display the lack of an obvious trend in the estimated coefficients on these dummy variables) and most have, for brevity, been omitted. A test of the null hypothesis that all of these year-dummy coefficients are zero (using the Stata "test" command and listing all 156 variables: d1952, d1953, ... d2007) rejects this null hypothesis with p-value less than .00005. Consequently, these dummy variables allowing for time variation in the model intercept are routinely included in the models from here on, but (again, for brevity) most of the output lines for the coefficient estimates on these explanatory variables will be omitted below.

Some of this Stata output deserves particular comment here.

First, the total number of sample observations (8,180) is comfortably large, but note that the sample is not "balanced." That is, while there are observations on 187 countries, there are substantially fewer observations on some countries than on others. In particular, the growth rate data on Belarus does not begin until 1993 (yielding only 13 annual observations) and that on 10 other countries (including Armenia, Georgia, Kyrgyzstan, and Latvia, for example) the sample does not begin until 1994, yielding only 14 annual observations. On the other hand, the data for many countries goes all the way back to 1951, yielding – as the output indicates – an average of 43.7 annual observations per country.

The unbalanced nature of this panel suggests an additional motivation for the diagnostic checking in Section 15.6 to address the stability of the key slope estimates in the model. The usual motivation, of course, is that the underlying slope coefficients may themselves may simply vary over time. This relates to the issue of whether the inclusion of the year-dummy variables, which only allow the model intercept to shift over time, is sufficient to allow for all of the heterogeneity in the actual relationships over time. Second – aside from that issue – the unbalanced nature of the data set raises the possibility that the data (on a limited number of countries) in the early parts of the sample might constitute a less representative sample of countries than do the data in the later parts of the sample. In other words, the specific relationships investigated in this example might be systematically different for countries which were only added to the PWT data set later on in the sample period.

Next, note that three different R^2 estimates are quoted in this regression output – R^2_{within}, $R^2_{overall}$, and $R^2_{between}$. None of these needs to be "corrected for degrees of freedom" – as was the case for R_c^2 defined in Equation 9.41 – because the sample is supposed to be large enough that this is not an issue. So why are there three of them? All three of these R^2 estimates are firmly rooted in the second interpretation of R^2 derived in Section 8.2: i.e., each one is the square of the sample correlation between a version of the dependent variable and its model-predicted value. All three of the R^2 values in the Stata output above use the same (Fixed Effects Model) estimates of α, β_{open}, β_{cshare}, β_{ishare}, β_{gshare}, and $\lambda_{1952} \ldots \lambda_{2007}$; they only differ in how the dependent and explanatory variable values used in calculating this squared sample correlation are calculated.

The most useful of these R^2 estimates is R^2_{within}. It is just the R^2 for the regression equation actually estimated – i.e., Equation 15-13, using the transformed data. It can thus be calculated as the square of the sample correlation between the transformed dependent variable data $\left(y_{i,t}^{FE}\right)$ and the predicted values of $y_{i,t}^{FE}$ obtained from the (estimated) right-hand side of Equation 15-13. Or it can equally well be calculated using the sum of squared fitting errors, using Equation 9-40. Because it is the R^2 from an OLS-estimated regression model, it is also a goodness-of-fit measure, constrained to lie in the interval [0, 1]. And – also because it is the R^2 from an OLS-estimated regression model – R^2_{within} is additionally interpretable as the fraction of the sample variation of the observed values of $y_{i,t}^{FE}$ around their sample mean attributable to the sample variation in $open_{i,t}^{FE}$, $cshare_{i,t}^{FE}$, $ishare_{i,t}^{FE}$, $gshare_{i,t}^{FE}$, and the (transformed) dummy variables for the different years.

In contrast, the value of $R^2_{overall}$ is calculated as the square of the sample correlation between the original (*un*transformed) dependent variable data – $y_{i,t}$ – and the predicted values of $y_{i,t}$ obtained by substituting the original (*un*transformed) explanatory variable data into the (estimated) right-hand side of Equation 15-13. The calculation of $R^2_{overall}$ uses the same parameter estimates as does the calculation of R^2_{within}, but $R^2_{overall}$ clearly pertains more closely to the fit of the model to the original data. On the other hand, because it is not the R^2 from an OLS-estimated regression model, it is not constrained to lie in the interval [0,1] and it is not the fraction of the sample variation of the observed values of $y_{i,t}^{FE}$ around their sample mean. Consequently, $R^2_{overall}$ is not as interpretable as R^2_{within}.

Like the other two reported R^2 values, $R^2_{between}$ is calculated as the square of the sample correlation between the dependent variable data and the predicted values of it obtained from the (estimated) right-hand side of Equation 15-13, so it too uses the coefficient estimates from the Fixed Effects Model. However, in calculating $R^2_{between}$, the original data are transformed in a different way: each observation (on $Y_{i,t}$, and on each of the explanatory variables) is replaced by its average over all T_i time periods available for country *i*. Thus, there will be only 187 sample values for the dependent variable and for each of the explanatory variables – one for each country. These are, in fact, the variables defined in Equation 15-12 as $\overline{Y}_i$, $\overline{OPEN}_i$, $\overline{CSHARE}_i$, $\overline{ISHARE}_i$, and $\overline{GSHARE}_i$. $R^2_{between}$ is therefore the square of the sample correlation between the data on $\overline{Y}_i$ and a weighted sum of the data on $\overline{OPEN}_i$, $\overline{CSHARE}_i$, $\overline{ISHARE}_i$, and $\overline{GSHARE}_i$, where the weights are the coefficient estimates on the analogous explanatory variables $\left(OPEN_{i,t}^{FE}, CSHARE_{i,t}^{FE}, ISHARE_{i,t}^{FE}, \text{and } GSHARE_{i,t}^{FE}\right)$ in the Fixed Effects Model. (Clearly the Fixed Effects Model estimates of $\lambda_{1952} \ldots \lambda_{2007}$ are irrelevant in the computation of $R^2_{between}$, since the data have been averaged over all of the time periods.)

R^2_{within} is the sensible "figure of merit" for an estimated Fixed Effects Model; $R^2_{overall}$ is less useful; and $R^2_{between}$ is hardly useful at all. So why even mention it? One reason is that all three of these R^2 values are commonly computed and displayed. And the variables $\overline{Y}_i$, $\overline{OPEN}_i$, $\overline{CSHARE}_i$, $\overline{ISHARE}_i$, and $\overline{GSHARE}_i$ had to be defined in any case: partly because they are needed for the "within" transformation and partly because they are also used in what will be called the "random effects" transformation discussed in the next section. More importantly, however, the OLS regression of $\overline{Y}_i$ on $\overline{OPEN}_i$, $\overline{CSHARE}_i$, $\overline{ISHARE}_i$, and $\overline{GSHARE}_i$ is of some interest in its own right: it is called the "Between Effects Model."

The Between Effects Model forms a kind of complement to the Fixed Effects Model: it is a bit like a cross-sectional model – where this exposition began – but it uses data which are averaged over all of the observations for a given country – $\overline{Y_i}$, $\overline{OPEN_i}$, $\overline{CSHARE_i}$, $\overline{ISHARE_i}$, and $\overline{GSHARE_i}$ – rather than just using the data for a single, arbitrarily chosen, year.

One can usefully view the Between Effects Model as quantifying what one would lose (in estimation precision) by, in effect, discarding the time-variation in a panel data set. On the other hand, the aggregation over time in the Between Effects Model also averages out some of the noise in the model error term, which somewhat mitigates this efficiency loss. Nevertheless, the estimates from the Between Effects Model are generally substantially less precise than those obtained using the Fixed Effects Model.

The big advantage to the Between Effects Model is that it allows one to include explanatory variables in the model which do not vary over time, such as the race of an individual or the land area of a country. The coefficients on such variables cannot be estimated at all in the Fixed Effects Model, because such time-invariant explanatory variables are eliminated by the "within" transformation.[24] Another way of putting this is to note that the Fixed Effects model cannot include such variables because they are perfectly collinear with the unit – i.e., individual or country – dummy variables; Exercise 15-1 illustrates this point.

If, on the other hand, one or more of the slope coefficients in the full model varies substantially over time – as is likely the case with the relatively long time-series in the present example – then the time-aggregation of the Between Effects Model is itself problematic and the resulting estimated coefficients are not very meaningful. The estimated coefficients in the Fixed Effects Model are problematic in that case, also, but the Fixed Effects Model can be diagnostically checked for parameter instability and, if necessary, respecified to allow for such variation; the Between Effects Model cannot.

The software syntax for estimating the Between Effects Model is typically almost identical to that for estimating the Fixed Effects model, so estimating it requires virtually no additional effort. For example, in Stata one simply re-executes the "xtreg" command, replacing the "fe" option by "be" and dropping the (now irrelevant) dummy variables for the various years. In the present example this yields the output:

```
. xtreg  y open cshare ishare gshare , be

Between regression (regression on group means)  Number of obs      =      8180
Group variable: countrynum                      Number of groups   =       187

R-sq:  within  = 0.0811                         Obs per group: min =        13
       between = 0.2262                                        avg =      43.7
       overall = 0.0818                                        max =        57

                                                F(4,182)           =     13.30
sd(u_i + avg(e_i.))=   1.7513                   Prob > F           =    0.0000

------------------------------------------------------------------------------
           y |      Coef.   Std. Err.      t    P>|t|     [95% Conf. Interval]
-------------+----------------------------------------------------------------
        open |   .2059842   .0614819     3.35   0.001     .0846753    .3272931
      cshare |  -1.309027   .1958416    -6.68   0.000    -1.695439   -.9226153
      ishare |   .5165507   .3012994     1.71   0.088    -.0779383     1.11104
      gshare |  -1.131013   .2812689    -4.02   0.000    -1.685981   -.5760463
       _cons |   1.530827   .1665751     9.19   0.000      1.20216    1.859493
------------------------------------------------------------------------------
```

[24] The Between Effects Model is not the only option in this regard, however: the Random Effects Model and the Hausman-Taylor estimator discussed in the next section both also allow for consistent estimation of coefficients on explanatory variables which are not time-varying.

Table 15-1 Fixed Effects and Between Effects Model Estimation Results Summary

	Fixed Effects Model			Between Effects Model		
	coefficient	std. error	*p*-value	coefficient	std. error	*p*-value
β_{open}	−.031	.017	.066	.206	.061	.001
β_{cshare}	−.337	.045	< .0005	−1.309	.196	< .0005
β_{ishare}	.023	.068	.730	.537	.301	.088
β_{gshare}	−.400	.091	< .0005	−1.131	.281	< .0005

The results from applying these two estimation methods are summarized in Table 15-1. Note that the estimated standard errors are two to four times larger for the Between Effects Model estimates; this greatly reduced estimation precision reflects the fact that the Between Effects Model is discarding the time variation in the data – and thus effectively reducing the sample size from to 8,180 observations to just 187.[25]

Turning to the parameter estimates themselves, note that the estimates of β_{cshare} and β_{gshare} are negative and very significantly different from zero using either estimation method; neither estimate of β_{ishare} is significant at the 5% level. The largest discrepancy in the results from these two models is in the estimates of β_{open}. This coefficient estimate is negative, but not significant at the 5% level in the Fixed Effects Model, whereas the estimate of β_{open} in the Between Effects Model is positive and so large that it is significant at the .1% level despite the larger standard error. This discrepancy could be due to the fact that the sample (of only 187 observations) for estimating $\hat{\beta}^{BE}_{open}$ (and its standard error) in the Between Effects Model is perhaps a bit skimpy; more likely it is due to the fact that the $\hat{\beta}^{BE}_{open}$ is estimating a coefficient in a model controlling for time (using the dummy variables dl952 through d2007), whereas the Between Effects Model is in essence averaging this coefficient over the 57 time periods.

15.5 THE RANDOM EFFECTS MODEL

While the Between Effects Model is obviously profligate in aggregating away all of the time variation in the panel data set, the Fixed Effects Model would appear to be an inefficient way to estimate the parameters of Equation 15-11 also, because it is – either explicitly or implicitly – estimating *M* country-specific dummy variable coefficients, and the value of *M* is typically substantial. Also, the Fixed Effects Model makes it impossible to estimate (or control for) the impact on $E(Y_{i,t})$ of a time-invariant explanatory variable, such country *i*'s land area, or number of trading-partner neighbors, or physical climate. Moreover, as will become apparent in Section 16.1, one cannot use lagged values of the dependent variable as explanatory variables in the Fixed Effects Model – inclusion of such explanatory variables renders the Fixed Effects Model parameter estimators inconsistent. But inclusion of lagged dependent variables can be essential in modeling economic dynamics – e.g., habit formation or brand loyalty in a demand function.

[25] A comparison of the standard error estimates from the two models is complicated, however, by the fact that the "vce(robust)" option is not available for the "xtreg" command in estimating the Between Effects Model.

This section introduces the Random Effects Model. The Random Effects Model resolves all of these defects in the Fixed Effects Model framework.[26] The price paid for this is that the Random Effects Model requires a further strengthening of the strict exogeneity assumption in order to provide consistent parameter estimates: one must additionally assume that the explanatory variables are also exogenous with respect to the country-specific component of the model error term, ν_i. This additional exogeneity assumption is stated more explicitly below (as Equation 15-18) and discussed at some length at that point. Remarkably, this assumption is empirically testable: material at the end of this section shows how to test whether violations of this assumption have a significant impact on the parameter estimates of economic interest, thereby making it possible to choose between the Random Effects Model and the Fixed Effects Model in practice.[27] The first order of business, however, is to describe and motivate the Random Effects Model itself.

Referring back to Equation 15-10, the overall model error $\left(U_{i,t}\right)$ is decomposed into a country-specific component (ν_i), a time-specific component (λ_t), and an idiosyncratic component $\left(\varepsilon_{i,t}\right)$. The time-specific component will again be taken here to have been modeled by the inclusion of time dummy variables as explanatory variables in the regression model, leaving $U_{i,t}$ equal to the sum of ν_i and $\varepsilon_{i,t}$. Whereas the Fixed Effects Model in essence estimates M dummy variables to account for variation in ν_i, the Random Effects Model finesses this problem by instead treating ν_i as a single *random* variable.[28]

It can be fairly innocuously assumed that this – now random – ν_i variate is distributed $\text{IID}\left(0, \sigma_\nu^2\right)$, independently of $\varepsilon_{i,t}$. Consequently, the remaining specification of the joint distribution of ν_i and $\varepsilon_{i,t}$ reduces to the determination of a single parameter. It will shortly become apparent that this single parameter is most gracefully expressed as $\sigma_\nu^2/\sigma_\varepsilon^2$, the ratio of the variance of the country-specific component of the model error to the variance of the idiosyncratic component. The calculation of the Random Effects Model parameter estimators hinges on "knowing" the value of $\sigma_\nu^2/\sigma_\varepsilon^2$, which, of course, one doesn't. Fortunately, however, this ratio is quite easy to estimate consistently and – because the value of M is taken to be very large here – that suffices.

The variance σ_ν^2 can be consistently estimated from the sample variance of the M dummy variable coefficients implicitly obtained in estimating the Fixed Effects Model. Stata, for example, reports the square root of this estimate as "sigma_*u*" at the foot of the regression output; the estimate of σ_ν^2 for the present model is thus $(1.8469114)^2$, using the Stata output from the Fixed Effects Model estimation quoted in the previous section. Assuming that $\varepsilon_{i,t}$ is uncorrelated with ν_i, σ_ε^2 is just equal to the difference between the variance of $U_{i,t}$ and σ_ν^2. The variance of $U_{i,t}$ is consistently estimated by the value of s^2 obtained from the estimated Fixed Effects Model; as with any regression model,

---

[26] The assertion that the Random Effects Model estimators are still consistent in the presence of lagged dependent variables will surprise many knowledgeable readers. The validity of this assertion for a simple model is demonstrated in Section 16.1, but one might note at the outset that this result does require that the idiosyncratic error $\left(\varepsilon_{i,t}\right)$ must be both non-autocorrelated and homoscedastic. Non-autocorrelation can be ensured by including sufficient dynamics in the model; the heteroscedasticity assumption is often problematic, however. One must, in that case, resort to instrumental variables estimation of the First-Differences Model when a model uses lagged dependent variables; this topic is taken up in Section 16.2.

[27] Because it makes such inefficient use of the data, the Between Effects Model is rarely competitive except in the occasional instance where the coefficient on a time-invariant explanatory variable is essential to the analysis but the Random Effects Model turns out to be inappropriate to the data. Even then, most analysts would turn to the Hausman-Taylor estimator described in Section 15.5. Note that the pooled model is not a contender either: OLS parameter estimators are inconsistent in the pooled model unless the Random Effects Model Assumption (Equation 15-18, described below) is satisfied, but in that case the Random Effects Model estimators are both consistent and more efficient.

[28] Recall that, in the Fixed Effects Model, the ν_i are taken to explicitly vary (with i) across the M countries, but they are assumed to be "fixed in repeated samples." Thus, in the Fixed Effects Model $\nu_{1i} \dots \nu_M$ are taken to be M fixed parameters, which could be estimated as the coefficients on these M dummy variables. That, of course, is the reason the word "fixed" is used in denoting this model in the first place.

this is calculated as the sum of the squared fitting errors, divided by the number of degrees of freedom. The difference between the estimated value of s^2 and the aforementioned estimate of σ_v^2 thus provides a consistent estimate of σ_ε^2.

Stata quotes the square root of this estimate as "sigma_e" at the foot of the regression output; the estimate of σ_ε^2 for the present model is thus $(6.806955)^2$, using the Stata output from the Fixed Effects Model estimation quoted in the previous section. The ratio of the estimate of σ_v^2 to this estimate of σ_ε^2 then yields a consistent estimate of $\sigma_v^2/\sigma_\varepsilon^2$; this estimate is quoted by Stata as "rho" at the foot of its regression output; here it equals .0685. Thus, for sufficiently large samples, the ratio $\sigma_v^2/\sigma_\varepsilon^2$ can be taken as known.[29]

To summarize, then, the Random Effects Model avoids the efficiency loss in the Fixed Effects Model (due to the estimation of the *M* country-specific components) by treating these as a random component in the model error term $(v_i + \varepsilon_{i,t})$ of the regression equation

$$\begin{aligned} Y_{i,t} &= \alpha + \beta_{open} OPEN_{i,t} + \beta_{cshare} CSHARE_{i,t} + \beta_{ishare} ISHARE_{i,t} \\ &\quad + \beta_{gshare} GSHARE_{i,t} + \lambda_{1952} \mathrm{D1952}_{i,t} + \ldots + \lambda_{2007} \mathrm{D2007}_{i,t} + v_i + \varepsilon_{i,t} \end{aligned} \tag{15-17}$$

with a known (or, at least, consistently estimated) value for the ratio $\sigma_v^2/\sigma_\varepsilon^2$. The inclusion of v_i in this model error term causes it to become autocorrelated, however, even though the idiosyncratic component $(\varepsilon_{i,t})$ is itself assumed to be independently distributed for all values of *i* and *t*. The exact form of this autocorrelation will be explicitly discussed shortly. For now, note that – for any given value of *i* – a positive realization of v_i will make all T_i realizations of $v_i + \varepsilon_{i,t}$ tend to be positive; similarly, a negative realization of v_i will make all T_i realizations of $v_i + \varepsilon_{i,t}$ tend to be negative. Thus, deviations of $v_i + \varepsilon_{i,t}$ from its mean (of zero) will tend to persist over all T_i of the observations for country or individual *i;* ergo, $v_i + \varepsilon_{i,t}$ is positively autocorrelated.

As with any regression equation for which the assumption of nonautocorrelation in the model errors is invalid, this serial correlation in $v_i + \varepsilon_{i,t}$ renders the OLS estimators of the parameters in Equation 15-17 inefficient and makes the usual OLS standard error estimators inconsistent. The cluster-robust standard error estimates discussed in Section 15.4 (Equation 15-16) are, of course, consistent; but the parameter estimation inefficiency still remains. The strategy here is to exploit the consistent estimate of $\sigma_v^2/\sigma_\varepsilon^2$ discussed above to "undo" this serial correlation in $v_i + \varepsilon_{i,t}$ and thereby obtain both efficient parameter estimators and consistent standard error estimators.

The first priority, however, is to ensure that OLS still at least provides consistent estimates of the model parameters $(\alpha,\ \beta_{open},\ \beta_{cshare},\ \beta_{ishare},\ \beta_{gshare},\ \text{and}\ \lambda_{1952} \ldots \lambda_{2007})$ in Equation 15-17. It is not obvious that it does so. In fact, the OLS estimators of these coefficients will be consistent only if all of the explanatory variables $(OPEN_{i,t},\ CSHARE_{i,t},\ ISHARE_{i,t},\ \text{and}\ GSHARE_{i,t})$ are uncorrelated with the "new" model error term $(v_i + \varepsilon_{i,t})$ implied by treating $v_1 \ldots v_M$ as random variables. Assuming, as with the Fixed Effects

[29] Technical note: Actual implementations of the Random Effects Model estimate this variance ratio a bit more efficiently, using either a method proposed by Swamy and Arora (1972) or an improved version (for unbalanced, relatively small data sets) suggested later by Baltagi and Chang (1994). The former method is the usual default; in the Stata "xtreg" command it is specified by appending the "re" instead of the "fe" option, or – since "re" is the default option for the "xtreg" command – by appending neither option specifier. The Baltagi/Chang version is used if one specifies "sa" instead of "fe" or "re." (See the Stata documentation for specific implementation details.) While the panel data set used in the present instance is quite unbalanced, it is not small; consequently, the Baltagi/Chang adjustment here doubles the computation time but does not noticeably affect the estimation results. Note also that, regardless of the method used, the estimator of $\sigma_v^2/\sigma_\varepsilon^2$ necessarily contributes additional sampling errors to the Random Effects Model parameter estimators in finite samples, thereby to some extent diminishing their efficiency advantage over the Fixed Effects Model estimators. Swamy, P. A. V. B., and S. S. Arora (1972), "The Exact Finite Sample Properties of the Estimators of Coefficients in the Error Components Regression Models," *Econometrica 40,* 643–57. Baltagi, B. H., and Y. Chang (1994), "Incomplete Panels: A Comparative Study of Alternative Estimators for the Unbalanced One-Way Error Component Regression Model," *Journal of Econometrics 62,* 67–89.

Model, that $OPEN_{i,t}$, $CSHARE_{i,t}$, $ISHARE_{i,t}$, and $GSHARE_{i,t}$ are all strictly exogenous – i.e., uncorrelated at all relative lags with $\varepsilon_{i,t}$, per Equation 15-14 – this consistency requires the additional assumption that all of these explanatory variables are also uncorrelated with the v_i:

Random Effects Model Assumption

$$\begin{aligned} \text{corr}(OPEN_{i,t},\ v_i) &= 0 \\ \text{corr}(CSHARE_{i,t},\ v_i) &= 0 \\ \text{corr}(ISHARE_{i,t},\ v_i) &= 0 \\ \text{corr}(GSHARE_{i,t},\ v_i) &= 0 \end{aligned} \tag{15-18}$$

Of course, this assumption would be stated differently for a different set of explanatory variables, but the essence would be identical: the Random Effects Model Assumption is valid if and only if the value of each observation on every explanatory variable for country i is uncorrelated with the country-specific error component for country i.

This assumption is not likely to be precisely valid in any particular empirical context. Here, for example, v_i is a measure of the impact on $Y_{i,t}$ (the real per capita GDP growth rate of country i in year t) of some intrinsic quality of country i which is not modeled by the growth rate in trade openness or by the changes in the GDP share of consumption, investment, and government expenditures. If these four explanatory variables capture *all* of the "country-effect" on $Y_{i,t}$, then $v_1 \ldots v_M$ are all zero – i.e., σ_v^2 must be zero – and, in that case, there is no need to go beyond the pooled model. If these four explanatory variables completely capture *none* of the "country-effect" on $Y_{i,t}$, then the assumptions embodied in Equation 15-18 are clearly reasonable. And these variables could in that case still be quite useful in modeling the "idiosyncratic" variation in $Y_{i,t}$, which is (by definition) not country-related.

But if these four explanatory variables explain some, but not all, of the "country-effect" on $Y_{i,t}$, then a problem arises.[30] This problem can be expressed in several ways.

The first way is to note that, if the sample variation in these explanatory variables is capturing some of the country-to-country variation in $Y_{i,t}$ then their sample variation must to some extent be correlated with which country a particular observation pertains to. But if v_i is defined as a "country-effect" itself, then it must, in that case, be correlated with some of these explanatory variables, thus violating Equation 15-18. Whereas, if one defines v_i – per the previous paragraph – as the sample variation in $Y_{i,t}$ which is *not* modeled by the variation in these explanatory variables, then Equation 15-18 is necessarily valid but the meaning of v_i becomes a bit murky.

A second – better – way of explaining this problem is to begin with a consideration of why an error component like v_i is part of the model specification in the first place. It must be because variables whose sample variation is, to some extent, country-specific have been wrongly omitted from the model – due to inadvertence, theoretical proscription, or a lack of data. Thus, it is the country-specific portion of the sample variation in these wrongly omitted variables which constitutes v_i. Therefore, if all of these wrongly omitted variables are uncorrelated with the included explanatory variables – $OPEN_{i,t}$, $CSHARE_{i,t}$, $ISHARE_{i,t}$, and $GSHARE_{i,t}$ – then v_i must be uncorrelated with these included explanatory variables also, and the Random Effects Model Assumption (Equation 15-18) is satisfied.[31]

[30] Advanced Note: A somewhat analogous problem arises with the inclusion of lagged dependent variables in an ordinary time-series model for Y_t with serially correlated model errors: OLS yields consistent parameter estimators if no lags in Y_i are included and also if a sufficient number of lags in Y_t are included so as to render the model errors serially uncorrelated. Introduction of some, but not enough, lags in Y_t yields inconsistent OLS estimation, however, because the included lagged dependent variables are then necessarily correlated with the (in that case still serially correlated) model errors.

[31] If the time dummy variables – $D1952_{i,t} \ldots D2007_{i,t}$ – are taken as fixed in repeated samples, then their correlations with any random variables are zero; if not, then their correlations with the wrongly omitted variables (and hence with v_i) are at issue also.

In contrast, if any of the wrongly omitted variables *are* correlated with any of these included explanatory variables, then the assumptions in Equation 15-18 are invalid. In that case, these (correlated) included explanatory variables will proxy for the wrongly omitted variables, yielding least squares parameter estimates which are realizations of inconsistent estimators.

Suppose, for example, that σ_v^2 is positive partly because a religion variable – e.g., $MUSLIM_{i,t}$, the fraction of the populace in country i which identifies itself as Muslim – has been incorrectly omitted from the model specification. $MUSLIM_{i,t}$ no doubt varies little over time, so its variation almost entirely contributes to v_i. If $CSHARE_{i,t}$, say, is correlated with $MUSLIM_{i,t}$, then any least-squares estimator of β_{cshare} will be inconsistent – as an estimator of $\partial E[Y_{i,t}]/\partial CSHARE_{i,t}$ – because $CSHARE_{i,t}$ will partly proxy for the omitted variable $MUSLIM_{i,t}$. This causes the least-squares estimator of β_{cshare} to actually be a consistent estimator for some mixture of β_{cshare} and β_{muslim}, the coefficient with which $MUSLIM_{i,t}$ would have entered the model. In contrast, if $OPEN_{i,t}$, say, is *not* appreciably correlated with $MUSLIM_{i,t}$, then any inconsistency in the least-squares estimator of β_{open} will be very minor. Thus, the wrongful omission of $MUSLIM_{i,t}$ from this model renders the Random Effects Model Assumption (Equation 15-18) invalid and causes inconsistency in any least-squares estimator of Equation 15-17 – including the Random Effects Model estimators described below. But the actual importance of this inconsistency depends on which coefficients we are interested in.[32]

Clearly, it would be preferable to simply include all such wrongly omitted variables in the model. On the other hand, we might not know what they are and, even if we did, we might not have data on them. In other words, if it were feasible to include these wrongly omitted variables in the model, then they probably would not have been omitted! Indeed, this argument displays the fact that these omissions are the entirety of why σ_v^2 is positive and of why there is a heterogeneity problem with panel data in the first place.

It is obvious, then, that the Random Effects Model Assumption is almost certainly false if σ_v^2 is positive. But so are almost all of the other assumptions made in empirical regression analysis. The practical issue is whether or not the assumptions embodied in Equation 15-18 are sufficiently invalid as to materially affect the parameter estimates which are of importance to the analysis at hand.

Remarkably, it is possible to test this proposition using the sample data. The reasoning behind this test is as follows: Conditional on the validity of both the Strict Exogeneity Assumption (Equation 15-14) and the Random Effects Model Assumption (15-18), it turns out to be fairly easy to use a consistent estimate of $\sigma_v^2/\sigma_\varepsilon^2$ to obtain asymptotically efficient estimates of the model parameters (β_{open}, β_{cshare}, β_{ishare}, β_{gshare}, and $\lambda_{1952} \ldots \lambda_{2007}$); the demonstration of this proposition is laid out in the remainder of this section. Moreover, note that any empirically relevant violation of the Random Effects Model Assumption must inherently be leading to statistically significant *in*consistency in the Random Effects Model parameter estimates – otherwise, the violation is not empirically relevant. In contrast, the coefficient estimators from the Fixed Effects Model require only the validity of the Strict Exogeneity Assumption (Equation 15-14) in order to be consistent. (The $v_1 \ldots v_M$ are essentially modeled with dummy variables in the Fixed Effects Model; hence v_i is not part of the Fixed Effects Model error term and thus this proxying issue does not arise.) The only problem with the Fixed Effects Model estimators is that they are inefficient. Consequently, a test of whether the economically important Random Effects Model coefficient estimates differ significantly from the corresponding Fixed Effects Model coefficient estimates amounts to a test of the practical validity of the Random Effects Model Assumption.

The strategy, then, is to obtain the (efficient, if they are consistent) Random Effects Model coefficient estimates and test whether they differ significantly from the (inefficient, but clearly consistent) Fixed Effects Model coefficient estimates. If these estimates do not differ significantly

[32] And it also depends on why we are interested in them: if the reason we want a consistent estimator of β_{cshare} is for forecasting purposes and we have no data on $MUSLIM_{i,t}$, then the inconsistent estimator may be more useful. Note also that this is precisely why the OLS estimator of a coefficient on $MUSLIM_{i,t}$ in the pooled model would be inconsistent.

for the coefficients of economic interest, then it is sensible to use the Random Effects Model coefficient estimators, as they are more efficient. If they do differ significantly, then one must content oneself with the Fixed Effects Model estimates.[33]

Presuming, for now, that explanatory variables are all strictly exogenous (Equation 15-14) and that the Random Effects Model Assumption (Equation 15-18) is valid, also, then all of the explanatory variables in Equation 15-17 are uncorrelated with the error term, $v_i + \varepsilon_{i,t}$, so OLS estimation of Equation 15-17 as it stands does lead to consistent estimates of the model parameters: α, β_{open}, β_{cshare}, β_{ishare}, β_{gshare}, and $\lambda_{1952} \ldots \lambda_{2007}$.

However, as noted earlier in this section, the model error term in Equation 15-17$(v_i + \varepsilon_{i,t})$ necessarily violates the non-autocorrelation assumption. In particular – because they both share the same value for v_i – the error term $v_i + \varepsilon_{i,t}$ for a given country i is positively correlated with the error term in every other period for that same country. More specifically, Exercise 15-5 shows that the covariance between such error terms is

$$\operatorname{cov}\left(v_i + \varepsilon_{i,\tau_1},\, v_i + \varepsilon_{i,\tau_2}\right) = E\left(v_i^2\right) = \sigma_v^2 \tag{15-19}$$

where τ_1 and τ_2 are different time periods; the correlation between any two model error terms in Equation 15-17 which correspond to observations in different years for the same country is thus

$$\operatorname{corr}\left(v_i + \varepsilon_{i,\tau_1},\, v_i + \varepsilon_{i,\tau_2}\right) = \frac{\sigma_v^2}{\sqrt{\left(\sigma_v^2 + \sigma_\varepsilon^2\right)\left(\sigma_v^2 + \sigma_\varepsilon^2\right)}} = \frac{\sigma_v^2}{\sigma_v^2 + \sigma_\varepsilon^2} = \frac{\left(\sigma_v^2/\sigma_\varepsilon^2\right)}{\left(\sigma_v^2/\sigma_\varepsilon^2\right) + 1} \tag{15-20}$$

which is positive so long as σ_v^2 is non-zero and increases as $\sigma_v^2/\sigma_\varepsilon^2$, the relative amount of heterogeneity across countries, becomes larger.

Thus, OLS directly applied to Equation 15-17 yields inefficient parameter estimators (and inconsistent standard error estimates for use in inference), just as in any regression equation for which the model errors violate the non-autocorrelation assumption.[34] This problem can be easily corrected, however, because – as discussed above – the variance ratio $\sigma_v^2/\sigma_\varepsilon^2$ can be consistently estimated and hence (for sufficiently large samples) can be taken as known. Consequently, the form of the serial correlation in $v_i + \varepsilon_{i,t}$ is – per Equation 15-20 – completely known also. Given $\sigma_v^2/\sigma_\varepsilon^2$, asymptotically efficient estimators (of α, β_{open}, β_{cshare}, β_{ishare}, β_{gshare}, and $\lambda_{1952} \ldots \lambda_{2007}$) – along with asymptotically valid standard error estimators – can be obtained by applying OLS to a simple transformation of Equation 15-17.[35]

The required transformation is called a "quasi-difference." And it is actually quite similar to the "within" transformation (Equation 15-12), which was used in order to obtain a transformed regression equation (Equation 15-13) for estimating the Fixed Effects Model. In fact, the only difference between the two transformations is that, whereas the "within" transformation subtracts off the country-specific (time-averaged) mean from each observation, the "quasi-difference" transformation subtracts off a country-specific constant (θ_i) times this country-specific mean

[33] Or – if one really needs to include time-invariant explanatory variables in the model – one would, if possible, use estimates from the Hausman-Taylor estimator described at the end of this section or, at worst, fall back to the Between Effects Model estimator of Section 15.4.

[34] Again, the cluster-robust standard error estimates discussed in Section 15.4 (Equation 15-16) can be used to obtain consistent standard error estimates regardless, but the parameter estimates are still unnecessarily inefficient.

[35] Technical Note: This comment presumes that it is appropriate to assume that $\lambda_{1952} \ldots \lambda_{2007}$ are fixed in repeated samples. Relaxing this assumption and instead modeling λ_t as a random variable, in much the same way that v_i is being modeled here in the Random Effects Model, yields what is called the "Two-Way Random Effects Model." This "two-way" model can then provide even more efficient parameter estimators, but it is primarily useful only where the number of time periods is relatively large, which is not the typical case. See Cameron and Trivedi (2009, pp. 304–05) for further discussion of this topic.

from each observation. The "quasi-differenced" values of the dependent and explanatory variables are denoted with an "RE" superscript below because the Random Effects Model will be estimated by applying OLS to these transformed variables:

$$
\begin{aligned}
Y_{i,t}^{RE} &= Y_{i,t} - \theta_i \overline{Y_i} \\
OPEN_{i,t}^{RE} &= OPEN_{i,t} - \theta_i \overline{OPEN_i} \\
CSHARE_{i,t}^{RE} &= CSHARE_{i,t} - \theta_i \overline{CSHARE_i} \\
ISHARE_{i,t}^{RE} &= ISHARE_{i,t} - \theta_i \overline{ISHARE_i} \\
GSHARE_{i,t}^{RE} &= GSHARE_{i,t} - \theta_i \overline{GSHARE_i} \\
D1952_{i,t}^{RE} &= D1952_{i,t} - \theta_i \overline{D1952_i} \\
&\dots \\
D2007_{i,t}^{RE} &= D2007_{i,t} - \theta_i \overline{D2007_i}
\end{aligned}
\tag{15-21}
$$

The time averages $\overline{Y_i}$, $\overline{OPEN_i}$, $\overline{CSHARE_i}$, $\overline{ISHARE_i}$, and $\overline{GSHARE_i}$ and the time-averaged values of the year-dummy variables for country $i\left(\overline{D1952_i} \dots \overline{D2007_i}\right)$ in Equation 15-21 were defined in Equation 15-12 for use in the "within" transformation. The parameter θ_i is defined as

$$
\theta_i \equiv 1 - \sqrt{\frac{1}{T_i \dfrac{\sigma_v^2}{\sigma_\varepsilon^2} + 1}}
\tag{15-22}
$$

This expression for θ_i is not as arbitrary as it at first appears: it will turn out (below) that this is precisely the formula needed in order for the "quasi-difference" transformation of Equation 15-21 to yield efficient estimators in the Random Effects Model.

The parameter estimates for the Random Effects Model are then obtained by simply applying OLS to the transformed model:

$$
\begin{aligned}
Y_{i,t}^{RE} = {} & \alpha(1-\theta_i) + \beta_{open} OPEN_{i,t}^{RE} + \beta_{cshare} CSHARE_{i,t}^{RE} + \beta_{ishare} ISHARE_{i,t}^{RE} \\
& + \beta_{gshare} GSHARE_{i,t}^{RE} + \lambda_{1952} D1952_{i,t}^{RE} + \dots + \lambda_{2007} D2007_{i,t}^{RE} + \gamma_{i,t}
\end{aligned}
\tag{15-23}
$$

where $\gamma_{i,t}$, then, must equal this same transformation applied to $v_i + \varepsilon_{i,t}$:

$$
\gamma_{i,t} \equiv \left(v_i + \varepsilon_{i,t}\right)^{RE} = v_i + \varepsilon_{i,t} - \theta_i \frac{1}{T} \sum_{s=1}^{T_i} \left(v_i + \varepsilon_{i,s}\right)
\tag{15-24}
$$

Note that the intercept (α) in Equation 15-23 is multiplied by $(1 - \theta_i)$ because, for an unbalanced panel, T_i is not the same for all countries and therefore θ_i is not the same for all countries. In that case the "quasi-difference" transformation has a nontrivial impact on the variable (usually set equal to one for every observation) used to create an intercept in the Multiple Regression Model.

The strict exogeneity of the original explanatory variables ($OPEN_{i,t}$, $CSHARE_{i,t}$, $CISHARE_{i,t}$, and $GSHARE_{i,t}$) and the Random Effects Model Assumption (Equations 15-14 and 15-18, respectively) together imply that the transformed explanatory variables in Equation 15-23 are uncorrelated with the transformed model error term, $\gamma_{i,t}$.[36] Consequently, OLS estimation of Equation 15-23 yields consistent parameter estimators. But the point of the transformation is not just that: it is to ensure that $\gamma_{i,t}$ is also both homoscedastic and non-autocorrelated. Only then does OLS estimation of α, β_{open}, β_{cshare}, β_{ishare}, β_{gshare}, and $\lambda_{1952} \ldots \lambda_{2007}$ in Equation 15-23 yield both efficient parameter estimators and asymptotically-valid standard error estimators.

A bit of algebra (Exercise 15-6) shows that the peculiar-looking definition of θ_i given in Equation 15-22 is in fact exactly what is necessary in order to make $\gamma_{i,t}$ homoscedastic and non-autocorrelated. In particular, this definition for θ_i implies that

$$\text{var}\left(\gamma_{i,t}\right) = \sigma_{\varepsilon}^2 \tag{15-25}$$

for all values of i and t, and that

$$\text{cov}\left(\gamma_{i,t}, \gamma_{j,s}\right) = 0 \tag{15-26}$$

for all values of i, t, j, and s; except, of course, for where i equals j and s equals t, in which case Equation 15-26 is not a covariance at all, but is instead the variance of $\gamma_{i,t}$.[37]

Of course, as with the "within" transformation in the Fixed Effects Model, one need not explicitly apply the transformation of Equation 15-21: these calculations are preprogrammed into modern econometric software. Indeed, in Stata, the random effects transformation is the default option; consequently, the Stata command for estimating Equation 15-23 is just:

```
xtreg y open cshare gshare ishare d1952-d2007, vce(robust)
```

The results from this command are summarized, for easy comparison with the estimation results from the Fixed Effects Model, in Table 15-2:[38]

Table 15-2 Fixed Effects and Random Effects Model Estimation Results Summary

	Fixed Effects Model			Random Effects Model		
	coefficient	std. error	*p*-value	coefficient	std. error	*p*-value
β_{open}	−.031	.017	.066	−.029	.017	.078
β_{cshare}	−.337	.045	< .0005	−.341	.036	< .0005
β_{ishare}	.023	.068	.730	.023	.048	.625
β_{gshare}	−.400	.091	< .0005	−.400	.075	< .0005

[36] Strict exogeneity (Equation 15-14) suffices, and is apparently necessary, because $\gamma_{i,t}$ (like $\varepsilon_{i,t}^{FE}$) depends on the country i idiosyncratic errors for *all* time periods. It will be demonstrated in Section 16.1, however, that strict exogeneity is not quite necessary: so long as $\varepsilon_{i,t}$ is both homoscedastic and serially uncorrelated, the quasi-difference of a lagged dependent variable – e.g., $Y_{i,t-1}$ here – turns out to be uncorrelated with the quasi-differenced error term, $\gamma_{i,t}$, despite the fact that it is only pre-determined, not strictly exogenous.

[37] The effectiveness of the "quasi-difference" transformation in yielding a homoscedastic and non-autocorrelated model error term is simply verified here, in Exercise 15-6. Its original derivation proceeds from the GLS/Aitken estimator and requires a goodly dollop of linear algebra, which is side-stepped in the present treatment.

[38] Per Footnote 15-22, the "vce(robust)" option computes cluster-robust standard error estimates, as described in Section 15.4; these are quoted here for both models. Also, the Random Effects Model estimates of $\lambda_{1952} \ldots \lambda_{2007}$, as with the estimates for the Fixed Effects Model, vary substantially (and significantly), but not in an obviously trended fashion; these estimates are, for brevity, not quoted in Table 15-2.

These results are exactly what one might expect if the Random Effects Model Assumption (Equation 15-18) is reasonably valid for these data: the coefficient estimates from the Random Effects Model are very similar to those obtained from the Fixed Effects Model, but a bit more precise.

In fact, the parameter estimates from the two models are so similar that it would seem to be unnecessary to formally test whether they are equal. But in general it *is* necessary to test this proposition, and there are some useful lessons to be learned from explicitly illustrating the process. The standard test for this equality is called a "Hausman test" after the author of the paper who first introduced tests of this type into the literature.[39] This test is so standard that most econometric software implements it conveniently, but the usual Hausman test assumes that the model errors are homoscedastic, which is not the case here. If one ignores this complication, the Stata commands for the Hausman test are:

```
xtreg y open cshare gshare ishare d1952-d2007, fe
estimates store fe_estimates
xtreg y open cshare gshare ishare d1952-d2007, re
estimates store re_estimates
hausman fe_estimates re_estimates, sigmamore
```

The "estimates store" command saves regression estimates under whatever name one specifies, for use in subsequent commands; note that the "robust" option has been omitted from the estimation commands as it is not consistent with (nor allowed in) the Stata implementation of the Hausman test. The "sigmamore" option instructs Stata to use only the estimated variance-covariance matrix from the Random Effects Model estimates; this option makes the test computationally more stable and is generally the best practice.[40] The output from this sequence of commands – condensed a bit, for brevity – is:

```
. hausman fe_estimates re_estimates , sigmamore

Note: the rank of the differenced variance matrix (20) does not equal the
number of coefficients being tested (60); be sure this is what you expect, or
there may be problems computing the test.  Examine the output of your
estimators for anything unexpected and possibly consider scaling your
variables so that the coefficients are on a similar scale.

                 ---- Coefficients ----
             |      (b)          (B)            (b-B)     sqrt(diag(V_b-V_B))
             | fe_estimates re_estimates    Difference          S.E.
-------------+----------------------------------------------------------------
        open |    -.031497    -.0291595       -.0023376        .0006608
      cshare |   -.3367431    -.3414845        .0047414        .0009583
      ishare |    .0234417     .0233063        .0001354        .0013174
      gshare |   -.3997391    -.4004656        .0007265        .0028134
       d1952 |   -2.447967    -2.415771       -.0321951        .0243623
       d1953 |   -2.003874    -1.961279       -.0425946        .0256798
```

[39] See Hausman, J. A. (1978), "Specification Tests in Econometrics," *Econometrica 46,* 1251–71, and a related discussion in Section 12.6.

[40] It is also fundamentally appropriate under the null hypothesis being tested – that the two sets of parameter estimates are equal, so that there is no evidence in favor of rejecting the Random Effects Model Assumption.

[Multiple lines of output omitted, for brevity.]

```
   d2006 |       .32892      .2981582        .0307617          .08259
   d2007 |     .1516318      .1265445        .0250873        .0826743
------------------------------------------------------------------------------
                           b = consistent under Ho and Ha; obtained from xtreg
            B = inconsistent under Ha, efficient under Ho; obtained from xtreg

    Test:  Ho:  difference in coefficients not systematic

                  chi2(20) = (b-B)'[(V_b-V_B)^(-1)](b-B)
                           =       60.81
                Prob>chi2 =      0.0000
                (V_b-V_B is not positive definite)
```

The "Prob>chi2" entry at the foot of this output is the p-value at which the null hypothesis that the two sets of parameter estimates are equal can be rejected. Here, of course, this rejection is meaningless, for several reasons. First of all, the model errors are substantially heteroscedastic in the present example, which is in conflict with the assumptions underlying this test.[41] Second, the output is giving fair warning that the computations did not go well. In fact, this kind of result is quite common: the standard Hausman test is prone to numerical problems, even in what would appear to be reasonably large samples.[42]

Fortunately, a "generalized" Hausman test is available which is both numerically stable and valid for models with heteroscedastic errors. The strategy of the test is straightforward: OLS is used to estimate both the Fixed Effects Model (Equation 15-13) and the Random Effects Model (Equation 15-23); the resulting parameter estimation results are then combined using the Stata "suest" command. This command computes an estimate of the joint sampling distribution of all of the parameter estimators for both equations, allowing for heteroscedasticity within each estimated equation, for correlations of the parameter estimator sampling errors across the two equations, and (if the "vce(robust)" option is specified) for heteroscedasticity and for intracountry serial correlation of the idiosyncratic errors. The usual Stata "test" command can then be applied to test a joint null hypothesis test that a particular set of parameters is equal across the two estimated equations.

The only problem in implementing this generalized Hausman test using Stata is that the "xtreg" command does not compute some of the information which the "suest" routine needs. Fortunately, the OLS regression command ("regress") does compute this information, however. Consequently, one can still do the test, but one must calculate both sets of transformed variables oneself and apply OLS to Equation 15-13 (for the Fixed Effects Model) and to Equation 15-23 (for the Random Effects Model). The resulting parameter estimation results are then saved (as with the Hausman test) using the "estimates store" command and combined using the Stata "suest" command. A set of Stata commands which implements all this, allowing for both an unbalanced panel data set and heteroscedastic model errors, is given in Appendix 15.1; these Stata commands can be entered directly into the Stata do file editor.[43]

The results from this generalized Hausman test, applied to the present model, are summarized in Table 15-3. There is no evidence in these results for rejecting the null hypothesis that the parameter estimates from the Fixed Effects Model and the Random Effects Model are equal, either

---

[41] Formal evidence for heteroscedasticity in $\varepsilon_{i,t}$ is given in the diagnostic checking described in Section 15.6.

[42] This is the reason that the "sigmamore" option was used; the results are even worse without it.

[43] The Stata syntax for computing and appropriately storing the country-specific means is a bit opaque. But once one has seen working code – as in Appendix 15.1 – it is very easy to modify it for doing the same thing to one's own data. For unbalanced panel data, it is necessary to include a variable *T_subi* in the data set whose (i, t)th value is T_i, the number of observations on country i.

Table 15-3 Generalized Hausman Test Results Summary

	Rejection P-value
$\beta^{FE}_{open} = \beta^{RE}_{open}$	.129
$\beta^{FE}_{cshare} = \beta^{RE}_{cshare}$	.111
$\beta^{FE}_{cshare} = \beta^{RE}_{cshare}$	.972
$\beta^{FE}_{cshare} = \beta^{RE}_{cshare}$	.918
All four equalities	.411

individually or as a group. Therefore, the more efficient Random Effects Model results are preferable to those of the Fixed Effects Model in this particular case.

At this point, however, one might want to confirm that the country-specific heterogeneity is sufficiently important that the Random Effects Model is actually superior to the pooled model. Baltagi and Li (1990) provide a test of the null hypothesis that $v_1 \ldots v_M$ are all equal to zero; their test is implemented in the Stata "xttest0" command.[44] After estimation of the Random Effects Model, this command is invoked by simply entering the "xtest0" command; in the present example, this command produces the output

```
. xttest0

Breusch and Pagan Lagrangian multiplier test for random effects

        y[countrynum,t] = Xb + u[countrynum] + e[countrynum,t]

        Estimated results:
                         |       Var     sd = sqrt(Var)
                ---------+-----------------------------
                       y |   55.58737       7.455694
                       e |   46.33464       6.806955
                       u |   1.408569       1.186831

        Test:   Var(u) = 0
                              chi2(1) =   193.34
                          Prob > chi2 =     0.0000
```

The null hypothesis that $v_1 \ldots v_M$ are all equal to zero is very strongly rejected here, with p-value $< .00005$. In fact, the observed test statistic (193.34) is a realization of a $\chi^2(1)$ variate under the null hypothesis; hence, this statistic only needed to be above 16.5 to yield this rejection p-value.

Thus, the Random Effects Model is most appropriate for this particular data set. But it is not prudent to accept this model – and, in particular, it is not prudent to take seriously any inference results from it with regard to hypotheses on β_{open}, β_{cshare}, β_{ishare}, and β_{gshare} – until the model has been diagnostically checked. Nor, as has been illustrated by the diagnostic checking in previous chapters, is this just a matter of prudence: diagnostic checking can lead to a fundamentally better model specification. The diagnostic checking of panel data models in general – and of the particular Random Effects Model specified and estimated above – is the topic of the next section.

[44] Baltagi, B. H., and Q. Li (1990), "A Lagrange Multiplier Test for the Error Components Model with Incomplete Panels," *Econometric Reviews* 9, pp. 103–7.

Before going on to the topic of diagnostic checking, however, it is important to touch on an additional panel-data technique – the Hausman-Taylor estimator – which, while a bit too intricate to cover in detail here, is easy to use and partially resolves some of the key defects of both the Random Effects Model and the Fixed Effects estimator. The crucial problem with the Random Effects Model is that it requires that all of the explanatory variables must be uncorrelated with the country-specific error component, v_i. (Or, at least, it requires that they are sufficiently uncorrelated with v_i that such correlation as exists does not significantly impact the coefficient estimates of interest.) Of course, this is not an issue with the parameter estimates from the (less efficient) Fixed Effects Model: it requires no assumptions regarding the correlations of the explanatory variables with v_i, as the "within" transformation eliminates v_i altogether. In some settings, however, the fact that the Fixed Effects Model cannot deal at all with estimating coefficients on explanatory variables which do not vary over time is a crucial defect.

The Hausman-Taylor (1981) approach requires that one be able to partition the explanatory variables into four mutually exclusive groups:

- k_1 time-varying variables which are *not* correlated with v_i
- k_2 time-varying variables which are unrestricted in their correlation with v_i
- g_1 time-invariant variables which are *not* correlated with v_i
- g_2 time-invariant variables which are unrestricted in their correlation with v_i

with the value of k_1 required to both exceed zero and also be at least as large as g_2. Thus, the method will yield consistent estimates of the coefficients on *all* of these explanatory variables – even the ones which are time invariant or correlated with v_i – so long as there is at least one variable which is *both* time-varying and uncorrelated with v_i and so long as there are not too many time-invariant variables which might be correlated with v_i.

The Stata implementation – using the "xthtaylor" command – is very simple: one need only specify a list of the $k_2 + g_2$ variables which are no longer assumed to be uncorrelated with v_i. (Stata can figure out which explanatory variables do not vary over time on its own.) Thus, for the PWT example considered here, one could include a time-invariant explanatory variable $LAND\_AREA_{i,t}$ in the model and also allow for the possibility that $OPEN_{i,t}$ violates the Random Effects Model Assumption by using the command:

```
xthtaylor open cshare gshare ishare d1952-d2007 land_area, endog(open)
```

The Hausman-Taylor estimator is not the panacea it might at first appear to be, however: there are two serious problems with using it. First, this estimation approach is not compatible with the computation of cluster-robust standard error estimates. If heteroscedasticity in $\varepsilon_{i,t}$ is a problem – which is quite common in panel data settings, and is problematic in the PWT model, in particular – then one must either resolve that issue oneself or not use the Hausman-Taylor estimator. (For example, one might respecify the functional forms with which the variables enter the model, or one might adjust all of the data for country i using an *ad hoc* multiplicative constant, or – had it not already been used in the PWT model – one might try using per capita rather than raw data.) Similarly, if serial correlation is a problem, then one can try to eliminate it by including lagged values of the explanatory variables. But this may well be insufficient to eliminate the serial correlation, and the Hausman-Taylor estimator does not allow for the inclusion of lagged values of the dependent variable. Thus, the infeasibility of computing cluster-robust standard error estimates for the Hausman-Taylor parameter estimators can be quite problematic.[45] The second big problem with the Hausman-Taylor estimator is that it yields quite imprecise parameter estimators unless the g_2 time-invariant variables which are allowed to be correlated with v_i are substantially correlated

[45] Research in progress by the author indicates that it may be possible to relax this limitation of the Hausman-Taylor estimation approach, but this work is insufficiently complete (at this writing) as to be confident that it will succeed.

with at least some of the $k_1 + g_1$ variables which are still assumed to be uncorrelated with v_i. In other words, one must sometimes pay a large efficiency price for using the Hausman-Taylor estimator to relax part of the Random Effects Model Assumption while still trying to estimate the coefficients on time-invariant explanatory variables.

15.6 DIAGNOSTIC CHECKING OF AN ESTIMATED PANEL DATA MODEL

The basic concerns, ideas, and techniques underlying the diagnostic checking of a model using panel data are very similar to those used in the diagnostic checking of a Multiple Regression Model (Equation 9-1) or in the diagnostic checking of a Dynamic Multiple Regression Model (Equation 14–3). In fact, the diagnostic checking summary given in Table 14-3 is still relevant and useful here, in the context of a panel data model. The diagnostic checking process is also much the same for the Fixed Effects Model as for the Random Effects Model, so it will be illustrated here by checking the particular Random Effects Model specified and estimated in Section 15.5 as Equation 15-23.

There *are* a few issues unique to panel data, however. These will, of course, be highlighted below, but it is well to foreshadow them at the outset. First, there are now *two* model errors for which non-normality – especially in the form of indications that the data are non-homogeneous across sub-samples – is of concern (or interest): the country-specific error component (v_i) and the idiosyncratic error component (ε_{it}). Similarly, in checking for parameter stability across the sample, homogeneity across countries is now an issue as well as homogeneity across time.

Second, it should be noted that the inclusion of lagged values of the dependent variable as explanatory variables in a Fixed Effects Model is problematic, because the "within" transformed values of such variables are no longer strictly exogenous. Thus, model respecification to include dynamic terms – suggested in Chapter 13 as the most appropriate response to the detection of serial correlation in the model errors – requires the application of instrumental variables estimation in a Fixed Effects Model and is hence not as attractive an option as in the pure time-series context of Chapter 13. This issue is only briefly raised in the present section, as dynamic modeling in the context of the Fixed Effects Model and the Random Effects Model is the topic of Section 16.1.[46]

Finally, the issue of endogenous explanatory variables in a panel data setting requires special treatment – and an additional model formulation, the First-Differences Model. This material is developed in Section 16.2.

That said, the remainder of this section illustrates diagnostic checking for a panel data model in general by applying it to the particular Random Effects Model estimated in Section 15.5 above. Specifically, this model is checked (per Table 14-3) for

- Model error normality (and outliers)
- Heteroscedastic model errors
- Non-autocorrelated model errors
- Nonlinearities
- Parameter instability across the sample

The issue of checking for normality of the model errors is taken up first. As noted previously – in Chapter 11 – once the assumption that the explanatory variables are fixed in repeated samples is abandoned, one's aspirations with regard to estimator properties are usually reduced to a desire for

[46] Interestingly, inclusion of lagged dependent variables is not a problem in the Random Effects Model formulation, so long as the idiosyncratic error term $(\varepsilon_{i,t})$ is serially uncorrelated and homoscedastic and so long as the other explanatory variables are strictly exogenous; see Section 16.1.

consistent parameter estimation and asymptotically valid parameter inference. From that perspective, normally distributed model errors are not required: all that needed to be assumed in Chapters 11 and 13 in order to show that OLS estimation provides both consistent parameter estimation and asymptotically-valid parameter inference was that the model errors have zero mean and are identically and independently distributed. Still, it was apparent in Chapter 10 that major departures from normality can be indicative of model misspecification: e.g., a need to apply the logarithm transformation, non-homogeneities across subsamples of the data, or the presence of an observation or two which are overly influential outliers. It can therefore be quite informative to check this aspect of a model nevertheless.

Per the decomposition in Equation 15-10, in a panel data setting there are actually two model error components to check: the idiosyncratic error component $(\varepsilon_{i,t})$ and the country-specific error component (v_i). Econometric software generally makes it easy to examine model fitting errors which are asymptotically equivalent to each of these components.[47] In Stata, for example, the command sequence:

```
xtreg y open cshare ishare gshare d1952-d2007, vce (robust)
predict epsilon_resid , e
predict nu_resid , u
histogram epsilon_resid , normal
histogram nu_resid , normal
```

fits the Random Effects Model to the data and stores the estimates of ε_{it} as $epsilon\_resid_{i,t}$ and the estimates of v_i as variable nu_resid_i. Figures 15-1 and 15-2 plot the histograms produced by the last two lines given above; note that the "normal" option causes Stata to overlay a plot of the density function for a normally distributed variate whose population mean and variance match the sample mean and variance of the data.

Outliers (influential or otherwise) do not appear to be a serious problem in either error distribution for this data set. Examining these fitting errors more closely, however, the distribution of the estimates of ε_{it} appears to have substantially more values which are very small or very large in magnitude than does a normally distributed variate. This relatively abundant set of large values should not be viewed as outliers, however; rather, one should simply recognize this as evidence that ε_{it} is simply non-normally distributed.[48] In contrast, the distribution of the estimates of v_i is roughly normal, but shows signs of multimodality – that is, the histogram looks like what one might observe in draws from a distribution with several peaks.

This aspect of the histogram of the estimates of v_i suggests that perhaps some of the non-homogeneity across countries is related to the unbalanced nature of the panel. Figure 15-3 displays a histogram of the values of T_i. The pattern in this histogram is indicating that the breadth of the PWT data set expanded in four distinct "waves" – corresponding to T_i ranges of [13, 20], [36, 37], [46, 48], and [52, 57] or, almost equivalently, to "sample entrance year" ranges of [1987,1994], [1970, 1970], [1959,1961], and [1950,1955].[49] Including dummy variables ($d\_13to20yrs_{it}$, $d\_36to37yrs_{it}$,

[47] More precisely, these estimates are realizations of estimators whose (stochastic) probability limits are equivalent to these components of the model error term, $U_{i,t}$; one could alternatively, more loosely, just say that these are consistent estimates of $\varepsilon_{i,t}$ and v_i.

[48] Random variables such as this are called "leptokurtic" and their distributions characterized as "thick-tailed," even though (as Figure 15-1 makes plain) leptokurtosis also involves an abundance of values with very small values, relative to what one would expect from a normally distributed variate. Leptokurtic random variables are not uncommon; for example, drawings from the Student's *t* distribution with a small value for the "degrees of freedom" parameter are leptokurtic and sample data on returns to financial assets are usually leptokurtic.

[49] This equivalence is not exact because the 2007 data are missing for one country (Bahrain); otherwise each country entered the sample in year 2007 – T_i. That is why the T_i range [36, 37] maps into the single year. This detail is pointed out here, not because it is so very important to the description of this particular example, but because it is broadly illustrative of exactly the kind of finicky little detail which one needs to confront and resolve in analyzing a real-world data set.

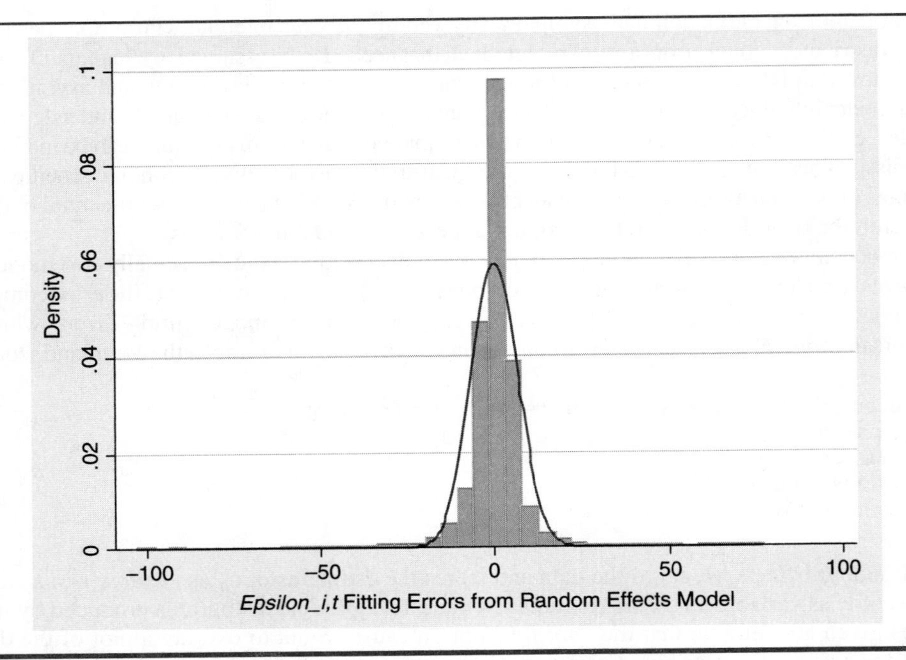

Figure 15-1 Histogram of ε_{it} Estimates (with Normal Density Overlay)

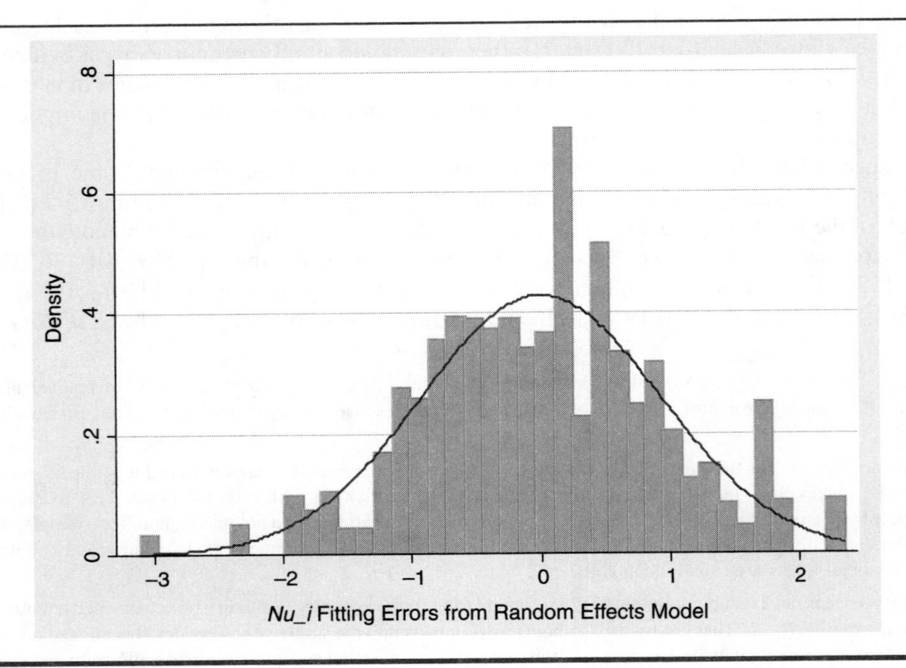

Figure 15-2 Histogram of ν_i Estimates (with Normal Density Overlay)

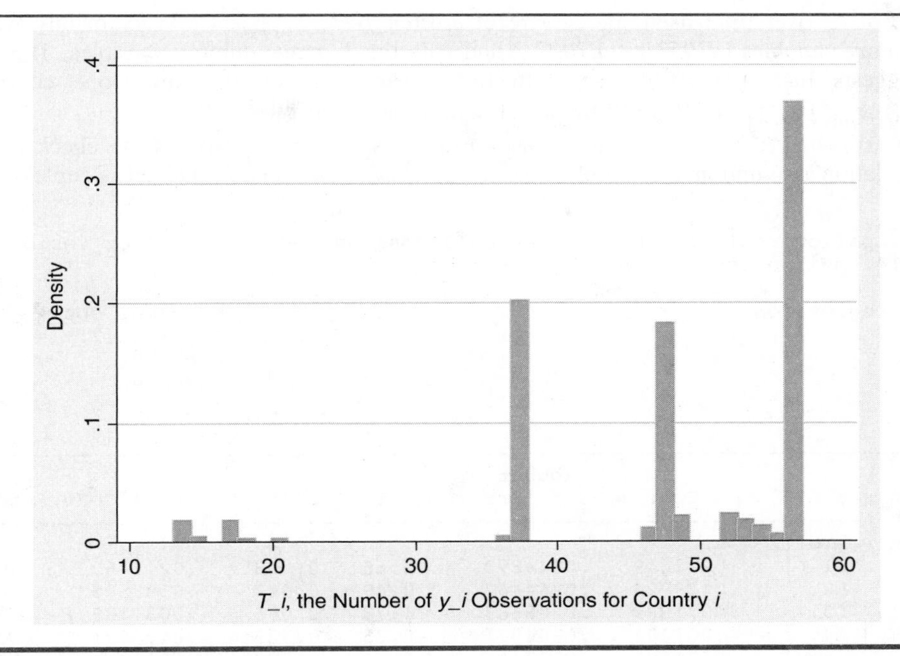

Figure 15-3 Histogram of T_i values

and $d\_46to48yrs_{it}$) to allow the intercept in the model to adjust for heterogeneity associated with country i's "sample entrance wave" is quite feasible; but it is really not necessary, as the Random Effects Model already accounts for general country-specific heterogeneity in the error term.[50] These results suggest, however, that it will probably be useful, later in this section, to test whether or not the key slope coefficients $(\beta_{open}, \beta_{cshare}, \beta_{ishare}, \text{ and } \beta_{gshare})$ are stable across these four "waves."

Next it is useful to test for heteroscedasticity in ε_{it}, the idiosyncratic error component of the model error term. Useful, but not essential. After all, standard error estimates which are robust to heteroscedasticity are already being estimated, and the sample is so large that these are very reasonable to use. Nevertheless, it is still worthwhile (in part because it is very easy) to specify and estimate the auxiliary regression discussed in Section 10.7, because it can potentially yield insights leading to an improved model specification. The potential for such improvements is limited here, however, because some care was taken with regard to this issue at the outset, by using the sample histograms to specify the output and openness variables in growth rate terms and the "share" variables in terms of their annual changes.

To estimate the heteroscedasticity-related auxiliary regression, one simply generates a variable which is the square of the fitting error estimates of ε_{it} – i.e, the square of $epsilon\_resid_{i,t}$ discussed above. This squared residual variable is then regressed against the likely sources of heteroscedasticity. Here, these sources would include the model explanatory variables, the T_i range dummy variables ($d\_13to20yrs_{it}$, $d\_36to37yrs_{it}$, and $d\_46to48yrs_{it}$), and perhaps other variables. The result of this exercise is strong evidence that the heteroscedasticity in ε_{it} is arising due to variations in the

[50] Indeed, accounting for such heterogeneity is the point of panel data methods, so this comment would be equally applicable if the model being diagnostically checked was an estimated Fixed Effects Model or (see Section 16.2) an estimated First-Differences Model.

variance of ε_{it} over time itself: the square of $epsilon\_resid_{i,t}$ appears to vary mainly with the year-dummy variables ($d1952_{i,t}$ ... $d2007_{i,t}$) and with the T_i range dummy variables. This result, too, suggests that it will be useful to test whether or not the key slope coefficients (β_{open}, β_{cshare}, β_{ishare}, and β_{gshare}) are stable across these four "waves."

Since estimates of ε_{it} are available – as $epsilon\_resid_{i,t}$ – it is also easy to check the non-autocorrelation assumption: one merely regresses $epsilon\_resid_{i,t}$ on itself lagged a couple of years:

```
. reg  epsilon_resid l1.epsilon_resid l2.epsilon_resid l3.epsilon_resid
     l4.epsilon_resid, robust

Linear regression                                      Number of obs =     7432
                                                       F(  4,   7427) =     3.44
                                                       Prob > F      =   0.0081
                                                       R-squared     =   0.0110
                                                       Root MSE      =   6.4825

------------------------------------------------------------------------------
             |               Robust
epsilon_resid |      Coef.   Std. Err.      t    P>|t|     [95% Conf.Interval]
-------------+----------------------------------------------------------------
epsilon_resid |
          L1. |   .0917849   .0344893     2.66   0.008     .0241762    .1593937
          L2. |   .0129924   .0264467     0.49   0.623    -.0388506    .0648354
          L3. |   .0371889   .0208683     1.78   0.075    -.0037189    .0780968
          L4. |   -.007201   .0204971    -0.35   0.725    -.0473811     .032979
        _cons |   .0421188   .0757146     0.56   0.578    -.1063034    .1905409
------------------------------------------------------------------------------
```

The only term in this estimated AR(4) model which is statistically significant is the one at a lag of one year; thus, these results indicate that there is mild positive autocorrelation in ε_{it} at lag one. Thus, it would appear that an AR(1) model (Equation 13-1) with the parameter φ_1 approximately equal to 0.1 would in this case adequately model the serial correlation in the idiosyncratic model errors.

The reason that this serial correlation is so mild is that the data for this model are in differenced form – i.e., these data are being modeled "in changes" rather than "in levels," using the terminology of Chapter 13.[51] In contrast, a model for real per capita GDP itself – i.e., $RGDPL_i$, or $\log(RGDPL_{it})$, or its deviation from trend – would have yielded very highly autocorrelated idiosyncratic model errors. However, from the discussion in Chapter 13, modeling "in changes" risks creating an error term which is "overdifferenced;" it also carries with it the need (and opportunity) to explore the data set for evidence of cointegration.

As to cointegration, in the model "in changes" one must consider whether there is a weighted sum of the I(1) variable $\log(RGDPL_{it})$ with one or more other I(1) variables such that this weighted sum is itself I(0) – i.e., is not wandering around like a random walk. If such a cointegrating relationship exists *and* if the errors in a model for this relationship (the "error correction term") are significantly related to $Y^{RE}_{i,t}$, then one is omitting a potentially important and informative explanatory variable in the model for $Y^{RE}_{i,t}$. One should in that case be including this I(0) weighted sum in the model for $Y^{RE}_{i,t}$ as an "error-correction term" in what would then be called a "panel vector error-correction model."[52] The exploration of possible error-correction term specifications is not pursued here.

[51] See the discussion immediately following Equation 15-8 in Section 15.3.

[52] In contrast, the discussion in Section 14.6 shows that the model "in levels" automatically subsumes such cointegrating variables, so there is no possibility of such wrongful omission. On the other hand, it is only in the model "in changes" where one can explicitly model – and thereby gain insight from – the cointegration, if it is statistically significant, by specifying and estimating an error-correction model.

The possibility that a model for $Y_{i,t}^{RE}$ is overdifferenced needs to be considered also. As discussed in Chapter 14 – especially in Sections 14.3 and 14.6 – the issue is whether the "levels" series – log($RGDPL_{i,t}$) – has a unit root, as was implicitly assumed here when it was decided to model $Y_{i,t}^{RE}$, which was defined (Equation 15-4) as the first difference of log($RGDPL_{i,t}$). (Thus, the issue is whether log($RGDPL_{i,t}$) is an I(1) time-series or whether it is instead generated by an AR(1) model with φ_1 – the coefficient on log($RGDPL_{i,t-1}$) – less than one.[53] For an ordinary time-series of reasonable length one can (per Section 14.2) test for a unit root using the Augmented Dickey-Fuller Test; and analogous tests are available which are specially adapted to panel data like log($RGDPL_{i,t}$). These tests have low power to distinguish a unit root from a large value of φ_1, however, so they are generally not very informative or reliable in practice.[54]

A more useful – albeit informal – approach is to observe, from Equations 14-18 to 14-20 in Section 14.6 (and from Exercise 14-9) that an autoregressive model for an overdifferenced AR(1) time-series – i.e., for a time-series which is the change in the I(0) series generated by an AR(1) model with parameter φ_1 less than one – will be of the form given in Equation 14-20:

$$Z_t = (\varphi_1 - 1)Z_{t-1} + (\varphi_1 - 1)Z_{t-2} + (\varphi_1 - 1)Z_{t-3} + (\varphi_1 - 1)Z_{t-4} + \ldots + U_t \qquad (14\text{-}20)$$

Thus, if Y_{it} in the present instance were overdifferenced, one would expect the estimated autoregressive model for the fitting errors (*epsilon_resid*$_{i,t}$) of the idiosyncratic model error component to have a significantly negative coefficient estimate on the lagged value of *epsilon_resid*$_{i,t}$ whereas, in the estimated AR(4) for *epsilon_resid*$_{i,t}$ discussed earlier, this coefficient estimate is significantly positive. Consequently, it seems highly unlikely that the model "in changes" considered here (Equation 15-17) is overdifferenced.

As noted above, however, the idiosyncratic error component in the present model is apparently somewhat autocorrelated. So it is appropriate to worry that any inferences obtained using it are importantly distorted by the consequent inconsistency in the estimated standard errors for the sampling distributions of the estimators of β_{open}, β_{cshare}, β_{ishare}, and β_{gshare}. The impact of this serial correlation can be dealt with in three different ways.

The simplest, most flexible, and most standard approach for dealing with serially correlated idiosyncratic model errors is to estimate cluster-robust standard error estimates, as was routinely done in Section 15.5, using the "vce(cluster countrynum)" option for the Stata "xtreg" command. Cluster-robust standard error estimators were described and motivated in some detail in the context of the Fixed Effects Model (Section 15.4, Equation 15-16), but are not any different for the Random Effects Model being diagnostically checked here. These standard error estimators are consistent regardless of any pattern of heteroscedasticity and/or within-country serial correlation. In particular, they do not assume that the serial correlation is of AR(1) form, nor do they assume that the serial correlation is of the same form for all countries: all that is assumed is that the idiosyncratic errors are uncorrelated across different countries. The use of cluster-robust standard error estimates is nowadays common practice, to the point where recent versions of Stata will automatically compute them (rather than White-Eicker standard errors) when one specifies the "vce(robust)" option with a panel-data specific regression command, such as "xtreg".

Cluster-robust standard error estimates are not a panacea, however. In particular, as in Section 13.7 and as in the pure time-series models considered in Chapter 17, one can – and should – take serial correlation in the $\varepsilon_{i,\,t}$ as an indication that some relevant dynamics have been omitted from the model

[53] Or, more precisely, a "stationary" AR(p) model – autoregressive models (and the conditions for them to be stationary) are discussed in Sections 17.3 and 18.1.

[54] See Cameron and Trivedi (2009, pp. 272–73) for a less jaundiced discussion of panel unit roots methods. Note also that a number of such tests are implemented in Stata 11, so the author's lack of enthusiasm for these tests is clearly not universally shared.

specification. Thus, the presence of serial correlation in the idiosyncratic errors suggests that it might be helpful to include lagged values of the dependent variable and/or the explanatory variables in the model specification: this respecification will likely both eliminate the serial correlation and yield a richer, better model. Such a respecification is trouble-free in the context of a Random Effects Model only when the idiosyncratic errors are both serially uncorrelated and homoscedastic, and the latter is certainly not the case for this model.[55] Inclusion of lagged dependent variables in a Fixed Effects Model always problematic, because the "within" transformation of a lagged dependent variable is no longer strictly exogenous. Consequently, if one has been forced to reject the Random Effects Model in favor of the Fixed Effects Model formulation – or if the idiosyncratic errors are heteroscedastic – then such dynamic model specifications will require the First-Differences Model (and instrumental variables estimation) described in Section 16.2.[56]

Finally, note that the use of cluster-robust standard error estimates does not at all modify the coefficient estimates obtained from applying OLS to either Equation 15-13 (for the Fixed Effects Model) or Equation 15-23 (for the Random Effects Model). Consequently, the estimation inefficiency induced in these parameter estimates by serial correlation in the $\varepsilon_{i,t}$ still remains. The dynamic model respecification discussed immediately above, of course, eliminates this inefficiency, but (as noted) is awkward in the Fixed Effects Model or if heteroscedasticity is present. In the Fixed Effects Model case – and if the serial correlation in ε_{it} appears to be generated by an AR(1) model – then one might want to consider using the estimator proposed by Baltagi and Li (1991) and conveniently implemented in the Stata "xtregar" routine.[57] Baltagi and Li are basically just implementing the Feasible Generalized Least Squares (FGLS) estimation approach described in Section 13.7 for the special case of the Bivariate Regression Model. The Baltagi/Li estimator is specific to serial correlation of AR(1) form, however. Moreover, it does not allow for the computation of cluster-robust standard errors, so it is not appropriate to the present example, in which heteroscedasticity in ε_{it} is an important feature.[58]

So far then, the diagnostic checking of the model specified and estimated in Section 15.5 has revealed that outliers are not a problem, but suggested that heterogeneity corresponding to which "wave" of the PWT a country entered in might be problematic. Heteroscedasticity and at least mild serial correlation both seem to be present also. The impact of these on the consistency of the standard

---

[55] See Footnote 15-46.

[56] Absent model features which in essence require the use of the First-Differences Model of Section 16.2 – such as endogenous regressors or a positive need to include dynamics in the form of lagged dependent variables (e.g., because modeling such dynamics is the point of the analysis) – one is usually better off using the Fixed Effects Model and cluster-robust standard standard error estimates. This is because the First-Differences Model typically yields substantially less precise estimators. The one likely exception to this is when the serial correlation is quite strong, as simulation results in Reed and Ye (2009) suggest that none of the various FE estimators they consider consistently provide reasonably accurate standard error estimates when $\text{corr}(\varepsilon_{i,t},\ \varepsilon_{i,t-1})$ substantially exceeds 0.30. Reed, W. R., and H. Ye (2009), "Which Panel Data Estimator Should I Use?" *Applied Economics,* first published on July, 16 2009 (iFirst).

[57] Baltagi, B. H., and Q. Li (1991), "A Transformation That Will Circumvent the Problem of Autocorrelation in an Error-Component Model," *Journal of Econometrics 48(3),* pp. 385–93. This is extended to unbalanced panels and panels with unequally spaced data in Baltagi, B. H., and P. X. Wu (1999), "Unequally Spaced Panel Data Regressions with AR(1) Disturbances," *Econometric Theory 15(6),* pp. 814–23 and to MA(q) serial correlation in Baltagi, B. H., and Q. Li (1994), "Estimating Error Components Models with General MA(q) Disturbances," *Econometric Theory 10(2),* pp. 396–408.

[58] Generalized Method of Moments (GMM) is not covered in this chapter – see Section 19.4. But GMM is the appropriate method to use (instead of the Baltagi/Li estimator) when heteroscedasticity as well as serial correlation is important and/or when the serial correlation is not of AR(1) form. The GMM estimator produces parameter estimates which are asymptotically efficient in the presence of heteroscedasticity and/or serial correlation, whereas the "xtreg" command with the vce(chister countrynum) option only adjusts the standard error estimates to be consistent. At this writing, GMM is not implemented for panel data in Stata, so one must either download a user-written routine ("xtivreg2") or perform the data transformation (for either the FE or RE model) oneself and then use the Stata "ivregress gmm" command. (One could easily modify the Stata do file routine given in Appendix 15.1 to perform either of these transformations.) In the present example, one would then invoke the "ivregress gmm" command, with no endogenous variables specified and with the "wmatrix(cluster countrynum)" option. Most likely, however, Stata will have already conveniently implemented GMM in its panel data regression routines by the time this book appears in print.

error estimators is already dealt with through the use of cluster-robust standard error estimates, but the diagnostic checking suggests that the three PWT "wave" dummy variables are significant in explaining the sample pattern of heteroscedasticity; this underlines the need to consider possible model coefficient heterogeneity of this form later in the diagnostic checking process.

The next diagnostic check is to consider the possibility that the relationship between $Y_{i,t}$ and the explanatory variables ($OPEN_{i,t}$, $CSHARE_{i,t}$, $ISHARE_{i,t}$, and $GSHARE_{i,t}$) is not linear. The simple way to check this is to include squared terms in the regression model specification. Defining such variables ($opensqr_{i,t}$, etc.) and augmenting the model specification in this way yields:

```
. xtreg  y open cshare gshare ishare opensqr csharesqr isharesqr gsharesqr
    d1952-d2007, vce(cluster countrynum)

Random-effects GLS regression                   Number of obs      =      8180
Group variable: countrynum                      Number of groups   =       187

R-sq:  within  = 0.1469                         Obs per group: min =        13
       between = 0.1995                                        avg =      43.7

       overall = 0.1453                                        max =        57

Random effects u_i ~ Gaussian                   Wald chi2(64)      =    930.33
corr(u_i, X)       = 0 (assumed)                Prob > chi2        =    0.0000

                          (Std. Err. adjusted for 187 clusters in countrynum)
------------------------------------------------------------------------------
             |               Robust
           y |      Coef.   Std. Err.      z    P>|z|     [95% Conf. Interval]
-------------+----------------------------------------------------------------
        open |  -.0155898   .0187572    -0.83   0.406    -.0523533    .0211737
      cshare |  -.3506977   .0473871    -7.40   0.000    -.4435747   -.2578207
      gshare |  -.3967428   .0909339    -4.36   0.000    -.5749699   -.2185156
      ishare |   .0202383   .0679339     0.30   0.766    -.1129098    .1533864
     opensqr |  -.0003593   .0001529    -2.35   0.019    -.0006589   -.0000596
   csharesqr |  -.0000113    .000583    -0.02   0.985     -.001154    .0011314
   isharesqr |  -.0014213   .0035514    -0.40   0.689    -.0083819    .0055393
   gsharesqr |  -.0029346   .0048496    -0.61   0.545    -.0124397    .0065705
       d1952 |  -2.374686   1.006127    -2.36   0.018    -4.346659   -.4027119
       d1953 |  -1.947373   1.071674    -1.82   0.069    -4.047815    .1530689
       d1954 |  -1.165503   .9541515    -1.22   0.222    -3.035606     .704599
       d1955 |  -1.039566   .7725091    -1.35   0.178    -2.553656    .4745243

  [lines omitted for brevity]

       d2005 |  -.1841072   .8108803    -0.23   0.820    -1.773403    1.405189
       d2006 |   .2563775   .8266411     0.31   0.756    -1.363809    1.876564
       d2007 |   .0740202   .8476204     0.09   0.930    -1.587285    1.735326
       _cons |   3.852884   .7760681     4.96   0.000     2.331819     5.37395
-------------+----------------------------------------------------------------
     sigma_u |  1.0105214
     sigma_e |  6.7952113
         rho |  .02163642   (fraction of variance due to u_i)
------------------------------------------------------------------------------
```

Evidently, there is some nonlinearity in the relationship between $Y_{i,t}$ and $OPEN_{i,t}$. That the form of this nonlinear relationship corresponds to a quadratic polynomial is doubtful, but it is something to consider in either interpreting the quantified relationship and/or in using it to inform or suggest theoretical modeling. Also, note that a test of the null hypothesis that the coefficient on $OPEN_{i,t}$ is zero in the linear model rejects this null hypothesis with a p-value of .078, so β_{open} is not statistically significant at the 5% level. In contrast, testing the joint null hypothesis that the coefficients on both $OPEN_{i,t}$ and $(OPEN_{i,t})^2$ are both zero is rejected at the .1% level:

```
. test open opensqr
( 1) open = 0
( 2) opensqr = 0

      chi2( 2) = 13.82
    Prob > chi2 = 0.0010
```

Thus, by considering the possibility of a nonlinear relationship, a strong relationship is uncovered, which was apparently insignificant in the linear specification. Pending a specification with a deeper theoretical foundation, then, the term in $(OPEN_{i,t})^2$ is added to the model specification.

Finally – and particularly in view of the evidence in Figure 15-3 – it seems prudent to investigate whether any of the model coefficients differ significantly across the four "waves" with which countries were added to the PWT sample. This is easily checked by including the fifteen variables in the model specification which are the products of $OPEN_{i,t}$, $(OPEN_{i,t})^2$, $CSHARE_{i,t}$, $ISHARE_{i,t}$, and $GSHARE_{i,t}$ with the three dummy variables ($d\_13to20yrs_{i,t}$, $d\_36to37yrs_{it}$, and $d\_46to48yrs_{it}$) corresponding to T_i ranges of [13, 20], [36, 37], and [46, 48]. Inclusion of these fifteen variables allows the five coefficients to differ for the countries in these three T_i ranges, compared to the countries with T_i in the range [52, 57]. Estimating this model, none of the explanatory variables involving $(OPEN_{i,t})^2$ remain statistically significant once the interactions between the other variables ($CSHARE_{i,t}$, $ISHARE_{i,t}$, and $GSHARE_{i,t}$) and the PWT wave dummy variables are controlled for. Dropping these variables yields the output:

```
. xtreg y open cshare gshare ishare  open_d13to20 cshare_d13to20
ishare_d13to20 gshare_d13to20  open_d36to37 cshare_d36to37 ishare_d36to37
gshare_d36to37 open_d46to48 cshare_d46to48 ishare_d46to48 gshare_d46to48
d1952-d2007, vce(robust)

Random-effects GLS regression                   Number of obs      =      8180
Group variable: countrynum                      Number of groups   =       187

R-sq:  within  = 0.1722                         Obs per group: min =        13
       between = 0.2062                                        avg =      43.7
       overall = 0.1692                                        max =        57

Random effects u_i ~ Gaussian                   Wald chi2(72)      =   1368.00
corr(u_i, X)       = 0 (assumed)                Prob > chi2        =    0.0000

                          (Std. Err. adjusted for 187 clusters in countrynum)
------------------------------------------------------------------------------
             |               Robust
           y |      Coef.   Std. Err.      z    P>|z|     [95% Conf. Interval]
-------------+----------------------------------------------------------------
        open |    -.02751   .0265724    -1.04   0.301    -.0795908    .0245709
      cshare |  -.3766822   .0459483    -8.20   0.000    -.4667391   -.2866252
      gshare |  -.9011705   .1341514    -6.72   0.000    -1.164102   -.6382386
      ishare |   .3260468   .0952319     3.42   0.001     .1393957     .512698
open_d13to20 |   -.012718    .032937    -0.39   0.699    -.0772733    .0518372
 cshare_d1~20|  -.0569323   .1727745    -0.33   0.742     -.395564    .2816994
 ishare_d1~20|    .062495   .2482019     0.25   0.801    -.4239718    .5489618
 gshare_d1~20|    .954043   .1900937     5.02   0.000     .5814663     1.32662
open_d36to37 |   .0236131   .0485348     0.49   0.627    -.0715134    .1187395
 cshare_d3~37|   .0782517   .1162765     0.67   0.501     -.149646    .3061495
 ishare_d3~37|  -.4146049   .1348138    -3.08   0.002     -.678835   -.1503747
 gshare_d3~37|   .6159666   .1876006     3.28   0.001     .2482761    .9836571
open_d46to48 |  -.0139674   .0367397    -0.38   0.704    -.0859759    .0580411
 cshare_d4~48|   .0555773   .0781315     0.71   0.477    -.0975576    .2087122
 ishare_d4~48|  -.5835868   .1360433    -4.29   0.000    -.8502267   -.3169468
 gshare_d4~48|   .4768788   .1831247     2.60   0.009     .1179609    .8357967
```

```
    d1952 |   -1.63011   1.017445    -1.60   0.109    -3.624265    .3640448
    d1953 |  -1.865488   .9921253    -1.88   0.060    -3.810018    .0790418
    d1954 |  -1.012071   .9110296    -1.11   0.267    -2.797657    .7735139
    d1955 |    -1.1474   .7082107    -1.62   0.105    -2.535467    .2406679

  [lines omitted for brevity]

    d2005 |   .2149171   .7734378     0.28   0.781    -1.300993    1.730827
    d2006 |   .5821905   .8083703     0.72   0.471    -1.002186    2.166567
    d2007 |   .3529513    .823062     0.43   0.668    -1.260221    1.966123
    _cons |   3.483988   .7388304     4.72   0.000     2.035907    4.932069
-------------+----------------------------------------------------------------
  sigma_u |  1.1590133
  sigma_e |  6.6972557
      rho |  .02907819   (fraction of variance due to u_i)
------------------------------------------------------------------------------
```

which indicates that the trade openness variable is actually not significant, at least not at the 5% level:

```
. test open  open_13to20  open_d36to37  open_d46to48
( 1) open = 0
( 2) open_13to20 = 0
( 3) open_36to37 = 0
( 2) open_46to48 = 0

         chi2( 4) = 7.81
       Prob > chi2 = 0.0988
```

Dropping the PWT wave interaction terms with $OPEN_{i,t}$ and testing just the coefficient on $OPEN_{i,t}$ itself yields similar results. The nonlinear dependence of $Y_{i,t}$ on $OPEN_{i,t}$ – and, indeed, any dependence of $Y_{i,t}$ on $OPEN_{i,t}$ at all – is thus quite possibly an artifact of lumping together countries which entered the PWT sample in the different waves.

This is probably a good place to stop with the analysis of this example. It seems reasonable to conclude from these results that – within the limited framework of the explanatory variables considered here – $Y_{i,t}$ appears to have a strong inverse dependence on $CSHARE_{i,t}$ and $GSHARE_{i,t}$ and a strong direct dependence on $ISHARE_{i,t}$; in contrast, the evidence for $Y_{i,t}$ depending on $OPEN_{i,t}$ is very weak. There also appears to be substantial time-dependence in the intercept, and the relationships with $ISHARE_{i,t}$ and $GSHARE_{i,t}$ (but not $CSHARE_{i,t}$) appear to depend strongly on the wave in which a country entered the PWT data set.

In some ways this PWT model is a good and useful example; in other ways it definitely is not. The good features to this example include the fact that it illustrates the specification and estimation of four of the five commonly considered kinds of panel data models (Pooled, Fixed Effects, Between Effects, and Random Effects) and how to choose between them.[59] It also provides a good illustration of the diagnostic checking of such a model and how the diagnostic checking process can cause a model (and its conclusions) to evolve.

On the other hand, this example has so far completely ignored the likely endogeneity of the explanatory variables due to joint determination. From that perspective, one would surely want to either estimate the model using the instrumental variables techniques described in Chapter 16 or respecify $Y_{i,t}$ as depending only on lagged values of these explanatory variables before taking any of the model's results very seriously.

Furthermore, on a deeper level, the estimation results from this model fail to provide credibly interesting economic conclusions. Fundamentally, this is because very little economics went into the model in the first place: this model is only loosely based on the Summers and Heston (1991) work, which

[59] The fifth panel data framework is the First-Differences Model; it is discussed in Section 16.2.

itself did not have particularly deep theoretical roots. This deficiency is amply reflected in the nature of the results: we end up with a model which (except for endogeneity issues) is likely an adequate statistical model of this particular data set, but the underlying intercept is very unstable over time and several key underlying coefficients are unstable with respect to when the country entered the sample. This strongly indicates that this model is mostly describing – rather than explaining – the relationships.

This failure of the model is not entirely a bad thing. For one thing, the primary intent of presenting this model here is to illustrate the basics of the econometric techniques used to analyze panel data, not really to further our understanding of the way, for example, that investment spending impacts growth. Moreover – as an initial semi-descriptive "pass" at the data set, the model does at least raise some interesting questions: e.g., why is it that the countries which entered the PWT in different waves differ so much, and in this way? Thus, in a crude way, this simple model illustrates yet another important characteristic of empirical work: often its most important contribution is to raise new questions (about the data set and/or about the economic phenomenon) rather than to provide settled conclusions with regard to the underlying economic theories.

KEY TERMS

For each term or concept listed below, provide a working definition or explanation:

Balanced vs. Unbalanced Panel Data
Heterogeneity – Across Units, Periods, or Explanatory Variable Values
Pooled Regression Model
Model Error Decomposition into v_i, λ_t, and $\varepsilon_{i,t}$
Fixed Effects Model
Strict Exogeneity Assumption
Endogenous vs. Exogenous Explanatory Variable
Strictly Exogenous vs. Predetermined Explanatory Variable
Strictly Exogenous vs. Weakly Exogenous Explanatory Variable
Cluster-Robust Standard Error Estimates
Between Effects Model
R^2_{within}
Random Effects Model
Random Effects Model Assumption
"Within" Transformation vs. Random Effects Transformation (Quasi-Difference)
Generalized Hausman Test

EXERCISES

15-1. For the model of $Y_{i,t}$ specified in Equation 15-9, let the sample data on $Y_{i,t}$, $OPEN_{i,t}$, and $one_{i,t}$ be

i	t	$y_{i,t}$	$open_{i,t}$	$one_{i,t}$	$open^{FE}_{i,t}$	$one^{FE}_{i,t}$
1	1	0.15	0.08	1		
1	2	0.17	0.08	1		
1	3	0.12	0.08	1		
2	1	0.08	0.11	1		
2	2	0.16	0.11	1		
2	3	0.20	0.11	1		

where M equals two and both T_1 and T_2 are equal to three. The "variable" denoted $one_{i,t}$ in this table is the explanatory variable implicitly multiplying the intercept coefficient (α) in Equation 15-9.

a. Calculate the values of $one_{i,t}^{FE}$, the result of applying the "within" transformation to $one_{i,t}$. What does this result imply about the feasibility of estimating the intercept (α) of Equation 15-9 in the Fixed Effects Model, Equation 15-13?

b. Calculate the values of $open_{i,t}^{FE}$, the result of applying the 'within' transformation to the sample data on $OPEN_{i,t}$. What does this result imply about the feasibility of estimating a coefficient on any time-invariant explanatory variable potentially considered for inclusion in the Fixed Effects Model, Equation 15-13?

15-2. For the model of $Y_{i,t}$ specified in Equation 15-9, let the sample data on $Y_{i,t}$, $OPEN_{i,t}$, and $CSHARE_{i,t}$ be the unbalanced panel – $T_1 = 3$ and $T_2 = 2$ here – given below. Report all calculations to four decimal places:

i	t	$y_{i,t}$	$open_{i,t}$	$cshare_{i,t}$	$y_{i,t}^{FE}$	$open_{i,t}^{FE}$	$cshare_{i,t}^{FE}$	$y_{i,t}^{RE}$	$open_{i,t}^{RE}$	$cshare_{i,t}^{RE}$
1	1	0.15	0.08	0.20						
1	2	0.17	0.08	0.35						
1	3	0.12	0.08	0.18						
2	1	0.08	0.11	0.32						
2	2	0.16	0.11	0.25						

a. Calculate the values of $y_{i,t}^{FE}$, $open_{i,t}^{FE}$, and $cshare_{i,t}^{FE}$, the result of applying the "within" transformation, for use in estimating the Fixed Effects Model, Equation 15-13.

b. Supposing that the Random Effects Model Assumption (Equation 15-18) is valid, prepare to estimate the Random Effects Model (Equation 15-23) by calculating the values of $y_{i,t}^{RE}$, $open_{i,t}^{RE}$, and $cshare_{i,t}^{RE}$. Briefly describe the ratio $\sigma_v^3/\sigma_\varepsilon^2$ in words; you may assume that its value is 0.75 here.

15-3. Let $logwage_{i,t}$ be the observed logarithm of wages for worker i in period t and let $edu_{i,t}$ denote the observed education level for this worker in period t, with sample data given by the following table:

i	t	$logwage_{i,t}$	$edu_{i,t}$	$logwage_{i,t}^{FE}$	$edu_{i,t}^{FE}$	$logwage_{i,t}^{RE}$	$edu_{i,t}^{RE}$
1	1	14	9				
1	2	16	10				
1	3	4	11				
2	1	7	11				
2	2	9	12				

a. Reporting your results to four decimal places, calculate the values of $logwage_{i,t}^{FE}$ and $edu_{i,t}^{FE}$, the result of applying the "within" transformation, for use in estimating the Fixed Effects Model.

b. Supposing that the Random Effects Model Assumption (Equation 15-18) is valid for this model, prepare to estimate the Random Effects Model (Equation 15-23) by calculating the values of $logwage_{i,t}^{RE}$ and $edu_{i,t}^{RE}$. Briefly describe the ratio $\sigma_v^2/\sigma_\varepsilon^2$ in words; you may assume that its value is 0.60 here.

15-4. Assuming that $\varepsilon_{i,t} \sim \text{IID}(0,\, \sigma_\varepsilon^2)$ for $t = 1 \ldots T_i$, show that

$$\text{corr}\left(\varepsilon_{i,t}^{FE},\, \varepsilon_{i,\tau}^{FE}\right) = \frac{-1}{T_i - 1} \tag{15-15}$$

for all $t \neq \tau$; that is, derive Equation 15-15. What does this result imply about the parameter estimators and standard error estimators obtained from applying OLS to the Fixed Effects Model (Equation 15-13)?

15-5. Assuming that the explanatory variables are all strictly exogenous (Equation 15-14) and that the Random Effects Model Assumption (Equation 15-18) is valid also, show that the error term $(v_i + \varepsilon_{i,t})$ in Equation 15-23 – the regression equation for the Random Effects Model – is serially correlated for any pair of observations on the same country. You can further assume that $v_i \sim \text{IID}(0,\, \sigma_v^2)$ independently of $\varepsilon_{i,t} \sim \text{IID}(0,\, \sigma_\varepsilon^2)$. That is, derive Equations 15-19 and 15-20:

$$\text{cov}\left(v_i + \varepsilon_{i,\tau_1}, v_i + \varepsilon_{i,\tau_2}\right) = E\left(v_i^2\right) = \sigma_v^2 \tag{15-19}$$

and

$$\text{corr}\left(v_i + \varepsilon_{i,\tau_1},\; v_i + \varepsilon_{i,\tau_2}\right) = \frac{\sigma_v^1}{\sqrt{\left(\sigma_v^2 + \sigma_\varepsilon^2\right)\left(\sigma_v^2 + \sigma_\varepsilon^2\right)}} = \frac{\sigma_v^2}{\sigma_v^2 + \sigma_\varepsilon^2} = \frac{\left(\sigma_v^2/\sigma_\varepsilon^2\right)}{\left(\sigma_v^2/\sigma_\varepsilon^2\right) + 1} \tag{15-20}$$

where τ_1 and τ_2 are different time periods. Assuming that σ_v^2 is positive, what do these results imply about the parameter estimators (and about the estimators of their sampling variances) obtained by applying OLS to Equation 15-17? What does this imply about the application of OLS estimation to the pooled model of Equation 15-9?

15-6. Show that the quasi-differenced error term $\gamma_{i,t}$,

$$\gamma_{i,t} = v_i + \varepsilon_{i,t} - \theta_i \frac{1}{T_i} \sum_{s=1}^{T_i} \left(v_i + \varepsilon_{i,s}\right) \tag{15-24}$$

induced in Equation 15-23 by applying the random effects transformation to Equation 15-17 is homoscedastic and non-autocorrelated. This is equivalent to showing that the results in Equations 15-25 and 15-26 are correct. Hint: Use Equation 15-22 to obtain an expression for $(\theta_i - 1)^2$; you will find it helpful to substitute $(\theta_i - 1)^2 - 1$ for $\theta_i^2 - 2\theta_i$. The point of doing the algebra for this exercise is to make it explicitly clear that the (otherwise somewhat cryptic-looking) formula for θ_i given in Equation 15-22 is in fact exactly what is needed in order to make $\gamma_{i,t}$, the error term in Equation 15-23, homoscedastic and non-autocorrelated.

Assuming that σ_v^2 is positive, what does this result imply about the parameter estimators (and about the estimators of their sampling variances) obtained by applying OLS to Equation 15-23? What, then is the advantage of the Random Effects Model over the Fixed Effects Model, presuming that the Random Effects Model Assumption (Equation 15-18) is valid?

APPENDIX 15.1: STATA CODE FOR THE GENERALIZED HAUSMAN TEST

The code listed below implements the generalized Hausman test described in Section 15.5, by estimating both the Fixed Effects Model and the Random Effects Model and testing the equality of a particular coefficient estimate (or a group of coefficient estimates) across the two estimated models. The routine automatically corrects for any heteroscedasticity/autocorrelation in the model errors and appropriately accounts for the (likely) cross-equation correlations in the estimator sampling errors. Since both models yield consistent parameter estimators if the Random Effects Model Assumption (Equation 15-18) is valid, it is this assumption which is being tested – assuming, of course, that the models are both otherwise well specified. Rejection thus implies that one cannot use the Random Effects Model; failure to reject indicates that one ought to use the Random Effects Model estimators, as they are more efficient.

This code can be entered directly into the Stata "do file" editor. It assumes that the units (countries, in the present example) are denoted by the variable *countrynum* and that the time periods are denoted by the variable *year*. Of course, one would need to modify the line specifying the location of the Stata file containing the data and one would also need to appropriately modify the variable names for the dependent and explanatory variables. (Because there are quite a number of year-dummy variables in the present example, some repetitious lines of the code were omitted, as indicated below.) So as to deal with an unbalanced panel, this Stata file needs to contain a variable (called *T_i* here) which, for each observation, is the number of time periods of data available for the unit (country) to which this observation belongs.[60]

```
*                          GENERALIZED HAUSMAN TEST
*                              (April 28, 2010)
*
*
* This routine tests whether the Random Effects Model is appropriate for a panel data set -
* balanced or unbalanced - in a way which is robust to heteroscedastic or serially
* correlated model errors. It works by estimating both the Fixed Effects Model and the
* Random Effects Model and testing the null hypothesis that selected coefficients (or
* groups of coefficients) are equal across the two models;
*
* This routine handles unbalanced samples by assuming that variable "Ti" in the data set
* specifies the number of periods for ith unit in the panel. As written, the countries are
* indexed by variable "countrynum" and the time periods are indexed by the variable "year".
* The user will need to replace the variable name for the dependent variable (here called
* "y") and for the explanatory variables (called "open", "cshare", "ishare", "gshare",
* and "d1952" ... "d2007" here).;
*
* set command line delimiter to ";"
*
#delimit;
* specifies where to find the data
*;
set mem 15m;
use "e:\Chapter14_PWT_example_data.dta", clear;
*
* specifies variable names for units and time periods;
```

[60] For a balanced panel, the variable *T_i* is a constant (equal to the number of observations per unit) and it is not necessary to include the variable re_ones in the Random Effects Model regression command.

```
*;
xtset countrynum year;
*
* Calculate theta_i for use in applying Random Effects transformation;
*
* This routine first uses xtreg to obtain estimates of the variance of nu (Stata reports the
* estimated standard deviation of nu as "sigma_u") and of the variance of epsilon (Stata
* reports the standard deviation of epsilon as "sigma_e"). The routine then combines this
* with T_subi to calculate the variable theta, which is the weight on the country-specific
* mean in the Random Effects transformation for each observation.
*;
quietly xtreg y open cshare ishare gshare d1952-d2007, robust re;
gen sigsquarenu = e(sigma_u)^2;
gen sigsquareepsilon = e(sigma_e)^2;
gen theta = 1 - sqrt(sigsquareepsilon/(T_subi*sigsquarenu + sigsquareepsilon));
*
* The next section computes the country-specific means for each variable, for use in
* constructing the Fixed Effects and Random Effects transformations of them. {Note that
* "ones" is a variable which is one for every observation. Its coefficient corresponds to
* the intercept in the un-transformed regression equation.}
*;
sort countrynum;
by countrynum: egen mean_y = mean(y);
by countrynum: egen mean_open = mean(open);
by countrynum: egen mean_cshare = mean(cshare);
by countrynum: egen mean_ishare = mean(ishare);
by countrynum: egen mean_gshare = mean(gshare);
by countrynum: egen mean_d1952 = mean.(d1952);
by countrynum: egen mean__d1953 = mean(d1953);

{Similar lines for 1954 through 2005 are omitted here, for brevity.}

by countrynum: egen mean_d2G06 = mean(d2006);
by countrynum: egen mean_d2007 = mean(d2007);
*
* Code below constructs the Fixed Effects transformed variables:
*;
generate fe_y = y_- mean_y;
generate fe_open = open - mean_open;
generate fe_cshare = cshare - mean_cshare;
generate fe_ishare = ishare - mean_share;
generate fe_gshare = gshare - mean_gshare;
generate fe_d1952 =d1952 - mean _d1952;
generate fe_d1953 =d1953 - mean_d1953;

{Similar lines for 1954 through 2005 are omitted here, for brevity.}

generate fe_d2006 =d2006 - mean_d2006;
generate fe_d2007 =d2007 - mean_d2007;
```

```
*
* Code below constructs the Random Effects transformed variables.
* Note that Random Effects transformation of the "ones" variable is needed
* if (and only if) the panel is unbalanced.
*;
generate re_y   = y - theta*mean_y;
generate re_ones = 1.   - theta;
generate re_open = open - theta*mean_open;
generate re_cshare = cshare - theta*mean_cshare;
generate re_ishare = ishare - theta*mean_ishare;
generate re_gshare = gshare - theta*mean_gshare;
generate re_d1952 =d1952 - theta*mean_d1952;
generate re_d1953 = d1953 - theta*mean_d1953;

{Similar lines for 1954 through 2005 are omitted here, for brevity.}

generate re_d2006 =d2006 - theta*mean_d2006;
generate re_d2007 =d2007 - theta*mean_d2007;
*
*
* Next, estimate both the Fixed Effects Model and the Random Effects Model and store the
* estimates. Note that robust or cluster-robust standard error estimates are not specified
* for either model because this is specified (using the robust or the cluster-robust vce
* option) in the suest procedure itself.
*
* Note also that the "noconstant" option is specified for the Random Effects Model because the
* "re_ones" explanatory included in this regression equation explicitly allows for the
* intercept-term variable, which is not all ones in an unbalanced panel.
*;
quietly regress fe_y fe_open fe_cshare fe_ishare fe_gshare fe_d1 952-fe_d2007, noconstant;
quietly estimates store fe_coefs;
quietly regress re_y re_ones re_open re_cshare re_ishare re_gshare re_d1952-re_d2007,
noconstant;
quietly estimates store re_coefs;
*
* The "suest" command computes a combined sampling variance-covariance matrix for all of the
* coefficient estimates from both models, using model fitting errors from the two models to
* estimate the cross-equation error correlations. The "vce(cluster countrynum)" option should
* be substituted for "vce(robust)" where there is substantial serial correlation in the
* model errors.
*
* {The "_mean" appended to the equation names assigned by the suest routine is an artifact of
* the historical development of the this Stata command.}
*;
quietly suest fe_coefs re_coefs, vce (robust);
*
* First, test each (interesting) coefficient separately for equality across the two equations;
*;
test [re coefs_mean]re_open = [fe_coefs_mean]fe_open;
test [re_coefs_mean]re_cshare = [fe_coefs_mean]fe_cshare;
test [re_coefs_mean]re_ishare = [fe_coefs_mean]fe_ishare;
```

```
test [re_coefs_mean]re_gshare = [fe_coefs_mean]fe_gshare;
*
* Finally, test all four coefficients simultaneously:
*;
quietly test [re_coefs_mean]re_open = [fe_coefs_mean]fe_open;
quietly test [re_coefs_mean]re_cshare = [fe_coefs_mean]fe_cshare, accumulate;
quietly test [re_coefs_m.ean]re_ishare = [fe_coefs_mean]fe_ishare, accumulate;
test [re_coefs_mean]re_gshare = [fe_coefs_mean]fe_gshare, accumulate;
```

16

Regression Modeling with Panel Data (Part B)

16.1 RELAXING STRICT EXOGENEITY: DYNAMICS AND LAGGED DEPENDENT VARIABLES

Both the Fixed Effects Model and the Random Effects Model require that all of the explanatory variables be "strictly exogenous," as defined by Equation 15-14:

Strict Exogeneity Assumption

$$\begin{aligned} \text{corr}(OPEN_{i,\tau},\ \varepsilon_{i,t}) &= 0 \\ \text{corr}(CSHARE_{i,\tau},\ \varepsilon_{i,t}) &= 0 \\ \text{corr}(ISHARE_{i,\tau},\ \varepsilon_{i,t}) &= 0 \\ \text{corr}(GSHARE_{i,\tau},\ \varepsilon_{i,t}) &= 0 \\ \text{for } \textbf{\textit{all}} \text{ values of } \tau \text{ and } t \end{aligned} \tag{15-14}$$

Thus, strict exogeneity of $OPEN_{i,t}$ requires that an explanatory variable such as $OPEN_{i,t}$ is uncorrelated with $\varepsilon_{i,\tau}$ for *all* values of τ, not just for τ equal to t, and similarly for the other explanatory variables in a panel data model. As noted at various points in Chapter 15, this assumption is quite restrictive. This chapter completes the treatment of panel data models by relaxing this assumption to account for model dynamics in the form of lagged values of the dependent variable (in the present section) and to allow for endogeneity in the explanatory variables, in Section 16.2.

A "dynamic" regression model quantifies the time-evolution of the dependent variable by including one or more lagged values of it as explanatory variables in the model. Such inclusion might be motivated by an effort to respecify the model so as to eliminate serial correlation in the idiosyncratic model errors. More typically, however, a single lag in the dependent variable is included in the model because it is intrinsic to the economic theory being quantified and/or tested.

For example, consider the following simple model of state-level cigarette demand, where $CIG_{i,t}$ is annual per capita cigarette consumption in state i, the intercept is omitted (for simplicity of exposition only), and $TAX_{i,t}$ is the current tax rate on a pack of cigarettes:

$$CIG_{i,t} = \beta_{cig} CIG_{i,t-1} + \beta_{tax} TAX_{i,t} + \nu_i + \varepsilon_{i,t} \tag{16-1}$$

The parameter β_{cig} in this model embodies the degree to which cigarette smoking is habitual or addictive, as it quantifies the degree to which cigarette consumption in period t depends on its value in the previous period; thus, the value of β_{cig} must clearly be non-negative. The value of β_{cig} must also be strictly less than one or else the dynamics of this model are not well behaved. That is essential here because it is assumed that the dynamic adjustment process described by Equation 16-1 has been ongoing for a substantial period of time – i.e., the model is assumed to also apply to time periods previous to the observed sample.

The parameter β_{tax} quantifies the impact of a potential policy variable, $TAX_{i,t}$. $TAX_{i,t}$ is, perhaps somewhat heroically, assumed to be strictly exogenous here: $P_{i,t}$, the price of a pack of cigarettes, will replace $TAX_{i,t}$ in this model in Section 16.2, where the discussion turns explicitly to a consideration of endogenous explanatory variables.[1]

The error components ν_i and $\varepsilon_{i,t}$ in Equation 16-1 are assumed to be independent of one another for all values of i and t, including, as noted above, for time periods previous to the observed sample.[2] The resulting implication that $\varepsilon_{i,t}$ is serially uncorrelated turns out to be essential in the development below. Were this not the case, however, then this non-autocorrelation could be easily induced by including lags in $TAX_{i,t}$ and additional lags in $CIG_{i,t}$ in the model. Such inclusions would increase the algebra involved, but not materially affect any of the conclusions reached here.

Obtaining the Fixed Effects Model or Random Effects Model estimates of β_{cig} and β_{tax} is trivially easy in Stata, using the commands:

```
xtreg cig L1.cig tax , fe
xtreg cig L1.cig tax , re
```

respectively, where *cig* is the Stata variable name for the data on $CIG_{i,t}$ and *tax* is the Stata variable name for the data on $TAX_{i,t}$. But are the resulting estimates realizations of consistent estimators in either case? Because of the dynamics induced by Equation 16-1, it will shortly become apparent that $CIG_{i,t-1}$ cannot be strictly exogenous. Therefore, the consistency of both the fixed-effects estimators $\left(\hat{\beta}_{cig}^{FE} \text{ and } \hat{\beta}_{tax}^{FE}\right)$ and the random-effect estimators $\left(\hat{\beta}_{cig}^{RE} \text{ and } \hat{\beta}_{tax}^{RE}\right)$ is in serious doubt.

The strategy for this section is as follows. First, the model for $CIG_{i,t}$ (Equation 16-1) will be re-written in terms of lags in the idiosyncratic error ($\varepsilon_{i,t}$) instead of in terms of $CIG_{i,t-1}$. This will be done via repeated substitution, much the same as in the analysis of the Autoregressive Model of Order One in Chapter 13. This result will then be used to show that

- $CIG_{i,t-1}$ is not strictly exogenous.
- $\hat{\beta}_{cig}^{FE}$ and $\hat{\beta}_{tax}^{FE}$ are not consistent estimators β_{cig} and β_{tax}.
- $\hat{\beta}_{cig}^{RE}$ and $\hat{\beta}_{tax}^{RE}$, in contrast, *are* consistent estimators β_{cig} and β_{tax}.

[1] Equation 16-1 – augmented with $P_{i,t}$, an income variable, some smuggling-related variables, and a tax revenue (rather than a tax rate) variable – is a subset of the "myopic" model considered in the Becker, Grossman, and Murphy (1994) analysis of cigarette addiction. The point of their paper, however, is a "rational" model of addiction, which is quite a bit different from (and more sophisticated than) the simple examples analyzed here and in Section 16.2. Also, note that both the intercept and the time-dependent component of the model error term (denoted λ_t in Equation 14-10) have been suppressed in these examples, so as to simplify and focus the exposition. Becker, G. S., M. Grossman, and K. M. Murphy (1994), "An Empirical Analysis of Cigarette Addiction," *The American Economic Review 84(3)*, pp. 396–418.

[2] Similar assumptions need to be made in "starting up" dynamic panel data models in a maximum likelihood framework – e.g., Bhargava and Sargan (1983). The exposition here, however, focuses solely on the Fixed Effects Model and the Random Effects Model in this dynamic context. Bhargava, A., and J. D. Sargan (1983), "Estimating Dynamic Random Effects Models from Panel Data Covering Short Time Periods," *Econometrica 51*, 1635–59.

This last result is a bit remarkable, but it is often of limited usefulness because its derivation depends on homoscedasticity in $\varepsilon_{i,t}$, which is often problematic in practice. Also, note that one needs an alternative estimator whose consistency does not rest on the Random Effects Model Assumption in order to test the practical validity of this assumption using the generalized Hausman Test described at the end of Section 15.5. The parameter estimators from the Fixed Effects Model played this role in the version of the test given at that point. With the inclusion of a lagged dependent variable, however, the Fixed Effects Model estimators are no longer consistent, and hence can no longer be used for this purpose. Fortunately, IV estimation of the "First-Differences Model" does provides a consistent – albeit not very efficient – estimator in this context: that model is introduced in Section 16.2, where the estimation of panel data models with endogenous explanatory variables is described.

Notation aside, Equation 16-1 actually differs only a little from the Autoregressive Model of Order One, the AR(1) model of Equation 13-11 in Chapter 13. In particular, Equation 16-1 drops the intercept term, but includes the explanatory variable $TAX_{i,t}$ and the country-specific term, ν_i. Proceeding as per the development of Equation 13-17, this is a straightforward matter of successively eliminating lagged values of the dependent variable from the right-hand side of the equation by repeated substitution – using Equation 16-1 itself, but rewritten for differing time periods.

The process begins by rewriting Equation 16-1 for period $t-1$:

$$CIG_{i,t-1} = \beta_{cig} CIG_{i,t-2} + \beta_{tax} TAX_{i,t-1} + \nu_i + \varepsilon_{i,t-1} \tag{16-2}$$

Substituting Equation 16-2 into the right-hand side of Equation 16-1 yields

$$\begin{aligned} CIG_{i,t} &= \beta_{cig}\left[\beta_{cig} CIG_{i,t-2} + \beta_{tax} TAX_{i,t-1} + \nu_i + \varepsilon_{i,t-1}\right] + \beta_{tax} TAX_{i,t} + \nu_i + \varepsilon_{i,t} \\ &= \beta_{cig}^2 CIG_{i,t-2} + \beta_{tax}(TAX_{i,t} + \beta_{cig} TAX_{i,t-1}) + (1+\beta_{cig})\nu_i + (\varepsilon_{i,t} + \beta_{cig}\varepsilon_{i,t-1}) \end{aligned} \tag{16-3}$$

Next, one uses Equation 16-1 to express $CIG_{i,t-2}$ in terms of its own past:

$$CIG_{i,t-2} = \beta_{cig} CIG_{i,t-3} + \beta_{tax} TAX_{i,t-2} + \nu_i + \varepsilon_{i,t-2} \tag{16-4}$$

and substitutes this expression for $CIG_{i,t-2}$ into Equation 16-3. This yields

$$\begin{aligned} CIG_{i,t} &= \beta_{cig}^3 CIG_{i,t-3} + \beta_{tax}(TAX_{i,t} + \beta_{cig} TAX_{i,t-1} + \beta_{cig}^2 TAX_{i,t-2}) \\ &\quad + (1 + \beta_{cig} + \beta_{cig}^2)\nu_i + (\varepsilon_{i,t} + \beta_{cig}\varepsilon_{i,t-1} + \beta_{cig}^2\varepsilon_{i,t-2}) \end{aligned} \tag{16-5}$$

Evidently, after $t-1$ such substitutions

$$\begin{aligned} CIG_{i,t} &= \beta_{cig}^t CIG_{i,0} + \beta_{tax}(TAX_{i,t} + \beta_{cig} TAX_{i,t-1} + \ldots + \beta_{cig}^{t-1} TAX_{i,1}) \\ &\quad + (1 + \beta_{cig} + \ldots + \beta_{cig}^{t-1})\nu_i + (\varepsilon_{i,t} + \beta_{cig}\varepsilon_{i,t-1} + \ldots + \beta_{cig}^{t-1}\varepsilon_{i,1}) \end{aligned} \tag{16-6}$$

or, in summation notation,

$$CIG_{i,t} = \beta_{cig}^t CIG_{i,0} + \beta_{tax}\sum_{\tau=0}^{t-1}\beta_{cig}^{\tau} TAX_{i,t-\tau} + \nu_i\sum_{\tau=0}^{t-1}\beta_{cig}^{\tau} + \sum_{\tau=0}^{t-1}\beta_{cig}^{\tau}\varepsilon_{i,t-\tau} \tag{16-7}$$

Presuming (as assumed at the outset of this example) that the dynamic adjustment embodied in Equation 16-1 has been in operation for a long time and that $0 \leq \beta_{cig} < 1$, this expression for $CIG_{i,t}$ becomes essentially indistinguishable from

$$CIG_{i,t} = \beta_{tax} \sum_{\tau=0}^{\infty} \beta_{cig}^{\tau} TAX_{i,t-\tau} + \left(\frac{1}{1-\beta_{cig}}\right) \nu_i + \sum_{\tau=0}^{\infty} \beta_{cig}^{\tau} \varepsilon_{i,t-\tau} \tag{16-8}$$

The lagged dependent explanatory variable, $CIG_{i,t-1}$, in the model for $CIG_{i,t}$ can therefore be written as

$$CIG_{i,t-1} = \beta_{tax} \sum_{\tau=0}^{\infty} \beta_{cig}^{\tau} TAX_{i,t-\tau-1} + \left(\frac{1}{1-\beta_{cig}}\right) \nu_i + \sum_{\tau=0}^{\infty} \beta_{cig}^{\tau} \varepsilon_{i,t-\tau-1} \tag{16-9}$$

The deviation of $CIG_{i,t-1}$ from its expected value (conditional on current and past values of the strictly exogenous variable, $TAX_{i,t}$) is thus

$$CIG_{i,t-1} - E\left[CIG_{i,t-1} | TAX_{i,t},\ TAX_{i,t-1},\ \ldots\right] = \left(\frac{1}{1-\beta_{cig}}\right) \nu_i + \sum_{\tau=0}^{\infty} \beta_{cig}^{\tau} \varepsilon_{i,t-\tau-1} \tag{16-10}$$

which depends on ν_i (and on $\varepsilon_{i,t-1}, \varepsilon_{i,t-2}, \ldots$), but not on $\varepsilon_{i,t}$ or on future values of $\varepsilon_{i,t}$.

Since ν_i is assumed to be independent of (and hence uncorrelated with) $\varepsilon_{i,t-1}, \varepsilon_{i,t-2}, \ldots$ and using the fact that the serial independence of $\varepsilon_{i,t}$ implies that it is serially uncorrelated, Equation 16-10 implies (after a bit of algebra, which constitutes Exercise 16-1), that the covariance of $CIG_{i,t-1}$ with $\nu_i + \varepsilon_{i,t}$, the model error term in Equation 16-1, is just

$$\text{cov}(CIG_{i,t-1},\ \nu_i + \varepsilon_{i,t}) = \frac{\sigma_\nu^2}{1-\beta_{cig}} \tag{16-11}$$

Thus, if σ_ν^2 is positive – i.e., in the Random Effects Model – then $CIG_{i,t-1}$ is endogenous as a regressor in Equation 16-1. In contrast, if σ_ν^2 is zero – i.e, in the Fixed Effects Model, wherein $\nu_1 \ldots \nu_M$ are taken as fixed in repeated samples – then $CIG_{i,t-1}$ is not endogenous. However, because $CIG_{i,t-1}$ is clearly correlated with the idiosyncratic error components from previous periods ($\varepsilon_{i,t-1} \ldots \varepsilon_{i,1}$), $CIG_{i,t-1}$ is not strictly exogenous. In fact, per the discussion in Section 15.4 after Equation 15-14, $CIG_{i,t-1}$ is "predetermined" in Equation 16-1. That is, $CIG_{i,t-1}$ is uncorrelated with current and future values of $\varepsilon_{i,t}$, albeit correlated with past values of it.

However, what's really at issue for consistent parameter estimation in the context of the Fixed Effects Model is not the correlation of $CIG_{i,t-1}$ with $\nu_i + \varepsilon_{i,t}$, but rather the correlation of the "within" transformed value of $CIG_{i,t-1}$ with the "within" transformed value of $\nu_i + \varepsilon_{i,t}$, as these are the relevant explanatory variable and error term in the regression equation actually estimated when one estimates this model. Similarly, the consistency of estimation in the Random Effects Model hinges on the correlation between the "quasi-differenced" value of $CIG_{i,t-1}$ with the "quasi-differenced" value of $\nu_i + \varepsilon_{i,t}$. Each of these estimating equations is now considered, in turn.

As in Equation 15-13, the equation for estimating the parameters in Equation 16-1 in the Fixed Effects Model is

$$CIG_{i,t}^{FE} = \beta_{cig} CIG_{i,t-1}^{FE} + \beta_{tax} TAX_{i,t}^{FE} + \varepsilon_{i,t}^{FE} \tag{16-12}$$

where, as in Equation 15-12,

$$\begin{aligned} CIG_{i,t}^{FE} &= CIG_{i,t} - \overline{CIG_i^{\text{lag}=0}} \quad \text{with} \quad \overline{CIG_i^{\text{lag}=0}} \equiv \frac{1}{T_i}\sum_{s=1}^{T_i} CIG_{i,s} \\ CIG_{i,t-1}^{FE} &= CIG_{i,t-1} - \overline{CIG_i^{\text{lag}=1}} \quad \text{with} \quad \overline{CIG_i^{\text{lag}=1}} \equiv \frac{1}{T_i}\sum_{s=1}^{T_i} CIG_{i,s-1} \\ TAX_{i,t}^{FE} &= TAX_{i,t} - \overline{TAX_i^{\text{lag}=0}} \quad \text{with} \quad \overline{TAX_i^{\text{lag}=0}} \equiv \frac{1}{T_i}\sum_{s=1}^{T_i} TAX_{i,s} \end{aligned} \tag{16-13}$$

These are the same definitions used in Equation 15-12 for the model analyzed in Section 15.4, except that the notation for the sample means is now adjusted to reflect the slightly different data used in calculating the sample mean for the lagged variable $CIG_{i,t-1}$.[3] Similarly, the transformed error term is

$$\varepsilon_{i,t}^{FE} = \varepsilon_{i,t} - \overline{\varepsilon_i^{\text{lag}=0}} \quad \text{with} \quad \overline{\varepsilon_i^{\text{lag}=0}} \equiv \frac{1}{T_i}\sum_{s=1}^{T_i} \varepsilon_{i,s} \tag{16-14}$$

As in Equation 15-13, ν_i^{FE} does not appear in Equation 16-12 because the "within" transformation eliminates any variable (such as ν_i) which does not depend on time – this, of course is precisely how the Fixed Effects Model deals with the heterogeneity across countries of the model posited in Equation 16-1.

The Fixed Effects Model yields consistent estimators of β_{cig} and β_{tax} if and only if OLS yields consistent estimators for Equation 16-12. Which it will not, because $CIG_{i,t-1}^{FE}$ is correlated with the model error term $\varepsilon_{i,t}^{FE}$. To see that this must be the case, the first step is to rewrite the deviation of $CIG_{i,t-1}^{FE}$ from its conditional mean in terms of the idiosyncratic model errors. This sequence of steps is very similar to that embodied in Equations 13-12 to 13-17; it begins with a rewrite of Equation 16-12 for period $t-1$:

$$CIG_{i,t-1}^{FE} = \beta_{cig} CIG_{i,t-2}^{FE} + \beta_{tax} TAX_{i,t-1}^{FE} + \varepsilon_{i,t-1}^{FE} \tag{16-15}$$

Substituting Equation 16-15 into the right-hand side of Equation 16-12 yields

$$\begin{aligned} CIG_{i,t}^{FE} &= \beta_{cig}\left[\beta_{cig} CIG_{i,t-2}^{FE} + \beta_{tax} TAX_{i,t-1}^{FE} + \varepsilon_{i,t-1}^{FE}\right] + \beta_{tax} TAX_{i,t}^{FE} + \varepsilon_{i,t}^{FE} \\ &= \beta_{cig}^2 CIG_{i,t-2}^{FE} + \beta_{tax}(TAX_{i,t}^{FE} + \beta_{cig} TAX_{i,t-1}^{FE}) + (\varepsilon_{i,t}^{FE} + \beta_{cig}\varepsilon_{i,t-1}^{FE}) \end{aligned} \tag{16-16}$$

Next, one uses Equation 16-12 to express $CIG_{i,t-2}^{FE}$ in terms of its own past:

$$CIG_{i,t-2}^{FE} = \beta_{cig} CIG_{i,t-3}^{FE} + \beta_{tax} TAX_{i,t-2}^{FE} + \varepsilon_{i,t-2}^{FE} \tag{16-17}$$

and substitutes this expression for $CIG_{i,t-2}^{FE}$ into Equation 16-16. This yields

$$\begin{aligned} CIG_{i,t}^{FE} = {} & \beta_{cig}^3 CIG_{i,t-3}^{FE} + \beta_{tax}(TAX_{i,t}^{FE} + \beta_{cig} TAX_{i,t-1}^{FE} + \beta_{cig}^2 TAX_{i,t-2}^{FE}) \\ & + (\varepsilon_{i,t}^{FE} + \beta_{cig}\varepsilon_{i,t-1}^{FE} + \beta_{cig}^2\varepsilon_{i,t-2}^{FE}) \end{aligned} \tag{16-18}$$

[3] A somewhat hidden cost of estimating a model including variables lagged j periods is that the first j sample observations are used to generate lagged variables rather than in estimating parameters; here the value of j is one and, for simplicity, the period of data used up is denoted as period zero. The value $CIG_{i,0}$ used in calculating $\overline{CIG_i^{\text{lag}=1}}$ is thus actually available.

After $t-1$ such substitutions,

$$\begin{aligned} CIG_{i,t}^{FE} &= \beta_{cig}^{t} CIG_{i,0}^{FE} + \beta_{tax}(TAX_{i,t}^{FE} + \beta_{cig} TAX_{i,t-1}^{FE} + \dots + \beta_{cig}^{t-1} TAX_{i,1}^{FE}) \\ &\quad + (\varepsilon_{i,t}^{FE} + \beta_{cig}\varepsilon_{i,t-1}^{FE} + \dots + \beta_{cig}^{t-1}\varepsilon_{i,1}^{FE}) \end{aligned} \tag{16-19}$$

or, in summation notation,

$$CIG_{i,t}^{FE} = \beta_{cig}^{t} CIG_{i,0}^{FE} + \beta_{tax}\sum_{\tau=0}^{t-1} \beta_{cig}^{\tau} TAX_{i,t-\tau}^{FE} + \sum_{\tau=0}^{t-1} \beta_{cig}^{\tau}\varepsilon_{i,t-\tau}^{FE} \tag{16-20}$$

Presuming again that the dynamic adjustment embodied in the model has been in operation for a long time and that $0 \leq \beta_{cig} < 1$, this expression for $CIG_{i,t}^{FE}$ becomes essentially indistinguishable from

$$CIG_{i,t}^{FE} = \beta_{tax}\sum_{\tau=0}^{\infty} \beta_{cig}^{\tau} TAX_{i,t-\tau}^{FE} + \sum_{\tau=0}^{\infty} \beta_{cig}^{\tau}\varepsilon_{i,t-\tau}^{FE}. \tag{16-21}$$

Hence, $CIG_{i,t-1}^{FE}$ can be written as

$$CIG_{i,t-1}^{FE} = \beta_{tax}\sum_{\tau=0}^{\infty} \beta_{cig}^{\tau} TAX_{i,t-\tau-1}^{FE} + \sum_{\tau=0}^{\infty} \beta_{cig}^{\tau}\varepsilon_{i,t-\tau-1}^{FE} \tag{16-22}$$

and the deviation of $CIG_{i,t-1}^{FE}$ from its conditional mean is thus

$$CIG_{i,t-1}^{FE} = E\left[CIG_{i,t-1}^{FE} \middle| TAX_{i,t-1}^{FE},\, TAX_{i,t-2}^{FE},\, \dots\right] = \sum_{\tau=0}^{\infty} \beta_{cig}^{\tau}\varepsilon_{i,t-\tau-1}^{FE} \tag{16-23}$$

Substituting Equation 16-14, rewritten for period $t-\tau-1$, into Equation 16-23 yields

$$\begin{aligned} & CIG_{i,t-1}^{FE} - E\left[CIG_{i,t-1}^{FE} \middle| TAX_{i,t-1}^{FE},\, TAX_{i,t-2}^{FE},\, \dots\right] \\ &= \sum_{\tau=0}^{\infty} \beta_{\text{cig}}^{\tau}\left(\varepsilon_{i,t-\tau-1} - \overline{\varepsilon_{i}^{\text{lag}=\tau+1}}\right) \end{aligned} \tag{16-24}$$

The covariance of $CIG_{i,t-1}^{FE}$ with the model error term $\varepsilon_{i,t}^{FE}$ in Equation 16-12 is thus

$$\begin{aligned} \operatorname{cov}\left(CIG_{i,t-1}^{FE}, \varepsilon_{i,t}^{FE}\right) &= E\left[\left\{\sum_{\tau=0}^{\infty} \beta_{cig}^{\tau}\left(\varepsilon_{i,t-\tau-1} - \overline{\varepsilon_{i}^{\text{lag}=\tau+1}}\right)\right\}\left(\varepsilon_{i,t} - \overline{\varepsilon_{i}^{\text{lag}=0}}\right)\right] \\ &= \sum_{\tau=0}^{\infty} \beta_{cig}^{\tau} E\left[\left(\varepsilon_{i,t-\tau-1} - \overline{\varepsilon_{i}^{\text{lag}=\tau+1}}\right)\left(\varepsilon_{i,t} - \overline{\varepsilon_{i}^{\text{lag}=0}}\right)\right] \end{aligned} \tag{16-25}$$

which (after a good deal of algebra, constituting Exercise 16-2) yields a complicated (and opaque) expression depending on t, T_i, and β_{cig}. For small values of β_{cig}, this expression reduces to

$$\lim_{\beta_{\text{cig}} \to 0}\left[\operatorname{cov}\left(CIG_{i,t-1}^{FE}, \varepsilon_{i,t}^{FE}\right)\right] = -\frac{\sigma_{\varepsilon}^{2}}{T_i}\left(2 - \frac{T_i - 1}{T_i}\right) < 0 \tag{16-26}$$

so it is evident that $CIG^{FE}_{i,t-1}$ is generally correlated with the model error term $\left(\varepsilon^{FE}_{i,t}\right)$ in Equation 16-12. Thus, the Fixed Effects Model in general yields inconsistent parameter estimators when a lagged dependent variable is included in the model.

Next, consider the consistency of the parameter estimators obtained from the Random Effects Model for estimating β_{cig} and β_{tax}:

$$\begin{aligned} CIG^{RE}_{i,t} &= \beta_{cig} CIG^{RE}_{i,t-1} + \beta_{tax} TAX^{RE}_{i,t} + (\nu_i + \varepsilon_{i,t})^{RE} \\ &= \beta_{cig} CIG^{RE}_{i,t-1} + \beta_{tax} TAX^{RE}_{i,t} + \gamma_{i,t} \end{aligned} \tag{16-27}$$

where, as in Equation 15-21,

$$\begin{aligned} CIG^{RE}_{i,t} &= CIG_{i,t} - \theta_i \overline{CIG_i^{\text{lag}=0}} \\ CIG^{RE}_{i,t-1} &= CIG_{i,t-1} - \theta_i \overline{CIG_i^{\text{lag}=1}} \\ TAX^{RE}_{i,t} &= TAX_{i,t} - \theta_i \overline{TAX_i^{\text{lag}=0}} \end{aligned} \tag{16-28}$$

and the parameter θ_i is defined as

$$\theta_i \equiv 1 - \sqrt{\frac{1}{T_i \frac{\sigma_\nu^2}{\sigma_\varepsilon^2} + 1}} \tag{16-29}$$

Per Equations 15-25 and 15-26 in Section 15.5, this expression for θ_i is exactly the weight in the quasi-difference transformation which makes $\gamma_{i,t}$, the implied the error term in Equation 16-2,

$$\begin{aligned} (\nu_i + \varepsilon_{i,t})^{RE} = \gamma_{i,t} &= (\nu_i + \varepsilon_{i,t}) - \theta_i \left(\overline{\nu_i^{\text{lag}=0}} + \overline{\varepsilon_i^{\text{lag}=0}} \right) \\ &= \left(\nu_i - \theta_i \overline{\nu_i^{\text{lag}=0}} \right) + \left(\varepsilon_{i,t} - \theta_i \overline{\varepsilon_i^{\text{lag}=0}} \right) \\ &= (1 - \theta_i)\nu_i + \left(\varepsilon_{i,t} - \theta_i \overline{\varepsilon_i^{\text{lag}=0}} \right) \end{aligned} \tag{16-30}$$

homoscedastic and serially uncorrelated.[4]

Considering now the Random Effects Model (Equation 16-27, for $CIG^{RE}_{i,t}$) instead of the Fixed Effects Model (Equation 16-12, for $CIG^{FE}_{i,t}$), the derivation of an expression for the deviation of $CIG^{RE}_{i,t-1}$ from its conditional mean – analogous to Equation 16-24 – proceeds in a very similar fashion. One begins by rewriting Equation 16-27 for period $t-1$:

$$CIG^{RE}_{i,t-1} = \beta_{cig} CIG^{RE}_{i,t-2} + \beta_{tax} TAX^{RE}_{i,t-1} + \gamma_{i,t-1} \tag{16-31}$$

Substituting Equation 16-31 into the right-hand side of Equation 16-27 yields

$$\begin{aligned} CIG^{RE}_{i,t} &= \beta_{cig} \left[\beta_{cig} CIG^{RE}_{i,t-2} + \beta_{tax} TAX^{RE}_{i,t-1} + \gamma_{i,t-1} \right] + \beta_{tax} TAX^{RE}_{i,t} + \gamma_{i,t} \\ &= \beta^2_{cig} CIG^{RE}_{i,t-2} + \beta_{tax} \left(TAX^{RE}_{i,t} + \beta_{cig} TAX^{RE}_{i,t-1} \right) + \left(\gamma_{i,t} + \beta_{cig} \gamma_{i,t-1} \right) \end{aligned} \tag{16-32}$$

[4] Note that $\overline{\nu_i^{\text{lag}=0}}$ in Equation 14-55 is just $\frac{1}{T_i} \sum_{s=1}^{T_i} \nu_i = \nu_i$, since ν_i is the same for all T_i periods.

Next, use Equation 16-27 to express $CIG^{RE}_{i,t-2}$ in terms of its own past:

$$CIG^{RE}_{i,t-2} = \beta_{cig} CIG^{RE}_{i,t-3} + \beta_{tax} TAX^{RE}_{i,t-2} + \gamma_{i,t-2} \quad (16\text{-}33)$$

and substitute this expression for $CIG^{RE}_{i,t-2}$ into Equation 16-32. This yields

$$\begin{aligned} CIG^{RE}_{i,t} &= \beta^3_{cig} CIG^{RE}_{i,t-3} + \beta_{tax}\left(TAX^{RE}_{i,t} + \beta_{cig} TAX^{RE}_{i,t-1} + \beta^2_{cig} TAX^{RE}_{i,t-2}\right) \\ &\quad + \left(\gamma_{i,t} + \beta_{cig}\gamma_{i,t-1} + \beta^2_{cig}\gamma_{i,t-2}\right) \end{aligned} \quad (16\text{-}34)$$

After $t-1$ such substitutions,

$$\begin{aligned} CIG^{RE}_{i,t} &= \beta^t_{cig} CIG^{RE}_{i,0} + \beta_{tax}\left(TAX^{RE}_{i,t} + \beta_{cig} TAX^{RE}_{i,t-1} + \dots + \beta^{t-1}_{cig} TAX^{RE}_{i,1}\right) \\ &\quad + \left(\gamma_{i,t} + \beta_{cig}\gamma_{i,t-1} + \dots + \beta^{t-1}_{cig}\gamma_{i,1}\right) \end{aligned} \quad (16\text{-}35)$$

or, in summation notation,

$$CIG^{RE}_{i,t} = \beta^t_{cig} CIG^{RE}_{i,0} + \beta_{tax}\sum_{\tau=0}^{t-1}\beta^{\tau}_{cig} TAX^{RE}_{i,t-\tau} + \sum_{\tau=0}^{t-1}\beta^{\tau}_{cig}\gamma_{i,t-\tau} \quad (16\text{-}36)$$

Presuming again that the dynamic adjustment embodied in the model has been in operation for a long time and that $0 \le \beta_{cig} < 1$, this expression for $CIG^{RE}_{i,t}$ becomes essentially indistinguishable from

$$CIG^{RE}_{i,t} = \beta_{tax}\sum_{\tau=0}^{\infty}\beta^{\tau}_{cig} TAX^{RE}_{i,t-\tau} + \sum_{\tau=0}^{\infty}\beta^{\tau}_{cig}\gamma_{i,t-\tau} \quad (16\text{-}37)$$

Hence, $CIG^{RE}_{i,t}$ can be written as

$$CIG^{RE}_{i,t-1} = \beta_{tax}\sum_{\tau=0}^{\infty}\beta^{\tau}_{cig} TAX^{RE}_{i,t-\tau-1} + \sum_{\tau=0}^{\infty}\beta^{\tau}_{cig}\gamma_{i,t-\tau-1} \quad (16\text{-}38)$$

and the deviation of $CIG^{RE}_{i,t-1}$ from its conditional mean is thus

$$CIG^{RE}_{i,t-1} - E\left[CIG^{RE}_{i,t-1} \middle| TAX^{RE}_{i,t-1}, TAX^{RE}_{i,t-2}, \dots\right] = \sum_{\tau=0}^{\infty}\beta^{\tau}_{cig}\gamma_{i,t-\tau-1} \quad (16\text{-}39)$$

The covariance of $CIG^{RE}_{i,t-1}$ with the Random Effects Model equation error term – $\gamma_{i,t}$, equal to $(\nu_i + \varepsilon_{i,t})^{RE}$ in Equation 16-27 – is therefore just

$$\begin{aligned} \text{cov}\left(CIG^{RE}_{i,t-1}, (\nu_i + \varepsilon_{i,t})^{RE}\right) &= E\left[\left(\sum_{\tau=0}^{\infty}\beta^{\tau}_{cig}\gamma_{i,t-\tau-1}\right)\gamma_{i,t}\right] \\ &= \sum_{\tau=0}^{\infty}\beta^{\tau}_{\text{cig}} E\left[\gamma_{i,t-\tau-1}\gamma_{i,t}\right] \\ &= 0 \end{aligned} \quad (16\text{-}40)$$

since the quasi-difference transformation forces $\gamma_{i,t}$ to be serially uncorrelated.

Thus, the nature of the quasi-difference transformation makes $\hat{\beta}^{RE}_{cig}$ and $\hat{\beta}^{RE}_{cig}$ consistent estimators of β_{cig} and β_{tax}, presuming that the Strict Exogeneity Assumption (Equation 15-14) and the Random

Effects Model Assumption, Equation 15-8 – rewritten in terms of the explanatory variables $CIG_{i,t-1}$ and $TAX_{i,t}$ – are both valid.

Recall, however, that the derivation above (Equations 16-27 to 16-40) requires that the original idiosyncratic model error term ($\varepsilon_{i,t}$ in Equation 16-1) is homoscedastic and serially uncorrelated: only in that case do Equations 15-25 and 15-26 in Section 15.5 make the quasi-differenced model error term $(\nu_i + \varepsilon_{i,t})^{RE}$ serially uncorrelated, as needed for Equation 16-40. One can force $\varepsilon_{i,t}$ to be serially uncorrelated, by simply including a sufficient number of lags of the dependent and explanatory variables in the model specification, but there is no straightforward way to ensure that $\varepsilon_{i,t}$ is homoscedastic.

The consistency of $\hat{\beta}_{cig}^{RE}$ and $\hat{\beta}_{cig}^{RE}$ is excellent, but note that – since $\hat{\beta}_{cig}^{FE}$ and $\hat{\beta}_{cig}^{FE}$ are no longer consistent estimators of β_{cig} and β_{tax} with the lagged dependent variable included in the model – it is no longer possible to use these estimators from the Fixed Effects Model in a generalized Hausman Test to check on the validity of the Random Effects Model Assumption. That is because the Hausman Test requires the availability of a second estimator of β_{cig} and β_{tax}, whose consistency does not depend on the validity of the Random Effects Model Assumption.[5]

Moreover, the assumption made above that the explanatory variable $TAX_{i,t}$ is strictly exogenous – i.e., uncorrelated with $\varepsilon_{i,t}$ for all values of τ – is actually quite a restrictive one in actual economic applications. Both of these issues are addressed in the next section, where a final major approach for estimating regression models using panel data is introduced, the First-Differences Model.

16.2 RELAXING STRICT EXOGENEITY: THE FIRST-DIFFERENCES MODEL

So far two main approaches for modeling panel data heterogeneity have been considered: the Fixed Effects Model and the Random Effects Model. Each of these has been analyzed under the Strict Exogeneity Assumption (Equation 15-14), which requires that all of the explanatory variables are uncorrelated with the idiosyncratic component of the model error, $\varepsilon_{i,t-\tau}$, for all values of τ. The Random Effects Model additionally makes the Random Effects Model Assumption (Equation 15-18), which requires that all of the explanatory variables are also uncorrelated with the country-specific model error component, ν_i.

The analysis in Sections 15.4 and 15.5 shows that both of these models yield consistent parameter estimates where these assumptions are valid. Where the assumption of strict exogeneity is relaxed so as to include the use of lagged dependent variables as explanatory variables, the analysis in Section 16.1 shows that only the Random Effects Model still yields consistent parameter estimates, and even then only when $\varepsilon_{i,t}$ is both serially uncorrelated and homoscedastic and when all of the other explanatory variables are strictly exogenous.

It should be noted, however, that most empirical economists are in practice quite skeptical as to the validity of the Random Effects Model Assumption. Consequently, the use of the Random Effects is often considered reasonable only following a Hausman Test result which fails to reject the null hypothesis of practical importance: this is the null hypothesis that the parameters of crucial economic importance are the same regardless of whether they are estimated using the Random Effects Model estimators or whether they are obtained using estimators whose consistency does not hinge on the validity of the Random Effects Model Assumption.

Where it can sensibly be used, however, the Random Effects Model does have distinct advantages over the Fixed Effects Model: it produces more efficient parameter estimates, it allows the use of explanatory variables which do not vary over time, and it can still provide consistent parameter estimates in dynamic models including lagged dependent variables – at least so long as the Random Effects Model Assumption is valid and the idiosyncratic errors are both serially uncorrelated and homoscedastic.

[5] The Random Effects Assumption here amounts to assuming that $CIG_{i,t-1}$ and $TAX_{i,t}$ are both uncorrelated with ν_i. See Equation 15-18 and the discussion immediately following.

However – with the sole exception of a lagged dependent variable in such a Random Effects Model – neither of these models yields consistent parameter estimates if any of the explanatory variables in the model violate the Strict Exogeneity Assumption. How, then, can one obtain consistent parameter estimates in a model with lagged dependent variables irrespective of the validity of the Random Effects Model Assumption, so that the Hausman Test alluded to above can be used to address the validity of this assumption? More important: how can one obtain consistent parameter estimates in a panel data model at all when one or more of the explanatory variables are simply endogenous? After all, the analysis in Chapter 11 makes it quite clear that such endogeneity can easily arise in actual economic data: due to omitted variables, measurement error, or joint determination.

These questions are addressed in this section by modifying the cigarette consumption model (Equation 16-1) introduced in Section 16.1. That model was designed to allow for the combination of a lagged dependent variable and a strictly exogenous explanatory variable in the simplest possible way. The modification introduced here is to augment Equation 16-1 by the inclusion of an arguably endogenous explanatory variable: $P_{i,t}$, the price of a pack of cigarettes in state i and period t. The model then becomes

$$CIG_{i,t} = \beta_{cig} CIG_{i,t-1} + \beta_{tax} TAX_{i,t} + \beta_{price} P_{i,t} + \nu_i + \varepsilon_{i,t} \qquad (16\text{-}41)$$

It is reasonable to think that $P_{i,t}$ is endogenous because one would expect its value to be jointly determined with that of $CIG_{i,t}$ in some sort of market equilibrium. Thus, the model is now formulated so as to allow for two kinds of explanatory variable which are not strictly exogenous: a lagged dependent variable and an explicitly endogenous variable.

As in the version of this model used in Section 16.1, the parameter β_{cig} embodies the degree to which cigarette smoking is habitual or addictive, as it quantifies the degree to which cigarette consumption in period t depends on its value in the previous period; thus, the value of β_{cig} must still be non-negative. The value of $|\beta_{cig}|$ must also still be strictly less than one so as to ensure that the dynamics of the model are well-behaved.[6]

The parameter β_{tax} again quantifies the impact of a potential policy variable, $TAX_{i,t}$. $TAX_{i,t}$ is still, and again perhaps somewhat heroically, assumed to be strictly exogenous; its presence in the model identifies Equation 16-41 as an equation modeling the demand for cigarettes. Had, say, the wholesale price of tobacco been included in this model instead of $TAX_{i,t}$, then Equation 16-41 would arguably be modeling the supply of cigarettes.

The new parameter, β_{price}, is quantifying the impact of the own-price on the quantity of cigarettes demanded; hence, it is directly related to the price elasticity of the demand for cigarettes. The parameter β_{price} would equal the price elasticity of demand if $CIG_{i,t}$ and $P_{i,t}$ had been defined as the logarithms of the quantity of cigarettes sold and of the unit price; as specified here, $\beta_{price}\,(P_{i,t}/CIG_{i,t})$ is the price elasticity of demand.[7]

As in the previous model for $CIG_{i,t}$, estimating β_{cig}, β_{tax}, and β_{price} in either the Fixed Effects Model or the Random Effects Model is practically trivial. For example, where the variable p denotes the data on $P_{i,t}$, the Stata command:

```
xtreg cig L1.cig tax p , fe
```

yields the parameter estimates for the Fixed Effects Model. That's not the problem. The challenge is to obtain *consistent* estimators for these parameters: testing hypotheses about any one, or all three, of

[6] See Exercise 16-3. Also – as with Equation 16-1 – the intercept is omitted, for simplicity of exposition only.

[7] Per Footnote 16-1, Equation 16-41 is a subset of the "myopic" model considered in the Becker, Grossman, and Murphy (1994) analysis of cigarette addiction. Again, however, the point of their paper was the analysis of a "rational" model of addiction, which is substantially more sophisticated than the example used here. In particular, their "rational" model of addiction implies the additional inclusion of $CIG_{i,t}+1$ as an explanatory variable.

the parameters (β_{cig}, β_{tax}, and β_{price}) might constitute the economic motivation for estimating Equation 16-41, but the validity of such testing first requires consistent estimation of these parameters.

As usual, the conclusions one can reach about estimator consistency – and about the validity of the asymptotic sampling distributions underlying the reported standard errors used in obtaining hypothesis testing and confidence interval results – in practice depend on additional model assumptions about the model errors.

In particular, the same assumptions are made here regarding the error components ν_i and $\varepsilon_{i,t}$ in Equation 16-41 as were made for the similarly named error components in Equation 16-1 of Section 16.1: they are assumed to be independent of one another for all values of i and t, including, where necessary, for time periods previous to the observed sample. (The resulting implication that $\varepsilon_{i,t}$ is serially uncorrelated could, where necessary, be readily induced by including additional lags of $CIG_{i,t}$, $TAX_{i,t}$, and $P_{i,t}$ in the model.) Also, since $TAX_{i,t}$ is again assumed to be strictly exogenous, it is uncorrelated with ν_j, and with $\varepsilon_{j,\tau}$ for every possible value of τ and of j.

Turning to the newly included explanatory variable, $P_{i,t}$, it is – like $TAX_{i,t}$ – assumed to be uncorrelated with all of the error components (ν_j, and $\varepsilon_{j,\tau}$) for every time period τ in other countries – i.e., for all values of j not equal to i. Since $P_{i,t}$ is endogenous, however, it is clearly allowed to be – indeed, it is expected to be – correlated with $\varepsilon_{i,t}$, and perhaps with ν_i as well. If $P_{i,t}$ is correlated with *future* values of $\varepsilon_{i,t}$, then lagged values of $P_{i,t}$ have been wrongly omitted from the model specification. Such lagged values could be readily included in the model specification so as to eliminate such correlations – it would only complicate the example a bit. Consequently, it can be assumed here that $P_{i,t}$ is uncorrelated with future values of $\varepsilon_{i,t}$ with no real loss of generality. Similarly, if $P_{i,t}$ is correlated with *past* values of $\varepsilon_{i,t}$, then this correlation can be eliminated by including *future* values of $P_{i,t}$ in the model as explanatory variables. Indeed, such variables frequently appear in model specifications derived from rational expectations models. Or one can just allow for the possibility that $P_{i,t}$ is correlated with past values of $\varepsilon_{i,t}$. The latter option is taken here. Thus, $P_{i,t}$ is assumed to be uncorrelated with future values of $\varepsilon_{i,t}$, but correlated with current and past values of $\varepsilon_{i,t}$. Correlation between $P_{i,t}$ and ν_i is not ruled out, but is assumed to be independent of t. More compactly,

$$\begin{aligned} \pi^{P\varepsilon}_{P\tau} &\equiv \text{Cov}(P_{i,t},\, \varepsilon_{i,t-\tau}) = E[P_{i,t}\, \varepsilon_{i,t-\tau}] \\ \pi^{P\nu} &\equiv \text{Cov}(P_{i,t},\, \nu_i) \quad = E[P_{i,t}\, \nu_i] \end{aligned} \tag{16-42}$$

with $\pi^{P\varepsilon}_{P\tau}$ equal to zero for negative values of τ.

Consider now the prospects for consistently estimating β_{cig}, β_{tax}, and β_{price} in either the Fixed Effects Model,

$$CIG^{FE}_{i,t} = \beta_{cig} CIG^{FE}_{i,t-1} + \beta_{tax} TAX^{FE}_{i,t} + \beta_{price} P^{FE}_{i,t} + \varepsilon^{FE}_{i,t} \tag{16-43}$$

or in the Random Effects Model,

$$\begin{aligned} CIG^{RE}_{i,t} &= \beta_{cig} CIG^{RE}_{i,t-1} + \beta_{tax} TAX^{RE}_{i,t} + \beta_{price} P^{RE}_{i,t} + (\nu_i + \varepsilon_{i,t})^{RE} \\ &= \beta_{cig} CIG^{RE}_{i,t-1} + \beta_{tax} TAX^{RE}_{i,t} + \beta_{price} P^{RE}_{i,t} + \gamma_{i,t} \end{aligned} \tag{16-44}$$

where all of these transformed variables are defined in Equations 16-13 and 16-28 of Section 16.1, except for the transformed values of $P_{i,t}$. These transformed values of $P_{i,t}$ are defined, analogously, as

$$\begin{aligned} P^{FE}_{i,t} &= P_{i,t} - \overline{P^{\text{lag}=0}_i} = P_{i,t} - \frac{1}{T_i}\sum_{s=1}^{T_i} P_{i,s} \\ P^{RE}_{i,t} &= P_{i,t} - \theta_i \overline{P^{\text{lag}=0}_i} = P_{i,t} - \frac{\theta_i}{T_i}\sum_{s=1}^{T_i} P_{i,s} \end{aligned} \tag{16-45}$$

Each value of both $P_{i,t}^{FE}$ and $P_{i,t}^{RE}$ clearly depends on all T_i values of $P_{i,t}$: $P_{i,1}$ ... $P_{i,Ti}$. And – from their definitions, in Equations 16-14 and 16-30, respectively – each value of both $\varepsilon_{i,t}^{FE}$ and $(\nu_i + \varepsilon_{i,t})^{RE}$ clearly depends on all T_i values of $\varepsilon_{i,t}$: $\varepsilon_{i,1}$ ... $\varepsilon_{i,Ti}$. Since $P_{i,t}$ is assumed to be correlated with current and past values of $\varepsilon_{i,t}$, it follows that $P_{i,t}^{RE}$ is correlated with $\varepsilon_{i,t}^{FE}$ and that $P_{i,t}^{RE}$ is correlated with $(\nu_i + \varepsilon_{i,t})^{RE}$. More explicitly,

$$\operatorname{cov}\left[P_{i,t}^{FE},\, \varepsilon_{i,t}^{FE}\right] = \left(1 - \frac{1}{T_i}\right)^2 \pi_0^{P\varepsilon} + \text{terms involving } \pi_1^{P\varepsilon},\, \pi_2^{P\varepsilon},\, \pi_3^{P\varepsilon} \ldots \tag{16-46}$$

$$\operatorname{cov}\left[P_{i,t}^{RE},\, (\nu_i + \varepsilon_{i,t})^{RE}\right] = (1-\theta_i)^2 \pi_0^{P\nu} + \left(1 - \frac{2\theta_i}{T_i} + \frac{\theta_i^2}{T_i}\right)\pi_0^{P\varepsilon} + \text{terms involving } \pi_1^{P\varepsilon},\, \pi_2^{P\varepsilon},\, \pi_3^{P\varepsilon} \ldots$$

where the full expression for $\operatorname{cov}\left[P_{i,t}^{RE},\, (\nu_i + \varepsilon_{i,t})^{RE}\right]$ is derived in Exercise 16-4 and $\operatorname{cov}\left[P_{i,t}^{FE},\, \varepsilon_{i,t}^{FE}\right]$ is equal to this expression with $\pi^{P\nu}$ set to zero and θ_i set to one. Because the assumed endogeneity in $P_{i,t}$ make these two covariances differ from zero, it renders the parameter estimators in both the Fixed Effects Model and the Random Effects Model inconsistent.

From the exposition of instrumental variables (IV) estimation in Chapter 12, it is easy enough to obtain consistent estimators of β_{cig}, β_{tax}, and β_{price} – but only if one has a sufficient number of valid instruments for use in the first-stage regressions. In particular, two-stage least squares estimation of the Fixed Effects Model (Equation 16-43) and the Random Effects Model (Equation 16-44) each requires at least two valid instruments (and two first-stage regression equations) because both the transform of $CIG_{i,t-1}$ and the transform of $P_{i,t}$ are in each case now correlated with the transformed model error term.[8] Valid instruments for $CIG_{i,t-1}^{FE}$ and $P_{i,t}^{FE}$ must be correlated with these two variables, yet must themselves be strictly exogenous – that is, uncorrelated with $\varepsilon_{i,1}$ ... $\varepsilon_{i,Ti}$. Similarly, valid instruments for $CIG_{i,t-1}^{RE}$ and $P_{i,t}^{RE}$ must be correlated with these two variables, yet must themselves be both strictly exogenous and also uncorrelated with ν_i.

Suppose – just for the moment – that one had on hand, say, three such valid instruments for $CIG_{i,t-1}^{FE}$ and $P_{i,t}^{FE}$. It would be straightforward, in that case, to obtain consistent two-stage least squares estimates of the model parameters using the Stata "ivregress" command. In particular, letting z1, z2, and z3 denote the variable names for these three instruments – and letting cig_fe, cig_lag1_fe, tax_fe, and p_fe denote the variable names for the corresponding "within" transformed variables – then the Stata command:

```
ivregress 2sls cig_fe (cig_lag1_fe p_fe = z1 z2 z3) tax_fe , vce(cluster statenum)
```

yields consistent two-stage least squares estimates of β_{cig}, β_{tax}, and β_{price}.[9] Similarly, supposing that q1, q2, and q3 are valid instruments for $CIG_{i,t-1}^{RE}$ and $P_{i,t}^{RE}$, and letting cig_re, cig_lag1_re, tax_re,

[8] The derivation in Section 16.1 to the effect that $\operatorname{cov}\left(CIG_{i,t-1}^{RE},\, (\nu_i + \varepsilon_{i,t})^{RE}\right)$ is zero – Equation 16-40 – is no longer valid when an endogenous explanatory variable is added to the model. This is because the expectation in Equation 14-64 must now account for the fact that $CIG_{i,t-1}^{RE}$ in the present model depends also on lagged values of $P_{i,t}^{RE}$.

[9] This command syntax assumes that "statenum" indexes the state for each observation. At this writing, the Stata "xtivreg" command eliminates the hassle of transforming the variables and instruments oneself – e.g., using code such as that in Appendix 15.1 – but does not compute cluster-robust standard errors. Stata is improving all the time, however, so the "xtivreg" command could be substantially more capable in this regard by the time you read this. Also, as in earlier references to the use of the "ivregress" command, Generalized Method of Moments (GMM) estimation is not covered here until Section 19.4, but those estimates are generated by simply replacing "2sls" by "gmm" in the "ivregress" command. The big advantage to GMM estimation is that the estimated weighting method can be specified – here using the "wmatrix(cluster statenum)" option – to produce parameter estimates which are asymptotically efficient despite any heteroscedasticity or serial correlation in $\varepsilon_{i,t}$, whereas two-stage least squares estimation with the "vce(cluster statenum)" option only adjusts the standard error estimates to be consistent.

and p_re denote the variable names for the corresponding "quasi-differenced" variables, then the Stata command:

```
ivregress 2sls cig_re (cig_lag1_re p_re = q1 q2 q3) tax_re , vce(cluster statenum)
```

also yields consistent two-stage least squares estimates of β_{cig}, β_{tax}, and β_{price}, presuming that the variables and instruments are all uncorrelated with ν_i. As in Section 16.1, if the parameter estimates of greatest interest are not significantly different across these two models, then one would prefer the more efficient Random Effects Model estimates.

Unfortunately, it is not immediately obvious what actual variables one could credibly use as the instruments $Z1_{i,t}$, $Z2_{i,t}$, and $Z3_{i,t}$ (or $Q1_{i,t}$, $Q2_{i,t}$, and $Q3_{i,t}$) in these models. In some regression models the underlying economic theory implies that certain variables will be exogenous; utilizing those implications in justifying the estimation procedure, however, makes the consistency of the model parameter estimators conditional on the validity of the theory.[10] This is fine for testing the theory – but only if one can also consistently estimate the model's parameters in a separate fashion that is *not* conditional on the theory's validity. Which leaves the analyst, again, needing credibly valid instruments.

Fortunately, there is an alternative approach, the "First-Differences Model," which provides a solution – albeit an imperfect one – to the problem of consistently estimating coefficients such as β_{cig}, β_{tax}, and β_{price} in a model like Equation 16-41.

Aside from the pooled regression model, which basically ignores the heterogeneity induced by the country/state/individual-specific component (ν_i) altogether, the First-Differences Model is actually the simplest framework so far considered. In the vocabulary of Chapter 13, it consists of simply considering the model "in changes." Thus, for the cigarette consumption model considered here (Equation 16-41), the First-Differences Model is just

$$\begin{aligned}\Delta CIG_{i,t} &= \beta_{cig}\Delta CIG_{i,t-1} + \beta_{tax}\Delta TAX_{i,t} + \beta_{price}\Delta P_{i,t} + \Delta\nu_i + \Delta\varepsilon_{i,t} \\ &= \beta_{cig}\Delta CIG_{i,t-1} + \beta_{tax}\Delta TAX_{i,t} + \beta_{price}\Delta P_{i,t} + \Delta\varepsilon_{i,t}\end{aligned} \tag{16-47}$$

where $\Delta CIG_{i,t}$ is $CIG_{i,t} - CIG_{i,t-1}$, $\Delta CIG_{i,t-1}$ is $CIG_{i,t-1} - CIG_{i,t-2}$, $\Delta TAX_{i,t}$ is $TAX_{i,t} - TAX_{i,t-1}$, and so forth for the other variables.

Note that ν_i, the state-specific component of the error term in Equation 16-41, is eliminated by this transformation, along with the intercept (had there been one in Equation 16-41) and any explanatory variables which do not vary over time. Thus, the first-difference transformation at one stroke eliminates the non homogeneity induced by the panel nature of the state-level cigarette consumption data, but – like the "within" transformation of the Fixed Effects Model – it also eliminates the possibility of quantifying how $CIG_{i,t}$ varies with any time-invariant explanatory variables.[11]

Also, one can (and ordinarily should) still include an intercept (α) and a set of year-dummy variables in a model specification like Equation 16-47. The inclusion of these terms guarantees that

---

[10] For example, as noted in Footnotes 16-1 and 16-7, Equation 16-41 is a subset of the "myopic" model considered in the Becker, Grossman, and Murphy (1994) analysis of cigarette addiction. Their more sophisticated ("rational") theory of addiction – which was the point of their paper – implies the additional inclusion of $CIG_{i,t+1}$ as an explanatory variable. Moreover, their theory also implies that current cigarette consumption, $CIG_{i,t}$, depends on past and future values of $P_{i,t}$ only through their impact on $CIG_{i,t-1}$ and $CIG_{i,t+1}$. Consequently – conditional on CIG_{t-1} and $CIG_{i,t+1}$ – both past and future values of $P_{i,t}$ provide valid instruments for use in estimating the regression parameters in their "rational" model setting.

[11] The Hausman-Taylor estimator discussed at the end of Section 14.5 allows for some time-invariant explanatory variables, but assumes that all of the explanatory variables are strictly exogenous with respect to $\varepsilon_{i,t}$ and also does not allow for heteroscedasticity and/or serial correlation in $\varepsilon_{i,t}$; work on generalizing this approach is currently in progress.

$E[\Delta\varepsilon_{i,t}]$ is zero for all values of i and t. These terms are omitted from Equation 16-47 (and, earlier, from Equations 16-1 and 16-41) solely so as to simplify the exposition.

The first-differencing transformation clearly eliminates any intercept term which might have been necessary in the original model, Equation 16-41. But what if Equation 16-41 had included a term λ_t to model deterministic shifts in $E[CIG_{i,t}]$ over time? In that case, the first-differencing also eliminates λ_t – *but only if this deterministic time dependence in the original error term ($U_{i,t}$, as defined in Equation 15-10) was a linear time trend with the same slope in every state or country.* Suppose instead, however, that the λ_t component of the model error term in the original model is of the form

$$\lambda_{i,t} = \ell_i t \tag{16-48}$$

Equation 16-48 allows for a linear time trend whose slope (ℓ_i) is distinct for state i. The first-difference (i.e., the change) in $\lambda_{i,t}$ is then

$$\begin{aligned}\Delta\lambda_{i,t} = \lambda_{i,t} - \lambda_{i,t-1} &= \ell_i t - \ell_i(t-1) \\ &= \ell_i t - \ell_i t - \ell_i \\ &= -\ell_i\end{aligned} \tag{16-49}$$

Thus, the First-Differences Model would in this case still need to include an intercept (if ℓ_i is a non-zero constant) and would still feature a state (or country) specific error component if the trend-slopes ($\ell_1 \ldots \ell_M$) are not all equal.

Evidently, then, there is no guarantee that first-differencing one's data will eliminate panel-specific heterogeneity. It might. But it also might not. Indeed, this has already occurred in the PWT example analyzed here in Sections 15.3 through 15.6. In fact, the model defined in Equation 15-9 of Section 15.3 (using the variable definitions given in Equations 15-4 through 15-8) is actually already a first-differenced model: it is the first-difference of an underlying model in terms of log($RGDPL_{i,t}$), log([$EXPORTS_{i,t} + IMPORTS_{i,t}$]/$RGDPL_{i,t}$), $C_{i,t}/RGDPL_{i,t}$, $I_{i,t}/RGDPL_{i,t}$, and $G_{i,t}/RGDPL_{i,t}$. Yet this first-differenced model still, as was quite clear from the Baltagi/Li test results at the end of Section 15.5, shows substantial heterogeneity across the countries. Log($RGDPL_{i,t}$) is evidently trended in each country, but the slope of the trend varies substantially from country to country. First-differencing is still exceedingly useful in modeling log($RGDPL_{i,t}$), in that it reduces a group of M trended – and hence I(1) – time-series to an I(0) data set whose intercountry heterogeneity can be handled using standard panel-data techniques. But it also serves as a warning: first-differencing does not, in itself, allow one to safely assume that the resulting data are homogeneous.

Assuming here that the first-difference transformation embodied in Equation 16-47 does in fact eliminate the heterogeneity across the states, the first question to ask is: does OLS estimation of this first-differenced equation yield consistent estimators for β_{cig}, β_{tax}, and β_{price}? Unfortunately, it does not. This is because one of the first-differenced explanatory variables ($\Delta P_{i,t}$) is correlated with the first-differenced error term:

$$\begin{aligned}\text{cov}\left[\Delta P_{i,t}, \Delta\varepsilon_{i,t}\right] &= \text{cov}\left[\left(P_{i,t} - P_{i,t-1}\right), \left(\varepsilon_{i,t} - \varepsilon_{i,t-1}\right)\right] \\ &= E\left[\left(P_{i,t} - P_{i,t-1}\right)\left(\varepsilon_{i,t} - \varepsilon_{i,t-1}\right)\right] \\ &= E\left[P_{i,t}\varepsilon_{i,t}\right] - E\left[P_{i,t}\varepsilon_{i,t-1}\right] - E\left[P_{i,t-1}\varepsilon_{i,t}\right] + E\left[P_{i,t-1}\varepsilon_{i,t-1}\right] \\ &= \pi_0^{P\varepsilon} - \pi_1^{P\varepsilon} - \pi_{-1}^{P\varepsilon} - \pi_0^{P\varepsilon} \\ &\neq 0\end{aligned} \tag{16-50}$$

since $\pi_0^{P\varepsilon}$ and $\pi_1^{P\varepsilon}$ are non-zero.

But do not be discouraged: the First-Differences Model will yield consistent parameter estimation in a different way, by providing a plethora of valid instruments for variables like

$\Delta P_{i,t}$ and $\Delta CIG_{i,t-1}$. In particular, consider instead the covariance of *lagged* values of $\Delta P_{i,t}$ with the model error term $\Delta\varepsilon_{i,t}$:

$$\begin{aligned}
\text{cov}\left[\Delta P_{i,t\text{-}j}, \Delta\varepsilon_{i,t}\right] &= \text{cov}\left[\left(P_{i,t-j} - P_{i,t-j-1}\right), \left(\varepsilon_{i,t} - \varepsilon_{i,t-1}\right)\right] \\
&= E\left[\left(P_{i,t-j} - P_{i,t-j-1}\right)\left(\varepsilon_{i,t} - \varepsilon_{i,t-1}\right)\right] \\
&= E\left[P_{i,t-j}\varepsilon_{i,t}\right] - E\left[P_{i,t-j}\varepsilon_{i,t-1}\right] - E\left[P_{i,t-j-1}\varepsilon_{i,t}\right] + E\left[P_{i,t-j-1}\varepsilon_{i,t-1}\right] \\
&= \pi_{-j}^{P\varepsilon} - \pi_{-j+1}^{P\varepsilon} - \pi_{-j-1}^{P\varepsilon} - \pi_{-j}^{P\varepsilon}
\end{aligned} \tag{16-51}$$

Note that Equation 16-51 implies that

$$\text{cov}\left[\Delta P_{i,t-1}, \Delta\varepsilon_{i,t}\right] = \pi_{-1}^{P\varepsilon} - \pi_{0}^{P\varepsilon} - \pi_{-2}^{P\varepsilon} - \pi_{-1}^{P\varepsilon} \tag{16-52}$$

which is still non-zero, because $\pi_0^{P\varepsilon}$ is non-zero, but that

$$\begin{aligned}
\text{cov}\left[\Delta P_{i,t-2}, \Delta\varepsilon_{i,t}\right] &= \pi_{-2}^{P\varepsilon} - \pi_{-1}^{P\varepsilon} - \pi_{-3}^{P\varepsilon} - \pi_{-2}^{P\varepsilon} \\
&= 0
\end{aligned} \tag{16-53}$$

since $\pi_\tau^{P\varepsilon}$ is assumed to be zero for all negative values of τ. Evidently, any value of $\Delta P_{i,t}$ which is lagged at least two periods will be uncorrelated with $\Delta\varepsilon_{i,t}$. Hence, any value of $\Delta P_{i,t}$ which is lagged at least two periods qualifies as a valid instrument for $\Delta CIG_{i,t-1}$ and/or for $\Delta P_{i,t}$ in Equation 16-47 so long as this lagged value of $\Delta P_{i,t}$ is still at least somewhat correlated with these two variables.[12]

Similarly, any value of $\Delta CIG_{i,t}$ which is lagged at least two periods will be also be uncorrelated with $\Delta\varepsilon_{i,t}$ (and hence qualify as another valid instrument for $\Delta P_{i,t}$), so long as this lagged variable is still at least somewhat correlated with $\Delta P_{i,t}$. Demonstrating this requires a bit more algebra. In particular, repeated substitution of lagged values of Equation 16-47 into itself yields the following expression for $\Delta CIG_{i,t}$, which no longer depends on any lagged values of $\Delta CIG_{i,t}$:[13]

$$\Delta CIG_{i,t} = \beta_{tax}\sum_{\tau=0}^{\infty}\beta_{cig}^{\tau}\Delta TAX_{i,t-\tau} + \sum_{\tau=0}^{\infty}\beta_{cig}^{\tau}\Delta P_{i,t-\tau} + \sum_{\tau=0}^{\infty}\beta_{cig}^{\tau}\Delta\varepsilon_{i,t-\tau}. \tag{16-54}$$

Thus, $\Delta CIG_{i,t}$ depends on current and lagged values of $\Delta TAX_{i,t}$, $\Delta P_{i,t}$, and $\Delta\varepsilon_{i,t}$. Consequently, $\Delta CIG_{i,t}$ lagged two or more periods depends only on values of $\Delta P_{i,t}$ and $\Delta\varepsilon_{i,t}$ lagged two or more periods. But, from the development above, these lagged values of $\Delta P_{i,t}$ are uncorrelated with the current value of $\Delta\varepsilon_{i,t}$. And – per the results obtained in Exercise 16-6 – values of $\Delta\varepsilon_{i,t}$ lagged two or more periods are uncorrelated with the current value of $\Delta\varepsilon_{i,t}$ also. Therefore, $\Delta CIG_{i,t}$ lagged two or more periods is also a valid instrument for $\Delta P_{i,t}$ in Equation 16-47, so long as such a lagged value of $\Delta CIG_{i,t}$ is still at least somewhat correlated with $\Delta P_{i,t}$.

[12] Recall that $\pi_\tau^{P\varepsilon}$ from Equation 16-42 is the covariance of $P_{i,t}$ with $\varepsilon_{i,t}$ lagged τ periods; thus, $\pi_{-j}^{P\varepsilon}$ is the covariance of the current value of $\varepsilon_{i,t}$ with $P_{i,t}$ lagged j periods. If any such covariances were actually non-zero, they could be eliminated by simply including lagged values of $P_{i,t}$ in the original model – Equation 16-41 – so it is reasonable to assume that $\pi_j^{P\varepsilon}$ is zero for negative values of j. On the other hand, note that including $P_{i,t-1}$ in the original model implies that $\Delta P_{i,t-1}$ is in the revised First-Differenced Model. From Equation 16-52, $\Delta P_{i,t-1}$ is itself endogenous, so a third first-stage regression would then be necessary. Going further and including P_{t-2} in the original model implies that $\Delta P_{i,t-2}$ is an explanatory variable in the revised First-Differenced Model and hence cannot be used as an instrument; in that case only values of $\Delta P_{i,t}$ which are lagged at least three periods could be used as instruments, and so forth.

[13] This sequence of steps is very similar to that used to obtain Equations 16-8, 16-21, and 16-38 in Section 16.1; this derivation is consequently left for Exercise 16-5.

Thus, the application of two-stage least squares to Equation 16-47 so as to obtain consistent estimators for β_{cig}, β_{tax}, and β_{price} is very feasible: one can use lags of $\Delta P_{i,t-1}$ and lags of $\Delta CIG_{i,t-1}$ as instruments for $\Delta P_{i,t}$. These are used as explanatory variables (along with any strictly exogenous variables, such as $TAX_{i,t}$ in the present example) in a first-stage regression model for $\Delta P_{i,t}$. The predicted value of $\Delta P_{i,t}$ from this model are then substituted for $\Delta P_{i,t}$ in Equation 16-47, which is then estimated via OLS; this last regression constituting the second-stage regression. If there is a second endogenous variable in the model, then it gets its own first-stage regression equation, but the process is otherwise identical.

It also turns out to often be helpful to use nonlinear functions of these variables, such as $(\Delta P_{i,t-2})^2$ or $\Delta P_{i,t-2}\Delta CIG_{i,t-2}$, as additional instruments. For an arbitrarily large sample – which is to say, letting the value of M become arbitrarily large compared to the values of T_1 ... T_M – the precision of the two-stage least squares estimators always increases as one includes more variables in the first-stage regression equations. With finite M, however, one reaches a point of diminishing (and then negative) returns if one pushes too hard in this direction.

However, there are two problems with these two-stage least squares parameter estimators of β_{cig}, β_{tax}, and β_{price}. The first of these problems is easily fixed; the other is inherent to the two-stage least squares approach and has motivated the development of more sophisticated procedures for use in practice.

The first problem is that, since $\varepsilon_{i,t}$ is assumed to be serially independent, $\Delta\varepsilon_{i,t}$ is serially correlated. (Indeed, in the terminology of Section 14.6, $\Delta\varepsilon_{i,t}$ is clearly "overdifferenced.") Consequently, the usual expressions for the standard error estimates for the two-stage least squares parameter estimators described above are not consistent. This is not much of a problem in practice because modern software readily produces consistent cluster-robust standard errors which "correct" for this serial correlation. These cluster-robust standard error estimates are indeed consistent, but they do not affect the parameter estimates themselves and hence cannot possibly correct for the estimation inefficiency caused by the serial correlation in $\Delta\varepsilon_{i,t}$.

Remarkably, however, such a correction is very easy to do, because the form of the serial correlation in $\Delta\varepsilon_{i,t}$ is simple and known, as $\Delta\varepsilon_{i,t}$ is just $(\varepsilon_{i,t} - \varepsilon_{i,t})$ and $\varepsilon_{i,t}$ is itself assumed to be serially uncorrelated. In particular, Arellano and Bover (1995) show that this serial correlation induced by differencing $\varepsilon_{i,t}$ can be effectively "un-done" by applying a straightforward additional transformation to all of the variables (and instruments) used in Equation 16-47. This transformation – which they call "forward orthogonal deviations" – is best described using a specific example. Letting a superscript FOD denote the transformed value,

$$(\Delta CIG_{i,t})^{FOD} \equiv c_t\left[\Delta CIG_{i,t} - \frac{1}{T_i - t}\left(\Delta CIG_{i,t+1} + \Delta CIG_{i,t+2} + \ldots + \Delta CIG_{i,T_i}\right)\right] \qquad (16\text{-}55)$$

where c_t is $\sqrt{(T_i - t)/(T_i - t + 1)}$.[14] Thus, the "forward orthogonal deviations" transformation amounts to something very like the "within" transformation defined in Equation 15-12, except that here the state-specific sample mean subtracted from the observation for state i in period t uses only future sample values for that state.[15]

[14] The reader may recall that the issue of overdifferencing an I(0) time-series arises if one (incorrectly) fails to reject the null hypothesis that the series is I(1) on a unit roots test was raised in Section 14.6. It was noted there that simulations reported in Ashley and Verbrugge (2009) indicate that such overdifferencing severely distorts some of the estimated dynamics for the series, as quantified in its MA(∞) or "impulse response function" form. The degree to which this kind of distortion is consequential in the context of the First-Differences Model is an open question, which is a topic of current research. Similarly, the further issue of whether something like a "forward orthogonal deviations" transformation can eliminate this kind of distortion in the pure time-series context – where T is large and one has overdifferenced a substantially autocorrelated series – is also under current investigation.

[15] Clearly, then, this transformation has no effect on the observations for the final observation (period T_i) for each state.

The second problem with the two-stage least squares estimation of Equation 16-47 is more troublesome. Yes, it has been shown above that multiply-lagged variables (such as $\Delta P_{i,t-2}$, $\Delta P_{i,t-3}$, $\Delta P_{i,t-4}$ ... and $\Delta CIG_{i,t-2}$, $\Delta CIG_{i,t-3}$, $\Delta CIG_{i,t-4}$ ...) are all valid instruments for $\Delta P_{i,t}$. But they are most likely not very strong instruments for $\Delta P_{i,t}$, especially because one lag has been "skipped." For example, even if $\Delta P_{i,t}$ is serially correlated – and hence likely to be correlated with $\Delta P_{i,t-1}$ to some degree – $\Delta P_{i,t}$ is may not be very correlated with $\Delta P_{i,t-2}$ and $\Delta P_{i,t-3}$. And values of $\Delta P_{i,t}$ which are lagged even more are most likely even more weakly correlated with $\Delta P_{i,t}$. This weakness in the instruments implies that, although the two-stage least squares estimators are consistent, they will probably be quite imprecise unless the sample is very large. Moreover, because the value of T_i is not itself very large, the $k+1$ observations consumed in calculating "startup" values for a lagged instrument like $\Delta P_{i,t-k}$ become quite problematic. For example, with T_i equal to six, using $\Delta P_{i,t-3} = P_{i,t-3} - P_{i,t-4}$ as an instrument effectively reduces the sample for state i to just two observations. Consequently, it is not possible to use a substantial number of lagged instruments to make up for the fact that each one is individually weak.[16]

Consequently, a good deal of attention has gone into – and continues to go into – the development of better ways to use instrumental variables techniques to estimate the First-Differences Model, embodied here as Equation 16-47. The current best-practice is to use the Arellano and Bond (1991) two-step GMM estimator with the Windmeijer (2005) bias-corrected standard error estimators.[17] This sounds complicated, but it is not as challenging as all that in practice, because the Arellano-Bond estimator is preprogrammed into modern econometric software – e.g., as the "xtabond" routine in Stata. Indeed, the remainder of this section is in large part just a guide to the syntax and choices involved in using the "xtabond" routine effectively.

The discussion above was essential, however: its purpose was to frame the problem, to show how the First-Differences Model implies a set of valid instruments (lags of $\Delta CIG_{i,t-1}$ and $\Delta P_{i,t-1}$) for an endogenous variable like $\Delta P_{i,t}$ – and to motivate why it is desirable to go beyond the simple application of two-stage least squares to Equation 16-47. The detailed econometric theory underlying the Arellano-Bond estimator is beyond the scope of the present treatment, but the essential character of this estimator is identical to what we have just done: The coefficients β_{cig}, β_{tax}, and β_{price} for the model in levels (Equation 16-41) are being estimated consistently by using instruments (lags of $\Delta CIG_{i,t-1}$ and $\Delta P_{i,t-1}$) which are valid instruments for the endogenous variable ($\Delta P_{i,t}$) in the First-Differenced Model, Equation 16-47.[18]

---

[16] The precision of the two-stage least squares estimator deteriorates long before one actually runs out of observations, however, since the point of the first-stage regression (for $\Delta P_{i,t}$, in this case) is to obtain a predicted value for $\Delta P_{i,t}$ to substitute for $\Delta P_{i,t}$ in the second-stage regression equation, which yields thereby consistent estimates of β_{cig}, β_{tax}, and β_{price}. But if most of the sample observations are used up in constructing the first-stage regressors, then the sample of predicted values for $\Delta P_{i,t}$ (and hence the sample for the second-stage regression) also has very few observations. Therefore, the use of too many instruments causes the precision of the two-stage least squares estimator to deteriorate for two reasons: with very few feasible observations left for estimating the coefficients in the first-stage regressions the estimated first-stage regression model is unable to produce very accurate predictors of $\Delta P_{i,t}$ for use in the second-stage regression *and* there are very few feasible observations left for estimating the second-stage regression anyway.

[17] A few years from now, however, a consensus may have built around a replacement for the Arellano-Bond estimator, probably from the Generalized Empirical Likelihood (GEL) class of estimators. Particularly for highly persistent data, the new "X-Differencing" estimator proposed by Han, Phillips, and Sul (2010) also looks promising. Han, C., P. C. B. Phillips, and D. Sul (2010), "X-Differencing and Dynamic Panel Model Estimation," mimeo.

[18] See Cameron and Trivedi (2009, Section 9.4) and the Stata manual "xtabond" entry – or the original articles – for more detailed treatments. Arellano, M., and S. Bond (1991), "Some Tests of Specification for Panel Data: Monte Carlo Evidence and an Application to Employment Equations." *Review of Economic Studies 58*, 277–297; and Windemeijer, F. (2005), "A finite Sample Correction for the Variance of Linear Efficient Two-Step GMM Estimators," *Journal of Econometrics 126*, 25–52.

Turning to the implementation of the Arellano-Bond estimator in Stata, the syntax for estimating Equation 16-41 as it stands is:

```
xtabond cig tax , lags(1) maxldep(4) twostep noconstant endogenous(p, lag(0 , 5))
  vce(robust)
```

Each of the specifications in this command will be discussed in turn, starting from the left. First, this command specifies that $CIG_{i,t}$ is the dependent variable and that $TAX_{i,t}$ can be treated as strictly exogenous.

The "lags(1)" option simply specifies that one lag in the dependent variable is included in the model. The "maxldep()" option limits the number of lags in $CIG_{i,t}$ that can be used in constructing instruments – in this particular example to a maximum of four periods, which allows the use of $\Delta CIG_{i,t-1}$, $\Delta CIG_{i,t-2}$, and $\Delta CIG_{i,t-3}$ as instruments, but not $\Delta CIG_{i,t-4}$, because its construction requires the use of $CIG_{i,t-5}$.

The "maxldep()" option can – and often should – be omitted, in which case every possible lag instrument is used. The Arellano-Bond estimator uses lagged variables as instruments in a more sophisticated way than does two-stage least squares – on a period-by-period basis – so this default choice does not reduce the sample length. But it can yield an uncomfortably large number of instruments if $T_1 \ldots T_M$ are not small. For example, suppose that T_i is 20. Note that the first two periods are used up in creating the lagged first difference of the explanatory variable $\Delta CIG_{i,t-1}$, so that t actually runs from 3 to 20 for state i in this case. Then, under the default option, the Arellano-Bond estimator uses the 17 variables $\Delta CIG_{i,t-1} \ldots \Delta CIG_{i,t-17}$ as instruments for the last observation in the sample on state i, where t equals T_i; the 17 instruments in that case are $\Delta CIG_{i,19} \ldots \Delta CIG_{i,3}$. For the second-to-last observation, where t equals 19, $\Delta CIG_{i,t-17}$ does not exist in the sample (as it requires knowledge of $CIG_{i,0}$), so the Arellano-Bond estimator just uses $\Delta CIG_{i,t-1} \ldots \Delta CIG_{i,t-16}$ in that case. Similarly, for t equal to 18, the Arellano-Bond estimator only uses $\Delta CIG_{i,t-1} \ldots \Delta CIG_{i,t-15}$. And so forth. Thus, in the Arellano-Bond approach, the sample length is unaffected by the number of lagged instruments used.[19] In the two-stage least squares approach, by way of contrast, specifying that $\Delta CIG_{i,t-1} \ldots \Delta CIG_{i,t-17}$ are to be used as instruments would reduce the sample on state i to a single observation, so the way the Arellano-Bond procedure handles instruments is tremendously more graceful. On the other hand – absent some restriction, via the "maxldep()" option – the Arellano-Bond approach will use something like $(T_i - 3)(T_i - 2)/2$ different lagged values of $\Delta CIG_{i,t}$ as instruments. For an arbitrarily large value of M this is not a problem, although many of these lagged values will be of very questionable value since they will be quite distant in time from whatever observation they are serving to instrument. For finite values of M, however – even pretty large ones – this profusion of instruments leads to unnecessarily imprecise estimators unless the values of $T_1 \ldots T_M$ are all quite small. Therefore, it is usually worth experimenting a bit with the "maxldep()" option when the panels are not very short.

The "twostep" option in the example "xtabond" command statement given above causes the procedure to correct for heteroscedasticity in $\varepsilon_{i,t}$. In particular, when this option is specified, the procedure first estimates the model parameters under the assumption that var($\varepsilon_{i,t}$) is a constant; it then uses the resulting model fitting errors to estimate how var($\varepsilon_{i,t}$) varies across i and t. Finally (in a second step) the model parameters are re-estimated more efficiently based on this estimated pattern of heteroscedasticity. Since substantial heteroscedasticity is typical in panel data sets, this option is usually worth specifying. Note, however, that it is essential to also specify the "vce(robust)" option when the "twostep" option is used, as the ordinary standard error estimates produced when the "twostep" option is used are known to be problematic.

[19] These are often called "GMM-style" instruments. GMM estimation – which is actually at the heart of the Arellano-Bond procedure – is described (for a simpler modeling context) in Section 19.4.

Whether the "no constant" option is included or not has no impact on the estimates of the slope parameters: β_{cig}, β_{tax}, and β_{price} in Equation 16-41 (the "levels" equation) and in Equation 16-47 (the "changes" equation). These are ordinarily the model parameters of sole economic interest, to the point that (to simplify the algebra later on) Equation 16-41 was actually specified here without an intercept. Ordinarily, the "levels" equation *will* include an intercept, however. But this intercept will be eliminated by the first-differencing which produces the "changes" equation, so an extra step in necessary in order to obtain an estimate of it – if one wants one. This step is not a big deal: in essence, the slope parameters are estimated first and then the intercept is estimated in the levels equation conditional on these slope estimates. This yields an estimate of the intercept (and an estimated standard error for same); these are quoted right alongside the slope estimates, as if they were all obtained in the same way, which is a bit misleading.

Clearly, it is actually simpler to omit the "noconstant" option, so long as one is clear on what this intercept estimate (which the omission of the "noconstant" option causes the command to produce) is – and what it is not. In particular, the foregoing discussion should make it clear that this is an estimate of the intercept in the "levels" equation. Thus, its size and statistical significance has no bearing on whether or not the "changes" equation actually itself needed an intercept – e.g., because the levels series for the M states had linear time trends (per Equation 16-48) with slopes $\ell_1 \ldots \ell_M$ that do not average to zero over the states. If such trends in the levels series are a worry, then this should be addressed by making time plots of the $CIG_{i,t}$ series: estimating an intercept for the "levels" equation (dropping the "noconstant" option) is in that case beside the point.

In addition, note that using the "predict resids, e" command after estimating a model using the "xtabond" command saves the implied fitting errors of the *"levels"* equation under the variable name *resids*. These fitting errors are valuable in diagnostic checking – as illustrated in Active Learning Exercises 16a and 16b (available at www.wiley.com/college/ashley) – regardless, but one should not expect them to have a negligible sample mean if the "noconstant" option has been specified.[20]

The option "endogenous(p, lag(0, 5))" in the example "xtabond" command statement specifies that the variable $P_{i,t}$ is endogenous, enters the model with lag zero, and that values of $P_{i,t}$ lagged at most five periods are to be used as instruments. Again, there is value in limiting the number of instruments used; the default option in this case would be to merely specify "endogenous(p)", in which case every possible lag of $P_{i,t-1}$ would be used in forming arguments. If there were a second endogenous variable in the model ($Y_{i,t}$, say), then one would just include a second "endogenous" term in the option list – e.g., "endogenous(y, lag(0, 5))".

One might also want to include one or more "predetermined" explanatory variables in the model. For example, if data are available for expenditures on anti-smoking classes in the high schools of state i in the previous year ($ANTI\_SMOKING\_EDU_{i,t-1}$), then one might want to include this as an explanatory variable in Equation 16-41. The current value of $ANTI\_SMOKING\_EDU_{i,t}$ would likely be endogenous – i.e., correlated with current and past values of $\varepsilon_{i,t}$. Arguably, however, lagged values of $ANTI\_SMOKING\_EDU_{i,t}$ are uncorrelated with the current value of $\varepsilon_{i,t}$, at least if enough lagged values of it are included in the model. Thus – like $CIG_{i,t-1}$ and $P_{i,t-1}$ – the lagged value $ANTI\_SMOKING\_EDU_{i,t-1}$ is not an endogenous variable, because it is not contemporaneously correlated with $\varepsilon_{i,t}$. But it is not strictly exogenous either, because at least some of its *future* values ($ANTI\_SMOKING\_EDU_{i,t}$, $ANTI\_SMOKING\_EDU_{i,t+1}$, $ANTI\_SMOKING\_EDU_{i,t+2}$, etc.) likely *are* correlated with the current value of $\varepsilon_{i,t}$. As noted earlier (in Section 15.4, just after Equation 15-14), such variables are called "predetermined."

The Arellano-Bond procedure can easily handle predetermined explanatory variables like $ANTI\_SMOKING\_EDU_{i,t-1}$; it treats them in much the same way that it handles lagged dependent variables, like $CIG_{i,t-1}$, and lagged endogenous variables, like P_{t-1}. But the implementing routine

[20] Also, note that the "predict" command requires that the data have been sorted, using the "xtset" command described in Section 15.4; the "xtabond" command does not.

must be informed that these variables are in fact predetermined, rather than strictly exogenous. The option "pre()" serves this purpose:

```
xtabond cig tax , lags(1) maxldep(4) twostep noconstant endogenous(p, lag(0 , 5))
  pre(lag_anti_smoking_edu, lag(0,4)) vce(robust)
```

where "lag_anti_smoking_edu" is generated as the lagged value of $ANTI\_SMOKING\_EDU_{i,t}$. Note that the syntax for the "pre()" option is very similar to that of the "endogenous" option – as used in the example above, it specifies that the variable enter $\Delta ANTI\_SMOKING\_EDU_{i,t-1}$ enters the (differenced) equation, and that up to four lags of $ANTI\_SMOKING\_EDU_{i,t-1}$ are used as instruments. As with the "endogenous()" option, one simply includes additional "pre()" option terms in the command if there is more than one predetermined variable in the model.

One might also be able to specify some additional instruments for use in the estimation process. The strictly exogenous variable $TAX_{i,t}$ (in the form of $\Delta TAX_{i,t}$) is automatically included in the list of instruments used in estimating Equation 16-47 because it enters the equation as an explanatory variable. If one wants Stata to also use, say, $\Delta TAX_{i,t-1}$ and $\Delta TAX_{i,t-2}$ as instruments, then one must explicitly generate the variable $\Delta TAX_{i,t}$ (e.g., with a variable name like "tax_change") and specify the option "inst(L1.tax_change L2.tax_change)" in the command; this option can also be used to specify any other variables one might want to include in the list of instruments the routine will use.[21]

Finally, the "vce(robust)" option in the "xtabond" command is effectively equivalent to specifying the computation of White-Eicker standard error estimates: i.e., allowing for an arbitrary pattern of heteroscedasticity, but still assuming that $\varepsilon_{i,t}$ is uncorrelated with its own past and with all errors from other states.[22] The Arellano-Bond procedure assumes, as did the derivation earlier in this section, that $\varepsilon_{i,t}$ is serially uncorrelated, so these robust standard error estimators are consistent only if the $\varepsilon_{i,t}$ actually are serially uncorrelated. It is consequently necessary to diagnostically check this assumption.

This diagnostic check is very easy: the post-estimation command "estat abond" performs a test of the null hypothesis that $\varepsilon_{i,t} - \varepsilon_{i,t-1}$ is serially uncorrelated at lags ("orders") one and two. If the reported rejection p-value ("Prob > z") is below .05 for the "order two" test, then one should include more lags in the model.[23] This is not difficult to do either. The analogous command for estimating a model including two lags in $CIG_{i,t}$ and both current and lagged values of $TAX_{i,t}$ and $P_{i,t}$ is just:

```
xtabond cig tax tax_lag , lags(2) maxldep(5) twostep noconstant
  endogenous(p, lag(1 , 6)) vce(robust)
```

where one has generated the variable "tax_lag" as TAX_{t-1} oneself. The "endogenous(p, lag(1, 6))" option in this example includes both lags in $P_{i,t}$ and allows the use of $P_{i,t-2}$ ... $P_{i,t-6}$ in the

[21] Technical Note: Unlike the "endogenous()" and "pre()" options, the "inst()" option can accept lag operators, such as the "L1." prepended to the variable name, which was *tax_change* in this example. Note, however, that the routine will use whatever variables one lists in the "inst()" option "as is" – i.e., without differencing them before using them as instruments in the estimation of Equation 16-47. The "inst()" option is defined this way so that one could explicitly specify a level variable, such as $TAX_{i,t-1}$ itself, to be used as an instrument. Similarly, an option "diffvars()" allows one to specify a list of strictly exogenous variables which are to be used "as is" – i.e., without differencing.

[22] The "twostep" option goes further and adjusts the estimation of the parameters themselves in view of whatever heteroscedasticity is estimated to be present in $\varepsilon_{i,t}$; this option is invoking the "two-step GMM" procedure described in Section 19.3. The "vce(robust)" standard error estimation option should still be invoked in this case also, however, as the default standard error estimators are known to be problematic in combination with the "twostep" estimator.

[23] The reported p-value for the test at order one is irrelevant, since one expects $\varepsilon_{i,t} - \varepsilon_{i,t-1}$ to be correlated with itself lagged one period.

construction of instruments. It is not necessary to separately specify that $P_{i,t-1}$ is actually only predetermined rather than endogenous. After this estimation one should check that sufficient dynamics have been included in the model by using the "estat, artests(3)" command to extend the serial correlation test to order three: the p-value for the test should now exceed .05 for both order two and order three.[24]

In summary, then, the Fixed Effects Model and Random Effects Model are very useful, so long as the explanatory variables are all strictly exogenous; but they no longer yield consistent parameter estimators once this restriction is relaxed. The only exception to this is that the Random Effects Model still provides consistent estimates with lagged dependent variables, so long as $\varepsilon_{i,t}$ is both serially uncorrelated and homoscedastic and so long as all of the remaining variables are strictly exogenous.[25] In contrast, the First-Differences Model described in this section – implemented as the Arellano-Bond estimator – allows one to gracefully deal with the problems arising from any kinds of explanatory variables which are not strictly exogenous: lagged dependent variables, predetermined variables, and endogenous variables.

This result basically arises from the fact that the structure of the First-Differences Model yields a large number of valid instruments for these not-strictly-exogenous explanatory variables. However, this same structure also inevitably leads to the two major limitations of the First-Differences Model approach.

First, as with the Fixed Effects Model, the First-Differences Model (estimated using the Arellano-Bond estimator or otherwise) does not allow one to estimate the impact on the dependent variable of explanatory variables which do not vary over time. If one has a pressing need to quantify/test the impact of such variables, then one has several choices, but each is unpalatable in its own way. One could, for example, turn to the Between Effects Model, but this choice essentially discards whatever time variation does exist in the data set, leaving one with only M observations. Alternatively, one could address this issue by using either the Random Effects Model estimator or – if the number of

[24] If one first re-estimates the model omitting the "vce(robust)" option, then one can also perform the Sargan test of the k over-identifying restrictions, where k is the excess of the number of instruments used over the number of parameters estimated, using the "estat sargan" command. If this test yields a p-value less than .05, then one or more of the k overidentifying restrictions is in conflict with the data. Of course, it is by no means clear which one or ones are problematic. As such it is a generalized test for model misspecification. Such misspecification could be in the form of an inappropriate specification of one or more variables as predetermined or strictly exogenous when it is really endogenous, or it could be due to unstable parameters, misspecified functional forms, etc. Failure to reject the null hypothesis that the overidentifying restrictions are correct does not, of course, imply that the model is well specified.

[25] Technical Note: This exception is only of practical value if the Random Effects Model estimator can be compared to an alternative estimator whose consistency does not hinge on the validity of the Random Effects Model Assumption – i.e., in the present instance, that $TAX_{i,t}$ in Equation 16-1 is uncorrelated with ν_i, as well as being uncorrelated with $\varepsilon_{i,\tau}$ for all values of τ. Only in that case can a generalized Hausman Test, as described at the end of Section 15.5, be used to assess the validity of the Random Effects Model Assumption. Because there is a lagged dependent variable in Equation 16-1, the Fixed Effects Model estimator no longer provides such a consistent alternative estimator, but the First-Differences Model described in the present section now does. Unfortunately, this alternative estimator is troublesome to obtain because, as of this writing at least, the Stata "suest" command does not work with stored parameter estimates from the "ivregress" or "xtabond" commands. But one could fairly easily generate and store estimates of Equation 16-1 using the two-stage least squares (ignoring the "forward orthogonal deviations" transformation) solely using the "regress" command; this would provide estimates which could be stored for use with the "suest" command. There would be one first-stage regression, which would regress $\Delta P_{i,t}$ against $\Delta TAX_{i,t}$ and all of the instruments; these instruments would here include lagged values of $\Delta CIG_{i,t-1}$, $\Delta TAX_{i,t}$, and various nonlinear functions of these. One would save the predicted values from this regression under some name – e.g., *lag_cig_hat* – using the "predict lag_cig_hat" command and substitute this predicted variable for $\Delta CIG_{i,t-1}$ in the second-stage regression. The second-stage regression would then yield consistent estimates of β_{tax} and β_{cig} from a regression of $\Delta CIG_{i,t}$ against $\Delta TAX_{i,t}$ and this *lag_cig_hat* variable. Newer versions of Stata will no doubt greatly simplify this sort of thing, at which point the Random Effects Model may become a more viable alternative for dynamic regression models whose other explanatory variables are strictly exogenous.

time-varying explanatory variables which are uncorrelated with ν_i is sufficiently large – by using the Hausman-Taylor estimator. However, the currently available implementations of both of these estimators require that the explanatory variables are all strictly exogenous with respect to $\varepsilon_{i,t}$. But this rules out precisely the lagged dependent variables, predetermined explanatory variables, and endogenous explanatory variables which are at issue when the assumption of strict exogeneity in the remaining explanatory variables is untenable. So, in effect, one is back looking at the Between Effects Model in this case.

Finally, the second major limitation of the First-Differences Model approach is that, as noted above, while the instruments it generates are numerous and valid, they may well be quite weak because of the additional lags involved. Thus, the resulting parameter estimators – e.g., of β_{cig}, β_{tax}, and β_{price} – may be very imprecise unless the sample is extremely large. On the other hand, as emphasized in Section 15.1, a very large sample is precisely what a panel data set can often provide – especially where the set of panel units consists of M individuals, rather than M states or countries.

16.3 SUMMARY

The recent availability of large-scale panel data sets is clearly a good development. These data sets enable an analyst to credibly utilize asymptotically justified methods to deal with violations of the basic assumptions of the Multiple Regression Model: that the model errors are homoscedastic and non-autocorrelated, and that the regressors are fixed in repeated samples.

On the other hand, the assumption that the model coefficients are homogeneous across the M units in a panel data set is itself obviously questionable. This problem has led to the development of the several estimation techniques described in this (and the previous) chapter for still obtaining consistent parameter estimates in spite of this heterogeneity: different techniques are necessary for modeling situations which differ in terms of what can be assumed about the explanatory variables and their relationships to the two components of the model error term. Table 16-1 summarizes this material.

Table 16-1 Summary of Panel-Data Estimation Methods and the Modeling Situations for Which They Yield Consistent Parameter Estimation

Estimation Model or Method	Explanatory Variable Complications Allowed				Availability of Cluster-Robust Standard Error Estimates	Section
	Lagged Dependent Variables	Regressors Correlated with ν_i	Regressors Correlated with $\varepsilon_{i,t}$	Time-Invariant Regressors		
Fixed Effects	No	Yes	No[b]	No	Yes	15.4 16.1
Random Effects	Yes[a]	No	No[c]	Yes	Yes	15.5 16.1
Hausman-Taylor	No	Yes[d]	No	Yes[d]	No	15.5
First-Differences (Arellano-Bond)	Yes	Yes	Yes	No	No[e]	16.2

[a]So long as the other explanatory variables are all strictly exogenous, $\varepsilon_{i,t}$ is homoscedastic, and a sufficient number of lagged variables are included in the model as to eliminate serial correlation in $\varepsilon_{i,t}$.
[b]Unless valid instruments are available for the "within" transformed variable, which is unlikely.
[c]Unless valid instruments are available for the "quasi-differenced" variable, which is unlikely.
[d]So long as there are enough time-varying variables which are uncorrelated with ν_i, a sufficient number of lagged variables are included in the model as to eliminate serial correlation in $\varepsilon_{i,t}$, and $\varepsilon_{i,t}$ is homoscedastic.
[e]The options "vce(robust)" and "vce(gmm)" produce standard error estimates which are robust to heteroscedasticity only; the user is responsible for including a sufficient number of lagged variables in the model so as to eliminate serial correlation in $\varepsilon_{i,t}$

The Fixed Effects Model and the Random Effects Model described in Sections 15.4 and 15.5 are arguably effective responses to this heterogeneity problem where it is reasonable to assume that the explanatory variables are strictly exogenous. The combination of panel-data heterogeneity with endogenous explanatory variables (or with dynamics in the form of lagged dependent variables) is a challenging one, however. The best practice at present is to apply instrumental variables methods to the First-Differences Model, using the Arellano-Bond formulation as described in Section 16.2. The First-Differences Model framework yields a substantial number of valid (albeit often quite weak) instruments, so that consistent parameter estimates and asymptotically valid standard error estimates for them can be obtained. These estimates provide a practical analytical tool where the number of units, M, is sufficiently large.

KEY TERMS

For each term or concept listed below, provide a working definition or explanation:

First-Differences Model
Arellano-Bond Estimator

EXERCISES

16-1. Using the cigarette consumption model from Section 16.1, start from Equation 16-9 and derive Equation 16-11; i.e., show that

$$\text{cov}(CIG_{i,t-1}, \nu_i + \varepsilon_{i,t}) = \frac{\sigma_\nu^2}{1 - \beta_{cig}} \tag{16-11}$$

16-2. Starting from Equation 16-25, show that

$$\text{cov}\left(CIG^{FE}_{i,t-1}, \varepsilon^{FE}_{i,t}\right) = -\frac{\sigma_\varepsilon^2}{T_i(1-\beta_{cig})}\left[2 - \beta_{cig}^{T_i - t} - \beta_{cig}^{t-1} - \frac{T_i - 1}{T_i}\left(1 - \beta_{cig}^{t-1}\right) + \frac{\beta_{cig} - (t-1)\beta_{cig}^{t-1} + \beta_{cig}^{t}}{T_i(1-\beta_{cig})}\right]$$

which is clearly not equal to zero. (You can show this by examining its limit as β_{cig} goes to zero, which is negative.) This result implies the Fixed Effects model in general yields inconsistent parameter estimators when a lagged dependent variable is included in the model, even if the other explanatory variables are strictly exogenous.[26]

16-3. Starting with Equation 16-41, the cigarette consumption model introduced in Section 16.2, use repeated substitutions (as in Equations 16-15 to 16-20) to show that

$$CIG_{i,t} = \beta_{cig}^{t} CIG_{i,0} + \beta_{tax}\sum_{\tau=0}^{t-1}\beta_{cig}^{\tau} TAX_{i,t-\tau} + \beta_{price}\sum_{\tau=0}^{t-1}\beta_{cig}^{\tau} P_{i,t-\tau} + \nu_i\sum_{\tau=0}^{t-1}\beta_{cig}^{\tau} + \sum_{\tau=0}^{t-1}\beta_{cig}^{\tau}\varepsilon_{i,t-\tau}$$

What will happen to the expected value of $CIG_{i,t}$ over time if β_{cig} exceeds one?

[26] You will need the result that the sum $\sum_{j=0}^{m} j\beta^j$ equals $(\beta - [m+1]\beta^{m+1} + \beta^{m+2})/(1-\beta)^2$, which is derived as β times the derivative of the sum $\sum_{j=0}^{m}\beta^j$ with respect to β.

16-4. Using the definitions of $P_{i,t}^{RE}$ in Equation 16-45 and the definition of $(\nu_i + \varepsilon_{i,t})^{RE}$ in Equation 16-30, show that

$$\text{cov}\left[P_{i,t}^{RE}, (\nu_i + \varepsilon_{i,t})^{RE}\right] = (1-\theta_i)^2 \pi^{P\nu} + \pi_0^{P\varepsilon} - \frac{\theta_i}{T_i}\sum_{j=1}^{t}\pi_{t-j}^{P\varepsilon} - \frac{\theta_i}{T_i}\sum_{s=t}^{T_i}\pi_{s-t}^{P\varepsilon} + \frac{\theta_i^2}{T_i^2}\sum_{s=1}^{T_i}\sum_{j=1}^{s-1}\pi_{s-j}^{P\varepsilon}$$

This reduces to the result in Equation 16-46 for the Fixed Effects Model case when θ_i is set equal to one. These results imply that the endogeneity of $P_{i,t}$ – i.e., $\pi_o^{P\varepsilon} \neq 0$ – in the original model (Equation 16-41) renders the transformed version of $P_{i,t}$ still endogenous in both the Fixed Effects Model and Random Effects Model.

16-5. Derive Equation 16-54 in Section 16.2,

$$\Delta CIG_{i,t} = \beta_{tax}\sum_{\tau=0}^{\infty}\beta_{cig}^{\tau}\Delta TAX_{i,t-\tau} + \sum_{\tau=0}^{\infty}\beta_{cig}^{\tau}\Delta P_{i,t-\tau} + \sum_{\tau=0}^{\infty}\beta_{cig}^{\tau}\Delta\varepsilon_{i,t-\tau}$$

using repeated substitution into Equation 16-47 to re-express $\Delta CIG_{i,t-1}$ in a form which no longer depends on any lagged values of $\Delta CIG_{i,t}$. {Hint: This derivation is very similar to those used to obtain Equations 16-8, 16-21, and 16-38.}

a. Use this expression to show that $\Delta CIG_{i,t-1}$ is a predetermined variable in Equation 16-47 – that is, $\Delta CIG_{i,t-1}$ is uncorrelated with the current and future values of the model error, $\Delta\varepsilon_{i,t}$. Thus, it is not the presence of $\Delta CIG_{i,t-1}$ in Equation 16-47 which makes the OLS parameter estimators for this equation inconsistent.[27]

b. Use this expression to show that $\Delta CIG_{i,t-2}$, $\Delta CIG_{i,t-3}$, etc. are uncorrelated with the current value of the model error, $\Delta\varepsilon_{i,t}$; this result implies that these variables are valid instruments for $\Delta P_{i,t}$, so long as these variables are at least somewhat correlated with $\Delta P_{i,t}$. ($\Delta CIG_{i,t-1}$ cannot be used as an instrument because it is already included in Equation 16-47 as an explanatory variable.)

16-6. Consider cov($\Delta\varepsilon_{i,t-j}$, $\Delta\varepsilon_{i,t}$), which equals $E[\Delta\varepsilon_{i,t-j}\ \Delta\varepsilon_{i,t}]$. Assuming that $\varepsilon_{i,t}$ is serially uncorrelated, with variance σ_ε^2, show that

a. Cov($\Delta\varepsilon_{i,t-1}$, $\Delta\varepsilon_{i,t}$) equals $-\sigma_\varepsilon^2$. (Hint: It is convenient to let γ_k denote cov($\varepsilon_{i,t-k}$, $\varepsilon_{i,t}$) = $E[\varepsilon_{i,t-k}\ \varepsilon_{i,t}]$.)

b. Cov($\Delta\varepsilon_{i,t-j}$, $\Delta\varepsilon_{i,t}$) equals zero for $j \geq 2$. Note that this result is necessary in order to use Equation 16-54 to conclude that $\Delta CIG_{i,t}$ lagged two or more periods is a valid instrument for $\Delta P_{i,t}$ in Equation 16-47.

[27] There is no need to explicitly specify $\Delta CIG_{i,t-1}$ are predetermined in the Stata "xtabond" statement – e.g., using the "pre()" option – because its presence and character are assumed.

Active Learning Exercise 16a: Assessing the Impact of 4-H Participation on the Standardized Test Scores of Florida Schoolchildren

Introduction

Assessing the effectiveness of social programs – public or private – is an important task for applied economic research. For example, Flores-Lagunes and Timko (FT, 2010) examine the impact of participation in the 4-H youth program on the academic performance of Florida schoolchildren.[28] Their study makes a good Active Learning Exercise for this chapter, since their sample data comprise a panel data set of exactly the sort covered here.

In particular, the FT data set includes observations on both the percentage of students who passed the Florida standardized math and reading tests (the "math FCAT" and "reading FCAT," respectively) and on the percentage of students who participated in the 4-H youth program, for each of the 67 counties in Florida and in each of five school-years: 2002/3, 2003/4, 2004/5, 2005/6, and 2006/7.[29] This yields a total of 335 observations on each variable. In addition, FT have also collected data on a number of other variables whose variation across time and/or county might explain variation in FCAT passage rates; these additional variables are listed in the next section.

Key questions to explore in this exercise are

- Is the estimated impact of 4-H participation misleading unless these covariates are used to control for heterogeneity across the 67 counties and five time periods?
- Are these covariates sufficient to control for heterogeneity across the 67 counties and five time periods, or are panel data methods necessary in order to obtain meaningful results?
- If panel-data methods are necessary, which method is best in this instance? And how does its use affect the conclusions which can be reached using these data?

This exercise also provides an opportunity to get some experience at diagnostically checking this kind of model, so as to enhance the credibility (and meaningfulness) of the resulting inferences on the impact of 4-H participation on educational outcomes.

Your Assignment:

1. Copy the data file ALE16a.csv (available at www.wiley.com/college/ashley) to your hard disk and read it into the econometrics software your course is using. (Or copy

[28] The nature and scope of 4-H is described at some length in their paper (FT, 2010, Section IIA); they note that "4-H is the largest youth development organization in the United States with over 6 million young Americans participating in the various programs it offers, such as organized clubs, day camps, and school enrichment programs." Flores-Lagunes, A., and T. Timko (FT, 2010), "Does Participation in 4-H Improve Schooling Outcomes?" Food and Resource Economics and Economics Department, University of Florida, mimeo.

[29] The Florida Comprehensive Assessment Test (FCAT) is described in detail in (FT, 2010, Section IIC). This test is taken by essentially all students in grade levels three through eight. FT analyze the FCAT score data for each county/school-year/grade-level; the data provided for this exercise are aggregated over students in all six grade levels which were tested.

ALE16a.dta if you are using Stata.) This file contains 335 observations on each of the following variables:

countynum	County number, from 1 to 67.
schoolyear	School year, entered as 200203, 200304, 200405, 200506, or 200607.
county_name	Non-numeric label for each county.
math_level1	Percentage of students whose math FCAT score was at the lowest level: "level 1." Analogous variables for students scoring up through the highest level ("level 5") – and for the reading FCAT – are included also.
mathpassrate	Percentage of students "passing" the math FCAT – i.e., who scored at "level 3" or higher.[30]
four_h_rate	Percentage of students (in all grade levels) who participated in 4-H, for this county and school-year.[31]
mathtestrate	Percentage of students who took the math FCAT.
teach_degree	Percentage of teachers with advanced degrees.
instruct_pct	Percentage of staff identified as "instructional."
disability	Percentage of students with any identified disability.
spending	Per-pupil expenditures.
absent_rate	Percentage of students absent more than 21 days during the school-year.
englishlearn	Percentage of students who are learning English.
teacherexper	Average teacher experience, in years.
gifted_pct	Percentage of students identified as "gifted."
white	Fraction of students identified as "white."
black	Fraction of students identified as "black."
hispanic	Fraction of students identified as "hispanic."
asian	Fraction of students identified as "asian."
native_amer	Fraction of students identified as "native American."[32]
unemployrate	County-level unemployment rate (%), averaged over the school-year.
unemp_prev	County-level unemployment rate (%), for the previous school-year.
urban	Dummy variable which equals *one* for urban counties.
year2	Dummy variable which equals *one* for the second school-year (2002/03). (The variables $year3_{i,t}$ ... $year5_{i,t}$ are defined analogously.)
year2_4h_rate	Product of dummy variable $year2_{i,t}$ with $four\_h\_rate_{i,t}$. (The variables $year3\_4h\_rate_{i,t}$ ... $year5\_4h\_rate_{i,t}$ are defined analogously.)
yearnum	Year number variable; takes on values 1, 2, 3, 4, or 5.
school_pop	Total number of students, for this county and school-year.

2. Estimate a bivariate OLS regression model relating $mathpassrate_{it}$ to $four\_h\_rate_{it}$, ignoring heterogeneity across the counties and time periods. Repeat, estimating cluster-

[30] The data set also includes a variable (*mathavgscore*) which is the average score on the math FCAT.

[31] Be aware that Stata variable names are case sensitive, so *four_H_rate* is not the same as this!

[32] The remaining fraction of the students were identified as "multiracial."

robust standard errors; does this much affect the standard error estimate for the coefficient on $four\_h\_rate_{it}$? Continuing to specify cluster-robust standard errors, now include the time-dummy variables, $year2_{i,t}$ ... $year5_{i,t}$ in the model, so as to allow for time variation in the intercept; do any of these enter with statistically significant coefficients? Would the folks at 4-H be happy with any of these results?

3. Now estimate a multivariate regression model relating $mathpassrate_{it}$ to $four\_h\_rate_{it}$, but this time allowing for the heterogeneity across counties by controlling for the county-specific variables: $mathtestrate_{i,t}$ through $urban_{i,t}$ in the list above, again using the cluster-robust standard errors and including the time-dummy variables, $year2_{i,t}$ ... $year5_{i,t}$. Focusing on the estimated coefficient with which $four\_h\_rate_{i,t}$ enters the model, should the folks at 4-H be any happier with these results? Do the signs on the estimated coefficients which are apparently statistically significant at least make sense?
4. Next allow for county-level heterogeneity in the model intercept by estimating the Fixed Effects Model relating $mathpassrate_{i,t}$ to $four\_h\_rate_{i,t}$, still including the explanatory variables $mathtestrate_{i,t}$ ... $urban_{i,t}$ and $year2_{i,t}$ ... $year5_{i,t}$.[33] Why does Stata drop the $urban_{i,t}$ dummy variable from the regression equation? Should the folks at 4-H be any happier with these results?
5. Next estimate the analogous Random Effects Model for these data.[34] Are the estimated coefficients – and, in particular, the coefficient on $four\_h\_rate_{i,t}$ – notably different from those obtained using the Fixed Effects Model? Is the Random Effects Model Assumption remotely reasonable in this context? Should the folks at 4-H be any happier with these results?
6. Now consider the possibility that the relationship between $mathpassrate_{i,t}$ and $four\_h\_rate_{i,t}$ is dynamic – i.e., the possibility that $mathpassrate_{i,t}$ might also depend on $mathpassrate_{i,t-1}$ and on $four\_h\_rate_{i,t-1}$. Why might one expect this to be the case? At the same time, allow for the possibility that the contemporaneous value of the $four\_h\_rate_{i,t}$ explanatory variable is endogenous – that is, the possibility that $four\_h\_rate_{i,t}$ is correlated with current (and possibly future) values of $\varepsilon_{i,t}$. Why might one expect this to be the case?

   To deal with these possibilities use the Arellano-Bond estimator, which estimates the First-Differences Model, relating $\Delta mathpassrate_{i,t}$ to $\Delta four\_h\_rate_{i,t}$ – and to $\Delta mathpassrate_{i,t-1}$, $\Delta four\_h\_rate_{i,t-1}$, and the changes in all of the other explanatory variables FT consider – i.e., $mathtestrate_{i,t}$, ... $year5_{i,t}$.[35] This estimation requires only three changes relative to estimating the Fixed Effects Model:
   a. First, one must use the "xtabond" command instead of the "xtreg" command.
   b. Second, the *four_h_rate* variable is dropped from the list of explanatory variables. It now enters the command as the option, "endogenous(four_h_rate, lag(1,2))". This

[33] Use the "xtreg" command for this, with the "fe" option; it is no longer necessary to specify the computation of cluster-robust standard error estimates for the "xtreg" command when using versions of Stata more recent than 10.1, as these are the default option.

[34] Use the "xtreg" command for this, now omitting the "fe" option; as before, it is no longer necessary to specify the computation of cluster-robust standard error estimates for the "xtreg" command when using versions of Stata more recent than 10.1, as these are the default option.

[35] You will find again that Stata insists on dropping the *urban* variable – for the same reason as in the Fixed Effects Model. One must also drop an additional year-dummy variable because of the differencing, so only include $year3_{i,t}$, $year4_{i,t}$, and $year5_{i,t}$. Stata will automatically drop these exactly collinear explanatory variables from the model anyway, but one must explicitly drop these two variables from the list of explanatory variables in order to get Stata to perform the autocorrelation diagnostic check using the "estat abond" post-estimation command.

option specifies that $four\_h\_rate_{i,t}$ is to enter the model contemporaneously and with one lag; it also specifies that at most two additional lags of $mathpassrate_{i,t-1}$ are to be used as instruments in the differenced equation. (The variable $\Delta mathpassrate_{i,t-2}$ is used as an instrument for $\Delta four\_h\_rate_{i,t}$ in the differenced equation which is analogous to Equation 16-47 in Section 16.2; with only five school-years of data available in the panel, this is anyway the maximum lag of $\Delta four\_h\_rate_{i,t}$ that can be constructed, so it makes no difference to the estimation if more than two additional lags are specified in this part of the command.)

c. Finally, replace the "fe" option by the string of options: "lags(1) noconstant twostep vce (robust)". The "lags(1)" specifies that just one lag in the dependent variable is to be included in the model; this option could actually be omitted, since including one lag in the dependent variable is the default.[36] The "noconstant" option instructs Stata to not bother estimating an intercept for the "levels" regression equation.[37] And the "twostep vce(robust)" options cause the procedure to correct the parameter estimation for possible heteroscedasticity in the $\Delta\varepsilon_{i,t}$.

Note that the estimated coefficient on the lagged dependent variable is larger than one, but not significantly so. The Arellano-Bond estimator assumes that enough lags have been included in the model so that $\Delta\varepsilon_{i,t}$ is serially uncorrelated; check this by using the "estat abond" command and examine the p-value for the "order 2" test.[38] Why do you think that the estimated coefficient on the county-level unemployment rate is negatively related to $mathpassrate_{i,t}$? Is the estimated coefficient on $four\_h\_rate_{i,t}$ notably different from that obtained using the Fixed Effects Model? Is it statistically significant in this estimated model, even though 67 observations (one for each county) are lost to the differencing? Why? Should the folks at 4-H be any happier with these results?

7. Finally, run some diagnostic checks on the estimated model from Part 6:

a. Save the fitting errors under the name "xtabond_resids".[39] Obtain a histogram of these fitting errors (using the "histogram xtabond_resids" command) and also plot them against observation number (using the "scatter xtabond_resids obsnum" command). Are outliers a problem here? List the values of $county\_num_{i,t}$, $schoolyear_{i,t}$, $school\_pop_{i,t}$, $spending_{i,t}$, $english\_learn_{i,t}$, and $urban$ – just for the observations for

---

[36] Eliminating the lagged dependent variable from the model is not feasible, by the way, because its change is needed as an instrument; specifying "lags(0)" just generates an error message.

[37] Recall, from the discussion in Section 16.2, that this option has no effect on the slope parameter estimates: better yet, try it both ways and confirm this for yourself. Do not expect the fitting errors ("resids") produced by the "predict resids , e" to have a sample mean of zero if this option is included, however.

[38] The variables "$urban_{i,t}$" and "$year2_{i,t}$" must be omitted from the model: the xtabond command will drop these collinear variables and still function to produce parameter estimates, but the "estat abond" routine will fail to run if there are any such "dropped" variables in the model. If the p-value for the "order 2" were less than .05 – which it is not, with this data set – then one would need to include an additional lag of mathpassrate$_{i,t}$ in the model, using the "lags(2)" option, and possibly additional lags in other explanatory variables as well. Including two lags in $mathpassrate_{i,t}$ here yields "nicer-looking" parameter estimates on the lags of $mathpassrate_{i,t}$. But with only five observations for each county to begin with, a model using $\Delta mathpassrate_{t-2}$ as an explanatory variable will have only two observations per county; with this particular data set, that is not enough sample data to obtain statistically significant parameter estimates for any of the model parameters.

[39] Use the "e" option in the "predict" command, so as to save the fitting errors – these are estimates of $\varepsilon_{i,t}$ in the original ("levels") model. The "xtabond" command does not require that the data have been sorted (using the "xtset countynum schoolyear" command), but the "predict" post-estimation command will require this.

which $xtabond\_resids_{i,t}$ is greater than 65.[40] Are these values notably different from their means over the entire sample?

b. Investigate the possible importance of nonlinearity in some of the relationships incorporated into this model by including the squares of some of the explanatory variables – e.g., $englishlearn_{i,t}$ and $spending_{i,t}$ – in the regression equation.

c. Investigate the possibility that the coefficient on $four\_h\_rate_{i,t}$ depends linearly on the value of the $englishlearn_{i,t}$ variable, by constructing the product variable and including it in the regression equation.

d. Apply the Sargan test of the overidentifying restrictions in this model. As noted in Footnote 16-24, this is testing the restrictions the model is placing on the data; as such, it is best viewed simply as a general test of model misspecification. If the test fails to reject its null hypothesis, however, this does not imply that the model is correctly specified: this result merely indicates that the test failed to detect any model misspecification. Similarly, if the test *does* reject its null hypothesis, then this result indicates that there is something significantly wrong with the model specifation, but it is completely uninformative as to what is wrong. Therefore, the test is worth doing only because it is very easy: one just re-estimates the model without the "vce(robust)" option – which is incompatible with the Sargan test – and issues the "estat sargan" command.

Concluding Comments:

Contrary to the impression one might glean from the particular results of this exercise, the impact of 4-H participation on FCAT pass rates is actually very significant, and FT's full results make the folks at 4-H very happy indeed. This impact is only significant at the 5% (and not at the 1%) level in the aggregated summary of FT's data set used here for two reasons. First, the sample size here is six times smaller than the full sample used by FT, because the data for grade levels 2 through 8 were aggregated for use here.[41] Second – and perhaps of equal importance – FT find that it is very important to allow for heterogeneity in the intercept term which is not estimatable using data aggregated over the grade levels. In particular, their results with the full data set indicate that it is essential to include interaction terms in the model specification which allow the coefficients on the year-dummies to vary with both county and with grade level and to also include interaction terms allowing the county-specific intercept to vary with grade level. The aggregated data set does, however, provide a nice illustration of the panel-data methods covered here – and also abides by the memory limits of the student version of Stata.

[40] The needed Stata command for this is "list countynum county_name schoolyear xtabond_resids if xtabond_resids >= 65 & xtabond_resids != ". The variable "$school\_pop_{i,t}$" is the total number of students enrolled in county i in schoolyear t; it is included in the data set, but it is not included in the regression models as an explanatory variable because all of the other variables are on a per-pupil basis.

[41] Indeed, a sample of just 335 observations is perhaps a bit skimpy for the use of the Arellano-Bond procedure.

17

A Concise Introduction to Time-Series Analysis and Forecasting (Part A)

17.1 INTRODUCTION: THE DIFFERENCE BETWEEN TIME-SERIES ANALYSIS AND TIME-SERIES ECONOMETRICS

Except for forecasting, all of the usual aspects of regression modeling which are specific to data sets which are in time order – i.e., "time-series" data sets – were discussed fairly thoroughly in Chapters 13 and 14. How is "time-series analysis" any different from ordinary econometrics applied to time-series data?

The first point to mention is that these two topics are not, in fact completely distinct. Both deal with time-series data and both typically lead to the estimation of one or more instances of the Dynamic Multiple Regression Model, Equation 14-3. The difference is a matter of emphasis.

For example, time-series econometrics is primarily concerned with estimation and inference, on models whose specification (at least in principle) is primarily derived from economic theory. Such model specifications usually involve a number of explanatory variables and quite often address issues of endogeneity – especially that due to joint determination via simultaneous equations, as described in Chapters 11 and 12 – and/or issues of panel data heterogeneity, as described in Chapters 15 and 16. Time-series analysis, in contrast, explicitly looks to the data itself for the model specification, and is usually more concerned with forecasting than with inference.[1]

Where time-series analysis does turn its attention to inference, the typical object of interest is an attempt to determine the direction of Granger-causality between a set (often just a pair) of time-series. Even there, however, the focus is still on forecasting, as the definition of Granger-causality is usually (and most appropriately) couched in terms of relative forecasting effectiveness. (Granger causality was introduced in Section 12.2; its practical implementation will be described in Section 18.5.) Of course, inference is still essential and useful in time-series analysis: in testing the statistical significance of estimated coefficients (as part of the model-building/model-evaluation

[1] Looking back at the examples in Sections 14.4 to 14.6, the reader might well observe that very little theory was used in their construction. In part that is because applied economists often rely less on economic theory than we say we do, and less than we probably should. In principle, each econometric model should begin from a well-developed economic theory and adapt this theory-derived specification to the exigencies of the data only insofar as is necessary in order to yield a regression model which passes all of its diagnostic checks. On the other hand, economic theory is usually silent about many of the crucial specification issues – e.g., which data series are most appropriate and in what ways they should enter the model. Also, the model respecifications suggested by the diagnostic checking process described in Chapters 10, 13, and 14 – which are usually the most effective responses to model deficiencies – in fact amount to adopting the "time-series analysis" point of view and using the sample data to guide the specification of the model.

process), and in estimating confidence intervals for forecasts. But, except where testing for the Granger-causality is the motivating issue, inference is generally a means to an end in time-series analysis, rather than the end itself: that "end" is usually forecasting.

In contrast, in time-series econometrics it is forecasting which is (if considered at all) typically a means to an end, rather than the end itself. A forecast in the time-series econometrics framework is usually a "conditional" forecast, where – for example – the dependent variable might be tax revenues collected by some level of government in period t and the explanatory variables might include a tax rate, the growth rate in the money supply, etc. True, the forecast itself is important in such a setting, but the main point of computing it is to examine the impact of the proposed (or anticipated) tax or monetary policies, rather than to forecast tax revenues.

The primacy of forecasting in time-series analysis profoundly influences the way that models are both specified and evaluated.

Regarding model specification, in time-series analysis one is more likely to frame the model using a smaller number of explanatory variables which are sampled more frequently – i.e., daily or monthly; quarterly or annual data is more commonly used in time-series econometric modeling. A smaller number of explanatory variables is typically considered in a time-series analysis model because the (always limited) information in the data set is being openly used to obtain the model specification as well as for parameter estimation. Consequently, there is a premium on keeping that specification relatively simple. The higher sampling frequency is essential so as to increase the amount of sample data available – for both model specification and parameter estimation – but it also enhances the prospects for short-term forecasting. For example, with monthly data one might uncover a relationship which is useful in forecasting a variable's value in the ensuing couple of months, based on correlations between this variable and the values of itself (and a few other variables) in the past month or two. In contrast, the annual average of this same variable might not be substantially related to its own (or the other variables') previous annual values. Thus, forecasting models attempting to exploit the correlations of variables with their own recent past – which is a lot of what models based on the time-series analysis framework do – are more likely to be effective with data which are frequently sampled.

In contrast, higher frequency (e.g., monthly) data are often unavailable for some or all of the variables useful – in the time-series econometrics setting – for making policy-relevant conditional forecasts. For example, national income accounting data – GDP, government spending, net exports, etc. – are only compiled on a quarterly basis. Thus, a model produced in the time-series analysis framework using monthly data might well be unable to even include the relevant policy-control variables as explanatory variables, and hence be inherently irrelevant to the task of policy analysis based on conditional forecasting.

Model evaluation is also influenced by the primacy of forecasting in time-series analysis. A model produced within the time-series econometrics framework will, in a high-quality analysis, be diagnostically checked in multiple ways using the sample data before being accepted for use. For example – referring to the summary of diagnostic checking listed in Table 15-3 of Section 15.6 – one would check the model for normality (especially outliers), heteroscedasticity and/or serial correlation in the errors, nonlinearity in the relationship, and parameter instability across the sample. An ample consideration of these issues is necessary in order make credible – even approximately – the validity of the model assumptions underlying the usual statistical inference machinery. Similar diagnostic checking is done in a high-quality time-series analysis application. But the ultimate test of a model formulated within the time-series analysis framework is always its ability to forecast post-sample – which is to say, over a set of observations held out and not already "used up" in specifying and estimating it.[2] After the model is accepted for use, one typically re-estimates the parameters using all of the available data.

[2] In principle, one could instead test one's model on data prior to sample data used for specifying and estimating it, but post-sample data are usually considered more relevant. An analogous diagnostic check is an excellent idea in building models with cross-sectional data also; it is called "out-of-sample" testing in that context, and the data so used is often called a "hold-out" sample.

In summary, then, the defining features of time-series analysis – that distinguish it from the time-series econometrics of Chapters 13 and 14 – are:

- Time-series analysis focuses on relatively simple models, whose dynamic specification is explicitly obtained from the sample data.
- The emphasis, in time-series analysis, is on forecasting – usually as an end in itself, but sometimes with regard to an inference as to Granger causality.

Because forecasting is so essential to time-series analysis, this chapter first addresses the question of what constitutes a "good" or even "optimal" forecast, in Section 17.2. As with the (somewhat related) issue in Chapter 3 of defining what is meant by a "good" parameter estimator, it is very worthwhile to pay some careful attention to this topic at the outset.[3] The exposition then turns, in Section 17.3, to a crucial concept underlying most of time-series analysis: the "stationarity" assumption. Getting this right turns out to be half the battle in producing a high-quality model in time-series analysis. This section also introduces the basic "tools of the trade" in time-series analysis: a time-plot of the sample data and the sample "correlogram."

The remainder of Chapter 17 describes how to specify, estimate, and diagnostically check univariate (one-variable) linear time-series models. Chapter 18 then extends this discussion to the modeling of integrated – i.e., I(1) – time-series, seasonality in time-series, multiple time-series, testing for Granger-causation, and modeling nonlinear serial dependence in a time-series. Chapter 18 closes with a treatment of two additional topics in time-series forecasting: how one can recognize a forecast which is worse than no forecast at all and how to combine several disparate forecasts in order to form a forecast which is more accurate than any of its component parts.[4]

17.2 OPTIMAL FORECASTS: THE PRIMACY OF THE CONDITIONAL-MEAN FORECAST AND WHEN IT IS BETTER TO USE A BIASED FORECAST

Suppose that one wants to forecast Y_{N+h} at time N, where h is a positive integer. Such a forecast is called an "h-step-ahead" forecast, and h is known as the "forecast horizon." Often, the value of h is one – and one is making a "one-step-ahead" forecast; but multi-step-ahead forecasts can be important also. The forecast of Y_{N+h} analyzed below is assumed to be some specific function of a set of sample data which are realizations of the random variables $Y_1, Y_2, \ldots, Y_N$ – and sometimes also a function of realizations of other random variables, such as $X_1 \ldots X_N$ and $Z_1 \ldots Z_N$.

This forecasting function is denoted $F_{N,h}(Y_1, Y_2, \ldots, Y_N)$ here. Additional arguments (e.g., for past values of other variables, such as X_t or Z_t) will be included in this function explicitly when they are applicable, but even the arguments $Y_1, Y_2, \ldots, Y_N$ will be dropped from the notation whenever they are not necessary. Where needed for clarity, a superscript – consisting of a number or a descriptive string in brackets (e.g., $F_{N,h}{}^{\{AR1CM\}}$ below) will be added, so as to distinguish the forecasting function provided by one model from that provided by another.

[3] If one wants to produce good forecasts, it is essential to understand what constitutes "goodness" in a forecast: in the words of the great Yankees baseball player (and philosopher) Yogi Berra, "If you don't know where you're going, chances are you will end up somewhere else."

[4] These two chapters constitute only a brief introduction to a large topic; there are several book-length treatments of time-series analysis which are well worth knowing about. Enders (2010) provides an excellent and accessible treatment of the current state of time-series analysis; Granger and Newbold (1977) and Box and Jenkins (1976) are the classic books in the field; and Hamilton (1994) is useful for the clarity with which it covers topics in a technically sophisticated way. Enders, W. (2010), *Applied Econometric Time-Series*, Wiley: Hoboken. Granger, C. W. J., and P. Newbold (1977), *Forecasting Economic Time-Series*, Academic Press: New York. Box, G. E. P., and G. M. Jenkins (1976), *Time-Series Analysis: Forecasting and Control*, Holden-Day: San Francisco. Hamilton, J. D. (1994), *Time-Series Analysis*, Princeton University Press: Princeton.

The derivation of specific expressions for the forecasting functions appropriate to specific models for how Y_t depends on its own past – and possibly on the pasts of other variables, also – will be taken up later in this chapter. For now, so as to claim the additional clarity of an explicit example, a possible form for $F_{N,1}$ – based on the AR(1) model analyzed as Equation 13-11 in Section 13.4 – will be used as an illustrative example:

$$
\begin{aligned}
F_{N,1}^{\{AR1CM\}} &\equiv \varphi_1 Y_N \\
f_{N,1}^{\{AR1CM\}} &\equiv \varphi_1 y_N
\end{aligned} \tag{17-1}
$$

It will be shown (later in the chapter) that the analogous h-step-ahead forecast functions for this model are

$$
\begin{aligned}
F_{N,h}^{\{AR1CM\}} &\equiv \varphi_1^h Y_N \\
f_{N,h}^{\{AR1CM\}} &\equiv \varphi_1^h y_N
\end{aligned} \tag{17-2}
$$

where φ_1^h denotes φ_1 raised to the power h. The superscript "$\{AR1CM\}$" is included above solely to explicitly specify that this particular forecast function corresponds to the conditional-mean forecast obtained from an AR(1) model – i.e., this forecast is $E[Y_{N+1}|Y_N = y_N]$.[5]

Also, note that (as usual) lowercase letters are used in Equations 17-1 and 17-2 to denote the sample realizations of random variables. In contrast to the analyses of model prediction in time-series econometrics – as in Sections 8.4 and 9.6, and in Appendix 9.1 – the analogous analysis in the time-series analysis framework quite often assumes that the sample length (N) is sufficiently large that $\hat{\varphi}_1^{OLS}$ need not be distinguished from its probability limit, φ_1. Consequently, this section will mostly – but not entirely – be analyzing forecasts ($f_{N,h}$) which are based on realized sample data and population values of the model parameters; hence these forecasts are non-random.[6]

Now return to the general case of $f_{N,h}$ – the realized forecast of Y_{N+h}. The h-step-ahead prediction error made by this forecast is the random variable $\varepsilon_{N,h}$ defined by

$$\varepsilon_{N,h} \equiv f_{N,h} - Y_{N+h} \tag{17-3}$$

The perfect forecast, of course, is the forecast $f_{N,h}$ which always yields $\varepsilon_{N,h}$ equal to zero. But $f_{N,h}$, as noted above, is fixed and Y_{N+h} is a random variable; thus, "perfect" forecasts are obviously not possible.

The next best forecast is the "optimal" forecast, defined as the $f_{N,h}$ which minimizes the expected value of the "losses" associated with using $f_{N,h}$ as one's predicted value for the realization of Y_{N+h}. Here, of course, one must specify a loss function – Loss($\varepsilon_{N,h}$) – which quantifies the dis-utility caused by the forecast error, $\varepsilon_{N,h}$. If Loss($\varepsilon_{N,h}$) is proportional to $(\varepsilon_{N,h})^2$, then this is called the "squared-error loss function" and the expected loss is then proportional to the mean square error, which will be denoted MSE($f_{N,h}$) here.

It was necessary to specify a very similar kind of loss function in Section 3.2. "Loss" occurs in that context because of a sampling error made by an estimator ($\hat{\mu}$) of the population mean of a random variable. (For examples, see Figures 3-3 and 3-4.) Loss($\varepsilon_{N,h}$) is different, however, because the forecast $f_{N,h}$ is a fixed number, whereas the prediction error $\varepsilon_{N,h}$ is a random variable because the

[5] As noted earlier, the form of the conditional-mean forecasting function will be derived for this (and a number of other) specific models in later sections of this chapter. See Appendix 2.1 for an explicit discussion of the conditional mean concept in the context of a pair of discretely distributed random variables.

[6] Theorem 17-4 is an exception to this. Also, note that plim($\hat{\varphi}_1^{OLS}$) will not in general be equal to φ_1 if Y_t actually depends on its own past in a more complicated fashion than is specified by the AR(1) model; that is being glossed over here.

value being forecast (Y_{N+h}) is a random variable. By way of contrast, in the parameter estimation problem, the parameter being estimated (μ) is a fixed (albeit unknown) number, whereas the estimator is a random variable – whose sampling distribution quantifies the uncertainty in $\hat{\mu}$, due to the finite amount of sample of data available for use in this estimator.[7]

Econometricians working in the time-series analysis area – notably including recent Nobel Prize winner Clive Granger – have obtained a number of useful theoretical results on optimal forecasting. Each of these results is based on a different set of assumptions regarding either the form of the loss function – Loss ($\varepsilon_{N,h}$) – or regarding the form of the distribution of Y_{N+h} conditional on $Y_1, Y_2, \ldots, Y_N$ – i.e., on the form of the conditional density function, $g_c(Y_{N+h}|Y_1 = y_1, Y_2 = y_2, \ldots, Y_N = y_N)$.

Five of these results on optimal forecasting will be described here. Most of these involve – and are couched in terms of – M_h, the "conditional-mean forecast":[8]

$$\begin{aligned} M_h &\equiv E[Y_{N+h}|Y_1 = y_1, Y_2 = y_2, \ldots, Y_N = y_N] \\ &\equiv \int_{-\infty}^{\infty} Y_{N+h}\, g_c(Y_{N+h}|Y_1 = y_1, Y_2 = y_2, \ldots, Y_N = y_N)\, dY_{N+h} \end{aligned} \tag{17-4}$$

M_h is usually extremely easy to calculate for a given time-series model of Y_t. Indeed, M_h for an AR(1) model of Y_t is precisely the example forecast given above in Equation 17-2:

$$f_{N,h}^{\{ARICM\}} \equiv \varphi_1^h y_N \tag{17-5}$$

for this AR(1) model, assuming that N is sufficiently large that sampling errors in the estimator of φ_1 can be neglected. The first two results set out conditions under which it can be shown that M_h is the optimal forecast of Y_{N+h}; the last three results give insights into reasonable circumstances where M_h is *not* the optimal forecast of Y_{N+h}:

***Theorem 17-1** {M_h **is optimal for the squared-error loss function**}*

If Loss($\varepsilon_{N,h}$) is proportional to $(\varepsilon_{N,h})^2$, then M_h is the optimal forecast of Y_{N+h}.

Proof: See Granger and Newbold (1977, p. 116) for a proof of this proposition.

The proof given in Granger and Newbold (1977) depends on the assumption that $f_{N,h}$ is nonrandom. In fact, as shown in Theorem 17-4, M_h in general is *not* optimal when sampling errors in estimated coefficients cause substantial violations of this assumption.

[7] Returning to the AR(1) h-step-ahead forecast example, recall that (as noted above) it is commonplace (in the time-series analysis literature) to assume that N is so large that the sampling errors in the model parameter ($\hat{\varphi}_1^{OLS}$) can be ignored. If this is not the case, then one must account for replacing the (fixed) forecast, $f_{N,h}^{(ARICM)} = \varphi_1^h y_N$ by the (random) estimator $\hat{f}_{N,h}^{(ARICM)} = \hat{\varphi}_1^n y_N$, in which case both terms in $\varepsilon_{N,h}$ are random; forecasts like this are considered in Theorem 17.4. In some contexts – notably, the forecasting of financial asset volatility – the true (population) value of the time-series is never known, and must be replaced by "proxy measures." This complication raises additional issues in evaluating a forecast, even well after the fact; see Patton (2010) for a recent contribution in this area. Patton, A.J. (2010), "Volatility Forecast Comparison Using Imperfect Volatility Proxies" *Journal of Econometrics* (in press), doi:10.1016/j.jeconom.2010.03.034.

[8] Refer back to Equation 2-13 in Chapter 2 if the integral in this definition is confusing rather than clarifying. Note that, to be consistent with typical usage, an uppercase letter is used for the conditional mean, even though it is a fixed quantity.

***Theorem 17-2* {M_h can be optimal if Loss$(\varepsilon_{N,h})$ and $g_c(Y_{N+h}|Y_1 = y_1 \dots Y_N = y_N)$ are both symmetric}**

M_h is the optimal forecast of Y_{N+h} if Loss $(\varepsilon_{N,h})$ is symmetric around its minimum (at $\varepsilon_{N,h}$ equal to zero) *and* $g_c(Y_{N+h}|Y_1 = y_1 \dots Y_N = y_N)$ is symmetric around M_h *and* either

a. the derivative dLoss $(\varepsilon_{N,h})/d\varepsilon_{N,h}$ exists almost everywhere (i.e., it has a unique, bounded value for all values of $\varepsilon_{N,h}$ except at isolated points) and this derivative is monotonically increasing (i.e., d^2Loss $(\varepsilon_{N,h})/d(\varepsilon_{N,h})^2$ is strictly positive) for all values of $\varepsilon_{N,h}$ except at isolated points

or

b. the conditional density function $g_c(Y_{N+h}|Y_1 = y_1 \dots Y_N = y_N)$ is a continuous function of X_{N+h} and is unimodal.[9]

Proof: See Granger (1969).[10]

As conditions (a) and (b) in Theorem 17-2 are both a bit on the fussy-and-opaque side, it is productive to approximately restate this result in a more intelligible way. Basically, Theorem 17-2 says that M_h can still be an optimal forecast of Y_{N+h} with a loss function Loss $(\varepsilon_{N,h})$ which is only symmetric – but not necessarily proportional to $(\varepsilon_{N,h})^2$ – *if* one is able to also assume that conditional distribution for Y_{N+h} is symmetric around M_h, *plus* some smoothness and monotonicity in either Loss $(\varepsilon_{N,h})$ or in the cumulative conditional distribution of Y_{N+h}.[11]

The final three results provide some insights into how the optimal forecast of Y_{N+h} differs from M_h when the conditions of Theorems 17-1 and 17-2 are not necessarily met. Theorem 17-3 assumes nothing about the form of Loss $(\varepsilon_{N,h})$, but instead assumes that $Y_1, Y_2, \dots, Y_N$ are normally distributed:

***Theorem 17-3* {If $g_c(Y_{N+h}|Y_1 = y_1 \dots Y_N = y_N)$ is normal, then the optimal $f_{N,h}$ is $M_h + \alpha$.}**

If Y_{N+h} is normally distributed (conditional on $Y_1, Y_2, \dots, Y_N$), then the optimal forecast of Y_{N+h} is $M_h + \alpha$, where α is a constant that depends on the form of the loss function, Loss $(\varepsilon_{N,h})$, but not on $y_1, y_2, \dots, y_N$.

Proof: See Granger and Newbold (1977, p. 118).

Of course, the value of α is not known, except where it is zero due to Theorem 17-1 or 17-2. Still, it is useful to know that – for normally distributed data – the form of Loss $(\varepsilon_{N,h})$ only impacts this fixed deviation of the optimal forecast from M_h, not how the optimal forecast depends on recent observations:y_N, y_{N-1}, etc. It is also worth noting that M_h is a linear function of $Y_1, y_2, \dots, Y_N$ when the conditional distribution of Y_{N+h} is normal.[12]

The next result relaxes the assumption (Equation 17-5 and Footnote 17-7) that N is so large that the sampling errors in the model parameter (i.e., $\hat{\varphi}_1^{OLS} - \hat{\varphi}_1$) can be ignored, by allowing for the possibility that M_h must, in practice, be replaced by a noisy estimate, $\hat{M}_h$:

***Theorem 17-4* {Shrinkage of M_h is optimal for the squared-error loss function if $\hat{M}_h$ is noisy.}**

[9] "Unimodality" means that the conditional density function $g_c(Y_{N+h}|Y_1 = y_1 \dots Y_N = y_N)$ has only one "peak."

[10] Granger, C. W. J. (1969), "Prediction with a Generalized Cost Function," *Operations Research Quarterly 20*, pp. 199–207.

[11] Symmetry in Loss $(\varepsilon_{N,h})$ and $g_c(Y_{N+h}|Y_1 = y_1 \dots Y_N = y_N)$ are not, in and of themselves, sufficient to ensure that M_h is optimal: Granger (1969) provides a counterexample.

[12] M_h is also known to be a linear function of $y_1, y_2, \dots, y_N$ when $Y_1, Y_2, \dots, Y_N$ are jointly distributed as a multivariate Student's t – see Zellner (1971). The Student's t distribution is qualitatively similar to the normal distribution, except that it has more weight in both the peak (right around the mean) and in the tails. A good deal of financial returns data are distributed like this. But M_h is not known to be a linear function for other joint distributions. Zellner, A. (1971), *An Introduction to Bayesian Inference in Econometrics.* Wiley: New York.

If M_h is not known, but must be replaced by a noisy estimate, $\hat{M}_h$ – due, for example, to substantial sampling variance in estimated model coefficients – which is uncorrelated with $M_h - Y_{N+h}$, then the optimal forecast of Y_{N+h} under a squared-error loss function will be of form λM_h with $0 < \lambda < 1$; in other words, the minimum-MSE forecast of Y_{N+h} is shrunk from M_h toward zero. In particular, the optimal value of λ is

$$\lambda^* = \frac{M_h^2}{M_h^2 + \text{var}(\hat{M}_h - M_h)} \tag{17-6}$$

Proof: This proposition is proven in Section 18.7, where simulation results from Ashley (2006, Tables 1 and 2) are quoted which indicate that this result is of some practical use.[13]

Note that $\text{var}(\hat{M}_h - M_h)$ is the variance of the errors made in estimating M_h. For the one-step-ahead $(h=1)$ forecasts from the AR(1) model illustrative example (Equation 17-1), this variance is just $y_{N+h}^2\ \text{var}(\hat{\varphi}_1 - \varphi_1)$. Because it depends on the ratio of ${M_h}^2$ to the sampling variance of $\hat{\varphi}_1$, λ^* is clearly not known with certainty. Nevertheless, it is evident from Equation 17-6 that λ^* is less than one in any practical circumstance – substantially so, if the model parameter estimates are very noisy.

The simulation results discussed in Section 18.7 address the issue of the degree to which errors in estimating λ^* reduce the MSE improvement provided by this kind of shrinkage. For now, the point to note is that the optimal forecast is always to some degree shrunk down from M_h toward zero, even with a squared-error loss function. In other words – even though we may not be certain of exactly how much it should be shrunk – the optimal forecast is generally biased toward zero, even under the assumption of a symmetric loss function.[14]

In practice, however, people usually have *asymmetric* preferences over forecast errors: either over-forecasts of Y_{N+h} or underforecasts of Y_{N+h} are generally more consequential. The final theorem of this section gives the most useful known result on optimal forecasting with an asymmetric loss function:

***Theorem 17-5* {Optimal forecasting with a bilinear loss function on forecast errors}**

If the loss function on forecast errors is the bilinear function,

$$\begin{aligned} \text{Loss}\,(\varepsilon_{N,h}) &= a\,\varepsilon_{N,h} && \text{for } \varepsilon_{N,h} > 0 \text{ and } a > 0 \\ &= 0 && \text{for } \varepsilon_{N,h} = 0 \\ &= -\,b\,\varepsilon_{N,h} && \text{for } \varepsilon_{N,h} < 0 \text{ and } b > 0 \end{aligned} \tag{17-7}$$

then the optimal forecast is the $a/(a+b)$ fractile of the cumulative (conditional) distribution of Y_{N+h} – i.e., the value such that predicted probability that Y_{N+h} is no larger than this is just the fraction $a/(a-b)$.

Proof: See Granger and Newbold (1977, p. 118).[15]

For example, under the symmetric bilinear loss function – i.e., the special case where the parameters b and a are equal – the bilinear loss function is proportional to the absolute value function: i.e., $\text{Loss}\,(\varepsilon_{N,h})$ in that case just equals the positive parameter a times $|\varepsilon_{N,h}|$. In that instance Theorem 17-5

[13] Ashley (2006) additionally applies stochastic dominance ideas to characterize a forecast which is "better than optimal," in that it provides a forecast with lower expected loss than M_h over a sensible *class* of loss functions. Unfortunately, the simulation work indicates that this stochastic dominance result – while of intellectual interest – is not very useful in practice, so that result is only alluded to here. Ashley, R. (2006), "Beyond Optimal Forecasting," (mimeo), available at ashleymac.econ.vt.edu/working_papers/beyond_optimal_shrinkage.pdf.

[14] Note that this result implies that the usual assumption to the effect that the rational expectation of a variable is its conditional mean is actually almost always incorrect.

[15] This proof is not difficult, but involves some basic integral calculus; it is omitted here for brevity.

says that the optimal forecast is just the median of $g_c(Y_{N+h}|Y_1 = y_1, Y_2 = y_2, \ldots, Y_N = y_N)$ rather than its mean, M_h.[16]

As another example, suppose that negative forecast errors are given triple weight in the loss function, so that the parameter b is three times as large as the parameter a. In that case Theorem 17-5 gives the optimal forecast as the 75% fractile of $g_c(Y_{N+h}|Y_1 = y_1 \ldots Y_N = y_N)$.[17] The sense of this result is that the optimal forecast is chosen so that there is only a 25% chance of incurring the large cost of a negative realization of $\varepsilon_{N,h}$.

The upshot of these results is that the conditional-mean forecast (M_h) is likely to be a good – even a close-to-optimal – forecast, unless either

- The sample length (*N*) is so small that sampling errors in the estimates of the model coefficients are substantial – in which case M_h should be shrunk to some degree toward zero.
- Or one's loss function on forecast errors, Loss ($\varepsilon_{N,h}$), is so asymmetric that biased forecasting is called for – in which case the result of Theorem 17-5 might be quite useful.

17.3 THE CRUCIAL ASSUMPTION (STATIONARITY) AND THE FUNDAMENTAL TOOLS: THE TIME-PLOT AND THE SAMPLE CORRELOGRAM

For time-series modeling purposes, "stationarity" is the most fundamental and necessary property that a time-series – or set of time-series – can have. Or fail to have. Like many quintessentially important properties, it embodies a very simple idea. Yet, in large part because the same word is used to denote several different properties, there is much confusion about it. And, as with diagnostic checking of the Multiple Regression Model assumptions, checking on the stationarity assumption is inherently a data-based endeavor which requires some enterprise, some common sense, and some of the courage which is always necessary in confronting decision-making under uncertainty. The payoff is large, however, because time-series modeling (especially linear modeling) is fairly easy and effective if one does a good job with this first step.

The most fundamental aspect of this assumption about (or property of) a time-series rests on the following simple idea: The population quantities which specify what one would want to estimate using a sample of data on a time-series – even an extremely lengthy sample over time – can only be sensibly estimated if these quantities are themselves independent of time – that is, the same for all parts of the sample data set.

Thus, it makes little sense to even speak of the population mean or population variance of a time-series Y_t – much less expect to consistently estimate these population quantities using the sample mean or sample variance calculated over $y_1 \ldots y_N$ – unless $\mu \equiv E[Y_t]$ and $\sigma^2 \equiv /E[(Y_t - \mu)^2]$ are constants over the entire sample, from $t = 1$ to $t = N$. This consideration motivates the first concept usually called "stationarity":

Covariance Stationarity

A time-series $Y(t)$ is said to be "covariance stationary" if and only if

- $\mu \equiv E[Y_t]$
- $\gamma_0 \equiv \sigma^2 \equiv \text{var}(Y_t) \equiv E[(Y_t - \mu)^2]$
- $\gamma_k \equiv \text{cov}(Y_t, Y_{t-k}) \equiv E[(Y_t - \mu)(Y_{t-k} - \mu)] \quad (k \geq 1)$

are all bounded constants, which do not depend on the value of t

(17-8)

[16] Note that the mean and median coincide for a normally distributed variate.

[17] That is, the optimal forecast in that case is the value x such that the integral $\int_{-\infty}^{x} g_c(Y_{N+h}|Y_1 = y_1 \ldots Y_N = y_N)dY_{N+h}$ equals 0.75.

Only for $Y(t)$ covariance stationary can μ, σ^2, the autocovariance at lag k (γ_k), and also the population autocorrelation at lag k – i.e., $\rho_k = \gamma_k/\gamma_o$ – possibly be consistently estimated by the corresponding sample moments. Indeed, covariance stationarity is necessary in order for these population quantities to even be well-defined constants.

If, in addition, a mild limitation is placed on the degree of serial dependence in $Y(t)$, then R_k, the sample autocorrelation at lag k:

$$R_k = \frac{\frac{1}{N-k}\sum_{t=k+1}^{N}(Y_t - \overline{Y})(Y_{t-k} - \overline{Y})}{\frac{1}{N-1}\sum_{t=1}^{N}(Y_t - \overline{Y})^2} \tag{17-9}$$

is a consistent estimator of ρ_k.[18] The realized value of this estimator is usually denoted r_k:

$$r_k = \frac{\frac{1}{N-k}\sum_{t=k+1}^{N}(y_t - \overline{y})(y_{t-k} - \overline{y})}{\frac{1}{N-1}\sum_{t=1}^{N}(y_t - \overline{y})^2} \tag{17-10}$$

R_k is often instead defined using $(1/N)$ to premultiply both sums. The sampling properties of R_k (which will be described shortly) are all asymptotic, so there is no need to worry this distinction: if the difference is consequential, then N is too small for the sensible use of the estimator R_k anyway.

Unfortunately, the word "stationarity" is also commonly used with reference to two other concepts. Each of these concepts is related to covariance stationarity, but distinct from it, creating a good deal of unnecessary confusion.

The first of these related concepts is "strict stationarity." A time-series is strictly stationary if it is covariance stationary and if, in addition, all possible third, fourth, and higher moments are also all constants – i.e., independent of time, t.[19] Covariance stationarity is all that is needed for making linear time-series models – in other words, in order to make models expressing $Y(t)$ as a linear function of its own past values, plus an error term. The stronger assumption of strict stationarity is necessary when making nonlinear time-series models, so this concept will come up (briefly) in Section 18.6. Throughout the exposition here, in the interest of clarity, the terms "covariance stationarity" and "strict stationarity" will generally be spelled out completely wherever they appear.[20]

The second confusingly related usage of the word "stationarity" has to do with the concept of I(1) – "integrated of order 1" – time-series, discussed at some length in Section 14.3 in the context of testing for a "unit root" in a time-series; this topic will be taken up again in Section 18.1. In essence, an I(1) time-series needs to be first-differenced in order to be covariance stationary. Such time-series are quite often called "non-stationary." This statement is correct: I(1) time-series really are neither strictly stationary nor covariance stationary, as they do not have a well-defined (bounded) variance. However, this usage of the term "non-stationary" is unfortunate in that it fails to recognize that this is only one of many ways that a time-series can fail to be covariance stationary. Hence, this verbalism will usually be avoided here: instead, a time-series which is I(1) will typically be referred to as "integrated" here – not as "non-stationary."

[18] This "mild limitation" is that the sum $\sum_{j=0}^{\infty}|\gamma_j|$ is bounded; this (plus covariance stationarity) suffices in order for a "law of large numbers" to hold. See Hamilton (1994, p. 186).

[19] Examples of such higher-order moments include $E[(Y_t - \mu)(Y_{t-k} - \mu)^2]$, $E[(Y_t - \mu)(Y_{t-k} - \mu)^2(Y_{t-j} - \mu)]$, $E[(Y_t - \mu)^3(Y_{t-k} - \mu)^2(Y_{t-j} - \mu)^4]$, $E[(Y_t - \mu)^3(Y_{t-k} - \mu)^2(Y_{t-j} - \mu)^2(Y_{t-\ell} - \mu)^2]$, and so forth.

[20] To compound the notational confusion, some authors use the term "wide-sense stationarity." This is simply a synonym for "covariance stationary" and will not be used here.

How can one tell whether a particular, realized, time-series – for example, $y_1 \dots y_N$ – is or is not covariance stationary? Just as with diagnostically checking the assumptions of the Multiple Regression Model – e.g., of homoscedastic and serially uncorrelated model errors – one can never tell for sure. Still, sensible and useful diagnostic checking of these regression assumptions is possible in practice, so long as one has a reasonable amount of data.[21]

Checking a time-series for covariance stationarity is a similar enterprise. The regression model diagnostic checking used data plots and auxiliary regressions; covariance stationarity checking concentrates on two tools: a time-plot of the sample data and a "sample correlogram."

The sample correlogram is simply a plot (and/or tabulation) of the sample autocorrelations – i.e., $r_1, r_2, r_3 \dots r_k$, where $k \leq 20$ is usually plenty for quarterly data and $k \leq 60$ – so as to include lags up to five years – is usually plenty for monthly data. A sample correlogram for a time-series is very easy to produce in most econometric software packages; for a time-series named *ydat*, for example, the commands in Stata are:[22]

```
tsset tee
ac ydat, lags(60)
corrgram ydat, lags(60)
```

Before looking as some illustrative sample output from these commands, it is helpful to first examine some useful results on the asymptotic sampling distribution of the estimator R_k, obtained by Bartlett (1946) and Marriot and Pope (1954).[23] Understanding these results – and their limitations – is essential to effectively interpreting the estimates, $r_1 \dots r_k$. In the way of "limitations," please note at the outset that these results were all derived under the assumption that N is large and that the time-series $Y_1 \dots Y_N$ is covariance stationary and (jointly) normally distributed. As we will see, a bit can be said about how large N needs to be, but the best advice with regard to data which are highly nonnormal is to pretty much ignore the Bartlett results.[24]

Assuming, then, that the time-series $Y_1 \dots Y_N$ is covariance stationary and (jointly) normally distributed, Bartlett (1946) finds that the asymptotic sampling distribution of R_k is

$$\sqrt{N}(R_k - \rho_k) \xrightarrow{d} N\left[0, \sum_{i-0}^{\infty} \rho_i^2\right] \tag{17-11}$$

Thus, R_k is consistent (as an estimator of ρ_k), asymptotically normal, and has an asymptotic variance of $(1/N) \sum_{i=0}^{\infty} \rho_i^2$. It is commonplace, therefore, for econometric software to blithely replace ρ_i by r_i in

---

[21] For example, using the plots and auxiliary regressions summarized in Equation 15-3 of Section 15.6. Note that the homoscedasticity assumption corresponds precisely to a portion of what is required for covariance stationarity. In fact – to make the connection explicit – the assumptions made about the model error term (U_t) in the Multiple Regression Model correspond precisely to assuming that U_t is covariance stationary, serially uncorrelated, and normally distributed.

[22] As noted in earlier chapters, Stata needs to be informed (once) that the data are in time order, using the "tsset" command to specify a variable which increases monotonically with time; here, it is assumed that a user-created variable named *tee* has this property. These commands compute $r_1 \dots r_{60}$; 40 lags is the default value; the "ac" command makes the plot and the "corrgram" command makes the tabulation; most people find the plot far more useful than the tabulation.

[23] See also discussion in Kendall and Stuart (1963, Volume 1). Bartlett, M. S. (1946), "On the Theoretical Specification of Sampling Properties of Autocorrelated Time-Series," *Journal of the Royal Statistical Society B 8*, pp. 27–41; Marriott, F. H. C., and J. A. Pope (1954), "Bias in the Estimation of Autocorrelations," *Biometrika 41(3)*, pp. 390–402; Kendall, M. G., and A. Stuart (1963), *The Advanced Theory of Statistics 1*, Griffin: London.

[24] Non-normality becomes a substantial issue when working with dispersion data – such as volatility measures for financial returns data. It is also an issue for nonlinear time-series modeling, because nonlinear generating mechanisms generally induce non-normality in the data. In this regard, note that transforming each observation in a non-normally distributed time-series so that a histogram of the observations looks normally distributed does not eliminate any nonlinearity in the way the time-series relates to its own recent past; it also does not induce *joint* normality in the time-series.

these expressions and compute an estimated 95% confidence interval for ρ_k as

Estimated Bartlett 95% Confidence Interval for ρ_k
(Assuming $\rho_k, \rho_{k+1}, \rho_{k+2}, \ldots$ are all zero.)

$$\left[-1.96\sqrt{\frac{1}{N}\sum_{i=0}^{k-1} r_i^2},\ 1.96\sqrt{\frac{1}{N}\sum_{i=0}^{k-1} r_i^2} \right] \tag{17-12}$$

under the tacit assumption that $\rho_k, \rho_{k+1}, \rho_{k+2}$, etc. are all zero. That assumption may or may not be remotely reasonable, but it is probably the only reasonable assumption to build into the software.

Of course, using Equation 17-11, one can easily compute one's own Bartlett-based asymptotic 95% confidence interval for ρ_k as

Bartlett 95% Confidence Interval for ρ_k
(Assuming $\rho_m, \rho_{m+1}, \rho_{m+2}, \ldots$ are all zero.)

$$\left[r_k - 1.96\sqrt{\frac{1}{N}\sum_{i=1}^{m} r_i^2},\ r_k + 1.96\sqrt{\frac{1}{N}\sum_{i=1}^{m} r_i^2} \right] \tag{17-13}$$

which is asymptotically valid so long as $Y_1 \ldots Y_N$ are covariance stationary and (jointly) normally distributed, with ρ_k equal to zero for values of k greater than a value of m one would have to choose. In practice, the squared sample autocorrelations become small at large lags – i.e., for large values of k – for data on time-series which are clearly covariance stationary, so the value of m one chooses to use in estimating such a confidence interval is actually not critical, so long as one makes it fairly large.[25]

The sample autocorrelation (R_k) is a consistent estimator of ρ_k for any covariance stationary time-series – and follows the asymptotic sampling distribution of Equation 17-11 for jointly normal time-series – but R_k is not generally an unbiased estimator. A bit is known about this finite-sample bias in R_k, however. In particular, Marriot and Pope (1954) looked at the *asymptotic* bias in R_k for time-series generated by several simple processes. For jointly normal Y_t generated by an AR(1) model with parameter value φ_1, they find that R_1, for example, is biased downward in amount equal to $3\rho_1/N$ in large samples.[26] Based on these results (and considerable experience with simulated data) it seems likely that R_k is always biased downward – i.e., toward zero – at low lags when the time-series is positively autocorrelated at low lags, and probably in greater degree for small N than the Marriott-Pope result suggests.

Finally, Bartlett (1946) also provides an expression for the correlation between the sampling errors made by R_k and those made by $R_{k+\ell}$ – i.e., at a different lag – assuming, as before, that the sample is large and that the time-series Y_t is both covariance stationary and jointly normally distributed. Their general expression for this correlation is a bit opaque, but it is worthwhile looking at a special case of it – which is by no means misleading – in which the difference in the two lags is one and the population autocorrelations are assumed to all be zero for lags larger than three. In that case, the Bartlett result is

$$\text{corr}\,(R_k, R_{k+1}) = 2\frac{(\rho_1 + \rho_1\rho_2 + \rho_2\rho_3)}{(1 + \rho_1^2 + \rho_2^2 + \rho_3^2)}. \tag{17-14}$$

[25] The reason for this is that the value of $(\rho_k)^2$ must dwindle to zero for large k in order for the variance of the time-series to be bounded; this will be demonstrated in Section 17.5, when the MA(∞) representation of a time-series is examined.

[26] Again, see Equation 13-11 in Section 13.4 for the definition of the AR(1) model (and φ_1); autoregressive models are analyzed more completely in Section 17.6.

This result says that the sampling errors made by "adjacent" correlogram estimators will all be positively correlated if the series itself is substantially positively correlated at low lags. In other words, if low-order autocorrelations like ρ_1, ρ_2, (and so forth) are strongly positive, then we should expect that the sampling errors $R_8 - \rho_8$ and $R_9 - \rho_9$ will tend to have the same sign, as will $R_9 - \rho_9$ and $R_{10} - \rho_{10}$, $R_{10} - \rho_{10}$ and $R_{11} - \rho_{11}$, and so forth.

Suppose, then, that ρ_1 (and perhaps ρ_2 as well) are substantially positive for the covariance stationary time-series $Y_1 \ldots Y_N$ and N is fairly large – several hundred, say.[27] What should one expect the sample correlogram of the observed data $y_1 \ldots y_N$ to look like? If a time plot of the sample data indicates that it is not unreasonable to assume that Y_t is covariance stationary, then – in view of the consequent conclusion that r_1 and r_2 are realized values of consistent estimators for ρ_1 and ρ_2 – one would expect these estimates to be positive. If, in addition, the sample histogram of $y_1 \ldots y_N$ is not indicative of wild non-normality in Y_t, then it is reasonable to compare the (probably fairly small) values of r_3, r_4, r_5, etc. to the Bartlett 95% confidence intervals, computed by the software using Equation 17-12. One would expect most of these r_k values (for $k \geq 3$) to lie within the Bartlett intervals.[28] But one should also expect to see a *pattern* in these r_3, r_4, r_5, ... values: they will not look like NIID(0, v^2) variates, with v^2 roughly equal to $(1/N)(1 + r_1^2 + r_2^2)$. Instead, from the result quoted as Equation 17-14, they will *smoothly* "wiggle around," albeit mostly inside the Bartlett confidence interval. Clearly, this apparent pattern in the sample autocorrelation estimates is not something to worry about – nor is it something to remotely contemplate trying to model: it is the ordinary and expected consequence of the strong positive serial correlation in Y_t at low lags.

With that preamble, now consider a few illustrative examples. The sample data $y_1^{\{NIID\}} \ldots y_{500}^{\{NIID\}}$ were generated as NIID(0, 1) variates using a random number generator.[29] Figures 17-1a and 17-1b display a time-plot and a plot of the sample correlogram for these data.

The time-plot in Figure 17-1a is exactly as one might expect from NIID data: the mean and variance appear to be constant across the sample. The data are quite noisy – as one should expect with data which are serially independent – and note that the degree of "unsmoothness" in the time plot seems similar in all parts of the sample: this is consistent with the population autocovariances (γ_1, γ_2, etc.) and population autocorrelations (ρ_1, ρ_2, etc.) at low lags all being homogeneous over time. There are no obvious outliers or "weird" subperiods in which the data appear to be distinct in their generating mechanism. In other words, these data "look" covariance stationary.

Formal tests for homogeneity in mean and variance are certainly possible. Two such tests were described in detail in Sections 4.8 and 4.9, for example, but the analysis in subsequent chapters indicates that it is easier and more effective to do testing of this sort using regression analysis.[30] And one could formally test the hypothesis that ρ_1 is constant across the sample by estimating an AR(1) model using $y_1^{\{NIID\}} \ldots y_{500}^{\{NIID\}}$ and including appropriately defined dummy variables to test the null hypothesis that the coefficient on $y_{t-1}^{\{NIID\}}$ is constant across several preselected subperiods.

Is such testing worthwhile? Within the "time-series analysis" framework, probably not: the time-plot seems convincing enough in this instance. Where such tests might be worthwhile is with a data

[27] Note that covariance stationarity must be assumed or else the symbols ρ_1 and ρ_2 are not meaningful.

[28] Here, "most" means something not terribly different from 19 out of 20, right?

[29] These data were generated with variable name "noise" in a Stata data set already of length 500, using the "drawnorm noise" command. Virtually any program makes this easy enough, however: e.g., the worksheet function normdist(rand(),0,1) inserts an NIID(0,1) variate in a given cell in an Excel spreadsheet. All such data are really "pseudo-random numbers." The ideas underlying the generation of such numbers are discussed in Active Learning Exercise 3a.

[30] That is, test for variation in the mean by regressing $y_t^{\{NIID\}}$ on an intercept plus dummy variables for subperiods; or test for variation in the variance by regressing $(y_t^{\{NIID\}})^2$ on an intercept plus dummy variables for subperiods.

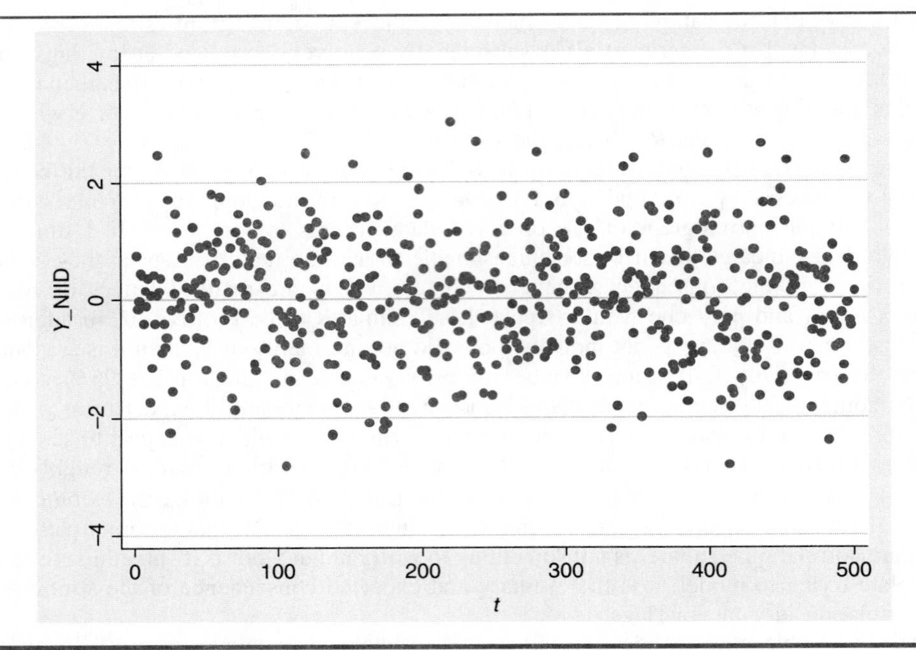

Figure 17-1a Time Plot of $y_1^{\{NIID\}} \ldots y_{500}^{\{NIID\}}$

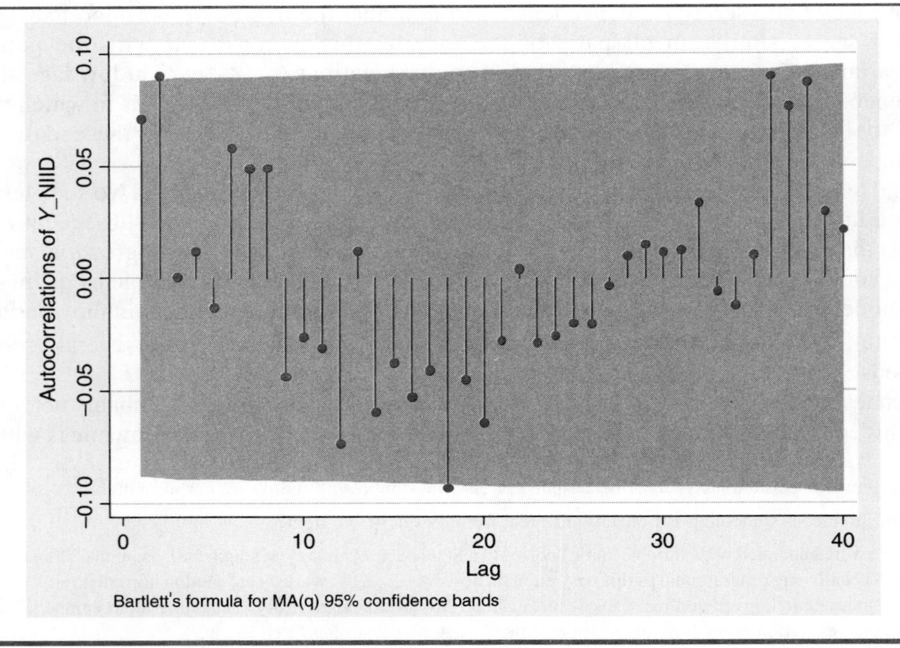

Figure 17-1b Sample Correlogram of $y_1^{\{NIID\}} \ldots y_{500}^{\{NIID\}}$

set for which the time-plot suggests that perhaps the mean, variance, or autocorrelations are a bit different over some subsample and one wants to quantify for oneself the degree to which such apparent departures from covariance stationarity are within the realm of the ordinary sampling fluctuations one might expect to see. Note, however, that such testing will give useful information only if one tests in a reasonably objective way. For example, if it appears that the mean is higher in observations 100 to 199, then it would be reasonable to estimate a regression model with just an intercept and dummy variables to shift the intercept for each of four 100-period long subperiods and to test the null hypothesis that all four dummy variable coefficients are zero. The p-value for that test would convey some information as to the frequency with which the kind of fluctuation you "saw" in the time-plot would occur due to chance. In contrast, just testing the statistical significance of the dummy variable corresponding to observations 100 to 199 yields a procedure which is quite over-likely to reject covariance stationarity in this sample and almost certain to reject it in sufficiently lengthy samples.

Turning to the sample correlogram of $y_1^{\{NIID\}} \dots y_{500}^{\{NIID\}}$ plotted in Figure 17-1b, note that all of the sample autocorrelations $r_1 \dots r_{40}$ are quite small. But how small is "negligible"? That is the issue which the (shaded) Bartlett 95% confidence interval addresses. Note that most – but not all – of the sample autocorrelations lie inside the interval. (The value of r_2 is a bit too large and the value of r_{18} is a bit too small.) Here it is known that $\rho_1 \dots \rho_{40}$ are all exactly zero and that the data are gaussian so – presuming (as is reasonable) that 500 observations qualifies as a large sample – the assumptions underlying the Bartlett 95% confidence interval are basically satisfied. Consequently, one would expect a couple of these 40 estimates to lie outside the interval. It was simply a chance event that exactly 5% of the 40 estimates were outside the 95% confidence interval in this particular case: it could just as easily have been 1 or 3 instead of two r_k values that were outside the interval.

Suppose that several of the r_k values are outside the Bartlett interval and one is concerned that this might be significant evidence against the null hypothesis that $\rho_1 \dots \rho_{40}$ are all zero. There are two sensible ways to address this concern. The null hypothesis that population autocorrelation (ρ_k) is zero is clearly rejected (at the 5% level) for each of these sample autocorrelations (r_k) lying outside the 95% confidence interval. But serial correlation is not equally likely at every value of k. With monthly data, for example, the values of k most likely to correspond to a non-zero value for ρ_k are small values (corresponding to serial correlation at one, two, or three months) and the seasonal value of 12, corresponding to correlation with the value one year previous. So it is a very good idea to pay attention when an r_k estimate at one of these lags appears to be statistically significant. When a handful of r_k estimates at "oddball" lags appear to be individually significant it is almost always a better idea to ignore them. This is because such estimates are typically artifacts of either bad luck or of a failure in one of the assumptions underlying the validity of the Bartlett result (For example, N is not large enough, or the data are not normally distributed, or the data are not actually covariance stationary.) In particular, illustrative examples are given later in this section demonstrating how even a modest trend or shift in the mean of a time-series can distort the sample autocorrelations at moderate-to-large lags.

Still, before ignoring them, it is a good idea to at least consider (and report) the p-value for what is called a "portmanteau" or "Q" test of the null hypothesis that the entire set of population autocorrelations considered are all zero. A simple test is easily constructed from the Bartlett asymptotic sampling distribution results given in Equations 17-11 and 17-14. Under the null hypothesis that all of the population autocorrelations are zero, each of $\sqrt{N}r_1 \dots \sqrt{N}r_{40}$ is (asymptotically) an independent unit normal variate. Consequently, $Q \equiv N \sum_{i=1}^{40} r_i^2$ is asymptotically distributed $\chi^2(40)$ under this null hypothesis, so the relevant p-value is just the probability that a $\chi^2(40)$ variate exceeds the observed value of Q by chance. The values of this Q statistic – and the corresponding p-values – are of course computed automatically by any software package that estimates sample correlograms.[31]

Finally, notice in Figure 17-1b that, as k increases, r_{k+1} strongly tends to have the same sign as r_k. This would seem to be clear evidence that the sampling error made by R_{k+1} – which is just r_k itself, since ρ_k is zero in this example – is positively correlated with that made by R_k. This is just what one would predict from the Bartlett covariance result in Equation 17-14 if ρ_1, ρ_2, etc. were positive, but that is not in fact the case: all of these population autocorrelations are zero here. This is an artifact of r_1 and r_2 being positive – when additional samples are generated for which r_1 and r_2 are negligible or somewhat (albeit insignificantly) negative, this apparent positive correlation between adjacent sample autocorrelations disappears.

All of this work with the sample correlogram is predicated on the assumption that the underlying time-series $Y_1 \ldots Y_N$ is covariance stationary and, in fact, the time plot of the sample realizations $y_1^{\{NIID\}} \ldots y_{500}^{\{NIID\}}$ in Figure 17-1a appears to be quite consistent with this assumption. But what if the time plot had given ample evidence that covariance stationarity is not a viable assumption for these data?

If this evidence is concentrated in the early part of the sample, then such a time-plot would suggest dropping the early observations altogether: better to have a shorter, but homogeneous sample. For example, quarterly data from the U.S. national income accounts generally begins in the first quarter of 1947, but many of these time-series exhibit strange-looking fluctuations until 1953. Apparent non-stationarity is more problematic, however, when it occurs in the middle of the sample period.

For example, Figure 17-2a plots the annualized growth rate in U.S. GNP from 1947II through 2010II.[32]

Starting the sample in 1953 (Figure 17-2b) avoids the typical 1947–1952 turbulence in this kind of data, but makes it all the more clear that the variance of this time-series dropped in the early 1980s.[33] Again paring down the sample – now to begin in 1981II – leaves one with what appears to be a covariance stationary time-series, with a single (possible) outlier in 2008IV, but only 117 remaining sample observations.[34] Holding out the last 20 observations for post-sample model evaluation, the remaining 97 observations yield the sample correlogram in Figure 17-3.

Even though a sample of only 97 observations is a bit skimpy for this sort of analysis, the two apparently significant autocorrelation estimates at lags of one and two quarters in this sample

[31] This is the main reason to issue the Stata "corrgram" command as well as specifying production of a plot of the correlogram. This test was originally proposed by Box and Pearce (1970); a somewhat more sophisticated version of the test, due to Ljung and Box (1978), weights the squared sample autocorrelations for larger lags somewhat more heavily. This improved test is not emphasized here because the correction is probably important only for values of N sufficiently small that the sample correlogram is of doubtful utility anyway. Box, G. E. P., and D. A. Pierce (1970), "Distribution of Residual Autocorrelations in Autoregressive Integrated Moving Average Time-Series Models," *Journal of the American Statistical Association 65,* pp. 1509–26; Ljung, G. M., and G. E. P. Box (1978), "On a Measure of Lack of Fit in Time-Series Models," *Biometrika* 65, pp. 297–303.

[32] Using GDP instead of GNP in this example would yield very similar results. GNP equals GDP plus net income from assets abroad; U.S. GDP is a better measure of the value of U.S. production, whereas U.S. GNP is a better measure of the value of U.S. production by U.S. nationals. These data were obtained from the FRED database at the St. Louis Federal Reserve Bank, at research.stlouisfed.org/fred2/. The annualized quarterly growth rate is calculated as $400\ln(GNP_t/GNP_{t-1})$.

[33] This variance drop seems obvious from the time-plot, but the null hypothesis of a stable variance is easily tested formally by regressing the square the GNP growth rate against a dummy variable defined to be one beginning in 1981II. The fitting errors for such a regression exhibit significant serial correlation at lag one, so the estimation was repeated specifying the computation of Newey-West standard errors, but this made no essential difference in the results: the coefficient estimate on the dummy variable is negative and the null hypothesis that this parameter is zero is rejected (on the two-tailed test, of course) with p-value $< .0005$.

[34] Setting the 2008IV observation to zero does not substantially alter the sample correlogram, although a dummy variable for this time period would clearly enter with a significant coefficient in a model for this time-series. Surely it is obvious why there is an outlier in these data for this particular quarter.

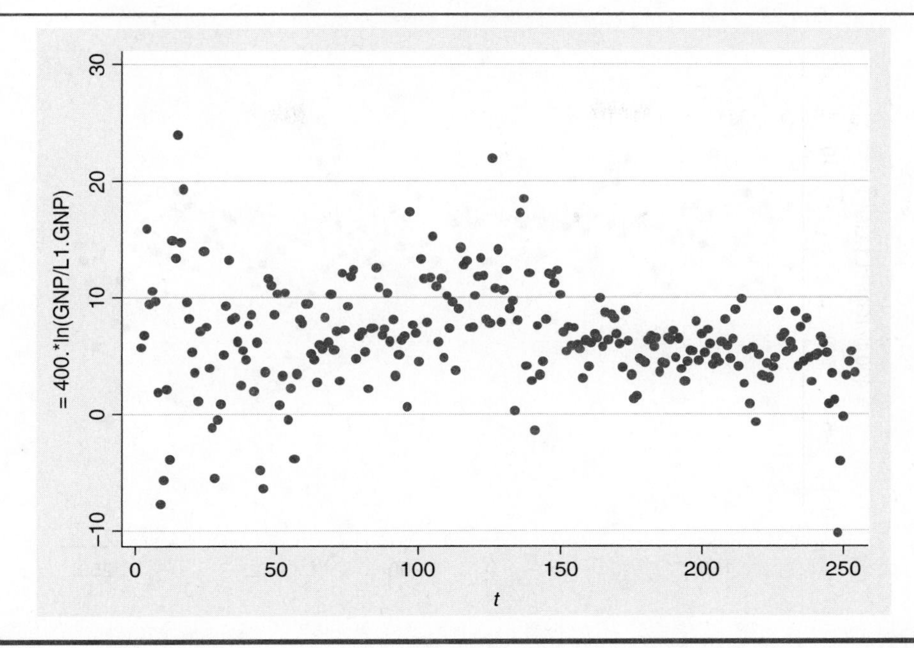

Figure 17-2a Time Plot of Annualized Quarterly Growth Rate in U.S. GNP from 1947II to 2010II

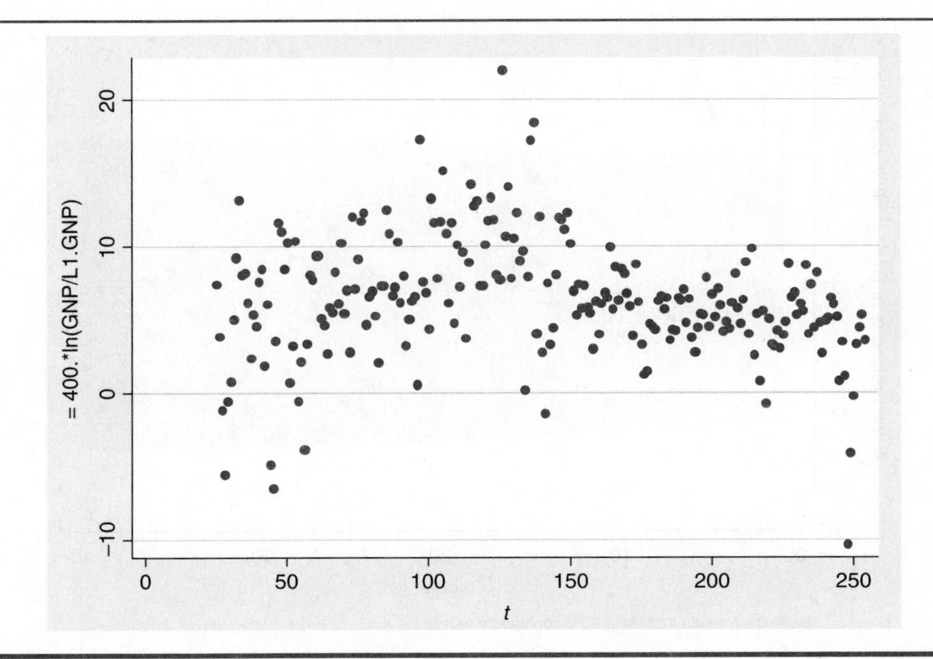

Figure 17-2b Time Plot of Annualized Quarterly Growth Rate in U.S. GNP from 1953I to 2010II

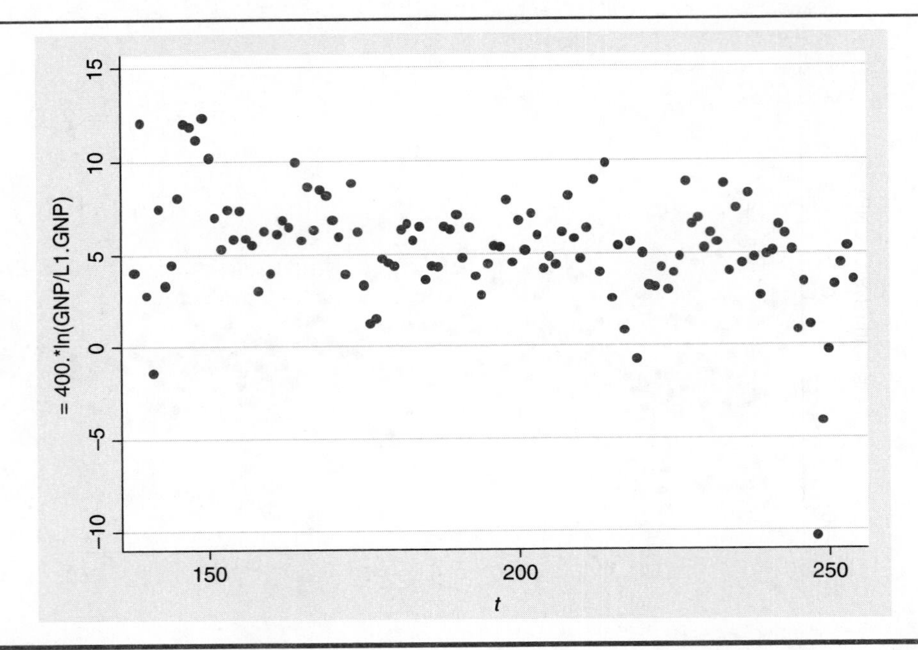

Figure 17-2c Time Plot of Annualized Quarterly Growth Rate in U.S. GNP from 1981II to 2010II

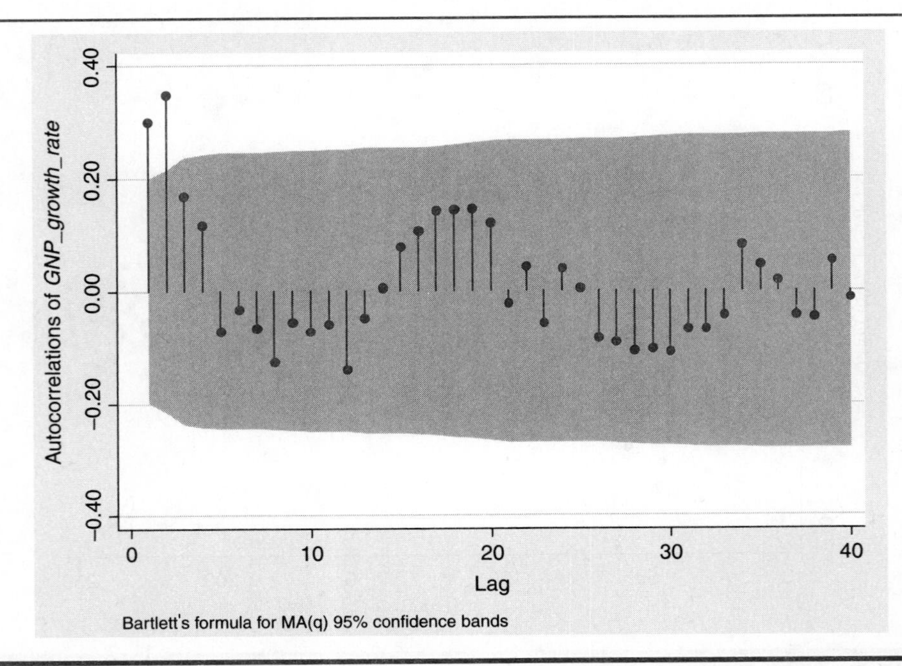

Figure 17-3 Sample Correlogram of Annualized Quarterly Growth Rate in U.S. GNP from 1981II to 2005II

correlogram will prove useful in specifying a linear time-series model for these data in Active Learning Exercise 17b.[35]

Before proceeding, however, it is useful to look at a few more sample correlogram examples. Each of these is based on a sample of 500 realizations of a time-series X_t generated from the zero-mean AR(1) model:

$$\begin{aligned} X_t &= \varphi_1 \quad X_{t-1} + U_t \\ &= 0.70\, X_{t-1} + U_t \end{aligned} \tag{17-15}$$

where $U_t \sim \text{NIID}(0, 1)$. This model is the same as the AR(1) model defined in Equation 13-11 of Section 13.4, only the parameter φ_0 has been set to zero so that X_t has zero mean.[36]

Figures 17-4a and 17-4b display a time-plot and sample correlogram of these data. The fairly strong serial correlation in X_t is, of course, reflected in the positive and statistically significant r_1, r_2, r_3, and r_4 estimates and in the positive correlations among the sampling errors of adjacent autocorrelation estimators at larger lags. The AR(1) model was analyzed in Section 13.4; referring

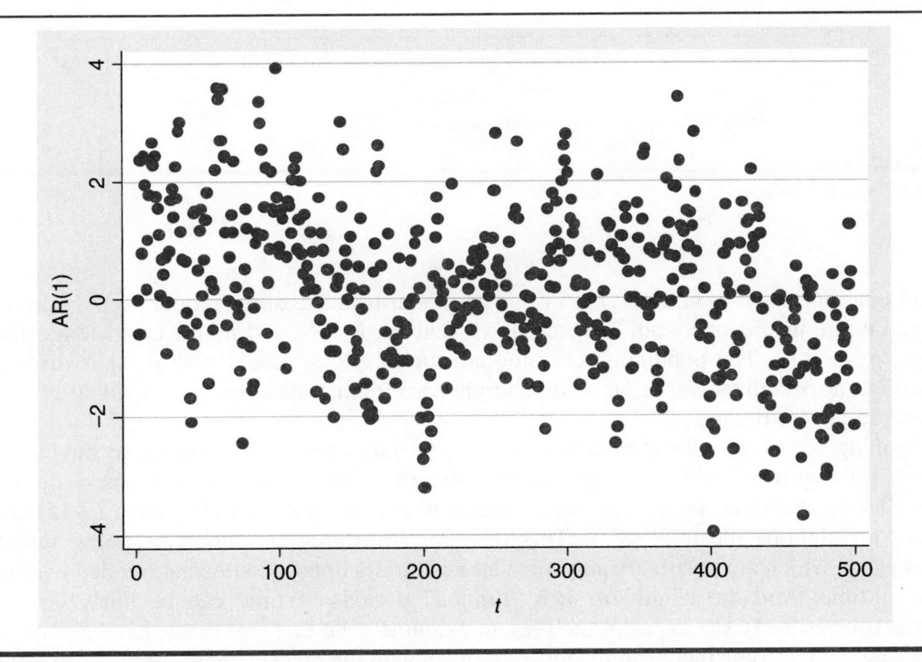

Figure 17-4a Time-Plot of AR(1) Generated Data

[35] This Active Learning Exercise is available at www.wiley.com/college/ashley. Note that the happiest solution to this apparent dilemma – sample length versus stable variance – would be to specify a theoretical model which *explains* the drop-off in the variance after 1981I. (This shift is called "The Great Moderation" in the macroeconomics literature, so a number of such models are no doubt already being fought over.) Such a model would not only allow the use of the entire sample (starting in 1953, at least) but also utilize this shift in the data to help estimate some of the key model parameters.

[36] This is the *un*conditional mean of X_t – i.e., $\mu = E[X_t] = \varphi_0/(1 - \varphi_1)$, from Equation 13-18 – which is distinct from the *conditional* mean of X_t. It was the conditional mean of X_t – which typically varies over time, because it is usually a function of x_{t-1}, x_{t-2}, etc. – whose optimality as a forecast of future values of X_t was discussed in Section 17.2.

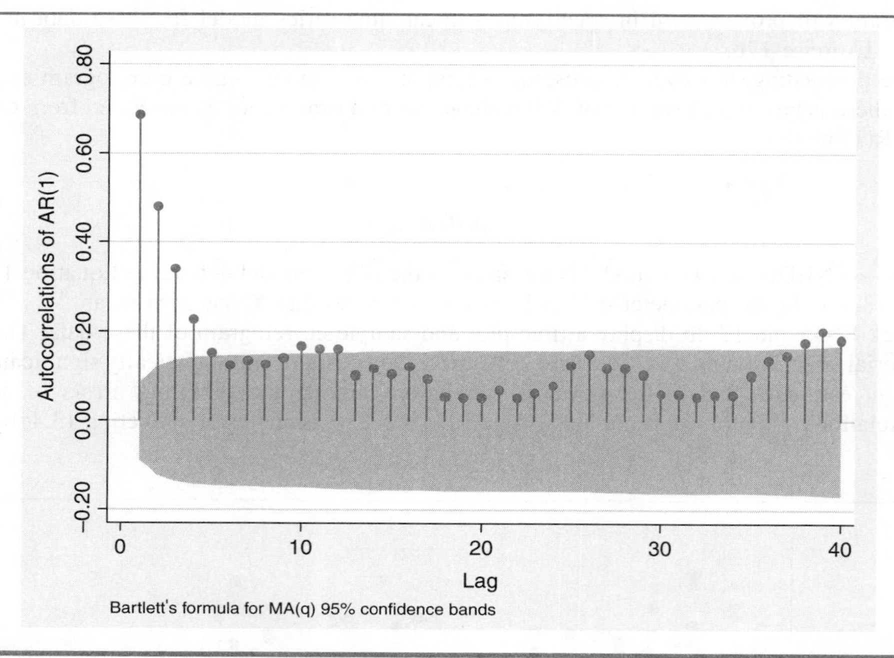

Figure 17-4b Sample Correlogram of AR(1) Generated Data

back to Equation 13-21, ρ_k equals $(.7)^k$ for this particular instance of the model, so the estimates r_1, r_2, r_3, and r_4 are just as one would expect, given that R_1, R_2, R_3, and R_4 are consistent estimators of ρ_1, ρ_2, ρ_3, and ρ_4. The population correlogram for an AR(p) model with $p \geq 1$ is discussed in Section 17.6; a specialized variation on the sample correlogram, designed to help identify the order p, is derived at that point.

Just looking at its time-plot in Figure 17-4a, many analysts might interpret X_t as having a slight (downward) linear trend, which becomes especially noticeable over the last 150 observations in the sample. Clearly, that is an artifact here, as these data were generated (from Equation 17-15) to have a constant (population) mean of zero. This data set illustrates an important point: covariance stationary data which are positively autocorrelated naturally appear somewhat trended over limited periods of time. And the length of such "limited" periods of time can be fairly large if the autocorrelation is fairly strong, as in the present example. The fact that these data have no overall trend at all would become increasingly apparent (even with the present degree of autocorrelation) as the length of the sample increases from its present value of 500 to 5,000 or 50,000 observations.

However, in any single realized time-series – even one which is 500 periods long – it is difficult to distinguish this weak (apparent) trend from the positive autocorrelation actually present. Indeed, "difficult" is putting it mildly: "practically impossible" is closer to the mark. For example, using this particular data set to estimate any regression model for X_t including a linear trend term will find a highly significant negative estimate for the coefficient on the trend term, even if one includes multiple lags of X_t in the regression equation, so as to allow for possible serial correlation in the model errors:[37]

[37] Including more lags (or using Newey-West standard error estimates) does not materially alter these results.

```
reg   ar1 t L1.ar1 l2.ar1 l3.ar1

      Source |       SS       df       MS              Number of obs =     497
-------------+------------------------------           F(  4,   492) =  119.24
       Model |  463.818212     4  115.954553           Prob > F      =  0.0000
    Residual |  478.461715   492  .972483161           R-squared     =  0.4922
-------------+------------------------------           Adj R-squared =  0.4881
       Total |  942.279927   496  1.89975792           Root MSE      =  .98615

------------------------------------------------------------------------------
         ar1 |      Coef.   Std. Err.      t    P>|t|     [95% Conf. Interval]
-------------+----------------------------------------------------------------
           t |  -.0011679   .0003358    -3.48   0.001    -.0018275   -.0005082
         ar1 |
         L1. |   .6575418   .0448045    14.68   0.000     .5695099    .7455736
         L2. |   .0005296   .0536117     0.01   0.992    -.1048064    .1058657
         L3. |  -.0163573   .0448947    -0.36   0.716    -.1045662    .0718516
       _cons |   .3415757   .0978928     3.49   0.001     .1492362    .5339152
------------------------------------------------------------------------------
```

Of course, the next set of 500 observations generated might appear to have a positive trend. Moreover, if one estimates a trend term in such a data set – i.e., one whose time-plot appears to be somewhat trended – then the coefficient on this trend term will be about as statistically significant as this one. A time-plot of a generated data set with 50,000 observations would likely have a less noticeable apparent trend than did this data set. On the other hand, because the sample is 10 times larger, an even smaller apparent trend observed in the time-plot might still appear to be statistically significant.

In actuality, of course, one does not get to generate one's data set over again. (Nor is it an effective modeling strategy to plan on petitioning an otherwise beneficent Deity for an additional 49,500 observations.) We must work with the data that we have. If these data are fairly autocorrelated, then it is quite likely that a time-plot of the data will appear to be somewhat trended, at least over sub-periods of the sample. And – just as in the present example – if a trend appears to be present in the time-plot, then a regression equation allowing for it will almost certainly find a statistically significant coefficient on the trend term, whether the data are actually covariance stationary or not. (Moreover, note that an even larger sample just makes this all worse, as a still-larger sample will merely cause a still-fainter apparent trend in the time-plot to be statistically significant.)

So how can one tell the difference in practice? One approach that would ordinarily help in detecting a regression coefficient which is actually zero but whose sample estimate appears to be statistically significant due to bad luck is to note that such coefficient estimates tend to be unstable over the course of the sample. One can test for that as part of the usual diagnostic checking framework. That isn't so helpful here because the sample time-plot has already revealed that the trend coefficient is not terribly unstable across the sample. (Otherwise, one would not be thinking that this time-series is trended in the first place!) A truly helpful tactic – which is particularly relevant for time-series analysis, but involves a good deal of trouble – is to ask whether the estimated model which includes the time trend is better able to forecast X_t in a post-sample period; tests to implement such comparisons are described below, in Section 18.5.[38]

Figures 17-5a and 17-5b display the time-plot and sample correlogram of the same data (generated using the AR(1) model of Equation 17-15), but now with an outlier introduced into the data set. Notice that the presence of the outlier notably diminishes the sizes of the sample autocorrelations at low lags (r_1, r_2, r_3, and r_4), but does not otherwise distort the sample correlogram.

Figures 17-6a and 17-6b display the time-plot and sample correlogram of these same AR(1) data, but now with a shift in the mean of the data introduced into the data set instead of an outlier. The

[38] One can still in this way reach an incorrect conclusion if one is so unlucky that the post-sample period by accident has a similar apparent trend: the risk of bad luck can only be quantified (using p-values), it cannot be eliminated.

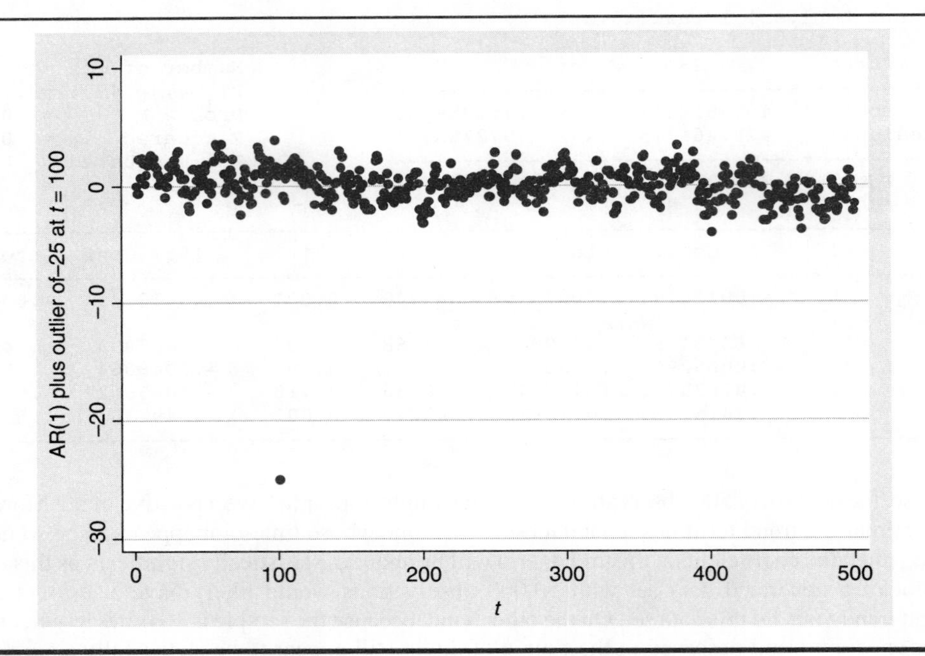

Figure 17-5a Time-Plot of AR(1) Generated Data Plus an Outlier

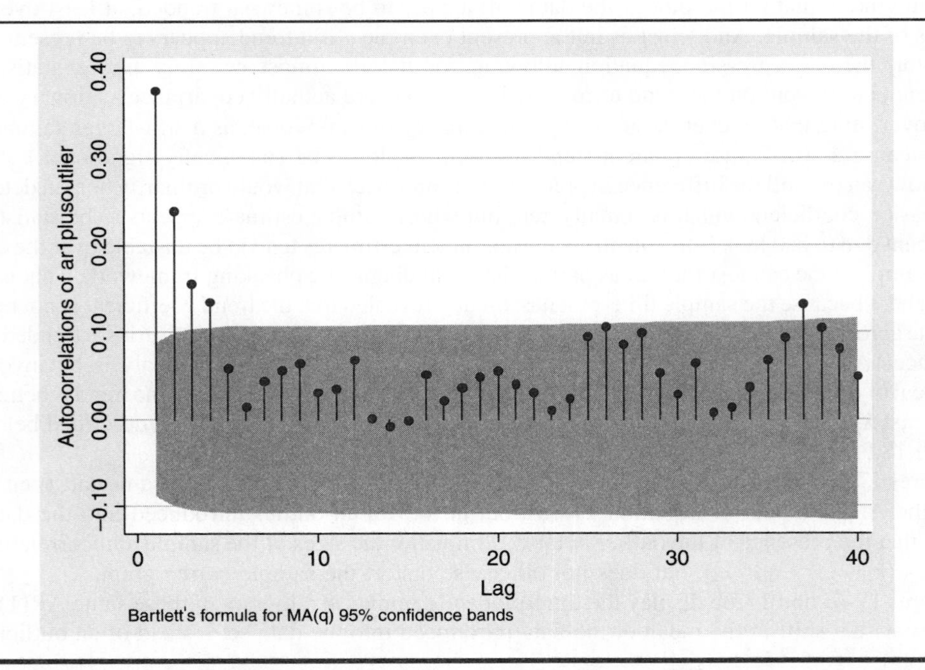

Figure 17-5b Sample Correlogram of AR(1) Generated Data Plus an Outlier

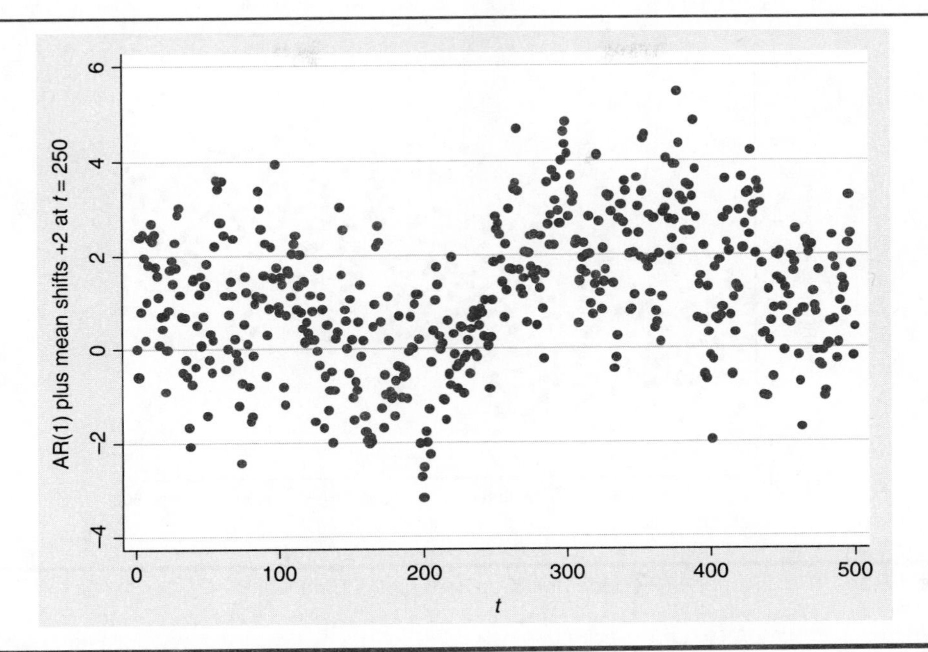

Figure 17-6a Time-Plot of AR(1) Generated Data Plus a Shift in the Mean

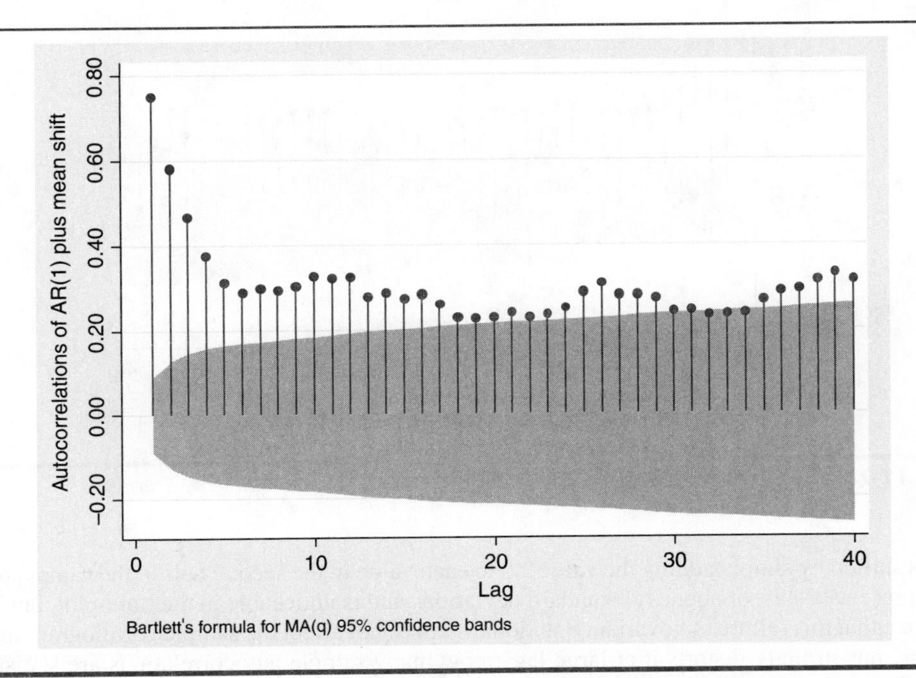

Figure 17-6b Sample Correlogram of AR(1) Generated Data Plus a Shift in the Mean

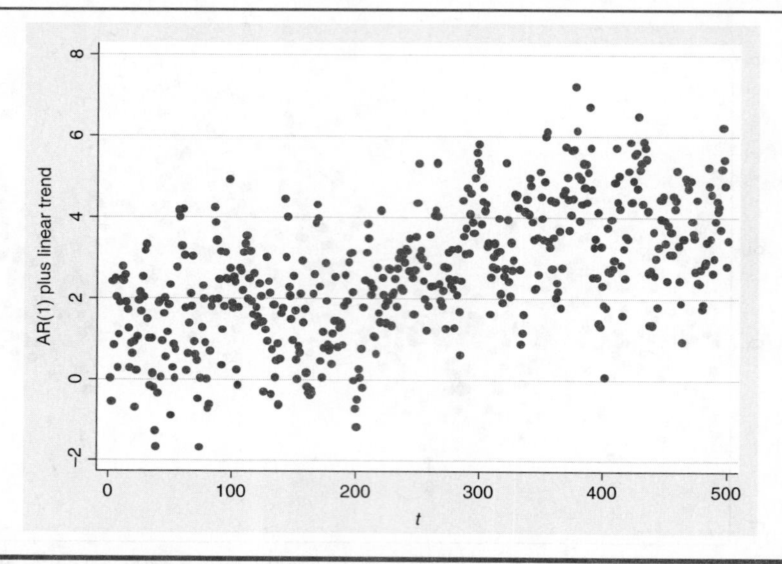

Figure 17-7a Time-Plot of AR(1) Generated Data Plus a Mild Time Trend

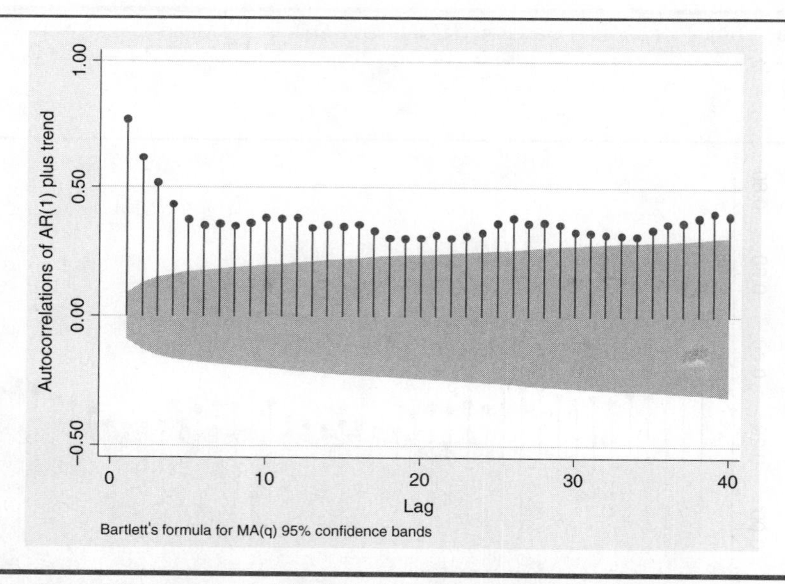

Figure 17-7b Sample Correlogram of AR(1) Generated Data Plus a Mild Time Trend

mean is shifted by simply adding the value 2.0 to each value in the second half of the sample period. This represents a shift of about 1.4 standard deviations and is noticeable in the time-plot, but barely so. Notice that this failure of covariance stationarity does not affect the sample correlogram much at low lags, but strongly distorts it at large lags: now many sample autocorrelations are statistically significant at most lags from 10 to 40. Introducing an actual, but modest, linear time trend into the data – Figures 17-7a and 17-7b – has a similar impact on the sample correlogram.

The main moral to be drawn from this last set of examples is this: it is the tail of the sample correlogram which is most sensitive to failures of covariance stationarity in the form of persistent changes in the mean, such as mean shifts and trends.[39] Fortunately, the tail of the sample correlogram is not its most important and informative part; this will become apparent after the specification of MA(q) and AR(p) models is discussed in Sections 17.5 and 17.6. First, however, it is necessary to introduce the twin of a polynomial in the lag operator and its inverse: this idea is crucial to understanding these two models and the relationship between them.

17.4 A POLYNOMIAL IN THE LAG OPERATOR AND ITS INVERSE: THE KEY TO UNDERSTANDING AND MANIPULATING LINEAR TIME-SERIES MODELS

Section 13.4 introduced the AR(1) model for a time-series and showed, in Equations 13-13 through 13-17, how it could be converted into an MA(∞) form which is superficially quite different, but actually equivalent. This MA(∞) form made it much easier to calculate the mean, variance, and autocorrelations for such a time-series generated by an AR(1) model. MA(q), AR(p), and related models for time-series will be examined in some detail in the sections to follow; the material in the present section shows how these models, too, can be inter-converted at will, using the concept of inverting a polynomial in what is called the "lag operator." This ability to convert one kind of time-series model into another is exceptionally useful because, as with the AR(1) model, what is challenging in one representation can be easy in the other.

The term "lag operator" sounds potentially difficult, but it merely consists of an explicit symbol representing the operation of lagging a time-series. The conventional notation for the lag operator is either the symbol L (for "lagging") or the symbol B (for "backshifting"); here, B is used. Thus, BX_t is just X_{t-1}. And applying B to BX_t is just B^2X_t, which is simply X_{t-2}.

A weighted sum of current and past values of X_t is called a "distributed lag" in X_t; a distributed lag in X_t can thus be written as a polynomial in B "operating" on X_t. Such a polynomial itself is frequently referred to as "lag structure." Equation 17-16 illustrates these concepts with a pth order polynomial in B:

$$
\begin{aligned}
\Omega(B)X_t &\equiv (\omega_0 B^0 + \omega_1 B^1 + \omega_2 B^2 + \omega_p B^p)X_t \equiv \sum_{i=1}^{p} \omega_i B^i \\
&= (1 + \omega_1 B + \omega_2 B^2 + \omega_p B^p)X_t \\
&= X_t + \omega_1 X_{t-1} + \omega_2 X_{t-2} + \omega_p X_{t-p}
\end{aligned}
\tag{17-16}
$$

Notice that, by convention, a uppercase letter (often Greek) is used to denote a polynomial in the lag operator and the corresponding lowercase letter is used (with an appropriate subscript) to denote each of the weights on the powers of B in the lag structure. Thus, the notation itself indicates that ω_3 – which stands for an ordinary number – is the coefficient on B^3 in a lag structure which would be denoted $\Omega(B)$.[40] The coefficient on B^0 (which has no actual effect on a time-series) is equal to one in a typical lag structure; that is why this coefficient (ω_0, in the present instance) is replaced by one in Equation 17-16, and – quite often – below.

For example, the one-period change in X_t can be written as $(1 - B)X_t$ in this notation. And an equally weighted average of a quarterly time-series over the previous year corresponds to the lag structure $\frac{1}{4}(B^0 + B + B^2 + B^3) = (\frac{1}{4} + \frac{1}{4}B + \frac{1}{4}B^2 + \frac{1}{4}B^3)$. The particular zero-mean AR(1) model of Equation 17-15 – i.e., $X_t = \varphi_1 X_{t-1} + U_t = 0.70\,X_{t-1} + U_t$ – provides an even more useful

[39] Indeed, this is the genesis of apparent "long memory" or "fractional integration" in time-series. See Footnote 18-1.

[40] Ω is the uppercase symbol for the last letter in the Greek alphabet, "omega." The corresponding lowercase symbol for omega is ω. Analogous pairs of uppercase and lowercase Greek letters which are frequently used in time-series analysis are (Γ, γ), (Θ, θ), (Φ, φ), and (Ψ, ψ).

example. Using the lag operator notation, it can be written as

$$\begin{aligned} \Omega(B)X_t &= U_t \\ (1+\omega_1 B)X_t &= U_t \\ (1-0.70\,B)X_t &= U_t \end{aligned} \tag{17-17}$$

where $U_t \sim \text{NIID}[0,1]$ and the parameter ω_1 in $\Omega(B)$ is clearly identical to minus parameter φ_1 in the AR(1) model.

Thus, a polynomial in the lag operator allows models involving distributed lags (i.e., lag structures) to be written more compactly. The real value in the concept arises, however, once one recognizes that a polynomial in the lag operator can have an inverse, defined as follows:

The Inverse of a Polynomial in the Lag Operator

The polynomial

$$\Lambda(B) \equiv \sum_{i=0}^{\infty} \lambda_i B^i$$

is $\Omega^{-1}(B)$, the inverse of the polynomial $\Omega(B)$, if and only if (17-18)

$$(a)\ \Lambda(B) \times \Omega(B) = 1 + 0B^1 + 0B^2 + 0B^3 + \ldots$$

and

(*b*) $|\lambda_i|$ approaches zero for sufficiently large values of *i*.

The inverse of $\Omega(B)$ is said "to exist" – so that this lag structure "has an inverse" – if and only if both conditions in Equation 17-18 hold. Strangely, as we will soon see, finding weights $\lambda_0, \lambda_1, \lambda_2, \lambda_3, \ldots$ such that condition (a) is satisfied is very easy; it is a bit more challenging to make sure ahead of time that the weights eventually die out, per condition (b).

Why is the inverse of a lag structure so useful? Supposing that $\Lambda(B) = \Omega^{-1}(B)$ exists, then one can multiply both sides of Equation 17-17 by it. This yields

$$\begin{aligned} \Lambda(B)\Omega(B)X_t &= \Lambda(B)U_t \\ \Omega^{-1}(B)\Omega(B)X_t &= \Lambda(B)U_t \\ X_t &= \Lambda(B)U_t \end{aligned} \tag{17-19}$$

where $U_t \sim \text{NIID}(0,1)$. Thus, the inverse of $\Omega(B)$ allows one to convert the AR(1) model of Equation 17-17 into the MA(∞) form of Equation 13-17 with no fuss whatsoever.[41] Indeed, one can let $\Omega(B)$ instead be a polynomial of *any* positive order *p* – with $\Omega(B)X_t$ still equal to U_t, a mean-zero and serially uncorrelated time-series, so that X_t is generated by an AR(*p*) model. In that case Equation 17-19 still shows that $\Omega^{-1}(B)$ gives all the weights for the MA(∞) form of X_t – at least, so long as $\Omega^{-1}(B)$ exists.

Thus, the two key questions are: Does $\Lambda(B) = \Omega^{-1}(B)$ exist? And – if it does – how can the weights $\lambda_0, \lambda_1, \lambda_2, \ldots$ be calculated? This second question turns out to be very simple to answer, so it is addressed first.

[41] The MA(∞) Model is first defined at Equation 13-17 in Section 13.4, but it is more thoroughly discussed below in Section 17.5. Note that a good deal of the "fuss" in Equations 13-12 to 13-17 is due to the fact that what amounts to the inverse of the relevant lag structure is explicitly obtained there – and will be again, as an example later in this section – whereas it has so far only been treated symbolically here.

Let $\Omega(B)$ be a given finite-order polynomial in the lag operator. The order of this polynomial will be called "p" here and the term "given" means that the weights $\omega_1 \ldots \omega_p$ are known numbers. (The weight ω_0 is taken, as is usual, to be one.) From part (a) of the definition of $\Omega^{-1}(B)$ given in Equation 17-18, the weights λ_0, λ_1, λ_3, (and so forth) defining the polynomial $\Lambda(B)$ must be such that the multiplying the polynomial $\Lambda(B)$ times the polynomial $\Omega(B)$ yields the very simple polynomial, $1B^0 + 0B^1 + 0B^2 + 0B^3 + \ldots$. Writing this out more explicitly:

$$\begin{aligned}(\lambda_0 B^0 + \lambda_1 B^1 + \lambda_2 B^2 + \lambda_3 B^3 + \ldots) \times (B^0 + \omega_1 B^1 + \omega_2 B^2 + \cdots + \omega_p B^p) \\ = (1B^0 + 0B^1 + 0B^2 + 0B^3 + \ldots)\end{aligned} \tag{17-20}$$

Multiplying out the two polynomials in the left-hand side of Equation 17-20, note that the coefficient on B^0 in the polynomial that results is just λ_0. Thus, the coefficient λ_0 itself must equal one, the coefficient on B^0 in the polynomial on the right-hand side of Equation 17-20. Similarly, the terms involving B^1 in the resulting polynomial on the left-hand side are just $\lambda_0\omega_1 B^1$ and $\lambda_1 B^1$. As λ_0 is now known to be one, this result implies that $\omega_1 + \lambda_1$ must be equal to the coefficient of B^1 in the polynomial on the right-hand side of the Equation 17-20: i.e., $\omega_1 + \lambda_1$ must be equal to zero. Hence, λ_1 must equal $-\omega_1$. Similarly, once one starts writing out the terms in the product indicated on the left-hand side of Equation 17-20, it is evident that the resulting coefficient on B^2 is just $\omega_2 + \lambda_1\omega_1 + \lambda_2$. Therefore, $\omega_2 + \lambda_1\omega_1 + \lambda_2$ must be zero, since the coefficient on B^2 in the polynomial on the right-hand side of Equation 17-20 is zero. Hence, λ_2 must be equal to $-\omega_2 - \lambda_1\omega_1$.

Summarizing and extending this reasoning – and writing out the resulting equations for the particular case where $p = 4$, so that ω_i equals zero for $i > 4$–

$$\begin{aligned}
\omega_1 + \lambda_1 &= 0 \\
\omega_2 + \lambda_1\omega_1 + \lambda_2 &= 0 \\
\omega_3 + \lambda_1\omega_2 + \lambda_2\omega_1 + \lambda_3 &= 0 \\
\omega_4 + \lambda_1\omega_3 + \lambda_2\omega_2 + \lambda_3\omega_1 + \lambda_4 &= 0 \\
\lambda_1\omega_4 + \lambda_2\omega_3 + \lambda_3\omega_2 + \lambda_4\omega_1 + \lambda_5 &= 0 \\
\lambda_2\omega_4 + \lambda_3\omega_3 + \lambda_4\omega_2 + \lambda_5\omega_1 + \lambda_6 &= 0 \\
\lambda_3\omega_4 + \lambda_4\omega_3 + \lambda_5\omega_2 + \lambda_6\omega_1 + \lambda_7 &= 0
\end{aligned} \tag{17-21}$$

Each of these equations allows one to calculate one value of λ_j. Moreover, if one sets λ_0 equal to one and λ_j equal to zero for $j < 0$, then all of these equations have exactly the same form:

$$\lambda_j = -\omega_1\lambda_{j-1} - \omega_2\lambda_{j-2} - \omega_3\lambda_{j-3} - \omega_4\lambda_{j-4} \quad \text{for all } j > 1 \tag{17-22}$$

Hence, in an obvious extension, where $\Omega(B)$ is a pth-order instead of a fourth-order polynomial, these equations can all be written as

$$\lambda_j = -\omega_1\lambda_{j-1} - \omega_2\lambda_{j-2} - \omega_3\lambda_{j-3} - \ldots\ \omega_p\lambda_{j-p} \quad \text{for all } j > 1 \tag{17-23}$$

where λ_0 equals one and λ_j is set to zero for j equal to $-1, -2, \ldots 1-p$.

Equation 17-23 can be easily be programmed into a spreadsheet.[42] Thus, the coefficients which make up the inverse lag polynomial – $\Lambda(B)$ – are very easy to obtain numerically. In the context of these

[42] This calculation only requires one spreadsheet column. Enter the value zero in this column for the first *1-p* cells and enter the value one in the next cell. Now move one cell down and use Equation 17-23 to create a formula for this cell; that formula will calculate λ_1. Finally, "fill down" from this cell to produce the values of λ_2, λ_3, and so forth.

numerical calculations it is straightforward to determine whether or not the inverse of $\Omega(B)$ exists: $\Lambda(B) = \Omega^{-1}(B)$ "exists" if and only if the magnitudes of these calculated coefficients become negligible as j becomes sufficiently large. This is very plain to see – one way or the other – when one looks at such a spreadsheet. Exercises 17-5 through 17-8 illustrate this calculation for several simple examples.

But how can one know whether or not the inverse of $\Omega(B)$ exists – i.e., that these $|\lambda_j|$ values will eventually decay to zero as j increases – in general, without specifying particular numerical values for the lag structure weights $\omega_1 \dots \omega_p$? This question turns out to be rather easily answered, because Equation 17-23 is a particular instance of what is called a "linear difference equation" and the form of the solutions to such equations is well known:

$$\lambda_j = c_1\left(\frac{1}{v_1}\right)^j + c_2\left(\frac{1}{v_2}\right)^j + \dots + c_p\left(\frac{1}{v_p}\right)^j \quad \text{for all } j \geq 1 \tag{17-24}$$

Here $c_1 \dots c_p$ are particular constants – determined by the conditions that λ_0 is one and that $\lambda_{-1}, \lambda_2, \dots, \lambda_{1-p}$ are all zero – and $v_1 \dots v_p$ are the roots of the polynomial equation

$$\omega_p z^p + \omega_{p-1} z^{p-1} + \omega_{p-2} z^{p-2} + \dots + \omega_2 z^2 + \omega_1 z + 1 = 0 \tag{17-25}$$

in the ordinary algebraic variable, z. This polynomial is called the "characteristic polynomial" for Equation 17-23; its roots are simply the values of z for which Equation 17-25 is satisfied. As with any pth order polynomial, Equation 17-25 will have at most p distinct roots, some of which may be complex-valued if p exceeds one.

From the form of the solution for λ_j given in Equation 17-24, the value of $|\lambda_j|$ will eventually decay to zero as j increases – regardless of the values of $c_1 \dots c_p$ – if and only if all p roots of this characteristic polynomial are greater than one in magnitude. In contrast, $|\lambda_j|$ will blow up as j increases if any of these roots is less than one in magnitude. And the value of $|\lambda_j|$ will approach a constant if all of the roots are greater than or equal to one in magnitude, but at least one of them is exactly one.[43] Thus, the inverse $\Omega(B)$ exists only if all p of these roots exceed one in magnitude.[44]

It is easy to confirm that the expression for λ_j in Equation 17-24 does indeed provide solutions for the difference equation of Equation 17-23 if and only $v_1 \dots v_p$ are the roots of the polynomial in Equation 17-25; this is done in Exercise 17-4. But it is only easy to explicitly solve Equation 17-24 for its roots in the two special cases where p equals either one or two.[45]

Where p equals one, Equation 17-25 reduces to

$$\omega_1 z + 1 = 0 \tag{17-26}$$

which has the single root $-1/\omega_1$. Thus, in this case λ_j equals $c_1\,(-\omega_1)^j$. Since λ_0 equals one, this implies that c_1 must equal one. Note that, since ω_1 equals $-\varphi_1$, this result yields the same MA(∞) form for the AR(1) model as was derived in Equation 13-17 in Section 13.4 and the same restriction on φ_1: it must be less than one in magnitude.

The other analytically tractable setting is the special case where p equals two. The characteristic polynomial defined in Equation 17-25 in this case reduces to

$$\omega_2 z^2 + \omega_1 z + 1 = 0 \tag{17-27}$$

[43] This is the source of the term "unit root" used in Sections 13. 4 and 14.3 to describe integrated – I(1) or "random walk" – time-series; this topic will be addressed more deeply as part of the discussion of integrated time-series in Section 18.1.

[44] Sometimes this is expressed in terms of all p roots lying "outside of the unit circle" because the roots are not necessarily all real-valued.

[45] Analytic expressions can be found for the roots of cubic and quartic polynomials also, but they are too complicated to yield any useful insights.

which, per the usual formula for the roots of a quadratic polynomial equation, has roots

$$z_{root} = \frac{-\omega_1 \pm \sqrt{\omega_1^2 - 4\omega_2}}{2\omega_2} \tag{17-28}$$

These two roots may both exceed one in magnitude, in which case the inverse $\Lambda(B)$ exists, or they may not – it depends on the values of ω_1 and ω_2. Box and Jenkins (1976, p. 58) state that the inverse will exist if and only if the three conditions

$$\begin{aligned} -\omega_2 - \omega_1 &< 1 \\ -\omega_2 + \omega_1 &< 1 \\ |\omega_2| &< 1 \end{aligned} \tag{17-29}$$

are met, but Equation 17-28 makes it easy enough to just calculate the two roots. Both roots are clearly complex-valued if ω_1^2 is less than $4\omega_2$; in that case the expression for λ_j given in Equation 17-24 can be rewritten in terms of sines and cosines and the values of λ_j oscillate as j increases.[46]

In summary, then, it is easy enough to characterize whether or not the inverse of a particular pth degree lag structure exists: it exists if and only if all p roots of the corresponding characteristic polynomial exceed one in magnitude. But the trouble involved in finding those roots is substantial for values of p greater than two.

In any case, explicitly solving for these roots is never necessary in practice if what one wants is the inverse of a particular lag structure: in that case one need only substitute the given values for $\omega_1 \ldots \omega_p$ into Equation 17-23 and numerically calculate the λ_j weights. If these weights eventually decay to zero, then the inverse $\Lambda(B)$ exists. (And this is it!) If these calculated weights explode as j increases, then the inverse clearly does not exist. And if the calculated weights approach a constant, then the inverse does not exist and there is at least one "unit root" in the characteristic polynomial. Thus, the analytic solution of the difference equation (involving the roots of the characteristic polynomial) is unnecessary in order to actually compute the inverse of $\Omega(B)$. On the other hand, it is very helpful in understanding why and how the inverse might fail to exist, and therefore be uncomputable.

The inverse of the pth order polynomial $\Phi(B)$ defining an AR(p) model for a time-series allows one to easily convert it into an equivalent moving average model. The material in the next section makes it clear why moving average models are important and useful.

17.5 IDENTIFICATION/ESTIMATION/CHECKING/FORECASTING OF AN INVERTIBLE MA(q) MODEL

The AR(1) model for a time-series, first introduced in Equation 13-11 of Section 13.4 and then used repeatedly as an example, makes a great initial illustration of a time-series model. And the AR(p) models are attractive in general, simply because they are so clearly related to the regression models described in Chapters 1 through 12.

But the most natural and fundamental linear model for a time-series analysis is actually the "moving average process" or "MA(q) model," first introduced as the MA(∞) model in

[46] Actually doing this involves rewriting a complex-valued z_{root} in the form re^{is}, where r is the magnitude of z_{root}, s is called its "phase," and i denotes $\sqrt{-1}$. The sines and cosines enter into this because e^{is} can also be written as $\cos(s) + i\sin(s)$. The algebra of complex numbers is a bit beyond the scope of the present treatment, but the reader can consult Pemberton and Rau (2007, Chapter 23) for an accessible treatment. Pemberton, M., and N. Rau (2007), *Mathematics for Economists*, Manchester University Press: Manchester.

Equation 13-17 of Section 13.4:[47]

The Moving Average – MA(q) or MA(∞) – Model for a Time-Series

Y_t is generated by a moving average process of order q – or, equivalently, Y_t follows an MA(q) model – if and only if

$$Y_t \sim \text{MA}(q) \;\Leftrightarrow\; Y_t = \Theta(B)U_t \;\Leftrightarrow\; Y_t = \sum_{j=0}^{q} \theta_j U_{t-j}$$

where the "innovation" U_t is serially uncorrelated, with mean zero and bounded variance (σ_u^2), and where $\Theta(B)$ is a polynomial of order q in the lag operator. The order q may be taken to be unboundedly large, in which case Y_t is an MA(∞) process and the lag operator polynomial is usually denoted $\Psi(B)$ instead of $\Theta(B)$: (17-30)

$$Y_t \sim \text{MA}(\infty) \Leftrightarrow Y_t = \Psi(B)U_t \Leftrightarrow Y_t \sum_{j=0}^{\infty} \psi_j U_{t-j}$$

In this case it must be assumed that $\sum_{j=0}^{\infty} \psi_j^2$ is bounded.

An MA(q) or MA(∞) process is called "invertible" – and is applicable to forecasting Y_t – if and only if $\Theta^{-1}(B)$ or $\Psi^{-1}(B)$ exists, so that Y_t can also be written in AR(∞) form, as a weighted sum of past values of Y_t, with eventually declining weights. (From Equations 17-20 to 17-25 in Section 17.4, this is equivalent to requiring that all q roots of the polynomial equation $\Theta(z) = 0$ lie outside of the unit circle.)

Notice that no intercept is included in either the MA(q) or the MA(∞) process defined in Equation 17-30; unless otherwise stated, it will be assumed throughout the rest of this chapter that Y_t is a covariance stationary process whose (consequently time-invariant) mean has already been eliminated by subtracting off its sample mean; of course, one could alternatively include an intercept in the model. Also, the assumption that $\sum_{j=0}^{\infty} \psi_j^2$ is bounded in the definition of an MA(∞) process given above is necessary because, as is shown in Equation 17-32, the variance of the time-series Y_t is just $\sigma_u{}^2$ times this sum.

The "invertibility" property of an MA(q) or MA(∞) process mentioned in Equation 17-30 – and in the title of this section – is necessary so as to ensure that Y_t can be rewritten in what is called "AR(∞)" form, as either $\Theta^{-1}(B)Y_t = U_t$ or as $\Psi^{-1}(B)Y_t = U_t$. In that case – and only in that case – can $E[Y_t | Y_{t-1} = y_{t-1}, Y_{t-2} = y_{t-2}, Y_{t-3} = y_{t-3} \ldots]$ be represented as a weighted sum of $Y_{t-1}, Y_{t-2}, y_{t-3}, \ldots$ with weights eventually decaying to zero for sufficiently large lags. It will become apparent later in this section that this invertibility property is both a necessary and a sufficient condition for the model to yield sensible expressions for M_h, the conditional-mean h-step-ahead forecast of Y_{N+h}. AR(∞) and AR(p) models will be discussed in the next section, however: the focus of the present section is on MA(∞) and MA(q) models.

The primacy of moving average models arises from a foundational result originally due to Wold (1938) and reproven in Sargent (1987, pp. 285–90):[48]

Wold's Decomposition

Any covariance stationary time-series Y_t can be written in the form of an MA(∞) process plus κ_t, an uncorrelated linearly-deterministic time-series. (17-31)

[47] The terms "process" and "model" are used interchangeably, here and below.

[48] See also Hamilton (1994, p. 109); Wold, H. (1938), *A Study in the Analysis of Stationary Time-Series*, Almqvist and Wiksell: Uppsala; Sargent, T. J. (1987), *Macroeconomic Theory*, Academic Press: Boston.

The "linearly-deterministic" component κ_t in Equation 17-31 can be ignored here; the essence of Wold's result is that *any* covariance stationary time-series can be exactly represented as an MA(∞) process.[49] Wold's Decomposition does not guarantee that this representation is unique, and, indeed, it is not: in addition to a unique invertible MA(∞) representation, there are also a multiplicity of non-invertible MA(∞) representations for a time-series.[50] But the existence of a unique invertible MA(∞) representation for a time-series is hugely important: it implies that, for any covariance stationary time-series, there always exists at least one linear model – the AR(∞) model corresponding to this invertible MA(∞) model – which exactly represents the time-series as a linear function of its own past, plus a serially uncorrelated model error, or "innovation."[51]

The MA(∞) process is extremely easy to analyze because its "innovations" – $U_t, U_{t-1}, U_{t-2} \ldots$ – are, by definition, serially uncorrelated. For example, if $Y_t \sim$ MA(∞), then the variance of Y_t is

$$\begin{aligned}
\text{var}(Y_t) &= E\left[(Y_t - E[Y_t])^2\right] = E\left[\left(\sum_{j=0}^{\infty}\psi_j U_{t-j}\right)^2\right] \\
&= E\left[\sum_{i=0}^{\infty}\psi_i U_{t-i}\sum_{j=0}^{\infty}\psi_j U_{t-j}\right] \\
&= E\left[\sum_{i=0}^{\infty}\sum_{j=0}^{\infty}\psi_i\psi_j U_{t-i}U_{t-j}\right] \\
&= \sum_{i=0}^{\infty}\sum_{j=0}^{\infty}\psi_i\psi_j E\left[U_{t-i}U_{t-j}\right] \\
&= \sum_{i=0}^{\infty}E\left[U_{t-i}^2\right]\psi_i^2 = \sigma_u^2\sum_{i=0}^{\infty}\psi_i^2
\end{aligned} \tag{17-32}$$

where the double sum reduces to a single sum because U_t is serially uncorrelated. This result for the variance of Y_t explains why it must be assumed in Equation 17-30 that $\sum_{i=0}^{\infty}\psi_i^2$ is bounded. Also, note that it is only possible for $\sum_{i=0}^{\infty}\psi_i^2$ to have a finite value if $|\psi_i|$ eventually decays to zero as i becomes arbitrarily large.

[49] Technical Note: This linearly deterministic time-series κ_t is assumed to be uncorrelated at all lags with U_t and perfectly forecastable as a linear function of y_{t-1}, y_{t-2}, etc. That is, $E[\kappa_t | Y_{t-1} = y_{t-1}, Y_{t-2} = y_{t-2}, \ldots]$ – the conditional mean of κ_t – is exactly equal to κ_t itself. No one has ever come up with an example of such a κ_t – theoretical or empirical – which is not hopelessly artificial; consequently, this component does not seem worthy of much attention here. For example, the weighted sum of trigonometric functions posited as an example of a linearly deterministic time-series by Sargent (1987, p. 289) is formally valid, but only a theoretical curio. (If the trigonometric weights $(a_1, b_1) \ldots (a_n, b_n)$ in his example are constant over time, then it seems bizarre to take them as unknown i.i.d. variates except in a very short sample. Whereas, to the extent that these weights are known, then the posited linearly deterministic time-series induces time variation in the mean of the series, which is hence no longer covariance stationary.)

[50] Exercise 17-10g will make this point clear in the simple context of an MA(1) process.

[51] Another way of putting this is to say that the Wold result guarantees the existence of a polynomial in the lag operator – often also called a "linear filter" – with eventually declining weights, which reduces Y_t to the serially uncorrelated innovation series, U_t. Because they are serially uncorrelated, such innovations are not *linearly* forecastable from their own past. Note, however, that this result does not preclude the possibility that there exists a *nonlinear* function of powers of the lag operator – a "nonlinear filter" – which reduces Y_t to a serially *independent* innovation series that is *completely* unforecastable from its own past. This topic is taken up in Section 18.6.

Similarly,

$$\begin{aligned}
\text{cov}(Y_t, Y_{t-k}) = \text{cov}(Y_{t+k}, Y_t) &= E\left[\sum_{i=0}^{\infty}\psi_i U_{t-i+k}\sum_{j=0}^{\infty}\psi_j U_{t-j}\right] \\
&= E\left[\sum_{m=-k}^{\infty}\psi_{m+k}U_{t-m}\sum_{j=0}^{\infty}\psi_j U_{t-j}\right] \\
&= E\left[\sum_{m=-k}^{\infty}\sum_{j=0}^{\infty}\psi_{m+k}\psi_j U_{t-m}U_{t-j}\right] \qquad (17\text{-}33) \\
&= \sum_{m=-k}^{\infty}\sum_{j=0}^{\infty}\psi_{m+k}\psi_j E\left[U_{t-m}U_{t-j}\right] \\
&= \sigma_u^2\sum_{j=0}^{\infty}\psi_{j+k}\psi_j
\end{aligned}$$

where i has been replaced by $m+k$ in the left-hand sum of the first line in Equation 17-33 and, because U_t is serially uncorrelated, only the terms where $m=j$ in the double-sum are non-zero.

Consequently, the correlogram for the MA(∞) process can be expressed rather simply in terms of the weights $\psi_1, \psi_2, \psi_3, \ldots$ as

$$\text{corr}(Y_t, Y_{t-k}) = \rho_k = \frac{\sum_{j=0}^{\infty}\psi_{j+k}\psi_j}{\sum_{j=0}^{\infty}\psi_j^2} \qquad (17\text{-}34)$$

Note that this result implies that the autocorrelation at lag k of any covariance stationary time-series must eventually decay to zero as the value of lag k increases, since the finite variance of Y_t implies that the MA(∞) weights $\psi_1, \psi_2, \psi_3, \ldots$ must decay to zero. (Otherwise $\sigma_u^2 \sum_{i=0}^{\infty} \psi_i^2$ cannot possibly be bounded.)

Because its autocorrelations must become negligible at sufficiently large lags, it follows that any covariance stationary process can be arbitrarily well approximated by a finite-order MA(q) process, by simply choosing q sufficiently large that $\psi_{q+1}, \psi_{q+2}, \psi_{q+3}$ (and so forth) are essentially negligible.

Making that approximation, then, suppose that Y_t is generated by the finite-order MA(q) process

$$Y_t = \Theta(B)U_t \Leftrightarrow Y_t = \Theta(B)U_t = \sum_{j=0}^{q}\theta_j U_{t-j} \qquad (17\text{-}35)$$

This MA(q) process is clearly a special case of the MA(∞) process; in particular, it corresponds to where the MA(∞) weights for Y_t are $\psi_j = \theta_j$ for $j \le q$ and $\psi_j = 0$ for $j > q$. Consequently, using Equation 17-34, the population correlogram for any such MA(q) process is

$$\begin{aligned}
\text{corr}\,(Y_t, Y_{t-k)} = \rho_k &= \frac{\sum_{j=0}^{q-k}\theta_{j+k}\theta_j}{\sum_{j=0}^{q}\theta_j^2} \qquad \text{for } k \le q \qquad (17\text{-}36) \\
&= 0 \qquad \text{for } k > q
\end{aligned}$$

where the terms in each sum which are now zero have been dropped. The population correlogram $\rho_1, \rho_2, \rho_3, \ldots, \rho_k, \ldots$ for any covariance stationary time-series therefore eventually decays to become negligible for a sufficiently large value of k.

Thus, any covariance stationary time-series can be approximated arbitrarily well by an MA(q) process – whose population correlogram cuts off completely for lags greater than q – so long as q is chosen to be sufficiently large.[52]

The selection ("identification") of the order q of an MA(q) model for Y_t is thus very straightforward if N is sufficiently large that r_k is a good estimate of ρ_k – and also sufficiently large that the Bartlett result for the asymptotic sampling distribution of R_k given in Equation 17-11 is useful.[53] Assuming that q is surely no larger than some value m – set sufficiently large that the observed sample correlogram has clearly decayed to the point where the r_k values for larger values of k are non-zero solely due to sampling errors – this Bartlett result, as used in practice, is that R_k is asymptotically distributed,

$$\sqrt{N}(R_k - \rho_k) \xrightarrow{d} N\left[0, \sum_{i=1}^{m} r_i^2\right] \tag{17-37}$$

Thus, the – under the assumptions that the Y_t are normally distributed, that N is sufficiently large, and that ρ_k is zero for all values of $k \geq m$ – the realized autocorrelation estimate (r_k) for any value of $k \geq m$ can be compared to $\sqrt{(1/N) \sum_{i=1}^{m} r_i^2}$, the estimated standard error from Equation 17-37. Equivalently, one could use the estimated 95% confidence interval given in Equation 17-13.

And the null hypothesis that a group of j r_k estimates (all for k greater than the posited value for q) are all zero can be tested by constructing a "portmanteau" or "Q" test statistic. In this case, $Q \equiv N \sum_{i=q+1}^{q+j} r_i^2$ is asymptotically distributed $\chi^2(j)$ under the null hypothesis that $\rho_{q+1} \ldots \rho_{q+j}$ are all zero, so the relevant rejection p-value is just the probability that a $\chi^2(j)$ variate exceeds the observed value of Q by chance.[54]

This operation of using the sample data to select a tentative value for q, the order of the MA(q) model, is called "model identification" in time-series analysis.[55] Note that model identification in the time-series analysis framework is thus completely data-based. But this model identification is only tentative, pending the estimation and diagnostic checking of a model. These topics (and forecasting Y_t) are developed for this tentatively-identified MA(q) model in the remainder of this section.

Foreshadowing the remainder of this chapter, this same set of topics (identification, estimation, diagnostic checking, and forecasting) is then taken up with regard to related – AR(p) and AR(p, q) – models in Sections 17.6 and 17.7. At that point the Box-Jenkins modeling algorithm is

[52] Not every population correlogram that becomes zero for lags larger than q corresponds to a meaningful MA(q) process, however: see Exercise 17-10e and 17-10f, which explores the MA(1) process in this regard.

[53] The Bartlett result also requires normality, so if $Y_1 \cdots Y_N$ are distributed in a highly non-normal way, then no value of N is sufficiently large as to guarantee that the Bartlett standard error and confidence interval estimates are valid.

[54] Such portmanteau test results are frequently quoted, but the reader is cautioned that they are really a bit misguided, as they treat $(r_{q+1})^2 \ldots (r_{q+j})^2$ symmetrically. Surely, if the value of q has been set too low, this error is most likely due to a failure to recognize that the time-series is actually also autocorrelated at lag $q+1$ or at the seasonal lag. For example, the seasonal lag is four for quarterly data, 12 for monthly data, etc. "Q" is the standard notation for this test statistic, so it is used here, despite the fact that (as a sample realization) it really should be denoted with a lowercase letter; using q instead would make the notation for this realized test statistic indistinguishable from the typical notation for the order of an MA(q) model.

[55] The reader is warned that the term "identification" is used differently elsewhere in econometric analysis, to specify that a particular model parameter uniquely minimizes the fit of model to the data. In fact, it will become apparent in Exercise 17-10g that the parameter θ_1 in the MA(1) model is not "identified" in this sense.

summarized for the entire class of models considered in this chapter: linear models for a single, covariance stationary time-series. The Box-Jenkins algorithm is then extended (in Section 18.1) to a time-series which needs to be first-differenced in order to be covariance stationary. Section 18.2 describes a worked example of the whole procedure, using data on the U.S. Treasury Bill rate; Active Learning Exercises 17b, 18a, and 18b (available at www.wiley.com/college/ashley) provide opportunities to apply these techniques oneself. The rest of Chapter 18 then surveys a selection of more advanced topics in time-series analysis, including seasonal adjustment, multivariate modeling, the testing of post-sample model forecasting accuracy (Granger-causality testing), and nonlinear modeling.

Returning to the MA(q) model, the estimation of the parameters $\theta_1 \dots \theta_q$ in an MA(q) model appears to be very easy in one sense, but is a bit fraught in another. MA(q) model parameter estimation looks (and, often, is) very easy in practice, simply because the necessary numerical procedures are already conveniently programmed into most econometric software. In Stata, for example, the command "arima ydat, arima(0,0,4)" estimates an MA(4) model for the sample data on the variable called "ydat". This routine can (and usually does) promptly produce consistent estimates of $\theta_1 \dots \theta_q$ and σ_u^2, so long as the value of q is set sufficiently high. On the other hand, the nonlinear least squares procedures used for estimating MA(q) models do not necessarily converge at all and can converge to a non-invertible model; such estimation procedures (and their potential problems) are examined in Exercise 17-11 for the particular case of an MA(3) model. Generally speaking, these estimation problems arise only when the MA(q) order is set higher than necessary or when the true process generating the data is close to being non-invertible.[56]

Once the model parameters, $\theta_1, \theta_1, \dots \theta_q$ have been estimated, the next step is to diagnostically check this estimated MA(q) model. The first question to ask is whether the fitting errors appear to be covariance stationary and serially uncorrelated. This is done by instructing the estimation software to save the fitting errors under some particular variable name and examining their time plot and sample correlogram, as in Section 17.3.[57] In essence, this sample correlogram is checking whether this tentative identification of the value of q was chosen to be sufficiently large: if it was not, then the fitting errors will still be serially correlated. One checks whether the value of q was tentatively set overlarge by comparing $\hat{\theta}_q$ to its estimated standard error, so as to test the null hypothesis that θ_q is zero. Obviously, one adjusts this tentative model identification accordingly, if need be. This diagnostic checking procedure is illustrated using monthly data on the U.S. Treasury Bill rate in Section 17.9.

Note, however, that the meaningfulness of these in-sample diagnostic checks is subverted to some extent by the fact that they are applied to models estimated using the same data which were used to estimate the sample correlogram from which this tentative model identification – i.e., the value of q – was obtained in the first place. The only way to avoid this dilemma is to reserve some data for use in model evaluation at the very outset. Thus, while the entire sample is generally used in obtaining what sensibly appears to be a covariance stationary data set, a restricted "identification/ estimation" sample should be used to compute the sample correlogram used to identify the model and to estimate the model parameters. This procedure leaves a post-sample model evaluation data set otherwise untouched.

[56] See Equation 17-30, and the text following it, regarding the definition of invertibility. Most MA(q) estimation routines will fail to converge rather than return parameter estimates corresponding to a non-invertible model. If in doubt, however, it is easy enough to check this oneself, by simply using the recursion method given in Equations 17-20 to 17-23 of Section 17.4 to calculate the inverse of the estimate of $\Theta(B)$: if the estimated model is non-invertible, then the calculated weights in this inverse will explode rather than decay.

[57] In Stata, the "predict" command works just as one might expect after the successful execution of the "arima" command: "predict residname, r" saves the fitting errors under the name "residname".

This reserved data set is variously called a "post-sample period," a "model prediction period," or a "hold-out" sample; its chosen length is nowadays usually denoted by the symbol P. Thus, having let N denote the length of the sample used for in the model identification and estimation procedure described above, the total data set must be of length $N+P$. Since increasing P by one observation necessarily decreases N by one observation, these two uses for the total data set obviously compete. It should be noted at the outset that there is no completely objective way to set a value for P, the length of the post-sample prediction period. Still, surprisingly enough, a good deal can nevertheless be said about how to make this decision in a reasonable fashion.

Regarding the first use of the sample data: the foregoing material has already described how to use N sample observations to identify and estimate an MA(q) process for Y_t. Clearly, N must be set sufficiently large that sample estimators of the autocorrelations $\rho_1, \rho_2, \ldots, \rho_m$ and of the model parameters $\theta_1 \ldots \theta_q$ are useful.[58] Moreover, the resulting sample estimates are valueless without usably small (and usably precisely estimated) estimates of their sampling variances; this clearly requires a *minimum* of 60 to 80 sample observations. On the other hand, note that sampling variances of almost all estimators (and, in particular, of $r_1, r_2, \ldots, r_m$ and of $\hat{\theta}_1 \ldots \hat{\theta}_q$), generally decline with sample length like $1/N$. Therefore, their estimated standard errors – which are what actually matter – decline with sample length proportionally to $1/\sqrt{N}$, at least for large N. The marginal usefulness of additional sample observations is thus declining as N increases: the first 80 observations are obviously crucial, and the next 80 observations are extremely useful, but the 80 observations increasing N from 320 to 400 are clearly not so important.

Regarding the second use of the sample data – to provide P post-sample Y_t observations for model evaluation – the considerations which apply to choosing a value for P are actually quite similar. But this requires a bit of discussion, as follows.

The last portion of this section will describe how to use an estimated MA(q) model to obtain a sequence of estimated one-step-ahead conditional mean (M_1) forecasts of Y_t in this post-sample period and – crucially – confidence interval estimates quantifying their accuracy. The widths of those confidence intervals will depend on how strong the MA(q) model is – i.e., on σ_u^2, which depends inversely on the R^2 of the estimated MA(q) model – but those widths do not depend on the size of P itself. However, any post-sample evaluation of the worth of this particular model for Y_t must, one way or another, involve comparing the average size of the P post-sample forecasting errors which it makes to the average size of the corresponding P forecasting errors made by some *other* model.

A "squared-error" loss function on forecasting errors is usually assumed – for lack of a credibly more appropriate criterion – so the "average size" of the P post-sample forecasting errors is almost always quantified by their mean square error or MSE. Mean square error was discussed in Section 3.6 and formally defined in Equation 3-20. There – in Equation 3-23 – the MSE of an estimator of the mean of a random variable was decomposed into the sum of its sampling variance and the square of its bias. The mean squared forecast error decomposes in exactly the same way into the sum of the forecast error variance and the square of the mean forecast error. Comparing the sizes of the P post-sample forecasting errors made by a tentatively identified MA(q) model to those of an "other" model usually amounts, then, to comparing the MSE of the errors made by this MA(q) model to the MSE of the errors made by an "other" model.

This "other" model might be an MA($\tilde{q}$)model with $\tilde{q} \neq q$, because the identification of the right value for q is in doubt. (That is where this discussion of setting a value for P started.) But a different value for q is not the only alternative to one might want to consider, however. This "other" model might be an MA(0) model – a "naive" model, acting as a benchmark for whether the MA(q) model

[58] None of these estimators are BLU or efficient: they are at best consistent. In particular, the estimators of $\rho_1, \rho_2 \ldots \rho_m$ are consistent so long as the data are covariance stationary; the estimators of $\theta_1 \ldots \theta_q$ are consistent also, but only if the value of q is set sufficiently high.

was worthwhile at all. Or this "other" model might be an AR(p) or an ARMA(p,q) model, as described in Sections 17.6 and 17.7. Or it might be some other kind of model altogether – such as a multivariate model (Section 18.4) or a nonlinear model (Section 18.6).

Regardless of the form this "other" model, takes, however, the essential task at hand practically always amounts to the same thing: a test of whether the mean square error (MSE) of the forecasts from one model exceed those of another, based on a set of P realized forecast errors from each model. For each model, this MSE is just the variance of the forecast errors plus the square of the mean error, so this task is closely related to that of using two samples, each of length P, to test for a difference in variance.

Recall that testing a null hypothesis with respect to the ratio of the population variances from which two samples are drawn was covered in Section 4.9 and it hinged on the sampling distribution of the variance estimator for each sample. That testing context (and the test obtained there, as Equation 4-60) was greatly simplified, however, because the observations from each sample were assumed to be NIID and the two samples were also assumed independent of one another. None of those assumptions can be maintained for the two sequences of P post-sample forecast errors generated by two different models for Y_t; consequently, testing whether one model provides smaller post-sample mean square forecasting errors than another is considerably more challenging, even aside from the fact that these MSEs involve the mean forecast errors as well as the variances of the forecast errors. If the "other" model is a multivariate model, then a comparison of the average size of the post-sample forecast errors made by this model to that of the analogous errors made by an MA(q) model has an interpretation in terms of the Granger-causality concept introduced in Section 12.2. Consequently, a description of the formal tests implementing this comparison is delayed to Section 18.5, which discusses how to implement the Granger-causation idea empirically. Here, this testing is discussed in general, intuitive terms.

An adequate minimum value for P, then, is equivalent to the amount of data required for the validity and effectiveness of such a test, comparing the post-sample MSE of the forecasts from one model to that of another. This value is not knowable in general. For errors which are roughly normally distributed, however, monte carlo simulations in Ashley (2003) indicate that – generally speaking – P needs to be on the order of 100 (or more) in order for an observed 20% difference in the post-sample MSE to be statistically significant at the 5% level; values of P less than, say, 40 appear unlikely to be very useful in practice.[59]

On the other hand, as with almost any kind of statistical testing, the effectiveness of these post-sample tests rises only as the square root of the sample length – P, in this context. Consequently, the marginal usefulness of post-sample observations – like estimation sample observations – is declining. Thus, again, the first 80 observations are crucial, and next 80 observations are very useful; but the improvement (in the ability to distinguish the post-sample MSE of one model from that of another) from increasing P from, say, 320 to 400 is not so important.

At first glance, these considerations would imply that one ought to set P equal to N and use half of one's total data set for model identification/estimation and the other half for post-sample testing. And that is a defensible viewpoint. In practice, however, most analysts are more comfortable setting P to an "adequate" value – which they often underestimate to be only 20 to 40 observations – and reserving the remainder of the total sample for model identification and estimation purposes. In view of the fact that the model identification is explicitly mined from the N sample observations, an adequate post-sample model evaluation check is extremely important in this modeling context. On the other hand, if N is not also set to an "adequate" value, then one will end up diagnostically checking a model whose specification was, perhaps unnecessarily, distorted. A reasonable compromise is probably to set P in the range 100 to 150, so long as $N + P$ *is* sufficiently large as to also

[59] Ashley, R. (2003), "Statistically significant forecasting improvements: how much out-of-sample data is likely necessary?" *International Journal of Forecasting 19*, 229–39.

yield N at least that large, and to start scrimping on P where the total sample $(N+P)$ is noticeably less than 300, so as to keep the value of N at least equal to 80 to 100. Clearly, where the total sample is much less than 150, effective post-sample model comparison/evaluation is not really feasible.

That said, once the model has been identified, estimated, and respecified (if need be) so as to pass its in-sample diagnostic checks, it is a good idea to subject the model to a post-sample diagnostic check, based on its ability to predict the observed post-sample data $y_{N+1} \dots y_{N+P}$.

The best such post-sample check for, say, a particular estimated MA(q) model is to compute the sequence of one-step-ahead forecast errors from the model

$$
\begin{aligned}
\hat{u}_{N+1}^{\text{MA}(q)} &\equiv \left(f_{N+1,1}^{\text{MA}(q)} - y_{N+1}\right) \\
\hat{u}_{N+2}^{\text{MA}(q)} &\equiv \left(f_{N+2,1}^{\text{MA}(q)} - y_{N+2}\right) \\
&\dots \\
\hat{u}_{N+P}^{\text{MA}(q)} &\equiv \left(f_{N+P,1}^{\text{MA}(q)} - y_{N+P}\right)
\end{aligned}
\tag{17-38}
$$

one for each of the P post-sample periods. The average squared value of these forecast errors – $(1/p)\sum_{t=N+1}^{N+P}\left(\hat{u}_t^{\text{MA}(q)}\right)^2$ – can then be compared to the average squared value of the errors made by some sort of "naive" model for Y_t – most typically, an MA(0) model. Here it is assumed that the sample mean $\left(\frac{1}{N}\sum_{t=1}^{N} y_t\right)$ has already been subtracted from the sample data, so that these "naive" forecasts are all zero – i.e., $f_{N+1,1}^{\text{naive}} = 0 \dots f_{N+P,1}^{\text{naive}} = 0$. Thus, the average squared forecast errors from this "naive" model is just $(1/P)\sum_{t=N+1}^{N+P} y_t^2$.

The analysis of the prediction errors made by the Bivariate Regression Model (Equation 5-10), the Multiple Regression Model (Equation 9-1), and even the Dynamic Multiple Regression Model (Equation 14-3) usually take explicit account of the sampling errors made by the OLS estimators of the model parameters.[60] In contrast, when model prediction errors are analyzed in the context of time-series analysis, it is usually assumed that N is sufficiently large that these sampling errors in the estimated model coefficients can be ignored. This convention is adopted here; partly so as to adhere to common practice and partly so as to keep the exposition as simple as possible. This is why Equation 17-38 is couched in terms such as $f_{N+1,1}^{\text{MA}(q)}$ rather than $\hat{f}_{N+1,1}^{\text{MA}(q)}$ and it is also why $\frac{1}{N}\sum_{t=1}^{N} y_t$ is not being distinguished from $E(Y_t)$ in the description of the "naive" forecasts.

In practice, however, most every analyst is well aware that N is hardly ever as large as we would like. Consequently, although N is routinely taken to be sufficiently large that it makes sense to use r_k as a surrogate for ρ_k, and even to use the expression for the Bartlett asymptotic sampling distribution of r_k as a reasonable approximation to its actual sampling distribution, it is common practice to update the parameter estimates (of $\theta_1 \dots \theta_q$) used in calculating $f_{N+1,1}^{\text{MA}(q)} \dots f_{N+P,1}^{\text{MA}(q)}$ in Equation 17-38 so that the model parameter estimates used in actually calculating $f_{N+j,1}^{\text{MA}(q)}$ are estimated using sample data up through period $N+j$.[61] For clarity of exposition, however, this complication – and (as noted

[60] For example, see the expressions for the variance of the regression model prediction errors given in Section 8.4 and in Appendix 9.1.

[61] Specialized software for working with time-series models will take care of such estimation updating automatically. Stata does not; one would have to implement this in a Stata do file using a program loop.

earlier) the sampling variation in the estimators of the model parameters altogether – is ignored in the description which follows.

In addition – although not included in the definitions of the MA(q) and MA(∞) processes in Equation 17-30 – it is conventional in the analysis of the forecasts obtained from these kinds of models to assume that the model errors ("innovations") are normally distributed.[62] Thus, from this point on, $\theta_1 \ldots \theta_q$ and $\sigma_u{}^2$ are taken to be known – based on a tacit assumption that N is sufficiently large that sampling errors in the estimators of these parameters can be neglected – and U_t is taken to be NIID(0, $\sigma_u{}^2$).

Finally, again for clarity of exposition, the remaining discussion will focus on the explicit special case where q equals three; this value of q is large enough to illustrate the important points, yet sufficiently small that the expressions are not overly cluttered. Thus, the MA(q) model definition given in Equation 17-30 implies that the model generating Y_t in this special case is

$$\begin{aligned} Y_t &= \Theta(B)U_t \quad \text{with} \quad U_t \sim \text{NIID}(0, \sigma_u^2) \\ &= \sum_{j=0}^{3} \theta_j U_{t-j} \\ &= U_t + \theta_1 U_{t-1} + \theta_2 U_{t-2} + \theta_3 U_{t-3} \end{aligned} \tag{17-39}$$

where $\theta_1 \ldots \theta_3, \sigma_u^2$, and the P post-sample observations, $y_{N+1} \cdots y_{N+P}$, are all taken as known.

From the discussion following Equation 17-30 – which defines the term "invertible" with respect to an MA(q) model – the MA(3) model of Equation 17-39 is invertible if and only if $\Theta^{-1}(B)$, the inverse of $\Theta(B)$ exists. And, per the material in Section 17.4 on obtaining the inverse of any particular lag structure, $\Theta^{-1}(B)$ exists if and only if there is a polynomial $\tilde{\Phi}(B) = \Theta^{-1}(B)$ such that $\tilde{\Phi}(B)\Theta^{-1}(B) = 1$ *and* the weights $\tilde{\varphi}_j$ in $\tilde{\Phi}(B)$ eventually decay to zero as j increases without bound. The recursion equation derived as Equation 17-23 allows one to easily calculate weights $\tilde{\varphi}_j$ in $\tilde{\Phi}(B)$; and the analysis in Equations 17-24 to 17-29 shows that these weights will eventually decay to zero if and only if all three roots of the characteristic polynomial equation $\theta_3 z^3 + \theta_2 z^2$ $\theta_1 z + 1 = 0$ exceed one in magnitude.[63]

Presuming, from here on in this example, that this MA(3) process is, in fact, invertible, so that the weights $\tilde{\varphi}_j$ in $\tilde{\Phi}(B) = \Theta^{-1}(B)$ do in fact eventually decay to negligible values, then the MA(3) process given in Equation 17-39 can be written in AR(∞) form as

$$\begin{aligned} \tilde{\Phi}(B)Y_t &= \tilde{\Phi}(B)\Theta(B)U_t \quad \text{with} \quad U_t \sim \text{NIID}(0, \sigma_u^2) \\ &= \Theta^{-1}(B)\Theta(B)U_t \\ &= U_t \end{aligned} \tag{17-40}$$

This AR(∞) model can be written out as

$$\begin{aligned} \tilde{\Phi}(B)Y_t &= U_t \quad \text{with} \quad U_t \sim \text{NIID}(0, \sigma_u^2) \\ Y_t + \tilde{\varphi}_1 Y_{t-1} + \tilde{\varphi}_2 Y_{t-2} + \ldots &= U_t \\ Y_t &= -\tilde{\varphi}_1 Y_{t-1} - \tilde{\varphi}_2 Y_{t-2} + \cdots + U_t \\ Y_t &= \varphi_1 Y_{t-1} - \varphi_2 Y_{t-2} + \cdots + U_t \end{aligned} \tag{17-41}$$

[62] This assumption primarily only impacts the critical point (1.96) used in the 95% confidence intervals for Y_{N+h} derived below; one would want to modify that appropriately for substantially non-normally distributed data.

[63] For this particular case, one would substitute $p = 3$, $\omega_1 = \theta_1$, $\omega_2 = \theta_2$, and $\omega_3 = \theta_3$ into Equation 17-23 and obtain λ_1, λ_2, λ_3, ... from the recursions; λ_1, λ_2, λ_3, ... are precisely the weights $\tilde{\varphi}_1, \tilde{\varphi}_2$, and $\tilde{\varphi}_2$, ... in the polynomial $\tilde{\Phi}(B) = \Theta^{-1}(B)$.

where the weights on the lagged values of Y_t eventually decay to negligible values so long as the MA(3) model was invertible.

Note that the last step in Equation 17-41 is only included so as to introduce the standard nomenclature for the "AR(∞) weights": these are defined so that the autoregressive coefficients multiplying the lagged values of Y_t in equations do not collect a negative sign when moved over to the right-hand side of the equation. Unfortunately, this notational convention somewhat complicates the expression for $\Phi(B)$ – when the AR(∞) model is written as $\Phi(B)Y_t = U_t$ – because $\Phi(B)$ must then be defined as $(1 - \varphi_1 B - \varphi_2 B^2 - \varphi_3 B^3 - \ldots)$. The only defense for this notational complication is that AR(p) models had been in use for many years prior to the invention of the lag operator technology for more conveniently expressing and manipulating lag structures; this notational infelicity is mentioned here only so that the reader is forewarned – and hopefully thereby forearmed – against it.

Either way in which the coefficients in $\Phi(B)$ are notated, Equation 17-41 makes it clear that Y_t generated by this – indeed, by any – MA(q) process can always be rewritten as a linear function of its own past values, but that Y_t so expressed will depend substantially on its own distant past unless this MA(q) process is invertible.

Consequently, it is only possible to forecast Y_t sensibly in terms of its own past using the MA(3) process given in Equation 17-39 if this MA(3) process is invertible. Therefore – as noted above – it is assumed that the particular MA(3) process being consider here in fact *is* invertible. This presumption is, of course, easy to check: if the model is not invertible, then the numerical recursion for obtaining the weights in $\Theta^{-1}(B)$ will fail to decay.

The next step in obtaining $f_{N,h}$ – the forecast of Y_{N+h} which can be made at time period N – is to use Equations 17-39 and 17-41 to derive the probability distribution of Y_{N+h}, conditional on the observed data $y_1 \ldots y_N$. The density function for this conditional distribution was denoted $g_c(Y_{N+h}|Y_1 = y_1, Y_2 = y_2, \ldots, Y_N = y_N)$ in Section 17.2 – just before its population mean (M_h, the conditional mean of Y_{N+h}) was defined, in Equation 17-4.

Evaluating Equations 17-39 and 17-41 for period $t = N + h$,

$$
\begin{aligned}
Y_{N+h} &= U_{N+h} + \theta_1 U_{N+h-1} + \theta_2 U_{N+h-2} + \theta_3 U_{N+h-3} \\
U_t &\sim \text{NIID}(0, \sigma_u^2)
\end{aligned}
\tag{17-42}
$$

and, equivalently,

$$
\begin{aligned}
Y_{N+h} &= \varphi_1 Y_{N+h-1} + \varphi_2 Y_{N+h-2} + \varphi_3 Y_{N+h-3} + \varphi_3 Y_{N+h-3} + \cdots + U_{N+h} \\
U_t &\sim \text{NIID}(0, \sigma_u^2)
\end{aligned}
\tag{17-43}
$$

Since Equation 17-42 expresses Y_{N+h} as a weighted sum of normally distributed variates, Y_{N+h} is evidently itself normally distributed, regardless of whether or not it is conditioned on observed values of Y_N, Y_{N-1}, Y_{N-2}, etc. Therefore, $g_c(Y_{N+h}|Y_1 = y_1, Y_2 = y_2, \ldots, Y_N = y_N)$ is just the usual normal density function (as specified in Equation 2-47) here, and is thus completely characterized by its mean (M_h) and its variance (σ_h^2).

From Theorem 17-1 of Section 17.2, the optimal forecast of Y_{N+h} is equal to M_h when the loss function on forecast error is proportional to the squared error, and also in the cases given in Theorem 17-2. In contrast, for an asymmetric loss function on forecast errors of the bilinear form considered in Theorem 17-5, the optimal forecast of Y_{N+h} is the $\alpha\%$ fractile of the conditional distribution of Y_{N+h}. This fractile is just the value of Y_{N+h} such that $\alpha\%$ of the area under the density function $g_c(Y_{N+h}|Y_1 = y_1, Y_2 = y_2, \ldots, Y_N = y_N)$ lies to the left of this value. Theorem 17-5 specifies exactly how the value of α yielding the optimal forecast depends on the relative slopes of the loss function for positive versus negative errors.[64] In practice, of course, M_h is almost always used, as – even though most forecast error loss functions are in fact asymmetric – one rarely knows much about this asymmetry. Be that as it may, since $g_c(Y_{N+h}|Y_1 = y_1,\, Y_2 = y_2, \ldots, Y_N = y_N)$ is completely determined by M_h and σ_h^2, any of these other forecasts can be fairly easily computed once M_h and σ_h^2 are obtained. The calculation of M_h is addressed first.

At the outset, note that M_h is the *conditional* mean of Y_{N+h} – the expected value of Y_{N+h} conditional on $(y_N,\, y_{N-1},\, y_{N-2}, \ldots)$, which are the observed values of the random variables $(Y_N,\, Y_{N-1},\, Y_{N-2}, \ldots)$. Hence, in general, M_h is a function of $(y_N,\, y_{N-1},\, y_{N-2}, \ldots)$.[65] In contrast, the unconditional mean of Y_{N+h} is just $E(Y_{N+h})$. This unconditional mean is a constant because Y_t is covariance stationary; in fact, Equation 17-42 makes it immediately plain that this constant value of $E(Y_{N+h})$ is zero.

Once one is conditioning on the values of $(Y_N,\, Y_{N-1},\, Y_{N-2}, \ldots)$, this set of random variables can be treated as fixed, and equal to the corresponding set of observed values, $(y_N,\, y_{N-1},\, y_{N-2}, \ldots)$. What about U_t? Solving Equation 17-41 for U_t, it equals $(\tilde{\varphi}_1 Y_{t-1} + \tilde{\varphi}_2 Y_{t-2} + \tilde{\varphi}_3 Y_{t-3} + \cdots)$. Consequently, U_N can be taken to be fixed, at the value u_N equal to $(\tilde{\varphi}_1 Y_{N-1} + \tilde{\varphi}_2 Y_{N-2} + \tilde{\varphi}_3 Y_{N-3} + \cdots)$; note that, as usual, the lowercase letter is being used to denote the (fixed) realization of the variable denoted by an uppercase letter. Similarly, U_{N-1} can be taken to be fixed, at the value u_{N-1} equal to $(\tilde{\varphi}_1 y_{N-2} + \tilde{\varphi}_2 y_{N-3} + \tilde{\varphi}_3 Y_{N-4} + \cdots)$, and so forth. In contrast, the "future" values of U_t – i.e., $(U_{N+1},\, U_{N+2},\, U_{N+3}, \ldots)$ are all still random variables, each of which (from Equation 17-39) is independently distributed as an $N(0, \sigma_u^2)$ variate.

Thus, conditioning on the observed values of $(Y_N,\, Y_{N-1},\, Y_{N-2}, \ldots)$, the future values of the time-series – i.e., $(Y_{N+1},\, Y_{N+2},\, Y_{N+3}, \ldots)$ – can be written

$$\begin{aligned}
Y_{N+1} &= U_{N+1} + \theta_1 u_N + \theta_2 u_{N-1} + \theta_3 u_{N-2} \\
Y_{N+2} &= U_{N+2} + \theta_1 U_{N+1} + \theta_2 u_N + \theta_3 u_{N-1} \\
Y_{N+3} &= U_{N+3} + \theta_1 U_{N+2} + \theta_2 U_{N+1} + \theta_3 u_N \\
Y_{N+4} &= U_{N+4} + \theta_1 U_{N+3} + \theta_2 U_{N+2} + \theta_3 U_{N+1} \\
Y_{N+5} &= U_{N+5} + \theta_1 U_{N+4} + \theta_2 U_{N+3} + \theta_3 U_{N+2}
\end{aligned} \tag{17-44}$$

Clearly, the expressions for Y_{N+h} will continue this pattern for all values of h which are greater than three. It follows immediately that, for Y_t generated by this particular MA(3) model, the values of the h-step-ahead conditional-mean forecasts of Y_t at time period N (i.e., $f_{N,h} = M_h$) and the variances of the consequent forecast errors (i.e., $\text{var}(Y_{N+h} - M_h) = \sigma_h^2$) are as given in Table 17-1.[66]

Evidently, this MA(3) process provides nontrivial forecasts only up to three steps ahead. Moreover, looking at Table 17-1, the pattern for a more general moving average model is obvious: if Y_t is generated by an MA(q) process and forecast using the conditional mean, then it can be forecast, to some degree, q steps ahead. As the conditional-mean forecast (M_h) becomes less and less

[64] Note that the optimal shrinkage of M_h toward zero in Theorem 17-4 does not occur here, since the sampling variance in the estimators of θ_1, θ_2, and θ_3 is being taken as negligible.

[65] Since N is assumed large – and the MA(q) model is assumed invertible – the distinction between "$Y_N,\, Y_{N-1},\, Y_{N-2}, \ldots$" and "$Y_N,\, Y_{N-1},\, Y_{N-2}, \ldots Y_1$" is negligible here.

[66] Recall, from Equation 2-19, that subtracting a fixed constant (such as M_h) from a random variable does not change its variance; thus, the forecast error variance is the same as the conditional variance of Y_{N+h}, σ_h^2.

Table 17-1 Conditional-Mean Forecast of Y_{N+h} and Its Error Variance {For $Y_t \sim MA(3)$, as given in Equation 17-39}[a]

h	$f_{N,h} = M_h$	$\sigma_h^2 \equiv \text{var}(Y_{N+h} - M_h)$
1	$\theta_1 u_N + \theta_2 u_{N-1} + \theta_3 u_{N-2}$	$\text{var}(U_{N+1}) = \sigma_u^2$
2	$\theta_1 u_N + \theta_3 u_{N-1}$	$\text{var}(U_{N+2} + \theta_1 U_{N+1}) = \sigma_u^2(1+\theta_1^2)$
3	$\theta_3 u_N$	$\text{var}(U_{N+3} + \theta_1 U_{N+2} + \theta_2 U_{N+1}) = \sigma_u^2(1+\theta_1^2+\theta_2^2)$
4	0	$\text{var}(U_{N+4} + \theta_1 U_{N+3} + \theta_2 U_{N+2} + \theta_3 U_{N+1}) = \sigma_u^2(1+\theta_1^2+\theta_2^2+\theta_3^2)$
$h \geq 4$	0	$\text{var}(U_{N+h} + \theta_1 U_{N+h-1} + \theta_2 U_{N+h-2} + \theta_3 U_{N+h-1}) = \sigma_u^2(1+\theta_1^2+\theta_2^2+\theta_3^2)$

[a]Because the conditioning in M_h is on the observed realizations of $(Y_N, Y_{N-1}, Y_{N-2}, \ldots)$, the realizations of $(U_N, U_{N-1}, U_{N-2}, \ldots)$ – denoted $(u_N, u_{N-1}, u_{N-2}, \ldots)$ – are observed also, whereas $U_t \sim \text{NIID}(0, \sigma_u^2)$ for all $t > N$.

distinct from the unconditional-mean forecast, the variance of the forecast errors (σ_h^2) rises – becoming equal to the variance of Y_t itself for values of h greater than q.[67]

This same set of results is reflected in confidence intervals for Y_{N+h}: if, as is typical practice, the model errors are assumed to be normally distributed, then the conditional distribution of Y_{N+h} is normal also, with mean M_h and variance $\sigma_h^2 = \sigma_u^2 \sum_{j=0}^{h-1} \theta_j^2$. Consequently, a 95% confidence interval for Y_{N+h} is $M_h \pm 1.96\sqrt{\sigma_h^2}$.[68]

17.6 IDENTIFICATION/ESTIMATION/CHECKING/FORECASTING OF A STATIONARY AR(p) MODEL

From Wold's Decomposition (Equation 17-31), any covariance stationary time-series Y_t can be expressed as an MA(∞) process, $Y_t = \Psi(B)U_t$. Moreover, from the expression for the variance of an MA(∞) process derived in Equation 17-32, the weights in $\Psi(B)$ must eventually decline in order for $\text{var}(Y_t)$ to be bounded. If, in addition, this MA(∞) process is invertible, then an inverse for $\Psi(B)$ exists, with – necessarily – eventually declining weights.[69]

Letting this inverse be denoted $\Phi(B)$ – as is customary – the existence of $\Psi^{-1}(B)$ implies that any invertible MA(∞) process can alternatively be expressed as the AR(∞) process, defined as follows:

[67] The general formulas for $Y_t \sim \text{MA}(q)$ are that M_h equals $\sum_{j=1}^{q-h+1} \theta_j u_{N-j+1}$ and that $\sigma_h^2 = \text{var}(Y_{N+h}) = \sigma_u^2 \sum_{j=0}^{h-1} \theta_j^2$; these can be easily verified by writing them out explicitly for small values of q.

[68] One of the reasons U_t is typically assumed to be normally distributed is that the derivation of 95% confidence intervals otherwise becomes substantially more complicated. Weighted sums of normally distributed random variables are normally distributed, but this property does not carry over to most other distributions.

[69] Recall that the definition of the inverse of a polynomial in the lag operator (Equation 17-18) requires that the weights in the inverse eventually decay to zero as the lag increases without bound.

The Autoregressive – AR(p) or AR(∞) – Model for a Time-Series

Y_t is generated by an autoregressive process of order p – or, equivalently, Y_t follows an AR(p) model – if and only if

$$Y_t \sim \text{AR}(p) \quad \Leftrightarrow \quad \Phi(B)Y_t = U_t \quad \Leftrightarrow \quad Y_t = \sum_{j=1}^{p} \varphi_j Y_{t-j} + U_t$$

where the "innovation" U_t is serially uncorrelated, with mean zero and bounded variance (σ_u^2), and where $\Phi(B)$ is a polynomial of order p in the lag operator. The order p may be taken to be unboundedly large, in which case Y_t is an AR(∞) process, but (unlike with moving average processes) the notation for the infinite-order lag operator polynomial is not distinct from that usually used for the pth order lag operator, $\Phi(B)$. (17-45)

An AR(p) process – or an AR(∞) process for which $|\varphi_j|$ eventually becomes negligible as j becomes sufficiently large – is inherently invertible, as its MA(∞) representation lag operator obviously has an inverse. A particular AR(p) or AR(∞) process is called "stationary" if and only if $\Phi^{-1}(B)$ exists, so that Y_t can also be written in MA(∞) form, as a weighted sum of past values of U_t with eventually declining weights. From Equations 17-20 to 17-25 in Section 17.4, this is equivalent to requiring that all p roots of the polynomial equation $\Phi(z) = 0$ lie outside of the unit circle.

Recall, from Equation 17-41 (where it first appeared) that this way of defining the AR(p) or AR(∞) lag polynomial weights makes the expression of the model as a regression equation simpler, but implies that the $\Phi(B)$ itself then has minus signs on each of its coefficients:

$$Y_t - \varphi_1 Y_{t-1} - \varphi_2 Y_{t-2} - \varphi_3 Y_{t-3} - \ldots = U_t \tag{17-46}$$

Box and Jenkins (1976) designated any autoregressive process as "stationary" if and only if the lag structure $\Phi^{-1}(B)$ exists.[70] If, as above, $\Phi(B)$ in Equation 17-45 is obtained as the inverse of $\Psi(B)$, the lag structure characterizing the presumed-invertible MA(∞) representation of the covariance stationary time-series Y_t, then the inverse of $\Phi(B)$ clearly exists – it is $\Psi(B)$!

But it is easy to imagine instead starting out with a time-series Y_t and trying to express it, in the first place, as an AR(∞) process of the form given in Equation 17-45. In that case, it is necessary to require that $\Phi^{-1}(B)$ exists – i.e., to require that this AR(∞) model is "stationary" – in order to ensure that Y_t can also be expressed in MA(∞) form: i.e., as $\Phi^{-1}(B)U_t$, with the finite (and time-independent) variance and autocorrelations then implied by Equations 17-32 and 17-34.

It is always possible to set up a recursion equation (completely analogous to Equations 17-20 to 17-23 in Section 17.4) to numerically calculate weights in a lag structure $\Psi(B)$ guaranteeing that $\Phi(B)\,\Psi(B)$ equals one, but this $\Psi(B)$ is a true inverse of $\Phi(B)$ only if its weights ψ_j eventually decay away for sufficiently large values of j. However, if Y_t has finite variance, then the weights ψ_j must eventually decay away for sufficiently large values of j, as (from Equation 17-32) the variance of Y_t is equal to $\sigma_u^2 \sum_{j=0}^{\infty} \psi_j^2$. Consequently, if one starts out with an AR(∞) process for Y_t – and Y_t at least has a finite variance – then $\Phi^{-1}(B)$ does exist and Y_t is "stationary." Since $\Phi^{-1}(B)$ thus provides the $\Psi(B)$ lag structure for a legitimate MA(∞) representation for Y_t, its mean, variance, and all of its autocovariances can easily be calculated (e.g., from Equations 17-32 and 17-33) and are

[70] Recall that "existing" means that the polynomial $\Phi^{-1}(B)$ not only yields $\Phi^{-1}(B)\Phi(B)$ equal to one, but also has weights which eventually become arbitrarily small at arbitrarily large lags.

independent of time. Therefore, if Y_t has finite variance and has a well-defined AR(∞) representation – i.e., one with eventually declining weights – then Y_t is covariance stationary. Indeed, this is why Box and Jenkins gave the name "stationary" to this property of an autoregressive model.

But not all AR(∞) models with eventually declining weights are stationary. In particular, time-series which need to be first-differenced in order to be covariance stationary are designated "ARIMA(p,d,q)" processes; these will be discussed in Section 17.8.

Note that – because the existence of $\Psi^{-1}(B)$ implies that its weights must eventually decay to become negligible at large lags – it is always possible to truncate the representation of the AR(∞) representation of a covariance stationary time-series with an invertible MA(∞) representation at some finite lag, p, with negligible error if p is chosen sufficiently large. Thus, to an arbitrarily good approximation, any covariance stationary Y_t with an invertible MA(∞) representation can be represented as a the finite-order AR(p) process:

$$\begin{aligned} Y_t - \varphi_1 Y_{t-1} - \varphi_2 Y_{t-2} - \varphi_3 Y_{t-3} - \ldots - \varphi_{pY_{t-p}} &= U_t \\ Y_t = \varphi_1 Y_{t-1} + \varphi_2 Y_{t-2} + \varphi_3 Y_{t-3} + \cdots + \varphi_{pY_{t-p}} &+ U_t \end{aligned} \tag{17-47}$$

Therefore, so long as Y_t is covariance stationary, it can always be represented arbitrarily well as an MA(q) process or (so long as its moving average representation is invertible) it can equally well be represented as an AR(p) process. We have our choice![71]

Box and Jenkins (1976) observed this and, because the time-series sample lengths available in those days were relatively small, suggested choosing whichever representation involves estimating the smallest number of parameters.[72] They named this notion the principle of "parsimonious representation" and placed a great deal of weight on it in their hugely influential book.

Where the values of p and q differ quite substantially, then this principle still makes a good deal of sense: all other things equal, a smaller number of parameters can be estimated more precisely for any given sample length. On the other hand, in practice, the values of p and q typically don't differ all that much. Moreover, all of this analysis – both inference about the population correlogram using sample autocorrelations and estimation/inference of the parameters in the models themselves – is justified only for large values of N. And the fact of the matter is that both of these activities actually do require fairly large samples in order to work well. Thus, large samples are necessary in order to do this kind of modeling effectively. In that case, however, N almost certainly dwarfs the value of $|p - q|$. Hence, it seems unreasonable to elevate model parsimony to the level of importance it is frequently accorded.

Moreover, the "all other things equal" alluded to in the previous paragraph are *not* equal.

For example, MA(q) models are potentially troublesome to estimate. In particular, Exercise 17-11 makes it plain that the estimating an MA(q) model involves a numerical calculation which might not converge at all or might converge to a non-invertible model – even though an invertible MA(q) model for the time-series does exist. Numerical problems in estimating MA(q) models are especially likely with highly autocorrelated data or where the value of q has been initially set too high. Equation 17-47 for the AR(p) model, in contrast, is just an ordinary regression equation, albeit one for which the Chapter 9 assumption that the explanatory variables are "fixed in repeated samples" is not tenable. Consequently, OLS provides fast, reliable, and (so long as p is set sufficiently large) consistent estimation of the parameters in AR(p) models.

[71] Exercise 17-10g shows – in the simple special case of an MA(1) process – that an invertible moving average model always exists for a covariance stationary time-series Y_t. The problem is that there are also non-invertible moving average models which yield the same population autocorrelations, so one's estimation routing may converge to a non-invertible moving average model. The non-invertible moving average representations do not have AR(∞) representations with eventually declining weights, so they don't make much sense as models for forecasting Y_t.

[72] They also earnestly urged consideration of the mixed (ARMA) models discussed in Section 17.7; these processes can sometimes represent a time-series using even fewer than the q parameters required for an MA(q) process or the p parameters required for an AR(p) process.

On the other hand, another aspect which is not equivalent across the two kinds of models is the ease with which the model order can be identified from the sample correlogram. In particular, identification of an adequate value for p in the AR(p) representation is not as straightforward as is the identification of an adequate value for q in the MA(q) representation. Equation 17-36 showed that there is a simple population correlogram signature for the order q of an MA(q) process: $|\rho_q| \neq 0$ and $\rho_k = 0$ for all values of $k > q$. In contrast, the pattern in ρ_1, ρ_2, ρ_3, etc. for an AR(p) process conveys only one little nugget of information with regard to the size of p.

To at least obtain this one nugget, multiply Equation 17-47 by Y_{t-k} and take the expectation of both sides:

$$
\begin{aligned}
E[Y_t Y_{t-k}] &= E\left[\left(\varphi_1 Y_{t-1} + \varphi_2 Y_{t-2} + \varphi_3 Y_{t-3} + \cdots + \varphi_p Y_{t-p} + U_t\right) Y_{t-k}\right] \\
E[Y_t Y_{t-k}] &= \varphi_1 E[Y_{t-1} Y_{t-k}] + \varphi_2 E[Y_{t-2} Y_{t-k}] + \varphi_3 E[Y_{t-3} Y_{t-k}] + \cdots + \varphi_p E\left[Y_{t-p} Y_{t-k}\right] + E[U_t Y_{t-k}] \\
\gamma_k &= \varphi_1 \gamma_{k-1} + \varphi_2 \gamma_{k-2} + \varphi_3 \gamma_{k-3} + \cdots + \varphi_p \gamma_{k-p} + E[U_t Y_{t-k}] \\
\gamma_k &= \varphi_1 \gamma_{k-1} + \varphi_2 \gamma_{k-2} + \varphi_3 \gamma_{k-3} + \cdots + \varphi_p \gamma_{k-p} \quad \text{for } k \geq 1
\end{aligned} \tag{17-48}
$$

Note that the third step in Equation 17-48 is simply using the definition of γ_k, the autocovariance of Y_t at lag k – from Equation 13-2, as repeated in Equation 17-8. The last step – observing that $E[U_t Y_{t-k}]$ is zero for $k \geq 1$ – follows because the MA(∞) representation of Y_t implies that it can be written as a weighted sum of U_t, U_{t-1}, U_{t-2}, and so forth. For values of $k \geq 1$, then, Y_{t-k} depends only on innovations which are prior to (and hence uncorrelated with) U_t.

Dividing both sides of Equation 17-48 by γ_0, the variance of Y_t, converts each of these autocovariances into the corresponding population autocorrelation:

$$
\begin{aligned}
\frac{\gamma_k}{\gamma_0} &= \varphi_1 \frac{\gamma_{k-1}}{\gamma_0} + \varphi_2 \frac{\gamma_{k-2}}{\gamma_0} + \varphi_3 \frac{\gamma_{k-3}}{\gamma_0} + \cdots + \varphi_p \frac{\gamma_{k-p}}{\gamma_0} \quad \text{for } k \geq 1 \\
\rho_k &= \varphi_1 \rho_{k-1} + \varphi_2 \rho_{k-2} + \varphi_3 \rho_{k-3} + \cdots + \varphi_p \rho_{k-p}
\end{aligned} \tag{17-49}
$$

These equations – plural because they hold for all values of $k \geq 1$ – are called the "Yule-Walker" equations. They imply that the autocorrelations for an AR(p) process follow a difference equation similar to the one already discussed (Equation 17-23) in deriving a recursion to calculate the coefficients in the inverse of a lag structure.

In fact, Equation 17-49 is precisely the same recursion relation one would use in numerically calculating the weights in the inverse of the polynomial $\Phi(B)$. The main difference is that the "initial conditions" for the recursion equation in Equation 17-49 specify that ρ_0 is one and that ρ_{-k} equals ρ_k, whereas the initial conditions for the (otherwise identical) recursion one would use in numerically calculating the weights in $\Phi^{-1}(B)$ consist of specifying that these weights are zero at negative lags.

Equations 17-24 and 17-25 show that the solutions to Equation 17-49 are of the form

$$
\rho_k = c_1 \left(\frac{1}{v_1}\right)^k + c_2 \left(\frac{1}{v_2}\right)^k + \cdots + c_p \left(\frac{1}{v_p}\right)^k \quad \text{for all} \quad k \geq 1 \tag{17-50}
$$

where $v_1 \ldots v_p$ are the roots of the "characteristic polynomial"

$$
\varphi_p z^p + \varphi_{p-1} z^{p-1} + \varphi_{p-2} z^{p-2} + \cdots + \varphi_2 z^2 + \varphi_1 z - 1 = 0 \tag{17-51}
$$

in the ordinary algebraic variable, z.[73] Thus, so long as the magnitudes of all p roots of Equation 17-51 exceed one, then $|\rho_k|$ decays eventually to zero as k becomes large. This is precisely the same

[73] As noted earlier, here the values of constants $c_1 \ldots c_p$ are determined by the requirements that ρ_0 must equal one and that $\rho_{-j} = \rho_j$ for $j = -1 \ldots 1-p$; thus, for example, the sum $c_1 + c_2 + \cdots + c_p$ must equal one.

condition needed in order for the recursions defining $\Phi^{-1}(B)$ to converge, and hence for this AR(p) process to be stationary. Unfortunately, however, this result on the eventual decay of the $|\rho_k|$ values implies nothing about the value of p, as the discussion of this point using Equation 17-34 showed the autocorrelations for *any* covariance stationary process must become negligible for sufficiently large lags.

More usefully, note that the solution for ρ_k given in Equation 17-50 shows that the autocorrelations of an AR(p) process decay exponentially if all of the roots $v_1 \ldots v_p$ are real-valued, whereas they can oscillate as they decay if some of these roots are complex-valued. This latter point leads to the one "nugget" of additional insight referred to above: since the possibility of complex-valued roots in a pth order polynomial requires $p > 1$, one can infer that the value of p must at least equal two if the population correlogram oscillates as it decays. Therefore, if one observes such oscillations in the statistically significant portion of the sample correlogram for a particular sample of data, then an AR(1) model is unlikely to provide an adequate representation for the process generating it.

Thus, the population correlogram is not very informative as to the order of an AR(p) model; it follows that the sample correlogram is not of much practical use in identifying the order of AR(p) processes. But it would be nice to have an analogue or modification of the sample correlogram which *is* useful for that purpose. For this reason, the Yule-Walker equations are also used to derive what are called "partial autocorrelations" and customarily denoted $\varphi_{1,1}, \varphi_{2,2}, \varphi_{3,3}$, and so forth. (The reason why the subscripts are "doubled up" in this notation will become evident shortly.) These partial autocorrelations are specifically defined so as to play the same role in identifying the order of an AR(p) process that the ordinary autocorrelations $(\rho_1, \rho_2, \rho_3, \ldots)$ play in identifying the order of an MA(q) process. In other words, the partial autocorrelations are defined in such a way that – if $Y_t \sim \text{AR}(p)$ – then $\varphi_{p,p} \neq 0$ and $\varphi_{j,j} = 0$ for all $j > p$.

The way this works is most clearly explained using an example with a specific value for p, so it is assumed (for this illustration) that $Y(t)$ is generated by an AR(3) process. Also, for the moment, it will be assumed that the population autocorrelations $(\rho_1, \rho_2, \rho_3, \ldots)$ are all known. (One could imagine that they have been consistently estimated using a huge sample; this assumption will, in any case, be relaxed shortly.) Since $Y(t)$ is actually generated by an AR(3) process, it must be that φ_j is zero for $j > 3$. Suppose, however, that one does not know that and writes down the Yule-Walker equations (Equation 17-49) for $k = 1, 2, 3$, and 4 under the mistaken assumption that $Y(t)$ is an AR(4) process. Replacing ρ_{-1} by ρ_1, ρ_{-2} by ρ_2, and ρ_{-3} by ρ_3, these four equations would be

$$\begin{aligned}
\rho_1 &= \varphi_1\rho_0 + \varphi_2\rho_1 + \varphi_3\rho_2 + \varphi_4\rho_3 \\
\rho_2 &= \varphi_1\rho_1 + \varphi_2\rho_0 + \varphi_3\rho_1 + \varphi_4\rho_2 \\
\rho_3 &= \varphi_1\rho_2 + \varphi_2\rho_1 + \varphi_3\rho_0 + \varphi_4\rho_1 \\
\rho_4 &= \varphi_1\rho_3 + \varphi_2\rho_2 + \varphi_3\rho_1 + \varphi_4\rho_0
\end{aligned} \tag{17-52}$$

where, of course, ρ_0 is just one. Since ρ_1, ρ_2, ρ_3, and ρ_4 are all known, Equation 17-52 actually constitutes four linear equations in the four unknowns: φ_1, φ_2, φ_3, and φ_4. Since true values for the population autocorrelations are used, solving these four equations yields the actual values for φ_1, φ_2, φ_3, and φ_4 – including a value of zero for φ_4, since the process is actually an AR(3).

In general, then – presuming that one knew all of the population autocorrelations – one could solve the first j Yule-Walker equations for $\varphi_1, \varphi_2, \varphi_3, \ldots \varphi_j$, *define* $\varphi_{j,j}$ (the "partial autocorrelation at lag j") to be the resulting solution value for φ_j, and obtain the order p of the AR(p) process generating Y_t as the smallest value of j such that $\varphi_{j,j}$ equals zero for all $j > p$. More explicitly, $\varphi_{1,1}$ is obtained by solving the equation

$$\rho_1 = \varphi_{1,1}\rho_0 \tag{17-53}$$

for $\varphi_{1,1}$, given the value of ρ_1. For $j = 2$, $\varphi_{2,2}$ is obtained by solving the pair of equations

$$\begin{aligned}
\rho_1 &= \varphi_{2,1}\rho_0 + \varphi_{2,2}\rho_1 \\
\rho_2 &= \varphi_{2,1}\rho_1 + \varphi_{2,2}\rho_0
\end{aligned} \tag{17-54}$$

for $\varphi_{2,2}$, given the values of ρ_1 and ρ_2. The value of $\varphi_{2,1}$ is discarded. For $j = 3$, $\varphi_{3,3}$ is obtained by solving the three equations

$$\begin{aligned} \rho_1 &= \varphi_{3,1}\rho_0 + \varphi_{3,2}\rho_1 + \varphi_{3,3}\rho_2 \\ \rho_2 &= \varphi_{3,1}\rho_1 + \varphi_{3,2}\rho_0 + \varphi_{3,3}\rho_1 \\ \rho_3 &= \varphi_{3,1}\rho_2 + \varphi_{3,2}\rho_1 + \varphi_{3,3}\rho_0 \end{aligned} \tag{17-55}$$

for $\varphi_{3,3}$, given the values of ρ_1, ρ_2, and ρ_3. Here the values of $\varphi_{3,1}$ and $\varphi_{3,2}$ are discarded. For $j = 4$, $\varphi_{4,4}$ is obtained by solving the equations

$$\begin{aligned} \rho_1 &= \varphi_{4,1}\rho_0 + \varphi_{4,2}\rho_1 + \varphi_{4,3}\rho_2 + \varphi_{4,4}\rho_3 \\ \rho_2 &= \varphi_{4,1}\rho_1 + \varphi_{4,2}\rho_0 + \varphi_{4,3}\rho_1 + \varphi_{4,4}\rho_2 \\ \rho_3 &= \varphi_{4,1}\rho_2 + \varphi_{4,2}\rho_1 + \varphi_{4,3}\rho_0 + \varphi_{4,4}\rho_1 \\ \rho_4 &= \varphi_{4,1}\rho_3 + \varphi_{4,2}\rho_2 + \varphi_{4,3}\rho_1 + \varphi_{4,4}\rho_0 \end{aligned} \tag{17-56}$$

for $\varphi_{4,4}$, given the values of ρ_1, ρ_2, ρ_3, and ρ_4. Here the values of $\varphi_{4,1}$, $\varphi_{4,2}$, and $\varphi_{4,3}$ are discarded. And so forth.

In this way – by construction – if Y_t is actually generated by an AR(p) process, then $\varphi_{j,j}$ would have to be non-zero for $j = p$ and zero for all $j > p$. Thus, one could use knowledge of the population correlogram to identify the order p of an AR(p) by solving the Yule-Walker equations first for $j = 1$, then for $j = 2$ – and so forth – until (for all $j > p$) the resulting $\varphi_{j,j}$ values become zero.

Of course, the population autocorrelations are not known in practice. But one could complete the same calculations, substituting the sample autocorrelations (r_1, r_2, $r_3 \ldots$) for the corresponding population autocorrelations (ρ_1, ρ_2, ρ_3, …), thereby obtaining estimates of $\varphi_{1,1}$, $\varphi_{2,2}$, $\varphi_{3,3}$, and so forth; these estimators are called the "sample partial autocorrelations" and denoted $\hat{\varphi}_{1,1}$, $\hat{\varphi}_{2,2}$, $\hat{\varphi}_{3,3}$, and so forth. What makes these estimates useful is that it can be shown that, if Y_t is normally distributed and generated by an AR(p) process, then the asymptotic sampling distribution of $\hat{\varphi}_{j,j}$ is $N(0, 1/N)$ for all $j > p$. Consequently, the procedure for identifying the order of an AR (p) process is to look at a plot or tabulation of these partial autocorrelation estimates and compare them to their asymptotic standard error, of $1/\sqrt{N}$. A reasonable tentative identification for p, then, is to choose the smallest value for p such that the all of the $\hat{\varphi}_{j,j}$ estimates appear to be statistically insignificant for $j > p$.[74]

Of course, one could instead simply estimate a sequence of models: AR(1), AR(2), AR(3), etc. and use the estimated t-ratio on the estimated coefficient at the largest lag to test the null hypothesis that this largest-lag coefficient is actually zero. But the computation of the partial autocorrelations is preprogrammed into most software packages, so it is considerably more convenient to use these estimates.[75]

---

[74] A portmanteau χ^2 test is usually reported, precisely analogous to the Q test described for the sample correlogram, to assess whether a group of sample partial autocorrelations is significantly different from zero.

[75] Many packages in fact calculate $\hat{\varphi}_{11}$, $\hat{\varphi}_{22}$, $\hat{\varphi}_{33}$ (and estimates of their standard errors) in exactly this way: i.e., by estimating a sequence of AR(j) models for j equal to 1, 2, 3, etc. This procedure likely gives higher-quality estimates in finite samples than solving a sequence of sets of Yule-Walker equations, as described above; nowadays the computations are so fast that estimating this sequence of AR(j) models is very feasible; this was not the case in the 1970s when Box and Jenkins were writing their book.

For example – augmenting the example given in Section 17.3 – the Stata commands:

```
tsset tee
ac ydat, lags(60)
pac ydat, lags(60)
corrgram ydat, lags(60)
```

compute and display an estimated partial correlogram as well as an ordinary correlogram for a time-series named "ydat".

Forecasting with an estimated AR(p) model is fairly straightforward under the same set of assumptions utilized in the analogous discussion of MA(q) model forecasts in Section 17.5: that $U_t \sim N(0, \sigma_u^2)$ and that N is sufficiently large that the model parameters ($\varphi_1 \ldots \varphi_p$ and σ_u^2) can be taken as known. In that case the conditional-mean forecast of Y_{N+1} (using Equation 17-4) is just

$$
\begin{aligned}
f_{N,1} = M_1 &= E[Y_{N+1}|Y_1 = y_1, Y_2 = y_2, \ldots, Y_N = y_N] \\
&= \varphi_1 y_N + \varphi_2 y_{N-1} + \varphi_2 y_{N-2} + \cdots + \varphi_p y_{N-p}
\end{aligned}
\tag{17-57}
$$

The conditional-mean forecast of Y_{N+2} is very similar, but uses this value of $f_{N,1}$ to replace Y_{N+1}:

$$
\begin{aligned}
f_{N,2} = M_2 &= E[Y_{N+2}|Y_1 = y_1, Y_2 = y_2, \ldots, Y_N = y_N] \\
&= \varphi_1 f_{N,1} + \varphi_2 y_N + \varphi_2 y_{N-1} + \cdots + \varphi_p y_{N-p+1}
\end{aligned}
\tag{17-58}
$$

Similarly,

$$
\begin{aligned}
f_{N,3} = M_3 &= E[Y_{N+2}|Y_1 = y_1, Y_2 = y_2, \ldots, Y_N = y_N] \\
&= \varphi_1 f_{N,2} + \varphi_2\, t_{N,1} + \varphi_2 y_N + \cdots + \varphi_p y_{N-p+2}
\end{aligned}
\tag{17-59}
$$

and so forth.

These forecasts decay to the unconditional mean (zero) as the value of h becomes large. In fact, these forecasts are precisely equal to those one would obtain from numerically inverting $\Phi(B)$ to obtain the equivalent MA(∞) model – truncating it at a lag q sufficiently large that ψ_{q+j} are negligible for all positive values of j – and forecasting Y_{N+1}, Y_{N+2}, Y_{N+3}, ... using this approximating MA(q) model, as in Table 17-1. This inversion is actually quite useful because Equations 17-57, 17-58, and so forth do not yield convenient expressions for the forecast error variances; consequently, conversion of the AR(p) into the equivalent (truncated) MA(∞) process is the sensible way to obtain these variances, and the concomitant 95% confidence intervals for $Y_{N+1}, Y_{N+2}, Y_{N+3}$, etc.

As with the MA(q) model identification procedure in Section 17.5, an application of this AR(p) model identification procedure to data on the U.S. Treasury Bill rate is explicitly worked out in Section 18.2. Active Learning Exercises 17b, 18a, and 18b (available at www.wiley.com/college/ashley) provide an opportunity to apply these techniques oneself. Before going on to that application, however, a variation on the MA(q) and AR(p) processes just described needs to be introduced: the "mixed" or ARMA(p,q) processes.

17.7 ARMA(p,q) MODELS AND A SUMMARY OF THE BOX-JENKINS MODELING ALGORITHM

In large part because of their intense (and likely, in retrospect, overblown) concern for parsimony in modeling, Box and Jenkins (1976) proposed a new kind of linear univariate time-series model; their new model subsumed the MA(q) and AR(p) models discussed above as special cases, but potentially involves estimating a smaller number of parameters than are required for either. This generalization of the MA(q) and AR(p) processes is called the "mixed" or "ARMA(p,q)" model, and is defined in Equation 17-60:

The "Mixed" or ARMA(p, q) Model for a Time-Series

Y_t is generated by an ARMA or 'mixed' process of order (p, q) – or, equivalently, Y_t follows an ARMA(p, q) model – if and only if

$$
\begin{aligned}
Y_t \sim \text{ARMA}(p,q) \;&\Leftrightarrow\; Y_t = \sum_{j=1}^{p} \varphi_j Y_{t-j} + \sum_{j=0}^{q} \theta_j U_{t-j} \\
&\Leftrightarrow\; \Phi(B) Y_t = \Theta(B) U_t \\
&\Leftrightarrow\; Y_t = \Phi^{-1}(B)\Theta(B) U_t \\
&\Leftrightarrow\; Y_t = \frac{\Theta(B)}{\Phi(B)} U_t
\end{aligned} \tag{17-60}
$$

where the "innovation" U_t is serially uncorrelated, with mean zero and bounded variance (σ_u^2), where $\Phi(B)$ is a polynomial of order p in the lag operator, and where $\Theta(B)$ is a polynomial of order q in the lag operator. This equation defines what is meant by the quotient of two polynomials in the lag operator.

An ARMA(p, q) process is called "invertible" – and is applicable to forecasting Y_t – if and only if $\Theta^{-1}(B)$ exists, so that Y_t can also be written in AR(∞) form, as a weighted sum of past values of Y_t, with eventually declining weights. An ARMA(p, q) process is called "stationary" if and only if $\Phi^{-1}(B)$ exists, so that Y_t can also be written in MA(∞) form, as a weighted sum of past values of U_t, with eventually declining weights; any ARMA(p, q) process which does not have this property cannot have a finite variance. From Equations 17-20 to 17-25 in Section 17.4, "invertibility" is equivalent to requiring that all q roots of the polynomial equation $\Theta(z) = 0$ lie outside of the unit circle, and "stationarity" is equivalent to requiring that all p roots of the polynomial equation $\Phi(z) = 0$ lie outside of the unit circle.

It is in fact sometimes the case that an ARMA(1,1) process can fit (i.e., model) the data just as well as, say, an AR(3) or an MA(4) process, allowing one to estimate a model with somewhat fewer parameters. As noted in Section 17.6, however, this hardly seems a crucial advantage when the estimation sample length N needs to be well over 100 in order to proceed effectively.

And the mixed model in every other way inherits the worst aspects of its constituent parts. First of all, there is no simple relationship between the defining order values (p and q) in the ARMA(p, q) model and either the correlogram ($\rho_1, \rho_2, \rho_3, \ldots$) or the partial correlogram ($\varphi_{1,1}, \varphi_{2,2}, \varphi_{3,3}, \ldots$) of Y_t. Consequently, the values of p and q are not easy to obtain from the sample data. Moreover, estimation of the model parameters ($\varphi_1 \ldots \varphi_p$ and $\theta_1 \ldots \theta_p$) in the ARMA(p,q) model is, if anything, more fraught than the estimation of the MA(q) model parameters, as the relevant numerical procedures are practically certain to be problematic if the values of both p and q are set too high.[76]

Why mention mixed models at all, then? For one thing, an ARMA(p,1) or an ARMA(1, q) model is sometimes useful; and it is not difficult to explore this modeling avenue using modern software. For another, the ARMA(p, q) model is the first context in which the quotient of two polynomials in

[76] Invoking these numerical estimation procedures, however, is no more difficult for estimating an ARMA(p, q) model than for estimating an MA(q) or $AR(p)$ model. Using Stata, for example, the command "arima ydat, arima(1,0,2)" estimates an ARMA(1, 2) model for the sample data on the variable called "ydat".

the lag operator, defined in Equation 17-60, arises; this notation is compact and can be useful in describing more complicated models. Finally, the time-series literature has made such a fuss over this wider class of models that no account of this topic can (or should) avoid at least mentioning it: indeed, this entire topic of linear, univariate time-series modeling is typically referred to as "ARMA modeling" whenever it is not denoted "Box-Jenkins modeling," after its founders.

Box and Jenkins did, indeed, found time-series analysis in its modern incarnation, but the mixed model is not their most enduring legacy.[77] Rather, their two main contributions were the notion of an "integrated" time-series – to be described in Section 18.1 – and their coherent, step-by-step, "algorithm" for modeling a time-series.

The elements of this Box-Jenkins modeling algorithm have all appeared in the previous sections of this chapter: Section 17.3 on covariance stationarity, Section 17.5 on MA(q) models, and Section 17.6 on AR(p) models.[78] Having now described the entire ARMA(p, q) class of processes, this is a good point at which to briefly summarize the results on these models and to provide a tightly organized description of the Box-Jenkins algorithm for specifying and using this set of processes to model and forecast a single time-series as a linear function of its own past.

First, a summary. The MA(q) model is guaranteed to suffice in modeling for any covariance stationary time-series (so long as the order q is chosen to be sufficiently large) and such a value for q can be easily ascertained from the sample correlogram. Because of the nonlinear relationship between the MA(q) model parameters and the population correlogram, however, the MA(q) representation is not unique. Consequently, model estimation can fail altogether or simply fail to converge to the single (invertible) MA(q) which yields an AR(∞) representation making the model useful in forecasting. The AR(p) model is guaranteed to yield a forecasting model, but it might not be "stationary," which is necessary in order for it to have an MA(∞) representation and finite variance – that issue will need to be dealt with in Section 18.1. AR(p) models are easy to estimate, but the order "p" cannot be determined from the correlogram; the partial correlogram was consequently defined for this purpose. Mixed – i.e., ARMA(p, q) – are difficult to identify, but there is no problem trying out a sequence of ARMA(1, q) or ARMA(p, 1) models. Mixed models can be problematic to estimate if they are overly complex, however. M_h, the h-step-ahead conditional mean forecast of Y_t – and the variance of the errors it makes – are easily obtained from any of these models, as they are all easily interconverted by numerically inverting the relevant lag operator polynomial.

Next, now that almost all of the bits and pieces have been carefully explained, it is time to summarize the full Box-Jenkins modeling algorithm:

Step 1: Using time plots and sample correlograms, force Y_t to be apparently covariance stationary.

This might involve dropping some data at the beginning of the sample or considering whether the logarithm of the data appears to have a more stable variance across the sample. If truly necessary, an outlier can be eliminated temporarily at this point.[79] The issue of what to do with "trendlike" behavior in the time plot (typically resulting in a sample correlogram which does not promptly decay to statistical insignificance) will be discussed in Section 18.1.

[77] Prior to Box and Jenkins (1976), time-series analysis was a fairly obscure branch of statistics mostly concerned with spectral analysis.

[78] Section 17.4 developed the necessary material on inverting lag structures, enabling us to interconvert the AR and MA representations of a time-series.

[79] At this point one would just set such an observation equal to its sample mean; if that does not make a major change in the sample correlogram, then re-include the datum and ignore the outlier. (If N is reasonably large, even a fairly prominent outlier will quite often be largely inconsequential to the identification and estimation of an ARMA model.) It is rarely useful or necessary to eliminate an outlier; it is almost *never* appropriate or useful to eliminate more than one "outlier": in such cases one merely has non-normally distributed data. Generally speaking, it is better to ignore an outlier unless it is so extreme as to seriously distort the model identification. On the other hand, it is useful to observe that an outlier (or other structural shift) exists, as these can be dealt with in the multivariate modeling described in Section 18.4, particularly if there is a plausible reason for such a shift.

Step 2: Partition the entire – now covariance stationary – data set into an identification/estimation sample of length N and a post-sample model evaluation period of length P.

The issues involved in this choice were discussed at length in Section 17.5, ending with the advice: "A reasonable compromise is probably to set P in the range 100 to 150, so long as $N+P$ is sufficiently large as to also yield N at least that large, and to start scrimping on P where the total sample $(N+P)$ is noticeably less than 300, so as to keep the value of N at least equal to 80 to 100. Clearly, where the total sample is much less than 150, effective post-sample model comparison/evaluation is not really feasible."

Step 3: Tentatively identify several models for the data – typically, an MA(q) *and an* AR(p) *model and make sure they pass the usual in-sample diagnostic checks.*

Utilizing the N "sample" observations, estimate a sample correlogram and use it to tentatively identify an MA(q) model; use the sample partial correlogram to tentatively identify an AR(p) model.[80] Eliminate the largest-lag coefficient in each estimated model (thereby reducing the value of q or p) if the estimate of this coefficient is statistically insignificant; do *not* eliminate statistically insignificant regressors inside of a lag-structure. For example, if the estimates of θ_1 and θ_3 in an MA(3) model are statistically significant, do not drop U_{t-2} from the model – the least-squares estimate of θ_2 is likely more accurate than arbitrarily setting it to zero.[81]

At this point the sample correlogram of the fitting errors for each model should be examined. If – for an MA(q) model, say – these r_j estimates are not consistent with the model errors being serially uncorrelated, then the value of q needs to be increased, especially if the statistically significant rj estimate is at lag $j+1$ or (with seasonal data) at the seasonal lag.

Step 4: Choose between the tentatively identified models using in-sample and, if possible, post-sample diagnostic checking.

The models being considered will typically have different numbers of parameters – e.g., $p \neq q$. Consequently, it is not appropriate to compare the sample fit of the models using the estimated variance of the fitting errors (s^2) or, equivalently, R_c^2 from Equation 9-41, as these measures are known to underadjust for model complexity. Most commonly – and appropriately – tentatively identified time-series models are nowadays compared using the Schwarz Criterion, also called the "Bayesian Information Criterion" or BIC, defined in Equation 9-42 as:[82]

$$\text{SC} = \text{Schwarz Criterion (BIC)} = \ln\left(\frac{1}{N}\sum_{i=1}^{N}\left(u_i^{\text{fit}}\right)^2\right) + \frac{k\ln(N)}{N} \tag{17-61}$$

Here $u_1^{\text{fit}} \dots u_N^{\text{fit}}$ are the model fitting errors and k is the number of parameters estimated in this particular model – e.g., $q+1$ for an MA(q) model including an intercept. Clearly, a smaller value of the BIC statistic is desirable.

[80] As noted above, some people will also experiment with estimating a sequence of ARMA(1, q) or ARMA(p, 1) models.

[81] On the other hand, with monthly data, if the estimates of θ_3 and θ_{12} are both statistically significant, but the estimates of $\theta_4 \dots \theta_{11}$ are not, then it is sensible to drop $U_{t-4} \dots U_{t-11}$ from the model and estimate what is called an "additive seasonal MA" model. This topic is taken up in Section 18.3.

[82] The AIC criterion is well known to underpenalize model complexity, so the SIC criterion is now widely preferred. The Stata postestimation command "estat ic" computes the BIC statistic.

The observed value of the BIC criterion is uninterpretable, of course, so people also look at the adjusted R^2 value as well:

$$R_c^2 \equiv 1 - \frac{\frac{1}{N-k}\sum_{i=1}^{N}\left(u_i^{\text{fit}}\right)^2}{\frac{1}{N-1}\sum_{i=1}^{N}(y_i - \bar{y})^2} = 1 - \frac{s^2}{\frac{1}{N-1}\sum_{i=1}^{N}(y_i - \bar{y})^2} \tag{17-62}$$

but model choice is more reliable using the BIC criterion.

Presuming that it was feasible to also allocate P observations to a post-sample model evaluation period, one should then also compute a sequence of one-step-ahead prediction errors from each of the top candidate models over this post-sample period. Ideally, the model parameters should be re-estimated ("updated") as this process moves through the post-sample period, but this parameter updating is not implemented in typical econometric software; if it is, then it is also useful to compute analogous (updated) forecast errors from a naive MA(0) model. The updated M_1 forecast of Y_{t+1} from this naive model is then just the sample mean of all the data up through period t; the mean squared forecast errors from this naive model over the P post-sample periods makes a good "benchmark" to which one can compare the analogous post-sample mean square forecast error values produced by the tentatively identified models.

Generally speaking, one should prefer (and choose) the tentatively identified model which provides the smallest post-sample mean square forecasting errors – even if it is the naive MA(0) model.[83] Where this choice differs from that which one would have made by choosing the model with the smallest in-sample value of the BIC criterion, it is legitimate to ask whether the difference in post-sample mean squared forecasting error between these two models is statistically significant; such testing is described in Section 18.5.[84]

Step 5: Re-estimate the chosen model using all $N+P$ sample observations.

This modeling algorithm is actually fairly easy to implement; an example is given in Section 18.2. First, however, the issue of "trendlike" behavior in the time-plot of the time-series – which was glossed over in describing Step 1 – must be addressed. This is done in Section 18.1.

KEY TERMS

For each term or concept listed below, provide a working definition or explanation:

Time-Series Econometrics vs. Time-Series Analysis

h-Step-Ahead Forecast

Loss Function on Forecast Errors, Loss($\varepsilon_{N,h}$)

Optimal Forecast and Conditional-Mean Forecast, M_h

[83] Unless, of course, per Section 17.2, one's loss function on prediction errors differs from the squared-error loss function in some moderately knowable way. For example, if one's loss function on forecast errors is known to be asymmetric, then one might want to approximate it by Equation 17-7 and use the $a/(a-b)$ fractile of the conditional distribution of Y_{t+1} implied by each model to compute its one-step-ahead forecast errors in the post-sample period. In that case one would also want to compare the post-sample average value of the losses given by Equation 17-7 rather than the post-sample mean square error from each model. This is almost never done in practice, mostly because analysts rarely have sufficient confidence as to the manner in which their actual loss function deviates from the squared-error loss function.

[84] The reason that such testing is delayed to Section 18.5 is that tests regarding the post-sample forecast MSE implied by different models first become crucial in multivariate settings, where the issue is whether certain explanatory variables are actually useful or merely appear to be useful in the sample period. With P set at a reasonable length, the forecasting results from various univariate models usually do not differ sufficiently for these tests to be able to distinguish between them; this makes sense in that the MA(q) and AR(p) models are both approximating the same MA(∞) process.

Sample Correlogram versus Population Correlogram
Covariance Stationarity versus Strict Stationarity
Bartlett Sampling Distribution for R_k and 95% Confidence Intervals for ρ_k
Portmanteau (or Q) Test
Polynomial in the Lag Operator and Its Inverse
Characteristic Polynomial for Inversion of Lag Structure
Wold Decomposition and MA(∞) Process
Invertibility of an MA(q) Model
AR(p) Model
Yule-Walker Equations and Partial Autocorrelations
ARMA(p, q) Model

EXERCISES

17-1. Assume that $X_1 \dots X_N$ are jointly normally distributed, that N is 200 – which you can take as "large" – and that the following sample autocorrelations have been observed:

k	r_k
1	0.70
2	0.30
3	−0.09
4	0.06
5	0.02
6	−0.03

a. Compute Bartlett 95% confidence intervals for ρ_1, ρ_2, and ρ_3 – first using Equation 17-12 and then using Equation 17-13 with $m = 5$. {Hint: Entering $r_1 \dots r_6$ into a spreadsheet will substantially expedite your calculations; r_0 is, of course, one. Report your results to six decimal places (for checking purposes), even though these figures are clearly only meaningful to two decimal places.}

b. Compute the Bartlett estimates of the asymptotic correlations between the sampling errors in r_k and r_{k+1}, approximating ρ_1, ρ_2, and ρ_3 by r_1, r_2, and r_3 and assuming that ρ_k is zero for values of k exceeding three.

17-2. Not all population correlograms are possible. In particular, the requirement that the variance of any non-zero weighted sum of X_t, X_{t-1}, and X_{t-2} must necessarily be positive implies that the value of ρ_2 is both less than one and greater than $2(\rho_1)^2 - 1$. Calculate the allowed interval for ρ_2, given that ρ_1 is equal to 0.9. Repeat your calculation for ρ_1 values of 0.2, 0.3, ..., 0.8. Intuitively, why does it make sense that a time-series which is highly positively correlated with itself at lag one cannot be negatively correlated with itself at lag two?

17-3. It is observed that the time-plot of $x_1 \dots x_{1000}$ indicates that the mean and/or variance of X_t are apparently unstable for the first 50 time periods in the sample. Why is this observation important and what should one do about it? How would your answer change if the sample consists of just $x_1 \dots x_{80}$?

17-4. For the special case of p equal to four, confirm (by substitution) that $\lambda_j = c(1/v)^j$ does solve Equation 17-22 for the weights in the inverse of $\Omega(B)$ for any constant c, so long as v is a root of the polynomial equation given as Equation 17-25.

17-5. For lag structure $\Omega(B) = 1 - 1.10B + 0.24B^2$,

a. What equation must the weights λ_j in the lag structure $\Lambda(B) = \Omega^{-1}(B)$ satisfy?

b. Does this lag structure satisfy the Box and Jenkins (1976, p. 58) conditions for the existence of an inverse given in Equation 17-29?

c. Obtain the weights λ_j in $\Lambda(B)$ numerically, or show that $\Omega^{-1}(B)$ does not exist because these numerical weights do not eventually converge to zero as j increases. (See Footnote 17-41 for material on how to program this calculation into a spreadsheet.) Print out a plot of λ_j versus j for $1 \leq j \leq 30$.

d. State the characteristic polynomial equation and solve for its roots. Do these roots exceed one in magnitude? Are any of these roots complex-valued? Relate these analytic results to your numerical results in part c.

17-6. For lag structure $\Omega(B) = 1 - 1.30B + .30B^2$,

a. What equation must the weights λ_j in the lag structure $\Lambda(B) = \Omega^{-1}(B)$ satisfy?

b. Does this lag structure satisfy the Box and Jenkins (1976, p. 58) conditions for the existence of an inverse given in Equation 17-29?

c. Obtain the weights λ_j in $\Lambda(B)$ numerically, or show that $\Omega^{-1}(B)$ does not exist because these numerical weights do not eventually converge to zero as j increases. (See Footnote 17-41 for material on how to program this calculation into a spreadsheet.) Print out a plot of λ_j versus j for $1 \leq j \leq 30$.

d. State the characteristic polynomial equation and solve for its roots. Do these roots exceed one in magnitude? Are any of these roots complex-valued? Relate these analytic results to your numerical results in part c.

17-7. For lag structure $\Omega(B) = 1 + 0.50B + 0.50B^2$,

a. What equation must the weights λ_j in the lag structure $\Lambda(B) = \Omega^{-1}(B)$ satisfy?

b. Does this lag structure satisfy the Box and Jenkins (1976, p. 58) conditions for the existence of an inverse given in Equation 17-29?

c. Obtain the weights λ_j in $\Lambda(B)$ numerically, or show that $\Omega^{-1}(B)$ does not exist because these numerical weights do not eventually converge to zero as j increases. (See Footnote 17-41 for material on how to program this calculation into a spreadsheet.) Print out a plot of λ_j versus j for $1 \leq j \leq 30$.

d. State the characteristic polynomial equation and solve for its roots. Do these roots exceed one in magnitude? Are any of these roots complex-valued? Relate these analytic results to your numerical results in part c.

17-8. For lag structure $\Omega(B) = 1 + 0.50B - 0.50B^2$,

a. What equation must the weights λ_j in the lag structure $\Lambda(B) = \Omega^{-1}(B)$ satisfy?

b. Does this lag structure satisfy the Box and Jenkins (1976, p. 58) conditions for the existence of an inverse given in Equation 17-29?

c. Obtain the weights λ_j in $\Lambda(B)$ numerically, or show that $\Omega^{-1}(B)$ does not exist because these numerical weights do not eventually converge to zero as j increases. (See Footnote 17-41 for material on how to program this calculation into a spreadsheet.) Print out a plot of λ_j versus j for $1 \leq j \leq 30$.

d. State the characteristic polynomial equation and solve for its roots. Do these roots exceed one in magnitude? Are any of these roots complex-valued? Relate these analytic results to your numerical results in part c.

17-9. Assuming that Y_t is covariance stationary, and can be represented as the MA(q) process, $Y_t = \sum_{j=0}^{q} \theta_j U_{t-j}$, as given by Equation 17-30,

a. Derive the expression (analogous to Equation 17-32) for the variance of Y_t.

b. Derive the expressions (analogous to Equations 17-33 and 17-34) for the autocovariance of Y_t at lag k (γ_k) and the autocorrelation at lag k (ρ_k).

c. Now assume that q equals 3, with $\theta_1 = 0.45$, $\theta_2 = 0.15$, and $\theta_3 = 0.05$, with σ_u^2 equal to 5. Calculate the variance of Y_t and its population correlogram. What is the correlogram "signature" of an MA(3) process? What is the correlogram "signature" of an MA(q) process?

17-10. Suppose that Y_t is covariance stationary, and can in fact be represented as the MA(1) process, $Y_t = (1 + \theta_1 B)U_t$.

a. Using the MA(∞) representation for Y_t obtained as Equation 17-32, show that the variance of Y_t is just $\sigma_u^2(1 + \theta_1^2)$.

b. Using the result in Equation 17-36, show that

$$\text{corr}(Y_t, Y_{t-1}) = \rho_1 = \frac{\theta_1}{1 + \theta_1^2} \tag{17-63}$$

and that ρ_k is equal to zero for all $k > 1$.

c. Show that, so long as $|\theta_1| < 1$,

$$(1 + \theta_1 B)^{-1} = 1 + (-\theta_1)B + (-\theta_1)^2 B^3 + (-\theta_1)^2 B^3 \ldots$$

What happens to this expression when $|\theta_1|$ equals or exceeds one?

d. Use the result of part c to rewrite Y_t in AR(∞) form – that is, write an expression for Y_t in terms of U_t and past values of Y_t. Then use this to obtain an expression for Y_{t+1} in terms of U_{t+1}, Y_t, Y_{t-1}, Y_{t-2}, etc. Also obtain an expression for $E[Y_{N+1}|Y_N = y_N, Y_{N-1} = y_{N-1}, Y_{N-2} = y_{N-2} \ldots]$, the one-step-ahead conditional mean forecast of Y_{N+1} (or $f_{N,1} = M_1$). As $|\theta_1|$ approaches one, what happens to the way in which this forecast of Y_{N+1} depends on realized past values of Y_t?

e. Using the result from part b, what is the maximum possible value of ρ_1 which can be attained with $|\theta_1| < 1$?

f. In view of your answer to part e, what does it imply about Y_t if its population correlogram is $\rho_1 = 0.60$, with ρ_k is equal to zero for all $k > 1$?

g. Suppose further that the value of ρ_1 is known to equal 0.30. Using the result from part b, does this value for ρ_1 uniquely determine the value of θ_1? Does your answer change if attention is restricted solely to invertible models?

17-11. Consider the estimation of θ_1, θ_2, and θ_3 via least squares fitting in an MA(3) model for $Y(t)$, using sample data $y_1 \ldots y_5$. Thus, one is choosing $\hat{\theta}_1^{\text{guess}}$, $\hat{\theta}_2^{\text{guess}}$, and $\hat{\theta}_3^{\text{guess}}$ to minimize the sum of the squared fitting errors, $\sum_{t=1}^{5} \left(u_t^{\text{fit}}\right)^2$.

a. Use the model equation – $Y_t = \Theta(B)U_t$ – to write out expressions for $u_1^{\text{fit}}, \ldots u_5^{\text{fit}}$ in terms of y_1, y_2, y_3, y_4, y_5, $\hat{\theta}_1^{\text{guess}}$, $\hat{\theta}_2^{\text{guess}}$, and $\hat{\theta}_3^{\text{guess}}$. What problem arises?

b. Suppose that one conditions the estimation on the (incorrect) assumption that U_0, U_{-1}, and U_{-2} are zero. Does this help?

It turns out that this all works out fine – including the approximation of arbitrarily setting u_0^{fit}, u_1^{fit}, and u_{-2}^{fit} to zero – so long as the actual sample length N is sufficiently large and, importantly, so long as both the actual values of θ_1, θ_2, and θ_3 (and any values of $\hat{\theta}_1^{guess}$, $\hat{\theta}_2^{guess}$, and $\hat{\theta}_3^{guess}$ posited by the numerical optimization routine) are well away from values such that the model is non-invertible. Major numerical awkwardness ensues for values of $\hat{\theta}_1^{guess}$, $\hat{\theta}_2^{guess}$, and $\hat{\theta}_3^{guess}$ such that any of the roots of the corresponding characteristic polynomial relating to the inverse of $\hat{\Theta}(B)$ are close to one or below one in magnitude. Absent such proximity to non-invertibility, however, the nonlinear least squares estimation pointed at in this exercise is usually numerically trouble-free and yields consistent and asymptotically normal estimates of θ_1, θ_2, and θ_3. These estimates are then of reasonably good quality so long as N is sufficiently large. Where problems do arise, they can often be resolved by starting the estimation routine from a better initial guess for the parameters; one way to obtain such a better initial guess is to first estimate a large-order AR(p) model for the time-series and then numerically invert the resulting estimated lag-structure.

Active Learning Exercise 17a: Conditional Forecasting Using a Large-Scale Macroeconometric Model

Introduction

This Active Learning Exercise provides an opportunity to explore the use of what is arguably the best – albeit not the most complicated – large-scale econometric model of the U.S. economy. This model is typically called "FAIRMODEL" after its creator, Professor Ray Fair at Yale University, who also maintains and updates the model continuously on his Web page for anyone to use.[85] This model's *forte* is in producing credible one-quarter-ahead through forty-quarter-ahead forecasts of the most important U.S. macroeconomic variables, conditional on posited time paths for a number of exogenous variables, including spending levels and tax rates set at both the Federal and State/Local levels.[86]

One can sensibly examine the likely consequences of alternative macroeconomic policies by re-forecasting the model using different assumptions about these time paths. Indeed, in this Active Learning Exercise you will boost federal government spending on goods by $10B

[85] See fairmodel.econ.yale.edu/main3.htm; detailed directions on using this Web site for this particular exercise are given below. Fair himself refers to this model as the "US Model," so as to distinguish it from his multicountry model, also available on this site.

[86] All states and localities are aggregated together into one sector in FAIRMODEL; this sort of aggregation is one of the reasons FAIRMODEL is a relatively small macroeconometric model. Similarly, consumption spending in FAIRMODEL is modeled as three separate components (services, durable goods, and non-durable goods). Thus, FAIRMODEL is not the right tool to use if one needs forecasts of consumption spending more finely dis-aggregated.

over that assumed in the baseline forecast and compare the forecast time path of several macroeconomic variables – e.g., real GDP, the unemployment rate, and the federal government deficit – to that of the baseline forecast, under two different assumptions about the behavior of the U.S. central bank, the "Fed."

Such policy simulation exercises are only meaningful if the macroeconometric model's conditional forecasts are reasonably accurate. FAIRMODEL shines in this regard, notably outperforming a seven-variable VAR model for forecasts horizons of four quarters or more.[87] Arguably FAIRMODEL is relatively accurate at postsample forecasting because it incorporates a good deal of reasonable (if not particularly fashionable) macroeconomic theory and because it is fairly carefully specified and estimated. The theory underlying the model is described at length in Fair (2004) and is summarized in Chapter 2 of the online workbook.[88] Another source of FAIRMODEL's forecasting accuracy is that it incorporates the full "flow of funds" accounting framework. Thus, the model is financially self-consistent: any deficit in one sector of the model must be matched with saving in the others.

The model currently consists of 123 equations, including 27 estimated equations; the latter are estimated using two-stage least squares, so as to account for the simultaneity in the system of equations. These equations are estimated also accounting for possible AR(p) serial correlation in the errors, as needed; but most of the estimated equations do not require such corrections, due to the judicious use of lagged explanatory variables. The 96 non-estimated equations are identities. Most of these are definitional – e.g., calculating the government surplus as receipts minus expenditures, converting nominal wages into real wages, or converting GDP into GNP – and others incorporate the "budget constraints" of the flow-of-funds accounting framework, alluded to above.

For example, the FAIRMODEL equation for the services component of aggregate consumption, as estimated on October 29, 2010 using data from 1954I through 2010III, is[89]

---

[87] "VAR" stands for "vector autoregression." A VAR model is the multivariate analogue of the AR(p) discussed in Section 17.6 – a variable Y_t is modeled as a linear function of p lags of itself and of each of the other variables in the model; VAR modeling is covered briefly in Section 18.4 above and at length in Enders (2010, Sections 5.5-5.13). In four-quarter-ahead post-sample forecasting over the period 1983:1 to 2002:3, for example, the MSE of FAIRMODEL's forecasts of real GDP, the unemployment rate, and the short-term interest rate is smaller than that of a seven-variable VAR model by 54%, 41%, and 16%, respectively. On the other hand, the VAR model is better (by 28%) for the GDP deflator, and is generally more competitive for one-quarter-ahead forecasts. These figures are calculated using the "US+" results in Table 14-1 of Fair (2004); the VAR model Fair used in these comparisons is described in Section 14.3 of Fair (2004). See Fair, R. C. (2004), *Estimating How the Economy Works*, Harvard University Press: Cambridge, and also fairmodel.econ.yale.edu/rayfair/pdf/2003a.htm.

[88] This workbook is posted at Web site fairmodel.econ.yale.edu/wrkbook/wb.htm; a key excerpt (quoted with permission) is: "The theoretical work stressed three ideas: 1) basing macroeconomics on solid microeconomic foundations, 2) allowing for the possibility of disequilibrium in some markets, and 3) accounting for all balance sheet and flow of funds constraints. The stress on microeconomic foundations for macroeconomics has come to dominate macro theory, and this work in the early 1970s is consistent with the current emphasis. The introduction of disequilibrium possibilities in some markets provides an explanation of business cycles that is consistent with maximizing behavior. The model explains disequilibrium on the basis of non rational expectations. Agents must form expectations of the future values of various variables before solving their multiperiod maximization problems. It is assumed that no agent knows the complete model, and so expectations are not rational. Firms, for example, make their price and wage decisions based on expectations that are not rational, which can cause disequilibrium in the goods and labor markets."

[89] These estimates are taken from Table A1 in fairmodel.econ.yale.edu/wrkbook/xatapa.pdf at the time of this writing; by the time you read this, the contents at this link (labeled "Appendix A: the US Model ... ") will have changed, but the link itself will (hopefully) still be valid. So as to facilitate comparison of this equation to the display of the $\log(CS_t/POP_t)$ equation under the "Modify Equations" option of the "home" menu, note that – within the software – the variables $\log(CS_t/POP_t)$, $\log(YD_t/[POP_t{\cdot}PH_t)$, and $\log(AA_t/POP_t)$ are denoted *LCSZ*, *LYDZ*, and *LAAZ*, respectively.

$$\log\left(\frac{CS_t}{POP_t}\right) = \underset{(-1.92)}{-0.47} + \underset{(25.0)}{.838}\log\left(\frac{CS_{t-1}}{POP_{t-1}}\right) + \underset{(0.87)}{.030}\log\left(\frac{YD_t}{POP_t PH_t}\right)$$

$$\underset{(-1.60)}{-.061}\, AG1_t - \underset{(-8.26)}{.529}\, AG2_t + \underset{(4.14)}{.363}\, AG3_t$$

$$\underset{(-5.05)}{-.00098}\, RSA_t + \underset{(7.37)}{.035}\log\left(\frac{AA_{t-1}}{POP_{t-1}}\right) + \underset{(4.98)}{.00048t} + U_t$$

where the figures in parentheses are the estimated t-ratios for the parameter estimates and the variables are defined, for quarter t, as follows:

CS_t	Consumer expenditures for services, in billions of 2005 dollars.
POP_t	Noninstitutional population, 16 years and older, in millions.
YD_t	Household disposable income, in billions of dollars.
PH_t	Price deflator for households.
$AG1_t$	Percent of POP_t aged 26–55 minus percent of POP_t aged 16–25.
$AG2_t$	Percent of POP_t aged 56–65 minus percent of POP_t aged 16–25.
$AG3_t$	Percent of POP_t aged 66 or older minus percent of POP_t aged 16–25.
RSA_t	After-tax 30-day Treasury bill rate.
AA_t	Household total net wealth, in billions of 2005 dollars.

Two of the explanatory variables in this equation – $\log[YD_t/(POP_t \cdot PH_t)]$ and RSA_t – are endogenous, so these are instrumented using first-stage regression equations, as noted above.[90]

This equation fits extremely well (and has fitting errors which appear to be non-autocorrelated) in large part because the dependent variable enters in lagged form with such a large coefficient: in fact, this equation is, in large part, an AR(1) model. But not entirely, as the current short-term interest rate, the lagged value of per-capita household wealth, a time trend, and the age-structure of the population also enter the regression equation significantly.[91] Note that the coefficient on real per-capita disposable income in this equation is positive, but not statistically significant. Fair evidently retained this explanatory variable in the services consumption equation because theory so strongly suggests its inclusion that he considered this to be a better estimate than zero; it enters the other two consumption equations (modeling the consumption of durable and of non-durable goods) with a positive and statistically significant coefficient.[92]

[90] Two-Stage Least Squares estimation was described in Section 12.5. The exogenous and predetermined variables used in the first-stage regressions for each equation in FAIRMODEL are listed in Table A.9 of the "Appendix A" link described in the previous footnote.

[91] Many FAIRMODEL equations heavily rely on a lagged dependent variable, but only three of the 27 estimated equations use time trend variables. The coefficient on the time trend is statistically significant, but very small. There is clearly a danger in extrapolating a substantial trend over a 40-quarter post-sample period; perhaps it is better to instead model the change in log (CS_t/POP_t), but this was Fair's choice. The age-structure of the household population enters significantly into all three of the FAIRMODEL consumption equations; thus, including these variables both improves the fit of the three consumption equations and also prevents inconsistency in the coefficient estimates on any explanatory variables in these equations which themselves are correlated with the age structure of the population.

[92] Also, Fair uses the most recently available data to update the parameter estimates quite frequently, but only respecifies the model equations at relatively lengthy intervals; thus, this coefficient may typically be larger relative to its estimated standard error than it is at this particular time.

A remarkable feature to FAIRMODEL is that Fair has implemented it on his Web page in such a way that it is very easy to use the current version of the model to calculate the impact of a posited change in economic policy on the model's forecast of the time path of key economic variables. For example, one can alter the posited time path for the total government purchases of goods (COG_t) or for the employee social security tax rate ($D4G_t$) and examine the impact of this alteration on the forecasted time paths of real GDP ($GDPR_t$), the price level as viewed by households (PH_t), the unemployment rate (UR_t), the government deficit ($-SGP_t$), or other variables in the model. In this way, one can explicitly calculate the dynamic government spending or tax multipliers for the model. This Active Learning Exercise will lead you through such a policy evaluation exercise.

Your Assignment:

1. Visit the FAIRMODEL Web site (at fairmodel.econ.yale.edu/main3.htm) and read the material in the first three links under the heading "Getting Started." (These links are about halfway down the page.) The link labeled "About US Model User Datasets" is particularly important because your task in this exercise revolves around making your own changes to the assumptions in the "BASE" dataset, recalculating the model's forecasts, and comparing these results. On the other hand, don't be surprised or dismayed as you encounter some details in these links which are not obvious: the directions below will lead you through what you need to do.
2. Next follow either of the two links labeled "The US Workbook." The "Preface" gives an overview of the entire workbook, but what is probably most useful is to just read sections 1.1 through 2.3 at this point: this material will make better sense to you after you have worked with FAIRMODEL a bit in the steps below.
3. Now return to the Web address at which you began (fairmodel.econ.yale.edu/main3.htm) and select the link immediately under the heading "The US Model." This link is labeled "(Solve the current version (October 29, 2010) of the model)" at the moment; the date, of course, will be different when you reach it.
4. The resulting screen will ask you to type in a dataset name and password. These are your choice, except that the dataset name can be at most eight characters in length and both are apparently case-insensitive. You might want to note down the dataset name and password that you choose so that you can return to this dataset at a later time – i.e., when you are sitting down with your instructor and puzzling over your results.[93]
5. At this point you will be prompted as to whether or not to copy the BASE dataset into yours; you want to do that for this exercise, so press the "Copy" button. At this point the program should display a screen indicating that it is "attempting to create your dataset" and then prompt you to click on the "Proceed" button shortly thereafter.[94] Doing so should yield a screen with "The US Model" at the top. This screen will be called the "main menu" below; you can return to it by selecting the "home" link in the upper-right corner of subsequent FAIRMODEL screens.

[93] It is a good idea to choose a separate dataset name for each of the forecasting exercises you do. Fair's program will prompt you to choose a different name if your choice already exists on the system – you may need to include a number in order to find a unique name.

[94] If nothing happens, it probably means that your Web browser is not allowing Javascript. Javascript does not seem to be an issue in the current version of Internet Explorer, even with the security level set to "High" or to the default value of "Medium-High" using the Tools|Internet Options| Security menu. The "Enable JavaScript" option is a checkbox in the Tools|Options|Content menu in most versions of Firefox.

6. Select the "Change exogenous variables" link. The right-hand side of the screen lists all of the exogenous variables in FAIRMODEL whose assumed time paths can be modified from those specified in the BASE simulation. These are all listed (along with the equation estimates, etc.) in Appendix A of the US Model Workbook, but the variable you are going to modify in this exercise is COG, which is right at the top of the list.[95]
7. The variable COG denotes Federal government purchases of goods in billions of inflation-adjusted dollars in FAIRMODEL. Selecting the COG link replaces the list of variables by a set of input boxes allowing you to individually change each value of COG in the dataset from its (listed) BASE value. Instead of doing that, however, for this exercise you will type the value 10 in the box immediately to the right of the "Add to each of the existing values" label and press the Return ("Enter") key. The display on the right-hand side of the screen should immediately change to indicate that each "New" value of COG (after the first eight periods, which are used for "starting up" the simulations) is now either 10 or 9.99999 larger than that listed for the "BASE" simulation. No change is made to your dataset until the "Commit to Changes" button on the left hand side of the screen is selected, however. After checking (on the right-hand side of the screen) that the values of COG are now indeed larger by 10 billion dollars, click on this "Commit to Changes" button. Now return to the main menu by selecting the "Home" link at the top of the screen.
8. Next select the "Change assumptions about monetary policy" link and read the material displayed. You will be using the default option in this first simulation: this means that FAIRMODEL Equation 30 – which determines the Treasury Bill rate (RS) endogenously, based on Fair's model of the Fed's past behavior – is used to calculate RS. Press the "Return" button to return to the main menu.
9. Next select the "Solve the model and examine the results" link in the main menu. The equations of FAIRMODEL are solved numerically for each of the 40 forecast periods using an iterative process called the Gauss-Seidel method. Basically, an initial guess for each variable is substituted into the right-hand side of each model equation; this yields a new value of the variable determined by this equation, for use in the next iteration.[96] If the changes one has made in the model are not too large, this solution method usually converges after 9 or 10 iterations: the screen will indicate how many iterations were needed for each period. If it indicates "Solution done," then the process converged and the new values for the endogenous variables have been written to your dataset. At this point, press the "Proceed" button.
10. At this point you can select how to display the results of your new simulation, here with COG larger by \$10B in each simulation period. For the purposes of this exercise, select the radio button labeled "Use BASE" in the "Comparison Dataset" box, so that your results will be compared to those of the BASE simulation. You can type whatever variable names you want into the "List of Variables for Output" box (separated by spaces) or you can select variable names from the list at the bottom of the page and press the "Add to Current List" button. (See Section 2.2 of the US Workbook for more information about the variables.) For this exercise, however, it suffices to select COG,

[95] Appendix A can be accessed directly at fairmodel.econ.yale.edu/wrkbook/xatapa.pdf or by selecting the "Appendix A" link at fairmodel.econ.yale.edu/main3.htm.

[96] See the "Solutions" portion of Section 1.1 of the US Model Workbook for a more detailed description of how this iterative solution process works.

GDPR, UR, and SGP from the list. (Or you can just type these into the box.) COG is included so as to confirm that you did indeed increase it by $10B; GDPR is real GDP; UR is the unemployment rate, and SGP is the total government surplus.[97] Once these four variable names are entered in the "List of Variables for Output" box, press the "Display Output" button.

11. First confirm that the value of COG is indeed $10B larger in the column labeled with the name of your dataset. Now look at the results for real GDP (i.e., for GDP) and note that it is larger in your simulation than in the BASE simulation – and by more than the $10B increase in government spending. Evidently, a Keynesian fiscal stimulus does have an impact on real output, in FAIRMODEL, at least. Each of these increments to RGDP, divided by 10, is the "dynamic multiplier" for that period. Print out this table; also, copy and paste the increment column into a spreadsheet and make a plot of the dynamic multiplier versus the number of periods since the increase in COG began. How large does the dynamic multiplier on government spending get? What happens to it over time?
12. What impact does this fiscal stimulus have on the unemployment rate over time?
13. What impact does this fiscal stimulus have on the Federal government deficit (-SGP) over time?
14. Repeat this simulation exercise assuming that the Fed employs accommodating monetary policy to keep the interest rate (RS) from changing in response to the $10B increase in COG. To do this, begin with a new dataset, again increase COG and now additionally select the "Drop or add equations" link from the main menu, uncheck the box in front of "RS – Bill rate", and press the "Save Changes" button. How does the dynamic multiplier now obtained compare to that in which the Fed behaves as usual, as modeled by Equation 30?

[97] Thus, −SGP is the federal government deficit.

18

A Concise Introduction to Time-Series Analysis and Forecasting (Part B)

18.1 INTEGRATED – ARIMA(*p,d,q*) – MODELS AND "TRENDLIKE" BEHAVIOR

The most fundamental requirement in order to model a time-series Y_t using the Box-Jenkins algorithm given at the end of the previous chapter is that the time-series must be covariance stationary – including a finding that the time-series is I(0). An assumption of covariance stationarity can be violated in a number of ways, as was described (at some length) in Section 17.3; here the focus is on violations due to "trendlike" behavior. Covariance stationarity of Y_t implies that both $E[Y_t]$ and $\text{var}(Y_t)$ are well-defined constants over time. Trendlike behavior in a time-series, in contrast, can lead to a time-varying value of $E[Y_t]$ and/or to an unbounded (ill-defined) value of $\text{var}(Y_t)$, either of which strongly violates an assumption of covariance stationarity.

Trendlike behavior in a time-series Y_t is variation which changes so smoothly (and slowly) over the length of the observed sample that one cannot discern multiple cycles or oscillations in Y_t during the course of this sample, as such cycles are either not occurring at all or are occurring too slowly as to be apparent in a record of this length. Clearly, then, variation which appears to be a smooth upward or downward trend-like variation over a sample of 100 observations could be part of a lengthy set of random, noise-like cycles, whose presence only becomes obvious over a sample of 10,000 or 100,000 observations. Or, alternatively, the mean value of the time-series might continue to smoothly rise – due to some exogenous influence – over the longer sample. In fact, absent the longer sample period, there is no way to know with any certainty whether one is in the midst of a "global" trend which will continue on indefinitely or whether one is instead at the top of a "local" trend which will soon, smoothly, change direction.[1]

Such considerations point at the huge dangers inherent in extrapolating trendlike behavior substantially into the future. The ARMA modeling described in Chapter 17, in contrast, is focused

[1] Ashley and Patterson (2010, Section 3) illustrate how this occurs in a record of long-term data on the Earth's average temperature, measured at 2,000 year (2 kyr.) intervals over the last 3,264 kyrs. Based on this sample, the average planetary temperature is clearly trending downward over this period, with noisy cycles ("ice ages") apparent in the data set if one looks at 100 kyr. subsamples. There is even simple geological theory supporting such a trend: one expects the Earth's core heat to be slowly leaking away over time. Interestingly, a data set discussed in Phillips (2010) going much farther back in time (ca. 540,000 kyr.) immediately refutes this notion: numerous noisy-looking cycles appear in this longer record. What is trend-like in a sample of one length can clearly be a sequence of noisy cycles in a sample that is 100 times longer! Ashley, R., and D. M. Patterson (2010), "Apparent Long Memory in Time-Series as an Artifact of a Time-Varying Mean: Considering Alternatives to the Fractionally Integrated Model," *Macroeconomic Dynamics 14*, 59–87. Phillips, P. C. B. "The Mysteries of Trend" Cowles Foundation Discussion Paper #1771. URL: cowles.econ.yale.edu/.

on using low-lag serial correlations in a time-series – i.e., ρ_1, ρ_2, ρ_3, etc. – to modeling the short-term evolution mechanism of Y_t. Here, trendlike behavior in the time-series is more of a distortionary nuisance: we need to eliminate any trendlike behavior in the time-series so as to obtain covariance stationary data for which ρ_1, ρ_2, ρ_3, etc. can be consistently estimated and then be used to construct MA(q), AR(p), or ARMA(p, q) models useful for short-term forecasting.

Unfortunately, trendlike behavior comes in two, fundamentally distinct, varieties: deterministic and stochastic. Each of these sources of trendlike behavior can be handled; the problem is identifying which one is present.

Each of these two sources of trendlike behavior is illustrated below, using three simple examples based on generated data: two with deterministic trends and one with a stochastic trend. These examples are then used to illustrate the relative desirability of three feasible modeling strategies:

- Box-Jenkins Approach: "difference (or not) based on the sample correlogram."
- Unit-Roots Test Approach: "difference (or not) based on the outcome of a unit roots test."
- Hybrid Approach: "decide based on the totality of the symptoms."

The "Hybrid Approach" turns out to be the most useful of the three for producing short-term forecasting models. With regard to producing long-term forecasts which attempt to exploit trend-like patterns in a time-series, it should be emphasized at the outset that the best policy for an analyst is actually a simple refusal to participate in such an endeavor, as it can very easily produce disastrously poor results.

The first two examples illustrate deterministic trendlike behavior. In both of these cases, Y_t is taken to be a smooth (non-random) function of time, $f(t)$, plus a covariance stationary model error term. The "Deterministic Trend #1" example illustrates the case of notably autocorrelated model errors; the "Deterministic Trend #2" case, in contrast, illustrates the case of *quite* highly autocorrelated model errors. This latter case is in keeping with what one often sees in practice with data exhibiting trendlike behavior. The function $f(t)$ could be any smooth function; a simple linear time trend is used here in both of these examples:

{Deterministic Trend #1}

$$\begin{aligned} Y_t^{\text{det.trend \#1}} &= 0.02\,t + v_t \\ v_t &= 0.7 v_{t-1} + U_t \\ U_t &\sim \text{NIID}(0,1) \quad t = 1 \ldots 500 \end{aligned} \tag{18-1}$$

{Deterministic Trend #2}

$$\begin{aligned} Y_t^{\text{det.trend \#2}} &= 0.05\,t + v_t \\ v_t &= 0.9 v_{t-1} + U_t \\ U_t &\sim \text{NIID}(0,1) \quad t = 1 \ldots 500 \end{aligned} \tag{18-2}$$

Note that neither $Y_t^{\text{det.trend \#1}}$ nor $Y_t^{\text{det.trend \#2}}$ is covariance stationary: in both cases this is because the expected value of Y_t clearly depends on time. Figures 18-1a,b and 18-2a,b display time-plots and sample correlograms for these two time-series. Note that, indeed, both of these series display clear evidence of trendlike behavior and both have sample correlograms which start quite close to one at lag one – i.e., for r_1 – and decay very slowly for larger lags.[2]

[2] The time trends in these two time-series are both intentionally more marked than that plotted in Figure 17-7 in Section 17.3: that example was intended to illustrate something different: how even a modest time trend distorts the decay of the sample correlogram at large lags.

(a) Time Plot

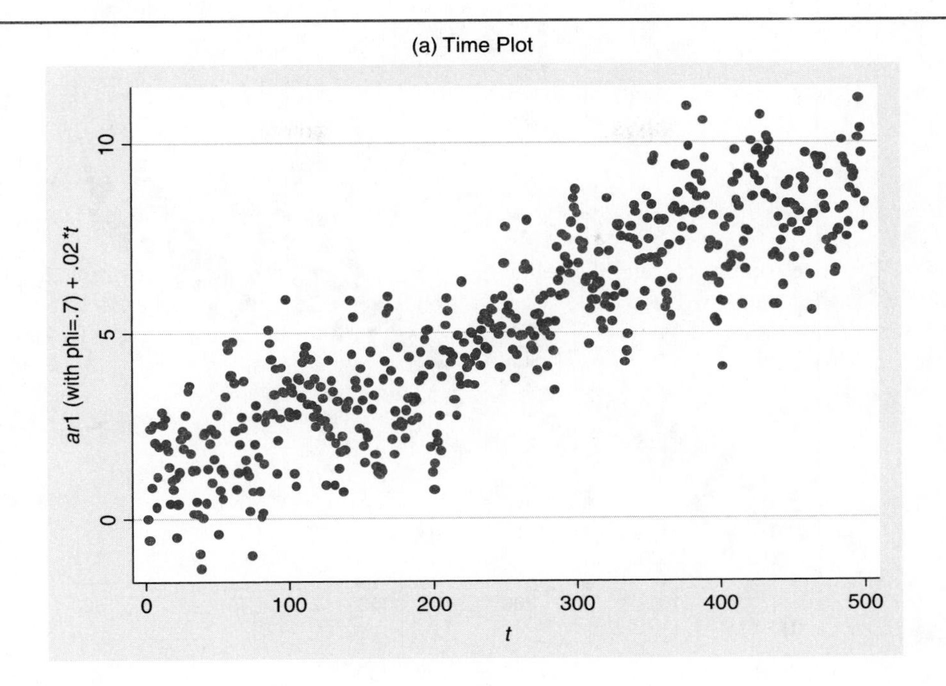

(b) Sample Correlogram

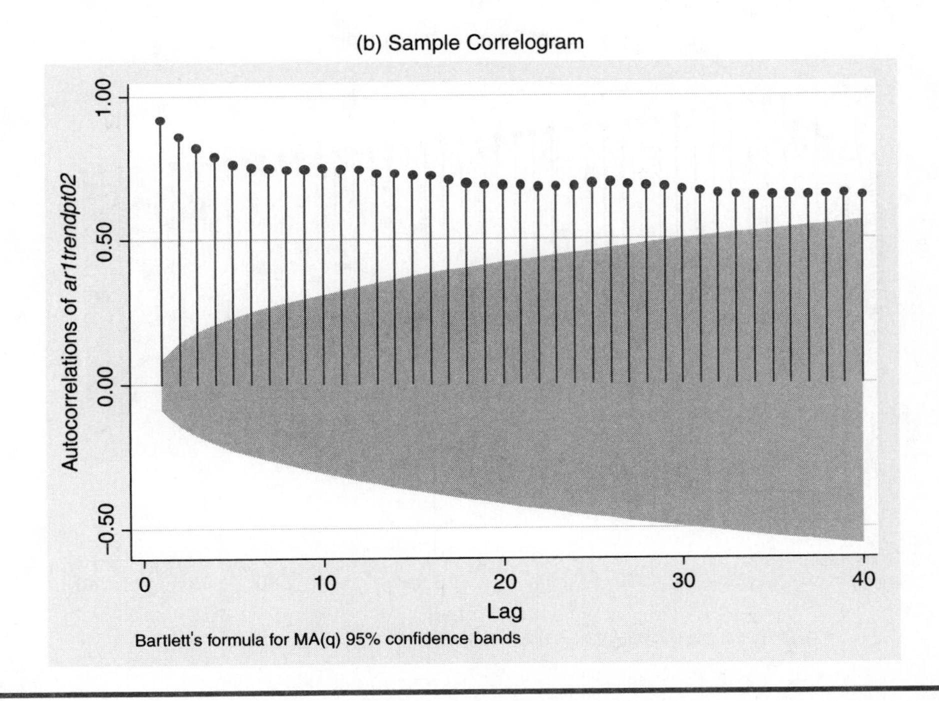

Figure 18-1 Generated Time-Series with Deterministic Time Trend #1

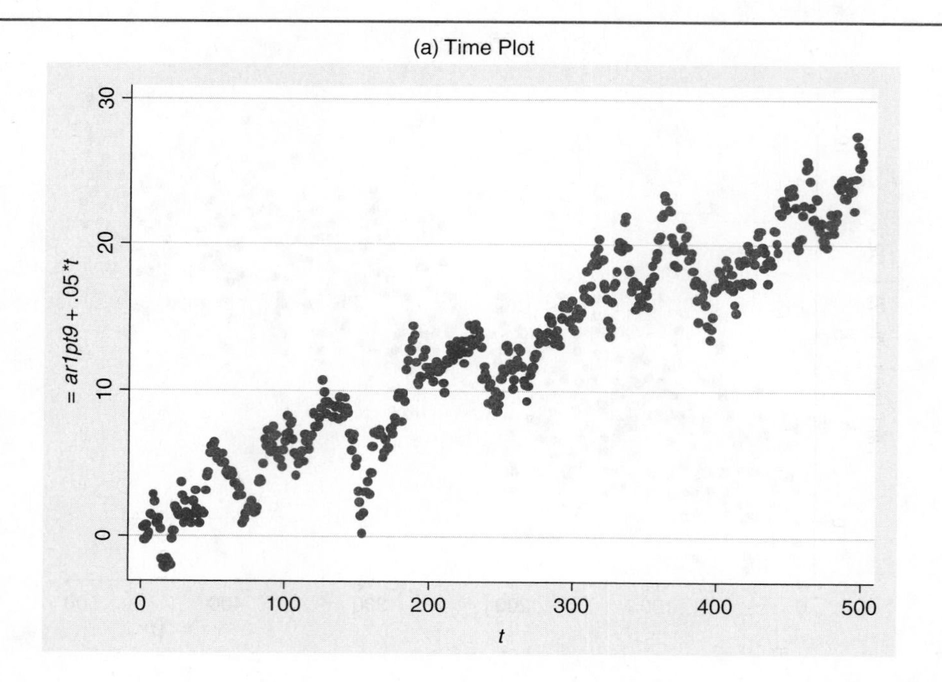

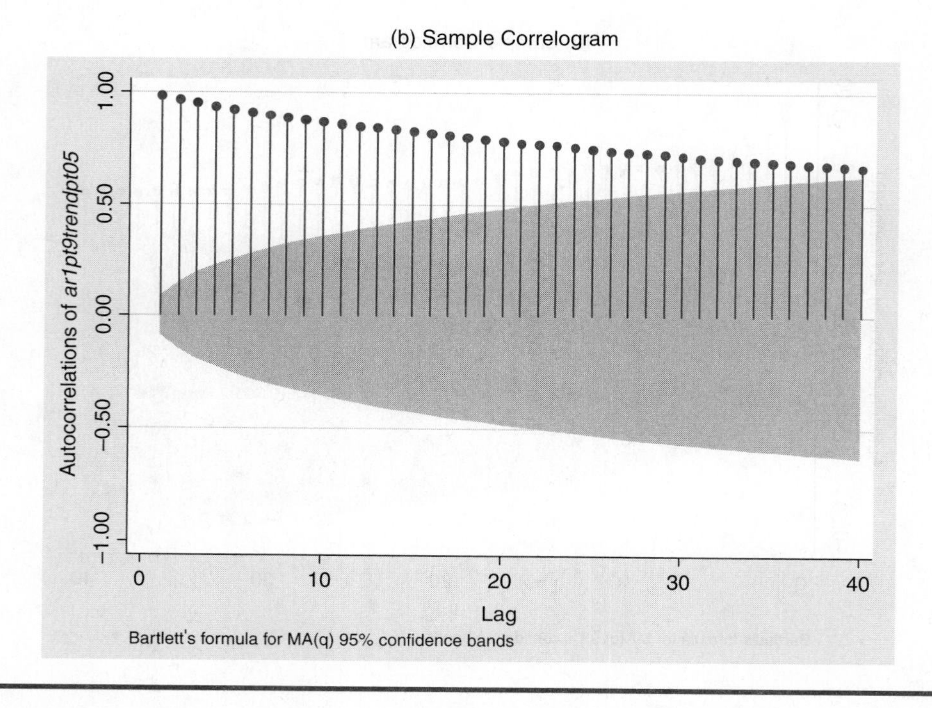

Figure 18-2 Generated Time-Series with Deterministic Time Trend #2

The third example illustrates stochastic trendlike behavior. The data in this case are generated from a "random walk" model:

$$\{\text{Stochastic Trend}\} \qquad \begin{aligned} Y_t^{\text{stoch.trend}} &= Y_{t-1}^{\text{stoch.trend}} + U_t \\ U_t &\sim \text{NIID}(0,1) \quad t = 1 \ldots 500 \end{aligned} \tag{18-3}$$

This random walk model was investigated at some length in Section 14.3 – as the limiting case of the AR(1) process given in Equation 14-4, where the parameter φ_1 goes to one. There it became evident (from Equation 14-8) that the variance of such a process becomes unboundedly large in this limit. Alternatively, taking the value of $Y_0^{\text{stoch.trend}}$ as fixed (i.e., known) in period zero, Equation 14-10 showed that the variance of $Y_t^{\text{stoch.trend}}$ increases linearly with time thereafter. Either way, $Y_t^{\text{stoch.trend}}$ defined in this way cannot be covariance stationary, because it does not have a well-defined, constant variance.

A time plot of the 500 generated values of $Y_t^{\text{stoch.trend}}$, and its sample correlogram, are given in Figure 18-3. Note that $Y_t^{\text{stoch.trend}}$ exhibits trendlike behavior also, even though Equation 18-3 does not include a linear time trend term.

In fact, the behavior over the sample period of all three of these time-series is pretty much the same: all three time-series appear to be somewhat noisy, but dominated by an upward trend. Indeed, the behavior of $Y_t^{\text{stoch.trend}}$ seems even more "trendlike" than the behavior of $Y_t^{\text{det. trend \#1}}$ and $Y_t^{\text{det. trend \#2}}$ in that it appears to rise more smoothly and predictably over time. The time-series $Y_t^{\text{det. trend \#1}}$ varies less smoothly around its trend; the trendlike behavior in $Y_t^{\text{stoch.trend}}$ and in $Y_t^{\text{det. trend \#2}}$ on the other hand appear to be almost identical.

Yet, knowing their generating mechanisms, it is obvious that these data sets ideally ought to be treated quite differently in order to produce a covariance stationary time-series suitable for use in identifying and estimating any kind of ARMA(p, q) model. In particular, $Y_t^{\text{det. trend \#1}}$ and $Y_t^{\text{det. trend \#2}}$ ought to be regressed against some function of time; the fitting errors from such a regression will likely be covariance stationary. In contrast, a first difference of $Y_t^{\text{stoch.trend}}$ will clearly be covariance stationary.

But how can one distinguish deterministic trendlike behavior from stochastic trendlike behavior? In theory, it is very easy: one merely "runs the world over again" by generating new sequences of 500 observations. $Y_t^{\text{det. trend \#1}}$ and $Y_t^{\text{det. trend \#2}}$ will be dominated by an upward trend every single time one does that. In contrast, while $Y_t^{\text{stoch.trend}}$ will be dominated by some kind of trend almost every single time, the *character* of the trend will be different for each newly generated time-series: some of these newly generated time-series will still be trended upward, but just as many will be trended downward.[3] The difference will be quite obvious after a handful of repetitions.

Of course, such repetitions are impossible in the real world. So what is to be done in practice? Three possible stategies are listed at the beginning of this section; each will now be discussed in turn.

The "Box-Jenkins Approach" is very straightforward. On this view, if the sample correlogram of Y_t starts out with r_1 large – i.e., greater than 0.90, say – and r_j decays very slowly as j increases over the next 20 to 40 (or more) lags, then Y_t should be differenced. In this view, if the sample correlogram of $(1–B)Y_t$ still has a large value for r_1 and r_j is still slowly decaying as j increases, then $(1–B)Y_t$ needs to itself be differenced: in that case perhaps $(1–B)^2Y_t$ will have a sample correlogram that promptly decays into the noise level, quantified, of course, by the Bartlett standard error estimates. And so forth. Eventually, under this approach, the data will have been differenced 'd' times and one will have thereby produced a time-series which is covariance stationary and can thus be modeled as an ARMA(p, q) process. As noted in Section 14.3, such a time-series is said to be

[3] And the trendlike behavior in some of these newly-generated series will also look less linear than the particular $Y_t^{\text{stoch. trend}}$ realization used here.

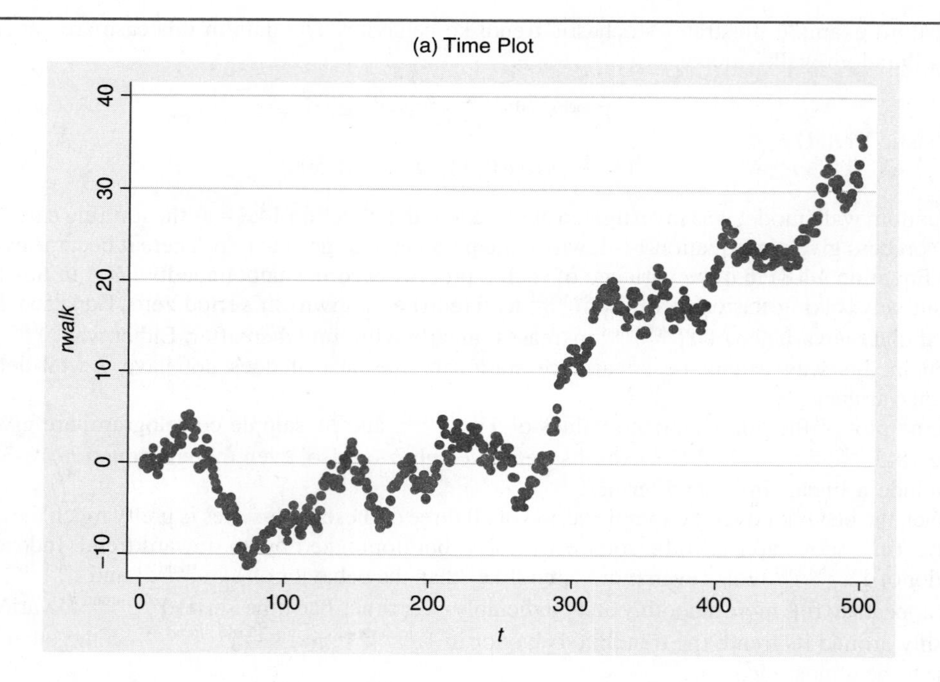

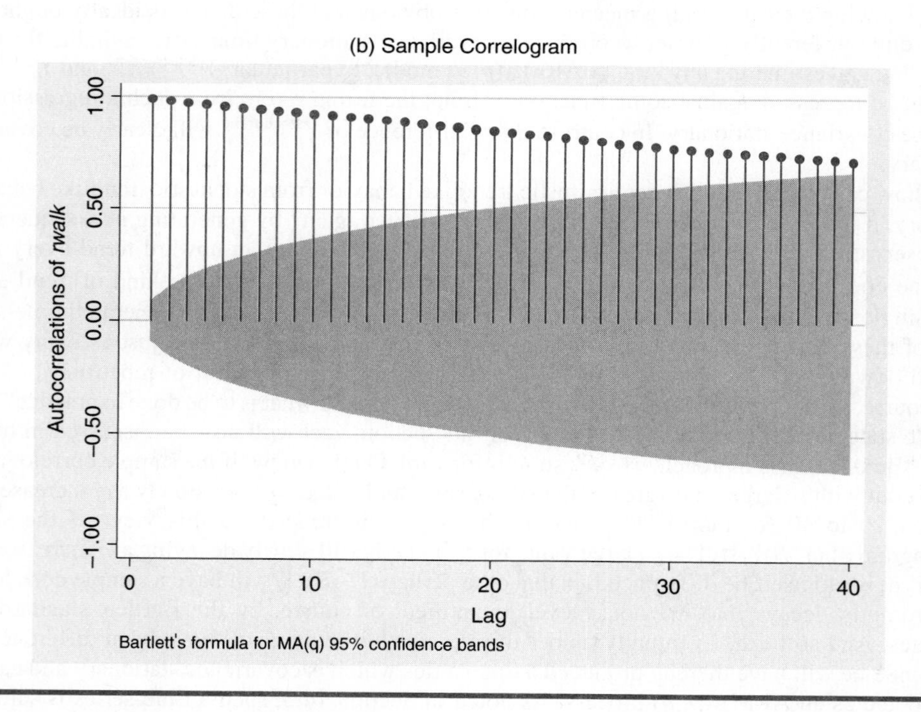

Figure 18-3 Stochastic Time Trend (Random Walk)

"integrated of order d" or, more compactly: $Y_t \sim I(d)$. In an intuitively obvious notation, then, Box and Jenkins denoted such a Y_t as generated by an "ARIMA(p, d, q)" model.[4]

One might fear, at first glance, that this approach would suffer from the subjectivity involved in deciding whether or not the sample correlogram "looks like" it is starting at a high level and failing to decay. Usually, however, this decision is pretty obvious, as in Figures 18-1, 18-2, and 18-30 illustrate: all three of these time-series should clearly be differenced on the Box-Jenkins criterion. Of course, that decision is incorrect in the cases of $Y_t^{\text{det. trend \#1}}$ and $Y_t^{\text{det. trend \#2}}$. Thus, the "Box-Jenkins Approach" can give a clear indiction as to when a difference is necessary, but this clear indication is sometimes false, leaving one with over-differenced model errors.

Using the second decision approach mentioned at the beginning of this section – the "Unit-Roots Test Approach" – one performs a unit root test on Y_t and makes the differencing decision based on the outcome of the test. The unit root test almost always used for this purpose in the Augmented Dickey Fuller (ADF) test, described in Section 14.3. The null hypothesis for this test is that Y_t does in fact have a unit root, so that it needs to be differenced in order to be covariance stationary. If the ADF test rejects this null hypothesis, then that is a clear indication that the time-series should *not* be differenced.

Here the ADF test does clearly reject the unit root null hypothesis for both $Y_t^{\text{det. trend \#1}}$ and $Y_t^{\text{det. trend \#2}}$. For example, denoting $Y_t^{\text{det. trend \#2}}$ by $Y2$ and $(1-B)Y_t^{\text{det. trend \#2}}$ by $\Delta Y2$, the regression output for an ADF unit root test with respect to $Y_t^{\text{det. trend \#2}}$ is:

```
      Source |       SS       df       MS              Number of obs =     497
-------------+------------------------------           F(  4,   492) =    6.62
       Model |  23.6253679     4  5.90634196           Prob > F      =  0.0000
    Residual |  438.756575   492  .891781657           R-squared     =  0.0511
-------------+------------------------------           Adj R-squared =  0.0434
       Total |  462.381943   496   .93222166           Root MSE      =  .94434

------------------------------------------------------------------------------
ΔY2          |      Coef.   Std. Err.      t    P>|t|     [95% Conf. Interval]
-------------+----------------------------------------------------------------
           t |   .0047635   .0010072     4.73   0.000      .0027845    .0067426
Y2           |
         L1. |  -.1019033   .0207675    -4.91   0.000     -.1427072   -.0610993
ΔY2          |
         L1. |   .0344028   .0451776     0.76   0.447      -.054362    .1231675
         L2. |  -.0155969   .0450845    -0.35   0.730     -.1041789    .0729851
       _cons |   .1234784   .0871367     1.42   0.157     -.0477276    .2946843
------------------------------------------------------------------------------
```

where coefficient estimates on several lags in $(1-B)Y_t^{\text{det. trend \#2}}$ are included to show that a sufficient number were included in the model. Since the estimated t-ratio on $Y_{t-1}^{\text{det. trend \#2}}$ (of -4.91) is less than the relevant 1% critical point (-3.96, from Table 14-1), the ADF test rejects the null hypothesis of a

[4] Box and Jenkins (1976) came up with an example or two of chemical engineering process data for which an ARIMA(p, 2, q) might be appropriate, but this almost never occurs with economic or financial data; in practice, the issue is always just a choice between $d = 0$ and $d = 1$. Also, as noted in Section 17.3, where r_i is *not* particularly large but the sample correlogram still fails to decay promptly, this too is an indication of some type of failure of the covariance stationary assumption – e.g., a structural shift or a weak trend – but it does not indicate that a difference is necessary. Tests for "fractional integration" – where $(1-B)^{\delta}Y_t$ is covariance stationary for δ in the interval (0, 1) – have been studied quite a lot in recent years; where such tests reject H_o: $\delta = 0$ it is an indication of weak long-term trends in the data, not of either "fractional integration" or "long memory." See Ashley and Patterson (2010) for details. Ashley, R., and D. M. Patterson (2010), "Apparent Long Memory in Time-Series as an Artifact of a Time-Varying Mean: Considering Alternatives to the Fractionally Integrated Model." *Macroeconomic Dynamics 14:* 59–87. ashleymac.econ.vt.edu/working_papers/long_memory.pdf.

unit root for this series. So the "Unit-Roots Test approach" corrects the false indications from the "Box-Jenkins Approach."

Turning to the time-series generated to actually have a stochastic trend, $Y_{t-1}^{\text{stoch. trend}}$, the "Box-Jenkins Approach" clearly and correctly indicates that this time-series should be differenced.

But the "Unit-Roots Test approach" does not give such a clear-cut answer. Denoting $Y_t^{\text{stoch.trend}}$ by Ystoch and $(1-B)Y_t^{\text{stoch.trend}}$ by ΔYstoch, the regression output for an ADF unit root test with respect to $Y_t^{\text{stoch.trend}}$ is:

```
      Source |       SS       df       MS              Number of obs =     497
-------------+------------------------------           F(  4,   492) =    2.10
       Model |  8.35368147     4  2.08842037           Prob > F      =  0.0799
    Residual |  489.693123   492  .995311226           R-squared     =  0.0168
-------------+------------------------------           Adj R-squared =  0.0088
       Total |  498.046804   496  1.00412662           Root MSE      =  .99765

------------------------------------------------------------------------------
     ΔYstoch |      Coef.   Std. Err.      t    P>|t|     [95% Conf.Interval]
-------------+----------------------------------------------------------------
           t |   .0018715   .0006896     2.71   0.007     .0005166    .0032265
      Ystoch |
         L1. |  -.0184073   .0081487    -2.26   0.024    -.0344179   -.0023966
     ΔYstoch |
         L1. |   .0286545   .0450132     0.64   0.525    -.0597874    .1170964
         L2. |  -.0312832   .0453108    -0.69   0.490    -.1203096    .0577433
       _cons |  -.2595269   .1291822    -2.01   0.045    -.5133437   -.0057101
------------------------------------------------------------------------------
```

again including several lags in $(1-B)Y_t^{\text{stoch.trend}}$ in the model to show that a sufficient number were included in the model.[5] The null hypothesis of a unit root in $Y_t^{\text{stoch.trend}}$ is not rejected at even the 10% level here – from Table 14-1, the estimated t-ratio on $Y_{t-1}^{\text{stoch.trend}}$ would have needed to be considerably more negative (−3.13) for such a rejection.

It is encouraging, of course, that the ADF test does not (incorrectly) reject the null hypothesis of a unit root in this instance. On the other hand, this failure to reject the null hypothesis is actually not all that informative – it is really more of a nonresult. In theory, a failure to reject the null hypothesis on a hypothesis test does not actually imply that one is justified in inferring that the null hypothesis is true: all it means is that the evidence against it was insufficient to reject the null hypothesis with the specified probability of being incorrect in so rejecting. The ADF test is designed so as to have low power to reject the null hypothesis when that hypothesis is true – indeed, by construction, a 5% ADF test should only reject the null hypothesis (of a unit root) incorrectly 5% of the time. But the ADF test is also known to have low power to reject the null hypothesis where it is actually false, but the data are simply highly autocorrelated. Notably, the ADF test is also known to have particularly small power to reject the null hypothesis of a unit root where there is a structural break in a time-series – i.e., where there is a sudden and permanent shift in the mean of the time-series.[6] Thus, the result of the ADF unit root test on $Y_t^{\text{stoch.trend}}$ – a failure to reject the null hypothesis of a unit root – is consistent with $Y_t^{\text{stoch.trend}}$ needing to be differenced, but this result is not really clear on the point.

Thus, the "Box-Jenkins Approach" and the "Unit-Roots Test Approach" each has its own drawbacks: the "Box-Jenkins Approach" can easily recommend differencing incorrectly and the "Unit-Roots Test Approach" will never actually, clearly recommend a difference. In addition, the "Unit-Roots Test Approach" will often fail to reject the difference in the presence of structural shifts

[5] Their presence does not materially alter the results.

[6] P. Perron (1989), "The Great Crash, the Oil Price Shock, and the Unit Root Hypothesis," *Econometrica 57*, 1361–1401.

– either sudden or smooth – or just through low power. Therefore the third – "Hybrid Approach" – listed above is the one advocated here. It combines all of the information at hand to make a more balanced decision, as follows:

Hybrid Approach:

1. First examine both the time-plot and the sample correlogram for Y_t.
   If Y_t looks very smooth and has a correlogram which starts out large and does not decay promptly, then tentatively decide to difference it. In the present examples, this would tentatively indicate that $Y_t^{\text{det. trend \#2}}$ and $Y_t^{\text{stoch.trend}}$ both need to be differenced; the need for a difference in $Y_t^{\text{det. trend \#1}}$ is bit less clear, as its time variation is not all that smooth.
2. In any cases where one tentatively decides to difference Y_t, go on to do the unit root test.
   a. If the unit root test rejects the null hypothesis of a unit root, then a difference is not called for: the sample correlogram behavior was due to a deterministic trend, which should be modeled.
   b. If the unit root test does *not* reject the null hypothesis of a unit root, then look at the time plots of Y_t and $(1–B)Y_t$ for evidence of a structural shift in Y_t which might explain this failure to reject the null hypothesis. If one is found, then it should be modeled; if no convincing evidence for a structural shift is found, then look for evidence that $(1–B)Y_t$ is over-differenced. (Such evidence would include significantly negative autocorrelation in $(1–B)Y_t$ at lag one (approaching -0.50) and/or an estimated AR(p) model for $(1–B)Y_t$ which drags out to long lags.) Absent such evidence for an overdifference in $(1–B)Y_t$, then one should go ahead and use the differenced series.

For the three examples given here, on would probably tentatively decide to difference all three series on Step 1. The unit root test would make it clear (Step 2a) that a difference is inappropriate for both $Y_t^{\text{det. trend \#1}}$ and $Y_t^{\text{det. trend \#2}}$. One would go on to Step 2b for $Y_t^{\text{stoch.trend}}$. Time plots of Y_t and $(1–B)Y_t$ convey no evidence that the failure to reject the unit root is an artifact of structural shifts. Further, the sample correlogram of $(1–B)Y_t^{\text{stoch.trend}}$ shows no evidence of significant serial correlation at lag one and AR(p) models for $(1–B)Y_t^{\text{stoch.trend}}$ are very weak and unexceptional. Thus, there is no evidence of overdifferencing in $(1–B)Y_t^{\text{stoch.trend}}$. Therefore, the procedure would (correctly) conclude that the evidence in the original sample correlogram for differencing $Y_t^{\text{stoch.trend}}$ is valid.

Thus, this "Hybrid Approach" yields good decisions in exchange for a modest additional effort, at least for the present examples, although one might complain that is a bit biased toward differencing rather than detrending. This is a good and appropriate tendency, in the author's view, however, as the downside risk of wrongly differencing is lower than that of wrongly detrending.[7]

Finally, from a "time-series analysis" point of view, one might naturally consider making this decision by holding out the last 100 sample observations and asking whether an ARIMA(p, *1*, q) model does a better job of forecasting how Y_t or $(1–B)Y_t$ varies during this postsample period than does a model positing a deterministic trend, $f(t)$. This comparison is usually not all that helpful in univariate modeling, as considered so far in this chapter, but can be valuable in the multivariate settings considered later in this chapter, in Section 18.4.

The key problem in forecasting any model positing a deterministic trend is specifying the trend values; these would be notated $f(401)$ ... $f(500)$ for the final 100 sample periods in the present context. Simply extrapolating the smooth behavior of $f(350)$ through $f(400)$ to continue on for the next 100 time periods would have worked fine in the three particular examples examined here, but would have been disastrous if the (actually) stochastic trend in Y_t had started randomly trending downward after period 400. For this reason – and especially in view of how difficult it is to

[7] Also, appropriate to its location in this chapter, the "Hybrid Approach" is a particularly reasonable strategy from the "time-series analysis" approach. In this regard, note that Chapter 14 tackles this same set of issues from the "time-series econometrics" point of view and reaches a somewhat different *modus operandi.*

distinguish deterministic trendlike behavior from stochastic trendlike behavior – extrapolation of trends very far beyond the sample data is an extraordinarily dangerous practice. Better to simply not do that.

18.2 A UNIVARIATE APPLICATION: MODELING THE MONTHLY U.S. TREASURY BILL RATE

Figure 18-4 plots monthly data on the three-month U.S. Treasury Bill Rate, $tb3ms_t$, obtained from the St. Louis Federal Reserve bank[8] for the period January 1934 through September 2010.

The data on $tb3ms_t$ itself are so thoroughly dominated by trendlike behavior in this series as to obscure all else. The time-plot of $(1\text{–}B)tb3ms_t$, however, makes it plain that the character of the data changes markedly in the middle of the time period – very roughly, from 1974 through 1983. A theoretically richer, multivariate framework might be able to make good use of this sample variation in the character of the data to estimate structural parameters; a univariate ARMA framework cannot. Consequently, the sample period here is restricted to just the 321-month period starting in period number 601, which corresponds to January 1984.

Figures 18-5 and 18-6 display a time-plot and sample correlogram for both the level series – $tb3ms_t$ – and its first-difference – $(1\text{–}B)tb3ms_t$ – over this restricted sample. The monthly change in the Treasury bill rate looks so smooth that the first-difference is probably necessary in order to make these data covariance stationary, but this is checked – per the "Hybrid Approach" of Section 18.1 – by applying (over this restricted sample) the Augmented Dickey Fuller (ADF) test, described in Section 14.3. The estimated ADF regression output is:

```
      Source |       SS       df       MS              Number of obs =     321
-------------+------------------------------           F(  5,    315) =   23.87
       Model |  4.67192788     5  .934385576           Prob > F      =  0.0000
    Residual |   12.328579   315  .039138346           R-squared     =  0.2748
-------------+------------------------------           Adj R-squared =  0.2633
       Total |  17.0005069   320  .053126584           Root MSE      =  .19783

------------------------------------------------------------------------------
  (1-B)tbill |      Coef.   Std. Err.      t    P>|t|     [95% Conf. Interval]
-------------+----------------------------------------------------------------
           t |  -.0004135   .0001964    -2.11   0.036    -.0007999   -.0000271
       tb3ms |
         L1. |  -.0207864   .0076171    -2.73   0.007    -.0357732   -.0057996
  (1-B)tbill |
         L1. |   .5248709   .0549139     9.56   0.000     .4168266    .6329152
         L2. |  -.1293497   .0616686    -2.10   0.037    -.2506841   -.0080153
         L3. |   .1771411   .0549667     3.22   0.001     .0689929    .2852893
       _cons |   .3957453   .1784047     2.22   0.027     .0447298    .7467607
------------------------------------------------------------------------------
```

The estimated t-ratio for the coefficient on $tb3ms_t$ in this regression equation (-2.73) exceeds even the 10% ADF test statistic critical point, of -3.13, from Table 14-1. Thus, the null hypothesis of a unit root in $tb3ms_t$ cannot be rejected at even the 10% level. This result only says that the null hypothesis of a unit root cannot be rejected, not that the alternative hypothesis is true. Nevertheless, in combination with the very smooth time plot, a sample correlogram which starts out extremely high and decays fairly slowly, and no evidence of overdifferencing in the sample correlogram of $(1\text{–}B)tb3ms_t$, the "Hybrid Approach" of the previous section indicates that the analysis should continue with the differenced data.

[8] research.stlouisfed.org/fred2/categories/116.

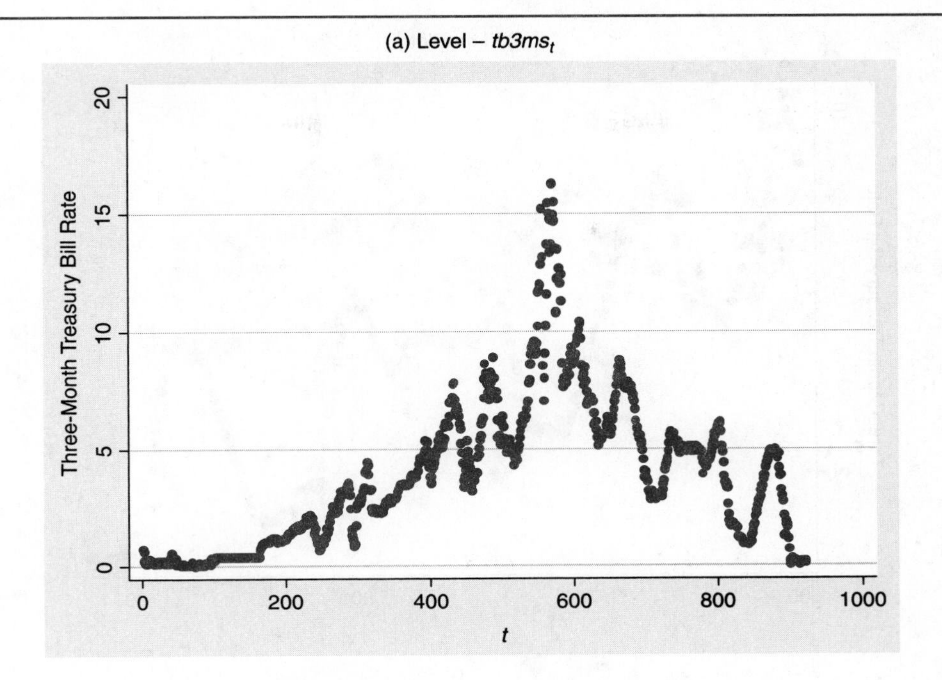

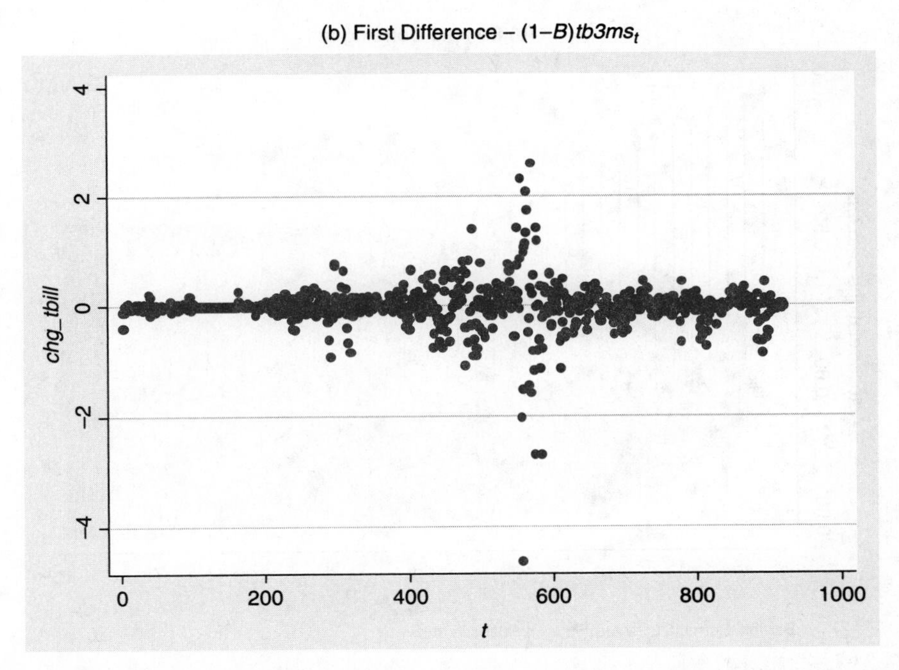

Figure 18-4 U.S. Treasury Bill Three-Month Rate January 1934 to September 2010

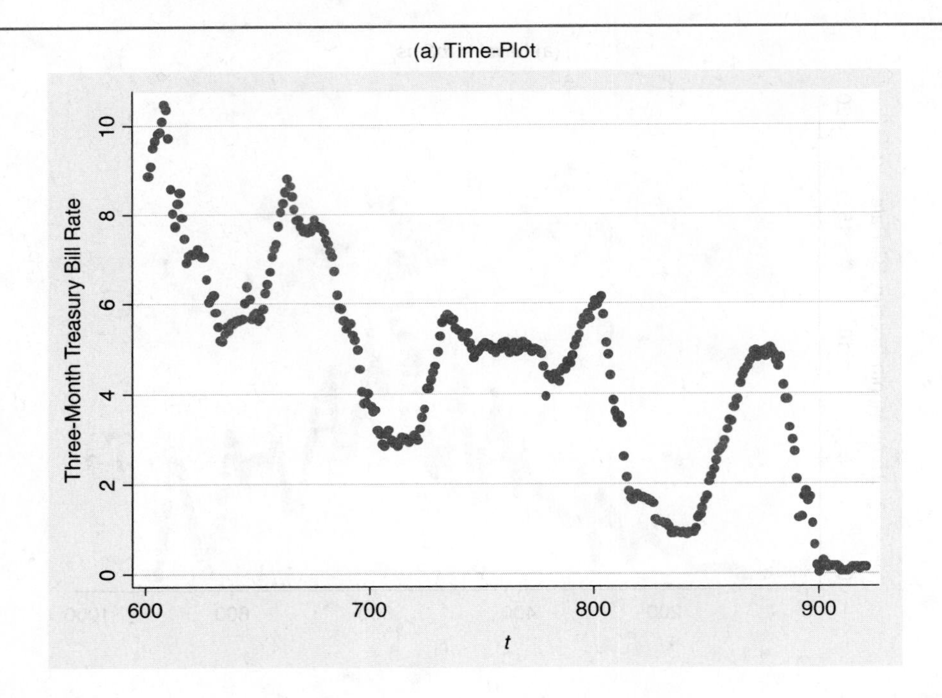

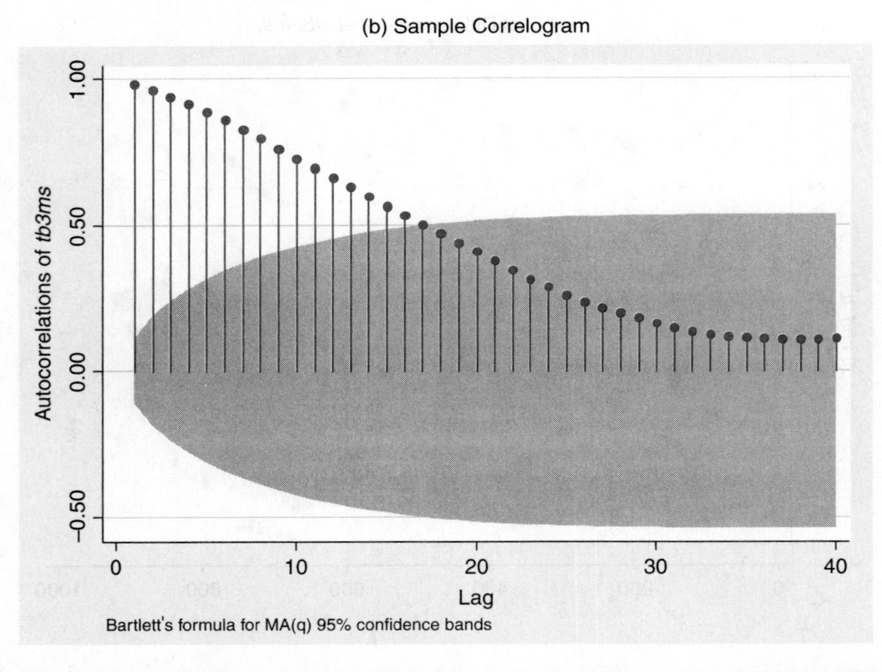

Figure 18-5 U.S. Treasury Bill Three-Month Rate – $tb3ms_t$ January 1984 to September 2010

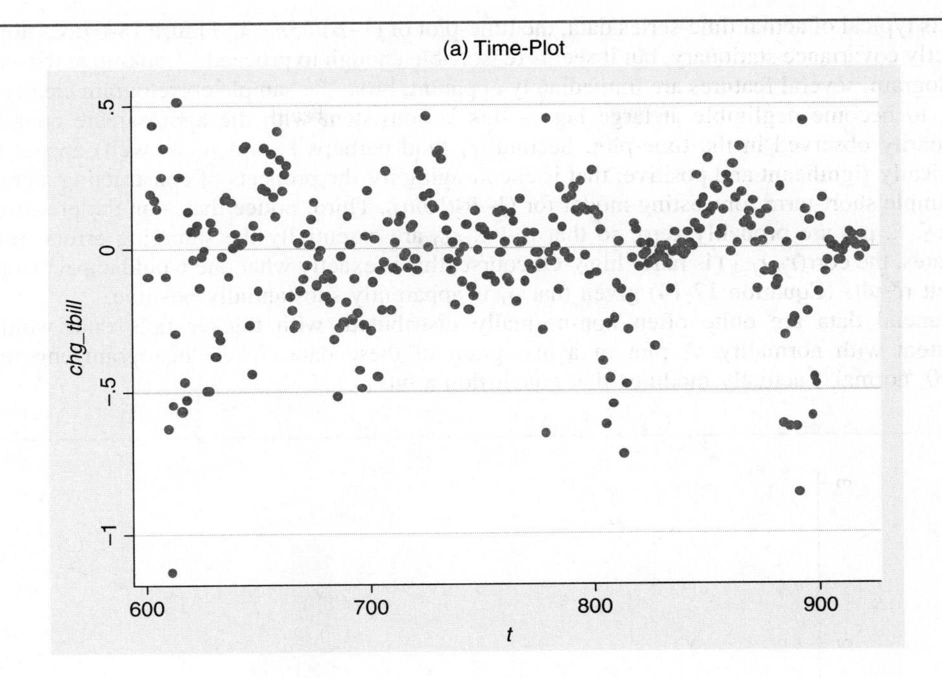

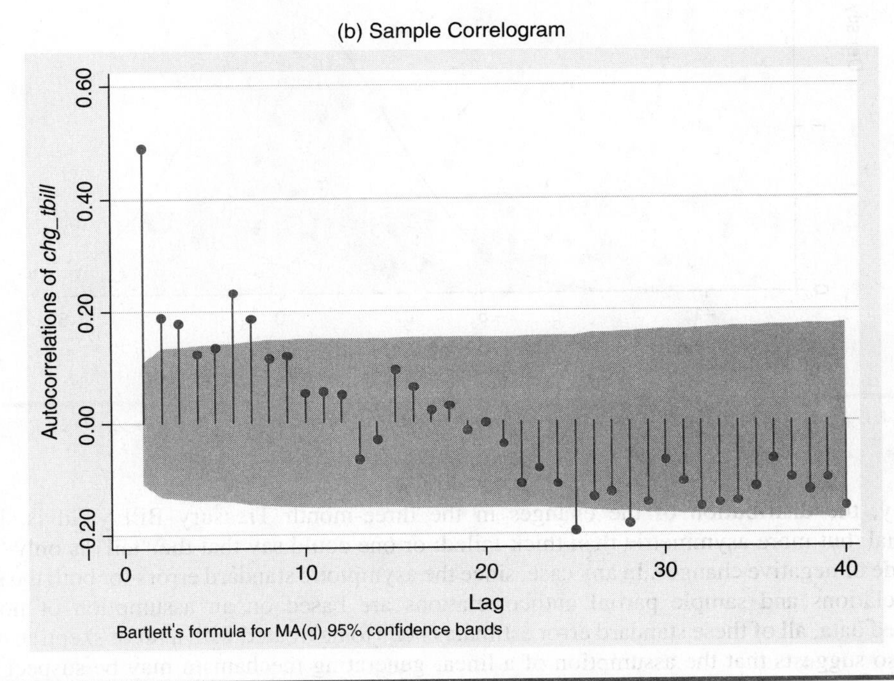

Figure 18-6 Change in U.S. Treasury Bill Three-Month Rate – $(1-B)\,tb3ms_t$ January 1984 to September 2010

As is typical of actual time-series data, the time-plot of $(1-B)tb3ms_t$ in Figure 18-6 does not look perfectly covariance stationary, but it seems reasonable enough to proceed.[9] Looking at the sample correlogram, several features are immediately apparent. First, the sample correlogram clearly does decay to become negligible at large lags – this is consistent with the approximate covariance stationarity observed in the time-plot. Second, r_1 (and perhaps r_2 and r_3, as well) appear to be statistically significant and positive; that is encouraging for the propects of constructing a credible and simple short-term forecasting model for $(1-B)tb3ms_t$. Third, notice that – on the presumption that ρ_{10} ... ρ_{40} are probably zero, so that r_{10} ... r_{40} are essentially the sampling errors in these estimates, the corr(r_j, r_{j+1}) is fairly high. Of course, this is exactly what one would expect from the Bartlett results (Equation 17-14) given that ρ_1 is apparently substantially positive.

Financial data are quite often non-normally distributed, with thicker tails than would be consistent with normality. A plot of a histogram of these data (from "histogram chg_tbill if $t > 600$, normal") actually modifies that conclusion a bit:

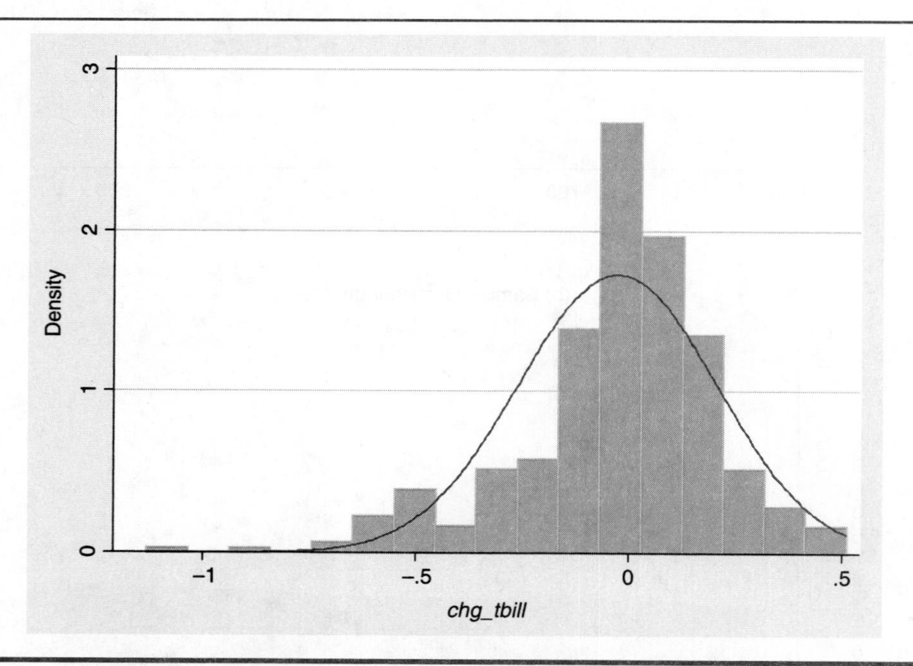

Figure 18-7 Histogram of the Change in U.S. Treasury Bill Three-Month Rate January 1984 to September 2010

Evidently, the distribution of the changes in the three-month Treasury Bill yield is, indeed, nonnormal, but more asymmetric than thick-tailed: or one could say that the "tail" is only "thick" on the side of negative changes. In any case, since the asymptotic standard errors for both the sample autocorrelations and sample partial autocorrelations are based on an assumption of normally distributed data, all of these standard error estimates need to be treated with a bit of skepticism. This result also suggests that the assumption of a linear generating mechanism may be suspect here – nonlinear modeling is discussed in Section 18.6.

[9] One could avoid the relatively large negative value for $(1-B)tb3ms_t$ in November 1984 – a drop of 1.12 percent in the three-month yield – but it wouldn't make all that much difference with a sample this long. Moreover, there will always be something else to drop if one is too finicky.

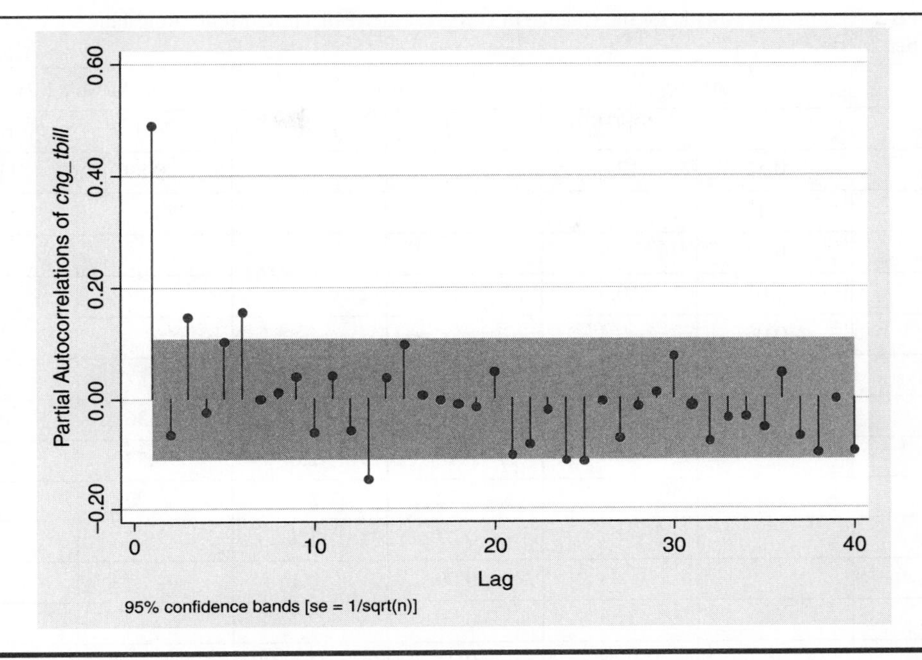

Figure 18-8 Partial Correlogram of Change in U.S. Treasury Bill Three-Month Rate

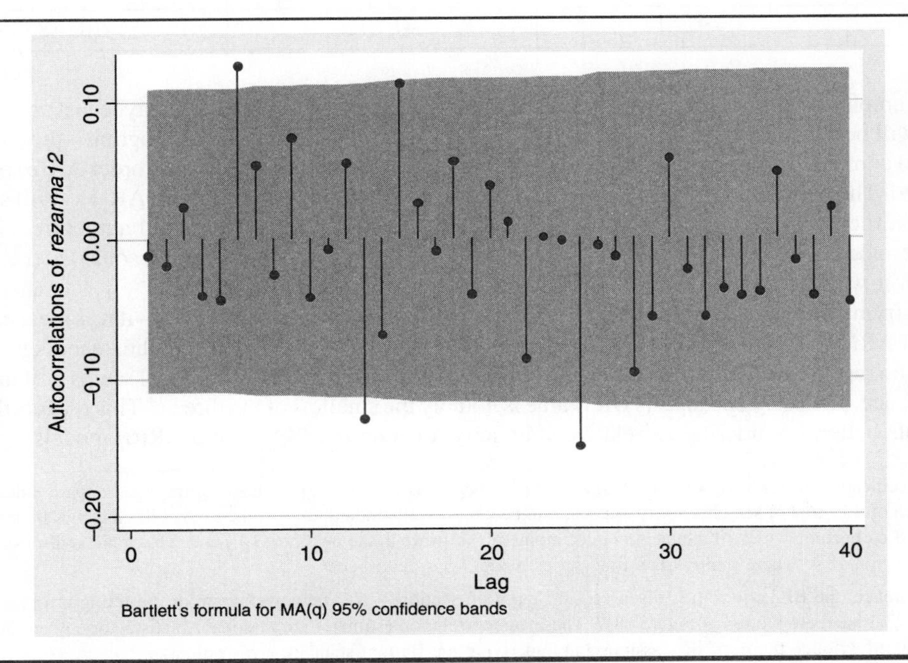

Figure 18-9 Sample Correlogram of Fitting Errors for ARMA(1,2) Model for the Change in U.S. Treasury Bill Three-Month Rate

Table 18-1 Estimated Models for the Change in U.S. Treasury Bill Three-Month Rate January 1984 to September 2010

	AR(6)		MA(7)		ARMA(1,2)	
	Coef.	|t-ratio|	Coef.	|t-ratio|	Coef.	|t-ratio|
φ_1	0.52	12.0			0.89	11.3
φ_2	−0.15	2.7				
φ_3	0.15	2.8				
φ_4	0.05	0.9				
φ_5	0.02	0.4				
φ_6	0.15	3.4				
θ_1			0.50	11.4	−0.36	4.1
θ_2			0.10	2.0	−0.34	4.2
θ_3			0.12	2.3		
θ_4			0.07	1.4		
θ_5			−0.00	0.1		
θ_6			0.16	2.7		
θ_7			0.21	4.4		
s	0.1948		0.1947		0.1972	
R^2_c	0.286		0.287		0.268	
BIC	−92.61		−87.12		−102.18	

The sample correlogram (Figure 18-6b) seems to indicate that an MA(7) – or maybe just an MA(1) – model will be adequate for these data. Figure 18-8 plots the sample partial correlogram – produced by the Stata command, "pac chg_tbill if $t > 600$" – which speaks to the issue of what order AR(p) process is needed. The partial autocorrelations indicates that an AR(6) – or maybe just an AR(1) – will suffice. Note that the value of $\hat{\varphi}_{13,13}$ is actually just as large in magnitude as the partial autocorrelations at lags five and six, but it is out "in the middle of nowhere": if this term were at the seasonal lag (i.e., at lag 12) then it would – quite possibly due to poor luck – be attractive to model.

After trying several AR(p) and MA(q) models – and finding them a bit complex – it was reasonable to consider ARMA(1, q) and ARMA(p, 1) models also. This led, finally, to three candidate models, whose estimation results are summarized in Table 18-1.[10] Overall, the ARMA(1,2) model seems preferable in this instance, primarily because its BIC value is notably the smallest of the three.[11] This reflects the fact that it fits better, considering its relative simplicity, than do the MA(7) and AR(6) models.[12]

[10] This specification search was fairly mechanical – e.g., it began with an MA(7) model and proceeded to pare it down. The automation of this kind of search activity is starting to become a well-studied topic in the time-series analysis literature and will, I predict, become widely implemented in econometric software in the next 5 to 10 years. This topic is discussed more fully in Section 18.4, where multivariate time-series modeling is described.

[11] For reference, the BIC criterion is discussed in Step 4 of Section 17.7. The correlogram of the fitting errors from this ARMA(1, 2) model are plotted in Figure 18-9. These autocorrelation estimates are reasonably satisfactory, given that these data apparently violate the normality assumption underlying the Bartlett standard error estimators.

[12] It is worth noting that this result is somewhat unusual: more typically one winds up with the AR(p) or the MA(q) model, as was indicated in Section 17.7.

Had a *P*-observation post-sample model evaluation been "held-out," then the post-sample forecasting performance of these three models could have been examined and compared to that of a "naive" MA(0) model, which would simply forecast $(1{-}B)tb3ms_t$ using its sample mean. The values of *s* and R_2 in Table 18-1 display the analogous in-sample information in this regard. S^2 is a consistent estimator of the variance of the model error term, so the *s* estimate of 0.1948 for the AR(6) model could be taken as an estimated standard deviation for the one-step-ahead (i.e., M_1) forecast errors this model would make, presuming that this sample length of 321 observations is sufficiently large that sampling error in $\hat{\varphi}_1 \ldots \hat{\varphi}_6$ can be neglected. The analogous statistic for the MA(0) model is the sample standard deviation of $(1{-}B)tb3ms_t$ itself, which is 0.2305. Indeed, the entries in the R^2 row of this table are in essence making precisely this comparison. Thus, these in-sample results indicate that these simple models for $(1{-}B)tb3ms_t$, just in terms of its own recent past, can explain something like 25% of the sample variation in $(1{-}B)tb3ms_t$ and (potentially) also reduce the post-sample forecast MSE by something like 25%.

The actual post-sample forecasting performance one obtains from models like these is generally less good than the in-sample fit would lead one to expect: approximately quantifying this diminution is perhaps the real value of postsample model evaluation, not using it to choose between alternative univariate models. Still, a forecasting improvement of even half this size seems notable, considering that these univariate models use no "actual" explanatory variables. Multivariate time-series modeling is taken up in Section 18.4. First, however, one last univariate-modeling topic deserves attention: the usefulness of ARMA models for seasonally adjusting a time-series.

18.3 SEASONAL TIME-SERIES DATA AND ARMA DESEASONALIZATION OF THE U.S. TOTAL NONFARM PAYROLL TIME-SERIES

It is well known that a very substantial number of Frenchmen go on holiday in August.[13] Thus, if one observes a drop in the growth rate of some component of French output in the third quarter of the year, that does not necessarily imply that France is headed into a growth recession. Clearly, for some (but not all) uses, one wants to use French data which have been adjusted to account for this seasonal pattern; such data are said to have been "deseasonalized."

Deseasonalizing time-series data properly poses a number of thorny statistical problems. Some of the issues are quite similar to those involved in dealing with trendlike behavior in a time-series, which were discussed in Section 18.1 above. In particular, is the seasonal pattern in a particular time-series substantial? Is it stable over time? If it is not stable over time, does it evolve in a deterministic or a stochastic way? Some macroeconomic time-series – e.g., aggregate price indices – are not very seasonal; others are. If the seasonal pattern in a time-series is not at least somewhat stable over time, then it would not be a 'pattern' at all; on the other hand, there is no reason to think that the such patterns are precisely stable, either.

The issue of "deterministic" versus "stochastic" evolution of a seasonal patterns – like that of trendlike patterns – is fundamentally unknowable for any particular time-series, simply because we inherently only have one realization of the time-series. Still, as with trendlike patterns, one can – to some extent – in practice detect the difference between stochastic ("random-walk-like," or "unit root") drift in a seasonal pattern and a pattern that changes linearly over time. We will return to this issue shortly.

For obvious reasons, several government agencies (notably the U.S. Bureau of the Census and the Bank of Spain) have devoted considerable resources to addressing these problems and to embodying solutions in the software – denoted "X-12-ARIMA" at this writing – used to produce most publicly available deseasonalized macroeconomic time-series.[14] As must also be evident (from the name

[13] This is merely an observation, not a criticism.

[14] For example, see the U.S. Bureau of the Census Web site – www.census.gov/srd/www/x12a/ – for working papers, downloadable software, etc.

given to the software) this state-of-the-art deseasonalization procedure in part draws on the same modeling ideas covered in Chapter 17.

Nevertheless, it is worthwhile saying a bit here about how one can use the ARMA(p, q) procedure to de-seasonalize a time-series oneself. For one thing, this description will provide at least a start on understanding what the X-12-ARIMA algorithm is doing in producing the sea of deseasonalized macroeconomic data that surrounds us.[15] For another, while X-12-ARIMA is really quite excellent – particularly in its effort to continually update the estimates of how the seasonal patterns are evolving through time – the deseasonalized data that it produces have one property which makes them quite awkward for some uses.

This undesirable property is that, using X-12-ARIMA, seasonally adjusted historical data have been subjected to what is known as a "two-sided filter," which uses both past and future data to estimate the current seasonal pattern in the time-series. This means, for example, that the deseasonalized values for U.S. GDP in the various quarters of 2005 depend, in part, on values of actual GDP for the four quarters in 2006. This is a feature (not a "bug") for many purposes, as it reflects the fact that X-12-ARIMA is using all of the historical information at its disposal to estimate the seasonal pattern for GDP in 2005. On the other hand, it also implies that information on future values of GDP is getting mixed up with the data on current GDP in historical data which have been deseasonalized in this way. This explains why "officially" deseasonalized data are commonly observed to be somewhat autocorrelated at the seasonal lag. This autocorrelation is usually negative, corresponding to X-12-ARIMA "overadjusting" in some sense. It is never very large in magnitude, but this autocorrelation at the seasonal lag is often statistically significant in a sample of typical length; most people find this a bit disconcerting once they notice it. More importantly, this mixing up of future with current values can distort econometric estimates of dynamic relationships; in particular, it is problematic for the Granger-causality analysis introduced in Section 12.2 and taken up in detail in Section 18.5.[16] Consequently, for that sort of analysis it is necessary to obtain the raw ("not seasonally adjusted" or "NSA") data and deal with its seasonality oneself, as part of the modeling process.

Suppose, for the sake of definiteness, that the data on a time-series Y_t are monthly and do exhibit a substantial seasonal pattern. In addition, for simplicity, any "ordinary" serial correlation in Y_t – i.e., at lags 1, 2, 3, ... ,11 – will be ignored at first. In that case, one can easily imagine two distinct – but not mutually exclusive – forms of seasonal serial dependence in Y_t. The first form assumes a deterministic seasonal pattern:

$$Y_t^{\text{deterministic seasonal}} = \alpha_{\text{jan}} D_t^{\text{jan}} + \alpha_{\text{feb}} D_t^{\text{feb}} + \ldots \alpha_{\text{dec}} D_t^{\text{dec}} + U_t \tag{18-4}$$

where D_t^{jan} is a dummy variable that is one for every January observation and zero otherwise; the other 11 monthly dummies are defined analogously; they could also, of course, be obtained as lags of D_t^{jan}. In this case the coefficients $\alpha_{\text{jan}} \ldots \alpha_{\text{dec}}$ are consistently estimated by simply applying OLS regression to Equation 18-4; the fitting errors from this regression model are then the de-seasonalized version of Y_t.[17]

[15] You'll know it by the acronym "saar" attached to an official time-series; this stands for "seasonally adjusted, at annual rates." The "annual rates" part refers to taking a monthly growth rate, for example, and inferring what annual growth rate would be implied by growth at this rate for 12 months in a row.

[16] See Wallis (1974) for details on how such two-sided seasonal adjustment can distort the apparent dynamic relationships between time-series. Wallis, K. F. (1974), "Seasonal Adjustment and Relations between Variables," *Journal of the American Statistical Association 69(345)*, pp. 18–31.

[17] Equation 18-4 assumes that the seasonal pattern is completely fixed, but it is actually easy to allow the seasonal coefficients to vary over time in a model such as this. The simplest way to do this is by using what is called an "exponential smoothing" model. Such a model formulates $\alpha_{\text{jan},t}$ as a weighted sum of its estimated value for the previous period and the sample mean of all previous estimates of it: i.e., $\alpha_{\text{jan},t}$ for the current period is set equal to $\lambda\ \alpha_{\text{jan},t-1} + (1-\lambda)\bar{\alpha}$ where λ is a constant (between zero and one) and $\bar{\alpha}$ is defined to be the sample mean of the previous values of $\alpha_{\text{jan},t}$. The weighting constant λ can be set to a "reasonable" value or estimated to fit the sample data. See Granger and Newbold (1977, pp. 163–70) for a complete exposition; the command "tssmooth" in Stata provides a convenient implementation.

The second way of formulating a seasonal pattern is stochastic:

$$(1 - \gamma B^{12})Y_t^{\text{stochastic seasonal}} = V_t \qquad \gamma \leq 1 \tag{18-5}$$

Note that Equation 18-4 is positing that January values have a different mean value than do February values (and so forth), whereas Equation 18-6 is positing that every value of Y_t is related (in the same way) to its value one year previous. If this latter pattern is correct, then one can more or less identify the value of γ from the sample correlogram by considering how r_{12}, r_{24}, r_{36} decay: if they decay rapidly, then γ is less than one; if they decay very slowly, then a value of one for γ is appropriate. If γ does equal one, then this lag operator is called a "seasonal difference." It is actually quite common for a strongly seasonal time-series to require a seasonal difference; typically, in that case, the seasonal difference substitutes for an ordinary difference.

Which model is best? In other words, is the seasonal pattern in Y_t deterministic or stochastic? Absent a set of repeated samples on Y_t, there is no way to answer this question with any generality or certainty. For any given time-series, however, the best suggestion is to simply look at some time-plots. Often, this will make the reasonable course of action fairly obvious.

For example, Figure 18-10 plots not-seasonally-adjusted data on U.S. Total Nonfarm Payrolls from January 1939 through September 2010, in both differenced and seasonally differenced forms.[18] Looking at these two time-plots, it is evident that the seasonal difference is not producing an I(0) time-series. More importantly, however, note that the time-plot of the monthly growth rate in payrolls – i.e., $(1\!-\!B)\log(payroll_t)$ – has separated into several "threads," each with its own, fairly

(a) $(1\!-\!B)\log(payroll_t)$

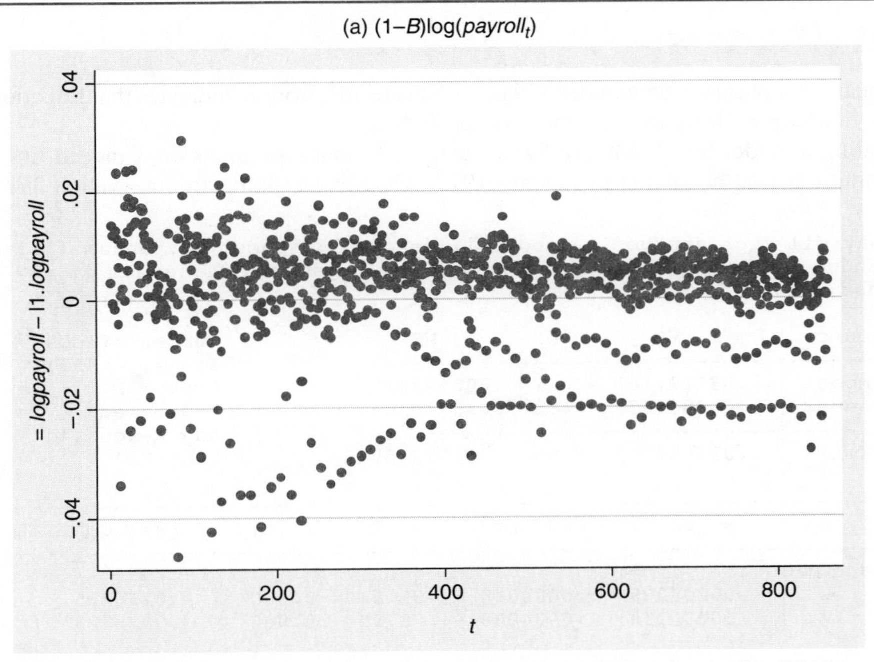

Figure 18-10 Time-Plot of U.S. Total Nonfarm Payrolls January 1939 to September 2010

[18] Source: http://research.stlouisfed.org/fred2/categories/11.

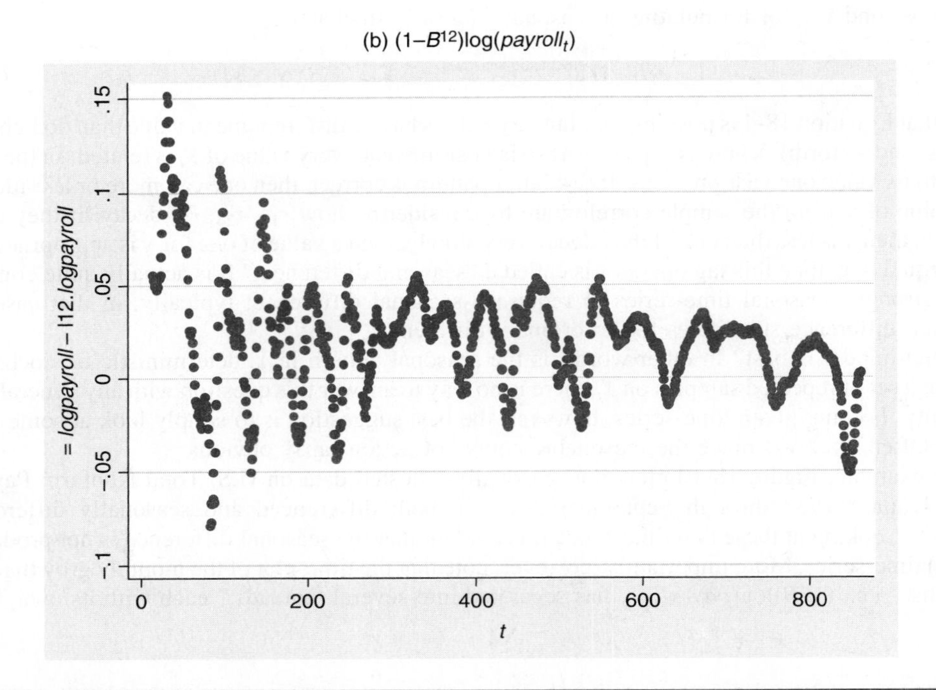

Figure 18-10 *(Continued)*

stable, mean after observation number 400 or so. This result strongly indicates that Equation 18-4 is likely to yield a good way to deseasonalize these data.

Estimating a model for (1–*B*)log($payroll_t$) using 12 month-dummies does indeed fit very well over a sample period beginning in January 1972, which corresponds to observation 397:[19]

```
reg  lpayroll_chg  jandum l1.jandum l2.jandum l3.jandum l4.jandum l5.jandum
   l6.jandum l7.jandum l8.jandum l9.jandum l10.jandum l11.jandum if t > 396,
   noconst

      Source |       SS       df       MS              Number of obs =     465
-------------+------------------------------           F( 12,    453) =  407.91
       Model |  .031127101    12  .002593925           Prob > F      =  0.0000
    Residual |  .002880651   453  6.3591e-06           R-squared     =  0.9153
-------------+------------------------------           Adj R-squared =  0.9131
       Total |  .034007752   465  .000073135           Root MSE      =  .00252

------------------------------------------------------------------------------
lpayroll_chg |      Coef.   Std. Err.      t    P>|t|     [95% Conf. Interval]
-------------+----------------------------------------------------------------
      jandum |
         --. |  -.0208389   .0004038   -51.61   0.000    -.0216325   -.0200454
         L1. |   .0036158   .0004038     8.95   0.000     .0028223    .0044094
```

[19] The variable $jandum_t$ is a dummy variable which is one for January values and zero otherwise. Because an intercept is not estimated in this regression equation, each of the 12 dummy coefficient estimates can be interpreted as an estimate of the mean payroll growth rate for the corresponding month. Evidently, January and July are relatively bad months for payroll growth; these two months no doubt yield the two "threads" apparent in Figure 18-10a.

L2.	.0062384	.0004038	15.45	0.000	.0054449	.0070319
L3.	.0074115	.0004038	18.35	0.000	.006618	.0082051
L4.	.0071119	.0004038	17.61	0.000	.0063183	.0079054
L5.	.0056606	.0004038	14.02	0.000	.0048671	.0064542
L6.	-.0097397	.0004038	-24.12	0.000	-.0105333	-.0089462
L7.	.0015017	.0004038	3.72	0.000	.0007082	.0022953
L8.	.0067205	.0004038	16.64	0.000	.0059269	.007514
L9.	.0052476	.0004091	12.83	0.000	.0044437	.0060515
L10.	.0023108	.0004091	5.65	0.000	.0015069	.0031148
L11.	-.000099	.0004091	-0.24	0.809	-.000903	.0007049

Saving the fitting errors from this regression equation as $resids\_paygrow_t$ and plotting them over this sample period yields Figure 18-11. These fitting errors appear to be reasonably covariance stationary after observation number 537, which corresponds to September 1983.

Figure 18-12 plots a sample correlogram and partial correlogram for $resids\_paygrow_t$ over the sample period for which it appears to be covariance stationary – i.e., beginning in September 1983. These fitting errors are clearly significantly autocorrelated; the sample correlogram promptly decays, however, confirming that $resids\_paygrow_t$ is approximately covariance stationary over this period.

The sample partial correlogram of $resids\_paygrow_t$ is particularly informative in this case. Note that it indicates that an AR(3) model would suffice for these data, but would be ignoring autoregressive terms at lags 12, 13, and 14 which appear likely to be statistically significant. Ordinarily, terms at lags like 13 and 14 would not be appetizing to model, but such terms are in fact quite natural in a monthly model with significant autoregressive terms at lags one and two. To see this, consider the following

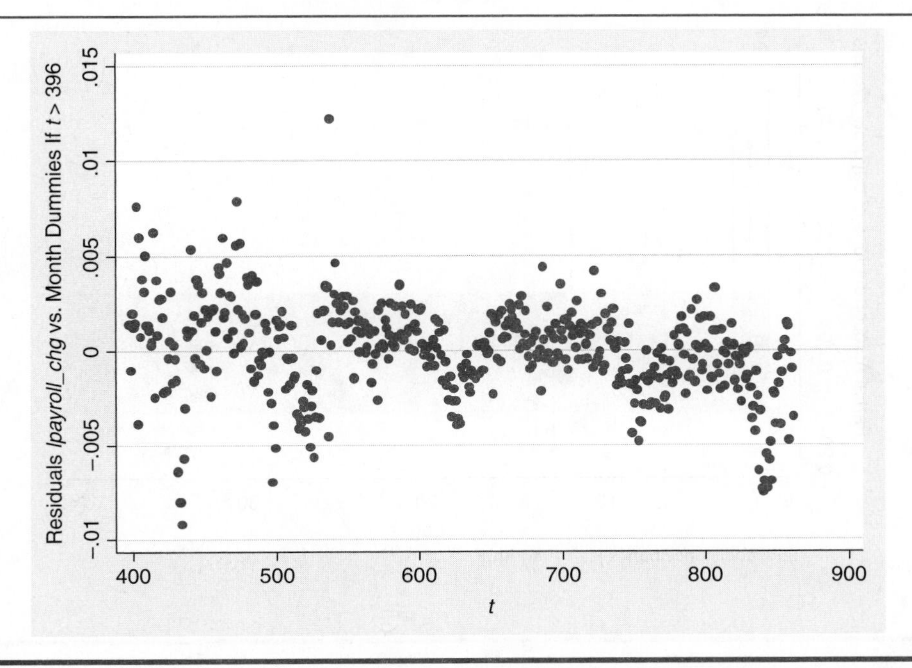

Figure 18-11 Fitting Errors from Regression of $(1-B)\log(payroll_t)$ on Monthly Dummy Variables September 1983 to September 2010

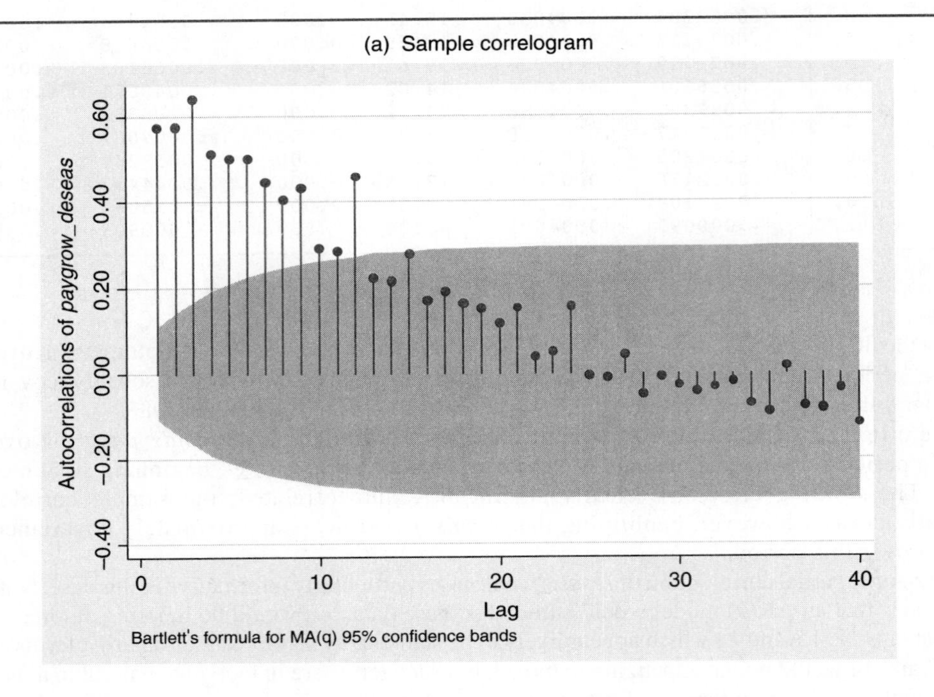

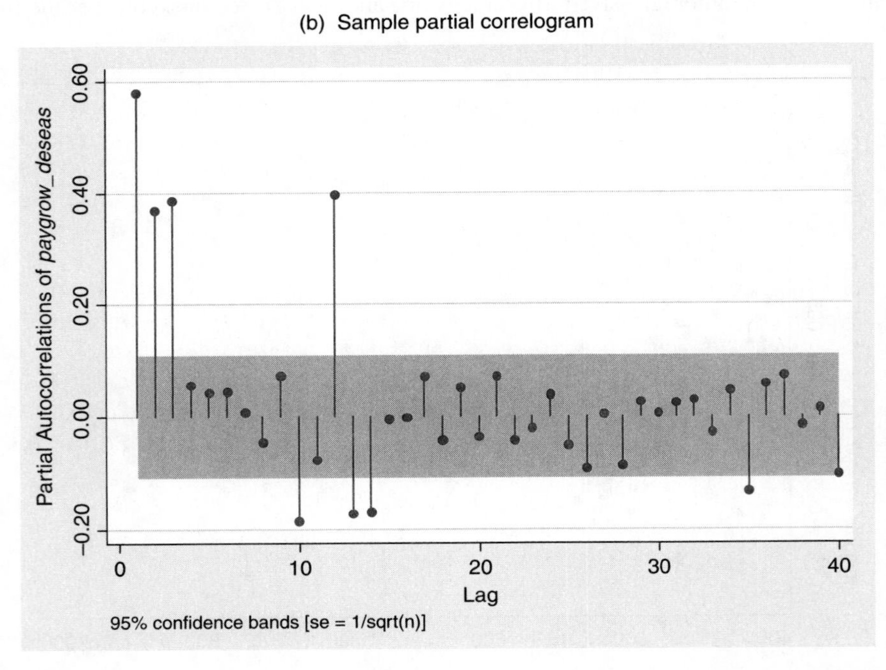

Figure 18-12 Correlogram and Partial Correlogram of Fitting Errors from Regression of $(1-B)\log(payroll_t)$ on Monthly Dummy Variables September 1983 to September 2010

multiplicative autoregressive model for $resids\_paygrow_t$:

$$\left(1 - \varphi_1^{\text{seasonal}} B^{12}\right)\left(1 - \varphi_1 B - \varphi_2 B^2\right) resids\_paygrow_t = \eta_t \tag{18-6}$$

which, on multiplying out the terms, is equivalent to the AR(14) model,

$$\left(1 - \varphi_1 B - \varphi_2 B^2 - \varphi_1^{\text{seasonal}} B^{12} + \varphi_1 \varphi_1^{\text{seasonal}} B^{13} + \varphi_2 \varphi_1^{\text{seasonal}} B^{14}\right) resids\_paygrow_t = \eta_t \tag{18-7}$$

Most software implementations of Box-Jenkins modeling make it very convenient to estimate models like Equation 18-6, but one could (in any case) easily estimate the AR(14) model of Equation 18-7, dropping the terms at lags three through 11. If one also drops the terms at lags one and two, then one could then use the fitting errors from this model as the "ARMA de-seasonalized" version of the time-series $paygrow_t$.

Notice how much more straightforward this example of ARMA deseasonalization is than one might have expected from the initial discussion of the problems involved. This example was not "cherrypicked": U.S. Total Nonfarm Employment was literally the first nonseasonally adjusted monthly time-series the author encountered in the St. Louis Federal Reserve Bank database when looking for an example. On the other hand, perhaps this particular time-series was, to some extent, a lucky choice. Moreover, notice that a government agency producing a seasonally adjusted version of U.S. Nonfarm Employment does not have the luxury of restricting its attention to a sample period beginning in September 1983: it needs to deal with the entire data set.

18.4 MULTIVARIATE TIME-SERIES MODELS

One might naturally think that multivariate modeling, especially from the time-series analysis perspective, is going to be a lot more challenging than univariate modeling or that it will be much more difficult than is multivariate modeling from the time-series econometrics perspective taken in Chapter 14. Strangely, these expectations are largely false.

It is certainly true that a modeler using the time-series analysis perspective is liable to be much more concerned about the possible distortions introduced into a dynamic model by two-sided seasonal adjustment methods, whereas modelers working from the time-series econometrics perspective typically ignore this. On the other hand, dealing with this issue merely involves a concerted effort, at the data collection phase of a project, to obtain data which are not seasonally adjusted.

Also, generally speaking, a modeler approaching the problem from the time-series analysis perspective is liable to be more concerned about forming relationships solely between covariance stationary time-series. However, this more-intense concern with regard to covariance stationarity actually simplifies matters in a way. In particular, the analysis of the "capstone" example in Sections 14.4 to 14.6 involved quite a bit of hand-wringing about whether to model the data in levels or in differences. From the time-series analysis perspective, in contrast, there is much more of a tendency to simply difference the data to apparent covariance stationary unless there is substantial evidence to the contrary. (Per the "hybrid approach" of Section 18.1, such contrary evidence might arise in the form of a rejection of the null hypothesis by a unit root test, or through sample evidence of overdifferencing in the differenced data, but compelling evidence of either of these sorts is the exception rather than the rule.) Consequently, the time-series analyst is more likely to, with a lot less fussing, just difference the data and then focus on other crucial issues.

One such crucial issue is the very fact that, especially once no longer masked by the overwhelming impact of a stochastic trend, other deviations of a time-series from apparent covariance stationarity commonly become apparent. In particular, it frequently then becomes evident that either the variance or the mean of a time-series is not stable over time. Each of these departures from covariance stationarity is a very serious problem in constructing an ARMA(p, q) model for the single variable of a univariate model. But such departures are actually less crucial a problem when they occur in the dependent or explanatory variables of a multivariate model, for the reasons next discussed.

First consider the case of a time-series whose variance is finite, but unstable over time. Substantial variation in the apparent variance of a time-series across the sample can be an indication that some of the functional forms with which the data enter the model are misspecified. Thus, framing some variables in per capita terms or expressing their time variation in terms of growth rates – $(1-B)\ln(X_t)$ – rather than as changes – $(1-B)X_t$ – can sometimes eliminate problems of this nature. In a more subtle fashion, it is shown in Section 18.6 that inclusion of nonlinear dynamic terms as explanatory variables can eliminate certain forms of conditional heteroscedasticity in the error term – where the variance of the error-term depends on its own recent past. Or this conditional heteroscedasticity can be modeled directly in the model error term, as in the ARCH models also introduced in Section 18.6. Thus, covariance nonstationarity in the form of explanatory variable (and error) variances which, while finite, are not stable over time can often be productively dealt with in a multivariate setting, even though this form of nonstationarity is problematic in a univariate modeling framework.

Time-variation in the means of the variables used in a model is also inherently less problematic in a multivariate setting. This insight is even more straightforward: the time variation in the mean of an explanatory variable can model (or "explain") the time-variation in the mean of a dependent variable. This renders the nonstationarity of the mean in both time-series benign.

The "intervention analysis" framework of Box and Tiao (1975)[20] provides a good illustration of this. Suppose that Y_t could be modeled as an ARMA(p, q) process except for the fact that an "intervention" is known to have occurred in time period τ, which caused $E(Y_t)$ to temporarily shift in an unknown manner. Y_t is clearly not covariance stationary in that case because covariance stationarity requires that $E(Y_t)$ is a constant independent of t. One might also be keenly interested in the degree to which this particular intervention shifted the mean of Y_t and the dynamics by which $E(Y_t)$ completely (or perhaps only partially) relaxed back to its original value in the periods subsequent to period τ. Supposing, for example, that a complete relaxation in the mean of Y_t does take place – and using the notation of Equation 17-60 – Box and Tiao proposed the following multivariate variation on an ARMA(p, q) representation for Y_t:

$$
\begin{aligned}
Y_t &\sim \text{ARMA}(p,q) + \text{Intervention}_\tau \\
Y_t &= \frac{\Theta(B)}{\Phi(B)} U_t + \text{Intervention}_\tau \\
Y_t &= \frac{\Theta(B)}{\Phi(B)} U_t + \frac{\omega_o}{1-\delta B} D_t^\tau
\end{aligned}
\tag{18-8}
$$

A multivariate time-series model in this format is called a "transfer function model." If the parameter ω_o is positive and δ is a positive fraction which is strictly less than one, then Box and Tiao show that the impact an intervention term of this form is that $E(Y_t)$ immediately rises by an amount ω_o in period τ, but the effect of the intervention decays geometrically at rate δ. That is, Equation 18-8 implies that $E(Y_{\tau+j}) = \omega_o\, \delta^j$ for $j \geq 0$.

These two additional parameters – ω_o and δ – can easily be estimated. To see this, first multiply Equation 18-8 though by the lag polynomial $(1 - \delta B)\Phi(B)$, yielding the regression equation

$$
(1-\delta B)\Phi(B)Y_t = (1-\delta B)\Theta(B)U_t + \omega_o \Phi(B) D_t^\tau
\tag{18-9}
$$

[20] Box, G. E. P., and G. C. Tiao (1975), "Intervention Analysis with Applications to Economic and Environmental Problems," *Journal of the American Statistical Association 70(349)*, pp. 70–79.

Note that Equation 18-9 is actually just an ARMA($p+1$, $q+1$) model plus the $(p+1)$ dummy variables, $D_t^\tau \ldots D_{t-p}^\tau$. For example, if $Y_t \sim$ ARMA(2, 0), then Equation 18-9 is:

$$\left(1-(\delta+\varphi_1)B-(\varphi_2-\delta\varphi_1)B^2+\delta\varphi_2 B^3\right)Y_t = (1-\delta B)U_t+\omega_o\left(1-\varphi_1 B-\varphi_2 B^2\right)D_t^\tau \quad (18\text{-}10)$$

The four unknown parameters – φ_1, φ_2, δ, and ω_o – in Equation 18-10 can then be consistently estimated using nonlinear least squares. This amounts to numerically choosing $\hat{\varphi}_1$, $\hat{\varphi}_2$, $\hat{\delta}$, and $\hat{\omega}_o$ to minimize $\text{SSE}\left(\hat{\varphi}_1, \hat{\varphi}_2, \hat{\delta}, \hat{\omega}_o\right) = \sum_{t=4}^{N} \hat{u}_t^2$ where the fitting error $\hat{u}_t$ is defined by

$$\hat{u}_t \equiv y_t-(\hat{\delta}+\hat{\varphi}_1)y_{t-1}-(\hat{\varphi}_2-\hat{\delta}\hat{\varphi}_1)y_{t-2}+\hat{\delta}\hat{\varphi}_2 y_{t-3}+\hat{\delta}\hat{u}_{t-1}-\hat{\omega}_o D_t^\tau+\hat{\omega}_o\hat{\varphi}_1 D_{t-1}^\tau+\hat{\omega}_o\hat{\varphi}_2 D_{t-2}^\tau \quad (18\text{-}11)$$

Box and Tiao (1975) give details on how to similarly formulate (and estimate) all sorts of variations on this theme: e.g., where a portion of the impact never decays away completely, where the intervention itself is a permanent increase in the mean of Y_t, etc. Thus, if one is able to assume at least something about the manner in which $E(Y_t)$ varies over time, then this form of nonstationarity in Y_t – which was problematic in univariate modeling – can be readily handled in a multivariate modeling framework.

Consequently, so long as all of the variables used are I(0), it is not necessary that they all be covariance stationary as well: in a multivariate setting, variation in their means and variances over time is all right. Indeed, it is just such variation in the means and variances of explanatory variables which allows for such variation in the dependent variable to be modeled.

The big problem, of course, lies in deciding what set of explanatory variables to consider. This problem was trivial for univariate – i.e., ARMA(p, q) – modeling, because only lagged values of Y_t (and of the model errors) were to be considered. Intervention analysis provides a good first example of the expansion of one's purview in this respect. Note that the idea of considering the possibility that an intervention occurred in a particular period τ has to arise from a combination of economic theory and of one's historical knowledge with regard to the sample period. And, clearly, the set of other variables to be considered as possible explanatory variables must similarly arise from a combination of these same two sources: first, some level of economic theory to which one is willing to give at least tentative credence and, second, what one already thinks likely about the historical context.

The *kinds* of variables one might include in a set of potential explanatory variables are

- I(0) variables suggested by theory and/or experience
- I(0) error-correction terms[21]
- Intervention (dummy variable) terms
- Nonlinear functions and lags of the above

Generally speaking, inclusivity in this choice of potential explanatory variables is a good thing, for several reasons. First, one frequently needs to include a sufficiently rich set of explanatory variables so as to cope with nonstationarity in the mean and/or variance of the dependent variables, as described above. Second, a multivariate model which includes explanatory variables which are potentially controllable can be useful in formulating and evaluating economic policies which manipulate future values of such variates; such policy analysis simply cannot be done using simpler models. Third, as usual, wrongly omitting explanatory variables which are correlated with included ones renders the estimated coefficients on the included variables inconsistent. Finally, of course, the inclusion of additional explanatory variables which are actually relevant to the variation in the dependent variable yield models which both fit and forecast better.

---

[21] Recall, from Section 14.5, that an error-correction term is a function (most typically just a linear function) of several I(1) variables which – theoretically and empirically – is itself I(0).

However, inclusivity in the set of explanatory variables to be considered for the model also creates some complications:

1. For example, multivariate models in time-series econometrics settings frequently include simultaneously determined explanatory variables, but inclusion of these variables raises the kinds of endogeneity issues addressed in Chapter 11. This can require the use of the instrumental variables methods discussed in Chapter 12. Indeed, it is in large part to avoid these complications that multivariate models in time-series analysis settings almost always eschew such simultaneous explanatory variables and only include lagged explanatory variables, as in the "capstone" examples given in Sections 14.4 through 14.6.
2. Overcomplicating a model can also lead to multicollinearity issues – as discussed in Section 9.8 – if the sample variation in one explanatory variable strongly resembles that of another.
3. If a potential explanatory variable (call it Q_{t-1} here) which is correlated with Y_t (but not actually related to it) and which is correlated with an explanatory variable (call it Z_{t-1}, with coefficient β_z) already used in the model for Y_t, then wrongly including Q_{t-1} in the model renders the estimates of all of the other model coefficients inconsistent as estimators for the coefficients they are ostensibly estimating.

   This last point is a bit subtle, but it is fundamental and important. Suppose that a variable X_{t-1}^{omitted} has been omitted from the model, and even from the list of explanatory variables potentially to be included in the model. This omission might be because the economic (or other) phenomena quantified by X_{t-1}^{omitted} are simply beyond the ken of the kinds of theory (and/or historical sensibilities) being used to guide the selection of variables for inclusion in this set of potential explanatory variables. Or it might be the case that historical data on X_{t-1}^{omitted} is either currently or inherently unavailable. Now additionally suppose that an available time-series, $Q_{t-1}^{\text{available}}$, is actually correlated with X_{t-1}^{omitted}. If $Q_{t-1}^{\text{available}}$ is included in the set of potential explanatory variables in the model *and* it is correlated with the dependent variable Y_t, then it will likely end up entering the model for Y_t. However, just as in the discussion of Section 9.6, $Q_{t-1}^{\text{available}}$ will in that case not only model/explain the sample variation in Y_t which is actually driven by fluctuations in $Q_{t-1}^{\text{available}}$: it will also "explain" a portion of the sample variation in Y_t which is actually driven by fluctuations in X_{t-1}^{omitted}. Thus, the estimated coefficient on $Q_{t-1}^{\text{available}}$ will be a consistent estimator of some mixture of the "true" coefficients on both $Q_{t-1}^{\text{available}}$ *and* X_{t-1}^{omitted}. If one is in a position to understand and recognize the fact $Q_{t-1}^{\text{available}}$ is partly proxying for X_{t-1}^{omitted} in the model, then this can be an excellent thing: the resulting model will fit and forecast better because the effect of X_{t-1}^{omitted} has thus been at least partially modeled. If, in contrast, one mistakes the estimator of the coefficient on $Q_{t-1}^{\text{available}}$ for a consistent estimator of the actual impact of variation in $Q_{t-1}^{\text{available}}$ on $E(Y_t)$, then this is a bad thing: one might, for example, in this way substantially mis-estimate the actual impact of a policy variable and thereby obtain misleading inferences regarding this impact.[22]
4. Finally, as one allows the set of potentially included explanatory variables to become more inclusive, one runs into practical problems with how to search effectively over the resulting plethora of potential models and into worries about the possibility that one has "data mined" a great fit to the sample data but produced a model which only fits (rather than "explains") the sample data.

[22] In a larger sense, this same point alternatively reflects the fact that including any additional explanatory variable in a regression model fundamentally affects the *meaning* of the population coefficients on all of the other variables. For example, the population coefficient β_z on variable Z_{t-1} is $\partial E(Y_t)/\partial Z_{t-1}$, but this expectation is conditional on $Q_{t-1}^{\text{available}}$ (and the partial derivative is holding $Q_{t-1}^{\text{available}}$ constant) if and only if $Q_{t-1}^{\text{available}}$ is included in the model.

The remainder of this section briefly describes two approaches which have been devised for addressing this last set of issues: VAR modeling and a new generation of search algorithms suggested by Doornick and Hendry (2007).

The Vector Autoregression or "VAR" model, first suggested in a seminal paper by Sims (1980)[23] resolves these issues by, from the outset, restricting the set of dependent variables modeled to M selected time-series variables and the explanatory variables to exactly p lags in each of M these variables. Thus, each of the M equations in the VAR model is essentially an instance of the Dynamic Multiple Regression Model considered in Chapter 13 (as Equation 13-40), with the contemporaneous values of the explanatory variables omitted and each explanatory variable lag length specified to be the same value, p. The issue of endogeneity in the explanatory variables due to simultaneous determination is thus avoided and the issue of choosing the explanatory variables is reduced to choosing the order p; the latter choice is often made using multivariate generalizations of the AIC and/or BIC criterion. As with the Dynamic Multiple Regression Model, there is still the issue of whether to formulate the model in levels or in changes, and additional explanatory variables are sometimes added to the mix.[24]

Once an inclusive set of potentially explanatory variables has been specified, the rest of the modeling process – as the reader may have noted in the "capstone" examples given in Sections 14.4 through 14.6 – is fundamentally mechanical: one is searching for the model with the best adjusted fit, typically based on a criterion such as the BIC.[25] The problem is that this mechanical search in principle involves the estimation of an impractically large number of models and, as noted above, can easily lead to a model which (because the sample has been so thoroughly "mined") fits the sample data very well but means very little. Remarkably, both of these problems have been largely overcome in recent work by Doornick and Hendry (2007) and described/evaluated in Doornick (2009) and Ericsson (2010).[26] This search algorithm – dubbed "Autometrics" by Doornick and Hendry – effectively reduces the computational load of such specification searches to a very manageable level and almost completely resolves the "data mining" issue. Consequently, although this approach is currently only available in one software package, I believe that something akin to this modeling technique will eventually become widely used.[27]

Even using the Doornick and Hendry procedure, however, there is still the distinct possibility that one has overfit the data by choosing too wide a set of possible explanatory variables. The "gold standard" for checking this sort of thing is to examine the forecasting performance of a final

---

[23] Sims, C. (1980), "Macroeconomics and Reality," *Econometrica 48*, 1–49.

[24] In particular, it is common to include a time trend in VAR models formulated in levels, whereas error correction terms can be added to VAR models in changes. And some authors will pare down some of the lag structures to eliminate insignificant terms at the largest lags. Clearly, at some point in all that, the distinction between the VAR model and the Dynamic Multiple Regression becomes lost. In another set of generalizations, a literature on "structural VAR" models has arisen, in which one or more assumptions are made about the VAR model coefficients and error terms based on economic theory. This material will not be covered here, but the interested reader can consult Enders (2010, Sections 5.5-5.13).

[25] It is also nice to end up with a model whose lag structures have only seasonally-related "holes" in them. For example, with monthly data, a sensible lag structure might include terms at lags one, two, and 12, but not an isolated term at lag nine.

[26] Doornik, J. A., and D. F. Hendry (2007), *PcGive 12*, Timberlake Consultants, Ltd.: London. Doornick, J. A. (2009), "Autometrics" (Chapter 4, pp. 88–121), *The Methodology and Practice of Econometrics; A Festschrift in Honour of David F. Hendry* (Castle, J. L., and N. Shephard, eds.), Oxford University Press: Oxford. Ericsson, N. R. (2010), "Empirical Model Selection: Friedman and Schwartz Revisited," mimeo, www.gwu.edu/~forcpgm/NeilEricsson-FSGets-March2010.pdf.

[27] The "Autometrics" procedure is available in the program PcGIVE, version 13 or later. The OxMetrics software package provides a commercially available front-end for PcGIVE; it runs on all of the usual platforms (Windows, Linux, Mac) and is available at www.doornik.com/products.html.

selection of candidate model over a post-sample period of P observations held out from the model identification procedure. The issue then becomes one of testing whether the post-sample mean square forecasting errors from one model are significantly smaller than those of another; that is the topic of the next section.

18.5 POST-SAMPLE MODEL FORECAST EVALUATION AND TESTING FOR GRANGER-CAUSATION

The topic (and desirability) of model validation via post-sample forecasting has come up repeatedly in this chapter. Principally this is because, the more intensely we use the sample data to obtain the model specification, the more crucial it is to test the model (and its specification) out on a separate data set. The notion of post-sample forecasting also arose in Section 12.2, where the concept of Granger-causality was introduced. In that context, a time-series X_t is said to "Granger-cause" Y_t if and only if widening the information set used in forecasting Y_t to include past values of X_t improves the Y_t forecasts.[28]

Generally speaking, most people are content to quantify "better forecasting" by the operational concept of "smaller mean square error," or "MSE," although this would surely not be the right criterion if one's preferences were asymmetric over positive versus negative forecast errors. Thus, in practice, most people routinely use the conditional mean forecast (M_h) discussed (among other forecast possibilities) in Section 17.2. In particular, post-sample forecasting for model validation purposes is almost always carried out by computing a sequence of one-step-ahead forecasts (estimates of M_1) through the P observations in the post-sample period, usually updating the model parameter estimates at each forecast. This is usually called a "recursive" forecast if the estimation sample is allowed to increase as the process moves through the post-sample period; it is called a "rolling window forecast" if observations are peeled off of the beginning of the sample so as to keep the estimation sample of constant length. These choices are usually not crucial to the qualitative result as to whether one model "forecasts better" than another.

Sometimes post-sample model forecasting evaluations or comparisons are frustratingly easy: when the model is confronted with new (post-sample) data its sequence of P one-step-ahead forecast errors has a larger average squared error than that obtained from a "naive" model in which the forecasting regression model contains only an intercept. This can easily occur if the actual relationships are quite unstable over time (due to unmodeled changes in the world around us) or where the model was substantially misspecified because we simply tried too hard to fit a model to the data. Sample data can be tortured into submission in this way, but it tends to snap back in the post-sample period![29] Of course, it is precisely the ability of post-sample forecasting to provide this kind of check on our work that makes post-sample model validation such a useful exercise.

One might predict that – once one has settled on a forecasting accuracy criterion (MSE), decided upon a partitioning of the data set into N specification/estimation observations and P post-sample evaluation periods, and dealt with the issues of covariance stationarity and model specification – that assessing whether the post-sample MSE from one model formulation is significantly less than that of another would be straightforward.

[28] Recall that this definition of Granger-causation tacitly assumes that both Y_t forecasting information sets are sufficiently inclusive as to not be omitting some variable Z_t whose fluctuations drive both X_t and Y_t, but at differing relative lags.

[29] Testing for unstable parameter estimates across the sample period will frequently reveal the tell-tale signs of such torture ahead of time but, for obvious reasons, the same people who do not test their models via post-sample forecasting tend to also not test for unstable parameter estimates within the sample. Also, it is worth noting that nonlinear models tend to be more susceptible to post-sample forecasting failure than linear models. Nonlinear modeling – discussed in Section 18.6 – is obviously the only way to exploit nonlinear serial dependence for forecasting purposes, but nonlinearity seems to substantially enhance the power of model misspecification to ruin forecasting effectiveness.

Unfortunately, that is not the case. For example, in principle, each one-step-ahead forecast error generated using M_1 should be equivalent to the model error U_t for the period being forecast, and hence both homoscedastic and serially uncorrelated. In practice, however, one cannot count on that. Consequently, the sampling distributions of the post-sample test statistics used must be obtained using bootstrap techniques designed, in particular, to cope with heteroscedastic forecast errors.

Similarly, one would expect that, even if the sampling distribution of the relevant test statistic must be obtained by simulation (bootstrap) methods, at least the test statistic itself would be simply the ratio of the post-sample average squared forecast error from one model to that of the other. Not so: it turns out to matter (noticeably) whether or not the two models being compared are "nested" or not.[30]

In fact, exactly how to do this testing appropriately is still an area of current research and a bit beyond the purview of the present treatment. Ashley and Ye (2011) provides a detailed example of how to conduct this sort of post-sample forecast analysis – and test for Granger causation in practice – at present; Clark and McCracken (2010) points at how post-sample forecast accuracy analysis will likely evolve in the next few years.[31]

18.6 MODELING NONLINEAR SERIAL DEPENDENCE IN A TIME-SERIES

This section extends the discussion of time-series analysis to nonlinear models, which capture/model nonlinear serial dependence in a time-series. For economic and financial data, this extension has modest implications with regard to our ability to make good forecasting models and huge implications with regard to our understanding of the nature of how the current value of a time-series evolves out of its past.

In order to understand nonlinear serial dependence in time-series, it is essential to first consider the concept of "serial dependence" itself in more depth. This is very fundamental – and the discussion of this topic below will initially seem a bit impractically-abstract – but the reader's patience will be rewarded.

"Serial dependence" in a time-series is the relatedness of the period-t value of a time-series – e.g., Y_t – to its past values, generally to its *recent* past values: Y_{t-1}, Y_{t-2}, Y_{t-3}, and so forth. The detection and modeling of such serial dependence is the very essence of time-series analysis. In fact, it is because (and only because) the data are in time-order – i.e., because they form a "time-series" – that the concepts "past" and "recent" have meaning in the context of the data. And it is only because (and to the degree) that Y_t is *dependent* on its past that these concepts are of any importance. In some contexts – e.g., in testing the "efficient markets" hypothesis in finance – the focus is on a finding of *lack* of serial dependence, but it is still serial dependence which is at issue.

Indeed, if $Y_1 \ldots Y_N$ are serially independent, then it would be entirely inconsequential if the data on Y_t were to be re-ordered at random; time-series data are in that case really no different from cross-sectional data. For example, sorting or re-ordering the log-wages data on a cross-sectional sample of N individuals has no effect whatever on any of the regression modeling results for these data. In contrast, such a random reshuffling of time-series data *is* consequential for a number of its

[30] Model A is said to "nest" Model B if Model B corresponds precisely to a special case of Model A with some parameter values set to specific values, usually zero. The key papers in this literature are Clark and West (2006, 2007), McCracken (2007), and Clark and McCracken (2010). Clark, T., and K. West (2006), "Using Out-of-Sample Mean Squared Prediction Errors to Test the Martingale Difference Hypothesis," *Journal of Econometrics,* 135(1–2): 155–86. Clark, T. and K. West (2007), "Approximately Normal Tests for Equal Predictive Accuracy in Nested Models," *Journal of Econometrics,* 138(1): 291–311. McCracken, M. W. (2007), "Asymptotics for Out of Sample Tests of Granger Causality," *Journal of Econometrics,* 140(2), 719–52. Clark, T. E, and M. W. McCracken (2010), "Reality Checks and Nested Forecast Model Comparisons," Federal Reserve Bank of St. Louis Working Paper 2010-032A, research.stlouisfed.org/wp/2010-032.pdf.

[31] Ashley, R., and H. Ye (2011). "On the Granger Causality between Median Inflation and Price Dispersion," *Applied Economics* (in press). Note also that it may before long become standard practice to use mechanized model specification search procedures to assess Granger causation, per Doornick (2009) and Ericsson (2010) referenced in Section 18.4.

observable properties if – and to the degree to which – these data are *not* serially independent. In fact, this observation is the basis for a fundamental statistical test for serial independence proposed by Ashley and Patterson (1986).[32]

It is thus the time-ordering of Y_t which makes any serial dependence in it – or even a lack of serial dependence in it, as noted above – meaningful. Serial dependence is not necessarily restricted to dependence only on the recent past, however: it is not impossible for Y_t to depend on its distant past or on its future. In fact, each of these phenomena commonly occurs in economic and financial time-series data. For example, the AR(∞) representation, available for any invertible ARMA(p, q) process, in general does imply that Y_t depends on its own distant past; invertibility implies, however, that this dependence of Y_t on Y_{t-j} fairly promptly becomes negligible as j becomes unboundedly large. And, even though the AR(∞) representation of a time-series necessarily expresses its current value only in terms of past values, it is well-known that rational expectations models of all sorts typically imply that current values of time-series variables are correlated with future values.

Indeed, since "dependence" does not imply "causation," there is no inherent problem with past values of a time-series being dependent on future values. In fact, we will see shortly that any relation between a time-series and its past necessarily implies a concomitant dependence on the future. So where and how do concepts like "past," "future," and "history" ever enter time-series analysis in a necessary and meaningful way? This requires a bit of discussion.

First, let's reconsider the concept of ρ_k, the serial correlation of a time-series Y_t with fixed mean (μ) at lag k:

$$\rho_k \equiv \text{corr}(Y_t,\, Y_{t-k}) \equiv E([Y_t - \mu]\,[Y_{t-k} - \mu]) \tag{18-12}$$

This serial correlation has everything to do with a kind of serial dependence – the linear kind, as will become apparent below – but nothing to do with concepts like "past," "future," and the like. To see this, merely observe that the definition of ρ_k in Equation 18-12 ensures that ρ_k and ρ_{-k} are indistinguishable. For example, if corr(Y_t, Y_{t-1}) is positive, then so is corr(Y_t, Y_{t+1}). In that case, observing that y_{t+1} exceeds μ implies that y_t most likely exceeds μ. Or perhaps it would be most accurate to say that, if corr(Y_t, Y_{t-1}) is positive and observation number t in an observed sequence y_1 ... y_N notably exceeds μ, then most likely both y_{t-1} and y_{t+1} one will exceed μ also. Thus, knowing that ρ_1 is positive then allows one to "predict" that $y_t > \mu$ (on average) from knowing that $y_{t+1} > \mu$, in exactly the same sense (and to the same degree) that knowing $y_{t-1} > \mu$ allows one to predict that $y_t > \mu$.

Note that all of the above reasoning would thus be exactly the same if time were flowing "backward," in the sense that the subscript t were to decrease, rather than increase, over time. This is not quite as odd a concept as it might first appear. For example, historical climatological data is often plotted and analyzed in opposite time-order. Thus, Y_τ might well be expressing average global temperature τ thousands of years ago in such a data set, in which case τ becomes *smaller* over time.

We see, then, that the concept of "serial correlation" is completely oblivious to what one might call, "the arrow of time." In contrast, the "arrow of causation" is – by definition – *not* oblivious to the "arrow of time." At least, not on Granger's definition of "causality." In his view, future fluctuations in a time-series are inherently incapable of causing – "Granger-causing," if you will – current or past fluctuations in the series. Future fluctuations can spuriously *appear* to cause fluctuations in the past of another time-series if an intervening time-series variable has been wrongly omitted from the analysis, however. See Ashley, Granger, and Schmalensee (1980) for a more extensive discussion of this issue.[33]

The ARMA(p, q) processes described so far in this chapter are similarly oblivious to the order in which time proceeds – i.e., whether time increases or decreases as the subscript t increases – because

[32] Ashley, R., and D.M. Patterson (1986), "A Non-Parametric, Distribution-Free Test for Serial Independence in Stock Returns," *Journal of Financial and Quantitative Analysis 21*: 221–27.

[33] Ashley, R., C.W.J. Granger, and R. Schmalensee (1980), "Advertising and Aggregate Consumption: An Analysis Of Causality," *Econometrica 48*, 1149–68.

these models are completely determined by the autocorrelations – ($\rho_1, \rho_2, \rho_3, \ldots$) – in Y_t. Note that any particular ARMA(p, q) model for Y_t is backward-looking – i.e., it expresses Y_t in terms of Y_{t-1}, $Y_{t-2}, \ldots, Y_{t-p}$ and $U_t, U_{t-1}, \ldots, U_{t-q}$. Presuming that the model is stationary, it has an MA(∞) representation yielding (from Equation 17-34) a particular set of values for the autocorrelations (ρ_1, $\rho_2, \rho_3, \ldots$) of Y_t. But the same model – only rewritten with the subscript "$t+1$" replacing "$t-1$," "$t+2$" replacing "$t-2$", and so forth – will imply exactly the same set of autocorrelations for Y_t.

ARMA(p, q) processes are called *linear* processes because they express Y_t as a linear function of $Y_{t-1}, Y_{t-2}, \ldots, Y_{t-p}$ and $U_t, U_{t-1}, \ldots, U_{t-q}$. The kind of dependence in a time-series which can be modeled in this way is thus called "linear serial dependence." However, since these processes are actually just modeling the autocorrelations of Y_t – and these autocorrelations are inherently oblivious to the direction in which time flows – it follows that a linear ARMA(p, q) model must be inadequate to describe the time-evolution of a time-series for which this direction of time-flow matters.

But the direction time runs in *does* matter for quite a number of economically important time-series. For example, Figure 18-13 plots the monthly observations on $UNRATE_t$, the U.S. Civilian Unemployment rate first (in panel a) from January 1948 to September 2010 and then (in panel b) in opposite time-order, from September 2010 to January 1948. Examining panel a, note that the unemployment rate rises sharply in a recession, but then declines much more slowly during the

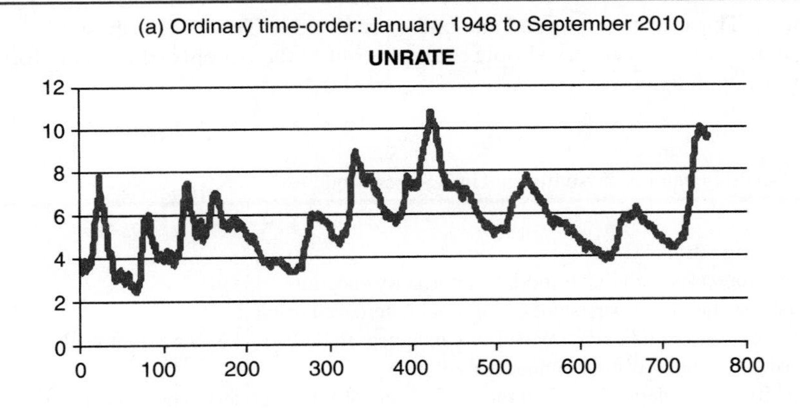

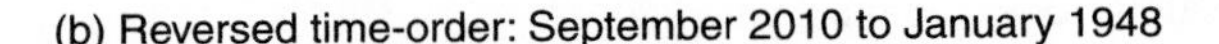

(b) Reversed time-order: September 2010 to January 1948

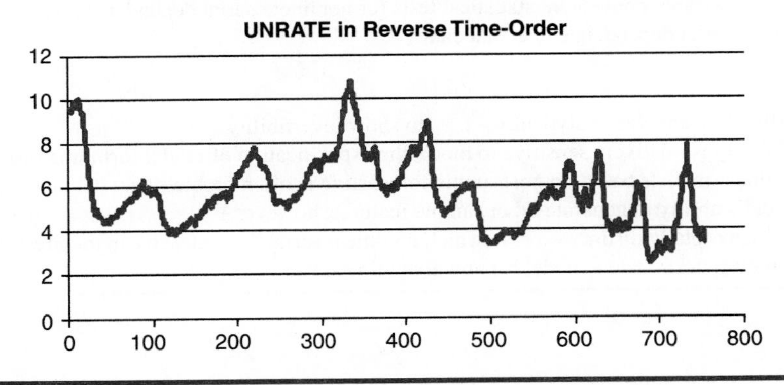

Figure 18-13 U.S. Civilian Unemployment Rate[a]

[a]Data are from research.stlouisfed.org/fred2/series/UNRATE?cid=12.

economic recovery which follows. Because of this asymmetry over time, the time-reversed plot of these same data, in panel b, is therefore a bit different. Until one knows to look for it, this difference in character between these two time-plots is visually subtle, but the economic and social impact of this asymmetry is immense.[34]

Clearly, a linear ARMA(p, q) model for $UNRATE_t$ will inherently be unable to capture or reproduce this asymmetry in the time-pattern of movements in the U.S. unemployment rate, since the structure and coefficients of such models arise from the autocorrelations of $UNRATE_t$, which we have seen are invariant to the direction in which time runs.

A linear ARMA(p,q) model for $UNRATE_t$ inherently reduces this time-series to the serially uncorrelated model error U_t. Indeed, the point of Wold's Decomposition (Equation 17-31) is that *any* covariance stationary time-series can be represented as a (linear) MA(∞) process with serially uncorrelated errors – i.e., errors which are not themselves linearly related to their own past values. But this does not rule out the possibility that these model errors are related to their own past in a *nonlinear* way: this possibility would be ruled out only if these model errors were serially independent as well as serially uncorrelated. Thus, Wold's Decomposition does not eliminate the possibility that there might exist a nonlinear model expressing $UNRATE_t$ in terms of its own past which is a better model in that it yields model errors which are serially independent. Indeed, the asymmetry we observe in the data plotted in Figure 18-13 implies that such a better, but nonlinear, model for $UNRATE_t$ must exist.

As a group, nonlinear time-series models have some very excellent features and some very difficult features. These features – good and bad – are listed in Table 18-2; these are illustrated and discussed below, using several very simple examples out of the panoply of possible formulations of nonlinear serial dependence.

Table 18-2 General Features of Nonlinear Time-Series Models

Good Points:

- Can exhibit asymmetry.
- Provide better forecasts than linear models if correctly specified.
- Endogenously explain time-persistent conditional heteroscedasticity.
- Can endogenously explain how a time-series can appear to be I(1) – i.e., a random walk with unbounded variance – yet not wander off unboundedly over time.
- Explain the "frequency dependence" in the coefficients of linear models, where the apparent permanence of a fluctuation in an explanatory variable affects its impact.
- Suggest richer directions for economic theorizing.
- Motivated by reasonably convenient statistical tests for nonlinear serial dependence, which frequently detect nonlinear serial dependence in actual data.

Bad Points:

- Are often difficult to analyze analytically – e.g., to show invertibility.
- Forecasting ability is relatively sensitive to modest misspecification of model form; therefore choosing between nonlinear models based on postsample forecasting is often problematic. (Choices can be made based on model's ability to generate other sample features, however.)
- There are so many totally distinct ways in which nonlinear serial dependence can manifest that it is difficult to credibly formulate a model for any given time-series.

[34] The political repercussions of this particular asymmetry can be intense also; these words are being written on Election Day (November 2, 2010) and the fact that the unemployment rate is only very slowly coming down, a number of quarters after the end of the sharp recession of 2008–9, is having a massive impact on the makeup of the next U.S. Congress.

The first model to be discussed is one of the simplest possible members of the "bilinear" family of nonlinear models. In this model, the time-series Y_t^{BILINEAR} is taken to be generated by the bilinear model:

$$\begin{aligned} Y_t^{\text{BILINEAR}} &= \beta Y_{t-2}^{\text{BILINEAR}}\,\varepsilon_{t-1} + \varepsilon_t \qquad \varepsilon_t \sim \text{IID}(0,1) \qquad \beta^2 < \tfrac{1}{2} \\ &= (\beta\varepsilon_{t-1})Y_{t-2}^{\text{BILINEAR}} + \varepsilon_t \end{aligned} \tag{18-13}$$

where Y_t^{BILINEAR} is assumed to be strictly stationary.[35]

Note that the error term in this model (ε_t) is assumed to be identically and *independently* distributed in each period. This symbol was chosen – instead of the U_t notation used to denote a serially uncorrelated error term in previous models – so as to emphasize this distinction. In particular, recall that serial independence implies that there is no relationship *at all* between ε_t and its past (or future) values, whereas the serial uncorrelatedness which has been assumed for U_t only implies that there is no *linear* relationship between U_t and its past (or future) values.

Where, earlier on, U_t was assumed to be normally distributed, as well as serially uncorrelated, these together implied that U_t was also serially independent. This reflects the fact that multivariate (i.e., joint) normality in a set of random variables implies that they are either linearly related (correlated) or completely unrelated (independent). Thus, if two variables are related in a nonlinear way, then they cannot be jointly normally distributed. This result does not rule out the possibility that the model errors in a nonlinear model could be jointly normally distributed. But the dependent variable generated by such a model will surely be non-normally distributed; indeed, any dependent variable produced by a non-trivial nonlinear generating mechanism must be non-normally distributed. Typically, this non-normality in a time-series with nonlinear serial dependence will exhibit itself in its marginal distribution – i.e., in a histogram of the data – as asymmetry around the mean or as thick tails.[36]

Returning to Equation18-13, this family of bilinear models was first described and analyzed by Granger and Anderson (1978),[37] who named them "bilinear" because all of these models can be re-written, as in the second part of this equation, to look like an AR(p) model whose coefficients are linear functions of lagged values of the model error term. In this particular case, Y_t^{BILINEAR} looks a lot like an AR(2) model, but differs from an actual AR(2) model in that the coefficient on the time-series lagged twice – which would be just the constant φ_2 in a linear AR(2) model – itself depends linearly on a past value of the model error term. This complication allows the bilinear model to generate asymmetric data – fundamentally, because the sign of "AR(2) parameter" itself depends on whether a positive or negative shock has recently occurred. This illustrates how asymmetry naturally arises out of a nonlinear generating mechanism.

[35] As noted in Section 17.3, strict stationarity of a time-series Y_t is a stronger assumption about the time independence of its population moments than is covariance stationarity. Covariance stationarity requires (and implies) that the mean, the variance, and all of the covariances of a time-series all have fixed (i.e., time-constant) population values across the entire sample. Strict stationarity extends this requirement to all of Y_t's population moments, including higher-order moments such as $E(Y_t\,Y_{t-1}Y_{t-2})$. Covariance stationarity ensures that the population coefficients of a correctly specified linear model are constants, which can therefore potentially be consistently estimated. Strict stationarity of Y_t ensures that a parameter like β in Equation 18-13 is a constant; thus, β in that case could be consistently estimated via nonlinear least squares, at least if the form of the model equation is correctly specified and, as described below, $|\beta|$ is sufficiently small that this bilinear model is invertible.

[36] Normality in the marginal distributions does not inherently imply joint (multivariate) normality, however, as any time-series can be transformed so as to have a normally distributed marginal distribution. Specifically, one can do this by merely first transforming the data by applying its own cumulative distribution function; this operation renders the data uniformly distributed on the interval (0, 1). Applying the inverse cumulative distribution function of the normal distribution to these uniformly distributed variates then, by construction, yields a set of observations with a normal marginal distribution. These data are not necessarily multivariate (jointly) normally distributed, however, and could be nonlinearly related to their own past, despite their normally distributed appearance. Most tests for normality only examine the marginal distribution; Hinich (1982) provided a notable exception, based on the estimated bispectrum of a time-series. Hinich, M. J. "Testing for Gaussianity and Linearity of a Stationary, Time-Series" *Journal of Time-Series Analysis 3*, 169–76.

[37] Granger, C. W. J., and A. A. Anderson (1978), *An Introduction to Bilinear Time-Series Models.* Vandenheur and Ruprecht: Gottingen.

This particular bilinear model also provides perhaps the simplest possible example of three additional features – two of which are very useful and one of which is very awkward – which nonlinear models frequently exhibit. The two highly useful features it illustrates consist of how a nonlinear model can provide better forecasts than a linear model and how nonlinear serial dependence can endogenously generate the substantial conditional heteroscedasticity often found in financial data.

Each of these two useful features are described, in turn, below. First, however, it must be noted that the entire family of bilinear models also exhibits a third – also illustrative, but not at all useful – property. Because the bilinear models share this awkward characteristic property in common with many other kinds of nonlinear models, it deserves mention here. This infelicitous property is that, despite its simple appearance, some important aspects of this bilinear model in particular – and nonlinear models in general – are quite challenging to analyze. In particular, it is not straightforward to derive conditions on the model parameters – just β in this simple example – which guarantee that a bilinear model is "invertible."

"Invertibility" in a nonlinear modeling context is fundamentally the same concept as for the linear MA(q) model discussed in Section 17.5: a model for Y_t is invertible if and only if it can be rewritten to express Y_t as a function only of model parameters and of the past values Y_{t-1}, Y_{t-2}, Y_{t-3}, and so forth – with no explicit dependence on past values of the model error term and with eventually declining weights on values of the time-series in the distant past. Recalling the numerical recursion results obtained as Equations 17-20 to 17-23 in Section 17.4, an MA(q) model can always be formally inverted to obtain an AR(∞) representation for a time-series. The issue in that case is to ensure that this representation has eventually declining weights on values of Y_{t-j} for increasingly large values of j. But invertibility in an MA(q) model turned out to be easy to characterize: any particular MA(q) model is invertible if and only if all of the roots of the qth order characteristic polynomial corresponding to it lie outside of the unit circle.

With bilinear models, in contrast, it is generally *not* so easy characterize whether a particular model is or is not invertible. In particular, while Granger and Anderson (1978) did give a proof that the particular bilinear model in Equation 18-13 is invertible if and only if the parameter β satisfies the condition $\beta^2 < ½$, their proof is substantially too difficult to discuss here. Moreover, extending their proof to provide invertibility conditions for more complex bilinear models is, to put it mildly, not straightforward. Invertibility is very consequential because this property is necessary in order to forecast with the model – or even to calculate fitting errors, so that parameters like β can be estimated. Thus, it is quite easy to run into numerical issues in estimating all but the simplest bilinear models, as it is usually not clear how to steer the nonlinear least squares routine well clear of parameter estimates corresponding to non-invertible models.

Because of these nagging invertibility issues, bilinear models are not widely used in practice.[38] So why is it brought up here? The bilinear model is discussed here because it illustrates four key points about nonlinear time-series models in a straightforward way. Two of these points have now been made: First, this model clearly illustrated how a nonlinear model can generate the asymmetry we observe in some important economic time-series data. And second, the bilinear model illustrated the analytic downside of nonlinear models: not only are they non-invertible for some parameter values, but it can be infeasible to even analyze them well enough to simply characterize ahead of time whether a particular model is or is not invertible.[39]

The third point which is well illustrated by this particular nonlinear model (Equation 18-13) arises from its implication that, while the values of Y_t generated by this model are clearly not serially

[38] See Rothman (1998) for a rare example. Rothman, P. (1998), "Forecasting Asymmetric Unemployment Rates," *The Review of Economics and Statistics* 80, 164–68.

[39] It is always easy to determine non-invertibility of a particular model after the fact: if one tries to simulate data from a non-invertible model, the numerical results eventually (and usually quickly) explode. This observation still leaves the design of a numerically stable estimation procedure highly problematic, however.

independent, it is easy to show that they are serially uncorrelated. First, note that the unconditional mean of Y_t is zero:[40]

$$\begin{aligned} E\left(Y_t^{\text{BILINEAR}}\right) &= E\left(\beta Y_{t-2}^{\text{BILINEAR}}\,\varepsilon_{t-1} + \varepsilon_t\right) \\ &= \beta E\left(Y_{t-2}^{\text{BILINEAR}}\,\varepsilon_{t-1}\right) + E(\varepsilon_t) \\ &= \beta E\left(Y_{t-2}^{\text{BILINEAR}}\right)E(\varepsilon_{t-1}) + E(\varepsilon_t) \\ &= 0 \end{aligned} \tag{18-14}$$

where $E\left(Y_{t-2}^{\text{BILINEAR}}\,\varepsilon_{t-1}\right)$ factors into the product of $E\left(Y_{t-2}^{\text{BILINEAR}}\right)$ and $E(\varepsilon_{t-1})$ because ε_{t-1} arises subsequent to $Y_{t-2}^{\text{BILINEAR}}$, and hence is independent of it; ε_t is assumed to be IID(0,1) for all time periods in Equation 18-13.

Since $E\left(Y_t^{\text{BILINEAR}}\right)$ and $E\left(Y_{t-k}^{\text{BILINEAR}}\right)$ are thus both equal to zero, the autocovariance of Y_t at positive lag k is just $E\left(Y_t^{\text{BILINEAR}}\,Y_{t-k}^{\text{BILINEAR}}\right)$:

$$\begin{aligned} &\operatorname{cov}\left(Y_t^{\text{BILINEAR}}, Y_{t-k}^{\text{BILINEAR}}\right) = E\left(Y_t^{\text{BILINEAR}}\,Y_{t-k}^{\text{BILINEAR}}\right) \\ &= E([\beta Y_{t-2}\,\varepsilon_{t-1} + \varepsilon_t]\,[\beta Y_{t-2-k}\,\varepsilon_{t-1-k} + \varepsilon_{t-k}]) \\ &= E\left(\beta^2\varepsilon_{t-1}\varepsilon_{t-1-k}Y_{t-2}Y_{t-2-k} + \beta\varepsilon_{t-1}\,\varepsilon_{t-k}\,Y_{t-2} + \beta\,\varepsilon_t\varepsilon_{t-1-k}Y_{t-2-k} + \varepsilon_t\varepsilon_{t-k}\right) \\ &= \beta^2 E(\varepsilon_{t-1})E(\varepsilon_{t-1-k}Y_{t-2}Y_{t-2-k}) + \beta E(\varepsilon_{t-1})E(\varepsilon_{t-k}Y_{t-2}) + \beta E(\varepsilon_t)E(\varepsilon_{t-1-k}Y_{t-2-k}) + E(\varepsilon_t)E(\varepsilon_{t-k}) \\ &= 0 \end{aligned} \tag{18-15}$$

where the superscript "BILINEAR" was dropped after the first line for easier readability. Note that the expression on the right-hand side of the first line of this equation is just multiplied out and rearranged in the next two lines. On the fourth line, the expected value of the weighted sum of terms is re-expressed as the weighted sum of the individual terms (using the usual linearity property of expectations) and each expectation is factored into two terms. This factorization is based on the fact that ε_τ is independent of all previous values of both itself (i.e., $\varepsilon_{\tau-1}$, $\varepsilon_{\tau-2}$, $\varepsilon_{\tau-3}$, etc.) and of Y_t (i.e., $Y_{\tau-1}$, $Y_{\tau-2}$, $Y_{\tau-3}$, etc.).

Thus, Y_t^{BILINEAR} generated by the nonlinear model of Equation 18-13 is serially uncorrelated with its own past values. Consequently, there is no nontrivial ARMA(p, q) model which can be made for these data: Y_t^{BILINEAR} is thus unforecastable using linear models. Yet, $Y_{N+1}^{\text{BILINEAR}}$ is clearly forecastable, by simply using Equation 18-13 to provide a nonlinear forecast. Denoting this nonlinear forecast $f_{N,1}^{\text{BILINEAR}}$,

$$f_{N,1}^{\text{BILINEAR}} = \hat{\beta} y_{N-1}\hat{\varepsilon}_N \tag{18-16}$$

where $\hat{\beta}$ is the sample estimate of β, y_{N-1} is the second-to-last observed sample value of Y_t, and $\hat{\varepsilon}_N$ is the last sample fitting error. The error made by this forecast is just ε_{N+1}, so its variance is given by the model as equal to one. It is easy to show, however – e.g., in Exercise 18-1 – that the variance of Y_t^{BILINEAR} itself is

$$\operatorname{var}\left(Y_t^{\text{BILINEAR}}\right) = E\left(\left[Y_t^{\text{BILINEAR}}\right]^2\right) = \frac{1}{1-\beta^2} \tag{18-17}$$

Under the Granger and Anderson (1978) invertibility result for this model, the maximum allowed value for β^2 is ½. Consequently, this very simple nonlinear model can reduce the forecasting error variance (over the linear forecast) by as much as 50%!

[40] "Unconditional" means that past values of Y_t – such as Y_{t-1}, Y_{t-2}, etc. – are not being taken as given in evaluating this expectation.

Finally, this simple bilinear model also illustrates a fundamental source of another feature of many economic time-series: autoregressive conditional heteroscedasticity, or "ARCH." The homoscedasticity assumption in a regression model is the assumption that the variance of the model error term is a constant, whereas heteroscedasticity is the failure of this assumption. Here the issue is homoscedasticity or heteroscedasticity of the time-series itself, which is the dependent variable in the model. The assumption that this dependent variable is strictly stationary (and hence also covariance stationary) implies that the *unconditional* variance of the time-series is a constant over time; hence, the time-series is unconditionally homoscedastic. This result, however, does not rule out the possibility that the *conditional* variance of a time-series – and, in particular, its variance conditional on having observed its own recent past – might vary over time.

Indeed, it has become well known in the last 15 years that the variance of the daily and monthly returns to many financial asset time-series vary over time and, moreover, vary in such a way as to be positively correlated with the magnitude of recent returns fluctuations. Predicting the variance of a financial return time-series is crucial to pricing related financial assets – "options" and the like – so a great deal of effort has gone into producing such variance prediction models. One of the most popular of these is the GARCH(p, q) model, where the current variance in the model error term is taken to be a function of the squares of model errors in the recent past:

$$
\begin{aligned}
Y_t &= \mu + \sqrt{h_t}\, U_t \\
h_t &= \alpha_o + \sum_{i=1}^{q} \alpha_i\, U_{t-i}^2 + \sum_{j=1}^{q} \beta_j\, h_{t-j}
\end{aligned}
\tag{18-18}
$$

Here U_t is taken to be serially uncorrelated – with mean zero and unit variance – and the variance of Y_t, conditional on its own past, is then given by the value of h_t. Much attention has gone into estimating and utilizing GARCH(p, q) models, and a number of variations on this theme have been elaborated and applied; Enders (2010, Chapter 3) provides an excellent introduction to this literature.[41]

The GARCH(p, q) model (and its variants) are usually considered to be nonlinear models in their own right, but usually do not allow for nonlinear serial dependence in the conditional mean of Y_t – only in its conditional variance – and hence are generally not helpful in forecasting Y_t itself. This is because the GARCH(p, q) formulation is fundamentally a "tack on" to the model for Y_t, focusing solely on the variance of the model error term. In contrast, it is easy to show that the bilinear model of Equation 18-13 *endogenously* induces positive conditional heteroscedasticity in Y_t^{BILINEAR}:[42]

$$
\begin{aligned}
\text{var}\left(Y_{N+1}^{\text{BILINEAR}} | y_N, y_{N-1}, \ldots\right) &= 1 \\
\text{var}\left(Y_{N+2}^{\text{BILINEAR}} | y_N, y_{N-1}, \ldots\right) &= \beta^2 y_N^2 + 1
\end{aligned}
\tag{18-19}
$$

Thus, if Y_t is generated by Equation 18-13, then the conditional variance of Y_t one period hence is still a constant, but the conditional variance of Y_t two periods hence is automatically a direct

[41] Note that the parameters $\alpha_1 \ldots \alpha_q$ are generally constrained to be positive, the parameter p is often set to one, and the estimated value of the parameter β_1 is usually close to one: this yields values of h_t which are positive and smoothly varying over time. See also: Heracleous and Spanos (2006) for a fundamentally better approach. Enders, W. (2010), *Applied Econometric Time-Series*, Wiley: Hoboken. Heracleous, M., and A. Spanos (2006), "The Student's t Dynamic Linear Regression: Re-examining Volatility Modeling," in *Econometric Analysis of Financial and Economic Time-Series (Part A); Advances in Econometrics 20.* Elsevier: Amsterdam.

[42] The derivation of Equation 18-19 is not very difficult, but a bit too challenging for a chapter exercise here. Consequently, this derivation – and the generalization of this result about the endogenous origin of conditional heteroscedasticity in nonlinear models – are both left to Ashley (2010). Ashley, R. (2010), "On the Origins of Conditional Heteroscedasticity in Time-Series," available at Web sites econpapers.repec.org/paper/vpiwpaper/e07-23.htm and ashleymac.econ.vt.edu/working_papers/origins_of_conditional_heteroscedasticity.pdf.

function of the most recently observed value of $(Y_t)^2$. This kind of result is generally the case for practically all nonlinear models: the nonlinear serial dependence itself inherently induces conditional heteroscedasticity in Y_{t+h} for some or all values of h greater than one.

Consequently – and despite the fact that this is very frequently done in practice – it is in most cases not actually necessary to "tack on" a GARCH(p, q) model to generate observed conditional heteroscedasticity: specifying an appropriate nonlinear model will automatically model this aspect of the time-series' behavior. More fundamentally, this kind of result shows that any observation of more-than-one-step-ahead conditional heteroscedasticity in one's data is an indication that the actual generating mechanism for the time-series is nonlinear; in that case the GARCH(p, q) model is unnecessarily giving up on forecasting Y_t itself.

The bilinear model of Equation 18-13 just described is a good example of a "smooth" nonlinear model. Here is another:

$$Y_t^{\text{EAR}} = \alpha + \left[\beta_o + \beta_1 e^{-\left(Y_{t-1}^{\text{EAR}}\right)^2}\right] Y_{t-1}^{\text{EAR}} + \varepsilon_t \tag{18-20}$$

Equation 18-20 is an example of what is called the "Exponential AR(1) model."[43] Many such models have been proposed – too many, in fact: the problem is in figuring out which one is best for the data at hand.

A whole genre of distinctly *non*-smooth nonlinear models has been proposed also. These models assume at the outset that the generating mechanism of the observed time-series depends on which of several "states" the world is in. It is typically assumed that the time-series evolves according to a linear AR(p) process in each state, but that the coefficients defining this model are distinct for each state. The specific nonlinearity in these time-series models arises from the ways in which the switching from one state to another is formulated.

One set of such formulations – "Markov switching models," originally proposed in Hamilton (1989) – posits that the state switches at random at the end of each period and estimates the switching probabilities. For example, Lam (2004) estimates the following two-state Markov switching model for the growth rate in U.S. real GNP over the sample period 1952II to 1996IV:

$$\begin{aligned} Y_t^{\text{Markov}} = & \left\{ \underset{(.093)}{.852} \text{ (State I) or } - \underset{(.453)}{1.500} \text{ (State II)} \right\} \\ & + \underset{(.084)}{.388}\, Y_{t-1}^{\text{Markov}} + \underset{(.102)}{.097}\, Y_{t-2}^{\text{Markov}} - \underset{(.099)}{.106}\, Y_{t-3}^{\text{Markov}} - \underset{(.083)}{127}\, Y_{t-4}^{\text{Markov}} + \varepsilon_t \end{aligned} \tag{18-21}$$

where the figures in parentheses are estimated standard errors for these coefficient estimates and Lam estimates that the system remains in State I with probability .966 and remains in State II with probability .208. These two "states" for the U.S. economies are easily interpreted in this case: State I clearly corresponds to what one might call "normal growth," whereas State II corresponds to "recession."[44]

Tong (1983) proposed a different multistate nonlinear model. His formulation is called the "Threshold Autoregression" or "TAR" model, because the state of the system depends on whether

[43] This family of smooth nonlinear models was first proposed by Haggan and Ozaki (1981); Rothman (1998) estimates a version of this model for the U.S. unemployment rate time-series. Haggan, V., and T. Ozaki (1981), "Modelling Nonlinear Random Vibrations Using an Amplitude-Dependent Autrogressive Time-Series Model," *Biometrika 68*, 189–196.

[44] Lam (1998) follows Hamilton (1989) in (rather artificially) constraining the non-intercept AR(4) parameters to be the same in both states. This is in part because his main interest is in extending Hamilton's formulation to allow both the intercept and the transition probabilities to depend parametrically on how long the economy has been in a particular state; in fact, one can allow the transition probabilities to depend on any observable variable of interest. Hamilton, J. (1989), "A New Approach to the Economic Analysis of Non-Stationary Time-Series and the Business Cycle" *Econometrica 57*, 357-84. Lam, P. (2004), "A Markov-Switching Model of GNP Growth with Duration Dependence," *International Economic Review 45*, 174–204.

an observable variable – usually a lagged value of the time-series itself – has exceeded a "threshold" value.[45] For example, Potter (1995) estimated the following two-state TAR model for the growth rate of U.S. real GNP:

$$\begin{aligned} Y_t &= \underset{(.423)}{-.808} + \underset{(.185)}{.516}\ Y_{t-1} - \underset{(.353)}{.946}\ Y_{t-2} + \underset{(.216)}{.352}\ Y_{t-5} + \varepsilon_t \qquad \text{for} \quad Y_{t-2} \leq 0 \\ Y_t &= \underset{(.161)}{.517} + \underset{(.080)}{.299}\ Y_{t-1} + \underset{(.107)}{.189}\ Y_{t-2} + \underset{(.069)}{1.143}\ Y_{t-5} + \eta_t \qquad \text{for} \quad Y_{t-2} > 0 \end{aligned} \tag{18-22}$$

Here the two states again correspond to normal growth versus recession, so it was natural to take the threshold value as zero; Potter presumably chose a threshold lag of two periods because it fit the data better. The number of states, threshold lag, and threshold lag values would nowadays typically be chosen to minimize the BIC criterion.[46]

A three-state TAR model provides a compellingly simple (and illuminating) rationale for the frequent observation that the level of a macroeconomic or financial time-series appears to be I(1) in its strong short-term serial dependence, yet these time-series also appear to revert over time to their mean (or trend-line) value – rather than wandering off over time, as would be implied by an I(1) process. For example, let $\log(P_t)$ denote the logarithm of the price of a financial asset; a reasonable model for $\log(P_t)$ might then be given by the TAR model:

$$\begin{aligned} \log(P_t) &= 0.5\log(P_{t-1}) + \varepsilon_t \quad \text{for} \qquad\qquad \log(P_{t-1}) > 1.0 \\ \log(P_t) &= \log(P_{t-1}) + \varepsilon_t \quad \text{for} \quad -1.0 \leq \log(P_{t-1}) \leq 1.0 \\ \log(P_t) &= 0.5\log(P_{t-1}) + \varepsilon_t \quad \text{for} \qquad\qquad \log(P_{t-1}) < -1.0 \end{aligned} \tag{18-23}$$

Notice that this nonlinear model allows for $\log(P_t)$ to evolve as a unit root – i.e., I(1) or random walk – process during every period in which $\log(P_t)$ remains in the interval $[-1.0, 1.0]$; and this might well constitute the bulk of the sample period. Yet the value $|\log(P_t)|$ does not become unboundedly large – nor is its variance unbounded – because the nature of the generating process switches to a stationary AR(1) model, which reverts fairly quickly to its unconditional mean of zero, whenever $|\log(P_t)|$ exceeds one. The two threshold values in Equation 18-23 were set here (for simplicity) to ± 1.0, but these could just as easily have been estimated from the sample data. Moreover, these estimates would have a sensible and interesting economic interpretation, as they clearly relate to the minimum departures of the asset price from its trend value necessary in order to yield a profitable arbitrage opportunity.[47]

TAR modeling has met with some success in practice, but the assumption of sudden transitions among discrete states seems artificial in many settings. For this reason Teräsvirta and Anderson (1992) proposed a variation on this family of models in which the transition from one state to another is "smoothed out."[48,49] This family of models – denoted "STAR" or "Smooth Transition Autoregression Models" – is best illustrated with an example. Letting Y_t^{STAR} denote the growth rate of U.S. real GNP,

[45] Tong, H. (1983), *Threshold Models in Non-linear Time-Series Analysis*, Springer-Verlag: New York.

[46] On this basis – and on common-sense considerations, as coefficients at lags three and four are not included – the terms at lag five would probably omitted from the model.

[47] See Dwyer, Locke, and Yu (1996) for an application of three-state TAR modeling to arbitrage in a real-world financial setting. Dwyer, G. P., P. Locke, and W. Yu (1996), "Index Arbitrage and Nonlinear Dynamics Between the S&P 500 Futures and Cash," *The Review of Financial Studies 9(1)*, 301–32.

[48] Enders (2010, Chapter 7) describes the several varieties of STAR models – and a number of other nonlinear model families – in some detail.

[49] Teräsvirta, T., and H. Anderson (1992), "Characterising Nonlinearities in Business Cycles Using Smooth Transition Autoregressive Models," *Journal of Applied Econometrics 7*, 119–36.

then a simple STAR model for Y_t^{STAR}, estimated using data from 1953I to 1993III, is

$$\begin{aligned} Y_t^{\text{STAR}} &= \underset{(.131)}{.226} + \underset{(.154)}{F}\left(Y_{t-2}^{\text{STAR}}\right)\left[\underset{(.183)}{.158}\ Y_{t-1}^{\text{STAR}} - .363\ Y_{t-2}^{\text{STAR}}\right] \\ &\quad + \left[1 - F\left(Y_{t-2}^{\text{STAR}}\right)\right]\left[\underset{(.090)}{.315}\ Y_{t-1}^{\text{STAR}} - \underset{(.115)}{.262}\ Y_{t-2}^{\text{STAR}}\right] + \varepsilon_t \end{aligned} \tag{18-24}$$

where $F(x)$ is the logistic function, $1/(1+e^{0.589\,x})$. The coefficient (0.589) in this function – as well as the other parameter estimates – were obtained from least squares regression.[50] Note that realized values of $F(Y_{t-2}^{\text{STAR}})$ vary smoothly from zero – when y_{t-2}^{STAR} is very negative – to one – when y_{t-2}^{STAR} is very positive. Thus, Equation 18-24 allows the sample data to quantify a smooth transition between these two AR(2) models for the time evolution of Y_t^{STAR}.[51]

Lastly, it is well worth noting that a nonlinear generating mechanism for a time-series – and only a nonlinear generating mechanism – can model what is called "frequency dependence" in a relationship. "Frequency dependence" sounds a bit arcane, but this is really exactly the same idea embodied in the well-known Permanent Income Hypothesis (PIH) of macroeconomic consumption theory, first proposed by Modigliani and Brumberg (1954) and Friedman (1957). Quoting from Ashley and Verbrugge (2009):[52]

> The PIH theory predicts that the partial derivative of aggregate consumption spending with respect to disposable income – which Keynes called the "marginal propensity to consume" – will differ across frequencies. In particular the PIH theory predicts that this coefficient will be large for slowly-varying (persistent or low frequency) fluctuations in household income, because these fluctuations are likely to be identified by the agents as primarily corresponding to changes in "permanent" income. In contrast, the theory predicts that the marginal propensity to consume will be small for quickly-varying (non-persistent or high frequency) fluctuations in household income, as these transitory fluctuations will be identified as primarily corresponding to changes in "temporary" income. Thus, the marginal propensity to consume – which would be a fixed parameter in an ordinary consumption function specification – is posited to be larger at low frequencies than at high frequencies: in other words, frequency dependence in this coefficient is the embodiment of the PIH theory.

Thus, if one considers a linear formulation of a simple Keynesian consumption relation, such as

$$\begin{aligned} C_t &= \lambda_1 Y_{t-1} + \lambda_2 C_{t-1} + \varepsilon_{c,t} \\ Y_t &= \alpha_1 Y_{t-1} + \alpha_2 C_{t-1} + \varepsilon_{y,t} \end{aligned} \tag{18-25}$$

then one might expect the parameter λ_1 – which one would identify (in Keynesian terms) as the short-run marginal propensity to consume – to be larger in time periods during which y_{t-1} is

[50] The transition lag (of two quarters) was lifted from Potter's TAR specification; the extraneous terms at lag five were omitted as their inclusion merely increased the BIC value for the fitted model; this particular sample period was used because this example is taken from Ashley and Patterson (2006), cited in Footnote 18-55.

[51] The general STAR framework provides for the possibility of more than two states. It also allows for other transition functions; in fact, the model given in Equation 18-24 is usually denoted L-STAR ("logistic-STAR") to explicitly indicate this particular transition function choice. See Granger and Teräsvirta (1993) or Enders (2010, Chapter 7.7) for more detail on STAR modeling. Granger, C.W.J., and T. Teräsvirta (1993), *Modelling Nonlinear Economic Relationships*. Oxford University Press: Oxford.

[52] Ashley, R., and R. Verbrugge (2009), "Frequency Dependence in Regression Model Coefficients: An Alternative Approach for Modeling Nonlinear Dynamic Relationships," *Econometric Reviews 28*: 4–20. Working paper available at Web site ashleymac.econ.vt.edu/working_papers/freq_depend.pdf.

primarily part of a smooth fluctuation over time – identified in the theory as a change in permanent income – and smaller in periods where during which y_{t-1} is a sudden fluctuation, corresponding in the theory to a change in temporary income. One could identify these as "low-frequency" and "high-frequency" changes in income, respectively, so that λ_1 is indicated to be a function – in this case, an inverse function – of the degree to which y_{t-1} is a high-frequency fluctuation.

One might model this kind of frequency dependence in λ_1 by observing that this dependence implies that the value of λ_1, rather than being a constant, depends on the recent history of Y_{t-1}. For example, a crude model for λ_1 exhibiting history-dependence consistent with frequency dependence (and the PIH theory) might parametrize λ_1 as

$$\begin{aligned}\lambda_1 &= \ell_o / \left\{1 + \ell_1 \left(Y_{t-1} - Y_{t-1}^{\text{smoothed}}\right)^2\right\} \\ &= \ell_o / \left\{1 + \ell_1 \left(Y_{t-1} - \left[\frac{1}{2} Y_{t-1} + \frac{1}{2} Y_{t-2}\right]\right)^2\right\} = \ell_o / \left\{1 + \frac{1}{4} \ell_1 (Y_{t-1} - Y_{t-2})^2\right\}\end{aligned} \tag{18-26}$$

with ℓ_1 a positive constant. This particular formulation specifies that λ_1 is smaller to the extent that the current value of lagged income represents a deviation from its average over the previous two periods. Clearly, this particular way of parameterizing λ_1 implies that

$$C_t = \left\{\frac{\ell_o}{1 + \frac{1}{4}\ell_1 (Y_{t-1} - Y_{t-2})^2}\right\} Y_{t-1} + \lambda_2 C_{t-1} + \varepsilon_{c,t} \tag{18-27}$$

so that, in the context of this particular example, the relationship between C_t and Y_{t-1} is nonlinear if and only if λ_1 is frequency dependent in the sense used here.[53]

Ashley and Verbrugge (2009) shows how to display (and test for) frequency dependence in estimated linear regression coefficients without making specific assumptions such as Equation 18-26, but those details are beyond the scope of the present treatment. The point here is to display how this kind of parameter instability in linear models – which theory suggests will be common in many economic settings – is actually just a reflection of nonlinear dynamics.

Thus, a nonlinear formulation of serial dependence in a time-series offers some important positive features for empirical modeling. Table 18-2 also, however, lists three major downsides to nonlinear time-series modeling. The first of these – the difficulty of analyzing nonlinear models – has already been mentioned above in the discussion of the opaque invertibility condition for the bilinear model of Equation 18-13. The second generic problem with nonlinear modeling is that the forecasting performance of nonlinear models is frequently sensitive to minor errors in misspecifying the form of the model. Consequently, it is all the more important to check the forecasting performance of such models in a post-sample evaluation period. Unfortunately, the results of such exercises are often disappointing. The survey of proposed nonlinear time-series models given above makes the third generic problem with nonlinear time-series modeling plain, however: there is a plethora of different ways that a time-series can be nonlinearly serially dependent. This multiplicity of possibilities greatly complicates the task of formulating an appropriate such model for any particular time-series a challenging one; this problem is returned to at the close of this section.

First, however, it is worth noting that the *detection* of nonlinear serial dependence in a particular time-series, somewhat surprisingly, is not such a difficult problem. Perhaps because nonlinear dependence in some kinds of economic data is quite strong, testing for nonlinear serial dependence has turned out to be reasonably feasible. Indeed, a number of useful statistical tests have been proposed and analyzed. The details of a representative (but by no means all-inclusive) group of such

[53] Equations 18-26 and 18-27 are intended only to illustrate how coefficient frequency dependence corresponds to nonlinearity in the relationship, not to be taken seriously as a model.

tests have been described elsewhere – e.g., Patterson and Ashley (2000) and Ashley and Patterson (2006, Appendix 1) – and even implemented in downloadable software, so only a few descriptive comments are warranted here.

First, almost all of the available tests for nonlinear serial dependence are actually tests for serial dependence of any kind; consequently, any linear serial dependence must first be removed before the tests are applied.[54] This removal is almost always accomplished by first making an AR(p) model for the time-series and then applying the tests to the fitting errors from the resulting estimated model; this process is called "pre-whitening" the time-series.

Second, while many tests for nonlinear serial dependence are still quite useful in modest samples, the asymptotic critical points for the test statistics are often not reliable – regardless of what the authors of the tests claim – unless the sample lengths are *quite* large. Thus, any credible application of these tests will routinely obtain critical points for the test statistics by simulation methods – usually the bootstrap, as covered in Section 11.8.

That said, a few of the best and/or most popular tests for nonlinear serial dependence are[55]

- BDS Test {Brock, Dechert and Scheinkman (1996)}[56]
  This test examines a large selection of what are called "m-histories" of the time-series – which are just sequences out of the sample of the form (y_t, y_{t-1}, ... , y_{t-m}) – and evaluates whether these sequences are "closer" to one another, on average, than one would expect if Y_t were serially IID.[57]
- McLeod-Li Test {McLeod and Li (1983)}[58]
  The McLeod-Li test was originally developed as a test for autoregressive conditional heteroscedasticity (ARCH) in a time-series. Fundamentally, it squares the (pre-whitened) sample data and examines the sample correlogram of this squared data. By construction, these pre-whitened data are serially uncorrelated. If they are serially independent as well, then the correlogram of their squared values should be zero at all non-zero lags. The McLeod-Li approach simply tests this hypothesis, using a portmanteau test essentially identical to that described in Section 17.3 – only applied to the sample correlations of the squared data, after it has first been pre-whitened. This portmanteau test statistic is asymptotically distributed as a χ^2 variate but, in practice, the critical points must be obtained using the bootstrap.

---

[54] The bispectrum test, originated in Hinich (1980), is the only exception: it tests directly for nonlinear (and solely nonlinear) serial dependence.

[55] Implementing software for these, and several additional tests for nonlinear serial dependence, is downloadable at Web site ashleymac.econ.vt.edu. This software both pre-whitens the data and bootstraps the critical points for the relevant test statistics; its usage is primarily documented in Patterson and Ashley (2000, Chapter 3). Numerous tests beyond this group have been proposed; e.g., see Barnett et al. (1997). Patterson, D. M., and R. Ashley (2000), *A Nonlinear Time-Series Workshop: A Toolkit for Detecting and Identifying Nonlinear Serial Dependence.* Kluwer Academic Publishers: Boston. Ashley, R., and D. M. Patterson (2006), "Evaluating the Effectiveness of State-Switching Models for U.S. Real Output," *Journal of Business and Economic Statistics 24(3):* 266–77. Barnett, W. A., A.R. Gallant, M.J. Hinich, J.A. Jungeilges, D.T. Kaplan, and M.J. Jensen (1997), "A Single-Blind Controlled Competition Among Tests for Nonlinearity and Chaos," *Journal of Econometrics 82*, 157–92.

[56] Brock, W. A., Dechert W., and Scheinkman J. (1996), "A Test for Independence Based on the Correlation Dimension," *Econometric Reviews 15*, 197–235.

[57] Choosing a value for m turns out to be easy, since setting m equal to one makes no sense and simulations in Ashley and Patterson (2006) show that the test is so sensitive to minor errors in the pre-whitening process that the choice of any value for m exceeding two is unwise. The BDS test with m set to two actually works quite well, so long as the test statistic is bootstrapped – otherwise extremely large samples are required. The BDS test operationalizes "closeness" by means of an m-dimensional hypercube with edge-length equal to a multiple (ε) of the sample standard deviation of the data; setting ε equal to one works well in practice.

[58] McLeod, A. I., and W. K. Li (1983), "Diagnostic Checking ARMA Time-Series Models Using Squared-Residual Autocorrelations," *Journal of Time-Series Analysis 4*, 269–73.

- Hinich Bicovariance Test {Hinich and Patterson (1995), Patterson and Ashley (2000)}[59]

  Recall that the sample correlogram is basically considering the sample autocovariance at lag j,

$$\gamma_k = \frac{1}{N-k} \sum_{t=k+1}^{N} (y_t - \bar{y})(y_{t-k} - \bar{y}) \quad k \geq 0 \tag{18-28}$$

  only scaled (by the sample variance) to convert it into a sample autocorrelation. The Hinich bicovariance test computes what is called the sample 'bicovariance' at lag pair (j, k):

$$\gamma_{j,k} \equiv \frac{1}{N-k} \sum_{t=k+1}^{N} (y_t - \bar{y})(y_{t-j} - \bar{y})(y_{t-k} - \bar{y}) \quad k \geq j \geq 0 \tag{18-29}$$

  Autocovariances are second moments of the data, and speak to how Y_t depends linearly on its own past. The bicovariances, in contrast, are third moments and consequently are related to asymmetries in the data; they are particularly relevant to how Y_t depends quadratically on its own past. These sample bicovariances are consistent estimates of the corresponding population bicovariances – which should all be zero, so long as j and k are not both zero, under the null hypothesis that $Y_t \sim \text{IID}(\mu, \sigma^2)$. Consequently, Hinich and Patterson (1995) were able to show that a portmanteau test statistic based on squares of $\gamma_{j,k}$ for various values of (j, k) is asymptotically distributed as a χ^2 variate under this null hypothesis. As with the McLeod-Li test, however, the critical points for this test statistic must in practice be obtained using the bootstrap.

And so forth: there are numerous additional tests for nonlinear serial dependence out there in the literature; several more are included in even the limited set implemented in Patterson and Ashley (2000) and Ashley and Patterson (2006); and new ones are constantly appearing.[60]

As a group, these tests work pretty well and have led to the detection of nonlinear serial dependence in a wide variety of economic and financial time-series.[61] Thus, detecting nonlinear serial dependence is not very difficult. And modeling nonlinear serial dependence is not really that difficult either – once one has specified the kind, as well as the existence, of the dependence.

The tough problem, as noted above, is that there are so many different kinds of nonlinear serial dependence that it is difficult to settle on the "right" specification – and no credible, comprehensive method exists for using the data itself to guide that specification. And it matters: as also noted above, even fairly modest defects in the specification of the form of the nonlinear dependence present will often have a serious impact on the postsample forecasting performance of the resulting model. Consequently, the nonlinear modeling choice issue does not usually boil down to testing whether the postsample forecasts from one model are significantly better than those of another: quite often, neither model being considered forecasts all that well post-sample.

---

[59] Hinich, M., and D. M. Patterson (1995), "Detecting Epochs of Transient Dependence in White Noise," unpublished manuscript.

[60] For example, Castle and Hendry (2010). Castle, J.L., and D. F. Hendry (2010), "A Low-Dimension Portmanteau Test for Non-Linearity," *Journal of Econometrics 158*, 231–245.

[61] For example, see Tong (1983), Hinich and Patterson (1985), Tsay (1986), Hamilton (1989), Ashley and Patterson (1989), Brock, Hsieh, and LeBaron (1991), Rothman (1991), Potter (1995), Verbrugge (1997), Altug, Ashley, and Patterson (1999), and a host of other studies. Hinich, M., and D. M. Patterson (1985), "Evidence of Nonlinearity in Daily Stock Returns," *Journal of Business and Economic Statistics 3*, 69–77. Tsay, R. S. (1986), "Nonlinearity Tests for Time-Series," *Biometrika 73*, 461–66. Hamilton, James (1989), "A New Approach to the Economic Analysis of Non-Stationary Time-Series and the Business Cycle," *Econometrica 57*, 357–84. Ashley, R., and D. M. Patterson (1989). "Linear Versus Nonlinear Macroeconomies" *International Economic Review 30*, 685–704. Brock, W. A., D. A. Hsieh and B. D. LeBaron (1991), *A Test of Nonlinear Dynamics, Chaos, and Instability: Theory and Evidence*, MIT Press: Cambridge. Rothman, P. "Further Evidence on the Asymmetric Behavior of Unemployment Rates Over the Business Cycle," *Journal of Macroeconomics 13*, 291–98. Potter, S. M. (1995), "A Nonlinear Approach to U.S. GNP," *Journal of Applied Econometrics 10*, 109–25. Verbrugge, R. (1997), "Investigating Cyclical Asymmetries," *Studies in Nonlinear Dynamics and Econometrics 2*, 15–22. Altug, S., R. Ashley, and D. M. Patterson (1999). "Are Technology Shocks Nonlinear?" *Macroeconomic Dynamics 3(4)*, 506–33.

Ashley and Patterson (2006) attempt to address this model-choice issue – in the face of poor post-sample forecasting performance from all of the posited models – by examining simulated data generated by each of the several estimated models. The issue then becomes one of testing whether the simulated data from one model is better able to reproduce "features of interest" – such as a pattern of results on a set of tests for nonlinear serial dependence, turning point behavior, and the like.

But this is not really a satisfactory solution. What is needed is an objective, well-defined method which uses the sample data to, at least in large samples, lead us to a nearly-correct model of nonlinear serial dependence: a nonlinear analogue to the Box-Jenkins algorithm for specifying linear time-series models. Unfortunately, it must be admitted that – despite a number of ambitious attempts[62] – such a comprehensive nonlinear model specification algorithm is at present still a research goal rather than a settled technique.

18.7 ADDITIONAL TOPICS IN FORECASTING

This final section returns to the general topic of forecasting, to briefly discuss three additional topics:

- Are there practical forecast accuracy gains to be had from shrinking the conditional mean forecast (M_h) toward zero?
- Is it possible to characterize a forecast of a time-series X_t which is so inaccurate that one is actually better off ignoring a strong relationship between X_t and some other time-series variable – Y_t, say – rather than model the Y-X relationship, but in practice replace X_t by this inaccurate forecast?

and

- Is it possible to combine several individual, disparate forecasts of a time-series Y_t, so as to obtain a forecast which is more accurate than any of them individually?

Each of these questions is taken up, in turn, below. Surprisingly, the answer to all three questions is, "Yes."

Practical Shrinkage Forecasting

First, a brief proof of Theorem 17-4 from Section 17.2 is in order. Defining some notation,

$$\begin{aligned} \varepsilon_{N+h} &\equiv M_h - Y_{N+h} \\ \nu_{N+h} &\equiv \hat{M}_h - M_h \end{aligned} \tag{18-30}$$

The random variable ε_{N+h} is the error made by the conditional-mean forecast. $E(\varepsilon_{N+h})$ is thus zero by construction; presuming that Y_t is covariance stationary, the variance of ε_{N+h} is a finite constant and here denoted as σ_ε^2. The random variable ν_{N+h} is the error made in estimating M_h, the conditional mean of Y_{N+h}, using the estimator $\hat{M}_h$. It will be assumed here that this estimator of M_h is unbiased – so $E(\nu_{N+h})$ is thus zero – and that the variance of the sampling errors is finite, so that this variance can be denoted σ_ν^2.

Theorem 17-4 also assumes that these two errors are uncorrelated, so that

$$\text{cov}(\varepsilon_{N+h}, \nu_{N+h}) = E(\varepsilon_{N+h}, \nu_{N+h}) = 0 \tag{18-31}$$

[62] For example, Gallant and Nychka (1987) and Priestley (1988). Perhaps the Doornick and Hendry (2007) automated model selection procedure alluded to in Section 18.4 will help resolve this issue. Gallant, A. R., and D. W. Nychka (1987), "Seminonparametric Maximum Likelihood Estimation," *Econometrica 55*, 363–90. Priestley, M. B. (1988), *Nonlinear and Non-stationary Time-Series Analysis.* Academic Press: London.

This is a nontrivial, but reasonable, assumption, in that there is no plausible reason to suppose that future fluctuations in Y_t are correlated with the sampling errors made in estimating the model parameters, which are presumably the source of the variance in $\hat{M}_h$.

The forecast errors made by the "shrinkage forecast" $\lambda\hat{M}_h$ are thus

$$\begin{aligned}\lambda\hat{M}_h - Y_{N+h} &= \lambda(\nu_{N+h} + M_h) - (M_h - \varepsilon_{N+h}) \\ &= (\lambda - 1)M_h + \lambda\nu_{N+h} + \varepsilon_{N+h}\end{aligned} \tag{18-32}$$

so that

$$\begin{aligned}\text{MSE}\left[\lambda\hat{M}_h\right] &= E\left(\left[(\lambda - 1)M_h + \lambda\nu_{N+h} + \varepsilon_{N+h}\right]^2\right) \\ &= (\lambda - 1)^2 M_h^2 + \lambda^2\sigma_\nu^2 + 2\,\lambda\text{cov}(\varepsilon_{N+h}, \nu_{N+h}) + \sigma_\varepsilon^2 \\ &= (\lambda - 1)^2 M_h^2 + \lambda^2\sigma_\nu^2 + \sigma_\varepsilon^2\end{aligned} \tag{18-33}$$

Setting the derivative of $\text{MSE}\left[\lambda\hat{M}_h\right]$ with respect to λ equal to zero and solving for λ^{minMSE} yields

$$\lambda^{\text{minMSE}} = \frac{M_h^2}{M_h^2 + \sigma_\nu^2} = \frac{1}{1 + \left(\sigma_\nu^2/M_h^2\right)} \tag{18-34}$$

which is equivalent to the result given in Theorem 17-4 of Section 17.2. Clearly, λ^{minMSE} is always strictly less than one, so long as σ_ν^2 is positive – i.e., whenever there is any noise in the estimator $\hat{M}_h$.

Evidently, some degree of shrinkage is always beneficial. But too much shrinkage could worsen the forecasts. Moreover, in order to implement this result in practice, one must estimate σ_ν^2/M_h^2. This leads to an estimator of λ^{minMSE} – here denoted $\hat{\lambda}^{\text{minMSE}}$ – which is itself a random variable because of its sampling errors in estimating λ^{minMSE}. This randomness in $\hat{\lambda}^{\text{minMSE}}$ clearly implies that $\text{MSE}\left(\hat{\lambda}^{\text{minMSE}}\hat{M}_h\right)$ exceeds $\text{MSE}\left(\lambda^{\text{minMSE}}\hat{M}_h\right)$ – i.e., the need to use an estimate of σ_ν^2/M_h^2 instead of its true value to some extent reduces the forecasting accuracy gains obtainable from using $\lambda^{\text{minMSE}}\hat{M}_h$ instead of $\hat{M}_h$. The practical question is this: Given that σ_ν^2/M_h^2 must be estimated, so that λ^{minMSE} must be estimated using $\hat{\lambda}^{\text{minMSE}}$, is the mean square error of $\hat{\lambda}^{\text{minMSE}}\hat{M}_h$ actually smaller than that of the unbiased forecast, $\hat{M}_h$?

Table 18-3 reports the results of a set of monte carlo simulations (per Section 11.8) which shed light on this question. In each of 10,000 trials, $y_1 \ldots y_{N+1}$ were generated from the usual Multiple Regression Model – Equation 9-1 – with k regressors, one of which corresponded to an intercept term. The other k–1 regressors were generated (on each trial) as independent unit normals, with each regressor entering the model multiplied by a population regression coefficient set to one. The regression model error term – identical to ε_t – was generated as an $\text{NIID}\left(0, \sigma_\varepsilon^2\right)$ variate, with σ_ε^2 adjusted so that R_c^2 for the resulting estimated regression models – for given (N, k) – averaged to a specified value in the range 0.15 to 0.95 over the 10,000 trials.[63] The regression model was estimated on each trial – using the N generated observations on the dependent variable and the N generated observations on the k–1 non-intercept regressors – to obtain the k coefficient estimates for the model.

This estimated model was then combined with the $k-1$ values of the explanatory variables in period $N+1$ generated for this trial so as to compute the unbiased forecast of Y_{N+1} and (since Y_{N+1} itself was generated also) the forecast error made by $\hat{M}_1$ in this trial. The value of $\text{MSE}\left(\hat{M}_1\right)$ was then obtained by simply averaging the squares of these forecast errors over the 10,000 trials. The

[63] Per Equation 9-41, R_c^2 is "R^2 corrected for the number of degrees of freedom."

Table 18-3 Simulated Average Values of $\text{MSE}\left(\hat{\lambda}^{\text{minMSE}}\hat{M}_{\text{h}}\right)/\text{MSE}(\hat{M}_{\text{h}})$

R_c^2	$N=10$	$N=20$	$N=40$	$N=60$	$N=80$
	$k=3$	$k=5$	$k=8$	$k=10$	$k=10$
Full Shrinkage					
0.15	0.835	0.885	0.923	0.943	0.964
0.35	0.892	0.935	0.962	0.975	0.988
0.55	0.941	0.975	0.988	0.994	1.000
0.75	0.986	1.002	1.002	1.004	1.004
0.95	1.027	1.016	1.010	1.006	1.004
Half Shrinkage					
0.15	0.901	0.930	0.952	0.964	0.977
0.35	0.929	0.955	0.972	0.981	0.989
0.55	0.955	0.976	0.986	0.991	0.996
0.75	0.979	0.991	0.995	0.997	0.999
0.95	1.004	1.002	1.001	1.001	1.000

shrinkage forecast for each trial, $\hat{\lambda}^{\text{minMSE}}\hat{M}_1$, was obtained by using the sample data for the trial to estimate σ_ν^2/M_1^2 and substituting this estimate into Equation 18.34 to obtain $\hat{\lambda}^{\text{minMSE}}$; averaging the squared errors from this forecast over the trials yielded an estimate of $\text{MSE}\left(\hat{\lambda}^{\text{minMSE}}\hat{M}_1\right)$.[64]

Each figure given in the top portion of Table 18-3 is the ratio of $\text{MSE}\left(\hat{\lambda}^{\text{minMSE}}\hat{M}_1\right)$ – the mean square error from the feasibly-shrunken forecast – to $\text{MSE}(\hat{M}_1)$, the mean square error of the usual, unbiased, forecast of Y_{N+1}. These mean square error values are obtained (as described above) using 10,000 generated data sets – each with the values of (N, k) specified by this column of the table and each generated using a value for σ_ε^2 adjusted so that the average R_c^2 value across the 10,000 estimated regression models has the value specified for this row of the table.

A value less than one for an entry in Table 18-3 implies that the shrinkage forecast is outperforming the unbiased forecast (on a squared-error loss function criterion), despite the additional noise inserted in the shrinkage forecast by the sampling errors involved in estimating λ^{minMSE}. Note that noticeable MSE improvements are possible for weak models – i.e, where R_c^2 is fairly small – but that the shrinkage forecast can slightly worsen the forecast accuracy for strong models. The bottom portion of Table 18-3 repeats the calculation, but shrinking the unbiased forecast by only half as much. This more conservative amount of shrinkage still provides modest MSE improvements – so long as the sample length is not too

[64] Ashley (2006, p. 10) provides an expression for a consistent estimator of σ_ν^2/M_1^2 based on the N values of Y_t and $X_{t,2} \ldots X_{t,k}$ and the $k-1$ values of $X_{t+1,2} \ldots X_{t+1,k}$. This estimator – details on which are omitted here, for brevity – was used in obtaining the estimates used in the simulation results reported below. However, as the shrinkage forecasts are clearly most useful where the ratio σ_ν^2/M_h^2 is sizeable – which is most likely to occur with relatively small values of N – some other estimator of this ratio might well yield better results than those quoted here. Ashley, R. (2006), "Beyond Optimal Forecasting," available at Web site ashleymac.econ.vt.edu/working_papers/beyond_optimal_shrinkage.pdf; this paper also explores shrinkage forecasts which stochastically dominate the conditional mean forecast.

large or the regression model too strong – but with little apparent risk of ever actually worsening the forecasts.[65]

One might justifiably remark that the forecast MSE improvements from this sort of shrinkage forecast are rather minor. On the other hand, these MSE improvements are "free": they require no additional sample data and precious little effort.

A Forecast "Beneath Contempt"

Quite often the motivation for forecasting a time-series is to provide an input to an existing forecasting model which exploits a relationship between this time-series and some other variable. This is an extremely common situation in regional or urban economic analysis, where local incomes, employment, tax collections, etc. are strongly linked to state-level or national-level economic conditions. In such cases one needs a forecast of the state or national input variable in order to predict the regional or local variable. However, the errors made by this forecast of the state-level or national-level input variable then contribute to the errors in forecasting the regional variable.

For example, suppose that one's actual interest is in forecasting the regional time-series Y_t^{region}, which is known to be related to a national-level variable X_t^{US} via the model

$$
\begin{aligned}
Y_t^{\text{region}} &= \alpha + \beta X_t^{\text{US}} + U_t^{\text{region}} \qquad U_t^{\text{region}} \sim \text{IID}(0, \sigma_u^2) \\
E\left(X_t^{\text{US}}\right) &= 0 \qquad \text{Var}\left(X_t^{\text{US}}\right) = \sigma_x^2 > 0 \\
\text{cov}\left(X_t^{\text{US}}, U_t^{\text{region}}\right) &= 0
\end{aligned}
\tag{18-35}
$$

where, for simplicity, the coefficients α and β are taken as given. The presence of the intercept α in Equation 18-35 implies that $E\left(X_t^{\text{US}}\right)$ and $E\left(U_t^{\text{region}}\right)$ can both be taken to be zero with no loss of generality. Also – for simplicity – this model abstracts away from any relationships between Y_t^{region} and other time-series, including its own past. Thus, U_t^{region} is assumed to be serially independent and independent of X_t^{US}. (The resulting implication that $\text{cov}\left(X_t^{US}, U_t^{\text{region}}\right)$ is zero is simply asserting that the value of β is given correctly.) Nothing specific needs to be assumed about the form of the distributions of X_t^{US} and U_t^{region} except that both have bounded variances (so that expressions involving σ_x^2 and σ_u^2 can make sense) and that σ_x^2 is strictly positive, so that X_t^{US} does actually vary. If the value of β is substantial, then this $Y_t^{\text{region}} - X_t^{\text{US}}$ relationship (coupled with the variation in X_t^{US}) could be highly useful in predicting Y_t^{region}, but only if the time path of X_t^{US} is known.

Suppose, however – as is commonly the case in such settings – that the time path of X_t^{US} is *not* known and must itself be forecast, using the forecast $\hat{X}_t^{\text{US}}$. If the errors made by this forecast $\hat{X}_t^{\text{US}}$ are uncorrelated with the model errors U_t^{region}, then these forecast errors in $\hat{X}_t^{\text{US}}$ will clearly worsen the

[65] The figures in Table 18-3 summarize a portion of Tables 1 and 2 in a preliminary (unpublished) study posted as Ashley (2006). The manner in which these results would change if the explanatory variables and/or the error term were non-normally distributed is an open question at this time.

quality of the Y_t^{region} forecasts obtainable, in practice, from Equation 8-35. Is it possible for these errors in forecasting X_t^{US} to so worsen the quality of the resulting Y_t^{region} forecasts as to make it preferable to ignore the $Y_t^{region} - X_t^{US}$ relationship altogether?

The forecast of Y_t^{region} which ignores the $Y_t^{region} - X_t^{US}$ relationship will be denoted $\hat{Y}_t^{region-naive}$ here. Because $E(X_t^{US})$ is zero, this forecast is simply equal to α; its mean square forecasting error (MSE) is thus given by

$$\begin{aligned}
\text{MSE}\left(\hat{Y}_t^{region-naive}\right) &= E\left[\left(\hat{Y}_t^{region-naive} - Y_t^{region}\right)^2\right] \\
&= E\left[\left(\alpha - \left[\alpha + \beta X_t^{US} + U_t^{region}\right]\right)^2\right] \\
&= E\left[\beta^2 (X_t^{US})^2 + 2\,\beta X_t^{US} U_t^{region} + \left(U_t^{region}\right)^2\right] \\
&= \beta^2\sigma_x^2 + 2\,\beta \text{cov}\left(X_t^{US}, U_t^{region}\right) + \sigma_u^2 \\
&= \beta^2\sigma_x^2 + \sigma_u^2
\end{aligned} \tag{18-36}$$

The forecast of Y_t^{region} which *does* exploit the $Y_t^{region} - X_t^{US}$ relationship, but replaces X_t^{US} with the forecast $\hat{X}_t^{US}$, is equal to $\alpha + \beta\hat{X}_t^{US}$. Its mean square forecasting error is given by

$$\begin{aligned}
\text{MSE}\left(\hat{Y}_t^{region}\right) &= E\left[\left(\hat{Y}_t^{region} - Y_t^{region}\right)^2\right] \\
&= E\left[\left(\left[\alpha + \beta\hat{X}_t^{US}\right] - \left[\alpha + \beta X_t^{US} + U_t^{region}\right]\right)^2\right] \\
&= E\left[\beta^2\left(\hat{X}_t^{US} - X_t^{US}\right)^2 - 2\,\beta\left[\hat{X}_t^{US} - X_t^{US}\right]U_t^{region} + \left(U_t^{region}\right)^2\right] \\
&= \beta^2\text{MSE}\left(\hat{X}_t^{US}\right) - 2\beta\text{cov}\left(\left[\hat{X}_t^{US} - X_t^{US}\right], U_t^{region}\right) + \sigma_u^2 \\
&= \beta^2\text{MSE}\left(\hat{X}_t^{US}\right) + \sigma_u^2
\end{aligned} \tag{18-37}$$

where $\text{cov}\left(\left[\hat{X}_t^{US} - X_t^{US}\right], U_t^{region}\right)$ is set to zero because the X_t^{US} forecast errors are assumed to be uncorrelated with the errors in the model for the regional variable.

Combining these two results, the improvement in the mean square forecasting error from trying to exploit the $Y_t^{region} - X_t^{US}$ relationship is

$$\text{MSE}\left(\hat{Y}_t^{region}\right) - \text{MSE}\left(\hat{Y}_t^{region-naive}\right) = \beta^2\sigma_x^2\left\{\frac{\text{MSE}\left(\hat{X}_t^{US}\right)}{\sigma_x^2} - 1\right\} \tag{18-38}$$

Thus, if the mean square error in forecasting X_t^{US} exceeds the variance of the X_t^{US} itself, then one is actually better off ignoring the $Y_t^{region} - X_t^{US}$ relationship altogether, even though this relationship might be very strong if $|\beta|$ is substantial. Indeed, Equation 18-38 implies that, if the forecasts of X_t^{US} which will be used are this inaccurate, then the stronger this $Y_t^{region} - X_t^{US}$ relationship is, the more

Table 18-4 Estimated Ratio of Forecast MSE to Variance of Actual Variable {1976I through 1980III – One-Quarter-Ahead and Four-Quarter-Ahead Forecasts}[a]

	Real GNP		GNP Deflator		CPI		Fixed Investment	
	1	4	1	4	1	4	1	4
CHASE	0.9	1.0	0.3	1.9	0.7	1.6	1.1	1.1
DRI	0.7	0.7	0.4	1.4	0.5	1.8	1.0	0.9
WEFA	0.8	0.9	0.4	1.6	0.2	1.3	0.7	0.9
RSQE	0.6	0.7	0.2	1.0			0.9	1.0
UCLA	0.5	1.0	0.3	0.9	0.3	1.6	1.0	1.0
ASA	0.6	0.7	0.5	1.6				
BEA	0.8	0.6	0.2	1.3	0.7	1.6		

[a]All variables are in growth rate form. The commercial forecasters included Chase Econometric Associates, Data Resources, Inc., and Wharton Econometric Forecasting Associates, Inc. Academic forecasting units included the Research Seminar on Quantitative Economics at the University of Michigan and the University of California at Los Angeles Business Forecasting Project. The acronym ASA denotes the median forecast from the American Statistical Association and National Bureau of Economic Research Survey of Regular Forecasters; the acronym BEA refers to the Bureau of Economic Analysis at the U.S. Department of Commerce. Figures are taken from Ashley (1983); data were unavailable for some forecaster/variable combinations. Ashley, R. (1983), "On the Usefulness of Macroeconomic Forecasts as Inputs to Forecasting Models," *Journal of Forecasting* 2, 211–223.

important it is to not try to utilize it! Thus, one might fairly characterize a forecast of X_t^{US} for which $\mathrm{MSE}\left(\hat{X}_t^{\mathrm{US}}\right)/\sigma_x^2$ exceeds one as "beneath contempt."

Note that Equation 18-37 used the assumption that the forecast errors made by $\hat{X}_t^{\mathrm{US}}$ are uncorrelated with the model errors for the regional variable, Y_t^{region}. But this assumption is actually stronger than necessary, as values of $\beta\mathrm{cov}\left(\left[\hat{X}_t^{\mathrm{US}} - X_t^{\mathrm{US}}\right],\, U_t^{\mathrm{region}}\right)$ which are negative will make the mean square error of the forecast attempting to exploit the $Y_t^{\mathrm{region}} - X_t^{\mathrm{US}}$ relationship even larger. Moreover, this result ignores the impact of likely sampling errors in estimates of β, which will only further increase the mean square error of $\hat{Y}_t^{\mathrm{region}}$. Thus any forecast $\hat{X}_t^{\mathrm{US}}$ for which $\mathrm{MSE}\left(\hat{X}_t^{\mathrm{US}}\right)/\sigma_x^2$ is even close to one is of highly dubious utility.

Of course, one might expect that no reputable source of national-level forecasts would produce $\hat{X}_t^{\mathrm{US}}$ forecasts this inaccurate – and that no one would utilize such low-quality forecasts if these sources did produce them. But one would be incorrect in both of those expectations.

For example, Table 18-4 quotes estimates of the ratio $\mathrm{MSE}\left(\hat{X}_t^{\mathrm{US}}\right)/\sigma_x^2$ for one-quarter-ahead and four-quarter-ahead forecasts of a number of important U.S. macroeconomic variables, as produced by a variety of commercial, academic, and government forecasters over the period 1976I through 1980III. The figures tabulated are, of course, only sample estimates of this ratio – and over a sample of just 19 quarters. A number of these figures could thus be overestimating the true (population) value of this ratio due to sampling errors; on the other hand, some of these tabulated estimates are no doubt underestimates.

Note that a good many of these ratio estimates either exceed or approach the "contemptibility" criterion value, where $\mathrm{MSE}\left(\hat{X}_t^{\mathrm{US}}\right)/\sigma_x^2$ is equal to one, especially at the four-quarter-ahead forecast horizon. On the other hand, this sample period was quite a while ago. Would similar results, perhaps taking into account the likely sampling properties of such ratio estimates, hold for more recent macroeconomic forecasts? Pending further research, one can hope that they would not, but fear that they would.

Gains from Combining Forecasts

Perhaps the most upbeat idea in all of economics is the Ricardian notion of the "gains from trade": if two individuals or nations are different from one another, then they will mutually benefit from specializing and trading with each other. Moreover, these gains from trade fundamentally arise from (and monotonically depend upon) how intrinsically different the two trading partners are. Interestingly, something quite similar occurs when one has two distinctly different forecasts – $F^A_{N,h}$ and $F^B_{N,h}$– available for use in forecasting Y_{N+h}: it is possible to combine them into a single forecast which is guaranteed to be an improvement over either one used separately, and the accuracy "gains" from this combined forecast rest squarely on how different the two original forecasts are.

The capitalization of $F^A_{N,h}$ and $F^B_{N,h}$ above is not a typographical error; these two forecasts are being treated here as a pair of random variables. For example, $F^A_{N,h}$ might be a forecast of Y_{N+h} made using an estimated MA(q) model for Y_t, in which case (presuming that $q \geq h$, so that the forecast $F^A_{N,h}$ is nontrivial) its randomness would arise from sampling errors in the estimates of $\hat{\theta}_h \ldots \hat{\theta}_q$. And $F^B_{N,h}$ might be a forecast of Y_{N+h} made using an estimated Dynamic Multiple Regression Model, as specified in Equation 14-3; its randomness might then arise from both sampling errors in estimated model coefficients and from random variation in the explanatory variables. Or $F^A_{N,h}$ and $F^B_{N,h}$ might be forecasts of Y_{N+h} made using two different estimated instances of the Dynamic Multiple Regression Model, where each is specified using somewhat (or entirely) different explanatory variables. Alternatively, either $F^A_{N,h}$ or $F^B_{N,h}$ might be a forecast obtained from an econometric model whose outputs are judgmentally tweaked by an experienced user, based on a multitude of random variables from a variety of sources.

Regardless of how this randomness in the forecasts arises, the forecast errors made by these two forecasts – $(F^A_{N,h} - Y_{N+h})$ and $(F^B_{N,h} - Y_{N+h})$ – are thus random variables for two reasons: first because the forecasts $F^A_{N,h}$ and $F^B_{N,h}$ are random variables, and second because the value being forecast(Y_{N+h}) is a random variable.

If $F^A_{N,h}$ and $F^B_{N,h}$ are both unbiased forecasts of Y_{N+1} and the forecast error variance of each is a positive, finite constant, then

$$\begin{aligned} E\left(F^A_{N,h} - Y_{N+h}\right) &= 0 \\ E\left(F^B_{N,h} - Y_{N+h}\right) &= 0 \end{aligned} \tag{18-39}$$

and

$$\begin{aligned} \operatorname{var}\left(F^A_{N,h} - Y_{N+h}\right) &= E\left(\left[F^A_{N,h} - Y_{N+h}\right]^2\right) = \sigma^2_A > 0 \\ \operatorname{var}\left(F^B_{N,h} - Y_{N+h}\right) &= E\left(\left[F^B_{N,h} - Y_{N+h}\right]^2\right) = \sigma^2_B > 0 \end{aligned} \tag{18-40}$$

It will be assumed here that these two forecasts are distinct from one another, so that the variance of $F^A_{N,h} - F^B_{N,h}$ is strictly positive. But the errors made by $F^A_{N,h}$ and $F^B_{N,h}$ are not assumed to be uncorrelated; the covariance between them is denoted σ_{AB} below, but its value is not restricted:

$$\sigma_{AB} \equiv \operatorname{cov}\left(\left[F^A_{N,h} - Y_{N+h}\right], \left[F^B_{N,h} - Y_{N+h}\right]\right) \equiv E\left(\left[F^A_{N,h} - Y_{N+h}\right]\left[F^B_{N,h} - Y_{N+h}\right]\right) \tag{18-41}$$

Now consider what is called a "combination" forecast of Y_{N+h}; such a forecast is defined as a weighted sum of $F^A_{N,h}$ and $F^B_{N,h}$:

$$F_\omega \equiv \omega F^A_{N,h} + (1-\omega)F^B_{N,h} \tag{18-42}$$

Because the weights in F_ω add to one, it is still an unbiased forecast of Y_{N+h}. The mean square error of this combination forecast can be obtained (Exercise 18-2) in just a few lines of algebra; the resulting expression is

$$\text{MSE}(F_\omega) = \omega^2\left[\sigma_A^2 - 2\sigma_{AB} + \sigma_B^2\right] - 2\omega\left[\sigma_B^2 - \sigma_{AB}\right] + \sigma_B^2 \tag{18-43}$$

Thus,

$$\frac{d\,\text{MSE}(F_\omega)}{d\omega} = 2\omega\left[\sigma_A^2 - 2\sigma_{AB} + \sigma_B^2\right] - 2\left[\sigma_B^2 - \sigma_{AB}\right] \tag{18-44}$$

Setting this derivative equal to zero and solving for the optimal weight, ω^{minMSE}, yields

$$\omega^{\text{minMSE}} = \frac{\sigma_B^2 - \sigma_{AB}}{\sigma_A^2 - 2\sigma_{AB} + \sigma_B^2} \tag{18-45}$$

This value for ω^* is the global minimum of $\text{MSE}(F_\omega)$, since

$$\frac{d^2\text{MSE}(F_w)}{d\omega^2} = 2\left[\sigma_A^2 - 2\,\sigma_{AB} + \sigma_B^2\right] = \text{var}\left(F^A_{N,h} - F^B_{N,h}\right) > 0 \tag{18-46}$$

and $\text{var}\left(F^A_{N,h} - F^B_{N,h}\right)$ must be strictly positive so long as $F^A_{N,h}$ and $F^B_{N,h}$ are both random and are distinct from one another.

Thus, there always exists a weighted combination of two distinct, unbiased forecasts which has a smaller mean square error than does either one separately. This result extends fairly easily to weighted combinations of any number of forecasts; the analysis was restricted to two forecasts here solely to keep the notation as simple as possible.

These combination forecasts are not directly applicable in practice, however, because the forecast error variance and covariance terms needed in order to compute the optimal combining weights are unknown. These terms can be estimated, of course, but the additional sampling variation in the resulting estimators then typically eliminates the MSE improvement in the combined forecast. Inspired by this optimal combination result, however, it has been found that *equally* weighted combination forecasts in practice usually provide a noticeable improvement in forecast quality.[66]

[66] For empirical examples of forecast combining, see Stock and Watson (2004) and Rapach and Strauss (2008, 2010). Rapach and Strauss apply a wide variety of combining methods to the forecasting of the growth rate in U.S. employment. Where a substantial number of different forecasts are available, they find that first using principal components analysis to aggregate the forecasts is quite helpful and that bootstrap-based aggregation ("bagging") can also yield improved forecasts. Stock, J. H., and M. W. Watson (2004), "Combination Forecasts of Output Growth in a Seven-Country Data Set," *Journal of Forecasting 23*, 405–430; Rapach, D. E., and J. K. Strauss (2008), "Forecasting US Employment Growth Using Forecast Combining Methods," *Journal of Forecasting 27*, 75–93; Rapach, D. E., and J. K. Strauss (2010), "Bagging or Combining (or Both)? An Analysis Based on Forecasting U.S. Employment Growth," *Econometric Reviews 29*, 511–33.

KEY TERMS

For each term or concept listed below, provide a working definition or explanation:

ARIMA(p, d, q) Model
Deterministic vs. Stochastic Trend
Seasonally Adjusted vs. Not Seasonally Adjusted Data
Non-autocorrelation vs. Serial Independence
Bilinear vs. GARCH vs. TAR Models

EXERCISES

18-1. Using Equation 18-13 – and the Equation 18-14 result that the unconditional mean of Y_t^{BILINEAR} is zero – show that

$$\text{var}\left(Y_t^{\text{BILINEAR}}\right) = e\left(\left[Y_t^{\text{BILINEAR}}\right]^2\right) = \frac{1}{1-\beta^2} \tag{18-17}$$

Hint: Your derivation will utilize the fact that the unconditional variance of Y_t^{BILINEAR} is the same for all time periods and that $\varepsilon_t \sim \text{IID}(0, 1)$.

18-2. Using Equations 18-39 to 18-42, show that

$$\text{MSE}(F_\omega) = \omega^2\left[\sigma_A^2 - 2\sigma_{AB} + \sigma_B^2\right] - 2\,\omega\left[\sigma_B^2 - \sigma_{AB}\right] + \sigma_B^2 \tag{18-43}$$

Active Learning Exercise 18a: Modeling the South Korean Won – U.S. Dollar Exchange Rate

Introduction

This Active Learning Exercise provides some practice in specifying ("identifying"), estimating, and diagnostically checking a univariate model for the South Korean Won–U.S. Dollar exchange rate.

Your Assignment:

1. Copy the data file ALE18a.csv (available at www.wiley.com/college/ashley) to your hard disk and read it in to the econometrics software your course is using. (Or copy file ALE18a.dta, if you are using Stata.) This file contains monthly data on the won–dollar exchange rate, from April 1998 through November 2010.[67]
2. Plot the exchange rate data against the observation number variable. Do these data appear to be covariance stationary?

[67] The source of these data is the Board of Governors of the U.S. Federal Reserve System; they were downloaded from www.federalreserve.gov/datadownload, ("Foreign Exchange Rates (G.5 / H.10)"). The data set begins in 1998, when South Korea moved to a floating exchange rate. Each observation is the number of won needed in order purchase one U.S. dollar, averaged over the month.

3. Compute the annualized monthly growth rate in the won-dollar exchange rate and plot this growth rate data against the observation number variable. Do these data appear to be covariance stationary?[68] Using a histogram, do these data appear to be normally distributed?[69]
4. In practice one would likely want to include a dummy variable for the October 2008 observation in one's models. Here, for simplicity, the sample will be truncated immediately prior to this observation. Using, from this point on, just the observations with "obs" less than 127, replot the growth rate data and its histogram. Do the data appear to be covariance stationary over this period?
5. Compute and plot a sample correlogram and partial correlogram for the growth rate data prior to October 2008. What models do these results suggest?
6. Estimate the suggested models, just using the data prior to October 2008. Which model would you choose, based on the BIC value?[70]
7. Re-estimate your chosen model over the entire data set, including the large value in October 2008. Does it differ notably?[71]
8. Diagnostically check your chosen model (estimated using the data prior to October 2008) by examining a time plot and sample correlogram of its fitting errors and by fitting a slightly more complicated model to check that the additional coefficient is statistically insignificant.[72]

[68] In Stata, the command "gen rategrow = 1200*(log(x)/log(L1.x))" produces the annualized monthly growth rate of the variable "x."

[69] Use the "normal" option in the Stata histogram command.

[70] In Stata you can use commands "arima rategrow if obs < 127, arima(p,0,0)" followed by "estat ic" to estimate an AR(p) model and compute the BIC criterion.

[71] Because October 2008 corresponds to a clearly identifiable event which will (hopefully) not be regularly repeated in future months, it is clearly appropriate to remove its influence on the model parameter estimates by including a dummy variable in the model specification. This is very easy in an AR(p) model because this is just a linear regression model; Stata makes it fairly easy to include additional explanatory variables in an ARMA(p, q) setting, but not all programs are so accommodating.

[72] The Stata command "predict resids, r" saves the fitting errors under the name "resids", but note that these fitting errors are calculated for the entire data set, so you must still restrict the sample to the time periods of interest when you make the plot and sample correlogram.

19

Parameter Estimation beyond Curve-Fitting: MLE (with an Application to Binary-Choice Models) and GMM (with an Application to IV Regression)

19.1 INTRODUCTION

The foregoing chapters have explained the essentials of regression parameter estimation and inference, basically in the context of modeling a linear parameterization of how the conditional mean of the dependent variable depends on a set of explanatory variables. In the Bivariate Regression Model setting, this amounts to fitting a straight line to the sample data so as to minimize the sum of the squared fitting errors – i.e., to OLS estimation. This chapter ends the main exposition of the book with a brief look at two alternative approaches to regression parameter estimation: Maximum Likelihood Estimation (MLE) and the Generalized Method of Moments (GMM). These two approaches conceptualize regression parameter estimation quite differently from OLS; each is illustrated within an empirically important context in which it is preferable to least-squares curve-fitting.

More specifically, the Multiple Regression Model of Equation 9-1 formulates the expected value of the dependent variable (Y_i) as a linear function of the k explanatory variables ($x_{i,1} \ldots x_{i,k}$). The accompanying regression model coefficients ($\beta_1 \ldots \beta_k$) are then estimated by choosing $\hat{\beta}_1^{guess} \ldots \hat{\beta}_k^{guess}$ to minimize the observed sum of squared fitting errors, SSE($\hat{\beta}_1^{guess} \ldots \hat{\beta}_k^{guess}$). In essence, a ($k$–1)-dimensional hyperplane is "fit" to the sample data ($y_1 \ldots y_N$), so as to minimize the sample average of the squared vertical distance of these N observations above (or below) this hyperplane. The solution to this minimization problem is $\hat{\beta}_1^* \ldots \hat{\beta}_k^*$, the OLS ("ordinary least squares") estimates of the parameters $\beta_1 \ldots \beta_k$.

Hyperplanes are a bit challenging to consider, but this curve-fitting approach is very easy to visualize in the special case where k equals two: the Bivariate Regression Model of Equation 5-10. As described in Section 5.5, this (k–1)-dimensional hyperplane is in that case just a straight line which is fit to a scatterplot of the sample data. The mean of a random variable (such as the dependent variable in the model, Y_i) is a reasonable measure of its size. It is therefore intuitively appealing to view the height of the fitted line (over the point specified by the value of x_i) as an estimate of the mean value of Y_i, conditional on the explanatory variable having taken the value x_i. And, indeed, the close relationship between fitting this line to the sample data and estimating the conditional mean of Y_i stands out when one observes that the expression in Equation 5-33 for the OLS model intercept parameter estimate reduces to just $\bar{y}$, the sample mean of the observations on Y_i, when $\bar{x}$ is zero.[1]

The OLS curve-fitting approach yields practical regression parameter estimators of generally good quality. Indeed, if the assumptions of the basic Multiple Regression Model of Equation 9-1 are satisfied, then $\hat{\beta}_1^{ols} \ldots \hat{\beta}_k^{ols}$ are BLU and efficient estimators of the parameters $\beta_1 \ldots \beta_k$. The material in Chapters 10 to 16 shows how to apply this estimation approach in more general settings, so as to still at least obtain consistent estimators for the parameters $\beta_1 \ldots \beta_k$ and asymptotically valid inference results (confidence intervals and hypothesis tests) regarding their values.

But least-squares curve-fitting is not the only way to estimate regression parameters such as $\beta_1 \ldots \beta_k$. Nor is it always the best way. Indeed, in one of the two examples described below – a "binary-choice" regression model – direct OLS estimation of the model coefficients is simply not feasible. And in the other example – instrumental variables (IV) regression with heteroscedastic errors – OLS estimation is feasible, but inefficient.

Moreover, while it is possible to show that $\hat{\beta}_1^{ols} \ldots \hat{\beta}_\kappa^{ols}$ are optimal (efficient) estimators of $\beta_1 \ldots \beta_k$ in the simple fixed-regressors setting of Chapters 5 through 9, least-squares regression parameter estimation inherently guarantees only one estimator property: the OLS parameter estimates yield the model which best fits the observed sample data in a least-squares sense. Everything else – unbiasedness, consistency, BLUness, efficiency – must be derived (at some effort), based on additional assumptions about the explanatory variables and the distribution of the model error term.

This chapter provides a brief introduction to two alternative regression parameter estimation frameworks: Maximum Likelihood Estimation (MLE) and Generalized Method of Moments estimation (GMM). Under fairly mild conditions, the parameter estimators from each of these frameworks are guaranteed to have good large-sample properties: consistency, asymptotic unbiasedness, asymptotic normality, and asymptotic efficiency. And each of these estimation approaches shines (relative to OLS curve-fitting) in its own natural setting. MLE and GMM are also just as easy to apply in practice as OLS in many circumstances, because they have been implemented in modern econometric software for these particular settings. The purpose of this chapter is to introduce the ideas underlying each of these approaches so that the reader can sensibly look for and utilize these implementations in the circumstances where they are preferable.

19.2 MAXIMUM LIKELIHOOD ESTIMATION OF A SIMPLE BIVARIATE REGRESSION MODEL

The idea underlying maximum likelihood estimation (MLE) in a regression model context will first be illustrated in the simplest imaginable setting:[2]

[1] The reader might find it helpful to reread Section 3.2 at this point and to also note that LAD ("Least Absolute Deviations" or "robust") regression estimation is still fitting a straight line (or hyperplane, for k greater than two) to the sample data. LAD estimation simply quantifies the vertical distance of the sample data from the hyperplane using the absolute value of the discrepancy rather than the square of the discrepancy. The LAD estimator is thus still curve-fitting; the difference is that LAD estimation is linearly parameterizing the conditional median of Y_i rather than its conditional mean.

[2] Of course, one would include an intercept in virtually any model estimated for practical use, so that $E[U_i] = 0$ can be assumed without any loss of generality. The intercept is omitted here solely to clarify the exposition; it was also omitted – so as to yield illustrative exercises involving a minimum of algebra – when this same model was analyzed in Exercises 6-11, 7-12, and 8-2.

The Bivariate Regression Model
{No Intercept; σ^2 known}

$$
\begin{gathered}
Y_i = \beta x_i + U_i \qquad i = 1 \dots N \\
x_1 \dots x_N \text{ fixed in repeated samples} \\
U_i \sim \text{NIID}[0, \sigma^2] \\
\textbf{Equivalently,} \\
Y_i \text{ is independently distributed } \text{N}[\beta x_i,\ \sigma^2] \\
\text{for } i = 1 \dots N
\end{gathered}
\tag{19-1}
$$

Because $Y_1 \dots Y_N$ are assumed to be independently distributed, the joint density function for this set of N random variables is just the product of the density functions for each one. In other words, the relative likelihood of observing the sample values $y_1 \dots y_N$ – a particular set of realizations of the random variables $Y_1 \dots Y_N$ – is

$$
\text{Likelihood}\,(y_1 \dots y_N) = f_1(y_1) \times f_2(y_2) \times \dots \times f_N(y_N) \tag{19-2}
$$

where $f_i(y_i)$ here is the density function for a normally distributed variate with mean βx_i and variance σ^2. Substituting into Equation 2-47 from Section 2.10 (with the mean value set to βx_i), this density function is

$$
f_i(y_i) = \frac{1}{\sqrt{2\pi\sigma^2}} e^{-\frac{(y_i - \beta x_i)^2}{2\sigma^2}}. \tag{19-3}
$$

Thus, the likelihood of observing the sample data $(y_1,\ x_1) \dots (y_N,\ x_N)$ is

$$
\begin{aligned}
&\text{Likelihood}\,(y_1 \dots y_N;\quad \beta,\ \sigma^2,\ x_1 \dots x_N) \\
&= \frac{1}{\sqrt{2\pi\sigma^2}} e^{-\frac{(y_1 - \beta x_1)^2}{2\sigma^2}} \times \frac{1}{\sqrt{2\pi\sigma^2}} e^{-\frac{(y_2 - \beta x_2)^2}{2\sigma^2}} \times \dots \times \frac{1}{\sqrt{2\pi\sigma^2}} e^{-\frac{(y_N - \beta x_N)^2}{2\sigma^2}}
\end{aligned}
\tag{19-4}
$$

given the model parameters β and σ^2, and given that the N values of the explanatory variable are fixed at $x_1 \dots x_N$.

Equation 19-4 could be used to calculate the value of this likelihood function for any particular data set $(y_1,\ x_1) \dots (y_N,\ x_N)$ – using a spreadsheet, say – for any given values of β and σ^2. Thus, if these two underlying model parameters were both known, then one could directly calculate the likelihood of observing the actually observed sample. In practice, however, these parameter values are not known. Indeed, estimating the unknown value of β is the point of this enterprise. (For simplicity of exposition, the value of σ^2 is taken as given in the present model – Equation 19-1 – but this artificial assumption is relaxed in Exercise 19-1.)

The value of β is unknown in the present model. However, a simple variation on Equation 19-4 can be still be used to calculate the likelihood of observing the actually-observed sample data for any particular guessed-at value for β, $\hat{\beta}^{\text{guess}}$:

$$
\begin{aligned}
&\text{Likelihood}(y_1 \dots y_N; \hat{\beta}^{\text{guess}}, \sigma^2, x_1 \dots x_N) \\
&= \frac{1}{\sqrt{2\pi\sigma^2}} e^{-\frac{(y_1 - \hat{\beta}^{\text{guess}} x_1)^2}{2\sigma^2}} \times \frac{1}{\sqrt{2\pi\sigma^2}} e^{-\frac{(y_2 - \hat{\beta}^{\text{guess}} x_2)^2}{2\sigma^2}} \times \dots \times \frac{1}{\sqrt{2\pi\sigma^2}} e^{-\frac{(y_N - \hat{\beta}^{\text{guess}} x_N)^2}{2\sigma^2}}
\end{aligned}
\tag{19-5}
$$

where σ^2, as noted above, is being taken as given in the model of Equation 19-1 analyzed here. The maximum likelihood estimate of β – i.e., $\hat{\beta}^{MLE}$ – is then defined as the value of $\hat{\beta}^{guess}$ which maximizes the likelihood function given in Equation 19-5. In other words, $\hat{\beta}^{MLE}$ is the value of $\hat{\beta}^{guess}$ which maximizes the likelihood that one would have observed the sample actually observed.[3]

Since Equation 19-5 is in the form of an extended product of terms, it is virtually always more convenient to maximize the logarithm of the likelihood it defines, rather than the likelihood function itself. The logarithm is monotonically increasing in its argument, so the same value of $\hat{\beta}^{guess}$ maximizes both functions, but this "log-likelihood" function is much simpler to analyze, because the logarithm function turns the extended product of Equation 19-5 into a sum:

$$\begin{aligned} L(y_1 \dots y_N; \hat{\beta}^{guess}, \sigma^2, x_1 \dots x_N) &= \ln\left\{\text{Likelihood}\,(y_1 \dots y_N; \hat{\beta}^{guess}, \sigma^2, x_1 \dots x_N)\right\} \\ &= \ln\left\{\frac{1}{\sqrt{2\pi\sigma^2}} e^{-\frac{(y_1-\hat{\beta}^{guess}x_1)^2}{2\sigma^2}} \times \frac{1}{\sqrt{2\pi\sigma^2}} e^{-\frac{(y_2-\hat{\beta}^{guess}x_2)^2}{2\sigma^2}} \times \dots \times \frac{1}{\sqrt{2\pi\sigma^2}} e^{-\frac{(y_N-\hat{\beta}^{guess}x_N)^2}{2\sigma^2}}\right\} \\ &= -\tfrac{1}{2}\ln(2\pi\sigma^2) - \frac{(y_1 - \hat{\beta}^{guess}x_1)^2}{2\sigma^2} - \dots - \tfrac{1}{2}\ln(2\pi\sigma^2) - \frac{(y_N - \hat{\beta}^{guess}x_N)^2}{2\sigma^2} \\ &= -\frac{N}{2}\ln(2\pi\sigma^2) - \sum_{i=1}^{N} \frac{(y_i - \hat{\beta}^{guess}x_i)^2}{2\sigma^2} \\ &= -\frac{N}{2}\ln(2\pi\sigma^2) - \frac{1}{2\sigma^2}\sum_{i=1}^{N}(y_i - \hat{\beta}^{guess}x_i)^2 \end{aligned} \tag{19-6}$$

Note that the log-likelihood function for this particular model is simply equal to a constant $\left\{-\frac{N}{2}\ln(2\pi\sigma^2)\right\}$ minus $1/(2\sigma^2)$ times the very same function – the "sum of squared fitting errors" or SSE – which is minimized in obtaining the OLS estimator of β for this model. Thus, without further algebra, it is evident that the maximum likelihood estimator of β for this particular model is identical to the OLS estimator of β:

$$\hat{\beta}^{MLE} = \hat{\beta}^{OLS} = \frac{\sum_{i=1}^{N} x_i Y_i}{\sum_{j=1}^{N} x_j^2} \tag{19-7}$$

and hence shares the same sampling distribution, properties, inference results, etc., obtained when this no-intercept model was analyzed using least-squares fitting in Exercises 6-11, 7-12, and 8-2.

Since $\hat{\beta}^{MLE}$ and $\hat{\beta}^{OLS}$ are identical in this case, why consider Maximum Likelihood Estimation? What advantages does it confer over just using OLS? The Maximum Likelihood Estimation framework is superior to OLS in three ways.

First, OLS actually only provides an estimator of the model slope parameter, β. The model error variance (σ^2) has to be estimated also in order to obtain any practical inference results, such as

[3] Strictly speaking, $\hat{\beta}^{MLE}$ should be stated at this point with an asterisk superscript, as it is actually the (fixed) sample realization of the estimator $\hat{\beta}^{MLE}$. This estimator is itself a random variable, with a sampling distribution discussed later.

confidence interval estimates and p-values for hypothesis tests. But OLS does not provide an estimator of σ^2; the estimator S^2 is tacked on separately.

In contrast, the MLE framework generates an estimator for σ^2 in a graceful and natural way. In the present example – but now no longer artificially assuming that the value of σ^2 is known – σ^2 in the log-likelihood function is simply replaced by $\hat{\sigma}^2_{guess}$ and $L(y_1 \ldots y_N; \hat{\beta}^{guess}, \hat{\sigma}^2_{guess}, x^1 \ldots x_N)$ is now maximized with respect to both $\hat{\beta}^{guess}$ and $\hat{\sigma}^2_{guess}$. The MLE estimator of σ^2 is thus just the value of $\hat{\sigma}^2_{guess}$ for which

$$\left(\frac{\partial L(y_1 \ldots y_N; \hat{\beta}^{guess}, \hat{\sigma}^2_{guess}, x_1 \ldots x_N)}{\partial \hat{\sigma}^2_{guess}} \right)_{\hat{\beta}^{guess} = \hat{\beta}^{MLE}} = \frac{\partial}{\partial \hat{\sigma}^2_{guess}} \left[-\frac{N}{2} \ln\left(2\pi\hat{\sigma}^2_{guess}\right) - \frac{1}{2\hat{\sigma}^2_{guess}} \sum_{i=1}^{N} \left(y_i - \hat{\beta}^{guess} x_i\right)^2 \right] \tag{19-8}$$

equals zero. After just a bit of algebra (Exercise 19-1), this yields the MLE estimator of σ^2:

$$\hat{\sigma}^2_{MLE} = \frac{1}{N} \sum_{i=1}^{N} (y_i - \hat{\beta}^{MLE} x_i)^2 = \frac{1}{N} \text{SSE} = \left(\frac{N-1}{N}\right) S^2 \tag{19-9}$$

Thus, the Maximum Likelihood Estimation framework leads to an estimator of σ^2 in a coherent, logically consistent way. Unlike S^2 – which was constructed so as to be an unbiased estimator of σ^2 – $\hat{\sigma}^2_{MLE}$ is clearly biased; but $\hat{\sigma}^2_{MLE}$ turns out to have very nice large-sample (asymptotic) properties.

In fact, this is the second big advantage of MLE over OLS estimation: the MLE estimator of *any* model parameter – call it θ – can be shown to have every good asymptotic property one could think of, just by virtue of being a maximum likelihood estimator:[4]

- $\hat{\theta}_{MLE}$ is a consistent and (asymptotically) unbiased estimator of θ.
- $\hat{\theta}_{MLE}$ is an asymptotically efficient estimator of θ – that is, there is no consistent estimator of θ with a smaller asymptotic variance than that of $\hat{\theta}_{MLE}$:
- The asymptotic sampling distribution of $\hat{\theta}_{MLE}$ is easy to obtain, because $\hat{\theta}_{MLE}$ is (asymptotically) normally distributed with (asymptotic) mean θ and (asymptotic) sampling variance equal to $-1/E[\partial^2 L(\theta)/\partial\theta^2]$, which is usually easy to calculate – see Exercises 19-1 and 19-2 for illustrative examples.[5]
- If $g(\cdot)$ is a continuous function, then $g(\hat{\theta}_{MLE})$ is the maximum likelihood estimator of $g(\theta)$, and hence partakes of all the nice asymptotic properties listed above.

---

[4] Theil (1971, Sections 8.4 and 8.5) gives a particularly accessible derivation of all of the results given below for the scalar (i.e., one-parameter) case. He also discusses the very mild regularity conditions (basically on the smoothness of the underlying density function) which are needed to support these results; these are all satisfied by regression models with normally distributed errors. Except for the more sophisticated notation, these conditions (and results) are very similar where $k > 1$ coefficients are estimated, except that the value of k must be finite; that is, k cannot rise with the sample length, N. Theil, H. (1971), *Principles of Econometrics*, Wiley: New York.

[5] Note that the log-likelihood function in the foregoing expression is in terms of the population parameter, θ – e.g., see Exercise 19-1b. The indicated second partial derivative is generally easy to obtain whenever (as here) one has an analytic expression for $L(\theta)$; its dependence on the model errors is also usually simple, so evaluating the expectation is generally easy. Estimated asymptotic variances for MLE estimators are readily obtained where $L(\hat{\theta})$ must be maximized numerically, using related results.

Moreover,

- If θ is actually a vector of parameters, then all of the results given above still apply.[6]

And, finally,

- If $\hat{L}_{H_o}$ is the value of the log-likelihood function obtained by imposing a set of r restrictions on θ specified by a particular null hypothesis (H_o), then the decrease in the value of log-likelihood function due to imposing these constraints $\left(\text{i.e., } L(\hat{\theta}^{MLE}) - \hat{L}_{H_o}\right)$ is asymptotically distributed $\chi^2(r)$ under H_o.

This last result is called a "likelihood ratio test" because the difference in the two log-likelihood functions equals the logarithm of the ratio of the two likelihood function values. This result makes hypothesis testing in the context of models estimated using maximum likelihood very easy. One simply computes the magnitude of the difference between the log-likelihood value obtained with and without the r constraints of the null hypothesis imposed; the p-value for rejecting H_o is then just the probability that a $\chi^2(r)$ variate exceeds this value.[7]

With all of this in its favor, one would think that Maximum Likelihood Estimation would be very commonly used in regression analysis. But it is not. The MLE framework does rely more heavily than OLS on the distributional assumption that the model errors are normally distributed, but this assumption can (and has) been relaxed – e.g., substituting the Student's t distribution for the normal distribution in contexts where the model errors show clear signs of leptokurtosis.[8] The real reason that MLE is relatively underutilized is mainly social rather than statistical, however: Maximum Likelihood Estimation can be difficult to implement in a "prepackaged" way. This is because one generally needs to program a small routine to compute the relevant log-likelihood function, a prospect which many people find daunting.

For example, one potential application for MLE is in dealing with model error heteroscedasticity of some specified form – such as where $\text{var}(U_i) = \sigma^2 z_i^\delta$, with $z_1 \dots z_N$ fixed and given. It is easy enough to modify the log-likelihood function of Equation 19-6 to accommodate heteroscedasticity of this form. (See Exercise 19-4.) In the Maximum Likelihood Estimation framework one can then simply estimate δ along with β and σ^2. In contrast to using OLS parameter estimation (which is only consistent for β) and computing White-Eicker standard errors, the $\hat{\beta}^{MLE}$ estimator obtained in this way is asymptotically efficient. Moreover, the maximum likelihood estimator of δ would be potentially informative, as well as asymptotically efficient. But actually implementing $\hat{\beta}^{MLE}$ in this case requires the numerical maximization of $L(y_1 \dots y_N;\ \hat{\beta}^{guess}, \hat{\delta}^{guess}, \hat{\sigma}^2_{guess}, x_1 \dots x_N, z_1 \dots z_N)$ over the parameter "guesses" ($\hat{\beta}^{guess}, \hat{\delta}^{guess}$, and $\hat{\sigma}^2_{guess}$), which requires a bit of programming; consequently, one never sees this done.[9]

[6] Except that, where $\hat{\theta}$ is a vector, then the asymptotic variance-covariance matrix of $\hat{\theta}^{MLE}$ is minus the expectation of the inverse of $\partial^2 L(\theta)/\partial\theta^2$, which is now a matrix. Where – as in the no-intercept version of the Bivariate Regression Model considered here – this matrix is diagonal, this distinction is inconsequential.

[7] See Exercise 19-3. Also, note that tail areas for the χ^2 distribution are easily obtained: e.g., in Excel, the worksheet function chidist(x, k) returns the probability that a $\chi^2(k)$ variate will exceed the particular value x.

[8] A leptokurtic distribution – such as the Student's t distribution – is usually characterized as having "fat tails" compared to the normal distribution; such a distribution generally also has an excess likelihood of realizations which are very small in magnitude. Much data on returns to financial assets are leptokurtic.

[9] GMM is used instead – see Section 19.3. The GMM approach requires no (possibly fallacious) assumption about the form of the heteroscedasticity but, as a consequence, requires more data for a given level of estimation precision and also provides no estimate of parameters like δ.

Thus, in practice, Maximum Likelihood Estimation is typically used only where people have no choice. This brings up the third big advantage of MLE over OLS estimation: in quite a substantial number of economically important contexts one *does* have no other choice. In particular, the MLE framework makes it feasible to still estimate model parameters like β and σ^2 even when some of the data which OLS estimation would require are missing or distorted, so that the direct application of OLS estimation is simply infeasible. Sometimes this infeasibility is due to gaps in the data set – i.e., to partially missing observations. But the most common application of Maximum Likelihood Estimation is in a set of very empirically relevant circumstances where the data on the actual dependent variable is so fragmented that one might almost characterize it as missing altogether. Remarkably, the MLE framework can allow for parameter estimation and inference in such regression models quite gracefully; that is the topic of the next section.

19.3 MAXIMUM LIKELIHOOD ESTIMATION OF BINARY-CHOICE REGRESSION MODELS

Sometimes the economic data we observe (and seek to model) are not really numbers at all. For example, an individual might choose to enter the labor force and seek employment – or not. Or an individual might choose to enter college and seek a Bachelor's Degree – or not. Data on explanatory variables potentially relevant to explaining the determinants of such a choice might well be available, so that multiple regression would appear to be the analytical tool of choice here – particularly in contexts where the data have been collected in a non-experimental setting.[10] On the other hand, direct application of the Multiple Regression Model of Equation 9-1 is awkward in this setting, because the dependent variable data $(y_1 \ldots y_N)$ are "yes- no" decisions, rather than numbers. And much of the awkwardness remains, even if one assigns the number one to a positive decision – e.g., choosing to enter the labor force – and the number zero to a negative decision, because no weighted sum of the explanatory variable values will produce only ones and zeros as its predicted values.

Suppose, for example, that one could observe m independent repeats of the ith household's decision, where m equals, say, 20. It would in that case make sense to use the fraction of these m decisions which were positive as y_i, the observed value of Y_i; and one could then sensibly interpret a weighted sum of the explanatory variables as the probability of a positive decision on the part of the ith household. There is still the awkward possibility that the weighted sum of the explanatory variables might produce a predicted probability less than zero or greater than one. But one could hope that the coefficient estimates would make such predicted outcomes rare; or one could parameterize the right-hand side of the regression equation as a nonlinear function of the explanatory variables (and the model error) in such a way as to rule out the possibility of such predicted outcomes. In practice, however, the value of m is just one and the observed dependent variable values $(y_1 \ldots y_N)$ are consequently just ones and zeros; thus, this interpretation of the model is not very appealing.

In contrast, there is a more sophisticated regression model – the "probit" model – which provides a truly graceful resolution of this estimation problem. But the probit regression model requires the

[10] Of course, one can easily envision more complex choice milieux – e.g., modeling the number of children a household decides to have – and a number of such empirical settings are briefly described at the close of this section. The central intent here, however, is to explicitly illustrate the simplest and most common setting where Maximum Likelihood Estimation is the estimation technique of choice, so attention at this point is restricted to binary-choice models.

use of Maximum Likelihood Estimation in order to estimate the regression parameters: OLS regression will not do. A very simple example of such a model is a conceptual extension of the no-intercept Bivariate Regression Model of Equation 19-1:[11]

The Bivariate Binary – Choice Regression Model
The "Probit" Model

Observed-Variable Model:

$$Y_i = 1 \text{ (positive decision)}$$
$$= 0 \text{ (negative decision)}$$

with Y_i independently distributed for $i = 1 \ldots N$. The value of Y_i is dependent, however, on the latent variable $\tilde{Y}_i$: Y_i equals one if and only if $\tilde{Y}_i > 0$. (19-10)

Latent-Variable Model:

$$\tilde{Y}_i = \alpha + \beta x_i + U_i \qquad i = 1 \ldots N$$
$$x_1 \ldots x_N \text{ fixed in repeated samples}$$
$$U_i \sim \text{NIID}[0, 1]$$

In this model $\tilde{Y}_i$ can be interpreted as the "propensity to make a positive decision." It is modeled as a linear function of the observed explanatory variable, plus an independently distributed unit normal model error term, U_i. The value of $\tilde{Y}_i$ completely determines the individual's decision in this model: if $\tilde{Y}_i$ is positive, then a positive decision is made, otherwise a negative decision is made. The "catch" is that $\tilde{Y}_i$ is not observed; data are available only on $(y_1, x_1) \ldots (y_N, x_N)$, where $y_1 \ldots y_N$ are sample realizations of $Y_1 \ldots Y_N$ – ones and zeros, corresponding to the two possible decisions. That is why $\tilde{Y}_i$ is called a "latent" variable. Since only the sign of $\tilde{Y}_i$ is consequential to the observed decisions, $\tilde{Y}_i$ is estimatable only up to an arbitrary multiplicative factor; consequently, the variance of U_i is set to one, rather than estimated.[12]

The economically interesting parameter (β) in Equation 19-10 clearly cannot be sensibly estimated using OLS, simply because the necessary data on the latent dependent variable, $\tilde{Y}_i$, are not observed. Nevertheless – remarkably enough – an asymptotically efficient estimate of β *can* be obtained using Maximum Likelihood Estimation, since the log-likelihood of observing the sample data $(y_1, x_1) \ldots (y_N, x_N)$ can be expressed explicitly as a function of these data and of the posited parameter values $\hat{\alpha}^{guess}$ and $\hat{\beta}^{guess}$. Maximizing the log-likelihood function over these two parameter values yields a maximum likelihood estimate of β. This MLE estimate of β also makes it possible to test the null hypothesis H_o: $\beta = 0$ and allows the estimation of a confidence interval for the impact of a change in x_i on the probability of a positive decision being made.

The derivation of the required log-likelihood function proceeds as follows: Suppose that y_i – the observed value of Y_i – happens to be one. In that case, the latent variable, $\tilde{Y}_i$, must be positive, which (according to the model, Equation 19-10) occurs with probability equal to the probability that

[11] This extended model is actually of practical use, so a model intercept is included from the outset.

[12] The variance of U_i is said to be "unidentified" in this model.

$\alpha + \beta x_i + U_i$ is positive. This probability can thus be expressed (in terms of α, β, and x_i) as

$$\begin{aligned}
\text{Prob}(Y_i = 1|x_i, \alpha, \beta) &= \text{Prob}(\tilde{Y}_i > 0|x_i, \alpha, \beta) \\
&= \int_0^{\infty} \frac{1}{\sqrt{2\pi}} e^{\frac{-(\tilde{Y}_i - \alpha - \beta x_i)^2}{2}} d\tilde{Y} \\
&= \int_{\alpha+\beta x_i}^{\infty} \frac{1}{\sqrt{2\pi}} e^{\frac{-z^2}{2}} dz \\
&= 1 - F(\alpha + \beta x_i)
\end{aligned} \tag{19-11}$$

where $F(\cdot)$ is the cumulative density function for the unit normal distribution.

In contrast, if y_i is zero, then the latent variable must be non-positive, which (according to Equation 19-10) occurs with probability equal to the probability that $\alpha + \beta x_i + U_i$ is non-positive. This probability is

$$\begin{aligned}
\text{Prob}(Y_i = 0|x_i, \alpha, \beta) &= \text{Prob}(\tilde{Y}_i \leq 0|x_i, \alpha, \beta) \\
&= \int_{-\infty}^{0} \frac{1}{\sqrt{2\pi}} e^{\frac{-(\tilde{Y}_i - \alpha - \beta x_i)^2}{2}} d\tilde{Y} \\
&= \int_{-\infty}^{\alpha+\beta x_i} \frac{1}{\sqrt{2\pi}} e^{\frac{-z^2}{2}} dz \\
&= F(\alpha + \beta x_i)
\end{aligned} \tag{19-12}$$

Thus, the likelihood of observing the value y_i can be written as

$$\{F(\alpha + \beta x_i)\}^{1-y_i}\{1 - F(\alpha + \beta x_i)\}^{y_i} \tag{19-13}$$

Hence, replacing α by $\hat{\alpha}^{\text{guess}}$ and β by $\hat{\beta}^{\text{guess}}$, the log-likelihood of observing the entire sample, $y_i \ldots y_N$, is

$$\begin{aligned}
&L\left(y_1 \ldots y_N; \hat{\alpha}^{\text{guess}}, \hat{\beta}^{\text{guess}}, x_1 \ldots x_N\right) \\
&= \sum_{i=1}^{N} \left[(1 - y_i) \ln\left\{F(\hat{\alpha}^{\text{guess}} + \hat{\beta}^{\text{guess}} x_i)\right\} + y_i \ln\left\{1 - F(\hat{\alpha}^{\text{guess}} + \hat{\beta}^{\text{guess}} x_i)\right\}\right]
\end{aligned} \tag{19-14}$$

Excellent computing approximations for the cumulative distribution function of the normal distribution (and its derivatives) are readily available and $L\left(y_1 \ldots y_N; \hat{\alpha}^{\text{guess}}, \hat{\beta}^{\text{guess}}, x_1 \ldots x_N\right)$ is very well-behaved as an optimand, so it is not difficult to numerically maximize it over $\hat{\alpha}^{\text{guess}}$ and $\hat{\beta}^{\text{guess}}$ to obtain $\hat{\alpha}^{\text{MLE}}$ and $\hat{\beta}^{\text{MLE}}$. This procedure is called "Probit Regression."

The estimation of such probit regression models is extremely easy in practice, because all of the numerical manipulations for maximizing log-likelihood functions like Equation 19-14 are already programmed into modern econometric software. For example, the Stata command for estimating the model of Equation 19-10 is just "probit *y x*". The Stata syntax for including additional explanatory variables (e.g., $z1_i$ and $z2_i$) in the latent variable model is straightforward: "probit *y x z1 z2*".

The "probit *y x*" command not only directs Stata to calculate the maximum likelihood estimates $\hat{\alpha}^{MLE}$ and $\hat{\beta}^{MLE}$, it also causes the program to calculate consistent standard error estimates for α and for β. As one might expect, given the third asymptotic MLE estimator property listed in the previous section, these standard error estimates are based on the curvature (second partial derivatives) of Equation 19-14, evaluated at its maximum – i.e., where $\hat{\alpha}^{guess}$ equals $\hat{\alpha}^{MLE}$ and where $\hat{\beta}^{guess}$ equals $\hat{\beta}^{MLE}$. This estimated standard error for $\hat{\beta}^{MLE}$ can be used to readily test the null hypothesis H_o: $\beta = 0$.[13]

The magnitude of the parameter β depends on the (arbitrary) assumption of unit-variance for U_i, so an estimated confidence interval for β itself is of no direct interest. What *is* useful, however, is an estimated confidence interval for what is called the "marginal effect" of the variable x_i. This marginal effect is the rate at which the probability of a positive choice varies with the value of x_i.

The marginal effect is conceptually simple where x_i is a dummy variable, so that its takes on only the values zero and one. In that case, Equation 19-11 implies that x_i equaling one implies that the probability of a positive decision increases by $[1 - F(\alpha + \beta)] - [1 - F(\alpha)]$ or $[F(\alpha) - F(\alpha + \beta)]$. Dummy variables are quite commonly used in probit models – e.g., for gender, high school graduation, etc. *A set* of dummy variables is used for "categorical" variables, where the relevant variable can take on *m* values – e.g., for a racial/ethnicity variable or an education-level variable which takes on one value for high school graduates, another value for respondents with some college, another for college graduates, etc.

In that case, *m*–1 dummy variables are needed in order to model the effect of *m* distinct categories. Such a set of dummy variables can still be a good choice even with *m* "evenly-spaced" categories in situations where one fears that the relationship is strongly nonlinear, but the value of *m* can start to become substantial in such cases. For example, in the labor force participation model analyzed in Active Learning Exercise 19a, the variable "age_i" takes on the value 5 for respondents aged 0 to 5 years old, the value *10* for respondents aged 6 to 10 – and so forth – so that there are 17 categories, which requires the estimation of 16 dummy variable coefficients.[14] In contrast, including an $(age_i)^2$ variable yields a model requiring the estimation of only two age-related coefficients; but this risks misspecifying the form of the relationship, rendering all of the model coefficient estimates inconsistent. The Current Population Survey for June 2010 yields a probit regression for this Active Learning Exercise with over 108,000 observations, so estimating a few additional coefficients hardly seems problematic, but this would certainly be a concern if there were only 108 sample observations.

Where x_i is not a dummy variable, the definition of the marginal effect is a bit more complex and – what's worse – implementing it involves making choices. The marginal effect is in that case equal to $\beta\varphi(\beta x_i)$, where $\varphi(\cdot)$ is the density function for the unit normal distribution. Thus, the value of the marginal effect of an explanatory variable such as x_i clearly depends substantially on the value of x_i at which the marginal effect is calculated. In a model like Equation 19-10, in which there is a single explanatory variable in the latent variable model, it is usually sensible to evaluate the estimated marginal effect of this single explanatory variable at the sample mean of $x_1 \dots x_N$, and this is the

[13] The Stata probit command also accepts the "vce(robust)" option, but heteroscedastic errors are inherently non-problematic in Equation 19-10, as nothing observable would change if the variance of U_i was parameterized as ω_i (with $\omega_1 \dots \omega_N$ equal to fixed constants) rather than set to one. However, any notable sensitivity of the estimation results to the specification of this option is a potentially useful indication that the model is misspecified – i.e., that some important explanatory variable has been wrongly omitted from the latent variable model. That is worth noting and trying to correct. The Stata "hetprob" command can be used to explicitly test the proposition that var(U_i) depends on a specified set of additional variables – presumably because they were wrongly omitted from the latent variable model – but it actually makes better sense to simply try including these additional variables in the model.

[14] All respondents more than 84 years old are lumped together in the CPS survey results; this is called "top-coding."

default option in most computer programs. But other choices might be preferable in any given modeling circumstance. If the distribution of X_i is highly non-gaussian, for example, the mean might be a poor choice – one might better compute the marginal effect at the median value of the observed x_i in that case. And in a model with k explanatory variables $(x_{i,1} \dots x_{i,k})$, an observation for which every explanatory variable is at its mean value – i.e., with $(x_{i,1} \dots x_{i,k})$ equal to $(\bar{x}_1 \dots \bar{x}_k)$ – might be quite rare. In such a circumstance it would make better sense to pick a typical value for $(x_{i,1} \dots x_{i,k})$ and evaluate all k marginal effects at this point.

Either way, the calculations are not difficult in most software implementations. In Stata, specifying the probit regression command as "dprobit" instead of as "probit" directs the program to display marginal effects (and estimated 95% confidence intervals for same) instead of the underlying coefficient estimates; Stata figures out on its own which explanatory variables are dummy variables and which are not.[15] Active Learning Exercise 19a illustrates how all of this works.

The binary-choice probit model described above provides the simplest possible example out of a large class of latent variable econometric models. These are collectively called "limited dependent variable" models and provide the econometric basis for a good deal of applied economic analysis. Some other examples include

- Multinomial probit
  Here multiple choices are possible, as when a consumer chooses from among a number of product types or brands.
- Ordered probit
  This is like multinomial probit, except that there is a natural ordering to the choices, as in an opinion survey with several choices, from "least agree with" to "most agree with." In this case a continuous latent variable is used to model this integer-valued choice.
- Censored regression
  Censoring occurs when the actual observations on the dependent variable are limited in value and hence "pile up" at the top and/or bottom limit. The data obtained from experiments on the Voluntary Contribution Mechanism – as considered in Active Learning Exercise 16b, provides a good example.[16] It is not possible to observe subjects contributing more than all or less than none of their endowment of tokens to the "public good," so observed contributions tend to pile up both at zero and at the endowment level. Here an unrestricted latent variable is used to model the subject's "desire to contribute."[17]
- Truncated regression
  Truncation occurs when data are inherently unobservable for a portion of the sample. For example, if log(wages) is the dependent variable in a model, then data will clearly only be available for individuals who are employed. Wherever an individual's presence in the sample is based on their own decisions, this can cause what is known as "selection bias" in the regression results. The latent variable in this example is the value of log(wages) which would have been earned by the remainder of the individuals in the full sample.

[15] The Stata command "probit y x $z1$ $z2$" followed by "mfx, at(1.2, 3.0, 5.2)" specifies that the marginal effects for $(x, z1, z2)$ are to be calculated at this particular triplet of values. Instead following with "mfx, at(median)" would specify that all of the marginal effects for $(x, z1, z2)$ are to be calculated at the point where each of these variables equals its median value.

[16] Available at www.wiley.com/college/ashley.

[17] Where the dependent variable is limited in range – e.g., it is a proportion, and hence inherently restricted to the interval [0, 1] – but the observed data never actually reach either limit, what is called a "logit" regression model can be estimated. In the logit regression model, Y_i is modeled as $\exp(\alpha + \beta x_i + U_i)/[1 + \exp(\alpha + \beta x_i + U_i)]$ and the parameters α and β can be estimated using MLE – e.g., see Kmenta (1986, Section 11-5). Kmenta, J. (1986), *Elements of Econometrics*, Macmillan: New York.

OLS estimation can be used to estimate the parameters in all of these models. But its use doesn't really make sense in these contexts, so there is good reason to expect OLS to produce notably inconsistent parameter estimates and invalid inference results. In contrast, in each case of these cases an appropriately specified latent-variable model can be estimated using Maximum Likelihood Estimation to obtain asymptotically efficient parameter estimates and asymptotically valid inference results.[18] Thus, these "limited dependent variable" models provide a natural setting wherein MLE shines.

On the other hand, in all honesty it must be noted that – as conceptually coherent and intellectually satisfying as these latent-variable models are – the MLE results obtained using them quite frequently do not differ all that substantially from those obtained by crudely applying OLS to a regression model which substitutes the actual decisions – e.g., ones and zeros – for the latent variables. The resulting regression equation is called the "Linear Probability Model" in settings such as Equation 19-10, where the unobserved latent variables, $\tilde{Y}_1 \dots \tilde{Y}_N$, are simply replaced by the ones and zeros of $y_1 \dots y_N$. Of course, one can't know to what degree the probit regression model results differ from those of the Linear Probability Model until one has estimated both.

19.4 GENERALIZED METHOD OF MOMENTS (GMM) ESTIMATION

Frequently, what makes it possible to estimate the coefficients in a regression model is a set of equations specifying the expected values of particular functions of the dependent variable and/or the explanatory variables and/or the model errors. These equations are generically called "moment conditions " or "population moment conditions," as any function of random variables is itself just a random variable and – per the discussion following Equation 2-5 – its expectation can be thought of as the first population moment of this random variable around zero. Such expectations can be compared to the corresponding sample statistics; these sample statistics are accordingly designated the "sample moments." The "method-of-moments" approach to parameter estimation exploits the fact that the numerical values of these sample moments are calculated from the sample data, whereas the corresponding population moments depend on posited values of the unknown model parameters. Thus, comparing the population moments to the sample moments says something about the plausibility of these posited values of the underlying parameters.

More specifically, parameter estimates based on the method-of-moments approach are chosen so as to minimize a measure of the discrepancy between such population moments and the observed values of the analogous sample moments, where the latter are explicit functions of the posited values of the model parameters. Method-of-moments estimation can be shown to provide consistent and asymptotically normal estimators in a wide variety of circumstances – including some in which the least-squares curve fitting and maximum likelihood estimation approaches are awkward or infeasible. The "generalized method of moments" (or "GMM") approach, described below, is an extension of method-of-moments estimation framework which in addition yields asymptotically efficient estimation.[19] For large samples, this asymptotic optimality is a strong advantage for GMM estimation.

In some applied settings, the aforementioned population moment conditions are the consequence of a theoretical presumption that the agents whose behavior is being modeled are "rational" – i.e., acting in such a way as to maximize the expected value of appropriately discounted future profits or utility. The first-order conditions for the relevant optimization problem in such cases imply exactly the kind of population moment conditions alluded to above. For

[18] For example, see Long (1997) or Cameron and Trivedi (2009, Chapters 14–16). Long, J. Scott, *Regression Models for Categorical and Limited Dependent Variables* (Advanced Quantitative Techniques in the Social Sciences, Volume 7), Sage Publications: London.

[19] An estimator is asymptotically efficient if it is consistent and no other consistent estimator has a smaller asymptotic variance; see Footnote 11-12.

example, a rational household's utility-maximizing choice of the sequence $\{X_t, X_{t+1}, \dots\}$ must satisfy conditions related to

$$\frac{\partial E\left[\sum_{\tau=t}^{\infty}\left(\frac{1}{1+r}\right)^{\tau} V_{\tau}(Y_{\tau}, X_{\tau}, \beta_1 \dots \beta_k)\right]}{\partial X_t} = 0 \qquad \text{(19-15)}$$

where V_τ is the period-τ utility function (V_τ), $[1/(1+r)]^\tau$ is a discount factor, and the optimization is constrained to respect an appropriately-specified multi-period budget constraint. Either the utility function itself and/or the budget constraint would typically depend on the unknown parameters $\beta_1 \dots \beta_k$ in a setting such as this one.[20] Consequently, a sample analogue of the expectation constituting the left-hand side of Equation 19-15 will depend on the posited values for $\beta_1 \dots \beta_k$. Thus, for "good" estimates of $\beta_1 \dots \beta_k$, this sample analogue ought to yield an observed value close to that of the right-hand side of Equation 19-15 – i.e., it ought to be close to zero.

Another common source of population moment conditions – and the basis for the illustrative example used below – naturally arises when the instrumental variables (IV) technique is used to estimate regression model parameters because one or more of the explanatory variables are endogenous. Recall, from Sections 11.5 to 11.7, that an explanatory variable is endogenous if – due to omitted variables, measurement error, or joint determination – it is correlated with the model error term. In that case, per the analysis in Section 11.4, OLS yields inconsistent parameter estimators. IV estimation, in contrast, is shown (in Section 12.3) to yield consistent parameter estimators – but only if the instruments used are all "valid." In order to be valid, the covariances of these instruments with the model error term must be zero. Thus, if Z_i is a valid instrument for use in estimating a regression with model error term U_i, then $E[(Z_i - \mu_z)(U_i - \mu_u)]$ must equal zero; this implies that $E[Z_i U_i]$ must equal zero if the model is specified with an intercept, ensuring that $E[U_i]$ is zero.[21] Consequently, the presumed validity of each instrument directly implies a corresponding population moment condition of this form.

Section 12.5 describes how IV regression parameter estimation can be implemented to obtain consistent parameter estimates using two-stage least squares (2SLS), given a sufficiently large number of valid instruments. And two-stage least squares estimation is, indeed, a good first step in implementing IV regression estimation. However, where (as is commonly the case in practice) the model errors are substantially heteroscedastic, 2SLS does not yield asymptotically efficient estimators. In contrast, the two-step GMM estimator described below uses the moment conditions implied by the assumption of valid instruments to yield regression parameter estimators which are identical to the 2SLS estimators on the first step, and which are asymptotically efficient estimators on the second step.[22]

Because of its applicability in a number of applied economic settings – and its relative efficiency in large samples – GMM is very useful. Inspired by this observation, the method-of-moments approach – and its extension to GMM estimation – are described here by applying them to the simplest empirically relevant circumstance in which GMM is uniquely advantageous: the IV estimation of a regression model with a single endogenous explanatory variable, two valid

[20] Equation 19-15 is the correct moment condition if and only if V_τ is specified so as to appropriately incorporate the budget constraint; otherwise, the actual population moment condition derives from the first-order condition for the constrained maximization – e.g., an Euler equation. Those details are intentionally glossed over here, for the sake of brevity.

[21] Recall from Equations 2-38 to 2-40 that $\text{cov}(Z_i, U_i]$ equals $E[Z_i U_i]$ minus $E[Z_i] E[U_i]$.

[22] Technical Note: The term "asymptotically efficient" in this context means that an estimator of a parameter β is consistent and that no other consistent estimator has a smaller asymptotic sampling variance than it does – *for this particular set of instruments*. This usage does not rule out the possibility that a wider (or better) set of instruments might yield a consistent estimator for β with an even smaller asymptotic variance. Also, GMM allows for more graceful usage of lagged values of endogenous variables as instruments, as noted in Section 16.2.

instruments, and model errors which exhibit heteroscedasticity of unknown form:[23]

Bivariate Regression Model with an Endogenous Explanatory Variable and Heteroscedastic Model Errors: The Two-Instrument Case

Regression Model:

$$\begin{gathered} Y_i = \beta X_i + U_i \qquad i = 1 \ldots N \\ U_i \sim \text{IID}\,[0,\, \omega_i] \\ \omega_i > 0;\ U_i \text{ is heteroscedastic if } \omega_1 \ldots \omega_N \text{ are not all equal.} \\ X_i \sim \text{IID}[0,\, \sigma_x^2]\, \sigma_x^2 > 0 \\ \text{Cov}(X_i, U_i) \neq 0 \quad (X_i \text{ endogenous}) \end{gathered} \tag{19-16}$$

Two Valid Instruments: Z_i and Q_i:[a]

$$\begin{array}{ccc} Z_i \sim \text{IID}[0, \sigma_z^2] & \text{and} & Q_i \sim \text{IID}[0, \sigma_z^2] \\ \text{cov}(Z_i,\, X_i) \neq 0 & \text{and} & \text{cov}(Q_i,\, X_i) \neq 0 \\ \text{cov}(Z_i,\, U_i) = 0 & \text{and} & \text{cov}(Q_i,\, U_i) = 0 \\ \text{cov}(Z_i^2,\, U_i^2) = 0 & \text{and} & \text{cov}(Q_i^2,\, U_i^2) = 0 \end{array}$$

[a] The variables X_i, Z_i, and Q_i are assumed to be zero-mean and IID for simplicity of exposition. As in the analogous model with homoscedastic errors analyzed in Section 12.3 and Appendix 12.1, consistent IV estimation of β requires only that the probability limits of the sample covariances of Z_i and Q_i are zero. $\text{Cov}(Z_i,\, U_i) = \text{cov}(Q_i,\, U_i) = 0$ is needed in order to also obtain asymptotic normality of the estimator from a Central Limit Theorem argument, however. The additional assumption that $\text{cov}(Z_i^2,\, U_i^2) = \text{cov}(Q_i^2,\, U_i^2) = 0$ is needed in order to obtain the usual asymptotic variance expressions.

The derivation of the IV estimator of β – and the proof of the consistency of $\hat{\beta}^{IV}$ as an estimator of β – is detailed in Section 12.3 for a similar one-parameter model (Equation 12-6), but one in which there is only a single instrument and in which the model errors are assumed to be homoscedastic. The consistency proof given there is actually still valid in the case of heteroscedastic model errors. And, as noted in Equation A12-9 of Appendix 12.1, it is also not difficult to extend the derivation of the asymptotic sampling distribution of $\hat{\beta}^{IV}$ to a model with heteroscedastic errors. Moreover, per the discussion in Section 12.5, similar results can be obtained for $\hat{\beta}^{2SLS}$, the two-stage least squares estimator needed in order to deal with the second instrument in the model of Equation 19-16. But $\hat{\beta}^{2SLS}$ is merely consistent, not asymptotically efficient.

The method-of-moments approach to estimating the parameter β in Equation 19-16 begins from the two instrument-validity assumptions, which require that the population covariances between the two instruments (Z_i and Q_i) and the model error (U_i) are both zero. Combining these with the assumption that $E[U_i]$ is zero, the two population moment conditions thus assert that $E[Z_i\, U_i]$ and $E[Q_i\, U_i]$ both equal zero for all values of i in the interval $[1, N]$:

$$\begin{aligned} E[Z_i\, U_i] &= E[Z_i(Y_i - \beta X_i)] = 0 \\ E[Q_i\, U_i] &= E[Q_i(Y_i - \beta X_i)] = 0 \end{aligned} \tag{19-17}$$

[23] A model with only one instrument is even simpler, but it does not provide a usable example here, because the heteroscedasticity does not in that case affect the expression for the asymptotically efficient IV estimator: i.e., the 2SLS and GMM estimators do not actually differ in that case. Also, note that the regression model intercept is omitted in Equation 19-16 – as it would not (and should not) be in any actual application – so that only one parameter (β) is being estimated. This omission greatly simplifies the algebra, but the assumption that $E[U_i]$ is zero could be made at no loss of generality if an intercept were included in the model.

These population moment conditions must hold exactly for the true model errors, $U_1 \dots U_N$, but sample realizations of these errors are not observable unless the value of β were known, which – of course – it isn't.

What *is* observable is the set of the sample data: $(y_1, x_1, z_1, q_1) \dots (y_N, x_N, z_N, q_N)$. And, for a given estimate of the model parameter β – denoted $\hat{\beta}^{guess}$ here – one can easily calculate an implied set of fitting errors: $u_1^{fit} = y_1 - \hat{\beta}^{guess} x_1 \dots u_N^{fit} = y_N - \hat{\beta}^{guess} x_N$, which are sample realizations of fitting errors which are asymptotically equivalent to $U_1 \dots U_N$. Conditional on $\hat{\beta}^{guess}$ being a reasonable estimate of β, these are reasonable estimates of $U_1 \dots U_N$, allowing one to calculate sample analogues of the population moments $E[Z_i\, U_i]$ and $E[Q_i\, U_i]$ in Equation 19-17. The "method-of-moments" estimator of β, then, is the value of $\hat{\beta}^{guess}$ which minimizes a measure of the overall discrepancy between these two sample analogues of $E[Z_i\, U_i]$ and $E[Q_i\, U_i]$ and the population values – zero, in both cases – which are implied for them by the model, Equation 19-16. Letting the parameter λ_{qq} stand for the relative penalty-weight attached to "matching" the $E[Q_i\, U_i]$ moment, an explicit formulation of $[\hat{\beta}^{MM}(\lambda_{qq})]^*$ – the sample realization of the method-of-moments estimator, $\hat{\beta}^{MM}(\lambda_{qq})$ – is given by

The Method-of-Moments Estimator of β in the Model of Equation 19-16

$[\hat{\beta}^{MM}(\lambda_{qq})]^*$ is the value of $\hat{\beta}^{guess}$ which minimizes $g(\hat{\beta}^{guess}; \lambda_{qq})$, the weighted squared discrepancy between the two sample moments (implied by $\hat{\beta}^{guess}$ and the sample data) and their corresponding population values, which are both zero. Thus, $g(\hat{\beta}^{guess}; \lambda_{qq})$ is

$$\begin{aligned} g(\hat{\beta}^{guess}; \lambda_{qq}) &= \left\{ \frac{1}{N} \sum_{i=1}^{N} z_i u_i^{fit} - E[Z_i\, U_i] \right\}^2 + \lambda_{qq} \left\{ \frac{1}{N} \sum_{i=1}^{N} q_i\, u_i^{fit} - E[Q_i\, U_i] \right\}^2 \\ &= \left\{ \frac{1}{N} \sum_{i=1}^{N} z_i u_i^{fit} - 0 \right\}^2 + \lambda_{qq} \left\{ \frac{1}{N} \sum_{i=1}^{N} q_i u_i^{fit} - 0 \right\}^2 \\ &= \left\{ \frac{1}{N} \sum_{i=1}^{N} z_i (y_i - \hat{\beta}^{guess} x_i) \right\}^2 + \lambda_{qq} \left\{ \frac{1}{N} \sum_{i=1}^{N} q_i\, (y_i - \hat{\beta}^{guess} x_i) \right\}^2 \end{aligned} \tag{19-18}$$

$[\hat{\beta}^{MM}(\lambda_{qq})]^*$ is the value of $\hat{\beta}^{guess}$ for which $d\left\{ g(\hat{\beta}^{guess}; \lambda_{qq}) \right\} / d\hat{\beta}^{guess}$ equals zero.

The use of squared discrepancies in Equation 19-18 substantially penalizes any large deviations between the two sample moments and their corresponding population moments. This specification of the minimand also penalizes positive and negative discrepancies symmetrically, but that is ordinarily innocuous, absent some sensible reason to impose an asymmetry.[24] The algebra involved

[24] Technical Note: This formulation of the method-of-moments estimation approach has been generalized in the literature in two directions which are instructive to think about at this point – but not until one is on at least their second reading of this chapter. De Jong and Han (2002) analyze GMM-type parameter estimation where these discrepancies are raised to a specific power p, which is still assumed to be positive but might not equal two; they call this the L_p-GMM estimator. De Jong and Han show that the L_p-GMM estimator is still consistent, but that this estimator is in general neither asymptotically normal nor asymptotically efficient. Of course, efficiency is defined in terms of the sampling variance, which is inherently an L_2-norm measure of the size of a random variable; so perhaps asymptotic efficiency is not an appropriate criterion for an estimator based on an L_p distance measure. Another generalization of the framework modifies the way the population and sample moments themselves are defined, so as to make what would otherwise be the usual L_2-GMM estimator more robust to outliers – e.g., see Gagliardini et al. (2005) and Park (2009). De Jong, R., and C. Han (2002), "The Properties of L_p-GMM Estimators," *Econometric Theory 18*, pp. 491–504; Galiardini, P., F. Trojani, and G. Urga (2005), "Robust GMM Tests For Structural Breaks," *Journal of Econometrics 129*, pp. 139–82; Park, B. (2009), "Risk-Return Relationship in Equity Markets: Using a Robust GMM Estimator for GARCH-M Models," *Quantitative Finance 9*, pp. 93–104.

in taking the indicated derivative in Equation 19-18, setting it equal to zero, and solving that equation for $\hat{\beta}^{guess}$ to obtain an explicit expression for $\left[\hat{\beta}^{MM}(\lambda_{qq})\right]^*$ is straightforward – see Exercise 19-5 – and yields the result

$$\left[\hat{\beta}^{MM}(\lambda_{qq})\right]^* = \sum_{i=1}^{N} m_i\{\lambda_{qq}\}y_i \tag{19-19}$$

with method-of-moments estimator weights, $m_1(\lambda_{qq})\dots m_N(\lambda_{qq})$, which are

$$m_i(\lambda_{qq}) = \frac{z_i\Sigma_{zx} + \lambda_{qq}q_i\Sigma_{qx}}{\Sigma_{zx}^2 + \lambda_{qq}\Sigma_{qx}^2} \tag{19-20}$$

where Σ_{zx} is defined as $\sum_{j=1}^{N} z_j x_j$ and Σ_{qx} is defined as $\sum_{j=1}^{N} q_j x_j$ so as to simplify the expressions. Note that the values $m_1\{\lambda_{qq}\}\dots m_N\{\lambda_{qq}\}$ are fixed numbers, which can – for any given value of λ_{qq} – be calculated from the sample observations on the explanatory variable and the two instruments, $(x_1, z_1, q_1)\dots(x_N, z_N, q_N)$.

Equation 19-19 gives the realized method-of-moments estimate of β, which is just an ordinary number. The method-of-moments estimator of β itself is thus

$$\hat{\beta}^{MM}(\lambda_{qq}) = \sum_{i=1}^{N} m_i\{\lambda_{qq}\}Y_i \tag{19-21}$$

where y_i, the realized value of the dependent variable, has been replaced by Y_i itself.

It can be shown that $\hat{\beta}^{MM}(\lambda_{qq})$ is a consistent estimator of β and also that it is asymptotically normally distributed. But the fact that its defining weights – $m_1\{\lambda_{qq}\}\dots m_N\{\lambda_{qq}\}$ – depend on an apparently arbitrary choice for the value of the penalty-weight λ_{qq} is a fatal flaw: no one wants an estimator of β which is not well-defined.

The "generalized method-of-moments" or "GMM" estimation approach eliminates this predicament by "generalizing" $\left[\hat{\beta}^{MM}(\lambda_{qq})\right]^*$ and $\hat{\beta}^{MM}(\lambda_{qq})$ in two ways. First, it recognizes that there was actually no good reason for excluding a cross-term of the form

$$\lambda_{zq}\left\{\frac{1}{N}\sum_{i=1}^{N} z_i u_i^{fit} - E[Z_i\,U_i]\right\}\left\{\frac{1}{N}\sum_{i=1}^{N} q_i u_i^{fit} - E[Q_i\,U_i]\right\} \tag{19-22}$$

from the minimand in Equation 19-18. Here λ_{zq} is a second penalty-weight, which quantifies the relative weight with which this moment-deviation cross-term enters the minimand. This additional term complicates the algebra of solving for the method-of-moments estimate, but only a bit; see Exercise 19-6. The resulting estimator weights for this "improved" method-of-moments estimator now depend on the additional penalty-weight λ_{zq}, as well as on λ_{qq}:

$$\hat{\beta}^{MM-improved}(\lambda_{qq}, \lambda_{zq}) = \sum_{i=1}^{N} \tilde{m}_i\{\lambda_{qq}, \lambda_{zq}\}Y_i \tag{19-23}$$

with estimator weights $\tilde{m}_1\{\lambda_{qq}, \lambda_{zq}\} \dots \tilde{m}_N\{\lambda_{qq}, \lambda_{zq}\}$ given by

$$\tilde{m}_i\{\lambda_{qq}, \lambda_{zq}\} = \frac{z_i\Sigma_{zx} + \lambda_{qq}q_i\Sigma_{qx} + 2\lambda_{zq}[z_i\Sigma_{qx} + q_i\Sigma_{zx}]}{\Sigma_{zx}^2 + \lambda_{qq}\Sigma_{qx}^2 + 4\lambda_{zq}\Sigma_{zx}\Sigma_{qx}} \tag{19-24}$$

At first glance, $\hat{\beta}^{MM-improved}(\lambda_{qq}, \lambda_{zq})$ hardly seems an improvement over $\hat{\beta}^{MM}(\lambda_{qq})$: now the estimator depends on two apparently arbitrary penalty-weight choices instead of on one! The second "generalization" is the charm, however: once the cross-term of Equation 19-22 is included in the minimand, it is possible to derive estimation formulas for the *optimal* values of the penalty-weights λ_{zq} and λ_{qq} – i.e., explicit, computable expressions of the values for these weights which yield an asymptotically efficient estimator of β. The derivation of these two optimal-weight functions – $\lambda^*_{zq}(\omega_1 \dots \omega_N)$ and $\lambda^*_{qq}(\omega_1 \dots \omega_N)$ – is beyond the scope of the present treatment, as it requires a substantial investment in matrix algebra, but these two functions themselves are fairly simple:[25]

$$\lambda^*_{zq}(\omega_1 \dots \omega_N) = -\frac{2\sum_{i=1}^{N} \omega_i z_i q_i}{\sum_{i=1}^{N} \omega_i q_i^2} \tag{19-25}$$

$$\lambda^*_{qq}(\omega_1 \dots \omega_N) = -\frac{\sum_{i=1}^{N} \omega_i z_i^2}{\sum_{i=1}^{N} \omega_i q_i^2} \tag{19-26}$$

Note that these formulas for the optimal values of λ_{zq} and λ_{qq} depend on the model error variances $(\omega_1 \dots \omega_N)$ in Equation 19-16) and on the sample data for the instruments z_i and q_i, but not on the values of the dependent or explanatory variables in the model. The dependence of $\lambda^*_{zq}(\omega_1 \dots \omega_N)$ and $\lambda^*_{qq}(\omega_1 \dots \omega_N)$ on $\omega_1 \dots \omega_N$ is essential to the discussion which now follows, so the notation emphasizes this; their dependence on the sample values of $(z_1, q_1) \dots (z_N, q_N)$ is not so essential, and has consequently been suppressed in the notation.

Substituting $\lambda^*_{zq}(\omega_1 \dots \omega_N)$ and $\lambda^*_{qq}(\omega_1 \dots \omega_N)$ into Equations 19-23 and 19-24 yields the GMM estimator of β:

$$\hat{\beta}^{GMM}(\omega_1 \dots \omega_N) = \sum_{i=1}^{N} \tilde{m}_i\left\{\lambda^*_{qq}(\omega_1 \dots \omega_N), \lambda^*_{zq}(\omega_1 \dots \omega_N)\right\} Y_i \tag{19-27}$$

with estimator weights

$$\tilde{m}_i\left\{\lambda^*_{qq}(\omega_1 \dots \omega_N), \lambda^*_{zq}(\omega_1 \dots \omega_N)\right\} = \frac{z_i\Sigma_{zx} + \lambda^*_{qq}(\omega_1 \dots \omega_N)q_i\Sigma_{qx} + \tfrac{1}{2}\lambda^*_{zq}(\omega_1 \dots \omega_N)\left[z_i\Sigma_{qx} + q_i\Sigma_{zx}\right]}{\Sigma_{zx}^2 + \lambda^*_{qq}(\omega_1 \dots \omega_N)\Sigma_{qx}^2 + \lambda^*_{zq}(\omega_1 \dots \omega_N)\Sigma_{qx}\Sigma_{zx}} \tag{19-28}$$

which thus depend explicitly on the variances of the model errors, $\omega_1 \dots \omega_N$.

[25] See Appendix 19.1. The optimal weights in the method-of-moments minimand for the general case of a Multiple Regression Model with k regressors (g of which are endogenous) and j instruments are derived in a number of places – e.g., Davidson and MacKinnon (2004, Section 7.2). Couched in matrix algrebra, this result is compact, albeit a bit opaque. Appendix 19.1 quotes this formula and unpacks it for the present model to obtain Equations 19-25 and 19-26. Davidson, R., and J. G. MacKinnon (1993), *Econometric Theory and Methods*, Oxford University Press: Oxford.

Conditional on the values of $\omega_1 \ldots \omega_N$, $\hat{\beta}^{GMM}(\omega_1 \ldots \omega_N)$ can be shown to be an asymptotically efficient estimator of β. Of course, the model error variances $\omega_1 \ldots \omega_N$ are not known. And, with only the N sample observations – $(y_1, x_1, z_1, q_1) \ldots (y_N, x_N, z_N, q_N)$ – it is clearly not possible to estimate $\omega_1 \ldots \omega_N$. What *is* feasible, however, is an iterative procedure for successively approximating $\omega_1 \ldots \omega_N$ which yields a GMM estimator for β that is asymptotically equivalent to $\hat{\beta}^{GMM}(\omega_1 \ldots \omega_N)$.

All values pertaining to the first iteration of this procedure are denoted with a superscript {1}, so the first-iteration approximations to the model error variances are called $\omega_1^{\{1\}} \ldots \omega_N^{\{1\}}$. Homoscedasticity is assumed on the first iteration, so these variances are assumed equal on this first pass. In fact, they can all be set to any convenient value on the first iteration, since only the parameter estimate is used from this first pass; a value of one works fine. The first-iteration estimate of β replaces $Y_1 \ldots Y_N$ in Equation 19-27 with the sample realizations $y_1 \ldots y_N$ and replaces the unknown values of $\omega_1 \ldots \omega_N$ by their first-iteration value; this estimate is denoted $\left[\hat{\beta}^{GMM}(\omega_1^{\{1\}} \ldots \omega_N^{\{1\}})\right]^*$. This initial estimate of β turns out to be identical to what one would obtain from 2SLS, ignoring the heteroscedasticity in $U_1 \ldots U_N$.

This first-iteration parameter estimate $\left[\hat{\beta}^{GMM}(\omega_1^{\{1\}} \ldots \omega_N^{\{1\}})\right]^*$ is then used to obtain an initial set of fitting errors:

$$
\begin{aligned}
(u_1^{fit})^{\{1\}} &\equiv y_1 - \left[\hat{\beta}^{GMM}(\omega_1^{\{1\}} \ldots \omega_N^{\{1\}})\right]^* x_1 \\
(u_2^{fit})^{\{1\}} &\equiv y_2 - \left[\hat{\beta}^{GMM}(\omega_1^{\{1\}} \ldots \omega_N^{\{1\}})\right]^* x_2 \\
(u_3^{fit})^{\{1\}} &\equiv y_3 - \left[\hat{\beta}^{GMM}(\omega_1^{\{1\}} \ldots \omega_N^{\{1\}})\right]^* x_3 \\
&\ldots \\
(u_1^{fit})^{\{1\}} &\equiv y_n - \left[\hat{\beta}^{GMM}(\omega_1^{\{1\}} \ldots \omega_N^{\{1\}})\right]^* x_N
\end{aligned}
\tag{19-29}
$$

The square of $(u_i^{fit})^{\{1\}}$ is certainly not a consistent estimate of $\text{var}(U_i) = \omega_i$, since it is using only one sample datum. Nevertheless, setting

$$
\begin{aligned}
\omega_2^{\{2\}} &\equiv \left\{(u_2^{fit})^{\{1\}}\right\}^2 \\
\omega_3^{\{2\}} &\equiv \left\{(u_3^{fit})^{\{1\}}\right\}^2 \\
&\ldots \\
\omega_N^{\{2\}} &\equiv \left\{(u_N^{fit})^{\{1\}}\right\}^2
\end{aligned}
\tag{19-30}
$$

yields a "second-pass" estimate of β – $\left[\hat{\beta}^{GMM}(\omega_1^{\{2\}} \ldots \omega_N^{\{2\}})\right]^*$ – which can be shown to be asymptotically efficient even though the true values of $\omega_1 \ldots \omega_N$ were never specified.[26]

That is the two-step GMM estimator of β in the model of Equation 19-16. Note that this particular model is just an illustrative example: as indicated earlier in this section, the Generalized Method of Moments is not specific to IV estimation. In fact, the term "GMM estimation" is generically used to denote the second (or subsequent) step in any iterative method-of-moments estimation procedure in which the first-iteration weights on the moment-deviations (analogous to λ_{qq} and λ_{zq} here) are set to

[26] This process can be iterated further. The resulting sequence of estimators are all asymptotically equivalent. Most users stop at the first iteration, but an argument can be made for iterating this process until either the parameter estimates or the sum of squared fitting errors becomes essentially constant. An option of this form is usually built into software implementing GMM estimation.

the optimal values based on an oversimplified model assumption (e.g., homoscedastic errors) and are then updated on subsequent iterations using the resulting fitting errors. The model assumption for the first iteration need only be sufficiently good as to yield consistent parameter estimates.[27]

The two-step GMM estimator described above provides an intellectually satisfying solution to the problem of estimating the coefficients in IV regression models like Equation 19-16 – if N is sufficiently large. The required numerical computations for this estimator might at first glance appear daunting, but they are actually very easy in practice. This is because the computations for the GMM estimator (formulated in matrix form as Equation A19-1 in Appendix 19.1) are easy to program in any computer language designed to accommodate matrix manipulations.[28] Moreover, the estimator has already been programmed up for convenient use in econometric packages like Stata.

For example, it is illuminating at this point to reconsider the Angrist-Krueger (1991) model of weekly log wages ($LWKLYWG_i$) described in Section 12.6. Two-stage least squares (2SLS) estimates were obtained there – along with White-Eicker standard error estimates, which are consistent in the presence of heteroscedastic model errors – for the intercept, for the coefficient on years of schooling (EDU_i), and for the nine birth-year dummy variables ($YR1_i$ ... $YR9_i$). The 2SLS estimation begins with a first-stage regression of edu_i on all 30 of the instruments ($QTR220_i$ ... $QTR429_i$) specified by Angrist and Krueger. (Their rationale for these instruments – and the consequent critiques in the literature – were discussed at that point.) The predicted values of EDU_i from this estimated first-stage regression model were then used to replace EDU_i in the second-stage regression equation.

All of this was implemented using the Stata command:

```
ivregress 2sls lwklywge (edu = qtr220 qtr221 qtr222 qtr223 qtr224 qtr225
      qtr226 qtr227 qtr228 qtr229 qtr320 qtr321 qtr322 qtr323 qtr324 qtr325
      qtr326 qtr327 qtr328 qtr329 qtr420 qtr421 qtr422 qtr423 qtr424 qtr425
      qtr426 qtr427 qtr428 qtr429) yr1 yr2 yr3 yr4 yr5 yr6 yr7 yr8 yr9 ,
      robust
```

and the sample observations: ($lwklywge_1$, edu_1, $qtr220_1$ ... $qtr429_1$, and $yr1_1$ ... $yr9_1$) ... $lwklywge_{329509}$, $qtr220_{329509}$ ... $qtr429_{329509}$, and $yr1_{329509}$ ... $yr9_{329509}$. This yields a 2SLS estimate of the coefficient on edu_i of $.089 \pm .016$ and an estimated 95% confidence interval for this coefficient of [.057, .121], thus providing empirical support for a positive return to education, even after (more or less credibly) allowing for possible endogeneity in edu_i due to the omission of confounding variables, such as a measure of an individual's innate ability.

If the 30 Angrist-Krueger instruments are actually uncorrelated with the model errors, then this parameter estimate is the sample realization of a consistent estimator; and the heteroscedasticity-robust standard error estimator quoted above is, in that case, consistent also. But, because there is evidence of statistically significant heteroscedasticity in the model errors, this estimator of the coefficient on edu_i is *only* consistent: it is not asymptotically efficient.

In contrast, the two-step GMM estimator described earlier in this section – suitably extended to deal with estimating multiple coefficients, based on a much larger number of population moment conditions – yields asymptotically efficient parameter estimators for all 11 coefficients, including the one on edu_i. These asymptotically efficient parameter estimators are obtained by minimizing the (weighted) squared deviations of the sample moments from the values of the corresponding population moments, which are specified by the population moment conditions. There are 40 – not

---

[27] See Davidson and MacKinnon (1993, pp. 586–87) for a good description of the intellectual origins and early applications of GMM estimation. Davidson, R., and J. G. MacKinnon (1993), *Estimation and Inference in Econometrics*, Oxford University Press: Oxford.

[28] For example, *MATLAB*, *GAUSS*, or *R*.

30 – of these population moment conditions; they are

$$\begin{aligned} E[U_i] &= 0 \\ E[YR1_i\, U_i] &= 0 \\ E[YR2_i\, U_i] &= 0 \\ &\cdots \\ E[YR9_i\, U_i] &= 0 \\ E[QTR220_i\, U_i] &= 0 \\ E[QTR221_i\, U_i] &= 0 \\ &\cdots \\ E[QTR429_i\, U_i] &= 0 \end{aligned} \quad (19\text{-}31)$$

Note that the first of these moment conditions is just asserting that the model errors have mean zero; the validity of this moment condition is guaranteed by the inclusion of an intercept in the model. The next nine conditions are asserting that the birth-year dummy variables are truly exogenous – that is, uncorrelated with the model errors. And the final set of population moment conditions are asserting that the 30 Angrist-Krueger instruments ($QTR220_i$ ... $QTR429_i$) are all valid instruments – i.e., that they, also, are uncorrelated with the model errors.[29]

The analogous sample moments substitute averages over the sample data for the expectations in the population moments. Thus, the deviations of the sample moments from the corresponding population moments are

$$\begin{aligned}
&\left(\frac{1}{329509}\right)\sum_{i=1}^{329509}[u_i^{\text{fit}}] - E[U_i] &&\Rightarrow \left(\frac{1}{329509}\right)\sum_{i=1}^{329509}[u_i^{\text{fit}}] - 0 \\
&\left(\frac{1}{329509}\right)\sum_{i=1}^{329509}[yr1_i u_i^{\text{fit}}] - E[YR1_i U_i] &&\Rightarrow \left(\frac{1}{329509}\right)\sum_{i=1}^{329509}[yr1_i u_i^{\text{fit}}] - 0 \\
&\left(\frac{1}{329509}\right)\sum_{i=1}^{329509}[yr2_i u_i^{\text{fit}}] - E[YR2_i U_i] &&\Rightarrow \left(\frac{1}{329509}\right)\sum_{i=1}^{329509}[yr2_i u_i^{\text{fit}}] - 0 \\
& &&\cdots \\
&\left(\frac{1}{329509}\right)\sum_{i=1}^{329509}[yr9_i u_i^{\text{fit}}] - E[YR9_i U_i] &&\Rightarrow \left(\frac{1}{329509}\right)\sum_{i=1}^{329509}[yr9_i u_i^{\text{fit}}] - 0 \\
&\left(\frac{1}{329509}\right)\sum_{i=1}^{329509}[qtr220_i u_i^{\text{fit}}] - E[QTR220_i U_i] &&\Rightarrow \left(\frac{1}{329509}\right)\sum_{i=1}^{329509}[qtr220_i u_i^{\text{fit}}] - 0 \\
&\left(\frac{1}{329509}\right)\sum_{i=1}^{329509}[qtr221_i u_i^{\text{fit}}] - E[QTR221_i U_i] &&\Rightarrow \left(\frac{1}{329509}\right)\sum_{i=1}^{329509}[qtr221_i u_i^{\text{fit}}] - 0 \\
& &&\cdots \\
&\left(\frac{1}{329509}\right)\sum_{i=1}^{329509}[qtr429_i u_i^{\text{fit}}] - E[QTR429_i U_i] &&\Rightarrow \left(\frac{1}{329509}\right)\sum_{i=1}^{329509}[qtr429_i u_i^{\text{fit}}] - 0
\end{aligned} \quad (19\text{-}32)$$

[29] Recall (from Chapter 9) that a simple way to include an intercept in the Multiple Regression Model is to define an additional explanatory variable whose value is one for each sample observation; thus, there are actually 10 exogenous explanatory variables in this model. (This count does not include EDU_i, of course, because it is endogenous.) These 10 variables – being exogenous – are all uncorrelated with the model error term, which yields these first 10 population moment conditions. Alternatively, one could view these 10 explanatory variables as instruments for themselves, in which case all 40 population moment conditions are "instrument validity" conditions here.

Crucially, note that each of the sample moments used in defining the 40 moment-deviations given above substitutes the realized fitting errors ($u_1^{\text{fit}} \dots u_{329509}^{\text{fit}}$) – which are observable, contingent on the parameter estimates – for $u_1 \dots u_{329509}$, the unobserved realizations of the model errors. The realized fitting error for observation i is calculated using the sample datum on the dependent variable ($lwklywge_i$), the data on the explanatory variables (edu_i and $yr1_i \dots yr9_i$), and the 11 model parameter estimates. (See Exercise 19-7 for an explicit example.)

Consequently, "poor" guesses at these model parameter values yield a set of realized fitting errors for which some or all of these 40 sample moments will deviate substantially from their corresponding population moment values, all 40 of which are equal to zero here. In contrast, "good" guesses at these parameter values yield a set of fitting errors such that these 40 sample moments will each deviate only a minimal amount from the posited value for the corresponding population moment value. Indeed, it is this very fact that – taking the sample data as given – better parameter estimates yield a set of smaller deviations between the implied sample moments and their population analogues that provides the basis for the estimating these model parameters.[30]

As in Equation 19-18, this concept of "smaller deviations" is operationalized by minimizing a weighted sum quantifying the overall size of these 40 deviation terms. This sum includes weighted terms involving both the squares of the 40 moment deviations given in Equation 19-32 and the 780 distinct moment deviation *cross-products.*[31]

A choice to place equal weights on the 40 squared deviations and no weight at all on the 780 distinct deviation cross-products yields parameter estimates identical to the 2SLS estimates. This is the first step in the two-step GMM estimation process. On the second step, optimal values for these 820 weights are calculated using the matrix expression quoted as Equation A19-1 in Appendix 19.1. Equation A19-1 requires a set of values for $\omega_1 \dots \omega_{329509}$, specifying the relative sizes of $var(U_1) \dots var(U_{329509})$ in the original regression model.[32] Each of these $\omega_1 \dots \omega_{329509}$ values is approximated by setting it equal to the square of the corresponding 2SLS fitting error. If the GMM estimation procedure is iterated beyond two steps, then the optimal set of weights for each subsequent step is calculated using the squares of the fitting errors implied by the parameter estimates obtained in the immediately preceding step. This procedure can be shown to produce asymptotically efficient estimators for the 11 model parameters and consistent estimates of their sampling distribution.[33]

The foregoing computation sounds complicated but, in practice, it is hardly more difficult than obtaining the 2SLS estimates: the Stata command for estimating this model using GMM

[30] Because $yr1_i \dots yr9_i$ and $qtr220_i \dots qtr429_i$ are all dummy variables in this particular model, these sample moments are just sample means of the fitting errors over various subsets of the observations in this case. For example, $(1/N)\sum_{i=1}^{N}[yr2_i u_i^{\text{fit}}]$ is the sample mean of u_i^{fit} over all of the respondents born in 1932 and $(1/N)\sum_{i=1}^{N}[qtr429_i u_i^{\text{fit}}]$ is the sample mean of u_i^{fit} over all of the respondents born in the fourth quarter of 1939. Thus, in this particular example the estimation procedure is actually matching sample means to population means; that is clearly not always the case in GMM estimation. (See Section 12.6 for a more detailed description of the Angrist-Krueger model and variables.)

[31] There are 40^2 possible products of the 40 moment deviations. Since 40 of these are the squared terms, there are $40^2 - 40$ possible cross-product terms. Each of the cross-product terms in this set of 40^2 possible is duplicated once, however, so the total number of distinct cross-product terms is $\frac{1}{2}(40^2 - 40)$, or 780.

[32] These correspond to the N elements of the diagonal matrix Ω. in Equation A19-1.

[33] The 820 optimal weights are estimated consistently, but are not directly used in estimation and inference on the 11 model parameters. Note that, as with the White-Eicker robust standard errors in Section 10.7, the N model error variances – $\text{var}(U_1) \dots \text{var}(U_{329509})$ – cannot be consistently estimated. As in that case, however, this does not matter: it is consistent estimation of the 11 model parameters (and their sampling distribution) which is needed.

is simply:

```
ivregress gmm lwklywge (edu = qtr220 qtr221 qtr222 qtr223 qtr224 qtr225
     qtr226 qtr227 qtr228 qtr229 qtr320 qtr321 qtr322 qtr323 qtr324 qtr325
     qtr326 qtr327 qtr328 qtr329 qtr420 qtr421 qtr422 qtr423 qtr424 qtr425
     qtr426 qtr427 qtr428 qtr429) yr1 yr2 yr3 yr4 yr5 yr6 yr7 yr8 yr9
```

(19-33)

and yields the output:

```
Instrumental variables (GMM) regression           Number of obs =   329509
                                                  Wald chi2(10) =    41.94
                                                  Prob > chi2   =   0.0000
                                                  R-squared     =   0.1088
GMM weight matrix: Robust                         Root MSE      =   .64084

------------------------------------------------------------------------------
             |               Robust
    lwklywge |      Coef.   Std. Err.      z    P>|z|     [95% Conf. Interval]
-------------+----------------------------------------------------------------
         edu |   .0906954   .0162087     5.60   0.000     .0589269    .1224639
         yr1 |  -.0090602   .0056166    -1.61   0.107    -.0200686    .0019483
         yr2 |  -.0177272   .0058081    -3.05   0.002    -.0291108   -.0063436
         yr3 |  -.0219337   .0063386    -3.46   0.001    -.0343572   -.0095102
         yr4 |  -.0261761    .006666    -3.93   0.000    -.0392412    -.013111
         yr5 |  -.0393061   .0073579    -5.34   0.000    -.0537274   -.0248849
         yr6 |  -.0390383   .0080384    -4.86   0.000    -.0547932   -.0232833
         yr7 |  -.0454522   .0088103    -5.16   0.000    -.0627201   -.0281843
         yr8 |  -.0473694   .0099433    -4.76   0.000    -.0668578   -.0278809
         yr9 |  -.0593177   .0105178    -5.64   0.000    -.0799322   -.0387033
       _cons |   4.773051   .2019225    23.64   0.000      4.37729    5.168812
------------------------------------------------------------------------------
Instrumented:  edu
Instruments:   yr1 yr2 yr3 yr4 yr5 yr6 yr7 yr8 yr9 qtr220 qtr221 qtr222
               qtr223 qtr224 qtr225 qtr226 qtr227 qtr228 qtr229 qtr320
               qtr321 qtr322 qtr323 qtr324 qtr325 qtr326 qtr327 qtr328
               qtr329 qtr420 qtr421 qtr422 qtr423 qtr424 qtr425 qtr426
               qtr427 qtr428 qtr429
```

Thus, the analogous GMM estimate of the coefficient on edu_i is $.091 \pm .016$ and an estimated 95% confidence interval for this coefficient of [.059, .122]. The GMM and 2SLS estimates are in this instance very, very similar: evidently, the heteroscedasticity in $U_1 \ldots U_N$ – while highly significant statistically – is not as consequential for the parameter estimation as all that. Of course one could not know that without obtaining the GMM estimates on the second step.

This GMM estimated model can (and should) be diagnostically checked. This is done in much the same way as was illustrated for the model estimated using 2SLS. In particular, the command "predict gmm_resids, r" can be used to store the fitting errors under the name *gmm_resids*; they can then be plotted, and so forth.[34]

[34] Had these been time-series data, then one of those diagnostic checks would be to regress the fitting errors on their own recent past, so as to test for the presence of serial correlation in the model errors. Analogous asymptotically efficient GMM estimators are readily available in the presence of serial correlation of arbitrary form up to a prespecified lag p. Now terms like $u_t^{\text{fit}}\, u_{t-j}^{\text{fit}}(\text{for } |j| \leq p)$ in addition to terms like $(u_t^{\text{fit}})^2$ are used in estimating the optimal weights for use in the moment deviations. The analogous Stata command is simple enough: one merely specifies the option "wmatrix(hac nwest)", where "#" is replaced by the value $p+1$. There are two reasons why this aspect is not emphasized above. First, the treatment here is designed to focus on the basic idea of GMM estimation, in as simple and clear a way as possible. Second, in the author's opinion the use of such "HAC" weighting matrices is really not a very good idea: it is better to take the existence of serial correlation in the model errors as a suggestion from Mother Nature that one ought to be including more dynamics – i.e., more lags in the dependent and explanatory variables – in the model specification.

GMM estimation also provides an additional diagnostic check, called "Hansen's *J* Test" or, sometimes, just a "test of the overidentifying restrictions." The derivation of this test is somewhat technical – e.g., see Davidson and MacKinnon (2004, Section 9.4) – but the underlying idea is simple and the test is easy to perform.

Applying Hansen's *J* test to the Angrist-Krueger model, for example, the null hypothesis for the test assumes that all 40 population moment conditions are exactly true. Consequently, the deviations of the 40 sample moments from the values (all zero) specified by the corresponding population moment conditions must all be due to sampling variation in the model errors, $U_1 \dots U_{329509}$. Because 11 coefficients are being estimated, these would suffice to force 11 of the moment condition discrepancies to equal zero, regardless of the validity (or falsity) of the population moment conditions. Consequently, there are effectively only 29 "free" moment conditions; these are called the "overidentifying restrictions." Under the null hypothesis, where all 40 restrictions are true, one would expect that the sample value of the GMM minimand – the (optimally) weighted sum of the squared (and cross-product) moment condition discrepancies – would be "small." In contrast, one would expect the sample value of this minimand to be "large" if the null hypothesis is false – i.e., if one or more of the 40 population moment conditions is false.

Thus, one should reject this null hypothesis – that both the 11 identifying restrictions and the 29 overidentifying restrictions are all true – if the GMM minimand is sufficiently large. As usual in hypothesis testing, the crucial point is to determine the sampling distribution of the relevant test statistic – here, the GMM minimand itself, evaluated using the GMM parameter estimates – so that one can compute the *p*-value at which the sample evidence allows one to reject this null hypothesis. An incorrect rejection of this null hypothesis will occur if and only if the GMM minimand turns out "too large" due to sampling variation. Consequently, the *p*-value of the test is simply the probability that the GMM minimand would, under the null hypothesis, exceed the observed value. Hansen showed that GMM minimand is asymptotically distributed $\chi^2(r)$ under the null hypothesis that all of the population moment conditions are valid, where r is the number of overidentifying restrictions.

The test statistic for Hansen's *J* test is thus very easy to calculate, once the parameter estimates have been obtained. But even that effort is generally unnecessary, as typical econometric software does this for us. For example, in Stata issuing the command "estat overid" after the GMM estimation command directs the program to compute the number of overidentifying restrictions (r), the *J* test statistic, and the relevant tail area for the $\chi^2(r)$ distribution. For the Angrist-Krueger model, this is:

```
. estat overid

  Test of overidentifying restriction:
  Hansen's J chi2(29) =  24.653 (p = 0.6961)
```

Thus, the null hypothesis (that all 40 population moment conditions, including the 29 overidentifying restrictions, are all valid) is not particularly close to being rejected in this particular case.

Hansen's *J* test is in such common use that it is important to know about it and to report its *p*-value in practice, lest one appear ignorant. But this test is actually of only very limited value: A failure to reject the null hypothesis – as in the present instance – means almost nothing, as the test is known to have rather low power. (That is, it often fails to reject the null hypothesis, even though the null hypothesis is false.) Moreover, even when the test *does* reject the null hypothesis, this rejection is usually not very informative, because the test only indicates that *something* is amiss with the model specification – for example, it gives no indication as to which moment conditions are problematic.[35]

Three salient features to this example are important to discuss at this point. First, note that the more efficient (and more sophisticated) GMM estimation results are not in this case substantially different from the 2SLS results. This is sometimes – but not always – the case with GMM estimation. Unfortunately, one cannot be sure of that without estimating the model both ways. Then, too, GMM is sometimes the *only* way to estimate the model parameters – as with the estimation of economic models characterized as in Equation 19-15.[36]

The second feature to point out is that the actual trouble involved in applying this more sophisticated – and arguably preferable – econometric technique is actually very minor. That is often the case, both with GMM and with other advanced techniques. This is because these estimators are often already implemented in commercially available software (such as Stata) or in freeware (such as *R*); other advanced techniques are available as user-written add-ons to such programs. Clearly, the issue at that point is knowing about the existence of the technique and enough about it so as to be able to apply it intelligently; hopefully the material presented in the chapters here is helpful in that regard.

Finally, note that – with GMM estimation – the scalar algebra which has formed the backbone of the present treatment has reached its limit. For the one-parameter two-instrument IV regression model of Equation 19-16 – which is arguably the simplest nontrivial GMM application imaginable – deriving the optimal moment-deviation weights which are at the heart of the GMM estimator is too complicated, using scalar algebra, to yield much insight.

Consequently, this is a good place to stop with the present exposition of the theory and practice of econometrics. There is a great deal of econometrics beyond what has been covered here; Chapter 20 addresses this, among other issues.

[35] See Exercise 19-8. Relatedly, in new research, Ashley and Parmeter (2011) show how to quantify the sensitivity of GMM inference to likely failures in the model assumptions underlying the GMM population moment conditions. In particular, this work shows how to calculate the minimum-length vector of instrument-error correlations such that a GMM-based inference (like that of Angrist and Krueger on the edu_i coefficient) is no longer significant at, say, the 1% level. This sensitivity analysis finds that the Angrist-Krueger result is quite fragile with respect to minor instrument flaws and also indicates that the inference is much more sensitive to flaws in some of the instruments – e.g., $qtr320_i$ and $qtr321_i$ – than to others. See also Footnotes 12-2 and 12-13, and also discussions related to sensitivity analysis in Sections 20.2 and 20.3. Ashley, R., and C. Parmeter (2011), "Sensitivity Analysis of GMM Inference" can be found at Web site ashleymac.econ.vt.edu/working_papers/Ashley_Parmeter_Credible_GMM.pdf.

[36] For now. But GMM in general has some unlovely properties – e.g., bias and imprecision in modest samples, especially when incorporating relatively large numbers of weak instruments in its moment conditions. Consequently, research in this area continues and new techniques which transcend GMM are under development. The most likely replacement for GMM (in the next five to ten years) is some variation on Generalized Empirical Likelihood (GEL) modeling. Note that in equations like 19-18 and 19-22, the sums quantifying the deviations of the sample moment conditions from the corresponding population moment conditions weight each of the N sample observations equally, with weight $(1/N)$. In GEL these weights are constrained only to add up to one, allowing for another level at which the model parameter estimation can be optimized. Some recent references to look at are Newey and Smith (2004), Newey and Windmeijer (2010), and Eryűrűk (2010). Newey, W., and R. J. Smith (2004), "Higher-Order Properties of GMM and Generalized Empirical Likelihood Estimators," *Econometrica* 72, 219–55. Newey, W., and F. Windmeijer (2010), "GMM with Many Weak Moment Conditions," *Econometrica 77*, 687–719. Eryűrűk, G. (2010), "The Time-Series and Cross-Section Asymptotics of Empirical Likelihood Estimators in Dynamic Panel Models," Instituto Tecnológico Autónomo de México, mimeo.

KEY TERMS

For each term or concept listed below, provide a working definition or explanation:

Curve-Fitting vs. OLS Estimation of Parameterized Conditional Mean
Likelihood of Observing Sample Data as Function of Parameter Values
Log-Likelihood Function vs. Likelihood Function
Properties of MLE Estimators
Likelihood Ratio Test
Marginal Effects
Method of Moments Estimation
Generalized Method of Moments Estimation
Sample Moment Conditions vs. Population Moment Conditions
Optimal GMM Weights
Two-Step vs. Multi-Step GMM Estimation
Hansen's J Test

EXERCISES

19-1. Using the no-intercept Bivariate Regression Model specified as Equation 19-1 and the log-likelihood function for the sample data derived as Equation 19-6:

a. Calculate $\partial L(y_i \dots y_N; \hat{\beta}^{guess}, \sigma^2, x_1 \dots x_N)/\partial\hat{\beta}_{guess}$ and set the resulting expression to zero to obtain $[\hat{\beta}^{MLE}]^*$, the maximum likelihood estimate of β. Then state $\hat{\beta}$,^{MLE} the maximum likelihood estimator of β. How does this estimator relate to $\hat{\beta}^{OLS}$?

b. Obtain the asymptotic sampling distribution of $\hat{\beta}^{MLE}$ using the general results given in Section 19.1, just after Equation 19-9. {Hint: Rewriting the log-likelihood function in terms of $Y_1 \dots Y_N$ instead of $y_1 \dots y_N$ and in terms of β instead of $\hat{\beta}^{guess}$ yields

$$L(Y_1 \dots Y_N;\ \beta,\ \sigma^2,\ x_1 \dots x_N) = -\frac{N}{2}\ln(2\pi\sigma^2) - \frac{1}{2\sigma^2}\sum_{i=1}^{N}(Y_i - \beta x_i)^2$$

The first partial derivative of this function is very similar to the result in part a; the required second partial derivative is obtained by simply taking another partial derivative with respect to β. Calculating the expectation is trivial in this case because the resulting expression does not depend on the random variables $U_1 \dots U_N$.}

19-2. Again use the no-intercept Bivariate Regression Model specified as Equation 19-1, but now drop the assumption that σ^2 is known and address the following questions:

a. Calculate $\partial L(y_i \dots y_N; \hat{\beta}^{guess}, \hat{\sigma}^2_{guess}, x_1 \dots x_N)/\partial\hat{\beta}_{guess}$ and set the resulting expression to zero to obtain $[\hat{\beta}^{MLE}]^*$, the maximum likelihood estimate of β. Then state $\hat{\beta}^{MLE}$, the maximum likelihood estimator of β. How does this estimator relate to $\hat{\beta}^{OLS}$?

b. Calculate $\partial L(y_i \dots y_N; \hat{\beta}^{guess}, \hat{\sigma}^2_{guess}, x_1 \dots x_N)/\partial\hat{\sigma}^2_{guess}$ and set the resulting expression to zero to obtain $[\hat{\sigma}^2_{MLE}]^*$, the maximum likelihood estimate of σ^2. Then state $\hat{\sigma}^2_{MLE}$, the maximum likelihood estimator of $\hat{\sigma}^2_{MLE}$. How does this estimator relate to the OLS estimator of the model error variance in the no-intercept case, $S^2 \equiv [1/(N\!-\!1)] \sum_{i=1}^{N} (Y_i - \hat{\beta}^{OLS} x_i)^2$? Exercise 7-12b shows that S^2 is an unbiased estimator for σ^2 in this model; what does this result imply about the unbiasedness of $\hat{\sigma}^2_{MLE}$?

c. As in Exercise 19-1b, Equations 19-5 and 19-6 imply that the log-likelihood of the variables $Y_1 \ldots Y_N$, given the fixed (albeit unknown) parameter values β and σ^2, is the random variable

$$L(Y_1 \ldots Y_N;\ \beta,\ \sigma^2,\ x_1 \ldots x_N) = -\frac{N}{2}\ln(2\pi) - \frac{N}{2}\ln(\sigma^2) - \frac{1}{2\sigma^2}\sum_{i=1}^{N}(Y_i - \beta x_i)^2$$

Calculate the mixed second partial derivative of $L(Y_1 \ldots Y_N;\ \beta,\ \sigma^2,\ X_1 \ldots x_N)$:

$$\frac{\partial^2 L(Y_1 \ldots Y_N;\ \beta,\ \sigma^2, x_1 \ldots x_N)}{\partial\beta\partial\sigma^2}$$

and take the expected value of this expression (over $U_1 \ldots U_N$) to confirm that this expectation is zero. This result implies that $\hat{\beta}^{MLE}$ and $\hat{\sigma}^2_{MLE}$ are asymptotically uncorrelated.[37]

d. Because $\hat{\beta}^{MLE}$ and $\hat{\sigma}^2_{MLE}$ are asymptotically uncorrelated, the asymptotic variance of $\hat{\beta}^{MLE}$ can be obtained from the expression

$$\frac{-1}{E[\partial^2 L(Y_1 \ldots Y_N;\ \beta,\ \sigma^2,\ x_1 \ldots x_N)/\partial\beta^2]}$$

and the asymptotic variance of $\hat{\sigma}^2_{MLE}$ can be obtained from the expression:[38]

$$\frac{-1}{E[\partial^2 L(Y_1 \ldots Y_N;\ \beta,\ \sigma^2,\ x_1 \ldots x_N)/\partial(\sigma^2)^2]}$$

Obtain these two second partial derivatives and take their expectations, over $U_1 \ldots U_N$. Use these results to state the asymptotic sampling distributions of $\hat{\beta}^{MLE}$ and $\hat{\sigma}^2_{MLE}$.

Because $\hat{\beta}^{MLE}$ and $\hat{\sigma}^2_{MLE}$ are both maximum likelihood estimators, they are both asymptotically efficient. (Under mild additional assumptions, all maximum likelihood estimators have this property.) It is possible to take this argument farther, however. In particular, the information matrix results obtained in parts c and d above can be used to prove

[37] This result is important because minus one times the expectation of this mixed second partial derivative is the off-diagonal element of what is called the "information matrix." (The information matrix is two-dimensional in the present instance, because there are only two coefficients.) It is the off-diagonal element of the *inverse* of this matrix which equals the asymptotic covariance of $\hat{\beta}^{MLE}$ and $\hat{\sigma}^2_{MLE}$, but the fact that this off-diagonal element is zero implies that both the information and its inverse are diagonal. Consequently, the reciprocals of the two diagonal elements of the information matrix are the diagonal elements of the inverse of the information matrix – i.e., the two asymptotic variances obtained in part d. See Footnote 19-6.

[38] Because the information matrix is diagonal, the diagonal elements of its inverse are just the reciprocals of its diagonal elements. See Footnote 19-37.

(fairly easily) that $\hat{\beta}^{MLE}$ is efficient in finite samples and to prove – not so easily – that and $\hat{\sigma}^2_{MLE}$ also is efficient in finite samples.[39]

It was shown in Exercise 6-11f that $\hat{\beta}^{OLS}$ is a BLU estimator for β in this model. BLUness is a weaker property than efficiency. On the other hand, the derivation in Exercise 6-11f did not require that the U_i be normally distributed. This normality assumption is explicitly needed here, in contrast, in order to write out the log-likelihood function. Thus, a stronger assumption regarding the model errors yields a stronger optimality property for the estimator.

19-3. The parameters $\beta_1 \ldots \beta_4$ in a model have been estimated, using a large sample, with maximum likelihood estimation (MLE). This yielded a value of -6.23 for the log-likelihood function.

a. Suppose that one wants to test the null hypothesis $H_o : \beta_2 = 0$ and therefore repeats the maximization of the log-likelihood function, restricting $\hat{\beta}_2^{guess}$ to equal zero. The maximum value of the log-likelihood function falls to -7.80. At what p-value can the null hypothesis be rejected? What is the implicit alternative hypothesis?

b. Suppose that one wants to test the joint null hypothesis $H_o : \beta_2 = 0$ and $\beta_3 = 2\beta_4 + 1$. How would one impose this pair of restrictions on the maximization of the log-likelihood function? Suppose that, on imposing these restrictions, the maximum value of the log-likelihood function falls to -8.80. At what p-value can the null hypothesis be rejected? What is the implicit alternative hypothesis?[40]

19-4. Rewrite the log-likelihood function of Equation 19-6 to accommodate heteroscedasticity of the particular form $\text{var}(U_i) = \sigma^2 z_i^\delta$, with both σ^2 and $z_1 \ldots z_N$ fixed and given. (The variables $Z_1 \ldots Z_N$ might be the population of country i or a gender dummy variable for individual i.) How can one estimate δ? What properties would the maximum likelihood estimator of δ have? How can one test the null hypothesis that the original model errors are homoscedastic? Supposing that z_i is the square of the population of country i, what value of δ corresponds to modeling the original variables in *per capita* terms?

19-5. Starting from Equation 19-18, take the indicated derivative of $g(\hat{\beta}^{guess}; \lambda_{qq})$ with respect to $\hat{\beta}^{guess}$ and set it equal to zero. Explicitly solve this equation – taking the sample data and the penalty-weight parameter λ_{qq} as given – for the expression given in Equations 19-19 and 19-20 for $\left[\hat{\beta}^{MM}(\lambda_{qq})\right]*$, the method-of-moments estimate of the parameter β in the regression model of Equation 19-16.

19-6. Augment the minimand in Equation 19-18 to include the cross-term specified in Equation 19-21, take the indicated derivative of $g(\hat{\beta}^{guess}; \lambda_{qq}, \lambda_{zq})$ with respect to $\hat{\beta}^{guess}$, and set it equal to zero. Explicitly solve this equation – taking the sample data and the penalty-weight parameters λ_{qq} and λ_{zq} as given – for the expression given in Equations 19-23 and 19-24 for

[39] In fact, these two asymptotic variances just calculated are what is known as the Cramér-Rao lower bounds on the sampling variance of any unbiased estimator for each of these two parameters. Because the OLS estimator of β is unbiased and has sampling variance equal to this lower bound, this result shows that it is an efficient estimator of β. S^2 is unbiased, but has a sampling variance which exceeds the Cramér-Rao lower bound. However, although the derivation is considerably more involved, it can be shown that no unbiased estimator for σ^2 in this model attains the Cramér-Rao lower bound; consequently, S^2 turns out to be efficient also. See Theil (1971, pp. 384–91) for details. He also states the "mild additional assumptions" alluded to above, but note that these need to also include an additional assumption that the number of coefficients being estimated remains finite as the sample size increases without bound. Theil, H. (1971), *Principles of Econometrics*, Wiley: New York.

[40] A given set of g nonlinear restrictions can be tested in much the same way, so long as they can be solved uniquely to eliminate g of the parameters near the log-likelihood maximum.

$\hat{\beta}^{MM-improved}(\lambda_{qq}, \lambda_{zq})$, the (improved) method-of-moments estimate of the parameter β in the regression model of Equation 19-16.

19-7. In the Angrist and Krueger (1991) data set, respondent number 111,930 was born in 1933 (so that $yr3_{111930}$ is one), is a high school graduate (so that edu_{111930} is 12) and reports log-wages (weekly) as 5.075775. Show that the 2SLS fitting error for this observation is –.76454 and that the two-step GMM fitting error for this observation is −.76369. Describe how each of these fitting errors is used in calculating the optimal weights for quantifying the overall size of the forty moment-deviations. {Hint: These optimal weights are then used in obtaining the second-step and third-step GMM estimates of the model parameters.}

19-8. Suppose that GMM has been used to estimate 14 parameters in a regression model, based on 23 moment restrictions and 14,320 sample observations.

a. How many overidentifying restrictions are there in this model?

b. After estimating this model in Stata, how would one use Hansen's J test to test the null hypothesis that these overidentifying restrictions are valid?

c. Under this null hypothesis (and assuming that a sample length of 14,320 observations is sufficiently large), from what distribution is the test statistic for Hansen's J test drawn?

d. Does one reject the null hypothesis – at the 1% level, say – if the observed value of the test statistic exceeds the 1% critical value for this sampling distribution? Or does one reject this null hypothesis if the observed test statistic fails to exceed this value?

e. If one cannot reject the null hypothesis at even a fairly large significance level – e.g., the 10% level – what can one conclude about the identifying restrictions and the over-identifying restrictions imposed by the model specification?

f. If one *can* reject the null hypothesis at a small significance level – such as the 1% or 0.1% level – what can one conclude about the identifying restrictions and the overidentifying restrictions imposed by the model specification?

Active Learning Exercise 19a: Probit Modeling of the Determinants of Labor Force Participation

Introduction

Labor force participation is the choice an individual makes to be a part of the labor force – i.e, to either work or actively seek paid employment. As this is a binary choice, the probit model introduced in Section 19.2 is well suited to quantifying the impact of explanatory variables on this decision. In this exercise you will use data from the June 2010 Current Population Survey (CPS) to assess the impact of various demographic variables – marital status, gender, educational attainment, and age – on this choice.

Key questions to explore in this exercise are

- Do these variables "matter" in ways that make sense?
- Does probit estimation yield notably different results from those one would have naively obtained by simply applying OLS to the Linear Probability Model?

Your Assignment:

1. Copy the data file ALE19a.csv – available at www.wiley.com/college/ashley – to your hard disk and read it into the econometrics software your course is using. (Or copy ALE19a.dta if you are using Stata.) This file contains 1,000 observations on each of the following variables:[41]

lforce	Dummy variable for labor force participation. Set to one if *PRMLR*=1 ("employed") or *PRMLR*=2 ("unemployed"); set to zero if *PRMLR* = 3 ("not in labor force").
married	Dummy variable for "married with spouse present." Set to one if *PEMARITL* = 1; otherwise set to zero.
male	Dummy variable for gender. Set to one if *PESEX* = 1; otherwise set to zero.
hsgrad	Dummy variable for high school graduates. Set to one if *PEEDUCA* ≥39; otherwise set to zero.
collegegrad	Dummy variable for college graduates. Set to one if *PEEDUCA* ≥43; otherwise set to zero. (So if this variable equals one, then the respondent holds at least a bachelor's degree.)
age	Age of respondent, as recorded in *PRTAGE*.[42]
age_sqr	Squared value of "age" variable.
age20	Dummy variable for age group 16–20 years old; otherwise set to zero. (Variables *age25* ... *age85* are defined analogously.)

2. Estimate a probit model for $lforce_i$, using $marriedi_i$, $male_i$, $hsgrad_i$, and $collegegrad_i$ as explanatory variables. Use the "dprobit" command in Stata so that estimates (and 95% confidence intervals) are computed and displayed for the marginal effects of each explanatory variable. Enter these estimated coefficients (and their estimated standard errors) into Table ALE19a-1 and their estimated confidence intervals into Table ALE19a-2; some results are already entered so as to make the answer format plain. Which of the variables appear to have an impact on the choice to enter the labor force which is statistically significant at the 5% level? Denoting an impact that, on average, raises the probability of entering the labor force by at least 0.10 as "economically significant" and an impact that raises this probability by at least 0.20 as "economically very significant," which of these explanatory variables are economically significant?[43] Do the estimated signs on the effects make sense?

   Repeat the probit analysis, but now controlling for the respondent's age by including age_i in the model as an additional explanatory variable. Does this change the results noticeably? Enter these estimation results into Tables ALE19a-1 and ALE19a-2.

[41] Variable names in capital letters refer to the CPS names; in each case any observations corresponding to "−1 – not in universe" are omitted. The raw data (on variables *PEEDUCA*, *PEMARITL*, *PESEX*, *PRTAGE*, and *PRMLR*) were downloaded from the U.S. Census Bureau Web site (www.census.gov/cps/) and were extracted from the Current Population Survey (Basic, for June 2010) using the "Data Ferrett" application available there. The full data set contains 108,007 usable observations; these data are in files ALE19a_full_sample.csv and ALE19a_full_sample.dta.

[42] This variable is "topcoded" at age 85 starting in April 2004; thus, all respondents with age greater than 85 are coded as being 85 years old.

[43] These designations are just a convenience for this exercise: there is by no means any general agreement on what size change in a marginal effect is economically significant.

Table ALE19a-1 Probit and OLS Coefficient Estimates (with Estimated Standard Errors and with rejection p-value for H_o that the coefficient is zero)

(1,000 observations)		$married_i$	$male_i$	$hsgrad_i$	$collegegrad_i$
Probit estimates:					
	gender/education	$.02 \pm .03$ $p = .506$	$.13 \pm .03$ $p < .0005$	$.25 \pm .04$ $p < .0005$	$.13 \pm .03$ $p < .0005$
	$+ age_i$				
	$+ age_i$ & age_sqr_i				
	$+ age20_i$ ... $age85_i$				
OLS estimates:					
	gender/education				
	$+ age_i$				
	$+ age_i$ & age_sqr_i				
	$+ age20_i$ ... $age85_i$				
(108,007 observations)		$married_i$	$male_i$	$hsgrad_i$	$collegegrad_i$
Probit estimates:					
	gender/education $+ age20_i$ ... $age85_i$	$.016 \pm 004$ $p = .002$	$.139 \pm .003$ $p < .0005$	$.205 \pm .005$ $p < .0005$	$.106 \pm .004$ $p < .0005$
OLS estimates:					
	gender/education $+ age20_i$ ... $age85_i$	$.008 \pm .003$ $p < .0005$	$.102 \pm .002$ $p < .0005$	$.162 \pm .004$ $p < .0005$	$.080 \pm .003$ $p < .0005$

Table ALE19a-2 Probit and OLS Estimated 95% Confidence Intervals

(1,000 observations)		$married_i$	$male_i$	$hsgrad_i$	$collegegrad_i$
Probit estimates:					
	gender/education	[−0.04, 0.08]	[0.07,0.19]	[0.17,0.34]	[0.06, 0.20]
	$+ age_i$				
	$+ age_i$ & age_sqr_i				
	$+ age20_i$ ... $age85_i$				
OLS estimates:					
	gender/education				
	$+ age_i$				
	$+ age_i$ & age_sqr_i				
	$+ age20_i$ ... $age85_i$				
(108,007 observations)		$married_i$	$male_i$	$hsgrad_i$	$collegegrad_i$
Probit estimates:					
	gender/education $+ age20_i$ ... $age85_i$	[.008, .023]	[.133, .146]	[.195, .214]	[.099, .113]
OLS estimates:					
	gender/education $+ age20_i$ ... $age85_i$	[.003, .014]	[.097, .107]	[.155, .169]	[.070, .081]

3. Next check for nonlinearity in the relationship by including age_sqr_i (in addition to age_i) in the model specification. Again, enter these estimation results into Tables ALE19a-1 and ALE19a-2. Is the relationship nonlinear in age? What does this imply about your estimates and conclusions in Question #2?
4. Next check for nonlinearity in the relationship in a more flexible way by including the age category dummy variables ($age20_i$ ... $age85_i$) in the model.[44] Again, enter these estimation results into Tables ALE19a-1 and ALE19a-2. Does this model fit the data better relative to the model using the squared age term? Does this more flexible way of controlling for age change the results notably, relative to those obtained using the squared age term? Does controlling for age in this way notably change the results, relative to those obtained in Question #1, not controlling for age at all?
5. Re-estimate the four regression models above, only using OLS instead of probit estimation, and enter these results into Tables ALE19a-1 and ALE19a-2. Are the results much different from those obtained using probit estimation? Is there any way to know this without estimating the model both ways?
6. The full sample extracted from the June 2010 CPS data set contains 108,007 observations. If your software is capable of handling this amount of data, re-estimate the model both ways – in each case controlling for age using the age-category dummy variables, to confirm the estimates listed in Tables ALE19a-1 and ALE19a-2. In each case, test the null hypothesis that the coefficient on the marriage dummy variable is zero.
   a. Is the marriage variable coefficient statistically significant? Is it economically significant?
   b. In what ways do the parameter estimates from the probit and OLS regressions differ using the full sample?

[44] In Stata one can include the entire set of variables – with less typing (and less chance of a typographical error) – by simply adding "age20-age85" to the regression command.

APPENDIX 19.1: GMM ESTIMATION OF β IN THE BIVARIATE REGRESSION MODEL (OPTIMAL PENALTY-WEIGHTS AND SAMPLING DISTRIBUTION)

The no-intercept Bivariate Regression Model of Equation 19-16 allows for endogeneity in the explanatory variable X_i by using two instruments, Z_i and Q_i. The improved version of the method-of-moments estimator of the slope parameter in this model (β) is given by Equations 19-23 and 19-24:

$$\hat{\beta}^{\text{MM-improved}}(\lambda_{qq}, \lambda_{zq}) = \sum_{i=1}^{N} \tilde{m}_i\{\lambda_{qq}, \lambda_{zq}\} Y_i \tag{A19-1}$$

with estimator weights $\tilde{m}_1\{\lambda_{qq}, \lambda_{zq}\} \dots \tilde{m}_N\{\lambda_{qq}, \lambda_{zq}\}$ given by

$$\tilde{m}_i\{\lambda_{qq}, \lambda_{zq}\} = \frac{z_i\Sigma_{zx} + \lambda_{qq} q_i \Sigma_{qx} + \tfrac{1}{2}\lambda_{zq}\left[z_i\Sigma_{qx} + q_i\Sigma_{zx}\right]}{\Sigma_{zx}^2 + \lambda_{qq}\Sigma_{qx}^2 + \lambda_{zq}\Sigma_{qx}\Sigma_{zx}} \tag{A19-2}$$

The estimate $\left[\hat{\beta}^{\text{MM-improved}}(\lambda_{qq}, \lambda_{zq})\right]^*$ leading to this estimator is given by the equation

$$\left[\hat{\beta}^{\text{MM-improved}}(\lambda_{qq}, \lambda_{zq})\right]^* = \sum_{i=1}^{N} \tilde{m}_i\{\lambda_{qq}, \lambda_{zq}\} y_i \tag{A19-3}$$

(using the observed sample realizations of $Y_1 \dots Y_N$), which is the value of $\hat{\beta}^{\text{guess}}$ which minimizes the weighted penalty function:

$$\begin{aligned} g(\hat{\beta}^{\text{guess}}; \lambda_{qq}, \lambda_{zq}) = {} & \left\{\frac{1}{N}\sum_{i=1}^{N} z_i(y_i - \hat{\beta}^{\text{guess}} x_i)\right\}^2 + \lambda_{qq}\left\{\frac{1}{N}\sum_{i=1}^{N} q_i(y_i - \hat{\beta}^{\text{guess}} x_i)\right\}^2 \\ & + \lambda_{zq}\left\{\frac{1}{N}\sum_{i=1}^{N} z_i(y_i - \hat{\beta}^{\text{guess}} x_i)\right\}\left\{\frac{1}{N}\sum_{i=1}^{N} q_i(y_i - \hat{\beta}^{\text{guess}} x_i)\right\} \end{aligned} \tag{A19-4}$$

Substituting the *optimal* penalty-weights, $\lambda_{zq}^*(\omega_1 \dots \omega_N)$ and $\lambda_{qq}^*(\omega_1 \dots \omega_N)$, into Equations A19-2 and A19-3 yields the GMM estimator of β:

$$\hat{\beta}^{\text{GMM}}(\omega_1 \dots \omega_N) = \sum_{i=1}^{N} \tilde{m}_i\left\{\lambda_{qq}^*(\omega_1 \dots \omega_N),\ \lambda_{zq}^*(\omega_1 \dots \omega_N)\right\} Y_i \tag{A19-5}$$

The derivation of these two optimal-weight functions – $\lambda_{zq}^*(\omega_1 \dots \omega_N)$ and $\lambda_{qq}^*(\omega_1 \dots \omega_N)$ – is beyond the scope of the present treatment. It *is* feasible, however, to quote the standard result for the optimal weight matrix in the general case of a Multiple Regression Model with *j* instruments and to "unpack" this result for the particular special case considered here.[45]

However, this "unpacking" process – indeed, even comprehending the terms in the formula being unpacked – does require some fundamental concepts from linear algebra:

- The definition of a symmetric matrix
- The definition of a diagonal matrix
- The definition of the transpose of a matrix

[45] Derivations of the general results quoted below can be found in a number of places – e.g., Davidson and MacKinnon (2004, Section 7.2); Davidson, R., and J. G. MacKinnon (1993), *Econometric Theory and Methods*, Oxford University Press: Oxford.

- The mechanics of multiplying two matrices to obtain their product
- The definition of the inverse of a matrix

These elements of linear algebra are not covered here, but these topics are described in any standard exposition of the topic, such as Pemberton and Rau (2007, Chapters 11 and 12).[46]

That said, the *optimal* penalty-weights are given by the $j \times j$ matrix Λ:

$$\Lambda = [W^t \operatorname{diag}(\omega_1 \ldots \omega_N) W]^{-1} \tag{A19-6}$$

where the superscript "−1" denotes a matrix inverse and diag $(\omega_1 \ldots \omega_N)$ is the $N \times N$ diagonal matrix whose diagonal elements are the model error variances – i.e., $\operatorname{var}(U_1) \ldots \operatorname{var}(U_N)$ – in Equation 19-16. There are two instruments used in the model analyzed here, so Λ is a 2×2 matrix, and here W is an N×2 matrix whose two columns consist of the data on the two instruments:

$$W = \begin{bmatrix} z_1 & q_1 \\ z_2 & q_2 \\ z_3 & q_3 \\ \ldots & \ldots \\ z_N & q_N \end{bmatrix} \tag{A19-7}$$

Thus, Equation A19-6 can be rewritten

$$\Lambda = \left\{ \begin{bmatrix} z_1 & z_2 & z_3 & \ldots & z_N \\ q_1 & q_2 & q_3 & \ldots & q_N \end{bmatrix} \operatorname{diag}(\omega_1 \ldots \omega_2) \begin{bmatrix} z_1 & q_1 \\ z_2 & q_2 \\ z_3 & q_3 \\ \ldots & \ldots \\ z_N & q_N \end{bmatrix} \right\}^{-1} \tag{A19-8}$$

which, multiplying out the three matrices, is

$$\Lambda = \begin{bmatrix} \sum_{i=1}^{N} \omega_i z_i^2 & \sum_{i=1}^{N} \omega_i z_i q_i \\ \sum_{i=1}^{N} \omega_i z_i q_i & \sum_{i=1}^{N} \omega_i q_i^2 \end{bmatrix}^{-1} \tag{A19-9}$$

The inverse of a symmetric 2×2 matrix is relatively simple:

$$\begin{bmatrix} a & b \\ b & c \end{bmatrix}^{-1} = \begin{bmatrix} \frac{c}{\Delta} & -\frac{b}{\Delta} \\ -\frac{b}{\Delta} & \frac{a}{\Delta} \end{bmatrix} \tag{A19-10}$$

where Δ is the determinant of the matrix, which in this case equals $ac - b^2$.[47]

[46] Pemberton, M., and N. Rau (2007), *Mathematics for Economists*, Manchester University Press: Manchester.

[47] This inverse is easily confirmed: multiply it by the original matrix and the result is just diag(1,1).

Therefore, the optimal weighting matrix Λ can be written

$$\Lambda = \begin{bmatrix} \frac{1}{\Delta}\sum_{i=1}^{N}\omega_i q_i^2 & -\frac{1}{\Delta}\sum_{i=1}^{N}\omega_i z_i q_i \\ -\frac{1}{\Delta}\sum_{i=1}^{N}\omega_i z_i q_i & \frac{1}{\Delta}\sum_{i=1}^{N}\omega_i z_i^2 \end{bmatrix} \tag{A19-11}$$

where Δ is now the determinant of the matrix being inverted in Equation A19-9. This determinant is easy enough to write out, but there is little reason to do so, as Δ cancels out of the expressions for $\lambda_{zq}^*(\omega_1 \dots \omega_N)$ and $\lambda_{qq}^*(\omega_1 \dots \omega_N)$. In particular, letting Λ_{ij} denote the (i, j)th element of Λ, these two penalty-weights are thus[48]

$$\begin{aligned} \lambda_{zq}^*(\omega_1 \dots \omega_N) &= \frac{2\Lambda_{1,2}}{\Lambda_{1,1}} = -\frac{2\sum_{i=1}^{N}\omega_i z_i q_i}{\sum_{i=1}^{N}\omega_i q_i^2} \\ \lambda_{qq}^*(\omega_1 \dots \omega_N) &= \frac{\Lambda_{2,2}}{\Lambda_{1,1}} = \frac{\sum_{i=1}^{N}\omega_i z_i^2}{\sum_{i=1}^{N}\omega_i q_i^2} \end{aligned} \tag{A19-12}$$

The above expressions for $\lambda_{zq}^*(\omega_1 \dots \omega_N)$ and $\lambda_{qq}^*(\omega_1 \dots \omega_N)$ are to be substituted into Equations 19-27 and 19-28 to yield $\hat{\beta}^{\mathrm{GMM}}(\omega_1 \dots \omega_N)$.

Having gone to this much trouble to calculate the matrix Λ, it is worthwhile noting that – under the assumptions of Equation 19-16 – the asymptotic distribution of $\hat{\beta}^{\mathrm{GMM}}(\omega_1 \dots \omega_N)$ is given by:

$$\sqrt{N}\left(\hat{\beta}^{\mathrm{GMM}}(\omega_1 \dots \omega_N) - \beta\right) \Rightarrow N\left(0, \sigma_{\hat{\beta}}^2\right) \tag{A19-13}$$

where

$$\begin{aligned} \sigma_{\hat{\beta}}^2 &= \begin{bmatrix} \frac{1}{N}\Sigma_{zx} & \frac{1}{N}\Sigma_{qx} \end{bmatrix} \Lambda \begin{bmatrix} \frac{1}{N}\Sigma_{zx} \\ \frac{1}{N}\Sigma_{qx} \end{bmatrix} \\ &= \Lambda_{1,1}\left(\frac{1}{N}\Sigma_{zx}\right)^2 + 2\Lambda_{1,2}\left(\frac{1}{N}\Sigma_{zx}\right)\left(\frac{1}{N}\Sigma_{qx}\right) + \Lambda_{2,2}\left(\frac{1}{N}\Sigma_{qx}\right)^2 \end{aligned} \tag{A19-14}$$

and where Σ_{zx} and Σ_{qx} are defined – as in Equations 19-20, 19-24, and 19-28 – as $\sum_{j=1}^{N} z_j x_j$ and $\sum_{j=1}^{N} q_j x_j$, respectively.

---

[46] The factor of two in the expression for $\lambda_{zq}^*(\omega_1 \dots \omega_N)$ comes about because the cross-term in A19-4 occurs twice in the matrix version, which is a quadratic form in the matrix Λ. The same thing happens in Equation A19-14.

20

Concluding Comments

20.1 THE GOALS OF THIS BOOK

If the reader has now completed at least one pass through the chapters of this book, then we are at the end of a substantial intellectual journey together. The point of this enterprise has been to introduce the reader to the theory and practice of modern econometrics and empirical analysis, basically following the dictum: "Everything should be made as simple as possible, but no simpler."[1]

The scope of the coverage here – while actually quite broad – has been limited in two notable ways. First, several empirically relevant areas of econometrics were omitted, notably non-parametric regression, Bayesian methods, "spatial" regression modeling, and much of the "limited dependent variables" area. A discussion of some of these topics might find its way into a subsequent edition of this book. Second, the exposition here has intentionally eschewed the use of matrix algebra in favor of analyzing in models which are sufficiently simple that they can be analyzed in depth in a very transparent way, using ordinary (scalar) algebra. The insights gained in this way were then extended heuristically to more complex empirical settings.

With just a few exceptions, this didactic strategy has been extremely effective. For example, there has been a good deal of ferment in applied econometrics recently, sparked by an article – Angrist and Pischke (2010) – basically celebrating the progress made in the last decade or so using data sets intentionally collected with subsequent empirical analysis in mind, in some cases using experimental or quasi-experimental methods. The ensuing papers in response to Angrist and Pischke make it quite plain that there is widespread disagreement with regard to (among other things) the value of using robust (White-Eicker) standard error estimates in regression analysis.[2] The derivation and meaning of robust standard error estimates were discussed in Section 10.7, without any use of the matrix algebra which would be needed for a formal derivation. Yet the three key points necessary for an intelligent understanding of this technique were clearly brought out:

1. Robust standard error estimators can provide consistent standard error estimates (and hence asymptotically valid inference machinery) even where the model errors are heteroscedastic in a manner whose form is completely unknown.

[1] This approximate restatement of Occam's Razor is widely mis-attributed to Albert Einstein. Einstein did express somewhat similar sentiments, but never – to be precise – quite this one: see a discussion by Will Fitzgerald at www.entish.org/wordpress/?p=638 for details.

[2] These responses appear in the *Journal of Economic Perspectives* immediately following the Angrist and Pischke (2010) article. Angrist, J. D., and J. Pischke (2010), "The Credibility Revolution in Empirical Economics: How Better Research Design is Taking the Con out of Econometrics," *Journal of Economic Perspectives 24*, pp. 3–30.

2. Their validity, on the other hand, essentially rests on using the squared fitting errors as proxies for the squared model errors, the appropriateness of which (from Section 10.2) rests on the consistency of the parameter estimation used to obtain those fitting errors.[3]
3. Further, while coping with heteroscedasticity effectively is certainly a good thing, the very best response to an observation of notable discrepancies between the robust and the ordinary standard errors is to view this as a signal from Mother Nature that significant nonlinearity and/or heterogeneity in the data's actual generating mechanism has likely been left unmodeled.[4] In that case there are model improvements potentially available whose importance likely dwarfs the inference accuracy increase that is obtained from the robust standard errors – which also (per point two above) might not even be consistent in that circumstance.

On the other hand, this strategy of eliminating the need for linear algebra by thoroughly examining very simple models basically "hit the wall" in Chapter 19: there is no way to get around the fact that a reasonably complete derivation of the GMM estimator requires the liberal use of linear algebra.[5] This is the point, then, where it is sensible to end the present treatment and transfer the reader to one of a number of textbooks – e.g., Davidson and MacKinnon (2004) or Greene (2007)[6] – which present econometrics almost exclusively in terms of linear algebra. In that way one gets the best of both worlds.

While an appropriate simplicity has been a conscious goal throughout this book, complications and sophistication have clearly not been entirely avoided in the foregoing chapters.[7] The idea here, however, is that such acumen is not desirable in and of itself. Rather, it is necessary and useful as a means to an end, where that end is the ability to produce high-quality empirical results.

And, finally, "quality" is what it is all about: regardless of whether the "it" is the efficiency of one's parameter estimates, the meaningfulness of the p-values one estimates for the relevant hypothesis tests, or – for that matter – any other part of one's life. After all, one of the key points raised in the Chapter 3 discussion of the possible properties of a parameter estimator is that there is no real problem in producing low-quality results. Obtaining low-quality results is very easy!

For example, it is no trouble to extend the zero-variance estimator of the mean of a normally distributed variate – denoted $\hat{\mu}_a$ in Table 3-1 of Section 3.7 – to regression analysis: one can simply use the estimator $\tilde{\beta} = 15$ as one's estimate for all regression parameters. This estimator is extremely simple and very convenient: no messing around with data entry or with sophisticated econometric theory is required. We can all agree, however, that this "just use 15" estimator in general produces low-quality results. Alternatively, as a less extreme example, one can just enter one's sample data into a program like Stata, pick a reasonable-sounding estimation command, and copy out the resulting estimation output – without further consideration as to what assumptions underlie the estimates and inference results produced by this command or as to whether one's data and regression model specification are remotely consistent with those assumptions. And in fact – whether through fear, ignorance, or laziness – that is what a lot of people do.

[3] See Equations 10-20 to 10-25, and especially Equation 10-22.

[4] Sims (2010) emphasizes this point also. Sims, C. A. (2010), "But Economics Is Not an Experimental Science," *Journal of Economic Perspectives 24,* pp. 59–68.

[5] Linear algebra is also necessary for deriving the small-sample distribution of the variance estimator S^2, but this could be (and was) replaced in Sections 4.5 and 7.7 by a reasonably useful large-sample argument. Similarly, in Chapter 9 the restriction to scalar algebra implied that the OLS parameter estimator weights could be explicitly stated (Equation 9-17) for at most the three-variable model; but the derivation of the OLS estimator for the full model was still feasible and informative. By way of contrast, scalar algebra is simply not up to the task of deriving the GMM optimal moment-weighting matrix, even for the simplest possible nontrivial IV regression problem, Equation 19-16.

[6] Greene, W. H. (2007), *Econometric Analysis*, Prentice-Hall: Upper Saddle River, NJ.

[7] They have often been relegated to footnotes, however.

In contrast, the fundamental goal here, as noted at the outset of this section, has been to make things as simple as possible – albeit no simpler! – so as to dramatically reduce the intellectual (and emotional) cost of producing reasonably high-quality results. What constitutes such high-quality results? And what does one need to do in order to obtain them in real life?

In order to convince others (and, most importantly, oneself) that the data have been well-analyzed, one wants to obtain one's parameter estimates from estimators which are credibly at least consistent (in happier circumstances, asymptotically efficient) and one wants to obtain one's inferences from estimated sampling distributions which are at least asymptotically valid. This does not generally happen by accident or without some concerted, engaged effort – even if the sample data were generated/collected in a conscientious and modern fashion. On the other hand, obtaining a reasonable approximation to consistent parameter estimation and asymptotically valid inference is not hopelessly difficult either: one can make a pretty good job of it by systematically diagnostically checking one's model and using the results to improve its specification.

20.2 DIAGNOSTIC CHECKING AND MODEL RESPECIFICATION

The basic idea of diagnostic checking is first introduced in Sections 4.8 and 4.9 in the simple context of estimation/inference on the mean of a normally distributed variate. Later on, Chapter 10 is entirely devoted to diagnostically checking a Multiple Regression Model and to using the insights thus gained to improve the model by appropriately respecifying it. This material is expanded in Chapters 13 and 14 to address the dynamic specification issues arising in time-series models with possibly autocorrelated model errors. At that point the entire diagnostic checking procedure is summarized in a very organized fashion in Table 14-3 of Section 14.6. This diagnostic checking process is sensible and feasible – it is also reasonably effective at producing what might be called "statistically adequate" models. Diagnostic checking is especially effective insofar as one uses it to focus on model respecification, as distinct from mere model criticism.

This diagnostic checking mainly consists of making some plots and estimating some auxiliary regressions – all of which are easy enough to do using typical econometric software. And it involves thinking, in an engaged and responsive way, about what these results mean and about what, perhaps, one should do about any problems that have thereby surfaced. This process involves a good deal of decision-making under uncertainty, with no explicit stopping criterion – just like most significant activities in life. As in these other life activities, one's effective marginal product of labor in this endeavor declines as more and more time and effort are expended. Consequently, there is a personally and situationally optimal (or "reasonable") amount of diagnostic checking and model respecification activity appropriate to each empirical project – and this optimal amount is clearly not the same in each instance.

Thus, "high-quality" does not mean "perfect." Indeed, "medium-quality" is sometimes optimal. And – regardless of the amount of effort expended – one can never be certain that one's model is okay – or even that one has "done enough." Again, this is just like all those other significant activities in life. On the other hand, it seems obvious that "none" is neither an optimal nor a reasonable amount.

Because Table 14-3 does a good job of summarizing the steps in a fairly complete diagnostic checking effort, that material will not be repeated at his point. Several potential model problems are more challenging to check (or ameliorate) than others, however. These each merit additional comment here:

- **Omitted Variables**
  This problem is discussed in Section 9.7 and again – and in more depth – later in this chapter, in the "Big Mistake #4" portion of Section 20.3. In the most favorable variety of this predicament, one can simply try including the omitted variables – ideally, as a group – into the model and

testing an appropriate joint null hypothesis as to whether they "belong." Of course, that advice is beside the point if these variables were omitted in the first place because one failed to think of them or if the requisite sample data on these variables are unavailable.

Particularly in the case of data unavailability, however, one can at least be explicitly aware – and make one's reader aware – of the potential (or likely) impact of these omissions on the *interpretation* of one's coefficient estimates. In this context, recall that the population coefficient on the *j*th explanatory variable in the model (i.e., X_{ij}) amounts to $\partial E\left[Y_i | x_{i,1} \ldots x_{i,k}\right] / \partial x_{i,j}$, the partial derivative of the conditional mean of the dependent variable with respect to the realized value of this explanatory variable – *holding the other explanatory variables fixed and averaging over all of the omitted variables.* Omitting some explanatory variables is basically all right then, so long as one keeps in mind what variables are being held fixed – or "conditioned upon," or "controlled for" – and what variables are not. And, crucially, so long as one recognizes that included explanatory variables will do their best to "proxy" for omitted ones to the maximum extent that they can. It is this proxying that leads to biased and inconsistent parameter estimators, if one is omitting variables which are correlated with included ones. That proxying is actually a good thing when one is making a forecasting model, but it is something to keep always in mind if parameter inference is the underlying purpose of the modeling activity.[8]

- **Sample Length Sufficiency**

  Per the results in Chapters 11 through 19, real-world empirical results are virtually always (at best) only asymptotically justified. Consequently, a perennial worry is whether the sample length is sufficiently large that the relevant asymptotic concepts (consistency, asymptotic variances, asymptotic efficiency) are meaningful. The diagnostic checking summarized in Table 14-3 incorporates one useful approach to resolving this always challenging worry, by examining the degree to which the model results are stable across subsets of the full sample. If the sample is too small for the large-sample results to apply, then one might expect this to observably worsen in using a collection of smaller sample subsets instead. On the other hand, results from such subsamples may be too imprecise to speak effectively to the issues and, in any case, one could worry even more about the validity of *those* results, as they are arising from the application of large-sample methods to what are, in essence, even smaller samples. If the results do fall apart in subsamples, one is left hanging as to whether maybe the full sample is nevertheless sufficient.

  Simulation methods – as covered in Section 11.8 – provide another useful approach. Because some aspects of it have been incorporated into mainstream econometric packages, simulation is nowadays no longer anything like as much trouble as it used to be. These methods allow one to vary the sample length at will, in a setting which is similar to that which generated the actual sample *if* one's estimated model is any good. One can in that context directly observe how the asymptotic variances compare to the actual variances, etc. Where the (now often modest) amount of additional trouble is warranted, this can be a very useful exercise, but the reader is cautioned that simulation methods have problems of their own: they are no panacea.[9]

[8] Note also the supposedly robust standard error estimates and otherwise-efficient parameter estimation are of no avail if the parameter estimates are biased and inconsistent. Nor does restricting oneself to experimental or quasi-experimental sample data necessarily eliminate this problem.

[9] In particular, recall that the generated model errors used to drive the simulations will necessarily be independently and identically distributed – i.e., IID – so simulations will be of very limited value unless the model credibly yields IID errors. (Or unless one uses one of the more sophisticated bootstrap methods cited in Footnote 11-29.) More troublingly, the finite-sample properties of some important econometric estimators – notably, ones based on instrumental variables – are so poor that simulation results based on them yield nonsense results; see Footnotes 11-30 and 11-39. This may reflect more on the value of these estimators than on the simulation methods; nevertheless, it limits our ability to do this kind of check in one of the circumstances where it would be most helpful.

- **Instrument Validity**
  Instrumental variables (IV) regression is described in Chapter 12. This is the key econometric technique for dealing with endogeneity in the explanatory variables – due to measurement error, to joint determination, or to the omitted variables alluded to above. However, IV estimation yields consistent parameter estimation and asymptotically valid inference machinery only if all of the instruments used are "valid" – that is, uncorrelated with the model errors. But, even for large samples, these model errors are unobservable unless one has consistent parameter estimates. Sounds circular, doesn't it? And it is: if the model has g endogenous explanatory variables and uses j instruments, then one must assume that g of the instruments are valid in order to test the validity of the remaining g–j instruments.[10]

  So diagnostically checking the instrument validity assumptions is effectively impossible. Consequently, the best that one can do along these lines is to check the sensitivity of one's key inferential conclusions (p-values and the like) to likely levels of correlation between the instruments and the model error term. New work is just now coming out – i.e., Ashley and Parmeter (2011) – which makes this sort of sensitivity analysis feasible for GMM-based IV regression; this work is described in a bit more detail in the final portion of Section 20.3.[11]

Diagnostic checking is necessary in order to credibly obtain high-quality results and, despite the difficulties discussed above, it is both reasonably easy and reasonably effective. Thus, the diagnostic checking described and recommended here is clearly worth doing – with an intensity and to an extent which is situationally specific. But it is also by no means perfectly effective, and some aspects of a regression model are not so feasible to check. In that context, it seems worthwhile to end by counseling the reader with regard to avoiding the four "Big Mistakes."

20.3 THE FOUR "BIG MISTAKES"

Of all the things that can go wrong in regression analysis, there are just four "Big Mistakes." These are not new items: all of these issues have already been discussed at some point (or points) above – in some cases, at considerable length! Still, it is these four mistakes which make a really big difference in the quality of the results; indeed, they can lead to disastrously poor results. And all four of them are reasonably avoidable. Consequently, this exposition will end by highlighting and discussing each:

- **Big Mistake #1: The Danger of Neglecting Trends and/or Strong Serial Dependence**
  All trended time-series will appear to be closely related. Even a simple scatterplot will be completely flummoxed by unrelated (but trended) data; this was amply illustrated in Active Learning Exercise 1d, available at www.wiley.com/college/ashley. Moreover, even the temporary "local" trends caused by strong serial dependence in untrended time-series will yield highly distorted parameter inference results unless this serial dependence is recognized and modeled.[12]

[10] See Keane (2010, Footnote 10). Moreover, one must explicitly specify which g of the instruments are being assumed valid in order to obtain informative results. A general test of these g–j "overidentifying restrictions" – such as the Hansen J test described in Section 19.4 – only requires that some unspecified set of g instruments are valid, but the results of such tests are not very useful: if the null hypothesis (that all j instruments are valid) is rejected, then all that one can really conclude is that the model is somehow misspecified. And, since these tests do not have very large power to reject when the null hypothesis is false, a failure to reject does not really allow one to conclude anything at all. Keane, M. P. (2010), "Structural vs. Atheoretic Approaches in Econometrics," *Journal of Econometrics 156*, pp. 3–20.

[11] See Ashley, R. and C. Parmeter (2011), "Sensitivity Analysis of GMM Inference," available at Web site ashleymac.econ.vt .edu/working_papers/Ashley_Parmeter_Credible_GMM.pdf.

[12] See Section 13.3 for an illustrative example. Similar issues will arise in "spatial" models where an observation in one location is strongly related to its value in adjacent locations, unless this dependence is appropriately modeled.

This mistake is easy to recognize: the plots and auxiliary regressions of the usual diagnostic checking procedure will clearly signal this set of problems – if the diagnostic checking is actually done. And, once recognized, it is not usually difficult to fix this sort of problem: one simply respecifies the regression equation with trend terms or dynamics. Of course it is always possible to respecify the model dynamics incorrectly, but the "Big Mistake" will generally have been averted.[13]

- **Big Mistake #2: The Tyranny of the Vocal (but Temporary) Minority**
  Both econometrically and economically, what is most important and meaningful to recognize and quantify are what one might call "stable statistical regularities." These are relationships which are broadly characteristic of the entire sample data set, rather than apparent relationships which are only valid for a couple of observations or whose intensity/character drifts around substantially over differing parts of the sample.

  A few unusual fluctuations in $X_{i,j}$ (the *j*th explanatory variable) are usually a good thing. These are generically the result of what one might call "natural experiments" and sharpen the parameter estimates: i.e, such fluctuations in $X_{i,j}$ reduce the sampling variance in a parameter estimator such as $\hat{\beta}_j^{OLS}$.[14] On the other hand, it is well to be aware of a very unusual fluctuation in either the dependent variable or in an explanatory variable like $X_{i,j}$, so that one at least has the opportunity to question whether this is a valid observation, as opposed to a bizarre, never-to-be-repeated incident or to a transcription error at some point in the data collection/analysis process.

  In contrast, fluctuation or drift in the coefficient β_j is an unalloyed bad thing: it means that the relationship at issue is itself unstable across the sample. Such instability is generically a symptom of either a misspecified functional form (e.g., per Equation 9-3, the linear approximation to a nonlinear relationship will have an unstable slope), or a symptom of the estimation of an empirical model based on a seriously incomplete or inadequate economic theory. It is also a common symptom of the misbegotten results of overzealous data mining.

  Diagnostic checking looks for influential outliers and parameter instability, so it will alert one to problems of this nature – again, if the diagnostic checking is actually done. Once recognized one can "fix" this sort of problem in a number of different ways – and some work (and judgment) are generally needed in order to choose between them. But, at worst, one will at least then have a good idea of how sensitive which parts of one's results are to what choice one makes in this regard: the "Big Mistake" will have been averted.[15]

- **Big Mistake #3: The Danger of Overextrapolation**
  Out-of-sample prediction – whether from a time-series, panel, or cross-sectional model – is both a sensitive diagnostic check and, in some cases, the primary use of an empirical model.

[13] It may not have been averted if linear dynamics have been included where the actual serial dependence is highly nonlinear – see Section 18.6 – but there is a reasonable chance that the diagnostic checking will pick this up. Also, note that there is an ample literature now on "long memory" (fractionally integrated) time-series models. Per Ashley and Patterson (2010), such models are best viewed as an overly sophisticated response to weak time trends in the data. Ashley, R., and D. M. Patterson (2010), "Apparent Long Memory in Time Series as an Artifact of a Time-Varying Mean: Considering Alternatives to the Fractionally Integrated Model," *MacroeconomicDynamics 14:* 59-87.

[14] For example, see Equation 6-25 for the sampling variance of $\hat{\beta}$OLS in the Bivariate Regression Model.

[15] New work by the author converts one kind of time-series model parameter instability – instability of a regression coefficient across frequency instead of across time – from a problem into an opportunity, by making the frequency dependence analysis simple and easy. Frequency dependence can be closely linked to economic theory, as when the Permanent Income Hypothesis predicts that the marginal propensity to consume in an aggregate consumption function ought to vary with the persistence of an income fluctuation. See Ashley and Verbrugge (2009) and Ashley, Verbrugge, and Tsang (2011). Ashley, R., and R. Verbrugge (2009), "Frequency Dependence in Regression Model Coefficients: An Alternative Approach for Modeling Nonlinear Dynamic Relationships." *Econometric Reviews 28:* 4-20. Ashley, Verbrugge, and Tsang (2011), "Frequency Dependence in a Real-Time Monetary Policy Rule" mimeo. url: ashleymac.econ.vt.edu/working_papers/freq_dependent_realtime_monetary_policy_Jan_2010.pdf.

As with parameter estimates, a model prediction is of little use without an accompanying estimated confidence interval to quantify its uncertainty due to sampling errors. The regression analysis technology itself provides the means to estimate such confidence intervals. For example, Equation 8-23 gives an estimated 95% confidence interval for an out-of-sample prediction of Y_{N+1}, the dependent variable from a Bivariate Regression Model estimated using the sample data $(y_1, x_1) \ldots (y_N, x_N)$, conditional on an observed or assumed value for x_{N+1}. Confidence interval estimates of this sort are extremely useful if the underlying model assumptions have been diagnostically checked. And Equation 8-23 clearly indicates that the 95% confidence interval for Y_{N+1} widens as $|x_{N+1} - \bar{x}|$ increases, where $\bar{x}$ is the sample mean of $x_1 \ldots x_N$. This result appropriately reflects the fact that larger values of $|x_{N+1} - \bar{x}|$ magnify the impact on the prediction errors of any sampling errors in the estimate of the model slope parameter.

Nevertheless, it is still extremely foolhardy to use a predicted value of Y_{N+1} based on any observed or assumed value for x_{N+1} such that $|x_{N+1} - \bar{x}|$ is notably larger than the values of $|x_1 - \bar{x}| \ldots |x_N - \bar{x}|$ observed in the actual sample data set. That is because the use of such a value for x_{N+1} is "betting the farm" on the model assumption that Y_i is in fact a linear function of x_i, so that the value of the population of the slope coefficient (β) is a well-defined constant. This assumption may be a reasonably accurate approximation to reality within the range of sample values of x_i actually observed. And the diagnostic checking can fairly easily spot a failure of this assumption, but only if it is apparent within the observed sample range of x_i values. *The diagnostic checking is inherently unable to detect failures of this assumption which are only substantial outside this range.*

Thus, the estimated confidence interval for Y_{N+1} emphatically does not incorporate any adjustment for uncertainty in the population value of the coefficient β itself: it only quantifies the uncertainty in the predicted value of Y_{N+1} arising from the model error term which will occur in period $N+1$ and arising from the fact that the estimate of the (presumed constant) slope parameter β is based on just these N sample observations. Therefore, while the length of such a confidence interval estimate might not be too far off, if $|x_{N+1} - \bar{x}|$ is notably larger than the observed values of $|x_i - \bar{x}| \ldots |x_N - \bar{x}|$, then the confidence interval for Y_{N+1} could easily be centered on a substantially incorrect value. None of this, of course, is any less problematic in models with multiple (or stochastic) explanatory variables.

In summary, then, diagnostic checking for model nonlinearity is a good and useful thing. And it is both reasonable and useful to estimate confidence intervals for regression model predictions. But relying on such confidence intervals when the prediction depends on an observed or assumed value of any explanatory variable which departs substantially from the sizes observed in the estimation sample is potentially – indeed, likely – a "Big Mistake" and could easily lead to terribly poor results.

- **Big Mistake #4: The Wrongly-Omitted-Variable Trap**

In a sense, *all* regression model deficiencies can be viewed as arising from wrongful omission of one or more explanatory variables from the model. Consequently, this "omitted variables" topic has arisen multiple times – equivalently, but in multiple guises – in Chapters 9 through 19, and even in Section 20.2. Failure to deal with wrongly omitted variables is not typically the source of the worst disasters in empirical analysis: "Big Mistake #1" and "Big Mistake #3" doubtless share that dubious distinction. But it is a common enough cause of very poor results for those who are oblivious with regard to it. And it is also a common source of angst (and, often enough, rather poor results) even for those who *are* aware of it.

In fact, the problem of wrongly omitted variables is a lot like "ageing" in medicine: We know that it is consequential. And we know something about how to detect, prevent, and (to a modest extent) deal with it. But we don't know enough to consider that the problem is really "under control."

As a result, the problem of wrongly omitted variables is still under active investigation. Indeed, some new work in this area by the author helps resolve part of this issue and is consequently briefly described below, in "Tactic #4" and "Tactic #5." Also as a result, this problem – which can easily become a "Big Mistake" if not understood and attended to – merits the more extensive discussion accorded it in this final section.

One useful way to frame this problem is to note – per Section 9.7 – that the explanatory variables which are included in the model will "proxy" for any omitted variables with which they are correlated – leading to biased and inconsistent parameter estimators for these included variables. Another useful frame for the problem is to observe that the model error term, by definition, is the sum of the impacts of all the explanatory variables omitted from the model: that is what the model error term *is*. Therefore, any explanatory variable included in the model which is correlated with an omitted one is inherently correlated with the model error term – i.e., any such explanatory variable is endogenous. (This argument was made in Section 11.5.) Either way, the impact of an omitted variable on the consistency of the model coefficient estimates and on the validity of the inference machinery – even in large samples – can be very substantial. In fact, this impact is worse with a large sample, because that is the context in which the regression results demand (and receive) more credence.

These two formulations of the omitted-variables problem yield a total of five reasonably straightforward ameliorative tactics. None of these tactics "fixes" the problem in the same sense (or to the same degree) that including more dynamic terms in a regression model "fixes" the problems caused by serially correlated model errors. It is fair to say, however, that last two of these tactics, at least, reduce the problem from a potential "Big Mistake" into a transparently quantified limitation on the empirical results achieved. Each of these five tactics is now described in turn.

Omitted-Variables Tactic #1: Include the Omitted Variable

The "proxying" formulation of the problem suggests two solutions: since the problem can be ascribed to an included explanatory variable which is correlated with an omitted one, one can either include the omitted variable in the model or drop the included one. Including the omitted variable certainly resolves the problem. On the other hand, the reason it was omitted in the first place might well be that one either didn't think of it or that the requisite sample data on this variable are unavailable. Clearly, if either of these conditions is the case, including the omitted variable is infeasible.

On the other hand, one oftentimes has a considerable amount of usable information on an omitted variable, even though it is omitted because it is unobservable. Consider, for example, a model explaining an individual's log-wages in terms of education level, such as the Angrist and Krueger (1991) study discussed in Section 12.6. It's a good bet that the education variable is endogenous because such models cannot include an explanatory variable separately measuring the individual's "ability." Yet it is reasonably obvious that ability is positively correlated with both education level and log-wages. Thus, the (included) education level is almost certainly "proxying" for the (wrongly omitted) ability variable in such a way as to bias the estimated coefficient on the education variable upward. One can therefore infer that the "ability" variable – had it been possible to include it in the model – would likely have made a positive coefficient on education level smaller. Consequently, if one does not reject the null hypothesis that the coefficient on education level is zero, then the wrongful omission of the ability variable is likely inconsequential to one's inference. If one *does* reject this null hypothesis, on the other hand, then the omission might well be consequential; in this latter case one still knows quite a bit about the likely omitted variable, but this knowledge is not as useful.

Omitted-Variables Tactic #2: Drop the Problematic Included Variables

This tactic has several undesirable features. For starters, it is not exactly clear which explanatory variables should be dropped, since it is clearly infeasible to check on which explanatory variables are correlated with any important omitted ones, for the same reasons that Tactic #1 is generally infeasible. Suppose, nevertheless, that one strongly suspects that a particular explanatory variable $(X_{i,j})$ is correlated with some omitted explanatory variable. Three problems with dropping $X_{i,j}$ from the model still remain. First, $X_{i,j}$ must surely be notably correlated with the dependent variable (Y_i), or else $X_{i,j}$ didn't belong in the model in the first place. Thus, dropping $X_{i,j}$ from the model must definitely worsen the model's fit to the data, decreasing the precision of any inferential or predictive results the model might otherwise produce with regard to the coefficients on the still-included explanatory variables.[16]

The second problem with dropping $X_{i,j}$ from the model is that the *meaning* of the coefficient on each of the remaining explanatory variables changes, as each one of these is now parameterizing the expected value of Y_i conditional on a different (smaller) set of other explanatory variables. That is not necessarily a fatal flaw for this tactic; this issue will be taken up below, with regard to "Tactic #3."

The third problem with this tactic, however, is often overwhelming: commonly enough, it is estimation and inference with respect to β_j, the coefficient on $X_{i,j}$, which is the point of the analysis in the first place. In that case, dropping $X_{i,j}$ from the model is tantamount to simply giving up. That would certainly be the case if one dropped the education level variable in the log-wages model alluded to above.

Omitted-Variables Tactic #3: Reinterpret the Estimated Coefficients

As noted in Section 20.2 $\beta_1 \ldots \beta_k$ are, by definition, the partial derivatives of the conditional expectation of Y_i with respect to $x_{i,1}$, with respect to $x_{i,2}$, and so forth. Each of these partial derivatives holds all of the other explanatory variables in the model fixed at their realized values. However, this conditional expectation of Y_i is always averaging over the values of all other variables which have any effect on Y_i, but which were not included in the model. What does it mean, then, to have "wrongly omitted" a variable $X_{i,j}$ from a regression model for Y_i? Presumably, this "wrongness" implies that β_j would not equal zero in a model including $X_{i,j}$, which means that variation in $X_{i,j}$ does in fact impact the mean of Y_i conditional on an information set expanded to include realized values of this additional explanatory variable. We also know that this "wrongful omission" is consequential for the coefficients on the already-included explanatory variables to the extent that (and only to the extent that) these other explanatory variables are correlated with the omitted variable, $X_{i,j}$.

Note, however, that the omission of $X_{i,j}$ from the model also changes the meaning of the coefficients on all of the explanatory variables which are still included in the model. These coefficients on the remaining variables are still the partial derivatives of the conditional expectation of Y_i with respect to each of the still-included explanatory variables. But this expectation is now the mean of the distribution of Y_i conditional on the realized values of a smaller set of random variables, which no longer includes $X_{i,j}$. That conditional distribution of Y_i is, in general a different probability distribution than the original conditional distribution, so it will in general have a different mean. In particular, the conditional mean of Y_i no longer depends on the realized value of $X_{i,j}$, and the partial derivatives of this conditional mean are no longer holding $x_{i,j}$ constant: now the values of $X_{i,j}$ are being averaged over in

[16] Of course, highly precise (but inconsistent) estimates and/or predictions are hardly more desirable than imprecise ones, so one might still be better off with the simpler model. See also "Tactic #3."

the expectation itself. In other words, the meaning of the coefficients on the still-included variables – $\beta_1, \ldots, \beta_{j-1}, \beta_{j+1}, \ldots, \beta_k$ – is now different. Consequently, each of these symbols now has a different meaning and could easily (and properly) have a different value than in the model including $X_{i,j}$ as an explanatory variable.

From this perspective, the entire problem with respect to inconsistent parameter estimation when $X_{i,j}$ is "wrongly omitted" from the model is just a misunderstanding based on inadequate notation: properly speaking, the symbols for the population parameters ($\beta_1 \ldots \beta_k$) should themselves each be explicitly labeled with the list of all k explanatory variables which are included in the model, and which are hence included in the conditioning used in defining the conditional mean of Y_i. Thus, $\hat{\beta}_1 \ldots \hat{\beta}_{j-1}$ and $\hat{\beta}_{j+1} \ldots \hat{\beta}_k$ obtained from estimating a model "wrongly" omitting $X_{i,j}$ are consistent estimators – and the inference machinery with respect to hypotheses concerning $\beta_1 \ldots \beta_{j-1}, \beta_{j+1} \ldots \beta_k$ is still asymptotically valid – so long as one correctly interprets these coefficient estimates and the null hypotheses couched in terms of their values.

Such careful interpretation is healthy, informative, and appropriate – where it is not tedious, cluttered, and unnecessarily confusing, of course. In the case where one knows that a probably important explanatory variable has to be omitted from the regression model (due to data unavailability, for example) explicitly labeling and reinterpreting the model coefficients keeps one honest and informative – with both oneself and one's readers. It also converts what would have otherwise been "Big Mistake #4" into what is, at worst, a complication in the discussion of the regression results.

Unfortunately, that complication may well so diminish the economic meaningfulness of the results as to reduce them to pap. For instance, returning to the log-wage model example, one could explicitly note that the estimated coefficient on education level is quantifying how the conditional mean of log-wages varies with education level but not conditioning on ("controlling for" or "holding constant") the individual's ability. Thus, the education level variable is proxying for all of the things (such as ability) that tend to "go along" with an additional year of schooling and is thus quantifying their joint impact on an individual's expected log-wages. As noted above, that careful re-interpretation of the population coefficient on education level is forthcoming and informative. And a consistent estimate of this coefficient is still useful for some purposes. For example, it could be used to predict how much higher the average log wages of a randomly chosen group of individuals with 10 years of schooling will be compared to the average log wages of a randomly chosen group of individuals with, say, eight years of schooling. But this coefficient estimate will at best be silent (and at worst be misleading) if the question is whether an additional two years of education will – even on average – benefit either any particular individual or individuals in general. Thus, either a consistently estimated 95% confidence interval for this reinterpreted coefficient or a rejection of the null hypothesis that this coefficient is zero are of little use in a policy debate as to the benefits of increasing education levels in a community.

Omitted-Variables Tactic #4: Attempt to Fix the Problem Using IV Regression

If one has on hand a sufficient number of reasonably strong and credibly valid instruments for the explanatory variables potentially made endogenous by any wrongly omitted variables, then this endogeneity is readily both detected and corrected: just use two-stage least squares (2SLS) estimation instead of OLS estimation, as described in Chapter 12.

The strength of an instrument can be readily assessed by looking at its contribution to the R^2 of the first-stage regressions. Testing a putative instrument for correlation with the model errors, however, is generally infeasible, because the model fitting errors are good large-sample approximations to the actual model errors only when the model parameter estimators are consistent – e.g., see Equation 10-2. And, of course, consistent parameter estimation is exactly what one doesn't have if IV estimation is necessary and if the validity of the instruments is in doubt.[17]

Until recently one had just two choices at this point. One choice was to "hold one's nose" and hope that the instruments were "valid enough." The other choice was to try out various combinations of explanatory variables and consider whether such changes in the set of other variables being conditioned upon caused the results to change much. Having thought about "Omitted-Variables Tactic #3," the reader will recognize this second option as irrelevant: one *expects* the population value of the coefficient on any particular variable to change as the set of other variables in the model is varied, simply because the meaning of this coefficient is changing. Thus, either variation or stability in possibly inconsistent OLS estimates of these distinct coefficient values is completely beside the point.

Neither of those two choices is remotely satisfying but, as mentioned in Section 20.2, there is now a third option available. It is still true that there is no way to test whether a particular instrument is correlated with the model errors, because these errors are unobserved. What one *can* now do, however, is quantify the sensitivity of any particular hypothesis test rejection p-value to such correlations. In other words, it is not possible to estimate the sizes of the instrument-error correlations, but one can quantify the degree to which likely levels of such correlations *matter* to the particular inference results one cares about most.

In particular, as noted in Chapter 12 and in Sections 19.4 and 20.2, Ashley and Parmeter (2011) show how to calculate the minimal amount of correlation between an instrument (or a set of instruments) and the model errors which suffices to "overturn" any particular inference result – e.g., that is sufficient to cause the rejection p-value for some particular null hypothesis which was below .05 to exceed .05.[18] An inference which is easily overturned – by instrument-error correlations which are small in magnitude, and hence easily envisioned – could be called "fragile." In contrast, one could term a particular inference "robust" if it remains valid (at, say, the 5% level) even when the instruments are correlated with the model errors to a substantial degree – e.g., even with correlations larger than, say, 0.30 in magnitude.

Returning, for example, to the Angrist and Krueger (1991) log-wages study, those authors proposed a set of instruments for their education variable; these instruments – and the arguments for and against their validity – are discussed in Section 12.6. The 2SLS estimate of the coefficient on their years-of-schooling variable obtained using these instruments is $.089 \pm .016$. This estimate is actually larger than the OLS estimate of $.071 \pm .0003$, contrary to what one would expect if a wrongly omitted "ability" variable was biasing the OLS estimator upward. But the difference is not statistically significant, because the weak correlations between the Angrist-Krueger instruments and the schooling variable make the 2SLS estimator relatively imprecise. Most importantly, the crucial null hypothesis – that the coefficient on years-of-schooling is zero – is still easily rejected (with a p-value less than .000005) using the 2SLS estimates.

But are the Angrist-Krueger instruments valid? The arguments against their exact validity – summarized, as noted, in Section 12.6 – have some merit. Nevertheless, it is difficult to imagine

[17] As noted in Footnote 20-10, tests of overidentifying restrictions (such as Hansen's J test, mentioned in Section 19.4) can test the validity of some instruments, but only under the assumption that a sufficient number of the rest are valid – see Keane (2010, Footnote 10).

[18] The fragility or robustness of an inference consisting of a *failure* to reject the null hypothesis can also be assessed using this sensitivity analysis framework. For example, one can calculate the minimal instrument-error correlation magnitude necessary in order to reduce an inference p-value which exceeded 0.01 to a value below 0.01. The calculations themselves are neither complex nor computationally burdensome; they are currently implemented in software written in *R*, but could easily be programmed up in any matrix-oriented language – e.g., *MATLAB* or *GAUSS*. See Footnotes 12-2, 12-13, and 19-33 and also the discussion in Section 20.2.

these instruments being *substantially* correlated with the model error term. But how much such correlation would be needed in order to overturn the Angrist-Krueger inference result with regard to the years-of-schooling variable? That is exactly the kind of question addressed by the Ashley and Parmeter (2011) sensitivity analysis, and – in this particular case – it yields a very clear answer: The Angrist-Krueger result appears to be very strong, but it is actually very fragile with respect to even minor flaws in their instruments. In fact, instrument-error correlations of just 0.01 to 0.02 suffice to reverse the result that the years-of-schooling variable is statistically significant at even the 5% level.[19]

Thus, where good instruments are available, IV regression can reduce or eliminate the risk of making a "Big Mistake" due to wrongly omitting an important explanatory variable. But this tactic might not work if (as in the Angrist-Krueger example) the instruments are not credibly valid with respect to the inference at issue – i.e., if this particular inference is "fragile" with respect to likely levels of instrument-error correlation. On the other hand, at least we now have stronger tools for assessing that validity, so the IV tactic itself is promising – at least, where reasonably suitable instruments are available.

Omitted-Variables Tactic #5: Use Sensitivity Analysis to Assess Whether the Induced Endogeneity Matters

But what if one has no instruments to propose – credibly valid or not? Tactic #4 is obviously infeasible in that case. But a sensitivity analysis using the Ashley and Parmeter (2011) algorithm is still potentially quite useful.

For example, in a now-classic paper in the growth and development literature, Mankiw, Romer, and Weil (1992) estimate a model for real per capita GDP growth in a country using a human-capital explanatory variable – the average percentage of the country's working-age population in secondary school – and find that the growth rate in human capital is indeed important: they reject the null hypothesis of a zero coefficient on this variable with p-value less than 0.00005. But their human capital variable is arguably endogenous – due to both wrongly omitted variables and also to measurement error.[20] However, Ashley and Parmeter (2011) find that this endogeneity would need to induce a correlation larger than 0.46 between the Mankiw et al. human capital variable and the model error term in order to make the p-value for rejecting their null hypothesis exceed 0.05. In other words, their particular inference is sufficiently "robust" with respect to endogeneity in this explanatory variable – arising from wrongly omitted variables or other sources – that it is very unlikely that their inferential result is mistaken.

That ends this exposition. To find out more about the underpinnings of applied econometrics, one must go on to a broader and more mathematically sophisticated treatment of this topic, couched liberally in matrix algebra.[21] In the meantime, the other good way to learn more is to make actual models using real data – and to critically examine these models, using a good deal of mindful diagnostic checking (of the model assumptions which *can* be checked) and a dollop of sensitivity analysis with respect to the model assumptions which cannot be checked.

[19] This sensitivity result is probably related to the fact that the Angrist-Krueger instruments are only weakly correlated with the education variable – see Bound et al. (1995) – but it is not a "weak instruments" problem *per se,* as reference to the definition of the instruments in Section 12.6 shows that the number of instruments will not increase as the sample size grows. Bound, J., D. Jaeger, and R. Baker (1995), "Problems with Instrumental Variables Estimation When the Correlation between the Instruments and the Endogenous Explanatory Variables Is Weak," *Journal of the American Statistical Association 90,* pp. 443–450.

[20] Referring to Section 11.6, measurement error in an explanatory variable induces endogeneity because the measurement error augmenting the variable-as-measured thus also appears, with the opposite sign, in the model error term.

[21] For example, Davidson and MacKinnon (2004) or Greene (2007).

MATHEMATICS REVIEW

SUMMATION NOTATION

1. Single Sum Examples:

$$\sum_{i=3}^{6} y_i = y_3 + y_4 + y_5 + y_6$$

$$\sum_{i=1}^{N} y_i = y_1 + y_2 + ... + y_{N-1} + y_N$$

2. Comments on Single Sums:

   a. Summation notation is inherently just bookkeeping.

   b. This notation is not necessary for adding up a handful of values, but is useful when things get more complicated, or when the number of terms is large, or when the number of terms needs to be left in symbolic form – e.g., as N.

   c. If one has already been exposed to a programming language (e.g., BASIC, FORTRAN, C, MATLAB, etc.), it is useful to think of summation notation as defining a loop which explicitly increments a variable at each pass through the loop. For example, in FORTRAN one would implement the sum illustrated above with the DO loop:

```
sumvar=0.
DO i=1, N
  sumvar=sumvar + y(i)
ENDDO
```

   Every programming language worthy of the name will have a similar construct.

      i. Thus, the name of the running index for a sum – exactly like the index variable in a program loop – is a choice up to the user.

      ii. This program-loop metaphor for summation notation is helpful for single sums. It is even more useful in understanding the double sums, which are described in the next section.

d. Whenever a sum with an upper limit of N for the sum index becomes confusing, one can almost always retrieve comprehension by simply writing out the sum for the special case of N equal to two or three. This will usually dramatically clarify the situation.

3. Algebra with Single Sums

a. In the context of summation notation, the word "constant" means "does not depend on the running index of the sum."

b. Where g is a constant:

$$\sum_{i=1}^{N} g = Ng$$

c. Where k is a constant:

$$\sum_{i=1}^{N} ky_i = k\sum_{i=1}^{N} y_i$$

d. The summation of the sum of two variables equals the sum of the summations of the two variables:

$$\sum_{i=1}^{N} \{y_i + z_i\} = \sum_{i=1}^{N} y_i + \sum_{i=1}^{N} z_i$$

e. Thus, combining Section 3c and Section 3d,

$$\sum_{i=1}^{N} \{cy_i + \mathrm{d}z_i\} = c\sum_{i=1}^{N} y_i + \mathrm{d}\sum_{i=1}^{N} z_i$$

and, for the special case where $y_i = 1$ for all values of i,

$$\sum_{i=1}^{N}\{c1 + \mathrm{d}z_i\} = c\sum_{i=1}^{N} 1 + \mathrm{d}\sum_{i=1}^{N} z_i$$
$$= cN + \mathrm{d}\sum_{i=1}^{N} z_i$$

f. Let $y_1 \ldots y_N$ be observations on some economic variable (e.g., N observations on quarterly GDP) and let $c_1 \ldots c_N$ be N given numbers. Then the weighted sum of the N observations can be written

$$c_1y_1 + c_2y_2 + \cdots + c_Ny_N = \sum_{i=1}^{N} c_iy_i$$

Such a weighted sum is also called "a linear combination of the y_i's"

4. Double Sums

a. A good simple example of a double sum is

$$\sum_{i=1}^{2}\sum_{j=1}^{3} (a_i + b_j)^2$$

This double sum is equivalent to the ordinary sum

$$(a_1 + b_1)^2 + (a_1 + b_2)^2 + (a_1 + b_3)^2 + (a_2 + b_1)^2 + (a_2 + b_2)^2 + (a_2 + b_3)^2$$

b. Per Section 2c, if one has already been exposed to a programming language, it is useful to think of a double sum as a pair of nested loops. For example, using FORTRAN syntax, the double sum above is equivalent to the nested DO loops:

```
sumvar = 0.
DO i = 1,2
DO j = 1,3
  sumvar = sumvar + (a(i) + b(j))**2
ENDDO
ENDDO
```

i. Thus, as with a single sum, the choice of names for the two running indices (here i and j) is up to the user. These indices must clearly be distinct, however.

ii. Note that the index on the right-most sum (here, j) is just like the index for the inner-most loop – and it runs "fastest." That is, one sets the value of the index on the left-most sum (i) to one and adds up the "summand" – i.e., $(a_1 + b_j)^2$ – over the required values of j, from one through three here. Then the index on the left-most sum (i) is incremented (so that i equals two) and the summand $(a_2 + b_j)^2$ is added on to the total value of the sum for each required value of the index j. This process is repeated until it is no longer possible to increase the index on the left-most sum without exceeding its given upper limit, which is two in the present example.

c. Whenever a double sum with upper limits of N for each sum becomes confusing, one can almost always retrieve comprehension by simply writing out the double sum for the special case of N equal to two or three. This tactic is even more useful for double sums than for single sums because the potential for confusion is greater with double sums.

d. Double sums are more challenging to understand than single sums, but are useful (and, indeed, often necessary) in two circumstances:

i. In evaluating the expectation of a function of two discretely-distributed random variables. In that case – e.g., Equation 2-27 – the relevant expected value will be a double sum over the possible realized values for each of the two random variables.

ii. Whenever evaluating the population variance of an estimator which is a linear function of underlying random variables – as will typically be the case in bivariate regression analysis – one will have to deal with the square of a linear combination of N random variables:[1]

$$\{c_1 Y_1 + c_2 Y_2 + \ldots + c_N Y_N\}^2 = \left\{\sum_{i=1}^{N} c_i Y_i\right\}^2$$

The squared term on the right-hand side of this equation will almost always need to be re-expressed as a double sum.

e. In particular, the square of such a single sum can be re-expressed as the following double sum:

$$\left\{\sum_{i=1}^{N} c_i Y_i\right\}^2 = \sum_{i=1}^{N} c_i Y_i \sum_{j=1}^{N} c_j Y_j = \sum_{i=1}^{N}\sum_{j=1}^{N} c_i c_j Y_i Y_j$$

[1] Capital letters are used here because Y_i is explicitly a random variable in this example.

The special case with N equal to two provides a clarifying example,

$$\sum_{i=1}^{2} c_i Y_i \sum_{j=1}^{2} c_j Y_j = (c_1 Y_1 + c_2 Y_2)(c_1 Y_1 + c_2 Y_2)$$

and

$$\sum_{i=1}^{2}\sum_{j=1}^{2} c_i c_j Y_i Y_j = c_1 c_1 Y_1 Y_1 + c_1 c_2 Y_1 Y_2 + c_2 c_1 Y_2 Y_1 + c_2 c_2 Y_2 Y_2$$

To prove this result for any value of N, let the symbol "A" stand for $\sum_{j=1}^{N} c_j Y_j$ in the following derivation:

$$\left\{\sum_{i=1}^{N} c_i Y_i\right\}^2 = \sum_{j=1}^{N} c_j Y_j \sum_{i=1}^{N} c_i Y_i$$

$$= A \sum_{i=1}^{N} c_i Y_i$$

$$= \sum_{i=1}^{N} A\, c_i Y_i$$ (This expression is equivalent to that of the previous step because A does not depend on running the index i.)

$$= \sum_{i=1}^{N} c_i Y_i A$$ (Reversing the order of the multiplications.)

$$= \sum_{i=1}^{N} c_i Y_i \left\{\sum_{j=1}^{N} c_j Y_j\right\}$$ (Using the definition of A.)

$$= \sum_{i=1}^{N}\left\{\sum_{j=1}^{N} (c_i Y_i) c_j Y_j\right\}$$ (Because $c_i y_i$ does not depend on the running index j, it can be either inside or outside the sum over j.)

$$= \sum_{i=1}^{N}\sum_{j=1}^{N} c_i c_j\, Y_i Y_j$$ (Reversing the order of the multiplications.)

DIFFERENTIAL CALCULUS

1. Derivatives of simple functions:

   a. if $f(x) = x^k$ then $\mathrm{d}f(x)/\mathrm{d}x = kx^{k-1}$

   b. if $f(x) = x^{-1}$ then $\mathrm{d}f(x)/\mathrm{d}x = -x^{-2}$

   c. if $f(x) = \log(x)$ then $\mathrm{d}f(x)/\mathrm{d}x = 1/x$

2. Derivative of a linear combination of functions:

$$\frac{\mathrm{d}}{\mathrm{d}x}\{cf(x) + eg(x)\} = c\frac{\mathrm{d}f(x)}{\mathrm{d}x} + e\frac{\mathrm{d}g(x)}{\mathrm{d}x}$$

or

$$\frac{d}{dx}\sum_{i=1}^{N} c_i f_i(x) = \sum_{i=1}^{N} c_i \frac{df_i(x)}{dx}$$

3. Derivative of a composite function – i.e., the "chain rule":
   For example,

$$\frac{d}{dx}\log(f(x)) = \frac{1}{f(x)}\frac{df(x)}{dx}$$

4. Partial Derivatives:
   a. If a function depends on more than one variable, then the partial derivatives of the function with respect to each of these variables is just the ordinary derivative of the function, holding the other variables fixed. For example, the partial derivative of $f(x_1, x_2, x_3)$ with respect to x_1 is taken as if x_2 and x_3 are constants, and similarly for the partial derivatives with respect to x_2 and x_3.
   b. For example, if

$$g(x_1, x_2, x_3, x_4) \equiv x_1^2 + 3x_2^2 x_3 + x_4$$

then

$$\frac{\partial g(x_1, x_2, x_3, x_4)}{\partial x_1} = 2x_1$$

$$\frac{\partial g(x_1, x_2, x_3, x_4)}{\partial x_2} = 6x_2 x_3$$

$$\frac{\partial g(x_1, x_2, x_3, x_4)}{\partial x_3} = 3x_2^2$$

$$\frac{\partial g(x_1, x_2, x_3, x_4)}{\partial x_4} = 1$$

INDEX

P

Q

R

Y

Z